The Routledge Handbook of Second Language Acquisition

'The editors, Susan M. Gass and Alison Mackey, have done a sterling job with this Handbook. The biggest names and rising stars in the fields of second language teaching and language learning have contributed to this "magnum opus".'

Jean-Marc Dewaele, *Birkbeck, University of London, UK*

The Routledge Handbook of Second Language Acquisition brings together fifty leading international figures in the field to produce a state-of-the-art overview of second language acquisition.

The *Handbook* covers a wide range of topics related to Second Language Acquisition: language in context, linguistic, psycholinguistic, and neurolinguistic theories and perspectives, skill learning, individual differences, L2 learning settings, and language assessment. All chapters introduce the reader to the topic, outline the core issues, then explore the pedagogical application of research in the area and possible future development.

The Routledge Handbook of Second Language Acquisition is an essential resource for all those studying and researching second language acquisition.

Susan M. Gass is University Distinguished Professor in the Department of Linguistics and Languages at Michigan State University, USA. She is the author of many titles and co-author of *Second Language Acquisition: An Introductory Course*, Fourth Edition (Routledge, 2013), with Larry Selinker. She co-edits the series, *Second Language Acquisition Research* (with Alison Mackey, for Routledge).

Alison Mackey is Professor in the Department of Linguistics at Georgetown University, USA. She is the author of many titles, and co-author of *Data Elicitation for Second and Foreign Language Research* (Routledge 2007), with Susan M. Gass. She co-edits the series, *Second Language Acquisition Research* (with Susan M. Gass, for Routledge).

Routledge Handbooks in Applied Linguistics

Routledge Handbooks in Applied Linguistics provide comprehensive overviews of the key topics in applied linguistics. All entries for the handbooks are specially commissioned and written by leading scholars in the field. Clear, accessible and carefully edited *Routledge Handbooks in Applied Linguistics* are the ideal resource for both advanced undergraduates and postgraduate students.

The Routledge Handbook of Forensic Linguistics
Edited by Malcolm Coulthard and Alison Johnson

The Routledge Handbook of Corpus Linguistics
Edited by Anne O'Keeffe and Mike McCarthy

The Routledge Handbook of World Englishes
Edited by Andy Kirkpatrick

The Routledge Handbook of Applied Linguistics
Edited by James Simpson

The Routledge Handbook of Discourse Analysis
James Paul Gee and Michael Handford

The Routledge Handbook of Second Language Acquisition
Edited by Susan M. Gass and Alison Mackey

The Routledge Handbook of Multilingualism
Edited by Marilyn Martin-Jones, Adrian Blackledge, and Angela Creese

The Routledge Handbook of Translation Studies
Edited by Carmen Millan Varela and Francesca Bartrina

The Routledge Handbook of Language Testing
Edited by Glenn Fulcher and Fred Davidson

The Routledge Handbook of Language and Intercultural Communication
Edited by Jane Jackson

The Routledge Handbook of Language and Health Communication
Edited by Heidi Hamilton and Wen-ying Sylvia Chou

The Routledge Handbook of Language and Professional Communication
Edited by Vijay Bhatia and Stephen Bremner

The Routledge Handbook of Second Language Acquisition

Edited by Susan M. Gass and Alison Mackey

Routledge
Taylor & Francis Group

LONDON AND NEW YORK

First published in paperback 2014
First published 2012
by Routledge
2 Park Square, Milton Park, Abingdon, Oxon OX14 4RN

Simultaneously published in the USA and Canada
by Routledge
711 Third Avenue, New York, NY 10017

Routledge is an imprint of the Taylor & Francis Group, an informa business

British Library Cataloguing in Publication Data
A catalogue record for this book is available from the British Library

Library of Congress Cataloging-in-Publication Data
   The Routledge handbook of second language acquisition/edited by
Susan M. Gass and Alison Mackey.
      p. cm.
   Includes index.
   1. Second language acquisition--Handbooks, manuals, etc.
   2. Language and languages--Handbooks, manuals, etc.
   I. Gass, Susan M. II. Mackey, Alison.
   P118.2.R68 2011
   401'.93--dc22

                                         2011002649

ISBN: 978-0-415-47993-6 (hbk)
ISBN: 978-0-415-70981-1 (pbk)
ISBN: 978-0-203-80818-4 (ebk)

Typeset in Bembo
by Integra Software Services Pvt. Ltd, Pondicherry, India

Printed and bound in Great Britain by
TJ International Ltd, Padstow, Cornwall

Contents

Contents

PART III

Psycholinguistic and neurolinguistic perspectives   177

PART IV

Skill learning   301

Contents

Illustrations

Figures

Tables

Abbreviations

ACTFL	American Council on the Teaching of Foreign Languages
ADHD	attention-deficit hyperactivity disorder
AE	American English
AMTB	Attitude/Motivation Test Battery
AoA	age of arrival
ASL	American Sign Language
AV	auditory-visual
CA	Contrastive Analysis
CALL	computer-assisted language learning
CANAL-F	Cognitive Ability for Novelty in Acquisition of Language—Foreign
CATSS	Computer Adaptive Test of Size and Strength
CCSARP	Cross-Cultural Speech Act Realization Project
CHL	Chinese as a heritage language
CLS	complementary learning systems
CMC	computer-mediated communication
CPH	Critical Period Hypothesis
CS	conditioned stimulus
CV	consonant-vowel
ΔP	Delta P
DCTs	discourse completion tasks
DLAB	Defense Language Aptitude Battery
EAP	English for Academic Purposes
EFL	English as a Foreign Language
ESL	English as a second language
ELAN	early left anterior negativity
ERPs	event-related potentials
ESF	European Science Foundation
ESP	English for Specific Purposes
EWM	executive working memory
FDH	fundamental difference hypothesis
FLES	foreign language in the elementary school
fMRI	functional magnetic resonance imaging
FonF	Focus on Form
FonFs	Focus on Forms
FSI/ILR	Foreign Service Institute/Interagency Language Round Table
GJTs	Grammaticality Judgment Tests

GM	grammatical metaphor
HLA	Heritage Language Acquisition
HLLs	heritage language learners
IDI	Intercultural Development Inventory
ILs	interlanguages
IMRD	Introduction-Method-Results-Discussion
L1	first language
L2	second language
LANs	left-to-bilateral anterior negativities
LANs	local area networks
LCP	Language Contact Profile
LeaP	Learning Prosody in a Foreign Language
LFG	Lexical-functional Grammar
LMT	Lexical Mapping Theory
LOR	length of residence
MCS	memory for contingent speech
MEG	magnetoencephalography
MLAT	Modern Language Aptitude Test
MM	Multidimensional Model
MTM	multiple-trace memory
NHLRC	National Heritage Language Resource Center
NLP	natural language processing
NS	native speaker
NS-NNS	native speaker-non-native speaker
OM	Ontogeny Model
OPI	Oral Proficiency Interview
OT	optimality theory
PDH	Proceduralization Deficit Hypothesis
PET	Positron Emission Tomography
PLAB	Pimsleur's Language Aptitude Battery
PLD	primary linguistic data
P&P	principles and parameters
PSTM	phonological short-term memory
PT	Processability Theory
PWM	phonological working memory
RST	reading span task
SA	study abroad
SES	socio-economic status
SFL	systemic-functional linguistics
SILC	Strategic Inventory for Learning Culture
SILL	Strategic Inventory for Language Learning
SLA	second language acquisition
SLM	Speech Learning Model
SOPI	Simulated Oral Proficiency Interview
TBLT	Task-based Language Teaching
TMS	transcranial magnetic stimulation
TOEFL	Test of English as a Second Language
TOEIC	Test of English for International Communication

Abbreviations

UCM	Unified Competition Model
UG	Universal Grammar
US	unconditioned stimulus
VACs	verb-argument constructions
VOT	voice onset time
ZISA	Zweitspracherwerb Italienischer und Spanischer Arbeiter
ZPD	Zone of Proximal Development

Contributors

Rebekha Abbuhl is Assistant Professor of Linguistics at California State University Long Beach. Second language writing, interactionist approaches to second language acquisition, and teacher training are her main research areas.

Kathleen Bardovi-Harlig is Professor of Second Language Studies at Indiana University. Her research focuses on second language acquisition of temporal expression including tense-aspect and narrative development and acquisition of second language pragmatics including the acquisition of sociopragmatic rules, pragmalinguistic resources, and conventional expressions.

Robert Bayley is Professor of Linguistics at the University of California, Davis. He has conducted research on variation in L1 and L2 English, Spanish, and ASL as well as ethnographic research in US Latino communities.

Martha Bigelow is Associate Professor at the University of Minnesota. Her research focuses on the language learning and cultural adaptation of immigrant youth. She is co-author of *Literacy and Second Language Oracy* (2009) and author of *Mogadishu on the Mississippi: Language, Racialized Identity and Education in a New Land* (2010).

Heidi Byrnes is George M. Roth Distinguished Professor of German at Georgetown University. Her research focuses on the development of advanced L2 literacy. She has addressed that topic in edited and co-edited volumes and papers, most recently in the co-authored monograph *Realizing Advanced Foreign Language Writing Development in Collegiate Education: Curricular Design, Pedagogy, Assessment.*

Carol Chapelle is Distinguished Professor of Liberal Arts and Sciences at Iowa State University. She is editor of *The Encyclopedia of Applied Linguistics* (Wiley-Blackwell); co-editor of the *Cambridge Applied Linguistics Series*; past President of the American Association for Applied Linguistics (2006–2007); and former editor of *TESOL Quarterly* (1999–2004).

Robert DeKeyser is Professor of Second Language Acquisition at the University of Maryland, College Park. His research interests include age effects in second language learning, individual differences and their interaction with second language teaching methodology, the relationship between implicit and explicit learning, the role of negative feedback, and study abroad.

Kathleen Dillon is Associate Director of the University of California Consortium for Language Learning & Teaching. She has published on topics pertaining to the poetics of

Boris Pasternak, biography of Russian Women Poets, and heritage language acquisition and pedagogy.

Zoltán Dörnyei is Professor of Psycholinguistics at the School of English Studies, University of Nottingham. He has published widely on various aspects of second language acquisition and is the author of several books, including *The Psychology of Second Language Acquisition* and *Teaching and Researching Motivation* (Second Edition with Ema Ushioda).

Patricia Duff is Professor of Language and Literacy Education at the University of British Columbia, Canada, and Co-Director of the Centre for Research in Chinese Language and Literacy Education. Her recent publications deal primarily with language socialization in linguistically diverse communities and qualitative research methods in applied linguistics.

Fred Eckman is Professor of Linguistics and Chair of the Department of Linguistics at the University of Wisconsin-Milwaukee. His research focuses on second language (L2) acquisition theory, and on the explanation of interphonology and L2 syntax.

Nick Ellis is Research Scientist at the English Language Institute, Professor of Psychology, and Professor of Linguistics at the University of Michigan. His research interests include cognitive, psycholinguistic, complex systems, and emergentist aspects of language. He serves as general editor of *Language Learning*.

Susan Gass is University Distinguished Professor in the Department of Linguistics and Germanic, Slavic, Asian and African Languages at Michigan State University where she serves as Director of the English Language Center and Director of the Second Language Studies program. Her research focuses on second language input and interaction. She is co-author of *Second Language Acquisition: An Introductory Course*.

ZhaoHong Han is Professor of Language and Education at Teachers College, Columbia University. Her research interests lie broadly in second language learnability and teachability. Her latest book is *Linguistic Relativity in SLA: Thinking for Speaking* (co-edited with Teresa Cadierno, Multilingual Matters).

Debra Hardison is Associate Professor in the TESOL and Second Language Studies programs at Michigan State University. Her research focuses on auditory-visual integration in spoken language processing with an emphasis on second-language speech development. Studies include applications of technology for perception and production training of segmental and prosodic elements.

Trude Heift is Professor of Linguistics in the Department of Linguistics at Simon Fraser University, Canada. Her main research areas are computer-assisted language learning, applied and computational linguistics. She is currently associate editor of *Language Learning & Technology*.

Jörg-U. Keßler is Professor of English and Applied Linguistics at Ludwigsburg University of Education, Germany. He is editor of *Processability Approaches to Second Language Development and Second Language Learning* and co-editor of an introductory textbook on PT. His main research areas are (instructed) second language acquisition, early foreign language learning and immersion & CLIL.

Olga Kagan is Professor in the Department of Slavic Languages and Literatures at UCLA and Director of the National Heritage Language Resource Center. Her research focuses on heritage language learners. She co-edits the *Heritage Language Journal* and has co-authored eight textbooks of Russian, including two textbooks for heritage language learners.

Keiko Koda is Professor of Second Language Acquisition and Japanese in the Department of Modern Languages at Carnegie Mellon University. Her research focuses on second language reading and biliteracy development. She authored *Insights into Second Language Reading* and edited/co-edited *Reading* and *Language Learning* and *Learning to Read across Languages*.

Folkert Kuiken is Professor of Dutch as a Second Language at the University of Amsterdam, where he coordinates the Dual Master of Dutch as a Second Language. His research interests include the effect of task complexity and interaction on SLA, Focus on Form, and the relationship between linguistic complexity and communicative adequacy.

Barbara Lafford is Professor of Spanish in the School of International Letters & Cultures at Arizona State University. She is editor of the Monograph/Focus Issues Series for the *Modern Language Journal*. Her main research areas are second language acquisition in study abroad and classroom environments, applied linguistics, and CALL.

James Lantolf is Greer Professor in Language Acquisition and Applied Linguistics at Penn State University. His research focus is on sociocultural theory and second language acquisition. He co-authored *Sociocultural Theory and the Genesis of Second Language Development* and co-edited *Sociocultural Theory and the Teaching of Second Languages*.

Donna Lardiere is Professor of Linguistics at Georgetown University. She is author of *Ultimate Attainment in Second Language Acquisition: A Case Study* (Taylor & Francis/Routledge). Her research focuses on the role of linguistic theory in second language acquisition, particularly the acquisition of morphology and syntax.

Diane Larsen-Freeman is Professor of Education, Professor of Linguistics, and Research Scientist at the English Language Institute at the University of Michigan, Ann Arbor. She is also Distinguished Senior Faculty Fellow at the School for International Training in Brattleboro, Vermont. Her areas of interest are second language acquisition, English grammar, language teacher education, and language teaching methodology.

Batia Laufer is Professor of Applied Linguistics at the University of Haifa, Israel. Her research focuses mainly on areas in second language vocabulary acquisition: form-focused instruction, incidental learning, cross-linguistic influence, testing, reading, word difficulty and dicitonary use.

Shawn Loewen is Associate Professor in the Second Language Studies program at Michigan State University. His research interests include instructed second language acquisition, corrective feedback and L2 interaction. He teaches courses on second language acquisition and research methodology.

Alison Mackey is Professor in the Department of Linguistics at Georgetown University and Head of the Applied Linguistics Programs there. Her academic interests include input and interaction, research methodology, and adult and child L2 learning.

Brian MacWhinney is Professor of Psychology at Carnegie Mellon University and has formulated a model of language processing and learning called the Competition Model. He has also developed the CHILDES Project for the computational study of child language transcript data, and the TalkBank system for the study of adult conversational interactions.

Sally Magnan is Professor of French, Director of the Language Institute, Co-Chair of the Doctoral Program in Second Language Acquisition at the University of Wisconsin, Madison and past editor of the *Modern Language Journal*. Her recent research investigates language learning during study abroad and learner issues with the National Standards for Foreign Language Learning.

Kara Morgan-Short is Assistant Professor in the Departments of Hispanic and Italian Studies and Psychology at the University of Illinois at Chicago. Informed by the fields of linguistics, cognitive psychology and neuroscience, her research aims to elucidate the neurocognitive processes underlying late-learned second language acquisition and use.

I. S. P. Nation is Emeritus Professor of Applied Linguistics in the School of Linguistics and Applied Language Studies at Victoria University of Wellington, New Zealand. He has taught in Indonesia, Thailand, the United States, Finland, and Japan. His special interests are language teaching methodology and vocabulary learning.

John Norris is Associate Professor in the Department of Second Language Studies at the University of Hawaii at Manoa. His teaching and research focus on language pedagogy, program evaluation, educational assessment, and research synthesis.

Lourdes Ortega is Professor of Second Language Studies at the University of Hawaii at Manoa. Her research focuses on second language acquisition, L2 writing, foreign language education, and research methods. Her most recent book is *Understanding Second Language Acquisition* (2009, Hodder). She is editor of *Language Learning*.

Lucy Pickering is Associate Professor of Applied Linguistics at Texas A&M-Commerce. Her research explores second language oral discourse, the pedagogical applications of computer-assisted speech analysis, and the ways in which learners develop competence in relation to prosody.

Manfred Pienemann is Professor of Linguistics at Paderborn University, Germany and Visiting Professor at Newcastle University, UK. He was previously Professor of Applied Linguistics at the Australian National University. He founded the Language Acquisition Research Centre at Sydney University and was one of the founding members of PacSLRF. He has been involved in SLA research since the 1970s.

Charlene Polio is Associate Professor at Michigan State University, where she teaches in the TESOL and Second Language Studies programs. Her research interests include second language writing research methods and the relationship betwee writing and SLA. She is the editor of the *Annual Review of Applied Linguistics*.

Peter Robinson is Professor of Linguistics and SLA at Aoyama Gakuin University, Tokyo, Japan. He is editor of the book series, *Cognitive Science and Second Language Acquisition*, published by Routledge, and of the forthcoming *Routledge Encyclopedia of Second Language Acquisition*.

Richard Schmidt is Professor of Second Language Studies and Director of the National Foreign Language Resource Center at the University of Hawaii at Manoa. His research focuses on psychological and social factors in SLA and issues concerning the teaching and learning of less commonly taught and difficult languages.

Norman Segalowitz is Professor of Psychology at Concordia University in Montréal, Associate Director of the Centre for the Study of Learning and Performance, and author of *The Cognitive Bases of Second Language Fluency* (Routledge, 2010). He studies automatic and attention-based processes in L2 fluency and proficiency and their implications for language instruction.

Peter Skehan is Professor of Applied Linguistics at the University of Auckland. He has taught in the U.K. and Hong Kong. He has published and researched in second language acquisition, particularly foreign language aptitude and task-based performance, assessment, and instruction.

Roumyana Slabakova is Professor of Linguistics and Second Language Acquisition at the University of Iowa. She investigates the acquisition of meaning in its relation to linguistic structure, focusing on temporal, aspectual and nominal meanings, as well as pragmatic implicatures. She is a founding editor of the journal *Linguistic Approaches to Bilingualism*.

Elaine Tarone is Distinguished Teaching Professor of Second Language Studies and Director of the Center for Advanced Research on Language Acquisition (CARLA) at the University of Minnesota-Twin Cities; author of *Literacy and Second Language Oracy, Exploring Learner Language*, and author of publications on interlanguage variation, referential communication and language play.

Pavel Trofimovich is Associate Professor of Applied Linguistics in the Department of Education at Concordia University in Montreal, Canada. His research focuses on cognitive aspects of second language processing, second language phonology, sociolinguistic aspects of second language acquisition, and the teaching of second language pronunciation.

Michael Ullman is Professor in the Departments of Neuroscience, Neurology, Linguistics and Psychology at Georgetown University. His research examines the brain bases of first and second language, how language and memory are affected in various disorders, and how factors such as sex and genetic variability affect the neurocognition of language.

Ema Ushioda is Associate Professor in ELT and Applied Linguistics at the Centre for Applied Linguistics, University of Warwick. Her main research interests are language learning motivation, learner autonomy, sociocultural theory and teacher development.

Bill VanPatten is Professor of Spanish and Second Language Studies at Michigan State University. His research has focused on morphological representation, input processing, language processing more generally, and instructed second language acquisition.

Ineke Vedder is Senior Researcher and Head of Education at the University of Amsterdam. Her research interests include instructed SLA, particularly Italian as a second language, the influence of task complexity and interaction on L2 performance, and the relationship between linguistic complexity and communicative adequacy in L2 writing.

Jill Watson is Lecturer in French at Cornell University in the Department of Romance Studies. She has done research in a range of foreign language and English as a second language settings with a focus on refugee adolescents who are becoming literate for the first time. She applies her work to language teacher development and school reform initiatives.

Jessica Williams is Professor of Linguistics at the University of Illinois at Chicago. She has published on variety of topics, including second language writing, lexical acquisition, and the effect of focus on form. Her books include *Teaching Writing in Second and Foreign Language Classrooms* and *Theories in Second Language Acquisition* (edited with Bill VanPatten).

John Williams is Reader in Applied Psycholinguistics at the University of Cambridge, UK. His research focuses on the cognitive mechanisms of second language learning, and second language lexical and syntactic processing.

Introduction

Susan M. Gass and Alison Mackey

Learning a second or foreign language is commonplace in today's world. In fact, recent estimates (Grosjean, 2010) suggest that more than half of the world's population knows more than one language. Some of this dual language knowledge comes from family or societal sources, that is, growing up in a dual-language family or a bi- or multilingual society; in other instances, second language knowledge comes from an instructional setting. In some instances, learning begins post-puberty; in other instances, it begins in childhood. Despite these varied facts, we are still a long way from understanding how second languages are learned, why many individuals have difficulty in reaching high levels of proficiency in a second language, or even what the best pedagogical approach might be. This *Handbook of Second Language Acquisition* provides comprehensive coverage of the field of second language acquisition (SLA) with an effort to incorporate a wide range of different approaches to understanding how languages are learned.

As an ever-growing body of research on SLA has indicated, numerous factors are involved in L2 learning (de Bot *et al.*, 2005; Gass and Selinker, 2008; Ortega, 2009; Mitchell and Myles, 1998). Put another way, the field of SLA is multi-faceted and interdisciplinary, a fact which also reflects the complexity of L2 development. The many factors involved in L2 learning (e.g., linguistic, psychological, sociological) are generally best viewed in combination. In other words, the highly complex phenomenon of second language learning can only be understood when all parts of the picture can be seen at the same time. A single approach (e.g., focusing only on linguistic aspects of learning, or focusing only on social aspects of learning) is too simplistic and is unlikely to move us toward our goal of understanding the entire phenomenon and, in particular, why and when language learning is successful, and why and when it is not.

This *Handbook* is designed to provide a state-of-the-art survey of L2 research exploring theoretical issues of particular significance in L2 learning and teaching. The *Handbook* is intended for SLA researchers, applied linguists, graduate students, upper-level undergraduate students, practitioners, and other professionals related to or interested in SLA. Accordingly, the topics discussed in the *Handbook* were selected in consideration of the needs of the intended audience. More importantly, the selections were also made based on the degree of significance and prominence to which each topic has contributed to L2 research. Some topics have already received book-length treatises (e.g., approaches related to sociocultural theories); other topics (e.g., issues related to heritage learners, study abroad, or education level) have not typically been included in an overall discussion of language learning prior to this *Handbook*.

Even though the primary scope of the *Handbook* is second language learning, authors were also asked to provide a section on how their approaches to learning a second language might be applied to an instructional context. We designed the *Handbook* this way because of our conviction that while these two disciplines (language teaching and language learning) are separate and each has its own research history and trajectories, there is, nonetheless, common ground and a need for strong cross-fertilization. Theories about learning are often tested in the classroom and understanding of classroom language and behavior can often feed into our theoretical notions. Below is a synopsis of the instructions provided to authors of the chapters in this volume concerning the structure of their chapters. To represent each area, we intentionally selected leading scholars and they, in turn, often selected rising stars as co-authors.

(1) Historical discussion
This section places the chapter in historical perspective and provides the reader with a sense of where the topic fits within the field as a whole, and how (when appropriate) it relates to other disciplines.

(2) Core issues in the area
This section presents and explains the major tenets of the topic and provides the reader with a commentary on the most up-to-date findings.

(3) Data and common elicitation measures
In this section, authors describe what types of data are used, how these data are typically gathered and how they are analyzed.

(4) Applications/instructional relevance
As discussed above, in the hope of bridging the divide between theory and practice, in this section, the authors discuss the impact that their approach has for instruction.

(5) Future directions
In the final section, authors point to the future of their approach and speculate where they see this area of research going both in the short and the longer term.

Quite clearly, this outline better suits some approaches better than others, but all authors were guided by this general outline. The book is divided into seven parts: (1) Language in context, (2) Linguistic perspectives—form and meaning, (3) Psycholinguistic and neurolinguistics perspectives, (4) Skill learning, (5) Individual differences, (6) The setting for learning and (7) Assessing learner knowledge.

The first section discusses how language use in context affects second language (L2) learning, dealing with three issues that have led to debates among researchers: the interactionist approach (including feedback), variationist perspectives, sociocultural theory, and complexity theory. This first section illustrates the dynamics involved in learning and emphasizes the need to understand the role that the context plays in learning. A particular focus is on how the context impacts learning and how learners take advantage of the opportunities that the context provides to further their learning.

In the second section, linguistic theories in SLA are presented, along with evidence for and/ or against relevant theories from research to date. In this section, there is an emphasis on language form (phonology and syntax), meaning and meaning-making (semantics, vocabulary, pragmatics), as opposed to language use, as was the case in some of the chapters in the first section.

The third section takes the reader to the area of language processing. All of the chapters in this section consider psycholinguistic and neurolinguistic accounts of L2 learning processes. Each of these chapters draws heavily on the field of psycholinguistics, cognitive psychology, or neurolinguistics. We do not intend the reader to infer that other chapters do not draw on these fields (e.g., speech perception); the organization was simply a heuristic for determining the main focus of chapters.

In the fourth section, we include chapters about L2 learning across the four traditional language skill areas: reading, writing, speech production, and speech perception, drawing attention to relevant research that elucidates how L2 learners can develop those skills and how they can benefit from particular (instructional) techniques designed to help improve the four skills. This section concludes with a comparison of spoken and written language production.

The fifth section reflects the fact that in SLA it has long been recognized that individuals vary in terms of how they learn, as well as their ultimate abilities in a second language. What is less clear is how to account for these differences. This section presents research on some of the proposed causes. The chapters in this section address a wide range of issues that may impact learning, some of which are commonly accepted (e.g., aptitude and motivation) and others which will provoke the reader to think about individual differences in a slightly different way (e.g., education level, home language background [language of one's heritage]).

In the sixth section, the focus is on the ways in which different settings affect L2 learning: study abroad, second language vs. foreign language environments, and language learning through technology. Each of these areas is important not only for our understanding of how languages are learned, but is also crucial to teachers, curriculum developers, and policy setters as they find footing in their decisions about numerous instances related to how to have a cutting-edge language program.

Last but not the least, in its final section, the *Handbook* brings to our attention the validity and reliability of various measures designed to assess L2 knowledge. We opened this introduction with an estimate of how much of the world's population is bilingual. There is no definitive answer for a variety of reasons, one of which is our inability to know how to make precise measurements. However, it is crucial to have a firm foundation in assessment, not only to measure pedagogical successes, also to measure SLA which is even more germane to the issues discussed in this book. In other words, in order to conduct sound SLA research, it is essential that we know how to measure knowledge and have a keen understanding of what it means to know a second language. The final chapter moves us in this direction.

In sum, this collection surveys the field of SLA with an eye on the history, the current practice, the applications, and the future, with an attempt to consider as many relevant factors as possible as we move toward an understanding of how, when, and where second languages are learned.

There are numerous individuals to whom we owe a debt of gratitude. First are the authors themselves. Because we wanted authoritative figures in the field, we invited scholars who have been asked many times before to write overview articles. But, we were asking them to reframe those earlier pieces. We recognize how difficult it is to write one more article on the same topic. They were patient with us as we sent chapters back for just "one more revision." Second are our graduate students who helped with many phases of this project. In particular, graduate students at Michigan State University and Georgetown helped us in the preparation of the manuscripts. Third are the reviewers of our initial proposal and of our entire final manuscript, all of whose comments were incorporated at almost every stage of the way, if not directly, at least implicitly. It is difficult to sufficiently express our gratitude to each of you for your careful reading of the manuscript. And, finally, Sophie Jaques from Routledge whose support, assistance and understanding were appreciated at each stage of this project. Producing a book with 35 chapters was almost a full-time job at some stages, and for allowing us time and providing encouragement, we are unceasingly grateful to our families and particularly our husbands, Josh Ard and David Yarowsky.

References

de Bot, K., Lowie, W., and Verspoor, M. (2005). *Second language acquisition: An advanced resource book*. New York: Routledge.

Gass, S. and Selinker, L. (2008). *Second language acquisition: An introductory course* (Third Edition). New York: Routledge.

Grosjean, F. (2010). *Bilingual: Life and reality*. Cambridge, MA: Harvard University Press.

Mitchell, R. and Myles, F. (1998). *Second language learning theories*. London: Edward Arnold.

Ortega, L. (2009). *Understanding second language acquisition*. London: Hodder Education.

Part I
Language in context

1

Interactionist approach

Alison Mackey, Rebekha Abbuhl, and Susan M. Gass

Introduction

In the 30 years since the initial formulations of the Interaction Hypothesis (Long, 1980, 1981), there has been an explosion of studies investigating the ways in which interaction can benefit second language acquisition (SLA), with the most recent work documenting its evolution from hypothesis to approach (Gass and Mackey, 2007a). This review begins with an overview of the historical background of the interactionist approach and then discusses the core issues surrounding it, examines some of the ways in which data are collected in this area of SLA, and explores the practical applications of the approach. Directions for future research will be addressed in the final section.

Historical discussion

The roots of the interactionist approach can be traced to several lines of research that began in the 1970s. At this time, researchers became increasingly interested in the types of discourse patterns found in native speaker and learner conversations. In particular, they examined "foreigner talk" and the ways in which native speakers modified their speech so as to make it more comprehensible for learners (e.g., Ferguson, 1971). Paralleling a similar line of work in first language acquisition (which examined caretaker talk and the ways in which parents modified their speech for young children), researchers in this area argued that modifications such as repetition and syntactic simplifications served to make the input more comprehensible to second language (L2) learners, and in this way promoted the acquisition of the target language.

This focus on input and comprehensibility could also be found in another strand of research that influenced the development of the interactionist approach: Krashen's Input Hypothesis (Krashen, 1977, 1980). According to this hypothesis, input that was comprehensible (but slightly above the learner's current level of proficiency) was the driving force behind language acquisition. In Krashen's view, if a learner was exposed to this type of input, and, at the same time, had a "low affective filter" (i.e., low levels of anxiety and negative feelings associated with learning the L2), acquisition of the non-native language would automatically (i.e., subconsciously) take place. For Krashen, any mechanism that served to make the input comprehensible (e.g., simplifying the grammar of a written or oral text) was of value; however, interaction between native speakers and learners did not hold any special place in his theories.

However, from the late 1970s researchers began to accord more importance to interaction itself. Wagner-Gough and Hatch (1975), for example, maintained that researchers needed to examine "the relationship between language and communication if we are looking for explanations of the learning process" (p. 307), while Hatch (1978a, 1978b) argued that interaction might be an actual site for L2 learning and not just a means of observing what had already been learned. In Hatch's (1978b) words, "one learns how to do conversation, one learns how to interact verbally, and out of the interaction syntactic structures are developed" (p. 404).

Drawing upon the work of these researchers, Long formulated his initial version of what became known as the Interaction Hypothesis (Long, 1980, 1981). In Long's view, both comprehensible input and L2 development stemmed from the conversational modifications that occurred when native speakers and non-native speakers (NNS) worked to resolve a communication difficulty. Although these modifications (commonly referred to as interactional adjustments during negotiation for meaning) were not, of course, the only means of achieving message comprehensibility, Long suggested these modifications were positioned to promote comprehensible input, and, ultimately, L2 acquisition.

Early research using the interactionist approach framework sought to describe the frequency and types of interactional modifications used in native speaker-learner and learner-learner pairings, examine the relationship between negotiation of meaning and learners' comprehension, and compare the effects of premodified and interactionally modified input (e.g., Doughty and Pica, 1986; Gass and Varonis, 1985, 1986; Long, 1983a, b; Loschky, 1994; Pica and Doughty, 1985; Pica et al., 1987; Porter, 1986; Varonis and Gass, 1985). As several researchers, including Mackey (1999), Ellis (1999) and Spada and Lightbown (2009), pointed out, this early research tended to be descriptive and did not seek to provide direct evidence that interaction was causally linked to L2 acquisition.

Early versions of the Interaction Hypothesis incorporated Krashen's claims about comprehensible input being necessary and sufficient for development in the L2: "Access to comprehensible input is a characteristic of all cases of successful acquisition, first and second ... greater quantities of comprehensible input seem to result in better (or at least faster) acquisition ... and crucially, lack of access to comprehensible input ... results in little or no acquisition" (Long, 1983b, p. 210). However, a number of researchers took issue with Krashen's claims about comprehensible input and SLA. Swain (1985, 1995), for example, argued that while comprehensible input was necessary for L2 acquisition to occur, it was far from sufficient. Based on her work with French immersion students in Canada, she argued that if learners do not have regular opportunities to speak or write the language (that is, to produce *output*), their production skills (speaking and writing) would lag considerably behind their comprehension skills (listening and reading). This observation served as the starting point for Swain's Output Hypothesis (1985), which posits that producing output plays a crucial role in the development of the L2, as it (a) gives learners the opportunity to practice and thus to automatize the production of the language; (b) allows learners to test hypotheses concerning the L2; (c) forces learners to focus on structure of the language; and (d) draws learners' attention to gaps in their interlanguage (1995; see also Swain, 2005). Swain suggested that second language learners need to be pushed to produce output, arguing that "being pushed in output, it seems to me, is a concept parallel to that of the *i + 1* of comprehensible input. Indeed, one might call this the comprehensible output" (1985, p. 249). As we discuss later in this chapter, Swain's Output Hypothesis is subsumed in later versions of the Interaction Hypothesis.

The idea of comprehensible input being insufficient for second language acquisition was also discussed by White (1991, 2003). Approaching the role of input from a different theoretical perspective, White claimed that it is unlikely that French learners of English acquire the rule that delimits adverb placement in English (the strict adjacency principle in case assignment) with positive evidence alone because the positive evidence they receive does not contain the information that what is acceptable in French adverb placement may not be acceptable in English. To elaborate, in English, adverbs cannot be placed between the verb and the direct object (thus "Mary watches often television" is ungrammatical). However, the same word ordering —V Adv O—is possible in French ("Mary regarde souvent la television"). Thus, drawing upon his/her L1, the native speaker of French learning English might assume that a sentence such as "Mary watches often television" is acceptable because positive evidence (i.e., English input) provides no information about non-acceptable utterances. White points out that if a learner were solely dependent on comprehensible input for making progress in the L2, they would have to notice the *absence* (referred to as indirect negative evidence) of a particular structure (for example, the V Adv O structure in English). While this is theoretically possible, the language acquisition process may be facilitated if the learner receives assistance in the form of correction or instruction. In essence, what White argued was that comprehensible input is insufficient for certain aspects of L2 development. However, as we will see below and in Chapter 2, the interactionist approach takes into account the important construct of feedback that helps to account for how learners receive information about incorrect utterances.

Other extensions of the Interaction Hypothesis grew out of points made about the role of attention in second language learning. Work in the early 1990s proposed that only *consciously* noticed features of the input became intake (e.g., Schmidt, 1990, 1993). According to Schmidt's Noticing Hypothesis, "subliminal language learning is impossible, and … noticing is the necessary and sufficient condition for converting input to intake" (1990, p. 129) (see also Chapter 15). Researchers were quick to point out, however, that L2 learners' input processing strategies might make certain portions of the L2 difficult to notice. As VanPatten (1989) noted, L2 learners typically practice a form of selective attention, focusing on a limited and thus less overwhelming portion of the input. Those aspects of the input that are salient and meaningful are typically those that draw the learners' attention; features that lack saliency or communicative value (such as determiners in English, gender agreement in Spanish, or postpositions in Japanese) may pass under the learner's radar, so to speak. For this reason, researchers argued, L2 learners might benefit from having their attention drawn to formal features of the target language. This claim, too, made its way into a later version of the Interaction Hypothesis.

Drawing upon the work of these researchers, Long presented a reformulated version of the Interaction Hypothesis in 1996, which stated that "Negotiation for meaning, and especially negotiation that triggers interactional adjustments by the native speaker or more competent interlocutor, facilitates acquisition because it connects input, internal learner capacities, particularly selective attention, and output in productive ways" (p. 451). The following section deals with the major tenets of the most recent updates of this approach (Gass and Mackey, 2007a), along with current research.

Core issues

In the most recent version of the interactionist approach, Gass and Mackey (2007a) note that, "it is now commonly accepted within the SLA literature that there is a robust connection between interaction and learning" (p. 176). The interactionist approach posits that the interactional "work" that occurs when a learner and his/her interlocutor (whether a native speaker or more proficient learner) encounter some kind of communication breakdown is beneficial for L2 development. For example, when a learner experiences difficulty understanding his/her interlocutor or making himself/herself understood, discourse strategies such as clarification requests, confirmation checks, repetitions, and recasts may be employed to help resolve the difficulty. In this manner, the learner may have received input that has been modified often in an effort to make it more comprehensible. The process of interacting with another individual may also serve to draw the learner's attention to some sort of "gap" (in Schmidt's terms, 1990) between his/her interlanguage and the target language. For example, the learner may become aware of a difficulty using a particular linguistic feature.

Aware of the gap, the learner may pay more attention to the subsequent input, something that is believed to be essential for L2 acquisition. The learner may also have his/her attention drawn to this gap through either explicit feedback (such as metalinguistic corrections) or potentially more indirect forms of feedback (such as recasts). Both of these terms will be explained in what follows, together with examples (also see Gass and Mackey, 2007a; Mackey and Abbuhl, 2006; Mackey, 2007 for recent overviews).

This constellation of features—interactionally modified input, having the learner's attention drawn to his/her interlanguage and to the formal features of the L2, opportunities to produce output, and opportunities to receive feedback—are the core components of the interactionist approach and have been investigated in nearly a hundred empirical studies since the mid-1990s. Researchers have found that interaction and its concomitant features are beneficial for a range of morphosyntactic features, including articles (Muranoi, 2000; Sheen, 2007), questions (Mackey and Philp, 1998; Mackey, 1999; Philp, 2003), past-tense formation (Doughty and Varela, 1998; Ellis, 2007; Ellis, Loewen, and Erlam, 2006; McDonough, 2007), and plurals (Mackey, 2006a). These results appear to hold true for children as well as adults (Mackey and Oliver, 2002; Mackey and Silver, 2005; Van den Branden, 1997), classroom as well as laboratory settings (Gass et al., 2005; see Mackey and Goo, 2007 for a meta-analysis in this regard), and for a range of languages, including French (Ayoun, 2001; Swain and Lapkin, 1998, 2002), Japanese (Ishida, 2004; Iwashita, 2003), Korean (Jeon, 2007), and Spanish (de la Fuente, 2002; Gass and Alvarez Torres, 2005, reprinted 2011; Leeman, 2003).

The current research agenda has moved away from investigating *whether* interaction impacts L2 outcomes to determining: (a) which aspects of the L2 benefit the most from interaction; (b) how individual difference variables mediate the relationship between interaction and L2 development; and (c) what forms of interaction (and in particular, what types of feedback) are the most beneficial for L2 learners (how various types of interactional feedback differentially impact various L2 forms).

The question of whether interaction differentially affects L2 development, in other words, whether interaction (more specifically, interactional feedback) works for all L2 forms or only for some forms, but not others, has been raised by a number of recent researchers (e.g., Jeon, 2007; Long, 2007; Long et al., 1998; Mackey et al., 2000). In particular, it has been proposed that aspects of the L2 that possess both transparency and high communicative value (such as lexis)—in comparison with less salient and more complex features such as morphosyntax—may receive the greatest benefit from interaction. For example, in one recent study, Jeon (2007) compared the effects of interaction on a range of morphosyntactic and lexical targets in Korean. Using a controlled pre-test-post-test design, Jeon found that her Korean as a foreign language learners experienced more gains with the lexical targets (concrete nouns and action verbs) and one of the morphosyntactic targets (object relative clause constructions) than with the highly complex morphosyntactic target of honorific subject-verb agreement. Jeon suggested that the low saliency and communicative value of the latter target might have mitigated the effect of interaction. In light of these and similar findings, as well as the fact that few studies investigating the effects of interaction have addressed pragmatic and phonological targets (Mackey, 2007), further research will be needed in order to determine *what* interaction impacts and *why* some features are more amenable to interaction-driven learning than others.

Another goal of recent interaction-related research has been to determine *how* learner-internal cognitive mechanisms (such as attentional control and working memory capacity) mediate the relationship between interaction and L2 learning. It has long been noted that some learners appear to benefit more from interaction than others, and recent researchers have zeroed in on working memory capacity (WM) as a possible explanatory variable. Mackey et al. (2002), for example, found that WM was positively associated with the noticing of recasts in their study of native speakers of Japanese learning English. A later study by Trofimovich *et al.* (2007) did not find such a relationship, but did report that WM (along with attention control and analytical ability) was positively related to their Francophone learners' production of English morphosyntax. In an investigation of computer-delivered oral recasts, Sagarra (2007) found that WM was related to the amount of modified output produced by learners who received recasts and also to their L2 Spanish morphosyntactic development. Taken together, these studies suggest that WM may play an important role in the processing and use of recasts by L2 learners, but clearly more research is warranted in this area.

Another promising line of research deals with the impact of affective states on the processing of interactional feedback. Although this is an underexplored area, a number of researchers have provided evidence that one affective state in particular, anxiety, may hinder learners' ability to learn from corrective feedback (e.g., Havranek and Cesnik, 2001; Havranek, 2002; Sheen, 2008). As Sheen (2008) notes, "language anxiety can be predicted to interfere with learning because it inhibits learners' capacity to notice recasts and to produce modified output" (p. 846). This assertion is in line with recent work on emotion and executive control, which suggests that negative affective states may impair attentional allocation and behavioral performance (e.g., Pessoa, 2009). In her own study, Sheen (2008) found a relationship between language anxiety and learners' responses to recasts and the degree to which they improved their use of English articles.

Another line of research that has been productive in recent years centers on the use of interactive feedback, and in particular, recasts, for L2 development (see Loewen, Chapter 2, this volume for a comprehensive review of interactional feedback). A number of studies have sought to compare recasts with other forms of corrective feedback, such as prompts (Ammar and Spada, 2006; Ammar, 2008; Lyster and Izquierdo, 2009; Lyster, 2004), metalinguistic explanations (Ellis, 2007; Ellis *et al.*, 2006), and elicitations (Nassaji, 2009). Other studies have addressed learners' perceptions of recasts (e.g., Kim and Han, 2007; Mackey *et al.*, 2000, 2007) and possible factors that may influence learners' noticing and use of this form of feedback (e.g., Bigelow *et al.*, 2006; Egi, 2007; Philp, 2003; Sheen, 2006; Trofimovich *et al.*, 2007). This line of research continues to be an important part of interaction researchers' attempts to fully understand *which aspects* of interaction are the most beneficial for second/foreign language learners.

Data and common elicitation measures

Common elicitation measures in interaction research

The majority of studies to date that seek to test the claims of the interaction approach have employed quantitative methods, often using controlled pre-test-post-test designs. An increasing number of studies is also examining learners' internal processes more qualitatively, often focusing on their perceptions about interaction (through some sort of recall process, see for example, Gass and Mackey, 2000, and Mackey *et al.*, 2000). And although the specific data elicitation measures used are as varied as the foci of the studies themselves, in general two types of quantitative studies can be distinguished in interaction research: those focusing on the learners' productions and those investigating their perceptions.

One common type of production-based study involves having learners engage in communicative tasks in a laboratory or classroom setting. In these tasks, such as a map task, spot-the-difference, and story completion, participants typically hold different pieces of information and must communicate with each other in order to complete the task (Gass and Mackey, 2007b; Mackey and Gass, 2006). For example, in a spot-the-difference task, each participant possesses a different picture (which the other individuals cannot see); by asking questions about the location of different objects (e.g., "is there a cat on your windowsill?") and describing what they see in their own picture (e.g., "in my picture, there is a ball under the chair"), the participants determine the number of differences between the two pictures. If carefully designed, these tasks can target and elicit specific language structures (such as questions and locatives), allowing researchers to determine, for example, how different kinds of feedback or input during the tasks affect the learner's use of the targeted structures.

In these experimental studies, researchers commonly transcribe the dyadic interaction and code the data for different measures of development, such as advances along a developmental continuum (e.g., Mackey and Oliver, 2002; Mackey and Silver, 2005; Mackey, 1999; McDonough, 2005), suppliance of the target structure in obligatory contexts (e.g., Leeman, 2003), or multiple measures designed to tap into both implicit and explicit knowledge of the target structure (such as a grammaticality judgment test combined with an oral imitation or free production test, e.g., Ellis, 2007; Loewen and Nabei, 2007).

Those data analysis methods are also used in studies that focus on intact classrooms. In experimental research involving intact classes, different classes are typically assigned to different treatment or control conditions. Learner performance on various written and/or oral tests is compared across the classrooms to determine whether, for example, feedback significantly impacts L2 development, or whether one kind of feedback is more beneficial than another (e.g., Ammar and Spada, 2006; Lyster, 2004; Mackey, 2006a; Sheen, 2007). In more descriptive research involving intact classes, researchers video- or audio-record multiple class sessions, transcribe those sessions, and then determine the distribution and frequency of various feedback types and/or uptake opportunities (e.g., Loewen, 2009; Lyster and Ranta, 1997; Lyster, 1998a, b; Sato and Lyster, 2007). This method has also been used in laboratory contexts to explore the effect of age or interlocutor status on the provision of feedback (e.g., Mackey et al., 2003; Oliver, 2000, 2009).

The second main focus of interaction-related studies has been to investigate learners' perceptions. As Loewen et al. (2009) point out, learner beliefs "underlie learner behavior to a large extent … [and] might help explain and predict behaviors that learners demonstrate when learning an L2" (p. 91). Researchers have probed learners' preferred feedback types (e.g., Loewen et al., 2009), explored whether learners notice corrective feedback (e.g., Kim and Han, 2007; Mackey et al., 2000; 2007; Nabei and Swain, 2002; Philp, 2003), and have also sought to determine what features of corrective feedback, and in particular, recasts, are salient for L2 learners (e.g., Carpenter et al., 2006).

Many of these perception-based studies have employed an elicitation procedure new to interaction research, the stimulated recall (Gass and Mackey, 2000). In this procedure, learners typically engage in a communicative task. This task is video-recorded, and immediately afterwards, the learner and the researcher watch the recording together. At certain "critical moments" (for example, when the learner receives feedback), the researcher may pause the tape and ask questions such as "What was going through your mind at that point in time?" The purpose of this line of questioning is to orient the student to the previous task and gain information about the learner's thought processes and attentional foci at the time of the original task. This increasing use of introspective measures reflects a renewed interest in "in-depth research on individuals within their social contexts" (Mackey, 2006b, p. 371), a point which will be addressed in more detail later in this chapter. Recent research has focused more explicitly on immediate recalls (e.g., Philp, 2003) versus stimulated recalls. However, using stimulated recall and/or immediate recall is not without controversy (for a relevant summary of think-alouds, see Bowles, 2010).

Empirical verification

In addition to the research described above, one of the main ways that researchers have sought to verify the claims of the interactionist approach is through meta-analyses. As Norris and Ortega note (2006), "meta-analyses are conducted (a) on 'quantitative' domains of inquiry in which (b) considerable replication of specific independent, dependent, and moderating variables has occurred, and (c) for the specific purposes of clarifying the actual relationship among main study variables, as well as potentially moderating effects of contextual and other variables on this relationship" (p. 9). Though still relatively new to the field of second language acquisition, these meta-analyses have allowed researchers to compare the results of individual studies, and in the process, evaluate the claims of particular theoretical frameworks, such as the interactionist approach.

One of the first meta-analyses to investigate the claims of the interactionist approach was carried out by Keck *et al.* (2006). Their research examined 14 studies on task-based interaction published between 1980 and 2003. The researchers noted that experimental groups receiving task-based interaction significantly outperformed control and comparison groups on both post-tests and delayed post-tests. In addition, large effect sizes were reported for lexis and grammar, although the scarcity of studies employing long-term delayed post-tests (30–60 days) led the researchers to conclude that more research is needed to assess the durability of interaction-driven learning. Keck *et al.* (2006) ultimately concluded that "interaction does in fact promote acquisition" (p. 120) but in light of the restricted number of studies examined, also noted that "the effect of interaction may not apply to educational settings, learner populations, and target languages that, as of 2003, were unrepresented in the research domain" (p. 123). Another meta-analysis of interaction research was reported by Mackey and Goo (2007). Focusing on 28 experimental or quasi-experimental studies published between 1990 and 2006, including 11 which were also examined by Keck *et al.*, Mackey and Goo also sought to investigate the relationship between interaction and L2 development. They found *inter alia* that interaction was significantly more effective in promoting lexical and grammatical development than no interaction. In addition, large effect sizes were found on both post-tests and delayed post-tests, leading them to conclude that there are "durable interaction effects on language learning" (p. 425). However, Mackey and Goo observed that the interactional treatments appeared to be more effective for lexis than for grammar, especially in the short term. They also noted that more studies are needed in order to draw firm conclusions about the long-term effect of interaction-driven learning, the relative value of interaction with feedback (in comparison to interaction without feedback), and the contribution of modified output to L2 learning.

Meta-analyses conducted by Russell and Spada (2006), Li (2010), and Lyster and Saito (2010) on corrective feedback are also relevant for evaluating the claims of the interactionist approach because corrective feedback is one of the key features involved in interaction. Russell and Spada (2006) examined 15 experimental or quasi-experimental studies published between 1977 and 2003 in order to investigate the link between corrective feedback and development in L2 grammar. The researchers reported large effect sizes for oral and written corrective feedback in both classroom and laboratory contexts. With respect to the durability of the effects, Russell and Spada noted that "although the sample size is too small to permit firm conclusions, it seems that the effects of [corrective feedback] have not been considerably reduced over time" (p. 152). Similarly, Li (2010) reported a meta-analysis of research findings on corrective feedback. Thirty-three primary studies were meta-analyzed; a medium overall effect for corrective feedback was found. Li's meta-analysis also showed that explicit feedback was more effective than implicit feedback on both immediate and short-delayed post-tests, and feedback in foreign language contexts produced larger effect sizes than did feedback in second language contexts. Lyster and Saito (2010) conducted a meta-analysis of 15 classroom-based studies with a focus on corrective feedback. They also found that corrective feedback had durable effects on target language development (more so for prompts than recasts). Interestingly, younger learners benefited more from corrective feedback than did older learners.

In summary, data collection measures have been utilized to investigate whether and how interaction facilitates L2 learning in a number of production- and perception-based studies. As shown in recent meta-analyses, the interactionist approach has strong empirical support with a clear, sustained link between interaction/corrective feedback and the development of lexis and grammar. It remains an open question as to whether interaction promotes L2 development in other areas, such as phonology and pragmatics. More research should be conducted on these underexplored areas so that a more comprehensive picture of the role that interaction plays in L2 learning can be obtained. In addition, as noted by the authors of the meta-analyses cited above, there is a dire need for more longitudinal research. Although the effect sizes reported for delayed post-tests give cause for optimism, the field would benefit from greater use of long-term delayed post-tests. Controversies also remain concerning optimal feedback types (see Loewen, Chapter 2, this volume) and the contribution of individual difference and contextual factors, a point to which we return below.

Applications

Drawing upon Schmidt's arguments for the importance of noticing and Long's hypothesis that interaction and feedback serve to promote this noticing, researchers working within the tradition of the interactionist approach have also sought to determine what forms of instruction best promote an attention to *form* (the formal features of the L2, such as grammatical rules) within a communicative setting. The two pedagogical concepts that have garnered the most attention are task-based learning and focus-on-form instruction.

Broadly speaking, a task refers to "an activity which requires learners to use language, with emphasis on meaning, to attain an objective" (Bygate *et al.*, 2001, p. 11). Task-based learning is usually described as a form of communicative language teaching in which the primary emphasis is not on decontextualized grammar drills or rote memorization, but rather on giving learners ample opportunities to receive meaningful input, produce the target language in context, and receive feedback on their efforts by working collaboratively on a task (Ellis, 2003, 2009; Long, 2000; Samuda and Bygate, 2008). Unlike more traditional forms of communicative language teaching that have little or no focus on grammar, task-based learning emphasizes the importance of drawing learners' attention to interlanguage "gaps." Long (1991) has described this as *focus on form*: "overtly draw[ing] students' attention to linguistic elements as they arise incidentally in lessons whose overriding focus is on meaning or communication" (pp. 45–46).

While task-based learning has been the subject of much recent discussion (see for example, Samuda and Bygate, 2008 and Bygate and Samuda, 2009 for an overview of task pedagogy), a number of researchers have noted that the relationship between research and pedagogy is not a simple one (e.g., Crookes, 1997). For example, some researchers have suggested that results obtained from laboratory-based studies may not be generalizable to and relevant for the classroom context (e.g., Foster, 1998; see however, Gass *et al.*, 2005). Thus, as Ellis (2005) notes, researchers can offer suggestions about pedagogical practice but only "so long as this advice does not masquerade as prescriptions or proscriptions ... and so long as it is tentative" (p. 210). Task-based learning with a focus on form should not be seen as the "ideal" teaching method, but rather one possibility of many that may help second/foreign language students reach their linguistic goals.

With respect to the particular advice that has emerged from research on task-based learning, researchers have argued that both interaction and acquisition can be promoted through the use of particular types of tasks. Tasks can vary along a number of dimensions, including the task type, participant roles, and methods of implementation; each of these dimensions in turn can affect the amount of negotiation of meaning and feedback that occurs, as well as the fluency, accuracy, and complexity of the language used (Ellis, 2003; Samuda and Bygate, 2008; Willis and Willis, 2007). For this reason, being aware of the probable effects a particular type of task can have on learner-to-learner interaction and language use can help the practitioner make more informed decisions about classroom practice.

Concerning task type, it has been argued that closed tasks (where learners are required to agree on a particular outcome, also known as "convergent tasks") are more effective in promoting both negotiation of meaning and feedback than open tasks (where learners are not required to reach any agreement, also known as "divergent tasks") (e.g., Duff, 1986; Garcia, 2007; Long, 1989; Pica et al., 1993). Thus, for example, a problem-solving task (a type of closed task), where learners need to reach a consensus about a particular problem, will likely lead to more instances of negotiation of meaning and feedback than an opinion exchange (a type of open task). Similarly, "required exchange tasks" (which require that either one participant give information to another participant in order to complete the task, as in a one-way task, or that both participants exchange information, as in a two-way task) may elicit more negotiation of meaning and greater accuracy and complexity than "optional exchange tasks" (which do not have a requirement that information be transferred or exchanged) (Doughty and Pica, 1986; Foster and Skehan, 1996, 1999; Foster, 1998; Long, 1980, 1983a; Samuda and Bygate, 2008; Skehan and Foster, 1997, 1999).

Taken together, these studies suggest that tasks that are interactive and that have a definite outcome are beneficial for L2 learners. However, a legitimate question to ask at this point is whether all learners benefit equally from these types of tasks, and whether, for example, proficiency affects learners' ability to negotiate for meaning. Yule and MacDonald (1990) investigated this question by comparing mixed proficiency pairs (pairs in which one student was of higher proficiency than the other). In one condition, the higher proficiency student assumed the dominant role (for example, describing a delivery route); in the other, the higher proficiency played the non-dominant role (e.g., drawing the delivery route on a map). The researchers found that when the higher proficiency student took the non-dominant role, not only were the conversations longer, but there were also more negotiations for meaning and greater cooperation between the students. Other research has provided evidence that, for adults, more negotiation of meaning occurs in mixed proficiency pairs than in pairs with similar proficiency levels (e.g., Doughty and Pica, 1986; Gass and Varonis, 1985; see, however, conflicting findings for child learners in Oliver, 2002). Research examining the frequency of language-related episodes (instances when learners "talk about the language they are producing, question their language use, or correct themselves or others," Swain and Lapkin, 1998, p. 326) has also provided evidence that mixed proficiency pairs can be beneficial for L2 learners (Watanabe and Swain, 2007, for example, found that participants achieved higher post-test scores when working with a lower proficiency rather than higher proficiency partner).

In addition to task type and participant proficiency, tasks can also vary in terms of their implementation, such as whether students are given planning time prior to the task (Crookes, 1989; Foster, 2001; Foster and Skehan, 1996, 2009; Skehan and Foster, 1997; Yuan and Ellis, 2003), whether task repetition is involved (Bygate, 2001, 2009; Gass and Varonis, 1985; Plough and Gass, 1993; Yule et al., 1992), whether the interlocutors are familiar with each other (Plough and Gass, 1993), and of course, what type of feedback is provided during the task. The latter has been particularly well investigated in recent years (Ellis, 2003) and a large body of literature has emerged on the effect of different types of feedback moves (e.g., clarification requests, recasts, prompts, and explicit metalinguistic corrections) on students' noticing of feedback, their production of modified output, and their target language development.

With respect to the salience of different types of feedback moves, there is growing evidence that recasts (and in particular, those that are long, not prosodically enhanced, contain one or more corrections, and are focused on morphological rather than lexical errors) may not be noticed by L2 learners, especially by those who are not developmentally ready or who possess relatively small WM capacities (e.g., Ammar, 2008; Ellis and Sheen, 2006; Leeman, 2003; Lyster and Ranta, 1997; Mackey *et al.*, 2000, 2002; Panova and Lyster, 2002). Additional research has sought to determine whether the degree of explicitness of the feedback technique affects either the amount of modified output produced or the degree of interlanguage development. These studies have reported conflicting results, with some supporting the use of more explicit techniques (e.g., Ammar and Spada, 2006; Ayoun, 2001; Carroll and Swain, 1993; Doughty and Varela, 1998; Ellis, 2007; Ellis *et al.*, 2006; Lyster, 2004; Nassaji, 2009; Sachs and Polio, 2007; Sauro, 2009) and others finding no difference (e.g., Loewen and Erlam, 2006; Loewen and Nabei, 2007; Lyster and Izquierdo, 2009; Sachs and Suh, 2007). On the whole, it appears that in meaning-focused classrooms (as opposed to laboratories), students notice and benefit from more explicit feedback techniques, but it needs to be kept in mind that there is no "one size fits all" form of feedback that will work for all learners in all contexts (Ammar and Spada, 2006).

Future directions

In the three decades since the formulation of the interactionist approach, a broad research agenda on interaction and L2 learning has emerged. In this section, we will provide some suggestions to push the field forward both in the short and long term, focusing on methodological issues and the role of context.

As reviewed above, there is now a solid body of literature linking the various components of interaction to L2 development. However, studies employing long-term delayed post-tests (30 or more days) remain relatively uncommon. For this reason, it remains an empirical question as to whether interaction leads to permanent restructuring of learner interlanguages (Spada and Lightbown, 2009). In addition, replication studies of interaction-related research, as is the case with replications in the field as a whole, are also rare. Given the increased importance the field of SLA is placing on replications and validating the findings of previous studies, we believe that greater emphasis should be placed on this form of research. As noted by the Language Teaching Review Panel (2008):

> Replication is even more needed today than before given that our field is becoming increasingly diverse in scope and investigation of topics, resulting in divergent and at times fragmented research results. Replication studies can verify and consolidate previous findings, helping results to be converged and extended. Thus, they must be more valued, encouraged and carried out in our field. (p. 11)

While a greater number of longitudinal and replication studies is (hopefully) easy to achieve in the short term, we also see a number of possible methodological advances on the (longer-term) horizon. As pointed out by Mackey (2006b), inter-disciplinary collaboration between interaction researchers and cognitive neuroscientists could facilitate the use of such technologies as electroencephalography (EEG) and functional magnetic resonance imaging (fMRI) to explore learners' responses to, and thus noticing of, recasts, for example, or issues related to the impact of individual variation in working memory capacity on the noticing and processing of interactional feedback.

With respect to the role of context, there are a number of research directions that would enrich our understanding of interaction and L2 learning. Traditionally, contextual factors (such as the social relationship between the interlocutors and the setting in which the conversation occurred) have not received focal attention in the interaction literature. Long (1998) has argued that "chang[ing] the social setting altogether, e.g., from street to classroom, or from a foreign to a second language environment, and, as far as we know, the way the learner acquires does not change much either" (p. 93). However, there is a growing suggestion that the interactionist approach might profitably expand its focus from the cognitive aspects of interaction to include more sociocognitive ones (e.g., Bayley and Tarone, Chapter 3, this volume; Tarone, 2009). As Philp and Mackey (in press) point out, the social relationship between interlocutors may influence the type of language the learner receives, the output the learner produces and the degree to which the learner pays attention to any feedback given. The context may also influence the degree to which learners pay attention to language forms (in an informal context, for example, learners are likely to privilege meaning and communication over grammatical accuracy, as pointed out by Tarone, 2009). Thus, further research exploring the mediating effect of context on interaction-driven learning would be a welcome development.

Questions concerning contextual influence have also arisen in recent studies on synchronous computer-mediated communication (SCMC) as well as research involving avatars as interactors (Petersen and Mackey, 2009). Recognizing the growing role that SCMC and other education technology is taking in the classroom, recent researchers have sought to determine whether the claims of the interactionist approach hold true in this new medium (see Ortega, 2009 for a recent overview). Unlike face-to-face interaction, SCMC involves less strict turn adjacency in conversation. The disrupted turn adjacency of SCMC is caused by "split negotiation routines" (Smith, 2003, p. 48), in other words, a long delay between the initial trigger and the indicator, and they produce multiple turn delays between each of the phrases of the routine (Smith, 2005). Additionally, the relatively less strict turn adjacency results in recasts not being provided immediately after the target turn but with 3–4 turns in between. Thus, the gap between the recasts and the target produce non-contingent recasts (Lai and Zhao, 2006). While recent studies have shed valuable light on how the disrupted turn adjacency of SCMC impacts interaction-driven L2 learning, the studies available at present are "insufficient in number and inconsistent in design and focus, and thus preclude firm conclusions" (Oretga, 2009, p. 245). For this reason, more research that explores negotiation of meaning, feedback, and output in this new medium would help us reach a deeper understanding of contextual factors in L2 learning.

In addition to these contextual matters, it is also of crucial importance to explore the many individual difference variables that mediate the relationship between interaction and learning. By investigating both learner-internal factors (such as WM and affect) and learner-external factors (such as the social context), researchers will be able to reach a deeper understanding of the complex role that interaction, feedback, output, and attention play in the development of a non-native language. As of now, we have "yet to achieve a complete understanding of what interaction can offer L2 learners and interaction interacts with other factors to impact the efficacy of interaction on L2 learning" (Mackey and Polio, 2009, p. 7). However, given the vitality of this area of research and the promising steps that have been made in the last 30 years, new insights and discoveries are doubtless close on the horizon.

References

Ammar, A. (2008). Prompts and recasts: Differential effects on second language morphosyntax. *Language Teaching Research*, *12*, 183–210.

Ammar, A. and Spada, N. (2006). One size fits all? Recasts, prompts, and L2 learning. *Studies in Second Language Acquisition, 28*, 543–574.

Ayoun, D. (2001). The role of negative and positive feedback in the second language acquisition of the *passé composé* and *imparfait. The Modern Language Journal, 85*, 226–243.

Bigelow, M., Delmas, R., Hansen, K., and Tarone, E. (2006). Literacy and the processing of oral recasts in SLA. *TESOL Quarterly, 40*, 665–689.

Bowles, M. (2010). *The think-aloud controversy in second language research.* New York: Routledge.

Bygate, M. (2001). Effects of task repetition on the structure and control of language. In M. Bygate, P. Skehan, and M. Swain (Eds.), *Task-based learning: Language teaching, learning and assessment* (pp. 23–48). London: Longman.

Bygate, M. (2009). Effects of task repetition on the structure and control of oral language. In K. Van den Branden, M. Bygate, and J. Norris (Eds.), *Task-based language teaching: A reader* (pp. 249–274). Amsterdam: John Benjamins.

Bygate, M. and Samuda, V. (2009). Creating pressure in task pedagogy: The joint roles of field, purpose, and engagement within the interaction approach. In A. Mackey and C. Polio (Eds.), *Multiple perspectives on interaction: Second language research in honor of Susan M. Gass* (pp. 93–116). New York: Routledge.

Bygate, M., Skehan, P., and Swain, M. (2001). *Researching pedagogic tasks: Second language learning, teaching and testing.* Harlow, England: Longman.

Carpenter, H., Jeon, K.S., MacGregor, D., and Mackey, A. (2006). Learners' interpretations of recasts. *Studies in second language acquisition, 28*, 209–236.

Carroll, S. and Swain, S. (1993). Explicit and implicit negative feedback: an empirical study of the learning of linguistic generalizations. *Studies in second language acquisition, 15*, 357–386.

Crookes, G. (1989). Planning and interlanguage variability. *Studies in second language acquisition, 11*, 367–383.

Crookes, G. (1997). SLA and language pedagogy: A socioeducational perspective. *Studies in second language acquisition, 20*, 93–116.

de la fuente, M. (2002). Negotiation and oral acquisition of L2 vocabulary: the roles of input and output in the receptive and productive acquisition of words. *Studies in second language acquisition, 24*, 81–112.

Doughty, C. and Pica, T. (1986). "Information gap" tasks: an aid to acquisition? *TESOL Quarterly, 20*, 305–325.

Doughty, C. and Varela, E. (1998). Communicative focus on form. In C. J. Doughty and J. Williams (Eds.), *Focus on form in classroom second language acquisition* (pp. 114–138). New York: Cambridge University Press.

Duff, P. (1986). Another look at interlanguage talk: Taking task to task. In R. Day (Ed.), *Talking to learn: Conversation in second language acquisition* (pp. 147–181). Rowley, MA: Newbury House.

Egi, T. (2007). Interpreting recasts as linguistic evidence: The roles of linguistic target, length, and degree of change. *Studies in Second Language Acquisition, 29*, 511–537.

Ellis, R. (1999). *Learning a second language through interaction.* Amsterdam: John Benjamins.

Ellis, R. (2003). *Task-based language learning and teaching.* Oxford: Oxford University Press.

Ellis, R. (2005). Principles of instructed language learning. *System, 33*, 209–224.

Ellis, R. (2007). The differential effects of corrective feedback on two grammatical structures. In A. Mackey (Ed.), *Conversational interaction in second language acquisition: A collection of empirical studies* (pp. 339–360). Oxford: Oxford University Press.

Ellis, R. (2009). Task-based language teaching: Sorting out the misunderstandings. *International Journal of Applied Linguistics, 19*, 221–246.

Ellis, R., Loewen, S., and Erlam, R. (2006). Implicit and explicit corrective feedback and the acquisition of L2 grammar. *Studies in Second Language Acquisition, 28*, 339–368.

Ellis, R. and Sheen, Y. (2006). Reexamining the role of recasts in second language acquisition. *Studies in Second Language Acquisition, 28*, 575–600.

Ferguson, C. (1971). Absence of copula and the notion of simplicity: A study of normal speech, baby talk, foreigner talk and pidgins. In D. Hymes (Ed.), *Pidginization and creolization of languages* (pp. 117–140). Cambridge: Cambridge University Press.

Foster, P. (1998). A classroom perspective on the negotiation of meaning. *Applied Linguistics, 19*, 1–23.

Foster, P. (2001). Rules and routines: A consideration of their role in task-based language production of native and non-native speakers. In M. Bygate, P. Skehan, and M. Swain (Eds.), *Researching pedagogic tasks, second language learning, teaching and testing* (pp. 75–97). Harlow: Longman.

Foster, P. and Skehan, P. (1996). The influence of planning and task type on second language performance. *Studies in Second Language Acquisition, 18,* 299–323.

Foster, P. and Skehan, P. (1999). The influence of planning and focus of planning on task-based performance. *Language Teaching Research, 3,* 215–247.

Foster, P. and Skehan, P. (2009). The influence of planning and task type on second language performance. In K. Van den Branden, M. Bygate, and J. Norris (Eds.), *Task-based language teaching: A reader* (pp. 275–300). Amsterdam: John Benjamins.

Garcia, M.F. (2007). Tasks, negotiation, and L2 learning in a foreign language context. In M. Mayo (Ed.), *Investigating tasks in formal language learning* (pp. 69–90). Clevedon, UK: Multilingual Matters.

Gass, S. and Mackey, A. (2000). *Stimulated recall methodology in second language research.* Mahwah, NJ: Lawrence Erlbaum.

Gass, S. and Mackey, A. (2007a). Input, interaction, and output in second language acquisition. In B. VanPatten and J. Williams (Eds.), *Theories in second language acquisition: An introduction* (pp. 175–200). Mahwah, NJ: Lawrence Erlbaum.

Gass, S. and Mackey, A. (2007b). *Data elicitation for second and foreign language research.* Mahwah, NJ: Lawrence Erlbaum.

Gass, S., Mackey, A., and Ross-Feldman, L. (2005). Task-based interactions in classroom and laboratory settings. *Language Learning (The best of Language Learning Series), 61,* 189–220.

Gass, S. and Alvarez Torres, M. (2005). Attention when? An investigation of the ordering effect of input and interaction. *Studies in Second Language Acquisition, 27,* 1–31.

Gass, S. and Varonis, E. (1985). Variation in native speaker speech modification to non-native speakers. *Studies in Second Language Acquisition, 7,* 37–58.

Gass, S. and Varonis, E. (1986). Sex differences in nonnative speaker—nonnative speaker interaction. In R. Day (Ed.), *Talking to learn: Conversation in second language acquisition* (pp. 327–351). Rowley, MA: Newbury House.

Hatch, E. (1978b). Discourse analysis and second language acquisition. In E. Hatch (Ed.), *Second language acquisition: A book of readings* (pp. 401–435). Rowley, MA: Newbury House.

Hatch, E. (1987a). Acquisition of syntax in a second language. In J. Richards (Ed.), *Understanding second and foreign language learning: Issues and approaches* (pp. 34–70). Rowley, MA: Newbury House.

Havranek, G. (2002). When is corrective feedback most likely to succeed? *International Journal of Educational Research, 37,* 225–270.

Havranek, G. and Cesnik, H. (2001). Factors affecting the success of corrective feedback. *EUROSLA Yearbook, 1,* 99–122.

Ishida, M. (2004). Effects of recasts on the acquisition of the aspectual form of *–te i (ru)* by learners of japanese as a foreign language. *Language Learning, 54,* 311–394.

Iwashita, N. (2003). Negative feedback and positive feedback in task-based interaction: Differential effects of L2 development. *Studies in Second Language Acquisition, 25,* 1–36.

Jeon, K. (2007). Interaction-driven L2 learning: Characterizing linguistic development. In A. Mackey (Ed.), *Conversation interaction in second language acquisition: A collection of empirical studies* (pp. 379–403). Oxford: Oxford University Press.

Keck, C., Iberri-Shea, G., Tracy-Ventura, N., and Wa-Mbaleka, S. (2006). Investigating the empirical link between task-based interaction and acquisition: A quantitative meta-analysis. In J. Norris and L. Ortega (Eds.), *Synthesizing research on language learning and teaching* (pp. 91–131). Amsterdam: John Benjamins.

Kim, J.-H. and Han, Z. (2007). Recasts in communicative EFL classes: Do teacher intent and learner interpretation overlap?. In A. Mackey (Ed.), *Conversational interaction in second language acquisition: A collection of empirical studies* (pp. 269–297). Oxford: Oxford University Press.

Krashen, S. (1977). Some issues relating to the monitor model. In H. Brown, C. Yorio, and R. Crymes (Eds.), *On TESOL '77* (pp. 144–158). Washington, D.C.: TESOL.

Krashen, S. (1980). The input hypothesis. In J. Alatis (Ed.), *Current issues in bilingual education* (pp. 168–180). Washington, D.C.: Georgetown University Press.

Language Teaching Review Panel. (2008). Replication studies in language learning and teaching: Questions and answers. *Language Teaching, 41,* 1–14.

Lai, C. and Zhao, Y. (2006). Noticing in text-based online chat. *Language Learning and Technology, 10*(3), 102–120.

Leeman, J. (2003). Recasts and L2 development: Beyond negative evidence. *Studies in Second Language Acquisition, 25,* 37–63.

Li, S. (2010). The effectiveness of corrective feedback in SLA: A meta-analysis. *Language Learning*, *60*(2), 309–365.

Loewen, S. (2009). Recasts in multiple response focus on form episodes. In A. Mackey and C. Polio (Eds.), *Multiple perspectives on interaction: Second language research in honor of Susan M. Gass* (pp. 176–196). New York: Routledge.

Loewen, S. and Erlam, R. (2006). Corrective feedback in the chatroom: An experimental study. *Computer Assisted Language Learning*, *19*, 1–14.

Loewen, S., Li, S., Fei, F., Thompson, A., Nakatsukasa, K., and Ahn, S. (2009). Second language learners' beliefs about grammar instruction and error correction. *The Modern Language Journal*, *93*, 91–104.

Loewen, S. and Nabei, T. (2007). Measuring the effects of oral corrective feedback on L2 knowledge. In A. Mackey (Ed.), *Conversational interaction in second language acquisition: A collection of empirical studies* (pp. 361–377). Oxford: Oxford University Press.

Long, M. (1980). *Input and interaction in second language acquisition*. Unpublished PhD dissertation. University of California at Los Angeles.

Long, M. (1981). Input, interaction, and second language acquisition. In H. Winitz (Ed.), *Native language and Foreign language acquisition: Annals of the New York Academy of Science* (Vol. *379*, 259–278).

Long, M. (1983a). Linguistic and conversational adjustments to non-native speakers. *Studies in Second Language Acquisition*, *5*, 177–193.

Long, M. (1983b). Native speaker/non-native speaker conversation in the second language classroom. In M. Clarke and J. Handscombe (Eds.), *Pacific perspective on language learning and teaching* (pp. 207–225). Washington, D.C.: TESOL.

Long, M. (1989). Task, group, and task-group interaction. *University of Hawaii Working Papers in English as a Second Language*, *8*, 1–26.

Long, M. (1991). Focus on form: A design feature in language teaching methodology. In K. de Bot, R. Ginsberg, and C. Kramsch (Eds.), *Foreign language research in cross-cultural perspective* (pp. 39–52). Amsterdam: John Benjamins.

Long, M. (1996). The role of the linguistic environment in second language acquisition. In W.C. Ritchie and T.K. Bhatia (Eds.), *Handbook of second language acquisition* (pp. 413–468). San Diego, CA: Academic Press.

Long, M. (1998). SLA: Breaking the siege. *University of Hawai'i Working Papers in ESL*, *17*, 79–129.

Long, M. (2000). Focus on form in task-based language teaching. In R. Lambert and E. Shohamy (Eds.), *Language policy and pedagogy: Essays in honor of A. Ronald Walton* (pp. 179–192). Amsterdam: John Benjamins.

Long, M. (2007). *Problems in SLA*. Mahwah, NJ: Lawrence Erlbaum.

Long, M., Inagaki, S., and Ortega, L. (1998). The role of implicit negative feedback in SLA: Models and recasts in japanese and spanish. *The Modern Language Journal*, *82*, 357–371.

Loschky, L. (1994). Comprehensible input and second language acquisition: What is the relationship?. *Studies in Second Language Acquisition*, *16*, 303–323.

Lyster, R. (1998a). Negotiation of form, recasts, and explicit correction in relation to error types and learner repair in immersion classrooms. *Language Learning*, *48*, 183–218.

Lyster, R. (1998b). Recasts, repetition, and ambiguity in L2 classroom discourse. *Studies in Second Language Acquisition*, *20*, 51–92.

Lyster, R. (2004). Differential effects of prompts and recasts in form-focused instruction. *Studies in Second Language Acquisition*, *26*, 399–432.

Lyster, R. and Izquierdo, J. (2009). Prompts versus recasts in dyadic interaction. *Language Learning*, *59*, 453–498.

Lyster, R. and Ranta, L. (1997). Corrective feedback and learner uptake: Negotiation of form in communicative classrooms. *Studies in Second Language Acquisition*, *19*, 27–66.

Lyster, R. and Saito, K. (2010). Oral feedback in classroom SLA: A meta-analysis. *Studies in Second Language Acquisition*, *32*, 265–302.

Mackey, A. (1999). Input, interaction, and second language development: An empirical study of question formation in ESL. *Studies in Second Language Acquisition*, *21*, 557–587.

Mackey, A. (2006a). Feedback, noticing and instructed second language learning. *Applied Linguistics*, *27*, 405–430.

Mackey, A. (2006b). From introspections, brain scans, and memory tests to the role of social context: Advancing research on interaction and learning. *Studies in Second Language Acquisition*, *28*, 369–379.

Mackey, A. (2007). Introduction: The role of conversational interaction in second language acquisition. In A. Mackey (Ed.), *Conversational interaction in second language acquisition: A collection of empirical studies* (pp. 1–26). Oxford: Oxford University Press.

Mackey, A. and Abbuhl, R. (2006). Input and interaction. In C. Sanz (Ed.), *Mind and context in adult second language acquisition: Methods, theory, and practice* (pp. 207–233). Washington, D.C.: Georgetown University Press.

Mackey, A., Al-Khalil, M., Atanassova, G., Hama, M., Logan-Terry, A., and Nakatsukasa, K. (2007). Teachers' intentions and learners' perceptions about corrective feedback in the L2 classroom. *Innovation in Language Learning and Teaching, 1,* 129–152.

Mackey, A. and Gass, S. (2006). *Second language research: Methodology and design.* Mahwah, NJ: Lawrence Erlbaum.

Mackey, A., Gass, S., and McDonough, K. (2000). How do learners perceive interactional feedback?. *Studies in Second Language Acquisition, 22,* 471–497.

Mackey, A. and Goo, J. (2007). Interaction research in SLA: A meta-analysis and research synthesis. In A. Mackey (Ed.), *Conversational interaction in second language acquisition: A collection of empirical studies* (pp. 407–452). Oxford: Oxford University Press.

Mackey, A. and Oliver, R. (2002). Interactional feedback and children's L2 development. *System, 30,* 459–477.

Mackey, A., Oliver, R., and Leeman, J. (2003). Interactional input and the incorporation of feedback: An exploration of NS-NNS and NNS-NNS adult and child dyads. *Language Learning, 53,* 35–66.

Mackey, A. and Philp, J. (1998). Conversational interaction and second language development: Recasts, responses, and red herrings? *The Modern Language Journal, 82,* 338–356.

Mackey, A., Philp, J., Egi, T., Fujii, A., and Tatsumi, T. (2002). Individual differences in working memory, noticing of interactional feedback, and L2 development. In P. Robinson (Ed.), *Individual differences and instructed language learning* (pp. 181–210). Amsterdam: John Benjamins.

Mackey, A. and Polio, C. (2009). Introduction. In A. Mackey and C. Polio (Eds.), *Multiple perspectives on interaction: Second language research in honor of Susan M. Gass* (pp. 1–10). New York: Routledge.

Mackey, A. and Silver, R. (2005). Interactional tasks and english L2 learning by immigrant children in singapore. *System, 33,* 239–260.

McDonough, K. (2005). Identifying the impact of negative feedback and learners' responses on ESL question development. *Studies in Second Language Acquisition, 27,* 79–103.

McDonough, K. (2007). Interactional feedback and the emergence of simple past activity verbs in L2 English. In A. Mackey (Ed.), *Conversational interaction in second language acquisition: A collection of empirical studies* (pp. 323–338). Oxford: Oxford University Press.

Muranoi, H. (2000). Focus on form through interaction enhancement: Integrating formal instruction into a communicative task in EFL classrooms. *Language Learning, 50,* 617–673.

Nabei, I. and Swain, M. (2002). Learner awareness of recasts in classroom interaction: A case study of an adult EFL student's second language learning. *Language Awareness, 11,* 43–63.

Nassaji, H. (2009). Effects of recasts and elicitations in dyadic interaction and the role of feedback explicitness. *Language Learning, 59,* 411–452.

Norris, J.M. and Ortega, L. (2006). The value and practice of research synthesis for language learning and teaching. In J.M. Norris and L. Ortega (Eds.), *Synthesizing research on language learning and teaching* (pp. 3–50). Amsterdam: John Benjamins.

Oliver, R. (2000). Age differences in negotiation and feedback in classroom and pairwork. *Language Learning, 50,* 119–151.

Oliver, R. (2002). The patterns of negotiation for meaning in child interactions. *The Modern Language Journal, 86,* 97–111.

Oliver, R. (2009). How young is too young? Investigating negotiation of meaning and feedback in children aged five to seven years. In A. Mackey and C. Polio (Eds.), *Multiple perspectives on interaction: Second language research in honor of Susan M. Gass* (pp. 135–156). New York: Routledge.

Ortega, L. (2009). Interaction and attention to form in L2 text-based computer-mediated communication. In A. Mackey and C. Polio (Eds.), *Multiple perspectives on interaction: second language research in honor of Susan M. Gass* (pp. 226–253). New York: Routledge.

Panova, L. and Lyster, R. (2002). Patterns of corrective feedback and uptake in an adult ESL classroom. *TESOL Quarterly, 36,* 573–595.

Pessoa, L. (2009). How do emotion and motivation direct executive control? *Trends in Cognitive Sciences, 13,* 160–166.

Petersen, K. and Mackey, A. (2009). Interaction, Modality and Learning: Comparing the Effectiveness of Computer-Generated and Face to Face Recasts. Paper presented at SLRF, October, Michigan State University.

Philp, J. (2003). Constraints on "noticing the gap": Non-native speakers' noticing of recasts in NS-NNS interaction. *Studies in Second Language Acquisition, 25,* 99–126.

Philp, J. and Mackey, A. (in press). Interaction research: What can socially informed approaches offer to cognitivists (and vice versa)? In R. Batstone (Ed.), *Sociocognitive aspects of second language learning and teaching.* Oxford: Oxford University Press.

Pica, T. and Doughty, C. (1985). The role of group work in classroom second language acquisition. *Studies in Second Language Acquisition, 7,* 233–248.

Pica, T., Kanagy, R., and Falodun, J. (1993). Choosing and using communication tasks for second language instruction and research. In G. Crookes and S. Gass (Eds.), *Tasks and language learning: Integrating theory and practice* (pp. 9–34). Clevedon, UK: Multilingual Matters.

Pica, T., Young, R., and Doughty, C. (1987). The impact of interaction on comprehension. *TESOL Quarterly, 21,* 737–758.

Plough, I. and Gass, S. (1993). Interlocutor and task familiarity: Effects on interactional structure. In G. Crookes and S. Gass (Eds.), *Tasks and language learning: Integrating theory and practice* (pp. 35–55). Clevedon, UK: Multilingual Matters.

Porter, P. (1986). How learners talk to each other: Input and interaction in task-centered discussions. In R. Day (Ed.), *Talking to learn: Conversation in second language acquisition* (pp. 200–222). Rowley, MA: Newbury House.

Russell, J. and Spada, N. (2006). The effectiveness of corrective feedback for the acquisition of L2 grammar: A meta-analysis of the research. In J. Norris and L. Ortega (Eds.), *Synthesizing research on language learning and teaching* (pp. 133–164). Amsterdam: John Benjamins.

Sachs, R. and Polio, C. (2007). Learners' uses of two types of written feedback on a L2 revision task. *Studies in Second Language Acquisition, 29,* 67–100.

Sachs, R. and Suh, B.-R. (2007). Textually enhanced recasts, learner awareness, and L2 outcomes in synchronous computer-mediated interaction. In A. Mackey (Ed.), *Conversational interaction in second language acquisition: A collection of empirical studies* (pp. 199–227). Oxford: Oxford University Press.

Sagarra, N. (2007). From CALL to face-to-face interaction: The effect of computer-delivered recasts and working memory on L2 development. In A. Mackey (Ed.), *Conversational interaction in second language acquisition: A collection of empirical studies* (pp. 229–248). Oxford: Oxford University Press.

Samuda, V. and Bygate, M. (2008). *Tasks in second language learning.* Hampshire, England: Palgrave Macmillan.

Sato, M. and Lyster, R. (2007). Modified output of japanese EFL learners: Variable effects of interlocutor vs. Feedback types. In A. Mackey (Ed.), *Conversational interaction in second language acquisition: A series of empirical studies* (pp. 123–142). Oxford: Oxford University Press.

Sauro, S. (2009). Computer-mediated corrective feedback and the development of L2 grammar. *Language Learning and Technology, 13,* 96–120.

Schmidt, R. (1990). The role of consciousness is second language learning. *Applied Linguistics, 11,* 129–158.

Schmidt, R. (1993). Awareness and second language acquisition. *Annual Review of Applied Linguistics, 13,* 206–226.

Sheen, Y. (2006). Exploring the relationship between characteristics of recasts and learner uptake. *Language Teaching Research, 10,* 361–392.

Sheen, Y. (2007). The effects of corrective feedback, language aptitude and learner attitudes on the acquisition of english articles. In A. Mackey (Ed.), *Conversational interaction in second language acquisition: A series of empirical studies* (pp. 301–322). Oxford: Oxford University Press.

Sheen, Y. (2008). Recasts, language anxiety, modified output and L2 learning. *Language Learning, 58,* 835–874.

Skehan, P. and Foster, P. (1997). Task type and task processing conditions as influences on foreign language performance. *Language Teaching Research, 1,* 185–211.

Skehan, P. and Foster, P. (1999). The influence of task structure and processing conditions on narrative retellings. *Language Learning, 49,* 93–120.

Smith, B. (2003). Computer-mediated negotiated interaction: An expanded model. *The Modern Language Journal, 87,* 38–57.

Smith, B. (2005). The relationship between negotiated interaction, learner uptake, and lexical acquisition in task-based computer-mediated communication. *TESOL Quarterly, 39,* 33–58.

Spada, N. and Lightbown, P. (2009). Interaction research in second/foreign language classrooms. In A. Mackey and C. Polio (Eds.), *Multiple perspectives on interaction: Second language research in honor of Susan M. Gass* (pp. 157–175). New York: Routledge.

Swain, M. (1985). Communicative competence: Some roles of comprehensible input and comprehensible output in its development. In S. Gass and C. Madden (Eds.), *Input in second language acquisition* (pp. 235–253). Rowley, MA: Newbury House.

Swain, M. (1995). Three functions of output in second language learning. In G. Cook and B. Seidlhofer (Eds.), *Principle and practice in applied linguistics: Studies in honour of henry G. Widdowson* (pp. 125–144). Oxford: Oxford University Press.

Swain, M. (2005). The output hypothesis: Theory and research. In E. Hinkel (Ed.), *Handbook of research in second language teaching and learning* (pp. 471–483). Mahwah, NJ: Lawrence Erlbaum Associates.

Swain, M. and Lapkin, S. (1998). Interaction and second language learning: Two adolescent french immersion students working together. *The Modern Language Journal, 82*, 320–337.

Swain, M. and Lapkin, S. (2002). Talking it through: Two french immersion learners' response to reformulation. *International Journal of Education Research, 37*, 285–304.

Tarone, E. (2009). A variationist perspective on the interaction approach. In A. Mackey and C. Polio (Eds.), *Multiple perspectives on interaction: Second language research in honor of Susan M. Gass* (pp. 41–57). New York: Routledge.

Trofimovich, P., Ammar, A., and Gatbonton, E. (2007). How effective are recasts? The role of attention, memory, and analytical ability. In A. Mackey (Ed.), *Conversational interaction in second language acquisition: A collection of empirical studies* (pp. 171–195). Oxford: Oxford University Press.

Van den Branden, K. (1997). Effects of negotiation of language learners' output. *Language Learning, 47*, 589–636.

VanPatten, B. (1989). Can learners attend to form and content while processing input?. *Hispania, 72*, 409–417.

Varonis, E. and Gass, S. (1985). Non-native/non-native conversations: A model for negotiation of meaning. *Applied Linguistics, 6*, 71–90.

Wagner-Gough, J. and Hatch, E. (1975). The importance of input data in second language acquisition studies. *Language Learning, 25*, 297–307.

Watanabe, Y. and Swain, M. (2007). Effects of proficiency differences and patterns of pair interaction on second language learning: Collaborative dialogue between adult ESL learners. *Language Teaching Research, 11*, 121–142.

White, L. (1991). Adverb placement in second language acquisition: Some effects of positive and negative evidence in the classroom. *Second Language Research, 7*, 133–161.

Yuan, F. and Ellis, R. (2003). The effects of pre-task planning and on-line planning on fluency, complexity and accuracy in L2 monologic oral production. *Applied Linguistics, 24*, 1–27.

White, L. (2003). *Second language acquisition and universal grammar*. Cambridge: Cambridge University Press.

Willis, D. and Willis, J. (2007). *Doing task-based teaching*. Oxford: Oxford University Press.

Yule, G. and Macdonald, D. (1990). Resolving referential conflict in L2 interaction: The effect of proficiency and interactive role. *Language Learning, 40*, 539–556.

Yule, G., Powers, M., and Macdonald, D. (1992). The variable effects of some task-based learning procedures on L2 communicative effectiveness. *Language Learning, 42*, 249–277.

2

The role of feedback

Shawn Loewen

Historical discussion

Negative feedback in second language (L2) learning has been of considerable interest to SLA researchers, generating a substantial amount of research (Ammar and Spada, 2006; Ellis *et al.*, 2001; Ellis *et al.*, 2006; Ishida, 2004; Iwashita, 2003; Leeman, 2007; Loewen, 2005; Loewen and Philp, 2006; Lyster and Izquierdo, 2009; Lyster and Ranta, 1997; Mackey, 1999; Mackey and Philp, 1998; Nassaji, 2009; Philp, 2003; Sheen, 2008; *inter alia*). Negative feedback, also known as corrective feedback and error correction, has typically been defined as information provided to learners about the ill-formedness of their L2 production. Feedback may occur in response to learners' oral or written production, with oral feedback usually occurring immediately during interaction while written feedback is often provided some time after a text has been produced. Because of the differences in modality and timing of feedback, only oral feedback will be considered in this chapter. For a comprehensive overview of written feedback, see Polio (Chapter 19, this volume).

Before considering the role of feedback in L2 acquisition, it is important to note that negative feedback, particularly recasts, has been investigated in first language (L1) acquisition. Studies of child-adult interaction have found corrective feedback to occur; nevertheless, considerable debate surrounds the efficacy of corrective feedback for L1 learning (e.g., Bohannon *et al.*, 1996; Farrar, 1992; Morgan *et al.*, 1995; Saxton, 2005). Similarly, negative feedback has assumed an important, although controversial, role within communicative approaches to L2 instruction as a means of drawing learners' attention to accurate language use without disrupting communicative classroom interaction. Historically, communicative language teaching generally rejected negative feedback because it was viewed as hindering learners' attempts to communicate freely as well as being ineffective for developing implicit L2 knowledge (e.g., Krashen, 1985). However, research in content-based and immersion instruction contexts revealed that while learners often reached high levels of L2 fluency, they did not achieve correspondingly high levels of grammatical accuracy, even on frequently occurring linguistic structures. Consequently, researchers began to reconsider the role of explicit attention to language in the classroom.

Negative feedback fits broadly within the research interests of instructed SLA (Williams, Chapter 33, this volume), with theoretical support coming from an information processing view of SLA, concerned with L2 input, intake, mental representations, and output. In particular, interactionist approaches to SLA value the role of negative feedback (Gass, 1997; Gass and Mackey, 2007). Additionally, several theoretical perspectives such as socio-cultural theory (Lantolf and Thorne, 2007; Ohta, 2000) and skill acquisition theory (DeKeyser, 2007) posit roles for feedback. However, because of the extensive investigation of feedback from an interactionist paradigm, this review will concentrate on that approach.

Early interactionist studies identified negotiation of meaning as an important component of the learning process, as L2 learners and their interlocutors interactionally modified their utterances in an attempt to achieve mutual understanding (e.g., Varonis and Gass, 1985). Negative feedback began to assume increased importance in this paradigm with the advent of focus on form (Long, 1991, 1996; Long and Robinson, 1998), which advocated spontaneous and brief attention to linguistic items in response to learners' problematic utterances within meaning-focused interaction. In this way, the use of negative feedback allowed L2 learners to integrate attention to meaning and form in ways that did not occur in focus on meaning instruction, which neglected linguistic accuracy, or in focus on forms instruction, which taught discrete linguistic forms apart from a communicative context. Following this early conceptualization of the importance of L2 interaction and focus on form, there has been a plethora of research investigating the occurrence and effectiveness of negative feedback. The next section discusses the core issues addressed by this research.

Core issues

Does feedback occur naturally in the L2 classroom?

An important initial question about L2 feedback regards its existence in L2 interaction. Descriptive studies of naturally-occurring feedback in L2 classrooms have examined a variety of contexts, including immersion, ESL, EFL, and university language classes. In both communicative and more traditional L2 instructional contexts, negative feedback has been found to occur (Ellis et al., 2001; Lyster and Ranta, 1997; Yoshida, 2008); however, studies have also shown that negative feedback does not occur with equal frequency in all contexts. For example, Zyzik and Polio (2008) found that feedback was virtually absent from content-based university Spanish classes. Furthermore, Loewen (2003) discovered differences in the amount of feedback within 12 different classes at the same language school. He also found that some students did not receive any feedback during his observations, whereas others received feedback on numerous occasions. Nevertheless, these descriptive studies demonstrate that negative feedback occurs, to varying degrees, in a variety of L2 classroom contexts.

What are the characteristics of naturally-occurring feedback?

Considerable research has investigated the features of negative feedback. In an early study, Chaudron (1977) developed an extensive negative feedback taxonomy, including categories such as repetition of the error with or without changes, prompts, and explanations. Lyster and Ranta (1997) refined these categories to six: recast, elicitation, repetition, metalinguistic feedback, explicit correction, and clarification requests. Subsequently, in an attempt to move from descriptive categorization of discourse features to a more psycholinguistically-motivated taxonomy, Ellis et al. (2001) identified three main types of negative feedback: recasts, elicitations, and metalinguistic feedback. Most recently, Ellis (2008) has reduced the categories to either input-providing feedback or output-promoting feedback. Definitions of several key feedback types will now be discussed.

Probably no type of feedback has received more attention than recasts, a type of input-providing feedback that correctly reformulates a learner's erroneous utterance but maintains the learner's intended meaning (Nicolas et al., 2001; Lyster and Ranta, 1997). Recasts are the most common feedback method in the classroom (Davies, 2006; Ellis et al., 2001; Havranek, 2002; Loewen and Philp, 2006; Lyster, 1998a; Lyster and Mori, 2006; Lyster and Ranta, 1997; Yoshida, 2008). Proponents of recasts argue that they are beneficial for L2 learning because they are unobtrusive, occur immediately after the error and provide the opportunity for learners to compare their erroneous utterances with target-like forms (Long, 2007). A recast is found in Example 1.

Example 1: Recast
S: to her is good thing (.) to her is good thing
T: yeah for her it's a good thing
S: because she got a lot of money there

(Loewen and Philp, 2006: p. 538)

Recent work (Ellis and Sheen, 2006; Loewen and Philp, 2006; Sheen, 2006) has suggested that recasts are non-monolithic in nature, and that they can differ in features such as length, prosody, and number of errors corrected. In general, recasts tend to isolate the error and to contain declarative intonation (Kim and Han, 2007; Loewen and Philp, 2006; Lyster, 1998b), although other patterns have also been observed.

Apart from recasts, elicitations are another relatively frequent type of negative feedback (Ellis *et al.*, 2001; Lyster and Mori, 2006; Lyster and Ranta, 1997). Also referred to as prompts (Ammar and Spada, 2006; Lyster, 2004) or negotiation of form (Lyster, 1998a; Lyster and Ranta, 1997), elicitations are output-prompting and consist of various feedback moves, such as repetitions or clarification requests, that encourage learners to self-correct without providing them with correct linguistic forms. Proponents of elicitations argue that elicitations are less ambiguous in their corrective intent and that they also involve the learner in deeper cognitive processing because they require learners to self-correct. Of course, learners must have some knowledge of the structure to be able to self-correct. A typical elicitation is shown in Example 2.

Example 2: Elicitation
Teacher: *Il vit où un animal domestique? Où est-ce que ça vit?*
"Where does a pet live? Where does it live?"
Student: *Dans un maison.* "In a (masc.) house."
Teacher: *Dans? Attention.* "In ...? Careful."
Student: *Dans une maison.* "In a (fem.) house."

(Lyster, 2004: p. 405)

A third category of negative feedback is explicit correction, which can involve a direct indication that an utterance is incorrect and/or the use of metalinguistic terminology to indicate the nature of the error. Both types of explicit correction have been observed in the L2 classroom (Ellis *et al.*, 2001; Lyster and Ranta, 1997). An explicit correction is shown in Example 3.

Example 3: Metalinguistic feedback
Learner: He kiss her.
Researcher: Kiss—you need past tense.
Learner: He kissed her.

(Ellis et al., 2006 p. 353)

An additional discoursal feature related to feedback is the learners' responses to feedback, referred to as uptake (Ellis *et al.*, 2001; Lyster, 1998a; Lyster and Ranta, 1997). Uptake is of interest because learners' successful production of the correct form may be a possible indication of the effectiveness of feedback (Chaudron, 1977; Lightbown, 1998) particularly in light of Swain's output hypothesis (1995). Uptake has been found to occur in response to negative feedback, although its occurrence and success have been found to vary (Ellis *et al.*, 2001; Loewen, 2005; Lyster and Ranta, 1997; Mackey and Philp, 1998; Sheen, 2004).

Is feedback effective for L2 learning?

The effectiveness of negative feedback for L2 learning is contentious, despite its frequent occurrence in the L2 classroom. In spite of contrary arguments (e.g., Krashen, 1985; Truscott,

1999), there is mounting evidence that negative feedback can be beneficial for learners. For example, several meta-analyses (Li, 2010; Mackey and Goo, 2007; Russell and Spada, 2006) have found overall positive effects for corrective feedback. Nevertheless, the necessity of feedback for learning remains disputed (Ellis, 2006; Long, 2007), although there is some evidence that it might be necessary for learning some linguistic structures that are otherwise non-salient in the input and do not hinder communication (White, 1991).

What characteristics of feedback influence its effectiveness?

If negative feedback can be beneficial for L2 learning, the next question to consider is which features influence its effectiveness. Given Schmidt's (1995) noticing hypothesis, it is argued that learners must notice negative feedback in order for it to be effective. As a result, numerous studies have investigated the salience of different types of feedback. In particular, controversy exists regarding the salience of recasts. On one hand, their implicit and unobtrusive nature does not interrupt the flow of communication, thereby allowing learners to pay attention to form and meaning at the same time (Long, 1991, 1996, 2007). On the other hand, recasts may go unnoticed because they are not salient enough (Lyster, 2004; Truscott, 1999). Furthermore, the corrective intent of recasts may be ambiguous because of their multiple discoursal functions (e.g., correction, confirmation check, or clarification request) and because teachers often repeat learners' correct utterances as well as recasting their incorrect ones. As a result, Nicholas et al. (2001) suggest that recasts are most effective when their ambiguity is diminished and their corrective intent is clear. Features that may influence recast salience include prosodic emphasis, intonation, segmentation, number of changes, recast length, and number of recasts (Loewen and Philp, 2006; Sheen, 2006).

In contrast to recasts, elicitations are generally viewed as a more explicit type of feedback, although it may be better to view explicitness as a continuum rather than a dichotomy. Elicitations are generally less ambiguous in their intent, and thus may be more salient as negative evidence. The most explicit type of feedback is explicit correction, and while detractors of explicit correction argue that it can be disruptive to communicative interaction, there is some evidence that more explicit feedback may be more effective for L2 learning (Ellis et al., 2006; Norris and Ortega, 2000).

In an attempt to provide an explanatory statement regarding the salience of feedback, Lyster and Mori (2006) have proposed the counterbalance hypothesis which suggests that feedback will be more effective when it contrasts with a class's predominant communicative orientation. Accordingly, the more communicatively-focused the class, the more explicit the feedback needs to be. This hypothesis is awaiting further investigation.

Another issue in considering the effectiveness of feedback is whether it is effective because it provides positive evidence, negative evidence, or both. On the one hand, negative evidence, indicating that a linguistic construction is not possible, is argued to be a central component of corrective feedback (Long, 2007; White, 1991). On the other hand, positive evidence, consisting of exemplars of what is possible in a language, has also been shown to be an important component of corrective feedback (Leeman, 2003).

The effectiveness of feedback may also be contingent on the linguistic items targeted by that feedback. Any aspect of language can receive feedback, although grammar, vocabulary, and pronunciation are the most common targets in classroom contexts (Ellis et al., 2001; Lyster and Ranta, 1997). In quasi-experimental studies, grammatical structures have been the primary focus, as can be seen in Table 2.1. Popular targets of inquiry have included English question formation and past tense, while fewer studies have been conducted in other languages or on other features. Furthermore, almost no research has investigated feedback on pragmatics or discourse features.

Table 2.1 Linguistic features targeted in quasi-experimental feedback studies

Linguistic Structure	Study
ENGLISH	
Regular past tense	Adams (2007); Dabaghi and Basturkmen (2009); Doughty and Varela (1998); Ellis (2007); Ellis *et al.* (2006); Loewen and Erlam (2006); Mackey (2006); McDonough (2007); Nobuyoshi and Ellis (1993); Yang and Lyster (2010)
Past progressive	Révész and Han (2006)
Past-tense conditionals	Doughty and Varela (1998)
Irregular past tense	Dabaghi and Basturkmen (2009); Yang and Lyster (2010)
Tense consistency	Han (2002)
Questions	Adams (2007); Loewen and Nabei (2007); Mackey and Philp (1998); Mackey and Silver (2005); Mackey (1999, 2006); McDonough and Mackey (2006); Philp (2003); Spada and Lightbown (1993)
Locatives	Adams (2007)
Vocabulary	Adams (2007); Alcón and García Mayo (2008); Trofimovitch *et al.* (2007)
Backshifted verbs	Sachs and Suh (2007)
Articles	Muranoi (2000); Sheen (2007)
Definite article	Dabaghi and Basturkmen (2009)
Indefinite article	Dabaghi and Basturkmen (2009)
Zero article with abstract count nouns	Sauro (2009)
Comparatives	Ellis (2007)
Plurals	Dabaghi and Basturkmen (2009); Mackey (2006)
Relative clause	Dabaghi and Basturkmen (2009)
Voice	Dabaghi and Basturkmen (2009)
Third-person–s	Dabaghi and Basturkmen (2009)
Possessive determiners	Ammar and Spada (2006); Ammar (2008); Lyster (2004); Trofimovitch *et al.* (2007)
Multiple, incidental forms	Havranek (2002); Loewen (2005); Nabei and Swain (2002)
FRENCH	
Gender marking on articles	Lyster and Izquierdo (2009)
Gender marking on nouns	Lyster (2004)
SPANISH	
Noun adjective agreement	Leeman (2003); Sagarra (2007)
Direct object placement	Long *et al.* (1998)
Adverb placement	Long *et al.* (1998)
KOREAN	
Object relative clauses	Jeon (2007)
Honorifics	Jeon (2007)
Verbs	Jeon (2007)
Nouns	Jeon (2007)
JAPANESE	
Locatives	Iwashita (2003); Long *et al.* (1998)
Aspectual *–te i-(ru)*	Ishida (2004); Iwashita (2003)

Learners' proficiency levels are also a consideration, with studies suggesting that learners need to be developmentally ready to benefit from feedback (Mackey, 1999; Mackey and Philp, 1998; Trofimovitch *et al.*, 2007). Additionally, there may be an interaction between proficiency and type of feedback. For example, Ammar and Spada (2006) found that higher proficiency students benefited equally from recasts and prompts, while lower proficiency learners benefited more from prompts than recasts.

The timing of feedback is also important. Generally, feedback occurs immediately after an error, and this juxtaposition of incorrect and correct forms is argued to benefit learners (Doughty, 2001; Long, 2007; Saxton, 1997, 2005). However, delayed feedback is also possible, particularly in computer-mediated communication (CMC) where the nature of synchronous written chat often means that feedback is not contingent to the error (Smith, 2003).

A final potentially influential characteristic of feedback is the amount of feedback provided to the targeted feature. Long's (1991, 1996) original definition of focus on form does not specify the ideal amount of feedback. Indeed, the construct of incidental focus on form (Ellis, 2001; Loewen, 2005) assumes that a linguistic structure may receive only one feedback episode. By contrast, feedback treatments in quasi-experimental studies have ranged from 30 minutes to 120 minutes. In his meta-analysis, Li (2010) found that treatments of 50 minutes or less were significantly more effective than were longer treatments. Additionally, Havranek (2002) found no advantage for correcting the same linguistic error multiple times as opposed to correcting it only once. Further investigations into the effects of the intensity of feedback are needed.

What contextual characteristics of feedback influence its effectiveness?

In addition to features of the feedback itself, there are also contextual features that may influence the effectiveness of feedback. These factors will be considered in turn.

Instructional variables. Negative feedback studies have been conducted in contexts, such as immersion classes, language school classes, and laboratories. One possible explanation for differences in results has been these varying contexts. For example, studies of immersion classes (Lyster 1998a,b; Lyster and Ranta, 1997) have found lower rates of feedback and uptake than studies conducted in communicative classes in language schools (Ellis *et al.*, 2001; Loewen, 2003; Sheen, 2004), and these differences have been suggested to be due to the learning goals of each environment. Additionally, concerns exist about the generalizability of laboratory studies to the classroom context; however, Gass *et al.*'s (2005) comparison of tasks in both a laboratory and classroom context found no differences in the interactional patterns between the two. Finally, studies have also begun to investigate, both descriptively and quasi-experimentally, negative feedback in CMC contexts (Loewen and Erlam, 2006; Sachs and Suh, 2007; Sagarra, 2007; Sauro, 2009).

Interlocutor variables. The role of the interlocutor in providing feedback can be another mediating variable. In most classroom studies, teachers have provided the majority of feedback (Oliver, 2000; Zhao and Bitchener, 2007). However, learners can and do provide feedback to each other, and while most of this feedback is accurate, there are instances of learners providing incorrect feedback (Adams, 2007). The accuracy of teacher feedback has not been investigated.

Other interlocutor variables, such as gender, L1 status, and age, have been investigated both separately and jointly. Studies of gender have found both differences between males and females (Ross-Feldman, 2007) and no differences (Oliver, 2002). Regarding the L1 or L2 speaker status of the interlocutor, several studies found differences, such as more negotiation in non-native speaker (NNS) dyads (Oliver, 2002) and more elicitations from L2 speakers and more reformulations from L1 speakers (Sato and Lyster, 2007). Additionally, age has been considered as a variable since it is possible that the differing cognitive aspects of children, adolescents, and adults may influence the effectiveness of feedback. Several feedback studies have investigated pre-adolescent learners and found that children can and do both provide and receive feedback (Mackey and Silver, 2005; Oliver, 2000, 2002) although it is not always in the same amount or type as adults (Oliver, 2000). Additionally, Mackey *et al.* (2003) found an interaction between L1 status and age, with adults native speakers providing significantly more feedback than NNS; however, for children there was no difference in the provision of feedback, although there was significantly more modified output in response to NNS.

One final interlocutor variable is whether learners are the direct recipients of feedback or merely observers of it. Some studies suggest that observers do not notice feedback as well as those who are the direct recipients of it (Mackey, 1999) while other studies suggest that observing feedback is as beneficial as receiving it (Havranek, 2002; Kim and Han, 2007; Ohta, 2000).

Data and common elicitation measures

In order to investigate these core issues, researchers have employed a number of different methodologies, which will be described in this section.

Oral production

One of the most important types of data for feedback research is oral production, with the utterances of both feedback provider and feedback recipient receiving attention. Considerable research has investigated the amount and types of feedback in naturally-occurring classrooms (Chaudron, 1977; Ellis *et al.*, 2001; Loewen, 2003; Lyster, 1998a,b; Lyster and Ranta, 1997; Sheen 2004; Yoshida, 2008). Such studies have high ecological validity because they describe actual classroom discourse. However, these studies are limited in the conclusions that they can draw about the effectiveness of feedback since they do not employ measures of L2 learning.

In addition to classroom observations, researchers have also investigated the occurrence of feedback in more controlled, laboratory contexts. In this way researchers have been able to investigate feedback variables in a more systematic and intentional manner. Laboratory-based studies can be either descriptive or quasi-experimental, with the former generally involving dyads of speakers that have been chosen according to specific characteristics, such as L1, age, sex, proficiency level, etc. Researchers then can describe the amount and types of feedback that occur given these different variables.

The utterances produced in both classroom and laboratory contexts have been analyzed using several similar taxonomies that take into account all or some of the following categories: the erroneous utterance that triggers the feedback, the feedback move itself, and the optional response to the feedback. The triggers are often coded for the general types of linguistic errors they contain, whether morphological, syntactic, phonological, or lexical. The feedback moves have been coded using taxonomies that attempt to categorize every type of feedback move or that attempt to differentiate only characteristics that may influence the learning potential of the feedback. Finally, some studies have investigated learners' responses to the feedback, which has alternatively been called repair, successful uptake, or modified output.

Measurements of learning

While descriptive studies of learner interaction have contributed to our understanding of how feedback occurs, these studies do not provide information about the effectiveness of the feedback, apart from learners' production of uptake. Therefore, quasi-experimental studies have used pre-test, treatment, post-test designs to investigate the issue of learning, which can be operationalized in terms of increased accuracy or progress along an acquisitional sequence (Ellis, 2006).

Measures of accuracy. The majority of the studies of negative feedback have operationalized learning as increased accurate use of the targeted linguistic items, with several different types of instruments used to measure accuracy (Doughty, 2003).

Production tests. A common method of measuring accuracy is by eliciting learner production of the targeted linguistic items. Oral production tests, some with the same design as the treatment tasks, are often used (Ammar and Spada, 2006; Loewen and Nabei, 2007; Long *et al.*, 1998; Lyster, 2004; Lyster and Izquierdo, 2009; Mackey and Silver, 2005; Mackey, 2006; Sachs and Suh, 2007; Spada and Lightbown, 1993; Trofimovitch *et al.*, 2007). Such tasks include information gap, picture description, and spot-the-differences tasks. After the learner production is recorded, it is generally coded using a target-like use analysis to arrive at a percentage of accurate use (Ellis and Barkhuizen, 2005). In addition to oral production tasks, some studies have also employed written production tasks (Han, 2002; Lyster, 2004; Révész and Han, 2006; Sagarra, 2007). Other types of production tests include sentence creation (Sagarra, 2007), fill-in-the-blank (Révész and Han, 2006), and meta-linguistic knowledge tests (Ellis, 2007). Finally, some studies have examined learners' subsequent production of targeted forms in classroom interaction (Havranek, 2002; Loewen, 2007).

A drawback of many production tests is that it is not always possible to ensure production of the desired linguistic items, as learners can be very adept at avoiding using them. Consequently another option is to use an elicited imitation test in which learners are provided with oral stimuli that include either grammatical or ungrammatical exemplars of the target structure; learners are then asked to repeat the items correctly (Ellis, 2007). Imitation tests arguably force learners to draw on their implicit L2 knowledge in order to reconstruct the sentence.

Grammaticality judgment tests. Numerous studies have used grammaticality judgment tests (GJTs) to measure gains in learners' ability to identify grammatical and ungrammatical sentences. An advantage of GJTs is that they can test the specific structures targeted in the feedback treatment; however, there has been concern that GJTs may be better measures of learners' explicit, rather than implicit, L2 knowledge. In addition, GJTs are receptive, decision-making tasks and do not elicit learner production of the target form. These limitations have been countered in numerous studies by the use of both GJTs and other types of tests (Ellis, 2007; Ellis *et al.*, 2006; Loewen and Nabei, 2007; Long *et al.*, 1998; Sachs and Suh, 2007).

Individualized, tailor-made tests. The previous tests are generally administered to measure the effects of feedback on a particular linguistic item. However, spontaneous feedback can target various and multiple linguistic items within one activity. In these instances the standard pre-test/post-test design is not feasible because the targeted linguistic items are not known ahead of time, and thus cannot be pre-tested. In these cases, post-hoc tailor-made tests have been used to specifically test individual students on the linguistic items that they themselves received feedback on (Adams, 2007; Dabaghi and Basturkmen, 2009; Egi, 2007b; Havranek, 2002; Loewen, 2005; Nabei and Swain, 2002; Williams, 1999). Test features may include production of the correct form, multiple choice, GJT, etc. Recently, Nassaji (2009) has attempted to pre-test linguistic items that subsequently receive spontaneous negative feedback by having learners perform the same task as a written pre-test and then an oral treatment session. This innovative design shows some promise, although not all linguistic errors in the pre-test received feedback during the oral interaction.

Measures of development

Developmental stages. Another way of investigating the effectiveness of feedback is by examining learners' progress through developmental stages (Pienemann and Keβler, Chapter 14, this volume). Often studies use similar language production instruments as those in studies that measure accuracy. In fact, both accuracy and development are sometimes investigated in the same study. Thus, it is the analysis of the data that differs. Rather than employing a target-like use analysis, researchers code the different linguistic stages found in the data. Increased use of higher stages, rather than increased accuracy, is viewed as a sign of learning. Studies have looked at learners' progression through stages of English question formation (Loewen and Nabei, 2007; Mackey, 1999; Mackey and Silver, 2005; Spada and Lightbown, 1993) and possessive determiners (Ammar, 2008).

Some studies distinguish between measuring learners' accurate production of linguistic stimuli that were used in the treatment (sometimes called "old" items) as well as novel stimuli that did not occur in the treatment session, in order to investigate learners' ability to generalize the feedback to new linguistic items (Ellis et al., 2006; McDonough, 2007; Sagarra, 2007; Sauro, 2009).

Timing of tests. Another issue, in addition to the types of instruments used to measure L2 learning, is the timing of their administration. Most quasi-experimental studies include, at minimum, a pre-test and a post-test. Immediate post-tests may occur up to one or two days after the treatment, while delayed post-tests may occur anywhere from one week to several months after the treatment. Given that several studies have found effects on delayed post-tests but not on immediate post-tests (Ellis et al., 2006; Mackey, 1999) and that some researchers argue that the effects of feedback may not be evident immediately, delayed post-testing is considered important.

Introspective measures

Because noticing is such an important construct in the theoretical support for negative feedback, recent research has begun to investigate the cognitive processes that learners engage in during negative feedback. Mackey (2006) operationalized noticing as "a learner's report indicating a mismatch between the target language form and the learner's non-target-like production or comprehension" (p. 413). Again, several different types of instruments have been used, sometimes within the same study, to elicit this information.

Sometimes learners are simply asked to report what they have noticed during interaction sessions by using learning journals or interview questions (Alcón and García Mayo, 2008; Mackey, 2006). Similar to self-report, stimulated recall has also been used to measure noticing (Gass and Mackey, 2000). While self-report relies entirely on learners' memories of the interaction, stimulated recall provides stimuli in the form of video or audio clips of negative feedback episodes that occurred in class. After viewing the clips, learners are asked to verbalize their thoughts at the time of feedback. If learners mention the targeted linguistic structure or the corrective nature of the interaction, this is taken to be evidence of noticing. There have been several studies employing stimulated recall of student's thoughts (Egi, 2004, 2007a, 2007b; Mackey et al., 2000; Mackey et al., 2002; Mackey et al., 2007).

In an effort to avoid the memory decay that can occur in stimulated recall, several studies (Bigelow et al., 2006; Philp, 2003) have used immediate repetition as a measure of learners' noticing of recasts. After a recast is given, the researcher knocks on the desk as a signal for the learner to repeat the last few words that they remembered hearing. If the repetition includes the correct form, this is taken as evidence of noticing.

Similar to immediate repetition, immediate report attempts to investigate learners' cognition as close to the time of feedback as possible. Learners also hear a knock after feedback, but instead of repeating what they just heard, they are asked to verbalize any thoughts they remember from the immediately preceding interaction. After the report, the communicative interaction continues.

Egi (2004, 2007a) has compared immediate report (occurring during the interaction) and stimulated recall (occurring after the interaction) and found that the two groups did not differ in subsequent production of the targeted form; however, stimulated recall protocols were longer than the immediate reports, and memory decay was an issue for stimulated recall participants.

Other measures

While noticing and learning have been the two main constructs investigated directly in negative feedback research, several additional constructs related to individual differences have been investigated as potential moderator variables in the effectiveness of negative feedback. These variables include analytical ability, phonological memory, working memory, and attention control (Mackey *et al.*, 2002; Trofimovitch *et al.*, 2007). It is beyond the scope of this chapter to discuss in detail the measurement of these constructs.

Empirical verification

Is feedback beneficial? There are three main indicators of the effectiveness of feedback which will be considered in this section: uptake, noticing, and learning.

Uptake. It has been argued that uptake/modified output is a possible indication that feedback has been noticed and a possible facilitator of learning (Chaudron, 1977; Ellis *et al.*, 2001; Lightbown, 1998; Swain, 1995). Studies have found that feedback can result in successfully modified output (Sagarra, 2007), although factors such as age (Oliver *et al.*, 2008) and instructional context (Lyster and Mori, 2006) can influence the amount of modified output. In addition, recasts generally have lower uptake rates than do elicitations or more explicit feedback moves (Davies, 2006; Lyster and Ranta, 1997). Some studies suggest a relationship between modified output in response to feedback and learning (Loewen, 2005; McDonough, 2005); however, other studies have not found such a relationship (Mackey and Philp, 1998) or have found it to be tenuous (Alcón and García Mayo, 2008).

Noticing. Given that noticing is argued to be an essential cognitive process for L2 learning, and since interaction and negative feedback are claimed to draw attention to linguistic items, a number of studies have investigated the noticeability of negative feedback. Several studies have shown that learners can notice recasts, with noticing operationalized as discussed earlier. Multiple studies have found that shorter recasts with fewer changes are more noticeable (Egi, 2007a; Kim and Han, 2007; Philp, 2003). Also, learners who were developmentally ready were more likely to notice recasts (Philp, 2003). Kim and Han (2007) found that students were largely able to identify the intent of the recasts, as indicated by the teachers. However, Mackey *et al.* (2007) found that learners noticed the correct intent more for explicit feedback and interrogative recasts, while declarative recasts and combinations of feedback had lower rates of noticing. Egi (2007a, b) found that feedback was more beneficial when learners noticed the linguistic nature of the feedback, as either positive or negative evidence, rather than viewing the feedback as a response to content alone. However, several studies have argued that recasts are less noticeable. For example, Lyster's (1998b) study found that teacher repetitions and teacher recasts occurred in roughly equal proportions, suggesting that the corrective nature of the recast is ambiguous. Nevertheless, Mackey (2006) found a significant association between reports of noticing and linguistic development, leading her to conclude that "these data seem to point to a relationship between noticing and learning of question formation" (p. 422).

Several studies have found that feedback on certain aspects of language are noticed more frequently than others, with most reporting that feedback targeting morphological and syntactic errors is more difficult to notice than lexical and phonological errors (Carpenter *et al.*, 2006; Gass and Lewis, 2007; Kim and Han, 2007; Mackey *et al.*, 2000; Trofimovitch *et al.*, 2007). However, Egi (2007a) found similar levels of perception for morphosyntax and lexis, with a possible explanation being that morphosyntactic recasts in her study were more frequent and more consistently targeting the same structures than were recasts in other studies. In Mackey *et al.* (2007) students recognized the corrective intent of feedback most for morphology/lexis, next for syntax, and least for phonology.

In addition, studies have investigated the role that the student plays in the discourse, whether they are the direct recipient of the feedback or only an observer. Mackey *et al.* (2007) found a higher percentage of recognition of feedback for primary recipients, although observers also indicated noticing feedback. In contrast, Ohta (2000) was more positive about the benefits of recasts for observers, finding that observers of negative feedback often produced the target form in private speech, suggesting that recasts can be salient, and that learners were sensitive to the corrective nature of the recasts. Kim and Han (2007) found no difference in receivers' or observers' ability to notice recasts.

Finally, as for the impact of individual differences on noticing, Trofimovitch *et al.* (2007) did not find that individual factors such as attention control, phonological/working memory, or analytical ability influenced the level of noticing. In contrast, Bigelow *et al.* (2006) and Tarone and Bigelow (2007) found that participants with higher alphabetic print literacy skills recalled recasts better. Mackey *et al.* (2002) found a positive correlation between noticing and working memory capacity.

L2 learning. Multiple studies have investigated the effects of negative feedback for L2 learning. In general, studies have found an effect for feedback, although there are exceptions (e.g., Loewen and Erlam, 2006). Some studies have investigated the effects of feedback without comparing them with other feedback groups or interaction-only groups and found that feedback improves learners' subsequent ability to use the structures. These studies include some of mixed types of feedback on various incidentally targeted linguistic items (Loewen, 2005), mixed types of feedback on specific linguistic structures (Adams, 2007), and specific types of feedback, such as recasts on specific linguistic structures (Révész and Han, 2006; Sachs and Suh, 2007; Trofimovitch *et al.*, 2007).

Other studies have found that feedback was more effective than interaction alone, but they did not compare different types of feedback (Mackey, 1999; Mackey and Silver, 2005). Several studies found that interaction with recasts or a combination of feedback types were better than interaction without feedback (Doughty and Varela, 1998; Han, 2002; Sagarra, 2007), and at least one small-scale study found that clarification requests were more effective than no feedback (Nobuyoshi and Ellis, 1993).

Additional research has compared different types of feedback along with a control group, and found that while feedback was effective, there was no difference for the type of feedback (Ammar and Spada, 2006; Loewen and Nabei, 2007; McDonough, 2007). However, not all studies have found feedback to be equally effective. Several studies have found metalinguistic feedback or explicit feedback to have a significantly larger effect on post-test performance than other types of feedback such as recasts (Dabaghi and Basturkmen, 2009; Ellis *et al.*, 2006; Sauro, 2009; Sheen, 2007). However, Sauro (2009) found that the effect for metalinguistic feedback was only present on test items that were included in the treatment sessions; learners were not able to generalize to novel items in the test stimuli.

Some studies have found an overall effect in favor of prompts, which elicit self-corrections from learners rather than providing them with the correct form (Ammar, 2008; Havranek, 2002; Yang and Lyster, 2010). However, at least one study (Nassaji, 2009) has found that recasts resulted in higher accuracy scores than did elicitations, particularly on immediate post-tests. He also found that more explicit types of feedback, whether recasts or elicitations, resulted in higher accuracy scores.

In addition to studies that have investigated the effects of feedback by itself, several studies have investigated the effects of feedback plus other instructional interventions. For example, Lyster (2004) included form-focused instruction (FFI), as well as prompts and recasts, as variables in his investigation of their effects on the learning of French gender. He found that while FFI was beneficial, FFI with prompts was the most effective. In contrast, Lyster and Izquierdo (2009) in a study that included FFI plus feedback (either recast or prompt) found no difference in their effectiveness.

Other factors influencing the effectiveness of feedback. In addition to types of feedback, some studies have investigated the moderating effects of other variables on L2 learning. For example, the proficiency level of learners appears to be an important factor, with higher proficiency learners more able to benefit from feedback (Ammar and Spada, 2006; Mackey and Philp, 1998; Trofimovitch et al., 2007).

Other individual difference variables have been investigated. For example, Mackey et al. (2002) suggest that low working memory scores were associated with initial interlanguage development, but learners with higher working memory scores showed more development on delayed tests. Sagarra (2007) found that higher working memory was associated with development of linguistic accuracy for the recast group but not the control group. Trofimovitch et al. (2007) found that, while phonological memory and analytical ability contributed to learners' improvement, attention control was the highest significant predictor of accuracy. Sheen (2007) found that language analytic ability correlated with accuracy scores for learners who received metalinguistic feedback but not for those who received recasts. Finally, Sheen (2008) found that, in general, feedback was more effective for learners with lower levels of anxiety. While these studies of individual differences are insightful, they are not sufficient in number to permit the types of generalizations made possible by synthetic analysis. As a result, meta-analyses such as Russell and Spada (2006), Mackey and Goo (2007) and Li (2010) have investigated the general effectiveness of corrective feedback; however, they have not been able to systematically explore such individual differences.

Applications

The role of negative feedback is highly relevant for instructional contexts, with existing research suggesting that teachers can effectively incorporate it into their more communicative activities. However, the question of what type of negative feedback is most effective is less clear, as the previous review of studies has shown. Given that there is no consensus on the superiority of one type of feedback over another, it could be best to include a variety of feedback options. In addition, there is some evidence that suggests that if teachers go to the effort of providing negative feedback, they should also ensure that students produce the correct forms.

One problem with using research as a guide for teaching is that much of the research focuses on planned focus on form in which one or two linguistic items are targeted intensively. However, descriptive research shows that negative feedback inside classrooms is generally more extensive and targets multiple forms on only one or two occasions.

Several studies also suggest that teachers' beliefs about negative feedback are important factors. For example, teachers may express their beliefs in the superiority of specific types of feedback; however, the types of feedback they provide in the classroom may not correspond with their expressed beliefs (Basturkmen et al., 2004; Yoshida, 2008). Mackey et al. (2004) suggest that providing workshops on negative feedback can help raise teachers' awareness of this issue and that teachers with more experience are likely to provide more feedback.

Learners' views on negative feedback are also worth considering. Different types of learners may have different opinions about feedback (Loewen *et al.*, 2009) and different views of feedback may affect its effectiveness. For example, Sheen (2007) found a correlation between learners' positive attitudes toward feedback and improved accuracy scores for learners who received metalinguistic feedback.

Future directions

While considerable research has investigated the role of negative feedback, there are still questions to which we do not have clear answers. For instance, although meta-analyses of negative feedback have found a significant main effect, these studies have commented on the lack of studies available to conduct secondary analyses. Therefore, more studies which compare the effects of different types of feedback will enhance future meta-analyses. Other issues to address include the intensity of feedback necessary for noticing and learning. Some studies of negative feedback have examined spontaneous, one-off episodes, while other studies have provided treatments of one hour or longer. Li's (2010) meta-analysis suggests that a medium duration of feedback was more beneficial than longer or shorter amounts; however, few studies have directly investigated this issue. Finally, it is also probable that different linguistic items may require more or less feedback. Given that many negative feedback studies have targeted one or two English structures, there is a need for additional studies of other languages and linguistic structures.

In sum, although considerable research has investigated the role of negative feedback, there are still numerous variables which are not well understood. Further research into the effects of negative feedback will continue to provide insight into both SLA theory and pedagogy.

References

Adams, R. (2007). Do second language learners benefit from interacting with each other? In A. Mackey (Ed.), *Conversational interaction in second language acquisition* (pp. 29–52). Oxford: Oxford University Press.

Alcón, E. and García Mayo, M. (2008). Incidental focus on form and learning outcomes with young foreign language classroom learners. In J. Philp, R. Oliver, and A. Mackey (Eds.), *Second language acquisition and the younger learner: Child's play?* (pp. 173–192). Amsterdam: John Benjamins.

Ammar, A. (2008). Prompts and recasts: Differential effects on second language morphosyntax. *Language Teaching Research*, 12(2), 183–210.

Ammar, A. and Spada, N. (2006). One size fits all? Recasts, prompts and L2 learning. *Studies in Second Language Acquisition*, 28(4), 543–574.

Basturkmen, H., Loewen, S., and Ellis, R. (2004). Teachers' stated beliefs about incidental focus on form and their classroom practices. *Applied Linguistics*, 25, 243–272.

Bigelow, M., Delmas, R., Hansen, K., and Tarone, E. (2006). Literacy and the processing of oral recasts in SLA. *TESOL Quarterly*, 40(4), 665–689.

Bohannon, J., Padgett, M., and Nelson, K. (1996). Useful evidence on negative evidence. *Developmental Psychology*, 32(3), 551–555.

Carpenter, H., Jeon, S., MacGregor, D., and Mackey, A. (2006). Learners' interpretations of recasts. *Studies in Second Language Acquisition*, 28(2), 209–236.

Chaudron, C. (1977). A descriptive model of discourse in the corrective treatment of learners' errors. *Language Learning*, 27(1), 29–46.

Dabaghi, A. and Basturkmen, H. (2009). The effectiveness of implicit and explicit error correction on learners' performance. *System*, 37(1), 82–98.

Davies, M. (2006). Paralinguistic focus on form. *TESOL Quarterly*, 40(4), 841–855.

DeKeyser, R. (2007). Introduction: Situating the concept of practice. In R. DeKeyser (Ed.), *Practice in a second language: Perspectives from applied linguistics and cognitive psychology* (pp. 1–18). Cambridge: Cambridge University Press.

Doughty, C. (2001). Cognitive underpinnings of focus on form. In P. Robinson (Ed.), *Cognition and second language instruction* (pp. 206–257). Cambridge: Cambridge University Press.

Doughty, C. (2003). Instructed SLA: Constraints, compensation, and enhancement. In C. Doughty and M. Long (Eds.), *The handbook of second language acquisition* (pp. 256–310). Malden, MA: Blackwell.

Doughty, C. and Varela, E. (1998). Communicative focus on form. In C. Doughty and J. Williams (Eds.), *Focus on form in classroom second language acquisition* (pp. 114–138). Cambridge: Cambridge University Press.

Egi, T. (2004). Verbal reports, noticing, and SLA research. *Language Awareness, 13*(4), 243–264.

Egi, T. (2007a). Interpreting recasts as linguistic evidence: The roles of linguistic target, length, and degree of change. *Studies in Second Language Acquisition, 29*(4), 511–537.

Egi, T. (2007b). Recasts, learners' interpretations, and L2 development. In A. Mackey (Ed.), *Conversational interaction in second language acquisition* (pp. 249–267). Oxford: Oxford University Press.

Ellis, R. (2001). Introduction: Investigating form-focused instruction. *Language Learning, 51*, 1–46.

Ellis, R. (2006). Researching the effects of form-focussed instruction on L2 acquisition. *AILA Review, 19*, 18–41.

Ellis, R. (2007). The differential effects of corrective feedback on two grammatical structures. In A. Mackey (Ed.), *Conversational interaction in second language acquisition* (pp. 339–360). Oxford: Oxford University Press.

Ellis, R. (2008). *The study of second language acquisition* (Second Edition). Oxford: Oxford University Press.

Ellis, R. and Barkhuizen, G. (2005). *Analysing learner language*. Oxford: Oxford University Press.

Ellis, R., Basturkmen, H., and Loewen, S. (2001). Learner uptake in communicative ESL lessons. *Language Learning, 51*(2), 281–318.

Ellis, R., Loewen, S., and Erlam, R. (2006). Implicit and explicit corrective feedback and the acquisition of L2 grammar. *Studies in Second Language Acquisition, 28*, 339–368.

Ellis, R. and Sheen, Y. (2006). Reexamining the role of recasts in second language acquisition. *Studies in Second Language Acquisition, 28*(4), 575–600.

Farrar, M. (1992). Negative evidence and grammatical morpheme acquisition. *Developmental Psychology, 28*(1), 90–98.

Gass, S. (1997). *Input, interaction, and the second language learner*. Mahwah, NJ: Lawrence Erlbaum Associates.

Gass, S. and Lewis, K. (2007). Perceptions about interactional feedback: Differences between heritage language learners and non-heritage language learners. In A. Mackey (Ed.), *Conversational interaction in second language acquisition* (pp. 79–100). Oxford: Oxford University Press.

Gass, S. and Mackey, A. (2000). *Stimulated recall methodology in second language research*. Mahwah, NJ: Lawrence Erlbaum Associates.

Gass, S. and Mackey, A. (2007). Input, interaction and output in second language acquisition. In B. VanPatten and J. Williams (Eds.), *Theories in second language acquisition: An introduction* (pp. 175–200). Mahwah, NJ: Lawrence Erlbaum Associates.

Gass, S., Mackey, A., and Ross-Feldman, L. (2005). Task-based interactions in classroom and laboratory settings. *Language Learning, 55*(4), 575–611.

Han, Z.-H. (2002). A study of the impact of recasts on tense consistency in L2 output. *TESOL Quarterly, 36*(4), 543–572.

Havranek, G. (2002). When is corrective feedback most likely to succeed?. *International Journal of Educational Research, 37*, 255–270.

Ishida, M. (2004). Effects of recasts on the acquisition of the aspectual form -te i-(ru) by learners of Japanese as a foreign language. *Language Learning, 54*(2), 311–394.

Iwashita, N. (2003). Negative feedback and positive evidence in task-based interaction. *Studies in Second Language Acquisition, 25*, 1–36.

Jeon, S. (2007). Interaction-driven L2 learning: Characterizing linguistic development. In A. Mackey (Ed.), *Conversational interaction in second language acquisition* (pp. 379–403). Oxford: Oxford University Press.

Kim, J. and Han, Z. (2007). Recasts in communicative EFL classes: Do teacher intent and learner interpretation overlap?. In A. Mackey (Ed.), *Conversational interaction in second language acquisition* (pp. 269–297). Oxford: Oxford University Press.

Krashen, S. (1985). *The input hypothesis: Issues and implications*. London: Longman.

Lantolf, J. and Thorne, S. (2007). Sociocultural theory. In B. VanPatten and J. Williams (Eds.), *Theories in second language acquisition: An introduction*. Mahwah, NJ: Lawrence Erlbaum Associates.

Leeman, J. (2003). Recasts and L2 development: Beyond negative evidence. *Studies in Second Language Acquisition, 25*, 37–63.

Leeman, J. (2007). Feedback in L2 learning: Responding to errors during practice. In R. DeKeyser (Ed.), *Practice in a second language: Perspectives from applied linguistics and cognitive psychology* (pp. 111–137). Cambridge: Cambridge University Press.

Li, S. (2010). The effectiveness of corrective feedback in SLA: A meta-analysis. *Language Learning, 60,* 309–365.

Lightbown, P. (1998). The importance of timing in focus on form. In C. Doughty and J. Williams (Eds.), *Focus on form in classroom second language acquisition.* Cambridge: Cambridge University Press.

Loewen, S. (2003). Variation in the frequency and characteristics of incidental focus on form. *Language Teaching Research, 7,* 315–345.

Loewen, S. (2005). Incidental focus on form and second language learning. *Studies in Second Language Acquisition, 27,* 361–386.

Loewen, S. (2007). The prior and subsequent use of forms targeted in incidental focus on form. In H. Nassaji and S. Fotos, (Eds.), *Form focused instruction and teacher education: Studies in Honour of Rod Ellis* (pp. 101–116). Oxford: Oxford University Press.

Loewen, S. and Erlam, R. (2006). Corrective feedback in the chatroom: An experimental study. *CALL, 19,* 1–14.

Loewen, S., Li, S., Fei, F., Thompson, A., Nakatsukasa, K., Ahn, S. and Chen, X. (2009). L2 learners' beliefs about grammar instruction and error correction. *The Modern Language Journal, 93*(1), 91–104.

Loewen, S. and Nabei, T. (2007). Measuring the effects of oral corrective feedback on L2 knowledge. In A. Mackey (Ed.), *Conversational interaction in second language acquisition* (pp. 361–378). Oxford: Oxford University Press.

Loewen, S. and Philp, J. (2006). Recasts in the adult english L2 classroom: Characteristics, explicitness, and effectiveness. *The Modern Language Journal, 90,* 536–556.

Long, M. (1991). Focus on form: A design feature in language teaching methodology. In K. de Bot, R. Ginsberg, and C. Kramsch (Eds.), *Foreign language research in cross-cultural perspective* (pp. 39–52). Amsterdam: John Benjamins.

Long, M. (1996). The role of the linguistic environment in second language acquisition. In W. Ritchie and T. Bhatia (Eds.), *Handbook of second language acquisition* (pp. 413–468). San Diego: Academic Press.

Long, M. (2007). Recasts in SLA: The story so far. In M. Long (Ed.), *Problems in SLA* (pp. 75–118). Mahwah, NJ: Lawrence Erlbaum Associates.

Long, M., Inagaki, S., and Ortega, L. (1998). The role of implicit negative feedback in SLA: Models and recasts in Japanese and Spanish. *The Modern Language Journal, 82,* 357–371.

Long, M. and Robinson, P. (1998). Focus on form: Theory, research and practice. In C. Doughty and J. Williams (Eds.), *Focus on form in classroom second language acquisition* (pp. 15–41). Cambridge: Cambridge University Press.

Lyster, R. (1998a). Recasts, repetition and ambiguity in L2 classroom discourse. *Studies in Second Language Acquisition, 20*(1), 51–81.

Lyster, R. (1998b). Negotiation of form, recasts, and explicit correction in relation to error types and learner repair in immersion classrooms. *Language Learning, 48*(2), 183–218.

Lyster, R. (2004). Differential effects of prompts and recasts in form-focused instruction. *Studies in Second Language Acquisition, 26,* 399–432.

Lyster, R. and Izquierdo, J. (2009). Prompts versus recasts in dyadic interaction. *Language Learning, 59*(2), 453–498.

Lyster, R. and Mori, H. (2006). Interactional feedback and instructional counterbalance. *Studies in Second Language Acquisition, 28,* 269–300.

Lyster, R. and Ranta, L. (1997). Corrective feedback and learner uptake: Negotiation of form in communicative classrooms. *Studies in Second Language Acquisition, 19*(1), 37–66.

Mackey, A. (1999). Input, interaction and second language development: An empirical study of question formation in ESL. *Studies in Second Language Acquisition, 21,* 557–587.

Mackey, A. (2006). Feedback, noticing and instructed second language learning. *Applied Linguistics, 27*(3), 405–430.

Mackey, A., Al-Khalil, M., Atanassova, G., Hama, M., Logan-Terry, A., and Nakatsukasa, K. (2007). Teachers' intentions and learners' perceptions about corrective feedback in the L2 classroom. *Innovations in Language Learning and Teaching, 1*(1), 129–152.

Mackey, A., Gass, S., and McDonough, K. (2000). How do learners perceive interactional feedback?. *Studies in Second Language Acquisition, 22*(4), 471–497.

Mackey, A. and Goo, J. (2007). Interaction research in SLA: A meta-analysis and research synthesis. In A. Mackey, (Ed.), *Conversational interaction in second language acquisition* (pp. 433–464). Oxford: Oxford University Press.

Mackey, A., Oliver, R., and Leeman, J. (2003). Interactional input and the incorporation of feedback: An exploration of NS-NNS and NNS-NNS adult and child dyads. *Language Learning*, *53*(1), 35–66.

Mackey, A. and Philp, J. (1998). Conversational interaction and second language development: Recasts, responses and red herrings?. *The Modern Language Journal*, *82*(3), 338–356.

Mackey, A., Philp, J., Egi, T., Fujii, A., and Tatsumi, T. (2002). Individual differences in working memory, noticing of interactional feedback and L2 development. In P. Robinson (Ed.), *Individual differences in L2 learning*. Amsterdam: John Benjamins.

Mackey, A., Polio, C., and McDonough, K. (2004). The relationship between experience, education and teachers' use of incidental focus on form techniques. *Language Teaching Research*, *8*(3), 301–327.

Mackey, A. and Silver, R. (2005). Interactional tasks and English L2 learning by immigrant children in Singapore. *System*, *33*, 239–260.

McDonough, K. (2005). Identifying the impact of negative feedback and learners' responses on ESL question development. *Studies in Second Language Acquisition*, *27*(1), 79–104.

McDonough, K. (2007). Interactional feedback and the emergence of simple past activity verbs in L2 English. In A. Mackey (Ed.), *Conversational interaction in second language acquisition* (pp. 323–338). Oxford: Oxford University Press.

McDonough, K. and Mackey, A. (2006). Responses to recasts: Repetitions, primed production and linguistic development. *Language Learning*, *56*(4), 693–720.

Morgan, J., Bonamo, K., and Travis, L. (1995). Negative evidence on negative evidence. *Developmental Psychology*, *31*(2), 180–197.

Muranoi, H. (2000). Focus on form through interaction enhancement: Integrating formal instruction into a communicative task in EFL classrooms. *Language Learning*, *50*, 617–673.

Nabei, T. and Swain, M. (2002). Learner awareness of recasts in classroom interaction: A case study of an adult EFL student's second language learning. *Language Awareness*, *11*(1), 43–63.

Nassaji, H. (2009). Effects of recasts and elicitations in dyadic interaction and the role of feedback. *Language Learning*, *59*(2), 411–452.

Nicolas, H., Lightbown, P. M., and Spada, N. (2001). Recasts as feedback to language learners. *Language Learning*, *51*, 719–758.

Nobuyoshi, J. and Ellis, R. (1993). Focused communication tasks and second language acquisition. *ELT Journal*, *47*(3), 203–210.

Norris, J. M. and Ortega, L. (2000). Effectiveness of L2 instruction: A research synthesis and quantitative meta-analysis. *Language Learning*, *50*, 417–528.

Ohta, A. S. (2000). *Re-thinking recasts: A learner-centered examination of corrective feedback in the Japanese language classroom*. Mahwah, NJ: Lawrence Erlbaum.

Oliver, R. (2000). Age differences in negotiation and feedback in classroom and pairwork. *Language Learning*, *50*, 119–151.

Oliver, R. (2002). The patterns of negotiation for meaning in child interactions. *The Modern Language Journal*, *86*, 519–533.

Oliver, R., Philp, J., and Mackey, A. (2008). The impact of teacher input, guidance and feedback on ESL children's task-based interactions. In J. Philp, R. Oliver, and A. Mackey (Eds.), *Second language acquisition and the younger learner* (pp. 131–147). Amsterdam: John Benjamins.

Philp, J. (2003). Constraints on "noticing the gap": Nonnative speakers' noticing of recasts in NS-NNS interaction. *Studies in Second Language Acquisition*, *25*(01), 99–126.

Ross-Feldman, L. (2007). Interaction in the L2 classroom: Does gender influence learning opportunities? In A. Mackey (Ed.), *Conversational interaction in second language acquisition* (pp. 29–52). Oxford: Oxford University Press.

Russell, J. and Spada, N. (2006). The effectiveness of corrective feedback for the acquisition of L2 grammar: A meta-analysis of the research. In J. Norris and L. Ortega (Eds.), *Synthesizing research on language learning and teaching* (pp. 133–164). Amsterdam: John Benjamins.

Révész, A. and Han, Z. (2006). Task content familiarity, task type and efficacy of recasts. *Language Awareness*, *15*(3), 160–178.

Sachs, R. and Suh, B. (2007). Textually enhanced recasts, learner awareness, and L2 outcomes in synchronous computer-mediated interaction. In A. Mackey (Ed.), *Conversational interaction in second language acquisition* (pp. 197–227). Oxford: Oxford University Press.

Sagarra, N. (2007). From CALL to face-to-face interaction: The effect of computer-delivere drecasts and working memory on L2 development. In A. Mackey (Ed.), *Conversational interaction in second language acquisition* (pp. 229–248). Oxford: Oxford University Press.

Sato and Lyster, R. (2007). Modified output of Japanese EFL learners: Variable effects of interlocutor versus feedback types. In A. Mackey (Ed.), *Conversational interaction in second language acquisition* (pp. 29–52). Oxford: Oxford University Press.

Sauro, S. (2009). Computer-mediated corrective feedback and the development of L2 grammar. *Language Learning and Technology, 13*(1), 96–120.

Saxton, M. (1997). The contrast theory of negative input. *Journal of Child Language, 24*, 139–161.

Saxton, M. (2005). "Recast" in a new light: Insights for practice from typical language studies. *Child Language Teaching and Therapy, 21*(1), 23–38.

Schmidt, R. (1995). *Attention and awareness in foreign language learning.* Honolulu: University of Hawai'i Press.

Sheen, Y. (2004). Corrective feedback and learner uptake in communicative classrooms across instructional settings. *Language Teaching Research, 8*(3), 263–300.

Sheen, Y. (2006). Exploring the relationship between characteristics of recasts and learner uptake. *Language Teaching Research, 10*(4), 361–392.

Sheen, Y. (2007). The effects of corrective feedback, language aptitude and learner attitudes on the acquisition of English articles. In A. Mackey (Ed.), *Conversational interaction in second language acquisition* (pp. 301–322). Oxford: Oxford University Press.

Sheen, Y. (2008). Recasts, language anxiety, modified output and L2 learning. *Language Learning, 58*, 835–874.

Smith, B. (2003). Computer-mediated negotiated interaction: An expanded model. *The Modern Language Journal, 87*, 38–57.

Spada, N. and Lightbown, P. M. (1993). Instruction and the development of questions in L2 classrooms. *Studies in Second Language Acquisition, 15*, 205–224.

Swain, M. (1995). Three functions of output in second language learning. In G. Cook and B. Seidlhofer (Eds.), *Principles and practice in the study of language: Studies in Honour of H. G. Widdowson.* Oxford: Oxford University Press.

Tarone, E. and Bigelow, M. (2007). Alphabetic print literacy and processing of oral corrective feedback in L2 interaction. In A. Mackey (Ed.), *Conversational interaction in second language acquisition* (pp. 101–121). Oxford: Oxford University Press.

Trofimovitch, P., Ammar, A., and Gatbonton, E. (2007). How effective are recasts? The role of attention, memory, and analytical ability. In A. Mackey (Ed.), *Conversational interaction in second language acquisition* (pp. 171–195). Oxford: Oxford University Press.

Truscott, J. (1999). What's wrong with oral grammar correction. *The Canadian Modern Language Review, 55*, 437–455.

Varonis, E. and Gass, S. (1985). Non-native/non-native conversations: A model for negotiation of meaning. *Applied Linguistics, 6*, 71–90.

White, L. (1991). Adverb placement in second language acquisition: Some effects of positive and negative evidence in the classroom. *Second Language Research, 7*, 133–161.

Williams, J. (1999). Learner-generated attention to form. *Language Learning, 49*(4), 583–625.

Yang, Y. and Lyster, R. (2010). Effects of form-focused practice and feedback on Chinese EFL learners' acquisition of regular and irregular past-tense forms. *Studies in Second Language Acquisition, 32*(2), 235–263.

Yoshida, R. (2008). Teachers' choice and learners' preference of corrective feedback types. *Language Awareness, 17*(1), 78–93.

Zhao, S.Y. and Bitchener, J. (2007). Incidental focus on form in teacher-learner and learner-learner interactions. *System, 35*, 431–447.

Zyzik, E. and Polio, C. (2008). Incidental focus on form in university Spanish literature courses. *The Modern Language Journal, 92*, 53–70.

3

Variationist perspectives

Robert Bayley and Elaine Tarone[1]

Historical discussion

After Corder (1967) proposed that second-language learners have a universal "built-in syllabus" that guides them in the systematic development of their own linguistic system, or "transitional competence," Selinker (1972) posited that this linguistic system (which he called "interlanguage") was variable, in that learner utterances could be expected to vary dramatically in form depending on whether the learner was trying to communicate meaning or was focused on form (as when responding to classroom drills and exercises or providing grammaticality judgments). Thus, variationist SLA began in 1972. Only three years later, Dickerson (1975), drawing upon the models of variation developed by Labov (1966, 1972a, 1972b), Wolfram (1969), and others for the study of variation in first languages, particularly in non-standard dialects, published the first variationist study of interlanguage. Her results showed systematic shifts in the accuracy of Japanese learners' production of English *z* depending on the degree of attention to form required by the task (e.g., reading a passage vs. reading a word list). Soon after, Beebe (1977, 1980) demonstrated the dramatic impact of the interlocutor on Thai English L2 learners' variable production of phonological forms. Early studies (Adamson, 1980; Ellis, 1985, 1987) explored the impact of social factors such as interlocutor and task on interlanguage variation and are summarized in Tarone (1988). Many early longitudinal case studies focusing on the spontaneous production of learner language in the daily life of individual learners, such as Schumann (1978) and Huebner (1983), also gathered data varying across a wide range of social situations.

However, in the 1980s, Krashen's (1981, 1982) Monitor Model portrayed a learner's attention to linguistic form as categorical, and not variably related to nuances of social context. In the mid-80s SLA researchers (most of whom had no background or interest in sociolinguistics) focused on learner cognition, using research designs based in experimental psychology. Such studies (e.g., Liceras, 1985; Zobl, 1985) ignored or even denied the relevance of social context to interlanguage development; they could be carried out in the convenience of on-campus labs and classrooms, assuming the irrelevance of social context. Selinker and Douglas (1985) urged that social context should be taken into account in interlanguage theory, but without much success. Generativists such as Gregg (1990) argued that variation was just a matter of performance that could be safely ignored by SLA researchers, whose focus of study should be competence, not performance. Perhaps the most explicit claim about the irrelevance of social context to learner language development in SLA is this one:

> Remove a learner from the social setting, and the L2 grammar does not change or disappear. Change the social setting altogether, e.g., from street to classroom, or from a foreign to a

second language environment, and, as far as we know, the way the learner acquires does not change much either, as suggested, e.g., by comparisons of error types, developmental sequences, processing constraints, and other aspects of the acquisition process in and out of classrooms .... (Long, 1998, p. 93)

This position, Tarone (2000a) argues, provides a useful set of hypotheses to be subjected to empirical verification by variationist SLA research carried out in a wide range of social contexts. Such research, she argues, has shown that cognition in SLA is affected by the social context (cf., Liu, 2000; Tarone, 2010). The SLA database is currently far too narrowly restricted in terms of the social status of learners studied (Bigelow and Tarone, 2004); for example, the vast majority of those who learn L2s worldwide are illiterate, yet almost no SLA research has been carried out in such populations or the social settings in which they live. Do we really intend to imply that illiterate L2 learners do not matter? A variationist approach to SLA calls for researchers to expand the study of social circumstances and learner types beyond school and academic settings and to study SLA as it occurs across the widest possible range of social settings and learner types.

Core issues

We will now examine some central theoretical assumptions of variationist L2 research.

An L2 Speaker produces a range of styles, depending on social context

This is one of the central assumptions of sociolinguistics, articulated by Labov (1972b): there are no single-style speakers. Tarone (1972) posited that there are no single-style L2 learners either. Every speaker has a range of styles that are appropriate for use in different social situations. According to Labov, these speech styles could be ranged on a continuum from informal (vernacular) to formal styles, where the speaker's attention to speech might cause a shift to more formal styles ("style shifting"). There is little doubt today that such variation is inherent in interlanguage, particularly at the level of phonology (Major, 2001). That said, it remains to be learned what a second language learner's set of interlanguage styles is, especially in the beginning stages of acquisition, and how different styles develop.

The most systematic style produced by the L2 Speaker is the vernacular

Although variationist methods have been successfully used in a substantial number of L2 studies, we cannot always take the methods developed in one discipline and apply them to another. Perhaps the most obvious problem concerns accessing the vernacular, or speakers' more unmonitored styles. Even when we design tasks to elicit different levels of L2 learner attention to speech, that is to elicit different speech styles, the results are often much more complex than usually found in L1 studies, which show a clear progression from casual speech to reading word lists. For example, Ellis (1985, 1987, 1989) has argued that free variation may be a characteristic of some interlanguage systems. In a study of syntactic and morphological variation in the interlanguage of L1 Arabic and L1 Japanese learners of English L2, Tarone (1985) found that their accuracy in the use of third-person singular verbal -s was greater in a multiple choice grammar test (where the entire focus was on form) than in a narrative task, which presumably required less attention to form. However, at the same time, and contrary to what one might expect, the same learners' accuracy in article use was *least* accurate on the multiple choice grammar task and *most* accurate on the oral narrative. In other words, in moving from one task to the next, the learners' accuracy in producing articles *increased* at the same time their third-person singular -*s* accuracy *decreased*.

The superordinate norm, or target, of interlanguage development can be idiosyncratic

Our interpretation of second-language speakers' responses is made difficult by the fact that we do not always know what their perception of the target language (TL) norm is. With native-language speakers, we interpret linguistic forms to mean what they seem to mean. In learner speech, however, a speaker's failure to use forms that are obligatory in the TL can easily lead to confusion. For example, in a sociolinguistic interview with an intermediate speaker of English, Bayley (1991) asked about the participant's family. The speaker offered a long account about his grandfather, a government official in China. All of the verbs in the account were unmarked for tense. Bayley then asked: "How old is your grandfather?" The response: "Oh, he die in 1969." It was fortunate that the interviewer thought to ask about the grandfather's age. Otherwise, the unmarked past-tense forms would simply have been coded as unmarked present-tense forms, with third-person singular -*s* missing.

The identity of the researcher has an impact on the speech of second-language learners

A problem in adapting sociolinguistic constructs to SLA research concerns the identity of the interviewer. Like many variationists who work with native language communities, some SLA scholars have elected to have interviews conducted by ethnically congruent fieldworkers. Beebe (1980) showed that Thai learners of English used more Thai variants when interviewed by ethnic Thais than by ethnic Chinese. In a study of English past-tense marking, Wolfram and Hatfield (1984) controlled this variable by hiring only ethnic Vietnamese to interview Vietnamese English L2 speakers in the Washington, D.C. area. However, such a decision presents problems because it takes away the need to use the TL rather than the interviewer's and interviewee's shared L1, which would be more natural (and easier) (see, e.g., Broner, 2001; Tarone and Swain, 1995).

It is unclear what categories define the speech community (and identity) of the L2 learner

In traditional sociolinguistics, researchers often aggregate speakers in a community according to social categories. Sociolinguists generally consider it axiomatic that constraints on variation have the same effect on all members of a speech community, although individuals may vary greatly in their use of a particular variant (Guy, 1991). For example, New Yorkers of all social classes are more likely to pronounce postvocalic /r/ in more careful than in more casual speech (Labov, 1966). Language change within a speech community may occur either "from above" (that is, begin with the most formal, superordinate style and over time spread downward into less formal styles) or "from below" (begin in an informal style and spread upward into more formal styles). Hence, if we are interested in the direction of language change within a community or in patterns of stable variation that distinguish one community from another, we are justified in aggregating speakers who belong to similar social categories (but see Johnstone, 1996).

However, when we attempt to identify the relevant speech communities of L2 speakers, the basis for aggregating speakers is much less firm. Preston (1989, p. 257) has proposed that the learners in an L2 classroom may constitute a speech community, and argued that both forces, of "change from above" and "change from below," apply in such communities. Tarone (2009, pp. 46–49) agrees, but more studies are needed to document the directionality of language change. Learner varieties change rapidly as acquisition proceeds and the same constraints on variability may not be operative at all stages of acquisition. In addition, the type of language that learners acquire is influenced by the context in which learning occurs, by opportunities for interactions with target language speakers, and by the varieties with which the learner comes into contact (Nagy et al., 2003). Moreover, although there are numerous similarities in the paths L2 acquirers take toward the target language, there is also considerable evidence that L2 acquirers pursue individually divergent learning strategies that may lead to differences in what is acquired (Bialystok, 1990). L2 learner identity and group orientation may be defined in terms of categories not traditionally used in sociolinguistics; for example, L2 learners entering academic disciplines may define themselves more in terms of membership in academic discourse communities than membership in traditional speech communities (Swales, 1990, pp. 23–27). Given current knowledge, we suggest that researchers need to examine individual patterns at various stages of acquisition rather than simply assume that learners, even learners from the same language background, will construct their identities according to traditional sociolinguistic categories, or that language change in learner communities will be analogous to that in the speech community in the Labovian sense.[2]

Data and common elicitation measures

Data

Since its inception as a subfield of linguistics in the 1960s with Labov's work on Martha's Vineyard and in New York City (1963, 1966, 1972a) and comparable studies in Detroit by Shuy et al. (1968) and Wolfram (1969), sociolinguistics has relied on natural speech data collected in the community. The centrality of this sort of data is based on the axiom described above that a speaker's vernacular, or the language variety learned first and spoken in the community, is more systematic than other more formal styles that may be susceptible to phenomena such as hyper-correction (e.g., the use of "I" in object position). According to Labov (1972b) this is the "the observer's paradox": our goal is to understand how speakers, including L2 speakers (Tarone, 1972), use informal language when they are not being observed; however, to obtain the data that we need, we must observe them. Although modern compact recording equipment has mitigated the paradox somewhat, making possible, for example, the nuanced identification of gender differences in the production of such informal L2 variants as -in' for -ing (Adamson and Regan, 1991), it has not done away with the problem.

Methodologies of data collection

Sociolinguists commonly conduct cross-sectional studies of a speech community to understand language change. Variationist SLA research also often uses this model, collecting data at a single time by sociolinguistic interviews or ethnographic observation. Typically, such studies include learners at different stages of acquisition.

The sociolinguistic interview. One solution to the observer's paradox is the sociolinguistic interview (Labov, 1972a, 1984), which contains modules dealing with topics designed to put the researcher in a "one-down" or less powerful position in relation to the speaker; such topics include childhood games, dating patterns, marriage and family, dreams, and (famously) danger of death (Have you ever been in a situation where you were in serious danger of getting killed?). Questions about these topics are brief and phrased in everyday speech. To elicit a wider range of speech styles and comparable data across speakers, sociolinguistic interviews may also include more formal tasks such as reading passages, word lists, and lists of minimal pairs; typically these are reserved for the end of the interview. The use of this same range of formal tasks to elicit L2 learner language has produced the same patterns of style shifting (Dickerson, 1975; Gatbonton, 1978).

The issue of researcher identity and community membership can affect outcomes in socio-linguistic interviews with both first and second language speakers: speakers use different speech styles with outsiders than with those they perceive to be community members. Rickford and McNair-Knox (1994), for example, report that a young female African American Vernacular English (AAVE) speaker spoke in a much less vernacular style with a white interviewer than with an African American interviewer from the community. As noted above, Beebe (1980) showed the same effect with Thai learners of English. However, sociolinguists who are not members of the community being studied may sometimes be able to establish a kind of insider-outsider role. Cukor-Avila and Bailey (2001), white linguists who have worked for many years in a rural African American community in Texas, argue that the effects of an interviewer's race can be minimized in the right circumstances: "familiarity with the informant and the use of peer groups ... can substantially ameliorate any effects that race of the fieldworker might have" (p. 267). The L2 learner vernacular use documented by Rampton (1995) suggests that this can also be the case in some SLA variationist research.

Ethnographic observation and the problem of identity. A number of early studies of sociolinguistic variation, including Labov's (1963) classic study of Martha's Vineyard, incorporated ethnographic observation and sought explanations for observed patterns of variation in the social categories that were meaningful to the community under observation. That is, they employed methods designed to assess speakers' views of meaningful social distinctions and interpretations of interactions. However, in the ensuing years, numerous variationist studies have relied primarily on quantitative analysis of linguistic variables and based their social analysis on externally prescribed social categories such as gender, social class defined in terms of indices of occupation and income, and ethnicity. Use of such externally derived categories provides us with an overall picture of changes occurring across the broad spectrum of a community, but it also has serious limitations. For example, large-scale studies that focus on pre-existing social and regional categories tend to view identities as static: constructed as membership in a particular class, with a particular regional identity, male or female, or a native or non-native speaker of a dominant language. However, identities are multifaceted and cannot be reduced to such predefined social categories; for example, gender is obviously distinct from biological sex. Moreover, as Bucholtz (1999) observed, by concentrating on core members of a group, traditional sociolinguistic studies tend to ignore marginal members. This dynamic becomes problematic when we deal with more fine-grained, individual-level nuances of language use and change, and particularly problematic in second-language acquisition research focused on immigrants. This is both because such speakers are often marginalized and because they may establish identities and social categories that do not accord with predefined categories in the host (TL) community (as in Bigelow, 2009 and Rampton, 1995). For example, Bigelow documents the hybrid identities being created by Somali adolescent immigrants in Minnesota and the creative mix of Somali and English language forms they produce. More such SLA research is needed.

To overcome some of the limitations of variationist approaches that emphasized recruiting individuals to represent predefined social categories, researchers have developed two main methods. The first, pioneered by Milroy (1987) in a study of Belfast, Northern Ireland, makes use of social networks. In her data collection, Milroy adopted an "emic" perspective and attempted to understand the social patterns of the community from participants' viewpoints, introducing herself to potential study participants as a "friend of a friend." Initial contacts led to other contacts with members of the participants' social networks until she had recruited a sufficient number of participants who met the study criteria. Crucially, "the unit of study was the pre-existing social group, rather than a series of isolated individuals as representatives of particular social categories" (Milroy, 2002, p. 553). Milroy's focus on pre-existing social groups opens up the possibility that such groups are organized using non-traditional categories that are meaningful to the members, and so must be used in understanding the group's language use.

The second approach is the community of practice (CofP), which, like the social network approach, ideally combines ethnographic observation and rigorous quantitative and linguistic analysis. Eckert's (2000) study of Detroit-area high school students is perhaps the best-known example. Based on extensive observations in the school, Eckert delineated a range of social practices engaged in by the two main identity categories identified by the students themselves (categories that did not correlate strictly with traditional, externally defined, social class categories): the "jocks," youth whose social lives centered around the school, and the "burnouts," youths whose social lives centered on activities outside the school. The students differed not only in pronunciation patterns such as their degree of participation in the Northern Cities Shift (with the burnouts being more advanced), but also in dress styles, places where members congregated, and whether they smoked. Other studies have examined communities of practice in a wide variety of settings. Bucholtz (1999) reports on an internally defined category of "nerd girls" in a northern California high school, who were distinguished not only by their language choices (precise diction, avoidance of slang, verbal play), but also by dress, taste in music, and academic orientation. Mendoza-Denton (2008) and Zhang (2005) employ the CofP approach to characterize Latina gang girls and Chinese yuppies respectively, and Haneda (1997) examines the CofP for SLA in a university Japanese foreign language setting.

Longitudinal research. Cross-sectional studies of speakers of different generations have served the field of sociolinguistics well. In fact, a number of scholars have returned to their original research sites and resurveyed the communities; for example, Cedergren (1988) found that her earlier study of Panamanians of different generations provided a generally accurate view of the direction of language change. However, since individuals acquiring second languages vary in their acquisitional trajectories and the same factors can affect learners at different levels of acquisition differently (Preston and Bayley, 2009), it is clear that variationist SLA research requires more longitudinal studies if we are to understand how patterns of variability change as acquisition proceeds.

Fortunately, a number of recent variationist SLA studies have been longitudinal in design. These include Liu's study of a Chinese immigrant to Australia (Liu, 1991, 2000; Tarone and Liu, 1995), Regan's (1996) study of variable *ne* deletion by Irish students before and after a year in France, Lybeck's (2002) study of the acquisition of Norwegian pronunciation by American sojourners in Norway, and Hansen's (2006) study of the acquisition of English syllable structure by a Vietnamese family in Arizona. We will use Liu (2000), Lybeck (2002) and Hansen (2006) to illustrate some of the advantages to be gained by longitudinal studies of L2 variation.

Liu (2000) compares the English language development of "Bob," a five-year-old Chinese immigrant to Australia, in three different situations over a period of two years: interactions with his teacher in class, with peers in classroom deskwork, and at home in play sessions with a family friend. With his teacher, Bob does not initiate turns and he produces only simple sentences or sentence fragments. However, with his peers and the family friend, he initiates more turns, produces more complex sentences, and assertively negotiates meaning. As Liu tracks Bob's acquisition of different stages of English questions across time and social context, he shows that almost every new stage is first produced with the family friend at home, then with his friends in desk work, and last with his teacher. Thus, the rate of acquisition of L2 is fastest in the at-home setting. Indeed, Liu (2000) argues that if Bob's only social setting for English use had been in interactions with his teacher, his progress in acquiring English L2 would have been much slower. Bob's pattern of language change is "change from below": development begins in the informal style and spreads over time to the formal style. Crucially, social setting also impacts Bob's *order of acquisition* of English questions. (According to Pienemann and Johnston, 1987, question stages are universal; they must always be acquired in numerical order, 1–5.) But for Bob, Stage 4 and 5 questions emerge at home before Stage 3 questions—and then when Stage 3 finally appears weeks later, it is not at home, but in deskwork with peers. This fact could only have been discovered by a variationist longitudinal case study of this design.

Lybeck (2002) tested Schumann's (1978) acculturation model, operationalized through social network theory (Milroy, 1987), to examine the extent to which acculturation patterns were correlated with success in the acquisition of pronunciation features by nine American women who had lived in Norway between one and three years. Participants were examined twice, once at the beginning of the study and once six months later, with a focus on two features, Norwegian *r*, pronounced as an alveolar trill or tap in native speech, and production of syllable length distinctions. As expected, speakers who were more integrated into Norwegian social networks increased in accuracy over the six months while those who were not integrated into native speaker networks showed little or no change. One participant's accuracy even decreased over time, including a decrease of 24.6 percent in her use of native-like *r* (Lybeck, 2002, p. 182) during a period when she experienced increased "dissatisfaction with her Norwegian exchange ties" (2002, p. 183). Even though Lybeck's study only spanned six months, she was able to demonstrate phonological change over time. Importantly, her longitudinal study, like Liu's, showed that change is not necessarily universally predictable and unidirectional, moving inexorably closer to target language norms; rather, change may involve movement away from target language norms.[3]

Hansen's (2006) study of the acquisition of syllable onsets and codas by a Vietnamese immigrant couple is among the few recent SLA studies that focus on working-class immigrants. The participants, Anh Nguyen, age 41, and her husband Nhi Nguyen, age 46, had been in the United States for less than a year when the study began. Although they had been teachers in Vietnam and members of their family who had immigrated earlier had achieved considerable success, their occupations in the U.S. conferred little status and limited income. Mrs. Nguyen worked as a nail technician and Mr. Nguyen as an order-filler for a factory. Hansen (2006) interviewed the Nguyens 28 times over a ten-month period, resulting in 42 hours of recording. Her detailed analysis of the Nguyens' phonological development is based on recordings of three sessions, one at the beginning of the data collection period, another from the middle, and a third at the end. Hansen's VARBRUL analysis shows the trajectory of acquisition, with fewer transfer effects over time, as well as the effect of social barriers.

Lybeck's (2002) and Hansen's (2006) studies provide valuable data on the acquisition of L2 phonology. As with any small-scale studies, it is difficult to generalize from their conclusions. While Hansen's working-class participants may be representative of a large number of adult immigrants, particularly those from Southeast Asia, it is not clear whether the processes Hansen identified would apply to Lybeck's (2002) middle-class participants. While Lybeck illustrates the effects of social networks on the acquisition of Norwegian phonological features, it is unclear whether similar findings would be found in less privileged immigrant communities such as the substantial Norwegian Filipino community examined in Lanza and Svendsen (2007). More longitudinal studies of SLA are needed to probe questions such as these, and to study further the way social factors influence the acquisition of L2 forms variably over time.

Methodology of data analysis

The main goal of variationist fieldwork is to collect a sufficient sample of the language variety being used by the community of interest, where "community" may be defined in a variety of ways described above. Normally this involves collecting many hours of natural speech, usually in sociolinguistic interviews but sometimes in ethnographic or other types of observations as well.

As we have shown in our discussion of the longitudinal studies summarized above, the process of data analysis involves establishing the linguistic or social categories that encourage or discourage the speaker's use of different variants of a relevant linguistic variable. For example, one variable in Lybeck's study was r, which had two variants: native-like Norwegian r and American r; the study identified linguistic and social contexts that favored either the Norwegian or the American variant. Such a process involves a detailed quantitative analysis: once the relevant linguistic variable has been identified, the researcher extracts all the relevant tokens of that variable in all relevant environments, i.e., in all linguistic or social contexts that may influence a speaker's choice of one or another variant. And, since variation is normally influenced not by one but by many contextual factors, any quantitative analysis of variation requires a very large number of tokens. Labov (1989, p. 90), for example, summarized the influences on t/d deletion (e.g., *west* → *wes'*) across all varieties of English, where each variable listed below has been demonstrated to encourage greater deletion:

(a) syllable stress (unstressed > stressed[4])
(b) consonant cluster length (CC$\underline{C}$ > C$\underline{C}$)
(c) the phonetic features of the preceding consonant, yielding the segmental order /s/ > stops > nasals > other fricatives > liquids
(d) the grammatical status of the final /-t,d/, with the order: part of -$\underline{n't}$ morpheme > part of stem > derivational suffix > past tense or past participial suffix
(e) the phonetic features of the following segment, yielding the order: obstruents > liquids > glides > vowels > pauses
(f) agreement in voicing of the segments preceding and following the /-t,d/ (homovoiced > heterovoiced).

Several of these influences on t/d deletion overlap in natural speech; for example, a three-consonant cluster always occurs in a syllable that is either stressed or unstressed. A moment's reflection should suffice to indicate that not all combinations of influencing factors occur equally in natural speech. For example, monomorphemic -t/d clusters occur much more frequently than past tense -t/d clusters. Furthermore, some combinations of factors are impossible. However, even if we exclude such categories, we are still left with a very large number of possible combinations. In the case of -t/d deletion, even if we eliminate -*n't* clusters, we are left with 600 possible cells in a spread sheet tabulating possible combinations, and we have yet to consider any possible social factors. If we add gender, three age groups, and two social classes, the number of possible cells increases to 7,200.

Given the number of possible cell combinations and the rarity of some combinations, conventional statistical methods that rely on balanced distribution derived from controlled experiments are unsuitable for the informal speech data gathered in sociolinguistic interviews. For many years, sociolinguists have relied on VARBRUL, a specialized application of logistic regression (Sankoff *et al.*, 2005).[5] As Young and Bayley (1996) note, "the programs known as VARBRUL have been used most extensively [in sociolinguistics] because they have been deliber-ately designed to handle the kind of data obtained in studies of variation. They also provide heuristic tools that allow the investigator to modify his or her hypotheses and reanalyze the data easily" (p. 256).

A substantial number of variationist studies of the acquisition of many L2s have used VARBRUL. These include, to name just a few, Young's (1991) work on the acquisition of English plural marking by Chinese native speakers, Bayley's (1994, 1996) studies of the acquisition of English past-tense morphology and variable consonant cluster reduction by native speakers of Chinese, and numerous studies of *ne* deletion by learners of Canadian and continental French (e.g., Regan, 1996, 2004; Rehner and Mougeon, 1999; Sax, 1999). Other work includes Jia and Bayley's (2008) study of the acquisition of aspectual marking by Chinese heritage language learners and Rau and colleagues' (2009) study of Chinese learners' acquisition of the English interdental fricative. Overall, these studies have provided a valuable perspective on a number of issues in SLA. For example, saliency seems to have a similar effect on tense marking in both L2 English and L2 Hungarian (Bayley and Langman, 2004), consistent with the hypothesis that noticing facilitates the learning of L2 forms (Schmidt, 2001). In addition, in both L2 Chinese and L2 French, speakers tend to use vernacular forms less frequently than native speakers—and follow classroom norms more closely than is typical of native speakers (Li, 2010; Mougeon *et al.*, 2004, 2010). Moreover, L2 speakers' social networks play an important role in the acquisition and use of variable target language features (Liu, 1991, 2000; Lybeck, 2002; Nagy *et al.*, 2003; Tarone and Liu, 1995). Learners acquire L2s at different rates across different social contexts, and social context may even alter developmental sequences in SLA, as in Liu's (1991, 2000) longitudinal study of English L2 question acquisition. Finally, quantitative variationist studies of SLA have shown convincingly, using VARBRUL and other statistical instruments, that learner varieties, like native languages, are likely to be systematic and that the examination of learners' variable departures from interlanguage norms can tell us a good deal about order of acquisition, the difficulty of various forms, and the impact of linguistic and social factors on cognitive processes of SLA over time.

Learner language may be studied in context using interactionist, sociocultural, and discourse approaches to SLA; such approaches document ways in which interlocutors may influence L2 input and output. However, the variationist approach to SLA is unique in its ability to offer powerful tools for the quantitative analysis of learner language in either cross-sectional or longitudinal studies, statistical tools that are capable of establishing the intricate and interacting relationships among a wide range of linguistic and social variables, many of which may not have been predetermined by the researcher, but all of which are shown to come together in patterned ways to influence development in a learners' production of specific linguistic forms.

Applications

Variationist studies of SLA raise a number of issues for instruction and assessment. These issues differ, however, depending on whether the focus is variability in the use of obligatory target language forms or the ability to style shift. We will consider each of these areas in turn.

Interlanguage variation, instruction, and assessment of obligatory forms

As illustrated in the previous sections, studies of interlanguage variation have amply demonstrated that linguistic and social context affects variable learner use and acquisition of forms that are obligatory in the target language. The degree of difference between present- and past-tense forms constrains past-tense marking (Bayley, 1994; Wolfram and Hatfield, 1984); past-tense marking in a number of interlanguages is constrained by lexical aspect (e.g., Ayoun and Salaberry, 2005, 2008; Bardovi-Harlig, 2000; Collins, 2002); redundancy appears to favor use of obligatory target language morphemes, as Young (1991) showed in his study of English plural marking by Chinese adult learners. And, finally, longitudinal studies that take social context into account show how social factors influence the acquisition of TL forms, both syntactic (Liu, 2000; Tarone and Liu, 1995) and phonological (Hansen, 2006; Lybeck, 2002). If learner language may change "from below" (beginning with learner vernaculars) as well as "from above" (beginning with formal instruction), then there are clear implications for classroom pedagogy. For example, it appears that not all learner language change begins with a focus on form, in the learner's most formal style, as predicted by sociocultural or interactionist theory. Rather some learner language changes may begin in the vernacular style, as the learner focuses on meaning in more relaxed settings, possibly through language play (Tarone, 2000b), and then spread to more formal styles. Classroom instruction should be set up to encourage both types of language change (for suggestions, see Tarone, 2000b).

Variationist studies also have implications for language assessment. First, learner accuracy in a testing situation changes considerably depending whether the question encodes general content or field-specific content (Smith, 1989). Second, different types of tasks can promote accuracy in the use of some forms while inhibiting accuracy in the use of other forms, as shown in the example from Tarone (1985), where a narrative task favored accuracy in English definite article use, but not in third-person singular -s, while a fill-in-the blanks test had the opposite effect. Third, the interlocutor can have an important effect on second language use and acquisition (Broner, 2000; Tarone and Liu, 1995). Fourth, most tests of language proficiency are based on the standard language. However, we have considerable evidence that the standard language is not the only—or even the main—target for many language learners. Goldstein (1987), for example, shows that the use of AAVE features by New York Puerto Ricans is influenced by speakers' degree of contact with African Americans and by affective factors. Thus, in interpreting learner performance on assessments, we might ask, for example, whether the absence of third-person singular -s, is evidence of a speaker's failure to acquire a form that is obligatory in the standard language or evidence of the speaker's success in acquiring a form in the English dialect that provides the bulk of the input.

Instruction and stylistic variation

Acquiring full proficiency in a language entails not only acquiring a native-like grammar, but also acquiring native speaker patterns of variation, including the ability to style shift in moving from formal to informal social situations, as, from the classroom to a range of social contexts outside the classroom. It is common for students to master new elements of the L2 in all classroom activities, but not be able use those same elements when they walk out the door of the classroom and try to use them in other social contexts. A fully proficient L2 speaker will be able to use the language when focused on meaning and not just when focused on form, be familiar with the use of a range of grammar and discourse markers, and be able to express emotions appropriately in a wide range of social contexts. However, as Tarone and Swain (1995) note, language classrooms are necessarily relatively formal environments where only certain forms of discourse are considered appropriate, and where a premium is usually placed on grammatical accuracy rather than communicative appropriateness. Indeed, this is a perennial problem for language teachers who hope to provide their students with the ability to actually use their L2 to communicate outside the classroom. Language classrooms naturally elicit formal styles of speech and encourage attention to formal accuracy; it is the purpose of schools and universities to foster the development of academic, formal styles of speech, and it is a primary purpose of classroom language teachers to offer accurate models of those styles, and, when students speak, to provide consistent corrective feedback on form. For this reason, students who learn L2s only in classrooms tend to learn to produce only academic and formal styles of those L2s (usually carefully-monitored), and usually find themselves at a loss when they need to use L2 in social situations outside the classroom where vernacular and informal L2 registers are more appropriate. For example, Dewaele (2005) documents the difficulties he experienced as a youthful speaker of L2 Spanish who was unable to move beyond the classroom register he had learned in school.

University language and K–12 language immersion teachers have struggled for decades to find ways to provide their students, proficient only in formal registers of the L2, with exposure to and practice in the less formal L2 registers. The importance of this exposure can hardly be over-emphasized. In just one example, Tarone and Swain (1995) found that pre-adolescent French immersion students who lacked a vernacular register of French appropriate for peer-peer inter-action, fell back on their native language, English, to talk among themselves and ultimately began using English more and more even in classroom academic discussions.

The question raised by studies such as Tarone and Swain (1995) and Dewaele (2005) is how to provide L2 learners in classroom contexts with sociolinguistically appropriate input. Teachers are not appropriate sources for the adolescent vernacular; adults who attempt to use adolescent language merely wind up sounding ridiculous. Indeed, classrooms are clearly not the place for most informal varieties suitable to the home, the street, or the blue collar workplace, or for topics such as pop culture or certain kinds of recreational activity[6]. Many teachers urge their students to leave the classroom and use their L2 in other social contexts—to study abroad, for instance, or to interact with heritage learners in the local community. For students who have no opportunity to study abroad, and no context for L2 use other than the classroom, a range of less-than-adequate tools exist. For example, Dewaele suggests the use of *telenovelas* in the foreign language classroom to expose language learners to the language of the home and of popular culture. Such sources, as well as films and short videos, can be used in the classroom to provide input on adolescent varieties, the language of popular culture, the language of sports, etc., and promote discussion of different types of language and their appropriateness to particular situations. We know that "input does not equal intake" (Corder, 1967)—that is, it will be difficult for learners to convert this informal input into intake so they can use it themselves in similar social situations—but some input is better than none. To encourage production of informal styles, students may be asked to do role-plays, imagining how they might use their L2s in a range of social situations, even though the undeniable fact is that their teachers are still there judging their performance inside the four walls of a classroom. Internet chat may offer classroom-bound learners the opportunity to engage in authentic interaction with L2 speakers who are not teachers, and expose them to the stylistic differences of L2 that vary according to context. Van Compernolle and Pierozak (2009), for example, examined the use of three widely studied French sociolinguistic variables—*on/nous*, *tu/vous*, and *ne* omission[7]—in 16 hours of moderated and un-moderated internet chat. They found that moderated chat closely approximated what L2 learners find in their textbooks and in teachers' speech. However, un-moderated chat presented quite a different picture. Second-person *vous* was used 99.5 percent of the time in moderated chat, while *tu* was used 99.8 percent of the time in un-moderated chat. Results for the other variables were almost as dramatic. First-person plural *nous*, the formal variant, was used at a rate of over 90 percent in moderated chat, but at a rate of less than 5 percent in un-moderated chat, where *on* was the preferred form. Similarly, *ne* was categorically present in moderated chat, but absent from 84 percent of the instances of negation in un-moderated chat.

Based on the pedagogical framework of the New London Group (1996), van Compernolle and Williams (2009) offer a four-stage model for instruction involving teacher-led whole group identification of relevant variants, small group discussions to give learners the opportunity to use new forms, comparison of patterns of variation in French and the students' native language, and finally participation in online French chat. (Online chat today can either be written or oral, asynchronous or synchronous; voice over internet protocol software such as Skype enables telephone-like synchronous voice interaction between foreign language learners and native speakers at minimal cost.) Participation in authentic communication through online chat may help meet L2 learners' need for authentic input from peers and opportunities for informal stylistic and vernacular L2 use.

Future directions

Despite the demanding nature of longitudinal studies, we need more such studies if we are to understand clearly how L2 users move from non-use to variable use to near native-like use of target language grammatical forms, and how social context affects that movement. The nature of longitudinal studies necessarily limits the number of participants in each study. Nevertheless, given a substantial number of longitudinal studies of speakers of different L1s acquiring different L2s, we will be in a position to understand more clearly what kinds of factors, both linguistic and social, constrain learners at all levels, what constraints are particular to speakers of different L1s, which to speakers of different L2s, and what factors impact learners differently at different stages of acquisition.

In addition, as noted above, a number of researchers in sociolinguistics have combined detailed qualitative studies of speakers' social groups with quantitative studies of linguistic variables. To understand fully the complex effects of social context on the L2 acquisition and use of language learners, we need similar studies of second language acquisition, particularly in immigrant communities. Variationist perspectives on SLA require that we move beyond the confines of the university, and conduct longitudinal, multiple-context studies of different types of learners, as they use and acquire L2s in the social contexts in which they live.

Notes

1 Authors' names are listed alphabetically. Both authors contributed equally to this chapter.
2 Although we have several studies that show that individual patterns of variation match group patterns (Bayley and Langman, 2004; Regan, 2004), the studies are small scale.
3 An interlanguage acquisition process termed "backsliding" in Selinker (1972).
4 For the syllable stress variable, unstressed > stressed means that unstressed syllables have significantly more t/d deletion than stressed syllables. For the next variable, consonant cluster length, three-consonant clusters have more t/d deletion than two-consonant clusters, and so on.
5 For detailed descriptions of the use of VARBRUL, see Bayley (2002), Tagliamonte (2006), and Young and Bayley (1996).
6 Dennis Preston (2002) has pointed out that he cannot use phrases from his academic register in Southern Indiana where he grew up without negative social consequences. Phrases like "Had I the ball," for example, are too "high-falutin" for talk on the basketball court.
7 *On/nous* are variants of the first-person plural pronoun, *tu/vous* of the second-person singular pronoun and *ne* is the first particle of negation. Use of *on, tu,* and omission of *ne* are characteristic of informal discourse.

References

Adamson, H. D. (1980). A study of variable syntactic rules in the interlanguage of Spanish-speaking adults acquiring English as a second language. Unpublished doctoral dissertation, Georgetown University.

Adamson, H. D. and Regan, V. (1991). The acquisition of community norms by Asian immigrants learning English as a second language: A preliminary study. *Studies in Second Language Acquisition, 13,* 1–22.

Ayoun, D. and Salaberry, M. R. (Eds.) (2005). *Tense and aspect in romance languages.* Amsterdam: John Benjamins.

Ayoun, D. and Salaberry, M. R. (2008). Acquisition of English tense-aspect morphology by advanced French learners. *Language Learning, 58,* 555–595.

Bardovi-Harlig, K. (2000). *Tense and aspect in second language acquisition: Form, meaning and use.* Oxford: Blackwell.

Bayley, R. (1991). Variation theory and second language learning: Linguistic and social constraints on interlanguage tense marking. Unpublished doctoral dissertation, Stanford University.

Bayley, R. (1994). Interlanguage variation and the quantitative paradigm: Past-tense marking in Chinese-English. In E. Tarone, S. M. Gass, and A. D. Cohen (Eds.), *Research methodology in second-language acquisition* (pp. 157–181). Hillsdale, NJ: Lawrence Erlbaum.

Bayley, R. (1996). Competing constraints on variation in the speech of adult Chinese learners of English. In R. Bayley and D. R. Preston (Eds.), *Second language acquisition and linguistic variation* (pp. 97–120). Amsterdam: John Benjamins.

Bayley, R. (2002). The quantitative paradigm. In J. K. Chambers, P. Trudgill, and N. Schilling-Estes (Eds.), *The handbook of language variation and change* (pp. 117–141). Oxford: Blackwell.

Bayley, R. and Langman, J. (2004). Variation in the group and the individual: Evidence from second language acquisition. *IRAL, 42,* 303–318.

Beebe, L. (1977). The influence of the listener on code-switching. *Language Learning, 27,* 331–339.

Beebe, L. (1980). Sociolinguistic variation and style-shifting in second language acquisition. *Language Learning, 30,* 433–447.

Bialystok, E. (1990). *Communication strategies: A psychological analysis of second language use.* Oxford: Blackwell.

Bigelow, M. (2009). Texts and contexts for cultural and linguistic hybridity in the diaspora. *MI TESOL Conference Proceedings,* East Lansing, Michigan.

Bigelow, M. and Tarone, E. (2004). The role of literacy level in SLA: Doesn't *who* we study determine *what* we know? *TESOL Quarterly, 38,* 689–700.

Broner, M. (2000). Impact of interlocutor and task on first and second language use in a Spanish immersion program. Unpublished doctoral dissertation, University of Minnesota, Minneapolis.

Broner, M. (2001). Impact of interlocutor and task on first and second language use in a Spanish immersion program. *CARLA Working Paper, 18.* Minneapolis: University of Minnesota.

Bucholtz, M. (1999). "Why be normal?" Language and identity practices in a community of nerd girls. *Language in Society, 28,* 203–223.

Cedergren, H. (1988). The spread of language change: Verifying inferences of linguistic diffusion. In P. Lowenberg, (Ed.), *Language spread and language policy: Issues, implications, and case studies. Georgetown University round table on languages and linguistics* (pp. 45–60). Washington, D.C.: Georgetown University Press.

Collins, L. (2002). The roles of L1 influence and lexical aspect in the acquisition of temporal morphology. *Language Learning, 52,* 43–94.

Corder, S. P. (1967). The significance of learners' errors. *IRAL, 5,* 161–170.

Cukor-Avila, P. and Bailey, G. (2001). The effects of the race of the interviewer on sociolinguistic fieldwork. *Journal of Sociolinguistics, 5,* 254–270.

Dewaele, J.-M. (2005). Investigating the psychological and emotional dimensions in instructed language learning: Obstacles and possibilities. *The Modern Language Journal, 89,* 367–380.

Dickerson, L. (1975). The learner's interlanguage as a system of variable rules. *TESOL Quarterly, 9,* 401–407.

Eckert, P. (2000). *Linguistic variation as social practice: The linguistic construction of identity in Belten High.* Oxford: Blackwell.

Ellis, R. (1985). Sources of variability in interlanguage. *Applied Linguistics, 6,* 118–131.

Ellis, R. (1987). Interlanguage variability in narrative discourse: Style-shifting in the use of the past tense. *Studies in Second Language Acquisition, 9,* 1–20.

Ellis, R. (1989). Sources of intra-learner variability in language use and their relationship to second language acquisition. In S. Gass, C. Madden, D. Preston, and L. Selinker (Eds.), *Variation in second language acquisition, vol. II: Psycholinguistic issues* (pp. 22–45). Clevedon, UK: Multilingual Matters.

Gatbonton, E. (1978). Patterned phonetic variability in second language speech: A gradual diffusion model. *Canadian Modern Language Review, 34,* 335–347.

Goldstein, L. M. (1987). Standard English: The only target for nonnative speakers of English?. *TESOL Quarterly, 21*, 417–436.

Gregg, K. (1990). The variable competence model and why it isn't. *Applied Linguistics, 11*, 364–383.

Guy, G. R. (1991). Explanation in variable phonology: An exponential model of morphological constraints. *Language Variation and Change, 3*, 1–22.

Haneda, M. (1997). Second language learning in a "community of practice": A case study of adult Japanese learners. *The Canadian Modern Language Review, 54*, 11–47.

Hansen, J. G. (2006). *Acquiring a non-native phonology: Linguistic constraints and social barriers.* London: Continuum.

Huebner, T. (1983). *A longitudinal analysis of the acquisition of English.* Ann Arbor, MI: Karoma.

Jia, L. and Bayley, R. (2008). The (re)acquisition of perfective aspect marking by Chinese heritage language learners. In A. W. He and Y. Xiao (Eds.), *Chinese as a heritage language: Fostering rooted world citizenry* (pp. 205–222). Honolulu: University of Hawai'i, National Foreign Language Resource Center.

Johnstone, B. (1996). *The linguistic individual: Self-expression in language and linguistics.* Oxford: Oxford University Press.

Krashen, S. (1981). *Second language acquisition and learning.* Oxford: Pergamon Press.

Krashen, S. (1982). *Principles and practice in second language acquisition.* Oxford: Pergamon Press.

Labov, W. (1963). The social motivation of a sound change. *Word, 19*, 273–309.

Labov, W. (1966). *The social stratification of English in New York city.* Washington, D.C.: Center for Applied Linguistics.

Labov, W. (1972a). *Language in the inner city: Studies in the Black English Vernacular.* Philadelphia: University of Pennsylvania Press.

Labov, W. (1972b). *Sociolinguistic patterns.* Philadelphia: University of Pennsylvania Press.

Labov, W. (1984). Field methods of the project on language variation and change. In J. Baugh and J. Sherzer (Eds.), *Language in use: Readings in sociolinguistics* (pp. 28–53). Englewood Cliffs, NJ: Prentice Hall.

Labov, W. (1989). The child as linguistic historian. *Language Variation and Change, 1*, 85–97.

Lanza, E. and Svendsen, B. A. (2007). Tell me who your friends are and I might be able to tell you what language(s) you speak: Social network analysis, multilingualism, and identity. *International Journal of Bilingualism, 11*, 275–300.

Li, X. (2010). Sociolinguistic variation in the speech of learners of Chinese as a second language. *Language Learning, 60*, 366–408.

Liceras, J. (1985). The role of intake in the determination of learners' competence. In S. M. Gass and C. G. Madden (Eds.), *Input in second language acquisition* (pp. 354–373). Rowley, MA: Newbury House.

Liu, G.-q (1991). Interaction and second language acquisition: A case study of a child's acquisition of English as a Second Language. Unpublished doctoral dissertation, Deakin University, Melbourne, Australia.

Liu, G.-q. (2000). *Interaction and second language acquisition: A longitudinal study of a child's acquisition of English as a second language.* Beijing: Beijing Language and Culture University.

Long, M. (1998). Breaking the siege. *University of Hawai'i Working Papers in ESL, 17*, 79–129.

Lybeck, K. (2002). Cultural identification and second language pronunciation of Americans in Norway. *The Modern Language Journal, 86*, 174–191.

Major, R. C. (2001). *Foreign accent: The ontogeny and phylogeny of second language phonology.* Mahwah, NJ: Lawrence Erlbaum.

Mendoza-Denton, N. (2008). *Homegirls: Language and cultural practice among Latina youth gangs.* Oxford: Blackwell.

Milroy, L. (1987). *Language and social networks* (second Edition). Oxford: Blackwell.

Milroy, L. (2002). Social networks. In J. K. Chambers, P. Trudgill, and N. Schilling-Estes (Eds.), *The handbook of language variation and change* (pp. 549–572). Oxford: Blackwell.

Mougeon, R., Nadasdi, T., and Rehner, K. (2010). *The sociolinguistic competence of immersion students.* Clevedon, UK: Multilingual Matters.

Mougeon, R., Rehner, K., and Nadasdi, T. (2004). The learning of spoken French variation by immersion students in Toronto, Canada. *Journal of Sociolinguistics, 8*, 408–432.

Nagy, N., Blondeau, H., and Auger, J. (2003). Second language acquisition and "real" French: An investigation of subject doubling in the French of Montreal Anglophones. *Language Variation and Change, 15*, 73–103.

New London Group (1996). A pedagogy of multiliteracies: Designing social futures. *Harvard Educational Review, 61*, 543–563.

Pienemann, M. and Johnston, M. (1987). Factors influencing the development of language proficiency. In D. Nunan (Ed.), *Applying second language acquisition research* (pp. 45–141). Adelaide: National Curriculum Research Centre, Adult Migrant English Program.

Preston, D. R. (1989). *Sociolinguistics and second language acquisition*. Oxford: Blackwell.

Preston, D. R. (2002). A variationist perspective on SLA: Psycholinguistic concerns. In R. Kaplan (Ed.), *Oxford Handbook of Applied Linguistics* (pp. 141–159). Oxford: Oxford University Press.

Preston, D. R., and Bayley, R. (2009). Variationist linguistics and second language acquisition. In W. Ritchie and T. Bhatia (Eds.), *The new handbook of second language acquisition* (pp. 89–113). Bingley, UK: Emerald Publishing.

Rampton, B. (1995). *Crossing: Language and ethnicity among adolescents*. New York: Longman.

Rau, D. V., Chang, H. A., and Tarone, E. (2009). Think or sink: Chinese learners' acquisition of the English voiceless fricative. *Language Learning, 59*, 581–621.

Regan, V. (1996). Variation in French interlanguage: A longitudinal study of sociolinguistic competence. In R. Bayley and D. R. Preston (Eds.), *Second language acquisition and linguistic variation* (pp. 177–201). Amsterdam: John Benjamins.

Regan, V. (2004). The relationship between the group and the individual and the acquisition of native speaker variation patterns: A preliminary study. *IRAL, 42*, 335–347.

Rehner, K. and Mougeon, R. (1999). Variation in the spoken French of immersion students: To *ne* or not to *ne*, that is the sociolinguistic question. *The Modern Language Journal, 56*, 124–154.

Rickford, J. R. and McNair-Knox, F. (1994). Addressee- and topic-influenced style shift: A quantitative sociolinguistic study. In D. Biber and E. Finegan (Eds.), *Sociolinguistic perspectives on register* (pp. 235–276). New York: Oxford University Press.

Sankoff, D., Tagliamonte, S. A., and Smith, E. (2005). GoldVarbX. Computer program. Department of Linguistics, University of Toronto.

Sax, K. (1999). Acquisition of stylistic variation by American learners of French. Unpublished doctoral dissertation, Indiana University.

Schmidt, R. (2001). Attention. In P. Robinson (Ed.), *Cognition and second language instruction* (pp. 3–32). Cambridge: Cambridge University Press.

Schumann, J. H. (1978). *The pidginization process: A model for second language acquisition*. Rowley, NA: Newbury House.

Selinker, L. (1972). Interlanguage. *IRAL, 10*, 209–241.

Selinker, L. and Douglas, D. (1985). Wrestling with "context" in interlanguage theory. *Applied Linguistics, 6*, 190–204.

Shuy, R., Wolfram, W., and Riley, W. (1968). *A study of social dialects in Detroit*. Washington, D.C.: Educational Resources Information Center.

Smith, J. (1989). Topic and variation in ITA oral proficiency: SPEAK and field-specific tests. *English for Specific Purposes, 11*, 99–124.

Swales, J. (1990). *Genre analysis: English in academic and research settings*. Cambridge: Cambridge University Press.

Tagliamonte, S. A. (2006). *Analysing sociolinguistic variation*. Cambridge: Cambridge University Press.

Tarone, E. (1972). A suggested unit for interlingual identification in pronunciation. *TESOL Quarterly, 6*(4), 325–331.

Tarone, E. (1985). Variability in interlanguage use: A study of style-shifting in morphology and syntax. *Language Learning, 35*, 373–404.

Tarone, E. (1988). *Variation in interlanguage*. London: Edward Arnold.

Tarone, E. (2000a). Still wrestling with "context" in interlanguage theory. *Annual Review of Applied Linguistics, 20*, 182–198.

Tarone, E. (2000b). Getting serious about language play: Language play, interlanguage variation and second language acquisition. In B. Swierzbin, F. Morris, M. Anderson, C. Klee, and E. Tarone (Eds.), *Social and cognitive factors in SLA: Proceedings of the 1999 second language research forum* (pp. 31–54). Somerville, MA: Cascadilla Press.

Tarone, E. (2009). A sociolinguistic perspective on interaction in SLA. In A. Mackey and C. Polio (Eds.), *Multiple perspectives on interaction: Second language research in honor of Susan M. Gass* (pp. 41–56). New York: Routledge.

Tarone, E. (2010). Social context and cognition in SLA: A variationist perspective. In R. Batstone (Ed.), *Sociocognitive perspectives on language use and language learning* (pp. 54–72). Oxford: Oxford University Press.

Tarone, E. and Liu, G.-q. (1995). Situational context, variation and SLA theory. In G. Cook and B. Seidlhofer (Eds.), *Principle and practice in applied linguistics: Studies in honour of H. G. Widdowson* (pp. 107–124). Oxford: Oxford University Press.

Tarone, E. and Swain, M. (1995). A sociolinguistic perspective on second language use in immersion classrooms. *The Modern Language Journal, 79*, 166–178.

van Compernolle, R. A. and Pierozak, I. (2009). Teaching language variation in French through authentic chat discourse. In L. Abraham and L. Williams (Eds.), *Electronic discourse for language learning and teaching* (pp. 111–126). Amsterdam: John Benjamins.

van Compernolle, R. A., and Williams, L. (2009). Learner versus non-learner patterns of stylistic variation in synchronous computer-mediated French: Yes/no questions and *nous* versus *on*. *Studies in Second Language Acquisition, 31*(3), 471–500.

Wolfram, W. (1969). *A sociolinguistic study of Detroit Negro speech*. Washington, D.C.: Center for Applied Linguistics.

Wolfram, W. and Hatfield, D. (1984). *Tense marking in second language learning: Patterns of spoken and written English in a Vietnamese community*. Washington, D.C.: Center for Applied Linguistics.

Young, R. (1991). *Variation in interlanguage morphology*. New York: Peter Lang.

Young, R. and Bayley, R. (1996). Varbrul analysis for second language acquisition research. In R. Bayley and D. R. Preston (Eds.), *Second language acquisition and linguistic variation* (pp. 253–306). Amsterdam: John Benjamins.

Zhang, Q. (2005). A Chinese Yuppie in Beijing: Phonological variation and the construction of a new professional identity. *Language in Society, 32*, 431–466.

Zobl, H. (1985). Grammars in search of input and intake. In S. M. Gass and C. G. Madden (Eds.), *Input in second language acquisition* (pp. 329–344). Rowley, MA: Newbury House.

4

Sociocultural theory

A dialectical approach to L2 research

James P. Lantolf

Historical discussion

Although sociocultural theory (SCT) is a general theory of human mental development, it has been productively extended to include the investigation of second language (L2) development. I think it is fair to say that the catalyst for SCT-informed L2 research (henceforth, SCT-L2) in the West was the publication of Frawley and Lantolf's (1985) study on the narrative performance of ESL speakers. Adopting the perspective of mediated-mind, the core concept of SCT (see below), Frawley and Lantolf showed how speakers lose, maintain, and regain control of their narrative performance through private speech.

One of the most influential SCT-L2 studies that followed Frawley and Lantolf's article was a paper by Aljaafreh and Lantolf (1994), which examined the relevance of the zone of proximal development (henceforth, ZPD) for L2 learning. The researchers argued that for feedback to be effective in promoting language development it had to be sensitive to a learner's ZPD, defined by Vygotsky (1978) as the difference between what individuals can do independently and what they can do with appropriate mediation from someone else. This is an important concept because the theory argues that development does not depend solely on internal mechanisms but on the quality and quantity of external forms of social interaction that is attuned to a learner's potential ability.

Lantolf and Thorne (2006) was the first book-length synthesis of SCT-L2 research. This work explained the core concepts of the theory, including mediation, internalization, ZPD, and activity theory, and discussed these in light of L2 research. It also laid the foundation for investigating the impact of SCT principles for language teaching programs. Lantolf and Poehner (2008) followed up on this aspect of the SCT-L2 research agenda with a collection of papers that report on the effects of SCT-L2 pedagogy on L2 development.[1]

SCT-L2 research encompasses an array of topics, all of which are connected to the basic concept of the general theory: human thinking is mediated by culturally organized and trans-mitted symbolic meaning. Vygotsky (1987, 1978) argued that the relationship between humans and the world is indirect and therefore mediated not only by physical tools, such as shovels, hammers, and saws, but also by symbolic tools, including art, numbers, and above all, language. Tools, physical and symbolic, empower humans to control and change the world in which they live. The latter, in particular, allow humans to intentionally control aspects of the neuropsychological functioning of their brains. Thus, when children master language as a meaning-making system they also master their own cognitive activity. This mastery gives rise to the mind, which for Vygotsky is not co-terminus with the brain, but extends into the body (e.g., gestures) and even into artifacts such as computers, with which we form functional systems that enhance our capacity to think (see Wertsch, 1998).

Core issues

Given the central tenet of the theory (i.e., that higher forms of thinking are symbolically mediated) two questions suggest themselves with regard to L2 learning: to what extent can learners deploy a new symbolic system to mediate their communicative and psychological behavior? How does this new system develop? A related question is whether or not there are significant differences between learning a new symbolic system on one's own versus learning the system with intentional guidance and support as occurs in the educational setting.

Cognitive use of L2

The SCT-L2 research that has addressed the first question shows that while learners can develop the ability to use a new language for communicative functions, using it for psychological mediation is quite a different matter. Pavlenko and Lantolf's (2000) analysis of the immersion experiences of immigrants provides evidence of the reorganization of the individual's inner order such that the person is able to mediate their thinking through the new language. Work carried out on classroom learners, including those with extended study abroad experiences (e.g., two to three years), however, has shown that even when learners are communicatively competent in the new language, they continue to think through their L1. Grabois (1997) for example found that the conceptual organization of L2 learners of Spanish with and without study abroad experiences was no different in their L2 than in their L1, English. Only learners who had been living in Spain for a minimum of ten years showed any indication of a shift away from their native pattern of lexical organization and toward an L2 pattern. The experimental study by Centeno-Cortés and Jiménez-Jiménez (2004) on the relationship between L2 private speech and completion of cognitive tasks found that when tasks become complex learners, including those at advanced levels of proficiency (i.e., graduate students in a Spanish doctoral program with extensive study-abroad experience) were unable to complete the tasks successfully if they used the L2 to regulate their cognitive functioning. They were only successful if they relied on private speech in their L1, English.

We now turn to the speech-gesture interface. Research carried out on the interface of speech and gesture within the "thinking for speaking" (TFS) framework proposed by Slobin (1996, 2003) has uncovered evidence that some L2 learners have shifted from an L1 to an L2 TFS pattern. McNeill (2005) proposes that speech and gesture form a dialectical unity of symbolic representation and material image where thinking finds its object. He calls this unity the Growth Point and argues that it can be observed at the point where hand movement synchronizes with speech. It turns out that synchronization patterns differently in different languages. Thus, when describing motion events (e.g., The cat crawled up the drainpipe) English speakers often focus on manner of movement (i.e., crawl) and manifest this not only in speech but in the synchronization of hand movements depicting the movement with the manner-conflated verb. In a language such as Spanish, which does not have a robust inventory of manner verbs, speakers more often focus on direction rather than on manner of movement and as such coordinate the movement of their hands in an upward direction with articulation of a verb such as *subir* (to ascend).

Research by Negueruela *et al.* (2004) on advanced Spanish and English L2 speakers and by Choi and Lantolf (2008) on advanced Korean and English L2 speakers report no evidence of a shift from L1 to L2 patterns for any of the speakers included in their respective projects. However, Gullberg (in press) does uncover some evidence of a shift in her study of Dutch learners of L2 French with regard to placement verbs (e.g., put, place, lay, set). Stam (2008) also reports evidence of a shift with regard to path, though not manner, of motion among Spanish learners of L2 English.

The learning process

Vygotsky proposed two related mechanisms to account for the emergence of psychological processes from social activity. The first is imitation and the second is the zone of proximal development. Imitation is understood not as mindless copying of patterns often associated with behaviorist psychology but as a uniquely human form of cultural transmission (Tomasello, 1999, p. 81) "aimed at the future" and which creates something new "out of saying or doing 'the same thing'" (Newman and Holzman, 1993, p. 151). Human imitation, as distinct from animal mimicry not only replicates the observed model but, unlike mimicry, it incorporates the intentions of the person producing the model (Gergely and Csibra, 2007). Thus, through imitation learners build up repertoires of resources for future performances, but these need not be precise replicas of the original model.

James Mark Baldwin, an early American social scientist distinguishes two types of imitation: *imitative suggestion* and *persistent imitation* (Sewny, 1945). Through the former an individual gradually moves closer to a given model over a series of trials resulting in a "faithful replication of the model" (Valsiner, 2000, p. 30). Through the latter an individual reconstructs "the model in new ways" enabling the person to "preadapt" to future performances (ibid.). The difference in outcome can be ascribed to the fact that in imitative suggestion the target is the original model, while in persistent imitation the target is the individual's imitation of the original model, which may or may not be fully accurate. In the case of language learning imitative suggestion would be more likely to occur when frequent exemplars of the model are available and are attended to either for internally motivated reasons (e.g., attaining target-like performance) or are pushed by someone else. This is particularly pertinent in traditional educational settings which value precision of imitation over transformation of a model (Valsiner, 2000, p. 30). Persistent imitation would be a more likely process when learners either do not have robust access to exemplars of the original model, for whatever reason fail to pay attention even if exemplars are available, or intentionally choose to ignore the original model because of perceived communicative needs.

The difference between imitative suggestion and persistent imitation has potentially interesting implications for the role of recasts in learning. As the literature documents, learners at times repeat recasts accurately, at other times they do not, and at still other times they fail to repeat the recast at all (see Loewen and Philp, 2006). Vygotsky (1987, p. 211) argues that development is a collaborative process in which individuals move from what they are incapable of to what they are able to do through imitation. This transition takes place in the ZPD—the collaborative activity where "imitation is the source of instruction's influence on development" (Vygotsky, 1987, pp. 211–212). In the ZPD teachers, or more capable peers, guide learners to carry out activities they are incapable of on their own. In so doing, however, the learners internalize the ability or knowledge, which allows them to perform independently of other-mediation. Crucially, according to Vygotsky (1987, p. 212), for instruction to be effective (i.e., to lead to development) it must be sensitive to what learners are able to imitate under other-mediation. This ability is an indication of their future development (i.e., what they will eventually know or be able to do on their own).

Thus, even less than precise imitation of a recast could signal future-oriented development, while failure to imitate could indicate that the model is not yet within a learner's ZPD.

To illustrate imitation as understood by Vygotsky, consider a learner of German who produces the following utterance: *Ich rufe meine Mutter jeden Tag "I call my mother every day" and then receives the partial recast from her teacher jeden Tag an (separable prefix of the verb anrufen "to call"). The student repeats the entire utterance with the correction "Ich rufe meine Mutter jeden Tag an." Later, the same student produces the following utterance: "*Ich empfehle das neues Buch an" "I recommend the new book," but incorporates an incorrect separable prefix. The verb in this case is empfehlen not *anempfehlen. One might argue that the student used analogy to create the innovative, though incorrect, verb. In other words, analogy is essentially an imitative process where one uses something already known to create something new.

Within SCT-L2 recasts are situated within a broader framework of mediation that is most effective when it is sensitive to learners' ZPD and as such they represent one type of mediation. One of the important findings of SCT-L2 research is that by focusing on the types of mediation negotiated between learners and others (teachers, peers, tutors, etc.) the process of development is understood in a different way than it is in other models of second language acquisition (SLA). This is because development begins as a social process and gradually becomes a psychological process. Thus, development it not only a matter of changes in the product of learning (i.e., moving from less to more accurate production) but it is also indicated by shifts in the quality and quantity of negotiated mediation (Aljaafreh and Lantolf, 1994). At one point a learner may require explicit mediation, as for instance when a teacher provides a recast or a recast accompanied by a metalinguistic explanation. At a later point the learner may still have problems using the feature but overcoming the problem no longer requires explicit mediation and may instead result from an implicit prompt such as pausing on the part of the teacher. The shift in mediation over time is a sign that development has taken place because control over the feature is moving from the intermental to the intra-mental plane.

Some researchers (e.g., Ellis et al., 2009) have proposed that because explicit feedback appears to be more effective than implicit feedback, it should be more efficient to always provide explicit feedback. However, development is not only about improvements in performance but also about control over the performance. Consequently, learners need to have the opportunity to take control of their behavior. Thus, mediation attuned to learner ability and responsivity is not only about feedback but it is also about helping learners attain a sense of agency in their new language (see Lantolf and Poehner, 2011). This is more difficult to achieve if corrective moves are not attuned to learner development and instead follow the same format (see Nassaji and Swain, 2000).

Although the most effective form of mediation is negotiated between learners and experts, it is also possible for peers to mediate each other's development in the ZPD. Donato (1994) was one of the first SCT-L2 researchers to provide support for peer mediation in his analysis of collective scaffolding among L2 learners of French. More recently, Swain (2006) has proposed the concept of languaging to describe the talk (it can also entail writing) learners engage in as a means of internalizing a new language. This talk is communicative in appearance but psychological in function because its focus is on language form rather than on message meaning. Essentially, "languaging serves to mediate cognition" (Swain, 2006, p. 97) about language and it enables learners to notice differences between their performance and a model and serves to resolve the differences; in other words, to create a more faithful imitation of the model. The process can involve collaborative dialog, as illustrated in much of the research of Swain and her colleagues (e.g., Swain and Lapkin, 2002; Watanabe, 2004; Swain et al., 2009), as well as private speech, as documented in Ohta (2001), Centeno-Cortés (2003), and Lantolf (2003).

Data and common elicitation measures

Vygotsky argued that it was necessary to develop a new research methodology to reflect the new theory of mind he proposed. The new methodology is referred to as the genetic method (Vygotsky, 1978; Wertsch, 1985). He reasoned that if researchers attempt to study mental processes after they have been fully formed, as is the case in normal adult cognition, it is impossible to observe anything other than something such as the pushing of a button in a laboratory experiment. He also was skeptical of methods that rely on introspection, such as think-aloud research because if language is implicated in the thinking process itself rather than simply a means of expressing fully formed thought, the very act of reflecting on a process through talking about it, in Swain's terms (2006), *languaging*, is likely to affect that process. As Smagorinsky (2001, p. 240) remarks, "If thinking becomes rearticulated through the process of speech, then the protocol is not simply representative of meaning. It is, rather, *an agent in the production of meaning*" (p. 240).

Vygotsky (1978) reasoned that because human thinking is mediated by what are originally external means (e.g., social communication involving symbolic artifacts), it would be possible to observe and study thinking as it is being formed in the early phases of human development when children are externally mediated. The method he and his colleagues proposed to carry out their research agenda is known as the *genetic method*, which incorporates what they called the "*functional method of double stimulation*" (Vygotsky, 1978, p. 74. Italics in original). The term "genetic" refers to the fact that the goal of research is to trace the development of thinking over time as it is being formed through external mediation.

In research with young children, they are given problems that are beyond their current abilities to solve. A neutral object is placed nearby and researchers then observe if and how children incorporate the object as a sign to mediate their thinking as they attempt to solve the problem. A classic study using "double stimulation" was Leontiev's forbidden color task, where children were asked a series of questions that were likely to elicit color terms in response. The children were to avoid specific colors. When asked the color of their house (assuming the forbidden color was white) very young children answered truthfully that it was white. Strips of differently colored paper, including white, were then placed next to the children and they were told they could use these to help them remember the forbidden color. Young children were unable to use the paper strips to mediate their thinking; that is, to remind themselves of the forbidden color. Older children, however, were able to mediate themselves by placing the relevant colored paper in a visible location and before responding to a question, they looked at the paper and successfully avoided the color. Older children, and adults, as with the youngest group, did not use the colored paper, but, unlike the youngest participants, they had no problem avoiding the forbidden color. This is because they had internalized the capacity to mediate their thinking covertly through inner speech and therefore had no need for external mediation. In such experiments Vygotsky and his colleagues were able to trace the transition of mediation from the external to the internal plane of processing over time, as represented in the different age groups participating in such studies.

The genetic method in SCT-L2 research

The genetic method has figured into SCT-L2 research in at least two ways. First is the intra-mental function language itself fulfills in learning a new language. The fact that individuals are confronted with the demanding task of learning a new language creates cognitive dissonance that is far more complex than the forbidden color task described above. To overcome the challenge, learners press their language system into service to mediate their own learning. Lantolf (1997) proposed that private speech serves as a cognitive tool to mediate L2 learning, just as it serves as a cognitive tool to learn other kinds of information. He also argued that learning, in the absence of audible private speech, is not possible and that in fact, private speech provides a glimpse into the learning process itself.

L2 private speech. Several studies have examined the role of private speech in L2 learning. Saville-Troike (1988) studied the private speech of children learning L2 English in a content classroom over a six-month period. The researcher was able to document a relationship between the patterns that children practiced in their private speech phase of development (i.e., the period of time from one to 23 weeks, depending on the child) and the patterns they produced when they began to use English in social interaction with their classmates and teacher. Ohta (2001), Lantolf and Yáñez-Prieto (2003), Lantolf (2003), and de Guerrero (2005) investigated the developmental function of private speech in adult L2 learners. The first three studies collected actual samples of private speech produced in learning environments; the fourth included a great deal of survey data in which learners were asked how they thought they used private speech to learn and think through the L2.

Ohta's study, by far the most robust investigation of adult classroom learners, tracked the private speech of L2 Japanese learners over the course of an entire academic year. The participants produced three different types of private speech: vicarious response, where an individual privately responds to a question directed to someone else, completes another's utterance, or repairs an error committed by someone else; repetition, where an individual repeats a word, phrase, or entire utterance produced by someone else or by the learner himself/herself; manipulation, where an individual modifies morphosyntactic or phonological patterns usually produced by someone else. The last two types, which in my view, qualify as imitation, were documented by Lantolf (2003), Lantolf and Yáñez-Prieto (2003) and Saville-Troike (1988). A significant difference between the adults and the children, however, is that the adults also used their L1 as metalanguage to organize and comment on their performance, while the children did not. For example, the learner studied by Lantolf and Yáñez-Prieto (2003, p. 106) when vicariously (to use Ohta's terminology) participating in an exchange between the instructor and another student regarding verb agreement in Spanish *se*-passive constructions, not only completes the instructor's utterance directed at another student ("*Se* what?") with the correct past-tense plural form of the verb *vendieron* "they sold," but also tells herself, quietly in English, "I knew it!" Lee (2006) documents use of L1 Korean and L2 English private speech among students enrolled in a US medical school. The students used L2 to work on correct pronunciation of new bio-medical terms but relied on their L1 to internalize the meanings of terms. Centeno-Cortés (2003) in a genetic study of Spanish L2 learners during study abroad was able to document the early appearance of specific features of Spanish in learner private speech and use of the same features in later social speech.

Social mediation. The genetic method has also been used in SCT-L2 research to explore the influence of social mediation on L2 development. The study reported in Aljaafreh and Lantolf (1994) analyzes the effects of learner-expert interaction in the ZPD among three L2 learners of English. In tracing the development of four high-frequency grammatical features (i.e., article use, tense marking, preposition use, and modal verbs) over a two-month period the study presents four significant findings. First, mediation negotiated in the ZPD between learner and expert varies across an explicit-implicit continuum, such that learner control over a particular L2 feature is a function of movement along the continuum, with less control being indicated by more explicit mediation and enhanced control by more implicit mediation on the part of the expert. Second, different linguistic features for the same learner may require different levels (explicit-implicit) of mediation, and mediation relative to the same linguistic feature may vary across learners. Third, microgenetic development passes through five different levels beginning at the lowest level where even with explicit mediation the learner has little if any awareness and virtually no control over use of a particular feature and culminating at the level where the learner uses the feature systematically and correctly with self-repair when necessary. Lantolf and Poehner (2006) refined the five-level developmental trajectory, when they discovered that even when learner performance is relatively error-free and when learners were able to self-correct mistakes, they continue to look to the mediator for confirmation that their performance was indeed appropriate. Fourth, effectiveness of mediation along the mediational continuum (or regulatory scale, to use Aljaafreh and Lantolf's terminology) is not a matter of whether it is implicit or explicit in any absolute sense, but what a particular learner needs as negotiated with a mediator.

Swain and her colleagues have investigated the effect of peer mediation on L2 learning. An important aspect of the languaging framework that informs Swain's research is the argument that even though speaking appears to be communicative it can, simultaneously have a psychological function. This notion is rooted in Vygotsky's (1987) claim that speech is a reflexive tool that can be directed outwardly at other individuals and inwardly at the speaker. Wells (1999) argues that this dual potential of speech (and writing) can occur simultaneously so that when talking to others, one can at the same time be talking to the self. Swain and Lapkin (2002) and Tocalli-Beller and Swain (2005) demonstrate the positive effects on learning of peer languaging activity. In both studies the researchers documented learning, at least in the short term, through use of post-tests developed on the basis of those language features that were in focus during language related episodes (LREs) (i.e., segments of dialog where learners negotiate form rather than meaning). They provide evidence that learners are able to mediate each other's as well as their own learning through talk. An especially important finding of this research is that even though learners ostensibly focus on the same language feature during LREs they do not necessarily appropriate precisely the same thing from the interaction. This can be explained by the fact that learners do not necessarily have the same ZPD. Finally, Swain and her colleagues observed that during LREs, the learners not only produced speech that was intended for their interlocutor, but they also generated talk that clearly displayed the profile of private speech (i.e., low volume, lack of eye contact, and no apparent expectation of a response; see Saville-Troike, 1988).

Applications

From the early days of the field SLA researchers have worried about the application of theory and research to pedagogical practice. Indeed, Crookes (1998, p. 6) notes that "If the relationship were simple, or not a source of concern, I do not think it would come up so often." The solution that most SLA researchers have proposed for addressing the research-practice gap has been focused on ways of making research findings and theoretical models comprehensible and usable for classroom teachers (see Erlam, 2008). Another way of dealing with the troubling situation is to propose an approach which unifies theory/research and practice into a single reciprocal system. In the following section, I consider such a solution in some detail.

L2 praxis

Vygotsky was a profoundly dialectical thinker, who understood the advantages of unifying rather than dichotomizing oppositional perspectives in the study of human psychological processes (Levitin, 1982). This not only enabled him to create a new psychology that overcame the crisis stemming from the long-standing Cartesian mind-body dualism that had afflicted psychology virtually from its inception, but it also allowed him to propose insightful solutions to specific problems within psychology. One of these had to do with the relationship between theory/research and practice, a dichotomy that was particularly problematic for education and which finds its contemporary instantiation in the theory/research-practice gap in applied linguistics.

According to Vygotsky, in dualistic approaches to science theory was "not dependent on practice" instead "practice was the conclusion, the application, an excursion beyond the boundaries of science, an operation which lay outside science and came after, which began after the scientific operation was considered completed" (Vygotsky, 1926/2004, p. 304). In dialectical epistemology, on the other hand, practice is integrated with theory in that it "sets the tasks and serves as the supreme judge of theory, as its truth criterion" (ibid.). On this view, theory without practice is verbalizm, while practice without theory is mindless activity (Vygotsky, 1987). The unity of theory and practice is known as *praxis* (see Sanchez Vazquez, 1977) as derived from Marx's well-known Eleventh Thesis on Feuerbach: "The philosophers have only *interpreted* the world, in various ways; the point, however, is to *change* it" (Marx, 1978, p. 145) [italics in original].

In praxis the unity of theory and practice means that each component necessarily informs and guides the other. The worry of whether or not theory/research applies to teaching is mitigated by the very nature of praxis itself. The research that tests the theory is practice and the process that guides practice is the theory. Hence, there is no gap between theory and practice to bridge because both the processes necessarily work in consort always and everywhere.

Beginning with Negueruela's (2003) dissertation, praxis has been taken seriously by SCT-L2 researchers. This research is carried out in real classrooms and is designed to implement and thereby test the principles of the theory in educational activity, while at the same time improving learning through theory-guided practice. Several other dissertations followed Negueruela's (see below), and Lantolf and Poehner (2008) published an edited volume, which is a collection of chapters reporting on praxis-based L2 research.

Concept-based instruction

Education, according to SCT, is, if properly organized, the activity that promotes a specific type of development—development that does not readily occur in the everyday world. Vygotsky (1926/2004) refers to education as the "artificial" development of individuals. It is artificial because it entails intentional explicit mediation, whereby specific signs are introduced into "an ongoing flow of activity by an 'external agent' (i.e., a teacher)" (Wertsch, 2007, p. 185). This is markedly different from the implicit, or spontaneous (Vygotsky's, 1987 term) development that generally occurs in the everyday world where "signs in the form of natural language that have evolved in the service of communication and are then harnessed in other forms of activity" (Wertsch, 2007, p. 185). This means that language development in and out of educational activity is a different process—a position that contrasts with SLA researchers who argue that development is psychologically the same process regardless of where or when it occurs (e.g., Long, 2007; Robinson and Ellis, 2008). The basic difference between everyday development, where learners are more or less left to their own devices, and *developmental education* (e.g., Davydov, 2004) is that the latter must be guided by well-organized and explicit scientific concepts, whereas in the former learners rarely have access to such knowledge and therefore must figure out on their own the patterns of the new language. Above all, rather than waiting for individuals to become developmentally ready to learn, in developmental education instruction itself "results in mental development and sets in motion a variety of developmental processes that would be impossible apart from learning" (Vygotsky, 1978, p. 90). The central unit of concept-based instruction (CBI), that is, instruction that leads development, is well-organized systematic knowledge, which is referred to as *scientific knowledge*.

Scientific knowledge, as contrasted with commonsense everyday knowledge, reflects the "generalizations of the experience of humankind that is fixed in science, understood in the broadest sense of the term to include both natural and social sciences as well as the humanities" (Karpov, 2003, p. 71). It manifests the "essential characteristics of objects or events" and presents these "in the form of symbolic and graphic models" (Karpov, 2003). Although L2 research has increasingly shown that explicit knowledge has a positive impact on learning (e.g., Ellis, 2006; Norris and Ortega, 2000), to my knowledge, only DeKeyser (1998) has argued that it is important to pay attention to the quality of this knowledge. Rules-of-thumb, for example, described by Hammerly (1982, p. 142) as "*simple, nontechnical, close to popular/traditional notions*" [italics in original], a staple of explicit instruction, do not qualify as scientific knowledge because they are superficial, non-generalizable, and more or less reflect commonsense understanding of language. Whitley (1986, p. 108) provides an example of a rule-of-thumb on verbal aspect typically found in Spanish L2 textbooks: preterit "reports, records, narrates, and in the case of certain verbs (e.g., *saber, querer, poder*) causes a change of meaning" and imperfect "tells what was happening, recalls what used to happen, describes a physical or mental emotion, tells time in the past, describes the background and sets the stage upon which another action occurred" (p. 108). According to Hammerly (1982, p. 142), rules-of-thumb are preferred over in-depth knowledge because the latter is usually complex and "too much for students to absorb" (Hammerly, 1982). The problem, however, is that rules-of-thumb are often vague and at best describe what is typical of a specific context and therefore have limited generalizability.

The challenge is to formulate appropriate scientific knowledge in a way that learners can understand it and use it to guide their own performance. Piotr Gal'perin, a leading pedagogical scholar of the SCT school (see Haenen, 1996) proposed that for systematic conceptual knowledge to be effectively appropriated and internalized by learners it had to be converted from verbal to visual form. Graphic depictions present knowledge holistically rather than sequentially and they mitigate against rote memorization without understanding (see Ausubel, 1970). In a series of studies, Talyzina (1981) demonstrated the superiority of graphically organized over verbally represented concepts on learner understanding in a wide array of school subjects.

The fact that SCT-L2 pedagogy relies on explicit conceptual knowledge as its unit of pedagogical action does not mean that communicative tasks or other activities designed to stimulate interaction among students is taken off the table. Quite the contrary, these remain as the centerpiece of practice, but the practice is guided by the concepts, which Gal'perin labels as schema of the orienting basis of action or SCOBA. An example of a SCOBA developed by Lee (in progress) is given in Figure 4.1 below. This SCOBA is intended for instruction on English phrasal verbs, a notoriously difficult feature of the language especially with regard to figurative meanings. The following sentences illustrate one literal and one figurative meaning depicted in each of the four subcomponents of Figure 4.1: (1) John was out of the house for the entire day; Patrick was out of his mind with fear when he read the threatening letter; (2) Mary picked out the dresses that she liked best; Rebecca laid out the optimal solution in clear terms; (3) The soldiers parachuted out of the airplane when it reached the target; Jack went out on a limb to convince the teacher of his perspective; (4) The explosion blew out the sides of the building; The union and the company worked out a contract that was good for both parties.

On the pre- and post-tests used in Lee's study, her students (N = 23) improved on their accurate interpretation of "out" constructions from 56 percent to 71 percent.

Swain *et al.* (2009) also report positive results in a developmental study of voice in L2 French where learners not only improved their performance but, as argued for by Negueruela (2008), they also improved their understanding of the concept of voice. On the other hand, a study discussed in Ferreira and Lantolf (2008) yielded mixed findings. The study was based on a

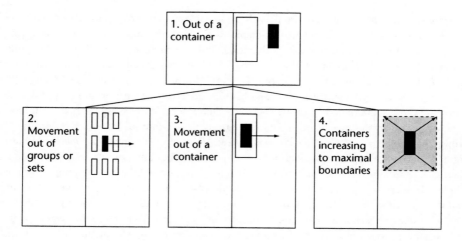

Figure 4.1   SCOBA for particle "out"
Source: (Lee, in progress)

semester-long university course on ESL writing in which genre as defined in Systemic-Functional Linguistics was the scientific concept around which the course was organized. Although some of the students improved in their writing, as assessed by independent judges, and in their understanding of the concept of genre, as determined by explanations of their own performance, other students were resistant to the praxis-based approach, because it seemed too "theoretical" and at odds with their previous heavily empirically based approach to instruction (i.e., "just tell me what to write and I'll write it").

Dynamic assessment

As with other aspects of the general theory, dynamic assessment (DA), which is the pedagogical instantiation of the ZPD, emerges naturally from the dialectical perspective. It merges teaching and assessment into a single pedagogical unity. In traditional assessments, the intrusion of someone else into the process is proscribed because it introduces an error factor, while in DA the intrusion, understood as mediation, is required. DA is based on the principle that human thinking develops in accordance with the quality of mediation afforded by social interaction. Thus, to miss opportunities to mediate the individual (or a group) is to miss opportunities to promote development. Effective assessment calls for mediation for without it development is inhibited. By the same token, effective instruction calls for assessment because the teacher needs to be aware of and bring to the surface those capacities that are ripening (Vygotsky's, 1987 terminology) and that often remain hidden from view in traditional assessment and instruction that is not sensitive to the ZPD. Said another way, in DA instruction leads development while at the same time development lays the foundation for further instruction.

Antón (2009) discusses the use of DA for advanced placement in a university Spanish L2 program. She showed that while students might exhibit similar independent (i.e., non-mediated) performance when narrating a video story, under mediation significant differences could emerge. Some students with mediation were able to repair many of their independently produced errors (e.g., marking tense and aspect), while others, even with mediation were unable to do so. The students projected differential future development and consequently were placed in different courses where instruction would be more appropriately tailored to their needs. Had the placements been made on the basis of independent performance alone, many of the learners would have been misplaced.

Ableeva (2010) conducted an in-depth study of listening comprehension, a relatively under-researched area of SLA. She carried out a four-month study of seven intermediate university learners of French. Using a series of video recall protocols to diagnose their abilities, Ableeva showed that learner performance determined by recall of the number of recalled propositions contained in the native speaker videos improved with statistical significance as a result of the DA sessions she conducted with the learners. This included not only the original video texts, but also more difficult texts, designed to assess learner ability to extend learning to new circumstances. Poehner (2007) stresses the importance of *transcendence*, or the capacity to transfer what is learned to different activities, as a true indication of development. In addition, and as in Antón's study of oral proficiency, mediation during listening comprehension was able to bring to the surface problem areas (i.e., phonology, lexicon, grammar, and cultural knowledge) that might otherwise have remained hidden from scrutiny.

A critique often leveled against DA, and against work on the ZPD in general, is that it requires a great deal of time and effort on the part of the mediator/teacher to support the development of individual learners. A response to the critique both within the general SCT (Newman, and *et al.*, 1989) and the SCT-L2 literature has been to show how DA and ZPD principles can be implemented at the group or even classroom level (see Gibbons, 2003; Guk and Kellogg, 2007; Lantolf and Poehner, 2009–2011).

Gibbons uses the ZPD as a lens for analyzing the interaction between elementary teachers of content-based ESL and their students. She documents how the teachers attempt in a whole-class format (following small group work by the students) to mediate the students into using appropriate scientific jargon instead of everyday terms. Guk and Kellogg (2007) analyze a fifth-year elementary school EFL class in Korea. The activity comprised two components: in the first the teacher explained and demonstrated a task to a group of students each of whom was then to explain the task to their respective groups. In teacher-student interaction the teacher provided analytical explanations of the language in the L2 with students responding appropriately in this language; whereas in the student- student interactions, most of the talk was conducted in the L1 with lengthier explanations. The authors propose that the teacher-student interactions served inter-mental functions and as such represented the upper limit of the ZPD, while the student-student interactions served intra-mental (i.e., internalization) functions and therefore represented the lower limit of the ZPD. However, neither study documents specific learning outcomes.

The study by Lantolf and Poehner (2009–2011) documents how an elementary school Spanish teacher effectively implements DA into her regular instructional program to promote learner development. Having worked through Lantolf and Poehner's (2006) *Teacher's Guide*, the teacher established a prefabricated menu of hints and prompts arranged from most implicit (i.e., pause in responding to student performance) to most explicit (i.e., providing the correct response with an appropriate explanation). She then designed a simple grid sheet that included the name of each student, the planned activities for each instructional session, along with the prompts and hints. She assigned a numerical score to each of these from 1 (pause) to 8 (correct response with explanation) with a 0 assigned if a student did not require any mediation. For each class activity students were assigned a score depending on the type of mediation needed. This allowed the teacher to compare students in a given activity as well as track the performance of individual students over time. Lantolf and Poehner (2009–2011) traced the improvement in performance of one student's use of noun-adjective agreement (number and gender). In addition, Poehner (2009) argues for the distributed effect of whole-class DA in that students not directly interacting with the teacher appear to have benefited by attending to the mediation provided to classmates.

Future directions

Future research within the SCT-L2 paradigm should address four general areas. The first is the relationship between private speech and internalization. To my knowledge since the publication of the research reviewed in this chapter no work has been conducted on this important topic. The research methodology should be based on that used by Ohta and Saville-Troike and should extend over a reasonably long time span (e.g., six months to a year, at least). This will be labor-intensive research but there is much to be gained from its outcome both for those interested in SCT research and also for those interested in the relationship between recasts and other forms of feedback and L2 learning. The particular importance of private speech is that it allows researchers a glimpse of language learning in "flight" (Vygotsky, 1987).

The second area is DA. Although of the four, this has received the lion's share of attention, there is still much work to be done. One of the most challenging, yet most important, topics is research on how to effectively implement DA in large group formats. The approach taken by the teacher in Lantolf and Poehner's study is only one way of tackling the problem. One can imagine technology-based approaches to mediation illustrated in a funded research project currently under way on computerized DA in French, Russian and Chinese (see Lantolf and Poehner, 2009–2011). An especially promising approach, which has been developed by Cole and Engeström (1993) in which reading instruction is based on the concept of division of labor, whereby the reading process is deconstructed with various of its subcomponents assigned to individual students as the whole class undertakes to collectively read a given text. Together the class, guided by the teacher, socially constructs expertise in reading and by participating in this process individual students develop through their particular ZPD.

Concept-based instruction is an extremely promising area for future SCT-L2 research. So far most of the work here has been concerned with grammar instruction. In this regard, there seems to be a natural fit between CBI and cognitive linguistics. In my view (see Lantolf, in press), cognitive linguistics is especially congruent with SCT-L2 pedagogy because of the kinds of theoretical/conceptual information it develops about language and because of its use of graphic depiction of theoretical statements about language that are potential candidates for SCOBAs (see Figure 4.1 above). To date, only one CBI study (Thorne et al., 2008) has addressed instruction in the domain of pragmatics and only one (Yáñez-Prieto, 2008) has dealt with learning of figurative language (see Littlemore and Low, 2006). Both areas are especially important for the development of advanced levels of L2 proficiency. I believe that SCT-L2, because of its concern with meaning, can make a significant contribution to helping learners develop proficiency in the area of conceptual fluency (see Danesi, 2008).

Finally, research on gesture has demonstrated that this mode of communication and thinking can have a powerful impact on learning (see Goldin-Meadow et al., 2009). Gesture, because it is imagistic, shares a great deal with SCOBAs. Some L2 researchers (Haught and McCafferty, 2008; Lantolf, 2010) have already shown that gesture has considerable potential for mediating L2 learning and performance. It is worth the effort for research to focus on ways of connecting SCOBAs with gesture so that learners can use their bodies (see Johnson, 1987) as an extension of their mind to help them learn and mediate their own performances in an L2. The advantage of introducing gesture as a pedagogical tool is that it is more portable than a SCOBA and as such would enable learners to transport conceptual meanings in a more efficient way than via a separate graphic depiction.

I have only been able to paint the history of SCT-L2 research with the broadest of brush strokes. The work is fleshed out in more chronological detail in Lantolf and Beckett (2009). The interested reader can also explore the searchable online bibliography on SCT-L2 research at http://language.la.psu.edu/SCTBIB/, which currently contains over 600 entries.

References

Ableeva, R. (2010). *Dynamic assessment of listening comprehension in L2 French*. Unpublished PhD dissertation. The Pennsylvania State University. University Park, PA.

Aljaafreh, A. and Lantolf, J. P. (1994). Negative feedback as regulation and second language learning in the zone of proximal development. *The Modern Language Journal, 78*, 465–483.

Antón, M. (2009). Dynamic assessment of advanced language learners. *Foreign Language Annals, 42*, 576–598.

Ausubel, D. P. (1970). Reception learning and the rote-meaningful dimension. In E. Stones (Ed.), *Readings in educational psychology. Learning and teaching* (pp. 193–206). London: Methuen.

Centeno-Cortés, B. (2003). *Private speech in the acquisition of Spanish as a foreign language*. Unpublished PhD dissertation. The Pennsylvania State University, University Park, PA.

Centeno-Cortés, B. and Jiménez-Jiménez, A. (2004). Problem-solving tasks in a foreign language: The importance of the L1 in private verbal thinking. *International Journal of Applied Linguistics, 14*, 7–35.

Choi, S. and Lantolf, J. P. (2008). The representation and embodiment of meaning in L2 communication: Motion events in speech and gesture in L2 Korean and L2 English speakers. *Studies in Second Language Acquisition, 30*, 191–224.

Cole, M. and Engeström, Y. (1993). A cultural-historical approach to distributed cognition. In G. Solomon (Ed.), *Distributed cognitions. Psychological and educational considerations* (pp. 1–46). Cambridge: Cambridge University Press.

Crookes, G. (1998). On the relationship between second and foreign language teachers and research. *TESOL Journal, 7*(3), 6–11.

Danesi, M. (2008). Conceptual errors in second-language learning. In S. De Koop and T. De Rycker (Eds.), *Cognitive approaches to pedagogical grammar* (pp. 231–256). Berlin: Mouton de Gruyter.

Davydov, V. V. (2004). *Problems of developmental instruction. A theoretical and experimental psychological study*. Translated by Peter Moxhay. Moscow: Academiya Press.

DeKeyser, R. M. (1998). Beyond focus on form: Cognitive perspectives on learning and practicing second language grammar. In C. Doughty and J. Williams (Eds.), *Focus on form in second language acquisition* (pp. 42–66). Cambridge: Cambridge University Press.

de Guerrero, M. (2005). *Inner speech—L2: Thinking words in a second language*. New York: Springer.

Donato, R. (2004). Collective scaffolding in second language learning. In J. P. Lantolf and G. Appel (Eds.), *Vygotskian approaches to second language research* (pp. 33–56). Norwood, NJ: Ablex.

Ellis, R. (2006). Current issues in the teaching of grammar: An SLA perspective. *TESOL Quarterly, 40*, 83–7.

Ellis, R., Loewen, S., Elder, C., Erlam, R., Philp, J., and Reinders, H. (2009). *Implicit and explicit knowledge in second language learning, testing and teaching*. Bristol, UK: Multilingual Matters.

Erlam, R. (2008). What do researchers know about language teaching? Bridging the gap between SLA research and language pedagogy. *Innovation in Language Learning and Teaching, 2*, 253–267.

Ferreira, M. and Lantolf, J. (2008). A concept-based approach to teaching writing through genre analysis. In J. P. Lantolf and M. E. Poehner (Eds.), *Sociocultural theory and second language teaching*. (pp. 285–320). London: Equinox.

Frawley, W. and Lantolf, J. P. (1985). Second language discourse: A Vygotskyan perspective. *Applied Linguistics, 6*, 19–44.

Gergely, G. and Csibra, G. (2007). The social construction of the cultural mind. Imitative learning as a mechanism of human pedagogy. In P. Hauf and F. Försterling (Eds.), *Making minds. The shaping of human minds through social context* (pp. 241–257). Amsterdam: John Benjamins.

Gibbons, P. (2003). Mediating language learning: Teacher interactions with ESL students in a content-based classroom. *TESOL Quarterly, 37*, 247–273.

Goldin-Meadow, S., Cook, S. W., and Mitchell, Z. A. (2009). Gesturing gives children new ideas about math. *Psychological Science, 20*, 267–272.

Grabois, H. (1997). *Love and power. Word association, lexical organization and second language acquisition*. Unpublished PhD dissertation. Cornell University, Ithaca, NY.

Guk, I. and Kellogg, D. (2007). The ZPD and whole class teaching: Teacher-led and student-led interactional mediation of tasks. *Language Teaching Research, 11*, 281–299.

Gullberg, M. (in press). Language-specific encoding of placement events in gestures. In E. Pedersen and J. Bohnemeyer (Eds.), *Event representations in language and cognition*. Cambridge: Cambridge University Press.

Haenen, J. (1996). *Piotr Gal'perin: Psychologist in Vygotsky's footsteps*. New York: Nova Science Publishers.

Hammerly, H. (1982). *Synthesis in language teaching: An introduction to linguistics*. Blaine, WA: Second Language Publications.

Haught, J. and McCafferty, S. G. (2008). Embodied language performance: Drama and the ZPD in the second language classroom. In J. P. Lantolf and M. E. Poehner (Eds.), *Sociocultural theory and the teaching of second languages* (pp. 139–162). London: Equinox.

Johnson, M. (1987). *The body in the mind. The bodily basis of meaning, imagination, and reason.* Chicago: University of Chicago Press.

Karpov, Y. V. (2003). Vygotsky's doctrine of scientific concepts: Its role for contemporary education. In A. Kozulin, B. Gindis, V. S. Ageyev, and S. Miller (Eds.), *Vygotsky's educational theory in cultural context* (pp. 39–64). Cambridge: Cambridge University Press.

Lantolf, J. P. (1997). The function of language play in the acquisition of L2 Spanish. In W. R. Glass and A. -T. Perez-Leroux (Eds.), *Contemporary perspectives on the acquisition of Spanish. Vol 2: Production, processing and comprehension* (pp. 3–24). Somerville, MA: Cascadilla Press.

Lantolf, J. P. (2003). Intrapersonal communication and internalization in the second language classroom. In A. Kozulin, B. Gindis, V. S. Ageyev, and S. Miller (Eds.), *Vygotsky's theory of education in cultural context* (pp. 349–370). Cambridge: Cambridge University Press.

Lantolf, J. P. (2010). Minding your hands: The function of gesture in L2 learning. In R. Batestone (Ed.), *Sociocognitive perspectives on language use and language learning* (pp. 131–150). Oxford: Oxford University Press.

Lantolf, J. P. (2011). Integrating sociocultural theory and cognitive linguistics in the second language classroom. In E. Hinkel (Ed.), *Handbook of research on second language teaching and learning vol. II* (Second Edition) (pp. 303–318). New York: Routledge.

Lantolf, J. P. and Beckett, T. (2009). Research timeline for sociocultural theory and second language acquisition. *Language Teaching, 42*(4), 1–19.

Lantolf, J. P. and Poehner, M. E. (2004). Dynamic assessment of L2 development: Bringing the past into the future. *Journal of Applied Linguistics, 1*, 49–72.

Lantolf, J. P. and Poehner, M. E. (Eds.). (2008). *Sociocultural theory and the teaching of second languages.* London: Equinox.

Lantolf, J. P. and Poehner, M. E. (2011). Dynamic assessment in the classroom: Vygotskian praxis for L2 development. *Language Teaching Research, 15*, 1–23.

Lantolf, J. P. and Poehner, M. E. (2009–2011). *Computerized dynamic assessment of language proficiency in French, Russian and Chinese.* Research project funded by a grant from the International Research Studies of the U.S. Department of Education Title VI program. Grant number P017A080071.

Lantolf, J. P. and Thorne, S. L. (2006). *Sociocultural theory and the genesis of second language development.* Oxford: Oxford University Press.

Lantolf, J. P. and Yáñez-Prieto, C. (2003). Talking yourself into Spanish: Intrapersonal communication and second language learning. *Hispania, 86*, 97–109.

Lee, J. (2006). *Talking to the self: A study of the private speech mode of bilinguals.* Unpublished PhD dissertation. University of Wisconsin-Madison, Madison, Wisconsin.

Lee, H. (in progress). *A concept-based approach to second language teaching and learning: Cognitive linguistics-inspired instruction of English phrasal verbs.* Ph.D. dissertation. The Pennsylvania State University, University Park, PA.

Levitin, K. (1982). *One is not born a personality. Profiles of Soviet education psychologists.* Moscow: Progress Press.

Littlemore, J. and Low, G. (2006). *Figurative thinking and foreign language learning.* Basingstoke, UK: Palgrave Macmillan.

Loewen, S. and Philp, J. (2006). Recasts in the adult English L2 classroom: Characteristics, explicitness, and effectiveness. *The Modern Language Journal, 90*, 536–556.

Long, M. (2007). *Problems in SLA.* Mahwah, NJ: Erlbaum.

Marx, K. (1978) Theses on feuerbach. In R. C. Tucker (Ed.), *The Marx-Engels reader* (Second Edition) (pp. 143–145).

McNeill, D. (2005). *Gesture and thought.* Chicago: University of Chicago Press.

Nassaji, H. and Swain, M. (2000). A vygotskian perspective on corrective feedback in L2: The effect of random versus negotiated help on the learning of English articles. *Language Awareness, 9*, 34–51.

Negueruela, E. (2003). *A sociocultural approach to the teaching-learning of second languages: Systemic-theoretical instruction and L2 development.* Unpublished Ph.D. dissertation. The Pennsylvania State University. University Park, PA.

Negueruela, E., Lantolf, J. P., Jordan, S. R. and Gelabert, J. (2004). The "private function" of gesture in second language communicative activity: A study of motion verbs and gesturing in English and Spanish. *International Journal of Applied Linguistics, 14*, 113–147.

Negueruela, E. (2008). Revolutionary pedagogies: Learning that leads (to) second language development. In J. P. Lantolf and M. E. Poenher (Eds.), *Sociocultural theory and the teaching of second languages* (pp. 189–227). London: Equinox.

Newman, D., Griffin, P., and Cole, M. (1989). *The construction zone: Working for cognitive change in school.* Cambridge: Cambridge University Press.

Newman, F. and Holzman, L. (1993). *Lev Vygotsky: Revolutionary scientist.* London: Routledge.

Norris, J. M. and Ortega, L. (2000). Effectiveness of L2 instruction: A research synthesis and quantitative meta-analysis. *Language Learning, 50,* 417–528.

Ohta, A. S. (2001). *Second language acquisition processes in the classroom: Learning Japanese.* Mahwah, NJ: Lawrence Erlbaum.

Pavlenko, A. and Lantolf, J. P. (2000). Second language learning as participation and the (re) construction of selves. In J. P. Lantolf (Ed.), *Sociocultural theory and second language learning* (pp. 155–178). Oxford: Oxford University Press.

Poehner, M. E. (2007). Beyond the test: L2 dynamic assessment and the transcendence of mediated learning. *The Modern Language Journal, 91,* 323–340.

Poehner, M. E. (2008). *Dynamic assessment: A Vygotskian approach to understanding and promoting L2 development.* Berlin: Springer.

Poehner, M. E. (2009). Group dynamic assessment: Mediation for the L2 classroom. *TESOL Quarterly, 43,* 471–492.

Robinson, P. and Ellis, N. (2008). Conclusion: Cognitive linguistics, second language acquisition and L2 instruction—issues for research. In P. Robinson and N. Ellis (Eds.), *Handbook of cognitive linguistics and second language acquisition* (pp. 489–545). New York: Routledge.

Sanchez Vazquez, A. (1977). *The philosophy of Praxis.* London: Merlin Press.

Saville-Troike, M. (1988). Private speech: Evidence for second language learning strategies during the "silent period". *Journal of Child Language, 15,* 567–590.

Sewny, V. D. (1945). *The social theory of James Mark Baldwin.* New York: King's Crown Press.

Slobin, D. I. (1996). From "thought and language" to "thinking for speaking". In S. Gumperz and S. Levinson (Eds.), *Rethinking linguistic relativity* (pp. 70–96). Cambridge: Cambridge University Press.

Slobin, D. I. (2003). Language and thought online: Cognitive consequences of linguistic relativity. In D. Gentner and S. Goldin-Meadow (Eds.), *Language in mind: Advances in the study of language and thought* (pp. 157–192). Cambridge, MA: MIT Press.

Smagorinsky, P. (2001). Rethinking protocol analysis from a cultural perspective. *Annual Review of Applied Linguistics, 21,* 233–245.

Stam, G. (2008). What gestures reveal about second language acquisition. In S. G. McCafferty and G. Stam (Eds.), *Gesture. Second language acquisition and classroom research* (pp. 231–256). New York: Routledge.

Swain, M. (2006). Languaging, agency and collaboration in advanced second language proficiency. In H. Byrnes (Ed.), *Advanced language learning. The contribution of Halliday and Vygotsky* (pp. 96–108). London: Continuum.

Swain, M. and Lapkin, S. (2002). Talking it through: Two French immersion learners' response to reformulation. *International Journal of Educational Research, 37,* 285–304.

Swain, M., Lapkin, S., Knouzi, I., Suzuki, W., and Brooks, L. (2009). Languaging: University students learn the grammatical concept of voice in French. *The Modern Language Journal, 93,* 5–29.

Talyzina, N. F. (1981). *The psychology of learning.* Moscow: Progress Press.

Thorne, S. L., Reinhardt, J., and Golombek, P. (2008). Mediation as objectification in the development of professional academic discourse: A corpus-informed curricular innovation. In J. P. Lantolf and M. E. Poehner (Eds.), *Sociocultural theory and the teaching of second languages* (pp. 256–284). London: Equinox.

Tocalli-Beller, A. and Swain, M. (2005). Reformulation: the cognitive conflict and L2 learning it generates. *International Journal of Applied Linguistics, 15,* 5–28.

Tomasello, M. (1999). *The cultural origins of human cognition.* Cambridge, MA: Harvard University Press.

Valsiner, J. (2000). *Culture and human development: An introduction.* London: Sage.

Vygotsky., L. S. (1926/2004). The historical meaning of the crisis in psychology: A methodological investigation. In R. W. Rieber and D. K. Robinson (Eds.), *The essential Vygotsky* (pp. 227–344). New York: Kluwer/Plenum.

Vygotsky, L. S. (1978). M. Cole, V. John-Steiner, S. Scribner, and E. Souberman (Eds.), *Mind in society. The development of higher psychological processes.* Cambridge, MA: Harvard University Press.

James P. Lantolf

Vygotsky, L. S. (1987). *The collected works of L. S. Vygotsky. Volume 1. Problems of general psychology. Including the volume Thinking and Speech* (R. W. Reiber and A. S. Carton (Eds.)). New York: Plenum Press.

Watanabe, Y. (2004). *Collaborative dialogue between ESL learners of different proficiency levels: Linguistic and affective outcomes.* Unpublished M.A. thesis. OISE, University of Toronto.

Wells, G. (1999). *Dialogic inquiry: Toward a sociocultural practice and theory of education.* Cambridge: Cambridge University Press.

Wertsch, J. V. (1985). *Vygotsky and the social formation of mind.* Cambridge, MA: Harvard University Press.

Wertsch, J. V. (1998). *Mind as action.* Oxford: Oxford University Press.

Wertsch, J. V. (2007). Mediation. In H. Daniels, M. Cole, and J. V. Wertsch (Eds.), *The Cambridge companion to Vygotsky* (pp. 178–192). Cambridge: Cambridge University Press.

Whitley, M. S. (1986). *Spanish/English contrasts.* Washington, D.C.: Georgetown University Press.

Yáñez-Prieto, C. M. (2008). *On literature and the secret art of invisible words: Teaching literature through language.* Unpublished doctoral dissertation. The Pennsylvania State University, University Park, PA.

5

Complexity theory

Diane Larsen-Freeman

Introduction

In a chapter discussing the recent major shift in the way language and language development have been viewed, child language researcher Evans (2007) wrote:

> Since the late 1950s the dominant metaphor for language and cognition has been the digital computer and the belief that human intelligence is a process of computations on symbolic representations—rule-based manipulation of symbols. Language, from this perspective, is a symbolic system that is innate, residing in the human genetic code. As a result, the focus of much language research has been on the universal, stable, orderly, stage-like patterns in learners' language and the discovery of these innate abstract linguistic structures.
>
> The emphasis of child language researchers has shifted recently to highlighting the flexible, transient, dynamic aspects of the emergence of language abilities ... From this perspective, language is no longer a static, abstract, symbolic system, but language patterns that emerge over time as a property of the self-organization of a complex system. Language development is no longer seen as a process of acquiring abstract rules, but as the *emergence* of language abilities in *real time*, where changes over days, months, and years and moment to-moment changes in language "processing" are the same phenomena, differing only in their timescales ... [With] its emphasis on the fluid, transient, contextually sensitive nature of behavior, the goal of this approach is to identify the mechanisms and states of the child's emerging language abilities that engender developmental change at all levels of real-time continuous processing. (p. 128).

The shift from innatism to emergence, from a top-down process of computation to a bottom-up process of self-organization, from rules to patterns, from a static system to a dynamic one, from universal to contextually sensitive behavior, and from stability to transience all reflect a profound shift of perspective, one that is applicable to second language acquisition (SLA), as well as to first. Although there is no doubt a confluence of post-structural accounts that one could point to that propelled this shift in perspective,[1] the new "science" of complexity theory (Gleick, 1987; Hall, 1993; Waldrop, 1992) has been a major contributor to this way of thinking.

Historical discussion[2]

One of the first to initiate the thinking that changed science was Warren Weaver (Érdi, 2007). Weaver is perhaps best known for his work with Claude Shannon on developing information theory. However, in an article that pre-dated his work with Shannon, Weaver (1948) distinguished between disorganized and organized complexity. Disorganized complexity, as the name implies, arises from random interactions of a large number of elements; gas molecules inside a container is an example. Organized complexity, on the other hand, also involves a large number of parts, but the parts work together to produce a coherent structure from their interaction, such as with individual birds coming together to form a flock. In Weaver's words "a sizable number of factors ... are integrated into an organic whole" (p. 539). The structure emerges and is not dictated to or embedded in any one part.

The idea of organized complexity is core to complexity theory (CT). Biologist von Bertalanffy (1950) applied this idea in his general systems theory. He sought to identify organizational principles that promote our understanding of the behavior of living systems and social groups. Of course living organisms and social groups, unlike my example involving a gas in a container, are open systems, which means that they are open to interacting with systems outside of themselves. They receive feedback from the environment and adapt as circumstances change.

As CT has been appropriated to deal with more human enterprises in the last 20 years or so, it has yielded insights into organizational development, economics, and epidemiology, to name but a few of its applications. Indeed, one of the strengths of CT is that it has been usefully applied to study different phenomena: traffic jams, stock markets, the growth of cancer tumors, the conservation and management of resources, and so on. A systems-level perspective also makes possible cross-disciplinary investigations, such as can be found in the work of Oxford University researchers Fricker, Efstathiou, and Reed-Tsochas (cited in Johnson 2007, p. 16), who analyzed the nutrient supply lines in a fungus in order to see whether lessons can be learned for supply-chain design in the retail trade.

Closer to our field, there has been a great deal of research in developmental psychology, based on principles from complexity theory and its close kin dynamic systems theory. Some of the pioneering work has been on investigating motor development in children (Thelen and Smith, 1994), modeling first language development (van Geert, 1991), and conceptualizing real-time language processing and the longer timescale of language development as integrated phenomena (Bates and Elman, 2000). In second language development, there is not a long history. Larsen-Freeman (1997) was the first to write about the value of seeing second language acquisition from a chaos/complexity theory perspective, following up in 2002a, 2007, and 2010 by showing how such a perspective can help to overcome the dualism that often besets our field. Larsen-Freeman (1997) and Larsen-Freeman and Cameron (2008a) have suggested that because CT features systems which are complex, dynamic, emergent, open, self-organizing, and adaptive, it holds great promise for inspiring innovative thinking concerning both first and second language development.

Also finding the perspective helpful, de Bot et al. (2005, 2007) applied dynamic systems theory to second language acquisition, and Herdina and Jessner (2002) used it to discuss changes in multilingual proficiency on an individual level and to provide a more dynamic description of multilingualism. Research reports based on this perspective are featured in special issues of *Applied Linguistics*, co-edited by Ellis and Larsen-Freeman (2006), *The Modern Language Journal*, edited by de Bot (2008), and *Language Learning*, co-edited by Ellis and Larsen-Freeman (2009). Given the date of these publications, it is clear, as I wrote earlier, that there is not a long history to CT nor to its use in SLA, but interest is growing.

Core issues

The association of CT and related theories, chaos theory and dynamic systems theory, with the new sciences stems from their common rejection of Newtonian linear determinism. Rather than seeing the world through a reductionist lens, CT and its relatives adopt a more holistic perspective. What this means is that they adopt a systems perspective and look for (nonlinear) relations among variables that have previously been separately studied for their linear cause and effect relationship. The new sciences have a great deal else in common. They focus on complex systems, those whose complexity results from many interacting elements or agents. Complex systems demonstrate an initial state dependence, in which even the smallest of differences can have a huge, amplifying effect on the subsequent behavior of the system, a phenomenon known as "the butterfly effect."

These systems are affected by "feedback." As a result of the feedback, the systems adapt to new conditions. The system is typically "open," which means it can be influenced by its environment. The system also exhibits emergent properties. It shows a mix of ordered and disordered behavior. Systems are said to operate at a number of different, but interconnected, levels, from a macro level, such as that of a whole ecosystem, all the way down to a micro level, such as subatomic particles. The system can thus be viewed at different levels of granularity, with each nested, one within another. The new sciences also focus on the dynamics of complex systems, making change, both gradual, and unpredictably sudden, a central focus of their investigation.

Perhaps its biggest contribution then is the shift of perspective it has ushered in. Not only is the perspective cross-disciplinary in scope, but it also makes possible a way to unify areas within language study. For instance, a CT perspective makes possible an integrated view across nested levels and across time scales from language processing in the brain, to language evolution and change, to language use, to language acquisition. To illustrate this, consider just one of these features of a complex system—its dynamism—and how it applies at different nested levels of scale.

At the level of language processing in the brain, cognitive scientist Spivey has developed a complex dynamic view of mind that he calls "continuity psychology" (Spivey, 2007). Spivey spurns cognitive psychologists' computer models of the mind, in which one discrete stable non-overlapping representational state gives way to another. He argues instead that the mind is in continual flux and that mental processes are continuously dynamic. Rather than "the assumption of stable symbolic internal representations ..." (2007, p. 332), we should think of internal representation as a process.

This same dynamism can be seen to apply to language evolution and change. Complexity theory sees language evolution as a dynamic process, characterized by continuous change. In other words, language is a complex adaptive system (Ellis and Larsen-Freeman, 2009; Kretzschmar, 2009). Lee and Schumann (2005, p. 2) propose that linguistic structure emerges as a complex adaptive system from the verbal interaction of hominids attempting to communicate with each other. What the interaction does is to insure that the forms that ultimately become part of the grammar are those that fit the cognitive and motor capacities of the brain. The adaptive process inherent in the interaction modifies the grammatical structures to fit the brain rather than requiring the brain to evolve a genetically based mechanism designed to specify the form of the language.

Thus, language has the shape that it does because of the way that it is used, not because of an innate bio-program or internal mental organ. Of course, there may be domain-general evolutionary prerequisites to language that support its use and acquisition. For instance, these might include the ability to imitate, to detect patterns, to notice novelty, to form categories, or the social drive to interact, to establish joint attention with another, to understand the communicative intention of others, etc. (Larsen-Freeman and Cameron, 2008a). However, language itself is an epiphenomenon, emerging from the interaction of its speakers (Hopper, 1988), a claim that Bybee (2006) has supported using diachronic data.

As I wrote, dynamism applies to real-time language use as well. Complexity theory maintains that because language is perpetually dynamic, every instance of language use contributes to language change. Thus, speakers' using a language at one time and at one level of scale (e.g., two speakers conversing) contributes to language change over time and at a higher level of scale, that is, the speech community. Of course, some emergent patterns in language become stable, for without stability, speakers of the same language would eventually be unable to understand one another. The stability is achieved as speakers adapt to each other. Resulting stable norms of the community, in turn, downwardly entrain emergent patterns, a process known as "reciprocal causality." As Gleick (1987, p. 24) has written of other dynamic systems occurring in nature: "The act of playing the game has a way of changing the rules." This does not assume, however, the existence of a homogeneous speech community. Language variation arises from language in use, from how people actually speak and write. Every group and every place, every situation, is different (Kretzschmar, 2009). For instance, phoneticians have long known that the same word is pronounced differently by the same person with every use (Milroy and Milroy, 1999).

The same dynamism also characterizes second language acquisition. Both the evolving language system of a speech community and the developing interlanguage system of individual language learners change through use. Language is an autopoietic system, not an entropic one.

As Evans (2007) writes:

> Developmental outcomes can be explained through the spontaneous emergence of more complex forms of behavior due to the cooperation of the multiple heterogeneous parts of the system that produce coherent complex patterned behavior. This process is known as *self-organization*. It occurs without pre-specification from internal rules or genetic code. Rather, development is truly self-organizing because it occurs through the recursive interactions of the components of the system. This process depends both on the organism itself and on the constraints put on the organism by the environment ... (p. 132)

Thus, from a CT perspective, an analogous process to real-time language change, self-organization in a dynamic system, occurs in first and second language development. During a particular communicative interaction, speakers *soft-assemble* their language resources. "Soft-assembly" refers to processes involving the articulation of multiple components of a system, where "each action is a response to the variable features of the particular task" (Thelen and Smith, 1994, p. 64). In other words, the assembly is said to be "soft" because the elements being assembled, as well as the specific ways in which they are configured, are adaptive; they can change at any point during the task. The soft-assembled patterns that arise from interaction are the products of dynamic adaptation to a specific context (Tucker and Hirsch-Pasek, 1993). The adaptation to a context includes the process of *co-adaptation* in which each individual in an interaction imitatively adapts to the language of another.

In communicative interactions, learners draw on what they know—the initial condition of their language systems. Given the pressures of responding in real time, they cobble together constructions (Goldberg, 2006; Tomasello, 2003)—form–meaning–use composites[3]: Words, phrases, idioms, metaphors, noncanonical collocations, grammar structures—a much more complex and diverse set of language-using patterns than the "core grammar" of formal approaches (Larsen-Freeman and Cameron, 2008, p. 99). By having an opportunity to repeatedly soft assemble, to revisit a similar semiotic space again and again, the language resources of learners are built up in an iterative fashion. Over time, those that occur frequently become emergent stabilities in a complex system. "Sequences of elements come to be automatized as neuromotor routines" in individuals. (Beckner *et al.*, 2009, p. 11).

Through this building up process, certain structures achieve stability. However,

> [w]hile achieving behavioral stability is critical in development, so is the need for flexibility and dissolution of old forms. With the emergence of novel, more complex forms, stable patterns must become unstable for change to occur. This instability itself allows the components of the system to reorganize in novel ways. From a [dynamic systems theory] perspective, *variability* is not simply "noise" in the system but instead provides valuable insights into the nature of language development and may in fact be the actual mechanism of change in development (Gershkoff-Stowe and Thelen, 2004, p. 13). (Evans 2007, p. 132)

The instability arises when two established patterns compete. This is signaled by a period of fluctuation between the competing patterns, followed by a phase shift in the system when a certain critical threshold is crossed, and some wider reorganization is triggered. The sudden discontinuity of the phase shift illustrates the non-linearity of complex systems, arising from the interaction of variables, whose modulating, mediating, attenuating, and amplifying effects on each other in positive feedback relationships (Ellis and Larsen-Freeman, 2006), cause a phase transition to be reached, which results in a change of state.

Moving between stability and instability, language can be seen as a "statistical ensemble" of interacting elements (Cooper, 1999, p. ix), and, similarly, a learner's language resources as "a network of dynamic language-using patterns" (Larsen-Freeman and Cameron, 2008). Through encounters with others, a process of co-adaptation takes place, in which each interlocutor's language resources are shaped and reshaped throughout the interaction (Larsen-Freeman and Cameron, 2008). Not only is "positive evidence" available in the interaction, so also is negative evidence. As Spivey (2007, p. 202) notes, learners can learn from the conspicuous absence of positive evidence. Its absence allows learners to decrement the probability of a relationship in the target language that they would have otherwise expected. Or, as Spivey puts it, "Negative evidence from the environment is not needed in such a situation because the predictive learner generates his or her own negative evidence."

Thus, it is not necessary to posit a central rule-governed mental grammar that applies in a top-down manner. The knowledge underlying fluent, systematic, apparently rule-governed use of language is the learner's entire collection of memories of previously experienced utterances, both the learner's own and what the learner has attended to in the learner's interlocutors' speech during co-adaptations. This socially situated view accords an active view of the learner—someone who learns from positive evidence, while generating her own negative evidence from her active noticing and exploration of the boundaries of the system.

As has been known for some time (Larsen-Freeman, 1976), frequency of occurrence has an important role in explaining the regularities that do exist in learner language (Ellis, 2002; Chapter 12, this volume). Of course, the language acquisition process is not mere imitation of frequently occurring forms. The failings of operant conditioning in language acquisition are well known. Therefore, it is not only frequency; development of a particular construction also depends on the degree to which the salience of a particular construction captures learner attention. Because learners must notice forms, and sometimes the forms are not very salient, factors relating to learner attention, such as automaticity, transfer, and blocking (Ellis, 2006), play a role in the development and use of any linguistic construction. Also important are a construction's cue contingency, the reliability with which learners can ascribe meaning or function to the construction in the language that flows about them, and its social value, and the role of particular constructions in organizing discourse (Celce-Murcia and Larsen-Freeman, 1999; Larsen-Freeman, 2002b, 2003). Another factor is the affective attachment learners have to certain patterns over others (Todeva, 2009). Learners thus exercise agency in the constructions they choose to use. With the ascription of meaning/function/value to forms, learners can begin to categorize them and generalize their meaning, often doing so around prototypes.

It is also true that learners do not merely reproduce what is said to them, or else, as Chomsky (1959) argued long ago, linguistic creativity would not take place. However, unlike the Chomskyan claim that a rule-governed process is required for novel forms to arise, CT offers morphogenesis through recombination and analogy (Larsen-Freeman, 1997, 2003). Indeed, connectionists' simulations show that generalizations can be formed from increasing experience of usage, which develop over time (Christiansen and Chater, 2001; Elman *et al.*, 1996), and that new forms, which are not present in the input data, can arise through overgeneralization, just as they do in natural language acquisition (Rumelhart and McClelland, 1986).

> These observations are consistent with a view of the social, discursive world as systematic—patterned and often predictable, but where the systems in play are open and dynamic, with human meanings and human agency not only reproducing familiar patterns, but also generating novelty and surprise. (Sealey, 2009, p. 216)

Ultimately, "It is the multiple integrations of many component processes in many different tasks that leads to a system that is flexible, inventive, and exquisitely adaptive" (Smith and Breazeal, 2007, p. 67).

Of course, learners do not immediately begin using new forms in a target-like manner. Learners design their own systems on the basis of the affordances in the language they are exposed to, so input does not lead directly to output; instead, L2 learners are known to adopt a frequently occurring or perceptually salient form, especially if it is prototypical, or similar to a form in their own language. Once a particular form has emerged, it stays around for a time. It does not suddenly disappear from a learner's repertoire. A hallmark of complex systems is their variable behavior at one point in time. Over time, increased variability is a sign that a sudden non-linear jump is about to take place (van Geert, 2003). The phase shift signals a restructuring of the learners' interlanguage. In fact, variation is essential for development to take place, just as it is for evolution in nature.

A very important caveat to all this, as always in SLA, is the powerful influence of what learners know of other languages. In a multilingual situation, there are multilingual norms instead of monolingual norms; furthermore, "the presence of one or more language systems influences the development not only of the second language, but also the development of the overall multilingual system" (Jessner, 2008, p. 274). In order to avoid the monolingual bias (Ortega, 2010), no longer can we assume language learners to be native speakers of a single national language, interacting with native speakers of another national language, and moving inexorably in a line from L1 to L2. Multilingualism is the norm.

Nor should we expect the processes of L1 and subsequent language development to be the same. Indeed, it is likely that SLA will need to be accomplished not only through implicit, but also through explicit, learning, at least for most older learners. In addition, languages are developed in local contexts of use. Because, from a CT perspective, open systems interact with the systems in their context of use, we should also not expect the details of SLA to be identical in all contexts.

As for the well-attested individual difference issue, individual difference factors are also seen to be dynamic (Dörnyei, 2009a; Ushioda and Dörnyei, Chapter 24, this volume), so that, for example, motivation is not static, but rather ebbs and flows and interacts with other factors. Moreover, there are so many individual differences, which are constantly changing and interacting, that it is difficult to separate the acquisition process from the one doing the acquiring (Kramsch, 2002). From a CT perspective, each individual is unique because he or she has developed his or her physical, affective, and cognitive self from a different starting point and through differing experience and history. Each individual thus acts as a unique learning context, bringing a different set of systems to a learning event, responding differently to it, and therefore, learning differently as a result of participating in it.

From this perspective, as heretical as it may seem to others, there is no end and there is no state to language or to its development (Larsen-Freeman, 2005). In fact, we would be better off using the term "second language development" rather than "second language acquisition" in that learners have "the capacity to create their own patterns with meanings and uses (morphogenesis) and to expand the meaning potential of a given language, not just to internalize a ready-made system" (Larsen-Freeman and Cameron, 2008, p. 116). Language acquisition is not a matter of conformity to uniformity. Thus, developmental change seems "not so much the stage-like progression of new accomplishments as the waxing and waning of patterns, some stable and adaptive and others fleeting and seen only under special conditions" (Thelen and Bates, 2003, p. 380). In conclusion:

> Embodied learners soft assemble their language resources interacting with a changing environment. As they do so, their language resources change. Learning is not the taking in of linguistic forms by learners, but the constant adaptation and enactment of language-using patterns in the service of meaning-making in response to the affordances that emerge in a dynamic communicative situation. (Larsen-Freeman and Cameron, 2008, p. 158)

Data elicitation and common measures

Characteristics

Complexity theory/second language acquisition researchers are primarily interested in learner performance data. Such data can be obtained from any language-using activity, inside or outside the classroom, which involves mental activity around language: understanding, speaking, recall of language, meaningful practicing, and so on. Language learning or development emerges with these adaptive experiences of language use.

In order to demonstrate endurance, and not only emergence of a form, longitudinal data would be desirable. In particular, dense corpora, with frequent samplings of learner language, are valuable in order to identify the "motors of change" (Thelen and Corbetta, 2002). Data are considered from an emic phraseological perspective (e.g., using "idea units" as the unit of analysis Ellis and Barkhuizen, 2005), seeking as much as possible to view learner performance from the learner's point of view, with comparison to the target language usually avoided.[4]

Furthermore, "Models which assume that speaker characteristics are 'independent variables', with linguistic features as 'dependent variables,' imply a linear model of causality. Such models do not allow for the interaction between the variables, and they do not model well the dynamic, systems-based realities" with which CT researchers are concerned (Sealey, 2009, p. 222).

Where to draw the ecological circuit (Atkinson et al., 2007) for a particular study and how to include enough detail for a rich, holistic account are challenges to doing research within this framework. This is because from a complexity perspective, context includes the physical, social, cognitive, and cultural, and is not separable from the system. That is, context cannot be seen as a frame surrounding the system that is needed to interpret its behavior (Goffman, 1974). The connection between system and context is shown by making contextual factors parameters of the system. We thus cannot separate the learner or the learning from context in order to measure or explain SLA. Rather we must collect data about and describe all the continually changing system(s) that are relevant to our research question, and be especially cautious about generalizing.

Another difference from traditional data is that since we are especially interested in change over time, CT changes what we look at in the behavior of systems: Flux and variability leading to stability signal self-organization and emergence; sudden phase shifts signal important instability in the system and can direct our attention to the conditions that lead up to them. Of course, the study of variability is not new in SLA. However, CT encourages us not to view variability as the result of some extrinsic factor, but rather to adjust our perspective so that we see the variability as necessary for learning to occur (Thelen and Smith, 1994). A complex system will show degrees of variability around stabilities, and the interplay of stability and variability offers potentially useful information about change in the system. From this perspective, variability in data is not noise to be discarded when averaging across events or individuals, or the result of measurement error (van Geert and van Dijk, 2002), but is part of the behavior of the system, to be expected around stabilities, and particularly at times of transition from one phase or mode of behavior to another. Changes in variability can be indicators of development. If we smooth away variable data by averaging, we lose the very information that may shed light on emergence (Larsen-Freeman, 2006). If, instead, we pay attention to the nature of changes in stability and variability, we may find new ways of understanding language learning processes.

Complex systems operate on a range of timescales, from the milliseconds of neural processing through the minutes of a classroom activity to change on an evolutionary timescale. They also operate on a number of nested levels. For a particular study, certain levels and scales will be focal, but they will be affected by what happens on other levels and scales. As Lemke (2002) pointed out, "certain events widely separated in linear time may be more relevant to meaningful behavior now than other events which are closer in linear time" (p. 80). Because activity on one level and scale influences, indeed is a part of what happens on other levels and scales (Kramsch and Whiteside, 2008; Kramsch, 2008), phenomena emerge at a particular level or scale as a result of activity at a lower level or from an earlier period. It is desirable, therefore, when researchers are conducting research within a complex systems approach that they seek to find relationships within and across different levels and timescales. When we are able to do so, the results will be all the more powerful.

Two new sources of SLA data, which are associated with CT, involve the use of computers. First, it is possible to use computer models to generate data—these are then checked for how closely they pattern with what would be expected in natural data (Ellis with Larsen-Freeman (2009). For example, Meara (2004, 2006) used dynamic modeling to describe vocabulary development and loss. Second, computer-searchable linguistic corpora have been used to chart the change in the use of a particular pattern over time in SLA research (Ellis and Ferreira-Junior, 2009; Ellis with Larsen-Freeman, 2009). While computer and corpus-based research has certain drawbacks, for example, the stripping away of context, they have the advantage of providing a way to model systems and condense time periods in the case of computer models and provide abundant exemplars in the case of corpora.

To summarize this section, complexity theory researchers search for ways to study the relational nature of dynamic phenomena, a search that is not the same as the pursuit of an exhaustive taxonomy of factors that might account for behavior of any given phenomenon. To do this, researchers must collect data that include the richness of the context, that do not strip away the variability, and that include data collected from different levels and timescales. All this is to avoid the reductionism that does not produce satisfying explanations, which are respectful of the holistic interconnectedness of complex dynamic systems.

Empirical verification

Port and van Gelder offer three methods of studying complex, dynamic systems: quantitative modeling, qualitative modeling, and dynamical description. The first is not appropriate for studying human behavior because it requires researchers to measure everything that could possibly influence a system, something that is not possible with humans. However, dynamical description and qualitative modeling have been used in our field, and I will give examples of each.

An example of a dynamical description is a classroom observation conducted by Cameron (Larsen-Freeman and Cameron, 2008) to study collaborative activity in an EFL classroom in Norway. I have chosen it to illustrate the notion of collective variables, an operational construct in the study of complex systems. Collective variables are "actions and responses that index the cooperativity of a multidimensional system" (Thelen and Smith, 1994, p. 99). They describe dynamic patterns, of varying and changing stabilities. The participants in the study were 11-year-old children in a rural classroom in northern Norway. The lesson Cameron observed began with the teacher asking the students to talk about polar animals in English, using content and language that they had encountered in previous lessons. To prompt them to speak, the teacher asked each student to select a particular animal and then to talk about it to the rest of the class.

The ecological circuit that Cameron drew centered on action on a task and so had the three components: teacher, students, and task. Relations among these components produced emergent "talk on task" that served as a learning opportunity or affordance for a particular individual. The trace of the talk, in the form of recording and transcription, represented the trajectory of the system over its state space landscape, that is, all possible outcomes of the task in that classroom. Each interactional episode with an individual learner showed the teacher's talk adapting to the learner's talk through interaction on the task. The data showed how the system started from the teacher's expectation that there would be extended talk, but quickly a not particularly helpful, but rather stable, attractor of limited questions and answers emerged.

In observing a series of such interactions between the teacher and other students, Cameron found that, with one exception, what started as an open invitation to students to speak about a polar animal transformed almost every time into a sequence of questions from the teacher followed by short answers from a student, sometimes added to by further comments from the teacher. In other words, it was the teacher who did much of the talking.

Applying a complex systems description to the unfolding lesson, the teacher-student interaction can be seen as co-adaptive, with each response constructing a feedback loop between participants. The move from an open description task to a series of questions and answers can be seen as a move to a stable attractor in state space landscape of talk on task, since most of the interactions between teacher and individual student ended up in this way. To describe the system in action, moving from the unstable interactional mode to the more stable, limited question and answer mode, Cameron needed to find a suitable collective variable for the system, that is, one that brings together teacher and learner talk on task into one collective variable (Thelen and Smith, 1994, p. 251). A collective variable for this interactional system was derived by comparing the actual language used by learner and with the expected language as set up by the teacher's utterances, something Cameron called the interaction differential.

This collective variable not only usefully described the shift from instability to stability, but it also showed how the trajectory was affected when a more advanced learner transformed the task to suit his own predilection. Rather than discussing a polar animal, he spoke about his pet tropical bird. By changing the task, the learner was able to use more complex language, and the teacher responded with fewer elicitations and more responsive language during his own turns. The result was that the interaction differential took on a wider range of values in this interaction, and did not follow the pattern of a large differential that was rapidly closed down.

Another dynamical description done recently illustrates the important process of adaptive imitation, where learners used an amalgam of old and new patterns to suit their communicative needs. Macqueen (2009) adopted a CT perspective in her investigation of the development of four ESL learners' writing. A qualitative methodology (lexical trail analysis) was used to capture a dynamic and historical view of the lexicogrammatical patterning in the learners' writing. Recurring patterns were traced, and the adaptations that learners made were noted. The newly adapted language-using patterns subsequently become part of the learners' language resources, available for further use and modification. Macqueen's results demonstrate learners' ability to imitate and to adapt, and thus transform their language resources. "Adaptive imitation is the means of gaining the power to conform and the power to create. This power is what enables reciprocal causality in language patterning where ... the communication patterns of individual people contribute to the prevailing norms of their discourse communities ... " (p. 266).

A study that illustrates qualitative modeling is one conducted by Ellis and Larsen-Freeman (2009). The focus of this study was on the acquisition of English verb–argument constructions (VACs) by EFL learners. As I mentioned earlier, first language acquisition researchers Tomasello (2003) and Goldberg (2006) had found support for the usage-based acquisition of constructions. They demonstrated that learners appear to induce categories from exemplars centered around verbs prototypical of a particular VAC.

What Ellis and Larsen-Freeman did was two-fold. First, they reviewed a corpus-based study conducted earlier by Ellis and Ferreira-Junior (2009), which analyzed the speech of seven second language learners of English and the language spoken to them as compiled in the European Science Foundation (ESF) corpus. They found that, just as was the case with L1 acquisition, L2 learners appear to encounter an overwhelming number of tokens of a given verb in a particular VAC. In turn, not surprisingly, when the learners began to produce VACs, the first verb to emerge for a VAC was the one with the highest frequency. Thus, the use of such exemplars by learners' interlocutors presumably facilitates comprehension of the learners in the micro-discursive moment, and perhaps their subsequent emergence and ultimate acquisition of VACs.

Ellis and Larsen-Freeman went on to use computer simulations to see if they would pattern VAC input data in a similar manner to the learners. Although decontexualized, computer simulation supports the investigation of the dynamic interactions of these factors in language learning, processing, and use. In fact, the simulations showed how simple general learning mechanisms, exposed to the co-adapted language usage typical of native speakers as they speak with non-native speakers, produced the same order of emergence as non-native speakers and used the same cues. In other words, the factors that were measured in the corpus study were corroborated in the computer simulations. Learning takes place through the continual revisiting of the same space over and over again.

Applications

From a CT perspective, teaching involves managing the dynamics of learning, exploiting the complex adaptive nature of action and language use while also working to see that co-adaptation works for the benefit of learning. It is not about bringing about conformity to uniformity through transmission. Teachers do not control their students' learning. Teaching does not cause learning; learners make their own paths. This does not mean that teaching does not influence learning, far from it; teaching and teacher-learner interaction construct and constrain the learning affordances of the classroom. What a teacher can do is manage and serve her or his students' learning in a way that is consonant with their learning processes. Thus, any approach consonant with CT would not be curriculum-centered nor learner-centered, but it would be learning-centered—where the learning guides the teaching and not vice versa.

Another implication for instruction, drawing on CT, is the acknowledgment that language is a dynamic system. Treating language more dynamically is an answer in part to the "inert knowledge problem," which arises when students are taught static rules of form using psychologically inauthentic activities. What students learn from traditional grammar drills is not available for use outside of the lesson. I have coined the term "grammaring" to suggest that grammar be treated in a more dynamic manner (Larsen-Freeman, 1995). Grammaring involves *using* grammar structures accurately, meaningfully, and appropriately (Larsen-Freeman, 2003). Students learn to do this when they are engaged in practice activities that are psychologically authentic, with the conditions of learning aligned with the conditions of use, when they are provided with appropriately tuned feedback, and when the activities are deliberately iterative, not repetitive (see Segalowitz and Trofimovich, Chapter 11 in this volume). In other words, from a CT perspective, language learning is seen as a process of meaningfully revisiting the same territory again and again, although each visit begins at a different starting point. In this way, language teaching is not about getting students to add knowledge to an unchanging system. It is about changing the system (Feldman, 2006).

Also implied is the idea of a more "organic" syllabus, which would evolve with learners' readiness to learn the particular form. Instead of a pre-determined sequence of language forms of any sort, learners would engage in tasks or activities that are designed to encourage the use of particular forms (task-essential use). From learners' use, teachers would offer feedback and diagnose the learners' readiness to learn a particular form. Notice that this approach calls for some pre-specification of the items to be learned, partly to fill in the gap and partly because without a teacher's monitoring language that arises in the classroom, certain language forms may never be used by learners who skillfully avoid them. Avoidance is, of course, a sign that learners are experiencing difficulty with particular language forms, and these, too, need attention—even though they are only detectable by their absence. Of course, what is being suggested is not easy to accomplish in a large class of students; nevertheless, it needs to be attempted because teaching students something they already know is not teaching.

Future directions

Complexity theory as applied to SLA is in its infancy; therefore, it is not difficult to imagine a robust research agenda for some time to come. Here are but four questions that would benefit from more exploration from a CT perspective:

(1) *Are there patterns in individual differences?* As is well known, there is a great deal of individual variation in SLA. However, to what extent are there patterns in the variation? There is reason to believe that even though each individual charts his/her own path uniquely, the variety among the paths is not infinite. While entertaining CT would suggest that there are few generalizations that would hold across learners, at best banal ones, for example, "motivation is important," there may well be configurations that capture generalizations among groups of learners or certain combinations of individual differences that act as integrated wholes (Dörnyei, 2009b). For example, Larsen-Freeman (2006) found that certain of the research participants were more analytically oriented and others more expressively oriented (also, see Meisel *et al.*'s multidimensional model (1981)).

(2) *Can we see the motors of change if our corpora are dense enough?* Not unlike any other SLA research effort, a CT approach would benefit from thick longitudinal descriptions, with many learners of many different languages in many contexts. Especially helpful would be dense corpora, which involve highly intensive sampling over short periods of time. Thelen and Corbetta (2002) suggest that the data which such an approach yields will not only allow us to fix the "when" of developmental milestones, but, importantly, the "how" of development by making development more transparent.

An assumption of researchers using a CT approach is that there are moments in the evolution of behavior where we can directly observe change happening. Furthermore, since change works at multiple time scales, these small-scale changes can illuminate change at a longer time scale. Microdevelopment, Thelen and Corbetta suggest, would allow us to dynamically describe important developmental differences among learners, both children and adults.

(3) *What are the potential and limitations of computer modeling?* As we have seen, van Gelder and Port (1995) make a distinction between two types of modeling for dynamic systems. Quantitative modeling cannot be undertaken in the human sciences, for in order to do so, numerical values would have to be assigned to all factors. Qualitative modeling, on the other hand, does lend itself to investigating SLA. Though it still involves quantification, qualitative modeling offers a way of exploring the dynamics of complex systems. Researchers build a computer model of the real world complex system under investigation and take it through multiple iterations, replicating change over time. The model is designed and adjusted so that the outcomes over time reflect what is known of the real world system. Further iterations or changes in parameters then allow the researcher to explore how the model system responds to changes in conditions.

Developing a computer model requires explicit statements of theory and the most accurate empirical knowledge about the real systems and processes being modeled. As a result, the model is only as good as the assumptions built into it. Inevitably, the model differs from the actual system, being idealized or simplified in some respects, approximated in others. Its potential and its limitations remain to be investigated.

(4) *To what extent is implicit learning responsible for SLA?* This is, of course, a question that has been circulating in the field since its inception. No longer can we be content with addressing this question in the absolute sense. There is a need "to create more fine-grained analyses that characterize precisely the ways in which basic implicit generalization mechanisms interact with higher level explicit control processes" (MacWhinney 1997, p. 280).

These are but four questions. With the change of perspective that CT offers, many more questions could easily be formulated and studied. And, I hope they are.

Notes

1 For example, this shift also, at least partly, overlaps with the assumptions of usage-based grammar, emergent grammar, cognitive linguistics, construction grammar, corpus linguistics, conversational analysis, computational linguistics, emergentism, and probabilistic linguistics.

2 For a more complete history see Larsen-Freeman and Cameron, 2008; van Geert, 2003; van Gelder and Port, 1995).

3 Construction grammarians and many others speak of form–meaning connections, but I have long maintained that the pragmatics governing the use of a particular structure is also part of knowing it. With this knowledge, speakers not only know how to form a structure and what it means, they also know when to use it, that is, on what particular occasion a particular form is appropriate.

4 I say, following Bley-Vroman (1983) "usually avoided," because sometimes, as in the study of instructed SLA, the directionality of the evolution of the interlanguage toward the target language merits consideration, even if the path is not a linear one.

References

Atkinson, D., Churchill, E., Nishino, T., and Okada, H. (2007). Alignment and interaction in a sociocognitive approach to second language acquisition. *The Modern Language Journal, 91*, 169–88.

Bates, E. and Elman, J. (2000). The ontogeny and phylogeny of language: A neural network perspective. In S. T. Parker and J. Langer (Eds.), *Biology, brains, and behavior: The evolution of human development* (pp. 89–130). Santa Fe, NM: School of American Research Press.

Beckner, C., Blythe, R., Bybee, J., Christiansen, M. H., Croft, W., Ellis, N. C., Holland, J., Ke, J., Larsen-Freeman, D., and Schonemann, T. (2009). Language is a complex adaptive system: Position paper. *Language Learning, 59* (Supplement 1), 1–27.

Bley-Vroman, R. (1983). The comparative fallacy in interlanguage studies: The case of systematicity. *Language Learning, 33*, 1–17.

Bybee, J. (2006). From usage to grammar: The mind's response to repetition. *Language, 82*, 711–733.

Celce-Murcia, M. and Larsen-Freeman, D. (1999). *The grammar book.* Boston: Heinle/Cengage.

Chomsky, N. (1959). A review of B. F. Skinner's *verbal behavior. Language, 34*(1), 26–58.

Christiansen, M. H. and Chater, N. (Eds.). (2001). *Connectionist psycholinguistics.* Westport, CO: Ablex.

Cooper, D. (1999). *Linguistic attractors: The cognitive dynamics of language acquisition and change.* Amsterdam/Philadelphia: John Benjamins.

de Bot, K. (2008). Second language development as a dynamic process. *The Modern Language Journal, 92*(2), 166–178.

de Bot, K., Lowie, W., and Verspoor, M. (2005). *Second language acquisition: An advanced resource book.* London: Routledge.

de Bot, K., Lowie, W., and Verspoor, M. (2007). A dynamic systems approach to second language acquisition. *Bilingualism: Language and Cognition, 10*, 7–21, 51–55.

Dörnyei, Z. (2009a). *The psychology of second language acquisition.* Oxford: Oxford University Press.

Dörnyei, Z. (2009b). Individual differences: Interplay of learner characteristics and learning environment. *Language Learning, 59*, 230–248.

Ellis, N. (2002). Frequency effects in language processing: A review with implications for theories of implicit and explicit language acquisition. *Studies in Second Language Acquisition, 24*, 143–88.

Ellis, N. C. (2006). Selective attention and transfer phenomena in SLA: Contingency, cue competition, salience, interference, overshadowing, blocking, and perceptual learning. *Applied Linguistics, 27*, 1–31.

Ellis, N. C. and Ferreira-Junior, F. (2009). Construction learning as a function of frequency, frequency distribution, and function. *The Modern Language Journal, 93*, 370–386.

Ellis, N. C. and Larsen-Freeman, D. (2006). Language emergence: Implications for applied linguistics. *Applied Linguistics, 27*(4), 558–589.

Ellis, N. C. and Larsen-Freeman, D. (2009). Constructing a second language: Analyses and computational simulations of the emergence of linguistic constructions from usage. *Language Learning, 59* (Supplement 1), 93–128.

Ellis, R. and Barkhuizen, G. (2005). *Analysing learner language,* Oxford: Oxford University Press.

Elman, J., Bates, E., Johnson, M., Karmiloff-Smith, A., Parisi, D., and Plunkett, K. (1996). *Rethinking innateness: A connectionist perspective on development.* Cambridge, MA: MIT Press.

Érdi, P. (2007). *Complexity explained.* New York: Springer.

Evans, J. (2007). The emergence of language: A dynamical systems account. In E. Hoff and M. Shatz (Eds.), *Handbook of language development.* Malden, MA: Blackwell.

Feldman, J. (2006). *From molecule to metaphor.* Cambridge, MA: Bradford/MIT Books.

Gershkoff-Stowe, L. and Thelen, E. (2004). U-shaped changes in behavior: A dynamic systems approach. *Journal of Cognition and Development, 5*, 11–36.

Gleick, J. (1987). *Chaos: Making a new science.* New York: Penguin Books.

Goffman, E. (1974). *Frame analysis.* London: Harper and Row.

Goldberg, A. (2006). *Constructions at work: The nature of generalization in language.* Oxford: Oxford University Press.

Hall, N. (Ed.). (1993). *Exploring Chaos: A Guide to the new science of disorder.* New York: Norton and Company.

Herdina, P. and Jessner, U. (2002). *A dynamic model of multilingualism*. Clevedon, UK: Multilingual Matters.

Hopper, P. (1988). Emergent grammar and the a priori grammar postulate. In D. Tannen (Ed.), *Linguistics in context: Connecting observation and understanding*. Norwood, NJ: Ablex Publishing Company.

Jessner, U. (2008). A DST model of multilingualism and the role of metalinguistic awareness. *The Modern Language Journal, 92*(ii), 270–283.

Johnson, N. (2007). *Simply complexity*. Oxford: Oneworld Publications.

Kramsch, C. (Ed.). (2002). *Language acquisition and language socialization*. London: Continuum.

Kramsch, C. (2008). Ecological perspectives on foreign language education. *Language Teacher, 41*(3), 389–408.

Kramsch, C. and Whiteside, A. (2008). Language ecology in multilingual settings: Towards a theory of symbolic competence. *Applied Linguistics, 29*(4), 645–671.

Kretzschmar, W. (2009). *The linguistics of speech*. Cambridge: Cambridge University Press.

Larsen-Freeman, D. (1976). An explanation for the morpheme acquisition order of second language learners. *Language Learning, 26*, 125–34.

Larsen-Freeman, D. (1995). On the Teaching and Learning of Grammar: Challenging the Myths. In F. Eckman, D. Highland, P. Lee, J. Mileham, and R. Rutkowski Weber (Eds.), *Second language acquisition theory and pedagogy*. Mahwah, NJ: Lawrence Erlbaum.

Larsen-Freeman, D. (1997). Chaos/complexity science and second language acquisition. *Applied Linguistics, 18*, 141–65.

Larsen-Freeman, D. (2002a). Language acquisition and language use from a chaos/complexity theory perspective. In C. Kramsch (Ed.), *Language acquisition and language socialization*. London: Continuum.

Larsen-Freeman, D. (2002b). The grammar of choice. In E. Hinkel and S. Fotos (Eds.), *New perspectives on grammar teaching*. Mahwah, NJ: Lawrence Erlbaum Associates.

Larsen-Freeman, D. (2003). *Teaching language: From grammar to grammaring*. Boston: Heinle/Cengage.

Larsen-Freeman, D. (2005). Second language acquisition and the issue of fossilization: There is no end, and there is no state. In Z-H. Han and T. Odlin (Eds.), *Studies of fossilization in second language acquisition*. Clevedon, UK: Multilingual Matters.

Larsen-Freeman, D. (2006). The emergence of complexity, fluency, and accuracy in the oral and written production of five Chinese learners of English. *Applied Linguistics, 27*, 590–619.

Larsen-Freeman, D. (2007). Reflecting on the cognitive-social debate in second language acquisition. *The Modern Language Journal, 91* (focus volume), 773–787.

Larsen-Freeman, D. (2010). The dynamic co-adaption of cognitive and social views: A complexity theory perspective. In R. Batstone (Ed.), *Sociocognitive perspective on language use and language learning*. Oxford: Oxford University Press.

Larsen-Freeman, D. and Cameron, L. (2008). *Complex systems and applied linguistics*. Oxford: Oxford University Press.

Lee, N. and Schumann, J. (2005). *Neurobiological and evolutionary bases for child language acquisition abilities*. Paper presented at the 14th World Congress of Applied Linguistics, AILA 2005, Madison, Wisconsin, July.

Lemke, J. (2002). Language development and identity: Multiple timescales in the social ecology of learning. In C. Kramsch (Ed.), *Language acquisition and language socialization*. London: Continuum.

MacWhinney, B. (1997). Implicit and explicit processes: Commentary. *Studies in Second Language Acquisition, 19*, 277–281.

Macqueen, S. M. (2009). *Patterns in second language writing*. Unpublished doctoral dissertation. University of Melbourne, Melbourne, Australia.

Meara, P. (2004). Modelling vocabulary loss. *Applied Linguistics, 25*, 137–55.

Meara, P. (2006). Emergent properties of multilingual lexicons. *Applied Linguistics, 27*, 620–44.

Meisel, J., Clahsen, H., and Pienemann, M. (1981). On determining developmental stages in second language acquisition. *Studies in Second Language Acquisition, 3*(2), 109–135.

Milroy, J. and Milroy, L. 1999. *Authority in language*. Third Edition, New York: Routledge.

Ortega, L. (2010). *The bilingual turn in SLA*. Plenary delivered at the Annual Conference of the American Association for Applied Linguistics. Atlanta, GA, March 8.

Rumelhart, D., and McClelland, J. (1986). On learning the past tenses of English verbs. In J. McClelland, D. Rumelhart, and the PDP Research Group (Eds.), *Parallel distributed processing: Explorations in the microstructure of cognition. Volume 2: Psychological and biological models* (pp. 216–271). Cambridge, MA: MIT Press.

Sealey, A. (2009). Probabilities and surprises: A realist approach to identifying linguistic and social patterns, with reference to an oral history corpus. *Applied Linguistics, 31*(2), 215–235.

Smith, L., and Breazeal, C. (2007). The dynamic lift of developmental process. *Developmental Science, 10*(1), 61–68.

Spivey, M. (2007). *The continuity of mind.* Oxford: Oxford University Press.

Thelen, E. and Bates, E. (2003). Connectionism and dynamic systems: Are they really different? *Developmental Science, 6,* 378–391.

Thelen, E. and Corbetta, D. (2002). Microdevelopment and dynamic systems: Applications to infant motor development. In N. Granott and J. Parziale (Eds.), *Microdevelopment.* Cambridge: Cambridge University Press.

Thelen, E. and Smith, L. (1994). *A dynamic systems approach to the development of cognition and action.* Cambridge, MA: MIT Press.

Todeva, E. (2009). Multilingualism as a kaleidoscopic experience: The mini universes within. In E. Todeva and J. Cenoz (Eds.), *The multiple realities of multilingualism* (pp. 53–74). Berlin: Mouton de Gruyter.

Tomasello, M. (2003). *Constructing a language.* Cambridge, MA: Harvard University Press.

Tucker, M., and Hirsh-Pasek, K. (1993). Systems and language: Implications for acquisition. In L. Smith and E. Thelen (Eds.), *A dynamic systems approach to development: Applications* (pp. 359–384). Cambridge, MA: The MIT Press.

Waldrop, M. (1992). *Complexity: The emerging science at the edge of order and chaos.* New York: Simon and Schuster.

Weaver, W. (1948). Science and complexity. *American Scientist, 36* (4), 536–544.

van Geert, P. (1991). A dynamic systems model of cognitive and language growth. *Psychological Review, 98,* 3–53.

van Geert, P. (2003). Dynamic systems approaches and modeling of developmental processes. In J. Valsiner and K. Connolly (Eds.), *Handbook of developmental psychology.* London: Sage.

van Geert, P. and van Dijk, M. (2002). Focus on variability: New tools to study intra-individual variability in developmental data. *Infant Behavior and Development, 25,* 340–374.

van Gelder, T. and Port, R. (1995). It's about time: An overview of the dynamical approach to cognition. In R. Port and T. van Gelder (Eds.), *Mind as motion: Explorations in the dynamics of cognition.* Cambridge, MA: MIT Press.

von Bertalanffy, L. (1950). An outline of general systems theory. *British Journal for the Philosophy of Science, 1,* 134–165.

Part II
Linguistic perspectives

6

Second language phonology

Fred R. Eckman

Introduction

The field of second-language (L2) phonology attempts to document and explain the pronunciation patterns of non–native learners of a language.[1] The purpose of this chapter is to describe this area of study through several steps. The first is to locate L2 phonology within the field of second language acquisition (SLA), and, in turn, to relate it to other disciplines. We will then consider a number of specific aspects of L2 phonology, including how it fits into a historical context, what its major findings have been, where the major questions and issues lie, and what kinds of data it seeks to use in order to test empirically the various hypotheses that one can postulate within the field. Finally, the chapter will take up the question of how the results of research on L2 phonology can be brought to bear on language pedagogy, and outline what some of the major questions are that need to be addressed by future research.

Because the field of SLA necessarily impinges on several academic areas, including psychology (SLA entails language contact within an individual), sociology (language contact within a society) and biology (the end state for acquisition seems to be different for older versus younger learners), L2 acquisition is naturally studied from a multidisciplinary perspective. Second-language phonology, by extension, is also of interest to researchers in several disciplines. Psycholinguistic perspectives on L2 phonology are concerned about, for example, the explicit and implicit learning of L2 phonemic categories; sociolinguistic approaches to L2 phonology, on the other hand, are interested is how L2 pronunciation patterns may vary according to social context in which a person is speaking; and from a biological viewpoint, L2 phonologists may investigate the acquisition of L2 sounds and contrasts as a function of age of first exposure to the target language (TL). L2 phonology is also studied from the point of view of phonological theory, placing it squarely within the domain of linguistics. The major distinction in the ways that L2 phonology is approached by the above-mentioned related disciplines, on the one hand, and the way it is investigated through a linguistic approach, on the other, is in the kinds of constructs and principles used to give explanations for the relevant L2 facts. Whereas psycholinguistic, sociolinguistic and biological approaches to L2 phonology employ constructs appropriate to their corresponding disciplines, such as short-term memory, prestigious dialect, and critical period hypothesis, respectively, linguistic approaches invoke concepts such as, for example, grammar, phoneme, devoicing, and derived environment. For a general discussion of these other perspectives, the reader is referred to the appropriate chapters in this volume. The focus of this chapter will be on a linguistic approach to L2 phonology.

Given this introduction, the remainder of the chapter is structured as follows. The next section places L2 phonology in its historical context by dividing the field into two distinct periods according to the objectives of the research carried out at the time. The section following that addresses several of the major models and approaches to L2 phonology, as well as some of the findings that derive from these different research programs. This is followed by a description of the kinds of studies that have been conducted in order to test the various hypotheses that these approaches have made, which leads naturally to a discussion of the instructional relevance of these findings. The chapter concludes with an outline of some of the important questions remaining to be addressed by future research.

An important caveat at the outset is that our discussion faces limitations of space that will necessarily curtail to some extent our treatment of all of these topics. Where possible the reader is referred to relevant chapters in this, or other volumes, or to the original work itself for more details.

Historical discussion

Although there are a number of ways in which one could structure the discussion of the historical context, we will, for our purposes, divide the study of L2 phonology into two major eras, the first being the time prior to the formulation of the interlanguage (IL) hypothesis, which we will designate as "pre-ILH," and the second being the period after the postulation of the IL hypothesis, which we term "post-ILH." The most salient characteristic of the pre-ILH approaches to explaining L2 pronunciation problems is that they focused on only two linguistic systems, the L2 learner's native language (NL) and TL. We turn first to the discussion of the pre-ILH period, after which we will define the term "interlanguage," and take up the post-ILH era.

Pre-ILH

The explanation of pronunciation patterns of L2 learners that we label as pre-ILH focused largely on explaining learners' errors in terms of the differences between the NL and TL, the underlying assumption being that the NL influenced the learning of the TL. The goal of SLA studies in general, and investigations into L2 phonology, in particular, was to explain learning difficulty, which, in turn, led to claims about degree of difficulty, and to the postulation of hierarchies of difficulty.

The best known and most explicit claim that the L2 learner's NL had a significant role to play in accounting for pronunciation errors dates from the middle of the last century. This work was carried out within the context of the contrastive analysis hypothesis (CAH), and claimed that NL-TL differences, along with L1 transfer, were paramount in accounting for L2 utterances. During this era, a phonological analysis of a language consisted of a description of the phonemes of that language along with the distribution of the allophones of those phonemes. L2 pronunciation errors were explained in terms of a comparison of the phonemes and their distribution within the respective NL and TL, and although phonemes figured prominently in the predictions of the CAH, a large role was also played by allophones. (See also Pickering, Chapter 20, this volume, for further discussion.) Thus, Lado's (1957) proposals concerning learning difficulty addressed the question of what constituted maximum phonological difficulty, and allophonic differences between the NL and TL were an important part of his predictions. For him, the greatest difficulty lay in the learner re-categorizing two or more allophones in the NL into different phonemic categories in the TL. An example, the one used by Lado, involved the sounds [d] and [ð], which are allophones of /d/ in Spanish, but which contrast as distinct phonemes in English. Lado claimed that assigning the allophones [d] and [ð] to separate phonemes in English by a learner whose native language is Spanish constituted maximum learning difficulty.

Important contributions to what constituted maximal learning difficulty in L2 pronunciation within the context of the CAH were made by Stockwell and Bowen (1965) and by Hammerly (1982). Stockwell and Bowen (1965) expanded and refined the predictions of the CAH by comparing the NL and TL in terms of whether any given sound was phonemic, allophonic, or absent in either language. Through these comparisons the authors constructed an eight-level hierarchy of difficulty in which maximum phonological difficulty was ascribed to a learner having to acquire a TL allophone that was absent in the NL. Work by Hammerly (1982) supported empirically some of the claims about learning difficulty made by the CAH and by Stockwell and Bowen's hierarchy. Hammerly's analysis showed that, of the six most problematic areas of pronunciation, the top three involved allophones. The greatest difficulty for his subjects was the suppression of NL allophones in pronouncing the TL; the second area of difficulty was producing NL allophones with a different distribution in the TL, including contrastive distribution; and the third most difficult aspect of L2 pronunciation was the production of a TL allophone that did not exist in the NL.

In the research that followed the postulation of the CAH in the ensuing decades, the results were mixed in terms of whether the hypothesis was confirmed. Although there were studies in which the findings were supportive of the CAH, there were many others that reported facts that were counter to the hypothesis, which led to the eventual demise of the CAH. Much of the work in this framework, while setting out to find support for the CAH, actually found that the role of developmental processes, patterns often found in first language acquisition, played a more significant role in the explanation of L2 sound patterns than did NL-TL differences. For example, Johannsson's (1973) study of 20 L2 learners of Swedish from eight different native-language backgrounds showed that, although some of the errors were predictable by the CAH, others were explainable in terms of articulation ease.

In sum, research within the CAH paradigm from this period showed that, whereas NL influence had a role to play in explaining some aspects of L2 pronunciation, the influence of the NL could not explain all of the facts. It became clear, therefore, that other principles were necessary to explain learning difficulty that could not be directly related to NL-TL differences. Over the decades since that time, numerous proposals have been made to account for facts that are not subsumed under the CAH. These include proposals pertaining to the similarities between the NL and TL, facts about the relationship between production and perception, and principles of markedness, each of which is briefly considered below.

Although the majority of work on L2 pronunciation during this time was done within the principles of the CAH, and attempted to explain L2 phonological difficulty on the basis of differences between the NL and TL, there are also frameworks that base the explanation of pronunciation problems on similarities between the NL and TL. Two such models that incorporate the role of L2 perception are the speech learning model (SLM) developed by Flege (1995), and the perceptual assimilation model (PAM), proposed by Best (1995). Pickering (Chapter 20, this volume) gives an in-depth discussion of Flege's SLM. For this reason, and because the topic of L2 speech perception is covered in Part IV of this volume, I will not discuss the SLM and PAM any farther here.

A principle that was introduced into SLA theory to help address problems with the CAH was typological markedness, a concept that was pioneered by the Prague School of Linguistics in the theories of Trubetzkoy (1939). The idea behind markedness is that binary oppositions between certain linguistic representations (e.g., voiced and voiceless obstruents, or open and closed syllables) are not simply polar opposites, but that one member of the opposition is assumed to be privileged in that it has wider distribution, both across languages and within a language. Assigning the term "unmarked" to this privileged member is a way of giving it special status, and indicating that it is considered to be, in some definable way, simpler, more basic, and more natural than the less widely occurring member of the opposition, which is designated as being "marked." Over the years, the term markedness has taken on a number of different definitions within several distinct approaches to linguistics (see Battistella, 1990 for discussion).

The proposal with respect to L2 phonology was that markedness, as defined in terms of cross-linguistic, implicational generalizations, as in (1) below, would be incorporated into the CAH as a measure of relative difficulty. According to this proposal, any given TL structure would be predicted to be more difficult if it was both different from the corresponding NL structure, and was also more marked than that structure. This claim was explicitly embodied in the markedness differential hypothesis (MDH) stated in Eckman (1977). Whereas the CAH attempted to explain L2 learning difficulty only on the basis of differences between the NL and TL, the claim behind the MDH is that NL-TL differences are necessary for such an explanation, but they are not sufficient, and that therefore one must incorporate into the hypothesis the concept of typological markedness as a measure of relative difficulty.

(1) Typological markedness

A structure X is typologically marked relative to another structure, Y if every language that has X also has Y, but every language that has Y does not necessarily have X.

Over the last three decades there have been a number of studies addressing the claims of the MDH, showing that typological markedness is a reliable predictor of difficulty, that there are cases where the directionality of difficulty between the NL and TL involved in a language-contact situation follows the predictions of the MDH, and that the relative degree of difficulty corresponds to the relative degree of markedness (Anderson, 1987; Carlisle, 1992; de Jong et al., 2009).

To sum up this sub-section, we have seen that several proposals have been developed over the years to address some of the perceived shortcomings of the CAH. Thus, it is fair to state that conventional wisdom within the field of L2 phonology is that, although the learner's NL has a role to play in explaining certain aspects of learning difficulty, NL influence is by no means sufficient to account for L2 pronunciation patterns. Rather, additional principles are necessary.

Post-ILH

Interlanguage. We now address the post-interlanguage hypothesis period of L2 phonology. Interlanguage (IL) is the term given to the mental system developed by L2 learners that enables them to produce and understand utterances of the TL. The idea behind this construct, which has been one of the key developments over the past few decades in SLA theory, in general, and in L2 phonology, in particular, is that L2 learners create their own version of the target language. The motivation for this idea, which was proposed independently by three different scholars (Corder, 1971; Nemser, 1971; Selinker, 1972), is the same as that invoked by a linguist postulating a mental grammar as underlying the ability of a native speaker of any language to speak and understand utterances of that language. Just as the patterns found in the productions of a native speaker of a language are assumed to derive from that speaker's mental system, so too, the patterns found in the utterances made by non-native speakers of a language are hypothesized to derive from a mental set of rules, viz. the interlanguage system that the learner has acquired.

It is important to note that, in linguistic discussions, the term "grammar" can be used with a systematic ambiguity, on the one hand referring to a description of sentence structure, and on the other hand indicating a mental system that relates meanings and utterances. It is in the latter, more general sense in which "grammar" includes phonological rules that the word is used in this chapter. Where these phonological rules characterize L2 patterns, the term "interphonology" is often used.

This IL system of the L2 learner must be at least partially different from the learner's NL grammar, because the L2 utterances produced by the learner of a language are different from that learner's NL utterances. By the same token, the IL grammar must be different in part from the TL grammar, because the L2 utterances of the learner are distinct from those produced by native speakers of the TL. Thus, a mental grammar that is in at least some respects different from both the NL and the TL must underlie the utterances of the L2 learners. On this view, the process of second language acquisition becomes the construction of a mental system of rules, the interlanguage. And although the acquisition of this IL may be based in part on structures transferred from the NL, and in part on input from the TL, it has also been shown that the IL is, to some extent, independent of both the NL and TL. This is true because studies have shown that some L2 patterns are not part of either the NL or TL.

The strongest argument for the postulation of an IL is an empirical one that requires providing evidence of what is acknowledged to be the most interesting of L2 data, viz., a pattern of utterances that, on the one hand, does not derive from NL transfer, because the NL does not evidence the regularity in question, and on the other hand could not be tied to TL input, because the TL does not exhibit the relevant pattern either. In other words, neither the NL nor the TL can explain the observed L2 patterns, but, as with all regularities, an explanation is required. Therefore, the interlanguage must be hypothesized to explain the observed systematicity.

The value of the construct of an IL is that it has allowed researchers to propose answers to questions that, before this notion was proposed, could not even be asked. Given the concept of IL, not only is it possible, but also reasonable, to raise the question of whether IL grammars are similar in important ways to native language grammars. It is this question which has driven many, if not most, of the research programs in L2 phonology over the last few decades, and on which we will focus in the following sections.

An example of this kind of IL pattern in L2 phonology was reported in Altenberg and Vago (1983) and in Eckman (1981). Altenberg and Vago found that their subjects who were native speakers of Hungarian learning English exhibited the kind of L2 pattern that would motivate a rule of word-final devoicing. What is particularly interesting about this outcome is that neither the phonology of the NL nor that of the TL has a devoicing rule, because both languages have a voice contrast in word-final position. Thus, the IL devoicing rule is independent of both the NL and TL. In the Eckman study, speakers of Spanish produced an IL pattern that motivated a rule of word-final devoicing. This was also a situation where the IL rule was independent of both the NL and TL in that Spanish did not exhibit the kind of evidence necessary to motivate such a rule. What is especially interesting is that the cases of the Hungarian and Spanish learners represent an example of an IL pattern that is not attributable to either NL transfer or TL input, but is attested in other languages of the world, including Catalan, German, Polish, and Russian, to name a few. See also Pickering (Chapter 20, this volume) for discussion of the relationship between the markedness differential hypothesis and the SCH.

To summarize this subsection, the concept of interlanguage led directly to the possibility that L2 patterns could emerge which were independent of both the NL and TL. This development allowed L2 researchers to question whether IL phonologies were in fact similar in important respects to L1 phonologies.

Constraints on IL grammars. With the postulation of the construct, interlanguage, the goal of SLA theory, and by inclusion, L2 phonology, changed from attempting to explain learning difficulty in L2 acquisition to the goal of addressing the question of why IL phonologies are the way they are, which is actually a subset of the question, "why is SLA the way it is?" The response that the research programs of this era have given is along these lines: "SLA is the way it is, because IL systems are they way they; and IL systems are as they are, because they are constrained by general, linguistic principles." In the case of interphonology, the constraints are principles of phonological theory, and within this context, it is also possible for explanations to hark back to the role of the learner's NL. Thus, a number of proposals hypothesized that various linguistic principles interacted with the NL phonology to explain L2 pronunciation patterns. Approaches to L2 phonology differed as to which kinds of theoretical principles the investigators proposed as constraining IL phonologies, and to the extent to which the learner's NL interacted with these principles. We now turn our discussion to the kind of principles that were proposed as constraining IL phonologies.

Constraining principles. The development of phonological theory during this period led to the use of a number of general principles and constructs from phonology to explain facts about L2 pronunciation patterns. These constructs included distinctive features, rule types, underlying representations, and derivations. Researchers viewed the application of these principles as a way, on the one hand, of testing the general claim that interphonologies are constrained in the same way as are native-language phonologies, and, on the other hand, as a way of accounting for different aspects of L2 pronunciation patterns. Whereas some of the constructs that were used to explain some aspect of L2 phonology may have overlapped in part with those invoked as an explanation in other areas, and although the application of some principles may have resulted in deeper explanations than the application of others, it is in general the case that the phonological principles in question did not conflict with each other, or create issues that had to be addressed.

As proposals for non-linear representations made their way into phonological theory, prosodic hierarchies (Zampini, 1997), metrical grids (Archibald, 1993, 1995), and feature geometry (Brown, 1998) were also employed as explanatory principles in L2 phonology. Likewise, as did phonologists focusing on NL phonologies, L2 phonologists appealed to linguistic universals, interpreted in the broadest sense of "universal," including typological generalizations and principles of Universal Grammar (UG), as sources of explanation for second-language pronunciation patterns. More recently, some L2 phonologists have turned from rule-driven grammars to constraint-based analyses within an Optimality Theory (OT) framework for analyzing L2 pronunciation patterns. OT is a framework in which constraints, constraint rankings and constraint re-rankings in the learner's interlanguage, rather than rules, determine the time course of acquisition (Broselow *et al.*, 1998; Hancin Bhatt, 2008). During this period, one of the important recurring themes in virtually all approaches to L2 phonology has been the reporting and explanation of L2 phonological patterns that are not directly attributable either to the learner's NL or to the TL, but may be attested in the phonologies of other languages of the world. Indeed, it is this kind of evidence that purports to show the fundamental properties involved in the acquisition of L2 phonology.

The first example of this involves the employment of prosodic hierarchies and metrical grids to account for the stress patterns of L2 learners. A prosodic hierarchy is a structural representation of the phonological domains that are relevant to the application of rules, with the phonetic segment being the smallest domain, the syllable the next larger, the foot the next larger, and so on, with the utterance being the largest and most inclusive domain. A metrical grid is a structural hierarchy of the syllables and prosodic feet of a given utterance from which properties of stress can be predicted. These constructs have been invoked by L2 phonologists (Archibald, 1993, 1995; Mairs, 1989) to account for the acquisition of stress patterns. Both Archibald and Mairs found that the TL had a role to play in the explanation of IL patterns in that L2 learners transferred some, or all, of their NL metrical grid into the IL grammar, but that the NL principles that applied to these grids may operate differently in the IL grammar than they do in the NL or in the TL.

Two other studies of note involving prosodic features are Nguyen and Macken (2008), and Zampini (1997). Nguyen and Macken analyzed the acquisition of the production of Vietnamese tones by American learners. The authors found the patterns of tone production to be influenced by several factors, including universal principles, NL structures, and TL-specific rules. Zampini studied the acquisition of Spanish spirantization, that is, the rule by which a stop becomes a fricative, by native speakers of English. She showed that the spirantization rule of Spanish must be formulated in terms of the prosodic hierarchy, with the domain of the rule being the intonational phrase. However, she found that the spirantization rule in the respective interlanguage grammars of her subjects applied in a more restrictive domain: only word-internally for most of her subjects, but in the phonological word for others.

Other kinds of phonological constructs have also been put forth as constraints on IL grammars; these include aspects of feature geometry and underspecification, along with principles governing the well-formedness of syllables.

Brown (1998) proposed that feature geometry and underspecification could be invoked as explanatory principles for L2 pronunciation patterns. Feature Geometry is a system of representing segments in which phonological features are not unordered bundles of properties, but are instead structured hierarchically so that some features are dependent on others. Underspecification is a system for representing the underlying representations of segments that takes advantage of the fact that some properties of sounds are predictable on the basis of other properties. These predictable properties are redundant for making contrasts, and are not represented underlyingly. All features are completely specified only when the segments are realized phonetically. Assuming that feature geometry and underspecification are principles that constrained IL phonologies, just as they constrain L1 grammars, Brown employed them in her analysis of the acquisition of several English contrasts by speakers of Japanese, Korean, and Mandarin.

Studies involving principles of syllable structure as a constraint on IL grammars have been carried out, for the most part using NLs which are much more restrictive than English in the kinds of syllable they allow. Sato (1984) conducted one such study of two Vietnamese-speaking brothers, aged 10 and 12, eliciting utterances exclusively through spontaneous conversations. Sato's data contained numerous tokens of syllable-initial and syllable-final consonant clusters, demonstrating that the subjects' difficulty with the TL clusters was reflected not in terms of vowel epenthesis, but in terms of reducing the length of the clusters in question, or in changing the features of one or both of the segments involved. Thus, bi-literal clusters were often reduced to single consonants, and voiced obstruents in the clusters were often devoiced. More recently, Hansen (2004) carried out a year-long study of two Vietnamese learners of English, mapping the development of onsets and codas as a function of several linguistic and contextual factors. Other longitudinal studies have raised the question of whether the development of L2 syllable structure is linear. Abrahamsson (2003) concluded that coda development over time was U-shaped rather than linear. One explanation proposed for this kind of development is that the subjects may tend to pay less attention to form as their fluency increases, and as their ability to control a more casual style of speaking develops.

We now focus our attention on the proposal that linguistic universals act as constraints on IL grammars, and then conclude this section with a discussion of the framework of Optimality Theory. See Pickering (Chapter 20, this volume) for discussion of the use of Optimality Theory in explaining L2 phonology.

One of the earliest studies in L2 phonology that utilized a parameter of UG as an explanatory principle was Broselow and Finer (1991). A parameter is a construct that specifies how grammars can differ from each other with respect to a given structure. The study by Broselow and Finer invoked the Minimal Sonority Distance (MSD) parameter to explain the performance of Korean and Japanese learners of English on the production of onset clusters.

This parameter uses a measure called the Sonority Index (SI), from Selkirk (1982), which assigns a numerical value to certain consonant types according to the consonant's sonority—the greater the sonority of the segment, the greater the value assigned by the SI. The idea is that the MSD parameter characterizes the systematic variation found in the kinds of onsets allowed cross-linguistically, specifying, for any given language the minimal difference in sonority that must exist between adjacent consonants in the onset of a syllable. This minimal difference is computed by subtracting the SI value of one consonant type from that of the other consonant type co-occurring in the onset. If the resulting value is equal to or greater than the value specified by the MSD for that language, then the onset cluster is allowed; if the resulting value is less than that number, the cluster is disallowed. The point of most interest in the Broselow and Finer (1991) study was the finding that their subjects did not simply transfer the value of the MSD parameter of the NL into the IL, nor did they evidence TL-like values of this parameter. Rather, the subjects evinced IL patterns that were somewhere in between the NL and TL settings, providing another instance in which interlanguage grammars obey general principles of phonological theory.

An approach to L2 phonology that invoked generalizations from the other school of universals, typological markedness is the Structural Conformity Hypothesis (SCH) (Eckman, 1991), stated as in (2).

(2) The Structural Conformity Hypothesis (Eckman 1991, p. 24)
    The universal generalizations that hold for primary languages hold also for interlanguages.

This hypothesis developed historically from the Markedness Differential Hypothesis (MDH), discussed briefly in the *Pre-ILH* section above, and it is part of the research program that invokes principles of linguistic typology to explain facts about L2 phonology. Thus, the universal generalizations that have been tested with respect to what the SCH asserts are typological universals. The crucial difference between the MDH and the SCH is that the former is relevant only in cases where the NL and TL are different with respect to some representation or structure, whereas the SCH is neutral on NL-TL differences. The MDH can be considered a special case of the SCH, viz., the case when the typological generalization in question involves an area of NL-TL difference. Consistent with the point made in the above section on *Interlanguage*, the strongest kind of support for the SCH is an L2 pattern in which the structures adhere to universals principles, but the patterns in question are not directly derivable from either the NL or the TL. This type of evidence has been adduced in a number of studies, including Altenberg and Vago (1983), Eckman (1991), Carlisle (1998), among others.

Two other proposals related to the topic of markedness, and also discussed by Pickering (Chapter 20, this volume), are the Similarity Differential Rate Hypothesis (SDRH) formulated by Major and Kim (1996), and Optimality Theory. The SDRH reprises an idea from earlier proposals in L2 phonology that sounds which are different from those in the NL may be easier to acquire, in that these sounds are acquired more quickly than sounds that are different. According to the hypothesis, "rate of acquisition" is the basis for explaining many L2 pronunciation errors, not difficulty, as is stated in both the CAH and the MDH.

The most significant difference between a phonology within the framework of Optimality Theory and phonologies within other approaches to sound systems is how well-formedness is described. In rule-based phonologies, a well-formed representation is characterized by constructing a set of rules, which, if adhered to, will yield well-formed utterances as judged by native speakers. Deviance is described by showing that unacceptable representations violate at least one of the principles of the phonology. Within OT, on the other hand, phonologies consist of a universal set of constraints instead of a set of rules. A good way to conceive of the constraints is as criteria for well-formedness, and the assumption is that no language can satisfy all of these criteria. Therefore, the constraints in question can be violated, and conflicts among constraints are resolved by ranking them in such cases in different orders for different languages. Within OT, therefore, well-formedness is not characterized on the basis of whether or not an utterance violates one or more of the constraints; instead, whether an utterance is well-formed is determined by an optimization procedure whereby well-formed utterances are those that conform to the highest ranked constraints. Thus, within the framework of OT, phonologies of particular languages result from different rankings of the universal constraints; any ranking of the universal constraints should yield a phonology of some language, and any phonological system of a language should conform to one of the possible rankings of the constraints.

In recent years there have been a few studies on L2 phonology done within an OT framework. One example is Broselow *et al.* (1998), in which the authors illustrated that the simplification strategies used to modify English codas by native speakers of Mandarin could be explained as what is termed "the emergence of the unmarked," one of the ways that OT phonologies can represent an L2 pattern that is independent of both the NL and TL. Another example is Lombardi (2003), who argued for an OT approach to the classical problem of "differential substitution," in which learners of L2 English substitute either [t] or [s] for [θ], depending on their NL background.

To summarize this section, the study of L2 pronunciation patterns can be insightfully divided into those that investigate the topic from the standpoint of the mental system of the L2 learner, that is, the interlanguage, and those that consider the patterns in terms of the native and target languages.

Core issues

This section is divided into two parts. First, we will outline the major tenets underlying research into L2 phonology, and then, we will discuss some of the major findings that have emerged from this research.

The principal postulation of virtually all, if not truly all, approaches to L2 phonology is the notion that each L2 learner must create an interlanguage system on the basis of whatever TL input is available. As discussed above, this mental system is the learner's version of the target language, and is used by the learner to produce and understand L2 utterances. Moreover, it is fair to say that the construct of an interphonology is the only tenet that is used in research on L2 pronunciation that is particular to L2 phonology. All of the other concepts that have been brought to bear on explaining patterns of L2 utterances are motivated also for the explanation of phonologies of L1 grammars. Where approaches to L1 phonology differ in their underlying assumptions and constructs, so, too, do the assumptions brought to bear on L2 phonologies.

In fact, one of the major underpinnings of approaches to L2 phonology is that interphonologies are subject to the same principles and constraints as are L1 phonologies. Whereas this claim is embodied implicitly in the analyses of L2 utterances that use principles that are motivated for L1s, it is made explicitly by the Structural Conformity Hypothesis in (2) above, and within the Optimality Theoretic approach to L2 phonology. The major premise of OT is that all phonologies are constructed in the same way; specifically, all phonologies, including interphonologies, must be one of the possible rankings of the universal set of constraints (Hancin Bhatt, 2008).

This brings us to the second point of this section: the major finding of research on L2 phonology over the decades is that IL phonologies are constrained by the same principles, and obey the same generalizations, as do phonologies of languages learned natively. In other words, the fundamental hypothesis that IL phonologies do not violate principles of native-language phonologies is supported, as is the claim that IL phonological systems are similar in important ways to native-language systems.

Therefore, the reasoning behind Zampini's (1997) and Archibald's (1993) respective claims that the prosodic hierarchy and the metrical grid could account for facts about the L2 acquisition of Spanish spirantization or English stress is that L2 phonologies adhere to the principles of the prosodic hierarchy and to metrical grids. Likewise, the rationale behind Brown (1998) invoking feature geometry, or Broselow and Finer (1991) appealing to the Minimal Sonority Distance parameter in their studies on the L2 acquisition of lateral contrasts or consonant clusters, is the assumption that IL systems will obey these principles. And these works are simply examples among many other studies pursuing the same general research program. And although this is a very general characterization of the findings of research on L2 phonology, we will see in the section below on applications that many of the pedagogical applications of this research hark back to this very point. We will consider this in more detail after we discuss the kind of data that is adduced by L2 phonologists.

Data and common elicitation measures

The kind of data that a researcher employs can be sorted along several dimensions, depending on the nature of the question being addressed, and the hypothesis being tested. One major distinction that can be made along these lines is whether the data to be gathered bear on the L2 learner's production versus perception of the TL sounds or contrasts. The second parameter by which the data can be characterized is the extent to which the researcher allows the speakers' utterances to be free ranging, or the extent to which the utterances are controlled.

For example, data gathered from L2 speakers in a casual conversation with another interlocutor are uncontrolled in the sense that the kinds of utterances produced by the speaker would be determined entirely by flow of the conversation topics, and by the speaker, rather than by the researcher. On the other hand, data elicited from L2 learners by having them read words on a list would be highly controlled in that the words produced by the speakers would be determined by the researcher. In a word-list recitation, the context for the productions would be the task itself, where words are produced one at a time, rather than as part of connected speech. Such elicited productions would represent a careful style of talking as opposed to a more casual style that one encounters during free conversation.

There are clear trade-offs as to which kind of elicitation methods are preferable. For example, if the researchers in question had not yet determined which kind of phonological structures to investigate, then it may well be worthwhile for them to simply "cast out a net" and record their subjects during an interview or some other extemporaneous form of speech. Free conversation might also be the task of choice if the researchers were investigating structures that would be likely to occur in all conversations, and would be likely to occur with sufficient frequency to allow analysis. This might not be the case with words containing consonant clusters in onsets or codas, as this type of phonological structure might not be very frequent. To ensure sufficient tokens of such words, a researcher might have to elicit them explicitly using a more controlled type of task.

Having considered some of the data used in L2 phonological studies, we turn to the applications of the results, more specifically, to the empirical testing of the hypotheses, and to the pedagogical implications of the findings. We begin with the empirical testing of hypotheses.

Empirical testing

The approach taken by virtually every L2 phonologist is that the claims that are made about IL phonologies are empirical in that they can be tested on the basis of facts about the real world. There are, however, several issues, listed in (3) below, that arise with respect to testing various hypotheses. We will address each in turn.

(3) Issues in empirical tests of hypotheses
  (a) How does one determine the kinds of facts that bear on a hypothesis?
  (b) Given that IL grammars are internal mental systems, what considerations must be taken into account?
  (c) What criteria does one invoke to conclude that a structure has been acquired?

Determining the kinds of data to bring to bear on a hypothesis involves a number of assumptions about what the objective of the research is. In the period that we referred to above as pre–ILH, the goal of studies on L2 phonology was to explain learning difficulty. Linguists posed the question as to why some aspects of the TL were difficult for a given learner, and why some structures were more difficult than others.

L2 phonologists generally agreed that errors that learners made were a reflection of difficulty, though there were other approaches, such as Schachter (1974), who proposed that difficulty could be reflected also in a learner's avoidance of a structure. Within this framework, to test empirically a hypothesis that structure A was more difficult to learn than structure B, the prediction would be, other things being equal, that a learner would make more errors on structure A than on structure B.

The second issue concerns the fact that hypotheses about the acquisition of aspects of L2 phonology are hypotheses about the state of an IL grammar, and as such, these hypotheses are claims about an individual's internal system. This system can be placed in time and space as existing in the mind of the L2 learner. Two conclusions follow immediately from this point. The first is that linguists cannot directly observe the workings of an internal IL grammar, and therefore must base their claims about an IL on the basis a speaker's utterances or behavior (but see the section Future directions below). The second conclusion is that linguists' claims about IL grammars must be tested against individual data, not against aggregate data. In other words, if second language acquisition is understood as the learning of an IL system, then a second language is learned by an individual. There is no IL grammar of a group of people, just as there is no mind of a group, at least not one that can be placed in time and space. In other words, a class or a group of people does not acquire the IL grammar collectively; rather, individuals in a class or a group acquire the IL grammar.

This leads directly to the third point: linguists formulating hypotheses about the acquisition of various TL structures must have a way of ascertaining when a structure has been acquired. As was true in the case of measuring difficulty, there have been several proposals for determining when a structure has been learned, but, in general, linguists consider a structure to be acquired when it is part of the IL grammar. A structure is assumed to be part of the IL grammar when it occurs systematically in the utterances of the learner. Finally, systematic occurrence is generally taken to be when the structure in question occurs with a relatively high percentage of occurrence, usually assumed to be around 80 or 90 percent.

Applications

The basis for the claim that research on L2 phonology has pedagogical implications is the conclusion, developed through studies on second-language pronunciation, that learning how to pronounce a TL involves much more than simply learning the sounds, that is, the phonetics, of the target language. In this subsection, we will illustrate this point using several examples, most importantly word-final devoicing discussed above in the section on *Interlanguage*. The idea we will attempt to get across in this discussion is that the pedagogical strategy devised to address at least some pronunciation errors must be based on the nature of the interlanguage phonological system, and should not simply be grounded on the sounds produced by the learner.

Within this context, let us consider an L2 pronunciation pattern in which a learner of English pronounces TL words containing word-final voiced obstruents such as [b], [d], and [g], as the corresponding voiceless sounds [p], [t], and [k]. In other words, the learner in question systematically pronounces the English words, [ɹɪb] "rib," [bɪd] "bid," and [pɪg] "pig" as [pɪk], [bɪt], [pɪk], respectively. Based on the sounds produced, and with no further analysis of the utterances, one might conclude that the learner in question needs to learn that these and similar TL words all have word-final voiced obstruents, and therefore must be distinguished from their minimal-pair counterparts "rip," "bit," and "pick." However, a deeper analysis of the IL systems of these learners reveals that they may already know that these words end in final voiced sounds, and instead that they need to acquire other aspects of TL pronunciation.

The crux of the matter, and what a deeper, phonological analysis would reveal, is the nature of the phonemic representation that the learners have stored in their mental lexicon, and that ultimately underlie the errors produced. There are two possibilities for this. On the one hand, the learners could have represented the words "rib," "bid," and "pig" phonemically in the IL lexicon as, respectively, /ɹɪb/, /bɪd/, and /pɪg/, in which case their ILs would also have to incorporate a word-final devoicing rule that systematically changes the pronunciation of all word-final voiced obstruents to voiceless. On the other hand, the learners' ILs could represent the relevant words in the lexicon as /ɹɪp/, /bɪt/, and /pɪk/, exactly as these words are pronounced, in which case the IL systems do not incorporate a rule of devoicing to yield the observed pronunciation pattern.

The differences between these two analyses, that is to say, the differences between the two IL systems, are not trivial, and they have different pedagogical implications. Moreover, it is an empirical matter as to which of the two IL grammar types a given learner has internalized. If a learner has acquired an IL system where the phonemic representations in the IL lexicon are /ɹɪb/, /bɪd/, and /pɪg/, in which case the IL contains a word-final devoicing rule, then the target-like pronunciation of the voiced obstruents should occur in morphologically-related forms of the words when the consonants in question are not in word-final position. For example, a learner with such an IL grammar should pronounce "ribbing" as [ɹɪbɪŋ] and "piggy" as [pɪgi], with voiced medial obstruents, whereas a learner who has internalized an IL system with the relevant words represented as /ɹɪp/, /bɪt/, and /pɪk/ in the IL lexicon should pronounce "ribbing" as [ɹɪpɪŋ] and "piggy" as [pɪki]. According to this analysis, a learner with the former IL grammar type knows, albeit implicitly, that the words in question end with a voiced obstruent, whereas a learner with the latter type of IL has not yet acquired this aspect of the TL. And based on this reasoning, the two learner types need to acquire different aspects of English in order for their pronunciation patterns to become more target-like. Specifically, the former needs to suppress the IL rule of devoicing, and the latter must learn that English has a word-final voice contrast. Without going into detail, it seems reasonable that different pedagogical strategies would be involved, depending on which IL grammar type confronted a teacher.

The point of our discussion is this. Although a teacher may observe L2 learners making the same kind of pronunciation errors (saying [bɪt] instead of [bɪd]), unless the analysis moves beyond the level of simply noting the sounds produced, the differences in the IL systems that the learners may have internalized and their concomitant pedagogical implications will not be revealed.

The same conclusion can be defended with respect to other aspects of L2 pronunciation. It has been shown that the phonetic properties of certain TL sounds do not have as great an impact on their acquisition as do the more abstract, phonological characteristics of a segment, such as whether the TL sounds to be learned are distributed as non-contrasting allophones or as phonemes. Studies have also confirmed that a learner's suppressing the pronunciation of NL allophones and learning to produce TL allophones can present significant difficulty, leading to later acquisition of these sound patterns (Flege, 1995; Stockwell and Bowen, 1965). Moreover, it is a serious learning problem when NL allophones correspond to TL phonemes. Well-known examples include Spanish [d] and [ð], which are allophones in Spanish but are phonemes in English, on the one hand, and Korean [s] and [š], which are allophonic in Korean but contrast in the English words "sip" and "ship." This is the area that Lado (1957) highlighted as being maximally difficult, and the intractable nature of this difficulty has also been borne out empirically, most recently by Eckman, Elreyes and Iverson (2003).

As a final example of the necessity to look beyond phonetics to more abstract representations in order to understand L2 pronunciation patterns, consider the role of the syllable in acquisition. Research into language typology has revealed that languages are much more restrictive with the sounds that can occur in syllable codas than they are with the sounds that can occur in onsets. Although all languages allow some consonants in onsets, some languages, such as Hawa'ian do not allow any consonants in coda position, while others such as Mandarin allow only sonorant consonants, and still others such as Spanish allow only the coronal consonants [s n l r ð]. It should not be surprising, then, when IL grammars adhere to the same constraints as L1 grammars, and L2 learners have more difficulty learning TL segments and contrasts in coda position than they do acquiring these aspects of the TL in onset position.

In sum, we are able to defend the position that learning to pronounce a target language involves the acquisition of an IL grammar, and therefore requires much more than simply learning the phonetics of the TL, and that these more abstract properties of L2 phonologies have implications for language pedagogy.

We conclude this chapter by speculating a bit on what important questions in L2 phonology will guide the future direction of research.

Future directions

Three important questions that confront future research in L2 phonology will, if on the mark, shape future work in the field. The first is what the place of heritage learners is within the study of L2 phonology; the second is whether it is possible for an L2 learner to achieve native-like competence or proficiency; and the third is what the role of cognitive neuroscience will be in L2 phonological research. Because the question of heritage learners is taken up in Section 5 of this volume, we will consider only the last two of these questions.

An issue that will likely continue to shape work in L2 phonology is how to measure whether an L2 learner can achieve native-like proficiency in a language. There are at least two methods in which this question has been addressed: one is to have the utterances of non-native speakers recorded and then evaluated as to how native-like the recordings sound, and the other method has been to measure the performance of the non-native speakers on various aspects of the TL and compare the results to the performance of native speakers on the same structures. Recent work by Abrahamsson and Hyltenstam (2009) used the second method, comparison of performance on a number of TL phonological structures and found that L2 speakers did not fall within the range of performance by natives.

The other important question for the future is whether developments in the field of cognitive neuroscience can confirm some of the constructs that L2 phonologists have postulated as part of their explanation for IL pronunciation patterns (Gollestani and Zatorre, 2002). In other words, can studies using neuro-imaging of the brain, such as through fMRI, provide independent evidence for underling representations, markedness, and phonemic contrasts, to cite just a few examples?

To conclude this subsection, postulating hypothetical constructs such as underlying forms and lexical representations has been part and parcel of L2 phonological analyses for decades. Thus, it is intriguing to consider whether advances in cognitive neuroscience will be able to provide more direct evidence for these constructs.

Conclusion

This chapter has characterized the field of second-language phonology from several perspectives. We have outlined the development of second-language phonology over the decades, and described its most significant findings. We have also reviewed, from an empirical standpoint, some of the most important questions in the field, and pointed out the kind of data that can be brought to bear on resolving these issues. Finally, we concluded our discussion with two additional points: the first, relating a number of pedagogical implications from the insights of theoretical research to instructional practice; and the second, pointing to what promise to be some of the important questions of the future.

Note

1 This work was supported in part by a grant from the National Institutes of Health R01 HD046908-05. The views and positions held in this work are those of the author. The NIH is not responsible for, nor does it necessarily agree with, any of the views taken in this chapter.

References

Abrahamsson, N. (2003). Development and recoverability of L2 codas: A longitudinal study of Chinese-Swedish interphonology. *Studies in Second Language Acquisition, 25*, 313–349.

Abrahamsson, N. and Hyltenstam, K. (2009). Age of onset and nativelikeness in a second language: Listener perception versus linguistic scrutiny. *Language Learning, 59*, 249–306.

Altenberg, E. and Vago, R. (1983). Theoretical implications of an error analysis of second language phonology production. *Language Learning, 33*, 427–447.

Anderson, J. (1987). The markedness differential hypothesis and syllable structure difficulty. In G. Ioup and S. Weinberger (Eds.), *Interlanguage phonology: The acquisition of a second language sound system* (pp. 279–291). Cambridge, MA: Newbury House.

Archibald, J. (1993). The learnability of English metrical parameters by Spanish speakers. *International Review of Applied Linguistics, 31*, 129–141.

Archibald, J. (1995). The acquisition of stress. In J. Archibald (Ed.), *Phonological acquisition and phonological theory* (pp. 81–109). Hillsdale, NJ: Lawrence Erlbaum Associates.

Battistella, E. (1990). *Markedness: The evaluative superstructure of language*. Albany: The State University of New York Press.

Best, C. T. (1995). A direct realist's view of cross-language speech perception. In W. Strange (Ed.), *Speech perception and linguistic experience: Issues in cross-language research* (pp. 171–204). Baltimore: York Press.

Broselow, E., Chen, S., and Wang, C. (1998). The emergence of the unmarked. *Studies in Second Language Acquisition, 20,* 261–280.

Broselow, E. and Finer, D. (1991). Parameter setting in second language phonology and syntax. *Second Language Research, 7,* 35–59.

Brown, C. (1998). The role of the L1 grammar in the acquisition of segmental structure. *Second Language Research, 14,* 139–193.

Carlisle, R. (1992). Environment and markedness as interacting constraints on vowel epenthesis. In J. Leather and A. James (Eds.), *New sounds 92: Proceedings of the Amsterdam symposium on the acquisition of second language speech* (pp. 64–75). Amsterdam: University of Amsterdam.

Carlisle, R. S. (1998). The acquisition of onsets in a markedness relationship: A longitudinal study. *Studies in Second Language Acquisition, 20,* 245–260.

Corder, S. P. (1971). Idiosyncratic dialects and error analysis. *International Review of Applied Linguistics, 9,* 149–159.

de Jong, K., Silbert, N. H., and Park, H. (2009). Generalizations across segments in second language consonant identification. *Language Learning, 59,* 1–31.

Eckman, F. (1977). Markedness and the contrastive analysis hypothesis. *Language Learning, 27,* 315–330.

Eckman, F. (1981). On the naturalness of interlanguage phonological rules. *Language Learning, 31,* 195–216.

Eckman, F. (1991). The Structural Conformity Hypothesis and the acquisition of consonant clusters in the interlanguage of ESL learners. *Studies in Second Language Acquisition, 13,* 23–41.

Eckman, F., Elreyes, A., and Iverson, G. (2003). Some principles of second language phonology. *Second Language Research, 19,* 169–208.

Flege, J. E. (1995). Second language speech learning: Theory, findings and problems. In W. Strange (Ed.), *Speech perception and linguistic experience: Issues in cross-language research* (pp. 233–277). Baltimore: York Press.

Gollestani, N. and Zatorre, R. J. (2002). Anatomical correlates of learning novel speech. *Neuron, 35,* 997–1010.

Hammerly, H. (1982). Contrastive phonology and error analysis. *International Review of Applied Linguistics 20,* 17–32.

Hancin Bhatt, B. (2008). Second language phonology in Optimality Theory. In J. Hansen Edwards and M. Zampini (Eds.), *Phonology and second language acquisition* (pp. 117–146). Amsterdam: John Benjamins.

Hansen, J. (2004). Developmental sequences in the acquisition of English L2 syllable codas: A preliminary study. *Studies in Second Language Acquisition, 26,* 85–124.

Johannsson, F. (1973). *Immigrant Swedish phonology: A study in multiple contact analysis.* Lund, Sweden: CWK Gleerup.

Lado, R. (1957). *Linguistics across cultures: Applied linguistics for language teachers.* Ann Arbor: University of Michigan Press.

Lombardi, L. (2003). Second language data and constraints on manner: Explaining substitutions for the English interdentals. *Second Language Research, 19,* 225–250.

Mairs, J. L. (1989). Stress assignment in interlanguage phonology: An analysis of the stress system of Spanish speakers learning English. In S. Gass and J. Schachter (Eds.), *Linguistic perspectives on second language acquisition* (pp. 260–283). Cambridge: Cambridge University Press.

Major, R. and Kim, E. (1996). The similarity differential rate hypothesis. *Language Learning, 46,* 465–496.

Nemser, W. (1971). Approximative systems of foreign language learners. *International Review of Applied Linguistics, 9,* 115–123.

Nguyen, H. and Macken, M. (2008). Factors affecting the production of Vietnamese tones: A study of American learners. *Studies in Second Language Acquisition, 30,* 49–78.

Sato, C. (1984). Phonological processes in second language acquisition: Another look at interlanguage syllable structure. *Language Learning, 34,* 43–57.

Schachter, J. (1974). An error in error analysis. *Language Learning, 24,* 205–214.

Selinker, L. (1972). Interlanguage. *International Review of Applied Linguistics, 10,* 209–231.

Selkirk, E. (1982). The syllable. In H. Van der Hulst and N. Smith (Eds.), *The structure of phonological representations Part II* (pp. 337–384). Dordrecht: Foris Publications.

Stockwell, R. and Bowen, J. (1965). *The sounds of English and Spanish.* Chicago: University of Chicago Press.

Trubetzkoy, N. (1939). *Principles of phonology.* Paris: Klincksieck.

Zampini, M. (1997). L2 Spanish spirantization, prosodic domains and interlanguage rules. In S. J. Hannahs and M. Young-Scholten (Eds.), *Focus on phonological acquisition* (pp. 263–289). Amsterdam: John Benjamins.

7

Linguistic approaches to second language morphosyntax*

Donna Lardiere

Introduction

The acquisition of the grammar—the morphology and syntax—of a second language (L2) lies at the heart of the study of second language acquisition (SLA) and consequently has generated, along with hundreds of studies, much heat as well as light. The study of L2 grammatical development, especially within the generative grammar tradition, proceeds from a core assumption shared by nearly all formal acquisitionists that an understanding of exactly *what* is to be acquired and how it is mentally represented is necessary in order to understand how it could come to be acquired (Chomsky, 1986a; Gregg, 1989, 1996). For this reason, most researchers who study L2 grammatical development in depth rely at least to some extent on highly articulated theoretical models of language form and its relation to meaning. In actual practice, this has meant that Chomsky's (1981) Principles and Parameters (P&P) framework, including subsequent revisions that have led to a radical theoretical overhaul known as the Minimalist Program (Chomsky, 1995a, 2001), has served as the linguistic basis for much of the work done in L2 morphosyntax and syntax over the past three decades. This chapter, therefore, reviews some of the key concepts and findings resulting from research in that framework, as well as touching on some of the different directions the study of the L2 acquisition of morphosyntax has more recently taken.

Core issues in historical context

Universal grammar

It is widely accepted that all normal children are ultimately successful at acquiring their native language(s). Moreover, native speakers of a language end up with a richer, more abstract system of knowledge than can be induced from the linguistic evidence directly observable in the environment, posing a learnability problem known as the *poverty of the stimulus*. In particular, they know that certain utterances may be ambiguous, or that others are impossible in their language. For example, English native speakers know that the sentence in (1) is ungrammatical, whereas (2) is perfectly fine:

(1) *Which professor* did John read the book about violent videogames had written?
(2) *Which professor* did John think had written the book about violent videogames?

Given that sentences like the one in (2) are present in the linguistic environment, what prevents an English language acquirer from overgeneralizing the movement of a question word to formulate questions like that in (1)? Or to put it another way, how does an English speaker learn that sentences like (1) are impossible? The answer given by Chomsky (1981, 1986a) was that such restrictions on possible *wh*-movement are not learned (and are certainly not taught); rather, they constitute part of the biological faculty of human language known as Universal Grammar (UG).[1] Chomsky's position thus represents a strong *nativist* view of language acquisition.

Many researchers who work on syntactic acquisition are committed to some form of nativism, at least for first language (L1) acquisition. This is essentially the idea that human children are genetically equipped to acquire language. All approaches to human cognition recognize the existence of innately guided learning of some sort (Eckman, 1996, p. 398; O'Grady, 2008, p. 620). However, acquisition researchers disagree on the extent to which the genetic capacity for language acquisition consists of mechanisms and categories that are specific to language (*special nativism*) or rather consists of more generalized learning mechanisms, such as a capacity for detecting distributional patterns in the environment and formulating categories based on them (*general nativism* and *emergentism*).[2]

Researchers working within the UG theoretical framework have largely embraced special nativism, analyzing their data in terms of certain formal constructs such as grammatical features, categories, and restrictions on operations that are thought to be specifically dedicated to language. In this framework, the study of syntax over the past three decades has focused on discovering universal linguistic constraints on possible human language grammars, and the study of the acquisition of syntax is largely devoted to investigating the effects of these constraints in learners' developing language.

What role, if any, does UG play in L2 acquisition, especially mature L2 acquisition? Note that, unlike native acquirers, it is not the case that all adult L2 learners, or even most of them, are ultimately successful (however we define "success.") This lack of a uniformly successful outcome, including the observation that L2 performance is often persistently variable in ways that L1 performance is not, has led many researchers to the conclusion that SLA, particularly adult SLA, is qualitatively "fundamentally" different from L1 acquisition, and that acquisition is based instead on general problem-solving abilities (Bley-Vroman, 1989, 2009; see also Clahsen and Muysken, 1986; Felix, 1985; Meisel, 1997; Newmeyer, 1998, among others).

Nonetheless, L2 learners—especially those who are immersed in the target language environment—are exposed to the same kind of linguistic stimuli as native speakers and thus also face a poverty of the stimulus problem (Schwartz and Sprouse, 2000; White, 1989, 2003). Therefore, one of the earliest and most enduring questions of the field of L2 syntax has been whether it is *possible* for mature L2 learners to end up with abstract knowledge of a second language that could not be induced from particular sets of utterances in the environment. If so, and if it could also be shown that such knowledge could not have been transferred from the L1, then researchers could conclude that UG constraints were still operational in mature SLA.

White (2003, p. 22) emphasizes that it is not necessary for L2 learners to acquire knowledge that is nativelike in all respects in order to demonstrate poverty of the stimulus effects which implicate continued access to UG constraints. In other words, even if learner interlanguages (ILs) are non-targetlike, they still exhibit many of the domain-specific properties of UG-constrained natural language grammars. However, even if it could be shown that the developing L2 grammar is UG-constrained, it is nonetheless striking that mature L2 learners often still ultimately fail to achieve nativelike performance in the target language. This is true even when the relevant stimuli in question (such as verbal inflections) are abundantly present in the linguistic environment and thus do not necessarily pose a learnability problem. R. Hawkins (2001a) argues that, in contrast to studies based on poverty of the stimulus that seek evidence for the fundamental similarities of L1 and L2 grammatical representations, the study of the *differences* between L1 and L2 acquisition within linguistic-based approaches could lead to a better understanding of the nature of the interaction or "interfaces" between UG and other components of the mind. This view reflects a shift that has taken place in generative SLA studies since the early 1990s, away from an earlier primary focus on "access to UG" debates, to seeking a greater understanding of the nature of IL grammatical representations in their own right, including potential sources of persistent morphosyntactic variability.

Principles and parameters theory

Because UG is a theory about the innate biological capacity for human language, its principles are invariant and apply to all human natural languages, delimiting the range of possible human languages. But the grammars of natural languages obviously differ from each other in striking ways, such as their sentential word orders, whether certain elements (such as subject pronouns) can be dropped, whether certain features are expressed inflectionally, whether thematic relations are determined by word order or case-marking, and so on. Interestingly, comparative typological research (e.g., Greenberg, 1963; see Biberauer, 2008 for a historical overview) strongly suggests that certain grammatical patterns and correlations recur throughout the world's languages, and that cross-linguistic syntactic differences are not limitless or random. This empirical observation has been captured within a UG framework by the notion of *parameters*. Parameters are considered to be an innately predetermined finite set of "limited options" whose values are fixed by the learner on the basis of having been exposed to some utterances of a particular language known as *primary linguistic data* (PLD). Together, principles and parameters were originally hypothesized to tightly restrict the range of cross-linguistic syntactic variation as well as the range of possible grammatical hunches entertained by child language learners, helping to account for the rapidity and relative ease with which children acquire language.

For example, one of the proposed principles of UG is that all sentences must have subjects.[3] However, languages differ in whether subjects must be expressed overtly or not—a parameterized option dubbed the Null Subject Parameter (Rizzi, 1982, 1986). In languages that select the (+) value of the parameter, such as Italian, the pronominal subject of a finite clause may consist of a null pronoun *pro*, whose person/number features are instead identifiable by verbal agreement morphology (3a). On the other hand, in languages that select the (–) null subject parameter value, such as English, overt pronouns are required (3b):

(3)

a. *pro* vorrei   parlare   con   Anna   Italian [+ null subject]
   pro would.like.1SG   speak-INF   with   Anna
   "I would like to speak with Anna."

b. **pro* would like to speak with Anna   English [– null subject]

Some properties that have been correlated with the positive setting of the null subject parameter include the possibility of null expletive subjects (4a), post-verbal subject inversion (5a), and the presence of an overt complementizer in subordinate clauses from which subject *wh*-movement has occurred (6a); languages with the negative setting, such as English, prohibit these:

(4)

(a) *pro* piove   Italian   [+ null subject]

     pro rain.3SG

     "it's raining"

(b) **pro* is raining   English   [− null subject]

(5)

(a) *pro* è   arrivato   un   uomo   Italian   [+ null subject]

     pro is   arrived   a   man

     "a man arrived"

(b) **pro* arrived a man   English   [− null subject]

(6)

(a) Chi   credi   *che*   verrà?   Italian   [+ null subject]

     Who   think.2SG   *that*   come.FUT

     "who do you think will come?"

(b) ★Who do you think *that* will come?   English   [− null subject]

At first glance, the contrasts shown above appear superficially unrelated to the option of having null subjects. There is nothing in the input, for example, that could indicate to a child learning English that (6b) is ruled out, especially since similar-sounding sentences like "Who do you think that Anna saw?" are acceptable. Yet, English native speakers do come to know this. Such associated properties, sometimes referred to as the "deductive consequences" of a parameter, were hypothesized to play a powerful role in language acquisition, in that learning one of the properties would automatically result in the acquisition of the others.

Parameter theory initially held great promise for formally describing the potential learning challenges facing the L2 acquirer as well. Since learners bring to the SLA task a fully developed L1 grammar with parameter values already fixed to their L1 settings, success or failure of grammatical acquisition might be attributed to learners' (in)ability to reset parameters from the L1 values to those of the L2. Moreover, researchers have wondered whether the cluster of properties associated with selecting a new parameter value would also automatically be acquired as they were hypothesized to for L1 acquisition. We return to this issue in the section entitled *Empirical Verification*.

Parameters in the minimalist program. Under early versions of P&P theory, as mentioned above, a limited number of parameters were hypothesized to be associated with invariant core principles of UG. The problem, as Chomsky (2005, p. 8) discusses, is that if language acquisition were just a matter of selecting among relatively few options attached to the invariant core principles of UG, then UG itself would have to be "rich and highly articulated." However, as wider ranges of languages were investigated and compared, it became clear that their properties could not be accommodated within relatively few, broadly general options. Instead, theories that could account for the data had to impose increasingly "varied and intricate" conditions that were necessarily formulated in language-specific terms that seemed unlikely to be built into the human genome.

The P&P framework, in attempting to move toward principles of ever-broader generality, represented a "radical break" from previous grammatical theories that relied on language-specific rules to account for particular grammatical constructions (Chomsky, 1995a, p. 170, 1995b,

p. 388). The Minimalist Program (Chomsky, 1995a, 2001) reflects a sharply intensified commitment to this ideal. It is an attempt to achieve maximum—in fact, universal—generality in its characterization of an invariant computational component of the human language faculty, using the fewest possible language-specific principles. With regard to language acquisition, Chomsky (2007, p. 4) observes that, whereas pre-Minimalist generative approaches asked "How much must be attributed to UG to account for language acquisition?," recent Minimalist approaches instead ask "How little can be attributed to UG while still accounting for the variety of I-languages attained?"

Under Minimalism, the locus of such "varied and intricate" cross-linguistic grammatical differences has been shifted to the lexicon—in particular, to grammatical features (such as [±wh], [±past], or [±definite]). These features are considered part of UG—specifically, part of a universal feature-set or inventory. Since not all languages make use of every feature in the inventory, "parameter-setting" within this framework consists of the learner identifying and selecting only that subset of features used in the target language. The selected features are assembled into language-specific morpholexical items, including free and affixal forms (e.g., *whether*, *-ed*, *the* in English). In other words, the burden of accounting for the acquisition of the features, categories and constraints of particular languages is largely shifted from the genetic endowment to language-independent mechanisms of data processing and computational efficiency (Chomsky, 2005).

For SLA, the learner's task is still couched in terms of the need to acquire the parameter values of the L2. In Minimalist, feature-based terms, this means that the learner must identify, select, and redistribute the required features among the lexical items of the L2. Recall that the learner brings to this task an already fully developed language in which the L1 features have already been selected and "packaged" into L1-specific grammatical categories and lexical items. In the following section, we consider more closely the role of prior-language knowledge in this process.

The role of L1 knowledge in acquiring the L2 grammar

Except for a relatively brief period (mainly through the 1970s) when the role of transfer was downplayed in favor of "natural order" approaches based primarily on morpheme-order studies,[4] the role of prior-language knowledge has been recognized by most generative researchers as a critically important factor in accounting for L2 grammatical acquisition. Within the L2 morpho-syntax literature of the past two decades, two broad questions regarding transfer clearly emerge: (1) To what extent (if any) does the grammar of the L1 constitute the initial "departure point" for a learner's assumptions and representation of the L2 grammar? and (2) To what extent (if any) is ultimate attainment of the L2 circumscribed by the categories and features of the L1?

Question (1) was addressed in the 1990s in the context of several studies examining the nature of the L2 initial state (e.g., Eubank, 1996; Schwartz and Sprouse, 1996; Vainikka and Young-Scholten, 1994, 1996). Assuming the existence of functional categories (such as case, tense, aspect, definiteness, etc.) in fully developed native-speaker grammars, the specific question asked was: At what point does knowledge of these categories become available to the learner? Do the functional categories and features of the L1 transfer, so that the L2 learner starts out with all (and only) those categories that make up the L1?[5]

Question (2) is important particularly in case the L1 has not selected a particular feature that is required by the L2: Are those previously unselected features still available? This question (at least tacitly) assumes that a constraining role of the L1 may persist through stages beyond the initial state, including the so-called "steady-" or end-state of acquisition. We briefly consider each of these questions in turn.

Partial vs. full transfer in the initial L2 state. Given that linguistically mature native speakers know which functional categories and features are required for producing and interpreting well-formed sentences in their L1, how much and which parts of this knowledge are used for constructing the grammar of the L2? And how can we tell? In other words, what counts as evidence for such knowledge?

The most conservative hypotheses about knowledge of the grammatical categories of the L2 are those which assume that a particular morphosyntactic category is not established in the learner's grammatical representation until the functor morphemes associated with that category are systematically produced at a certain criterial level in obligatory contexts. (Some researchers, following Brown's (1973) L1 study, employ a 90% criterion, but for L2 studies, the criteria vary and are typically relaxed somewhat.) Vainikka and Young-Scholten (1994, 1996) observed that naturalistic Turkish or Korean L1 speakers learning L2 German omitted many functional elements in early stages of their spoken German, or produced them only variably (at a rate lower than 60% suppliance in obligatory contexts), or produced default forms such as infinitive-inflected verbs where finite forms were required. They therefore hypothesized that only the open-class lexical categories of the L1 such as noun phrases (NPs) verb phrases (VPs) (including their subject-object-verb linear word order) carried over to the L2.

Under this view, dubbed the Minimal Trees Hypothesis (and in more recent work, Organic Grammar), the syntactic categories of the learners' L1, including those associated with case, tense, and subject-verb agreement (for the Turkish speakers), were argued not to transfer, even though learners obviously have knowledge of these categories in their L1. These would be acquired instead as a result of learning the language-specific morphemes associated with each category in the target L2. Moreover, Vainikka and Young-Scholten proposed that the acquisition of functional categories proceeded gradually and implicationally, such that "lower" categories in the phrase-structure hierarchy were acquired in successive stages before "higher" ones; that is, inflectional phrase (IP) related categories were acquired before complementizer phrase (CP) related ones. Note that, in principle, under Vainikka and Young-Scholten's approach there is no impediment to the eventual attainment of nativelike UG-constrained syntactic knowledge of the L2.

In a direct challenge to the Minimal Trees Hypothesis, Schwartz and Sprouse (1996) proposed a *full transfer* account, called the Full Transfer/Full Access Hypothesis (FT/FA), in which they argued that the morphosyntactic categories and features of the L1 grammar in its entirety constitute the initial state of the L2. In other words, learners initially assume that the L2 includes all the functional projections (e.g., CP, IP, determiner phrases (DP)) and their associated feature specifications (e.g., for tense, aspect, case, agreement, definiteness, etc.) of the L1, even though they have not yet acquired the specific functional morphemes that express these categories in the L2.

The FT/FA hypothesis does not imply that a learner is somehow stuck with the L1 grammar. Restructuring of the IL grammar is input-driven, occurring wherever there is a mismatch between the initial (L1) representation and what is needed to parse or accommodate the L2 input. Thus, arguments against FT/FA suggesting that a learner's L1 has little influence on syntactic aspects of the L2 that are readily accessible in the input (such as basic word order; see, e.g., Ellis, 2008, p. 362) are misconceived, especially for developmental stages beyond the initial state. According to Schwartz and Sprouse, there is, however, one circumstance under which a learner might indeed become stuck, and that is just in case (a) a particular parameter or feature specification has been set to a different value in the L1 than that required by the L2, and (b) there is *no* positive evidence in the input to force restructuring to the L2 value. In that case, assuming full transfer, the correct L2 value might never be acquired. (See Lardiere, 2007, pp. 216–229 for discussion of this issue.)

Note the similarities and differences between these hypotheses in terms of the types of evidence used to support their developmental claims. Both approaches assume that the productive use by the learner of functional elements (such as case, agreement, and finite-tense marking, the use of auxiliaries, complementizers, determiners, etc.) indicates that the corresponding functional syntactic categories have been acquired. In addition, functional categories in both approaches serve as landing sites for syntactic movement (such as *wh*-movement). Therefore, any evidence for syntactic movement in the learner IL, such as subject-auxiliary inversion in English questions or finite-verb raising in main clauses in German, may also be taken as evidence that higher functional structure is present. This creates something of an analytical dilemma for researchers examining early developmental stages in which grammatical morphology is variably omitted but constituents such as finite verbs in German or *wh*-question words in English appear in their correct (i.e., displaced) positions. Additionally, because the acquisition of a functional category higher in the clausal hierarchy is generally assumed to entail the acquisition of any lower categories as well, a similar kind of dilemma results when acquisition data appear to show that a learner produces the elements of a higher category (e.g., *wh*-question words, presumed to be in CP) well before producing (criterial) levels of grammatical morphemes associated with lower ones (e.g., correct subject-verb agreement marking, associated with IP). Yet, such data are common. For example, Gavruseva and Lardiere (1996) and Lardiere (2000) showed in two different longitudinal case studies that evidence for CPs was present despite the absence of inflectional morphology associated with IPs.

Each approach addresses these dilemmas somewhat differently, relying on contrasting views of the relation between morphology and syntax, or more precisely, between knowledge of morphemes—the language-specific realization of a functional feature (such as English -*ed*, *the*, or -*s*)—vs. knowledge of the abstract feature itself (such as PAST, DEFINITE, PLURAL). Schwartz and Sprouse argue that it is the latter—that is, knowledge of abstract morphosyntactic categories—that transfers. On the other hand, Vainikka and Young-Scholten believe that knowledge of the abstract grammatical properties of the L2 can only be acquired from actual, overt L2 morphemes, which need to be learned *before* a corresponding abstract category can be inferred and projected in the L2 syntax. (Neither approach assumes that actual morphemes transfer.) The Vainikka and Young-Scholten model, therefore, requires a more ad hoc sort of syntactic structure—one that is underspecified and more flexible with respect to particular functional categories but that can nonetheless still provide structural landing sites for displaced constituents in earlier stages of development.

The persistence of L1 influence in morphosyntactic development. As mentioned above, cross-linguistic "parametric" variation in the Minimalist Program arises because languages select different features and/or assemble them differently within their particular lexicons. For SLA, therefore, "parameter-resetting" requires that the learner (re)select and (re)assemble the features of the morphemes of the target language. Can L2 learners successfully accomplish this? In some recent proposals, prior-language knowledge plays a persistent and even deterministic role in the ultimate outcome of grammatical development in the L2.

One prominent feature-based line of inquiry attempts to predict the precise conditions under which parameter-resetting will fail, due to a mismatch between L1 and L2 feature selection. Referred to variously as the Failed Functional Features Hypothesis (Hawkins and Chan, 1997), the Representational Deficit Hypothesis (Hawkins, 2003; Hawkins and Liszka, 2003), or more recently, the Interpretability Hypothesis (Hawkins and Hattori, 2006; Tsimpli and Dimitrakopoulou, 2007—the cover term I adopt here to represent the approach), the specific prediction is that, in cases where a particular morphosyntactic feature is required in the L2 but was not previously activated in the learner's L1, that feature will no longer be acquirable, due to critical period effects. In the most recent studies, an additional condition is that the feature in question be *uninterpretable*—that is, a purely formal feature with no semantic content of its own, such as those that trigger movement and/or enter into agreement relations. (We return to an example below.)

Another type of approach that addresses ultimate acquirability and the persistent role of L1 influence in SLA is the Feature Reassembly Hypothesis of Lardiere (2008, 2009a). Under this proposal, difficulty in L2 grammatical acquisition is related to the extent to which formal features that have already been "packaged" or assembled into certain morphemes in the L1 must be isolated and redistributed among different morpholexical items in the L2. Additionally, the learner must acquire knowledge of the appropriate conditioning environment for expressing a certain feature, which may sharply differ from that of the L1 (e.g., what constitutes an *obligatory context* in the L1 vs. the L2).

To illustrate, consider the case of a native (Mandarin) Chinese speaker acquiring plural-marking in L2 English, or vice-versa. Both English and Chinese have morpholexical means for indicating plurality—the suffixes *-s* and *-men* respectively.[6,7] In English, plural-marking is obligatory on count nouns that denote "more-than-one" referents, especially in quantified contexts such as *several books* or *three students*. However, plural-marking in English is indiscriminate with regard to animacy (e.g., *books* vs. *students*) or definite/specific reference (e.g., *any students* vs. *those students*). In Chinese, on the other hand, plural-marking is optional (except on plural personal pronouns, where it is required) and quite restricted. It is explicitly prohibited in certain contexts in which it is required in English, namely, quantified contexts (e.g., **san-ge xuesheng-men* "three-CL student-PL"); it is typically only marked on nouns denoting humans; and, notably unlike English, its use on a noun requires that noun to be interpreted as definite. Thus, compare the Chinese sentences shown below in (7). Whereas (7a) is a perfectly good sentence in Chinese that is simply neutral or underspecified with regard to number and definiteness, (7b) is specified with regard to both. The plural-marked noun *haizi-men* "children" in (7b) must be interpreted as plural and definite; it cannot, for example, mean "I will go find (some) child(ren)" (examples from Li, 1999, p. 78):

(7)
(a) wo   qu   zhao   haizi
    I   go   find   child
    "I will go find the/some child/children."

(b) wo   qu   zhao   haizi-*men*
    I   go   find   child-PL
    "I will go find the children."

Although both Chinese and English could be argued to "parametrically select" the feature [+plural] and both have overt morphemes for expressing it, learners must still distinguish between optional vs. obligatory application, and consider additional syntactic and semantic restrictions (e.g., [±human], [±definite], co-occurrence with quantifiers). Grammatical acquisition, in other words, requires redistributing abstract features among the relevant morpheme(s) in the target language and learning the precise conditions under which these can or must (or must not) be expressed. There is nothing ultimately preventing a learner from accomplishing this; that is, unlike the Interpretability Hypothesis, successful acquisition of both interpretable and uninterpretable features is in principle possible, but is likely to be more difficult in cases where the features in question are configured quite differently and expressed under quite different grammatical and/ or discourse conditions. Because of this, the Feature-Reassembly approach offers less crisp predictions (of failure) than the Interpretability Hypothesis, but it is more compatible than parameter-setting models with the longstanding observation that for any given feature or category, any given learner's production of the corresponding inflection may be highly variable, and a learner's L2 grammatical idiolect may not exactly match that of either the native or the target language.

Finally, we consider another type of potentially persistent L1 influence on the acquisition (and certainly the spoken production) of grammatical morphemes in the L2—the effect of L1 phonology. The Prosodic Transfer Hypothesis of Goad and White (2004, 2006, 2008) proposes that L1 prosodic constraints may impede the spoken production of L2 functional morphemes, by restricting the kinds of phonological representations that can be built in the L2; as a result, L2 learners are sometimes forced to delete morphology or pronounce it in non-nativelike ways. At first glance, this proposal seems rather like a phonological equivalent to the morphosyntactic Interpretability Hypothesis, in that the (un)availability of L1 phonological structures plays a near-deterministic role in the attainment of L2 functional morphology. Goad and White, however, do not predict inevitable acquisition failure in cases where the prosodic representations required by the L2 are unavailable in the L1. Instead, they argue that, although acquisition will be more difficult, it is not impossible in cases in which L2 learners are able to "minimally adapt" appropriate pieces of their L1 prosodic structures in order to accommodate L2 requirements. However, representations that cannot be built from existing L1 structures will indeed be impossible to acquire, leading to fossilization (Goad and White, 2006, pp. 246–247).

To summarize this subsection, the effect of prior-language knowledge—L1 transfer—on L2 grammatical development has long played a central role in SLA theorizing. The two main issues discussed here were the extent to which the L1 grammar constitutes the initial "departure point" for a learner's assumptions and representation of the L2 grammar, and the extent to which ultimate attainment of L2 knowledge is affected by persistent L1 influence. The first issue carries important implications for our understanding of when and how knowledge of grammatical features and categories in the L2 arises in the course of development; the second bears on our ability to predict and account for the eventual outcome of the developmental process.

Data and common elicitation measures

The different kinds of data elicitation methods used to study morphosyntactic acquisition in SLA depend on the specific research questions being asked, but serve the shared common purpose of illuminating the nature of learners' L2 knowledge at particular stages of development. The grammatical systems of (all) language acquirers are part of their mentally represented idiolects and are largely inaccessible to direct inspection by researchers; therefore, conjectures about their nature must be indirectly inferred from observable performance.

The ability of learners to correctly produce grammatical morphemes (such as markers for case, tense/aspect, plurality, definiteness, negation, agreement, etc.) to some criterial degree in appropriate or obligatory contexts under real-time pressure in either naturalistic or experimental circumstances typically remains the standard for inferring that a learner has acquired the representation of morphosyntactic categories and features associated with the morphemes, along with the contextual conditions for their expression. There are many kinds of procedures for eliciting production data, ranging from collecting and transcribing spontaneous conversational and interview data, to narrative story or film retelling, to the use of tasks specifically designed to elicit targeted grammatical structures (for example, relative clauses). The latter are particularly useful in cases where the targeted elements might not be readily forthcoming in more naturalistic situations, due to lower frequency of occurrence or to learner avoidance. Such tasks include elicited imitation, picture description, sentence combining, and translation, among others. Some tasks, such as translation from the L2 into the L1, can be used to investigate L2 comprehension as well.

Furthermore, there are many circumstances in which researchers would like to know if learners have acquired knowledge of what is *not* possible in the L2, such as knowledge of the restrictions on *wh*-movement discussed earlier. For obvious reasons, such data do not occur in the L2 linguistic environment (the PLD) and the use of a production task alone would be uninformative and/or inappropriate. Additionally, learners might prefer one structure over another without ever indicating whether a particular unproduced structure or unselected task item is in fact ruled out by their IL grammar. In these cases, researchers are apt to make use of some type of *acceptability judgment task* (also commonly referred to as a *grammaticality judgment task*).[8] The ability to reject ungrammatical sentences is considered stronger evidence of knowledge of linguistic constraints and constitutes the primary rationale for the task.

Both the validity and reliability of acceptability judgment tasks have been widely discussed and criticized, although an in-depth discussion is beyond the scope of this chapter. (See Birdsong, 1989; Schütze, 1996; Sorace, 1996 for overviews and suggestions for improving the methodology.) In general, judgments by learners are clearly subject to extra-linguistic rating strategies unanticipated by the researcher (see Snyder, 2000 for discussion and examples). Nonetheless, with carefully designed studies, acceptability judgment tasks can provide researchers with valuable insights about learner grammars.

Another task that is fruitfully used especially to investigate the interpretive consequences of (morpho)syntactic relations and operations is the *truth-value judgment task*. Learners are presented with a brief context or scenario and then asked to make a simple "true" or "false" judgment about whether a statement accurately describes some aspect of the preceding context. Typically, the statement incorporates some syntactic structure that the learner must be able to parse and interpret appropriately in order to respond correctly. The great advantage of this task is that, unlike acceptability judgment tasks, it does not require the learner to make a metalinguistic judgment about whether the statement in question is grammatical or not, but rather simply to build a semantic representation for it on which to base a "true" or "false" response in relation to the context.

Finally, let us briefly consider the use of online language processing tasks that make use of reaction or reading time (RT) measures. One such task is sentence-matching, in which either a grammatical or ungrammatical sentence is presented on a computer screen followed by another; the participant is asked to simply record as quickly as possible whether the two sentences match or not. Again, no metalinguistic judgments are required regarding acceptability; instead, the reaction time of the response is measured. The assumption is that if L2 learners take significantly longer to respond to ungrammatical rather than grammatical sentences (as has been demonstrated for native speaker (NS) controls), then it is because their IL grammar has (tacitly) detected the ungrammaticality and has taken longer to parse or build a representation for the ungrammatical sentence. If there is no significant difference in reaction time for ungrammatical vs. grammatical pairs of sentences, however, then the assumption is that the learner has not detected any ungrammaticality and—rather more controversially—therefore must not mentally represent the grammatical contrasts under investigation.

Proponents of RT studies point out that such tasks show whether or not some grammatical contrast has been fully "integrated" into the IL representation—that is, automatized, whereas judgment and production data are more susceptible to metalinguistic monitoring of explicit knowledge (e.g., Jiang, 2004, 2007). Other researchers urge caution, observing that interpreting the data are tricky. Gass (2001, p. 439), for example, suggests that, especially for lower-proficiency learners with slower reading times, the sentence-matching task "may represent little more than word-by-word matching" rather than actual reading and processing. Ultimately, the strongest support for claims about L2 grammatical knowledge will be based on convergent data from multiple sources and different kinds of tasks.

Empirical verification

In this section, we consider findings from data-based studies that have investigated some of the core issues presented above (*Core issues in historical context*). As mentioned earlier, there have been literally hundreds of studies investigating various aspects of the acquisition of morphology and syntax within a formal linguistic framework; space constraints prevent us from looking at more than a representative handful of these.

Access to UG? The question of whether the grammatical representations of mature L2 acquirers are in some sense epistemologically equivalent to those of native language acquirers is of enduring interest for researchers seeking to understand the nature of L2 knowledge and the contribution such understanding could make to our overall picture of the components of human cognition. Schwartz and Sprouse (2000, p. 156) write: "The leading question animating generative research on non-native language (L2) acquisition is, presumably, whether Interlanguage 'grammars' fall within the bounds set by UG, and if they do not, then just what their formal properties are." Such studies are necessarily focused on testing predictions based on specific aspects of syntactic theory; however, the accumulated evidence amassed to date for a wide range of formal aspects of language suggests that knowledge of the essential formats of UG-constrained (morpho)syntactic representations (e.g., of hierarchical structure dependence, conditions on movement, knowledge of interpretive restrictions, the presence and acquirability of functional categories and features) remains intact in adult L2 acquisition (e.g., Anderson, 2008; Dekydtspotter and Sprouse, 2001; Dekydtspotter, 2001; Kanno, 1998; Lardiere, 1998; Martohardjono, 1993; Pérez-Leroux and Glass, 1999; White and Genesee, 1996; among many others). Carroll (2001, p. 107), though skeptical of a role for UG in SLA, observes that language is nonetheless apparently encoded in the "right" representational systems in the L2 as in the L1.

Empirical studies informed by formal linguistic theory are necessarily shaped by the details of a particular version of the theory in effect at the time of the study. As Schwartz and Sprouse (2000, p. 168) point out, the extent to which the conclusions of such studies are based on theory-internal technicalities is the extent to which they can also be undermined by revisions to that theory. They therefore advocate the investigation of clearcut poverty of the stimulus problems, for which positive evidence is unavailable either from the PLD or from properties of the L1, and for which attained knowledge thus necessarily implicates the availability of UG constraints regardless of changes to the "easily revisable details of particular hypotheses of specific syntactic theories." One such investigation is the widely cited study by Martohardjono (1993), who tested L1 speakers of Chinese, Indonesian, or Italian acquiring L2 English on their knowledge of the ungrammaticality of sentences such as the earlier example in (1) repeated below as (8):

(8) ★Which professor did John read the book about violent videogames had written?

Her results indicated that, like the NS controls, the L2 learners in all three L1 groups rejected these ("strong violation") sentences at a significantly higher rate than more weakly ungrammatical ("weak violation") sentences such as the one in (9):

(9) ★Which professor did John think that had written the book about violent videogames?

This distinction between strong and weak violations was motivated within the *Barriers* (Chomsky, 1986b) framework of generative syntactic theory. As Schwartz and Sprouse (2000) discuss, although the technical details of syntactic theory have changed considerably in the meantime, the conceptual problem addressed by Martohardjono remains the same:

> No matter how the constraints on [*wh-*]extraction are framed, there is a clear poverty-of-the-stimulus problem involved in acquiring the distinction between strong and weak violations, since they both refer to essentially non-occurring syntactic patterns. ... The fact that Martohardjono's L2 acquirers display knowledge not only of the unacceptability of strong violations, but also the distinction between strong and weak violations, is a very strong indication that L2 development is constrained by UG. (p. 177)

Deductive consequences in parameter resetting? Recall from the section *Principles and Parameters Theory* that the various seemingly unrelated properties associated with particular parameter values— so-called "deductive consequences"— were hypothesized to play a powerful role in L1 acquisition; SLA researchers have been interested in learning whether these properties would also automatically be acquired if and when L2 learners managed to select the appropriate parameter value for the L2. The acquisition of the correct L2 setting of the Null Subject Parameter, including its associated cluster of properties (discussed earlier), has been studied intensively in generative SLA research, and we briefly review the main empirical findings here. Along with the [+null subject] setting, including the absence of expletive subject pronouns, such related properties include the possibility of post-verbal subjects, and the possibility of extraction of *wh-*subjects from embedded clauses with an overt complementizer. Not all studies tested all properties, but overall, the findings indicate an absence of the expected clustering effects in SLA.

Phinney (1987) and Tsimpli and Roussou (1991) found that, whereas L1 Spanish and Greek speakers (respectively) acquiring L2 English were likely to supply overt referential subject pronouns and/or reject null referential subject pronouns where required, they failed to do so with expletive subjects; that is, they incorrectly allowed null expletive subjects in English. White (1985, 1986) reported that L1 Spanish/Italian ([+null subject]) speakers were significantly less accurate than L1 French ([−null subject]) speakers in rejecting null subjects in L2 English and more likely to allow *that-*trace violations, suggesting L1 transfer, although both groups were highly accurate in correctly rejecting post-verbal subjects. Reviews by Hawkins (2001b, p. 206) and Carroll (2001, p. 164) of the available evidence to date point to the conclusion that the hypothesized cluster of properties associated with this parameter do not emerge as a cluster in L2 development.

More recently, Belletti and Leonini (2004) found that, whereas null pronominal subjects were available to L2 learners of Italian, the grammatical option of post-verbal subjects was significantly less so, again suggesting a dissociation. Furkóné Banka (2006) found that L1 Hungarian learners of L2 English were able to acquire overt subjects and the ability to reject post-verbal subjects, but they were not able to accurately reject *that-*trace violations, even at advanced-proficiency levels. Sauter (2002) undertook a two-year longitudinal study of nine Romance learners of English or Swedish and found that, although the related properties appeared to transfer as a cluster, they were never "unlearned"; that is, the parameter value was never reset. All nine learners persisted (to varying degrees) in producing utterances with missing pronominal subjects in main and subordinate clauses as well as post-verbal subjects, and Sauter concluded that they were unable to acquire previously unactivated options of UG.

To summarize, then, the majority of SLA studies that have tested the hypothesized clustering of deductive consequences associated with parameter setting in general and the Null Subject Parameter in particular indicate that such clustering effects remain empirically unverified, if not outrightly disconfirmed. Bley-Vroman (2009, p. 184) goes so far as to state that "in 20 years of SLA research, not a single study has convincingly demonstrated the sort of triggering and clustering that might be expected." Moreover, as discussed in Lardiere (2009a, b; see also Carroll, 2001), within syntactic theory itself, the proposed clustering effects associated with most parameters have also failed over time to be empirically verified.[9] Such clustering effects have now been largely abandoned as a necessary condition for acquisition within much P&P research, especially in so-called "microparametric" research that investigates fine-grained differences between related languages (e.g., Kayne, 2005, p. 6). Consequently, the notion of parameter-setting as a useful explanatory construct for (second) language acquisition must be reconsidered in light of these developments within linguistic theory.

More on wh-features. Let us consider empirical verification within another area that has been intensively investigated in SLA syntactic research—that of *wh*-movement and constraints on *wh*-movement. Such constraints are broadly referred to as *subjacency* constraints, and have often been used as a kind of test case to verify whether adult learners have UG-constrained syntactic knowledge. The study by Martohardjono (1993) discussed above is one example of how demonstrated knowledge of the distinction between strong and weak violations of constraints on *wh*-movement has led to the claim that adult learner ILs are indeed constrained by conditions that are both underdetermined in the target language PLD and unavailable from the L1, and therefore pose a genuine learnability problem.

Several other studies have been carried out in this area, with conflicting results. Some have found that L1 speakers of *wh*-in-situ languages have difficulty rejecting subjacency violations in English, and have concluded from this that principles of UG are inaccessible to adults (e.g., Bley-Vroman *et al.*, 1988; Johnson and Newport, 1991; Schachter, 1989, 1990). Others have found evidence that subjacency-type constraints either still appear to be available or that they are simply not applicable because the (apparently) displaced *wh*-element may have instead been base-generated in clause-initial position or alternatively "scrambled" to that position via a different movement mechanism that is common in case-marking languages (see Belikova and White, 2009; Hawkins, 2001b for more thorough reviews of this literature). Although the latter type of claim is compatible with "access to UG" analyses, learner representations are nonetheless argued to be non-nativelike, because parameter-setting (in the form of [+wh] feature-selection mentioned earlier) fails. To illustrate, we briefly turn to a recent study that investigated the L2 knowledge of *wh*-movement constraints among Japanese-speaking learners of L2 English.

Hawkins and Hattori (2006) first observe that, in several previous studies, Japanese NSs acquiring L2 English appear able to converge on the same representation for *wh*-movement as English NSs on a number of different measures, such as targetlike *wh*-fronting and subject-auxiliary inversion, knowledge of the impossibility of contracting *is* to *'s* in cases like *Do you know where John is/*'s now?*, the ability to distinguish grammatical from ungrammatical long-distance *wh*-questions involving strong and weak violations, and so on. These findings suggest that Japanese NSs are ultimately able to acquire sophisticated intuitions about English syntax despite the absence of an uninterpretable [+wh]-feature in Japanese. Hawkins and Hattori argue, however, that such convergence is only apparent. They found that, although there was no significant difference between Japanese speakers and English NS controls in accepting responses that did not violate any movement constraints, the Japanese were significantly more likely than the English NS controls to also accept sentences that did violate interpretive constraints on English multiple *wh*-questions such as *Who did Sophie's brother warn Sophie would phone when?* They concluded that the learner group was drawing on the grammatical possibility of scrambling in Japanese, which is arguably not subject to subjacency constraints (Saito and Fukui, 1998), and that they had not selected the required uninterpretable [+wh] feature in their L2 English, thus supporting the

Interpretability Hypothesis discussed in the section *The role of L1 knowledge in acquiring the L2 grammar*. More generally, they caution against interpreting targetlike performance (found by many studies) as evidence that L2 speakers have the same underlying grammatical representations as native speakers or that their representations originate from the same source.

Note that the claim that the L1 Japanese speakers failed to reject violations in this study is not the same as arguing that they ultimately *could not* do so (say, if another group were more advanced than this group or if it could be established that their grammars were not yet endstate grammars), which is what the Interpretability Hypothesis requires. Therefore, Hawkins and Hattori are correct to claim that their results at this point are "consistent with" the hypothesis (p. 269). Moreover, this is an example of a study whose premises rest particularly heavily on theory-internal technical details, and the judgments obtained even from the English NS controls appear highly fragile. Thus, the conclusions from this and similar studies remain quite vulnerable to being undermined by ongoing revisions to Minimalist syntactic theory, as previously pointed out by Schwartz and Sprouse (2000). More recently, Belikova and White (2009) discuss this issue in particular relation to constraints on *wh*-movement. It is clear that the evidence for such constraints is underdetermined by the available PLD of the target language environment and acquiring them thus constitutes a genuine learnability problem. However, assuming the operation of the same few invariant computational principles in the grammars of all languages (as Minimalist theory now requires), they argue that it may not be possible to pinpoint the source of attained L2 knowledge of movement constraints, whether nativelike or not.

Applications

As mentioned earlier, a language acquirer's knowledge of abstract syntactic constraints and operations is tacit, considered largely inaccessible to introspection. The mechanisms of language processing are similarly not available to conscious awareness. Unlike, say, a knowledgeable poker player or basketball coach, who can readily transmit the rules of these games to other would-be players, theoretical linguists find themselves in the position of trying to infer what the "rules" of language are by observing whether the sentences the rules generate are well-formed or not. The formal nature of theoretical constructs, their level of abstraction and technical complexity, might render it difficult or even pointless to attempt to directly translate them into pedagogically useful guidelines. Chomsky (1966/71, pp. 152–155, cited in Widdowson, 2003) for example, noted the following:

> I am, frankly, rather skeptical about the significance, for the teaching of languages, of such insights and understanding as have been attained in linguistics and psychology. … It is possible—even likely—that principles of psychology and linguistics, and research in these disciplines, may supply insights useful to the language teacher. But these must be demonstrated, and cannot be presumed. …

But let us concentrate for the moment on the possibility of morphosyntactic research supplying insights that might be useful to the language teacher, as Chomsky mentions. Widdowson (2003, pp. 11–12) points out that theoretical linguists (rightly) develop their own specialist discourses to suit their own disciplinary perspectives on language, as do language teachers, and that insights from linguistic theory cannot simply be supplied or "retailed" from one discourse to the other. Rather, he argues, it is up to applied linguists to act as mediating agents in both directions: to make linguistic insights intelligible to language teachers, as well as to perceive and (re-)formulate the learning or teaching problems such insights could effectively address.

In considering the applicability of SLA morphosyntactic research to language instruction, two broad candidate areas come to mind. The first is obvious: The impact of L1 knowledge (and processing routines; see Carroll, 2001; Hopp, 2010) in acquiring a second language cannot be denied. Ringbom and Jarvis (2009) describe the notion of transfer as "an umbrella term" for a learner's reliance on perceiving L1–L2 similarities between individual items and also the functional equivalences between the two underlying grammatical systems. The fewer the similarities, as in the case of less-closely-related languages, then the more difficult it will be to establish "how different L2 units correspond to L1 units and how they relate to the underlying concepts" (pp. 112–113). (The Feature-Reassembly approach is just one way of more formally articulating this observation in terms of the distribution of formal features among lexical items in each language.) The implication for language teaching, Ringbom and Jarvis suggest, is that teachers should focus on similarities between the L1 and L2: "In general terms, a good strategy would be to make use of, and even overuse, actual similarities at early stages of learning" (p. 114). Implicit in this proposal, however, is the assumption that a teacher will be explicitly, metalinguistically *aware* of such similarities (and their limits). Therefore, a teacher who has been exposed to some training in morphosyntactic comparative research, particularly comparison of the L1(s) and L2(s) in question, will be in a better position to devise ways (in the mediating sense of Widdowson, cited above) of incorporating its constructs and findings into the classroom.

The second area of applicability to teaching—once teachers have become aware of the differing distributions of formal features among morpholexical items in the L1 and L2—is attention to the contextual conditioning environments for expressing those features. It is not enough to know *how* to spell out a particular feature or grammatical construction (although of course one should know that); one must also learn exactly *when* and under what conditions it is correct to do so. We asked earlier, for example: What constitutes an obligatory context? For features whose expression is considered optional (such as plural-marking in Chinese discussed earlier) when is it syntactically, discursively or pragmatically appropriate to express them? Such optionality poses a thorny and persistent learning problem for language students (see, e.g., Sorace, 2003).

Future directions: "The end of syntax"?

To conclude, we briefly consider a few key issues that seem likely to shape the direction of future research in formal linguistic approaches to the study of the L2 acquisition of syntax and morphosyntax. The first issue is whether acquisition researchers can continue to generate interesting testable hypotheses for language acquisition based on syntactic theory, especially Minimalist syntactic theory.

As R. Hawkins (2008, p. 445) points out, some of the properties that had been the basis for hypotheses about the availability of UG in SLA disappear under Minimalist assumptions. He cites Chomsky's (2001) suggestion that verb-raising, a formerly-parameterized core grammatical option that many generative SLA researchers have spent years intensively studying (see, e.g., Ayoun, 2003; R. Hawkins, 2001b; White, 2003 for discussion and summary overviews), is no longer a property of core or "narrow" syntax, but rather a consequence of linearization procedures at the interface with phonology (as are virtually all word-order phenomena now). If that is so, Hawkins writes, then L2 research on the acquisition of differences in verb-raising "would shed no light on the availability of innately determined features and computations in this domain" (p. 445).

Marantz (1995) refers to this ongoing relegation of formerly syntactic phenomena to the interfaces with phonology and semantics/pragmatics as "the end of syntax":

The syntactic engine itself—the autonomous principles of composition and manipulation Chomsky now labels "the computational system"– has begun to fade into the background. ... A vision of the end of syntax—the end of the sub-field of linguistics that takes the computational system, between the interfaces, as its primary object of study—this vision encompasses the completion rather than the disappearance of syntax. (pp. 380–381)

As Marantz points out, however, this shift has the positive consequence of forcing syntacticians to "renew their interface credentials" by paying serious attention to work in phonology and semantics (p. 381; see also Jackendoff, 2002). The same is true, of course, for the study of language acquisition, including L2 acquisition. If the Minimalist vision of syntax is too general and abstract to allow us to generate testable predictions for SLA grammatical research, then such predictions will have to come from our developing understanding of the interaction of syntactic computation with other components of language knowledge. (See White, 2009 for an overview of recent L2 research which addresses linguistic interfaces.)

Another question is the extent to which special and general nativist concerns will continue to converge, and the limits of each approach. As J. Hawkins (2004, p. 273) observes, regardless of whether UG constructs such as subjacency constraints fall by the wayside as possible grounds for innateness claims in formal linguistics (a conclusion he persuasively argues for), there nonetheless remains a poverty-of-the-stimulus problem in language acquisition that must be addressed, "since one does have to explain how the child learns the limits on the set of possible sentences that go beyond the positive data to which he or she has been exposed." We asked earlier: What can replace or recapture the original highly restrictive role of parameters in earlier UG theory? After all, a major motivation for positing parameters was to account not only for observed recurring cross-linguistic tendencies, but also for the observed rapid, uniformly successful acquisition of language by young children.

J. Hawkins' own general-nativist solution (like that of O'Grady, 1996, 2008) is that language learners will comprehend input and construct grammars in accordance with innate processing and learning mechanisms, and that hierarchies of processing ease vs. complexity may structure initial hypotheses about the target grammar. Extensions beyond these initial hypotheses will need to be justified by the data of experience, just as we have posited for parameters. Because Chomsky's own current (2005, 2007) agenda for Minimalist syntax encompasses pursuing this latter possibility to account for language acquisition, we can anticipate that a consideration of proposed processing constraints and hierarchies such as those proposed by Hawkins will become increasingly important to special nativists as well as to general nativists in future SLA research. More specifically, Hawkins suggests that it will be important to find out whether factors thought to facilitate L2 acquisition, such as frequency effects and L1–L2 similarities, also operate within the ease-of-processing hierarchies and constraints that are hypothesized to account for crosslinguistic variation and native language acquisition (p. 275).

A final, related question we might ask is whether the P&P/Minimalist approach offers the best analytical tools for the job to those of us who work on formal linguistic approaches to grammatical acquisition. The answer, of course, depends on precisely what we are interested in studying, but future research at the "interfaces" with morphosyntax will require increasing familiarity with additional frameworks that are better suited for analyzing the type of data that interact with the syntactic computational component. The (optimality-theoretic-based) work by Goad and White (2004, 2006, 2008) on phonological analyses of prosodic factors impinging on morphological production, discussed earlier in this chapter, offers a striking case in point. For the acquisition of morphosyntax in particular, Carroll (2009, p. 252) argues that categorial and phrase structure grammatical frameworks offer a far richer theory of features and categories than Minimalism, and suggests that the field of SLA would benefit from a broader, "less parochial" perspective on syntactic theoretical frameworks than it has held over the past two decades.

Notes

* I am grateful to Lydia White and the editors of this volume for comments on an earlier draft of this chapter.

1 For a useful historical summary of refinements to conditions on *wh*-movement and their applicability to SLA, see Belikova and White (2009).

2 See O'Grady (1999) for a discussion of nativism and points of consensus as well as differences between general and special nativism.

3 This principle was originally proposed as the Extended Projection Principle in Chomsky (1981) and has undergone considerable revision over the evolution of P&P theory. The requirement that all clauses have subjects has more recently been recast as the Subject Criterion (Rizzi, 2006).

4 From these (mainly grouped, cross-sectional) L2 studies of morpheme suppliance in obligatory contexts, a developmental sequence or "natural order" of morpheme acquisition was extrapolated that cut across the various L1 backgrounds of the study participants, thus apparently minimizing the role of L1 influence. See various comprehensive introductory SLA course texts (e.g., R. Ellis, 2008; Gass and Selinker, 2008; Larsen-Freeman and Long, 1991) for morpheme-order study references and an overview.

5 A mature grammatical representation includes knowledge of syntactic phrase structure in which open-class, lexical-headed constituents such as verb phrases (VPs) and noun phrases (NPs) are grammatically contextualized, or extended, by hierarchically nesting them within functional-category-headed phrases such as "Complementizer phrases" (CP), "Infl(ectional)" phrases (IP, later subdivided into Tense and Agreement (TP/AgrP) as well as other functional subcategories), "Determiner phrases" (DP), and "Number phrases" (NumP) that encode formal features related to clause type, tense and agreement, definiteness, and plurality, respectively. The derived syntactic structure could be modeled something like that shown in (i), where "Spec(ifier)" represents a type of subject position:

(i) [CP Spec [C] [IP Spec [I] [VP Spec [V] [DP [D] [NumP [Num] [NP]]]]]] The overall CP>IP >VP hierarchy for clauses shown in (i) is broadly accepted as universal among P&P researchers, although the many (possibly language-specific) subcategories associated with these more general categories are subject to considerable debate. (Haegeman, 2006 provides an accessible introductory overview.)

6 There is some question in the syntactic literature regarding the "true" plural status of *men* suffixation in Chinese; see Li (1999) for arguments in support of the "plural marker" view. See Lardiere (2009a) for additional discussion.

7 Of course, English has phonetically conditioned allomorphy, as well as irregular plural-marking on certain nouns, which is why it is necessary to posit an underlying abstract morphosyntactic feature [+plural] that may be spelled out differently for different lexical items depending on particular language-specific conditioning factors (such as particular lexical roots, e.g., *foot, ox, mouse, woman*, etc.).

8 Technically, these terms are not interchangeable, as noted as far back as Chomsky (1965), although in actual practice they often are. Linguists have mostly assumed that grammatical knowledge is categorical—sentences are either grammatical or ungrammatical—and that the continuous spectrum of acceptability is caused by extra-grammatical factors (plausibility, working memory limitations, etc.) (Sprouse, 2007, p. 118).

9 However, see Nicolis (2008) for one apparently exceptionless implicational correlation between referential and expletive null subjects in null-subject languages, and an explanation for the correlation.

References

Anderson, B. (2008). Forms of evidence and grammatical development in the acquisition of adjective position in L2 French. *Studies in Second Language Acquisition, 30,* 1–29.

Ayoun, D. (2003). *Parameter-setting theory in first and second language acquisition.* New York: Continuum.

Belikova, A. and White, L. (2009). Evidence for the fundamental difference hypothesis or not? Island constraints revisited. *Studies in Second Language Acquisition, 31,* 199–223.

Belletti, A. and Leonini, C. (2004). Subject inversion in L2 Italian. In S. Foster-Cohen, M. Sharwood Smith, A. Sorace and M. Ota (Eds.), *EuroSLA Yearbook 2004* (pp. 95–118). Amsterdam: John Benjamins.

Biberauer, T. (2008). Introduction. In T. Biberauer (Ed.), *The limits of syntactic variation* (pp. 1–72). Amsterdam: John Benjamins.

Birdsong, D. (1989). *Metalinguistic performance and interlanguage competence*. New York: Springer.

Bley-Vroman, R. (1989). What is the logical problem of foreign language learning? In S. M. Gass and J. Schachter (Eds.), *Linguistic perspectives on second language acquisition* (pp. 41–68). New York: Cambridge University Press.

Bley-Vroman, R. (2009). The evolving context of the fundamental difference hypothesis. *Studies in Second Language Acquisition, 31*, 175–198.

Bley-Vroman, R., Felix, S., and Ioup, G. (1988). The accessibility of universal grammar in adult language learning. *Second Language Research, 4*, 1–32.

Brown, R. (1973). *A first language: The early stages*. Cambridge, MA: Harvard University Press.

Carroll, S. E. (2001). *Input and evidence: The raw material of second language acquisition*. Amsterdam: John Benjamins.

Carroll, S. E. (2009). Re-assembling formal features in second language acquisition: Beyond minimalism. *Second Language Research, 25*, 245–253.

Chomsky, N. (1965). *Aspects of the theory of syntax*. Cambridge, MA: MIT Press.

Chomsky, N. (1966/71). In J. P. B. Allen and P. Van Buren (Eds.), *Chomsky: Selected readings*. New York: Oxford University Press.

Chomsky, N. (1981). *Lectures on government and binding*. Dordrecht: Foris.

Chomsky, N. (1986a). *Knowledge of language*. New York: Praeger.

Chomsky, N. (1986b). *Barriers*. Cambridge, MA: MIT Press.

Chomsky, N. (1995a). *The minimalist program*. Cambridge, MA: MIT Press.

Chomsky, N. (1995b). Bare phrase structure. In G. Webelhuth (Ed.), *Government and binding theory and the minimalist program* (pp. 385–439). Cambridge, MA: Blackwell.

Chomsky, N. (2001). Derivation by phase. In M. Kenstowicz (Ed.), *Ken Hale: A life in language* (pp. 1–52). Cambridge, MA: MIT Press.

Chomsky, N. (2005). Three factors in language design. *Linguistic Inquiry, 36*, 1–22.

Chomsky, N. (2007). Approaching UG from below. In U. Sauerland and H. -M. Gärtner (Eds.), *Interfaces + recursion = language?* (pp. 1–29). Berlin: Mouton de Gruyter.

Clahsen, H. and Muysken, P. (1986). The availability of universal grammar to adult and child learners: A study of the acquisition of German word order. *Second Language Research, 2*, 93–119.

Dekydtspotter, L. (2001). The universal parser and interlanguage: Domain-specific mental organization in the comprehension of *combien* interrogatives in English-French interlanguage. *Second Language Research, 17*, 91–143.

Dekydtspotter, L. and Sprouse, R. A. (2001). Mental design and (second) language epistemology: Adjectival restrictions of *wh*-quantifiers and tense in English-French interlanguage. *Second Language Research, 17*, 1–35.

Eckman, F. (1996). On evaluating arguments for special nativism in second language acquisition theory. *Second Language Research, 12*, 398–419.

Ellis, R. (2008). *The study of second language acquisition*. Oxford: Oxford University Press.

Eubank, L. (1996). Negation in early German-English interlanguage: More valueless features in the L2-initial state. *Second Language Research, 12*, 73–106.

Felix, S. (1985). More evidence on competing cognitive systems. *Second Language Research, 1*, 47–72.

Furkóné Banka, I. (2006). Resetting the null subject parameter by Hungarian learners of English. In M. Nikolov and J. Horváth (Eds.), *UPRT 2006: Empirical studies in English applied linguistics* (pp. 179–195). Pécs: Lingua Franca Csoport.

Gass, S. M. (2001). Sentence matching: A re-examination. *Second Language Research, 17*, 421–441.

Gass, S. M. and Selinker, L. (2008). *Second language acquisition: An introductory course* (3rd ed.). New York: Routledge.

Gavruseva, L. and Lardiere, D. (1996). The emergence of extended phrase structure in child L2 acquisition. In A. Stringfellow, D. Cahana-Amitay, E. Hughes, and A. Zukowski (Eds.), *BUCLD 20 Proceedings* (pp. 225–236). Somerville, MA: Cascadilla Press.

Goad, H. and White, L. (2004). Ultimate attainment of L2 inflection: Effects of L1 prosodic structure. In S. Foster-Cohen, M. Sharwood Smith, A. Sorace, and M. Ota (Eds.), *EuroSLA Yearbook* (Vol. 4, pp. 119–145). Amsterdam: John Benjamins.

Goad, H. and White, L. (2006). Ultimate attainment in interlanguage grammars: A prosodic approach. *Second Language Research, 22*, 243–268.

Goad, H. and White, L. (2008). Prosodic structure and the representation of L2 functional morphology: A nativist approach. *Lingua, 118*, 577–594.

Greenberg, J. H. (1963). Some universals of grammar with particular reference to the order of meaningful elements. In J. H. Greenberg (Ed.), *Universals of language* (pp. 73–113). Cambridge, MA: MIT Press.

Gregg, K. R. (1989). Second language acquisition theory: The case for a generative perspective. In S. Gass and J. Schachter (Eds.), *Linguistic perspectives on second language acquisition* (pp. 15–40). Cambridge: Cambridge University Press.

Gregg, K. R. (1996). The logical and developmental problems of second language acquisition. In W. C. Ritchie and T. K. Bhatia (Eds.), *Handbook of second language acquisition* (pp. 49–81). San Diego, CA: Academic Press.

Haegeman, L. (2006). *Thinking syntactically: A guide to argumentation and analysis*. Malden, MA: Blackwell.

Hawkins, J. A. (2004). *Efficiency and complexity in grammars*. Oxford: Oxford University Press.

Hawkins, R. (2001a). The theoretical significance of Universal Grammar in second language acquisition. *Second Language Research, 17*, 345–367.

Hawkins, R. (2001b). *Second language syntax: A generative introduction*. Malden, MA: Blackwell.

Hawkins, R. (2003). *"Representational deficit" theories of adult SLA: Evidence, counterevidence and implications*. Plenary paper presented at EuroSLA, Edinburgh, September 2003.

Hawkins, R. (2008). Current emergentist and nativist perspectives on second language acquisition. *Foreword to the special issue of Lingua, 118*, 445–446.

Hawkins, R. and Chan, C. Y. -H. (1997). The partial availability of universal grammar in second language acquisition: The "failed functional features hypothesis". *Second Language Research, 13*, 187–226.

Hawkins, R. and Hattori, H. (2006). Interpretation of English multiple wh-questions by Japanese speakers: A missing uninterpretable feature account. *Second Language Research, 22*, 269–301.

Hawkins, R. and Liszka, S. (2003). Locating the source of defective past tense marking in advanced L2 speakers. In R. van Hout, A. Hulk, F. Kuiken, and R. Towell (Eds.), *The lexicon-syntax interface in second language acquisition* (pp. 21–44). Amsterdam: John Benjamins.

Hopp, H. (2010) Ultimate attainment in L2 inflection: Performance similarities between non-native and native speakers. *Lingua, 120*, 901–931.

Jackendoff, R. (2002). *Foundations of language*. Oxford: Oxford University Press.

Jiang, N. (2004). Morphological insensitivity in second language processing. *Applied Psycholinguistics, 25*, 603–634.

Jiang, N. (2007). Selective integration of linguistic knowledge in adult second language learning. *Language Learning, 57*, 1–33.

Johnson, J. and Newport, E. (1991). Critical period effects on universal properties of language: The status of subjacency in the acquisition of a second language. *Cognition, 39*, 215–258.

Kanno, K. (1998). The stability of UG principles in second language acquisition. *Linguistics, 36*, 1125–1146.

Kayne, R. S. (2005). Some notes on comparative syntax, with special reference to English and French. In G. Cinque and R. S. Kayne (Eds.), *The Oxford handbook of comparative syntax* (pp. 3–69). New York: Oxford University Press.

Lardiere, D. (1998). Case and tense in the "fossilized" steady state. *Second Language Research, 14*, 1–26.

Lardiere, D. (2000). Mapping features to forms in second language acquisition. In J. Archibald (Ed.), *Second language acquisition and linguistic theory* (pp. 102–129). Malden, MA: Blackwell.

Lardiere, D. (2007). *Ultimate attainment in second language acquisition: A case study*. Mahwah, NJ: Lawrence Erlbaum Associates.

Lardiere, D. (2008). Feature assembly in second language acquisition. In J. M. Liceras, H. Zobl, and H. Goodluck (Eds.), *The role of formal features in second language acquisition* (pp. 106–140). Mahwah, NJ: Lawrence Erlbaum Associates.

Lardiere, D. (2009a). Some thoughts on the contrastive analysis of features in second language acquisition. *Second Language Research, 25*, 173–227.

Lardiere, D. (2009b). Further thoughts on parameters and features in second language acquisition. *Second Language Research, 25*, 409–422.

Larsen-Freeman, D. and Long, M. H. (1991). *An introduction to second language acquisition research*. Essex, UK: Longman.

Li, Y. -H. A. (1999). Plurality in a classifier language. *Journal of East Asian Linguistics, 8*, 75–99.

Marantz, A. (1995). The minimalist program. In G. Webelhuth (Ed.), *Government and binding theory and the minimalist program* (pp. 351–382). Cambridge, MA: Blackwell.

Martohardjono, G. (1993). *Wh-movement in the acquisition of a second language: A cross-linguistic study of three languages with and without overt movement*. Unpublished doctoral dissertation. Cornell University.

Meisel, J. M. (1997). The acquisition of the syntax of negation in French and German: Contrasting first and second language acquisition. *Second Language Research, 13*, 227–263.

Newmeyer, F. J. (1998). *Language form and language function*. Cambridge, MA: MIT Press.

Nicolis, M. (2008). The null subject parameter and correlating properties: The case of creole languages. In T. Biberauer (Ed.), *The limits of syntactic variation* (pp. 271–294). Amsterdam: John Benjamins.

O'Grady, W. (1999). Toward a new nativism. *Studies in Second Language Acquisition, 21*, 621–633.

O'Grady, W. (1996). Language acquisition without Universal Grammar: A general nativist proposal for L2 learning. *Second Language Research, 12*, 374–397.

O'Grady, W. (2008). Innateness, universal grammar, and emergentism. *Lingua, 118*, 620–631.

Phinney, M. (1987). The pro-drop parameter in second language acquisition. In T. Roeper and E. Williams (Eds.), *Parameter setting* (pp. 221–238). Dordrecht: Reidel.

Pérez-Leroux, A. T. and Glass, W. (1999). OPC effects in the L2 acquisition of Spanish. In A. T. Pérez-Leroux and W. Glass (Eds.), *Contemporary perspectives on the acquisition of Spanish, vol. 1: Developing grammars* (pp. 149–165). Somerville, MA: Cascadilla Press.

Ringbom, H. and Jarvis, S. (2009). The importance of cross-linguistic similarity in foreign language learning. In M. H. Long and C. J. Doughty (Eds.), *The handbook of language teaching* (pp. 106–118). Chichester, UK: Wiley-Blackwell.

Rizzi, L. (1982). *Issues in Italian syntax*. Dordrecht: Foris.

Rizzi, L. (1986). Null objects in Italian and the theory of *pro*. *Linguistic Inquiry, 17*, 501–557.

Rizzi, L. (2006). On the form of chains: Criterial positions and ECP effects. In L. L. -S. Cheng and N. Corver (Eds.), *Wh-movement: Moving on* (pp. 97–133). Cambridge, MA: MIT Press.

Saito, M. and Fukui, N. (1998). Order in phrase structure and movement. *Linguistic Inquiry, 29*, 439–474.

Sauter, K. (2002). Transfer and access to universal grammar in second language acquisition. *Groningen Dissertations in Linguistics* 41. University of Groningen.

Schachter, J. (1989). Testing a proposed universal. In S. M. Gass and J. Schachter (Eds.), *Linguistic perspectives on second language acquisition* (pp. 73–88). New York: Cambridge University Press.

Schachter, J. (1990). On the issue of completeness in second language acquisition. *Second Language Research, 6*, 93–124.

Schwartz, B. D. and Sprouse, R. A. (1996). L2 cognitive states and the Full Transfer/Full Access model. *Second Language Research, 12*, 40–72.

Schwartz, B. D. and Sprouse, R. A. (2000). When syntactic theories evolve: Consequences for L2 acquisition research. In J. Archibald (Ed.), *Second language acquisition and linguistic theory* (pp. 156–186). Oxford: Blackwell.

Schütze, C. (1996). *The empirical base of linguistics: Grammaticality judgments and linguistic methodology*. Chicago: University of Chicago Press.

Snyder, W. (2000). An experimental investigation of syntactic satiation effects. *Linguistic Inquiry, 31*, 575–582.

Sorace, A. (1996). The use of acceptability judgments in second language acquisition research. In W. C. Ritchie and T. K. Bhatia (Eds.), *Handbook of second language acquisition* (pp. 375–409). San Diego: Academic Press.

Sorace, A. (2003). Near-nativeness. In C. J. Doughty and M. H. Long (Eds.), *The handbook of second language acquisition* (pp.–130–151). Oxford: Blackwell.

Sprouse, J. (2007). Continuous acceptability, categorical grammaticality, and experimental syntax. *Biolinguistics, 1*, 118–129.

Tsimpli, I. -M. and Dimitrakopoulou, M. (2007). The interpretability hypothesis: Evidence from wh-interrogatives in second language acquisition. *Second Language Research, 23*, 215–242.

Tsimpli, I. -M. and Roussou, A. (1991). Parameter resetting in L2? *UCL Working Papers in Linguistics, 3*, 149–169.

Vainikka, A. and Young-Scholten, M. (1994). Direct access to X'-theory: Evidence from Turkish and Korean adults learning German. In T. Hoekstra and B. D. Schwartz (Eds.), *Language acquisition studies in generative grammar* (pp. 265–316). Amsterdam: John Benjamins.

Vainikka, A. and Young-Scholten, M. (1996). Gradual development of L2 phrase structure. *Second Language Research, 12*, 7–39.

White, L. (1985). The pro-drop parameter in adult second language acquisition. *Language Learning, 35*, 47–62.

White, L. (1986). Implications of parametric variation for adult second language acquisition: An investigation of the "pro-drop" parameter. In V. Cook (Ed.), *Experimental approaches to second language acquisition* (pp. 55–72). Oxford: Pergamon Press.

White, L. (1989). *Universal grammar and second language acquisition*. Amsterdam: John Benjamins.

White, L. (2003). *Second language acquisition and universal grammar*. Cambridge: Cambridge University Press.

White, L. (2009). Grammatical theory: Interfaces and L2 knowledge. In W. Ritchie and T. Bhatia (Eds.), *The new handbook of second language acquisition* (pp. 49–68). Leeds, UK: Emerald Group Publishing Limited.

White, L. and Genesee, F. (1996). How native is near-native? The issue of ultimate attainment in adult second language acquisition. *Second Language Research, 11*, 233–265.

Widdowson, H. G. (2003). *Defining issues in English language teaching*. Oxford: Oxford University Press.

8

L2 semantics*

Roumyana Slabakova

Introduction

Few people start learning a second language because it has exotic sounds, or elegant sentence structure. *Meaning* is what we are after. We would like to understand and to be able to convey thoughts and feelings and observations in another language the way we do in our native language. Ever since Aristotle, linguists have considered language to be the pairing of form (sounds or signs or written strings) and meaning. In this chapter, I examine the road to meaning, that is, how we come to understand and convey meaning in a second language, and where the pitfalls to that goal may lie. I will begin by distinguishing between several types of meanings: lexical, grammatical, and semantic. Next, I will situate them in the language architecture.

When language learners think of semantics, they think almost exclusively of the meaning of words. Semantics, however, involves much more than word meaning. Lexical meanings are stored in our mental lexicon while sentential semantics is compositional, based on combining the meanings of all the words in a sentence and taking their order into account. Take for example the English sentence *Someone criticized everyone*. Depending on the context, it may mean that there is a certain person who criticized every other person in a situation; in other words, everyone was criticized by one individual. The sentence may also mean that everyone was criticized by some person or other. In the first reading we have one critic, in the second we have possibly many critics. Of these two readings, only the first is available for the equivalent Japanese sentence *Dareka-ga daremo-o semeta* (Hoji, 1985, p. 336), while the second is not. Although the quantifiers *dareka* and *daremo* may be equivalent in meaning to *someone* and *everyone*, when used in speech, they give rise to two sentence meanings in English, only one sentence meaning in Japanese. This difference is captured and explained by the rules for calculating sentence meaning in the two languages, and is the research focus of (phrasal) semantics. The Principle of Compositionality (Frege, 1884) ensures that the meaning of the whole sentence (the proposition) is a function of the meanings of the parts and of the way they are syntactically combined.

Grammatical meaning also comes into consideration in calculating sentence interpretation. Consider the two sentences *Jane eats meat* and *Jane ate meat*. They contain two identical lexical items (*Jane, meat*) and the third, the verbal form, encodes a grammatical difference in tense and aspect. We understand that a present characteristic or habitual (but not an ongoing) event is meant by the first utterance (e.g., Jane is not a vegetarian) while a past habitual event or a past completed event is a possible reading of the second.[1] Grammatical meanings are mostly encoded in inflectional morphology (*-ed* for past simple, *-s* for third-person singular present simple, etc.), for more on their acquisition see Lardiere (Chapter 7, this volume).

When learning a second language, speakers are faced with different acquisition tasks regarding meaning: they have to learn the lexical items of the target language, that is, map linguistic form and lexical meaning one by one. This is certainly a laborious task but learners are facilitated in it by detecting semantic components, or primitives, that can combine to make up lexical meaning. Learning the functional morphology is not qualitatively different: abstracting away from irregular morphology, once learners learn that -*ed* in English encodes a past habit or a past completed event, they can apply this knowledge to all English regular verbs. As in lexical learning, primitives of grammatical meanings reflected singly or combined in various morphemes help learners in grammar acquisition. The aspectual meanings of habitual, ongoing and completed event constitute examples of such primitive grammatical meanings. Sentential meanings are calculated using universal mechanisms of human language.[2] Once the lexical and grammatical meanings are learned, sentential meanings are calculated using a universal procedure and do not constitute a barrier for acquisition. I will explain these claims based on current assumptions of the language architecture.

Historical discussion

Within lexical semantics, one fruitful approach has been to view lexical meanings as made up of primitives, or semantic components. This kind of analysis is called componential analysis (Katz, 1972; Katz and Fodor, 1963). For example, the meaning of *wife* is viewed as containing the components [human], [female], [adult], [married] while *spinster* contains the components [human], [female], [adult], [unmarried]. Semantic relations between words such as synonymy, hyponymy, etc., are easily explained by comparing sets of component meanings. Katz and colleagues aimed at establishing a semantic metalanguage through identifying recurring semantic components in words across languages. This type of analysis also highlights the selectional restrictions that we see in combining words into sentences. For example, why is the sentence in (1) perfectly grammatical, but doesn't make any sense? Because the selectional restrictions of the verb and the object require what is spread on the bread to be spreadable, and socks are not.

(1)   I spread my warm bread with socks.

Some linguists apply the component analysis of verb meanings to explain syntactic behavior, the intuition behind this approach being that employing semantic primitives in different combinations helps us describe grammatical processes correctly. The gist of this approach (Levin, 1993) is to set up verb classes with distinct syntactic behavior, for example, motion verbs, causative and inchoative verbs, etc. Furthermore, these linguists postulate different linking rules mapping grammatical functions (subject, object) with thematic roles (Agent, Theme, Goal, Location) (Levin and Rappaport Hovav, 1995, 2005). For example, in the locative alternation below, (2a) links the direct object to the Theme argument while (2b) links the object to the Goal argument, and these two linking rules apply to some verbs but not others (3a, b).

(2)   a.   She sprayed pesticide on the roses. AGENT—THEME—on GOAL
      b.   She sprayed the roses with pesticide. AGENT—GOAL—with THEME

(3)   a.   *She covered a blanket on the bed. AGENT—THEME—on GOAL
      b.   She covered the bed with a blanket. AGENT—GOAL—with THEME

A related research program is that of Talmy (e.g., Talmy, 1985) who studies how semantic components associated with verbs of motion (Figure, Ground, Path, Manner) are combined not only in single words but in phrases, and highlighted their different conflation patterns in different languages.[3] Both of these theoretical approaches to lexical semantics have been utilized in L2 acquisition research, to be reviewed in the next section.

Let us consider briefly the essential philosophical divide between theories of semantics without being able to do it justice: the divide between *representational* and *denotational* approaches to meaning. Within representational approaches, semanticists like Jackendoff and Cognitive Grammar proponents view semantic analysis as discovering the conceptual structure that underlies language; the search for meaning is the search for mental representations in the human mind/brain. Denotational, or formal semanticists, on the other hand, argue that understanding the meaning of an utterance is being able to match it with the situation it describes. In Portner's (2005, p. 9) example, one could think of the meaning of *dog* in terms of the concept DOG in the human mind (the representational approach), or in terms of the real-world animals represented by that word: Spot, Shelby, Ziggy, etc. (the denotational approach).

Formal semantics borrows from logic the notion of truth and the formalisms of propositional logic in order to calculate the truth value of sentences and to characterize semantic relations such as entailment, conjunction and disjunction. The meaning of the sentence is equivalent to its truth conditions. Thus, knowing the meaning of an English sentence such as (4) involves understanding what situation in the world this sentence would correspond to, or in what situation it would be true:

(4) It is sunny and warm in Iowa City.

Topics frequently discussed in formal semantics research and textbooks include the relationship between syntax and semantics (compositionality), types of predicates and modifiers, referring expressions, quantifiers, tense and aspect, modality, discourse representation structures, etc. Unlike cognitive semantics, which is more often than not concerned with lexical semantics (see below), formal semantics is predominately focused on the rules of computing meaning when words combine in sentences and discourse.

Cognitive semantics comes on the representational side of the philosophical debate of what is meaning.[4] Thus, proponents of cognitive semantics reject the correspondence theory of truth of formal semanticists (the meaning of a sentence is equal to its truth conditions) and argue that linguistic truth or falsity must be relative to the way an observer construes a situation, based on her or his conceptual framework. In other words, meaning is the product of the human mind. Human beings have no access to a reality independent of human categorization, and the real focus of semantics should be the human conceptual frameworks and how language reflects them. Rooted in this fundamental understanding of meaning, cognitive linguists (Lakoff, Johnson, Fauconnier, Langacker, Talmy, among others) study the mental categories that people have formed in their experience of acting in the world. Important topics in this theoretical approach are metaphor and metonymy as essential elements in our categorization of the world (Lakoff, 1993), image schemas which provide a link between bodily experience and higher cognitive functions (Johnson, 1987), mental spaces that speakers set up to manipulate reference to entities (Fauconnier, 1994), conceptual processes such as viewpoint shifting, figure-ground shifting, scanning and profiling (Langacker, 1993, 1999, 2002). In sum, cognitive semanticists take meaning to be an experiential phenomenon and argue that the human experience of interacting in society motivates basic conceptual structures, which in turn make understanding language possible.

Next, we shall survey another view of semantics, that of Jackendoff's (2002) Parallel Language Architecture. I have chosen to represent this theoretical model in more detail for several reasons. Firstly, Jackendoff's views of semantics, although highly idiosyncratic, bridge formal and cognitive semantics and pay particular attention to where the language variation lies. Secondly, he articulates a coherent picture of the grammar that takes into account psycholinguistic and neurolinguistic views. Most importantly for our purposes in this chapter, his views of the language architecture are used by L2 researchers to inform their research questions.[5]

The answer to the question "What is the architecture of the language faculty?" is crucial for understanding the L2 acquisition process, because it bears directly on what has to be learned and what can come for free in acquiring a second language. While looking at Jackendoff's theoretical assumptions, particular attention will be paid to how the different types of meaning (lexical, phrasal) are accessed and computed compositionally (Figure 8.1).

In his 2002 book *Foundations of Language*, Jackendoff argues that linguistic structure should be viewed as a collection of independently functioning layers, or levels, of structure: phonological structure (PS), syntactic structure (SS), and conceptual structure (CS), see Figure 8.1. In order to make linguistic theory more compatible with findings from neurolinguistics and psycholinguistics, Jackendoff proposes that all three modules (autonomous levels) of the grammar build structure by compositionally combining the units of the particular level. He calls his model the Parallel Architecture.

At each level of the language architecture, a number of rules and constraints operate, allowing the formation of fully-specified structure at that level. These are called *integrative* processes. SS, for example, works with objects like syntactic trees, their constituents and relations: noun phrases, verb phrases, grammatical features, etc. CS operates with events and states, agents and patients, individuals and propositions. It has three tiers, each of which conveys a different aspect of sentence meaning: predicate logic, reference, topic and focus. Although independent, the three linguistic levels are linked by interfaces. At the interfaces, we have another kind of process, a process that takes as input one type of linguistic structure and outputs another. These are called *interface* processes. Note that the interface processes are qualitatively different from the integrative ones.

In this chapter, we focus on the operations at the conceptual level and the syntax–semantics (SS–CS) interface.[6] Syntactic structure needs to be correlated with semantic structure and that correlation is not always trivial. The syntactic processor works with objects like syntactic trees and

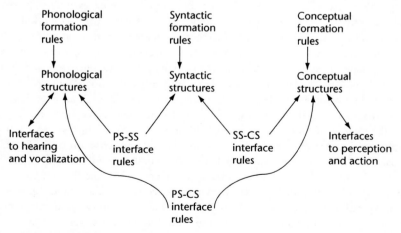

Figure 8.1 Tri-partite parallel architecture
Source: (Jackendoff (2002), Figure 5.4, p. 125)

their constituents: noun phrase, verb phrase, etc. In contrast, a semantic processor operates with events and states, agents and patients, individuals and truth of propositions. For example, in the sentence in (5), *the teacher* is a noun phrase in subject position in the syntax, but an Agent in the semantics.

(5) The teacher ate the apple.

The operations at the interface are limited precisely to those structures that need to be correlated and they do not see other structures and operations (like case-marking) that would have no relevance to the other module.

Core issues

When more than one language come into play, these different computations (lexical, syntactic, conceptual and interface) get even more complicated. Rooted in the language architecture, the core issue of the second language acquisition of meaning is how we come to possess the target meanings and to use them in comprehension and production. That is why it is crucial to identify the locus of language variation. The crucial question for L2 researchers of meaning then is: How much of semantic/conceptual structure is part of Universal Grammar and how much of it may be parameterized? Jackendoff argues that while the content of meaning is the same (concepts and relations between them), different linguistic forms map different natural groupings of meanings. (Jackendoff, 2002, p. 417). Let me illustrate a mismatch at the syntax-semantics interface with marking of politeness in languages like German, French, Bulgarian, and Russian, as opposed to English. German reserves the second-person plural pronoun *Sie* for situations when there is only one addressee, but the speaker wants to be polite, while using the singular *du* in all other cases. French, Bulgarian and Russian, among other languages, work similarly to German. English, however, does not reflect this distinction in the morphology of personal pronouns. This does not mean that English speakers have no concept of politeness; they express it differently.

Another example would be the grammaticalization of semantic concepts in inflectional morphology. Compare the marking of tense in English and Mandarin Chinese, Vietnamese and Thai. While English has a separate, productive piece of morphology (*-ed*) to indicate that an event or state obtained in the past, Chinese, Vietnamese, and Thai do not. This of course does not mean that these speakers have no concept of past; it is just expressed differently. The interpretation of a past event or state is based on the overt aspectual marking, time adverbials and monitoring of the discourse context.

Finally, let us take an example from lexical semantics. In English, verbs that express psychological states can appear with a Theme subject and an Experiencer object, as in (6) while in Chinese this usage is not possible, as (7) illustrates.

(6) The book disappointed Mary.

(7) *Nei ben shu shiwang le ZhangSan
    that CL book disappoint PERF Zhang San
    "That book disappointed Zhang San."

Of course, Chinese can express a similar meaning, but with another construction (Juffs, 1996). However, this gap in argument structures presents difficulties for L2 acquisition: in learning English, Chinese speakers have to learn the availability of constructions such as (6); in learning Chinese, English speakers have to de-learn, or acquire the fact that (7) is unavailable.

To recapitulate, most of the language variation in meaning, then, is found at the lexicon–syntax and at the syntax–semantics interfaces. Linguistic semantics is the study of the interface between conceptual structures and linguistic form. The operations at the interface are non-trivial computations. When learning a second language, a speaker may be confronted with different mappings between units of meaning on the conceptual level and units of syntactic structure.

Data and common elicitation measures

Before we look at concrete linguistic properties and their acquisition, a few remarks on the type of elicitation procedures used in this area of L2 acquisition are in order. How do we gain access to the linguistic interpretations learners attribute to input strings? The tasks for studying interpretive properties have evolved from the staple grammaticality judgment tasks assumed to be the main tool of the generative linguist. Most of the studies looking at L2 semantics use the Truth Value Judgment Task (TVJT) (Crain and McKee, 1985), especially versions adapted to the needs of adult L2 acquisition. In a TVJT, a story is supplied, sometimes in the native language of the learners to establish clear and unambiguous context.[7] A test sentence in the target language appears below the story. Learners are asked to judge whether the test sentence is appropriate, or fits (describes) the story well. Participants answer with Yes or No, True or False. Some test sentences are ambiguous so a story supplies only one of their two available interpretations; in such a case, those sentences appear under another story as well, supporting their second interpretation. Typically, stories and test sentences are squared in a 2 × 2 design, giving a quadruple of story–test sentence combinations, as illustrated below (Figure 8.2):

	Meaning 1	Meaning 2
Test sentence 1	√	√
Test sentence 2	√	*

Below is a quadruple of story–test sentence combinations from Slabakova (2003). The experiment investigates whether speakers of English know that a bare infinitive such as *eat* must refer to a complete event (*I saw him eat a cake*), while the gerund *eating* only refers to the process and need not refer to a complete event (*I saw him eating a cake*, see more on this study later on in this chapter). For lack of space, each story is followed by the two sentences here, but in the actual test each story-sentence pairing is judged on its own.

(9) Matt had an enormous appetite. He was one of those people who could eat a whole cake at one sitting. But these days he is much more careful what he eats. For example, yesterday he bought a chocolate and vanilla ice cream cake, but ate only half of it after dinner. I know, because I was there with him.

I observed Matt eat a cake.   True   (False)

I observed Matt eating a cake.   (True)   False

Alicia is a thin person, but she has an astounding capacity for eating big quantities of food. Once when I was at her house, she took a whole ice cream cake out of the freezer and ate it all. I almost got sick, just watching her.

I watched Alicia eat a cake.   (True)   False

I watched Alicia eating a cake.   (True)   False

The first story in the quadruple in (9) presents an unfinished event (the cake was half-eaten); consequently, only the sentence with the gerund describes it correctly; the sentence with the bare infinitive should be rejected by a speaker who knows the two meanings. The second story in (9) represents a complete event, so both the test sentence with a bare infinitive and the one with a gerund are true. Note that all the test sentences are grammatical under *some* interpretation in the target language, so learners are not invited to think about the form of the sentences but just to consider their meaning. Nevertheless, this task reveals much about the learners' grammars, and more specifically, about the interpretations they map onto linguistic expressions. Its main advantage is that learners do not access metalinguistic knowledge that may be due to language instruction but rather engage their true linguistic competence.

Another advantage of the TVJT is that it does away with judgment preference, since the expected answer is categorically True or False, and never both. In this respect, it is interesting to note that White *et al.* (1997), investigating the interpretation of reflexives in French-English and Japanese-English interlanguage, addressed the methodological question of which task, a TVJT or a picture selection task, better represented the interlanguage competence of the learners. Take the example in (10).

(10)   Mary$_i$ showed Susan$_j$ a portrait of herself$_{i/j}$

If we have to find out whether learners interpret *herself* to refer to *Mary* or to *Susan*, or possibly to either one, we can test their interpretation with a picture selection task.[8] Participants would be offered a picture in which Mary is showing Susan a prominent portrait of Susan, and a sentence underneath it like the one in (10) without the indexes. Participants have to indicate whether what is going on in the picture matches the sentence. If the learners allow *Susan*, the object of the sentence, and the reflexive to co-refer, they will answer positively. The same sentence will appear under another picture (not side by side but at another location in the test), this time of Mary showing Susan a portrait of Mary, to check whether learners allow binding to subject. It has been noticed (see White *et al.*, 1997, p. 148 for discussion) that these picture-selection tests reflect, for the most part, the linguistic preferences of the learners. In the case of (10), for example, learners prefer to interpret the reflexive as co-referring with the subject and not the object. This does not mean that the other interpretation is missing from their grammar, but it does mean that experimental results capturing this preference actually underestimate the learners' competence. White *et al.* (1997) used both a picture task and a TVJT. Results showed that both native speakers and L2 learners were significantly more consistent in accepting local objects as reflexive antecedents on the TVJT. Since the two tasks are arguably tapping the same linguistic competence, it is clear that the TVJT better deals with licit but dispreferred interpretations of ambiguous sentences, disposing of preferences to a larger degree. However, when we are not dealing with interpretive preferences, the picture selection task is appropriate and very useful for its clarity (see successful application of this task by Hirakawa, 1999; Inagaki, 2001; Montrul, 2000, and White *et al.*, 1999).

A third type of task tapping interpretive judgments (pioneered in Slabakova, 2001, but see also Gabriele and Martohardjono, 2005; Gabriele *et al.*, 2003; Montrul and Slabakova, 2002) is a sentence conjunction judgment task, in which the participants are asked to decide whether the two clauses in a complex sentence go well together or not. For example, take the sentences in (11).

(11)   a.   Allison worked in a bakery and made cakes.
       b.   Allison worked in a bakery and made a cake.

The first clause presents context and the felicity of combination of the first and the second clause is being judged. The two clauses in (11a) are a good fit because they represent two habitual activities, while the pairing in (11b) is less felicitous because a habitual and a one-time event are combined. This task could be used in learning situations where the TVJT is not appropriate, although the TVJT is superior to it because it establishes the context in a clearer way.

A fourth type of interpretation task (used in Gürel, 2006; Kanno, 1997; Slabakova, 2005) presents the learners with a test sentence and spells out the three (or more) interpretations, as the example in (12) from Kanno (1997, p. 269) illustrates. In this case, the instructions made clear that participants were allowed to choose both (a) and (b) as possible answers, if this seemed appropriate.

(12) Dare$_i$-ga [pro$_i$ kuruma-o katta to] itta no?
      who-NOM car-ACC bought that said Q
      "Who$_i$ said (he$_i$) bought a car?"

      (a) the same person as *dare*
      (b) another person

This task is also less effective than the TVJT because learners may find it more difficult to externalize how they interpret a particular structure. In a way, this task expects them *to think* about the meaning of the test sentence and then choose from a couple of provided interpretations, while the TVJT allows them to focus on the story context and then judge the test sentence in a more natural way, abstracting away from its grammatical form. However, Gürel (2006) used this task in conjunction with the TVJT to find out whether her learners allowed pronominal elements to be ambiguous, and her findings on the two tasks were similar, suggesting that her learners were able to overcome the problems mentioned above.

In summary, versions of these four tasks are predominantly used in the L2 literature to probe semantic interpretations. I have argued that the best one is the written TVJT with answers of True and False. Whenever test sentences are not ambiguous, the picture selection task is useful, followed by the sentence conjunction judgment task, and the multiple choice of explicitly spelled-out interpretations task.

Acquisition of lexical meaning

In this section, we turn to explorations of lexical semantic acquisition, both from the point of view of generative grammar and of cognitive semantics. Generative studies of lexical semantics explore the relationship between argument structure, lexical meaning and overt syntax. The theoretical foundation for much of this work is the semantic decomposition of lexical items into primitives or conceptual categories such as Thing, Event, State, Path, Place, Property, Manner (Grimshaw, 1990; Jackendoff, 1990; Pinker, 1989) and linking rules between arguments and thematic roles (Levin and Rappaport Hovav, 1995). In the mapping from the lexicon to syntax, there is a logical problem of L2 acquisition (Juffs, 1996; Montrul, 2001a): L2 learners have to discover the possible mappings between meaning and form in the absence of abundant evidence. There is rarely one-to-one relationship between syntactic frames and available meanings. Though some mappings may be universal, there is a lot of cross-linguistic variation in this respect. To take an example from the English double-object and dative alternation, it may seem that the two syntactic frames that alternate are completely semantically equivalent, but it is not really so.

(13) a. Mary sent the package to John. (Dative syntactic frame)
      b. Mary sent the package to Chicago.
      c. Mary sent John the package. (Double Object syntactic frame)
      d. *Mary sent Chicago the package.

In the double-object frame, it is necessary that at the end of the event, the Goal is actually in possession of the Theme, *the package*. While this is possible in the case of a Goal such as *John*, it is not possible for a Goal such as the city of *Chicago*. Furthermore, it is not the case that every verb that can take a dative argument alternates:

(14) *Sam pushed Molly the package.

For these reasons, it is very easy to overgeneralize lexical alternations and conflation patterns that appear in the native language, and it is not obvious how learners can retract from such overgeneralizations.

Such research questions inspired a lot of experimental studies in the 1980s and through the early 2000s. Mazurkewich (1984), White (1987), Bley-Vroman and Yoshinaga (1992), and Whong-Barr and Schwartz (2002) studied the dative-double object alternations. Findings of these studies are largely consistent with the claim that L2 learners initially adopt L1 argument structures. Cross-linguistic differences in conflation patterns (i.e., what primitives of meaning are conflated in a verb) as studied by Talmy and also illustrated by the Chinese and English examples in (6) and (7) were taken up by Juffs (1996) and Inagaki (2001). Juffs tested Chinese native speakers learning English in China on acceptance and production of psychological, causative, and locative verbs that do not have an equivalent in Chinese. He related these three types of verbs to a lexical conflation parameter. Results suggest that learners at low to advanced levels of proficiency are sensitive to the conflation pattern of English, having acquired structures unavailable in their native language. Inagaki (2001) is a bidirectional (English to Japanese and Japanese to English) study of motion verbs with Goal PPs. Using the same test in both learning directions, a picture followed by sentences to be judged for appropriateness, Inagaki found that there is evidence for directional differences in acquiring L2 conflation patters. English learners of Japanese overgeneralize their native pattern, which is unavailable in Japanese, but Japanese learners of English have no trouble learning the new pattern on the basis of positive evidence. While supporting L1 transfer in learning lexical form-meaning mappings, such results also highlight the issue of the availability of negative evidence in L2 acquisition.

Hirakawa (1999) tested knowledge of the unaccusative-unergative verb distinction[9] in the interlanguage of Chinese and English native speakers learning Japanese, using a TVJT with pictures. One of the properties she investigated was whether learners are aware of the fact that combined with unaccusative verbs, the adverb *takusan* "a lot" modifies the Theme, or underlying object, while combined with unergative verbs, the adverb modifies the Agent, or underlying subject. Again as in Juffs' and Inagaki's studies, the findings indicated successful acquisition. Finally, in a series of studies, Montrul (2000, 2001b) studied transitivity (the causative-inchoative) alternations as signaled by inflectional morphology in L2 Turkish, Spanish and English. The gist of her findings is that argument structure alternations are crucially dependent on argument-change signaling morphology. Learners who speak a language where alternations are overtly marked in the morphology (a suffix signaling the causative in Turkish, a clitic signaling the inchoative Spanish) are more sensitive to these alternations in a second language than learners whose native language has no overt morphological reflex of the alternation (English). These findings suggest that overt morphology facilitates the acquisition of argument structure alternations, highlighting the logical problem of lexical meaning acquisition in some languages that are poor in such morphology.

Within cognitive semantics, the influential work of Talmy (1991, 2000) has provided inspiration for much L2 acquisition research. Talmy (1991) suggests that languages can be divided into two typological groups depending on how Path of motion is lexicalized: in the verb (verb-framed) or outside the verb (satellite-framed).

(14)　Tama-ga saka-o kudaru
　　　 Ball-Nom hill-Acc descend
　　　 "The ball descends the slope"

(15)　The ball rolls down the hill.

In (14), a prototypical example from Japanese, Path is lexicalized in the verb *kudaru* "descend." In (15), a corresponding prototypical example from English, Path is lexicalized in the so-called "satellite," the verb particle *down*. The reader should be reminded of a very similar property tested by Inagaki (2001). It is important to note a significant difference: while generative studies on lexical meaning typically employ experimental methods for assessing comprehension, cognitive semantics studies typically scrutinize language production, either elicited or from corpora. In a series of studies, Cadierno and colleagues (Cadierno, 2004, 2008; Cadierno and Robinson, 2009; Cadierno and Ruiz, 2006) investigate this type of lexicalization pattern in L2 English and L2 Spanish by learners speaking typologically similar and typologically different languages. Findings indicate that even though intermediate and advanced L2 learners are generally able to develop the appropriate L2 lexicalization patterns, they still seem to exhibit some L1 transfer effects. In particular, in Cadierno and Robinson (2009), the two groups of learners (Danish-to English and Japanese-to-English) demonstrated possible successful acquisition, L1 effects, as well as some effects of task complexity. Brown and Gullberg (2010) argue that learning a second language affects the lexicalization pattern employed in the native language, so language transfer is not only unidirectional.

In a corpus-based study, Lemmens and Perez (2010) investigate the use of Dutch posture verbs (equivalents of *stand, lie* and *sit*) by French learners of Dutch. The authors come to the conclusion that the interlanguage system should be treated as a linguistic system in its own right, and that it shows both errors due to L1 transfer, in this case underuse of posture verbs, as well as errors due to overextension of the pattern that learners have acquired in the target language. Looking at the usage of similar verbs (*put* versus *set/lay*) in speech analysis as well as in gesture, Gullberg (2009) employed an elicited production task of describing placing events that English-native learners of Dutch have just seen on video. Their production was video-recorded. Gullberg also argues that her subjects show some sensitivity to the target semantic patterns of the L2.

In sum, research within cognitive linguistics more often scrutinizes production rather than measures comprehension as generative lexical semantic research does. Nevertheless, both research traditions come to very similar conclusions: lexical semantics presents significant difficulties to L2 learners when they have to restructure their lexical knowledge; however, these difficulties are not insurmountable and successful acquisition is attested.

Acquisition of sentence-level meaning

In their search of L2 (grammatical) meaning, learners can encounter complete overlap of L1 and L2 syntactic and conceptual structures. They can also encounter differences in interpretation which are due *only* to syntactic differences. I will illustrate with a property from French, which allows the interrogative *combien* "how many" to form either continuous or discontinuous constituents with its restriction *de livres* "of books" (Dekydtspotter, 2001; Dekydtspotter et al., 2001).

(16) Combien de livres est-ce que les étudiants achètent tous?
      how many of books is it that the students buy all
      "How many books are the students all buying?"

(17) Combien est-ce que les étudiants achètent tous de livres?
      how many is it that the students buy all of books
      "How many books are the students all buying?"

Although the questions in (16) and (17) look much alike, considering that French allows discontinuous constituents, their interpretive differences are reflected in the possible answers to them. Let us consider the following situation. There are two French students studying English literature, Jerome and Jacqueline, and they are buying a number of English books, with some overlapping titles. Jerome is buying *Moby Dick, Little Women,* and *The Age of Innocence,* while Jacqueline is buying *Moby Dick, Little Women,* and *The Scarlet Letter.* In this situation, one can truthfully answer both (16) and (17) with "three," that is, Jerome is buying three books and Jacqueline is buying three books. This is known as the distributive (books per student) answer. However, (16) can also be answered with "two," because there are two books that both Jerome and Jacqueline are buying in common, namely *Moby Dick,* and *Little Women.* This answer is known as the common answer. The discontinuous *combien* question in (17), however, cannot receive the common answer, only the distributive answer.

The explanation of these interpretive differences involves the interaction of the universal rules of semantic calculation and some language-specific syntactic properties of the French sentence. For example, French allows quantifiers such as *combien* "how many" to be displaced from its restriction *de livres* "of books." Note that this property is not difficult to deduce, since it is reflected in the word order of French questions, and in particular, in the word order of the test sentences in the experiment.

In order to test knowledge of this extremely subtle contrast, Dekydtspotter (2001) followed the trade-mark experimental designs of these researchers, namely, stories in the L1 of the learners, followed by a question and an answer in French. The participants had to indicate whether the supplied answer was appropriate for the question and the story. The quadruple design was implemented, wherein continuous and discontinuous questions were paired with distributive and common answers. Results showed that distributive answers were overwhelmingly preferred by the native speakers (see Dekydtspotter, 2001 for an explanation of this fact in terms of parsing complexity measured by the number of reanalysis steps that each interpretation necessitates). However, even with the depressed acceptance of the common answers, the native speakers demonstrated a significant contrast between continuous and discontinuous constructions, and between the two meanings paired with the discontinuous questions. The same crucial contrast appeared in the performance of the advanced learners. Results for the intermediate learners revealed a thoroughly different pattern. First of all, they did not show the expected contrast between the two interpretations of discontinuous interrogative and their means were in the wrong direction: higher acceptance for common answers. Secondly, they clearly preferred continuous interrogatives, probably because discontinuous interrogatives were not yet part of their (productive) grammar. Thus the relevant interpretive asymmetry was not attested in the grammar of intermediate French learners but was attested in the grammar of native speakers and advanced learners.

In sum, the interpretive mismatch exemplified above and those used in other experiments are based on quite complex syntax, in the sense that sentences involve less frequent constructions (double genitives in Dekydtspotter *et al.*, 1997; discontinuous constituents in Dekydtspotter and Sprouse, 2001; quantifiers at a distance in Dekydtspotter *et al.*, 1999/2000, scrambling[10] in Hopp, 2007; Song and Schwartz, 2009; Unsworth, 2005, etc.). Very often the native speakers in these experiments show far lower than the acceptance rates we are used to seeing in the L2 literature. In many cases, there are alternative ways of articulating the same message, making the tested constructions dispreferred. In most cases, the properties are not supported by positive evidence in the input; in other words, they present a poverty of the stimulus learning situations. However, at the syntax-semantics interface, these same properties do not present much difficulty, as there are no mismatches. Once learners have acquired the relevant functional lexicon item and have constructed the right sentence representation, the presence or absence of semantic interpretation follows straightforwardly without any more stipulations. In most studies[11] investigating such learning situations, learners demonstrate that a contrast exists in their grammar between the allowed and disallowed interpretations.

In contrast, the other learning situation that arises in acquiring L2 meanings is not characterized by poverty of the stimulus. The syntactic structure presents less difficulty to the learners. Quite often, these studies deal with properties related to truth-conditional meanings of common morphological forms, like the preterite and imperfect tenses in Spanish-English interlanguage (Montrul and Slabakova, 2002, 2003; Slabakova and Montrul, 2003), progressive tenses in Japanese-English interlanguage (Gabriele, 2005), reflexive pronouns in Japanese/French-English interlanuaage (White *et al.*, 1997), aspect-marking in Bulgarian-English (Slabakova, 2001) and English-Russian (Slabakova, 2005) interlanguage, article semantics in Korean/Russian-English interlanguage (Ionin *et al.*, 2004). Not surprisingly, native speakers in these experiments show the regular range of accuracy in the study of L2 acquisition (80–90 percent). The learning challenges lie, however, at the syntax-semantics mapping. Learners have to figure out what morphological forms are mapped onto what meanings in the target language, since there is no one-to-one correspondence at the syntax-semantics interface. When we consider results at all levels of proficiency from beginner to near-native, what crystallizes is that knowledge of these properties emerges gradually but surely. I will illustrate this learning situation with an aspectual syntax-semantics mismatch between Bulgarian and English.

Slabakova (2003) investigates linguistic properties related to grammatical aspect. English differs from German, Romance, and Slavic with respect to the semantics of the present tense, which can denote a present habit but not an ongoing event, see examples in (18).

(18)   a.   *She eats an apple right now.   #Ongoing event
       b.   She is eating an apple right now.   Ongoing event
       c.   She eats an apple (every day).   Habitual series of complete events

Furthermore, the English bare infinitive denotes not only the processual part of an event but includes the completion of that event.

(19)   a.   I saw Mary cross the street.   (completion entailed)
       b.   I saw Mary crossing the street.   (no completion entailed)

In trying to explain the facts illustrated in (18)–(19), many researchers have noticed that English verbal morphology is impoverished. For example, lexical roots such as *dress* or *play* can be verbs or nouns. The experimental study adopts Giorgi and Pianesi's (1997) proposal. English verbs, they argue, are "naked" forms that can express several verbal values, such as the bare infinitive, the first- and second-person singular, and the first- second- and third-person plural. Giorgi and Pianesi (1997) propose that verbs are categorially disambiguated in English by being marked in the lexicon with the aspectual feature [+perf], standing for "perfective." In Romance, Slavic, and other Germanic languages, on the other hand, all verbal forms have to be inflected for person, number, and tense. Thus, nouns and verbs cannot have the same forms. Bulgarian verbs are associated with typical verbal features as [+V, person, number] and they are recognizable and learnable as verbs because of these features. Bulgarian verbs are therefore not associated with a [+perf] feature. Consequently, Bulgarian equivalents to bare infinitives do not entail completion of the event, as (20) illustrates.

(20) Ivan vidja Maria da presiča ulicata.   (no completion entailed)
     Ivan saw Maria to cross street-DET
     "John saw Mary crossing the street."

Thus, Bulgarian and English exhibit a contrast in grammatical aspect. In the acquisition of English by Bulgarian native speakers, then, the learning task is to notice the trigger of this property: the fact that English inflectional morphology is highly impoverished, lacking many person–number–tense verb endings. The property itself, if Giorgi and Pianesi are correct, is the [+perf] feature that is attached to English eventive verbs in the lexicon. Knowledge of this property will entail knowledge of four different interpretive facts: (1) bare verb forms denote a completed event; (2) present tense has only habitual interpretation; (3) the progressive affix is needed for ongoing interpretation of eventive verbs; (4) states in the progressive denote temporary states. This is a syntax-semantics mismatch that relates a minimal difference between languages—the presence or absence of a feature in the lexicon—to various and superficially not connected interpretive properties. Importantly, of the four semantic properties enumerated above, the second, third, and fourth are introduced, discussed, and drilled in language classrooms, but the first one is not explicitly taught.

A hundred and twelve Bulgarian learners of English took part in the experiment, as well as 24 native speaker controls. All participants completed a production task to ascertain knowledge of inflectional morphology and a Truth Value Judgment Task with a story in their native language and a test sentence in English. Example (9) above illustrates a test quadruple.

Results on the acquisition of all four semantic properties pattern in the same way: initial L1 transfer and subsequent successful acquisition are clearly attested in the data. Advanced learners are even more accurate than native speakers in their knowledge that an English bare verb denotes a complete event, knowledge that cannot be transferred from the L1, as example (20) indicates. Considering the impact of the instruction variable, analysis of variance indicated that all groups performed equally well on all conditions. The theoretical implication of this finding is that all semantic effects of learning the trigger (English verbs are morphologically impoverished) and the related property ([+perf] feature attached to verbs in the lexicon) appear to be engaged at the same time. Even untaught syntax-semantics mismatches are learnable to a native-like level.

In this section, illustrative studies of two types of learning situations were reviewed. These are representative of a range of recent studies on the L2 acquisition of the syntax-semantics interface (for an extensive review, see Slabakova, 2006, 2008). Importantly, both types of studies attest to the fact that acquisition of meaning is not problematic in the second language, once the inflectional morphology is learned (see the Bottleneck Hypothesis presented in the next section).

Applications

It is fairly common to assert that the generative approach to L2 acquisition does not really have any predictions to make about teaching a language. As a cognitive discipline within a theoretical perspective inherently not interested in the process of instructed learning, this approach has frequently turned its attention to the L2 acquisition of subtle phenomena that are never discussed in language classrooms and that, in some cases, language teachers have no explicit knowledge of. Generative studies of L2 acquisition rarely incorporate classroom instruction as part of their design, the studies by White and colleagues (White, 1991) are a notable exception. Thus, it is generally believed that the generative framework has nothing valuable to offer to language teachers. In a break with tradition, however, I argue that the recent generative L2 research does have a pedagogical implication.

In this chapter, it was argued that the meaning computation mechanism is universal and should come for free in second language acquisition, transferred from the native language or Universal Grammar. What is to be learned then, and what should our instructional effort focus on? In both learning situations outlined above, the road to meaning passes through grammatical (inflectional) morphology and its features. In the French *combien* questions (Dekydtspotter, 2001; Dekydtspotter *et al.*, 2001), idiosyncratic properties of French inflectional morphology allow the possibility of discontinuous syntax, which in turn allows the different interpretations of the continuous and discontinuous *combien* questions. In the Bulgarian-English grammatical aspect contrast (Slabakova, 2003), the analysis argues for a [+perf] feature of English bare verbs, absent in the Bulgarian grammar, which brings forward the various interpretive differences between the two languages. Based on such considerations, Slabakova (2008) formulates the Bottleneck Hypothesis, which states that inflectional morphemes and their formal features present the most formidable challenge to learners while syntax and phrasal semantics pose less difficulty. The inflectional morphemes carry the features that are responsible for syntactic and semantic differences among languages of the world, so it is logical that once these morphemes and their features are acquired, the other linguistic properties (word order, interpretation, etc) would follow smoothly. The numerous empirical studies on the L2 acquisition of semantic properties, including the ones summarized in this chapter, indicate that there is no critical period for the acquisition of meaning (Slabakova, 2006). If inflectional morphology is the real bottleneck of L2 acquisition, what are the implications for teaching second languages?

In language classrooms, teaching techniques that emphasize communicative competence (Canale and Swain, 1980; Savignon, 1983) are very popular these days. Such techniques encourage learners to use context, world knowledge, argument structure templates, and other pragmatic strategies to comprehend the message, capitalizing on the fact that learners almost certainly use their expectations of what is said to choose between alternative parses of a sentence. In fact, Clahsen and Felser's (2006) Shallow Structure Hypothesis proposes that context, pragmatic knowledge, and argument structure are the only processing strategies available to adult learners. However, many second language researchers question the direct connection between comprehending the L2 message and figuring out how the L2 syntax works (Cook, 1996, p. 76; Gass and Selinker, 2008, p. 376). It is believed that some attention to, or focus on, *grammatical form* is beneficial and necessary for successful learning. In this respect, communicative competence approaches—with their exclusion of focus on form—may not be the best way to accomplish the ultimate goal of second language learning: building a mental grammar of the target language.

The Bottleneck Hypothesis supports such a conclusion and endorses increased emphasis on practicing grammar in the classroom, of course combined with other communication-based classroom activities. The functional morphology in a language has some visible and some hidden characteristics. It may have phonetic form, and if it does, its distribution is in evidence and learnable. Secondly, it carries syntactic features that are responsible for the behavior of other, possibly displaced elements and phrases in the sentence. Thirdly, it carries one or more universal units of meaning. While the first trait of functional morphology is observable from the linguistic input, the second and third characteristics may not be so easy to detect. The inflectional morphology presents considerable difficulty and leaves residual problems even in very advanced speakers, although there is a huge amount of evidence for it in the input to which the learners are exposed. On the other hand, semantic properties of the sort discussed in this chapter, that learners and teachers are not aware of and that are certainly obscure, are acquired without a problem. This discrepancy powers the Bottleneck Hypothesis. It is suggested here that practicing the inflectional morphology in language classrooms should happen in meaningful, plausible sentences where the syntactic effects and the semantic import of the morphology are absolutely transparent and non-ambiguous. Some controlled repetition of the inflectional morphology is inevitable if the form has to move from the declarative to the procedural memory[12] of the learner and then get sufficiently automatic for easy lexical access. Practicing inflectional morphology in context should be very much like lexical learning (because it *is* lexical learning), and, as everybody who has tried to learn a second language as an adult (or even a teenager) knows, no pain—no gain. This claim is obviously not new. Although rooted in a different theoretical foundation, the Bottleneck Hypothesis is akin in its pedagogical implications to the Focus on Form approach (Doughty, 2001; papers in Doughty and Williams, 1998), the Input Processing theory of VanPatten (1996, 2007, Chapter 16, this volume) and the Skill Acquisition theory of DeKeyser (1997, 2007).

Furthermore, we have been discussing ambiguous and polysemous morphemes in this chapter (for more discussion of the syntax-morphology interface, see Lardiere, Chapter 7, this volume, and Lardiere, 2009). Some meanings encoded in a morpheme appear with less frequency in the input, or in a more complex combination with other morphemes and lexical items. For example the progressive form *be* + *-ing* has the common "ongoing" meaning, but it denotes a "temporary state" when combined with a stative verb, the latter meaning being rarer in the input. Hence, the second morpheme meaning needs a clear presentation in disambiguating context and subsequent practice in addition to the first meaning. It is also important for teachers to highlight the connection between the two or more meanings, both in presentation and in practice. For this reason, teachers must be appropriately trained to be aware of grammatical morpheme polysemy (see also Lardiere, Chapter 7, this volume). Importantly, in acquisition research as well as in language teaching, we should always think of a morpheme as having phonetic form, carrying syntactic features and denoting potentially more than one meaning.

Future directions

Depending on the theoretical model, information structure (a.k.a. new and old information, topic and focus, theme and rheme) falls within the provenance of semantics (as in Jackendoff, 2002) or is at the syntax-pragmatics interface (as in Reinhart, 2006). Acquisition of the way the target language marks topic and focus is one of the hottest topics in current generative SLA research. The concepts of topic and focus are universal but languages may use word order, clitic-doubling, intonation, or a combination of all these to mark them. The logical prediction is that successful acquisition will be possible, as with the acquisition of purely semantic properties. Very recent work by Valenzuela (2006), Ivanov (2009), and Fruit Bell (2009) suggests that this is indeed the case.

However, a recent version of the Interface Hypothesis (Tsimpli and Sorace, 2006) proposes a principled distinction between internal interfaces, those between narrow syntax and the other linguistic modules (phonology, morphology, semantics) and external interfaces, those between syntax and other cognitive modules. As a primary example of such an external interface, researchers have concentrated on the syntax-discourse/pragmatics interface. The claim is that this interface is the major source of difficulty, causing delays in L1 acquisition, failure in bilingual and L2 acquisition, as well as indeterminacy of judgments and residual optionality even at near-native levels of acquisition. Research has supported this claim mostly with data on syntactic and discourse constraints on the usage of null subjects (Belletti *et al.*, 2007). It remains an open question, however, whether this theoretical proposal can be substantiated with data from other phenomena at the syntax-discourse interface and not just null subject use.

A fascinating research question at the syntax-semantics interface is to compare and contrast child L1, child L2, and adult L2 acquisition of semantic properties. A recent experimental study, Song and Schwartz (2009), investigates the development of Korean *wh*-constructions with negative polarity items (e.g., *anyone*) in these three populations and finds similar developmental paths. The authors argue that their findings militate against the Fundamental Difference Hypothesis (Bley-Vroman, 1990, see also *Studies in Second Language Acquisition* 2009 special issue). More generally speaking, whenever a specific property becomes part of the child grammar rather late (for example, scrambling is acquired at the age of 7 to 9), the question arises of whether this is due to some cognitive delay in child development or to difficulties in processing the specific construction. Comparing the ways children and adults acquire the same construction can tease these two explanations apart, because adults are already completely cognitively developed. If research finds a similar developmental pattern in children and adult L2 learners, then only processing remains as a viable explanation (Schwartz, 2003; Unsworth, 2005).

The final research question that I offer here concerns the relative difficulty of acquiring a meaning that is signaled by context versus the same meaning signaled by inflectional morphology. Let us take the example of tense marking in Mandarin Chinese, Vietnamese, or Thai introduced earlier. The meaning of past event or state has to be expressed in any language. While the English learner is exposed to (roughly) one meaning reflected in one morpheme (if we disregard irregular verbs), the Mandarin, Vietnamese, and Thai learner has to pay attention to context and the various lexical means of marking temporality. It is logical to predict that the English learner would arrive at a form-meaning mapping sooner and more easily than the Mandarin/Vietnamese/Thai learner. On the other hand, beginning learners of languages with tense morphology go through a stage where they use lexical means (such as adverbs and adverbial phrases) before they start utilizing the morphological means of tense marking (Dietrich *et al.*, 1995). This fact suggests that lexical marking of tense may be easier. This remains one of the many intriguing puzzles at the interface between morphosyntax and semantics that awaits its researchers.

Notes

* I am grateful to Susan Gass and Alison Mackey for inviting me to contribute to this handbook and for editing suggestions. Thanks go to all my students at the University of Iowa for being interested in and enthusiastic about generative L2A, and for asking hard questions. I am especially grateful to Jacee Cho and Tania Leal Mendez for reading and commenting on this chapter.

1 The context or the rest of the sentence will disambiguate: *Jane ate meat last night* versus *Jane ate meat when she was younger.*

2 I am abstracting away from pragmatic meaning, which is arguably regulated by a different module of the language architecture (Reinhart, 2006). See Bardovi-Harlig's chapter on the L2 acquisition of pragmatics, Chapter 9, this volume.

3 Jackendoff's Conceptual Semantics (Jackendoff, 1972, 1983, 1990) is another decompositional theory of meaning. Since the meaning of the sentence is composed from word meanings, a good deal of attention is

paid to lexical semantics in his approach. See his language architecture proposal later in this section. Other influential approaches in this vein include Pustejovsky's Generative Lexicon (Pustejovsky, 1995) and Role and Reference Grammar (Van Valin, 2005).

4 For a good introduction to cognitive semantics, see Chapter 11 in Saeed (2009).

5 For more discussion on this topic, see Slabakova (2008), Chapter 2.

6 Lexical items contain the same three structures, CS, SS, and PS, in miniature.

7 Dekydtspotter and Sprouse pioneered the presentation of the story in the native language, see also Borgonovo et al., 2006; Gürel, 2006; and Slabakova, 2003.

8 See a different version of this task in Belletti et al. (2007), where one test sentence appears above three pictures illustrating three different interpretations.

9 Unaccusative verbs are intransitive verbs whose only argument is a Theme, or underlying object (e.g., *fall, arrive*), while unergative verbs are intransitives with an Agent argument (e.g., *laugh, sneeze*).

10 "Scrambling" involves the displacement of constituents from their usual position in the sentence. It happens in languages without fixed word order and is determined mainly by pragmatic considerations such as topic and focus.

11 Hawkins and Hattori (2006) is an exception.

12 *Declarative* memory is the memory for repeatedly encountered facts and data such as who is president, what is the square root of 25, and where you were born. *Procedural* memory, by contrast, is memory for sequences of events, processes, and routines. Procedural memory is often not easily verbalized, but can be used without consciously thinking about it; procedural memory can reflect simple stimulus-response pairing or more extensive patterns learned over time. In contrast, declarative memory can generally be put into words.

References

Belletti, A., Bennati, E., and Sorace, A. (2007). Theoretical and developmental issues in the syntax of subjects: Evidence from near-native Italian. *Natural Language and Linguistic Theory*, *25*, 657–689.

Bley-Vroman, R. (1990). The logical problem of foreign language learning. *Linguistic Analysis*, *20*, 3–49.

Bley-Vroman, R. and Yoshinaga, N. (1992). Broad and narrow constraints on the English dative alternation: Some fundamental differences between native speakers and foreign language learners. *University of Hawai'i Working Papers in ESL*, *11*, 157–199.

Borgonovo, C., Bruhn de Garavito, L., and Prévost, P. (2006). Is the semantics/syntax interface vulnerable in L2 acquisition? Focus on mood distinctions in relative clauses in L2 Spanish. In V. Torrens and L. Escobar (Eds.), *The acquisition of syntax in romance languages* (pp. 353–369). Amsterdam: John Benjamins.

Brown, A. and Gullberg, M. (2010). Changes in encoding of Path of motion in a first language during acquisition of a second language. *Cognitive Linguistics*, *21*(2), 263–286.

Cadierno, T. (2004). Expressing motion events in a second language: A cognitive typological perspective. In M. Achard and S. Niemeier (Eds.), *Cognitive linguistics, second language acquisition and foreign language teaching* (pp. 13–49). Berlin: Mouton deGruyter.

Cadierno, T. (2008). Learning to talk about motion in a foreign language. In P. Robinson and N. C. Ellis (Eds.), *Handbook of cognitive linguistics and second language acquisition* (pp. 239–274). London: Routledge.

Cadierno, T. and Robinson, P. (2009). Language typology, task complexity and the development of L2 lexicalization patterns for describing motion events. *Annual Review of Cognitive Linguistics*, *7*, 245–276.

Cadierno, T. and Ruiz, L. (2006). Motion events in Spanish L2 acquisition. *Annual Review of Cognitive Linguistics*, *4*, 183–216.

Canale, M. and Swain, M. (1980). Theoretical bases of communicative approaches to second language teaching and testing. *Applied Linguistics*, *1*, 1–47.

Clahsen, H. and Felser, C. (2006). Grammatical processing in language learners. *Applied Psycholinguistics*, *27*, 3–42.

Cook, V. (1996). *Second language learning and language teaching* (Second Edition). London: Edward Arnold.

Crain, S. and McKee, C. (1985). The acquisition of structural restrictions on anaphora. In *Proceedings of NELS 16*, Amherst, MA: GLSA, University of Massachusetts.

DeKeyser, R. (1997). Beyond explicit rule learning: Automatizing second language morphosyntax. *Studies in Second Language Acquisition*, *19*, 195–221.

DeKeyser, R. (2007). Skill Acquisition Theory. In B. VanPatten and J. Williams (Eds.), *Theories in second language acquisition* (pp. 97–113). Mahwah, NJ: Erlbaum.

Dekydtspotter, L. (2001). Mental design and (second) language epistemology: Adjectival restrictions of *wh*-quantifiers and tense in English-French interlanguage. *Second Language Research, 17*, 1–35.

Dekydtspotter, L. and Sprouse, R. (2001). Mental design and (second) language epistemology: Adjectival restrictions of *wh*-quantifiers and tense in English-French interlanguage. *Second Language Research, 17*, 1–35.

Dekydtspotter, L., Sprouse, R., and Anderson, B. (1997). The Interpretive Interface in L2 Acquisition: The Process-Result Distinction in English-French Interlanguage Grammars. *Language Acquisition, 6*, 297–332.

Dekydtspotter, L., Sprouse, R., and Swanson, K. (2001). Reflexes of the mental architecture in Second Language Acquisition: The interpretation of discontinuous Combien extractions in English-French interlanguage. *Language Acquisition, 9*, 175–227.

Dekydtspotter, L., Sprouse, R., and Thyre, R. (1999/2000). The interpretation of quantification at a distance in English-French interlanguage: Domain-specificity and second language acquisition. *Language Acquisition,, 8*, 265–320.

Dietrich, R., Klein, W., and Noyau, C. (1995). *The acquisition of temporality in a second language*. Amsterdam: John Benjamins.

Doughty, C. (2001). Cognitive underpinnings of focus on form. In P. Robinson (Ed.), *Cognition and second language acquisition* (pp. 206–257). Cambridge: Cambridge University Press.

Doughty, C. and Williams, J. (Eds.) (1998). *Focus on form in classroom second language acquisition*. Cambridge: Cambridge University Press.

Fauconnier, G. (1994). *Mental spaces: Aspects of meaning construction in natural language* (Second Edition). Cambridge: Cambridge University Press.

Frege, G. (1884/1980). *The foundations of arithmetic*. Evanston, IL: Northwestern University Press.

Fruit Bell, M. (2009). Divergence at the syntax-discourse interface: Evidence from the L2 acquisition of contrastive focus in European Portuguese. In A. Pires and J. Rothman (Eds.), *Minimalist inquiries into child and adult language acquisition: Case studies across Portuguese* (pp. 197–219). Berlin: Mouton de Gruyter.

Gabriele, A. (2005). *The acquisition of aspect in a second language: a bidirectional study of learners of English and Japanese*. Unpublished PhD thesis. The City University of New York.

Gabriele, A. and Martohardjono, G. (2005). Investigating the role of transfer in the L2 acquisition of aspect. In L. Dekydtspotter *et al.* (Eds.), *Proceedings of the 7th generative approaches to second language acquisition conference (GASLA 2004)* (pp. 96–110). Sommerville, MA: Cascadilla Proceedings Project.

Gabriele, A., Martohardjono, G., and McClure, W. (2003). Why *dying* is just as difficult as *swimming* for Japanese learners of English. *ZAS Papers in Linguistics, 29*, 85–104.

Gass, S. and Selinker, L. (2008). *Second language acquisition: An introductory course*. New York and Abingdon: Routledge (Taylor and Francis).

Giorgi, A. and Pianesi, F. (1997). *Tense and aspect: From semantics to morphosyntax*. New York: Oxford University Press.

Grimshaw, J. (1990). *Argument structure*. Cambridge, MA: MIT Press.

Gullberg, M. (2009). Reconstructing verb meaning in a second language. How English speakers of L2 Dutch talk and gesture about placement. *Annual Review of Cognitive Linguistics, 7*, 221–244.

Gürel, A. (2006). L2 acquisition of pragmatic and syntactic constraints in the use of overt and null subject pronouns. In R. Slabakova, S. Montrul, and P. Prévost (Eds.), *Inquiries in linguistic development: Studies in honor of Lydia White* (pp. 259–282). Amsterdam: John Benjamins.

Hawkins, R. and Hattori, H. (2006).Interpretation of English multiple wh-questions by Japanese speakers: A missing uninterpretable feature account. *Second Language Research, 22*, 269–301.

Hirakawa, M. (1999). L2 acquisition of Japanese unaccusative verbs by speakers of English and Chinese. In K. Kanno (Ed.), *The acquisition of Japanese as a second language* (pp. 89–113). Amsterdam: John Benjamins.

Hoji, H. (1985). *Logical form constraints and configurational structures in Japanese*. Unpublished PhD dissertation. University of Washington.

Hopp, H. (2007). *Ultimate attainment at the interfaces in second language acquisition: Grammar and processing*. PhD dissertation. University of Groningen. Groningen Dissertations in Linguistics 65.

Inagaki, S. (2001). Motion verbs with goal PPs in the L2 acquisition of English and Japanese. *Studies in Second Language Acquisition, 23*, 153–170.

Ionin, T., Ko, H., and Wexler, K. (2004). Article semantics in L2 acquisition: The role of specificity. *Language Acquisition, 12*, 3–69.

Ivanov, I. (2009). *Second language acquisition of clitic doubling in L2 Bulgarian: A test case for the Interface Hypothesis*. Unpublished PhD dissertation. University of Iowa.

Jackendoff, R. (1972). *Semantic interpretation in generative grammar*. Cambridge, MA: MIT Press.

Jackendoff, R. (1983). *Semantics and cognition*. Cambridge, MA: MIT Press.

Jackendoff, R. (1990). *Semantic structures*. Cambridge, MA: MIT Press.

Jackendoff, R. (2002). *Foundations of language*. Oxford, UK: Oxford University Press.

Johnson, M. (1987), *The body in the mind: The bodily basis of meaning, imagination and reason*. Chicago, IL: University of Chicago Press.

Juffs, A. (1996). *Learnability and the lexicon: Theories and second language acquisition research*. John Benjamins: Amsterdam.

Kanno, K. (1997). The acquisition of null and overt pronominals in Japanese by English speakers. *Second Language Research, 13*, 299–321.

Katz, J. (1972). *Semantic theory*. New York: Harper and Row.

Katz, J. and Fodor, J. (1963). The structure of a semantic theory. *Language, 39*, 170–210.

Lakoff, G. (1993). The contemporary theory of metaphor. In A. Ortony (Ed.), *Metaphor and thought* (pp. 205–251). Cambridge: Cambridge University Press.

Langacker, R. (1993). Reference-point constructions. *Cognitive Linguistics, 4*, 1–38.

Langacker, R. (1999). *Grammar and conceptualization*. Berlin: Mouton de Gruyter.

Langacker, R. (2002). *Concept, image, symbol: The cognitive basis of grammar* (Second Edition). Berlin: Mouton de Gruyter.

Lardiere, D. (2009). Some thoughts on the contrastive analysis of features in second language acquisition. *Second Language Research, 25*, 173–227.

Lemmens, M. and Perez, J. (2010). On the use of posture verbs by French-speaking learners of Dutch: A corpus-based study. *Cognitive Linguistics, 20*(2), 315–347.

Levin, B. (1993). *English verb classes and alternations*. Chicago, IL: University of Chicago Press.

Levin, B. and Rappaport Hovav, M. (1995). *Unaccusativity: A the syntax-semantics interface*. Cambridge, MA: MIT Press.

Levin, B. and Rappaport Hovav, M. (2005). *Argument realization*. Cambridge: Cambridge University Press.

Mazurkewich, I. (1984) The acquisition of the dative alternation by second language learners and linguistic theory. *Language Learning, 34*, 91–109.

Montrul, S. (2000). Transitivity alternations in L2 acquisition: Toward a modular view of transfer. *Studies in Second Language Acquisition, 22*, 229–273.

Montrul, S. (2001a). Introduction. Special issue on the lexicon in SLA. *Studies in Second Language Acquisition, 23*, 145–151.

Montrul, S. (2001b). Agentive verbs of manner of motion in Spanish and English as a second language. *Studies in Second Language Acquisition, 23*, 171–206.

Montrul, S. and Slabakova, R. (2002). Acquiring morphosyntactic and semantic properties of preterite and imperfect tenses in L2 Spanish. In A. -T. Perez-Leroux and J. Liceras (Eds.), *The acquisition of Spanish morphosyntax: The L1–L2 connection* (pp. 113–149). Dordrecht: Kluwer.

Montrul, S. and Slabakova, R. (2003).Competence similarities between native and near-native speakers: An investigation of the preterite/imperfect contrast in Spanish. *Studies in Second Language Acquisition, 25*, 351–398.

Pinker, S. (1989). *Learnability and cognition: The acquisition of argument structure*. Cambridge, MA: MIT Press.

Portner, P. (2005). *What is meaning: Fundamentals of formal semantics*. Oxford: Blackwell.

Pustejovsky, J. (1995). *The generative lexicon*. Cambridge, MA: MIT Press.

Reinhart, T. (2006). *Interface strategies*. Cambridge, MA: MIT Press.

Saeed, J. (2009). *Semantics* (Third Edition). Chichester: Wiley-Blackwell.

Savignon, S. (1983). *Communicative competence: Theory and classroom practice*. Reading, MA: Addison-Wesley.

Schwartz, B. (2003). Child language acquisition: Paving the way. In B. Beachley, A. Brown, and F. Conlin (Eds.), *Proceedings of the 27th Boston University Conference on Language Development* (Vol. 1, pp. 26–50). Somerville, MA: Cascadilla Press.

Slabakova, R. (2001). *Telicity in the second language*. Amsterdam: John Benjamins.

Slabakova, R. (2003). Semantic Evidence for Functional Categories in Interlanguage Grammars. *Second Language Research, 19*(1), 42–75.

Slabakova, R. (2005). What is so difficult about telicity marking in L2 Russian? *Bilingualism: Language and Cognition, 8*(1), 63–77.

Slabakova, R. (2006). Is there a critical period for the acquisition of semantics. *Second Language Research, 22*(3), 302–338.

Slabakova, R. (2008). *Meaning in the second language*. Berlin: Mouton de Gruyter.

Slabakova, R. and Montrul, S. (2003). Genericity and aspect in L2 acquisition. *Language Acquisition*, *11*, 165–196.

Song, H. -S. and Schwartz, B. D. (2009).Testing the fundamental difference hypothesis: L2 adult, L2 child and L1 child comparisons in the acquisition of Korean wh-constructions with negative polarity items. *Studies in Second Language Acquisition, 31*, 323–361.

Talmy, L. (1985). Lexicalization patterns: Semantic structure in lexical forms. In T. Shopen (Ed.), *Language typology and syntactic description* (Vol. *3*, pp. 57–149). Cambridge: Cambridge University Press.

Talmy, L. (1991) Path to realization: A typology of event conflation. In *Proceedings of the 17th annual meeting of the Berkeley Linguistic Society* (pp. 480–519). Berkeley, CA: Berkeley Linguistic Society.

Talmy, L. (2000). *Toward a cognitive semantics* (Vol. *2*). Cambridge, MA: MIT Press.

Tsimpli, I. M. and Sorace, A. (2006). Differentiating interfaces: L2 performance in syntax-semantics and syntax-discourse phenomena. In D. Bamman, T. Magnitskaia, and C. Zaller (Eds.), *Proceedings of the 30th annual Boston University Conference on Language Development 30* (pp. 653–664). Somerville, MA: Cascadilla Press.

Unsworth, S. (2005). *Child L2, adult L2, child L1: Differences and similarities. A study on the acquisition of direct object scrambling in Dutch*. PhD dissertation. Utrecht University. Published by LOT, Trans 10, 3512 JK Utrecht, the Netherlands.

Valenzuela, E. (2006). L2 end state grammars and incomplete acquisition of Spanish CLLD constructions. In R. Slabakova, S. Montrul, and P. Prévost (Eds.), *Inquiries in linguistic development* (pp. 283–304). Amsterdam: John Benjamins.

Van Valin, R. (2005). *Exploring the syntax-semantics interface*. Cambridge: Cambridge University Press.

VanPatten, B. (1996). *Input processing and grammar instruction: Theory and research*. Norwood, NJ: Ablex.

VanPatten, B. (2007). Input processing in adult second language acquisition. In B. VanPatten and J. Williams (Eds.), *Theories in second language acquisition* (pp. 115–135). Mahwah, NJ: Lawrence Erlbaum Associates.

White, L. (1987). Markedness and second language acquisition: The question of transfer. *Studies in Second Language Acquisition, 9*, 261–286.

White, L. (1991). Adverb placement in second language acquisition: Some effects of positive and negative evidence in the classroom. *Second Language Research, 7*, 133–161.

White, L., Bruhn-Garavito, J., Kawasaki, T., Pater, J., and Prévost, P. (1997). The researcher gave the subject a test about himself: Problems of ambiguity and preference in the investigation of reflexive binding. *Language Learning, 47*, 145–172.

White, L., Brown, C., Bruhn de Graravito, J., Chen, D., Hirakawa, M. and Montrul, S. (1999). Psych verbs in second language acquisition. In G. Martohardjono and E. Klein (Eds.), *The development of second language grammars: A generative approach* (pp. 173–199). Amsterdam: John Benjamins.

Whong-Barr, M. and Schwartz, B. (2002). Morphological and syntactic transfer in child L2 acquisition of the English dative alternation. *Studies in Second Language Acquisition, 24*, 579–616.

9

Pragmatics in second language acquisition

Kathleen Bardovi-Harlig

Historical discussion

Interlanguage pragmatics, unlike other areas treated in this *Handbook*, can be related to second language acquisition (SLA), but also exists apart from SLA research. This chapter focuses on the intersection of pragmatics and SLA research. To this end, this section considers definitions of pragmatics as practiced in SLA, the development of interlanguage pragmatics and its affiliations with fields of inquiry in applied linguistics, and a brief history of pragmatics in SLA.

Definitions of pragmatics

Interlanguage pragmatics has been defined as "the study of non–native speakers' use and acquisition of L2 [second language] pragmatic knowledge" (Kasper, 1996, p. 145); however, the definitions of *pragmatics* used in L2 pragmatics have changed over the years. Levinson (1983) defined pragmatics as deixis, conversational implicature, presupposition, speech acts, and conversational structure. In practice, however, interlanguage pragmatics has focused largely on speech acts, with conversational structure and implicature trailing far behind and studies of deixis and presupposition rarely found. Interlanguage pragmatics has also included conversational management, discourse organization, and choice of address forms (Kasper and Dahl, 1991, p. 216), which are typically associated with sociolinguistics.

In their monograph on L2 pragmatic development, Kasper and Rose (2002) adopt definitions of pragmatics by Mey (1993) and Crystal (1997) which emphasize the social–interactional aspects of pragmatics: "the societally necessary and consciously interactive dimension of the study of language" (Mey, 1993, p. 315) and "the study of language from the point of view of users, especially of the choices they make, the constraints they encounter in using language in social interaction and the effects their use of language has on other participants in the act of communication" (Crystal, 1997, p. 301).

Affiliation of interlanguage pragmatics within applied linguistics

Although pragmatics is now considered an independent area of investigation in second language studies, it was originally affiliated with sociolinguistics. An early venue for L2 pragmatics papers was the Sociolinguistics and TESOL Colloquium, which began at the TESOL conference in 1980. Several of the papers in *Sociolinguistics and Language Acquisition*, the landmark book edited by

Wolfson and Judd (1983), came from the 1981 colloquium. Neither the foreword, preface, nor introduction mention *pragmatics*, using instead the terms *speech act, speech act theory, speech event, discourse analysis*, and *sociolinguistics*. Nevertheless, the titles of the papers reveal a distinctly pragmatic content. The papers themselves identify the ability to use speech acts as *sociolinguistic competence* (e.g., Schmidt, 1983). In 1987 co-organizers Lawrence Bouton and Yamuna Kachru launched the Conference on Pragmatics and Language Learning at the University of Illinois, Urbana-Champaign. The first volume of the selected proceedings, *Pragmatics and Language Learning*, was published in 1990 and the twelfth is due out in 2010. The early volumes included descriptions of L1 and L2 use, cross-linguistic comparisons, and L2 acquisition.

Comparative interlanguage pragmatics studies have contributed to applied linguistics by providing cross-cultural and cross-linguistic documentation of pragmatics where none existed previously. In addition, the comparisons of a variety of features in a range of languages, although far from comprehensive, provide the basis for acquisitional inquiries and models for pedagogical materials.

Pragmatics in second language acquisition

Along with early alignment of pragmatics with sociolinguistics, pragmatics was also linked with L2 acquisition, reflecting contemporary theories and analyses. A case in point is Schmidt's (1983) study of Wes which includes the first longitudinal study of the L2 pragmatics of an adult second language learner. A test of the acculturation model (Schumann, 1978), this study positioned pragmatics in mainstream SLA. By 1992, there had already been a noticeable bifurcation of the field—perhaps nonintegration of interlanguage pragmatics with SLA is more apt—as noted by Kasper (1992, p. 205) when she described interlanguage pragmatics as having studied "precisely the kinds of issues raised in comparative studies of different communities ... Interlanguage pragmatics has predominantly been the sociolinguistic, and to a much lesser extent a psycholinguistic [or acquisitional] study of NNS' linguistic action." Comparative studies typically compare the production of native speakers of the target language (L2), native speakers of the learners' first language (L1), and L2 learners of the same L1.

Interlanguage pragmatics has become increasingly concerned with SLA, although it is not the dominant orientation in interlanguage pragmatics given continued interest in comparative studies. Nonetheless, significant research agendas have positioned pragmatics acquisitionally. Kasper and Schmidt (1996) reviewed research in L2 pragmatics by posing 14 questions relevant to SLA addressing such issues as measurement, stages of L2 pragmatic development, mechanisms of change, comparison of L1 aquisition and L2 aquisition, comparison of pragmatics to other areas of the linguistic system, and the influence of individual differences, environment, and instruction. Two additional orienting papers appeared in 1999, a research agenda for investigating the interlanguage development that occurs with pragmatic development (Bardovi-Harlig, 1999) and a survey of pragmatics and SLA (Kasper and Rose, 1999). Finally, a book-length treatment of pragmatic development in second language was published in the *Language Learning* monograph series (Kasper and Rose, 2002), further anchoring pragmatics research in SLA.

Core issues

This section addresses general issues that L2 pragmatics shares with SLA more broadly, namely, environment, instructional influence, L1 transfer, and two areas of special concern to L2 pragmatics, data elicitation, and the relation of grammar to pragmatic development.

Data elicitation

Perhaps because of its hybrid origins in ordinary language philosophy, comparative pragmatics, sociolinguistics, and SLA, interlanguage pragmatics researchers have always investigated and discussed data collection. This is in part due to, on the one hand, conflicting goals and traditions among the contributing fields and audiences, and on the other hand, the lack of a prescribed or inherited method for speech act research (which dominates the field to this day). There is, however, another interpretation: One of the factors that drives the almost constant reflection on data elicitation in L2 pragmatics is that most studies use facsimiles of spontaneous oral conversation, and thus must reflect on whether alternative data collection methods can illuminate characteristics of conversation itself. Data collection is taken up in detail below (see Data and common elicitation measures).

Grammar and pragmatics: The development of pragmalinguistic resources

The development of L2 pragmatic competence involves the development of both L2 socio-pragmatic sensibilities and L2 pragmalinguistic resources. The development of L2 sociopragmatic knowledge, "the link between action-relevant context factors and communicative action (e.g., deciding whether to request an extension, complain about the neighbor's barking dog)" (Kasper, 2001, p. 51) has received more attention in the literature than the development of pragmalinguistic resources which include the various linguistic devices that allow speakers to implement their sociopragmatic knowledge. Investigating how pragmalinguistic resources develop involves investigating the development of L2 grammar and lexicon to understand how they interface with sociopragmatic knowledge; this is often referred to as the interface of grammar and pragmatics (Bardovi-Harlig, 1999). Although the specific concern of L2 pragmatics is pragmalinguistic knowledge, it is important to take into account that grammar (including prosody, morphology, syntax, semantics, and the lexicon) has important functions outside prag-matics. For example, although tense functions pragmatically as a mitigator, its primary function is referring to time; embedding pragmatically encodes conventional indirectness but primarily serves syntactic functions.

The segregation of pragmatic from grammatical inquiry in early work (Thomas, 1983) lent clarity to research in interlanguage pragmatics in its formative years. Nevertheless, even without focal research in the area, researchers observed the relationship between grammar and pragmatics reporting that L2 learners with high grammatical proficiency do not necessarily show equivalently high levels of L2 pragmatic competence (Bardovi-Harlig and Hartford, 1993; Olshtain and Blum-Kulka, 1985). Instead L2 learners show a range of L2 pragmatic competence, from divergence to convergence on targetlike norms, suggesting that the conditions that foster L2 pragmatic development are not the same as those that foster L2 grammatical development.

It is important to note that in the case of adult L2 acquisition the agenda of investigating L2 grammatical development in light of L2 pragmatics does not constitute the claim that grammar precedes pragmatics or that pragmatics precedes grammar. Applying the same functionalist frame-work employed in much tense-aspect research (Bardovi-Harlig, 2007) provides a useful perspec-tive. A basic tenet of the concept-oriented approach to L2 acquisition is that adult learners of second or foreign languages have access to the full range of semantic concepts from their previous linguistic and cognitive experience. Von Stutterheim and Klein argue that "a second language learner—in contrast to a child learning his first language—does not have to acquire the underlying concepts. What he has to acquire is a specific way and a specific means of expressing them" (1987,

p. 194). This applies equally to pragmatics where adults come to L2 acquisition with knowledge of what Kasper and Rose (2002, p. 165) characterize as implicit universal pragmatic competence which includes knowledge of and ability to use systems constraints including turn taking, repairs, and sequencing; conversational and institutional talk; main categories of illocutionary acts; specific communicative acts; politeness; indexicality; directness levels; routine formulas; contextual variability; discursive construction of social identity; and accomplishment of activities.

Another basic tenet of pragmatics is that all speakers—native speakers, non-native speakers, and learners—make choices among available linguistic forms to convey social meanings. The choice of an address term (*usted* versus *tú*), the use of a request strategy (*would you* versus *I was wondering if you would* ...), or the use of an aggravator rather than a mitigator (*I just decided that I will take syntax* versus *I was thinking about taking syntax*) all have meaning because there are other possible alternatives.

Examining a learner's grammatical and lexical development reveals what linguistic devices are available to that learner. Because pragmatic value is derived from the *choice* of available linguistic devices, if a learner has only one form available, then the use of that form lacks pragmatic significance, revealing only the learner's level of interlanguage development. Thus, the study of acquisition within the framework of interlanguage pragmatics is necessary because it is the study of the development of alternatives.

As an illustration of the interface between pragmatics and language development, consider L2 modality and conventional expressions (other areas of grammar are discussed in Bardovi-Harlig, 1999). The general prevalence of the modals "*would*" and "*could*" in American English contrasts with their relative absence in learner production at low to intermediate proficiency. A longitudinal investigation of modality in oppositional talk showed that the dearth of *would* and *could* was a result of late emergence in interlanguage (Salsbury and Bardovi-Harlig, 2000). Whereas the modal expressions *maybe* and *I think* emerged early and were used widely by all learners, *would* and *could* emerged at least six months later in the interlanguage of only a few learners and accounted for less that 1 percent of modal expressions. The learners with the greatest range in inventory also showed contextualized use. Moreover, learners showed awareness of the sociopragmatics of oppositional talk by using the linguistic means at their disposal.

A second example is the acquisition of conventional expressions. Pragmaticists have suggested that differences in L1 and L2 production result from learners' lack of access to or control of conventional expressions (Edmondson and House, 1991; Kasper and Blum-Kulka, 1993). Such hypotheses require direct investigation of both recognition and use of conventional expressions (Bardovi-Harlig, 2009). Comparing learner familiarity with conventional expressions to their production reveals that both knowledge of the conventional expressions (pragmalinguistics) and knowledge of their contexts of use (sociopragmatics) drive the production patterns that have been reported.

Environment: Second, foreign, and study abroad contexts

Once the general question addressed by L2 pragmatics, "Can L2 pragmatics be acquired?," is answered (if there is any doubt, the answer is "yes"), it is a natural extension to ask "Can L2 pragmatics be acquired better, faster, or more efficiently under different conditions?" Two conditions that have received the most attention in L2 pragmatics are environment and instruction.

The role of learning environment has received noticeable attention in the last decade. At the time of this writing, there have been more pragmatic study-abroad studies published in the seven years since Kasper and Rose's (2002) comprehensive review than the total number cited in their review of nearly 25 years of research. Most pragmatics research has been situated in host environments (countries in which the language is spoken by the population) and include studies of university students learning English in North America, for example. Foreign language contexts (in which learners study languages not spoken in the country) include the acquisition of languages other than English in the USA or English in non-English speaking countries (Cook, 2001, Japanese in Hawaii; Liddicoat and Crozet, 2001, French in Australia; Takahashi, 2005, English in Japan). The addition of study-abroad contexts to the literature began noticeably in the late 1990s and early 2000s with dissertations and later as published articles (see especially the thematic issue of *Intercultural pragmatics*, 4(2), 2007; DuFon and Churchill, 2006).

Adding the study abroad context brings the investigation of environment in pragmatics full circle (see Chapter 32). Many study-abroad studies focus exclusively on learners in the host environment (for French Warga and Schölmberger, 2007; for German, Barron, 2007; for Indonesian, DuFon, 2010; for Spanish, Félix-Brasdefer, 2007; and for Spanish and French, Cohen and Shively, 2007) whereas others compare learners doing the same tasks in the host and foreign environments (for English, Bardovi-Harlig and Dörnyei, 1998, and the replication studies by Niezgoda and Roever, 2001, and Schauer, 2006, pragmatic awareness; Davis, 2007, attitudes and willingness to communicate; Schauer, 2007, requests; T. Takahashi and Beebe, 1987, refusals; for French, Hoffman-Hicks, 1999, greetings, leave takings, and compliments; for Spanish, Rodriguez, 2001, perception of requests).

Learners in host environments typically show some aspect of pragmatic development that exceeds that of learners in foreign environments. For example, learners in France showed greater sensitivity to sociopragmatics of French compliments, greetings and leave-takings than classmates in the USA (Hoffman-Hicks, 1999) and Taiwanese learners of English in the USA showed greater sociopragmatic gains in using acceptances as compliment responses than classmates in Taiwan who used rejections (Yu, 2004). Pragmalinguistics also shows gains: Study-abroad learners used a boarder repertoire of external request modifiers at the end of their sojourn than the at-home learners (Schauer, 2007). The advantage of comparisons is noted by Hoffman-Hicks who characterizes the study-abroad group's progress as modest, but nevertheless significant in light of the fact that the at-home group showed no development during the same semester. In contrast, when study-abroad and at-home learners were compared only in academic contexts fewer differences were evident (Rodriguez, 2001).

Different results in a series of replications emphasizes the importance of viewing the environment as a set of features rather than as a single variable. Bardovi-Harlig and Dörnyei (1998) and Schauer (2006) reported higher awareness of pragmatic infelicities by English as a second language (ESL) learners in host environments than English as a foreign language (EFL) learners in foreign environments. Bardovi-Harlig and Dörnyei interpreted this as due to the cross-cultural interaction experienced in the host setting. In contrast, using the same task, Niezgoda and Roever (2001) reported that EFL learners in the Czech Republic were better able to identify pragmatic infelicities than ESL learners in Hawaii. The conflicting findings may be due to differences among learners. The Czech learners were the top 5 percent of university students training to be English teachers, and the ESL learners in Hawaii may not have been as academically oriented as learners in other studies. Taken together, these studies emphasize the interaction of the environment with other variables including contact with native speakers, proficiency, aptitude, engagement, proficiency and experience of teachers (in the case of instructed learners), and access to NS other than teachers.

Investigating length of stay is closely linked to studying host environments (Félix-Brasdefer, 2004). Highly salient conversational functions such as greetings and discourse markers appear to respond to relatively short lengths of stay as illustrated by L2 development of American learners of

Kiswahili who had visited Tanzania (Omar, 1992) and students of French who lived abroad for a semester (Hoffman-Hicks, 1999). In contrast, other areas take much longer to develop without instruction. The acceptance of positive request strategies and directness by Hebrew NNS increased as length of stay increased, but targetlike judgments developed only after ten years of residence (Olshtain and Blum-Kulka, 1985). Similarly, ESL learners enrolled at an American university without specific training in implicature became increasingly targetlike in their interpretations as length of stay increased, although some resolved only after three–four years (Bouton, 1994).

Influence of instruction

The interest in the effect of instruction on L2 pragmatics reflects the general interest in instructional effects in SLA and the specific demonstration that native and non-native pragmatics systems can vary significantly. The latter have encouraged researcher-teachers to undertake experiments in teaching pragmatics, both to test the efficacy of instruction and to develop means by which to assist learners gain knowledge in L2 pragmatics. (Comprehensive reviews can be found in Kasper and Rose, 2002; Kasper, 2001; Rose, 2005).

Instruction on a range of pragmatic targets has been investigated including discourse markers and pragmatic routines (House, 1996; Tateyama, 2001), speech acts (including compliments and compliment responses, Huth, 2006; Rose and Kwai-fun, 2001; directives, Pearson, 2006; requests, Safont Jordà, 2003; Takahashi, 2005; Takimoto, 2007), greetings (Liddicoat and Crozet, 2001), mitigators (Fukuya and Clark, 2001), lexical phrasal downgraders (Salazar, 2003), workplace speech events (Gibbs, 2005), terms of address including pronouns (Vyatkina and Belz, 2006), and strategies (Cohen and Shively, 2007).

Rose (2005, p. 239) characterizes research on instructional effects on L2 pragmatics as addressing three main questions, each of which have their own design. Studies addressing the first question—"Is the targeted pragmatic feature teachable at all?"—employ pre-test/post-test designs with intervening treatment (e.g., Huth, 2006; Liddicoat and Crozet, 2001; Vyatkina and Belz, 2006). In each of these studies learners responded favorably to instruction. Huth's learners compared authentic examples of American English, and German and received explicit information about, and practice on, compliment-response sequences. Role plays showed modest production gains in German compliment responses but follow-up interviews suggest that learners gained explicit knowledge about German compliment-acceptances. Vyatkina and Belz (2006) report the most robust results, but also had the most extensive intervention over the longest period which combined awareness-raising, explanation, and practice with form-focused instruction on modal particles in German over nine weeks. In seven weeks learners went from using four modal particles to using 89 at 84 percent accuracy.

Studies in the first group show that pragmatic features can be learned from instruction, but they do not test the possibility that learners at the same proficiency could make equivalent progress without instruction, which forms Rose's second question: "Is instruction in the targeted feature more effective than no instruction?" Studies in this group compare a control group that receives no specific pragmatic input to the treatment group. Bouton (1994) showed that implicatures that took up to four years to develop without instruction responded quickly to instruction.

Studies of this type suggest that instruction has an advantage, but leave open the question of whether another type of intervention would have produced different outcomes. Thus, studies addressing the third question—"Are different teaching approaches differentially effective?"—compare two or more interventions (often explicit and implicit conditions) and may include a control group with no pragmatics instruction (Pearson, 2006; Takimoto, 2007).

Takimoto (2007) evaluated the relative effectiveness of three types of input-based approaches for teaching polite request forms in an EFL setting. Performance of learners receiving (a) structured input tasks with explicit information, (b) structured input tasks without explicit information, or (c) problem-solving tasks was compared with control group performance on pre-tests, post-tests eight–nine days after instruction, and post-tests four weeks after instruction. These consisted of a discourse completion test, a role play test, a listening test, and an acceptability judgment test. The three treatment groups performed significantly better than the control group on all the measures, but there were no significant differences among the treatment groups. In contrast, Pearson (2006) reported no difference between two instructional approaches and no advantage for instruction in a study of directives in Spanish as a foreign language. Two second-semester classes received speech act lessons on Spanish expressions of gratitude, apologies, commands, and directives that included video segments from a pedagogical video series and role plays to practice directives and other speech acts. One class received metapragmatic discussions of the speech acts and the other received additional exposure to the speech acts through another viewing of the videos. A third second-semester class received no specialized instruction in Spanish pragmatics. The pre-test, post-test one week following instruction, and two delayed post-tests (at the end of the semester and six months later) showed no quantitative difference in the production of the groups when request forms were evaluated holistically. However, there were qualitative differences between the treatment groups and the control group (such as the use of *poder* statements), suggesting that the holistic measure (total/some/no variation) was too blunt to capture interlanguage change.

In sum, instruction appears to facilitate the development of L2 pragmatics. In addition, different teaching approaches may be differentially effective, but differences often disappear by the delayed post-test (Rose, 2005). However, the body of research on instruction to date is still quite small and operationalization of instruction is itself one of the variables. Instruction has ranged from learner-driven comparisons of NS-NNS talk-texts, which although provided by the instructor, display many natural features (S. Takahashi, 2005), individualized input showing learners specific features from their own computer-mediated communication (Vyatkina and Belz, 2006), to whole class activities which deliver linguistic resources such as pragmatic routines and rules of use (House, 1996) in lessons that range from as little as two 20-minute sessions (see Rose, 2005) to three interventions over a nine-week interval with continued opportunities for authentic use (Vyatkina and Belz, 2006).

Studies also vary in the target of instruction and thus the type of input: on one end of the continuum, an instructional target such as turn taking minimally requires timing examples, but no new linguistic resources, whereas biclausal request forms (*I was wondering if you could* or *Is it possible for me to*) require input on both form and use. Encouraging the use of a speech act in a range of contexts and promoting mitigation of a single speech act or semantic formula are targets of different magnitudes. Whether implicit or explicit conditions are selected for instruction (or both), the specific information about the target has to be determined; this is compounded in explicit conditions where appropriate explanations are given. Building linguistic resources for pragmatics (pragmalinguistics) may be able to draw on instruction in more formal areas of grammar whereas instruction on rules of use (sociopragmatics) has a shorter instructional history. In addition, all pedagogy interacts with a learner's stage of L2 development and is subject to constraints and principles of acquisition. This is an area where much exciting work remains to be done.

The means of evaluation in instructional studies range from written production for the assessment of oral features to conversation analytic assessments of talk to computer mediated communication (Huth, 2006; Vyatkina and Belz, 2006). Whereas implicitness/explicitness has been considered in terms of instructional delivery, it has not been considered widely in terms of pragmatic knowledge. Learners may show development of explicit knowledge, but not increased use (cf., House, 1996; Huth, 2006).

L1 influence

Among the questions identified by Kasper and Schmidt (1996), the most enthusiastically investigated has been the influence of the first language. Pragmatic transfer, "non-native speakers' use of L1 pragmatic knowledge to understand or carry out linguistic action in the L2" (Kasper, 1997, p. 119) may result in positive transfer leading to successful exchanges or negative transfer leading to non-native use (or avoidance) of speech acts, semantic formulas, content, or linguistic form based on an assumption that L1 and L2 are similar where, in fact, they are not. The main limitation of these studies has been that they are generally comparative, but as Rose (2000) has pointed out, the results from comparative studies on transfer may have to be reassessed when more acquisitional studies have been completed.

Determining the stage of interlanguage development at which L1 influence is most likely to occur has also inspired studies. T. Takahashi and Beebe (1987) posited a positive correlation between proficiency and transfer suggesting that "pragmatic transfer requires more fluency to surface" (p. 153). This echoed earlier observations by Blum-Kulka (1982) that Canadian learners of Hebrew did not transfer request strategies to Hebrew because they lacked the L2 knowledge necessary to implement indirectness. Similarly, Maeshiba et al. (1996) observed that in the case of positive transfer, advanced learners used the same strategies as native speakers in both the L1 and the L2, and they concluded that this "makes sense in light of the assumption that advanced learners are likely to be more acculturated, and have the linguistic facility to transfer pragmatic strategies from the native language" (p. 169). This issue is not settled, however, as instances of transfer have been identified at lower levels of proficiency (Kasper and Rose, 2002).

An important development in this area will be the adoption of designs specific to the investigation of transfer (Jarvis, 2000) in which learners from one L1 group are compared to learners from a typologically distinct group to determine which characteristics of development belong to L2 acquisition in general and which are shared exclusively by learners of distinct L1s. To my knowledge, such designs have not yet been implemented in L2 pragmatics.

Data and common elicitation measures

Reviews of tasks used for data collection have a long history in interlanguage pragmatics, beginning not even a decade after the field was established (Wolfson, 1986). The reviews are fueled by the range of tasks employed in interlanguage pragmatics, frequent innovations in tasks, and use of facsimiles of spontaneous oral conversation which in turn fuels additional reflection on method.

One means of evaluating tasks used in L2 pragmatics is to ask how well they illuminate the features attributed to pragmatics by current definitions (Bardovi-Harlig, 2010). Using the definition of pragmatics by Crystal (1997) (see above, Definitions of pragmatics), the most highly valued forms of data collection should be those that promote the investigation of users, choices, constraints, social interaction, effects on other participants, and acts of communication. A second means of evaluating tasks is to determine the degree to which tasks conform to the general principles of task construction in SLA research, considering mode (whether the oral or written mode of the task matches the stated mode of the object of inquiry), planning (whether the task realistically represents the amount of time a speaker has to plan utterances for communication in advance), and explicit knowledge (whether the task promotes the use of explicit knowledge).

A third means is to evaluate authenticity, consequentiality, and comparability (Bardovi-Harlig and Hartford, 2005).

Tasks utilized in L2 pragmatics can be divided into production tasks and nonproduction tasks. Data collection that focuses on production, and which accounts for about 60 percent of studies, (Bardovi-Harlig, 2010) observes or generates conversation or simulated conversation for primary analysis. Authentic speech such as informal conversation, institutional talk, or classroom discourse, as well as elicited talk including role plays and oral discourse completion tasks (DCTs) are examples of oral production; letters, computer-mediated communication (CMC), and written DCTs are examples of written production. Nonproduction tasks include judgment tasks of various types, rating and sorting tasks, and interpretation tasks. Figure 9.1 organizes common production tasks from most to least authentic according to the relevant characteristics.

Authentic discourse may be oral or written, monologic, dyadic, or multipartied, and with the advent of computer communication, synchronous or asynchronous. Conversational data constitute the most familiar form of authentic discourse and the one most generally referred to in interlanguage pragmatics; institutional talk is another source of authentic discourse.

Role plays are elicited through the presentation of a context called a *scenario* which typically includes information about speaker characteristics and setting. Role plays may ask participants to take on new roles or play themselves (the latter are *role enactments*). Kasper and Dahl (1991) argue that role plays "represent oral production, full operation of the turn-taking mechanism, impromptu planning decisions contingent on interlocutor input, and hence negotiation of global

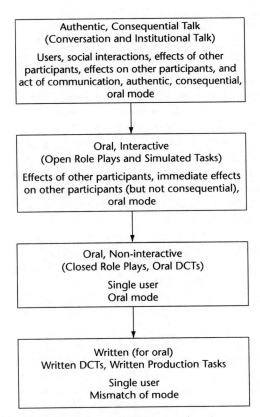

Figure 9.1 Oral tasks and simulations from most to least authentic

and local goals, including negotiation of meaning" (p. 228). Simulated tasks, in which speakers are brought together in an experimental setting to complete a task such as puzzle-solving or teaching a computer program, also yield experimenter-initiated interactive language samples. In simulated tasks participants speak as themselves. Some simulated tasks have been very successful in blurring the distinction between the authentic and simulated when they are employed in instructional settings where participants have existing social relations: Nguyen (2008), for example, had learners write essays, then meet with peer reviewers which facilitated the study of L2 criticism in context.

Oral DCTs (or closed role plays) provide scenarios to which participants respond. There is no interaction, although there may be an initiated turn provided by a recording. Participants respond orally and the production is recorded.

DCTs, unless otherwisely indicated, are written production questionnaires which provide scenarios to which participants respond (Example 1). DCTs that provide one or more turns are known as dialog completion tasks and those with no turns are called open questionnaires.

> It's your friend Anne's birthday party. Anne is one of your colleagues from university but you do not consider her to be a very close friend. In her invitation she asked you to bring something to eat for the buffet. You promised to prepare some Mousse au Chocolat, but you didn't manage to do it. You feel embarrassed. What do you tell her when she opens the door?

> *You*:   Hi Anne! Happy birthday!
> *Anne*:   Hi! Good to see you!
> *You*:   _____

> *(Warga and Schölmberger, 2007, p. 245, translated from French by the authors.)*

In SLA there is a clear divide between oral and written tasks, and yet in interlanguage pragmatics written tasks have been used to represent oral production for three decades. The mismatch of written-for-oral-production increases learners' opportunity to plan their responses and to draw on explicit knowledge. A recent review of data collection in L2 pragmatics in refereed journals shows that oral production is currently the dominant source of data, although this was not always the case (Bardovi-Harlig, 2010). Because written production generally stands in for oral production in interlanguage pragmatics, 90 percent of written tasks were written-for-oral and only 10 percent investigated authentic written communication. In contrast, written format is prevalent in non-production tasks. Only 29 percent utilize audio or audio-visual data for judgment tasks or rating, whereas 59 percent employ written transcripts. Acknowledging the general mismatch of mode, Cohen and Shively (2007, p. 196) described their written DCT as "an indirect means for assessing spoken language in the form of a written production measure."

Language samples may also be characterized by comparability, interactivity, and consequentiality (Bardovi-Harlig and Hartford, 2005). *Comparability* assures that language samples can be reasonably compared. *Interactivity* addresses speakers' opportunities to take turns. *Consequentiality* refers to the fact that there is a real world outcome to naturally occurring talk.

Production questionnaires are highly controlled tasks and yield language samples of high comparability. However, they are neither interactive nor consequential. Role plays retain the experimental control of production questionnaires resulting in language samples that are comparable and interactive, but not consequential. Conversation is both interactive and consequential with a range of outcomes. Like conversation, institutional talk is interactive and consequential, and in addition, the goal-oriented nature of institutional talk and the repetition of exchanges results in comparability.

The advantages of studying conversation and institutional talk for interlanguage pragmatics research derive from the fact that they are natural occurrences: spontaneous authentic language used by speakers who are speaking as themselves, in genuine situations, with socio-affective and real-world consequences. Unmonitored oral production has always been valued in SLA research; from the interlanguage pragmatics perspective, conversational data have been seen as lacking comparability except for the most routine and superficial exchanges, and role plays have been seen as more desirable for pragmatics research (Kasper and Dahl, 1991, p. 229). However, with the increased adoption of conversation analysis, it is expected that these purported disadvantages will be cited less often. Careful selection of interactive tasks (including authentic talk) in the mode that is being investigated, with multiple samples, should meet the multiple criteria for evaluation.

Analysis

The analyses used by particular studies depends on how they operationalize "pragmatics." Speech act studies may report whether or not a speech act has occurred, analyze the use of semantic formulas (presence, absence, order, and frequency), describe the form of the semantic formulas or head acts, or analyze the content; external and internal modifiers might be analyzed. Coding schemes for some speech acts have become standard, such as the Cross-Cultural Speech Act Realization Project (CCSARP) coding manual for requests and apologies (Blum-Kulka *et al.*, 1989) and refusal-coding of Beebe *et al.* (1990).

Other studies can be divided into four main groups: turn structure, grammatical and lexical devices including routines, interpretation, and discourse structure, with some remainders. Studies of turn structure investigate sequencing of turns, repair, and alignment. Studies that focus on grammar, lexicon, and routines investigate pragmalinguistic resources that speakers use to realize communication. Analyses include the use of modal particles in L2 German (Vyatkina and Belz, 2006), modals in L2 English (Salsbury and Bardovi-Harlig, 2000) and formulas (House, 1996; Tateyama, 2001). Studies of discourse structure include investigations of speech events, such as workplace calls (Gibbs, 2005), and written events such as letters of recommendation (Bouton, 1995). Studies that focus on interpretation included analyses of speakers' underlying knowledge including metapragmatic judgments, ranking, rating, comprehension, identification, and implicature.

An ongoing challenge in the analysis of L2 pragmatics is to determine which measures will capture change over time. Any nuanced interlanguage analysis could potentially serve if it is sufficiently sensitive to interlanguage development, but not all analyses were designed to do that. For example, the CCSARP coding manual places the use of "can" and "could" queries in the same category, whereas acquisitional studies show a significant developmental difference between them. Adopting classifications designed for other purposes require significant attention to L2 sequences of development.

Empirical verification

Closely related to data elicitation is the evidence taken by a field as empirical verification of its approach. At the level of data elicitation, features of monologic written responses have been accepted as evidence for features of spontaneous oral conversation. (The disadvantages of this were discussed above (Data and common elicitation measures)). However this has recently shifted with two-thirds of current studies drawing on oral production. Oral samples can be divided further:

About one-third consist of non-interactive oral samples, while the balance consists of interactive communication indicating a move toward increased interactivity.

Moving beyond task, L2 pragmatics has a relatively good record of longitudinal studies, ranging from two months (admittedly very short) to four years, with most around an academic year (eight–ten months). Taguchi (2010) provides a synthesis of 21 longitudinal studies of adult learners published up to 2008; Taguchi's review included studies that observed the development of participants over time, examined the development of specific pragmatic features, documented development by collecting data systematically over time (excluding ethnographic studies), did not involve intervention or training, and observed participants from secondary-school age to adult. Bardovi-Harlig (2010) included eight additional published longitudinal studies; Kasper and Rose's (2002) review included unpublished dissertations and studies of children. About 30 distinct longitudinal studies have been published; in total, about 36 have either been published or circulated.

Far fewer cross-sectional studies have been conducted in L2 pragmatics. Rose (2000; Kasper and Rose, 2002) surveys the cross-sectional literature, identifying six cross-sectional studies (including Rose, 2000) that focus on development of pragmatic features across levels, thus extrapolating a sequence of change across time. Like Taguchi, Rose distinguishes acquisitionally focused studies, pointing out that cross-sectional formats in L2 pragmatics often compare learner-knowledge at different levels with that of native speakers, but do not attempt to identify or document sequences of development between levels and thus differ from cross-sectional studies in SLA more broadly (Kasper and Rose, 2002, p. 14).

Although developmentally focused cross-sectional studies could, and probably should, be perfected, the promise of longitudinal studies is so much greater that it seems more profitable to pursue that approach. Longitudinal studies that collect authentic data (at best) or elicited interactive data (at least) are more valuable than studies with controlled written production or multiple choice tasks. Moreover, repeating the same tasks longitudinally runs the risk of introducing task learning.

Applications

Research in interlanguage pragmatics is directly relevant to second and foreign language instruction; moreover, effect of instruction constitutes an area of inquiry in pragmatics (see above, Core issues). Both acquisitional and comparative research offer a needs assessment for instruction (Bardovi-Harlig, 2001). Many researchers have also developed teaching activities, materials, and assessments. Pedagogically relevant publications include reviews of commercial materials (Bardovi-Harlig et al., 1991; Boxer and Pickering, 1995), innovative teaching units (*System*, 2005, 33 (3); Félix-Brasdefer, 2006), and books on classroom activities (Bardovi-Harlig and Mahan-Taylor, 2003; Tatsuki and Houck, 2010; Houck and Tatsuki, 2011). Other resources include extensive websites (CARLA at University of Minnesota and Indiana University's website by Félix-Brasdefer on the teaching of refusals (http://www.indiana.edu/~discprag/practice_refusals. html)), innovative activities found in research reports (use of conversational transcripts of American and Japanese speakers of English, S. Takahashi, 2005), and papers and colloquia at conferences to discuss the teaching of pragmatics.

The key barrier to wider presence of pragmatics in second and foreign language teaching is the general lack of commercially available materials based on authentic interaction. Reviews of published materials report that interactions are often incomplete, fail to show differences among alternatives, or neglect to provide examples of functions or outcomes. Such materials are necessary because as Wolfson (1986) pointed out, in the area of pragmatics native-speaker intuition is an insufficient basis for instruction. Using materials based on authentic interaction provides an opportunity for students and teachers (both native and non-native-speaker teachers!) to learn together, using transcripts, recordings, or audio-visual materials to guide the discovery process.

Future directions

A review of L2 pragmatics research suggests a range of areas for future investigations. A recurrent theme is the need for L2 pragmatics (as opposed to interlanguage pragmatics) to focus on acquisition: identifying and accounting for stages of development, testing various measures of development, and recognizing SLA's concern for task effect. Many of these directions were discussed in the preceding sections. "Be acquisitionally focused" is not an admonition that researchers will take lightly. Part of interlanguage pragmatics will always be comparative. The call to increase the acquisitional orientation is addressed to readers who would like to know more about how L2 pragmatics evolves during the course of adult L2 acquisition and who might find much of the published literature persuasive, but not as acquisitionally focused as other SLA inquiries.

Thus, to assist readers in conceiving of acquisitional approaches I offer the following suggestions:

(1) Explore the underpinnings of the production patterns reported in the literature. Comparative studies report multiple differences between native speakers and learners. What are the underlying causes? Is production limited by linguistic resources? By comprehension? By general proficiency?

(2) Investigate the relationships between the knowledge systems that contribute to pragmatic knowledge. How are sociopragmatic and pragmalinguistic knowledge related during different acquisitional stages? How are grammar and pragmatics related?

(3) Test the relation between general communicative success and the development of L2 pragmatics. How is general aural comprehension related to aural comprehension of pragmatics (including interpreting implicature, intended illocutionary force, and sincerity)?

(4) Spend less time investigating how "naturalistic" tasks compare to natural L2 encounters, and more time developing means of collecting natural communication. Develop more understanding of the effects of task, planning, explicit knowledge, and modality in pragmatics (see, for example, Taguchi, 2007).

(5) Expand the investigation: Add more target languages, include untutored learners, and incorporate more non-production tasks while addressing (1)–(4).

References

Bardovi-Harlig, K. (1999). The interlanguage of interlanguage pragmatics: A research agenda for acquisitional pragmatics. *Language Learning, 49*, 677–713.

Bardovi-Harlig, K. (2001). Evaluating the empirical evidence: Grounds for instruction in pragmatics? In K. Rose and G. Kasper (Eds.), *Pragmatics in language teaching* (pp. 13–32). Cambridge: Cambridge University Press.

Bardovi-Harlig, K. (2007). One functional approach to SLA: The concept-oriented approach. In B. VanPatten and J. Williams (Eds.), *Theories in second language acquisition* (pp. 57–75). Mahwah, NJ: Erlbaum.

Bardovi-Harlig, K. (2009). Conventional expressions as a pragmalinguistic resource: Recognition and production of conventional expressions in L2 pragmatics. *Language Learning, 59*, 755–795.

Bardovi-Harlig, K. (2010). Exploring the pragmatics of interlanguage pragmatics: Definition by design. In A. Trosborg (Ed.), *Pragmatics across languages and cultures* (Vol. 7 of *Handbooks of pragmatics*; pp. 219–259). Berlin: Mouton de Gruyter.

Bardovi-Harlig, K. and Dörnyei, Z. (1998). Do language learners recognize pragmatic violations? Pragmatic vs. grammatical awareness in instructed L2 learning. *TESOL Quarterly, 32,* 233–259.

Bardovi-Harlig, K. and Hartford, B. S. (1993). Learning the rules of academic talk: A longitudinal study of pragmatic development. *Studies in Second Language Acquisition, 15,* 279–304.

Bardovi-Harlig, K. and Hartford, B. S. (Eds.). (2005). *Interlanguage pragmatics: Exploring institutional talk.* Mahwah, NJ: Erlbaum.

Bardovi-Harlig, K., Hartford, B. A. S., Mahan-Taylor, R., Morgan, M. J., and Reynolds, D. W. (1991). Developing pragmatic awareness: Closing the conversation. *ELT Journal, 45,* 4–15.

Bardovi-Harlig, K. and Mahan-Taylor, R. (2003). *Teaching pragmatics.* Washington, D.C.: United States Department of State. http://draft.eca.state.gov/education/engteaching/pragmatics.htm

Barron, A. (2007). "Ah no honestly we're okay:" Learning to upgrade in a study abroad context. *Intercultural Pragmatics, 4,* 129–166.

Beebe, L. M., Takahashi, T., and Uliss-Weltz, R. (1990). Pragmatic transfer in ESL refusals. In R. Scarcella, E. Andersen, and S. D. Krashen (Eds.), *On the development of communicative competence in a second language* (pp. 55–73). Cambridge, MA: Newbury House.

Blum-Kulka, S. (1982). Learning to say what you mean in a second language: A study of the speech act performance of learners of Hebrew as a second language. *Applied Linguistics, 3,* 29–59.

Blum-Kulka, S., House, J., and Kasper, G. (Eds.) (1989). *Cross-cultural pragmatics: Requests and apologies.* Norwood, NJ: Ablex.

Bouton, L. F. (1994). Can non-native speakers' skill in interpreting implicature in American English be improved through explicit instruction? A pilot study. In L. F. Bouton (Ed.), *Pragmatics and language learning* (Vol. *5,* pp. 88–109). Urbana-Champaign, IL: University of Illinois, Division of English as an International Language.

Bouton, L. F. (1995). A cross-cultural analysis of the structure and content of letters of reference. *Studies in Second Language Acquisition, 17,* 211–244.

Boxer, D. and Pickering, L. (1995). Problems in the presentation of speech acts in ELT materials: The case of complaints. *ELT Journal, 49,* 44–58.

Cohen, A. D. and Shively, R. (2007). Acquisition of requests and apologies in Spanish and French: Impact of study abroad and strategy-building intervention. *The Modern Language Journal, 91,* 189–212.

Cook, H. M. (2001). Why can't learners of JFL distinguish polite from impolite speech styles? In K. Rose and G. Kasper (Eds.) *Pragmatics in language teaching* (pp. 80–102). Cambridge Cambridge University Press.

Crystal, D. (Ed.). (1997). *The Cambridge encyclopedia of language* (Second Edition). New York: Cambridge University Press.

Davis, J. (2007). Resistance to L2 pragmatics in the Australian ESL context. *Language Learning, 57,* 611–649.

DuFon, M. (2010). The socialization of leave-taking in Indonesian. In G. Kasper, D. Yoshimi, H. Nguyen, and J. Yoshioka (Eds.), *Pragmatics and language learning* (Vol. *12,* pp. 91–111). Honolulu: University of Hawai'i, National Foreign Language Resource Center.

DuFon, M. and Churchill, E. (2006). *Language learners in study abroad contexts.* Clevedon, UK: Multilingual Matters.

Edmondson, W. and House, J. (1991). Do learners talk too much? The waffle phenomenon in interlanguage pragmatics. In R. Phillipson, E. Kellerman, L. Selinker, M. Sharwood Smith, and M. Swain (Eds.), *Foreign/second language pedagogy research: A commemorative volume for Claus Faerch* (pp. 273–287). Clevedon, UK: Multilingual Matters.

Félix-Brasdefer, J. C. (2004). Interlanguage refusals: Linguistic politeness and length of residence in the target community. *Language Learning, 54,* 587–653.

Félix-Brasdefer, J. C. (2006). Teaching the negotiation of multi-turn speech acts: Using conversation-analytic tools to teach pragmatics in the classroom. In K. Bardovi-Harlig, K. C. Félix-Brasdefer, and A. S. Omar (Eds.), *Pragmatics and language learning* (Vol. *11,* pp. 165–197). Honolulu, HI: Second Language Teaching and Curriculum Center, University of Hawai'i at Manoa.

Félix-Brasdefer, J. C. (2007). Pragmatic development in the Spanish as a FL classroom: A cross-sectional study of learner requests. *Intercultural Pragmatics, 4,* 253–286.

Fukuya, Y. J. and Clark, M. K. (2001). A comparison of input enhancement and explicit instruction of mitigators. In L. F. Bouton (Ed.), *Pragmatics and language learning* (Vol. *10,* pp. 111–130). Urbana-Champaign, IL: University of Illinois, Division of English as an International Language.

Gibbs, T. (2005). Using moves in the opening sequence to identify callers in institutional settings. In K. Bardovi-Harlig and B. S. Hartford (Eds.), *Interlanguage pragmatics: Exploring institutional talk* (pp. 175–199). Mahwah, NJ: Erlbaum.

Hoffman-Hicks, S. (1999). *The development of pragmatic competence in learners of French.* Unpublished doctoral dissertation. Indiana University, Bloomington.

Houck, N. R. and Tatsuki, D. H. (Eds.) (2011). *Pragmatics: Teaching natural conversation.* New York: TESOL.

House, J. (1996). Developing pragmatic fluency in English as a foreign language: Routines and metapragmatic awareness. *Studies in Second Language Acquisition, 18,* 225–252.

Huth, T. (2006). Negotiating structure and culture: L2 learners' realization of L2 compliment-response sequences in talk-in-interaction. *Journal of Pragmatics, 38,* 2025–2050.

Jarvis, S. (2000). Methodological rigor in the study of transfer: Identifying L1 influence in the interlanguage lexicon. *Language Learning, 50,* 245–309.

Kasper, G. (1992). Pragmatic transfer. *Second Language Research, 8,* 203–231.

Kasper, G. (1996). Introduction: Interlanguage pragmatics in SLA. *Studies in Second Language Acquisition, 18,* 145–148.

Kasper, G. (1997). The role of pragmatics in language teacher education. In K. Bardovi-Harlig and B. S. Hartford, (Eds.), *Beyond methods: Components of language teacher education* (pp. 113–136). New York: McGraw Hill.

Kasper, G. (2001). Classroom research on interlanguage pragmatics. In K. Rose and G. Kasper (Eds.), *Pragmatics in language teaching* (pp. 33–60). Cambridge: Cambridge University Press.

Kasper, G. and Blum-Kulka, S. (1993). Interlanguage pragmatics: An introduction. In G. Kasper and S. Blum-Kulka (Eds.), *Interlanguage pragmatics* (pp. 1–17). Oxford: Oxford University Press.

Kasper, G. and Dahl, M. (1991). Research methods in interlanguage pragmatics. *Studies in Second Language Acquisition, 12,* 215–247.

Kasper, G. and Rose, K. (1999). Pragmatics and SLA. *Annual Review of Applied Linguistics, 19,* 81–104.

Kasper, G. and Rose, K. (2002). *Pragmatic development in a second language.* Malden, MA: Blackwell. ([also *Language Learning, 52* (Supplement 1)])

Kasper, G. and Schmidt, R. (1996). Developmental issues in interlanguage pragmatics. *Studies in Second Language Acquisition, 18,* 149–169.

Levinson, S. C. (1983). *Pragmatics.* Cambridge: Cambridge University Press.

Liddicoat, A. J. and Crozet, C. (2001). Acquiring French interactional norms through instruction. In K. Rose and G. Kasper (Eds.), *Pragmatics in language teaching* (pp. 125–144). Cambridge: Cambridge University Press.

Maeshiba, N., Yoshinaga, N., Kasper, G., and Ross, S. (1996). Transfer and proficiency in interlanguage apologizing. In S. M. Gass and J. Neu (Eds.), *Speech acts across cultures: Challenge to communication in a second language* (pp. 155–187). Berlin: Mouton de Gruyter.

Mey, J. L. (1993). *Pragmatics: An introduction.* Oxford: Blackwell.

Nguyen, T. T. (2008). Criticizing in an L2: Pragmatics strategies used by Vietnamese EFL learners. *Intercultural Pragmatics, 5,* 41–66.

Niezgoda, K. and Roever, C. (2001). Pragmatic and grammatical awareness: A function of the learning environment? In K. Rose and G. Kasper (Eds.), *Pragmatics in language teaching* (pp. 63–79). Cambridge: Cambridge University Press.

Olshtain, E. and Blum-Kulka, S. (1985). Degrees of approximation: Nonnative reactions to native speech act behavior. In S. M. Gass and C. Madden (Eds.), *Input in second language acquisition* (pp. 303–325). Rowley, MA: Newbury House.

Omar, A. S. (1992). Conversational openings in Kiswahili: The pragmatic performance of native and non-native speakers. In L. F. Bouton and Y. Kachru (Eds.), *Pragmatics and language learning* (Vol. 3, pp. 20–32). Urbana-Champaign, IL: University of Illinois, Division of English as an International Language.

Pearson, L. (2006). Patterns of development in Spanish L2 pragmatic acquisition: An analysis of novice learners' production of directives. *The Modern Language Journal, 90,* 473–495.

Rodriguez, S. (2001). *The perception of requests in Spanish by instructed learners of Spanish in the second- and foreign-language contexts: A longitudinal study of acquisition patterns.* Unpublished doctoral dissertation. Indiana University, Bloomington.

Rose, K. (2000). An exploratory cross-sectional study of interlanguage pragmatic development. *Studies in Second Language Acquisition, 22,* 27–67.

Rose, K. (2005). On the effects of instruction in second language pragmatics. *System, 33,* 385–399.

Rose, K. and Kwai-fun, C. N. (2001). Inductive and deductive teaching of compliments and compliment responses. In K. Rose and G. Kasper (Eds.), *Pragmatics in language teaching* (pp. 145–170). Cambridge: Cambridge University Press.

Safont Jordà, M. P. (2003). Instructional effects on the use of request acts modification devices by EFL learners. In A. Martinez, E. Usó Juan, and A. Fernández (Eds.), *Pragmatic competence and foreign language teaching* (pp. 211–232). Castellon, Spain: Servei de Publicacions de la Univerisitat Jaume I.

Salazar, P. (2003). Pragmatic instruction in the EFL context. In A. Martinez, E. Usó Juan, and A. Fernández (Eds.), *Pragmatic competence and foreign language teaching* (pp. 233–246). Castellon, Spain: Servei de Publicacions de la Univerisitat Jaume I.

Salsbury, T. and Bardovi-Harlig, K. (2000). Oppositional talk and the acquisition of modality in L2 English. In B. Swierzbin, F. Morris, M. E. Anderson, C. A. Klee, and E. Tarone (Eds.), *Social and cognitive factors in second language acquisition: Selected proceedings of the 1999 second language research forum* (pp. 57–76). Somerville: Cascadilla Press.

Schauer, G. A. (2006). Pragmatic awareness in ESL and EFL contexts: Contrast and development. *Language Learning, 56*, 269–318.

Schauer, G. A. (2007). Finding the right words in the study abroad context: The development of German learners' use of external modifiers in English. *Intercultural Pragmatics, 4*, 193–220.

Schmidt, R. (1983). Interaction, acculturation, and the acquisition of communicative competence: A case study of an adult. In E. Judd and N. Wolfson (Eds.), *Sociolinguistics and language acquisition* (pp. 137–174). Rowley, MA: Newbury House.

Schumann, J. H. (1978). The acculturation model for second language acquisition. In R. C. Gingras (Ed.), *Second language acquisition and foreign language learning* (pp. 27–50). Washington, D.C.: Center for Applied Linguistics.

Taguchi, N. (2007). Task difficulty in oral speech act production. *Applied Linguistics, 28*, 113–135.

Taguchi, N. (2010). Research synthesis of longitudinal studies in interlanguage pragmatics. In A. Trosborg (Ed.), *Pragmatics across languages and cultures* (Vol. 7 of *Handbooks of pragmatics*, pp. 333–361). Berlin: Mouton de Gruyter.

Takahashi, S. (2005). Pragmalinguistic awareness: Is it related to motivation and proficiency? *Applied Linguistics, 26*, 90–120.

Takahashi, T. and Beebe, L. M. (1987). The development of pragmatic competence by Japanese learners of English. *JALT Journal, 8*, 131–155.

Takimoto, M. (2007). The effects of input-based tasks on the development of learners' pragmatic proficiency. *Applied Linguistics, 28*, 1–25.

Tateyama, Y. (2001). Explicit and implicit teaching of pragmatic routines. In K. Rose and G. Kasper (Eds.), *Pragmatics in language teaching* (pp. 200–222). Cambridge: Cambridge University Press.

Tatsuki, D. H. and Houck, N. R. (Eds.) (2010). *Pragmatics: Teaching speech acts.* New York: TESOL.

Thomas, J. (1983). Cross-cultural pragmatics. *Applied Linguistics, 4*, 91–112.

von Stutterheim, C. and Klein, W. (1987). A concept-oriented approach to second language studies. In C. W. Pfaff (Ed.), *First and second language acquisition processes* (pp. 191–205). Cambridge, MA: Newbury House.

Vyatkina, N. and Belz, J. A. (2006). A learner corpus-driven intervention for the development of L2 pragmatic competence. In K. Bardovi-Harlig, C. Félix-Brasdefer, and A. Omar (Eds.), *Pragmatics and language learning* (Vol. *11*, pp. 293–329). Honolulu: University of Hawai'i, National Foreign Language Resource Center.

Warga, M. and Schölmberger, U. (2007). The acquisition of French apologetic behaviour in a study abroad context. *Intercultural Pragmatics, 4*, 221–252.

Wolfson, N. (1986). Research methodology and the question of validity. *TESOL Quarterly, 20*, 689–699.

Wolfson, N. and Judd, E. (Eds.). (1983) *Sociolinguistics and second language acquisition* (pp. 137–174). Rowley, MA: Newbury House.

Yu, M. -C. (2004). Interlinguistic variation and similarity in second language speech act behavior. *The Modern Language Journal, 88*, 102–119.

10

Vocabulary

Batia Laufer and I. S. P. Nation

Introduction

"The real intrinsic difficulty of learning a foreign language lies in that of having to master its vocabulary" (Sweet, 1899). More and more, language researchers and practitioners have come to realize the truth of Sweet's statement. Unlike grammar, which is a system of a limited number of rules, vocabulary is an open set of many thousands of items. Hence, one reason for the enormity of the vocabulary learning task lies in its quantity. Furthermore, word knowledge entails the mastery of numerous features of the word in question and of the patterns it can form with other words. Hence, the second intrinsic difficulty of vocabulary learning is qualitative. Finally, since vocabulary consists of a huge number of words of various degrees of usefulness, many of them will not appear frequently in the second language input, particularly in the context of instructed learning (i.e., in a regular classroom). Learners receive grammatical reinforcement by encountering grammatical structures in every phrase or sentence they are exposed to. They do not receive the same kind of reinforcement of a lot of the low frequency vocabulary, for which large quantities of input would be required. Hence, the third difficulty of learning foreign language vocabulary is environmental or situational. This paper provides an overview of vocabulary learning addressing the three dimensions stated above.

Historical discussion

Except for some brief times of activity, vocabulary teaching has been largely neglected and has been subordinated to other units of analysis in curriculum design, such as grammar, topics, or tasks. The noted exception to this was Michael West's (1931) *New Method Readers* which used vocabulary as the main unit of progression in the course.

There has, however, been a long history of creating word lists of the most useful vocabulary needed by second language learners of English. Since usefulness was considered to overlap with word frequency, word lists included the most frequent words in a language. The most influential of the word lists was the 2000 headword *General Service List of English Words* (West, 1953), which included frequency information and also provided relative frequencies of the major senses and meanings of the words that it contained. It was especially influential in the development of schemes for graded readers. There is still no equivalent adequate replacement for it.

Vigorous growth in research on L2 vocabulary learning has largely occurred since the 1990s when an increasing body of researchers made vocabulary research part of their continuing research agenda.

Core issues

Lexical selection

When selecting words for L2 vocabulary teaching, it is important to realize that non-native speakers operate with a limited vocabulary by comparison with native speakers. One must therefore make sure that this vocabulary will be as useful as possible and as accurate as possible when functioning in the language. Important words are of two kinds: those that are frequent in the language being learnt and therefore useful for all purposes, and words that may be infrequent, but are nevertheless useful for learners' particular needs, for example, academic reading, or tour guiding.

Frequent words and useful words. In recent years there has been an interest in creating specialized vocabulary lists. This reflects the realization that some words may be useful to some learners even if they are not generally frequent in the language, depending on the specific needs that learners may have. A good example is Coxhead's (2000) Academic Word List, which contains 570 words which are frequent in academic discourse, and has therefore provided a very useful source for designing instructional materials for academic purposes (see for example Schmitt and Schmitt, 2005).

In spite of the technological advances that led to the construction of corpora and subsequent collection of data on word frequency, range and dispersion, the creation of reliable and valid word lists is still problematical. Two methodological problems with creating word lists are distinguishing between various meanings of homonyms and including multiword units. Word frequency counting programs cannot distinguish *panel* (meaning a group of experts) from *panel* (as in *ceiling panel*, or a part of a car). With research into homonymy it may be possible to design programs that can search for known homonyms and tag them so that they can be counted as separate items. Typically, word lists do not contain multiword units. There is no consensus in either terminology or in criteria for deciding which multiword units should be counted with the same status as single words. Continuing research into multi-word units (Schmitt, 2004) provides convincing evidence that high frequency multiword units are stored as single choices and that use of multiword units is an indicator of proficiency development. It seems likely that most multiword units are largely lexically and grammatically regular, and lists of frequent multiword units (Biber *et al.*, 2004; Grant and Nation, 2006; Shin and Nation, 2008) are useful resources for teachers and curriculum designers.

Easy words and difficult words. Another criterion for deciding which vocabulary should be focused on, in addition to frequency and usefulness, is the word's learnability. Differences in word learning difficulty were realized by Lado (1972) and Higa (1965). Lado attributed learning difficulty to the formal and semantic congruence or lack thereof between L1 and L2. Thus, for example, cognates, words similar in form and meaning between two languages, are easy, while false cognates, words similar in form, but different in meaning, are difficult. Higa, on the other hand, emphasized the relationship between the new words and already known words in the L2, particularly the relationship between the way the new words were related to each other in terms of semantic sets for presentation for learning. For example, words presented at the beginning and the end of a word list are easier than those in the middle, and new words which are semantically related are more difficult to remember than semantically unrelated words (Tinkham, 1997).

Languages related genetically contain many cognates, and unrelated languages, too, borrow words from each other, particularly from English, albeit with some phonological adaptations (Daulton, 2008). These words are easy to learn and introducing them in large numbers can enrich learners' functioning in a foreign language and consequently positively affect their confidence and motivation.

Lexical competence and its measurement

Defining lexical competence and measuring it in a valid and reliable manner is crucial for conducting research in vocabulary acquisition and for setting the goals of lexical instruction in the L2. Both researchers and educators have to decide what about single words and vocabulary in general can and should be researched or taught, and what measurement techniques to employ for testing whether and how well a word is known. We will discuss the concept of lexical competence in connection with single words and total vocabulary, and later on describe several well-known vocabulary tests and the research they have generated.

Lexical knowledge has been defined in a number of ways. Some researchers (e.g., Nation, 2001) claim that knowing a word involves a range of inter-related *sub-knowledges*—knowledge of the spoken and written form, morphological knowledge, knowledge of word meaning, collocational and grammatical knowledge, connotative and associational knowledge, and the knowledge of social or other constraints to be observed in the use of a word. For each feature of knowledge, we can distinguish between receptive (passive) and productive (active) knowledge. All these components together constitute the depth of knowledge of a word. Some researchers (e.g., Wesche and Paribakht, 1996) claim that lexical knowledge constitutes a continuum, starting with a superficial familiarity with the word and ending with the ability to use the word correctly in free production.

Read (2004) distinguishes between several types of depth of lexical knowledge—precision of meaning, comprehensive word knowledge, and network knowledge. Precision of meaning relates to one aspect of knowledge, for example, how well the meaning of a word is known. Comprehensive knowledge involves knowing aspects of the form, meaning, and use of a word. Network knowledge involves incorporation of a word into a lexical network and also has connections with fluency of access.

Another way of describing lexical knowledge, in addition to depth of knowledge of individual words, is in terms of a person's total vocabulary, i.e., the number of words s/he is familiar with. This is called vocabulary breadth or size, and here, knowledge typically refers to the ability to associate word forms with their meanings, since it is impossible to measure many aspects of depth of knowledge when a large number of words are tested.

In spite of the very long history of interest in vocabulary measurement, there are remarkably few standard, well-researched vocabulary tests. The early interest in lexical measurement was in measuring the vocabulary size of native speakers. The earliest published research in this area dates from the 1890s (see for example Kirkpatrick, 1891). Unfortunately, the methodological issues involved in vocabulary testing, particularly those related to getting a representative sample of words to test, were not properly dealt with in most of the early studies. The results of such studies greatly overestimated vocabulary size, with studies like Seashore and Eckerson's (1940) claiming that university students had vocabulary sizes of 100,000 to 200,000 words. More recent research has dealt with these problems and thus we can have more faith in their results (Goulden *et al.*, 1990; Zechmeister *et al.*, 1995). In general research shows that native speakers acquire vocabulary at a rate of around 1000 word families per year, up to the age of around 20.

There has also been interest in measuring the vocabulary size of non–native speakers. One of the earliest systematically designed tests for measuring this was Meara and Jones (1990) which used a yes/no format. This involved learners looking at an isolated word and deciding if they could provide a meaning for that word (they did not actually have to provide the meaning). A proportion of the words in the test were nonsense words that looked as if they could be real words. These were used to adjust scores for learners overstating their knowledge. If a learner responded to a proportion of the nonsense words by saying he could give a meaning for those words, the score on the real words was reduced by this proportion.

More recently, a multiple-choice vocabulary size test has been developed (Beglar, 2009; Nation and Beglar, 2007) which appears to work well. The items for the test were selected on the basis of the British National Corpus. This test measures vocabulary size up to 14,000 word families. The target words appear in neutral, non-defining contexts and the distracters include words of higher frequency than, or similar to the tested item. Here is a sample item:

fragile: These things are very <fragile>.

    a   precious
    b   hard to find
    c   popular
    d   easily broken

There are two well-established diagnostic tests of vocabulary which can be used to decide which level of vocabulary learners need to work on: the Vocabulary Levels Test (Schmitt et al., 2001), which is a revised version of the original Vocabulary Levels Test (Nation, 1983) and the Productive Levels Test (Laufer and Nation, 1999).

The latest versions of the Levels Test, Computer Adaptive Test of Size and Strength (CATSS) (Laufer and Goldstein, 2004; Laufer et al., 2004) provide a finer picture of global vocabulary knowledge by testing four degrees of knowledge of the meaning-form connection: active recall, i.e., being able to supply the *form* for a given meaning, passive recall—supplying the *meaning* for a given form, active recognition—recognizing the word form among several options, and passive recognition—recognizing the word's meaning among several options. These degrees of knowledge were shown to constitute a hierarchy (with active knowledge as the most difficult to achieve) and to be implicationally scaled.

Finding out learners' global vocabulary in terms of size or level is important when we want to describe their state of knowledge, observe their lexical progress, or check whether their lexical level is adequate for a task we plan to assign, for an experiment we want to conduct, or for a course we are designing.

The ability to supply the word form when prompted does not necessarily imply that the learner will use the word in production. Confidence, lexical preferences, and avoidance strategies can play a role in the decision to use words. Hence, it is useful to separate active knowledge from use, which can be defined as lexical richness and diversity. Similarly, fluency, that is the speed with which the word form with its meaning can be retrieved, is not part of knowledge, but control over it (see also Henriksen, 1999; Laufer and Nation, 2001).

In measuring lexical richness in writing, we measure how broad a vocabulary learners use when they write. "Broad" is usually defined in relation to the word frequency levels of a language. Vocabulary richness from this perspective involves using words from the lower word frequency levels. Laufer and Nation (1995) developed a computer-based measure, the Lexical Frequency Profile using the Range program freely available at http://www.victoria.ac.nz/lals/staff/paul-nation.aspx. The profile has been developed for French by Cobb and is available at http://www.lextutor.ca. Following the development of the Lexical Frequency Profile, several investigations have been conducted showing that the measure could be used to measure change over time, that it could distinguish between learners at different proficiency levels, and that the use of infrequent vocabulary developed even more slowly than active knowledge, but better language proficiency would eventually lead to richer lexis in free production (Laufer, 1994; 1998; Laufer and Paribakht, 1998; Morris and Cobb, 2004; Ovtcharov et al., 2006).

Research on measuring lexical richness in writing has received a considerable boost with investigations through modeling (Meara, 2006), and the development of other measures such as D (D stands for diversity), which is a measure of the quantity of different words in a text that is independent of text length (Duran *et al.*, 2004). With the development of computer-based testing it becomes easily possible to gather data on fluency of access to vocabulary by getting the computer to measure reaction times to vocabulary items.

Lexical growth

In this section we will address one of the major issues regarding the learning of vocabulary: the main source of learning new words. Is it language input, or attending to words in communicative activities, or decontextualized word practice? Some related issues are the role of intentional versus incidental learning, the number of exposures to a word that learners need in order to acquire at least partial knowledge of a word, and the nature of activities that lead to effective learning.

Sources of vocabulary learning—language input. Even though vocabulary is considered to be one of the most important elements in language learning, it tends to be subordinated to the learning of grammar, and is largely left to take care of itself in language courses. These teaching practices are probably rooted in the belief that new words are acquired as a by-product of exposure to language input and language activities that do not necessarily focus on vocabulary. The vocabulary-through-input position assumes that on encountering an unfamiliar word, the learner notices it as unfamiliar, infers its meaning from context by using a variety of linguistic and non-linguistic clues, and may consequently retain a partial or precise meaning of the word. If the word is not remembered after the learner's first exposure to it, or if only partial information about the word has been acquired, additional encounters with the same word will increase the probability of retaining it and expanding its knowledge. Even if very few words are retained after one communicative activity or reading of a text, the cumulative gains over time may be quite remarkable if the learner reads regularly. Krashen and his colleagues have been particularly active in promoting the importance of reading for vocabulary acquisition, in naturalistic and instructed contexts (e.g., Cho and Krashen, 1994; Mason and Krashen, 2004).

Interesting questions are how many times a word has to be met in the input to be learnt with its meaning, and how much learners have to read to achieve this number of exposures. Researchers seem to agree that with ten exposures, there is some chance of recognizing the meaning of a new word later on (Brown *et al.*, 2008; Waring and Takaki, 2003). According to Nation and Wang (1999), in order to meet 108 words ten times, learners would need to read nine simplified readers. They suggest that for extensive reading to be effective, learners should read one–two books per week. Such ongoing exposure to vocabulary may not only result in learning, but, more importantly, prevent the forgetting of newly learnt words. However, Cobb (2007) computed, on the basis of corpus analysis, that most words beyond the most frequent 2,000 words will not be encountered at all in a year or two even if we assume the largest plausible amounts of free reading. Hence, if highly motivated L2 readers, let alone average students, do not meet new words frequently enough, an additional source of vocabulary learning is necessary—word-focused instruction.

Sources of vocabulary learning—word focused instruction. Word focused instruction, as with form-focused instruction in grammar, combines attention to form, i.e., to specific words, in authentic, communicative activities, as well as practice of decontextualized vocabulary. The first is known as Focus on Form (FonF) and the second as Focus on Forms (FonFs) (Ellis, 2001; Long, 1991). (For relating vocabulary instruction to form-focused instruction, see Laufer, 2005, 2009, 2010).

Even though the question of incidental versus intentional learning is still being debated, some researchers attach less importance to the type of learning, and more to the quality of processing of word information. Acknowledging the importance of the notions of depth of processing (Craik and Lockhart, 1972) and elaboration (Craik and Tulving, 1975), but feeling the need to translate and operationalize such general cognitive notions in terms of L2 vocabulary learning tasks, Laufer and Hulstijn (2001) developed a motivational-cognitive construct, the Involvement Load Hypothesis, for L2 vocabulary learning.

The Involvement Load Hypothesis provides a quantifiable way of examining teaching and learning procedures to try to predict the likelihood of learning occurring from the activities. The criteria used in the analysis are need, search, and evaluation, and if each of these three criteria are present in some form, then learning is highly likely to occur. There have now been several pieces of research investigating the hypothesis and largely confirming its predictive value (Barcroft, 2004; Keating, 2008; Kim, 2008).

A continuing issue in vocabulary learning which is related to form-focused instruction is the role of the first language in explaining and defining words. There is a belief among teachers that using the first language to explain the meaning of words is undesirable. There is however no evidence to support this claim. Earlier studies of error analysis, lexical elicitation studies, and more recent analyses of learner corpora have shown that many lexical errors and avoidance phenomena are a result of the influence of the first language (see the section on lexical selection). Evidence is available that the use of the first language is a very effective way of communicating word meaning (Laufer and Shmueli, 1997), and explanation of interlingual differences between new L2 words and expressions and corresponding L1 vocabulary may be more effective than other form-focused activities (Laufer and Girsai, 2008).

Data and common elicitation measures

Lexical selection

The construction of numerous corpora of various sizes and the development of computers has had significant effects on our ability to quickly gather data on word frequency, range, and dispersion. Many of the word counting and word searching programs are available as freeware (e.g., Range, AntConc, AntWordProfiler), as Web-based programs (e.g., Range, VocabProfile, Concordance), or as commercial programs (e.g., WordSmith Tools, MonoPro).

Word learnability data is available from early error analyses of written samples (Duškova, 1969; Laforest, 1980; Myint Su, 1971), elicitation studies (e.g., Biskup, 1992), and relatively recent analyses of large learner language corpora (Granger, 1998; Nesselhauf, 2005). Two major types of difficulty emerge from all the studies. The first one is interlingual, that is, it results from relating the new L2 words to L1 words which the learners take to be equivalent in meaning. The second one is intralingual, that is, stems from relating the new words to already familiar words within the foreign language (for reviews and summaries, see Laufer, 1990, 1997; Swan, 1997). Let us look at two examples: one interlingual and the other intralingual. Different languages lexicalize concepts differently and the result is lack of semantic overlap between words in L2 and their L1 equivalents. For example, *song* and *poem* are represented by one word *shir* in Hebrew, since Hebrew does not distinguish between rhyming words with or without music. Similarly *evaluate, appreciate*, and *estimate* are translated by one Hebrew word *leha'arich*. Each time learners speak or write in English, they have to make the choice between several variants that designate a concept represented by one lexical item in their L1. An example of an intralingual difficulty is synformy—similarity of form between different words. Pairs or groups of words can be similar in sound, script, and morphology and consequently confused by learners both in production and comprehension. (for definitions and classifications of synformy see Laufer, 1988, 1991). The following are examples of synforms:

conceal/cancel/counsel   embrace/embarrass   cute/acute   lunch/launch   industrious/industrial
exhausted/exhaustive   economic/economical   sensible/sensitive/sensual

Lexical problems have been found not only in single words, but also in multi-word units. Learners whose writing has no grammatical errors and no errors in the choice of single words may still sound odd or foreign because of lack of mastery of multi-word units, particularly collocations. The difficulties with collocations are both intra- and interlingual. Many errors can be traced to learners' L1 (Biskup, 1992; Kaszubski, 2000; Nesselhauf, 2005). Furthermore, by comparison with native speaker corpora, learners exhibit underuse of common collocations and overuse of certain collocations, particularly with the core verbs—*be, have, make,* etc. (Altenberg and Granger, 2001; Kaszubski, 2000). The overall picture that emerges on the basis of collocation studies is that the use of collocations is problematic for L2 learners, regardless of years of instruction they received in L2, their native language, or type of task they are asked to perform.

Lexical competence and its measurement

The availability of the receptive and productive forms of the Vocabulary Levels Test has resulted in studies on the development of passive and active vocabulary size using both measures (Laufer, 1998; Laufer and Paribakht, 1998). These studies show that active vocabulary is smaller than passive vocabulary, and the two do not develop at a similar pace. A very important line of research involving measures of global vocabulary has to do with the relationship between lexical knowledge and the ability to function in the L2. Some examples of passive vocabulary size of learners of English as an L2 include Japanese college learners of English as a Foreign Language (EFL) who were found to know 2,000–2,300 word families after receiving 800–1,200 hours of instruction (Barrow *et al.*, 1999; Shillaw, 1995), Israeli high school learners with 3,500 word families after 1,500 hours of instruction (Laufer, 1998), and Spanish university students in English philology with about 3,700 word families after 1,100 hours of instruction (Miralpeix, 2007). The vocabulary size of learners may be adequate for conducting a simple conversation, which can be done with 2,000 word families, but it is insufficient for listening and reading comprehension. To understand a radio interview with minimal support, i.e., without the necessity to use a dictionary too often, the listener would need to know 6,000–7,000 word families, to comprehend non-fiction and novels, the reader needs 8,000–9,000 word families (Nation, 2006). People with a vocabulary size above 8,000 words can usually comprehend 98 percent of the text's lexis. A lower level of comprehension can be achieved with a vocabulary size of around 5,000 word families and 95 percent of the text's lexis. These percentages and the vocabulary sizes that ensure them have been referred to as the lexical threshold of comprehension (Hazenberg and Hulstijn, 1996; Hu and Nation, 2000; Laufer, 1989).

Unlike the studies above, which examined global vocabulary, other researchers chose to focus on the depth of knowledge by using different tests formats that all test the same words (Pulido, 2004; Waring and Takaki, 2003), or that allow the allocation of partial or full credit to each word depending on the depth of knowledge (Nurweni and Read, 1999; Wesche and Paribakht, 1996). Webb (2007) measured knowledge of orthography, paradigmatic association, syntagmatic associations, grammatical functions, and meaning and form, both productively and receptively. His tests illustrate an attempt to measure comprehensive word knowledge and the study shows that different aspects of word knowledge are affected differently by learners' exposure to words.

Wesche and Paribakht (1996) used a group administered version of an interview test (Nagy *et al.*, 1985) where learners rate their knowledge of a word on a scale of statements.

(1) I don't remember having seen this word before.
(2) I have seen this word before, but I don't know what it means.
(3) I have seen this word before, and I think it means _____ (synonym or translation).
(4) I know this word. It means_____ (synonym or translation).
(5) I can use the word in a sentence: _____.

Scores can range from 0–4. This vocabulary knowledge scale has come in for a lot of criticism because it mixes aspects of knowledge (e.g., familiarity with word form, word meaning, word use), requires proof at some levels and not at others, and is not necessarily a truly progressive scale in that it is possible to use a word in a sentence without being very sure about its meaning.

Even though, according to most researchers, word knowledge involves more than just understanding the link between form and meaning, most studies on vocabulary learning investigate whether, at a certain point of time, or at the end of some intervention, learners can demonstrate understanding of the target words, or produce the target form for given meanings. The studies that do investigate several aspects of word knowledge (e.g., Pigada and Schmitt, 2006; Waring and Takaki, 2003; Webb, 2007) examine the acquisition of meaning as well.

The emphasis on meaning is inevitable given that words are, first and foremost, units of meaning. Moreover, for comprehension purposes, matching the meaning to form, spoken or written, will usually suffice since most of the word's other features are provided in the input. Hence, word meaning is arguably the central feature of word knowledge and vocabulary research should at least focus on the extent to which people can correctly associate the word form with the concept the form denotes.

Even though multi-word units are considered to be a part of lexical knowledge, we do not yet have standardized tests that measure global knowledge of these units.

Lexical growth

Most studies of the acquisition of words from reading used relatively short texts (up to 7,000 words) and measured short-term retention of meaning (recall or recognition). The gains were very small: 1–7 words per text, though Brown et al. (2008) found better recognition results (about 11 out of 28 words), but very low (less than 1) recall results. Most words that were recognized appeared more than 10 times in stories of about 5,000 words each. Acquisition from one graded reader (measured in terms of recall or recognition of meaning) was also low: 3–5 words per reader (Horst, 2005; Waring and Takaki, 2003).

There is a lot of empirical evidence showing that the acquisition of words attended to in communicative tasks (i.e., in FonF) is more effective than acquisition from input only. Thus, reading tasks where attention is drawn to words by dictionary use yielded better results than reading tasks with or without glosses (Hulstijn et al., 1996; Knight, 1994; Luppescu and Day, 1993). In oral interaction, whenever learners focused on unfamiliar vocabulary by asking for clarifications, they had a better chance of retaining these words than when they did not attend to words in this way (De la Fuente, 2002; Ellis and He, 1999; Newton, 1993; et al., 1994). There is also evidence that focusing on words in non-communicative, non-authentic language tasks (i.e., FonFs) yields better results than acquisition from input. These can be learning from word cards or exercises in matching words, various multiple-choice activities, filling in blanks, writing unrelated sentences, creating word banks, online concordances, and other computer-assisted practice, etc. (Cobb, 2007; Hill and Laufer, 2003; Horst et al., 2005; Kitajima, 2001; Laufer, 2003; Paribakht and Wesche, 1997). Particularly effective, for short- and long-term retention, are productive tasks, which require learners to retrieve the word forms and use them generatively, that is, in novel contexts (Ellis and He, 1999; Joe, 1995, 1998; Kitajima, 2001)

The studies above have an incidental design as defined earlier. Studies of intentional learning (e.g., using bilingual lists, word cards, or in minimal context in a computer environment) show very encouraging results: up to 99 percent on immediate tests of passive knowledge, up to 79 percent on immediate tests of active knowledge, and a loss of about 25 percent on delayed tests. Moreover, research by Elgort (2011) indicates that the deliberate study of vocabulary from word cards results in both explicit and implicit knowledge. Implicit knowledge been typified by being available through subconscious access, being fluently available, and being part of a lexical network. The deliberate teaching and learning of vocabulary can result in knowledge which is of immediate use for communication.

Applications

In the previous sections we discussed the advantages and shortcomings of input based learning and demonstrated the benefits of word-focused instruction. Our contention was that attention, operationalized as involvement, is a key factor in learning. Though there are promising movements in encouraging extensive reading (see for example the Extensive Reading Foundation website), extensive reading programs are more noticeable by their absence rather than presence in most courses. For extensive reading to be maximally effective, it should be combined with autonomous word-focused learning. Learners could be encouraged to read one or two books per week which are appropriate to their language proficiency, select a certain number of new words from the books and attend to them by using a dictionary, online concordances and other computer-assisted exercise, by creating word banks and word cards, and by using the new words in writing about the plots. If large quantities of input are unavailable and teacher designed word-focused practice is the major source of vocabulary growth, the guiding teaching principles could be variation in activities and periodic recycling of words. The activities could be communicative and non-communicative, contextualized and decontextualized, related to textbook and to novel contexts, focused on comprehension and production. They could make use of either L2 or L1 and could foster incidental or intentional learning. Periodic recycling can occur in the input, in word-focused activities and in tests.

Since there is sense in taking a balanced approach to language learning in general and vocabulary learning in particular, it is important to make use of input-based learning and form-focused instruction, incidental and intentional learning, contextualized and decontextualized teaching, the use of L2 and L1, and recycling vocabulary in language input and in teacher-designed tasks. Consequently, Nation (2007) argues that to create the best opportunities for well-balanced vocabulary learning, there should be a balance across four strands—meaning-focused input, meaning-focused output, language-focused learning, and fluency development, with each of these four strands gaining roughly equal time in a course. If this guideline was followed then in some courses there would be a large reduction of deliberate teaching and learning, and a corresponding increase in message-focused input, output and fluency development, for example, through extensive reading, while in some communicatively based courses, there would be an increase in language-focused learning (form-focused instruction) using, for example, word card study and vocabulary exercises. Although the idea behind balancing the four strands is not readily researchable, there is plenty of evidence to support the existence of each one of the strands. The idea of the four strands is intended largely as a guideline for course designers and teachers to ensure that the courses provide a good balance of opportunities for learning. Another guideline for course designers and material writers, at least at the beginning stages of language learning, or in specialized courses, could be a lexical syllabus, i.e., the specific number and type of words for a particular course. For example, material writers of an academic English course could benefit from an Academic Word List as the words on the list could serve as a target for word-focused practice.

A well-designed vocabulary learning program has sensible vocabulary selection procedures, gives attention to a range of aspects of vocabulary knowledge, monitors and tests this knowledge, and provides opportunities to learn through input, output, deliberate learning, and fluency development.

Future directions

While there is now a large amount of vocabulary-focused research, there are still areas that deserve further research.

(1) *Investigation of vocabulary learning tasks*. The Involvement Load Hypothesis has proved to be a useful stimulus for research on vocabulary teaching activities. However, other systems of analysis are possible and the testing of competing systems of analysis is likely to be a fruitful area of research. The experimental and observational study of both deliberate and incidental vocabulary learning activities is a much neglected area of vocabulary studies. Incidental vocabulary learning through extensive reading has received some attention, but beyond this and a few direct tests of the Involvement Load Hypothesis, much remains to be done. Research focuses could include studies of ways to build retrieval, generative use (Joe, 1998), negotiation and imaging into learning tasks; and ways to recycle vocabulary through the use of linked skills tasks and procedures such as reporting back on a task, the pyramid procedure (Jordan, 1990), and expert groups and family groups (Nation and Newton, 2009).

(2) *Deliberate learning*. A particular vocabulary learning task that deserves further experimental study is learning vocabulary using word cards. Although there has been a lot of research establishing the basic principles of spaced retrieval, use of mnemonic techniques, and receptive and productive learning (Griffin and Harley, 1996), there is still a need for research on making the beginning stages of such learning more immediately successful. For example, will learning words that are thematically related (Tinkham, 1997) greatly increase success rates? Will learning small groups of ten words at a time lead to greater early success rates than larger numbers of words? Will the use of cues on one side of the card which make retrieval easier result in faster learning and good long-term results?

(3) *Computer-assisted vocabulary learning*. There are now many word card programs in electronic format and they can be used very portably on cell phones and iPods. The potential of these programs is greater than that of word cards in that they can monitor and manage the spacing of repetitions, provide a variety of cues when needed, and provide the pronunciation of the words and phrases.

The investigation of vocabulary-learning activities now needs to work out criteria for evaluating computer-assisted activities that take account of their unique features and yet allow comparison with non-electronic alternatives. Similarly, there needs to be experimental research comparing and evaluating the various programs.

(4) *Partial knowledge*. One of the frontiers in vocabulary research involves the measurement of small amounts of learning of words. Most of the present vocabulary measures rely largely on conscious knowledge of word form and meaning. There is plenty of evidence that implicit knowledge of vocabulary, which is subconscious, results from both deliberate and incidental

learning and, in some case, is a precursor to explicit knowledge. Having practical ways of measuring such knowledge may reveal that many activities result in far more vocabulary learning than was previously thought.

(5) *Multiword units.* Where does vocabulary end and grammar begin? The vocabulary/grammar distinction is an arbitrary one and research on multiword units serves to underline this. If much of language use is instance-based and such instances (multiword units) can be learned as vocabulary then the deliberate learning of multiword units has a large role to play in a language course, and this role should largely replace much of what is included in grammar teaching. The two-way relationship between fluency and the use and storage of multiword units is a promising area of research.

(6) *Corpus-based research.* Corpus-based research on multiword units has largely taken practical paths rather than valid ones. There are however the beginnings of growth in the number of more rigorous studies using sensible criteria that combine computer-based analysis with the painstaking manual analysis that is necessary for good research in this area. This is likely to lead to findings that can be built upon.

(7) *Vocabulary size and growth.* We still know very little about the vocabulary growth of native speakers of English. This knowledge is very useful for setting goals in second language courses both in terms of rate of learning and amount of vocabulary to be learnt. Now that the methodology of vocabulary size testing is better understood, it is likely that this area of research will now yield results that we can have some faith in.

References

Altenberg, B. and Granger, S. (2001). The grammatical and lexical patterning of MAKE in native and non-native student writing. *Applied Linguistics, 22*(2), 173–195.

Barcroft, J. (2004). Effects of sentence writing in second language lexical acquisition. *Second Language Research, 20*(4), 303–334.

Barrow, J., Nakashimi, Y., and Ishino, H. (1999). Assessing Japanese college students' vocabulary knowledge with a self-checking familiarity survey. *System, 27,* 223–247.

Beglar, D. (2009). A Rasch-based validation of the Vocabulary Size Test. *Language Testing, 26*(4), 1–22.

Biber, D., Conrad, S., and Cortes, V. (2004). If you look at …: Lexical bundles in university teaching and textbooks. *Applied Linguistics, 25*(3), 371–405.

Biskup, D. (1992). L1 influence on learners' rendering of English collocations: A Polish/German empirical study. In P. J. L. Arnaud and H. Bejoint (Eds.), *Vocabulary and applied linguistics* (pp. 85–93). London: Macmillan.

Brown, R., Waring, R., and Donkaewbua, S. (2008). Incidental vocabulary acquisition from reading, reading-while-listening, and listening. *Reading in a Foreign Language, 20*(2), 136–163.

Cho, K. -S. and Krashen, S. D. (1994). Acquisition of vocabulary from the Sweet Valley Kids Series: Adult ESL acquisition. *Journal of Reading, 37*(8), 662–667.

Cobb, T. (2007). Computing the vocabulary demands of L2 reading. *Language Learning and Technology, 11*(3), 38–63.

Coxhead, A. (2000). A new academic word list. *TESOL Quarterly, 34*(2), 213–238.

Craik, F. I. M., and Lockhart, R. S. (1972). Levels of processing: A framework for memory research. *Journal of Verbal Learning and Verbal Behavior, 11*(6), 671–684.

Craik, F. I. M. and Tulving, E. (1975). Depth of processing and the retention of words in episodic memory. *Journal of Experimental Psychology: General, 104*(3), 268–294.

Daulton, F. E. (2008). *Japan's built-in lexicon of English-based loanwords.* Clevedon, UK: Multilingual Matters.

De la Fuente, M. J. (2002). Negotiation and oral acquisition of L2 vocabulary (The roles of input and output in receptive and productive acquisition of words). *Studies in Second Language Acquisition, 24*(1), 81–112.

Duran, P., Malvern, D., Richards, B., and Chipere, N. (2004). Developmental trends in lexical diversity. *Applied Linguistics, 25*(2), 220–242.

Duskova, L. (1969). On sources of errors in foreign language learning. *International Review of Applied Linguistics in Language Teaching, 7*(1), 11–36.

Elgort, I. (2011). Deliberate learning and vocabulary acquisition in a second language. *Language Learning, 61*, 367–413.

Ellis, R. (Ed.) (2001). *Form-focused instruction and second language learning*. Malden: Blackwell Publishers.

Ellis, R. and He, X. (1999). The roles of modified input and output in the incidental acquisition of word meanings. *Studies in Second Language Acquisition, 21*(2), 285–301.

Ellis, R., Tanaka, Y., and Yamazaki, A. (1994). Classroom interaction, comprehension and the acquisition of L2 word meanings. *Language Learning, 44*(3), 449–491.

Goulden, R., Nation, P., and Read, J. (1990). How large can a receptive vocabulary be? *Applied Linguistics, 11*(4), 341–363.

Granger, S. (1998). Prefabricated patterns in advanced EFL writing: Collocations and formulae. In A. P. Cowie (Ed.), *Phraseology: Theory, analysis and applications* (pp. 145–160). Oxford: Clarendon Press.

Grant, L. and Nation, I. S. P. (2006). How many idioms are there in English? *ITL—International Journal of Applied Linguistics, 151*, 1–14.

Griffin, G. F. and Harley, T. A. (1996). List learning of second language vocabulary. *Applied Psycholinguistics, 17*(4), 443–460.

Hazenberg, S. and Hulstijn, J. (1996). Defining a minimal second language vocabulary for non-native university students: An empirical investigation. *Applied Linguistics, 17*(2), 145–163.

Henriksen, B. (1999). Three dimensions of vocabulary development. *Studies of Second Language Acquisition, 21*(2), 303–317.

Higa, M. (1965). The psycholinguistic concept of "difficulty" and the teaching of foreign language vocabulary. *Language Learning, 15*(3–4), 167–179.

Hill, M. M. and Laufer, B. (2003). Type of task, time-on-task and electronic dictionaries in incidental vocabulary acquisition. *International Review of Applied Linguistics, 41*(2), 87–106.

Horst, M. (2005). Learning L2 vocabulary through extensive reading: A measurement study. *The Canadian Modern Language Review, 61*(3), 355–382.

Horst, M., Cobb, T., and Nicolae, H. (2005). Expanding academic vocabulary with an interactive on-line database. *Language Learning and Technology, 9*(2), 90–110.

Hu, H. -C. and Nation, P. (2000). Unknown vocabulary density and reading comprehension. *Reading in a Foreign Language, 13*(1), 403–430.

Hulstijn, J., Hollander, M., and Greidanus, T. (1996). Incidental vocabulary learning by advanced foreign language students: The influence of marginal glosses, dictionary use, and reoccurrence of unknown words. *The Modern Language Journal, 80*(3), 327–339.

Joe, A. (1995). Text-based tasks and incidental vocabulary learning. *Second Language Research, 11*(2), 149–158.

Joe, A. (1998). What effects do text-based tasks promoting generation have on incidental vocabulary acquisition? *Applied Linguistics, 19*(3), 357–377.

Jordan, R. R. (1990). Pyramid discussions. *ELT Journal, 44*(1), 46–54.

Kaszubski, P. (2000). *Selected aspects of lexicon, phraseology and style in the writing of Polish advanced learners of English: a contrastive, corpus-based approach*. Retrieved November 2004, from http://main.amu.edu.pl/~przemka/research.html.

Keating, G. (2008). Task effectiveness and word learning in a second language: The involvement load hypothesis on trial. *Language Teaching Research, 12*(3), 365–386.

Kim, Y. J. (2008). The role of task-induced involvement and learner proficiency in L2 vocabulary acquisition. *Language Learning, 58*(2), 285–325.

Kirkpatrick, E. A. (1891). Number of words in an ordinary vocabulary. *Science, 18*(446), 107–108.

Kitajima, R. (2001). The effects of instructional conditions on students' vocabulary retention. *Foreign Language Annals, 34*(5), 470–482.

Knight, S. M. (1994). Dictionary use while reading: The effects on comprehension and vocabulary acquisition for students of different verbal abilities. *The Modern Language Journal, 78*(3), 285–299.

Lado, R. (1972). Patterns of difficulty. In K. Croft (Ed.), *Readings on English as a second language: For teachers and teacher-trainees* (pp. 277–291). Cambridge, Massachusetts: Winthrop Publishers, Inc.

Laforest, M. H. (1980). Towards a typology of lexical errors. *Anglistica, 23*, 1–30.

Laufer, B. (1988). The concept of "synforms" (similar lexical forms) in L2 vocabulary acquisition. *Language and Education, 2*(2), 113–132.

Laufer, B. (1989). What percentage of lexis is essential for comprehension? In C. Lauren and M. Nordman (Eds.), *Special language: From humans thinking to thinking machines* (pp. 316–323). Clevedon, UK: Multilingual Matters.

Laufer, B. (1990). Words you know: How they affect the words you learn. In J. Fisiak (Ed.), *Further insights into contrastive linguistics* (pp. 573–593). Amsterdam: John Benjamins.

Laufer, B. (1991). Some properties of the L2 mental lexicon as evidenced by lexical confusions. *International Review of Applied Linguistics, 29*(4), 317–330.

Laufer, B. (1994). The lexical profile of second language writing: Does it change over time? *RELC Journal, 25*(2), 21–33.

Laufer, B. (1997). What's in a word that makes it hard or easy? Intralexical factors affecting the difficulty of vocabulary acquisition. In M. McCarthy and N. Schmitt (Eds.), *Vocabulary description, acquisition and pedagogy* (pp. 140–155). Cambridge: Cambridge University Press.

Laufer, B. (1998). The development of passive and active vocabulary: Same or different? *Applied Linguistics, 19*(2), 255–271.

Laufer, B. (2003). Vocabulary acquisition in a second language: Do learners really acquire most vocabulary by reading? *The Canadian Modern Language Review, 59*(4), 567–587.

Laufer, B. (2005). Focus on form in second language vocabulary learning. *EUROSLA Yearbook, 5*, 223–250.

Laufer, B. (2009). Second language vocabulary acquisition from language input and from form-focused activities. *Language Teaching, 42*(3), 341–354.

Laufer, B. (2010). Form focused instruction in second language vocabulary learning. In R. Chacón-Beltrán, C. Abello-Contesse, M. M. Torreblanca-López, and M. D. López-Jiménez (Eds.), *Further insights into non-native vocabulary teaching and learning*. Clevedon, UK: Multilingual Matters.

Laufer, B., Elder, C., Hill, K., and Congdon, P. (2004). Size and strength: Do we need both to measure vocabulary knowledge? *Language Testing, 21*(2), 202–226.

Laufer, B. and Girsai, N. (2008). Form-focused instruction in second language vocabulary learning: A case for contrastive analysis and translation. *Applied Linguistics, 29*(4), 694–716.

Laufer, B. and Goldstein, Z. (2004). Testing vocabulary knowledge: Size, strength, and computer adaptiveness. *Language Learning, 54*(3), 399–436.

Laufer, B. and Hulstijn, J. (2001). Incidental vocabulary acquisition in a second language: The construct of task-induced involvement. *Applied Linguistics, 22*(1), 1–26.

Laufer, B. and Nation, P. (1995). Vocabulary size and use: Lexical richness in L2 written production. *Applied Linguistics, 16*(3), 307–322.

Laufer, B. and Nation, P. (1999). A vocabulary-size test of controlled productive ability. *Language Testing, 16*(1), 33–51.

Laufer, B. and Nation, P. (2001). Passive vocabulary size and speed of meaning recognition: Are they related? *EUROSLA Yearbook, 1*, 7–28.

Laufer, B. and Paribakht, T. S. (1998). The relationship between passive and active vocabularies: Effects of language learning context. *Language Learning, 48*(3), 365–391.

Laufer, B. and Shmueli, K. (1997). Memorizing new words: Does teaching have anything to do with it? *RELC Journal, 28*(1), 89–108.

Long, M. (1991). Focus on form: A design feature in language teaching methodology. In K. de Bot, R. Ginsberg, and C. Kramsch (Eds.), *Foreign language research in cross-cultural perspective* (pp. 39–52). Amsterdam: John Benjamins.

Luppescu, S. and Day, R. (1993). Reading, dictionaries and vocabulary learning. *Language Learning, 43*(2), 263–287.

Mason, B. and Krashen, S. D. (2004). Is form-focused vocabulary instruction worthwhile? *RELC Journal, 35*(2), 179–185.

Meara, P. (2006). Emergent properties of multilingual lexicons. *Applied Linguistics, 27*(4), 620–644.

Meara, P. and Jones, G. (1990). *Eurocentres vocabulary size test. 10KA.* Zurich: Eurocentres.

Miralpeix, I. (2007, June). *Testing receptive vocabulary size: X_Lex and Y_Lex.* Paper presented at the 29th Language Testing Research Colloquium, Barcelona, Spain.

Morris, L. and Cobb, T. (2004). Vocabulary profiles as predictors of the academic performance of Teaching English as a Second Language trainees. *System, 32*(1), 75–87.

Myint Su (1971). *The analysis of lexical errors.* Unpublished master's thesis. University of Edinburgh: Edinburgh, UK.

Nagy, W. E., Herman, P. A., and Anderson, P. C. (1985). Learning words from context. *Reading Research Quarterly, 20*(2), 233–253.

Nation, I. S. P. (1983). Testing and teaching vocabulary. *Guidelines, 5*, 12–25.

Nation, I. S. P. (2001). *Learning vocabulary in another language.* Cambridge: Cambridge University Press.

Nation, I. S. P. (2006). How large a vocabulary is needed for reading and listening? *The Canadian Modern Language Review, 63*(1), 59–82.

Nation, I. S. P. (2007). The four strands. *Innovation in Language Learning and Teaching, 1*(1), 1–12.

Nation, P. and Beglar, D. (2007). A vocabulary size test. *The Language Teacher, 31*(7), 9–13.

Nation, P. and Newton, J. (2009). *Teaching ESL/EFL Listening and Speaking.* New York: Routledge.

Nation, P. and Wang, M. (1999). Graded readers and vocabulary. *Reading in a Foreign Language, 12*(2), 355–380.

Nesselhauf, N. (2005). *Collocations in a learner corpus.* Amsterdam: John Benjamins.

Newton, J. (1993). *Task based instruction among adult learners of English and its role in second language development.* Unpublished doctoral dissertation. Victoria University of Wellington, New Zealand.

Nurweni, A. and Read, J. (1999). The English vocabulary knowledge of Indonesian university students. *English for Specific Purposes, 18*(2), 161–175.

Ovtcharov, V., Cobb, T., and Halter, R. (2006). La richesse lexicale des productions orales: Mesure fiable du niveau de compétence langagière. *The Canadian Modern Language Review, 63*(1), 107–125.

Paribakht, T. S. and Wesche, M. (1997). Vocabulary enhancement activities and reading for meaning in second language vocabulary acquisition. In J. Coady and T. Huckin (Eds.), *Second language vocabulary acquisition: A rationale for pedagogy* (pp. 174–202). Cambridge: Cambridge University Press.

Pigada, M. and Schmitt, N. (2006). Vocabulary acquisition from extensive reading: A case study. *Reading in a Foreign Language, 18*(1), 1–28.

Pulido, D. (2004). The relationship between text comprehension and second language incidental vocabulary acquisition: A matter of topic familiarity? *Language Learning, 54*(3), 469–523.

Read, J. (2004). Plumbing the depths: How should the construct of vocabulary knowledge be defined? In P. Bogaards and B. Laufer (Eds.), *Vocabulary in a second language: Selection, acquisition and testing* (pp. 209–227). Amsterdam: John Benjamins.

Seashore, R. H. and Eckerson, L. D. (1940). The measurement of individual differences in general English vocabularies. *Journal of Educational Psychology, 31*, 14–38.

Schmitt, D. and Schmitt, N. (2005). *Focus on vocabulary: Mastering the academic word list.* New York: Longman Pearson Education.

Schmitt, N. (Ed.). (2004). *Formulaic sequences.* Amsterdam: John Benjamins.

Schmitt, N., Schmitt, D., and Clapham, C. (2001). Developing and exploring the behaviour of two new versions of the Vocabulary Levels Test. *Language Testing, 18*(1), 55–88.

Shillaw, J. (1995). Using a word list as a focus for vocabulary learning. *The Language Teacher, 19*(2), 58–59.

Shin, D., and Nation, I. S. P. (2008). Beyond single words: The most frequent collocations in spoken English. *ELT Journal, 62*(4), 339–348.

Swan, M. (1997). The influence of the mother tongue on second language vocabulary acquisition and use. In M. McCarthy and N. Schmitt (Eds.), *Vocabulary description, acquisition and pedagogy* (pp. 156–180). Cambridge: Cambridge University Press.

Sweet, H. (1899). *The practical study of languages: A guide for teachers and learners.* New York: Henry Holt and Company.

Tinkham, T. (1997). The effects of semantic and thematic clustering on the learning of second language vocabulary. *Second Language Research, 13*(2), 138–163.

Waring, R. and Takaki, M. (2003). At what rate do learners learn and retain new vocabulary from reading a graded reader? *Reading in a Foreign Language, 15*(2), 130–163.

Webb, S. (2007). The effects of repetition on vocabulary knowledge. *Applied Linguistics, 28*(1), 46–65.

Wesche, M. and Paribakht, T. S. (1996). Assessing second language vocabulary knowledge: Depth versus breadth. *The Canadian Modern Language Review, 53*(1), 13–40.

West, M. (1931). *New Method Readers* (Vol. 1–7). London: Longman.

West, M. (1953). *A general service list of English words.* London: Longman, Green and Co.

Zechmeister, E. B., Chronis, A. M., Cull, W. L., D'Anna, C. A., and Healy, N. A. (1995). Growth of a functionally important lexicon. *Journal of Reading Behavior, 27*(2), 201–212.

Part III

Psycholinguistic and neurolinguistic perspectives

11

Second language processing

Norman Segalowitz and Pavel Trofimovich

Introduction

> [T]o every outward voluntary action there correspond inner acts of volition … Therefore ordered expression of thought in speech corresponds as outward volitional activity.
>
> *(Wilhelm Wundt, 1912/1973, p. 146)*

The above quote from Wilhelm Wundt (1832–1920), a German psychologist considered to be the founder of modern psychology and psycholinguistics (Blumenthal, 1970), is remarkably relevant today. Wundt considered language comprehension and production as cognitive activities, driven by the "inner" train of thought. The speaker's verbal message starts with his or her "apperception" of the overall idea (concept or general impression) to be communicated. The speaker then organizes this mental content into structured, ordered linguistic constituents, which Wundt believed to be specific to a particular language, and prepares and articulates the phonetic detail of the message. The listener, whose aim is in turn to recover the speaker's overall idea, uses this phonetic detail as cues to reconstruct the structural relations in the speaker's message and to create his or her own "inner" thought.

Wundt's ideas about language have had a lasting impact on psycholinguistics. He provided an accurate description of the psycholinguistic processes involved in language comprehension and production. This description is now part of virtually all current theoretical frameworks of language processing (e.g., Bock and Levelt, 2002). He also conceptualized language within a broader context. For Wundt, language was a cognitive phenomenon, characterized by the transformation of mental representations into ordered linguistic elements. As can be seen from our opening quote, Wundt saw language as a volitional activity as well, suggesting that speakers use language as a tool to accomplish particular goals. Emphasizing both speaker and listener in his writings, Wundt most likely also viewed language as a social act.

These three dimensions of language so aptly captured by Wundt—cognitive, volitional, and social—in a nutshell characterize our approach to discussing processing research in this chapter. We first define language processing research and provide a brief historical discussion of it, with a particular focus on second language (L2) processing. We then discuss several core issues in L2 processing research and describe what we call a "traditional" view of L2 processing research, one that emphasizes language as a cognitive activity but largely overlooks its volitional and social dimensions. Finally, we outline an alternative view of L2 processing research that encompasses many language dimensions, including cognitive, volitional, social, and what we call variational.

Historical discussion

Before we identify some of the important issues in L2 processing research, we first describe L2 processing research in relation to psycholinguistics in general, and then we place L2 processing research in historical perspective (see Blumenthal, 1970, and Altmann, 2006, for a detailed history of psycholinguistics, and Dörnyei, 2009a, for an introduction to the psychology of L2 learning). Language processing is a term central to psycholinguistics. In fact, describing what psycholinguists do would be utterly impossible without referring to language processing in some form or fashion. In one of the first reviews of psycholinguistic literature, Ervin-Tripp and Slobin (1966) defined the challenge of psycholinguists to be "finding the processes by which the competence described by linguists ... is reflected in performance under a variety of conditions" (p. 436). More recently, Harley (2008) identified the need "to discover the actual processes involved in producing and understanding language" as the primary theme of psycholinguistics (p. 19). Explicit in these statements is the emphasis on language *in action*, that is, language as it is being used for comprehension and production. Psycholinguists are interested in what people do with the language: how they learn and use it, and ultimately what processes, mechanisms, or procedures underlie language learning and use. Language processing, therefore, has come to refer to research that aims to uncover these processes, mechanisms, and procedures, typically using the research techniques of experimental psychology.

Some of the first L2 processing experiments were carried out by Cattell (1886a, c, 1887), who worked in Wundt's psychological laboratory at the University of Leipzig. While in Leipzig, Cattell perfected the use of the chronoscope to study people's reaction times (RTs) to various stimuli, including letters and words. The chronoscope was a sophisticated device which allowed researchers to record participants' RTs with millisecond accuracy when participants pressed a telegraphic key or spoke in response to a stimulus (see Cattell, 1886b). In his L2 experiments (1887), Cattell hypothesized that speakers of two languages are slower at associating words and concepts in their L2 than in their native language (L1), and believed that the strength of this association depended on speakers' familiarity with the language. To test his ideas, Cattell measured the time it took his participants to name words and pictures in both the L1 and the L2 and to translate words in both directions. He found that it took longer to name pictures in the L2 than in the L1, and that it took longer to translate words from the L1 to the L2 than in the reverse direction. Cattell concluded that the processing in an L2 is often not as rapid (and perhaps not as efficient) as the processing in one's L1.

Many of Cattell's ideas are still pertinent. For example, researchers continue to investigate how L2 users associate words with concepts in each of their two languages (e.g., Kroll and Tokowicz, 2005), and how L2 skills develop as a result of language experience (e.g., Piske and Young-Scholten, 2009). Cattell is credited with the discovery of semantic priming (Harley, 2008), the phenomenon that a prior experience with a word facilitates recognition or production of a word related in meaning. Semantic priming has been used widely in processing research which focuses on how L2 users organize and use their lexicons (see McDonough and Trofimovich, 2008). Cattell also examined the effect of practice on processing colors, words, and letters (1886d), concluding that RTs "become shorter as they become more automatic but that a limit is reached beyond which further practice has little or no effect" (p. 536). This theme is central to current research on skill learning (e.g., DeKeyser, 2007a) and on processing efficiency and automaticity (e.g., Segalowitz and Hulstijn, 2005).

However, due to a shift in research paradigms in linguistics (see Blumenthal, 1970), L2 processing research of the kind conducted by Cattell would not resume until decades later, the 1950s to be exact. In that decade, Weinreich (1953) published a model of bilingual memory organization. Ervin and Osgood (1954) elaborated the distinction between compound and coordinate bilingual processing systems and, importantly, they did so using the theoretical constructs of internal mediating processes that came to characterize cognitive approaches of the day. Penfield and Roberts (1959) proposed a "language switch" to explain how L2 users can code-switch from one language to another. The details of these theoretical proposals are not relevant to the present discussion; what is important is that these and other publications spurred a flurry of processing research (e.g., Kolers, 1963, 1966a, 1996b; Lambert *et al.*, 1958; see Keatley, 1992, for review). This upsurge in interest occurred, in no small part, because it seemed that linguistic, psychological, and neuropsychological approaches to second language learning and bilingualism were successfully converging to make possible an integrated understanding of these phenomena. From then on, L2 processing has become an active and burgeoning area of research whose scope reaches far beyond these early investigations of language organization in L2 users.

Today, L2 processing research covers virtually all aspects of language. A number of major review chapters and edited books, in addition to the present volume, provide an excellent introduction to L2 processing in the areas of phonology (Cutler and Broersma, 2005; Sebastián-Gallés and Bosch, 2005), syntax (Clahsen and Felser, 2006a, b; Frenck-Mestre, 2002), and lexicosemantics (Kroll and Tokowicz, 2005). L2 processing research also deals with different levels of analysis: processing of words (Francis, 2005), sentences (Heredia and Altarriba, 2002), and larger discourse (Raney *et al.*, 2002; Roberts *et al.*, 2008). There is research on L2 processing in different skills: reading (Healy and Bourne, 1998), writing (Francis *et al.*, 2002), listening (Cutler, 2000), and speaking (Kilborn, 1994). Last but not least, L2 processing research also intersects with other areas of cognitive psychology: language and emotion (Altarriba *et al.*, 2008; Pavlenko, 2005a), cognitive development (Nicoladis, 2008), thought (Pavlenko, 2005b), attention and automaticity (Segalowitz and Hulstijn, 2005), memory (Heredia, 2008; John Williams, Chapter 26, this volume), and aging (Schrauf, 2008).

Core issues

In his overview of processing perspectives in the field of second language acquisition (SLA), Pienemann (2004) noted that "[l]anguage processing research has been a key aspect of SLA ... right from the beginning" (p. 37). The beginning is marked by the publication of Pit Corder's now classic 1967 paper "The significance of learner's errors" which, for Pienemann and others (e.g., Larsen-Freeman, 2002), defined SLA as an independent discipline. Corder argued that L2 learners' errors constitute a rich source of evidence of what strategies or procedures learners use in their language learning. He also argued that learners' performance is not simply a reflection of the language input they receive. Rather, learners' performance reflects the language input they can effectively *use* at a given stage of development. Corder suggested that L2 acquisition can be seen as a complex interaction between language input and learner-internal processes, and implied that understanding these learner-internal processes is key to explaining L2 acquisition. In a nutshell, these ideas defined what could be called the overall research agenda for L2 processing research in SLA: to determine how L2 learners process language input and, ultimately, to provide a theoretical description of the "L2 processor."

There is a rich body of published literature dealing with this goal of L2 processing research, including Krashen's Monitor Model (1985), Levelt's and McLaughlin's work on procedural skills (Levelt, 1978; McLaughlin, 1987), VanPatten's work on input processing (2007, Chapter 16, this volume), Andersen's conception of operating principles (1984), MacWhinney and Bates' Competition Model (1989) and MacWhinney's more recent Unified Model (2008; Chapter 13, this volume), Clahsen's writing on processing strategies (1984), Pienemann's Processability

Theory (2007; Pienemann and Keßler, Chapter 14, this volume), as well as Carroll's Autonomous Induction Theory (2007). Much of this work is described elsewhere in this volume (see also Pienemann, 2003). Current L2 processing research reaches far beyond SLA; we outline here several major strands of this processing research.

The goals of L2 processing research today are manifold. One strand of research, for example, investigates the organization of the two languages in L2 users, including L2 learners. Do L2 users represent and use the forms and meanings of words in a separate or a shared manner (e.g., Francis, 2005)? Do they use separate or shared syntax (e.g., Hartsuiker and Pickering, 2008)? Another strand of research focuses on documenting how L2 processing is different from L1 processing (e.g., De Bot, 1992; Levelt, 1999). There is a growing body of literature on language switching. For example, how do L2 users keep their two languages apart when they use them and yet seamlessly switch from one to the other (e.g., Gollan and Ferreira, 2009; Meuter, 2005)? Another active strand of research focuses on how innate language knowledge is, including L2 knowledge (e.g., Mehler *et al.*, 2005; see also DeKeyser, Chapter 27, this volume). Other researchers investigate how L2 processing (procedural) skills develop (e.g., DeKeyser, 2007b), whether and how explicit rules are involved in L2 processing (e.g., Hulstijn, 2005b; Paradis, 2009), and how L2 users allocate and use attentional resources (e.g., Taube-Schiff and Segalowitz, 2005; Tomlin and Villa, 1994). Yet others study relationships among different language processes and examine whether these processes are modular or interactive (e.g., Costa, 2005; Truscott and Sharwood Smith, 2004). Finally, there is some research investigating whether L2 learning relies on processing specific to language or, instead, on general cognitive processing capacity (e.g., DeKeyser, Chapter 27, this volume; Goldberg and Casenhiser, 2008).

As mentioned earlier, most L2 processing research has overwhelmingly focused on *cognitive* information processing issues and has characterized L2 processing as performance in well-controlled laboratory situations. However, as Wundt pointed out long ago, language also involves volitional and social dimensions. A lot has been learned about these dimensions since Wundt's time, and so these will be discussed here with respect to L2 processing. We also discuss a variational dimension that is important to consider in L2 processing.

Volitional

Wundt's idea that speech acts correspond to inner acts of volition has important implications for both L1 and L2 processing. The first and most central implication is that when speakers use a language, they behave as active agents, not passive recipients of messages or mechanical producers of speech. Being an active agent has consequences for processing. It means that the linguistic information being exchanged is embedded in a cognitive environment marked by communicative intentions. When an L2 user produces speech, the output is driven by communicative intentions (e.g., the speaker wants to persuade the listener of something). These intentions have their own underlying processing mechanisms that recruit appropriate linguistic resources so that the speech produced will serve to promote the speaker's goals. This means that the processing underlying speech output includes the processing underlying the formation of communicative intentions. Likewise, the perception of speech involves trying to understand the communicative intentions of the interlocutor. This is because the interlocutor's communicative intentions provide crucial contextual information that helps to constrain possible interpretations of the incoming speech and thereby facilitate accurate comprehension.

The importance of this last idea has been emphasized in usage-based (Barlow and Kemmer, 2000) accounts of L1 and L2 acquisition (Robinson and Ellis, 2008; Tomasello, 2003). For example, according to Tomasello, language use does not involve simply putting an acoustic message "out there" or taking in a message. It involves engaging with the interlocutor in joint attentional activities (in which each person monitors the other's attention and together they attend to the objects and events that are the focus of the communication) and in intention reading (in which each person engages in identifying the other person's communicative and social intentions). These attentional functions are just as important in L2 acquisition and use as they are in L1, and they point to the importance of thinking about how language involves attentional processing. Moreover, the use of an L2 to engage interlocutors in joint attention and intention reading can pose certain L2-specific challenges.

In terms of establishing joint attention with the interlocutor and trying to read his or her intentions, the L1 and L2 can in some ways be relatively congruent in how they afford possibilities for doing this and in other ways quite discrepant, giving rise to processing challenges. For example, one way a speaker can use language to harness a listener's attention is by naming the objects and events that the listener should attend to. There is usually a great deal of overlap in the way different languages allow one to do this and, other than having to learn the specific names for things and taking into account how the lexicons of the two languages are interconnected (Kroll and Tokowicz, 2005), the processing involved in L2 naming requires linking words to concepts, much as in the L1. The L2 should pose relatively little challenge in this case.

However, communication is not just about naming things. Speakers try to convey their *perspective* regarding the *relationships* between the things they are naming. Consider, for example, these sentences:

(1) John passed his exam and he had partied the night before.
(2) John passed his exams despite having partied the night before.
(3) John passed his exams despite supposedly having partied the night before.

The first sentence draws attention to two events, John's passing the exam and John's partying. The second sentence draws attention to the connection between the two events (partying was definitely not the reason for passing the exam). The third sentence conveys a message similar to the second but the focus here is to suggest that the speaker has doubts about the connection (perhaps John really did study the night before). The relational information in these sentences is conveyed by the use of grammaticized words (*and*, *despite*, *supposedly*), not by simple naming. In general, grammaticized words do not map onto translation equivalents from one language to another as directly as content words seem to do (which also is seldom in a clear one-to-one fashion).

These kinds of cross-linguistic differences, which have been especially well documented with respect to spatial prepositions (e.g., Levinson and Wilkins, 2006), can place a processing burden on the L2 user, particularly if knowledge of the L2 is relatively weak. The L2 user—whether speaking or listening—has to engage in extra processing in order to accurately insert or extract the appropriate perspective on the relational information in the message. There has been relatively little cognitive processing work on this topic in the L2. Taube-Schiff and Segalowitz (2005) and Segalowitz and Frenkiel-Fishman (2005) showed that attention focus in the processing of simple grammaticized aspects of language involved a greater cognitive load in the L2 than in the L1. The processing implication of these ideas is that speakers have to think about the perspective they wish to convey in a way that is compatible with how the language makes it possible for them to do so. Slobin (1996) referred to this as "thinking for speaking," a mode of thinking that can present a processing burden in the L2.

Social

The social dimension of L2 processing arises naturally from the fact that communication is a social process, as discussed in more detail by Lantolf, Chapter 4, in this volume. What is important to recognize is that there are specific types of social information that are always part of a speaker's communicative intentions. These types of information include knowing how to speak appropriately according to the social norms of the target language community (Hymes, 1967, 1972). Hymes commented that every L1 speaker acquires "the communicative competence that enables a member of the community to know when to speak and when to remain silent, which code to use, when, where and to whom, etc." (1967, p. 13). The communication of these types of social information draws upon particular features of language (Canale and Swain, 1980; Pawley and Syder, 1983; Wray, 2002). For example, interlocutors normally wish to maintain good social relations with each other. This usually involves speaking in an appropriate register and shifting from one register to another in a socially appropriate way, using correct forms of politeness, etc. Languages provide different ways of accomplishing such sociolinguistic functions, and L1 users normally process sociolinguistic information contained in the phonology, prosody, grammatical constructions, fixed expressions, and lexis of messages quite unconsciously. For L2 users, this can be a challenge if they are not as familiar with how the target language handles these sociolinguistic functions as they are in the L1 (e.g., Segalowitz, 1976).

This social dimension of communication has processing implications for speakers, especially in the L2. Wray (2002) describes some of these implications in her account of speaker-hearer alignment. Her idea is that L1 speakers try to help each other by minimizing the processing loads they place on each other. They can do this, for example, by using formulaic expressions and partially fixed strings: pre-assembled, lexicalized utterances and expressions that mark out the structure of the discourse to make it more predictable (e.g., *In the first place* ...). Speakers also often provide clues as to their place of origin, background, etc. (sometimes volitionally, sometimes not) by the expressions they use and through their accent, thereby informing the interlocutor about which fixed expressions they are likely to understand. All this helps reduce processing load. Of course, engaging in speaker-hearer alignment may be difficult for some L2 speakers; this activity, which lies behind the communication of the main cognitive content of the message, can thus constitute a processing burden for L2 speakers.

There is yet another processing challenge for L2 users, associated with the social dimension of L2 processing and its volitional nature. As mentioned earlier, the L2 speaker/listener's normal focus of attention will be on the establishment of joint attention with the interlocutor and reading that person's communicative and social intentions. Also, as mentioned, it will involve efforts to achieve speaker-hearer alignment. These will depend on correctly perceiving and interpreting subtle speech features. Because these aspects of speech are almost never taught explicitly, and because most proficient speakers of either an L1 or L2 are usually not consciously aware of how utterances systematically provide social messages alongside their cognitive content, the learning of these aspects of speech will be implicit rather than explicit. Hulstijn (2005a) defines this implicit/explicit distinction as follows: "Explicit learning is input processing with the conscious intention to find out whether the input information contains regularities and, if so, to work out the concepts and rules with which these regularities can be captured. Implicit learning is input processing without such an intention, taking place unconsciously" (p. 131). Thus, an important aspect of L2 ability involves the processing and learning of the implicit knowledge associated with the social dimension of communication (see also Ellis, 1994). This can be problematic for many L2 speakers.

Variational

By "variational" we mean that contexts in which the L2 is used—in the classroom, in natural settings, in laboratory studies—can be characterized in terms of variability features that establish the cognitive processing demand characteristics for L2 performance in a particular context. (This meaning is not to be confused with the important but quite different "variationist perspective" discussed by Bayley and Tarone, Chapter 3, this volume.) A variational continuum can be described ranging from closed to open skill environments (Allard and Starkes, 1991), although most communicative situations will include many characteristics of both. A closed skill environment is one where variability in the conditions under which performance takes place has negligible impact on performance, and where the goal of performance is to repeat some action (physical or cognitive) as precisely as possible to meet some standard. In sport, weight lifting and basketball free throws are often given as examples. In these cases, variability in the environment has a negligible impact on performance and the goal of performance is to execute the required movements as precisely as possible. A language-based example might be a (very narrowly conceived) L2 instruction requiring the recitation of memorized material or heavily scripted role play activities.

An open skill environment is one where there is a great deal of variability in the conditions under which performance takes place and where dealing with this variability is fully part and parcel of skilled performance. As well, the goal of an open skill is to bring about some change in the environment, as opposed to simply repeating an action precisely. Examples of open skill environments include competitive team sports such as basketball or hockey, where the goal is to place an object in a particular location (the puck into the net, the basketball through the hoop). Here the performance conditions change unpredictably from moment to moment as players try to out-maneuver each other, and achieving the performance goal requires overcoming this variability. A language-based example here would be L2 learning that takes place in naturalistic contexts (e.g., during stay abroad or in some immersion classrooms).

Natural communicative contexts are examples of open skill environments because the goal is to change the environment (e.g., persuade someone to believe or do something) in the face of the unpredictability of the interlocutor's reactions and of unanticipated interruptions and distractions from the environment. Open skills, in contrast to closed skills, carry processing demands that draw on attention, given how important it is to notice and then respond quickly to unexpected changes in the environment. Thus, not only does L2 processing in natural communicative contexts require the ability to harness linguistic resources in the social dimension of language as discussed earlier, but it also requires being able to handle changes as they occur in real time (e.g., adapting to an interlocutor who unexpectedly responds emotionally to a message, or who tries to change the topic, or refuses to yield the floor). Closed skill environments do not carry such demand characteristics and L2 learning that takes place in such environments is unlikely to elicit appropriate processing activities that will enable full transfer of learning outside the learning context (we return to this point below in the section on applications).

Data and common elicitation measures

What defines L2 processing research (and language processing research in general) is that it employs methodologies targeting the processes, mechanisms, and procedures that language users rely on in the many ways that they use language. Early L2 processing research, apart from Cattell's pioneering studies, employed two major methodologies (for review, see Keatley, 1992). These two methodologies were recall (in which participants retrieve from memory previously heard or seen words, sentences, or texts) and recognition (in which participants indicate whether or not they had previously heard or seen words, sentences, or texts). It was not until the late 1970s and early 1980s that what we now consider to be typical processing methodologies—those relying on timed responses—became mainstream. In the 1970s, researchers questioned whether recall and recognition provided an accurate depiction of how people access and use language (e.g., Posner and Snyder, 1975). These researchers reasoned that recall and recognition were examples of slow and consciously controlled language processing influenced by participants' test-taking strategies. They argued instead that only automatic processing accurately reflected how languages are organized and used. In the terminology of the day, processing was considered automatic when it was not subject to conscious control and when it proceeded without much attention or awareness (see Neely, 1977, and Favreau and Segalowitz, 1983, for examples of studies targeting automatic processing in L1 and L2, respectively).

Automatic processing can be elicited through methodologies requiring participants to respond to language stimuli as quickly as possible, under time pressure or in situations where more than one task competes for participants' attention. Examples of such methodologies, all using RT measures, include lexical decision, repetition priming, and phoneme detection. In lexical decision, participants indicate whether a letter string spells a word (e.g., *brain*) or nonword (e.g., *brone*). In repetition priming, participants perform the same or similar task more than once so that RTs can be compared. And in phoneme detection, they press a key as soon as they detect a particular target in a stimulus, for example, the phoneme /n/. The logic of all these and most other RT-based methodologies is the following: because the tasks are speeded (performed under time pressure), participants' reliance on test-taking strategies is minimized, and RTs become a measure of the time (and sometimes the effort) needed to complete a given language processing task (see Posner, 1978; Sternberg, 1969).

Of course, not all RT-based methodologies elicit automatic processing. For example, in self-paced reading or listening (the so-called moving window technique), participants read sentences or texts one word at a time so that the time required to read each word can be recorded. Depending on how the task is set up (i.e., whether participants read or listen under time pressure), it may not elicit automatic processing; nevertheless, the measures collected by researchers using such tasks will be "on-line," that is, reflecting processing in real time. For example, self-paced reading tasks are considered on-line, but grammaticality judgment tasks (in which participants read a sentence and then indicate, on paper, whether a sentence is acceptable in a language) are not.

Modern on-line processing techniques also include the use of eye-tracking and event-related brain potentials to study various aspects of L2 processing (e.g., Frenck-Mestre, 2005; Libben and Titone, 2009). We refer interested readers to the following additional references on the use of particular processing methodologies and tasks: auditory, semantic, and syntactic priming (McDonough and Trofimovich, 2008), lexical decision (Altarriba and Basnight-Brown, 2007; Goldinger, 1996), cross-modal priming (Marinis, 2003; Tabossi, 1996), various measures of speech processing (reviewed in Grosjean and Frauenfelder, 1997), picture-word interference (Costa *et al.*, 2003), translation recognition (de Groot, 1992), and self-paced reading and listening (Marinis, 2003).

Empirical verification

Hulstijn (2002), in a broad overview of processing issues in L2 acquisition, called for more attention to the emotional, motivational and social aspects of L2 processing. He wrote, "... eventually cognition should be conceived as a much broader construct, encompassing not only information or knowledge, but also *emotion and motivation ... and that cognition develops and exists in a social and cultural environment*" (emphasis added; p. 195).

Putting all these elements together will be a challenge. The challenge is all the greater because the different dimensions—cognitive, volitional, social, variational, emotional, and even motivational—will interact in complex ways. For example, the acquisition of L2 processing skills along the cognitive dimensions—say, highly efficient and rapid word retrieval, grammatical parsing, etc.—is likely to increase a person's motivation to engage in L2 contact compared to a person whose efficiency of L2 cognitive processing remains low. Increased motivation will lead to decisions that result in more frequent exposure to the L2 in communicative contexts where the learner experiences a great deal of language repetition that, in turn, will strengthen cognitive processing efficiency and the acquisition of the implicit linguistic knowledge. A number of self-reinforcing loops between the cognitive, motivational, social, and experiential aspects of L2 use can emerge, all leading to increased L2 processing skills (see Segalowitz, 2010). Very likely, a multidimensional, dynamic theoretical framework will be needed to capture these complex interactions among different dimensions of L2 processing (see De Bot *et al.*, 2007, and Larsen-Freeman and Cameron, 2008).

In addition to conceptual challenges of integrating several processing dimensions into a coherent (and testable) theoretical framework of L2 processing, an even greater challenge is for L2 researchers to identify appropriate methodologies for studying complex interactions among these dimensions. At the beginning of this chapter, we discussed several methodologies typically used in current L2 processing research. However, the more complex picture of L2 processing that emerged here will clearly require either using existing methodologies in novel ways or developing new ones capable of capturing subtle dynamic effects and interactions among the many different aspects of language processing. While we are unable to point to any such new methodologies at this time, we see great potential in using existing research tools in novel ways. The edited volume by Trueswell and Tanenhaus (2005) contains excellent examples of existing processing methodologies used to study what they term "world-situated language use," that is, language processing in contextually rich and socially appropriate environments. Some of these examples include the use of eye-tracking to study real-time reference resolution in an unscripted conversation, as participants perform a common task, or the use of syntactic priming to examine interlocutors' linguistic accommodation and alignment in a dialog. Although this volume focuses on L1 processing, many (if not all) methodologies described in it are appropriate to the study of L2 processing as well.

Applications

These L2 processing considerations have considerable instructional relevance with respect to a number of topics, including motivation and L2 learning (e.g., Dörnyei, 2009a, b; Ushioda and Dörnyei, Chapter 24, this volume), the transfer of learning from one context to another (e.g., Lightbown, 2007; Trofimovich and Gatbonton, 2006), and the promotion of automaticity and L2 processing efficiency within a communicative language teaching framework (Gatbonton and Segalowitz, 2005). At least one way to conceptualize the instructional relevance issue is to pose two questions about transfer: (a) What target L2 processing skills does the learner need to acquire during instruction for transfer later to different communicative situations both in and outside the classroom? (b) What is the best way for instruction to optimize this transfer?

From the account presented here, the target processing skills required for communication include the ability to process the basic cognitive information in a message, while at the same time participating in an exchange of sociolinguistic information. Moreover, this processing of cognitive and social information needs to take place while the speaker is engaged in trying to accomplish several other goals simultaneously: establishing joint attention with the interlocutor; trying to read the interlocutor's social and communicative intentions; and pursuing his or her own communicative intentions. All this has to be done in an open communicative environment characterized by variability that must be taken into account for communication to succeed.

How can instruction optimize successful acquisition and transfer of these L2 processing skills? According to the principle of transfer-appropriate processing (Morris *et al.*, 1977; see Lightbown, 2007, for L2-specific examples), learners need to engage in the kinds of cognitive processing that include establishing joint attention, reading communicative intentions, processing perspective/construal information, etc. because it is these aspects of L2 processing that will need to be transferred to other communicative settings. Perhaps the most direct way to accomplish this is for learning activities to require participants to engage in *authentic interaction*, where speakers have a psychologically genuine need to successfully receive and convey the cognitive information at the core of the communication (see Gatbonton and Segalowitz, 2005, for discussion of how to accomplish this). Instruction that includes activities imbued with authentic interaction will bring into the picture the volitional, social, and variational elements discussed earlier, because these elements are inherent to such communication, thereby eliciting more transfer appropriate L2 processing. Also, following from the earlier discussion, language instruction needs to promote the development of efficient L2 processing (DeKeyser, 2007b). For this, there must be ample repetition of the targeted L2 processing during communicative learning activities, in real time. The challenge here is to provide this repetition in a way that does not undermine the authenticity of the communication. This can be achieved by designing learning activities that are *inherently repetitive* (Gatbonton and Segalowitz, 2005), that is, activities that require the learner to repeat targeted L2 processing in order to achieve his or her genuine communicative goals (e.g., in gathering multiple pieces of information for a problem-solving activity).

In closing, if there is one overriding point to emphasize regarding the instructional relevance of the L2 processing issues discussed in this chapter, it is that successful use of the L2 requires cognitive multitasking in several dimensions of processing at once. That is why instructional settings need to promote L2 processing in a pedagogically sound and cognitively engaging multitasking context if learning is to transfer beyond the instructional setting.

Future directions

We began this chapter by citing Wilhelm Wundt's ideas on language as primarily a volitional activity, one that likely occurs in a constantly changing, and therefore highly variable, social environment. Our goal was to describe language processing, and L2 processing in particular, not only as a purely cognitive activity, a view that has dominated language processing research to date, but also as a phenomenon that involves volitional, social, and variational aspects. We conclude our chapter by citing Wundt again. In his lectures on psychology as a science, he wrote, "... [I]t is experience and reflection which constitute each and every science. Experience comes first; it gives us our bricks. Reflection is the mortar, which holds the bricks together. We cannot build without both ... It is therefore essential for scientific progress that the sphere of experience be enlarged, and new instruments of reflection from time to time invented" (Wundt, 1894/1977, pp. 8–9). This statement by Wundt aptly captures what we would like to identify as possible future directions of L2 processing research. For L2 processing to be understood more fully, in future studies researchers need to "enlarge" their research experience to include the study of L2 processing not only in decontextualized laboratory settings but also in real-life environments, those that involve the use of language as a volitional, social, and variational activity. Researchers may also need to expand their stock of research tools to enable the study of complex interactions among cognitive, volitional, social, variational, emotional, and motivational dimensions of language processing, to name a few. All these avenues of future research, we hope, will lead to coherent and testable theoretical conceptualizations of L2 processing and will allow for a greater understanding of how L2 processing issues relate to L2 acquisition in various instructional contexts.

References

Allard, F. and Starkes, J. L. (1991). Motor-skill experts in sports, dance, and other domains. In K. A. Ericsson and J. Smith (Eds.), *Toward a general theory of expertise* (pp. 126–152). Cambridge: Cambridge University Press.

Altarriba, J. and Basnight-Brown, D. M. (2007). Methodological considerations in performing semantic- and translation-priming experiments across languages. *Behavior Research Methods*, *39*(1), 1–18.

Altarriba, J., Pavlenko, A., and N. Segalowitz (Eds.) (2008). Emotion words in the monolingual and bilingual lexicon [Special issue]. *The Mental Lexicon*, *3*(1).

Altmann, G. T. M. (2006). History of psycholinguistics. In K. Brown (Ed.), *The encyclopedia of language and linguistics* (pp. 257–265). Oxford: Elsevier.

Andersen, R. (1984). The one-to-one principle of interlanguage construction. *Language Learning*, *34*(4), 77–95.

Barlow, M. and Kemmer, S. (Eds.) (2000). *Usage based models of language.* Stanford: CSLI Publications.

Blumenthal, A. L. (1970). *Language and psychology: Historical aspects of psycholinguistics.* New York: John Wiley.

Bock, K. and Levelt, W. J. M. (2002). Language production: Grammatical encoding. In G. T. M. Altmann (Ed.), *Psycholinguistics: Critical concepts in psychology* (Vol. 5, pp. 405–452). London: Routledge.

Canale, M. and Swain, M. (1980). Theoretical bases of communicative approaches to second language teaching and testing. *Applied Linguistics*, *1*(1), 1–47.

Carroll, S. E. (2007). Autonomous induction theory. In B. VanPatten and J. Williams (Eds.), *Theories in second language acquisition: An introduction* (pp. 155–173). Mahwah, NJ: Lawrence Erlbaum.

Cattell, J. M. (1886a). The time it takes to see and name objects. *Mind*, *11*, 63–65.

Cattell, J. M. (1886b). The time taken up by cerebral operations, Parts 1 and 2. *Mind*, *11*, 220–242.

Cattell, J. M. (1886c). The time taken up by cerebral operations, Part 3. *Mind*, *11*, 377–392.

Cattell, J. M. (1886d). The time taken up by cerebral operations, Part 4. *Mind*, *11*, 524–538.

Cattell, J. M. (1887). Experiments on the association of ideas. *Mind*, *12*, 68–74.

Clahsen, H. (1984). The acquisition of German word order: A test case for cognitive approaches to L2 development. In R. W. Andersen (Ed.), *Second languages: A cross-linguistic perspective* (pp. 219–242). Rowley, MA: Newbury House.

Clahsen, H. and Felser, C. (2006a). Grammatical processing in language learners. *Applied Psycholinguistics*, *27*(1), 3–42.

Clahsen, H. and Felser, C. (2006b). How native-like is non-native language processing? *Trends in Cognitive Sciences*, *10*(12), 564–570.

Corder, S. P. (1967). The significance of learner's errors. *International Review of Applied Linguistics*, *5*(4), 161–170.

Costa, A. (2005). Lexical access in bilingual production. In J. F. Kroll and A. M. B. de Groot (Eds.), *Handbook of bilingualism: Psycholinguistic approaches* (pp. 308–325). New York: Oxford University Press.

Costa, A., Colomé, A., Gómez, O., and Sebastián-Gallés, N. (2003). Another look at cross-language competition in bilingual speech production: Lexical and phonological factors. *Bilingualism: Language and Cognition*, *6*(3), 167–179.

Cutler, A. (2000). Listening to a second language through the ears of a first. *Interpreting*, *5*(1), 1–23.

Cutler, A. and Broersma, M. (2005). Phonetic precision in listening. In W. J. Hardcastle and J. M. Beck (Eds.), *A figure of speech: A festschrift for John Laver* (pp. 63–91). Mahwah, NJ: Lawrence Erlbaum.

De Bot, K. (1992). A bilingual production model: Levelt's "Speaking" model adapted. *Applied Linguistics*, *13*(1), 1–24.

De Bot, K., Lowie, W., and Verspoor, M. (2007). A dynamic systems theory approach to second language acquisition. *Bilingualism: Language and Cognition*, *10*(1), 7–21.

de Groot, A. M. B. (1992). Determinants of word translation. *Journal of Experimental Psychology: Learning, Memory, and Cognition*, *18*(5), 1001–1018.

DeKeyser, R. (2007a). Skill acquisition theory. In B. VanPatten and J. Williams (Eds.), *Theories in second language acquisition* (pp. 97–113). Mahwah, NJ: Lawrence Erlbaum.

DeKeyser, R. (Ed.). (2007b). *Practice in a second language: Perspectives from applied linguistics and cognitive psychology*. Cambridge: Cambridge University Press.

Dörnyei, Z. (2009a). *The psychology of second language acquisition*. Oxford: Oxford University Press.

Dörnyei, Z. (2009b). The L2 motivational self system. In Z. Dörnyei, E. Ushioda. (Eds.), *Motivation, language identity and the L2 Self* (pp. 9–42). Bristol, UK: Multilingual Matters.

Ellis, N. (1994). Implicit and explicit language learning: An overview. In N. Ellis (Ed.), *Implicit and explicit learning of languages* (pp. 1–32). London: Academic Press.

Ervin, S. and Osgood, C. E. (1954). Second language learning and bilingualism. *Journal of Abnormal Social Psychology, Supplement, 49*, 139–146.

Ervin-Tripp, S. M. and Slobin, D. I. (1966). Psycholinguistics. *Annual Review of Psychology, 17*, 435–474.

Favreau, M. and Segalowitz, N. (1983). Automatic and controlled processes in the first and second language reading of fluent bilinguals. *Memory and Cognition, 11*(6), 565–574.

Francis, W. S. (2005). Bilingual semantic and conceptual representation. In J. F. Kroll, A. M. B. de Groot (Eds.), *Handbook of bilingualism: Psycholinguistic approaches* (pp. 251–267). New York: Oxford University Press.

Francis, W. S., Romo, L. F., and Gelman, R. (2002). Syntactic structure, grammatical accuracy, and content in second-language writing: An analysis of skill learning and on-line processing. In R. R. Heredia and J. Altarriba (Eds.), *Bilingual Sentence Processing* (pp. 317–337). Amsterdam: Elsevier.

Frenck-Mestre, C. (2002). An on-line look at sentence processing in the second language. In R. R. Heredia and J. Altarriba (Eds.), *Bilingual Sentence Processing* (pp. 217–236). Amsterdam: Elsevier.

Frenck-Mestre, C. (2005). Ambiguities and anomalies: What can eye movements and event-related potentials reveal about second language sentence processing? In J. F. Kroll and A. M. B. de Groot (Eds.), *Handbook of bilingualism: Psycholinguistic approaches* (pp. 268–281). New York: Oxford University Press.

Gatbonton, E. and Segalowitz, N. (2005). Rethinking communicative language teaching: A focus on access to fluency. *The Canadian Modern Language Review, 61*(3), 325–353.

Goldberg, A. E. and Casenhiser, D. (2008). Construction learning and second language acquisition. In P. Robinson and N. C. Ellis (Eds.), *Handbook of cognitive linguistics and second language acquisition* (pp. 197–215). New York: Routledge.

Goldinger, S. D. (1996). Auditory lexical decision. *Language and Cognitive Processes, 11*(6), 559–567.

Gollan, T. H. and Ferreira, V. S. (2009). Should I stay or should I switch? A cost-benefit analysis of voluntary language switching in young and aging bilinguals. *Journal of Experimental Psychology: Learning, Memory, and Cognition, 35*(3), 640–665.

Grosjean, F. and Frauenfelder, U. (Eds.) (1997). *A Guide to spoken word recognition paradigms*. Hove, England: Psychology Press.

Harley, T. A. (2008). *The psychology of language: From data to theory* (Third Edition). New York: Psychology Press.

Hartsuiker, R. J. and Pickering, M. J. (2008). Language integration in bilingual sentence production. *Acta Psychologica, 128*(3), 479–489.

Healy, A. F. and Bourne, L. E., Jr. (Eds.) (1998). *Foreign language learning: Psycholinguistic studies on training and retention*. Mahwah, NJ: Lawrence Erlbaum.

Heredia, R. R. (2008). Mental models of bilingual memory. In J. Altarriba and R. R. Heredia (Eds.), *An introduction to bilingualism: Principles and processes* (pp. 39–67). Mahwah, NJ: Lawrence Erlbaum.

Heredia, R. and J. Altarriba (Eds.). (2002). *Bilingual sentence processing*. Amsterdam: Elsevier.

Hulstijn, J. (2002). Towards a unified account of the representation, processing and acquisition of second language knowledge. *Second Language Research, 18*(3), 193–223.

Hulstijn, J. H. (2005a). Theoretical and empirical issues in the study of implicit and explicit second-language learning: Introduction. *Studies in Second Language Acquisition, 27*(2), 129–140.

Hulstijn, J. H. (Ed.) (2005b). Implicit and explicit second-language learning [Special issue]. *Studies in Second Language Acquisition, 27*(2), 129–359.

Hymes, D. (1967). Models of the interaction of language and social setting. *Journal of Social Issues, 23*(1), 8–28.

Hymes, D. (1972). On communicative competence. In J. B. Pride and J. Holmes (Eds.), *Sociolinguistics* (pp. 269–293) Middlesex, UK: Penguin Books.

Keatley, C. W. (1992). History of bilingualism research in cognitive psychology. In R. J. Harris (Ed.), *Cognitive processing in bilinguals* (pp. 15–49) Amsterdam: Elsevier.

Kilborn, K. (1994). Learning a language late: Second language acquisition in adults. In M. A. Gernsbacher (Ed.), *Handbook of psycholinguistics* (pp. 917–944). San Diego, CA: Academic Press.

Kolers, P. A. (1963). Interlingual word associations. *Journal of Verbal Learning and Verbal Behavior, 2*(4), 291–300.

Kolers, P. A. (1966a). Interlingual facilitation of short-term memory. *Journal of Verbal Learning and Verbal Behavior, 5*(3), 314–319.

Kolers, P. A. (1966b). Reading and talking bilingually. *The American Journal of Psychology, 79*(3), 357–377.

Krashen, S. D. (1985). *The Input Hypothesis: Issues and implications.* London: Longman.

Kroll, J. F. and Tokowicz, N. (2005). Models of bilingual representation and processing: Looking back and to the future. In J. F. Kroll and A. M. B. de Groot (Eds.), *Handbook of bilingualism: Psycholinguistic approaches* (pp. 531–553). New York: Oxford University Press.

Lambert, W. E., Havelka, J., and Crosby, C. (1958). The influence of language acquisition contexts on bilingualism. *Journal of Abnormal and Social Psychology, 56*(2), 239–244.

Larsen-Freeman, D. (2002). Making sense of frequency. *Studies in Second Language Acquisition, 24*(2), 275–285.

Larsen-Freeman, D. and Cameron, L. (2008). *Complex systems and applied linguistics.* Oxford: Oxford University Press.

Levelt, W. J. M. (1978). Skill theory and language teaching. *Studies in Second Language Acquisition, 1*(1), 53–70.

Levelt, W. J. M. (1999). Producing spoken language: A blueprint of the speaker. In C. Brown and P. Hagoort (Eds.), *The neurocognition of language* (pp. 83–122). Oxford: Oxford UniversityPress.

Levinson, S. C. and Wilkins, D. (Eds.) (2006). *Grammars of space: Explorations in cognitive diversity.* Cambridge: Cambridge University Press.

Libben, M. R. and Titone, D. A. (2009). Bilingual lexical access in context: Evidence from eye movements during reading. *Journal of Experimental Psychology: Learning, Memory, and Cognition, 35*(2), 381–390.

Lightbown, P. (2007). Transfer appropriate processing as a model for classroom second language acquisition. In Z. Han (Ed.), *Understanding second language process* (pp. 27–44). Clevedon, UK: Multilingual Matters.

MacWhinney, B. (2008). A Unified Model. In P. Robinson and N. C. Ellis (Eds.), *Handbook of cognitive linguistics and second language acquisition* (pp. 341–371). New York: Routledge.

MacWhinney, B. and Bates, E. (Eds.). (1989). *The crosslinguistic study of sentence processing.* Cambridge: Cambridge University Press.

Marinis, T. (2003). Psycholinguistic techniques in second language acquisition research. *Second Language Research, 19*(2), 144–161.

McDonough, K. and Trofimovich, P. (2008). *Using priming methods in second language research.* New York: Routledge.

McLaughlin, B. (1987). *Theories of second language learning.* London: Edward Arnold.

Mehler, J., Sebastián-Gallés, N., and Nespor, M. (2005). Biological foundations of language acquisition: Evidence from bilingualism. In M. S. Gazzaniga (Ed.), *The cognitive neurosciences* (pp. 825–836). Cambridge, MA: MIT Press.

Meuter, R. (2005). Language selection in bilinguals: Mechanisms and processes. In J. Kroll and A. De Groot (Eds.), *Handbook of bilingualism: Psycholinguistic approaches* (pp. 349–370). Oxford: Oxford University Press.

Morris, C. D., Bransford, J. D., and Franks, J. J. (1977). Level of processing versus transfer appropriate processing. *Journal of Verbal Learning and Verbal Behavior, 16*(5), 519–533.

Neely, J. H. (1977). Semantic priming and retrieval from lexical memory: Roles of inhibitionless spreading activation and limited-capacity attention. *Journal of Experimental Psychology: General, 106*(3), 1–66.

Nicoladis, E. (2008). Bilingualism and language cognitive development. In J. Altarriba and R. R. Heredia (Eds.), *An introduction to bilingualism: Principles and processes* (pp. 167–182). Mahwah, NJ: Lawrence Erlbaum.

Paradis, M. (2009). *Declarative and procedural determinants of second languages.* Amsterdam: John Benjamins.

Pavlenko, A. (2005a). *Emotions and multilingualism.* New York: Cambridge University Press.

Pavlenko, A. (2005b). Bilingualism and thought. In J. F. Kroll and A. M. B. de Groot (Eds.), *Handbook of bilingualism: Psycholinguistic approaches* (pp. 433–453). New York: Oxford University Press.

Pawley, A. and Syder, F. (1983). Two puzzles for linguistic theory: Nativelike selection and nativelike fluency. In J. Richards and R. Schmidt (Eds.), *Language and communication* (pp. 191–226). London: Longman.

Penfield, W. and Roberts, L. (1959). *Speech and brain mechanisms.* Princeton, NJ: Princeton University Press.

Pienemann, M. (2003). Language processing capacity. In C. J. Doughty and M. H. Long (Eds.), *Handbook of second language acquisition* (pp. 679–713). Malden, MA: Blackwell.

Pienemann, M. (2004). Processing perspectives in SLA research and their compatibility. *Bilingualism: Language and Cognition, 7*(1), 37–39.

Pienemann, M. (2007). Processability theory. In B. VanPatten and J. Williams (Eds.), *Theories in second language acquisition: An introduction* (pp. 137–154). Mahwah, NJ: Lawrence Erlbaum.

Piske, T. and Young-Scholten, M. (Eds.). (2009). *Input matters in SLA*. Toronto: Multilingual Matters.

Posner, M. (1978). *Chronometric explorations of mind*. Hillsdale, NJ: Lawrence Erlbaum.

Posner, M. and Snyder, C. (1975). Facilitation and inhibition in the processing of signals. In P. Rabbitt and S. Dornic (Eds.), *Attention and performance V* (pp. 669–683). New York: Academic Press.

Raney, G. E., Obeidallah, S. M., and Miura, T. K. (2002). Text comprehension in bilinguals: Integrating perspectives on language representation and text processing. In R. R. Heredia and J. Altarriba (Eds.), *Bilingual sentence processing* (pp. 165–183). Amsterdam: Elsevier.

Roberts, L., Gullberg, M., and Indefrey, P. (2008). Online pronoun resolution in L2 discourse: L1 influence and general learner effects. *Studies in Second Language Acquisition*, 30(3), 333–357.

Robinson, P. and Ellis, N. (Eds.) (2008). *Handbook of cognitive linguistics and second language acquisition*. London: Routledge.

Schrauf, R. W. (2008). Bilingualism and aging. In J. Altarriba and R. R. Heredia (Eds.), *An introduction to bilingualism: Principles and processes* (pp. 105–127). Mahwah, NJ: Lawrence Erlbaum.

Sebastián-Gallés, N. and Bosch, L. (2005). Phonology and bilingualism. In J. F. Kroll and A. M. B. de Groot (Eds.), *Handbook of bilingualism: Psycholinguistic approaches* (pp. 68–87). New York: Oxford University Press.

Segalowitz, N. (1976). Communicative incompetence and the non-fluent bilingual. *Canadian Journal of Behavioural Science*, 8(2), 122–131.

Segalowitz, N. (2010). *Cognitive bases of second language fluency*. London: Routledge.

Segalowitz, N. and Frenkiel-Fishman, S. (2005). Attention control and ability level in a complex cognitive skill: Attention-shifting and second language proficiency. *Memory and Cognition*, 33(4), 644–653.

Segalowitz, N. and Hulstijn, J. (2005). Automaticity in bilingualism and second language learning. In J. F. Kroll and A. M. B. De Groot (Eds.), *Handbook of bilingualism: Psycholinguistic approaches* (pp. 371–388). Oxford: Oxford University Press.

Slobin, D. (1996). From "thought and language" to "thinking for speaking". In J. J. Gumperz and S. C. Levinson (Eds.), *Rethinking linguistic relativity* (pp. 70–96). Cambridge: Cambridge University Press.

Sternberg, S. (1969). Memory-scanning: Mental processes revealed by reaction-time experiments. *American Scientist*, 57(4), 421–457.

Tabossi, P. (1996). Cross-modal semantic priming. *Language and Cognitive Processes*, 11(6), 569–576.

Taube-Schiff, M. and Segalowitz, N. (2005). Within-language attention control in second language processing. *Bilingualism: Language and Cognition*, 8(3), 195–206.

Tomasello, M. (2003). *Constructing a language*. Cambridge, MA: Harvard University Press.

Tomlin, R. and Villa, V. (1994). Attention in cognitive science and second language acquisition. *Studies in Second Language Acquisition*, 16(2), 183–203.

Trofimovich, P. and Gatbonton, E. (2006). Repetition and focus on form in L2 Spanish word processing: Implications for pronunciation instruction. *The Modern Language Journal*, 90(4), 519–535.

Trueswell, J. C. and Tanenhaus, M. K. (Eds.). (2005). *Approaches to studying world-situated language use: Bridging the Language-as-Product and Language-as-Action traditions*. Cambridge, MA: MIT Press.

Truscott, J. and Sharwood Smith, M. (2004). Acquisition by processing: A modular perspective on language development. *Bilingualism: Language and Cognition*, 7(1), 1–20.

VanPatten, B. (2007). Input processing in adult second language acquisition. In B. VanPatten and J. Williams (Eds.), *Theories in second language acquisition: An introduction* (pp. 115–135). Mahwah, NJ: Lawrence Erlbaum.

Weinreich, U. (1953). *Languages in contact*. New York: The Linguistic Circle of New York.

Wray, A. (2002). *Formulaic language and the lexicon*. Cambridge: Cambridge University Press.

Wundt, W. (1912/1973). *An introduction to psychology*. New York: Arno Press.

Wundt, W. (1894/1977). *Lectures on human and animal psychology*. Washington, D.C.: University Publications of America.

12

Frequency-based accounts of second language acquisition

Nick C. Ellis

Historical discussion

Linguistic background

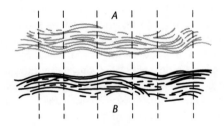

Language acts as an intermediary between thought and sound in such a way that the combination of both necessarily produces a mutually complementary delimitation of units. Thought, chaotic by nature, is made precise by this process of segmentation. But what happens is neither a transformation of thought into matter, nor a transformation of sound into ideas. What takes place is a somewhat mysterious process by which "thought-sound" evolves divisions, and a language takes place with its linguistic units in between these two amorphous masses.

(Saussure, 1916, pp. 110–111)

Saussure (1916) characterized language as thought organized in sound, and the units of language as linguistic signs, the signifiers of linguistic form and their associated signifieds, the functions, concepts or meanings. In Saussure's view:

(1) Linguistic signs arise from the dynamic interactions of thought and sound—from patterns of usage: "Everything depends on relations .... [1] Words as used in discourse, strung together one after another, enter into relations based on the linear character of languages ... Combinations based on sequentiality may be called *syntagmas* .... [2] Outside of the context of discourse, words having something [meaningful] in common are associated together in memory. This kind of connection between words is of quite a different order. It is not based

on linear sequence. It is a connection in the brain. Such connections are part of that accumulated store which is the form the language takes in an individual's brain. We shall call these *associative relations*" (pp. 120–121).

(2) Linguistic structure emerges from patterns of usage that are automatically memorized by individual speakers, and these representations and associations collaborate in subsequent language processing: "The whole set of phonetic and conceptual differences which constitute a language are thus the product of two kinds of comparison, associative and syntagmatic. Groups of both kinds are in large part established by the language. This set of habitual relations is what constitutes linguistic structure and determines how the language functions ..." (p. 126). "Any [linguistic] creation must be preceded by an unconscious comparison of the material deposited in the storehouse of language, where productive forms are arranged according to their relations." (p. 164).

(3) Regular schematic structures are frequency-weighted abstractions across concrete patterns of like-types. "To the language and not to speech, must be attributed all types of syntagmas constructed on regular patterns, ... such types will not exist unless sufficiently numerous examples do indeed occur" (pp. 120–121). "Abstract entities are based ultimately upon concrete entities. No grammatical abstraction is possible unless it has a foundation in the form of some series of material elements, and these are the elements one must come back to finally" (p. 137).

Thus began Structural Linguistics, the study of language as a relational structure, whose elemental constructions derive their forms and functions from their distributions in texts and discourse. This approach had significant impact upon applied linguistics and SLA too. Fries (1952) argued that language acquisition is the learning of an inventory of patterns as arrangements of words with their associated meanings. His (1952) *Structure of English* presented an analysis of these patterns, Roberts' (1956) *Patterns of English* was a textbook presentation of Fries's system for classroom use, and *English Pattern Practices, Establishing the Patterns as Habits* (Fries et al., 1958) taught beginning and intermediate EFL students English as patterns using audio-lingual drills. Harris (1955, 1968), founder of the first US linguistics department at the University of Pennsylvania, developed rigorous discovery procedures for phonemes and morphemes, based on the distributional properties of these units. For Harris too, form and information (grammar and semantics) were inseparable. He proposed that each human language is a self-organizing system in which both the syntactic and semantic properties of a word are established purely in relation to other words, and that the patterns of a language are learned through exposure to usage in social participation (Harris, 1982, 1991).

Structuralism was the dominant approach in linguistics for the earlier part of the twentieth century. It was overtaken in the 1960s by Generative approaches. Harris's student, Chomsky (1965, 1981) abandoned structure-specific rules and developed the Principles-and-Parameters approach, the general grammatical rules and principles of Universal Grammar. Grammar became top-down and rule-governed, rather than bottom-up and emergent. Structures and functional patterns were no longer interesting for such theories of syntax—instead they were epiphenomena arising from the interaction of more fundamental and universal principles. Chomsky (1981) classified grammatical phenomena into the "core" of the grammar and a "periphery," where the core phenomena were those describable by the parameterized principles of Universal Grammar, and peripheral phenomena were those marked elements and constructions that are not widespread. Grammar was modularized, encapsulated, and divorced from performance, lexis, social usage, and the rest of cognition. Patterns, structures, constructions, formulaic language, phraseology, all were peripheral. Since Universal Grammar was innate, Linguistics was no longer interested in frequency or learning.

Psychological background

> Perception is of definite and probable things.
>
> *(James, 1890, p. 82)*

From its very beginnings, psychological research has recognized three major experiential factors that affect cognition: frequency, recency, and context (e.g., Anderson, 2010; Bartlett, 1932/ 1967; Ebbinghaus, 1885). Learning, memory and perception are all affected by frequency of usage: the more times we experience something, the stronger our memory of it, and the more fluently it is accessed. The more recently we have experienced something, the stronger our memory of it, and the more fluently it is accessed. The more times we experience conjunctions of features, the more they become associated in our minds and the more these subsequently affect perception and categorization; so a stimulus becomes associated to a context and we become more likely to perceive it in that context. The power law of learning (Anderson, 1982; Ellis and Schmidt, 1998; Newell, 1990) describes the relationships between practice and performance in the acquisition of a wide range of cognitive skills—the greater the practice, the greater the performance, although effects of practice are largest at early stages of learning, thereafter diminishing and eventually reaching asymptote. The power function relating probability of recall (or recall latency) and recency is known as the forgetting curve (Baddeley, 1997; Ebbinghaus, 1885).

William James' words which begin this section concern the effects of frequency upon perception. There is a lot more to perception than meets the eye, or ear. A percept is a complex state of consciousness in which antecedent sensation is supplemented by consequent ideas which are closely combined to it by association. The cerebral conditions of the perception of things are thus the paths of association irradiating from them. If a certain sensation is strongly associated with the attributes of a certain thing, that thing is almost sure to be perceived when we get that sensation. But where the sensation is associated with more than one reality, unconscious processes weigh the odds, and we perceive the most probable thing: "*all brain-processes are such as give rise to what we may call* FIGURED *consciousness*" (James, 1890, p. 82). Accurate and fluent perception thus rests on the perceiver having acquired the appropriately weighted range of associations for each element of the language input.

It is human categorization ability which provides the most persuasive testament to our incessant unconscious figuring or "tallying" (Ellis, 2002a). We know that natural categories are fuzzy rather than monothetic. Wittgenstein's (1953) consideration of the concept *game* showed that no set of features that we can list covers all the things that we call games, ranging as the exemplars do from soccer, through chess, bridge, and poker, to solitaire. Instead, what organizes these exemplars into the *game* category is a set of family resemblances among these members—son may be like mother, and mother like sister, but in a very different way. And we learn about these families, like our own, from experience. Exemplars are similar if they have many features in common and few distinctive attributes (features belonging to one but not the other); the more similar are two objects on these quantitative grounds, the faster are people at judging them to be similar (Tversky, 1977). Prototypes, exemplars which are most typical of a category, are those which are similar to many members of that category and not similar to members of other categories. Again, the operationalization of this criterion predicts the speed of human categorization performance—people more quickly classify as *birds* sparrows (or other average-sized, average-colored, average-beaked, average-featured specimens) than they do birds with less common features or feature combinations like geese or albatrosses (Rosch and Mervis, 1975; Rosch *et al.*, 1976. Prototypes are judged faster and more accurately, even if they themselves have never been seen before—someone who has never seen a sparrow, yet who has experienced the rest of the run of the avian mill, will still be fast and accurate in judging it to be a bird (Posner and Keele, 1970) Such effects make it very clear that although people do not go around consciously counting features, they nevertheless have very accurate knowledge of the underlying frequency distributions and their central tendencies. Cognitive theories of categorization and generalization show how schematic constructions are abstracted over less schematic ones that are inferred inductively by the learner in acquisition (Harnad, 1987; Lakoff, 1987; Taylor, 1998). So Psychology has remained committed to studying these processes of cognition.

Core issues

Although, as we have seen, much of Linguistics post 1960 studiously ignored issues of learning and frequency, the last 50 years of Psycholinguistic research has demonstrated language processing to be exquisitely sensitive to usage frequency at all levels of language representation: phonology and phonotactics, reading, spelling, lexis, morphosyntax, formulaic language, language comprehension, grammaticality, sentence production, and syntax (Ellis, 2002a). Language knowledge involves statistical knowledge, so humans learn more easily and process more fluently high frequency forms and "regular" patterns which are exemplified by many types and which have few competitors. Psycholinguistic perspectives thus hold that language learning is the associative learning of representations that reflect the probabilities of occurrence of form-function mappings. Frequency is a key determinant of acquisition because "rules" of language, at all levels of analysis from phonology, through syntax, to discourse, are structural regularities which emerge from learners' lifetime analysis of the distributional characteristics of the language input. In James' terms, learners have to FIGURE language out.

It is these ideas which underpin the last 30 years of investigations of language cognition using connectionist and statistical models (Christiansen and Chater, 2001; Elman *et al.*, 1996; Rumelhart and McClelland, 1986), the competition model of language learning and processing (Bates and MacWhinney, 1987; MacWhinney, 1987b, 1997), the recent re-emergence of interest in how frequency and repetition bring about form in language (Bybee and Hopper, 2001) and how probabilistic knowledge drives language comprehension and production (Bod *et al.*, 2003; Ellis, 2002a, b; Jurafsky and Martin, 2000), and proper empirical investigations of the structure of language by means of corpus analysis (Biber *et al.*, 1999; Sinclair, 1991).

Frequency, learning, and language are now back together, no more so than in Usage-based approaches (Barlow and Kemmer, 2000) which hold that we learn constructions while engaging in communication, the "interpersonal communicative and cognitive processes that everywhere and always shape language" (Slobin, 1997, p. 267). Such beliefs, increasingly influential in the study of child language acquisition, have turned upside-down generative assumptions of innate language acquisition devices, the continuity hypothesis, and top-down, rule-governed, processing, bringing back data-driven, emergent accounts of linguistic systematicities. Constructionist theories of child language acquisition use dense longitudinal corpora to chart the emergence of creative linguistic competence from children's analyses of the utterances in their usage history and from their abstraction of regularities within them (Goldberg, 1995, 2006; Tomasello, 1998, 2003). Children typically begin with phrases and they are initially fairly conservative in extending the use of the particular verb within them to other structures. The usual developmental sequence is from formula to low-scope slot-and-frame pattern to creative construction.[1]

What in the 1950s were known as structural patterns would today also be referred to by other names—"constructions" or "phraseologisms." Constructions, a term used in Cognitive Linguistic circles, are form-meaning mappings, conventionalized in the speech community, and entrenched as language knowledge in the learner's mind. They are the symbolic units of language relating the defining properties of their morphological, syntactic, and lexical form with particular semantic, pragmatic, and discourse functions (Croft, 2001; Croft and Cruise, 2004; Goldberg, 1995, 2006; Langacker, 1987; Robinson and Ellis, 2008b; Tomasello, 2003). The term phraseologism, more the currency of Corpus Linguistics, adds an additional statistical emphasis to its definition as the co-occurrence of a lexical item and one or more additional linguistic elements which functions as one semantic unit in a clause or sentence and whose frequency of co-occurrence is larger than expected on the basis of chance (Gries, 2008; Howarth, 1998).

Goldberg's (1995, 2003) Construction Grammar argues that all grammatical phenomena can be understood as learned pairings of form (from morphemes, words, idioms, to partially lexically filled and fully general phrasal patterns) and their associated semantic or discourse functions: "the network of constructions captures our grammatical knowledge *in toto*, i.e., It's constructions all the way down" (Goldberg, 2006, p. 18). There are close relations here with Functional linguistic descriptions of the associations between particular lexico-grammatical patterns and their systemic functions (their propositional, interpersonal, and textual semantics) (Halliday, 1985; Langacker, 1987, 2000). Related developments with a typological perspective, Croft's Radical Construction Grammar (2001; Croft and Cruise, 2004) reject the idea that syntactic categories and relations are universal and argue instead that they are both language- and construction-specific, being induced from particular local frequencies of usage of thought-sound relations. What are universal are the patterns of ways that meanings map onto form.[2]

What of SLA? Language learners, L1 and L2 both, share the goal of understanding language and how it works. Since they achieve this based upon their experience of language usage, there are many commonalities between first and second language acquisition that can be understood from corpus analyses of input and cognitive- and psycho- linguistic analyses of constructions acquisition following associative and cognitive principles of learning and categorization. Thus usage-based approaches, Cognitive Linguistics and Corpus Linguistics are becoming increasingly influential in SLA research, too (Collins and Ellis, 2009; Ellis, 1998, 2003; Ellis and Cadierno, 2009; Robinson and Ellis, 2008b), albeit with the twist that since L2 learners have previously devoted considerable resources to the estimation of the characteristics of another language—the native tongue in which they have considerable fluency—their computations and inductions are often affected by transfer, with L1-tuned expectations and selective attention (Ellis, 2006b) blinding the acquisition system to aspects of the L2 sample, thus biasing their estimation from naturalistic usage and producing the limited attainment typical of adult L2 acquisition. Thus SLA involves processes of construction and *reconstruction*.

Data and common elicitation measures

Understanding the mysterious process by which "thought-sound" evolves divisions and a (second) language takes place with its linguistic units in between these two amorphous masses is a hugely interdisciplinary enterprise. As the diverse research cited in this chapter illustrates, it requires the full range of techniques of cognitive science: psycholinguistics, cognitive linguistics, corpus linguistics, connectionism, dynamic systems theory, educational evaluation, child language acquisition, psychology, and computational modeling. Language is a complex adaptive system involving interactions at all levels, and we need to measure these processes and try to understand its emergence thence (Ellis and Larsen-Freeman, 2006b, 2009b; Larsen-Freeman and Cameron, 2008; MacWhinney, 1999). The studies cited in more detail in the next section and elsewhere in this chapter illustrate some of the relevant techniques.

Empirical verification

Figure 12.1 tries to put some illustrative detail to Saussure's thought-sound interface by illustrating a variety of constructions as form-function mappings. If these are the units of language, then language acquisition involves learners infer these associations from their experience of language usage. Psychological analyses of the learning of constructions as form-meaning pairs is informed by the literature on the associative learning of cue-outcome contingencies where the usual determinants include: factors relating to the form such as frequency and salience; factors relating to the interpretation such as significance in the comprehension of the overall utterance, prototypicality, generality, redundancy, and surprise value; factors relating to the contingency of form and function; and factors relating to learner attention, such as automaticity, transfer, overshadowing, and blocking (Ellis, 2002a, 2003, 2006a, 2008c). These various psycholinguistic factors conspire in the acquisition and use of any linguistic construction. Constructionist accounts of language acquisition thus involve the distributional analysis of the language stream and the parallel analysis of contingent perceptual activity, with abstract constructions being learned from the conspiracy of concrete exemplars of usage following statistical learning mechanisms (Christiansen and Chater, 2001) relating input and learner cognition.

The determinants of learning include (1) input frequency (construction frequency, type-token frequency, Zipfian distribution, recency), (2) form (salience and perception), (3) function (prototypicality of meaning, importance of form for message comprehension, redundancy), and (4) interactions between these (contingency of form-function mapping). We will briefly consider each in turn, along with studies demonstrating their applicability:

(1) *Input frequency (construction frequency, type-token frequency, Zipfian distribution, recency)*

Construction frequency

Frequency of exposure promotes learning. Ellis' (2002a) review illustrates how frequency effects the processing of phonology and phonotactics, reading, spelling, lexis, morphosyntax, formulaic language, language comprehension, grammaticality, sentence production, and syntax. That language users are sensitive to the input frequencies of these patterns entails that they must have registered their occurrence in processing. These frequency effects are thus compelling evidence for usage-based models of language acquisition which emphasize the role of input.

Type and token frequency

Token frequency counts how often a particular form appears in the input. Type frequency, on the other hand, refers to the number of distinct lexical items that can be substituted in a given slot in a construction, whether it is a word-level construction for inflection or a syntactic construction specifying the relation among words. For example, the "regular" English past tense -ed has a very high type frequency because it applies to thousands of different types of verbs, whereas the vowel change exemplified in *swam* and *rang* has much lower type frequency. The productivity of phonological, morphological, and syntactic patterns is a function of type rather than token frequency (Bybee and Hopper, 2001). This is because: (a) the more lexical items that are heard in a certain position in a construction, the less likely it is that the construction is associated with a particular lexical item and the more likely it is that a general category is formed over the items that

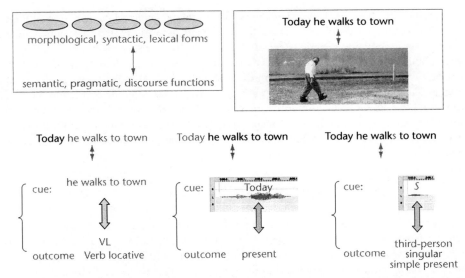

Figure 12.1 Constructions as form-function mappings. Any utterance comprises multiple nested constructions. Some aspects of form are more salient than others—the amount of energy in *today* far exceeds that in *s*

occur in that position; (b) the more items the category must cover, the more general are its criterial features and the more likely it is to extend to new items; and (c) high type frequency ensures that a construction is used frequently, thus strengthening its representational schema and making it more accessible for further use with new items (Bybee and Thompson, 2000). In contrast, high token frequency promotes the entrenchment or conservation of irregular forms and idioms; the irregular forms only survive because they occur with high frequency. These findings support language's place at the center of cognitive research into human categorization, which also emphasizes the importance of type frequency in classification.

Zipfian distribution

In the early stages of learning categories from exemplars, acquisition is optimized by the introduction of an initial, low-variance sample centered upon prototypical exemplars (Elio and Anderson, 1981, 1984). This low variance sample allows learners to get a fix on what will account for most of the category members. The bounds of the category are defined later by experience of the full breadth of exemplar types. Goldberg *et al.* (2004) demonstrated that in samples of child language acquisition, for a variety of verb–argument constructions (VACs), there is a strong tendency for one single verb to occur with very high frequency in comparison to other verbs used, a profile which closely mirrors that of the mothers' speech to these children. In natural language, Zipf's law (Zipf, 1935) describes how the highest frequency words account for the most linguistic tokens. Goldberg *et al.* (2004) show that Zipf's law applies within VACs too, and they argue that this promotes acquisition: tokens of one particular verb account for the lion's share of instances of each particular argument frame; this pathbreaking verb also is the one with the prototypical meaning from which the construction is derived (see also Ninio, 1999, 2006).

Ellis and Ferreira-Junior (2009a, b) investigate effects upon naturalistic second language acquisition of type/token distributions in the islands comprising the linguistic form of English VACs : VL verb locative, VOL verb object locative, VOO ditransitive) in the European Science

Foundation corpus (Perdue, 1993). They show that in the naturalistic L2 acquisition of English, VAC verb type/token distribution in the input is Zipfian and learners first acquire the most frequent, prototypical and generic exemplar (e.g., *put* in VOL, *give* in VOO, etc.). Their work further illustrates how acquisition is affected by the frequency and frequency distribution of exemplars within each island of the construction (e.g., [Subj V Obj Obl$_{path/loc}$]), by their prototypicality, and, using a variety of psychological and corpus linguistic association metrics, by their contingency of form-function mapping. Ellis and Larsen-Freeman (2009a) describe computational (emergent connectionist) serial-recurrent network models of these various factors as they play out in the emergence of constructions as generalized linguistic schema from their frequency distributions in the input.

Recency

Cognitive psychological research shows that three key factors determine the activation of memory schemata: frequency, recency, and context (Anderson, 1989; Anderson and Schooler, 2000). Language processing also reflects recency effects (Segalowitz and Trofimovich, Chapter 11, this volume). This phenomenon is known as priming and may be observed in phonology, conceptual representations, lexical choice, and syntax (McDonough and Trofimovich, 2008). Syntactic priming refers to the phenomenon of using a particular syntactic structure given prior exposure to the same structure. This behavior has been observed when speakers hear, speak, read, or write sentences (Bock, 1986; Pickering, 2006; Pickering and Garrod, 2006). For SLA, Gries and Wulff (2005) showed (i) that advanced L2 learners of English showed syntactic priming for ditransitive (e.g., *The racing driver showed the helpful mechanic*) and prepositional dative (e.g., *The racing driver showed the torn overall ...*) argument structure constructions in a sentence completion task, (ii) that their semantic knowledge of argument structure constructions affected their grouping of sentences in a sorting task, and (iii) that their priming effects closely resembled those of native speakers of English in that they were very highly correlated with native speakers' verbal subcategorization preferences whilst completely uncorrelated with the subcategorization preferences of the German translation equivalents of these verbs. There is now a growing body of research demonstrating such L2 syntactic priming effects (McDonough and Mackey, 2006; McDonough, 2006)

(2) Form (salience and perception)

The general perceived strength of stimuli is commonly referred to as their salience. Low salience cues tend to be less readily learned. Ellis (2006a, b) summarized the associative learning research demonstrating that selective attention, salience, expectation, and surprise are key elements in the analysis of all learning, animal and human alike. As the Rescorla-Wagner (1972) model encapsulates, the amount of learning induced from an experience of a cue-outcome association depends crucially upon the salience of the cue and the importance of the outcome.

Many grammatical meaning-form relationships, particularly those that are notoriously difficult for second language learners like grammatical particles and inflections such as the third-person singular *−s* of English, are of low salience in the language stream. For example, some forms are more salient: "*today*" is a stronger psychophysical form in the input than is the morpheme "*-s*" marking third-person singular present tense, thus while both provide cues to present time, *today* is much more likely to be perceived, and *-s* can thus become overshadowed and blocked, making it difficult for second language learners of English to acquire (Ellis, 2006b, 2008a; Goldschneider and DeKeyser, 2001).

(3) *Function (prototypicality of meaning, importance of form for message comprehension, redundancy)*

Prototypicality of meaning

Categories have graded structure, with some members being better exemplars than others. In the prototype theory of concepts (Rosch and Mervis, 1975; Rosch *et al.*, 1976), the prototype as an idealized central description is the best example of the category, appropriately summarizing the most representative attributes of a category. As the typical instance of a category, it serves as the benchmark against which surrounding, less representative instances are classified. The greater the token frequency of an exemplar, the more it contributes to defining the category, and the greater the likelihood it will be considered the prototype. The best way to teach a concept is to show an example of it. So the best way to introduce a category is to show a prototypical example.

Ellis and Ferreira-Junior (2009a) show that the verbs that second language learners first used in particular VACs are prototypical and generic in function (*go* for VL, *put* for VOL, and *give* for VOO). The same has been shown for child language acquisition, where a small group of semantically general verbs, often referred to as *light verbs* (e.g., *go, do, make, come*) are learned early (Clark, 1978; Ninio, 1999; Pinker, 1989). Ninio argues that, because most of their semantics consist of some schematic notion of transitivity with the addition of a minimum specific element, such verbs are semantically suitable, salient, and frequent; hence, learners start transitive word combinations with these generic verbs. Thereafter, as Clark describes, "many uses of these verbs are replaced, as children get older, by more specific terms .... General purpose verbs, of course, continue to be used but become proportionately less frequent as children acquire more words for specific categories of actions" (p. 53).

Redundancy

The Rescorla-Wagner model (1972) also summarizes how redundant cues tend not to be acquired. Not only are many grammatical meaning-form relationships low in salience, but they can also be redundant in the understanding of the meaning of an utterance. For example, it is often unnecessary to interpret inflections marking grammatical meanings such as tense because they are usually accompanied by adverbs that indicate the temporal reference. Second language learners' reliance upon adverbial over inflectional cues to tense has been extensively documented in longitudinal studies of naturalistic acquisition (Bardovi-Harlig, 2000; Dietrich *et al.*, 1995), training experiments (Ellis, 2007; Ellis and Sagarra, 2010), and studies of L2 language processing (VanPatten, 2006).

(4) *Interactions between these (contingency of form-function mapping)*

Psychological research into associative learning has long recognized that while frequency of form is important, so too is contingency of mapping (Shanks, 1995). Consider how, in the learning of the category of birds, while eyes and wings are equally frequently experienced features in the exemplars, it is wings which are distinctive in differentiating birds from other animals. Wings are important features to learning the category of birds because they are reliably associated with class membership, eyes are not. Raw frequency of occurrence is less important than the contingency between cue and interpretation. Distinctiveness or reliability of form-function mapping is a driving force of all associative learning, to the degree that the field of its study has been known as "contingency learning" since Rescorla (1968) showed that for classical conditioning, if one removed the contingency between the conditioned stimulus (CS) and the unconditioned (US), preserving the temporal pairing between CS and US but adding additional trials where the US appeared on its own, then animals did not develop a conditioned response to the CS. This result was a milestone in the development of learning theory because it implied that it was contingency, not temporal pairing, that generated conditioned responding. Contingency, and its associated aspects of predictive value, information gain, and statistical association, have been at the core of learning theory ever since. It is central in psycholinguistic theories of language acquisition, too (Ellis, 2006a, b, 2008c; Gries and Wulff, 2005; MacWhinney, 1987b), with the most developed account for second language acquisition being that of the Competition model (MacWhinney, 1987a, 1997, 2001). Ellis and Ferreira-Junior (2009b) use Delta P (ΔP) and collostructional analysis measures (Gries and Stefanowitsch, 2004; Stefanowitsch and Gries, 2003) to investigate effects of form-function contingency upon L2 VAC acquisition. Wulff *et al.* (2009) use multiple distinctive collexeme analyses to investigate effects of reliability of form-function mapping in the second language acquisition of tense and aspect. Boyd and Goldberg (2009) use conditional probabilities to investigate contingency effects in VAC acquisition. This is still an active area of inquiry, and more research is required before we know which statistical measures of form-function contingency are more predictive of acquisition and processing.

There is thus a range of frequency-related factors that influence the acquisition of linguistic constructions. For the example of verb-argument constructions illustrated to the left of Figure 12.1, there is:

(1) the frequency, the frequency distribution, and the salience of the form types,
(2) the frequency, the frequency distribution, the prototypicality and generality of the semantic types, and their importance in interpreting the overall construction,
(3) the reliabilities of the mapping between 1 and 2, and,
(4) the degree to which the different elements in the VAC sequence (such as Subj V Obj Obl) are mutually informative and form predictable chunks.

There are many factors involved, and research to date has tended to look at each hypothesis, variable by variable, one at a time. But they interact. And what we really want is a model of usage and its effects upon acquisition. We can measure these factors individually. But such counts are vague indicators of how the demands of human interaction affect the content and ongoing co-adaptation of discourse, how this is perceived and interpreted, how usage episodes are assimilated into the learner's system, and how the system reacts accordingly. We need a model of learning, development, and emergence that takes these factors into account dynamically. I will return to this prospect in the final section of this chapter.

Applications

Language learners have to acquire the constructions of their language from usage. Learning is dynamic, it takes place during processing, as Hebb (1949), Craik and Lockhart (1972), Elman *et al.* (1996) and Bybee and Hopper (2001) have variously emphasized from their neural, cognitive, connectionist, and linguistic perspectives, and the units of learning are thus the units of language processing episodes. Before learners can use constructions productively, they have to encounter useful exemplars and analyze them to identify their linguistic form, their meaning, and the mapping between these. Since every stimulus is ambiguous, forms, meanings, and their mappings have to be tallied—probabilistic statistical information is an inherent part of the representation of every construction. The tallying that provides this information takes place implicitly during processing. Implicit learning supplies a distributional analysis of the problem space: Frequency of usage determines availability of representation according to the power law of learning, and this process tallies the likelihoods of occurrence of constructions and the relative probabilities of their mappings between aspects of form and interpretations, with generalizations arising from conspiracies of memorized utterances collaborating in productive schematic linguistic constructions. Every language comprises very many constructions. It is no wonder then that the accomplishment of native levels of attainment involve thousands of hours on the task of language usage. There is no substitute for this. Learners' cognitive systems have to be allowed sufficient exposure to allow Saussure's somewhat mysterious process by which "thought-sound" evolves divisions, and language to take place with its linguistic units in between these two amorphous masses.

A language is not a fixed system. It varies in usage over speakers, places, and time. Yet despite the fact that no two speakers own an identical language, communication is possible to the degree that they share constructions (form-meaning correspondences) relevant to their discourse. Learners have to enter into communication from experience of a very limited number of tokens. Their limited exposure poses them the task of *estimating* how linguistic constructions work from an input sample that is incomplete, uncertain, and noisy. Native-like fluency, idiomaticity, and selection are another level of difficulty again. For a good fit, every utterance has to be chosen, from a wide range of possible expressions, to be appropriate for that idea, for that speaker, for that place, and for that time. And again, learners can only *estimate* this from their finite experience.

Language, a moving target then, can neither be described nor experienced comprehensively, and so, in essence, *language learning is estimation from sample*. Like other estimation problems, successful determination of the population characteristics is a matter of statistical sampling, description, and inference. For language learning the estimations include: What is the range of constructions in the language? What are their major types? Which are the really useful ones? What is their relative frequency distribution? How do they map function and form, and how reliably so? How can this information best be organized to allow its appropriate and fluent access in recognition and production? Are there variable ways of expressing similar meanings? How are they distributed across different contexts? And so on.

There are three fundamental instructional aspects of this conception of language learning as statistical sampling and estimation.

(1) The first and foremost concerns sample size: As in all surveys, the bigger the sample, the more accurate the estimates, but also the greater the costs. Native speakers estimate their language over a lifespan of usage. L2 and foreign language (FL) learners just don't have that much time or resource. Thus, they are faced with a task of optimizing their estimates of language from a limited sample of exposure. Broadly, power analysis dictates that attaining native-like fluency and idiomaticity requires much larger usage samples than does basic interpersonal communicative competence in predictable contexts. But for the particulars, the instructor must ask what sort of sample is needed to adequately assess the workings of constructions of, respectively, high, medium, and low base occurrence rates, of more categorical versus more fuzzy patterns, of regular vs. irregular systems, of simple vs. complex "rules," of dense versus sparse neighborhoods?

Corpus and Cognitive Linguistic analyses are essential to the determination of which constructions of differing degrees of schematicity are worthy of instruction, their relative frequency, and their best (= central and most frequent) examples for instruction and assessment (Biber *et al.*, 1998; 1999). Gries (2007) describes how the three basic methods of corpus linguistics (frequency lists, concordances, and collocations) inform the instruction of L2 constructions. Achard (2008), Tyler (2008), Robinson and Ellis (2008a) and other readings in Robinson and Ellis (2008b) show how an understanding of the item-based nature of construction learning inspires the creation and evaluation of instructional tasks, materials, and syllabi, and how cognitive linguistic analyses can be used to inform learners how constructions are conventionalized ways of matching certain expressions to specific situations and to guide instructors in precisely isolating and clearly presenting the various conditions that motivate speaker choice.

(2) The second concerns sample selection: Principles of survey design dictate that a sample must properly represent the strata of the population of greatest concern. Thus, Needs Analysis is relevant to all L2 learners. Thus, too, the truism that FL learners, who have much more limited access to the authentic natural source language than L2 learners, are going to have greater problems of adequate description. But what about learning particular constructions? What is the best sample of experience to support this? How many examples do we need? In what proportion of types and tokens? Are there better sequences of experience to optimize estimation? I will briefly consider the identification of the patterns to teach, and then suggestions for ordering exemplars to optimize schematic construction learning.

Corpus linguistics, genre analysis, and needs analysis have a large role to play in identifying the linguistic constructions of most relevance to particular learners. For example, every genre of English for Academic Purposes and English for Special Purposes has its own phraseology, and learning to be effective in the genre involves learning this (Swales, 1990). Lexicographers develop their learner dictionaries upon relevant corpora (Hunston and Francis, 1996; Ooi, 1998) and dictionaries focus upon examples of usage as much as definitions, or even more so. Good grammars are now frequency informed (Biber *et al.*, 1999). Corpus linguistic analysis techniques have been used to identify the words relevant to academic English (the Academic Word List, Coxhead, 2000) and this, together with knowledge of lexical acquisition and cognition, informs vocabulary instruction programs (Nation, 2001; Schmitt, 2000). Similarly, corpus techniques have been used to identify formulaic phrases that are of special relevance to academic discourse and to inform their instruction (the Academic Formulas List, Ellis *et al.*, 2008; Simpson-Vlach and Ellis, in preparation).

Cognitive linguistics and psycholinguistics have a role to play in informing the ordering of exemplars for optimal acquisition of a schematic construction. Current work in cognitive linguistics and child language acquisition (e.g., Bybee, 2008; Goldberg, 2008; Lieven and Tomasello, 2008) suggests that for the initial acquisition of a productive schematic construction, optimal acquisition should occur when the central members of the category are presented early and often. This initial, low-variance sample centered upon prototypical exemplars should allow learners to get a "fix" on the central tendency that will account for most of the category members. Tokens that are more frequent have stronger representations in memory and serve as the analogical basis for forming novel instances of the category. Then more diverse exemplars should be introduced in order for learners to be able to determine the full range and bounds of the category. It is type frequency which drives productivity of pattern. It seems that Zipfian distributions in the constructions of natural language naturally provide learners with such samples in natural language. As a general instructional heuristic then, this is probably a good rule-of-thumb, although further work is needed to determine its applicability in L2 acquisition to the full range of constructions, and to particular learners and their L1s (Collins and Ellis, 2009; Ellis and Cadierno, 2009).

(3) A final implication of language acquisition as estimation concerns sampling history: How does knowledge of some cues and constructions affect estimation of the function of others?

What is the best sequence of language to promote learning new constructions? And what is the best processing orientation to make this sample of language the appropriate sample of usage?

Cognitive Linguistics is the analysis of these mechanisms and processes that underpin what Slobin (1996) called "thinking for speaking." But learning an L2 requires "rethinking for speaking." In order to counteract the L1 biases to allow estimation procedures to optimize induction, all of the L2 input needs to be made to count (as it does in L1 acquisition), not just the restricted sample typical of the biased intake of L2 acquisition. Reviews of the experimental and quasi-experimental investigations into the effectiveness of L2 instruction (e.g., Doughty and Williams, 1998; Ellis and Laporte, 1997; Hulstijn and DeKeyser, 1997; Lightbown et al., 1993; Long, 1983; Spada, 1997), particularly the comprehensive meta-analysis of Norris and Ortega (2000), demonstrate that focused L2 instruction results in substantial target-oriented gains, that explicit types of instruction are more effective than implicit types, and that the effectiveness of L2 instruction is durable. Form-focused instruction can help to achieve this by recruiting learners' explicit, conscious processing to allow them to consolidate unitized form-function bindings of novel L2 constructions (Ellis, 2005). Once a construction has been represented in this way, so its use in subsequent processing can update the statistical tallying of its frequency of usage and probabilities of form-function mapping.

Future directions

The intuitions of Ferdinand de Saussure and William James were basically correct—we can count on that. Saussure (1916) said, "To speak of a 'linguistic law' in general is like trying to lay hands on a ghost ... Synchronic laws are general, but not imperative ... [they] are imposed upon speakers by the constraints of common usage ... In short, when one speaks of a synchronic law, one is speaking of an arrangement, or a principle of regularity" (pp. 90–91). The frequencies of common usage count in the emergence of regularity in SLA. Usage is rich in latent linguistic structure.

Nevertheless, as Einstein observed, "Everything that can be counted does not necessarily count; everything that counts cannot necessarily be counted." Corpus Linguistics provides the proper empirical means whereby everything in language texts can be counted. But counts on the page are not the same as counts in the head. Cognitive Linguistics, mindful of research on categorization, recognizes frequency as a force in linguistic representation, processing, and change, and psycholinguistic demonstrations of language users' sensitivity to the frequencies of occurrence of a wide range of different linguistic constructions suggests an influence of usage events upon the user's system. But not everything that we can count in language counts in language cognition and acquisition.

The study of SLA from corpus linguistic and cognitive linguistic perspectives is a two-limbed stool without triangulation from an understanding of the psychology of cognition, learning, attention, and development. Sensation is not perception, and the psychophysical relations mapping physical onto psychological scales are complex. The world of conscious experience is not the world itself but a perception crucially determined by attentional limitations, prior knowledge, and context. Not every experience is equal—effects of practice are greatest at early stages but eventually reach asymptote. The associative learning of constructions as form-meaning pairs is affected by: factors relating to the form such as frequency and salience; factors relating to the interpretation such as significance in the comprehension of the overall utterance, prototypicality, generality, redundancy, and surprise value; factors relating to the contingency of form and function; and factors relating to learner attention, such as automaticity, transfer, and blocking.

Even a three-limbed stool does not make much sense without an appreciation of its social use. The connectionist networks that compute these associations are embodied, attentionally and socially gated, conscious, dialogic, interactive, situated, and cultured (Ellis, 2008b). Language usage, social roles, language learning, and conscious experience are all socially situated, negotiated, scaffolded, and guided. They emerge in the play of social intercourse. All these factors conspire dynamically in the acquisition and use of any linguistic construction. The future lies in trying to understand the component dynamic interactions at all levels, and the consequent emergence of the complex adaptive system of language itself (Ellis and Larsen-Freeman, 2006a, 2009b).

Notes

1 Remember Saussure's "abstract entities are based ultimately upon concrete entities. No grammatical abstraction is possible unless it has a foundation in the form of some series of material elements, and these are the elements one must come back to finally."
2 Remember Saussure's "somewhat mysterious process by which 'thought-sound' evolves divisions, and a language takes place with its linguistic units in between these two amorphous masses."

References

Achard, M. (2008). Cognitive pedagogical grammar. In P. Robinson and N. C. Ellis (Eds.), *Handbook of cognitive linguistics and second language acquisition*. London: Routledge.

Anderson, J. R. (1982). Acquisition of cognitive skill. *Psychological Review, 89*(4), 369–406.

Anderson, J. R. (1989). A rational analysis of human memory. In H. L. I. Roediger and F. I. M. Craik (Eds.), *Varieties of memory and consciousness: Essays in honour of Endel Tulving* (pp. 195–210). Hillsdale, NJ: Lawrence Erlbaum Associates.

Anderson, J. R. (2010). *Cognitive psychology and its implications* (Seventh Edition). New York: Worth Publishers.

Anderson, J. R. and Schooler, L. J. (2000). The adaptive nature of memory. In E. Tulving and F. I. M. Craik (Eds.), *The Oxford handbook of memory* (pp. 557–570). London: Oxford University Press.

Baddeley, A. D. (1997). *Human memory: Theory and practice* Revised Edition. Hove: Psychology Press.

Bardovi-Harlig, K. (2000). *Tense and aspect in second language acquisition: Form, meaning, and use*. Oxford: Blackwell.

Barlow, M., and Kemmer, S. (Eds.). (2000). *Usage based models of language*. Stanford, CA: CSLI Publications.

Bartlett, F. C. ([1932] 1967). *Remembering: A study in experimental and social psychology*. Cambridge: Cambridge University Press.

Bates, E. and MacWhinney, B. (1987). Competition, variation, and language learning. In B. MacWhinney (Ed.), *Mechanisms of language acquisition* (pp. 157–193). Hillsdale, NJ: Lawrence Erlbaum Associates.

Biber, D., Conrad, S., and Reppen, R. (1998). *Corpus linguistics: Investigating language structure and use*. New York: Cambridge University Press.

Biber, D., Johansson, S., Leech, G., Conrad, S., and Finegan, E. (1999). *Longman grammar of spoken and written English*. Harlow, UK: Pearson Education.

Bock, J. K. (1986). Syntactic persistence in language production. *Cognitive Psychology, 18*, 355–387.

Bod, R., Hay, J., and Jannedy, S. (Eds.) (2003). *Probabilistic linguistics*. Cambridge, MA: MIT Press.

Boyd, J. K. and Goldberg, A. E. (2009). Input effects within a constructionist framework. *The Modern Language Journal, 93*(2), 418–429.

Bybee, J. (2008). Usage-based grammar and second language acquisition. In P. Robinson and N. C. Ellis (Eds.), *Handbook of cognitive linguistics and second language acquisition*. London: Routledge.

Bybee, J. and Hopper, P. (Eds.) (2001). *Frequency and the emergence of linguistic structure*. Amsterdam: Benjamins.

Bybee, J. and Thompson, S. (2000). Three frequency effects in syntax. *Berkeley Linguistic Society, 23*, 65–85.

Chomsky, N. (1965). *Aspects of the theory of syntax*. Boston, MA: MIT Press.

Chomsky, N. (1981). *Lectures on government and binding*. Dordrecht: Foris.

Christiansen, M. H. and Chater, N. (Eds.). (2001). *Connectionist psycholinguistics*. Westport, CO: Ablex.

Clark, E. V. (1978). Discovering what words can do. In D. Farkas, W. M. Jacobsen, and K. W. Todrys (Eds.), *Papers from the parasession on the lexicon, Chicago Linguistics Society April 14–15, 1978* (pp. 34–57). Chicago: Chicago Linguistics Society.

Collins, L. and Ellis, N. C. (2009). Input and second language construction learning: Frequency, form, and function. *The Modern Language Journal, 93*(2), Whole issue.

Coxhead, A. (2000). A new Academic Word List. *TESOL Quarterly, 34,* 213–238.

Craik, F. I. M. and Lockhart, R. S. (1972). Levels of processing: A framework for memory research. *Journal of Verbal Learning and Verbal Behavior, 11,* 671–684.

Croft, W. (2001). *Radical construction grammar: Syntactic theory in typological perspective.* Oxford: Oxford University Press.

Croft, W. and Cruise, A. (2004). *Cognitive linguistics.* Cambridge: Cambridge University Press.

Dietrich, R., Klein, W., and Noyau, C. (Eds.) (1995). *The acquisition of temporality in a second language.* Amsterdam: John Benjamins.

Doughty, C. and Williams, J. (Eds.) (1998). *Focus on form in classroom second language acquisition.* New York: Cambridge University Press.

Ebbinghaus, H. (1885). *Memory: A contribution to experimental psychology* (H. A. R. C. E. B. (1913), Trans.). New York: Teachers College, Columbia.

Elio, R. and Anderson, J. R. (1981). The effects of category generalizations and instance similarity on schema abstraction. *Journal of Experimental Psychology: Human Learning and Memory, 7*(6), 397–417.

Elio, R. and Anderson, J. R. (1984). The effects of information order and learning mode on schema abstraction. *Memory and Cognition, 12*(1), 20–30.

Ellis, N. C. (1998). Emergentism, connectionism and language learning. *Language Learning, 48*(4), 631–664.

Ellis, N. C. (2002a). Frequency effects in language processing: A review with implications for theories of implicit and explicit language acquisition. *Studies in Second Language Acquisition, 24*(2), 143–188.

Ellis, N. C. (2002b). Reflections on frequency effects in language processing. *Studies in Second Language Acquisition, 24*(2), 297–339.

Ellis, N. C. (2003). Constructions, chunking, and connectionism: The emergence of second language structure. In C. Doughty and M. H. Long (Eds.), *Handbook of second language acquisition.* Oxford: Blackwell.

Ellis, N. C. (2005). At the interface: Dynamic interactions of explicit and implicit language knowledge. *Studies in Second Language Acquisition, 27,* 305–352.

Ellis, N. C. (2006a). Language acquisition as rational contingency learning. *Applied Linguistics, 27*(1), 1–24.

Ellis, N. C. (2006b). Selective attention and transfer phenomena in SLA: Contingency, cue competition, salience, interference, overshadowing, blocking, and perceptual learning. *Applied Linguistics, 27*(2), 1–31.

Ellis, N. C. (2007). Blocking and learned attention in language acquisition. *CogSci 2007, Proceedings of the twenty ninth cognitive science conference. Nashville, Tennesse, August 1–4.*

Ellis, N. C. (2008a). The dynamics of language use, language change, and first and second language acquisition. *The Modern Language Journal, 41*(3), 232–249.

Ellis, N. C. (2008b). The psycholinguistics of the interaction hypothesis. In A. Mackey and C. Polio (Eds.), *Multiple perspectives on interaction in SLA: Second language research in honor of Susan M. Gass* (pp. 11–40). New York: Routledge.

Ellis, N. C. (2008c). Usage-based and form-focused language acquisition: The associative learning of constructions, learned-attention, and the limited L2 endstate. In P. Robinson and N. C. Ellis (Eds.), *Handbook of cognitive linguistics and second language acquisition.* London: Routledge.

Ellis, N. C. and Cadierno, T. (2009). Constructing a second language. *Annual Review of Cognitive Linguistics, 7*(Special section), 111–290.

Ellis, N. C. and Ferreira-Junior, F. (2009a). Construction learning as a function of frequency, frequency distribution, and function. *The Modern Language Journal, 93,* 370–386.

Ellis, N. C. and Ferreira-Junior, F. (2009b). Constructions and their acquisition: Islands and the distinctiveness of their occupancy. *Annual Review of Cognitive Linguistics, 7,* 188–221.

Ellis, N. C. and Laporte, N. (1997). Contexts of acquisition: Effects of formal instruction and naturalistic exposure on second language acquisition. In A. M. DeGroot and J. F. Kroll (Eds.), *Tutorials in bilingualism: Psycholinguistic perspectives* (pp. 53–83). Mahwah, NJ: Erlbaum.

Ellis, N. C. and Larsen Freeman, D. (2006a). Language emergence: Implications for Applied Linguistics. *Applied Linguistics, 27*(4), whole issue.

Ellis, N. C. and Larsen Freeman, D. (2006b). Language emergence: Implications for applied linguistics (introduction to the special issue). *Applied Linguistics, 27*(4), 558–589.

Ellis, N. C. and Larsen-Freeman, D. (2009a). Constructing a second language: Analyses and computational simulations of the emergence of linguistic constructions from usage. *Language Learning, 59* (Supplement 1), 93–128.

Ellis, N. C. and Larsen-Freeman, D. (2009b). Language as a complex adaptive system [Special issue]. *Language Learning, 59* (Supplement 1).

Ellis, N. C. and Sagarra, N. (2010). The bounds of adult language acquisition: Blocking and learned attention. *Studies in Second Language Acquisition, 32*(4), 553–580.

Ellis, N. C. and Schmidt, R. (1998). Rules or associations in the acquisition of morphology? The frequency by regularity interaction in human and PDP learning of morphosyntax. *Language and Cognitive Processes, 13*(2and3), 307–336.

Ellis, N. C., Simpson-Vlach, R., and Maynard, C. (2008). Formulaic language in native and second-language speakers: Psycholinguistics, corpus linguistics, and TESOL. *TESOL Quarterly, 42*(3), 375–396.

Elman, J. L., Bates, E. A., Johnson, M. H., Karmiloff-Smith, A., Parisi, D., and Plunkett, K. (1996). *Rethinking innateness: A connectionist perspective on development.* Cambridge, MA: MIT Press.

Fries, C. C. (1952). *The structure of English.* New York: Harcourt, Brace and Co.

Fries, C. C. and Lado, R. and the Staff of the Michigan English Language Institute (1958). *English pattern practices: Establishing the patterns as habits.* Ann Arbor: University of Michigan Press.

Goldberg, A. E. (1995). *Constructions: A construction grammar approach to argument structure.* Chicago: University of Chicago Press.

Goldberg, A. E. (2003). Constructions: A new theoretical approach to language. *Trends in Cognitive Science, 7,* 219–224.

Goldberg, A. E. (2006). *Constructions at work: The nature of generalization in language.* Oxford: Oxford University Press.

Goldberg, A. E. (2008). The language of constructions. In P. Robinson and N. C. Ellis (Eds.), *Handbook of cognitive linguistics and second language acquisition.* London: Routledge.

Goldberg, A. E., Casenhiser, D. M., and Sethuraman, N. (2004). Learning argument structure generalizations. *Cognitive Linguistics, 15,* 289–316.

Goldschneider, J. M. and DeKeyser, R. (2001). Explaining the "natural order of L2 morpheme acquisition" in English: A meta-analysis of multiple determinants. *Language Learning, 51,* 1–50.

Gries, S. T. (2007). Corpus-based methods in analyses of SLA data. In P. Robinson and N. C. Ellis (Eds.), *A handbook of cognitive linguistics and SLA.* Mahwah, NJ: Erlbaum.

Gries, S. T. (2008). Phraseology and linguistic theory: A brief survey. In S. Granger and F. Meunier (Eds.), *Phraseology: An interdisciplinary perspective.* Amsterdam: John Benjamins.

Gries, S. T. and Stefanowitsch, A. (2004). Extending collostructional analysis: A corpus-based perspective on "alternations". *International Journal of Corpus Linguistics, 9,* 97–129.

Gries, S. T. and Wulff, S. (2005). Do foreign language learners also have constructions? Evidence from priming, sorting, and corpora. *Annual Review of Cognitive Linguistics, 3,* 182–200.

Halliday, M. A. K. (1985). *An introduction to functional grammar.* London: E. Arnold.

Harnad, S. (Ed.). (1987). *Categorical perception: The groundwork of cognition.* New York: Cambridge University Press.

Harris, Z. (1955). From phoneme to morpheme. *Language, 31,* 190–222.

Harris, Z. (1968). *Mathematical structures of language.* New York: Wiley and Sons.

Harris, Z. (1982). *A grammar of English on mathematical principles.* New York: John Wiley and Sons.

Harris, Z. (1991). *A theory of language and information: A mathematical approach.* Oxford: Oxford University Press.

Hebb, D. O. (1949). *The organization of behaviour.* New York: John Wiley and Sons.

Howarth, P. (1998). Phraseology and second language proficiency. *Applied Linguistics, 19*(1), 24–44.

Hulstijn, J. and DeKeyser, R. (Eds.) (1997). Testing SLA theory in the research laboratory. *Studies in Second Language Acquisition, 19, 2* [Special issue].

Hunston, S. and Francis, G. (1996). *Pattern grammar: A corpus driven approach to the lexical grammar of English.* Amsterdam: Benjamins.

James, W. (1890). *The principles of psychology* (Vol. 1). New York: Holt.

Jurafsky, D. and Martin, J. H. (2000). *Speech and language processing: An introduction to natural language processing, speech recognition, and computational linguistics.* Englewood Cliffs, NJ: Prentice-Hall.

Lakoff, G. (1987). *Women, fire, and dangerous things: What categories reveal about the mind.* Chicago: University of Chicago Press.

Langacker, R. W. (1987). *Foundations of cognitive grammar: Vol. 1. Theoretical prerequisites.* Stanford, CA: Stanford University Press.

Langacker, R. W. (2000). A dynamic usage-based model. In M. Barlow and S. Kemmer (Eds.), *Usage-based models of language* (pp. 1–63). Stanford, CA: CSLI Publications.

Larsen-Freeman, D. and Cameron, L. (2008). *Complex systems and applied linguistics.* Oxford: Oxford University Press.

Lieven, E. and Tomasello, M. (2008). Children's first language acquisition from a usage-based perspective. In P. Robinson and N. C. Ellis (Eds.), *Handbook of cognitive linguistics and second language acquisition*. New York and London: Routledge.

Lightbown, P. M., Spada, N., and White, L. (1993). The role of instruction in second language acquisition. *Studies in Second Language Acquisition, 15* [Special issue].

Long, M. H. (1983). Does second language instruction make a difference? A review of research. *TESOL Quarterly, 17*, 359–382.

MacWhinney, B. (1987a). Applying the Competition Model to bilingualism. *Applied Psycholinguistics, 8*(4), 315–327.

MacWhinney, B. (1987b). The Competition Model. In B. MacWhinney (Ed.), *Mechanisms of language acquisition* (pp. 249–308). Hillsdale, NJ: Erlbaum.

MacWhinney, B. (1997). Second language acquisition and the Competition Model. In A. M. B. De Groot and J. F. Kroll (Eds.), *Tutorials in bilingualism: Psycholinguistic perspectives* (pp. 113–142). Mahwah, NJ: Lawrence Erlbaum Associates.

MacWhinney, B. (Ed.) (1999). *The emergence of language*. Hillsdale, NJ: Erlbaum.

MacWhinney, B. (2001). The competition model: The input, the context, and the brain. In P. Robinson (Ed.), *Cognition and second language instruction* (pp. 69–90). New York: Cambridge University Press.

McDonough, K. (2006). Interaction and syntactic priming: English L2 speakers' production of dative constructions. *Studies in Second Language Acquisition, 28*, 179–207.

McDonough, K. and Mackey, A. (2006). Responses to recasts: Repetitions, primed production and linguistic development. *Language Learning, 56*, 693–720.

McDonough, K. and Trofimovich, P. (2008). *Using priming methods in second language research*. London: Routledge.

Nation, P. (2001). *Learning vocabulary in another language*. Cambridge: Cambridge University Press.

Newell, A. (1990). *Unified theories of cognition*. Cambridge, MA: Harvard University Press.

Ninio, A. (1999). Pathbreaking verbs in syntactic development and the question of prototypical transitivity. *Journal of Child Language, 26*, 619–653.

Ninio, A. (2006). *Language and the learning curve: A new theory of syntactic development*. Oxford: Oxford University Press.

Norris, J. and Ortega, L. (2000). Effectiveness of L2 instruction: A research synthesis and quantitative meta-analysis. *Language Learning, 50*, 417–528.

Ooi, V. B. Y. (1998). *Computer corpus lexicography*. Edinburgh: Edinburgh University Press.

Perdue, C. (Ed.) (1993). *Adult language acquisition: Crosslinguistic perspectives*. Cambridge: Cambridge University Press.

Pickering, M. J. (2006). The dance of dialogue. *The Psychologist, 19*, 734–737.

Pickering, M. J. and Garrod, S. C. (2006). Alignment as the basis for successful communication. *Research on Language and Computation, 4*, 203–228.

Pinker, S. (1989). *Learnability and cognition: The acquisition of argument structure*. Cambridge, MA: Bradford Books.

Posner, M. I. and Keele, S. W. (1970). Retention of abstract ideas. *Journal of Experimental Psychology, 83*, 304–308.

Rescorla, R. A. (1968). Probability of shock in the presence and absence of CS in fear conditioning. *Journal of Comparative and Physiological Psychology, 66*, 1–5.

Rescorla, R. A. and Wagner, A. R. (1972). A theory of Pavlovian conditioning: Variations in the effectiveness of reinforcement and nonreinforcement. In A. H. Black and W. F. Prokasy (Eds.), *Classical conditioning II: Current theory and research* (pp. 64–99). New York: Appleton-Century-Crofts.

Roberts, P. (1956). *Patterns of English*. New York: Harcourt, Brace and World.

Robinson, P. and Ellis, N. C. (2008a). Conclusion: Cognitive linguistics, Second language acquisition and L2 instruction—issues for research. In P. Robinson and N. C. Ellis (Eds.), *Handbook of cognitive linguistics and second language acquisition*. London: Routledge.

Robinson, P. and Ellis, N. C. (Eds.) (2008b). *A handbook of cognitive linguistics and second language acquisition*. London: Routledge.

Rosch, E. and Mervis, C. B. (1975). Cognitive representations of semantic categories. *Journal of Experimental Psychology: General, 104*, 192–233.

Rosch, E., Mervis, C. B., Gray, W. D., Johnson, D. M., and Boyes-Braem, P. (1976). Basic objects in natural categories. *Cognitive Psychology, 8*, 382–439.

Rumelhart, D. E. and McClelland, J. L. (Eds.) (1986). *Parallel distributed processing: Explorations in the microstructure of cognition* (Vol. 2, Psychological and biological models) Cambridge, MA: MIT Press.

Saussure, F. D. (1916). *Cours de linguistique générale* (Roy Harris, Trans.). London: Duckworth.

Schmitt, N. (2000). *Vocabulary in language teaching*. New York: Cambridge University Press.

Shanks, D. R. (1995). *The psychology of associative learning*. New York: Cambridge University Press.

Simpson-Vlach, R. and Ellis, N. C. (2010). An Academic Formulas List (AFL). *Applied Linguistics, 31*, 487–512.

Sinclair, J. (1991). *Corpus, concordance, collocation*. Oxford: Oxford University Press.

Slobin, D. I. (1996). From "thought and language" to "thinking for speaking". In J. J. Gumperz and S. C. Levinson (Eds.), *Rethinking linguistic relativity* (pp. 70–96). Cambridge: Cambridge University Press.

Slobin, D. I. (1997). The origins of grammaticizable notions: Beyond the individual mind. In D. I. Slobin (Ed.), *The crosslinguistic study of language acquisition* (Vol. 5, pp. 265–323). Mahwah, NJ: Erlbaum.

Spada, N. (1997). Form-focused instruction and second language acquisition: A review of classroom and laboratory research. *Language Teaching Research, 30*, 73–87.

Stefanowitsch, A. and Gries, S. T. (2003). Collostructions: Investigating the interaction between words and constructions. *International Journal of Corpus Linguistics, 8*, 209–243.

Swales, J. M. (1990). *Genre analysis: English in academic and research settings*. Cambridge: Cambridge University Press.

Taylor, J. R. (1998). Syntactic constructions as prototype categories. In M. Tomasello (Ed.), *The new psychology of language: Cognitive and functional approaches to language structure* (pp. 177–202). Mahwah, NJ: Erlbaum.

Tomasello, M. (Ed.) (1998). *The new psychology of language: Cognitive and functional approaches to language structure*. Mahwah, NJ: Erlbaum.

Tomasello, M. (2003). *Constructing a language*. Boston, MA: Harvard University Press.

Tversky, A. (1977). Features of similarity. *Psychological Review, 84*, 327–352.

Tyler, A. (2008). Cognitive linguistics and second language instruction. In P. Robinson and N. C. Ellis (Eds.), *Handbook of cognitive linguistics and second language acquisition*. London: Routledge.

VanPatten, B. (2006). Input processing. In B. VanPatten and J. Williams (Eds.), *Theories in second language acquisition: An introduction*. Mahwah, NJ: Lawrence Erlbaum.

Wittgenstein, L. (1953). *Philosophical investigations* (G. E. M. Anscombe, Trans.). Oxford: Blackwell.

Wulff, S., Ellis, N. C., Römer, U., Bardovi-Harlig, K., and LeBlanc, C. (2009). The acquisition of tense-aspect: Converging evidence from corpora and telicity ratings. *The Modern Language Journal, 93*, 354–369.

Zipf, G. K. (1935). *The psycho-biology of language: An introduction to dynamic philology*. Cambridge, MA: The M.I.T. Press.

13

The logic of the Unified Model

Brian MacWhinney

Historical discussion

Many people believe that learning a second language (L2) is fundamentally different from learning a first language (L1). Evidence of this fundamental difference comes from the fact that first language acquisition almost invariably produces full native speaker competence, whereas many second language learners achieve only partial success in learning their new language. Some researchers believe that this difference in levels of ultimate attainment result arises because, after the expiration of a certain critical period, the learning mechanisms that subserve first language learning atrophy or expire.

The Unified Competition Model (UCM) (MacWhinney, 2008b) takes a different approach to this issue. Instead of attributing differences between first and second language learning to the effects of a critical period, these differences are attributed to the differential interplay between risk-generating processes and protective, support processes. For L1 learning, the five risk factors are entrenchment, parasitism, misconnection, negative transfer, and isolation. To overcome these five risk factors, adults can rely on the support processes of resonance, internalization, chunking, positive transfer, and participation. All of these risk factors and support processes are available to children, as well as adults. What differs between L1 and L2 learning is the way in which these processes are configured.

There are three obvious differences between L1 and L2 learners. First, while infants are learning language, they are also engaged in learning about how the world works. In contrast, L2 learners already have a full understanding of the world and human society. Second, infants are able to rely on a highly malleable brain that has not yet been committed to other tasks (MacWhinney et al., 2000). In contrast, second language learners have to deal with a brain that has already been committed to the task of processing the first language. Third, infants can rely on an intense system of social support from their caregivers (Snow, 1999). In contrast, L2 learners are often heavily involved in L1 social and business commitments that distract them from L2 interactions.

Together, these three differences might suggest that it would make little sense to try to develop a unified model of first and second language acquisition. In fact, many researchers have decided that the two processes are so different that they account for them with totally separate theories with separate processes. For example, Krashen (1994) sees L1 learning as involving "acquisition" and L2 learning as based instead on "learning." Clahsen and Muysken (1986) hold that Universal Grammar (UG) is available to children up to some critical age, but not to older learners of L2. Paradis (2004) and Ullman (2004) argue that children learn language implicitly as a proceduralized, automated skill, whereas adults learn language through explicit declarative controlled processes. Using analyses and arguments such as these, Bley-Vroman (1989, 2009) articulated the fundamental difference hypothesis (FDH), which holds that first and second language acquisition are so fundamentally different that trying to explain them through a single unified theory would make no sense. In this vein, Chomsky (Searchinger, 1995) remarks that learning to speak a second language is as unnatural as learning to ride a unicycle.

Despite these analyses, there are good reasons to question the FDH. The many parallels between L1 and L2 learning are more striking than the differences. Both groups of learners need to segment speech into words. Both groups need to learn the meanings of these words. Both groups need to figure out the patterns that govern word combination in syntactic constructions. Both groups have to interleave their growing lexical and syntactic systems to achieve fluency. Both groups are trying to learn the same target language. Thus, both the overall goal and the specific subgoals involved in reaching that goal are the same for both L1 and L2 learners. Both groups are enmeshed in social situations that require a continual back and forth of communication and learning. Furthermore, both groups of learners rely on the same underlying neuronal hardware.

One could recognize these parallels, but still emphasize the idea that the remaining differences are fundamental. The question is whether those remaining differences are great enough to motivate two separate theories for learning and processing. The thesis of the UCM is that the inclusion of L1 and L2 learning in a single unified model produces a more coherent and insightful analysis. The fact that L2 learning is so heavily influenced by transfer from L1 means that it would be impossible to construct a model of L2 learning that did not take into account the structure of the first language. Unless the two types of learning and processing share virtually no important commonalities, it is conceptually simpler to formulate a unified model within which the specific areas of divergence can be clearly distinguished from the numerous commonalities.

Core issues

The UCM is an extension of the Competition Model of the 1980s (Bates and MacWhinney, 1982; MacWhinney, 1987). The original model was designed to account for the end state of first and second language learning, but not the details of the learning process. The classic Competition Model dealt effectively with processes of transfer and the growth of cue strength. However, it had three major gaps. First, it was unable to provide insights into the ways in which proceduralization of language processes can lead to increases in fluency and the avoidance of fossilization. Second, it failed to incorporate information from our continually growing understanding of the neuroscience of language. Third, it provided no central role to social processes in L2 acquisition. In order to explain the workings of the newer version of the model, it is best to begin with a review of the core concepts of competition, cues, cue strength, and cue validity from the original Competition Model. These concepts remain unchanged in the new model, and the empirical basis of these concepts remains as it has been described in the literature. However, the processes of the classic version of the model are now supplemented by formulations of additional cognitive, neural, and social mechanisms. These additional mechanisms provide additional determination of cue strength, which is the major explanatory principle in the model.

Competition

Competition is a fundamental construct in many psychological theories. Freud viewed the ego as mediating a competition between the impulses of the Id and the restrictions of the superego.

Modern cognitive theories view competition as arising whenever two cues for a given decision point in opposite directions. When this occurs, the strength of the resultant decision is a function of the competing strengths of the input cues. A classic example is the Stroop effect (Stroop, 1935) in which the name for a word competes with the color in which that word is written. Theories based on competition have been articulated in areas as diverse as visual perception (Brunswik, 1956), reading (Seidenberg and McClelland, 1989), social psychology (Kelley, 1967), cognitive development (Anderson, 1981), infant attachment (van Geert, 1991), motor control (Carlson *et al.*, 1989), and auditory perception (Massaro, 1987).

Cues

Traditionally, the Competition Model has focused on the ways in which cues compete for thematic role assignment in sentences with transitive verbs. For example, in the sentence *the boys chase the ball*, the two nouns (*boys* and *ball*) are possible candidates for the role of the agent or subject of the verb. However, the candidacy of *the boys* for this role is favored by three strong cues—preverbal positioning, subject-verb agreement, and animacy. None of these cues favors the candidacy of *ball*. Therefore, native speakers uniformly conclude that *the boys* are the agents. However, in certain ungrammatical sentences, the competition between the noun phrases can become tighter. The ungrammatical sentence *the ball are chasing the boys* illustrates this effect. In this sentence, the strong cue of preverbal positioning favors *the ball* as agent. However, the cues of subject-verb agreement and animacy favor *the boys* as the agents. Given a competition sentence of this type, listeners are often quite unsure which of the two noun phrases to choose as agent, since neither choice is perfect. As a result, listeners, as a group, are slower to make this choice, and their choices are nearly evenly split between the two possibilities.

Competition Model experiments use sentences in which cues have been randomly combined to measure the strength of the underlying cues. The same method has been used in 92 empirical studies involving 18 different languages. Across these various experiments and languages, the cues involved come from a very small set of linguistic devices. Languages mark case roles using basically five possible cue types: word order, case marking, agreement, intonation, and verb-based expectations. For simple transitive sentences with two nouns and a verb, the possible word orders are NNV, NVN, and VNN. In addition, the marking of the cases or thematic roles of nouns can rely on affixes (as in Hungarian or Turkish), postpositions (as in Japanese), prepositions (as in Spanish), or articles (as in German). Agreement marking displays correspondences between the subject and the verb (as in English) or the object and the verb (as in Hungarian and Arabic). Some of the features that can be marked through agreement include number (as in English), definiteness (as in Hungarian), gender (as in Arabic), honorific status (as in Japanese), and other grammatical features. Intonation is seldom a powerful cue in thematic role identification, although we have found that it plays a role in some non-canonical word order patterns in Italian and in the topic marking construction in Hungarian. Verb-based expectations vary markedly across verb types. High activity transitive verbs like *push* and *hit* tend to serve as cues for animate agents and inanimate patients. Stimulus-experiencer verbs like *amaze* and *surprise* cue animate patients and either animate or inanimate agents.

Competition Model experiments put these various cues into systematic conflict with one another using orthogonalized analysis of variance designs. The extent to which cues dominate or control the choices of agent nouns in these experiments is the measure of their *cue strength*. The core claim of both the classic and revised versions of the Competition Model is that cue strength is determined by cue validity. Cue strength is defined through experimental results; cue validity is defined through corpus counts. Using conversational input data such as those available from the

CHILDES (http://childes.talkbank.org) or TalkBank (http://talkbank.org) corpora, we can define *cue reliability* as the proportion of times the cue is correct over the total number of occurrences of the cue (Ellis, Chapter 12, this volume). Cue *availability* is the proportion of times the cue is available over the times it is needed. The product of cue reliability and cue availability is overall *cue validity*.

Early in both L1 and L2 learning, cue strength is heavily determined by availability, because beginning learners are only familiar with cues that are moderately frequent in the language input (Matessa and Anderson, 2000; Taraban and Palacios, 1993). As learning progresses, cue reliability becomes more important than cue availability. In adult native speakers, cue strength depends entirely on cue reliability. In some cases, we can further distinguish the effects of *conflict reliability*. When two highly reliable cues conflict, we say that the one that wins is higher in conflict reliability. For example, in the case of Dutch pronouns, only after age 8 do L1 learners begin to realize that the more reliable cue of pronoun case should dominate over the more frequent, but usually reliable, cue of word order (McDonald, 1986).

When adult native speakers have sufficient time to make a careful decision, cue strength is correlated at levels above 0.90 with cue reliability. However, when cue strength is measured online during the actual process of comprehension, before the sentence is complete, other factors come into play. During online processing, listeners tend to rely initially on a single cue with good reliability and high availability without integrating the effects of that core cue with other possible cues. This happens, for example, during online processing of sentences in Russian (Kempe and MacWhinney, 1999). Cue strength is also heavily influenced during the early phases of learning by the factors of *cue cost* and *cue detectability*. Cue cost factors arise primarily during the processing of agreement markers, because these markers cannot be used to assign thematic roles directly. For example, in an Italian sentence such as *il gatto spingono i cani* (the cat push the dogs), the listener may begin by thinking that *il gatto* is the agent because it occurs in preverbal position. However, because the verb *spingono* requires a plural subject, it triggers a search for a plural noun. The first noun cannot satisfy this requirement and the processor must then hope that a plural noun will eventually follow. In this example, the plural noun comes right away, but in many cases it may come much later in the sentence. This additional waiting and matching requires far more processing than that involved with simple word order or case marking cues. As a result of this additional cost for the agreement cue, Italian children are slow to pick it up, despite its high reliability in the language (Bates *et al.*, 1982).

Cue detectability factors (VanPatten, Chapter 16, this volume) play a major role only during the earliest stages of learning of declensional and conjugational patterns. For example, although the marking of the accusative case by a suffix on the noun is a fully reliable cue in both Hungarian and Turkish, three-year-old Hungarian children show a delay of about ten months in acquiring this cue, when compared to young Turkish children. The source of this delay seems to be the greater complexity of the Hungarian declensional pattern and the weaker detectability of the Hungarian suffix. However, once Hungarian children have "cracked the code" of accusative marking, they rely nearly exclusively on this cue. Because of its greater reliability, the strength of the Hungarian case-marking cue eventually comes to surpass the strength of the Turkish cue.

Although Competition Model experiments have focused on the issue of thematic role assignment in simple transitive sentences, the principle of competition is a very general one that can be elaborated into a full model of language processing (MacDonald *et al.*, 1994; MacWhinney, 1987). For example, in a sentence, such as *the women discussed the dogs on the beach*, there is a competition between the attachment of the prepositional phrase *on the beach* to the verb or the noun *the dogs*. In this case, the competition can be resolved either way. However, in a sentence, such as *the communist farmers hated died*, the competition between the adjectival and nominal reading of *communist* is initially resolved in favor of the adjectival reading, because of the presence of the following noun *farmers* and then the verb *hated*. However, once the second verb is encountered, the listener realizes that the adjectival reading has taken them down a garden path. At that point, the weaker nominal reading of *communist* is given additional strength and the alternative reading is eventually obtained.

The view of language processing as fundamentally competitive has three important consequences for a variety of issues in second language learning. One consequence, which has already been discussed, is that second language learning is viewed as a data–driven process in which the forces of cue validity, detectability, and reliability play a major role. A second consequence is the learner's ability to recover from errors and overgeneralizations can be directly related to variations in the strengths of competing constructions, thereby resolving the core issue in the Logical Problem of Acquisition (MacWhinney, 2004). Finally, the fact that cue strength can be influenced by additional inputs from other factors allows us to extend the model, while still maintaining a focus on detailed studies of cue usage during language processing.

Inputs to competition

The unified version of the Competition Model (MacWhinney, 2008b) extends the basic model by providing characterizations of additional neurocognitive, developmental, and social (Bayley and Tarone, Chapter 3, this volume) forces that control the core competition. As MacWhinney (2005a) notes, these forces operate on very different time scales, varying from seconds to years. However, in the end, these forces have their effect at the moment of speaking by imparting strength to particular cues and by affecting the timing of the interaction between cues. Some of these forces operate to restrict the smooth acquisition of second languages. We can refer to these as "risk factors." Other forces serve to promote both first and second language learning. We can refer to these as support factors. Table 13.1 presents these factors in terms of these two dimensions.

Entrenchment and resonance

Entrenchment is a basic neurodevelopmental process. At birth, the cerebral cortex of the human infant is uncommitted to specific linguistic patterns. However, across the first years, neural territory becomes increasingly committed to the patterns of the first language. These processes of commitment and entrenchment can be modeled using self-organizing maps (SOMs) (Kohonen, 2001), a computational formalism that reflects many of the basic facts of neural structure. Simulations of lexical learning from real input to children (Hernandez *et al.*, 2005) have shown how the organization of lexical fields into parts of speech becomes increasingly inflexible across learning. If the structure of the second language is extremely close to that of the

Table 13.1 Risk factors and support factors for second language learning

Risk Factors	Support Factors
Entrenchment	Resonance
Misconnection	Proceduralization
Parasitism	Internalization
Negative transfer	Positive Transfer
Isolation	Participation

Table 13.2 Levels of linguistic processing

Map	Area	Processes	Theory
Audition	Auditory cortex	Extracting units	Statistical learning
Articulation	IFG, motor cortex	Targets, timing	Gating
Lexicon	Wernicke's area	Phonology to meaning	DevLex
Syntax	Inferior Frontal Gyrus	Slots, sequences	Item-based patterns
Gram. Roles	DLPFC	Role binding, lists	Attachment, roles
Mental Models	Dorsal cortex	Deixis, perspective	Perspective

first language, then this commitment to lexical structure will cause few errors. However, if the languages are very different, the entrenchment of grammatical categories in the lexicon can lead to problems.

The detailed operation of entrenchment has been modeled most explicitly for lexical (Li *et al.*, 2007) and auditory (Guenther and Gjaja, 1996) structure. However, the UCM holds that cortical maps exist for each of the structural levels recognized by traditional linguistics, including syntax (Pulvermüller, 2003), grammatical roles (Jackendoff, 1983), and mental models (MacWhinney, 2008a), as given in Table 13.2. Research has shown that entrenchment in cortical maps presents the greatest risk factor for second language learners in the areas of auditory phonology (Kuhl *et al.*, 2005), articulatory phonology (Major, 1987), and the interactions of syntax with the lexicon (DeKeyser, 2000).

Resonance

The risk factor of entrenchment can be counteracted by the support factor of resonance. Resonance provides new encoding dimensions to reconfigure old neuronal territory, permitting the successful encoding of L2 patterns. Because this encoding operates against the underlying forces of entrenchment, special configurations are needed to support resonance. Resonance can be illustrated most easily in the domain of lexical learning. Since the days of Ebbinghaus (1885), we have understood that the learning of the associations between words requires repeated practice. However, a single repetition of a new vocabulary pair such as *mesa–table* is not enough to guarantee robust learning. Instead, it is important that initial exposure be followed by additional test repetitions timed to provide correct retrieval before forgetting prevents efficient resonance from occurring (Pavlik and Anderson, 2005). Because robustness accumulates with practice, later retrieval trials can be spaced farther and farther apart. This is the principle of "graduated interval recall" that was formulated for second language learning by Pimsleur (1967).

The success of graduated interval recall can be attributed, in part, to its use of resonant neural connections between cortical areas. While two cortical areas are coactive, the hippocampus can store their relation long enough to create an initial memory consolidation. Repeated access to this trace (Wittenberg *et al.*, 2002) can further consolidate the memory. Once initial consolidation has been achieved, maintenance only requires occasional reactivation of the relevant retrieval pathway. This type of resonance can be used to consolidate new forms on the phonological, lexical (Gupta and MacWhinney, 1997), and construction levels.

The success of graduated interval recall also depends on correctly diagnosing the point at which a new memory trace is still available, albeit slightly weakened. At this point, when a learner attempts to remember a new word, sound, or phrase, some additional work will be needed to generate a retrieval cue. This retrieval cue then establishes a resonance with the form being retrieved. This resonant cue may involve lexical analysis, onomatopoeia, imagery, physical responses, or some other relational pattern. Because there is no fixed set of resonant connections (Ellis and Beaton, 1995), we cannot use group data to demonstrate the use of specific connections in lexical learning. However, we do know that felicitous mnemonics provided by the experimenter (Atkinson, 1975) can greatly facilitate learning.

Orthography provides a major support for resonance in L2 learning. When a learner of German encounters the word *Wasser*, it is easy to map the sounds of the word directly to the image of the letters. Because German has highly regular mappings from orthography to pronunciation, calling up the image of the spelling of *Wasser* is an extremely good way of activating its sound. When the L2 learner is illiterate, or when the L2 orthography is unlike the L1 orthography, this backup orthographic system is not available to support resonance. L2 learning of Chinese by speakers of languages with Roman scripts illustrates this problem. In some signs and books in mainland China, Chinese characters are accompanied by romanized Pinyin spellings. This provides the L2 learner a method for establishing resonant connections between new words, their pronunciation, and their representations in Chinese orthography. However, in Taiwan and Hong Kong, characters are seldom written out in Pinyin in either books or public notices. As a result, learners cannot develop resonant connections from these materials. In order to make use of resonant connections from orthography, learners must focus on the learning of Chinese script. This learning itself requires constructing other resonant associations, because the Chinese writing system is based heavily on radical elements that have multiple potential resonant associations with the sounds and meanings of words.

Connection and misconnection

The negative effects of entrenchment on L2 learning are amplified by the fact that the major language processing areas are connected across white matter tracts. Unlike the digital computer, the brain has no system for assigning absolute and constant addresses to individual neurons. Consider a sentence, such as *the black dog chased the white dog*. When processing the two instances of *dog* in this sentence, the same lexical item is responding. But the brain needs to keep the first mention of the noun distinct from the second, so it can know that the one who did the chasing was the black dog and not the white dog. This means that the head noun and all of its associated arguments have to be bound together to operate as a unit. Solving this "binding problem" is a fundamental challenge for neuronal computation. Within individual cortical maps, local regional self-organization can solve a part of the binding problem, because items that behave similarly tend to cluster near each other. Differences between these items can be resolved by short, local connections that are relatively inexpensive in metabolic terms (Buzsaki, 2006). However, the connections between separate cortical maps must rely on long-distance neuronal projections that are more expensive metabolically and more difficult to repair, if they are broken. As a result, these connecting pathways are relatively less plastic and more committed to L1 functions than the areas within individual maps. For the language areas, important connecting pathways include the *arcuate fasciculus*, the *superior longitudinalis*, and the several subsegments of these major pathways (Friederici, 2009).

When activation is passed along these long-distance connections, there must be some method for the receiving units to process the identity of the sending units. The brain can address this problem by applying a method of parallel *topological organization* that has been widely documented for sensory and motor systems. Within the lexical map, words that share a similar part of speech and a similar meaning, such as *cut*, *chop*, *slice*, and *hack*, are located topologically near each other.

When items in this area connect to other processing regions, topological organization can help the receiving area identify the general shape of the sending units.

In aphasia, lesions to white matter tracts can result in various forms of language loss, and disorganization in the formation of these tracts during early development can lead to Specific Language Impairment. The task of reorganizing communication across these connections presents a major challenge to L2 learners. If L1 and L2 use roughly similar systems for part-of-speech assignment, communication between L2 lexical items and L2 syntactic processes will be relatively smooth. However, if L2 is typologically quite different from L1, it will be difficult for a learner to acquire the new mapping and there will be a persistent tendency for L2 learners to rely on L1 pathways for composing sentences.

Proceduralization and chunking

Second language learners can address these connectivity problems by relying on the support factors of proceduralization and chunking. Proceduralization (Anderson, 1993) is a cognitive process that transfers newly learned material into a smoothly operating procedure which then requires minimal attentional control. Proceduralization is closely related to the process of chunking (Rosenbloom and Newell, 1987) that takes a series of separate elements and welds them into a single processing unit or chunk.

Chunks function as single, unanalyzed wholes, whereas procedures may have some room for flexible variation. For example, in Spanish, L2 learners can learn *muy buenos días* "very good morning" as a chunk. This chunk is based on a series of connections between preexisting lexical items, stored within the lexical map in the posterior cortical areas in the temporal lobe. However, this pattern could also be learned as a flexible procedure triggered by the word *muy* "very" that would allow other completions such as *muy buenas tardes* "good afternoon" or *muy buenas noticias* "very good news."

Second language learners often fail to pick up sufficiently large chunks, seeking instead to analyze the input into small easily managed segments. For example, learners of German often learn the word *Mann* "man" in isolation. If, instead, they would learn phrases such as *der alte Mann, meines Mannes, den jungen Männern*, and *ein guter Mann*, they would have a good basis for acquiring the declensional paradigm for both the noun and its modifiers. If learners were to store larger chunks of this type, then the rules of grammar could emerge from analogic processing of the chunks stored in feature maps (Bybee and Hopper, 2001; Ellis, 2002; MacWhinney, 1982; Tomasello, 2003). However, if learners analyze a phrase like *der alte Mann* into the literal string "the + old + man" and throw away all of the details of the inflections on "der" and "alte," then they will lose an opportunity to induce the grammar from implicit generalization across stored chunks.

Chunking focuses on storage in posterior lexical areas, whereas proceduralization relies on storage in frontal areas for sequence control (Broca's) that then point to lexical items in posterior areas. Proceduralization is initially less robust then chunking, but it is capable of greater extensibility and flexibility (Gobet, 2005) across constructions beyond the level of the item-based construction. For example, a Spanish phrase such as *quisiera comprar* … (I would like to buy …) can be used with any manner of noun to talk about things you would like to buy. In each of these cases, producing one initial combination, such as *quisiera comprar una cerveza* (I would like to buy a beer) may be halting at first. However, soon the result of the creation process itself can be stored as a chunk. In this case, it is not the actual phrase that is chunked, but rather the process of activating the predicate combination (*quisiera comprar*) and then going ahead and filling the argument. In other words, we develop fluency by repeated practice in making combinations.

Once learners have developed fluency in the combination of well-learned words, they can still experience disfluency when trying to integrate newly learned words into established constructions. For example, even if we have learned to use the frame *quisiera comprar* fluently with words such as *una cerveza* (a beer) or *un reloj* (a clock), we may still experience difficulties when we need to talk about buying "a round trip ticket to Salamanca" (*un billete de ida y vuelta para Salamanca*). In this selection, we might have particular problems when we hit the word "*para*" since the English concept of "for, to" can be expressed in Spanish using either *por* or *para* and our uncertainty regarding the choice between these two forms can slow us down and cause disfluency or error. In general, for both L1 and L2 learners, disfluencies arise from delays in lexical access, misordering of constituents, and selection of agreement markings. Fluency arises through the practicing of argument filling and improvements in the speed of lexical access and the selections between competitors.

Researchers such as Paradis (2004) or Ullman (2004) believe that L2 learners cannot effectively proceduralize their second language; and, as a result, L2 productions must remain forever slow and non-fluent. We can refer to this position as the Proceduralization Deficit Hypothesis (PDH). This hypothesis is a specific articulation of the general Critical Period Hypothesis (CPH) about which so much has been written in recent years (DeKeyser and Larson-Hall, 2005). Surveying this vast literature is beyond the scope of this brief review. However, we can point to a couple of recent findings that bear specifically on the PDH. Initial work by Hahne and Friederici (2001) indicated that, even after five or more years learning German, native Russian and Japanese speakers failed to show rapid early left anterior negativity (ELAN) responses to grammaticality violations in German sentences. These results suggested that, after the end of the critical period, comprehension could not be automated or proceduralized. However, further studies using artificial language systems (Friederici *et al.*, 2002; Müller *et al*, 2005) have shown that, if the rules of the target language are simple and consistent, L2 learners can develop proceduralization, as measured by ELAN, with a couple of months of training. Thus, it appears that proceduralization can be successful in adult learners, as long as cues are consistent, simple, and reliable (MacWhinney, 1997; Tokowicz and MacWhinney, 2005). This finding is in accord with the UCM analysis, rather than the PDH analysis, since it shows that the crucial factor here is not the age of the learner, but the shape of the input.

It is important not to confuse proceduralization with implicit learning. Although first language learning relies primarily on implicit learning, second language learning involves a complex interaction of both explicit and implicit learning (VanPatten, Chapter 16, this volume). In formal contexts such as classrooms, a second language may be learned through explicit methods. However, this knowledge can then become proceduralized and automatized, producing good fluency. A simple example of this process comes from a study by Presson and MacWhinney (under review) based on use of a computerized tutorial system for teaching the gender of French nouns. In this experiment, if naïve learners who have never studied French are given simple cues to gender, they are able to achieve 90 percent accurate gender assignment after only 90 minutes of computerized practice. Moreover, this ability is retained across three months without any further training.

In a review of the role of explicit rule presentation, MacWhinney (1997) argued that L2 learners can benefit from explicit cue instruction, as long as the cues are presented simply and clearly. Once a simple pattern has been established in explicit declarative form, repeated exposures to a cue can use the scaffolding of the explicit pattern to establish proceduralization. As in the case of lexical learning, the method of graduated interval recall can further support proceduralization. In addition, error correction can help to tune cue weights (McDonald and Heilenman, 1991). Of course, proceduralization can be achieved without scaffolding from explicit instruction. However, if explicit scaffolding is available, learning will be faster.

Positive and negative transfer

Entrenchment and connectivity have important consequences for L2 learning, because new forms must be entered into maps that are already heavily committed to L1 patterns. One way of solving this problem is by aligning L2 forms with analogous L1 forms. When the forms align well, mapping an L1 form to L2 will result in *positive transfer*. However, when there are mismatches, then the alignment produces at least some *negative transfer*. In the terms of the overall analysis of risk and support factors, negative transfer functions as a risk factor and positive transfer as a support factor.

The UCM holds that L2 learners will attempt to transfer any pattern for which there is some perceptual or functional match between L1 and L2. The match need not be exact or complete, as long as it is close enough. It is often easy to transfer the basic pragmatic functions that help structure conversations and the construction of mental models (Bardovi-Harlig, Chapter 9, this volume). The transfer of lexical meaning from L1 to L2 is also largely positive, although there will be some mismatches in meaning (Dong *et al.*, 2005) and translation ambiguities (Prior *et al.*, 2007). We also expect a great deal of transfer of L1 patterns stored on the auditory and articulatory maps. It is reasonable enough to map a Chinese /p/ to an English /p/, even though the Chinese sound has a different time of voicing onset and no aspiration. The result of this type of imperfect transfer is what leads to the establishment of a foreign accent in L2 learners. As Eckman (Chapter 6, this volume) explains, patterns in learners' phonologies are determined both by transfer and universal principles of markedness. Moreover, the unit of phonological transfer reaches beyond the segment, including syllable structure and other prosodic patterns.

Transfer is also easy enough for the semantics of lexical items (Kroll and Tokowicz, 2005). In this area, transfer is often largely positive, particularly between languages with similar linguistic and cultural patterns. In the initial stages of L2 word learning, this type of transfer requires very little reorganization, because L2 forms are initially parasitic upon L1 forms.

However, transfer is difficult or impossible for item-based syntactic patterns (MacWhinney, 2005b), because these patterns cannot be readily matched across languages. For the same reason, transfer is unlikely for the formal aspects of conjugational or declensional patterns and classes. The fact that transfer is difficult for these systems does not mean that they are easy for L2 learners, but rather that they must be learned from the bottom up without any support from the L1.

When learners have several possible L1 forms that can transfer to L2, they tend to prefer to transfer the least marked forms (Eckman, 1977; Major and Faudree, 1996). For example, as Pienemann *et al.* (2005) have noted, Swedish learners of German prefer to transfer to German the unmarked Swedish word order that places the subject before the tense marker in the German equivalent of sentences such as *Peter likes milk today*. Although Swedish has a pattern that allows the order *Today likes Peter milk*, learners tend not to transfer this pattern initially, because it is the more marked alternative.

Parasitism and internalization

In her Revised Hierarchical Model, Kroll has emphasized the extent to which beginning second language learners depend on preexisting L1 pathways for mediating the activation of L2 lexical items (Kroll and Sholl, 1992). For example, when hearing the word *perro* "dog" in Spanish, the learner may first translate the word into English and then use the English word to access the meaning. At this point, the use of the Spanish word is *parasitic* on English-based knowledge. Later on, the word *perro* comes to activate the correct meaning directly.

In order to move from this parasitic use of L2 to direct access of meaning, the learner needs to strengthen the direct pathways between the new forms and the preexisting functions. The process of internalization can serve to counteract the forces of parasitism. Internalization (Pavlenko and Lantolf, 2000) involves the use of L2 by learners in their inner speech (Vygotsky, 1934). When we activate inner speech, we are using language to build up mental models to control our thinking and plans. Vygotsky (1934) observed that young children would often give themselves instructions overtly. For example, a two-year-old might say, "pick it up" while picking up a block. At this age, the verbalization tends to guide and control the action. By producing a verbalization that describes an action, the child sets up a resonant connection between vocalization and action (Asher, 1969). Later, as Vygotsky argues, these overt instructions become inner speech and continue to guide our cognition. L2 learners go through a process much like that of the child. At first, they use the language only with others. Then, they begin to talk to themselves in the new language and start to "think in the second language." At this point, the second language begins to assume the same resonant status that the child attains for the first language.

Once a process of internalization is set into motion, it can also be used to process new input and relate new forms to other forms paradigmatically. For example, if I hear the phrase *ins Mittelalter* (in the Middle Ages) in German, I can think to myself that this means that the stem *Alter* must be *das Alter*. This means that the dative must take the form *in welchem Alter* (in which age) or *in meinem Alter* (in my age). These form-related exercises can be conducted in parallel with more expressive exercises in which I simply try to talk to myself about things around me in German, or whatever language I happen to be learning. Even young children engage in practice of this type (Berk, 1994; Nelson, 1998). Internalization also helps us understand the growth of the ability to engage in code switching. If a language is being repeatedly accessed, it will be in a highly resonant state. Although another language will be passively accessible, it may take a second or two before the resonant activation of that language can be triggered by a task (Grosjean, 1997). Thus, a speaker may not immediately recognize a sentence in a language that has not been spoken in the recent context. On the other hand, a simultaneous interpreter will maintain both languages in continual receptive activation, while trying to minimize resonant activations in the output system of the source language.

Isolation and participation

The fifth risk factor for older L2 learners is social isolation. As we get older, full integration into a second language community can become increasingly difficult. There are at least three reasons for this. First, as we age, it can become increasingly difficult to set aside L1 allegiances and responsibilities. Second, L2 communities tend to be more immediately supportive of younger L2 learners. As children get older, peer groups become increasingly critical of participants who fail to communicate in accepted ways. Third, as we age, we may develop images regarding our social status that make it difficult to accept corrective feedback, teasing, or verbal challenges, even though these are excellent sources of language input. The cumulative effect of these social factors is that positive support for language learning can decrease markedly across the lifespan. Unless older learners focus directly on making friends in the new community and developing a full L2 persona (Pavlenko and Lantolf, 2000), they can become isolated and cut off from learning.

The fifth support factor for older L2 learners is the obverse of the risk factor of social isolation. Older learners can increase their participation (Pavlenko and Lantolf, 2000) in the L2 community in a variety of ways. They can join religious groups, athletic teams, or work groups. Often these groups are highly motivated to improve the language abilities of new members, so that they can function smoothly within the group. Any method that can promote interaction with native speakers can facilitate learning (Mackey, Abbuhl, and Gass, Chapter 1, this volume).

Older learners can also engage in formal study and expose themselves to L2 input through books, films, and music. When these methods for increasing participation operate in concert with the processes of chunking, resonance, and internalization, L2 learning will lead to increasingly high levels of proceduralization and correctness. Instruction can also incorporate insights from activity theory (Engeström, 1999; Ratner, 2002) to guide a contextualized curriculum. Many syllabi already make use of a simple form of activity theory when they compose units based on specific activities such as ordering food at a restaurant, asking for directions, dealing with car problems, or transferring money across bank accounts. Multimodal video materials linked to transcripts can be used to further support this type of activity-based learning of vocabulary, pragmatics, and syntax.

Data and common elicitation measures

As we noted earlier, Competition Model studies place cues into competition using orthogonalized analysis of variance designs. Each factor in the design represents a particular cue. Consider the example of a study that examines the competition between word order, case marking, and agreement in Hungarian. The three levels of the word order factor will be NNV, NVN, and VNN with the verb in different positions vis-a-vis the two nouns. For example, the VNN sentence could be the Hungarian equivalent of *chases the dog the cat*. For the case-marking cue, the three levels would involve marking on the first noun, the second noun, or neither noun. For the agreement cue, the three levels would involve agreement of the verb with the first noun, the second noun, or neither noun. This combination of factors would then yield a $3 \times 3 \times 3$ design with 27 cells. In order to achieve greater reliability of measurement, the study might have three replications in each cell for a total of 81 trials. The dependent variables would be percentage choice of the first noun as agent and reaction time for this decision. In the 1980s, these studies were conducted using pictures; work with very young children still uses small toy objects. However, with adults we now use computers to present both the picture stimuli and the sentences. In this mode, subjects select one of two pictures on the screen by pressing a key corresponding to the selected picture. The results of these studies are analyzed using either analysis of variance or maximum likelihood analysis.

Competition Model work also involves computation of cue validity from texts. This is done by examining selected corpora and looking for each case of a relevant competition. To compute the validity of cues for agent choice, we examine sentences with a transitive verb. We then list for each cue whether it is (a) available in the sentence, (b) contrastive, (c) reliable, and (d) reliable in direct conflicts with other cues. In this way, we compute the proportions for simple availability, contrast availability, reliability, and conflict reliability. We then use these values as predictors of the relative strengths of the cues.

Apart from the data provided by the classic version of the Competition Model, the UCM relies on new data gathered from online studies of L2 learning. These studies are designed to examine the effects of resonance, chunking, and internalization on L2 learning. These studies have shown that methods that promote these three processes achieve higher levels of language learning for basic skills such as French nominal declension (Presson and MacWhinney, under review), Japanese sentence patterns (Yoshimura and MacWhinney (2007), vocabulary (Pavlik *et al.*, 2007), and pinyin dictation (Zhang 2009).

By looking at how children, adult monolinguals, and adult bilinguals speaking 18 different languages process various types of sentences, we have been able to reach these conclusions, regarding competition during sentence comprehension:

(1) When given enough time during sentence comprehension to make a careful choice, adults assign the role of agency to the nominal with the highest cue strength for that role.

(2) When there is a competition between cues, the levels of choice in a group of adult subjects will closely reflect the relative strengths of the competing cues.

(3) When adult subjects are asked to respond immediately, even before the end of the sentence is reached, they will tend to base their decisions primarily on the strongest cue in the language.

(4) When the strongest cue is neutralized, the next strongest cue will dominate.

(5) The fastest decisions occur when all cues agree and there is no competition. The slowest decisions occur when strong cues compete.

(6) Children begin learning to comprehend sentences by first focusing on the strongest cue in their language.

(7) As children get older, the strength of all cues increases to match the adult pattern with the most valid cue growing most in strength.

(8) As children get older, their reaction times gradually get faster in accord with the adult pattern.

(9) Compared to adults, children are relatively more influenced by cue availability, as opposed to cue reliability.

(10) Cue strength in adults and older children (8–10 years) is not related to cue availability (since all cues have been heavily encountered by this time), but rather to cue reliability. In particular, it is a function of conflict reliability, which measures the reliability of a cue when it conflicts directly with other cues.

(11) Older learners tend to transfer cue strengths from L1 to L2.

A bibliography of studies supporting these conclusions can be found on the Web at http://psyling. psy.cmu.edu/papers.

Applications

The findings and formulations of the UCM have important implications for the teaching of second languages. For learners in the pre-school and early school years, the risk factors of entrenchment, misconnection, transfer, and isolation are not yet serious concerns. Young learners can acquire additional languages using the same methods they used to pick up their first language. At this age, instruction should focus on providing rich input to implicit learning processes. The principle danger is that, once instruction or exposure to a language ceases, children will soon lose their ability to use that language (Burling, 1959). For immigrant children, the major challenge during this period is to provide social situations that allow them to integrate fully into peer group contexts (McLaughlin, 1985).

During the later school years, second language instruction should become increasingly explicit. For ten year olds, instruction can still rely principally on songs, phrases, and games. However, adolescents should begin to learn in adult mode by relying on chunking, resonance, internalization, and participation. For adolescent and adult learners, instruction should include both contextualized and decontextualized components. Decontextualized components should focus on the resonant practice of basic skills in auditory phonology, articulatory phonology, lexicon, and syntactic constructions. This type of basic skills practice can be controlled through computerized presentation with the results tailored to the individual student level (Pavlik et al., 2007) and relying on the method of graduated interval recall to maximize efficiency. We have implemented systems of this type (http://talkbank.org/SLA) for learning Chinese sound patterns through Pinyin dictation, Chinese vocabulary, French dictation, and French gender (Presson and MacWhinney, under review). These online systems automatically provide the instructor with students' scores to allow them to monitor students' progress through each phase of each module.

Basic skills training can focus first on chunking (Yoshimura and MacWhinney, 2007) and resonance. As these basic skills become consolidated, learners can begin to focus increasingly on internalization and participation for consolidating L2 fluency. For these levels, instruction should be increasingly contextualized. Methods that rely on computerized presentation of contextually realistic videotaped interactions linked to transcripts can be particularly effective, as in the DOVE transcript browser illustrated at http://talkbank.org/SLA.

Future directions

Further elaboration and testing of the UCM's approach to the issues of fluency, competition, transfer, entrenchment, and internalization will need to address the following high priority research questions:

(1) Competition Model experiments typically treat all transitive verbs as a single group. However, the model emphasizes the item-based nature of syntactic learning (MacWhinney, 2005b; McDonald and MacWhinney, 1995). This means that we need to devise experimental methods that can measure cue competition more accurately across smaller lexical groups for both nouns and verbs.

(2) To deepen the grounding of the model on neuroscience, we need to extend the DevLex model in three major ways. First, we need to show how morphological markers can emerge through the processing of lexical forms. Second, we need to develop a SOM model of the acquisition of syntactic patterns from item-based frames. Third, we need to construct DevLex simulations of early bilingual learning that show how the two languages are merged on the level of deep semantics, but separate on the level of lexical semantics.

(3) We need to devise methods for evaluating the mechanistic effects of the support factors of proceduralization, resonance, transfer, internalization, and participation. Much of this work is now in progress. We have some precise characterizations of some of these mechanisms, but a great deal of careful, empirical work will be needed to complete this picture.

(4) In terms of pedagogical applications, we need to parcel out the effects of transfer, markedness, and cue strength on early skill learning. For example, we know that beginning learners find some French gender cues easier than others (Carroll, 2005; Presson and MacWhinney, under review). Similarly, we know that learners with different L1 backgrounds face very different problems in the learning of Chinese phonology (Zhang, 2009). In order to maximize the efficiency of computerized instruction, we need to develop models that base training on information about these differences.

(5) We need to study the retention of items and basic skills across longer time spans, using standard pre-test/post-test designs. Specifically, we need to know whether emphases on chunking and resonance produce robust learning of L2 patterns.

References

Anderson, J. (Ed.) (1981). *Cognitive skills and their acquisition*. Hillsdale, NJ: Lawrence Erlbaum Associates.
Anderson, J. (1993). *Rules of the mind*. Hillsdale, NJ: Lawrence Erlbaum Associates.
Asher, J. (1969). The total physical response approach to second language learning. *The Modern Language Journal, 53*, 3–17.

Atkinson, R. (1975). Mnemotechnics in second-language learning. *American Psychologist, 30*, 821–828.

Bates, E. and MacWhinney, B. (1982). Functionalist approaches to grammar. In E. Wanner and L. Gleitman (Eds.), *Language acquisition: The state of the art* (pp. 173–218). New York: Cambridge University Press.

Bates, E., McNew, S., MacWhinney, B., Devescovi, A., and Smith, S. (1982). Functional constraints on sentence processing: A cross-linguistic study. *Cognition, 11*, 245–299.

Berk, L. E. (1994). Why children talk to themselves. *Scientific American, November, 273*, 78–83.

Bley-Vroman, R. (1989). What is the logical problem of foreign language learning? In S. Gass, and J. Schachter (Eds.), *Linguistic perspectives on second language acquisition*. Cambridge: Cambridge University Press.

Bley-Vroman, R. (2009). The evolving context of the fundamental difference hypothesis. *Studies in Second Language Acquisition, 31*, 175–198.

Brunswik, E. (1956). *Perception and the representative design of psychology experiments*. Berkeley, CA: University of California Press.

Burling, R. (1959). Language development of a Garo and English speaking child. *Word, 15*, 45–68.

Buzsaki, G. (2006). *Rhythms of the brain*. Oxford: Oxford University Press.

Bybee, J. and Hopper, P. (2001). *Frequency and the emergence of linguistic structure*. Amsterdam: John Benjamins.

Carlson, R., Sulllivan, M., and Schneider, W. (1989). Practice and working memory effects in building procedural skill. *Journal of Experimental Psychology: Learning, Memory and Cognition, 15*, 517–526.

Carroll, S. (2005). Input and SLA: Adults' sensitivity to different sorts of cues to French gender. *Language Learning, 55*, 79–138.

Clahsen, H. and Muysken, P. (1986). The availability of UG to adult and child learners: A study of the acquisition of German word order. *Second Language Research, 2*, 93–119.

DeKeyser, R. (2000). The robustness of critical period effects in second language acquisition studies. *Studies in Second Language Acquisition, 22*, 499–533.

DeKeyser, R. and Larson-Hall, J. (2005). What does the critical period really mean? In J. F. Kroll and A. M. B. de Groot (Eds.), *Handbook of bilingualism: Psycholinguistic approaches*. Oxford: Oxford University Press.

Dong, Y. -P., Gui, S. -C., and MacWhinney, B. (2005). Shared and separate meanings in the bilingual mental lexicon. *Bilingualism: Language and Cognition, 8*, 221–238.

Ebbinghaus, H. (1885). *Über das Gedächtnis*. Leipzig: Duncker.

Eckman, F. R. (1977). Markedness and the contrastive analysis hypothesis. *Language Learning, 27*, 315–330.

Ellis, N. (2002). Frequency effects in language processing. *Studies in Second Language Acquisition, 24*, 143–188.

Ellis, N. and Beaton, A. (1995). Psycholinguistic determinants of foreign language vocabulary learning. In B. Harley (Ed.), *Lexical issues in language learning* (pp. 107–165). Philadelphia: John Benjamins.

Engeström, Y. (1999). Activity theory and individual social transformation. In Y. Engeström, R. Miettinen, and R. L. Punamiki (Eds.), *Perspectives on activity theory* (pp. 1–15). New York: Cambridge University Press.

Friederici, A. (2009). *Brain circuits of syntax: From neurotheoretical considerations to empirical tests. Biological foundations and origin of syntax*. Cambridge, MA: MIT Press.

Friederici, A., Steinhauer, K., and Pfeifer, E. (2002). Brain signatures of artificial language processing: Evidence challenging the critical period hypothesis. *Proceedings of the National Academy of Sciences, 99*, 529–534.

Gobet, F. (2005). Chunking models of expertise: Implications for education. *Applied Cognitive Psychology, 19*, 183–204.

Grosjean, F. (1997). Processing mixed languages: Issues, findings and models. In A. M. B. de Groot and J. F. Kroll (Eds.), *Tutorials in bilingualism: Psycholinguistic perspectives* (pp. 225–254). Mahwah, NJ: Lawrence Erlbaum.

Guenther, F. and Gjaja, M. (1996). The perceptual magnet effect as an emergent property of neural map formation. *Journal of the Acoustical Society of America, 100*, 1111–1121.

Gupta, P. and MacWhinney, B. (1997). Vocabulary acquisition and verbal short-term memory: Computational and neural bases. *Brain and Language, 59*, 267–333.

Hahne, A. and Friederici, A. (2001). Processing a second language: Late learners' comprehension mechanisms as revealed by event-related brain potentials. *Bilingualism: Language and Cognition, 4*, 123–141.

Hernandez, A., Li, P., and MacWhinney, B. (2005). The emergence of competing modules in bilingualism. *Trends in Cognitive Sciences, 9*, 220–225.

Jackendoff, R. (1983). *Semantics and cognition*. Cambridge, MA: MIT Press.

Kelley, H. H. (1967). Attribution theory in social psychology. *Nebraska Symposium on Motivation, 15,* 192–238.

Kempe, V. and MacWhinney, B. (1999). Processing of morphological and semantic cues in Russian and German. *Language and Cognitive Processes, 14,* 129–171.

Kohonen, T. (2001). *Self-organizing maps* (Third Edition). Berlin: Springer.

Krashen, S. (1994). The input hypothesis and its rivals. In N. C. Ellis (Ed.), *Implicit and explicit learning of languages* (pp. 45–78). San Diego: Academic.

Kroll, J. and Sholl, A. (1992). Lexical and conceptual memory in fluent and nonfluent bilinguals. In R. Harris (Ed.), *Cognitive processing in bilinguals* (pp. 191–206). Amsterdam: North-Holland.

Kroll, J. and Tokowicz, N. (2005). Bilingual lexical processing. In J. F. Kroll and A. M. B. DeGroot (Eds.), *Handbook of bilingualism: Psycholinguistic approaches.* New York: Oxford University Press.

Kuhl, P., Conboy, B., Padden, D., Nelson, T., and Pruitt, J. (2005). Early speech perception and later language development: Implications for the "Critical Period". *Language Learning and Development, 1,* 237–264.

Li, P., Zhao, X., and MacWhinney, B. (2007). Dynamic self-organization and early lexical development in children. *Cognitive Science, 31,* 581–612.

MacDonald, M. C., Pearlmutter, N. J., and Seidenberg, M. S. (1994). Lexical nature of syntactic ambiguity resolution. *Psychological Review, 101*(4), 676–703.

MacWhinney, B. (1982). Basic syntactic processes. In S. Kuczaj (Ed.), *Language acquisition: Vol. 1. Syntax and semantics* (pp. 73–136). Hillsdale, NJ: Lawrence Erlbaum.

MacWhinney, B. (1987). The competition model. In B. MacWhinney (Ed.), *Mechanisms of language acquisition* (pp. 249–308). Hillsdale, NJ: Lawrence Erlbaum.

MacWhinney, B. (1997). Implicit and explicit processes. *Studies in Second Language Acquisition, 19,* 277–281.

MacWhinney, B. (2004). A multiple process solution to the logical problem of language acquisition. *Journal of Child Language, 31,* 883–914.

MacWhinney, B. (2005a). The emergence of linguistic form in time. *Connection Science, 17,* 191–211.

MacWhinney, B. (2005b). Item-based constructions and the logical problem. *ACL,* 46–54.

MacWhinney, B. (2008a). How mental models encode embodied linguistic perspectives. In R. Klatzky, B. MacWhinney, and M. Behrmann (Eds.), *Embodiment, Ego-Space, and Action* (pp. 369–410). Mahwah: Lawrence Erlbaum.

MacWhinney, B. (2008b). A unified model. In P. Robinson and N. Ellis (Eds.), *Handbook of Cognitive Linguistics and Second Language Acquisition.* Mahwah, NJ: Lawrence Erlbaum Associates.

MacWhinney, B., Feldman, H. M., Sacco, K., and Valdes-Perez, R. (2000). Online measures of basic language skills in children with early focal brain lesions. *Brain and Language, 71,* 400–431.

Major, R. (1987). The natural phonology of second language acquisition. In A. James and J. Leather (Eds.), *Sound Patterns in Second Language Acquisition* (pp. 207–224). Dordrect: Foris.

Major, R. and Faudree, M. (1996). Markedness universals and the acquisition of voicing contrasts by Korean speakers of English. *Studies in Second Language Acquisition, 18,* 69–90.

Massaro, D. (1987). *Speech perception by ear and eye.* Hillsdale, NJ: Lawrence Erlbaum.

Matessa, M. and Anderson, J. (2000). Modeling focused learning in role assignment. *Language and Cognitive Processes, 15,* 263–292.

McDonald, J. L. (1986). The development of sentence comprehension strategies in English and Dutch. *Journal of Experimental Child Psychology, 41,* 317–335.

McDonald, J. L. and Heilenman, K. (1991). Determinants of cue strength in adult first and second language speakers of French. *Applied Psycholinguistics, 12,* 313–348.

McDonald, J. L. and MacWhinney, B. J. (1995). The time course of anaphor resolution: Effects of implicit verb causality and gender. *Journal of Memory and Language, 34,* 543–566.

McLaughlin, B. (1985). *Second-language acquisition in childhood.* Hillsdale, NJ: Lawrence Erlbaum Associates.

Müller, J., Hahne, A., Fujii, Y., and Friederici, A. (2005). Native and nonnative speakers' processing of a miniature version of Japanese as revealed by ERPs. *Journal of Cognitive Neuroscience, 17,* 1229–1244.

Nelson, K. (1998). *Language in cognitive development: The emergence of the mediated mind.* New York: Cambridge University Press.

Paradis, M. (2004). *A neurolinguistic theory of bilingualism.* Philadelphia: John Benjamins.

Pavlenko, A. and Lantolf, J. (2000). Second language learning as participation and the (re)construction of selves. In A. Pavlenko and J. Lantolf (Eds.), *Sociocultural theory and second language learning* (pp. 155–178). Oxford: Oxford University Press.

Pavlik, P. and Anderson, J. (2005). Practice and forgetting effects on vocabulary memory: An activation-based model of the spacing effect. *Cognitive Science, 29,* 559–586.

Pavlik, P., Presson, N., Dozzi, G., Wu, S., MacWhinney, B., and Koedinger, K. (2007). The FaCT (Fact and Concept Training) System: A new tool linking Cognitive Science with educators. *Proceedings of the 29th Annual Conference of the Cognitive Science Society* (pp. 1379–1384). Nashville, TN: Cognitive Science Society.

Pienemann, M., Di Biase, B., Kawaguchi, S., and Håkansson, G. (2005). Processing constraints on L1 transfer. In J. F. Kroll and A. M. B. DeGroot (Eds.), *Handbook of bilingualism: Psycholinguistic approaches* (pp. 128–153). New York: Oxford University Press.

Pimsleur, P. (1967). A memory schedule. *The Modern Language Journal, 51*, 73–75.

Presson, N. and MacWhinney, B. (under review). Learning grammatical gender: The effects of rules and prototypes. *Applied Psycholinguistics*.

Prior, A., MacWhinney, B., and Kroll, J. (2007). Translation norms for English and Spanish: The role of lexical variables, word class, and L2 proficiency in negotiating translation ambiguity. *Behavior Research Methods, 37*, 134–140.

Pulvermüller, F. (2003). *The neuroscience of language*. Cambridge: Cambridge University Press.

Ratner, C. (2002). *Cultural psychology: Theory and method*. New York: Kluwer/Plenum.

Rosenbloom, P. S. and Newell, A. (1987). Learning by chunking: A production system model of practice. In D. Klahr, P. Langley, and R. Neches (Eds.), *Production system models of learning and development* (pp. 221–286). Cambridge, MA: MIT Press.

Searchinger, G. (1995). *The Human Language Series*. New York: Equinox Films.

Seidenberg, M. and McClelland, J. (1989). A distributed, developmental model of word recognition and naming. *Psychological Review, 96*, 523–568.

Snow, C. E. (1999). Social perspectives on the emergence of language. In B. MacWhinney (Ed.), *The emergence of language* (pp. 257–276). Mahwah, NJ: Lawrence Erlbaum Associates.

Stroop, J. R. (1935). Studies of interference in serial verbal reactions. *Journal of Experimental Psychology, 18*, 643–662.

Taraban, R. and Palacios, J. M. (1993). Exemplar models and weighted cue models in category learning. In G. Nakamura, R. Taraban, and D. Medin (Eds.), *Categorization by humans and machines*. San Diego: Acdemic Press.

Tokowicz, N. and MacWhinney, B. (2005). Implicit and explicit measures of sensitivity to violations in second language grammar: An event-related potential investigation. *Studies in Second Language Acquisition, 27*, 173–204.

Tomasello, M. (2003). *Constructing a first language: A usage-based theory of language acquisition*. Cambridge: Harvard University Press.

Ullman, M. (2004). Contributions of memory circuits to language: The declarative/procedural model. *Cognition, 92*, 231–270.

van Geert, P. (1991). A dynamic systems model of cognitive and language growth. *Psychological Review, 98*, 3–53.

Vygotsky, L. (1934). *Thought and language*. Cambridge: MIT Press.

Wittenberg, G., Sullivan, M., and Tsien, J. (2002). Synaptic reentry reinforcement based network model for long-term memory consolidation. *Hippocampus, 12*, 637–647.

Yoshimura, Y. and MacWhinney, B. (2007). The effect of oral repetition in L2 speech fluency: System for an experimental tool and a language tutor. *SLATE Conference*, 25–28.

Zhang, Y. (2009). A tutor for learning Chinese sounds through pinyin. *Applied Psycholinguistics*.

14

Processability theory

Manfred Pienemann and Jörg-U. Keßler

Historical discussion

The basic ideas underlying Processability Theory (PT) developed as a result of the shortcomings of older approaches which predate PT. The goal of PT as well as its predecessor approaches is to explain second language (L2) acquisition based on the following logic: at any stage of development the learner can process only those L2 linguistic forms which the current state of the language processor can handle.

The conceptual development from the Multidimensional Model (MM) (Meisel *et al.*, 1981) to Processability Theory (Pienemann, 1998a, 2005) has a 20-year history. There is a substantial difference between PT and ideas that precede it. Pienemann (1998a) took stock of the ideas predating PT, including the MM (Meisel *et al.*, 1981), Clahsen's (1984) Strategies Approach, the Teachability Hypothesis (Pienemann, 1984, 1989) and the Predictive Framework (Pienemann and Johnston, 1987). PT was designed to overcome the limitations of these earlier approaches. Table 14.1 presents information about PT as well as earlier versions that led up to PT.

As illustrated in Table 14.1, the MM focused on the issue of determining developmental sequences in second language acquistion (SLA) corpora. One has to bear in mind that this line of research addressed some of the key issues discussed in the late 1970s and early 1980s which focused on the relationship between data and their proper description. The issue was whether every change found in an interlanguage (IL) constitutes evidence of IL development and if the changes that can be found need to be measured in native language terms. As the name suggests, the MM assumes that IL development is not linear and that instead ILs contain at least two dimensions. This assumption has repercussions for determining stages of development, and IL differences can be understood to represent either development or inter- or intra-learner variation. The MM utilizes implicational scaling and probabilistic rules to operationalize the emergence criterion for acquisition. The MM has been criticized for a lack of falsifiability. Larsen-Freeman and Long (1991) note that there is no independent motivation for variational IL features and that as a result there is a problem in not being able to falsify a developmental sequence because any deviation from a predicted sequence can be considered a variational feature. This shortcoming was rectified in PT (Pienemann, 1998a) which formally constrains development as well as variation in a predictable and testable manner as further discussed below.

The Strategies Approach was developed by Clahsen (1984) to explain the development of German L2 word order. It is based on a set of processing constraints which are assumed to be shed as IL development progresses. In this way, the strategies approach complements the MM by providing an explanation of the developmental dimension. Nevertheless, the MM and the

Table 14.1 PT and its predecessors and relatives

Model	Key references	Key concepts	Scope

Multidimensional Model	• Meisel et al., 1981; Pienemann et al., 1993,	• implicational scaling,
		 • probabilistic rules,
		 • emergence criterion,
		 • two dimensions in L2 dynamics:
		   (1) development
		   (2) variation
			descriptive framework for dynamic processes in L2 development

Strategies Approach	Clahsen, 1984	development of L2 German word order determined by shedding of processing constraints	explanation of German L2 word order development
Predictive framework	Pienemann and Johnston, 1987	development of ESL morpho-syntax determined by incremental development of processing resources	Explains developmental patterns in ESL and GSL morpho-syntax
PT	Pienemann, 1998a, b, 2003, 2005; Pienemann et al., 2005	• processability hierarchy modeled in linguistic theory (LFG), • hypothesis space constrains development and variation (testable), • factorization and other refined descriptive methods, • partial transfer hypothesis (DMT), • task variation: steadiness hypothesis, • stabilization, • L1-L2 differences, • basis for L2 profiling	*explains* L2 development and variation in syntax and morphology cross-linguistically

Strategies Approach constitute two separate conceptual entities. Meisel (1983) produced his own version of the Strategies Approach that is more closely related to Slobin's (1973) and Andersen's (1984) acquisition strategies. Clahsen's strategies approach was subject to strong criticism (e.g., White, 1991). While some of these criticisms were refuted, the main limitations remained, including the problem with the model being restricted to constraints on L2 German word order and its undefined relationship to grammatical representation. These limitations were overcome in PT by utilizing a psychologically and typologically plausible theory of grammar (Lexical-functional Grammar [LFG], cf., Bresnan, 2001) that has been applied to a large variety of languages.

The Teachability Hypothesis (Pienemann, 1984, 1989) was based on the MM and the Strategies Approach. It predicts that stages of SLA cannot be skipped through teaching intervention because of the implicational nature of the processing strategies. It also predicts that variational features are not subject to the same constraints on teachability. In other words, the Teachability Hypothesis defines constraints on teachability; however, it does not predict sufficient conditions for teaching to be successful. The Teachability Hypothesis was later incorporated into PT (Pienemann, 1998a).

All of the critical points listed so far gave rise to the development of Processability Theory, especially with regard to the lack of falsifiability in the MM and the inability of the Strategies Approach to link up to grammatical knowledge and its lack of typological plausibility.

PT was designed to address the two key issues of a theory of language acquisition, (i) the developmental problem ("why do learners follow universal stages of acquisition?" cf., Clahsen, 1992) and (ii) the logical problem (i.e., "how do learners develop linguistic knowledge—given that it cannot be inferred from the input without innate knowledge?" cf., Wexler and Culicover, 1980; Wexler, 1982; cf., VanPatten, Chapter 16, this volume). The 1998 volume on PT focused on the first issue. The 2005 volume also addressed the logical problem. This modular approach to explaining SLA was possible because of the incorporation of a grammatical theory (i.e., LFG, cf., Bresnan, 2001). This approach also permitted a clear and falsifiable differentiation between the two dimensions of SLA postulated by the MM. Both dimensions are constrained by the hypothesis space defined by PT.

Core issues

The basic idea

The basic idea underlying PT (Pienemann, 1998a, b, 2005) is the following: at any stage of development the learner can process only those L2 linguistic forms which the current state of the language processor can handle. Therefore understanding the architecture of the language processor and the way in which it handles a second language enables one to predict the course of development of L2 linguistic forms.

The architecture of the language processor accounts for language processing in real time and within human psychological constraints. Incorporating the language processor in the study of SLA therefore brings to bear human psychological constraints that go beyond the logico-mathematical considerations of learnability theory.

The core of PT is formed by a universal processability hierarchy that is based on Levelt's (1989) approach to language production and that is modeled using LFG (Bresnan, 2001). This universal basis permits PT to predict developmental trajectories for any second language. The notion "developmental trajectory" implies a developmental dimension known as "staged development" as well as a variational dimension accounting for individual differences between developmental trajectories as illustrated in Figure 14.1.

Figure 14.1 shows two different developmental trajectories, T1 and T2, which are based on the same set of developmental stages (indicated by the dotted horizontal lines). The two developmental trajectories differ with respect to the IL varieties that are developed at each stage (indicated by vertical lines).

In this paradigm, each stage corresponds to a set of grammatical rules that share certain processing routines, and each IL variety represents a specific variant of the grammatical rules.

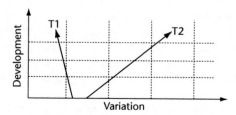

Figure 14.1   Different developmental trajectories

For instance, in English Second Language (ESL) question formation the following developmental sequence has been found (e.g., Pienemann, 1998a):

Structure	Example
▲ 5. Aux–second	What has she seen?
4. Copula	What is this?
3. WH+SVO	What this is?
2. SVO question	She see this?
1. Single words	This?

Learners attempting to produce "Aux-second" before level 5 (i.e., before they are ready for this structure) have been found to produce the following interlanguage variants:

A   What she seen?
B   What has seen?
C   What she has seen?
D   She seen this?

Variants A to D have in common that they get around placing the auxiliary before the subject. In other words, they constitute different solutions to the same learning problem. In Figure 14.1 each of the different solutions is represented by a vertical line. In the course of L2 development, learners accumulate grammatical rules and their variants, allowing them develop an individual developmental trajectory while adhering to the overall developmental schedule. In this way, PT defines a two-dimensional space (i.e. "Hypothesis Space"). Both dimensions of Hypothesis Space are constrained by the processability hierarchy.

Key claims and constructs

PT entails the following key claims:

(a) L2 development follows universal stages that are constrained by the processability hierarchy.
(b) IL variation is limited and regular, and this limitation and regularity is caused by the constraints inherent in the processability hierarchy.
(c) L1 transfer is constrained by processability. This implies that L1 forms can be transferred to the L2 only when they can be processed in the developing L2 system. In other words, this entails an operationalized "partial transfer" position (cf., Pienemann et al., 2005).
(d) Task variation is constrained by the processability hierarchy. This claim results in the "Steadiness Hypothesis" which predicts that a specific IL will be placed at one and the same stage of development in different tasks as long as they refer to the same skill type.
(e) Both, L1 and L2 acquisition is constrained by the processability hierarchy. Nevertheless, both types of acquisition may be associated with fundamentally different developmental trajectories.
(f) Bilingual language development can be compared across different languages on a universal scale using the processability hierarchy inherent in PT (Pienemann et al., 2011).

These claims are based on two key constructs: (a) The processability hierarchy and (b) Hypothesis Space. The *processability hierarchy* is based on a universal set of processing resources that is modeled using LFG (Bresnan, 2001). In Pienemann (1998a) the hierarchy was based solely on information exchange

	locus of exchange	example	illustration
sentence	within sentence	he talk-s	S / NPs — VP / Pro [3rd pers sg] — V [pres, non-cont, 3rd pers sg]
phrase	within phrase only	two kids	NP / Det [pl] — N [pl]
category	no exchange	talk-ed	V [past]

Figure 14.2 A simplified account of the processability hierarchy

the notion of transfer of grammatical information within constituent structure. The second theory module of PT (Pienemann *et al.*, 2005) the processability hierarchy covers the relationship between conceptual structure and surface grammatical structure which is also modeled using LFG.

A simplified account of the processability hierarchy (with a focus on constituent structure) is given in Figure 14.2 where three example constituent-structures are listed in the left-hand column. The second column specifies the type of information exchange possible at each stage. English morphological structures are given in the next column to exemplify the types of structures possible at each stage, and the information transfer involved in the generation of these structures is illustrated in the column on the right-hand side. For instance, for the noun phrase "two kids" (e.g., in the sentence "he has two kids") the information "plural" has to be exchanged between the determiner and the noun; this information does not need to be exchanged with any other constituent in the sentence.

The notion "Hypothesis Space" was mentioned above in the context of developmental trajectories (cf., Figure 14.1). The structures that are processable at any given stage are constrained by the available processing resources. As can be seen in Figure 14.2, at the stage "phrase" grammatical information can be exchanged only within phrases, not beyond the phrasal boundary. Subject–verb agreement cannot be processed at the stage "phrase" because this structure requires grammatical information to be exchanged beyond the phrasal boundary. In other words, processing resources define and constrain the range of possible production grammars for every level.

At the same time, these constraints leave sufficient leeway for learners to find different solutions to structural learning problems. We illustrated this above with the example of the position of auxiliaries in English WH-questions. This position requires processing procedures at the sentence level in the hierarchy. L2 learners can nevertheless produce WH-questions before these procedures are processable. When they attempt to do this, learners have four structural options (variants A–D above) that avoid the placement of the auxiliary before the subject (i.e., in second position). The options available are all processable using the resources available at the previous stage, and the number of options is limited because of the limited resources that are available. The fact that learners need to circumnavigate a structural problem (here Aux 2nd) is caused by the constraints inherent in the hierarchy. In this way, possible and predictable developmental trajectories are constrained by the processability hierarchy.

PT principles and hypotheses

PT is based on four psycholinguistic principles and hypotheses which will be summarized below: (i) transfer of grammatical information, (ii) a lexically driven grammar, (iii) lexical mapping, and (iv) the TOPIC Hypothesis.

As mentioned above, the 1998 PT module focused on constituent structure and the exchange of grammatical information within it, using feature unification. The modeling of feature unification, as envisaged in this approach, is illustrated in Figure 14.2. In the sentence "He talks" the insertion of the verbal affix "–s" relies on information contained in the subject-noun phrase, namely the features PERS(ON) and NUM(BER) and their values PERS=3 and NUM=SG. These features are unified in S as shown in Figure 14.2. In other words, the need to store grammatical information on PERS and NUM during sentence generation illustrates the non-linearity of this morphological process.

In the design of PT, the point of unification is related to a hierarchy of processability that reflects the time course of real time processing as detailed in Levelt (1989). In this way a range of morphological and syntactic processes can be aligned with a universal hierarchy of processability yielding developmental trajectories for the given target languages as shown in several chapters of Pienemann (2005). The hierarchy that results from a comparison of the points of feature unification can be illustrated on the basis of Figure 14.2 which shows that the example structures described in Figure 14.2 can be ordered as follows:

(1) No exchange of grammatical information (= no unification of features),
(2) Exchange of grammatical information within the phrase,
(3) Exchange of grammatical information within the sentence.

Once one applies this hierarchy to ESL morphology, the following developmental trajectory can be predicted:

(1) past –ed
(2) plural –s (det + N)
(3) third-person –s.

In order to appreciate the universal nature of PT, it is crucial to consider that the hierarchy illustrated in Figure 14.2 is not language-specific and that, in principle, it applies to the transfer of grammatical information in any language. The application of the full processability hierarchy to the syntax and morphology of specific languages will, of course, involve more detail of the LFG formalism. It should be noted here that PT does not predict morphology and syntax to develop in tandem. Instead, in L2 acquisition "developmental trailers" (Pienemann, 1998a) may develop which can be brought in line through formal intervention.

A *lexically driven grammar* (second principle) stores grammatical information in the lexicon. For instance, the lexical entry for "walked" is marked for past tense and it lists the core argument of the verb as "agent." This lexical information is required in the assembly of the sentence. The lexically driven nature of sentence generation is an integral part of Levelt's approach. LFG also encodes syntactic properties primarily in the lexicon (cf., Schwarze, 2002, pp. 148–149). This makes LFG particularly suitable for the study of dynamic linguistic systems such as developing learner grammars, because LFG affords a formal account of the linguistic dynamics present in developing learner grammars.

The lexically driven nature of sentence generation is supported by a wide range of psycho-linguistic empirical evidence including research on slips of the tongue and on-line experiments (cf., Levelt, 1989) and was demonstrated in experimental work on sentence production by Pickering *et al.* (2002, p. 127) which shows that "constituent structure is formulated in one stage" and thus supports the architecture of LFG. Pienemann (1998a, b) showed that every level of the PT hierarchy processing procedures can be captured through feature unification in LFG which in turn shares key characteristics with Kempen and Hoenkamp's (1987) procedural account of language generation.

The third PT principle, *lexical mapping*, is based on Lexical Mapping Theory (LMT) which is a component of LFG (cf., Bresnan, 2001). LFG has three independent and parallel levels of representation as shown in Figure 14.3: a(rgument) structure, f(unctional) structure and c(onsti-tuent) structure. A-structure is universal. The component parts of f-structure and c-structure are also universal, whereas the specific form of the latter two are language-specific.

Lexical mapping refers to the mapping of argument structure onto functional structure. In PT the default mapping principle is "unmarked alignment" which is based on the one-to-one mapping of semantic roles onto grammatical functions. Naturally, mature languages allow for a much wider range of relationships between argument structure and functional structure (including passives, topicalization etc), and these develop step-wise in SLA. Principles of lexical mapping can account for these developmental processes.

In other words, Unmarked Alignment is the initial state of L2 development. It is based on the one-to-one mapping of the three parallel levels of representation onto each other. Unmarked alignment results in canonical word order. For English this is SVO. Unmarked alignment simplifies language processing for the learner who, at this stage, will analyze the first noun phrase as the agent. This way, canonical word order avoids any kind of exchange of grammatical information during language processing.

It follows from the Unmarked Alignment hypothesis that L2 learners will not have access to L2-specific a-structures for predicates. This implies that in cases where L1 and L2 predicates have different a-structures, one can predict that L2 learners will initially have to map arguments canonically onto the LMT hierarchy of core grammatical functions.

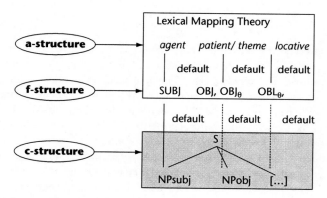

Figure 14.3 Unmarked alignment in LFG
Source: Pienemann *et al.*, 2005, p. 230.

The passive is a good example of this mapping process. In the passive the relationship between argument roles and syntactic functions may be altered as can be seen in the supression of argument roles and altered function-assignment. These alterations for passives are illustrated in examples (1)–(4).

(1) Peter sees a dog.

(2) see <experiencer, theme>
        | , |
    , , , SUBJ   OBJ

(3) A dog is seen by Peter.

(4) seen <experiencer, theme>
     | , , |,
    Ø   SUBJ , , (ADJ)

Sentences (1) and (3) describe the same event involving two participants. The difference between the two is that in (3) the constituent *a dog* that is OBJ in (1) is promoted to SUBJ, and the constituent *Peter* that is SUBJ in (1) is defocused and realized as ADJ. These alterations of the relationship between argument roles and syntactic functions constitute a deviation from Unmarked Alignment.

Similar predictions can also be derived from the relationship between f-structure and c-structure. One set of such predictions is "packaged" in the TOPIC Hypothesis. To account for developmental dynamics in the relationship between f-structure and c-structure Pienemann *et al.* (2005) propose the TOPIC hypothesis as in (6).

(6) The TOPIC hypothesis
In second language acquisition learners will initially not differentiate between SUBJ and other discourse functions (e.g., TOP). The addition of an XP to a canonical string will trigger a differentiation of TOP and SUBJ which first extends to non-arguments and successively to core arguments thus causing further structural consequences.

The mapping principles involved in the TOPIC Hypothesis and their structural outcomes are summarized in Table 14.2.

Table 14.2 The topic hypothesis

Discourse principle	c- to f- mapping	Structural outcomes
Topicalization of core arguments	TOP = OBJ	The TOP function is assigned to a *core* argument other than SUBJ.
↑	↑	↑
XP adjunction	TOP = ADJ	Initial constituent is a circumstantial adjunct or a FOCUS WH-word. TOPIC is differentiated from SUBJECT
↑	↑	↑
Canonical Order	SUBJ = default TOP	TOPIC and SUBJECT are not differentiated.

Data and common elicitation measures

Given that PT focuses on natural language production, the main type of data used in PT based research is conversational data – which are subject to the very time constraints in language production that are a crucial element in PT. In addition, reaction-time data have been used since they can potentially tap directly into the language production process.

Initially, conversational data were collected in "linguistic interviews" that followed thematic guidelines. These were conducted as participant observations where the interviewer actively participates in the discourse. It was found that this approach to data elicitation and data collection has a number of drawbacks. The formal drawback of interviews is the poverty of the data they elicit. Even very long interviews have been shown to elicit very small quantities of data that are relevant for a given research question.

Pienemann and Mackey (1993) and Mackey (1992) developed tasks that were designed on the basis of principles derived from task-based language teaching (Long, 1985) for the purpose of eliciting specific L2 grammatical contexts. Figure 14.4 shows the effect of elicitation tasks on the frequency of three grammatical forms in an ESL study with six informants. Even though the interview lasted longer than the two elicitation tasks, the tasks elicited more relevant structures, and they elicited those structures that were targeted (i.e., 3rd-person-s in "Habitual Actions" and questions in "Picture Differences.") In an extensive study Mackey (1992) demonstrated that these trends can be generalized and that tasks serve to speed up the data elicitation process.

As can be seen in Figure 14.4, elicitation tasks serve the purpose of eliciting relevant data (see also Mackey, 1992). For instance, the study of third-person-s marking requires a large set of contexts for third-person-s. This will allow the researcher to decide if the verbal marker is supplied or not. If no context appears, no conclusion can be drawn. However, even the presence of a number of morphological markers is no guarantee that these are based on productive IL rules. In order to exclude the use of formulae and chunks the researcher needs to check lexical and morphological variation (i.e., the same morpheme on different words and the same word with different morphemes). These descriptive methods are described in more detail in Pienemann (1998a).

The interpretation of corpus data depends on the acquisition criterion that is used. Pienemann (1998a) makes a case for the use of the emergence criterion. The basic point is this: Accuracy criteria (e.g., 80 percent suppliance) are arbitrary. This is illustrated in Figure 14.5 which shows

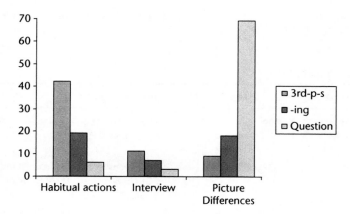

Figure 14.4 Frequency of obligatory contexts in tasks and interviews
Source: Pienemann and Mackey, 1993.

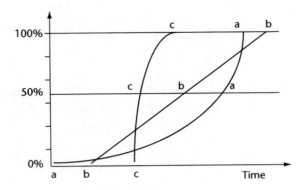

Figure 14.5 Accuracy and developmental trajectories

three different routes for the development of the rate of suppliance of grammatical structures. Obviously, the three routes have different gradients. Therefore the order of acquisition of the three structures is c > b > a using a 50 percent criterion and c > a > b using a 100 percent criterion. In other words, accuracy rates do not permit firm conclusions about the state of the IL. In contrast, the point of emergence (of a linguistic form) is not arbitrary. It also permits one to trace development over time, and it operationalizes the first point in time when a structure can be processed. The emergence criterion is operationalized differently for syntax and morphology, taking into account the status of formulae (cf., Pienemann, 1998a). Any test of the PT hierarchy would need to be based on the same definition of the acquisition criterion and on sufficiently large sets of relevant spontaneous production data. Naturally, spontaneous production data cannot be directly compared with other types of data, such as grammatical judgment data because both sets of data tap into different skills and /or types of knowledge.

We now turn to empirical verification. Since the publication of the first systematic presentation of PT (Pienemann, 1998a) the theory has been tested in many different contexts and has been applied to a range of typologically different L2s. For the purpose of this handbook chapter we will summarize one recent study in some detail and give an overview of some of key research projects that have been carried out within the PT framework.

Our exemplary study focuses on transfer. As mentioned above, PT implies that L1 forms can be transferred to the L2 only when they can be processed in the developing L2 system. Pienemann *et al.* (2011) tested this hypothesis in a cross-sectional study of Swedish SLA based on seven German *ab-initio* students who performed unseen communicative tasks eliciting V2 structures after only 30 minutes of exposure to Swedish (on a one-to-one basis). This intensive format of input was used with "square one beginners" to be sure to be tapping into the initial state. The study focuses on V2 because the L1 and the L2 are both V2 languages, and V2 appears at stage 5 in the PT hierarchy. Therefore, a full transfer hypothesis would predict that these learners will transfer V2 from their L1 (German) to L2 Swedish, whereas PT predicts that they won't because they are not ready to process V2 in the L2 system.

Figure 14.6 gives an overview of the results. All learners produced SVO sentences, and five of seven learners also produced the context for V2 in L2 Swedish (here: preposed adverbials). In other words, the intensive input session generated successful L2 learning at the initial state, and most learners "attempted" the V2 structure. However, none of the learners produced even a single instance of V2 in the L2.

	SVO	advSVO	V2
Swedish	+	–	+
German	+	–	+
English	+	+	–

Informant	SVO	*adv SVO	V2	L2 = V2?	Imitation of V2
C03	+	14	0.00	–	16
C05	+	25	0.00	–	14
C07	+	–	–	–	10
C04	+	–	–	–	20
C01	+	30	0.00	+	30
C02	+	15	0.00	+	15
C06	+	13	0.00	+	9

Figure 14.6 The effect of 30 minutes' exposure to L2 Swedish with L1 German

The non-application of V2 cannot be explained by transfer from English as the strongest L2 because three of the informants have a V2 language as their strongest L2. The study also focused on the position of the negator. The learners used proverbial negation but they could not transfer do-insertion from English.

We turn to a discussion of some of the key projects that utilize and support PT. Pienemann and Håkansson (1999) applied the PT hierarchy to Swedish L2 morpho-syntax. Their research is based on an extensive overview of the majority of studies carried out on Swedish SLA over a period of more than two decades. Testing this set of predictions in the large number of studies reviewed by Pienemann and Håkansson produced very solid empirical support for the overall approach. Glahn *et al.* (2001) tested PT with specific reference to affixation in attributive and predicative adjectives in Scandinavian languages (cf., also Hammarberg, 1996). When intervening variables, such as gender assignment, are "factored out" (cf., Pienemann, 1998a, pp. 159ff.) the data strongly support the predictions made by the theory.

The application of PT to Japanese SLA constitutes a crucial test case for the theory because all other languages PT had initially been applied to (i.e., German, English, and Swedish) are closely related to each other and share a number of typological features. For instance, they are all configurational languages with verb-second constraints. In contrast, Japanese is a non-configurational, agglutinative language. The crux of the typological plausibility test for PT is to demonstrate that the universal architecture of grammatical information flow entailed in PT can make testable and correct predictions for the course of Japanese L2 development. Kawaguchi (2005) demonstrated that the developmental predictions she made for Japanese as L2 on the basis of PT are bourne out by longitudinal and cross-sectional learner data.

Itani-Adams (2003) studied the bilingual first language acquisition of a Japanese-Australian child. Her work utilizes the developmental trajectory of English as a second language established by Pienemann (1998a) and the developmental trajectory of Japanese as a second language established by Di Biase and Kawaguchi (2002) and Kawaguchi (2005). Itani-Adams found that both languages develop following the hierarchy predicted by PT (lexical > phrasal > inter-phrasal). She used PT as a matrix for a comparison of language development across the two first languages of the informant. She found the three different types of morphology (i.e., lexical, phrasal, and interphrasal morphology) did not develop in synchrony in two languages. Iwasaki (2003) studied the acquisition of Japanese morphosyntax by a child a seven-year-old Australian boy in a naturalistic environment and found the same developmental trajectory as Di Biase and Kawaguchi (2002).

Zhang (2001 and 2005) applied PT to modern standard Chinese, another language that is typologically distant from Germanic languages. Modern standard Chinese is an isolating and topic-prominent language. Zhang identified five grammatical morphemes and related them to three different PT levels. Zhang carried out a one-year longitudinal study with five learners using communicative tasks. Her data show that the above-mentioned morphemes are acquired in the sequence predicted by PT. Gao's (2004) study supports these findings.

Di Biase (cf., Di Biase and Kawaguchi, 2002) applied the PT hierarchy to Italian as L2. One important corollary of his research is the conclusion that the mechanics of subject–verb agreement may vary between typologically different languages. This analysis is not only congruent with the data presented by Di Biase and with his implementation of PT into Italian, but also with cross-linguistic on-line studies of agreement in English and Romance languages by Vigliocco *et al.* (1996) and Vigliocco *et al.* (1995).

Empirical research carried out in the PT framework yielded precise descriptions of ESL and other developmental trajectories and of learner variation. This research has been used as an objective psycholinguistic basis of measurement in educational evaluation studies. For instance, Keßler (2006) compared levels of attainment in primary and secondary ESL programs in German schools utilizing PT-based descriptions of ESL development. Liebner (2006) studied the acquisition of English as L2 by German and Swedish primary school students in immersive and non-immersive contexts and compared learner variation in the different contexts demonstrating that non-immersive and non-communicative contexts are more likely to be associated with simplified varieties of learner language. Berti and Di Biase's (2002) and Di Biase's (2002) studies show the effectiveness of L2 teaching based on a syllabus informed by the PT hierarchy in conjunction with form-focused teaching. PT has also been used as a basis for profiling natural and formal L2 learners of Italian as an L2 (Bettoni and Di Biase, 2005). This study confirms the results of Di Biase's (2002) Australian study of Italian L2 development in a formal context.

Håkansson *et al.* (2003) utlized the cross-linguistic capacity of PT to measure the two languages of bilingual informants on one and the same scale. Håkansson *et al.* studied the acquisition of Swedish-Arabic bilingual children with and without specific language impairment. Based on the above PT hierarchy for Swedish, Mansouri's (2000) Arabic PT levels and further development of this research by Håkansson and Mansouri, Håkansson *et al.* (2003) were able to measure language development of bilingual informants using compatible scales for both languages. Key issues arising from the comparison between impaired and non-impaired language development are taken up by Håkansson (2001).

PT-based research is presented at annual international workshops which have generated several volumes on a variety of theoretical and applied topics, including aphasia, bilingual language development, Task-based Language Teaching (TBLT), transfer and testing (Keßler, 2008b; Keßler and Keatinge, 2009; Mansouri, 2007; Bettoni and Di Biase, under review). Work presented at these workshops and other PT-based research appears in a book series published by Benjamins.

Applications

From the outset, PT has been developed with applications to diagnosing language development and language teaching in mind. In this section we will briefly discuss the following practical applications of PT:

- Diagnosing language development,
- Developmental approaches to the L2 classroom,
- Interfaces between TBLT and PT.

Diagnosing language development

The connection between PT and diagnosing language development is obvious. A theory that can account for developmental trajectories and that is based on an abundance of empirical research detailing standard developmental trajectories for a range of L2s (e.g., Johnston, 1997; Keßler, 2006, 2007; Mansouri and Duffy, 2005; Pienemann and Johnston, 1987; Pienemann, 1998a, 2005; Pienemann et al., 2006) is in an excellent position to serve as a point of reference for developmental linguistic profiles.

The Rapid Profile procedure has been developed and refined over a number of years (Keßler, 2006, 2007, 2008a; Keßler and Keatinge, 2008; Mackey et al., 1991; Pienemann, 1990, 1992; Pienemann, 2003; Pienemann et al., 1988; Pienemann et al., 1993; Pienemann and Keßler, 2007;). In this approach a trained analyst identifies a set of 25 developmental features in the speech of a learner. This ocurrs on-line, using profiling software. The speech sample is elicited using communicative tasks as elicitation devices. After about 10–15 minutes a reliable profile of the learner's L2 can be obtained. Other L2s work in a similar manner. At this stage, Rapid Profile has been implemented for the following L2s: English, German, and Turkish.

The software serves the following functions. It records the observations made by the analyst and applies the emergence criterion that has been implemented into an expert system. In addition, it specifies the accuracy of IL structures in the given samples. On this basis it provides on-line feedback to the analyst about the current profile. The software also contains a training environment that can certify an analyst, a database of profiles that can be used in a school context, and a database of tasks that can be used in connection with on-line feedback. The analysis provided by the system also allows the analyst to assess aspects of the lexicon and of variational features as well as grammatical accuracy.

The refinement of Rapid Profile has been driven in part by studies of its reliability. The most recent study is that by Keßler (2006, 2007) who compared the Rapid Profile analysis of 21 samples by newly trained analysts with the the full linguistic analysis of the same samples. Overall, he found an 86 percent agreement on the level of acquisition between the on-line observation and the full analysis. The remaining 14 percent were due to under-observations by one level.

Since Rapid Profile is criterion-referenced, it identifies both what the learner can do as well as what he or she cannot do at a given point in the ESL learning process. The profile produced by this procedure permits the teacher to pinpoint those developmental features that are learnable by a particular student at the given point in time and that can thus be focused on in teaching.

A brief word about linguistic profiling and proficiency rating: As Brindley (1998) pointed out, current rating scales are not based on SLA research and they do not reflect L2 development even if their authors claim the opposite. This does not mean, however, that Rapid Profile was designed to replace rating scales. Such an undertaking would be pointless for the near future, because linguistic profiling and rating scales have rather different objectives. Profiling, by its very nature, aims at maximum precision whereas rating scales aim at maximum scope (Pienemann and Keßler, 2007). At the current state of our knowledge we cannot have both in one procedure. Therefore both are needed until we have a more complete understanding of SLA. Until that time the interface between the two approaches needs to be explored for the benefit of the practitioner (cf., Ferrari and Nuzzo, 2009; Lenzing and Plesser, 2010).

Developmental approaches to the L2 classroom

The Teachabilty Hypothesis (Pienemann, 1984, 1989, 1998a) is the second major theory-practice interface that is part of PT. The Teachability Hypothesis predicts that stages of SLA cannot be

Table 14.3 Studies relating to the Teachability Hypothesis

Study	TL	Learners' L1	Design	Findings
Pienemann (1984)	German	Italian	Pre-test, Post-test control group design: whether stages can be skipped	Stages of acquisition cannot be skipped
Ellis (1989)	German	English	Pre-test, Post-test control group design: formal versus naturalistic instruction	Support for the Teachability Hypothesis
Boss (1996)	German	English/ Chinese	Oral language production compared to taught syllabus as opposed to PT sequence	Learners progressed in the predicted order regardless of the taught syllabus
Spada and Lightbown (1999)	ESL	French	Pre-test, Post-test control group design: whether stage skipping is possible	Inconclusive: no support for Teachability Hypothesis[1]
Dyson (1996)	ESL	Spanish	Longitudinal study of ESL development with a syllabus based on teachable forms	Overall support for the Teachability Hypothesis despite inter-learner variation
Mansouri and Duffy (2005)	ESL	Chinese/ Korean/ Thai	Pre-test, Post-test control group design: developmental versus reversed order group	Support for the Teachability Hypothesis

Note:
[1] This study was inconclusive because the informants had already acquired the test structure in the pre-test. Also, the studyt is based on the false assumption that the Teachability Hypothesis predicts that "timed intervention" will promote acquisition.

skipped through formal intervention and that variational features are not subject to these constraints. The constraints implied in the Teachability Hypothesis have been tested and substantiated in a number of empirical studies which are listed in Table 14.3 (cf., Mansouri and Duffy, 2005 and Keßler *et al.*, 2011 for overviews).

Whereas the Teachability Hypothesis delineates constraints on teachability, "timed intervention" (Long, 1988) goes one step further by assuming that formal intervention will promote acquisition if it occurs at a time when the learner is developmentally ready for the taught form. Di Biase (2002, 2008) demonstrated that learners who received developmentally timed form-focused instruction (Long, 1991) traversed the developmental hierarchy more quickly and more successfully than learners without timed (and form-focused) instuction.

From a PT perspective, timed intervention needs to be driven by the developmental readiness of the learners. This approach is facilitated by assigning a developmental profile to every student using Rapid Profile. In this way, formal intevention can focus on developmentally relevant forms for every individual. As Pienemann (1985) pointed out, this approach does not imply the inclusion of non-target IL forms in the syllabus.

Interfaces between task-based language teaching and PT

Lightbown (1998, p. 179) raised the concern that the heterogeneity of learners' profiles in class "... would make developmentally targeted teaching very difficult to organize." Keßler (2008a) shows that the heterogeneity of linguistic profiles does not preclude developmentally timed intervention if it occurs in task-based language teaching (Long, 1985). Several studies (e.g., Keßler, 2008a; Mackey, 1992) have shown that learners at different levels of acquisition use different linguistic forms in the same task—nevertheless successfully communicating with each other. Therefore one syllabus can be used in heterogeneous classes enabling the teacher to focus on different forms for learners with different profiles while the negotiation of meaning is coherent for the whole group. In this context, the more advanced learner can also provide scaffolds for his/her partner while working on the same task (Keßler, 2008a), thus priming (McDonough and Mackey, 2008) the less developed learner.

Keßler (2008a) proposes a "diagnostic task cycle" for the implementation of developmentally timed instruction in TBLT. The cycle starts with the task-based elicitation of interlanguage samples for linguistic profiling. This first step generates the diagnostic basis that informs the design of tasks in the cycle. Once the teacher has ascertained the learners' developmental profiles, the task-as-workplan (cf., Seedhouse, 2005) phase begins with pre-task activities to provide the necessary preconditions for the learning task and interactive language learning to be successful – such as knowledge of the lexical fields relevant for the learning task. Once this preparatory work has been completed, the class proceeds to the actual task work which is now developmentally appropriate and communicatively manageable.

When the task-as-workplan-phase is completed the focus of instruction shifts from timed intervention to more conventional communicative activities that focus on the negotiation of meaning in order to use the newly acquired linguistic and communicative competence in new and different contexts. Given the developmental timing of the instruction, this phase also provides an opportunity for the teacher to give corrective feedback on learnable forms.

The diagnostic task cycle is completed by a new round of profiling. The second profiling exercise serves as an evaluation of language development and, at the same time, as a diagnostic basis for the next cycle of task-based activities.

Future directions

One key area that requires attention in the further development of PT is the interface between the learner's developmental grammar and its effect on discourse and interaction (cf., Mackey, Abbuhl and Gass, Chapter 1, this volume). The basic assumption is that the constraints on L2 grammar entailed in PT also constrain L2 discourse and interaction. For instance, the Unmarked Alignment Hypothesis and the TOPIC Hypothesis imply that at the initial state of L2 acquisition learners have no choice other than to produce sentences using canonical word order (SVO for English). This means that at the initial state learners lack the grammatical means to express information that is structured in a non-linear way. For instance, at this stage learners do not have the freedom to structure information according to "given" and "new" information. Instead, the agent-subject always needs to appear as the first constituent.

A further focus of future research on PT is on automatization. For instance, Kawaguchi and Di Biase (in press) carried out a number of experiments to study how L2 performance in the formation of passives improves due to automatization. Pienemann (2006) studied the relationship between level of acquisition and word access utilizing Segalowitz' (2003) operationalization of automatization (cf., Segalowitz and Trofimovich, Chapter 11, this volume). The purpose of this research is to gain a better understanding of the learner's development from the point of emergence to the mastery of linguistic forms.

In the area of diagnosing L2 development, software has been developed and trialled that permits a fully automatic analysis of written interlanguage samples. The software is based on the systematicity of L2 development and regularities in time-constrained L2 writing. This approach may serve to make profiling more accessible to practitioners.

As we pointed out above, PT derives hypotheses about the L2 initial state (and thus about the "logical problem") from constraints on processing, lexical mapping and the architecture of LFG. One example is L2 initial word order. This line of thought has great potential for further investigation which can be based on a systematic integration of the processing and mapping phenomena covered by PT as well as on the integration of universal principles inherent in LFG.

References

Andersen, R. (1984). The one-to-one principle. *Language Learning*, *34*, 77–95.

Berti, P. and Di Biase., B. (2002). Form-focused instruction and the acquisition of nominal morphology in primary school learners of Italian L2. *Italiano e Scuola NSW Italian Teachers Bulletin*, *7*(1), 10–14.

Bettoni, C. and Di Biase, B. (2005). Sviluppo obbligato e progresso morfosintattico – un caso di Processabilità in Italiano L2. *Italiano Lingua Seconda*, *3*(7), 27–48.

Bettoni B. and Di Biase B. (Eds.) (under review). *Processability theory: Current issues in theory and application*. Amsterdam: Benjamins.

Boss, B. (1996). German grammar for beginners – the teachability hypothesis and its relevance to the classroom. In C. Arbones Sola, J. Rolin-Ianziti, and R. Sussx (Eds.), *Proceedings of the conference on "Who's afraid of teaching grammar?" Working papers in applied linguistics* (Vol. *1*, pp. 93–103). Brisbane: Centre for Language Teaching and Research, University of Queensland, Australia.

Bresnan, J. (2001). *Lexical-functional syntax*. Malden, MA: Blackwell.

Brindley, G. (1998). Describing language development? Rating Scales and SLA. In L. F. Bachman and A. D. Cohen (Eds.), *Interfaces between second language acquisition and language testing research* (pp. 112–140). Cambridge: Cambridge University Press.

Clahsen, H. (1984). The acquisition of German word order: A test case for cognitive approaches to L2 development. In R. Anderson (Ed.), *Second Languages* (pp. 219–242). Rowley, MA: Newbury House.

Clahsen, H. (1992). Learnability theory and the problem of development in language acquisition. In J. Weissenborn, H. Goodluck, and T. Roeper (Eds.), *Theoretical issues in language acquisition: Continuity and change* (pp. 53–76). Hillsdale, NJ: Lawrence Erlbaum.

Di Biase, B. (2002). Focusing strategies in second language development: A classroom-based study of Italian L2 in primary school. In B. Di Biase (Ed.), *Developing a second language: Acquisition, processing and pedagogy issues in Arabic, Chinese, English, Italian, Japanese, Swedish* (pp. 95–120). Melbourne: Language Australia.

Di Biase, B. (2008). Focus-on-form and development in L2 learning. In J. U. Keßler (Ed.), *Processability approaches to second language development and second language learning* (pp. 197–219). Newcastle upon Tyne, UK: Cambridge Scholars Publishing.

Di Biase, B. and Kawaguchi, S. (2002). Exploring the typological plausibility of Processability Theory: Language development in Italian second language and Japanese second language. *Second Language Research*, *18*(3), 274–302.

Dyson, B. (1996). The debate on form-focused instruction: A teacher's perspective. *Australian Review of Applied Linguistics*, *19*(2), 59–78.

Ellis, R. (1989). Are classroom and naturalistic acquisition the same? A study of the classroom acquisition of German word order rules. *Studies in Second Language Acquisition*, *11*, 303–328.

Ferrari, S. and Nuzzo, E. (2009, July). *Exploring interfaces between PT and other SLA related measures*. Paper presented at the 9th International Symposium on Processability Theory, Bilingualism and Second Language Acquisition, Ludwigsburg, Germany.

Gao, X. (2004). *Noun phrase morphemes and topic development in L2 Mandarin Chinese: A processability perspective*. Unpublished doctoral dissertation. Victoria University of Wellington, New Zealand.

Glahn, E., Håkansson, G., Hammarberg, B., Holmen, A., Hvenekilde, A., and Lund, K. (2001). Processability in Scandinavian second language acquisition. *Studies in Second Language Acquisition*, *23*, 389–416.

Håkansson, G. (2001). Tense morphology and verb-second in Swedish L1 children, L2 children and children with SLI. *Bilingualism: Language and Cognition*, *4*, 85–99.

Håkansson, G., Salameh, E. -K., and Nettelbladt, U. (2003). Measuring language development in bilingual children: Swedish-Arabic children with and without language impairment. *Linguistics*, *41*, 255–288.

Hammarberg, B. (1996). Examining the processability theory: The case of adjective agreement in L2 Swedish. In E. Kellerman, B. Welters, and T. Bongaerts (Eds.), *Toegepaste taalwetenschap in artikelen 55: EUROSLA 6. A Selection of Papers, Nijmegen 1996* (pp. 75–88).

Itani-Adams, Y. (2003, September). *From word to phrase in Japanese-English bilingual first language acquisition.* Paper presented at the MARCS seminar, University of Western Sydney, Sydney, Australia.

Iwasaki, J. (2003, July). *The acquisition of verbal morphosyntax in JSL by a child learner.* Paper presented at 13th Biennial Conference of the JSAA, Brisbane, Australia.

Johnston, M. (1997). *Development and variation in learner language.* Unpublished doctoral dissertation. Australian National University, Canberra, Australia.

Kawaguchi, S. (2005). Argument structure and syntactic development in Japanese as a second language. In M. Pienemann (Ed.), *Cross-linguistic aspects of processability theory* (pp. 253–298). Amsterdam: John Benjamins.

Kawaguchi, S. and Di Biase, B. (in press). Emergence and automatization in second language development. In C. Bettoni and B. Di Biase (Eds.), *Processability theory: Current issues in theory and application.* Amsterdam: Benjamins.

Kempen, G. and Hoenkamp, E. (1987). An incremental procedural grammar for sentence formulation. *Cognitive Science, 11*, 201–258.

Keßler, J. -U. (2006). *Englischerwerb im Anfangsunterricht diagnostizieren. Linguistische Profilanalysen und der Übergang von der Primar- in die Sekundarstufe I. Giessener Beiträge zur Fremdsprachendidaktik.* Tübingen, Germany: Narr.

Keßler, J. -U. (2007). Assessing EFL-development online: A feasibility study of rapid profile. In F. Mansouri (Ed.), *Second language acquisition research: Theory-construction and testing* (pp. 119–143). Newcastle upon Tyne, UK: Cambridge Scholars Press.

Keßler, J. -U. (2008a). Communicative tasks and second language profiling: Linguistic and pedagogical implications. In J. Eckerth and S. Siepmann (Eds.), *Research on task-based language learning and teaching: Theoretical, methodological and pedagogical perspectives* (pp. 291–310). New York: Peter Lang.

Keßler, J. -U. (Ed.) (2008b). *Processability approaches to second language development and second language learning.* Newcastle upon Tyne, UK: Cambridge Scholars Publishing.

Keßler, J. -U. and Keatinge, D. (2008). Profiling oral second language development. In J. -U. Keßler (Ed.), *Processability approaches to second language development and second language learning* (pp. 167–197). Newcastle upon Tyne, UK: Cambridge Scholars Publishing.

Keßler, J. -U. and Keatinge, D. (Eds.) (2009). *Research in second language acquisition. Evidence across languages.* Newcastle upon Tyne, UK: Cambridge Scholars Publishing.

Keßler, J. -U., Liebner, M., and Mansouri, F. (2011). "Teaching". In M. Pienemann and J. -U. Keßler (Eds.), *Studying processability theory. An introductory textbook* (pp. 149–156). Amsterdam: John Benjamins.

Larsen-Freeman, D. and Long, M. H. (1991). *An introduction to second language acquisition research.* London: Longman.

Lenzing, A. and Plesser, A. (2010). "Challenging the Scope-Presission Dilemma in language testing. Paper presented at the 10th International Symposium on Processability Theory, Bilingualism and Second Language Acquisition, Sydney.

Levelt, W. J. M. (1989). *Speaking: From intention to articulation.* Cambridge, MA: MIT Press.

Liebner, M. (2006). Variationsverhalten in verschiedenen Lernergruppen. In M. Pienemann, J. -U. Keßler, and E. Roos (Eds.), *Englischerwerb in der Grundschule. Ein Studien- und Arbeitsbuch.* Paderborn, Germany: Schöningh/UTB.

Lightbown, P. M. (1998). The importance of timing in focus on form. In C. Doughty and J. Williams (Eds.), *Focus on form in second language acquisition* (pp. 177–196). Cambridge: Cambridge University Press.

Long, M. H. (1985). A role for instruction in second language acquisition: Task-based language teaching. In K. Hyltenstam and M. Pienemann (Eds.), *Modelling and assessing second language acquisition* (pp. 77–99). Clevedon, UK: Multilingual Matters.

Long, M. H. (1988). Instructed interlanguage development. In L. Beebe (Ed.), *Issues in second language acquisition: Multiple perspectives* (pp. 115–141). Cambridge, MA: Newbury House.

Long, M. H. (1991). Focus on Form: A design feature in language teaching methodology. In K. de Bot, R. Ginsberg, and C. Kramsch (Eds.), *Foreign language research in cross-cultural perspective* (pp. 39–52). Amsterdam: John Benjamins.

Mackey, A. (1992). Targeting morpho-syntax in children's ESL: An empirical study of the use of interactive goal-based tasks. *Working Papers in Educational Linguistics, 10*(1), 67–91.

Mackey, A., Pienemann, M., and Thornton, I. (1991). Rapid PROFILE: A second language screening procedure. *Language and Language Education: Working Papers of the National Languages Institute of Australia, 1,* 61–82.

Mansouri, F. (2000). *Grammatical markedness and information processing in the acquisition of Arabic as a second language* (pp. 1–260). Munich, Germany: LINCOM EUROPA Academic Publishers.

Mansouri, F. (2007). *Second language acquisition research: Theory-construction and testing.* Newcastle upon Tyne, UK: Cambridge Scholars Press.

Mansouri, F. and Duffy, L. (2005). The pedagogic effectiveness of developmental readiness in ESL grammer instruction. *Australian Review of Applied Linguistics, 28*(1), 81–99.

McDonough, K. and Mackey, A. (2008). Syntactic priming and ESL question development. *Studies in Second Language Acquisition, 30*(1), 31–47.

Meisel, J. M. (1983). Strategies of second language acquisition: More than one kind of simplification. In R. W. Andersen (Ed.), *Pidginisation and creolisation as language acquisition* (pp. 120–157). Rowley, MA: Newbury House.

Meisel, J. M., Clahsen, H., and Pienemann, M. (1981). Determining developmental stages in natural second language acquisition. *Studies in Second Language Acquisition, 3,* 109–135.

Pickering, M. J., Branigan, H. P., and McLean, J. F. (2002). Constituent structure is formulated in one stage. *Journal of Memory and Language, 46,* 586–605.

Pienemann, M. (1984). Psychological constraints on the teachability of languages. *Studies in Second Language Acquisition, 6*(2), 186–214.

Pienemann, M. (1985). Learnability and syllabus construction. In K. Hyltenstam and M. Pienemann (Eds.), *Modelling and assessing second language acquisition* (pp. 23–75). Clevedon, UK: Multilingual Matters.

Pienemann, M. (1989). Is language teachable? Psycholinguistic experiments and hypotheses. *Applied Linguistics, 10*(1), 52–79.

Pienemann, M. (1990). *LARC Research Projects 1990.* Sydney: NLIA/Language Acquisition Research Center.

Pienemann, M. (1992). *Assessing second language acquisition through rapid profile.* ms. Sydney.

Pienemann, M. (1998a). *Language processing and second language development - processability theory.* Amsterdam: John Benjamins.

Pienemann, M. (1998b). Developmental dynamics in L1 an L2 acquisition: Processability theory and generative entrenchment. *Bilingualism: Language and Cognition, 1*(1), 1–20.

Pienemann, M. (2003). Language processing capacity. In C. Doughty and M. Long (Eds.), *Handbook of second language acquisition theory and research* (pp. 679–714). Malden, MA: Blackwell.

Pienemann, M. (Ed.) (2005). *Cross-linguistic aspects of processability theory.* Amsterdam: John Benjamins.

Pienemann, M. (2006). "Applying SLA research to the measurement of bilingual proficiency". Paper read at the Conference on "Lexical organisation in bilinguals". University of the West of England, Bristol, 6 January, 2006.

Pienemann, M., Di Biase, B., and Kawaguchi, S. (2005). Extending processability theory. In M. Pienemann (Ed.), *Cross-linguistic aspects of processability theory* (pp. 199–251). Amsterdam: John Benjamins.

Pienemann, M., Di Biase, B., Kawaguchi, S., and Håkansson, G. (2005). Processing constraints on L1 transfer. In J. F. Kroll and A. M. B. DeGroot (Eds.), *Handbook of bilingualism: Psycholinguistic approaches* (pp. 128–153). New York: Oxford University Press.

Pienemann, M. and Håkansson, G. (1999). A unified approach towards the development of Swedish as L2: A processability account. *Studies in Second Language Acquisition, 21*(3), 383–420.

Pienemann, M. and Johnston, M. (1987). Factors influencing the development of language proficiency. In D.Nunan (Ed.), *Applying second language acquisition research* (pp. 45–141). Adelaide, Australia: National Curriculum Resource Centre.

Pienemann, M., Johnston, M., and Brindley, G. (1988). Constructing an acquisition-based procedure for second language assessment. *Studies in Second Language Acquisition, 10*(2), 217–243.

Pienemann, M., Johnston, M., and Meisel, J. (1993). The multidimensional model, linguistic profiling, and related issues. A reply to Hudson. *Studies in Second Language Acquisition, 15*(4), 495–503.

Pienemann, M. and Keßler, J.-U. (2007). Measuring bilingualism. In P. Auer and L. Wei (Eds.), *Handbook of applied linguistics: Vol. 5. Multilingualism and multilingual communication* (pp. 247–275). Berlin/New York: Mouton de Gruyter.

Pienemann, M. and Keßler, J.-U. (eds.) (2011). *Studying processability theory. An introductory textbook.* Amsterdam: John Benjamins.

Pienemann, M., Keßler, J. -U., and Itami-Adams, Y. (2011). Comparing levels of processability across languages [Special issue]. *International Journal of Bilingualism,* 128–146.

Pienemann, M., Keßler, J. -U., and Lenzing, A. (forthcoming). Transfer at the initial state. In J.-U. Keßler and M. Liebner (Eds.), *Developing and Assessing Second Languages*. Amsterdam: John Benjamins.

Pienemann, M., Keßler, J. -U., and Liebner, M. (2006). Englischerwerb in der Grundschule: Untersuchungsergebnisse im Überblick. In M. Pienemann, J.-U. Keßler, and E. Roos (Eds.), *Englischerwerb in der Grundschule. Ein Studien- und Arbeitsbuch* (pp. 67–88). Paderborn, Germany: Schöningh/UTB.

Pienemann, M. and Mackey, A. (1993). An empirical study of children's ESL development and *Rapid Profile*. In P. McKay (Ed.), *ESL development: Language and literacy in Schools*. Vol. 2 (pp. 115–259). Canberra: National Languages and Literacy Institute of Australia.

Schwarze, C. (2002). Representation and variation: On the development of Romance auxiliary syntax. In M. Butt and T. Holloway King (Eds.), *Time over matter: Diachronic perspectives in morphosyntax* (pp. 105–141). Stanford, California: CSLI Publications.

Seedhouse, P. (2005). "Task" as research construct. *Language Learning*, *58*(3), 533–570.

Segalowitz, N. (2003). Automaticity and second languages. In C. Doughty and M. Long (Eds.), *Handbook of second language acquisition theory and research* (pp. 382–408). Malden, MA: Blackwell.

Slobin, D. I. (1973). Cognitive prerequisites for the development of grammar. In C. A. Ferguson and D. I. Slobin (Eds.), *Studies of child language development* (pp. 175–208). New York: Holt, Rinehart and Winston.

Spada, N. and Lightbown, P. M. (1999). Instruction, first language influence and developmental readiness in second language acquisition. *The Modern Language Journal*, *83*(1), 1–22.

Vigliocco, G., Butterworth, B., and Garrett, M. F. (1996). Subject-verb agreement in Spanish and English: Differences in the role of conceptual constraints. *Cognition*, *61*, 261–298.

Vigliocco, G., Butterworth, B., and Semenza, C. (1995). Constructing subject-verb agreement in speech: The role of semantic and morphological factors. *Journal of Memory and Language*, *34*, 186–215.

Wexler, K. (1982). A principle theory for language acquisition. In E. Wanner and L. R. Gleitman (Eds.), *Language acquisition: The state of the art* (pp. 288–315). Cambridge: Cambridge University Press.

Wexler, K. and Culicover, P. (1980). *Formal principles of language acquisition*. Cambridge, MA: MIT Press.

White, L. (1991). Second language competence versus second language performance: UG or processing strategies? In L. Eubank (Ed.), *Point counterpoint. Universal grammar in the second language* (pp. 167–189). Amsterdam: John Benjamins.

Zhang, Y. (2001). *Second language acquisition of Chinese grammatical morphemes: A processability perspective.* Unpublished doctoral dissertation. The Australian National University, Canberra, Australia.

Zhang, Y. (2005). Processing and formal instruction in the L2 acquisition of five Chinese grammatical morphemes. In M. Pienemann (Ed.), *Cross-linguistic aspects of processability theory* (pp. 155–177). Amsterdam: John Benjamins.

15

Attention and awareness in second language acquisition

Peter Robinson, Alison Mackey, Susan M. Gass, and Richard Schmidt

Historical discussion

Attention and awareness in cognitive science and SLA

Issues of attention "bear on every area of cognitive science" (Allport, 1989, p. 631). Attention, however, is not a unitary construct; many mechanisms have been proposed to explain how it affects different aspects of behavior and learning. Attentional mechanisms have been invoked to explain such diverse phenomena in second language acquisition (SLA) as variation in the accuracy, fluency and complexity of second language (L2) use in different social environments, and the effects of pedagogic task demands on learners' spoken and written performance in experimental and classroom language learning settings. Availability of attentional resources has also been argued to predict the extent to which instructional conditions manipulating the focus of learners' attention affect the quality of perception, and, as a consequence, memory for targeted aspects of input. Explaining variational phenomena implicates mechanisms of attention which are used to *control* action while using the L2. Explaining perceptual, learning, and memory phenomena implicates mechanisms of attention which are used to select (or inhibit) and mentally rehearse information in the L2 input. These two broad classes of attentional mechanisms interact to affect SLA in ways that researchers have explored in both experimental and classroom settings.

Attentional mechanisms regulating the use and learning of L2s can be studied at a number of different levels. For example, at the neurobiological level (Schumann, 2004), research using functional magnetic resonance imaging (fMRI) shows changes in areas of neural activation during stages of behaviorally induced visual orienting (overt head and eye movement toward visual stimuli), as well as in subsequent stages of accurate discrimination between and in response to visual targets (Posner and Peterson, 1990). One aim of research at this level is to show how attentional networks in the brain give rise to *awareness*—the subjective, contentful "feel" of experience that can be reported to others, to varying extents. For example, Beck *et al.* (2001) found that the ability to successfully detect and report awareness of changes in a visual scene was associated not only with visual cortex activity related to the changing object, but also with additional activity in regions of the fronto parietal cortex commonly associated with directed attention. Neurobiological research has identified a number of these types of attentional networks (Raz and Buhle, 2006), and has begun to influence accounts of the neural components of attention to language (Arabski and Woltaszek, 2010; Chee, 2009; Green, 2003; Green *et al.*,

2006; Indefrey *et al.*, 2001) and how they interact with phonological working memory to affect such processes as rule-learning and fossilization (de Diego-Balaguer and Lopez-Barroso, 2010; Schuchert, 2004), language selection and control in bilinguals (Fabbro, 1999; Rodriguez-Fornells *et al.*, 2006), and the influence of selection and control on the attainment of varying levels of bilingual proficiency (Chee, 2005).

Attention can also be studied at the information processing level, in which performance on cognitively demanding tasks, rather than less demanding tasks, is thought to implicate mechanisms for attention allocation (e.g., automatic versus controlled responding) that differentiate performance on each of them. At this level, attention is conceptualized as having functions that regulate our actions in and facilitate our learning about the environment. These functions include selecting information for processing, focusing on it and inhibiting distractions, activating concepts in long-term memory, and coordinating participation in multiple simultaneous activities. Many of the models of attention that have guided SLA research have their origins in areas of cognitive science addressing one of these information-processing functions. These include models proposed for the study of selective attention in visual processing (Posner and Peterson, 1990); the study of mental workload and divided attention (Kahneman, 1973; Wickens, 1984, 2007); the relationship of focal attention to rehearsal in working memory (Cowan, 1995); conditioned attention and associative learning (Rescorla and Wagner, 1972); and the withdrawal of attention during the development of automaticity and skilled responding (Anderson, 1993; Logan, 1988; Shiffrin and Schneider, 1977). In order to address specific issues in SLA theory, some models of attention have been adapted from the form in which they were originally proposed (see Chaudron, 1985; Gass, 1997; McLaughlin *et al.*, 1988; Robinson, 1995). Debate continues about which models are most effective in their explanations of aspects of information processing during SLA, such as the allocation of attention to competing task demands and the resulting effects on second language (L2) production. In addition, there is disagreement regarding how detailed or "fine-grained" attentional models should be for explaining the effects of L2 instruction (Leow, 2002; Robinson, 2003; Simard and Wong, 2001).

Attention and awareness in SLA research

Input and intake. The distinction between what is available to be learned (input), and what is cognitively registered through learners' perceptions and further processing (intake), is one of the earliest psycholinguistic distinctions made in SLA theory, although Corder's terminology differs from what is used today:

> The simple fact of presenting a certain linguistic form to a learner in the classroom does not necessarily qualify it for the status of input, for the reason that input is "what goes in" not what is *available* for going in, and we may reasonably suppose that it is the learner who controls this input, or more properly his intake. This may well be determined by the characteristics of his language acquisition mechanism.
>
> *(Corder, 1967, p. 165)*

Discussing the "psychological variables that make up the learner's mechanisms for perception and learning," Chaudron (1985) further distinguished between an initial stage involving perception of input, or "preliminary intake," from a later stage involved in the "recoding and encoding of the semantic (communicated) information into long term memory" (1985, p. 2), leading to "final intake." Two issues much SLA research and theory has subsequently addressed are the attentional mechanisms responsible for learners' selective perception at the early stage of preliminary intake, and whether and to what extent, it is accompanied by awareness.

Implicit and explicit learning and knowledge. Throughout the 1970s and 1980s, research and theory in cognitive psychology increasingly addressed the role of awareness in learning. These early efforts aimed to reveal the extent that "consciousness" and the "cognitive unconscious" contribute to learning, and were highly influential on SLA research. This seminal work included research and theorizing about implicit, unaware learning of complex artificial grammars (Reber, 1967, 1993) and the relationship of conscious, "explicit" memory to "implicit" memory, which (in contrast to explicit memory) involves no deliberate conscious attempt at recall (Schacter, 1987). Reber and Schacter argued that there were two functionally independent learning and memory systems, since both implicit and explicit learning as well as implicit and explicit memory, could be dissociated from each other. Furthermore, Reber claimed that where a stimulus domain was complex, as in the case of natural language, it could only be learned implicitly, that is, without participants knowing what they learned or how they learned it. Implicit learning was operationalized by asking learners to memorize strings of letters, such as XVVXXZ, generated from the rules regulating a complex finite-state grammar. Learners' above chance accurate performance on post exposure grammaticality judgments, accompanied by the learners' inability to describe the knowledge guiding their judgments, led Reber to conclude that participants had unconsciously abstracted the underlying structural rules (for reviews of this research see Perruchet, 2008; Pothos, 2007; Shanks and St. John, 1994; Williams, 2009).

At the same time as these early publications on implicit learning and memory in cognitive psychology were appearing, Krashen (1982) put forward a similar proposal for a distinction between two dissociated language learning systems responsible for unconscious knowledge, or "acquisition," and conscious knowledge or "learning." Successful SLA, he claimed, was largely the result of unconscious "acquisition," since only simple aspects of an L2 can be consciously learned, and since access to what has been consciously learned is only possible under stringent conditions, that is, when learners have time to reflect, know the rule, and are focused on accuracy, or form. Krashen's "Monitor Model," and claims about the superiority of acquisition processes over conscious learning processes, prompted well over a decade of empirical research into the role of awareness in SLA. Bialystok (1978) proposed a model similar to Krashen's, distinguishing between an Explicit Linguistic Knowledge source, containing all the "conscious" facts the learner has about the L2, and an Implicit Linguistic Knowledge source, containing "intuitive information" that cannot be verbally described. The Explicit Knowledge source stores simple rules while the Implicit Knowledge source stores the complex ones. The implicit knowledge is drawn on in spontaneous language production, in the same way that acquired knowledge is used in spontaneous production in Krashen's model.

Consciousness raising and input enhancement. Sharwood Smith (1981) argued that "consciousness raising" activities could be potentially helpful for instructed L2 learners, distinguishing four types of intervention that could be used to direct learners' attention to language form. These activities ranged from the provision of pedagogic rules to "brief indirect clues" to the L2 target structure such as visually enhancing a particular structure in the input during language learning activities. A great deal of SLA research has investigated the effectiveness of what Sharwood Smith (1991) later called "input enhancement" techniques and the extent to which they influence learners' selective attention to forms. In addition, research has examined the effects of these interventions on learners' subsequent knowledge and performance. Two particularly interesting issues in this research are how explicit or attention-demanding the input enhancement techniques should be, as in Doughty and Williams' (1998) investigations of "focus on form" (Long, 1991), and whether input enhancement should be presented reactively (immediately following evidence that a learner has problems producing or comprehending the forms) or proactively, in anticipation of the problems learners are likely to have in selectively attending to form (R. Ellis, 2001).

Apperception. The late 1980s and early 1990s saw a great deal of theoretical debate about the role of attention and awareness in SLA, much of it reacting to Krashen's claim that unconscious acquisition processes are most influential on the levels of success learners reach. Gass (1988) proposed a framework for research which identified five levels, or processing stages, in the conversion of ambient speech (input) to output. The first of these stages, apperception, concerns attention to and selection of input: "the apperceived input is that bit of language which is noticed by the learner because of some particular features" (p. 202)—and apperception is "the process of understanding by which newly observed qualities of an object are related to past experiences … the selection of what we might call noticed (apperceived) material" (p. 201). It is clear that by apperception Gass means attention to and awareness of input. However, it is "not equivalent to perception" (p. 201), defined as a stimulus-driven process. Apperception involves "noticing" a form and consciously relating it to "some prior knowledge which has been stored in our experience" (p. 201).

For Krashen all that was necessary for acquisition processes to operate was comprehensible input, but Gass (1988) makes the distinction between this and *comprehended* input, which is controlled by the learner and is the processing stage preceded by apperception. Gass therefore suggests that consciousness is necessary for acquisition to take place. The extent of prior knowledge is one of the factors that determines whether apperception will select input for further processing, and which aspects of the input will be selected. Three others factors are frequency (both highly frequent, and highly infrequent input may result in apperception), affect, and attention, which is "what allows a learner to notice a mismatch between what he or she produces/knows and what is produced by speakers of the second language" (p. 203).

The "Noticing Hypothesis." At about the same time, Schmidt and Frota (1986) published the results of a diary study in which Schmidt argued for a close relationship between what he had "noticed" (operationalized as testimony to the occurrence of L2 forms, in written diary entries) about a language he was learning [Portuguese], and the subsequent appearance of some of those forms in his own production. Further pursuing the notion of noticing, Schmidt (1990) pointed out that the term "unconscious" (the defining feature of Krashen's "acquisition" process) is commonly used in three distinct senses: to describe learning without "intention," learning without metalinguistic "understanding," and learning without attention and "awareness." Schmidt argued that while L2 learning without intention or metalinguistic understanding is clearly possible, there can be no learning without attention, accompanied by the subjective experience of "noticing," or being *aware* of aspects of the "surface structure" of input. All L2 learning is conscious in this sense, since input does not become intake for learning unless it is noticed. Schmidt (1995) assumed that focal attention and the contents of awareness are essentially isomorphic. The "Noticing Hypothesis" continues to promote much research into the role of awareness in second language learning in instructed and experimental settings, using an increasingly sophisticated and sensitive range of measures of awareness, as will be described in the third section of this chapter.

Detection, noticing and working memory. In another widely cited paper, however, Tomlin and Villa (1994) argued that while attention was necessary for L2 learning, awareness was not. They argued that a more fine-grained analysis of the role of attention in SLA was necessary, and drew on Posner and Peterson's (1990) neurocognitive model of three interrelated networks, which function not only to detect stimuli (cognitive registration of them), but also to alert (prepare to attend) and orient (commit attentional resources) to stimuli. "None of the central components of attention—alertness, orientation or detection—require awareness" (p. 193), they claimed, and further, that detection was the initial, prerequisite level of processing needed for input selection and second language acquisition. Robinson (1995) described a model of attention and memory complementary to Schmidt's Noticing Hypothesis, which accommodated some details of Tomlin and Villa's proposal. In that model, noticing was defined as "detection plus rehearsal in short-term memory, prior to encoding in long-term memory" (1995, p. 296). Drawing on Cowan's (1988, 1995) embedded process model of attention and memory he argued that only a subset of input that is detected is focally attended and noticed. Detected input, which is in peripheral attention, enters into short-term memory. Focally attended input enters working memory, which is that part of long-term memory in a currently heightened state of activation. Further, the nature of the rehearsal processes operating on the contents of working memory help to differentiate the contents of what is noticed and, following rehearsal, permanently encoded in long-term memory—thus accommodating Gass's (1988) claim that prior knowledge and attention together help determine what is noticed and available for learning. Since there are differences between learners in the abilities drawn on in focusing (and inhibiting) attention, and maintaining and rehearsing information in short-term and working memory, Robinson argued that these differences should correspond to differences in learning under implicit, incidental and explicit conditions of exposure. Those higher in these abilities should be more successful at noticing, and learning than those lower in these abilities, whatever the condition of instructional exposure. To this extent, he argued (1997a), learning under any condition of exposure is fundamentally similar.

Selective attention and frequency effects. In a series of influential papers, first appearing in the mid-1990s, N. Ellis addressed the issue of selective attention in the context of "emergentism" (N. Ellis, 1998, and Chapter 12, this volume), and the role of frequency effects in second language learning and processing (N. Ellis, 1996, 2002, 2006a, 2006b). As has been previously shown (Rescorla and Wagner, 1972), human memory is sensitive to *recency*, the time since past occurrence of a stimulus, and *frequency*, the number of times it has previously occurred, with both of these positively affecting the "associative learning of representations that reflect the probabilities of occurrence of form-function mappings" (2006a, p. 8). Ellis interprets Goldschneider and DeKeyser's (2001) findings that perceptual salience, frequency, and morphophonological regularity of morphemes were the strongest predictors of their rank in morpheme acquisition orders as evidence that these are the factors contributing the most to the intensity with which learners attended to, and associatively learned, these forms. This work on associative, statistical learning, has been influential in research into child language acquisition (Conway and Christiansen, 2006; Gomez and Gerken, 1999; Saffran *et al.*, 1999), and is currently being drawn on in studies of implicit and explicit learning during adult SLA (Rebuschat, 2008; Williams, 2010).

Core issues

In this section, we deal with three issues related to attention and awareness in L2 research: (1) interface between implicit and explicit knowledge, (2) objects of attention (i.e., which aspects of language can or cannot be attended to), and (3) the role of attention to and awareness of output.

Interface between implicit and explicit knowledge

Within SLA research, the study of implicit and explicit learning, as well as the distinctions between implicit and explicit knowledge, is firmly rooted in cognitive psychology as discussed earlier. Disagreement regarding a number of factors, including the role of awareness, and the nature of knowledge acquired through different types of learning, became a source of debate in both SLA and cognitive psychology. Central to the implicit/explicit discussion is the question of whether or not implicit and explicit learning, and implicit and explicit knowledge, are two dissociated and distinct systems. If in fact two independent systems exist, what is the relationship, or interface, between these two learning and knowledge systems? Krashen (1982) has claimed that grammatical competence is acquired only through exposure and cannot be explicitly taught, that is, it is essentially implicit. Because learners rely on implicit knowledge for both comprehension and production, and explicit knowledge is used only for monitoring the accuracy of output, explicit instruction and the explicit knowledge gained through it are useful when responding to discrete items on tests, but play no real role when language is being used for real communication. Krashen also argued that these two types of language knowledge are stored and used differently by learners, and that explicit knowledge cannot become implicit knowledge. This position, that implicit knowledge is informationally encapsulated and unaffected by conscious knowledge, is referred to as the non-interface position.

Recent research in neuroscience and neurolinguistics has demonstrated the existence of two distinct and separate processes for developing and storing implicit and explicit knowledge (as described in Chapter 17 of this volume by Ullman and Morgan-Short), but the influence of explicit knowledge on the development of implicit knowledge remains a source of debate in the field of second language acquisition. DeKeyser (1997, 2003, 2009) argued that explicit declarative knowledge can provide a basis for repeated practice, which, if sufficient, leads to proceduralized and eventually automatized knowledge. Over time, proceduralized knowledge allows the learner to become faster and more consistent in their production and comprehension, thus devoting fewer attentional resources to form. This strong interface position claims that declarative knowledge resulting from explicit learning can directly result in the development of procedural knowledge that learners can subconsciously access in the same way as implicit competence. However, this position depends on excluding awareness as a crucial part of the definition of acquired knowledge, because learners do not become unaware of the rules through practice. Rather, DeKeyser argues that they can develop knowledge that is "functionally equivalent" (2003) to knowledge that is learned implicitly and suggests, moreover, that after automatization of the rules, learners may in fact forget previously known metalinguistic rules, since they are no longer needed.

Another perspective is the weak interface position, which holds that explicit knowledge can become implicit knowledge under the right conditions. R. Ellis (1993) has argued that the transformation of explicit to implicit knowledge through practice can only occur if the learner is developmentally ready to advance (see, for example, the developmental constraints on readiness proposed by Pienemann in his Processability Theory described in Chapter 14). Another possibility is that explicit knowledge can facilitate the growth of implicit knowledge by alerting learners to what they need to attend to when processing input. Indeed, explicit knowledge (whether gained through instruction or through conscious induction) should have mostly positive influences on learning through exposure and interaction, since "learning with advance organizers and clues is always better than learning without cues" (MacWhinney, 1997, p. 278). N. Ellis (2005, 2008) has argued for still another version of the weak interface position, stating that although explicit and implicit knowledge are distinct and dissociated systems, representing different types of knowledge supported in different areas of the brain, there is interaction between them. According to N. Ellis, explicit knowledge is developed through learners' conscious efforts to construct meaning, while implicit knowledge is developed during fluent language production and comprehension. Relying on implicit and automatized knowledge in predictable situations, we only draw on additional conscious resources, such as explicit knowledge, when these automatic abilities fail. Ellis provides the example of walking to illustrate his point. We do not think about walking until we take a misstep, at which point we use explicit knowledge to subsidize the failure of our implicit knowledge. These implicit and explicit processes connect in what Ellis (2005) refers to as a dynamic interface (p. 325), which is established during conscious processing in working memory. Thus consciousness plays a crucial role in enabling this interface, which then allows conscious and unconscious processes to operate in parallel in language learning as in any other cognitive performance task.

Paradis (2009) has argued that these various scenarios do not constitute an interface between two systems, but rather the replacement of one system with another. Paradis suggests that when instructed learners first begin to acquire a language, metalinguistic knowledge may be used almost exclusively. However, as learners progress, they begin to rely more on the implicit knowledge that has been developed and internalized through continued and extensive practice, with this knowledge eventually becoming automatized as implicit competence. Paradis provides the metaphor of someone recovering from blindness. As this person learns to read visually, he will gradually replace reading with Braille to reading with his eyes. The two systems, tactile and visual, are independent of each other, and although the knowledge of Braille still exists, it does not become visual reading. Within SLA, this can be interpreted to mean that metalinguistic knowledge remains available to language learners, even as they gradually develop automatic implicit competence as a separate and independent system. For instance, learners can use their explicit knowledge to produce monitored output, which then serves as the input for the development of the implicit knowledge system (as also argued by Gass and Mackey, 2006, Schmidt and Frota, 1986). As learners progress, they devote more attention to creating meaning while the structural processes become more automatic (Schmidt, 1995), gradually replacing reliance on the explicit system with implicit knowledge acquired through repetition and exposure to the form in context.

Objects of attention

So far, we have been referring to attention as if it were uniformly involved in all language learning and processing, but research suggests that learners pay more attention to some aspects of language than to others. It is well-established, for example, that learners are less sensitive to syntactic cues to grammatical gender than they are to morphophonological cues (noun endings) during processing. In particular, Bordag and Pechmann (2007); Bordag *et al.* (2006); Carroll (1999); Franceschina (2005); Holmes and de la Batie (1999) provided evidence to demonstrate that learners are sensitive to noun endings and make use of them in their determination of gender. On the other end of the spectrum, Lew-Williams (2009) and Guillelmon and Grosjean (2001) have shown that learners are insensitive to syntactic indicators of gender, such as agreement on determiners and adjectives. Most of this research has been examined through processing measures such as speed or accuracy of noun production or production using priming experiments, preferential looking tasks, and word recognition tasks. Diversity in cue sensitivity may be considered an indication of where attention is focused when processing a second language.

Mackey, *et al.*, (2000) indirectly investigated attention to different parts of language by looking at learners' perceptions of oral feedback. In this study, learners were given feedback on their production of target forms, and then were asked through retrospective interviews to comment on the feedback that they received. These learner-produced comments provide a way of examining learners' attentional focus on a particular area of production, in this case, a form that deviated from target language norms. Results indicated that feedback intended to correct lexical, semantic, and phonological errors was perceived more accurately than feedback intended for morphosyntactic errors. Related to these results is Jiang's (2004) study of Chinese ESL learners, and his finding that learners are not sensitive to morphology when processing L2 sentences. Possible explanations for this observed differential sensitivity to certain aspects of language are the phenomena of attentional blocking and learned attention (N. Ellis, 2006a, b). According to N. Ellis, when linguistic cues are redundant (e.g., in the sentence *He goes to the store*, both *He* and *−s* indicate the third-person singular) the learning of later experienced cues is blocked by earlier learned cues. For example, N. Ellis (2006b) found that for redundant cues, when learners were exposed to adverbial cues, the acquisition of verbal tense morphology was blocked, whereas earlier exposure to verbal tense morphology blocked the later acquisition of adverbs. In the case of L2 acquisition, speakers who do not have a certain linguistic cue in their L1 may fail to pay attention to, and subsequently learn, that cue in their L2. Indeed, N. Ellis (2006b) also found that L1 speakers of Chinese languages, which do not have verb tense morphology, were unable to acquire inflectional morphology in the presence of redundant adverbial and verbal cues. Other theoretical approaches to L2 learning (e.g., Lardiere, 1998; Prévost and White, 2000; Sprouse, 1998) also support the view of differential learning. However, in these studies, the explanations take a more formal direction with rare discussion devoted to the role or influence of attention.

Gass *et al.* (2003) investigated the role of focused attention on the learning of three areas of language: syntax, lexicon, and morphosyntax. The focus of attention was manipulated by under-lining words, phrases and sentences in stories that participants read on a computer screen and telling participants to pay attention to the underlined material. Findings indicated that although learners' attention was focused on all three parts of language, the greatest amount of learning took place in syntax. However, without focused attention, the greatest amount of learning took place in the lexicon, followed by morphosyntax, and then by syntax. In addition, the authors discussed the role of proficiency in relation to attention, finding a diminished impact of directed attention as a function of proficiency and in all language areas. However, "focused attention" in that study refers only to externally-manipulated attention, and does not necessarily correspond to internal attentional processes, which the authors cite as a limitation.

The role of attention to and awareness of output

Many of the issues we have described concern the role of attention and awareness in processing input, and the extent to which levels of attention and awareness are necessary for retention of input and further learning. Recently, however, there has been an increasing number of studies examining attention to and awareness of form in L2 production, or output, and the extent to which attention to and awareness of output can facilitate SLA. Swain (1995) argued that attention to output has a facilitating role, since "in producing the target language ... learners may notice a gap between what they want to say and what they can say, leading them to recognize what they do not know, or know only partially" (pp. 125–126). Producing language also offers opportunities for testing hypotheses about well-formedness, and for metalinguistic reflection on L2 form. Izumi (2003) and Kormos (2006) have described the stages of L2 speech production at which attention can operate to promote the three kinds of awareness that Swain described, and current research is concerned with the extent to which the attentional demands of pedagogic tasks promote these kinds of awareness, and so affect performance and learning.

The theoretical question of interest here is the notion of attention as "capacity." Clearly, the human information processing system is limited in its ability to process and respond to information in the environment; but are breakdowns in performance caused by limits on attentional capacity? Skehan (1998, 2009) argues for this position, claiming that capacity limits on a single pool of attentional resources will, in general, lead to decrements in the fluency, accuracy and complexity of L2 speech when tasks are high in their attentional, memory, and other cognitive demands. Skehan argues that certain task characteristics may "predispose learners to channel their attention in predictable ways, such as clear macrostructure toward accuracy, the need to impose order on ideas toward complexity, and so on" (Skehan, 1998, p. 112). However, tasks can lead either to increased complexity, or accuracy of production, but not to both. In Skehan's account, due to scarcity of attentional resources, attention to accuracy of speech takes place at the expense of attention to complexity of speech. A contrasting position has been proposed by Robinson (2003, 2007), who argues that attentional capacity limits are an unsatisfactory, post-hoc explanation for breakdowns in attention to speech. Following Neuman (1987) and Sanders (1998), Robinson suggests that breakdowns in "action-control," not capacity limits, lead to decrements in speech production, and learners' failure to benefit from the learning opportunities that attention directing provides. Consequently, increasing complexity along various dimensions of tasks, such as increasing the amount of reasoning the task requires or increasing the memory load of the task, promotes greater effort at controlling production and more vigilant monitoring of output. This increased task complexity leads to greater accuracy and complexity of L2 production when compared to performance on simpler task versions that require little or no reasoning. Furthermore, greater task complexity leads to increased noticing and improved uptake of task relevant input. Research into Skehan's and Robinson's contrasting predictions, and their theoretical underpinnings in models of attention and speech production, can be expected to continue in current SLA research.

Data and common elicitation measures

First-person verbal reports

First-person reports of experience, collected in the form of speech or writing, have been the major source of information on the contribution of attention and awareness to SLA, and have been elicited via a range of methodologies. These include diary entries, in which learners reflect on their experience over weeks or months (Schmidt and Frota, 1986; Warden et al., 1995); on-line "think-aloud" protocols, in which learners verbalize the contents of their experience while directly engaged in learning activities (Bowles, 2010; Leow, 1997, 2000; Leow and Morgan-Short, 2004); immediate off-line response prompts to recall experience (Philp, 2003); or somewhat more delayed responses to written questionnaires (Bell and Collins, 2009; Robinson, 1996, 2010a); stimulated recall, in which learners are prompted to report the thoughts they had while performing a task (Gass and Mackey, 2000; Mackey et al., 2000) or oral interview questions (Leow, 2000; Williams, 2004, 2005).

As Baars (2003) notes, the standard behavioral index for consciousness is the ability people have to report their experience (see also Weiskrantz, 1997). Conscious processes "can be operationally defined as events that: (1) can be reported and acted upon, (2) with verifiable accuracy, (3) under optimal reporting conditions, and (4) which are reported as conscious" (2003, p. 4). Optimal reporting conditions involve, for example, factors such as a minimum delay between the event and the report, and freedom from distraction. Because of the need for optimal conditions, immediate off-line measures, such as those collected by Philp (2003) and Mackey et al. (2000), have advantages over first-person reports collected after some period of delay, as in diary studies or during oral interviews, where learners may have simply forgotten what they were aware of during learning. Think-aloud protocols have been argued to be concurrent measures of awareness and, possibly, learning, and have the advantage of immediacy over all other methods for first-person reporting, but it has been argued that learning activities may distract attention from attempts to verbalize experience while thinking aloud, thereby reducing their faithfulness as records of what learners were aware of. On the other hand, the effort to verbalize thoughts may distract learners' attention from the learning activity, negatively affecting performance. This potential effect that the effort of verbalization may have on the cognitive processes of interest is referred to as the risk of "negative reactivity." Sachs and Polio (2007) found just such an effect, since a group instructed to think aloud while processing feedback in the form of reformulations provided on the drafts of essays they had written made a lower percentage of corrections to their revised essays than a group not instructed to think aloud while processing the feedback. On the other hand, Sanz *et al.* (2009) found that a group of English speaking students instructed to think aloud while participating in a computerized lesson on the Latin case system, in which they received explicit feedback about responses to the semantic functions of case markers, performed significantly better on post-test measures of grammaticality judgment and sentence production than a group not instructed to think aloud, but had no effect on the latency of response to grammaticality judgment items. Thus the observed reactivity was "positive" in this case (see Bowles, 2010 for extensive discussion of this issue of "reactivity").

Overall, although they differ in the optimality of the conditions they require for eliciting awareness, the first-person reports of experience described above are valuable sources of information about the facilitating effect (or not) of more versus less reported awareness on learning morpho-syntacic, lexical or phonological form (Mackey *et al.*, 2000) or pragmatic form (Felix-Brasdefer, 2008). In the classroom and laboratory studies referred to above, first-person reports are used to assess the relative "extent" of awareness of forms made salient through some instructional intervention intended to guide attention to them, such as input enhancement (Alanen, 1995; Jourdenais *et al.*, 1995; Robinson, 1997b), or recasting (Mackey, 2006; Philp, 2003), and the extent to which these "greater" levels of awareness did (more explicit learning) or did not (more implicit learning) accompany pre-to post-test gains in knowledge.

Subjective and objective behavioral tests of learning

First-person verbal reports, however, clearly may fail to include all of the information learners were aware of during learning (cf. Allport, 1988; Godfroid *et al.*, 2010; Jourdenais, 2001; Rosa and O'Neill, 1999). This lack of information may be due to some of the reasons provided above, such as the possibility of forgetting after a delay between experience and reporting, as well as for other reasons described below. In studies of implicit learning in cognitive psychology, first-person verbal reports have been criticized for failing to meet what Shanks and St. John (1994) have called the *information criterion*, and also the *sensitivity criterion*.

In the early studies of implicit learning conducted by Reber (see Reber, 1989), during training he asked participants to attend to, and copy down a series of letter strings they were presented with (e.g., XXVVZ). He then told them the strings they had seen followed certain rules, regulating permissible sequences, and asked them to judge which of a further series followed, or did not follow the same rules. Participants performed with above chance accuracy, but without being able to respond to requests to verbalize the rules they were following in making judgments. However, as Perruchet and Pacteau (1990) and Shanks and St. John (1994) argued, these results were not evidence that unconscious learning had taken place. Participants were asked to provide information in the verbal reports about their *knowledge of rules*, but even those who were completely unaware of and unable to verbalize *rules* could have been aware of and used other information (e.g., co-occurring bigrams and trigrams) to guide their perfor-mance. These verbal reports therefore violated the information criterion necessary in measures of implicit learning because they did not necessarily measure the knowledge responsible for guiding behavior.

The sensitivity criterion states that a measure of awareness should be *sensitive to all* of the conscious knowledge that could have guided learning. First-person verbal reports may fail to meet this criterion since participants may be insufficiently motivated to report knowledge which they have, but which they feel unsure of or lack confidence in. In short, when learners are asked to report first-person experiences, they may not be asked about the information they were aware of and which led to learning, or they may intentionally withhold knowledge they were aware of and which led to learning. For these reasons, researchers argue (e.g., Dienes and Scott, 2005; Merickle and Reingold, 1991; Tunney and Shanks, 1993) that both subjective and objective "behavioral tests" need to be employed as markers of awareness. These tests are necessary supplements to first-person reports of experience, such as protocols, in order to probe whether awareness is actually implicated in learning, even in the absence of learner failures to voluntarily self-report it.

An objective test of learning encourages learners to respond by consciously accessing the knowledge they need to perform the test or task. For example, after being trained on an artificial grammar in implicit or explicit learning conditions, learners are often asked to complete a grammaticality judgment task (i.e., indicate whether the new string follows the grammar of the strings encountered during training). When learners are required to underline or otherwise identify the information that guided their decisions, they are guided to consciously indicate the knowledge on which their judgments are based. Where the above chance accuracy of grammaticality judgments matches learners' underlining or other identification of the information that did occur during training, it is taken to be evidence that learning was the result of awareness. However, asking participants to engage in such a task may increase awareness of the target forms during testing, and does not necessarily reflect the level of awareness during the learning phase. Objective measures may also require learners to generate a sequence of letter strings or words based on learners' explicitly accessible knowledge and memory of their occurrence during trained exposure. Again, where the explicitly accessed knowledge used to generate strings or sentences in these tests matches the occurrence of those strings and sentences in training, then learning is judged to be the result of awareness. All of the direct measures for assessing reflective memory for prior exposure to grammatical strings during training described by Merikle and Reingold (1991) (and summarized in Robinson, 1995) are therefore objective tests. These measures include forced choice recognition tests of information presented during training, or responses to instructions to recall whether information in the test occurred during training.

In contrast, a subjective test of learning does not encourage learners to consciously reflect on their prior experience with—and so their explicit memory for—the stimulus during training, but rather requires them to respond on the basis of the degree of "feel," or certainty about intuitions guiding their responses during actual test performance. These subjective tests include those eliciting estimates of the confidence which learners have in making responses to a post-training exposure test of knowledge gained (Rebuschat and Williams, 2010; Shanks and Johnstone, 1998; cf., Krashen, 1982). Where learners themselves report to have no confidence in their responses, and so to be "guessing" versus "not guessing" (a dichotomous scale), and where there is also above chance accuracy in responding to the test of what was learned (another dichotomous scale), the knowledge guiding responding is then judged to be outside of awareness. According to Dienes et al. (1995), tests of implicit, unaware learning should meet this guessing criterion, which can be calculated using the chi-square statistic. This guessing criterion demonstrates the absence of awareness by showing a greater than expected proportion of guessing/above chance accurate responses compared to other responses in a 2 x 2 guessing/not guessing, above/below chance matrix. Similarly, when there is no significant positive correlation between learners' confidence ratings on the accuracy of their decisions, measured along some interval scale from "no confidence" to "absolute confidence," and their percentage of accurate decision-making on test items, the knowledge that guides performance on the tests is also judged to be outside of awareness. This is what Dienes et al. (1995) call the "zero correlation criterion" for demonstrating implicit learning.

Applications

Input enhancement

Many subfields of second language research are relevant to the instructional context (see Chapter 33). Significant amounts of research have investigated what Sharwood Smith (1991) referred to as input enhancement, or induced input salience (p. 121) and the extent to which it in fact induces selective attention. Polio (2007) provides a clear review of the input enhancement literature, including definitions, similarities, and correspondences with the term "focus on form" (see Chapter 33) as well as empirical evidence. She points to narrow definitions of input enhancement, in which instructors or materials developers visually enhance materials (e.g., colors, bold letters), as having been shown to have little effect. On the other hand, if a broader definition is taken, such as one that includes any effort to draw learners' attention to certain language features, then the impact on acquisition is broader (see also Han et al., 2008; Huang, 2008; Leow, 2007).

As was noted earlier, the significance of attention-drawing activities varies according to the structure involved. For example, Jeon (2007) designed communicative activities that were focused on lexical items (nouns and verbs) and morphosyntactic features (relative clauses and Korean honorifics). In the short-term, relative clauses, verbs, and nouns were impacted more than honorifics; in the long-term, attention-drawing activities had a greater impact on relative clauses than on honorifics within the category of morphosyntax. Comparing morphosyntax and the lexicon, verbs were more impacted than nouns and honorifics. Jeon's explanation for the differential effects of attention-focusing activities centers on the salience of form.

Individual differences and attention

Aptitude. Considered a strong indicator of academic success, aptitude has generally been regarded as a key factor in predicting learners' rate of development in second language learning contexts (DeKeyser, 2000; Dörnyei, 2005) and is discussed in Chapter 23 by Skehan in this volume. Early aptitude research (Carroll, 1973, 1981) identified four cognitive components related to predicting language learning potential: phonemic coding ability, grammatical sensitivity, associative memory ability, and inductive language learning ability. Recent research has also suggested that these aptitude components play an important role in learners' individual processing abilities (Dörnyei and Skehan, 2003; Robinson, 1996, 1997a). For instance, earlier sections of this chapter have addressed the importance of focusing learners' attention on form in order to facilitate acquisition. However, the success of focusing learners' attention is likely affected by learners' individual abilities to focus on form, abilities which are grounded in the aptitude components of grammatical sensitivity and inductive language learning ability.

Empirical research (de Graaff, 1997; Robinson, 1997a; Williams, 1999) has also demonstrated that individual differences in aptitude influence learning in both implicit and explicit conditions. For instance, in Robinson's studies examining the effects of varying learner / learning conditions (rule-search, instructed, incidental, and implicit) on acquisition (1996, 1997a), learners in the implicit group who demonstrated greater grammatical sensitivity were more likely to deduce and be able to verbalize explicit knowledge from language stimuli than those lower in grammatical sensitivity. Robinson (2002) also suggests that learning conditions that promote attention to and noticing of target forms (such as explicit conditions in which a pedagogic rule is presented to guide input processing, or in which learners are encouraged to search the input for grammatical rules) draw on different aptitude resources, or aptitude complexes, than learning that takes place during incidental (i.e., a comprehension activity) or implicit conditions (i.e., memorizing sentences and answering questions about the location of words in the sentences).

These differential relationships between aptitude complexes and psycholinguistic processing conditions, such as pedagogical tasks or instructional treatments, have significant implications for the language learning classroom (Robinson, 2002). For example, by profiling the strengths and weaknesses learners have in the abilities that contribute to language learning aptitude it should then be possible to match these profiles to tasks and input processing conditions that draw on the abilities learners are strong in, thereby optimizing their chances of success in L2 instructional programs.

Working memory. Another individual difference closely linked to attention, working memory is usually described as the processes used to temporarily store and manipulate information needed for both known and novel cognitive tasks and is discussed in Chapter 26 by John Williams in this volume. Working memory is often considered to be a central component of language aptitude (Miyake and Friedman, 1998; Robinson, 2001, 2002, 2005a; Skehan, 2002), and the relationship between working memory and attention has been a key area of research in SLA, with working memory capacity closely related to comprehension and processing skills. Although there are a number of working memory models (Baddeley and Hitch, 1974; Conway *et al.*, 2005; Engle, 2001; Miyake and Shah, 1999) defining the construct in variable ways, each model identifies a form of executive attention or coordination. This executive component supervises the distribution of attentional resources when more than one cognitive task or task dimension requires attention, maintaining access to relevant information and blocking access to irrelevant information (Kane *et al.*, 2007).

Considering the complexity and cognitive demands involved in second language learning, the link between working memory capacity and attention is an important one, and a number of empirical studies have demonstrated a connection between them. In an exploratory small-scale study, Mackey *et al.* (2002) examined the relationship between both phonological and verbal working memory and noticing, finding that learners who reported lower levels of noticing of questions during task performance also had low working memory capacities. Learners with high working memory capacities were more likely to have noticed more questions. Mackey *et al.* (2010) investigated the relationship between working memory and modified output during interaction. Because modified output can occur following corrective feedback on an utterance in interaction, the idea is that the learner must have, at some point, attended to the corrective feedback and in this study, working memory scores significantly predicted the production of modified output by learners (see also Mackey and Sachs, 2011, for similar working memory-learning patterns with older adults). Within instructional contexts, learners' individual capabilities to store and manipulate information, as well as manage and devote attentional resources to competing cognitive demands and suppress irrelevant information, are likely to be significant factors affecting learner success.

Tasks in language learning

Tasks are central to language learning in communicative classrooms. Arguments for their validity as a pedagogical tool come partially from the interactionist literature (see Mackey and Gass, 2006; Gass and Mackey, 2007; for reviews) which, in turn, relies heavily on the construct of attention and attention-drawing activities. As Schmidt noted, in summarizing conclusions drawn by Ericsson and Simon (1984), and others, "Task demands are a powerful determinant of what is noticed" in experimental settings, "and provide one of the basic arguments that what is learned is what is noticed ... the information committed to memory is essentially the information that must be heeded in order to carry out a task" (1990, p. 143). The extent to which this is true of second language learning tasks in classrooms is an important issue for materials and instructional design. Space limitations prevent us from a thorough discussion of tasks, and findings from research into their effects on learning, but, suffice it to say, proposals concerning task characteristics, task complexity and task sequencing (see e.g., Candlin, 1987; Robinson, 2001, 2007; Skehan, 1996, 1998) have proven to be central in discussions of classroom instruction. For example, are there certain task types or even feedback types that might result in implicit or explicit knowledge? In what way is it useful to manipulate the conceptual demands of tasks so as to direct attention to one part of language as opposed to another? What task characteristics promote output and noticing of forms in the input, and to what extent do attestations of noticing lead to greater retention and learning of those forms?

Feedback in interactive settings is an important factor that may guide attention since, in principle, feedback may focus attention on problematic parts of an utterance. Thirty years ago, Schachter (1981) engaged in a discussion of the role of feedback types and proposed hand signals that focused on specific error types. The underlying principle is similar to today's activities which focus on the extent to which learners can be trained to understand the intent of feedback and understand the function of feedback. Connecting task demands and attention to feedback, Robinson (2005b) has argued that complex tasks (compared to simpler counterpart tasks) lead learners to attend more closely to information provided in task input (such as corrective feedback), with the consequence that complex tasks will result in more uptake and retention of attended input than simple task versions. A final issue of instructional relevance is the extent to which preparatory attention, provided during planning time, facilitates task-based learning, and whether it is better to provide this before (pre-task) or during (within-task) task performance. Ellis (2009), provides a comprehensive summary of findings for this research to date.

Future directions

The area of attention and awareness in second language acquisition is growing in importance in second language research. Many of the areas discussed in this section are continuations and outgrowths of current research. Below we provide some suggestions for new research directions to continue to move the field forward.

(1) *Do different techniques for focusing attention on form draw on different sets of cognitive abilities?* The contribution of individual differences in cognitive abilities to attend to, be aware of, and successfully learn forms and meaning is an ongoing and important area of research, particularly regarding instructional attempts to make forms and meanings salient to learners. A research area of particular interest is whether different techniques for focusing attention on form (Doughty and Williams, 1998; Long and Robinson, 1998) draw on different sets of cognitive abilities. For example, do different sets of abilities promote successful attention to and noticing of recasts of problematic learner utterances, compared to the abilities that are involved in understanding metalinguistic explanations of the error? Research has shown that working memory capacity is related to the ability to notice and use the negative feedback provided in interaction (Mackey *et al.*, 2002, Mackey and Sachs, 2011). Learners with greater working memory capacity profit more from this feedback technique, and are also better able to attend to, notice and learn aspects of grammar while processing input for meaning. Findings such as these (see e.g., Sagarra, 2007; Trofimovich *et al.*, 2007) are prompting new proposals for comprehensive aptitude batteries (Robinson, 2002, 2005a, 2007) that sample the cognitive abilities learners draw on under a range of input processing conditions, and in response to a range of focus on form techniques, which aim to promote attention to

and noticing of instructionally targeted forms. For example, some learners may be more "prime-able" than others, such that previous recasts more successfully prompt later recollection, use and so longer-term retention of the recast forms in subsequent episodes inviting their use (McDonough and Trofimovitch, 2008; Robinson, 2005a). The prospect that this research offers, is that—if identified—the cognitive abilities that promote attention to, noticing and retention of form-meaning connections under differing task and processing conditions can be profiled in populations of learners, and instructional options can subsequently be matched to these profiles in order to optimize the probability of more successful allocation of attention to, noticing and elaborative processing of forms and their meanings (cf., Robinson, 2010b; Snow, 1994).

(2) *How do we increase the sensitivity of behavioral tests of the role of attention and awareness in learning?* Future research will likely adopt increasingly sensitive measures of the contents of awareness, and explore new methodologies for operationalizing this complex and multi-faceted construct. For example, Rebuschat (2008) has used, for the first time, subjective behavioral tests, such as confidence estimates and source attributions, described earlier, to examine the extent of implicit versus explicit L2 learning. Neurophysiological measures of physical changes in brain states will also be used increasingly to complement the behavioral and introspective methods for studying the relationship of attention and awareness to learning. Studies such as that of Godfroid *et al.* (2010) reported below, provide an example of how such converging behavioral and neurophysiological evidence for the influence of attention and awareness on L2 learning may be gathered in future studies.

(3) *How do we research situated and distributed cognition perspectives on the roles of attention and awareness?* Cognition, learning, and attention are always situated processes, occurring in sociocultural contexts which can be analyzed at different levels of granularity in instructional settings (Snow, 1994). This raises the question of the extent to which these contexts can be consistently reproduced (for purposes of instructional accountability, planning, and management) and matched to the abilities learners bring to them. One option is to reproduce instructional contexts by delivering tasks having the same or similar characteristics, and research the ways these task characteristics make demands on the abilities learners bring to them, and the consequences of these task characteristic—ability determinant coordinates for success or failure in learning (Ackerman and Ciancolo, 2002). Another option is to research how attention and noticing are deployed across sequences of such tasks, such that the distribution of attention and learning opportunities across task affordances is maximized. Sequences of tasks, appropriately distributed across timescales, have the capacity to afford opportunities to prime and prompt recollection of previously experienced language related episodes, thus strengthening memory for them. The theoretical constructs adopted in research into the role of "remindings" in other areas of instructional design (see Ross and Bradshaw, 1994) will be important to consider in SLA research into these issues.

(4) *Combining first-person verbal reports and physiological measures to study attention and awareness during second language acquisition.* A final issue for research that we raise here is important for operationally evaluating the results of future research into all the other issues raised above into the roles of attention and awareness in instructed SLA. We described the limitations of verbal reports as measures of attention to and awareness of learning targets above. Verbal reports are unlikely to faithfully reflect everything that learners are attending to and aware of. Consequently, supplementing these reports with physiological indices of on-line attention to learning targets such as eye movements (Scheiter and Van Gog, 2009), is a valuable way of attempting to establish more reliable, converging evidence for the roles of attention and

awareness in learning. Eye-tracking lines of research provide one such example of a converging physiological index of learning processes in what follows.

One might assume that longer length of eye gaze fixation indicates greater effort, and awareness of the fixated content (the eye-mind assumption; e.g., Reichle *et al.*, 2006). Godfroid *et al.* (2010) report the first SLA research to explore this procedure in the context of noticing. In their study of incidental learning of vocabulary, participants read short 9–11 line paragraphs on a computer screen for comprehension purposes (participants were told the aim of the exercise was to compare how people read on a computer screen and read on paper). Eight pseudo word target forms were embedded in the paragraphs. Following a post-exposure recognition test of knowledge of the pseudo words, Godfroid *et al.* used a stimulated recall procedure (Gass and Mackey, 2000) to elicit comments from learners about the words in the post-tests, and memories of their occurrence while reading. Accurate scores on the multiple choice post-test showed some learners recognized words they had been exposed to, and understood their meaning. The stimulated recall data also indicated that some learners remembered reading the target words, and provided information about how they dealt with them during the reading task. Godfroid *et al.* also collected information about four different measures of eye fixation time for the pseudo words and the immediately following words (the *spillover region*). Statistical analyses (reported in Godfroid, 2010) revealed that the total amount of time learners spent reading a pseudo word predicted the recognition of that pseudo word on the post-test, thereby lending support to the view that attention plays a crucial role in encoding stimuli in memory. However, some participants recognized words they had been exposed to (performing accurately on the post-test), even though fixation times were quite low (indicating lack of increased awareness). These findings led to the conclusion that the "mere perception of the target words sufficed to create a memory trace that enabled participants to discriminate them" (p. 185). This suggests that detection, not noticing, led to learning, as measured by post-test recognition of the words. The problem here, however, is in establishing a boundary of eye fixation time above which one can conclude attention was accompanied by awareness, and below which it was not. Although it might be possible to establish such a boundary for an individual by using a combination of the verbal reports, test performance, and eye tracking data, such an eye fixation threshold would likely differ across individuals. Furthermore, this type of threshold could possibly vary within individuals, given the levels of variation in the complexity of processing they are engaged in on any two tasks. As Godfroid *et al.* (2010) suggest, these remain important issues for future research.

Note

* Authors' note: This chapter benefited significantly from a great deal of insightful feedback and helpful suggestions provided by Aline Godfroid and editing assistance by Kaitlyn Tagarelli. Any errors that remain are the sole responsibility of the authors.

References

Ackerman, P. and Ciancolo, A. (2002). Ability and task determinants of complex task performance. *Journal of Experimental Psychology: Applied, 8*, 194–208.

Alanen, R. (1995). Input enhancement and rule presentation in second language acquisition. In R. Schmidt (Ed.), *Attention and awareness in foreign language learning and teaching* (pp. 259–302). Honolulu, HI: University of Hawai'i Press.

Allport, A. (1989). Visual attention. In M. Posner (Ed.), *Foundations of cognitive science*.MA: MIT Press: Cambridge.

Anderson, J. R. (1993). *Rules of the mind*. Hillsdale, NJ: Erlbaum.

Arabski, J. and Woltaszek, A. (Eds.) (2010). *Neurolinguistic and psycholinguistic perspectives on SLA*. Clevedon, UK: Multilingual Matters.

Baars, B. (2003). Introduction: Treating consciousness as a variable—The fading taboo. In B. Baars, W. Banks, and J. Newman (Eds.), *Essential sources in the scientific study of consciousness* (pp. 1–10). Cambridge, MA: MIT Press.

Baddeley, A. D. and Hitch, G. J. (1974). Working memory. In G. H. Bower (Ed.), *The psychology of learning and motivation* (Vol. 8, pp. 47–90). New York: Academic Press.

Beck, D., Rees, G., Frith, C., and Lavie, N. (2001). Neural correlates of change detection and change blindness. *Nature Neuroscience, 4*, 645–650.

Bell, P. and Collins, L. (2009). "It's vocabulary"/"It's gender": Learner awareness and incidental learning. *Language Awareness, 18*, 277–293.

Bialystok, E. (1978). A theoretical model of second language learning. *Language Learning, 28*, 69–83.

Bordag, D. and Pechmann, T. (2007). Factors influencing L2 gender processing. *Bilingualism: Language and Cognition, 10*(3), 299–314.

Bordag, D., Opitz, A., and Pechmann, T. (2006). Gender processing in L1 and L2: The role of noun termination. *Journal of Experimental Psychology: Learning, Memory, and Cognition, 32*(5), 1090–1101.

Bowles, M. (2010). *The think-aloud controversy in second language research*. New York: Routledge.

Candlin, C. (1987). Toward task-based learning. In C. Candlin and D. Murphy (Eds.), *Language learning tasks* (pp. 5–22). Englewood Cliffs, NJ: Prentice-Hall.

Carroll, J. B. (1973). Implications of aptitude test research and psycholinguistic theory for foreign-language teaching. *Linguistics, 112*, 5–14.

Carroll, J. B. (1981). Twenty-five years of research on foreign language aptitude. In K. C. Diller (Ed.), *Individual differences and universals in language learning aptitude* (pp. 83–118). Rowley, MA: Newbury House.

Carroll, S. (1999). Input and SLA: Adults' sensitivity to different sorts of cues to French gender. *Language Learning, 49*, 37–92.

Chaudron, C. (1985). Intake: On models and methods for discovering learners processing of input. *Studies in Second Language Acquisition, 7*, 1–14.

Chee, M. W. (2005). Brain differences between bilinguals of differing proficiency: An empirical look at an emotional issue. *Singapore Medical Journal, 46*, 49–53.

Chee, M. W. (2009). fMR-Adaptation and the bilingual brain. *Brain and Language, 109*, 75–79.

Conway, C. and Christiansen, M. (2006). Statistical learning within and between modalities. *Psychological Science, 17*, 905–912.

Corder, S. P. (1967). The significance of learners' errors. *International Review of Applied Linguistics, 5*, 161–170.

Cowan, N. (1988). Evolving conceptions of memory storage, selective attention, and their mutual constraints within the human information processing system. *Psychological Bulletin, 104*, 163–191.

Cowan, N. (1995). *Attention and memory: An integrated framework*. Oxford: Oxford University Press.

de Diego-Balaguer, R. and Lopez-Barroso, D. (2010). Cognitive and neural mechanisms sustaining rule-learning from speech. *Language Learning, 60* (Supplement 1), 151–182.

deGraaff, R. (1997). The eXperanto experiment: effects of explicit instruction on second language acquisition. *Studies in Second Language Acquisition, 19*, 249–275.

DeKeyser, R. (2000). The robustness of critical period effects in second language acquisition. *Studies in Second Language Acquisition, 22*, 499–533.

Dienes, Z., Altmann, G., Kwan, L., and Goode, A. (1995). Unconscious knowledge of artificial grammars is applied strategically. *Journal of Experimental Psychology. Learning, Memory and Cognition, 21*, 1322–1338.

Dienes, Z. and Scott, R. (2005). Measuring unconscious knowledge: Distinguishing structural knowledge and judgment knowledge. *Psychological Research, 69*, 338–351.

Dörnyei, Z. (2005). *The psychology of the language learner: Individual differences in second language acquisition*. Mahwah, NJ: Lawrence Erlbaum Associates.

Dörnyei, Z. and Skehan, P. (2003). Individual differences in second language learning. In C. J. Doughty and M. H. Long (Eds.), *The handbook of second language acquisition* (pp. 589–630). Malden, MA: Blackwell.

Doughty, C. and Williams, J. (1998). Pedagogical choices in focus on form. In C. Doughty and J. Williams (Eds.), *Focus on form in classroom second language acquisition* (pp. 197–262). New York: Cambridge University Press.

Ellis, N. C. (1993). Rules and instances in foreign language learning: Interactions of explicit and implicit knowledge. *European Journal of Cognitive Psychology, 5*, 289–318.

Ellis, N. C. (1996). Sequencing and SLA: Phonological memory, chunking and points of order. *Studies in Second Language Acquisition, 18*, 91–126.

Ellis, N. C. (1998). Emergentism, connectionism and language learning. *Language Learning*, *48*, 631–664.

Ellis, N. C. (2002). Frequency effects in language processing: A review with implications for theories of implicit and explicit acquisition. *Studies in Second Language Acquisition*, *24*, 143–188.

Ellis, N. C. (2005). At the interface: How explicit knowledge affects implicit language learning. *Studies in Second Language Acquisition*, *27*, 305–352.

Ellis, N. C. (2006a). Language acquisition as rational contingency learning. *Applied Linguistics*, *27*, 1–24.

Ellis, N. C. (2006b). Selective attention and transfer phenomena in L2 acquisition: Contingency, cue competition, salience, interference, overshadowing, blocking and perceptual learning. *Applied Linguistics*, *27*, 164–194.

Ellis, N. C. (2008). The dynamics of second language emergence: Cycles of language use, language change, and language acquisition. *The Modern Language Journal*, *92*, 232–249.

Ellis, R. (1993). A theory of instructed second language acquisition. In N. C. Ellis (Ed.), *Implicit and explicit learning of languages* (pp. 79–114). San Diego, CA: Academic Press.

Ellis, R. (Ed.), (2001). *Form-focused instruction and second language learning*. Malden, MA: Blackwell.

Ellis, R. (2009). The differential effects of three types of task planning on the fluency, accuracy and complexity of L2 oral production. *Applied Linguistics*, *30*, 474–509.

Engle, R. W. (2001). What is working memory capacity? In H. L. Roediger, J. S. Nairne, I. Neath, and A. M. Suprenant (Eds.), *The nature of remembering: Essays in honor of Robert G. Crowder* (pp. 297–314). Washington, D.C.: American Psychological Association Press.

Fabbro, F. (1999). *The neurolinguistics of bilingualism*. Hove: Psychology Press.

Felix-Brasdefer, J. C. (2008). Perceptions of refusals to invitations: Exploring the minds of foreign language learners. *Language Awareness*, *17*, 195–211.

Franceschina, F. (2005). *Fossilized second language grammars: the acquisition of grammatical gender*. Amsterdam and Philadelphia: J. Benjamins.

Gass, S. (1988). Integrating research areas: A framework for second language studies. *Applied Linguistics*, *9*, 198–217.

Gass, S. (1997). *Input, interaction, and the second language learner*. Mahwah, NJ: Erlbaum.

Gass, S. M. and Mackey, A. (2000). *Stimulated recall methodology in second language research*. Mahwah, NJ: Erlbaum.

Gass, S. M. and Mackey, A. (2006). Input, interaction and output: An overview. *AILA Review*, *19*, 3–17.

Gass, S., Svetics, I., and Lemelin, S. (2003). Differential effects of attention. *Language Learning*, *53*, 497–545.

Godfroid, A. (2010). Cognitive processes in second language acquisition: The role of noticing, attention and awareness in processing words in written L2 input. Unpublished PhD dissertation. Vrije Universiteit Brussels, Belgium.

Godfroid, A., Housen, A., and Boers, F. (2010). A procedure for testing the noticing hypothesis in the context of vocabulary acquisition. In M. Putz and L. Sicola (Eds.), *Cognitive processing in second language acquisition: Inside the learner's mind* (pp. 169–197). Amsterdam: John Benjamins.

Goldschneider, J. and DeKeyser, R. (2001). Explaining the "natural order of L2 morpheme acquisition" in English: A meta-analysis of multiple determinants. *Language Learning*, *51*, 1–50.

Gomez, R. and Gerken, L. (1999). Artificial grammar learning by 1-year olds leads to specific and abstract knowledge. *Cognition*, *70*, 109–135.

Green, D. (2003). The neural basis of the lexicon and the grammar in L2 acquisition. In R. van Hout, A. Hulk, F. Kuiken, and R. Towell (Eds.), *The interface between syntax and the lexicon in second language acquisition* (pp. 197–218). Amsterdam: Benjamins.

Green, D., Crinion, J., and Price, C. (2006). Convergence, degeneracy and control. *Language Learning*, *56* (Supplement 1), 99–125.

Guillelmon, D. and Grosjean, F. (2001). The gender marking effect in spoken word recognition: The case of bilinguals. *Memory & Cognition*, *29*, 503–511.

Holmes, V. M. and Dejean de la Batie, B. (1999). Assignment of grammatical gender by native speakers and foreign learners of French. *Applied Psycholinguistics*, *20*, 479–506.

Indefrey, P., Hagoort, P., Herzog, H., Seitz, R., and Brown, C. (2001). Syntactic processing in left prefrontal cortex is independent of lexical meaning. *Neuroimage*, *14*, 546–555.

Izumi, S. (2003). Comprehension and production processes in second language learning: In search of the psycholinguistic rationale of the output hypothesis. *Applied Linguistics*, *24*, 168–192.

Jiang, N. (2004). Morphological insensitivity in second language processing. *Applied Psycholinguistics*, *25*, 603–634.

Kahneman, D. (1973). *Attention and effort*. Englewood Cliffs, NJ: Prentice Hall.

Kormos, J. (2006). *Speech production in second language acquisition*. Mahwah, NJ: Erlbaum.

Krashen, S. (1982). *Principles and practice in second language acquisition*. Oxford: Pergamon.

Lardiere, D. (1998). Case and tense in the "fossilized" steady-state. *Second Language Research, 14*, 1–26.

Leow, R. (2000). A study of the role of awareness in foreign language behavior: Aware versus unaware learners. *Studies in Second Language Acquisition, 22*, 557–584.

Leow, R. (2002). Models, attention and awareness in SLA. *Studies in Second Language Acquisition, 24*, 113–119.

Leow, R. P. (2007). Input in the L2 classroom: An attentional perspective on receptive practice. In R. M. DeKeyser (Ed.), *Practice in second language: Perspectives from applied linguistics and cognitive psychology* (pp. 21–50). Cambridge: Cambridge University Press.

Leow, R. and Morgan-Short, K. (2004). To think aloud or not to think aloud: The issue of reactivity in SLA research methodology. *Studies in Second Language Acquisition, 26*, 35–58.

Lew-Williams, C. (2009). Real-time processing of gender-marked articles by native and non-native Spanish-speaking children and adults. PhD Dissertation. Stanford University.

Logan, G. D. (1988). Toward an instance theory of automatization. *Psychological Review, 95*, 492–527.

Long, M. H. (1991). Focus on form: A design feature in language teaching methodology. In K. de Bot, D. Coste, R. Ginsberg, and C. Kramsch (Eds.), *Foreign language research in cross-cultural perspective* (pp. 39–52). Amsterdam: Benjamins.

Long, M. H. and Robinson, P. (1998). Focus on form: Theory, research, and practice. In C. Doughty and J. Williams (Eds.), *Focus on form in classroom second language acquisition* (pp. 15–41). New York: Cambridge University Press.

Mackey, A. (2006). Feedback, noticing and instructed second language learning. *Applied Linguistics, 27*, 405–430.

Mackey, A., Adams, R., Stafford, C., and Winke, P. (2010). Exploring the relationship between modified output and working memory capacity. *Language Learning, 60*, 501–533.

Mackey, A., Gass, S., and McDonough, K. (2000). How do learners perceive interactional feedback? *Studies in Second Language Acquisition, 22*, 471–497.

Mackey, A., Philp, J., Egi, T., Fujii, A., and Tatsumi, T. (2002). Individual differences in working memory, noticing of interactional feedback and L2 development. In P. Robinson (Ed.), *Individual differences and instructed language learning* (pp. 181–210). Amsterdam: Benjamins.

Mackey, A. and Sachs, R. (2011). Older learners in SLA research: A first look at working memory, feedback, and L2 development. *Language Learning*.

MacWhinney, B. (1997). Implicit and explicit processes. *Studies in Second Language Acquisition, 19*, 277–281.

McDonough, K. and Tromfimovich, P. (2008). *Using priming methods in second language research*. London: Routledge.

McLaughlin, B., Rossman, T., and McLeod, B. (1988). Second language learning: An information-processing perspective. *Language Learning, 33*, 135–158.

Merikle, P. and Reingold, E. (1991). Comparing direct (explicit) and indirect (implicit) measures to study unconscious memory. *Journal of Experimental Psychology: Learning, Memory and Cognition, 17*, 224–233.

Miyake, A. and Shah, P. (Eds.) (1999). *Models of working memory: Mechanisms of active maintenance and executive control*. New York: Cambridge University Press.

Neumann, O. (1987). Beyond capacity: A functional view of attention. In H. Heuer and A. Sanders (Eds.), *Perspectives on perception and action* (pp. 361–394). Berlin: Springer.

Paradis, M. (2009). *Declarative and procedural determinants of second languages*. Amsterdam: Benjamins.

Perruchet, P. (2008). Implicit learning. In H. L. Roediger III (Ed.), *Learning and memory: Cognitive psychology of memory* (Vol. 2, pp. 597–621). Oxford: Elsevier.

Perruchet, P. and Pacteau, C. (1990). Synthetic grammar learning: Implicit rule abstraction or fragmentary knowledge? *Journal of Experimental Psychology: General, 119*, 264–275.

Philp, J. (2003). Constraints on "noticing the gap": Nonnative speakers' noticing of recasts in NS-NNS interaction. *Studies in Second Language Acquisition, 25*, 99–126.

Polio, C. (2007). A history of input enhancement: Defining an evolving concept. In C. Gascoigne (Ed.), *Assessing the impact of input enhancement in second language education* (pp. 1–17). Stillwater, OK: New Forums Press.

Posner, M. and Petersen, S. (1990). The attention system of the human brain. *Annual Review of Neuroscience, 13*, 25–42.

Pothos, E. (2007). Theories of artificial grammar learning. *Psychological Bulletin, 133*, 227–244.

Prévost, P. and White, L. (2000). Missing surface inflection or impairment in second language acquisition? Evidence from tense and agreement. *Second Language Research, 16*, 103–133.

Raz, A. and Buhle, J. (2006). Typologies of attentional networks. *Nature Reviews Neuroscience, 7*, 367–380.

Reber, A. S. (1967). Implicit learning of artificial grammars. *Journal of Verbal Learning and Verbal Behavior, 6*, 855–863.

Reber, A. S. (1989). Implicit learning and tacit knowledge. *Journal of Experimental Psychology: General, 118,* 219–235.

Reber, A. S. (1993). *Implicit learning and tacit knowledge: An essay on the cognitive unconscious.* Oxford: Oxford University Press.

Rebuschat, P. (2008). Implicit learning of natural language syntax. Unpublished PhD dissertation. University of Cambridge, UK.

Rebuschat, P. and Williams, J. (2010). Implicit learning of second language syntax. Manuscript submitted for publication.

Reichle, E., Pollatsek, A., and Rayner, K. (2006). E-Z reader: A cognitive-control, serial-attention model of eye-movement behavior. *Cognitive Systems Research, 7,* 4–22.

Rescorla, R. A. and Wagner, A. R. (1972). A theory of Pavlovian conditioning: Variations in the effectiveness of reinforcement and non reinforcement. In A. Black and W. Prokasy (Eds.), *Classical conditioning II: Current theory and research* (pp. 64–99). New York: Appleton-Century Crofts.

Robinson, P. (1995). Attention, memory and the "noticing" hypothesis. *Language Learning, 45,* 283–331.

Robinson, P. (1996). Learning simple and complex second language rules under implicit, incidental, rule search and instructed conditions. *Studies in Second Language Acquisition, 18,* 27–67.

Robinson, P. (1997a). Individual differences and the fundamental similarity of implicit and explicit adult second language learning. *Language Learning, 47,* 45–99.

Robinson, P. (1997b). Generalizability and automaticity of second language learning under implicit, incidental, enhanced and instructed conditions. *Studies in Second Language Acquisition, 19,* 223–247.

Robinson, P. (2001). Task complexity, task difficulty, and task production: Exploring interactions in a componential framework. *Applied Linguistics, 22,* 27–57.

Robinson, P. (2002). Learning conditions, aptitude complexes and SLA: A framework for research and pedagogy. In P. Robinson (Ed.), *Individual Differences and Instructed Language Learning* (pp. 113–133). Amsterdam: Benjamins.

Robinson, P. (2003). Attention and memory during SLA. In C. Doughty and M. Long (Eds.), *Handbook of second language acquisition* (pp. 631–662). Oxford: Blackwell.

Robinson, P. (2005a). Aptitude and second language acquisition. *Annual Review of Applied Linguistics, 25,* 46–73.

Robinson, P. (2005b). Cognitive complexity and task sequencing: A review of studies in a componential framework for second language task design. *International Review of Applied Linguistics, 43,* 1–32.

Robinson, P. (2007). Task complexity, theory of mind, and intentional reasoning: Effects on L2 speech production, interaction, uptake and perceptions of task difficulty. *International Review of Applied Linguistics, 45,* 193–213.

Robinson, P. (2010a). Implicit artificial grammar, and incidental natural second language learning: How comparable are they?. *Language Learning, 60* (Supplement 1), 245–264.

Robinson, P. (2010b). Situating and distributing cognition across task demands: The SSARC model of pedagogic task sequencing. In M. Putz and L. Sicola (Eds.), *Cognitive processing in second language acquisition: Inside the learner's mind* (pp. 243–268). Amsterdam: Benjaimins.

Rodriguez-Fornells, A., de Diego-Balaguer, R., and Munte, T. (2006). Executive control in bilingual processing. *Language Learning, 56* (Supplement 1), 133–190.

Ross, B. H. and Bradshaw, G. (1994). Encoding effects of remindings. *Memory & Cognition, 22* (5), 591–605.

Sachs, R. and Polio, C. (2007). Learners' uses of two types of written feedback on an L2 writing revision task. *Studies in Second Language Acquisition, 29,* 67–100.

Saffran, J., Johnson, E., Aslin, R., and Newport, E. (1999). Statistical learning of tone sequences by human infants and adults. *Cognition, 70,* 27–52.

Sagarra, N. (2007). From CALL to face-to-face interaction: The effect of computer delivered recasts and working memory on L2 development. In A. Mackey (Ed.), *Conversational interaction in second language acquisition* (pp. 229–248). Oxford: Oxford University Press.

Sanz, C., Lin, H.-J., Lado, B., Bowden, H. W., and Stafford, C. A. (2009). Concurrent verbalizations, pedagogical implications and reactivity: Two CALL studies. *Language Learning, 59,* 33–71.

Sanders, A. (1998). *Elements of human performance.* Mahwah, NJ: Lawrence Erlbaum.

Schachter, D. (1987). Implicit memory: History and current status. *Journal of Experimental Psychology: Learning, Memory and Cognition, 13,* 501–518.

Schachter, J. (1981). The hand signal system. *TESOL Quarterly, 15,* 125–138.

Scheiter, K. and Van Gog, T. (2009). Using eye tracking in applied research to study and stimulate the processing of information from multi-representational sources. *Applied Cognitive Psychology, 23,* 1209–1214.

Schmidt, R. (1990). The role of consciousness in second language learning. *Applied Linguistics, 11,* 129–158.

Schmidt, R. (1995). Consciousness and foreign language learning: A tutorial on the role of attention and awareness in learning. In R. Schmidt (Ed.), *Attention and awareness in foreign language learning and teaching* (pp. 1–64). Honolulu, HI: University of Hawai'i Press.

Schmidt, R. and Frota, S. (1986). Developing basic conversational ability in a second language: A case study of an adult learner of Portuguese. In R. Day (Ed.), *Talking to learn: Conversation in second language learning* (pp. 237–322). Rowley, MA: Newbury House.

Schuchert, S. (2004). The neurobiology of attention. In J. Schumann (Ed.), *The neurobiology of learning: Perspectives from second language acquisition* (pp. 143–174). Mahwah, NJ: Erlbaum.

Schumann, J. (Ed.) (2004). *The neurobiology of learning: Perspectives from second language acquisition.* Mahwah, NJ: Erlbaum.

Shanks, D. and Johnstone, T. (1998). Implicit knowledge in sequential learning tasks. In M. Stadler and P. Frensch (Eds.), *Handbook of implicit learning* (pp. 533–572).Thousand Oaks, CA: Sage.

Shanks, D. R. and St. John, M. F. (1994). Characteristics of dissociable human systems. *Behavioral and Brain Sciences, 17,* 367–447.

Sharwood-Smith, M. (1981). Consciousness-raising and the second language learner. *Applied Linguistics, 2,* 159–168.

Sharwood-Smith, M. (1991). Speaking to many minds: On the relevance of different types of language information for the L2 learner. *Second Language Research, 7,* 118–132.

Shiffrin, R. and Schneider, W. (1977). Controlled and automatic human information processing II: Perceptual learning, automatic attending and a general theory. *Psychological Review, 84,* 127–190.

Simard, D. and Wong, W. (2001). Alertness, orientation and detection: The conceptualization of attentional functions in SLA. *Studies in Second Language Acquisition, 23,* 103–124.

Skehan, P. (1996). A framework for the implementation of task-based instruction. *Applied Linguistics, 17,* 38–62.

Skehan, P. (1998). *A cognitive approach to language learning.* Oxford: Oxford University Press.

Skehan, P. (2009). Modeling second language performance: Integrating complexity, accuracy, fluency and lexis. *Applied Linguistics, 30,* 510–532.

Snow, R. E. (1994). Abilities in academic tasks. In R. Sternberg and R. Wagner (Eds.), *Mind in context: Interactionist perspectives on human intelligence* (pp. 3–37). New York: Cambridge University Press.

Sprouse, R. (1998). Some notes on the relationship between inflectional morphology and parameter setting in first and second language acquisition. In M. Beck (Ed.), *Morphology and its interfaces in second language knowledge* (pp. 41–67). Amsterdam: Benjamins.

Swain, M. (1995). Three functions of output in second language learning. In G. Cook and B. Seidlhoffer (Eds.), *Principle and practice in applied linguistics: Studies in honor of H. G. Widdowson* (pp. 125–144). Oxford: Oxford University Press.

Swain, M. and Lapkin, S. (1995). Problems in output and the cognitive processes they generate. *Applied Linguistics, 16,* 370–391.

Tomlin, R. and Villa, V. (1994). Attention in cognitive science and second language acquisition. *Studies in Second Language Acquisition, 15,* 183–203.

Trofimovich, P., Ammar, A., and Gatbonton, E. (2007). How effective are recasts? The role of attention, memory and analytical ability. In A. Mackey (Ed.), *Conversational interaction in second language acquisition* (pp. 171–196). Oxford: Oxford University Press.

Tunney, R., and Shanks, D. (1993). Subjective measures of awareness and implicit cognition. *Memory & Cognition, 31,* 1060–1071.

Warden, M., Lapkin, S., Swain, M., and Hart, D. (1995). Adolescent language learners on a three month exchange: Evidence from their diaries. *Foreign Language Annals, 28,* 537–549.

Weiskrantz, L. (1997). *Consciousness lost and found: A neuropsychological exploation.* New York: Oxford University Press.

Wickens, C. (1984). Processing resources and attention. In R. Parasuraman and D. Davies (Eds.), *Varieties of attention* (pp. 63–101). New York: Academic Press.

Wickens, C. (2007). Attention to the second language. *International Review of Applied Linguistics, 45,* 177–192.

Williams, J. (1999). Memory, attention and inductive learning. *Studies in Second Language Acquisition, 21,* 1–48.

Williams, J. (2005). Learning without awareness. *Studies in Second Language Acquisition, 27,* 269–304.

Williams, J. (2009). Implicit learning in second language learning. In W. Ritchie and T. J. Bhatia (Eds.), *The new handbook of second language acquisition* (pp. 319–353). Bingley, UK: Emerald Publishing.

Williams, J. (2010). Initial incidental learning of word order regularities: Is it just sequence learning?. *Language Learning, 60* (Supplement 1), 221–244.

16

Input processing

Bill VanPatten

Historical discussion

Input processing emerged as a field of inquiry in the mid-1980s. The central question it sought to address was "What linguistic data do learners process in the input and what constrains/guides that processing?" As such, research on input processing was a natural outgrowth of the importance given to input within the field of second language acquisition (SLA) during the 1970s and 1980s. At that time, research tended to focus on how input was negotiated by learners and/or modified by other speakers (e.g., Hatch, 1983; Long, 1983; and the many papers in Gass and Madden, 1985). The central concern of the time was what made input comprehensible and thus useable by second language (L2) learners. An underlying assumption of the research seemed to be that if input was comprehensible, learners would comprehend it correctly and get good linguistic data from that input (see, for example, Krashen, 1982).

But it became increasingly clear that although negotiation was probably important to SLA more generally, it was insufficient as a construct to account for acquisition. Something internal to the learner was interacting with input in particular ways, as some kind of filter or set of strategies that kept input from being completely useful. As I asked in the mid-1980s, why don't learners seem to pick up things that they hear in another person's question or statement, particularly when that statement is relatively short and should not tax working memory limitations (VanPatten, 1984a)? The reader is invited to examine the following interchange (E = experimenter, L = learner; all errors are original to learner):

E: ¿Cómo están ellos? "How are they?"
L: Ellos son contentos, "They're happy."
E: Y ellos, ¿cómo están?, "And them. How are they?"
L: Son contento también. "They're happy, too."

(from VanPatten, 1984a, p. 92)

Only *estar* can be used as a copular verb with predicate adjectives possessing the feature [+perfective], whereas *ser* is used with predicates that are [-perfective] in nature. In the above interchange, the experimenter uses the correct copular verb (*estar*) in Spanish to express a condition [+perfective] but the learner uses the incorrect copular (*ser*). Note that in his second question, the experimenter follows standard conventions for emphasis and change of topic and moves the copular to the end of the sentence, that is, *¿cómo están?* This second question is not long and there is no new information that the learner has to attend to: both speakers used the same words throughout the interchange. What is more, in the E's second question the copular verb now has two things going for it in terms of perceptual salience: it is in final position and it carries strong stress. Why can't the learner pick up the copular verb during this interchange? Is the learner even paying attention to it? If not, why not? As this example illustrates, exposure to a linguistic item in the input does not mean that item gets acquired at that time.

Work on child first language (L1) acquisition was also suggestive that learners somehow filter input (e.g., Bever, 1970; Slobin, 1966). For example, children learning their L1s seemed to misinterpret passive structures ("The lion was killed by the tiger") as active structures ("The lion killed the tiger"). What this suggested was that during acquisition, even though the input to children was "comprehensible," they didn't comprehend it correctly. In 1974, Ervin-Tripp demonstrated with child L2 learners that even if literal translations of passives existed in two languages (in her study, French and English) children who already have passives in their L1 do not use the syntactic information they possess to interpret passives early in their acquisition of the L2. Just like L1 children, they would misinterpret passive sentences as active sentences. Thus, even though English and French have word for word passive equivalents, her learners interpreted the L2 passives as actives, ignoring all the passive cues in the sentences.

The point here is that in the 1970s and 1980s, L2 researchers were looking at the role of input globally in terms of input modification and negotiation and not psycholinguistically in terms of processing. They were not asking the more micro-level question of how learners comprehended individual sentences and what elements of sentences learners attended to. Input processing as an area of research emerged to address this gap in the field.

To be sure, input processing has never been viewed as a model of acquisition per se, but as part of a larger acquisition puzzle. Thus, it is compatible with a variety of other approaches and frameworks. One way to conceptualize this is to consider that input processing research focuses on one and only one set of processes used by learners during the course of acquisition. There are other processes and factors that must be involved in order to have a full understanding of SLA (e.g., Universal Grammar, frequency).

Core issues

The core questions in input processing center on the psycholinguistic conditions under which learners initially connect formal features of language with their meanings and functions, why learners make some of these connections at a given moment and not others, and what the strategies are that learners use in comprehending sentences that affect making such these connections. Underlying, of course, is the idea that connecting formal features to their meanings and functions is part of acquisition. Research on these issues led to a set of principles that guide and constrain how learners—when left to their own devices—process input data. These principles and their motivation have been described in detail in a number of other places (e.g., VanPatten, 1996, 2004, 2007, 2008) and so I will provide only a brief overview of three of them.

I begin with a definition of processing that underlies the discussion in this chapter:

Definition of processing: Processing refers to making a connection between form and meaning/ function.

What this definition underscores is that in the present model of input processing, processing is not equivalent to perception, noticing, and other terms that are often used in the SLA literature (e.g., Schmidt, 1990). As I understand these other terms, they do not require that learners connect form to meaning or function. Thus, a learner may notice a third-person -s on the end of a verb, but not connect it to any function or meaning. In short, that learner may notice but not process that form. We note here that input processing is neutral on the role of noticing; that is, it is not necessary to posit a role for noticing in the current model of input processing.

At the heart of input processing have been two key issues. The first is that input processing is tied to comprehension and the drive for learners to get meaning from the input. That is, the point of comprehension from the learner's point of view is to try to understand what someone is saying. This led to what can be called "good enough for now" processing. By "good enough for now" we mean that learners would use the easiest most efficient strategies for coping with input, especially considering that in the early stages of acquisition comprehension is likely to require a good deal of mental effort and processing resources. From this observation comes a set of principles by which learners rely heavily on lexical cues in interpreting utterances. To put it briefly, L2 learners come to the task of SLA knowing there are such things as words; that is, learners have "names for things" and can ask "how do you say X?" when asking about a word. They also know that words carry meaning. Thus, learners initially approach input processing by searching for words as the easiest way to get meaning (leaving aside, for the moment, whether it is the best way to get meaning). In VanPatten (2004), I referred to this learner-centered strategy as "The primacy of content words":

> *Primacy of Content Words*: Learners process content words in the input before anything else.

What this principle means is not that learners know the words and are looking for them (although this may be true later in acquisition); it means that learners *begin* input processing in an L2 by trying to isolate words in the speech stream. While morphemes and inflections, for example, might be *perceived* and/or noticed, they are not *processed* (see definition above for processing).

So, what the principle of Primacy of Content Words suggests is that *initially*, learners connect lexical form to its meaning and function, but not grammatical form to its meaning or function. This idea is borne out in the acquisition literature in a number of ways. For example, in Gass's 2003 overview of interaction research, almost all research cited on the impact of interaction on learner development are vocabulary related (including the pronunciation of words that leads to misunderstanding) and Gass says that "[interaction and negative evidence] may be effective with low-level phenomena, such as pronunciation or basic meanings of lexical items" but not with morpo-syntax and certainly not with any abstractions related to syntax (Gass, 2003, p. 248). Additional evidence that learners put lexicon before morpho-syntax in a number of ways can be found in a variety of sources (e.g., Clahsen and Felser, 2006; Faerch and Kasper, 1986; Klein, 1986; Sharwood Smith, 1986; Truscott and Sharwood Smith, 2004; among others). In short, in the early stages, processing lexical items is "good enough" and gets the learners through most of the tasks they need to perform in and out of classrooms.

To be sure there are a few studies reporting learners "processing" of form before lexicon (e.g., Han and Peverly, 2007; Park, 2009), but as I have argued elsewhere (VanPatten, 2009a), such studies confuse noticing with processing (as defined here). To be sure, learners can notice just about anything, but do they connect what they notice with its meaning or function? In Park's study, for example, naïve learners of Korean report to a high degree that they kept seeing the morpheme -*ta* in a text they were reading. However, no learner reports that he or she knew what it meant or attached it to any function, and Park did not measure their processing. These learners simply saw it recurring in the written texts they were exposed to and noticed it.

A consequence of the Primacy of Content Words principle is another major principle, the Lexical Preference Principle. Because of my interpretation of the work of others (e.g., Carroll, 2001; Truscott and Sharwood Smith, 2004), as well as criticisms of an earlier version of this principle, (e.g., Carroll, 2004; Harrington, 2004), I have suggested that this principle ought to be stated as follows (VanPatten, 2007, 2009b):

> *Lexical Preference Principle*: If grammatical forms express a meaning that can also be encoded lexically (e.g., that grammatical marker is redundant), then learners will not initially process those grammatical forms until they have lexical forms to which they can match them.

What this principle attempts to capture is the observable delay that learners have in processing inflectional redundancies. A good deal of parsing and processing research as well as recent advances in syntactic theory suggest that part of the "agreement problem" (i.e., concordance between items in an utterance) involves checking one item against another. L2 learners can't begin to check anything against anything unless they have the basics against which to check something. In the case of redundant grammatical markers, lexical items must be acquired before learners can acquire the grammatical markers against which they must be checked. For input processing, this means that learners wouldn't normally process grammatical markers in the input until they've processed (and acquired) corresponding lexical items first. A consequence is that the consistently redundant grammatical markers get short shrift in early stage processing because of the "good enough" strategy that works for learners: reliance on lexical items (again, defined here as content words). This idea is borne out in the literature by the fact that consistently redundant grammatical items take the longest for learners to acquire (e.g., Ellis, 1994; Gass and Selinker, 2008). To be sure, there may be other internal factors that delay the acquisition of such features, factors which are covered elsewhere in this volume (e.g., Lardiere, Chapter 7, this volume).

In addition to processing lexical items and grammatical items, learners must determine basic meanings of sentences. In Ervin-Tripp (1974), cited earlier, even when the L1 and L2 passive structures coincide word for word, L2 learners initially interpret (read "process") passive sentences as actives. Thus, the learners tended to interpret "The lion was killed by the man" as "The lion killed the man." In my early research on Spanish L2, I found that learners have a protracted period of misinterpreting object-verb-subject (OVS) structures as SVO. Because Spanish has much more flexible word order as well as null subjects, OVS and OV structures are possible and sometimes required. Yet learners misinterpret clitic object pronouns (and case marked fronted full noun phrases) in preverbal position incorrectly. In the example *Lo vio María* "Him ACC saw Mary NOM" or "Mary saw him" learners misinterpret the sentence as "He saw Mary" (see, e.g., Lee, 1987; VanPatten, 1984b). In German, case marking allows flexible word order under certain discourse and syntactic conditions. The sentence *Den Jungen küsst die Frau* "The boy-ACC, kisses the girl-NOM" or "The girl kisses the boy" is often misinterpreted by learners as "The boy kisses the girl" (e.g., Henry *et al.*, 2009). Even though in natural L1 discourse such sentences might contain additional intonational cues that co-occur with these word orders, learners do not attend to them. This reliance on word order is captured by the First Noun Principle:

> *The First Noun Principle*: Learners tend to process the first noun or pronoun they encounter in the sentence as the subject.

To be sure, some have suggested that this is not a universal processing principle but is derived from L1 transfer (e.g., Carroll, 2004; Isabelli, 2008), mainly because the vast majority of L2 learners tested have English as their L1. For example, Isabelli's 2008 study shows that Italian L1 speakers do not have the same problems interpreting *Lo vio María* as learners with English L1. This is because Italian is like Spanish in its use of word order and also coincides with the same lexical forms for clitic object pronouns in the singular (e.g., *lo, la*). Thus, they are able to make use of their L1 in processing Spanish. By extension, it is the English speakers' L1 that gets in the way of processing Spanish because of the lack of flexible word order and OVS structures in English. This reasoning is sound but before we abandon the First Noun Principle in favor of L1 transfer, we must reconcile such findings with those of Ervin-Tripp (1974) in which L1–L2 passive equivalents did not aid L2 learners' processing of French with English L1. We must also see what L1 Italian learners of Spanish L2, for example, do with sentences in which the L1 and L2 do not coincide.

We also know that the First Noun Principle is attenuated by lexical semantics and event probabilities, captured by the following sub-principles:

> *The Lexical Semantics Principle*: Learners may rely on lexical semantics, where possible, instead of the First Noun Principle to interpret sentences.

> *The Event Probabilities Principle*: Learners may rely on event probabilities, where possible, instead of the First Noun Principle to interpret sentences.

What the first sub-principle addresses is that learners bring knowledge about the semantics of verbs to the task of processing. Thus, they know that when it comes to "biting" something, the action represented by the verb requires an agent that can bite. Thus, with the two nouns "boy" and "apple" in a sentence, learners will go for "the boy" as the one who bites (irrespective of word order) because apples are incapable of performing the action. So, learners are less likely to misinterpret "The apple was bitten by the boy" compared with "The lion was killed by the man." To be clear, this does not mean that in the "bite" sentence learners are actually processing the passive markers. They are using lexical semantics to derive meaning (see also work on the Competition Model by Bates and MacWhinney, 1984). The second sub-principle addresses what we see in acquisition in that some events are more likely than others. Returning to "bite," if we have "rattlesnake" and "man" in the same sentence, it is more likely that the rattlesnake bites the man than the other way around, even though both are capable of biting. These two sub-principles account for the fact that sometimes learners step outside of the First Noun Principle and seemingly interpret sentences correctly not because they paid attention to grammatical cues but because they relied on non-grammatical information (see also VanPatten and Houston, 1998, for work on how informational context can attenuate processing principles).

Data and common elicitation measures

The data used for input processing research are various kinds of listening and reading measures designed to elicit how learners understand sentences and what aspects of sentences learners rely on to make determinations such as tense, aspect, and others.

Off-line measures

Off-line measures refer to those in which learners hear or read sentences and then indicate what they think the sentence means (by selecting a picture, by selecting an L1 equivalent, by choosing the most logical follow-up, by matching it to another sentence or phrase and so on). For example, learners may hear *The lion was killed by the man* and then asked to select from two pictures: one in which the lion is alive and the man lies dead, and another in which the man is alive and the lion lies dead. These are called off-line measures because the measurement of comprehension occurs after the learner hears the entire sentence. As another example, a learner might hear *Right now the cowboy participated in the dance contest* and then asked which of the following two sentences "best completes the story": (a) *He won first place*. (b) *He will win first place*. The idea here is that the selection of *a* or *b* indicates whether the learner relied on the adverb (right now) or the verb form (participated) to assign tense to the sentence. Early research on input processing used off-line measures (e.g., Lee,

1987; VanPatten, 1984b; VanPatten and Houston, 1998). However, because off-line measures have been questioned in processing research, scholars have begun to incorporate on-line measures.

On-line measures

On-line measures refer to those in which measurements about learners' reactions to sentences are taken at particular points during their reading or listening of sentences. Such measurements include eye-tracking, self-paced reading, and ERPs (event-related potentials). The idea behind on-line measures is that they show what learners are doing *during* the act of comprehension. For example, in VanPatten and Keating (2007), we tracked learners eye movements as they read sentences in which there were "tense conflicts": sentences had inflected verbs that matched adverbials (e.g., *yesterday/he played*) or had inflected verbs that didn't match adverbials (e.g., *right now/he played*). Because we were investigating the Lexical Preference Principle which would predict that learners rely on adverbials to determine tense and not verbal inflections in the initial stages of processing, we compared native speakers of Spanish with advanced, intermediate, and beginning L2 learners. What we found was that native speakers of Spanish spend significantly more time reading verbs and not adverbs in non-match situations, suggesting a reliance on verb morphology to determine tense. Beginning and intermediate learners spent significantly more time reading adverbs rather than verbs, suggesting a reliance on adverbs to determine tense. Advanced learners patterned like native speakers. (Reading time here includes first pass on a verb/ adverb as well as subsequent additional passes, i.e., regressions.)

Applications

The basic constructs and principles of input processing have served as the basis for a pedagogical intervention known as *processing instruction* (sometimes referred to by others as "input processing instruction" or as simply "input processing"). The idea behind processing instruction is deceptively simple: if we know how learners approach input processing (i.e., what strategies they use, what principles underlie sentence interpretation), we might be able to construct an intervention that alters problematic processing. The result ought to be better grammatical intake for acquisition.

Although dozens of studies have now been conducted within the framework of processing instruction, the classic study often cited is VanPatten and Cadierno (1993). In that study, VanPatten and Cadierno compared two experimental groups to a control group (no instruction): processing group and a traditional group. The processing group received an input-oriented instruction in which they heard and read sentences designed to push them away from the First Noun Strategy and to interpret Spanish word order and object pronouns correctly. Thus, if they heard *Lo ve la chica* "The girl sees him" and incorrectly selected a picture in which the boy was looking at the girl, they were told "No, it's the other picture." The traditional group received what was then typical foreign language instruction in the USA: a movement from mechanical to meaningful to communicative drills or practice. Thus, they practiced producing object pronouns in a variety of exercises. Two assessment tasks were given: an interpretation task that biased for the processing group and a sentence-level production task that biased for the traditional group. What VanPatten and Cadierno found was quite interesting: the processing group improved significantly on both the interpretation and the production measures, even though during the treatment they did not practice producing object pronouns. The traditional group improved on the production measure but not on the interpretation measure. There was no difference in improvement between the traditional group and the processing group on the production test. VanPatten and Cadierno concluded that somehow the processing instruction must have resulted in a change in the underlying grammar of the learners that was available for production as well as interpretation. They questioned what internal changes happened to the traditional group, although in a subsequent study (VanPatten and Wong, 2004), it seemed that the traditional group gained some kind of conscious knowledge that they applied as a test-taking strategy for the post tests—a conscious knowledge that they couldn't apply to the interpretation tests. The processing group did not show signs of such a strategy.

Since VanPatten and Cadierno's original study, a number of studies have been conducted that have examined various issues related to processing instruction. I list them here.

- *Processing instruction versus some other kind of intervention* (e.g., traditional instruction, meaning-based output instruction, dictogloss). In sum, processing instruction is always as good as other interventions and often better (see, e.g., Benati, 2001, 2005; Cadierno, 1995; Collentine, 1998; Farley, 2001; Keating and Farley, 2008; Morgan-Short and Wood Bowden, 2006; Qin, 2008; VanPatten et al., 2009; VanPatten et al., 2009; and some of the studies in VanPatten, 2004). Some studies have contradictory findings (e.g., Allen, 2000, and Qin, 2008; VanPatten and Wong, 2004, and VanPatten et al., 2009 as well as Uludag and VanPatten, forthcoming), suggesting that replication from one study to another is difficult, especially depending on the materials and assessment tasks that researchers use.

- *Processing instruction and communicative assessment tasks*. In this line of research, several studies have shown that the results of processing instruction appear not just on sentence-level tasks but also on discourse level tasks such as video narration and text reconstruction (e.g., Sanz and Morgan-Short, 2004; Sanz and VanPatten, 1998; VanPatten and Uludag, forthcoming).

- *Explicit information is not a necessary or determinate variable within processing instruction*. This research has shown that providing learners with the particular kinds of activities used in processing instruction ("structured input," e.g., Farley, 2005; Lee and VanPatten, 1995, 2003; Wong, 2005) is sufficient to cause change in knowledge and behavior. These studies include Benati (2004), Sanz and Morgan-Short (2004), VanPatten (2009c), VanPatten and Oikkennon (1996), and various studies in VanPatten (2004). Because these studies all used pre-test/post-test designs, another line of research has emerged to demonstrate that perhaps explicit information isn't necessary, but it may be beneficial *during* treatment. This research uses an on-line technique to track learner responses as they participate in structured input activities. The results suggest that explicit information may be utilized by learners during structured input activities, but their ability to use that information may be constrained by either structure type or the intersection of a structure with a processing problem (e.g., Culman et al., 2009; Fernández, 2008; Henry et al., 2009). Still, these on-line studies do not find that explicit information is required within processing instruction, only that it is useful.

- *Durative effects of processing instruction*. One study has been conducted that demonstrates durable effects of processing instruction. After eight months, the effects of processing instruction were still evident; that is, final post-test scores were significantly greater than those of the pre-test, albeit there was some decline from the immediate post-test (VanPatten and Fernández, 2004). However, this is one study and replication on durative effects needs to be conducted.

- *Secondary effects of processing instruction*. Based on a hypothesis by Lee (2004), a series of studies have shown that the effects of processing instruction on one structure transfer to other structures. For example, processing instruction on English past-tense results in increased performance on English third-person -s in the present tense. A series of these studies can be found in Benati and Lee (2008).

To be sure, there have been some criticisms of the research on processing instruction. Early criticism suggested a misunderstanding of the nature of processing instruction in that it was not clear that processing instruction aimed to alter particular processing strategies and was mistaken as just another approach to input in the classroom. Accordingly, the criticism implied that VanPatten and Cadierno (1993) were focused on "input versus output" and were somehow contextualizing grammatical structures in input (e.g., DeKeyser and Sokalski, 1996; Erlam, 2004; Salaberry, 1997; Toth, 2000; but see the response by Sanz and VanPatten, 1998 as well as VanPatten, 2002 and 2009b). We hope it is clear now that processing instruction is a particular kind of intervention that does very particular things to alter underlying processing strategies. Thus, it is quite different in both theory and intent from text enhancement, recasts, input floods, and other types of input-oriented interventions.

Subsequently, other criticisms surfaced, namely in DeKeyser et al., (2002). The major thrust of these criticisms is that (a) the model of input processing is "meaning based" rather than structurally based as L1 parsing models are, (b) processing instruction contains an inherent contradiction in that it purports to aid acquisition (an unconscious process) and yet it contains both explicit information and form-focused activities, and (c) research on processing instruction suffers from problems of internal validity. I and others have addressed these criticisms in various ways elsewhere (e.g., Carroll, 2001; Doughty, 2003; Truscott, 2004; VanPatten, 2002, 2004, 2007; VanPatten and Leeser, 2006; Wong, 2004) but in this chapter I would like to focus on the first two.

That the model of input processing is meaning based is partly true (i.e., the Lexical Preference Principle is meaning based but not the First Noun Principle). However, the question is one of how parsing in an L2 is acquired and what learners begin with. My perspective has been that learners do not *begin* with target-like processors and parsers but must acquire them. While there are structural aspects of parsing and processing that L2 learners adhere to (e.g., the First Noun Principle), it is also clear that the concept of "good enough" with a priority of non-syntactic processing before syntactic processing for getting data from the input is not very radical. As Clahsen and Felser (2006) have argued, the "good enough" strategy exists in both L1 and L2 processing, but L2 learners make greater use of it. What is more, the research on how learners process and interpret morphological markings in the early stages of acquisition is relatively clear: they don't. Learners rely on lexicon (and the First Noun Principle) as opposed to morphological cues to understand sentences. What learners must eventually do is move to morpho-syntactic cues and abandon a strict reliance on lexical cues.

This line of reasoning is completely in synch with other perspectives about grammatical growth (e.g., lexical categories precede functional categories); however, the focus is on how learners interact with the external data rather than how the processed data interact with, say, Universal Grammar. The reader will note that I am not juxtaposing input processing and Universal Grammar by any means. It is clear to me that input processing and Universal Grammar are both implicated in grammatical development (see, for example, the discussion in VanPatten, 1996 as well as VanPatten, 2011.)

A second criticism, an inherent contradiction in processing instruction, is that acquisition cannot make use of explicit information and form-focused tasks., The problem here centers on the definition of acquisition and what Krashen has said about the role of instruction. Krashen's claims are quite clear: (1) acquisition involves unconscious processes; and (2) explicit instruction does not affect acquisition (e.g., Krashen, 1982). Strictly speaking then, the criticism that processing instruction cannot affect acquisition as I have claimed it does would be true. But the reading of Krashen's work requires a closer inspection. First, acquisition is comprehension dependent. That is, acquisition happens in one way: learners get input, they comprehend it, and through the processing of the data during comprehension, acquisition happens (other internal/external factors ceteris paribus). This is precisely what processing instruction aims to do. It improves comprehension by making sure comprehension is correct. By making sure comprehension is correct, one impacts the data that learners make available to other internal processors and knowledge sources (e.g., Universal Grammar). In short, any instruction that fosters good comprehension ought to foster acquisition. There is no contradiction in this position.

Second, Krashen's claim that explicit instruction doesn't aid acquisition refers to two ideas: (1) explicit knowledge cannot be turned into acquisition via practice; and (2) production practice does not lead to acquisition—only the processing of input leads to acquisition. Thus, what Krashen has always argued against is form without meaning, practice as production, the need for explicit information, and what generally characterized instruction at the time of his writings in the late 1970s and throughout the 1980s. Processing instruction is a direct reaction to that same kind of instruction, and it does not purport to do any of the things that Krashen railed against in his condemnations of language teaching. For this reason, early on I characterized processing instruction as an intervention for the "acquisition rich" classroom (VanPatten, 1993). What is more, as we have shown in at least one line of research within processing instruction, explicit information is not even needed in processing instruction (see above); appropriately crafted structured input alone is sufficient to cause the changes in learner knowledge and performance we see in our research. (For additional arguments on the implications for instruction from an acquisition/processing perspective, see Truscott and Sharwood Smith, 2004).

Future directions

One area in which input processing will change or evolve is in part determined by what I call the difference between processing as acquisition and processing as a by-product of acquisition (VanPatten and Jegerski, 2011). Processing as acquisition refers to how learners comprehend and process data in the input *to construct linguistic systems*. Processing as a byproduct refers to how learners *make use of that linguistic system to comprehend utterances*. I will illustrate with a simple example from null subjects in Spanish. Unlike English, Spanish is a null subject language, meaning that in simple declarative sentences overt subject pronouns are not necessary (e.g., *Habla/Él habla* "He speaks" are both grammatical) and in certain kinds of sentences overt subjects are disallowed (e.g., time expressions such as *Es la una/*Ello es la una* "It's one o'clock," weather expressions such as *Está lloviendo/Ello está lloviendo* "It's raining" and others). Processing for acquisition refers to how learners get data from the input that then informs the internal system that Spanish is a null subject language. This, of course, is relatively straightforward in that learners encounter early on subjectless sentences and the grammar is forced to posit Spanish as a null subject language. In short, the absence of an overt subject motivates projecting null subjects.

But once the grammar is established, how do learners subsequently interpret null and explicit pronouns they encounter in the input? This is processing as a by-product of acquisition in that the learner is no longer processing to create a system but is learning to equate new pragmatic meanings with the existing syntax. How does the learner interpret, for example, the embedded clauses in the two sentences *Juan vio a Roberto después que, regresó de Europa* ("John saw Robert after [null subject] returned from Europe") and *Juan vio a Roberto después que él regresó de Europa* ("John saw Robert after [él = 'he', explicit subject] returned from Europe"). Do learners distinguish between antecedents (e.g., John vs. Robert) when the pronoun in the second clause is either null or overt? Spanish speakers seem to but it is not clear that learners do (e.g., Sorace and Filiaci, 2006); but again, this is not related to the recreation of a linguistic system that permits null subjects. It is related to what learners do with a null and explicit pronoun system once they get it. (For a summary of work on null subjects and Spanish, see Montrul, 2004.)

The point of this distinction is that input processing cannot address the issue of what happens after grammatical features are acquired. It is not the point of input processing to address the resolution of, for example, ambiguity during comprehension. The point of input processing is to address how learners create a grammar. To be sure, the distinction between processing for acquisition and processing as a by-product of acquisition may not be so categorical for all areas of language (again, see the discussion in VanPatten and Jegerski) but I believe it is a useful distinction to keep in mind as we evaluate various models of processing and parsing applied to the L2 context.

This leads me to one future direction of input processing. In addition to the current principles it contains, input processing may have to branch out and include features of parsing. In the case of null subjects, in order for learners to grasp that Spanish is a null subject language, they must process *the absence of an overt subject* in the input. This can only be done by recurring to principles of parsing such as those in Pritchett (1992). According to Pritchett, during processing the parser attempts to meet the requirements of the theta criterion, that is, find and tag all required thematic elements of the verb (e.g., agent, theme, goal) in the sentence. If there is no overt subject in a sentence that corresponds to an underlying thematic element of the verb, then the parser must posit a null subject in order for the parse of the sentence to be accepted. Thus, learners at some point in SLA have to make use of such principles for a complete grammar to develop. In the case of null subjects, there is no foreseeable way that the learner would posit null subjects unless there was something in the parser that demanded that all thematic elements of the verb be represented somewhere in the sentence. I see, then, that input processing will expand to include not only those principles that currently comprise it, but others as well. These other principles may be some of those currently found in parsing models. I do not believe, however, that input processing will be replaced by parsing models. Again, such models do not address the initial drive to get lexicon before grammatical inflection, for example. Instead, I see input processing and parsing merging in some way to better account for how a grammar is acquired.

I also see an area of research that is still open to question; that is, the role of L1 in input processing. As currently formulated, the principles of input processing are universal in nature and apply to all learners of all languages in all contexts. Carroll (2001), on the other hand, has been a strong proponent of L1 processing underlying all initial L2 processing. The question, then is this: Do L2 learners transfer L1 processing routines and strategies to SLA? Or, is L2 input processing guided by universal principles? Alternatively, is there some mix of the two, such as, do learners start with universal principles but L1 processing routines "kick in" when triggered by certain data in the input? Some research on sentence processing more generally has suggested strong L1 influence (e.g., Frenck-Mestre, 2005; Serratrice, 2007; Sorace and Filiaci, 2006) while other research has not (e.g., Marinis *et al.*, 2005; Papadopoulou and Clahsen, 2003). However, these studies examine processing as by-product (how learners make use of grammar while processing) and thus do not address the initial stages of processing as acquisition (how learners get the grammar). In short, I see the role of L1 in processing for acquisition open for discussion and continued research.

Conclusion

Since the early 1990s, input processing has enjoyed a rigorous research agenda, in part due to the immediate instructional applications that arose (e.g, VanPatten and Cadierno, 1993). Like other aspects of acquisition, its relative merits have been questioned and debated, and it is clear that input processing will evolve. In some ways, it already has. For example, Truscott and Sharwood Smith's (2004) acquisition as processing subsumes/assumes the current model of input processing in that their perspective provides a much larger view of acquisition that includes processing. Yet, at the same time, their theory does not detail particular strategies that may or may not impede the processing of input data, as their main concern is overarching theoretical issues concerning how grammars change over time. Because of the strong line of application research that has emerged from input processing—namely processing instruction—it is likely that some version of the current model of input processing will remain in the mainstream for some time, perhaps side by side with other approaches to acquisition as processing and processing for acquisition.

References

Allen, L. (2000). Form-meaning connections and the French causative: An experiment in processing instruction. *Studies in Second Language Acquisition, 22,* 69–84.

Bates, E. and MacWhinney, B. (1984). Functionalism and the Competition Model. In B. MacWhinney and E. Bates (Eds.), *The cross-linguistic study of sentence processing* (pp. 3–73). Cambridge: Cambridge University Press.

Benati, A. (2001). A comparative study of the effects of processing instruction and output-based instruction on the acquisition of the Italian future tense. *Language Teaching Research, 5,* 95–127.

Benati, A. (2004). The effects of structured input activities and explicit information on the acquisition of the Italian future tense. In B. VanPatten (Ed.), *Processing instruction: Theory, research, and commentary* (pp. 207–225). Mahwah, NJ: Lawrence Erlbaum and Associates.

Benati, A. (2005). The effects of processing instruction, traditional instruction, and meaning–output instruction on the acquisition of the English past simple tense. *Language Teaching Research, 9,* 67–93.

Benati, A. and Lee, J. F. (2008). *Grammar acquisition and processing instruction.* Bristol, UK: Multingual Matters.

Bever, T. G. (1970). The cognitive basis for linguistic structures. In J. R. Hayes (Ed.), *Cognition and the development of language* (pp. 279–362). New York: John Wiley and Sons.

Cadierno, T. (1995). Formal instruction from a processing perspective: An investigation into the Spanish past tense. *The Modern Language Journal, 79,* 179–93.

Carroll, S. (2001). *Input and evidence: The raw material of second language acquisition.* Amsterdam: John Benjamins.

Carroll, S. (2004). Commentary: Some general and specific comments on input processing and processing instruction. In B. VanPatten (Ed.), *Processing instruction: Theory, research, and commentary* (pp. 293–309). Mahwah, NJ: Lawrence Erlbaum Associates.

Clahsen, H. and Felser C. (2006). Grammatical processing in language learners. *Applied Psycholinguistics, 27,* 3–42.

Collentine, J. (1998). Processing instruction and the subjunctive. *Hispania, 81,* 576–587.

Culman, H., Henry, N., and VanPatten, B. (2009). The role of explicit information in processing instruction: An on-line study with German accusative case inflections. *Die Unterrichtspraxis.*

DeKeyser, R., Salaberry, M. R., Robinson, P., and Harrington, M. (2002). What gets processing in processing instruction? A response to Bill VanPatten's "Update". *Language Learning, 52,* 805–823.

DeKeyser, R. and Sokalski K. (1996). The differential role of comprehension and production practice. *Language Learning, 46,* 613–642.

Doughty, C. J. (2003). Instructed SLA: Constraints, compensation, and enhancement. In C. J. Doughty and M. H. Long (Eds.), *The handbook of second language acquisition* (pp. 256–310). Oxford: Blackwell.

Ellis, R. (1994). *The study of second language acquisition.* Oxford: Oxford University Press.

Erlam, R. (2004). Evaluating the effectiveness of structured input and output-based instruction in foreign language learning. *Studies in Second Language Acquisition, 25,* 559–582.

Ervin-Tripp, S. M. (1974). Is second language acquisition really like the first?. *TESOL Quarterly, 8,* 111–127.

Faerch, C. and Kasper G. (1986). The role of comprehension in second language learning. *Applied Linguistics, 7,* 257–274.

Farley, A. P. (2001). Authentic processing instruction and the Spanish subjunctive. *Hispania, 84,* 289–299.

Farley, A. P. (2005). *Structured input.* New York: McGraw-Hill.

Fernández, C. (2008). Reexamining the role of explicit information in processing instruction. *Studies in Second Language Acquisition, 30,* 277–305.

Frenck-Mestre, C. (2005). Eye-movement recording as a tool for studying syntactic processing in a second language: A review of methodologies and experimental findings. *Second Language Research, 21,* 175–198.

Gass, S. M. (2003). Input and interaction. In C. Doughty and M. H. Long (Eds.), *The handbook of second language acquisition* (pp. 224–255). Oxford: Blackwell.

Gass, S. M. and Madden, C. G. (Eds.) (1985). *Input in second language acquisition*. Rowley, MA: Newbury House.

Gass, S. M. and Selinker, L. (2008). *Second language acquisition: An introductory course*. (Third Edition). New York: Routledge.

Han, Z. and Peverly, S. T. (2007). Input processing: A study of ab initio learners with multilingual backgrounds. *International Journal of Multilingualism, 4*, 17–37.

Harrington, M. (2004). Commentary: Input processing as a theory of processing input. In B. VanPatten (Ed.), *Processing instruction: Theory, research, and commentary* (pp. 79–92). Mahwah, NJ: Lawrence Erlbaum Associates.

Hatch, E. (1983). Simplified input. In R. W. Andersen (Ed.), *Pidginization and creolization as language acquisition* (pp. 64–88). Rowley, MA: Newbury House.

Henry, N., Culman, H., and VanPatten, B. (2009). More on the effects of explicit information in instructed SLA: A partial replication of and a response to fernández (2008). *Studies in Second Language Acquisition, 31*, 559–575.

Isabelli, C. (2008). First Noun Principle or L1 transfer principle in SLA? *Hispania, 2*, 463–476.

Keating, G. D. and Farley, A. P. (2008). Processing instruction, meaning-based output instruction, and meaning-based drills: Impacts on classroom L2 acquisition of Spanish object pronouns. *Hispania, 91*, 631–650.

Klein, W. (1986). *Second language acquisition*. Cambridge: Cambridge University Press.

Krashen, S. D. (1982). *Principles and practice in second language acquisition*. Oxford: Pergamon Press.

Lee, J. F. (1987). Morphological factors influencing pronominal reference assignment by learners of Spanish. In T. A. Morgan, J. F. Lee, and B. VanPatten (Eds.), *Language and language use: Studies in Spanish* (pp. 221–232). Lanham, MD: University Press of America.

Lee, J. F. (2004). On the generalizability, limits, and potential future directions of processing instruction research. In B. VanPatten (Ed.), *Processing instruction: Theory, research, and commentary* (pp. 311–323). Mahwah, NJ: Lawrence Erlbaum and Associates.

Lee, J. F. and VanPatten, B. (1995). *Making communicative language teaching happen* (First Edition). New York: McGraw-Hill.

Lee, J. F. and VanPatten, B. (2003). *Making communicative language teaching happen* (Second Edition). New York: McGraw-Hill.

Long, M. (1983). Native speaker/non-native speaker conversations and the negotiation of comprehensible input. *Applied Linguistics, 4*, 126–141.

Marinis, T., Roberts, L., Felser, C., and Clahsen, H. (2005). Gaps in second language processing. *Studies in Second Language Acquisition, 27*, 53–78.

Montrul, S. (2004). *The acquisition of Spanish: Morphosyntactc development in monolingual and bilingual L1 acquisition and adult L2 acquisition*. Amsterdam: John Benjamins.

Morgan-Short, K. and Wood Bowden, H. (2006). Processing instruction and meaningful output-based instruction: Effects on second language development. *Studies in Second Language Acquisition, 28*, 31–65.

Papadopoulou, D. and Clahsen, H. (2003). Parsing strategies in L1 and L2 sentence processing: A study of relative clause attachment in Greek. *Studies in Second Language Acquisition, 25*, 501–528.

Park, E. (2009). Learners' self-generated noticing of L2 written input: noticed features and processing strategies. Paper delivered at the annual meeting of the Georgetown University Roundtable on Linguistics.

Pritchett, B. L. (1992). *Grammatical competence and parsing performance*. Chicago: University of Chicago Press.

Qin, J. (2008). The effect of processing instruction and dictogloss tasks on acquisition of the English passive voice. *Language Teaching Research, 12*, 61–82.

Salaberry, M. R. (1997). The role of input and output practice in second language acquisition. *The Canadian Modern Language Review, 53*, 422–451.

Sanz, C. and Morgan-Short, K. (2004). Positive evidence vs. explicit rule presentation and explicit negative feedback: A computer assisted study. *Language Learning, 54*, 35–78.

Sanz, C. and VanPatten, B. (1998). On input processing, processing instruction, and the nature of replication tasks: A response to Salaberry. *The Canadian Modern Language Review, 54*, 263–273.

Schmidt, R. W. (1990). The role of consciousness in second language learning. *Applied Linguistics, 11*, 129–158.

Serratrice, L. (2007). Cross-linguistic influence in the interpretation of anaphoric and cataphoric pronouns in English-Italian bilingual children. *Bilingualism: Language and Cognition, 10*(3), 225–238.

Sharwood Smith, M. (1986). Comprehension versus acquisition: Two ways of processing input. *Applied Linguistics*, 7, 239–274.

Slobin, D. I. (1966). Grammatical transformations and sentence interpretation in childhood and adulthood. *Journal of Verbal Learning and Verbal Behavior*, 5, 219–227.

Sorace, A. and Filiaci, F. (2006). Anaphora resolution in near-native speakers of Italian. *Second Language Research*, 22(3), 339–368.

Toth, P. D. (2000). The interaction of instruction and learner-internal factors in the acquisition of L2 morphosyntax. *Studies in Second Language Acquisition*, 22, 169–208.

Truscott, J. (2004). The effectiveness of grammar instruction: Analysis of a meta-analysis. *English Teaching and Learning*, 28, 17–29.

Truscott, J. and Sharwood Smith, M. (2004). Acquisition by processing: A modular perspective on language development. *Bilingualism: Language and Cognition*, 7, 1–20.

Uludag, O. and VanPatten, B. (forthcoming). The comparative effects of processing instruction and dictogloss on the acquisition of the English passive by speakers of Turkish. *International Review of Applied Linguistics*.

VanPatten, B. (1984a). Processing strategies and morpheme acquisition. In F. R. Eckman, L. H. Bell, and D. Nelson (Eds.), *Universals of second language acquisition* (pp. 88–98). Rowley, MA: Newbury House.

VanPatten, B. (1984b). Learners' comprehension of clitic pronouns: More evidence for a word order strategy. *Hispanic Linguistics*, 1, 57–67.

VanPatten, B. (1993). Grammar instruction for the acquisition-rich classroom. *Foreign Language Annals*, 26, 433–450.

VanPatten, B. (1996). *Input processing and grammar instruction*. Norwood, NJ: Ablex.

VanPatten, B. (2002). Processing the content of input processing and processing instruction: A response to DeKeyser, Salaberry, Robinson, and Harrington. *Language Learning*, 52, 825–831.

VanPatten, B. (Ed.) (2004). *Processing instruction: Theory, research, and commentary*. Mahwah, NJ: Lawrence Erlbaum Associates.

VanPatten, B. (2007). Input processing in adult second language acquisition. In B. VanPatten and J. Williams (Eds.), *Theories in second language acquisition* (pp. 115–135). Mahwah, NJ: Lawrence Erlbaum Associates.

VanPatten, B. (2008). Processing matters. In T. Piske and M. Young-Scholten (Eds.), *Input Matters* (pp. 47–61). Clevedon, UK: Multilingual Matters.

VanPatten, B. (2009a.) Stubborn syntax. Plenary paper delivered at the annual meeting of the Georgetown University Roundtable on Linguistics.

VanPatten, B. (2009b). Processing matters in input enhancement. In. T. Piske and M. Young-Scholten (Eds.), *Input matters* (pp. 47–61). Bristol, UK: Multilingual Matters.

VanPatten, B. (2009c). Formal intervention and the development of proficiency: The role of explicit information. In A. Benati (Ed.), *Issues in attaining second language proficiency* (pp. 169–188). London: Continuum.

VanPatten, B. (2011). Stubborn syntax: How it resists explicit teaching and learning. In C. Sanz and R. Leow (Eds.), *Proceedings of the 2009 Georgetown University Roundtable on Linguistics*. Washington, D.C.: Georgetown University Press.

VanPatten, B. and Cadierno, T. (1993). Explicit instruction and input processing. *Studies in Second Language Acquisition*, 15, 225–243.

VanPatten, B. Farmer, J. L., and Clardy, C. L. (2009). Processing instruction and meaning-based output instruction: A response to Keating and Farley (2008). *Hispania*, 92, 116–126.

VanPatten, B. and Fernández, C. (2004). The long-term effects of processing instruction. In B. VanPatten (Ed.), *Processing instruction: Theory, research, and commentary* (pp. 273–289). Mahwah, NJ: Lawrence Erlbaum Associates.

VanPatten, B. and Houston, T. (1998). Contextual effects in processing L2 input sentences. *Spanish Applied Linguistics*, 2, 53–70.

VanPatten, B., Inclezan, D., Salazar, H., and Farley, A. P. (2009). Processing instruction and dictogloss: A study on word order and object pronouns in Spanish. *Foreign Language Annals*, 42, 558–576.

VanPatten, B. and Jegerski, J. (2011). L2 processing and parsing: The issues. In B. VanPatten and J. Jegerski (Eds.), *Second language processing and parsing* (pp. 3–23). Amsterdam: John Benjamins.

VanPatten, B. and Keating, G. D. (2007). The hidden problem of second language acquisition: Learners' processing of morpho-syntax during comprehension. Paper delivered at the annual meeting of the American Association of Teachers of Spanish and Portuguese, San Diego.

VanPatten B. and Leeser, M. J. (2006). Theoretical and research considerations underlying classroom practice: The fundamental role of input. In R. Salaberry and B. Lafford (Eds.), *The art of teaching Spanish: Second language acquisition from research to praxis* (pp. 55–77). Georgetown: Georgetown University Press.

VanPatten, B. and Oikkenon, S. (1996). Explanation versus structured input in processing instruction. *Studies in Second Language Acquisition, 18,* 495–510.

VanPatten, B. and Sanz, C. (1995). From input to output: Processing instruction and communicative tasks. In F. R. Eckman, D. Highland, P. W. Lee, J. Milcham, and R. Ruthkowski Weber (Eds.), *Second language acquisition theory and pedagogy* (pp. 169–85). Mahwah, NJ: Lawrence Erlbaum Associates.

VanPatten, B. and Uludag, O. (2011). Transfer of training and processing instruction: From input to output. *System, 39,* 44–53.

VanPatten, B. and Wong, W. (2004). Processing instruction and the French causative: Another replication. In B. VanPatten (Ed.), *Processing instruction: Theory, research, and commentary* (pp. 97–118). Mahwah, NJ: Lawrence Erlbaum Associates.

Wong, W. (2004). The nature of processing instruction. In B. VanPatten (Ed.), *Processing instruction: Theory, research, and commentary* (pp. 33–63). Mahwah, NJ: Lawrence Erlbaum Associates.

Wong, W. (2005). *Input enhancement: From theory and research to classroom practice.* New York: McGraw-Hill.

17

The neurocognition of second language

Kara Morgan-Short and Michael T. Ullman

Introduction

This chapter examines the neurocognition of second language, that is, the neural and cognitive (psychological and computational) bases of late-learned second or subsequent language (L2). The chapter focuses on lexical and grammatical processes. We first summarize the historical context of research related to the neurocognition of L2, and then examine current neurocognitive theories and their predictions. Next, we describe two common neurocognitive measures (Event-Related Potentials and functional Magnetic Resonance Imaging—that is, ERPs and fMRI) and review their extant neurocognitive empirical evidence for L2. Finally, we discuss the instructional relevance of such theories and evidence and suggest future directions for research.

Historical discussion

The field of second language acquisition (SLA) has examined, among other issues, the nature of the cognitive mechanisms underlying L2 learning and use, and the various intrinsic and extrinsic factors that may influence these mechanisms. The field has gained insight into these issues, primarily through behavioral approaches. However, the development of valid operationalizations and reliable measurements of the cognitive mechanisms of interest is often a complex task at best, as in the case of assessing implicit learning. Because of the difficulty of identifying underlying mechanisms with behavioral methods, interest is growing in more brain-based approaches, which can complement behavioral approaches in gaining an understanding of these issues. Importantly, this research may elucidate not only the cognitive mechanisms of L2, which have been one focus of SLA, but also its brain and biological bases, which are potentially important in their own right.

Brain-based research of L2 has experienced a virtual explosion in recent years—for several reasons, including recent advances both in neuroimaging techniques and in the development of neurocognitive theories of L2 acquisition and processing. Indeed, a search of the databases *Language and Linguistics Behavioral Abstracts* and *PsychINFO* using the search terms "second language," "neur*," and "ERP" or "fMRI" revealed only one publication in 1981–1990, 21 publications in 1991–2000, and an astounding 875 from 2001 to mid-2010.

However, the study of the neurocognition of L2, which has emerged mainly from the field of cognitive neuroscience, has developed largely independently from the field of SLA. Unlike SLA, it has focused almost exclusively on two questions: (1) whether the neurocognitive representation and processing of L2 are similar to or different from those of first language (L1); and (2) to what degree such similarities and differences are influenced by a small number of factors, in particular, L2 age of acquisition and proficiency, and to a lesser extent, transfer effects from the learner's L1 to the L2. The empirical focus on these factors is evident in a number of recent reviews of L2 neurocognitive research (Abutalebi, 2008; Hernandez and Li, 2007; Indefrey, 2006; Kotz, 2009; Mueller, 2005; Schmidt and Roberts, 2009; Steinhauer *et al.*, 2009; van Hell and Tokowicz, 2010). Perhaps most importantly, although this body of neurocognitive research has made a significant contribution to our understanding of *what* the neural representation and processing of L2 look like in comparison to L1, it is still in its infancy in understanding *why* L2 neural representation and processing look the way they do, and why various factors might affect them.

In this chapter we take a somewhat different approach from most previous overviews of L2 neurocognitive research. We focus not only on the L2 empirical evidence (the *what*), but also on the theoretical landscape and how the evidence constrains it (the *why*). Specifically, we present current neurocognitive theories of L2; discuss how their claims and predictions overlap or differ; review the L2 neurocognitive evidence from ERPs and fMRI; and finally discuss how these data do or do not fit current theories.

Core issues

Here we focus on four theories, all of which make claims about the neural as well as the cognitive basis of second language: the Declarative/Procedural model, Paradis' model, the Competition model, and the Convergence hypothesis. As we shall see below, these four theories are representative of two broad neurocognitive perspectives that make quite different claims and predictions. For reasons of space, we have left out other theories, including those of Clahsen (Clahsen and Felser, 2006a, b, c), whose theory shares many claims with those of the Declarative/Procedural model, and Ellis (Ellis, 2002a, b, 2006), whose view shares certain similarities with the Competition Model.

The declarative/procedural model

The Declarative/Procedural (DP) model (Ullman, 2001b, 2004) proposes that crucial aspects of language depend on two well-studied brain memory systems—declarative and procedural memory—that support non-language functions in humans and other animals (Eichenbaum and Lipton, 2008; Henke, 2010; Mishkin *et al.*, 1984; Squire and Schacter, 2002). Declarative memory, which stores knowledge about facts and events (semantic and episodic knowledge), is posited to also underlie the mental lexicon, including the conceptual meanings of words as well as their phonological forms and grammatical specifications (e.g., irregular morphology and argument structure). This lexical dependence on declarative memory is expected in both L1 and L2. Knowledge can be learned rapidly in declarative memory, and it is at least partly, but *not* completely (Chun, 2000) explicit, that is available to conscious awareness. Declarative memory relies on the hippocampus and other medial temporal structures for learning new knowledge, which eventually depends largely on neocortical regions, particularly in the temporal lobes. Other brain structures play a role in declarative memory as well, including a region in frontal neocortex corresponding to Brodmann's Areas (BAs) 45 and 47 (within and near classical Broca's area), which underlie the selection or retrieval of declarative memories. (Note that for both declarative and procedural memory, the DP model refers to the *entire* neurocognitive system involved in the learning, representation, and processing of the relevant knowledge, not just to those parts underlying learning and consolidating new knowledge, which is what some researchers refer to regarding the two memory systems.)

The procedural memory system, which is a distinct brain memory system from declarative memory, underlies the implicit learning and use of motor and cognitive skills, and may be specialized at least in part for sequences and rules (Henke, 2010; Mishkin *et al.*, 1984; Poldrack and Foerde, 2008; Squire and Schacter, 2002). Note that evidence suggests the existence of more than one non-declarative implicit memory system, only one of which is referred to as procedural memory by the DP model. Thus it is *not* the case that all implicit skills or knowledge are learned in the procedural memory system. According to the DP model (Ullman, 2001a, 2005), in L1 procedural memory is posited to also underlie aspects of a symbol-manipulating grammar, across grammatical sub-domains, including phonology, morphology, and syntax, in both expressive and receptive language. Procedural memory is posited to be especially important in the real-time sequential and hierarchical combination (e.g., Merge (Chomsky, 1995) or concatenation) of stored lexical forms and abstract representations into rule-governed complex structures (e.g., *the + cat, walk + -ed,* Noun Phrase + Verb Phrase)—that is, in grammatical structure-building. However, just as we can memorize lyrics, poems, and speeches, presumably in declarative memory, so complex structures can also be stored in declarative memory, for example as chunks ("*the cat*"). Unlike learning in declarative memory, learning in procedural memory requires repeated exposure to the stimulus, or practice with the skill, although once learned, skills seem to apply automatically, rapidly, and reliably. The procedural memory system is composed of a network of interconnected brain structures rooted in circuits connecting the basal ganglia (a set of structures deep within the brain, including the caudate nucleus and putamen) with certain frontal regions, in particular pre-motor regions and nearby BA 44 within Broca's area. The basal ganglia may be more important in learning new skills, while frontal regions are more important in representing and processing already-learned skills.

Crucial to the DP model's predictions about L2 is the fact that learning abilities in the declarative and procedural memory systems change differentially across the lifespan. Learning in declarative memory improves during childhood, and plateaus during adolescence and early adulthood, though it subsequently begins to decline (DiGiulio *et al.*, 1994; Graf, 1990; Vaidya *et al.*, 2007). In contrast, procedural memory learning abilities seems to be established early in childhood, with minimal subsequent changes into adulthood, including a possible decrement from childhood to adolescence (Bachevalier, 2001; Dorfberger *et al.*, 2007; Siegel, 2001). These changes in functionality during development lead to predicted changes in reliance on the two memory systems for later- vs. earlier-learned language. According to the DP model, later-learned L2s are expected to initially depend on the declarative memory system not only for *lexical* knowledge (which can only be learned in this system, and thus depends on it for both L2 and L1) but also for *complex forms*, which can be memorized as chunks (or processed in declarative memory in other ways, e.g., computed with rules learned in this system; Ullman, 2005, 2006). This dependence on declarative rather than procedural memory for complex forms is due both to the fact that knowledge is learned faster in declarative than procedural memory (and thus is learned initially in the former), and because later learners of language should have more developed declarative learning abilities than younger learners, and possibly also more attenuated procedural learning abilities. Thus complex forms in L2 should depend more on declarative memory than in L1, and the later the L2 is learned (up to young adulthood), the greater its dependence on this system.

However, the procedural memory system is not dysfunctional in adulthood. At worst, it is somewhat attenuated, and procedural learning can and does take place in adults. Thus, with increasing practice with the L2 (and accompanying proficiency), aspects of grammar are predicted to increasingly rely on the procedural memory system. Therefore, the DP model predicts that though the neurocognition of L2 is always L1-like for lexical/conceptual knowledge, it can also become L1-like for complex forms. The degree of this proceduralization of grammatical abilities is expected to be a function of multiple intrinsic and extrinsic factors, including not only the amount of L2 practice (experience), but also the type of input (see below) and the kinds of grammatical rules and relations (some may be easier to proceduralize), as well as intrinsic factors such as genotype and sex (male vs. female), which can modulate the functionality of the declarative and/or procedural memory systems (Ullman, 2004, 2005, 2007, 2008; Ullman *et al.*, 2008).

Note that although the improvement of declarative memory and possible worsening of procedural memory during childhood should lead to a greater reliance of complex forms on declarative than procedural memory in later than earlier learned language (e.g., in L2 vs. L1, and later- vs. earlier-learned L2), the *basic pattern of the trajectory* is predicted to be similar in L1 and L2 acquisition, that is, in both cases the rapid learning ability of declarative memory should lead to earlier learning of words as well as complex forms as chunks, with only later proceduralization of the grammar (Ullman, 2005).

Finally, note that it is *not* the case that such changes in the relative reliance on the two memory systems are due to any "transformation" of knowledge from one to the other system. The two systems can *independently* acquire knowledge, though knowledge acquired in one system can either enhance or inhibit learning analogous knowledge in the other system (Poldrack and Packard, 2003; Ullman, 2004). Thus proceduralization of grammar does *not* constitute the "transformation" of declarative into procedural representations, but rather the gradual acquisition of grammatical knowledge in procedural memory, which is increasingly relied on, with an accompanying decrease in reliance on declarative memory (Ullman, 2001a, 2004, 2005).

Paradis

Paradis' model also implicates notions of declarative and procedural memory in language acquisition (Paradis, 1994, 2004, 2009). Unlike the DP model, Paradis assumes isomorphic relations between declarative memory and explicit knowledge; that is, declarative memory only contains explicit knowledge, and all explicit knowledge is in declarative memory. Similar to the DP model, Paradis claims that procedural memory is necessarily implicit but that other types of implicit knowledge also exist (Paradis, 2009). He argues that explicit knowledge (stored in declarative memory) must be "learned," with attention directed to what is being learned, whereas implicit knowledge (stored in procedural memory) can only be "acquired" incidentally, without attention being paid directly to it. Paradis implicates hippocampal/medial-temporal structures and association cortex in declarative memory, and the basal ganglia, the cerebellum, and perisylvian neocortex (i.e., around the Sylvian fissure) in procedural memory (Paradis, 1994, 2009).

For L1, language acquisition is posited to depend on procedural memory for all aspects of language that are implicit. This includes all aspects of the grammar, including not only phonology, morphology, and syntax but also implicit grammatical properties of the lexicon (Paradis, 2009). In contrast, *consciously* accessible vocabulary items, specifically, the sound-meaning pairings of words, are stored in declarative memory, although their use in context, which requires automatic access to their representation, is "also implicit (i.e., non-conscious)" (Paradis, 2009, p. 12). Note a particular but important difference between Paradis and Ullman's positions. For both Paradis (Paradis, 1994, 2009) and Ullman (Ullman, 2001b, 2004), the "lexicon" is comprised of the sound-meaning pairings *and* the grammatical properties of words. Paradis claims that the sound-meaning pairings of words, that is, the "vocabulary," are explicit and are subserved by declarative memory, which is synonymous with explicit memory, whereas knowledge about the grammatical properties of words, also referred to as the "lexicon," is implicit and is subserved by procedural memory. In contrast, Ullman claims that both the sound-meaning pairings *and* the grammatical properties of words are part of the mental lexicon and are expected to rely on the declarative memory system, which is understood to underlie implicit as well as explicit knowledge.

Paradis accounts for differences between L1 and L2 in terms of brain maturation. Specifically, he claims that there is a decline in "the use" of procedural memory after the "optimal period" for language acquisition between two and five years of age (Paradis, 2009, pp. 114–118). Because declarative memory becomes more available during development (see above), older learners depend more on declarative-based learning as opposed to procedural-based acquisition. This reliance on declarative memory is predicted *across* various domains of language, including lexical knowledge and processing that is implicit in L1. Paradis states that, with sufficient practice, that is, "repeated use (involving both comprehension and production) in interactive communicative situations" (p. 4), it is theoretically possible, though very rare, for learners to *acquire* L2 grammar in its entirety (Paradis, 2009). More commonly, some specific elements of the grammar may become part of the implicit linguistic system and come to depend on procedural memory. A final key element of this model is that explicit, metalinguistic knowledge about the L2 grammar is expected to *indirectly* contribute to the process of acquiring elements of the L2 grammar, in that explicit knowledge may promote repeated use of the form, which in turn leads to the development of procedural knowledge for that form.

The competition model

According to the Competition Model (Hernandez *et al.*, 2005; MacWhinney, 2005, 2007), language comprehension is based on the detection of a set of cues whose strength is determined by their reliability and availability. Language acquisition in the Competition Model occurs as cue-driven learning, which is a "process of acquiring coalitions of form–function meanings, and adjusting the weight of each mapping until it provides an optimal fit to the processing environment" (MacWhinney and Bates, 1989, p. 59). This mechanism for acquisition is relevant for all aspects of language, including lexical, phonological, and grammatical forms, in both first and second language (MacWhinney, 2007).

Thus the Competition Model posits that L2 acquisition relies on the same mechanisms as does L1 acquisition. The difference between early L1 and late L2 acquisition is explained in terms of the concepts of competition, resonance, parasitism, and entrenchment (Hernandez *et al.*, 2005). Specifically, a learner's ability to engage in the process of cue-driven learning of an L2 is more difficult than in L1 because an entrenched set of L1 relationships is already established and resonant, that is, repeatedly coactivated. L2 learning is claimed to be parasitic on L1 because L2 associations are interspersed with L1 forms instead of being clustered in a separate L2 region. This parasitism would be expected to lead to L1 transfer effects. However, by using explicit metacognitive procedures such as rehearsal and recoding, L2 learners can increase the strength between relationships within L2, so that the L2 itself becomes more resonant and is able to compete with entrenched L1 forms and block L1 transfer effects more effectively. Additionally, high similarity between L2 and L1 forms is predicted to lead to positive overlap and to be facilitative for acquisition of the similar L2 form. In contrast, when L2 forms differ from those in L1, competition between the forms may negatively affect successful acquisition of the L2.

Consistent with these claims, on a neurocognitive level the Competition Model expects that L1 and L2 will show significant overlap in neural representation and processing, for example as measured by fMRI or ERP (Hernandez *et al.*, 2005)— especially when there is a lack of competition between the L1 and L2 forms, and even at lower levels of proficiency (Tokowicz and

MacWhinney, 2005). Thus few differences in the neural representation and processing of L1 and L2 are expected, apart for some neural separation that might be detectable at a local cortical level, as well as the activation of non-language brain areas, such as those recruited for explicit metacognitive processes (Hernandez et al., 2005, p. 223).

The convergence hypothesis

The Convergence Hypothesis (Abutalebi, 2008; Abutalebi and Green, 2007; Green, 2003; Green et al., 2006) is largely consistent with the Competition Model, in that it claims that L2 acquisition depends on the same neural mechanisms as does L1, and that these mechanisms operate in the context of the already-specified L1 neural system. Specifically, the Convergence Hypothesis expects that at initial stages of L2 acquisition, aspects of L2 (e.g., L2 semantics and syntax) will depend on the neural substrates that underlie parallel aspects of the learner's L1, and thus will arise in the context of the speaker's already-specified L1 system. Therefore initially the representation of L2 is "convergent" with the (already-specified) representation of the learner's L1. However, with increasing proficiency, the L2 is expected to "converge with the representation of that language learned as an L1" (Green, 2003, p. 204).

Although the model predicts that the neural representation of L2 converges to that of the same language in a native speaker, especially at higher levels of proficiency, the model also expects L2/L1 differences, possibly due to competition between the L2 and L1, particularly at lower levels of proficiency. This competition may lead to increased neural activation for L2 as compared to L1 in certain areas, particularly for those associated with language control (prefrontal cortex, basal ganglia, and anterior cingulate cortex; Abutalebi, 2008). In addition, the model also recognizes that "explicit, declarative representations of grammatical information" may play an initial role in on-line processing, and expects that different contexts of acquisition (e.g., "formal school setting versus immersion setting") should affect this initial registration of linguistic information" (Green, 2003, p. 205). Thus the model accounts not only for convergence between L1 and L2 but also offers a proficiency- and context-based account for differences between L1 and L2.

Distinguishing between theories

Ideally, in order to test these competing theories one would compare and contrast them on a range of issues, such as claims of domain generality, the specific implicated neural substrates and their functions, the roles for explicit metalinguistic L2 learning and knowledge, and so on. However, many of these comparisons are difficult to make because they are either specified to different levels by different models or not specified at all. Here we focus on two related issues that seem sufficiently well specified by each of the theories laid out above and that lead to different predictions, providing a means to help distinguish between two broad neurocognitive perspectives represented by these theories. Note that although there are clear differences between the theories within each broad perspective (e.g., between the DP model and Paradis, and between the Competition model and the Convergence hypothesis), we do not address these here. The two issues we examine in light of the theoretical perspectives are: *what* the neurocognition of L2 representation, processing and acquisition looks like in comparison to L1, and *why* it looks that way, including which factors affect it.

First, a clear difference emerges between two sets of theories regarding the assumptions underlying L2 vs. L1 (the why). On the one hand, the DP model and Paradis posit the involvement of two distinct neurocognitive systems that play somewhat different roles in L2 and L1, due primarily to the development or maturation of the declarative and procedural memory systems

(Paradis, 1994, 2004, 2009; Ullman, 2001a, 2005). On the other hand, the Competition and Convergence models posit the involvement of a single set of mechanisms that play similar roles in L2 and L1, with any differences emerging largely as a result of the neural commitment of L1, which competes with the establishment of an L2 (Green, 2003; Green et al., 2006; Hernandez et al., 2005).

Second, these different underlying assumptions lead to different predictions regarding the neurocognitive basis of L2 (the what). The DP model and Paradis both predict certain *qualitative* neurocognitive differences between L1 and L2, as well as between lower and higher exposure L2—that is, differences in which brain and cognitive systems are being relied on. In particular, both of these models expect that L1 will depend more on procedural memory, and L2 more on declarative memory, particularly at lower exposure L2. (Note that the specifics differ between the two models, both in which brain structures are involved, and in which linguistic forms and functions should show the qualitative differences. The DP model predicts that rule-governed relations and forms should show these differences, while idiosyncratic lexical knowledge should not. Paradis predicts these differences for all knowledge and processing that is implicit in L1, including both grammar and lexical knowledge. However, these specific differences are not addressed here. For further discussion, see e.g., Ullman, 2001a, 2005).

Both the Competition and Convergence models predict primarily either *no differences* or *quantitative* differences between L2 and L1: that is, L2 should activate largely the same set of neural structures as L1. At lower levels of proficiency, L2 learners may show increased brain activity in these structures as compared to L1, due to greater competition and difficulty. At higher proficiency levels, activation should decrease, perhaps to the level of L1 (Abutalebi, 2008; Green, 2003; Green et al., 2006; Hernandez et al., 2005). Note, however, that these models also provide some accounts of possible qualitative differences between L1 and L2. For example, at lower levels of proficiency, both models posit a reliance on explicit metalinguistic knowledge during lower levels of proficiency, and the Convergence Model emphasizes an increased reliance on neural structures involved in language control.

Data and common elicitation measures

These differing claims and predictions can be tested using a variety of different behavioral and brain measures. Consistent with this chapter's focus on brain-based approaches, here we provide a short overview of two brain-based methods, the most commonly used in neurocognitive L2 research: the electrophysiological technique of ERPs and the hemodynamic neuroimaging approach of functional fMRI. In our discussion of evidence below, we also present results from Positron Emission Tomography (PET), a more rarely used hemodynamic neuroimaging approach. Note that other methods, such as the lesion method, magnetoencephalagraphy (MEG), direct cortical brain stimulation, and transcranial magnetic stimulation (TMS), have also been used in L2 research but are beyond the scope of this chapter.

Event-related potentials

ERPs are scalp-recorded electrical potentials of the brain activity that takes place after subjects are presented with stimulus "events," such as words, pictures, or sounds. Language-related ERP research often employs a violation paradigm for presenting linguistic stimuli. In this paradigm the ERP response to a linguistic violation (e.g., lexical, syntactic, morphosyntactic) is compared to the ERP response of a matched control word or structure. As the stimuli are presented, electrophysiological activity is recorded at the scalp from electrodes that are bound to ERP caps. The precise time of each stimulus is marked in the ongoing electro-encephalogram (EEG). After the EEG is amplified, the time-locked signal for each stimulus is averaged by condition in order to detect that part of the wave-form related to that specific condition. This waveform is called the "event-related potential." Characteristic peaks (i.e., "bumps" or "dips") in the ERP wave-form that are consistently found in particular experimental conditions are referred to as "ERP components." Different ERP components can be identified and distinguished by various factors, including their latency (when they occur in the wave-form), amplitude (of the voltage), scalp distribution (which electrodes the component is strongest at and extends to), and polarity (whether their voltage is positive or negative).

A benefit that researchers gain when using ERPs is that, unlike other neuroimaging techniques (e.g., fMRI, MEG), ERP research has revealed a set of widely studied language-related ERP components in L1, whose characteristics and underlying functions are relatively well understood (Steinhauer and Connolly, 2008). These components thus provide a frame of reference for examining the attainment of native-language processing in L2. A second advantage of ERPs is that they reflect actual electrophysiological neuronal activity, which changes on the order of milliseconds, and thus provide us with excellent temporal information.

Unfortunately, ERPs' advantage in temporal resolution is accompanied by a strong disadvantage in spatial resolution. It is quite difficult, though not impossible, to identify the actual brain structures that generate scalp-recorded potentials. There are also other limitations to ERPs. The electrical activity of a single neuron firing is much too small to measure outside the brain, and ERPs are generally detectable only when hundreds or even thousands of neurons with a similar geometrical orientation are active at the same time. It also turns out that only certain types of neurons in the cortex tend to have these properties, and therefore it is mainly these cortical neurons that are captured by ERPs. Finally, ERP research is limited by the fact that participants must refrain from moving (even blinking their eyes) during the presentation of stimuli because of the electrical noise produced both by muscles and by motor neurons. So almost all ERP language studies are limited to language perception (reading or listening).

Functional magnetic resonance imaging

A second common elicitation method used for exploring the neurocognition of L2 is fMRI, a neuroimaging technique that emerged in the 1990s. In fMRI two images are recorded: (a) a structural image, which details the anatomical structures of the brain, and (b) a functional image, which typically reflects changes in blood oxygenation in the brain. These changes are thought to reflect increases or decreases in neuronal firing rates, which in turn are taken to be related to cognitive processes. When a functional image is aligned with a structural image, one can thus attempt to determine the location in the brain of neuronal activity related to a particular cognitive process.

The primary benefit of fMRI is that it provides superb spatial resolution. Indeed, it allows one to distinguish different areas of brain activation that are as little as a few millimeters apart. However, fMRI does have its limitations. First, the very strong magnetic fields of the MRI scanner can be quite dangerous in some circumstances (e.g., if you have metal in your body). Second, in fMRI studies, the participant must be lying down and must not move their head, limiting the nature of experimental paradigms. Finally, the hemodynamic changes that take place in response to neural activity are too slow to allow the detection of real-time processing changes, so one cannot use fMRI to measure the spatio-temporal dynamics of language. It is therefore important to test a given linguistic process not only with fMRI, but also with techniques such as ERPs that provide very high temporal resolution.

Empirical verification

Several reviews of ERP and hemodynamic (fMRI and PET) evidence have recently provided synthesis and insight on the neurocognition of L2 (Abutalebi, 2008; Hernandez and Li, 2007; Indefrey, 2006; Kotz, 2009; Mueller, 2005; Schmidt and Roberts, 2009; Steinhauer et al., 2009; Stowe and Sabourin, 2005; van Hell and Tokowicz, 2010). Thus the purpose of the current section is not to provide an exhaustive review of empirical studies, but rather to point out emerging patterns of evidence, and to consider these in light of the theories discussed above. Specifically, we consider ERP and hemodynamic studies of natural and artificial L2 in order to assess whether the extant evidence suggests qualitative or quantitative differences between L2 and L1 and between lower and higher exposure L2.

ERP evidence from natural language. In L1, different types of processing difficulties elicit different ERP components (for recent comprehensive reviews see Kaan, 2007; Steinhauer and Connolly, 2008). Difficulties in lexical/semantic processing in L1 elicit central/posterior bilaterally distributed negativities (N400s) that often peak about 400 ms after the onset of the word (Friederici et al., 1999; Kutas and Hillyard, 1980). N400s reflect aspects of lexical/semantic processing, and may depend on the declarative memory brain system (Lau et al., 2008; McCarthy et al., 1995; Simos et al., 1997; Steinhauer and Connolly, 2008; Ullman, 2001a). In contrast, difficulties in (morpho) syntactic processing often produce three components. First, such processing difficulties can, though do not always (Hagoort and Brown, 1999; Osterhout et al., 1997), elicit early (150–500 ms) left-to-bilateral anterior negativities (LANs) (Friederici et al., 1993; Neville et al., 1991). LANs appear to reflect aspects of rule-governed automatic structure-building (Friederici and Kotz, 2003; Hahne and Friederici, 1999) and have been posited to depend on the procedural memory brain system (Ullman, 2001a, 2004). Second (morpho)syntactic processing difficulties usually elicit late (600 ms) centro-parietal positivities (P600s) (Kaan et al., 2000; Osterhout and Holcomb, 1992) linked to controlled (conscious) processing and structural reanalysis (Hahne and Friederici, 1999; Kaan, 2007; Kaan et al., 2000). The biphasic pattern of a LAN followed by a P600 may be characteristic of native-speaker processing of (morpho)syntactic violations (Friederici et al., 1993; Steinhauer and Connolly, 2008). Finally, such violations may also elicit later (600–2000 ms) sustained anterior negativities ("late anterior negativities"), which generally show bilateral distributions, and may reflect increased working memory demands (Martin-Loeches et al., 2005).

In L2, ERP studies have revealed the following: Difficulties in lexical/semantic processing do not differ qualitatively between L1 and L2, reliably eliciting N400s in both cases, even after minimal L2 exposure (McLaughlin et al., 2004; Steinhauer et al., 2009; Ullman, 2001a). In contrast, L2 differs from L1 in aspects of (morpho)syntactic (grammatical) processing, in particular at lower levels of exposure and proficiency. At lower levels LANs are typically absent, with subjects instead showing no negativity at all (Hahne and Friederici, 2001; Ojima et al., 2005) or N400s or N400-like posterior negativities (Osterhout et al., 2008; Weber-Fox and Neville, 1996). However, recent studies have reported LANs in higher proficiency L2 (Gillon Dowens et al., 2009; Isel, 2007; Ojima et al., 2005; Rossi et al., 2006; Steinhauer et al., 2009) (but see Chen et al., 2007). These LANs are sometimes bilaterally distributed (Isel, 2007; Rossi et al., 2006), possibly due to lower L2 proficiency (Steinhauer et al., 2009). P600s are generally found in L2, particularly at higher proficiency (Gillon Dowens et al., 2009; Isel, 2007; Osterhout et al., 2008; Rossi et al., 2006; Steinhauer et al., 2009; Weber-Fox and Neville, 1996). In some studies of high proficiency L2, the LAN and P600 are both elicited in response to (morpho)syntactic violations (Gillon Dowens et al., 2009; Hahne et al., 2006; Rossi et al., 2006; Steinhauer et al., 2009). Finally, late anterior negativities have also been observed in L2, again mainly at higher proficiency (Gillon Dowens et al., 2009; Rossi et al., 2006).

Hemodynamic evidence from natural language. In L1, fMRI and PET research shows somewhat different activation patterns for lexical/semantic and grammatical processing (for a review see Hasson and Small, 2008). Brain structures in temporal/temporo-parietal regions, including the medial temporal lobe, are linked with lexical/semantic processing (Friederici *et al.*, 2003; Illes *et al.*, 1999; Kuperberg *et al.*, 2000; Newman *et al.*, 2001). In addition, BA 45 and 47 seem to underlie the selection, retrieval or integration of lexical and semantic knowledge (Dapretto and Bookheimer, 1999; Illes *et al.*, 1999; Poldrack *et al.*, 1999). In the (morpho)syntactic domain, activation of inferior frontal regions, in particular BA 44 and the frontal operculum, as well as of the superior temporal gyrus and the basal ganglia, are observed (Dapretto and Bookheimer, 1999; Friederici *et al.*, 2003; Newman *et al.*, 2001).

In L2, certain patterns are beginning to emerge from hemodynamic studies (for comprehensive reviews see Indefrey, 2006; Kotz, 2009; Stowe and Sabourin, 2005). First, tasks that involve *only* lexical processing typically depend on the same brain structures in L2 as in L1, and do *not* generally yield different activation patterns in L1 and L2 (Chee *et al.*, 1999; Klein *et al.*, 1999; Xue *et al.*, 2004), although some studies have reported greater activation in L1 compared to L2 (Pillai *et al.*, 2004) as well as in L2 compared to L1 (Perani *et al.*, 2003). In contrast, grammatical processing has thus far shown varied results in both region and level of activation. Some studies suggest that grammatical processing in L2 as compared to L1 elicits greater temporal lobe involvement, in both the left and right hemispheres (Dehaene *et al.*, 1997; Perani *et al.*, 1996; Perani *et al.*, 1998). The extent of temporal lobe involvement during these tasks also appears to be greater for later than earlier L2 learners, and for L2 speakers with less than more exposure, although confounds between age of exposure and amount of exposure complicate interpretation (Dehaene *et al.*, 1997; Perani *et al.*, 1996; Perani *et al.*, 1998). Greater frontal lobe involvement in L2 than L1 has also varied across studies. Although some studies have not found more frontal activation in L2 than L1 (Dehaene *et al.*, 1997; Perani *et al.*, 1996, 1998), others have found increased frontal activation in L2, albeit in different regions across studies, including BA 44, 45, and 47 (Golestani *et al.*, 2006; Hasegawa *et al.*, 2002; Nakai *et al.*, 1999; Ruschemeyer *et al.*, 2005; Wartenburger *et al.*, 2003).

ERP and hemodynamic evidence from artificial language. Examining artificial language learning and processing offers several important advantages over, and crucially complements, testing only natural language. These advantages include both very rapid learning (e.g., on the order of hours to days to reach high proficiency levels of production and comprehension) and the ability to control for a range of linguistic and other factors. If indeed it can be demonstrated that (at least certain types of) artificial languages constitute valid models for aspects of natural language, this will provide researchers in the study of language with an extremely useful tool, analogous to the reliance of many other scientific disciplines on simplified models to test complex phenomena.

An early ERP study examined a simple artificial language (Brocanto) whose syntactic rules conform to language universals (Friederici *et al.*, 2002). Adults listened to Brocanto sentences while playing a computer-based game until they reached high proficiency at the language, at which point syntactic violations elicited a LAN/P600, typical of L1 natural languages. This ERP pattern was found even for violations of rules that did not exist in any language known to the subjects, ruling out L1–L2 rule transfer.

More recent ERP research used a modified version of Brocanto to examine how L2 neuro-cognition might be differentially affected by explicit training (in which the rules of the language are explained to the learner) and implicit training (in which only meaningful phrases and sentences of the language are heard) (Morgan-Short, 2007; Morgan-Short *et al.*, 2010; Morgan-Short *et al.*, in press). The findings showed that for L2 syntax (Morgan-Short *et al.*, in press), learning under explicit and implicit training conditions led to similar performance on behavioral (performance) measures of the language. There were striking differences, however, in the ERPs elicited by syntactic violations. Implicitly but not explicitly trained learners showed evidence of (a) reliance on lexical/semantic processing, as evidenced by an N400, at low proficiency; and (b) an L1-like LAN/P600 biphasic pattern at high proficiency. For L2 morphosyntax (grammatical gender agreement) (Morgan-Short *et al.*, 2010), some ERP differences were also found between the explicit and implicit training conditions, although neither condition led to a fully native-like biphasic LAN-P600 response.

In an fMRI Brocanto study (Opitz and Friederici, 2003), adult Brocanto acquisition initially involved the hippocampus and temporal neocortical regions. While activation in these brain structures *decreased* during learning, activation *increased* in BA 44. This finding suggests a switch from declarative memory to L1-like (procedural memory) processing during L2 learning. Two other fMRI studies examined the acquisition of artificial grammatical rules that either do or do not follow natural-language universals (Musso *et al.*, 2003; Tettamanti *et al.*, 2002). In both studies, subjects learned both types of rules to high proficiency. In one study, activation increased in Broca's area (BA 45) as proficiency increased, but only for the rules following natural-language patterns (Musso *et al.*, 2003). Similarly, in the other study learners showed activation in Broca's area (BA 44) only for natural-language-like rules (Tettamanti *et al.*, 2002); moreover, those learners with the highest proficiency showed more such activation than learners with somewhat lower proficiency (Tettamanti *et al.*, 2002).

Discussion of ERP and hemodynamic evidence. We have summarized ERP and hemodynamic (fMRI and PET) evidence of lexical and grammatical aspects of L2, examining studies of both natural and artificial language. Studies of ERPs provide evidence for qualitative differences in (morpho)syntactic processing between (a) L2 at lower levels of exposure/proficiency and L1, with LAN/P600 responses typically found in the latter but not the former, for which N400s have been reported; and (b) lower and higher exposure/proficiency L2, with L1-like LAN/P600 responses found only in the latter case. In contrast, no such qualitative differences are found for lexical/semantic processing, which consistently yields N400s in both L1 and L2, irrespective of exposure and proficiency levels. Overall, this pattern is consistent with the qualitative differences predicted by the DP model and Paradis.

From hemodynamic studies perhaps the clearest findings are from lexical/semantic processing, which do not seem to show any qualitative differences between L1 and L2. For grammatical processing the pattern is less clear, with both differences and similarities between L1 and L2 reported across studies. Perhaps the clearest hemodynamic results seem to be found in studies of grammatical processing of artificial languages, for which the evidence appears to be largely consistent with that from ERPs: L1-like processing patterns at high but not low levels of exposure and proficiency, and declarative memory brain structures active only at low levels, as would be expected by the DP model and Paradis.

It is interesting to note that, to our knowledge, hemodynamic as well as ERP studies that employ longitudinal designs, in which between-subject variability is eliminated, consistently provide evidence of a qualitative neurocognitive shift in (morpho)syntactic processing with increasing exposure and proficiency (Morgan-Short, 2007; Morgan-Short *et al.*, 2010; Morgan-Short *et al.*, in press; Opitz and Friederici, 2003; Osterhout *et al.*, 2008; Osterhout *et al.*, 2006). Specifically, ERP studies with longitudinal designs report qualitative shifts of neural patterns with increasing L2 exposure and proficiency, either from one ERP component to others (e.g., from N400 to LAN/P600), or from an absence of components to their emergence (e.g., of a P600) (Morgan-Short *et al.*, 2010; Morgan-Short *et al.*, in press; Opitz and Friederici, 2003; Osterhout *et al.*, 2006; Osterhout *et al.*, 2008). Likewise, the one longitudinal fMRI study we are aware of reported a shift from declarative memory brain structures at low proficiency to BA 44 (implicated in L1 syntactic processing and procedural memory) at high proficiency. Thus longitudinal studies seem to support the DP model and Paradis.

In sum, although there appears to be a fair bit of variability in the findings of cross-sectional hemodynamic studies of L2 grammar, consistent findings can be found in various strands of L2 neurocognitive research: (a) in ERP studies, whether of natural or artificial language; (b) in hemodynamic as well as ERP studies of artificial language; (c) in longitudinal studies, again whether using ERP or hemodynamic methods; and (d) in hemodynamic studies of lexical/semantic processing. Overall, these consistencies support the qualitative neurocognitive L1/L2 differences and low/high exposure and proficiency shifts predicted by the DP model and Paradis.

Future research is necessary to understand why some strands of L2 neurocognitive research are more consistent than others. For example, it remains to be resolved why the ERP approach might yield much greater consistency across studies of grammatical processing than hemodynamic methods (e.g., perhaps the small number of ERP components leads to less variability than hemodynamic activation patterns; the violation paradigm used in ERPs is more consistent than the task paradigms used in fMRI or PET, etc.). Moreover, some of the consistent strands of research are still somewhat confounded. In particular, almost all longitudinal L2 studies examine artificial language, so it is remains unclear whether the consistency of such studies is due to their longitudinal design or to the fact that they examine artificial languages. Nevertheless, both artificial languages (see above) and longitudinal designs (de Bot, 2008; Green, 2003; Indefrey, 2006; Larsen-Freeman and Cameron, 2008; Ortega and Byrnes, 2008; Osterhout *et al.*, 2006; Steinhauer *et al.*, 2009) seem to offer clear advantages, and both seem worthwhile pursuing.

Applications

It is not yet clear to what extent L2 neurocognitive research has direct implications for L2 instruction. However, as researchers continue to adopt a more explanatory rather than descriptive approach, we will gain a deeper understanding of the neurocognition of L2 processing and acquisition, which should lead to clearer implications for instruction. In other words, as we come to understand *why* there are similarities or differences between L1 and L2, we may better be able to draw conclusions about *how* instruction can best be structured to promote successful L2 acquisition.

Based on current research, however, we can already draw a few cautious conclusions about the instructional relevance of L2 neurocognitive research. First, the neurocognitive evidence seems promising for adult L2 learners. It is not the case that such learners are unable to achieve L1-like neural processing. Rather increasing evidence suggests that they can do so, not only for lexical/semantics but also for at least some aspects of grammar. Of course native-like neurocognition does not imply native-like proficiency (conversely, high L2 proficiency does not necessarily suggest a dependence on native-language neurocognitive mechanisms; Ullman, 2005). Nevertheless, given that L1 mechanisms are evidently extremely well-suited to language, it is quite plausible that native-like proficiency might be reliably attained only with native-language neurocognitive mechanisms. Thus the achievement of such mechanisms by L2 learners is good news.

Second, as we have seen, some research suggests that the type of training and instruction can influence the achievement of L1-like neurocognitive mechanisms. Specifically, learning under more implicit contexts, such as immersion, may be more effective at promoting L1-like processing at higher levels of proficiency than more explicit contexts such as traditional grammar-focused classroom settings. This suggestion is based on two observations: (a) The only study to examine the effects of explicit and implicit training on the neurocognition of L2 found that when processing syntactic elements of an artificial L2, implicitly trained learners evidenced both the automatic and controlled processes (i.e., LAN-P600) seen in native speakers whereas explicitly trained learners evidenced controlled (i.e., P600) but not automatic processes (Morgan-Short et al., in press); and (b) an examination of neurocognitive studies of natural L2 showing L1-like grammatical processing suggests that these effects are generally found in L2 learners who have been immersed in their L2 for non-trivial amounts of time (e.g., Gillon Dowens et al., 2009; Hahne et al., 2006; Rossi et al., 2006; Steinhauer et al., 2009). Although additional studies are clearly needed (e.g., in these natural language studies immersion is not teased apart from other factors such as motivation and amount of exposure), the evidence suggests that immersion may be an important element in attaining native-like neurocognition.

Future directions

Neurocognitive L2 research has clearly contributed to our understanding of L2 acquisition and processing. The empirical research has begun to paint an increasingly detailed picture of the neurocognition of aspects of L2, and how it is affected by various factors, including age of acquisition, amount of exposure and proficiency, similarity of L1/L2 linguistic forms, and type of training. Moreover, neurocognitive theories of L2 and its relation to L1 are beginning to explain and, even more importantly, to *predict* the way in which L2 is acquired, represented, and processed in the brain and mind.

But many issues remain unresolved—issues that in some cases have been investigated by the field of SLA and have not been addressed by neurocognitive research, but in other cases have been left entirely unexamined. We strongly believe that the future of L2 research should be bi-directional in the sense that the fields of SLA and cognitive neuroscience should inform each other. Neurocognitive research may be able to shed light on central questions in SLA that are difficult to assess with behavioral methods alone. Neurocognitive researchers, moreover, would be wise to design their studies in a manner informed by theoretical perspectives and empirical findings from SLA (de Bot, 2008).

Following are some issues and questions that would greatly benefit from future investigations, and at least in some cases from an influence from SLA research:

(1) Although most neurocognitive L2 research has examined lexical and grammatical processing—the topic of this chapter—other L2 domains are also important, such as prosody and phonology. Indeed, some research has begun to examine these areas (Chandrasekaran et al., in Press; Sanders and Neville, 2003; Sanders et al., 2002; Song et al., 2008; Wong et al., 2008; Wong et al., 2007), though much work remains to be done.

(2) Most neurocognitive L2 studies to date have examined language processing. Future studies should begin to investigate the acquisition and learning of L2 (e.g., neuroimaging during the acquisition of an artificial language).

(3) As discussed in the introduction to this chapter, research on the factors affecting L2 neurocognition has been limited to a small number of factors, in particular age of acquisition and proficiency. However, many other intrinsic (e.g., sex, genotype) and extrinsic (e.g., type of training) factors need to be investigated, some of which are specifically predicted by neurocognitive theory to play important roles (see above). Additionally, the factors of proficiency and exposure, which have been confounded by most previous research, need to be teased apart.

Conclusion

In sum, the explosion of research in recent years on the neurocognition of L2 has begun to elucidate the neural and cognitive bases of L2 acquisition, representation and processing. These empirical and theoretical advances not only complement SLA research, but also crucially help to answer questions that have been difficult to address within the field of SLA as it has been traditionally defined. In the future, SLA and cognitive neuroscience will increasingly interact, and indeed a new area of research tightly integrating the two is likely to emerge.

References

Abutalebi, J. (2008). Neural aspects of second language representation and language control. *Acta Psychologica*, *128*(3), 466–478.

Abutalebi, J., and Green, D. (2007). Bilingual language production: The neurocognition of language representation and control. *Journal of Neurolinguistics*, *20*, 242–275.

Bachevalier, J. (2001). Neural bases of memory development: insights from neuropsychological studies in primates. In C. A. Nelson and M. Luciana (Eds.), *Handbook of developmental cognitive neurosience* (pp. 365–379). Cambridge: The MIT Press.

Chandrasekaran, B., Sampath, P. D., and Wong, P. C. M. (2010). Individual variability in cue-weighting and lexical tone learning. *Journal of the Acoustical Society of America*, 128(1), 456–465.

Chee, M. W., Tan, E. W., and Thiel, T. (1999). Mandarin and English single word processing studied with functional magnetic resonance imaging. *Journal of Neuroscience*, *19*(8), 3050–3056.

Chen, L., Shu, H., Liu, Y., Zhao, J., and Li, P. (2007). ERP signatures of subject-verb agreement in L2 learning. *Bilingualism: Language and Cognition*, *10*(2), 161–174.

Chomsky, N. (1995). *The minimalist program*. Cambridge, MA: The MIT Press.

Chun, M. M. (2000). Contextual cueing of visual attention. *Trends in Cognitive Sciences*, *4*(5), 170–178.

Clahsen, H., and Felser, C. (2006a). Continuity and shallow structures in language processing: A reply to our commentators. *Applied Psycholinguistics*, *27*(1), 107–126.

Clahsen, H., and Felser, C. (2006b). Grammatical processing in language learners. *Applied Psycholinguistics*, *27*(1), 3–42.

Clahsen, H., and Felser, C. (2006c). How native-like is non-native language proceessing? *Trends in Cognitive Science*, *10*(12), 564–570.

Dapretto, M., and Bookheimer, S. Y. (1999). Form and content: Dissociating syntax and semantics in sentence comprehension. *Neuron*, *24*(2), 427–432.

de Bot, K. (2008). The imaging of what in the multilingual mind?. *Second Language Research*, *24*(1), 111–133.

Dehaene, S., Dupoux, E., Mehler, J., Cohen, L., Paulesu, E., Perani, D. (1997). Anatomical variability in the cortical representation of first and second language. *NeuroReport*, *8*(17), 3809–3815.

DiGiulio, D. V., Seidenberg, M., O'Leary, D. S., and Raz, N. (1994). Procedural and declarative memory: A developmental study. *Brain and Cognition*, *25*(1), 79–91.

Dorfberger, S., Adi-Japha, E., and Karni, A. (2007). Reduced susceptibility to interference in the consolidation of motor memory before adolescence. *PLoS ONE*, *2*(2), 1–6.

Eichenbaum, H., and Lipton, P. A. (2008). Towards a functional organization of the medial temporal lobe memory system: Role of the parahippocampal and medial entorhinal cortical areas. *Hippocampus*, *18*(12), 1314–1324.

Ellis, N. C. (2002a). Frequency effects in language processing: A review with implications for theories of implicit and explicit language acquisition. *Studies in Second Language Acquisition*, *24*, 143–188.

Ellis, N. C. (2002b). Reflections on frequency effects in language processing. *Studies in Second Language Acquisition*, *24*, 297–339.

Ellis, N. C. (2006). Cognitive perspectives on SLA: The Associative-Cognitive CREED. *AILA Review*, *19*(1), 100–121.

Friederici, A. D., and Kotz, S. A. (2003). The brain basis of syntactic processes: Functional imaging and lesion studies. *NeuroImage*, *20* (Supplement 1), S8–S17.

Friederici, A. D., Pfeifer, E., and Hahne, A. (1993). Event-related brain potentials during natural speech processing: Effects of semantic, morphological and syntactic violations. *Cognitive Brain Research*, *1*(3), 183–192.

Friederici, A. D., Ruschemeyer, S. A., Hahne, A., and Fiebach, C. J. (2003). The role of left inferior frontal and superior temporal cortex in sentence comprehension: Localizing syntactic and semantic processes. *Cerebral Cortex*, *13*(2), 170–177.

Friederici, A. D., Steinhauer, K., and Frisch, S. (1999). Lexical integration: Sequential effects of syntactic and semantic information. *Memory and Cognition*, *27*(3), 438–453.

Friederici, A. D., Steinhauer, K., and Pfeifer, E. (2002). Brain signatures of artificial language processing: Evidence challenging the critical period hypothesis. *Proceedings of the National Academy of Sciences, 99*(1), 529–534.

Gillon Dowens, M., Vergara, M., Barber, H., and Carreiras, M. (2009). Morphosyntactic processing in late second-language learners. *Journal of Cognitive Neuroscience, 22*(8), 1870–1887.

Golestani, N., Alario, F. X., Meriaux, S., Le Bihan, D., Dehaene, S., and Pallier, C. (2006). Syntax production in bilinguals. *Neuropsychologia, 44*, 1029–1040.

Graf, P. (1990). Life-span changes in implicit and explicit memory. *Bulletin of the Psychonomic Society, 28*(4), 353–358.

Green, D. W. (2003). Neural basis of lexicon and grammar in L2 acquisition: The convergence hypothesis. In Rv. Hout, A. Hulk, F. Kuiken, and R. Towell (Eds.), *The lexicon-syntax interface in second language acquisition* (pp. 197–218). Amsterdam: John Benjamins.

Green, D. W., Crinion, J., and Price, C. J. (2006). Convergence, degeneracy, and control. *Language Learning, 56* (Supplement 1), 99–125.

Hagoort, P. and Brown, C. M. (1999). Gender electrified: ERP evidence on the syntactic nature of gender processing. *Journal of Psycholinguist Research, 28*(6), 715–728.

Hahne, A. and Friederici, A. D. (1999). Electrophysiological evidence for two steps in syntactic analysis: Early automatic and late controlled processes. *Journal of Cognitive Neuroscience, 11*(2), 194–205.

Hahne, A. and Friederici, A. D. (2001). Processing a second language: Late learners' comprehension mechanisms as revealed by event-related brain potentials. *Bilingualism: Language and Cognition, 4*, 123–141.

Hahne, A., Mueller, J. L., and Clahsen, H. (2006). Morphological processing in a second language: Behavioral and event-related brain potential evidence for storage and decomposition. *Journal of Cognitive Neuroscience, 18*(1), 121–134.

Hasegawa, M., Carpenter, P. A., and Just, M. A. (2002). An fMRI study of bilingual sentence comprehension and workload. *NeuroImage, 15*, 647–660.

Hasson, U., and Small, S. L. (2008). Functional magnetic resonance imaging (fMRI) research of language. In B. Stemmer and H. Whitaker (Eds.), *Handbook of the neuroscience of language* (pp. 81–89). Elsevier.

Henke, K. (2010). A model for memory systems based on processing modes rather than consciousness. *Nature Reviews Neuroscience, 11*, 523–532.

Hernandez, A., Li, P., and MacWhinney, B. (2005). The emergence of competing modules in bilingualism. *Trends in Cognitive Science, 9*(5), 220–225.

Hernandez, A. E., and Li, P. (2007). Age of acquisition: Its neural and computational mechanisms. *Psychological Bulletin, 133*(4), 638–650.

Illes, J., Francis, W. S., Desmond, J. E., Gabrieli, J. D., Glover, G. H., and Poldrack, R. (1999). Convergent cortical representation of semantic processing in bilinguals. *Brain and Language, 70*(3), 347–363.

Indefrey, P. (2006). A meta-analysis of hemodynamic studies on first and second language processing: Which suggested differences can we trust and what do they mean? *Language Learning, 56* (Supplement 1), 279–304.

Isel, F. (2007). Syntactic and referential processes in second-language learners: Event-related brain potential evidence. *NeuroReport, 18*(18), 1885–1889.

Kaan, E. (2007). Event-related potentials and language processing: A brief overview. *Language and Linguistics Compass, 1*(6), 571–591.

Kaan, E., Harris, A., Gibson, E., and Holcomb, P. (2000). The P600 as an index of syntactic integration difficulty. *Language and Cognitive Processes, 15*(2), 159–201.

Klein, D., Milner, B., Zatorre, R. J., Zhao, V., and Nikelski, J. (1999). Cerebral organization in bilinguals: A PET study of Chinese-English verb generation. *NeuroReport, 10*(13), 2841–2846.

Kotz, S. A. (2009). A critical review of ERP and fMRI evidence on L2 syntactic processing. *Brain and Language, 109*, 68–74.

Kuperberg, G. R., McGuire, P. K., Bullmore, E. T., Brammer, M. J., Rabe-Hesketh, S., and Wright, I. C., (2000). Common and distinct neural substrates for pragmatic, semantic, and syntactic processing of spoken sentences: An fMRI study. *Journal of Cognitive Neuroscience, 12*, 321–341.

Kutas, M. and Hillyard, S. A. (1980). Reading between the lines: Event-related brain potentials during natural sentence processing. *Brain and Language, 11*, 354–373.

Larsen-Freeman, D. and Cameron, L. (2008). *Complex systems and applied linguistics.* Oxford: Oxford University Press.

Lau, E. F., Phillips, C., and Poeppel, D. (2008). A cortical network for semantics: (de)constructing the N400. *Nature Reviews Neuroscience, 9*, 920–933.

MacWhinney, B. (2005). A unified model of language acquisition. In J. F. Kroll and A. M. B. Degroot (Eds.), *Handbook of bilingualism: Psycholinguistic approaches* (pp. 49–67). Oxford: Oxford University Press.

MacWhinney, B. (2007). A Unified Model. In N. Ellis and P. Robinson (Eds.), *Handbook of cognitive linguistics and second language acquisition*. Mahwah, NJ: Lawrence Erlbaum Press.

MacWhinney, B. and Bates, E. (Eds.) (1989). *The cross-linguistic study of sentence processing*. New York: Cambridge University Press.

Martin-Loeches, M., Munoz, F., Casado, P., Melcon, A., and Fernandez-Frias, C. (2005). Are the anterior negativities to grammatical violations indexing working memory? *Psychophysiology, 42*, 508–519.

McCarthy, G., Nobre, A. C., Bentin, S., and Spencer, D. D. (1995). Language-related field potentials in the anterior-medial temporal lobe: I. Intracranial distribution and neural generators. *Journal of Neuroscience, 15*(2), 1080–1089.

McLaughlin, J., Osterhout, L., and Kim, A. (2004). Neural correlates of second-language word learning: Minimal instruction produces rapid change. *Nature Neuroscience, 7*(7), 703–704.

Mishkin, M., Malamut, B., and Bachevalier, J. (1984). Memories and habits: Two neural systems. In G. Lynch, J. L. McGaugh, and N. W. Weinburger (Eds.), *Neurobiology of learning and memory* (pp. 65–77). New York: Guilford Press.

Morgan-Short, K. (2007). *A neurolinguistic investigation of late-learned second language knowledge: the effects of explicit and implicit conditions*. Dissertation. Georgetown University, Washington, D.C.

Morgan-Short, K., Sanz, C., Steinhauer, K., and Ullman, M. T. (2010). Second language acquisition of gender agreement in explicit and implicit training conditions: An event-related potential study. *Language Learning, 60*(1), 154–193.

Morgan-Short, K., Steinhauer, K., Sanz, C., and Ullman, M. T. (in press). Implicit but not explicit second language training leads to native-language brain patterns. *Journal of Cognitive Neuroscience*.

Mueller, J. L. (2005). Electrophysiological correlates of second language processing. *Second Language Research, 21*(2), 152–174.

Musso, M., Moro, A., Glauche, V., Rijntjes, M., Reichenbach, J., and Buchel, C. (2003). Broca's area and the language instinct. *Nature Neuroscience, 6*(7), 774–781.

Nakai, T., Matsuo, K., Kato, C., Matsuzawa, M., Okada, T., and Glover, G. H. (1999). A functional magnetic resonance imaging study of listening comprehension of languages in human at 3 tesla-comprehension level and activation of the language areas. *Neuroscience Letters, 263*(1), 33–36.

Neville, H. J., Nicol, J. L., Barss, A., Forster, K. I., and Garrett, M. F. (1991). Syntactically based sentence processing classes: Evidence from event-related brain potentials. *Journal of Cognitive Neuroscience, 3*(2), 151–165.

Newman, A. J., Pancheva, R., Ozawa, K., Neville, H. J., and Ullman, M. T. (2001). An event-related fMRI study of syntactic and semantic violations. *Journal of Psycholinguistic Research, 30*(3), 339–364.

Ojima, S., Nakata, H., and Kakigi, R. (2005). An ERP study on second language learning after childhood: Effects of proficiency. *Journal of Cognitive Neuroscience, 17*(8), 1212–1228.

Opitz, B., and Friederici, A. D. (2003). Interactions of the hippocampal system and the prefrontal cortex in learning language-like rules. *NeuroImage, 19*(4), 1730–1737.

Ortega, L., and Byrnes, H. (Eds.) (2008). *The longitudinal study of advanced L2 capacities*. New York: Routledge.

Osterhout, L., Bersick, M., and McLaughlin, J. (1997). Brain potentials reflect violations of gender stereotypes. *Memory and Cognition, 25*(3), 273–285.

Osterhout, L., and Holcomb, P. J. (1992). Event-related brain potentials elicited by syntactic anomaly. *Journal of Memory and Language, 31*, 785–806.

Osterhout, L., McLaughlin, J., Pitkänen, I., Frenck-Mestre, C., and Molinaro, N. (2006). Novice learners, longitudinal designs, and event-related potentials: A means for exploring the neurocognition of second language processing. *Language Learning, 56* (Supplement 1), 199–230.

Osterhout, L., Poliakov, A., Inoue, K., McLaughlin, J., Valentine, G., Pitkanen, I., Frenck-Mestre, C. and Hirschensohn, J. (2008). Second-language learning and changes in the brain. *Journal of Neurolinguistics, 21*(6), 509–521.

Paradis, M. (1994). Neurolinguistic aspects of implicit and explicit memory: Implications for bilingualism and SLA. In N. C. Ellis (Ed.), *Implicit and explicit learning of languages* (pp. 393–419). London, UK: Academic Press.

Paradis, M. (2004). *A neurolinguistic theory of bilingualism*. Amsterdam, Netherlands: John Benjamins.

Paradis, M. (2009). *Declarative and procedural determinants of second languages* (Vol. 40). John Benjamins Publishing Company.

Perani, D., Abutalebi, J., Paulesu, E., Brambati, S., Scifo, P., and Cappa, S. F. (2003). The role of age of acquisition and language usage in early, high-proficient bilinguals: An fMRI study during verbal fluency. *Human Brain Mapping, 19*(3), 170–182.

Perani, D., Dehaene, S., Grassi, F., Cohen, L., Cappa, S. F., and Dupoux, E. (1996). Brain processing of native and foreign languages. *NeuroReport*, 7(15–17), 2439–2444.

Perani, D., Paulesu, E., Galles, N. S., Dupoux, E., Dehaene, S., and Bettinardi, V. (1998). The bilingual brain. Proficiency and age of acquisition of the second language. *Brain*, 121(10), 1841–1852.

Pillai, J. J., Allison, J. D., Sethuraman, S., Araque, J. M., Thiruvaiyaru, D., and Ison, C. B. (2004). Functional MR imaging study of language-related differences in bilingual cerebellar activation. *AJNR Am J Neuroradiol*, 25(4), 523–532.

Poldrack, R. A. and Foerde, K. (2008). Category learning and the memory systems debate. *Neuroscience and Biobehavioral Reviews*, 32, 197–205.

Poldrack, R. A. and Packard, M. G. (2003). Competition among multiple memory systems: Converging evidence from animal and human brain studies. *Neuropsychologia*, 41(3), 245–251.

Poldrack, R. A. Wagner, A. D., Prull, M. W., Desmond, J. E., Glover, G. H., and Gabrieli, J. D. (1999). Functional specialization for semantic and phonological processing in the left inferior prefrontal cortex. *NeuroImage*, 10(1), 15–35.

Rossi, S., Gugler, M. F., Friederici, A. D., and Hahne, A. (2006). The impact of proficiency on syntactic second-language processing of German and Italian: Evidence from event-related potentials. *Journal of Cognitive Neuroscience*, 18(12), 2030–2048.

Ruschemeyer, S. A., Fiebach, C. J., Kempe, V., and Friederici, A. D. (2005). Processing lexical semantic and syntactic information in first and second language: FMRI evidence from German and Russian. *Hum Brain Mapp*, 25(2), 266–286.

Sanders, L. D., Neville, H., and Woldorff, M. G. (2002). Speech segmentation by native and non-native speakers: The use of lexical, syntactic, and stress-pattern cues. *Journal of Speech, Language, and Hearing Research*, 45(3), 519–530.

Sanders, L. D. and Neville, H. J. (2003). An ERP study of continuous speech processing. II. Segmentation, semantics, and syntax in non-native speakers. *Cognitive Brain Research*, 15(3), 214–227.

Schmidt, G. L. and Roberts, T. P. L. (2009). Second language research using magnetoencephalography: A review. *Second Language Research*, 25(1), 135–166.

Siegel, D. J. (2001). Memory: An overview, with emphasis on developmental, interpersonal, and neurobiological aspects. *Journal of the American Academy of Child and Adolescent Psychiatry*, 40(9), 997–1011.

Simos, P. G., Basile, L. F. H., and Papanicolaou, A. C. (1997). Source localization of the N400 response in a sentence-reading paradigm using evoked magnetic fields and magnetic resonance imaging. *Brain Research*, 762(1–2), 29–39.

Song, J. H., Skoe, E., Wong, P. C. M., and Kraus, N. (2008). Plasticity in the adult human auditory brainstem following short-term linguistic training. *Journal of Cognitive Neuoscience*, 20(10), 1892–1902.

Squire, L. R. and Schacter, D. L. (2002). *Neuropsychology of memory* (Third Edition.) New York: The Guildford Press.

Steinhauer, K. and Connolly, J. F. (2008). Event-related Potentials in the Study of Language. In B. Stemmer and H. A. Whitaker (Eds.), *Handbook of the neuroscience of language*. Oxford, UK: Elsevier.

Steinhauer, K., White, E. J., and Drury, J. E. (2009). Temporal dynamics of late second language acquisition: Evidence from event-related brain potentials. *Second Language Research*, 25(1), 13–41.

Stowe, L. A. and Sabourin, L. (2005). Imaging the processing of a second language: Effects of maturation and proficiency on the neural processes involved. *International Review of Applied Linguistics in Language Teaching*, 43(4), 329–353.

Tettamanti, M., Alkadhi, H., Moro, A., Perani, D., Kollias, S., and Weniger, D. (2002). Neural correlates for the acquisition of natural language syntax. *NeuroImage*, 17(2), 700–709.

Tokowicz, N. and MacWhinney, B. (2005). Implicit and explicit measures of sensitivity to violations in second language grammar: An event-related potential investigation. *Studies in Second Language Acquisition*, 27(2), 173–204.

Ullman, M. T. (2001a). The neural basis of lexicon and grammar in first and second language: The declarative/procedural model. *Bilingualism: Language and Cognition*, 4(1), 105–122.

Ullman, M. T. (2001b). A neurocognitive perspective on language: The declarative/procedural model. *Nature Reviews Neuroscience*, 2, 717–726.

Ullman, M. T. (2004). Contributions of memory circuits to language: The declarative/procedural model. *Cognition*, 92(1–2), 231–270.

Ullman, M. T. (2005). A cognitive neuroscience perspective on second language acquisition: The declarative/procedural model. In C. Sanz (Ed.), *Mind and context in adult second language acquisition: Methods, theory and practice* (pp. 141–178). Washington, D.C.: Georgetown University Press.

Ullman, M. T. (2006). The declarative/procedural model and the shallow-structure hypothesis. *Journal of Applied Psycholinguistics, 27*(1), 97–105.

Ullman, M. T. (2007). The biocognition of the mental lexicon. In M. G. Gaskell (Ed.), *The Oxford handbook of psycholinguistics* (pp. 267–286). Oxford, UK: Oxford University Press.

Ullman, M. T. (2008). The role of memory systems in disorders of language. In B. Stemmer and H. A. Whitaker (Eds.), *Handbook of the neuroscience of language* (pp. 189–198). Oxford, UK: Elsevier Ltd.

Ullman, M. T., Miranda, R. A., and Travers, M. L. (2008). Sex differences in the neurocognition of language. In J. B. Becker, K. J. Berkley, N. Geary, E. Hampson, J. Herman, and E. Young (Eds.), *Sex on the brain: From genes to behavior* (pp. 291–309). New York, NY: Oxford University Press.

Vaidya, C. J., Huger, M., Howard, D. V., and Howard, J. H. J. (2007). Developmental differences in implicit learning of spatial context. *Neuropsychology, 21*(4), 497–506.

van Hell, J. G. and Tokowicz, N. (2010). Event-related brain potentials and second language learning: Syntactic processing in late L2 learners at different L2 proficiency levels. *Second Language Research, 26*(1), 43–74.

Wartenburger, I., Heekeren, H. R., Abutalebi, J., Cappa, S. F., Villringer, A., and Perani, D. (2003). Early setting of grammatical processing in the bilingual brain. *Neuron, 37*, 159–170.

Weber-Fox, C. M. and Neville, H. J. (1996). Maturational constraints on functional specializations for language processing: ERP and behavioral evidence in bilingual speakers. *Journal of Cognitive Neuroscience, 8*(3), 231–256.

Wong, P. C. M., Perrachione, T. K., and Parrish, T. B. (2007). Neural characteristics of successful and less successful speech and word learning in adults. *Human Brain Mapping, 28*, 995–1006.

Wong, P. C. M., Warrier, C. M., Penhune, V. B., Roy, A. K., Sadehh, A., and Parrish, T. B. (2008). Volume of left Heschl's Gyrus and linguistic pitch learning. *Cerebral Cortex, 18*, 828–836.

Xue, G., Dong, Q., Jin, Z., Zhang, L., and Wang, Y. (2004). An fMRI study with semantic access in low proficiency second language learners. *Neuroreport, 15*(5), 791–796.

Part IV
Skill learning

18

Development of second language reading skills

Cross-linguistic perspectives

Keiko Koda

Introduction

Reading is a complex construct, involving multiple operations and a unique set of skills each of those operations entail. When learning to read occurs in a second language (L2), the complexity increases exponentially because each operation involves two languages (Koda, 2005). The primary objective of this chapter is to explore how the involvement of two languages affects L2 reading development. In probing highly complex issues, entailing multiple skills in multiple languages, it is important to clarify the basic assumptions underlying the conceptual explorations.

First, under the input driven view of learning (Ellis, 2002), learning—be it of language or reading—is regarded as the process of detecting, abstracting, and internalizing regularly co-occurring elements in input as corresponding units. Learning is achieved primarily through cumulative experience of mapping between corresponding elements. The more frequently particular patterns of mappings are experienced, the stronger the linkages holding them together. Under this view, reading skills are seen as an outcome of cumulative experience of symbol-to-sound, as well as symbol-to-morpheme, mappings.

Next, from a developmental perspective, Perfetti and associates (Perfetti, 2003; Perfetti and Dunlap, 2008) regard reading as a dynamic pursuit embedded in two interrelated systems: a language and its writing system. Because no writing systems directly encode meaning independent of language, reading acquisition involves making links between the two systems. In learning to read, therefore, children must uncover how spoken language elements are mapped onto the graphic symbols that encode them. It is hardly accidental that reading instruction does not commence until children acquire sufficient spoken language competence. Reading development thus necessitates substantial linguistic knowledge.

Transfer has been a major theoretical concept in second language (L2) research. Studies have repeatedly shown that L2 learning is affected by previously acquired competencies. Based on this notion of transfer, L2 reading research generally assumes that L2 reading skills are shaped jointly by transferred first language (*L1*) skills, *L2* linguistic knowledge and *L2* print input. In this regard, L2 reading is cross-linguistic, entailing continual interaction and assimilation of L1 and L2 factors. Theories of L2 reading must explain how the involvement of two languages affects

L2 reading development; how transferred L1 skills are assimilated in L2 reading; and how the resulting L2 skills vary across learners with diverse L1 backgrounds.

Historical discussion

L2 reading research has evolved both as an extension of L1 reading and as a branch of second language acquisition (SLA). Reflecting such subordination, impacts of major conceptual changes in the two fields are apparent in its theoretical orientations. In the sections below, those changes are briefly described and their relevance to the emergence of cross-linguistic perspectives in L2 reading research discussed.

Shifting views of reading

Over the past 40 years, L1 reading research has gone through dramatic changes in the way the very construct of reading is conceptualized. In the early days, under the premise that reading is a conceptually driven process, it was likened to a "psycholinguistic guessing game" (Goodman, 1973). In this view, readers were believed to engage in forming and confirming a series of hypotheses about up-coming text contents. Two assumptions underlie this top-down view of reading. First, as a communication (meaning-making) system, reading is an indivisible whole and should be treated as such in examining its process and development (Goodman, 1967). As a result, early reading studies treated reading as a single unitary construct, relegating all component skills to the periphery. Second, as a conceptually driven enterprise, the basic process of reading is largely unaffected by language elements and their properties (Goodman, 1969). Reading was thus considered universal across languages. However, both these assumptions were later challenged and largely discredited.

In the following decade, advances in technology made it possible to incorporate more sophisticated measurements and data collection techniques in reading research, and as a consequence, more complex models of reading began to emerge. Unlike the earlier view, these newer models uniformly regard reading as a complex, multi-faceted, construct. In the component skills approach (Carr and Levy, 1990), for example, reading is seen as the product of a complex information-processing system, involving a constellation of closely related mental operations. These operations are theoretically distinct and empirically separable. To fulfill the assigned function, each of these operations necessitates a set of processing skills, which interact and impact upon one another to facilitate perception, comprehension, and memory of visually presented language. The component approach further presumes variances in virtually all facets of reading ability. Studies conducted under this view aim to determine which particular variances are centrally related to reading competence by isolating component skills for inspection. The approach thus provides solid bases for determining the sources of reading problems attributable to a single deficiency or a combination of multiple deficiencies in specific skills.

The universality assumed in the top-down view of reading has also been contested. Experimental psychologists have repeatedly challenged language-processing theories based on data obtained exclusively from native English-speaking participants. Sentence processing research, for example, has shown that the cognitive strategies involved in sentence comprehension and production are heavily constrained by the syntactic properties of the language inspected (Bates and MacWhinney, 1989; Bates et al., 1982; Kail, 1989; Mazuka and Itoh, 1995). Word recognition studies have also reported that different procedures are used during print information processing by skilled readers of a wide variety of languages employing typologically diverse writing systems, and that those varied procedures are identifiable with the distinct properties of their respective writing systems (e.g., Katz and Frost, 1992; Saito *et al.*, 1999; Taft and Zhu, 1995; Vaid, 1995).

Of late, the notion of reading universals has reemerged. Unlike the earlier view, the current conceptualization (Perfetti and Dunlap, 2008; Perfetti and Liu, 2005; Perfetti, 2003) incorporates the multi-dimensionality of reading and cross-linguistic variations in its operations. By specifying the universally mandated demands for learning to read, imposed on all learners in all languages, the theory sets the limits on possible variations in learning to read across languages and in so doing, stipulates precisely where cross-linguistic variations occur. Such stipulation is critical because languages vary in virtually all aspects of meaning-making conventions, as well as in the methods of graphically encoding those conventions. Clearly, the theory laid a solid foundation on which the language-specific demands for learning to read can be identified and compared systematically across typologically diverse languages.

Changing conceptions of reading transfer

Although transfer has long been a major concern in L2 reading research, there is no explicit theory explaining how reading skills developed in one language affect learning to read in another. In the absence of general guiding principles, transfer studies pursued how L1 and L2 reading abilities are related primarily under the *developmental interdependence* hypothesis (Cummins, 1979, Cummins, 1991). The hypothesis posits that academic language competence is supported by a set of non language-specific capacities, referred to as "common underlying proficiency." Hence, the development of L2 academic language competence, including literacy skills, is determined, to a major extent, by the degree to which the "common underlying proficiency" has been established in the primary language. Although the hypothesis has prompted a significant amount of useful research, it offers little clarification as to what constitutes the core construct of "common underlying proficiency." As a result, subsequent studies examining the hypothesized interdependence vary in nearly all aspects of their design, including participants' characteristics (age, language background, ethnicity, academic status), "academic" skills measured and assessment tools used. These deviations make it difficult to consolidate empirical findings across studies to draw collective conclusions regarding the role of shared competencies in learning to read in an additional language.

In more recent studies, reading skills have been more clearly defined within the component approach and more accurately measured in two languages. Such refinements make it possible to clarify the fundamental notion of "common underlying proficiency" and to empirically examine cross-linguistic relationships in a variety of skills both in isolation and in tandem in the pursuit of "developmental interdependence." These newer studies have shown systematic connections in a still small, but critical, set of skills (e.g., phonological awareness, decoding, orthographic processing) across diverse combinations of languages (e.g., Spanish/English, Hebrew/English, Turkish/Dutch, English/Chinese) in school-age biliteracy learners.

Core issues

Over the years, the conceptual bases of L2 reading research have become increasingly more sophisticated. Under the more refined views of reading, a growing number of studies have begun to use programmatic approaches in addressing complex, cross-linguistic, issues in L2 reading development. In particular, three interrelated questions are currently being addressed: (1) how do reading skills in two languages relate to one another?; (2) which factors affect the way transferred L1 skills are assimilated in L2 reading?; and (3) how do the resulting L2 skills vary across learners with diverse L1 backgrounds?

Cross-linguistic relationships in reading skills

What is actually transferred is one of the most fundamental questions in reading transfer research. Within the component skills approach, many of the skills vital to successful reading have been identified. While some skills—for example, those involved in linguistic information processing—are language-specific, directly affected by linguistic properties, others are cognitive and do not vary across languages. Given these differences, it is critical to determine whether all transferred skills are assimilated in L2 reading in the same manner and to the same extent. If the answer is yes, all reading skills in one language should relate systematically and similarly to corresponding skills in the other. If, however, disparities exist, there should be parallel divergence in the way corresponding skills are related between two languages. Two hypotheses— "central processing" (Da Fontoura and Siegel, 1995) and "script-dependent" (Gholamain and Geva, 1999)—are useful in exploring variations in the way the two types of skills (language-specific and non language-specific) affect reading development in an additional language.

The "central processing" hypothesis posits that differences in underlying cognitive factors (such as working memory and coding speed) are primarily responsible for variances in reading achievements in school-age bilingual learners in both their languages. Its central claim is that children who are good readers in their L1 have a much better chance of achieving higher reading proficiency in a second language. Conversely, children with specific reading disability in one language are likely to experience similar difficulties in another language. Obviously, the notion of "central processing" originated in the concept of "common underlying proficiency" in Cummins' developmental inter-dependence hypothesis (1979, 1991). Grounded in the current theories of reading, however, the "central processing" hypothesis provides clear delineations of the skills that constitute the "central processing" capacity, making it possible to test the specific predictions the hypothesis has generated.

In contrast, the "script-dependent" hypothesis contends that decoding development is facili-tated by phonological transparency (i.e., degrees of regularity in symbol-sound correspondences) of the writing system. The hypothesis aims to explain why decoding skills are acquired more easily in some languages than in others. The formulation underscores the significance of phonological transparency and other language-specific properties as a critical factor explaining variations in reading acquisition.

Although the two formulations seem diametrically opposite in their core contentions, the two are complementary in that each explains the specific way in which two types of reading skills, language-specific (e.g., symbol-to-sound mappings) and non language-specific (e.g., word seg-mentation) affect L2 reading development. The distinction is important because the two types of skills presumably behave differently when transferred to L2 reading. To illustrate, non language-specific skills, once developed in one language, should be available and serviceable in learning to read in another language. In principle, these skills, if available, should provide all L2 learners, regardless of their L1 background, with direct and equal facilitation in L2 reading acquisition. However, such uniformity cannot be expected for language-specific skills because they are closely attuned to L1 properties, which may or may not be shared between two languages. For those skills to become functional in a second language, they need to undergo varying degrees of modification. The question then is what determines how much modification is necessary for such functional adjustment.

Factors affecting the assimilation of L1 skills in L2 reading

Once the involvement of L1 skills in L2 reading is established empirically, the next step is to uncover what happens to language-specific skills when they transfer across languages. Because no two languages are identical, transferred L1 skills must be adjusted to L2 properties. Given that some combinations of languages are more closely related than others, the amount of modification necessary for functional adjustment should vary. The second cross-linguistic issue deals with the factors explaining such variation.

Linguistic distance (degrees of similarity) between two languages is one such factor because it is responsible in large part for individual differences in the rate in which L2 reading skills develop. When the two languages share similar structural properties, what is required for linguistic information processing should also be similar—if not identical. Alphabetic writing systems, for example, share the basic unit of orthographic representation, requiring similar symbol-to-sound mapping procedures for decoding regardless of the graphic form of the symbols (e.g., the Roman script in English vs. the Cyrillic script in Russian). When transfer occurs between two alphabetic systems, therefore, L1 mapping skills should be functional in L2 decoding with minimum modification. Conversely, when two languages are distinct, transferred skills must be substantially modified. L1 and L2 distance thus determines the extent of adjustment necessary for the assimilation of transferred L1 skills in L2 reading.

Ultimately, however, it is the quality (linguistic/orthographic properties) and quantity (frequency) of L2 print input that determine the form and level of L2 skills emerging from a particular instance of L2 literacy learning (Koda, 2008). It is essential that the nature of L2 input be analyzed and documented. Despite its significance, limited attention has been give to input properties, such as structural transparency, frequency, and formation regularity. Investigations of L2 factors have focused mainly on the effects of general language proficiency. Of late, however, a small, but growing, number of studies have begun to incorporate detailed analysis of L2 input properties as the basis for generating hypotheses regarding the relative ease at which varying L2 skills are acquired. Properly sustained, these on-going studies will eventually yield far more specific information on how transferred skills are assimilated in L2 reading.

Variations in L2 reading skills

As mentioned earlier, dual-language involvement is the defining characteristic of L2 reading. It is vital to clarify how two languages interact during L2 print information processing. In the past decade, interest in such interactions has risen. The basic assumptions are two-fold: (1) L2 reading skills are shaped through continual cross-linguistic interactions between transferred L1 skills and L2 print input, and (2) such interactions induce sustained assimilation of print processing experiences in two languages. It follows then that the resulting L2 skills should reflect the major properties of the two languages involved, and therefore, vary systematically across learners with diverse L1 backgrounds. The third, and final, issue has to do with the empirical validation of such variations.

Data and common elicitation measures

Empirical explorations of the cross-linguistic issues outlined above necessitate at the minimum clear specification of focal skills and linguistic demands for their utilization in two languages. Such clarification requires a series of analyses, including construct analysis (isolating reading skills involved in a particular task in learning to read), linguistic analysis (identifying the properties of the linguistic facet directly related to the task under consideration), and cross-linguistic analysis (determining how the properties of the relevant linguistic facet vary between two languages). Sequentially, these analyses enable researchers to convert highly complex cross-linguistic issues into empirically testable hypotheses by allowing them to set the scope of their investigations. The sections below briefly describe these analyses, and then discuss the methodologies commonly used to test the hypotheses generated through the analyses.

Setting the scope: Generating hypotheses

Construct analysis. As a complex psycholinguistic construct, reading involves three major operations: (a) *decoding* (extracting linguistic information directly from print), (b) *text-information building* (integrating the extracted information into phrases, sentences, and paragraphs), and (c) *reader-model construction* (synthesizing the amalgamated text-information with prior knowledge). In examining the impacts of dual-language involvement on L2 reading development, it is essential to clarify the requisite skills for each operation. As an illustration, phonological and morphological information extraction constitutes the requisite *tasks* for *decoding*, and as such, the operation necessitates the skills to map phonological and morphological elements onto units of graphic symbols in the writing system. Because languages differ in the way they graphically represent sub-lexical information, the skills optimal for the required mappings vary across languages. Linguistic analysis is thus in order.

Linguistic analysis. In order to properly address cross-linguistic issues in L2 reading, we must establish reliable methods of comparing corresponding skills between two languages. One such method is to identify the language-specific demands for a particular task by analyzing the properties of the linguistic facet directly related to the task. Using decoding as an example again, efficiency in phonological information extraction in English is largely determined by the ability to manipulate intra-syllabic sounds, such as onset, rhyme, and phoneme, by assembling and dissembling letters and letter clusters (e.g., Ehri, 1998; Shankweiler and Liberman, 1972). It has been widely recognized that competent readers are uniformly adept at pronouncing both individual letters and nonsense letter-strings (e.g., Hogaboam and Perfetti, 1978; Siegel and Ryan, 1988; Wagner *et al.*, 1994); and that such ability depends on orthographic knowledge, that is, understanding the rules about how graphic symbols are used to represent speech sounds (e.g., Adams, 1990; Ehri, 1994, 1998; Seidenberg and McClelland, 1989). In principle, therefore, the linguistic demands for phonological information extraction can be identified by uncovering which phonological unit (e.g., syllable, phoneme) is directly encoded in each graphic symbol and how the symbols are combined to represent spoken words. Accurate descriptions of such demands in two languages make the subsequent, cross-linguistic, analysis possible.

Cross-linguistic analysis. Documentation of the linguistic demands for a particular task allows systematic comparisons of the requisite skills for the task in two languages. Such comparisons permit reasonably accurate estimates of the relative ease with which transferred skills gain functionality in a second language. Once again, using decoding as an illustration, cross-linguistic variation in the requisite skill for phonological information extraction can be identified by comparing the basic unit of orthographic representation in the two languages involved.

Korean children, for example, must develop sensitivity to both syllables and phonemes, because phonological information is encoded at these two levels in their writing system, Hangul. In the Hangul script, the graphic symbols, each representing a distinct phoneme, cannot appear on their own; instead, they must be packaged into blocks to form syllables. In learning to read, phoneme and syllable manipulation skills are both strong predictors of word reading ability in Korean children (McBride-Chan *et al.*, 2005). In contrast, in consonantal Hebrew, children develop stronger sensitivity to consonants than to vowels, and this sensitivity plays a pivotal role in Hebrew literacy development (Geva, 2008; Tolchinsky and Teberosky, 1998). In logographic Chinese, moreover, the grapheme-morpheme connections are more prominent than the grapheme-syllable linkages. Reflecting the stronger morpheme representation, morphological awareness has been found a more powerful predictor of initial reading success in Chinese than is phonological awareness (Ku and Anderson, 2003; Li *et al.*, 2002). Evidently, the requisite skill for a particular task is closely aligned with the properties of the linguistic facet directly related to the task. The incorporation of cross-linguistic analysis, thus, allows empirical examinations of the hypothesized variation in the way previously acquired reading skills affect L2 reading development.

Empirical examinations: Testing hypotheses

Correlational studies. The current views of transfer uniformly treat previously acquired skills as potential resources promoting reading acquisition in another language (August and Shanahan, 2006; Riches and Genesee, 2006). The first step in exploring facilitation benefits stemming from prior literacy experience is to determine whether L1 skills are indeed involved in L2 reading. If a new set of reading skills builds on previously acquired skills, there should be systematic connections between corresponding skills in two languages. Correlational analysis has been widely used to examine cross-linguistic relationships in a variety of reading skills (e.g., phonological awareness, morphological awareness, decoding).

Once the involvement of L1 skills is established empirically, the next step is to determine the directionality in the observed relationships. The problem is that the mere presence of a correlation between two variables does not indicate which of the two may be affecting the other. There is also a possibility that a correlation can be attributed to a "third" variable to which the two variables in the correlation are both related. For these reasons, correlational studies are limited in their simplest forms. They can be made more powerful, however, by incorporating statistical techniques that allow the partial control of "third" variables (Stanovitch and Cunningham, 2004). These techniques, including multiple regression, path analysis, and structural equation modeling, allow the recalculation of the correlation between two variables after the effect of other key variables (possible "third" variables) are removed.

In L2 reading research, hierarchical multiple regression has been used extensively in determining the relative contributions of a variety of competencies, such as oral vocabulary knowledge, phonological awareness and working memory, to L2 reading performance both within and across languages. In these studies, cognitive and maturational factors (e.g., non-verbal intelligence and age) are used as control variables. The inclusion of these and other control variables in the regression analysis ensures that the observed associations between any of the predictor variables (e.g., oral vocabulary knowledge, working memory) and the criterion variable (i.e., reading performance) are not mediated by other related factors. Given that a large proportion of data in educational research is correlational, this and other like techniques are highly advantageous in exploring the role of previously acquired skills in L2 reading development.

Group comparison studies. Another way of exploring the impact of prior literacy experience on L2 reading development is to demonstrate L1-induced variations in L2 processing behaviors among learners with diverse L1 backgrounds. Typically, empirical evidence for such variations is obtained through cross-linguistic experiments, wherein performances on experimental tasks are compared between two comparable L2 learner groups, differing only in their L1 backgrounds. Experimental tasks are designed to elicit particular processing behaviors, which are clearly identifiable with specific L1 properties. By design, experimental manipulations should induce a greater impact on the group whose L1 processing behaviors are targeted for manipulation. If the two groups respond differentially to such manipulations, the observed variation can be taken as an indication that L1 skills are indeed used during L2 print information processing.

To illustrate, L2 learners of English (ESL) with alphabetic and logographic L1 backgrounds can be contrasted in their reliance on phonemic analysis during phonological information extraction.

Because alphabetic literacy requires segmenting and assembling phonological information at the phonemic level, alphabetic readers rely heavily on phonemic analysis. In contrast, phonological decoding in logographic languages does not entail similar analysis because the spoken sound of a single morpheme corresponds holistically to a single graphic symbol. A word's phonology (usually a syllable) is mapped onto the visual display (a single character) as a whole. Hence, phonological information extraction in logographic writing systems requires no analysis or segmentation at the phonemic level. Instead, logographic readers are required to distinguish a large number of visually complex symbols. In light of these disparities, two experimental manipulations—one blocking a word's phonological information and the other distorting the visual configuration—should affect phonological decoding differently among ESL learners with alphabetic and logographic L1 backgrounds. When phonological information is made unavailable, decoding performance of alphabetic ESL learners will be more seriously disrupted, whereas visual distortion will impede phonological decoding among logographic learners to a greater extent.

These predictions have been tested using a variety of experimental manipulations, including case alterations (e.g., replacing "read" with "ReAd"; Akamatsu, 2003) and phonological information blocking (e.g., replacing words with unpronounceable symbols; Koda, 1990). Because these manipulations are designed to cause processing disruption by blocking the information presumed to be critical for phonological decoding in participants' respective first languages, performance decline, if occurred, can be taken as evidence for the presence of L1 decoding skills in L2 print information processing. The section that follows discusses empirical results from studies examining the three core issues.

Empirical verification

Cross-linguistic relationships in reading skills. On the assumption that L2 reading success depends largely on common underlying competencies, early bilingual studies investigated how L1 and L2 reading abilities are related (e.g., Cummins *et al.*, 1981; Legarretta, 1979; Skutnabb-Kangass and Toukomaa, 1976; Troike, 1978). Their results consistently showed that reading abilities among school-age children were strongly related in their two languages. Such a relationship was taken as indicating that L1 reading competence is the chief determinant of L2 reading achievement (Cummins, 1979, 1991). In these early studies, however, reading was uniformly treated as a single unitary construct, and the critical question—how corresponding skills are related between two languages–remained unaddressed.

Under the componential view of reading, more recent studies have begun to incorporate larger batteries of tasks designed to measure a variety of skills and cognitive capacities, including phonological awareness (Branum-Martin *et al.*, 2006; Durgunoglu *et al.*, 1993; Wade-Woolley and Geva, 2000; Wang *et al.*, 2006), decoding (Abu-Rabia, 1997; Da Fontoura and Siegel, 1995; Durgunoglu *et al.*, 1993; Geva and Siegle, 2000; Gholamain and Geva, 1999; Wade-Woolley and Geva, 2000), syntactic awareness (Abu-Rabia, 1995; Da Fontoura and Siegel, 1995), and working memory (Abu-Rabia, 1995; Da Fontoura and Siegel, 1995; Geva and Siegle, 2000; Gholamain and Geva, 1999).

Because these studies involved children learning to read two alphabetic languages, it is less certain whether the reported cross-linguistic relationships can be generalized to others whose literacy learning involves two typologically dissimilar languages. A small, but growing, body of evidence suggests that phonological awareness is systematically related in Chinese and English (Bialystok *et al.*, 2005; McBride-Chan *et al.*, 2006; Wang *et al.*, 2005), but phonological awareness in one language only minimally contributes to decoding in the other (Luk and Bialystok, 2008; Wang *et al.*, 2005). This makes a stark contrast with the strong functional relationship between L1 phonological awareness and L2 decoding skills found in Spanish–English bilingual children (e.g., Durgunoglu *et al.*, 1993). Unlike phonological awareness, moreover, other competencies, such as orthographic knowledge and morphological awareness, are not systematically related in Chinese and English in school-aged biliteracy learners (Wang *et al.*, 2005).

A sub-set of the biliteracy studies listed above further explored, within the "central processing" hypothesis, common deficiencies explaining reading failure in both languages in at-risk bilingual school-age readers. Their analyses revealed that poor readers are uniformly weak in phonological skills in both languages; and that their deficiencies usually are domain-specific and cannot be explained by non-phonological factors (e.g., Abu-Rabia, 1995; August *et al.*, 2002; Carlisle and Beeman, 2000; Cormier and Kelson, 2000; da Fontoura and Siegel, 1995; Gholamain and Geva, 1999; Verhoeven, 2000; Wade-Woolley and Geva, 2000). These results provide strong empirical support for the critical role that "central processing" capacities, or "common underlying proficiency" (Cummins, 1979), play in literacy learning in an additional languages.

Taken as a whole, these findings make it plain that L1 and L2 reading skills are systematically related; that, as in L1 reading, L2 decoding development depends on phonological awareness; and that such dependency occurs both within and across languages. Caution is necessary, however, in generalizing the reported cross-linguistic relationships because current studies have concentrated primarily on school-age children at the initial grades, as well as on the functional connection between phonological awareness and decoding between two alphabetic languages. Obviously, more studies are needed to expand the current data base on cross-linguistic relationships in reading skills.

Factors affecting the assimilation of L1 skills. Within the input driven view of learning, it is assumed that previously acquired reading skills continue to evolve through L2 print input processing until they reach optimal efficiency in the new language. The second cross-linguistic issue pertains to the factors affecting the assimilation of transferred L1 skills. Two factors are particularly germane: (1) L1 and L2 linguistic distance because it determines how much modification is necessary for L1 skills to be functional in L2 reading, and (2) L2 print pocessing experience because L2 input is the dominant force in reshaping transferred L1 skills.

Linguistic distance varies widely across diverse L2 learner groups. As noted earlier, it directly affects L2 processing efficiency at a given point in time among learners with similar and dissimilar L1 backgrounds. Although L2 studies have repeatedly shown faster and more accurate processing performance for learners from typologically related L1 backgrounds than those from unrelated backgrounds (e.g., Green and Meara, 1987; Hamada and Koda, 2008; Koda, 2000), to date, little is known about precisely *how* shared structural properties facilitate L2 reading development. Muljani and colleagues (1998) shed some light on the issue by testing orthographic distance effects on L2 intraword structural sensitivity. Comparing lexical-decision performance among proficiency-matched adult ESL learners with alphabetic (Indonesian) and logographic (Chinese) L1 orthographic backgrounds, the researchers demonstrated that only Indonesian participants benefited from intraword structural congruity (i.e., spelling-patterns consistent between English and Indonesian). However, their superiority was far less pronounced with incongruent items whose spelling patterns were unique to English. Thus, while orthographic distance appears to have a general facilitative impact, accelerated efficiency occurs only in the tasks whose demands are identical to those imposed by L1 properties.

Similar findings have been reported in studies comparing morphological segmentation skills among ESL learners with alphabetic (Korean) and logographic (Chinese) L1 backgrounds (Koda, 2000; Koda *et al.*, 1998). As does phonological decoding, morphological information extraction requires intraword segmentation and analysis in alphabetic languages, whereas morphological processing in logographic languages entails a more holistic operation, which does not involve segmentation or analysis. As predicted, Korean learners were more efficient in morphological segmentation than their proficiency-matched Chinese counterparts, but their efficiency gap was substantially reduced when the groups were confronted with the items whose structural properties are unique to English. Clearly, segmentation efficiency in the items structurally unique to the target language is far less affected by linguistic distance presumably because their analysis requires insights not yet available to either Korean or Chinese ESL learners. These findings corroborate the results from the Muljani *et al.*, study, suggesting that the distance effect is far more specific and localized than has been assumed.

Another factor directly affecting the assimilation of transferred reading skills is L2 print input. As noted earlier, reading skills are shaped through cumulative print processing experience. The nature of print input thus is a critical factor determining the level and form of the skills emerging from a particular instance of literacy learning. Documenting L2 input properties is crucial in predicting how transferred L1 skills are modified through L2 print processing experience. In a recent study (Koda *et al.*, 2007), the impact of print input has been examined with bilingual school-age children learning to read English as their primary language and Chinese as a heritage language (CHL). The researchers analyzed properties of the Chinese characters explicitly taught in grades 1 to 6 Language Arts textbooks specifically designed for CHL learners. Their analysis revealed that CHL students are taught roughly 35 percent of the characters and 20 percent of the radicals (i.e., graphic components in characters providing semantic information) that are introduced in grades 1 to 6 Language Arts textbooks for native Chinese-speaking children in China. Despite these quantitative differences, however, the types of characters and proportions of structurally and functionally regular characters were remarkably similar between the two textbook corpora. Based on the analysis, the researchers examined how the identified input (Chinese characters) properties related to morphological awareness among grade 3 to 5 CHL students. Their data demonstrated that CHL students in the three grade levels were similarly sensitized to the major properties of the morphologically complex characters, and that few children in any grade group showed sensitivity to refined facets of morphological awareness. Given that major growth in morphological awareness occurs between grades 2 and 5 among native Chinese-speaking children (Ku and Anderson, 2003; Shu and Anderson, 1999), these results are astonishing. Apparently, the input available to CHL students provided a sufficient basis for forming sensitivity to the major input properties, but it was too restricted to allow those children to refine their preliminary understanding, and as a result, their morphological awareness remained basic. Viewed as a whole, findings from this and other initial studies (e.g., Wang *et al.*, 2005) are illuminating, suggesting that input characteristics in the target language are directly related to the level and form of reading skills acquired through literacy learning in that language.

Cross-linguistic variations. The third and final cross-linguistic issue addressed in L2 reading research has to do with L1-induced variations in L2 reading skills. Two basic assumptions underlie empirical explorations of such variations: (1) L2 skills are shaped through cross-linguistic interactions between transferred L1 skills and L2 print input; and (2) the resulting L2 skills reflect both L1 and L2 linguistic properties. Consequently, studies aim to determine whether systematic differences exist in L2 print processing behaviors among learners with contrasting L1 backgrounds. Their results generally confirm that L2 learners respond differently to a variety of experimental manipulations (e.g., Akamatsu, 2003; Brown and Haynes, 1985; Green and Meara, 1987; Koda, 1998, 1999); and more critically, that the observed differences are attributable to the structural variations in participants' respective L1 writing systems (e.g., Koda, 1989, 1990, 1993; Ryan and Meara, 1991).

In more recent studies, an additional step has been taken to explore cross-linguistic interactions during L2 processing. These studies have examined the relative impacts of L1 and L2 factors on L2 lexical processing, using diverse experimental tasks, including semantic category judgment (Wang et al., 2003), associative word learning (Hamada and Koda, 2008), and word identification (Wang and Koda, 2005). To distinguish the impact stemming from L1 factors from that associated with L2 factors, in these studies, L2 stimulus words were manipulated in one way or another, and the effects of such manipulations were compared between two learner groups each representing a distinct first language. In such a design, the extent that a particular manipulation affects both groups is used as the basis for gauging the L2 impact, and the degree to which the effect of the manipulation varies between the participant groups serves as an index of the L1 impact.

Through semantic category judgments, for example, Wang et al., (2003) compared the relative impacts of phonological and graphic manipulations on judgment performance (both accuracy and speed) among ESL learners with alphabetic (Korean) and logographic (Chinese) L1 backgrounds. In the study, participants were first presented with a category description, such as "flower," and then showed a target word. They were then asked to decide whether the word was a member of the category. The trick was that the target words were manipulated either phonologically (using homophones as targets; e.g., "rows" for "rose") or graphically (using similarly spelled words as targets; e.g., "fees" for "feet"). The primary hypothesis was that the two ESL groups would respond differently to the two types of manipulation: Korean participants would be more likely to accept homophones as category members while Chinese would make more false positive responses to graphically similar targets. The data demonstrated that both phonological and graphic manipulations significantly interfered with category judgment performance among ESL learners regardless of their L1 backgrounds. However, the magnitude of interference stemming from each type of manipulation varied between the groups. As predicted, Korean learners made more errors with homophonic (phonologically manipulated) items, while similarly spelled (graphically manipulated) targets seriously affected judgment performance among Chinese learners. These results seem to suggest that (1) proficiency-matched ESL learners are similarly sensitized to L2 properties, (2) that the two groups rely on different information sources during L2 lexical processing, and (3) that these differences are consistent with the variations predicted from participants' L1 orthographic properties.

To summarize, the studies investigating cross-linguistic variations generally suggest that while L1 literacy experience has a long-lasting impact on L2 reading development, proficiency-matched L2 learners are similarly affected by L2 properties. These findings seem to imply that L2 input is a more dominant force in shaping L2 reading skills. In fact, in all studies comparing L1 and L2 impacts, L2 variables had stronger effects, reducing the *L1 background x stimulus manipulation* interaction effect. Viewed collectively, the empirical findings discussed above provide a sufficient basis for drawing two conclusions: (1) prior literacy experience affects L2 reading development, and therefore (2) previously acquired skills play a pivotal role in explaining individual differences in L2 print information processing. Beyond these, however, the currently available data indicate that cross-linguistic variations in L2 print processing behaviors are far more complex than previously assumed because they can be explained by a number of factors, including reading skills, linguistic distance, L2 input, experimental manipulations, and the tasks used for measuring the focal reading skills.

Applications

Translating research into practice is not an easy task because not all insights brought to light in empirical studies can be taught directly or even have direct utility in increasing instructional efficiency. Although there is an impressive body of information on L1 reading development, the information alone—without considering the unique nature of L2 reading—is not likely to improve reading proficiency among linguistically diverse L2 learners. Throughout the chapter, dual-language involvement has been underscored as the major characteristic of L2 reading. A great number of studies have repeatedly shown that both L1 and L2 factors play a role in shaping L2 reading skills. It is important therefore to reflect on how dual-language involvement can be dealt with effectively in L2 reading instruction.

The clear implication of L1-induced variations is that no one method works optimally for all learners. Teachers should be aware that previously acquired reading skills have lasting impacts on learning to read in a new language. Although it is virtually impossible for them to know every possible variation brought about through transferred L1 skills, the awareness is vital in accommodating the disparate needs of their students. For example, teachers could address the disparities by incorporating diagnostic reading assessments. Their awareness of long-term L1-impacts would guide them in two critical phases: constructing assessment tasks and interpreting assessment outcomes. In this way, diagnostic information could allow them to compare the requisite skills across diverse learner groups, and in so doing, identify deficiencies in any of those skills, and variations therein. It would also help teachers fine-tune their instruction to meet the specific challenges their students face in learning to read in the new language.

Given that reading skills are shaped through input exposure and experience, L2 reading development can be promoted by improving the quality and quantity of the L2 print input that can be incorporated in instruction. Although simulating the quantity of input typically available in L1 learning to read is not feasible within the L2 instructional context, it is certainly possible to maximize the quality of input experience by manipulating input presentation, as well as by increasing input processing experience. Input presentation can be enhanced by reorganizing instructional materials in such a way that cumulative input exposure leads to heightened awareness of the structural regularities (e.g., regularly spelled words and canonically ordered sentences) directly related to the requisite information processing for text meaning construction. Additionally, input experience can be enhanced by providing operations processing exercises carefully designed to engage students in input analysis in constructing local text meaning (e.g., word meaning inference).

Dual-language involvement has different implications for reading instruction for school-age children learning to read in two languages concurrently. Because reading skills in young learners are still developing in their primary language, we cannot assume that they all possess the requisite competencies for the initial tasks in learning to read in either language. This indicates that school-age learners may encounter reading difficulties fundamentally different from those experienced by adult L2 learners because their problems could stem from various combinations of multiple deficiencies, including underdeveloped L1 metalinguistic awareness, insufficient L2 linguistic knowledge, and inadequate "central processing" capacity. Here again, it is essential that teachers be clear about these multiple sources of difficulties their students might face in learning to read in their two languages.

Future directions

This chapter has explored how L2 reading development is jointly affected by L1 and L2 factors. The picture emerging from the existing database is extremely complex, showing reading skills developed in one language differentially affecting the formation of an additional set of skills in another language. Although the picture captures the multiple layers of diversities inherent in L2 reading, it is far from complete because the currently available data do not encompass the full spectrum of skills, a broad range of learners, and a sufficient variety of learning contexts. To gain a deeper understanding of L2 reading development, the scope should be extended to additional related factors. Future research directions can be set to purposefully expand the current scope in the following three areas: (a) incorporating a broader range of skills, (b) including a wider variety of languages, and (c) integrating learner-external factors into psycholinguistic accounts of L2 reading development.

Incorporating a broader range of reading skills

Reading transfer research of late has begun to address one of the most fundamental questions–the question of which skills are transferred. Currently, the investigative goal is focused primarily on cross-linguistic relationships in decoding and related skills. Successful text comprehension, however, entails far more than decoding. It is crucial to extend the investigative scope to higher-order operations, such as text information building and reader-model construction. Because the execution of the tasks involved in these higher-order operations depends on well-established decoding skills, future studies should probe the functional and developmental interconnections among skills at different processing levels both within and across languages. Such explorations could yield significant new insights into the cognitive and linguistic requisites for the execution of various higher-order tasks directly contributing to text comprehension.

Including a wider variety of languages

Although a solid body of evidence suggests that prior literacy experience does affect L2 reading development, little is known about how previously acquired skills become functional in a typologically distant second language. The information is vital in understanding the precise nature of facilitation stemming from reading skills transfer. Obtaining such information necessitates accurate descriptions of the language-specific demands for a particular operation (e.g., decoding) in two languages. Without clarifying what is required for the execution of the operation in both languages, it is virtually impossible to identify what has been previously established and then to deduce what has yet to be acquired. At present, however, only limited information is available in languages other than English on how learning to read is linguistically constrained. Clearly, we need more information on how reading skills develop in typologically diverse languages.

Integrating learner-external factors

Finally, literacy learning does not occur in a vacuum. A number of learner-external factors directly and indirectly contribute to reading development. Despite the obvious relevance, learner-external factors are rarely incorporated into psycholinguistic accounts of L2 reading development. Traditionally, L2 reading research has pursued learner-internal (e.g., cognitive and linguistic) and learner-external (e.g., contextual) factors separately under clearly distinct conceptual orientations, using widely disparate methodologies. Although the psycholinguistic focus informs us which factors promote reading acquisition, it does not explain how and why those factors that come into play in reading skills development. Much can be gained by examining learner-internal and learner-external factors in tandem under a single unified framework.

One way of achieving such integration is to incorporate input properties as the pivot connecting learner-internal and learner-external factors under the input-driven view of learning. Because this view assigns a vital role to linguistic input (both oral and print) in predicting and explaining variances in psycholinguistic outcomes, it mandates accurate descriptions of the qualitative (what kinds) and quantitative (how much) input characteristics available to a focal group of learners. Hence, a framework grounded in this view can easily incorporate learner-external factors in explaining how the cognitive and linguistic resources for reading acquisition vary across learners.

Obviously, integrating psycholinguistic and contextual factors in a coherent framework is challenging, but it is vital, if we are to gain a more comprehensive grasp of L2 reading development.

References

Abu Rabia, S. (1995). Learning to read in Arabic: Reading, syntactic, orthographic and working memory skills in normally achieving and poor Arabic readers. *Reading Psychology, 16*, 351–394.

Abu-Rabia, S. (1997). Verbal and working memory skills of bilingual Hebrew-English speaking children. *International Journal of Psycholinguistics, 13*, 25–40.

Adams, M. J. (1990). *Beginning to read.* Cambridge, MA: The MIT Press.

Akamatsu, N. (2003). The effects of first language orthographic features on second language reading in text. *Language Learning, 53*, 207–231.

August, D., Calderon, M., and Carlo, M. (2002). Transfer of skills from Spanish to English: A study of young learners (Final Report). Washington, D.C.: Center for Applied Linguistics.

August, D. and Shanahan, T. (Eds.). (2006). *Executive summary: Developing literacy in second-language learners: report of the National Literacy Panel on Language-Minority Children and Youth.* Mahwah, NJ: Lawrence Erlbaum.

Bates, E. and MacWhinney, B. (1989). Functionalism and the competition model. In B. MacWhinney and E. Bates (Eds.), *The crosslinguistic study of sentence processing* (pp. 3–73). Cambridge: Cambridge University Press.

Bates, E., McNew, S., MacWhinney, B., Devescovi, A., and Smith, S. (1982). Functional constraints on sentence processing: A cross-linguistic study. *Cognition, 11*, 245–299.

Bialystok, E., McBride-Chang, C., and Luk, G. (2005). Bilingualism, langue proficiency, and learning to read in two writing systems. *Journal of Educational Psychology, 97*, 580–590.

Branum-Martin, L., Fletcher, J. M., Carlson, C. D., Ortiz, A., Carlo, M., and Francis, D. J. (2006). Bilingual phonological awareness: Multilevel construct validation among Spanish-speaking kindergarteners in transitional bilingual education classrooms. *Journal of Educational Psychology, 98*, 170–81.

Brown, T. and Haynes, M. (1985). Literacy background and reading development in a second language. In T. H. Carr (Ed.), *The development of reading skills* (pp. 19–34). San Francisco, CA: Jossey-Bass.

Carlisle, J. F. and Beeman, M. M. (2000). The effects of language of instruction on the reading and writing achievement of first-grade Hispanic children. *Scientific Studies of Reading, 4*, 331–353.

Carr, T. H. and Levy, B. A. (Eds.). (1990). *Reading and its development: Component skills approaches.* San Diego: Academic Press.

Cormier, P. and Kelson, S. (2000). The roles of phonological and syntactic awareness in the use of plural morphemes among children in French immersion. *Scientific Studies of Reading, 4*, 267–294.

Cummins, J. (1979). Linguistic interdependence and educational development of bilingual children. *Review of Educational Research, 49*, 222–251.

Cummins, J. (1991). Interdependence of first- and second-language proficiency in bilingual children. In E. Bialystok (Ed.), *Language processing in bilingual children* (pp. 70–89). New York: Cambridge University Press.

Cummins, J., Swain, M., Nakajima, K., Handscombe, J., and Green, D. (1981). *Linguistic interdependence in Japanese and Vietnamese students.* Report prepared for the Inter-America Research Associates. June. Tronto: Ontario Institute for Studies in Education.

Da Fontoura, H. A. and Siegel, L. S. (1995). Reading syntactic and memory skills of Portuguese-English Canadian children. *Reading and Writing: An International Journal, 7*, 139–153.

Durgunoglu, A. Y., Nagy, W. E., and Hancin, B. J. (1993). Cross-language transfer of phonemic awareness. *Journal of Educational Psychology, 85*, 453–465, read (pp. 119–147). New York: Springer-Verlag.

Ehri, L. C. (1994). Development of the ability to read words: Update. In R. Ruddell, M. Ruddell, and H. Singer (Eds.), *Theoretical models and processes of reading* (Fourth Edition) (pp. 323–358). Hillsdale, NJ: Erlbaum.

Ehri, L. C. (1998). Grapheme-phoneme knowledge is essential to learning to read words in English. In J. L. Metsala and L. C. Ehri (Eds.), *Word recognition in beginning literacy* (pp. 3–40). Mahwah, NJ: Erlbaum.

Ellis, N. (2002). Frequency effects in language processing: A review with implications for theories of implicit and explicit language acquisition. *Studies in Second Language Acquisition, 24*, 143–188.

Geva, E. (2008). Facets of metalinguistic awareness related to reading development in Hebrew: Evidence from monolingual and bilingual and bilingual children. In K. Koda and A. M. Zehler (Eds.), *Learning to read across languages: Cross-linguistic relationships in first and second language literacy development.* New York: Routledge.

Geva, E. and Siegle, L. S. (2000). Orthographic and cognitive factors in the concurrent development of basic reading skills in two languages. *Reading and Writing, 12,* 1–30.

Gholamain, M. and Geva, E. (1999). Orthographic and cognitive factors in the concurrent development of basic reading skills in English and Persian. *Language Learning, 49,* 183–217.

Goodman, K. S. (1967). Reading: A psycholinguistic guessing game. *Journal of the Reading Specialist, 6,* 126–135.

Goodman, K. S. (1969). Analysis of oral language miscues: Applied psycholinguistics. *Reading Research Quarterly, 5,* 9–30.

Goodman, K. S. (1973). Psycholinguistic universals of the reading process. In F. Smith (Ed.), *Psycholinguistics and reading* (pp. 21–29). New York: Holt: Rinehart and Winston.

Green, D. W. and Meara, P. (1987). The effects of script on visual search. *Second Language Research, 3,* 102–117.

Hamada, M. and Koda, K. (2008). Influence of first language orthographic experience on second language decoding and word learning. *Language Learning, 58,* 1–31.

Hogaboam, T. W. and Perfetti, C. A. (1978). Reading skill and the role of verbal experience in decoding. *Journal of Educational Psychology, 70,* 717–729.

Kail, M. (1989). Cue validity, cue cost, and processing types in sentence comprehension in French and Spanish. In B. MacWhinney and E. Bates (Eds.), *The cross-linguistic study of sentence processing* (pp. 77–117). New York: Cambridge University Press.

Katz, L. and Frost, R. (1992). Reading in different orthographies: The orthographic depth hypothesis. In R. Frost and L. Katz (Eds.), *Orthography, phonology, morphology, and meaning* (pp. 67–84). Amsterdam: Elsevier.

Koda, K. (1989). The effects of transferred vocabulary knowledge on the development of L2 reading proficiency. *Foreign Language Annals, 22,* 529–542.

Koda, K. (1990). The use of L1 reading strategies in L2 reading. *Studies in Second Language Acquisition, 12,* 393–410.

Koda, K. (1993). Transferred L1 strategies and L2 syntactic structure during L2 sentence comprehension. *The Modern Language Journal, 77,* 490–500.

Koda, K. (1998). The role of phonemic awareness in L2 reading. *Second Language Research, 14,* 194–215.

Koda, K. (1999). Development of L2 intraword structural sensitivity and decoding skills. *The Modern Language Journal, 83,* 51–64.

Koda, K. (2000). Cross-linguistic variations in L2 morphological awareness. *Applied Psycholinguistics, 21,* 297–320.

Koda, K. (2005). *Insights into second language reading.* NY: Cambridge University Press.

Koda, K., Lu, C., and Zhang, Y. (2007). Properties of Characters in heritage Chinese textbooks and their implications for character knowledge development among Chinese heritage Language Learners. In A. W. He and Y. Xiao (Eds.), *Chinese as a heritage language.* Hawaii: University of Hawaii Press.

Koda, K., Takahashi, E., and Fender, M. (1998). Effects of L1 processing experience on L2 morphological awareness. *Ilha do Desterro, 35,* 59–87.

Ku, Y.-M. and Anderson, R. C. (2003). Development of morphological awareness in Chinese and English. *Reading and Writing: An Interdisciplinary Journal, 16,* 399–422.

Legarretta, D. (1979). The effects of program models on language acquisition of Spanish speaking children. *TESOL Quarterly, 13,* 521–534.

Li, W., Anderson, R. C., Nagy, W., and Zhang, H. (2002). Facets of metalinguistic awareness that contribute to Chinese literacy. In W. Li, J. S. Gaffiney, and J. L. Packard (Eds.), *Chinese children's reading acquisition: Theoretical and pedagogical issues* (pp. 87–106). Boston: Kluwer Academic.

Luk, G. and Bialystok, E. (2008). Common and distinct cognitive bases for reading in English–Cantonese bilinguals. *Applied Psycholinguistics, 29,* 269–289.

Mazuka, R. and Itoh, K. (1995). Can Japanese speakers be led down the garden path? In R. Mazuka and N. Nagai (Eds.), *Japanese sentence processing* (pp. 295–330). Hillsdale, NJ: Erlbaum.

McBride-Chan, C., Cheung, B. W. -Y., Chow, C. S. -L., and Choi, L. (2006). Metalinguistic skills and vocabulary knowledge in Chinese (L1) and English (L2). *Reading and Writing, 19,* 695–716.

McBride-Chan, C., Wagner, R. K., Muse, A., Chow, B. W. -Y., and Shu, H. (2005). The role of morphological awareness in children's vocabulary acquisition in English. *Applied Psycholinguistics, 26,* 415–435.

Muljani, M., Koda, K., and Moates, D. (1998). Development of L2 word recognition: A Connectionist approach. *Applied Psycholinguistics, 19,* 99–114.

Perfetti, C. A. (2003). The universal grammar of reading. *Scientific Studies of Reading, 7,* 3–24.

Perfetti, C. A. and Dunlap, S. (2008). Learning to read: General printiples and writing system variations. In K. Koda and A. M. Zehler (Eds.), *Learning to read across languages: Cross-linguistic relationships in first- and second-language literacy development.* Mahwah, NJ: Lawrence Erlbaum.

Perfetti, C. A. and Liu, Y. (2005). Orthography to phonology and meaning: Comparisons across and within writing systems. *Reading and Writing, 18,* 193–210.

Riches, C. and Genesee, F. (2006). Crosslanguage and crossmodal influences. In F. Genesee, K. Lindholm-Leary, W. Saunders, and D. Christian (Eds.), *Educating English language learners: A synthesis of research evidence.* New York: Cambridge University Press.

Ryan, A. and Meara, P. (1991). The case of invisible vowels: Arabic speakers reading English words. *Reading in a Foreign Language, 7,* 531–540.

Saito, H., Masuda, H., and Kawakami, M. (1999). Subword activation in reading Japanese single Kanji character words. *Brain and Language, 68,* 75–81.

Seidenberg, M. S. and McClelland, J. L. (1989). A distributed, developmental model of word recognition and naming. *Psychological Review, 96,* 523–568.

Shankweiler, D. and Liberman, I. Y. (1972). Misreading: A search for causes. In J. F. Kavanaugh and I. G. Mattingly (Eds.), *Language by eye and by ear* (pp. 293–317). Cambridge, MA: MIT Press.

Shu, H. and Anderson, R. C. (1999). Learning to read Chinese: The development of metalinguistic awareness. In A. Inhuff, J. Wang, and H. C. Chen (Eds.), *Reading Chinese scripts: A cognitive analysis* (pp. 1–18). Mahwah, NJ: Lawrence Erlbaum.

Siegel, L. S. and Ryan, E. B. (1988). Development of grammatical sensitivity, phonological, and short-term memory in normally achieving and learning disabled children. *Developmental Psychology, 24,* 28–37.

Skutnabb-Kangass, T. and Toukomaa, P. (1976). *Teaching migrant children's mother tongue and learning the language of the host country in the context of soci cultural situation of the migrant family.* Helsinki: The Finnish National Commission for UNESCO.

Stanovitch, K. E. and Cunningham, A. E. (2004). Inferences from correlational data: Exploring associations with reading experience. In N. K. Duke and M. H. Mallette (Eds.), *Literacy research methodologies.* New York: Guilford.

Taft, M. and Zhu, X. P. (1995). The representation of bound morphemes in the lexicon: A Chinese study. In L. B. Feldman (Ed.), *Morphological aspects of language processing* (pp. 109–129). Hillsdale, NJ: Erlbaum.

Tolchinsky, L. and Teberosky, A. (1998). The development of word segmentation and writing in two scripts. *Cognitive Development, 13,* 1–25.

Troike, R. C. (1978). Research evidence for the effectiveness of bilingual education. *NABE Journal, 3,* 13–24.

Vaid, J. (1995). Effect of reading and writing directions on nonlinguistic perception and performance: Hindi and Urdu data. In I. Taylor and D. R. Olson (Eds.), *Scripts and literacy: Reading and learning to read the world's scripts* (pp. 295–310). Dordrecht: Kluwer Academic.

Verhoeven, L. (2000). Components in early second language reading and spelling. *Scientific Studies of Reading, 4,* 313–330.

Wade-Woolley, L. and Geva, E. (2000). Processing novel phonemic contrasts in the acquisition of L2 word reading. *Scientific Studies of Reading, 4,* 295–311.

Wagner, R. K., Torgesen, J. K., and Rashotte, C. A. (1994). The development of reading-related phonological processing abilities: New evidence of bi-directional causality from a latent variable longitudinal study. *Developmental Psychology, 30,* 73–87.

Wang, M. and Koda, K. (2005). Commonalities and differences in word identification skills among learners of English as a second language, *Language Learning, 55,* 71–98.

Wang, M., Koda, K., and Perfetti, C. A. (2003). Alphabetic and non-alphabetic L1 effects in English semantic processing: A comparison of Korean and Chinese English L2 learners. *Cognition, 87,* 129–149.

Wang, M., Park, Y., and Lee, K. R. (2006). Korean-English biliteracy acquition: Cross language and orthography transfer. *Journal of Educational Psycholgy, 98*(1), 148–158.

Wang, M., Perfetti, C. A., and Liu, Y. (2005). Chinese-English biliteracy acquisition: Cross-language and writing system transfer. *Cognition, 97,* 67–88.

19

The acquisition of second language writing

Charlene Polio

Introduction

This chapter reviews what is known about the acquisition of written language by examining studies from both L2 acquisition and L2 writing pedagogy. I will focus here on the language used by learners as they learn to write in their L2. Thus, the scope of the chapter will be limited to linguistic issues such as accuracy, complexity, the lexicon, and, to a lesser extent, fluency and cohesion. It will not focus on higher level matters such as learning the structure of specific genres, understanding audience conventions, or adapting to cultural writing norms. This is not to say that such issues are not important. Indeed, Flowerdew and colleagues (Flowerdew 2001, Flowerdew and Li, 2009) have argued, for example, that Chinese scholarly writers and other non-native speakers face more obstacles with regard to content and discourse structure than language. In fact, when writing is used to accomplish certain goals in society, native-like proficiency may not be necessary. When viewed from a language development perspective, however, even such advanced writers may have problems that are interesting. For example, a lack of mastery of English articles reflects incomplete language development, and infelicitous collocations may shed light on frequency issues.

By written language, I refer to learner-produced texts of at least paragraph length. Research that examines cloze tests or sentence completion, for example, is not considered. And although language used in synchronous computer-mediated discourse is written and could have an impact on learners' subsequent oral production (e.g., Blake, 2009) or longer written texts, I will not consider that research because of space limitations.

Historical discussion

For years, the fields of second language acquisition (SLA) and second language (L2) writing did not overlap much. An examination of the research published in the *Journal of Second Language Writing*, since its inception in 1992, reveals few articles that would be of obvious interest to those studying what has traditionally fallen under the realm of SLA. Much of the research on L2 writing has grown out of first language (L1) composition studies, where researchers come from a more social, less cognitively oriented tradition. (For a concise yet clear historical perspective on traditions in L2 writing, see Ferris and Hedgcock, 2005. For a summary of social issues such as those related to identity and the political contexts of writing, see Leki *et al.*, 2008.)

Studies of SLA research published in what can be considered mainstream SLA journals (e.g., *Language Learning, Second Language Research, Studies in Second Language Acquisition*) have occasionally reported on research that used written data beyond the sentence level (e.g., Bardovi-Harlig, 1997), but little or no mention is made of the fact the studies might be useful to those interested in the teaching of L2 writing. Although SLA theory and research are relevant to L2 writing, and although L2 writing can affect how L2s are learned, only recently have such relationships been made explicit (e.g, Manchón, 2011; Williams, 2008).

I now turn to the relationship between writing and theories of SLA. Historically, L2 teaching and learning has been about the acquisition of spoken language. From structuralist approaches, such as the audio-lingual method, to more meaning-based methods, such as the natural approach, the focus was on teaching speaking. With regard to current theories or approaches in SLA—and I will use the terms interchangeably to avoid a discussion of which are considered theories—most do not explicitly deal with writing. In fact, in order to understand how various SLA theories might apply to writing, some speculation is inevitable. Nevertheless, it is important for those working in the area of L2 writing to have a theoretical framework in mind and to consider whether or not the various theories are applicable to what they want to know about L2 writing. Another way to approach the role of SLA theory in learning how to write in an L2 is to examine research that studies L2 writing and determine what approach or approaches are explicit or implicit in the researchers' framing of the research.

SLA approaches have been portrayed in different ways. Mitchell and Myles (1998) divided approaches to SLA into six categories. Norris and Ortega (2003) divided the approaches into four general categories. Later, VanPatten and Williams (2007) classified them into nine approaches or theories, and the current volume divides them differently. Most would agree that there is overlap and that these approaches are not mutually exclusive, hence the difficulty in classifying them. I have chosen to very briefly mention approaches labeled generative, emergentist/associative, processability, and functionalist regarding their possible relevance to L2 writing. I end with a more detailed description of the sociocultural and interactionist approaches as they are the most relevant.

A generative approach, which seeks to describe the mental representation of language, generally relies on the use of judgment tasks and acquisition is indicated by "nativelike levels of rejection of illegal exemplars of the target grammar" (Norris and Ortega, 2003, p. 727). It follows that generativists would not examine written essays as evidence of acquisition. White (2007) states that judgment tasks are the most common method of trying to tap into learners' underlying linguistic competence with a generativist approach, but also claims that judgment data are not privileged and that the data collection method must be tied to what is being investigated. Nevertheless, I know of no studies in this approach that examine written essays, since written production seems even less likely than spoken language to be a reflection of competence. In writing, one has more time to review and correct what has been written, thus drawing on explicitly learned rules; more accurate grammar in essays alone would not necessarily be seen as evidence of acquisition.

An emergentist/associative approach assumes that language is learned through usage and that learners make links among words and structures. The approach, in part, tries to determine what influences those links (e.g., frequency or saliency of the items). In a description of what N. Ellis (2007) calls the associative-cognitive CREED theory, he states that several sources of data, including learner production data, are relevant, but he does not specifically mention written data. N. Ellis (2005) acknowledges the role explicit knowledge may play in acquisition. Thus, written data, where a learner has time to consider explicit knowledge, may be relevant to acquisition.

Processability theory, best associated with Pienemann and Johnston (1987) and Pienemann (1998, 2005, 2007), describes stages of language development across languages and explains them as being a result of processing constraints. Pienemann (2007) claims that the data examining development can be cross-sectional or longitudinal and must contain enough examples of the phenomenon being studied. He states: "In such studies the researcher collects naturalistic or elicited speech data that form the corpus on which the study is based" (p. 146). Pienemann does not say why written data is not relevant, but his theory is based on a processing model of speech (Levelt, 1989). The extent to which this model can be applied to writing is open to discussion (Alamargot and Chanquoy, 2001), but it seems that in writing tasks, learned rules could overtake processing constraints.

Functional approaches are more problematic to characterize. In some ways, the interaction approach subsumes a functional approach because both are concerned with form-meaning mappings, and, in fact, Norris and Ortega (2003) state that the interaction approach is based on a functional view of language. Meanwhile, Tyler (2011) describes three different functional approaches: systemic functional linguistics, discourse functionalism, and cognitive linguistics. Cognitive linguistics is closely tied to an emergentist/associative approach. Another functional approach is what Bardovi-Harlig (2007) calls a concept-oriented approach. She states that it is not a theory but rather a "framework for analysis" (p. 60) with regard to form-meaning mappings, as opposed to accuracy per se. In her own work that includes both oral and written production data, Bardovi-Harlig's work (reviewed in Bardovi-Harlig, 2000) analyzes L2 learners' use of verb tenses. Work by Hinkel (2002) uses a related approach. Analyzing written essays, she describes functions of various forms (e.g., modals) in native speaker texts and then compares the frequency of use of those forms with regard to native non-native speaker differences. Instead of a detailed analysis of how learners develop with regard to a form or function, Hinkel paints a broader picture of the use of various forms in writing without discussing development.

Sociocultural SLA research, as described by Lantolf (Lantolf and Thorne, 2007; Chapter 4, this volume) is related to a Vygotskian theory of the mind and does not quantitatively measure acquisition. In fact, research in this framework investigates learning quite differently than other approaches. Lantolf and Thorne (2007) point out that if less assistance is needed in a task, as shown in a study of written error correction study by Aljaafreh and Lantolf (1994), then learning has occurred. Lantolf and Thorne (2007) also argue that although longitudinal evidence is preferable, learning can take place during a short-term interaction. This is not to be confused with development. As Brooks and Swain (2009) point out in their study of learner discussions of reformulation, learning precedes development. Although written error correction is not often addressed within a sociocultural approach, or at least not in the same way as other approaches, it would most definitely be appropriate to look at written language as an area of investigation. Even those who view speaking as an innate process governed by rules of Universal Grammar cannot deny that writing is a learned, social process (cf., Pinker, 1994), arguably facilitated by scaffolding. Features of a sociocultural approach are apparent in studies of discourse-level language functions used in writing (e.g., Nassaji and Cumming, 2000) and collaborative writing (e.g., Storch, 2005).

The interaction approach, as summarized by Gass and Mackey (2006, 2007) and Mackey and Polio (2009), clearly has its origins in oral language. Hatch (1978) claimed that acquisition resulted from "learning how to carry on conversation, learning how to communicate" (p. 63). The work was further investigated by Long (1981, 1983), who continued to investigate oral interaction. What happened, however, is that some researchers began to study written language drawing on concepts that are central to the interaction approach (e.g., Sachs and Polio, 2007; Swain and Lapkin, 1995; Swain, 1998).[1] These concepts, namely, input, output, feedback, and attention (Gass and Mackey, 2006, 2007) have all played a role in some L2 writing research, particularly attention. A discussion of each of these concepts is beyond the scope of this paper, but each is mentioned below with regard to L2 writing research.

This is not to say that everyone who works in this framework would agree that the interaction approach can be applied to writing, but one interpretation of the approach is that interactionists take a broad view of acquisition and that many types of changes in learner performance can be considered significant, even small or short-term changes[2] on a wide variety of data types (Norris and Ortega, 2003). In sum, if researchers are not interested in writing pedagogy per se, examining written texts, within some approaches to SLA, can be considered as a source of learner language and might help us better understand L2 development.

Core issues

Models of L2 writing, longitudinal language development, writing tasks variables, the relevance of the written medium to SLA, and the role of error correction are some of the core issues related to the acquisition of L2 writing. The extent to which the above theories are considered in each of the issues below is minimal, but certain studies do draw on some aspects of SLA theory.

Models of the L2 writing process

Although models of L2 writing process are central in understanding the acquisition of L2 writing, they have, arguably, had little influence over L2 writing research, perhaps because trying to model the L2 writing process is an ambitious endeavor. Models of the L1 writing process (Hayes, 1996) are quite complex; comprehensive models of L2 writing would be even more so. Flower and Hayes (1980) and Hays and Flower (1980) developed a model of the L1 writing process that included a recursive process of planning, text generation, and revision as well as the long-term memory factors (e.g., knowledge of the topic) and task environment factors (e.g., the writing assignment). Hayes (1996) modified the model to include more social and motivational factors (e.g., collaborators and goals, respectively). What is more relevant to the scope of this chapter is that he also included a working memory component and a linguistic knowledge component.

The few proposed models of the L2 writing process are not comprehensive. Zimmerman (2000) proposed a recursive model of the writing process suggesting that the L2 comes in at the formulation, repair, and reviewing stages, and that at least among his participants, writers were not translating from their L1 but rather using the L1 only at the planning stages. Wang and Wen (2002) proposed a model based on the language used by the participants at the various stages. For example, the writers in their study used their L1 to generate ideas and like the participants in Zimmerman's study, they did not generate text in their L1 and translate to their L2. Sasaki (2000) conducted a study that examined the writing processes of novice and expert L2 writers and provided a series of observations to be incorporated into a model, but she did not go so far as to propose one. Finally, the Dutch NELSON project, composed of several studies summarized in Schoonen *et al.*, (2009), attempted to provide "a blueprint of the writer" (p. 77) and examined a number of cognitive issues such as overall proficiency, lexical retrieval, and metacognitive knowledge.

What is missing from most of these models is a clear picture of the linguistic knowledge component and any close links to SLA theories. For example, SLA theories differ on the relationship of implicit and explicit knowledge. Any proposed model of L2 writing should address the role of implicit versus explicit linguistic knowledge. On one hand, we know that as learners compose, they use metalanguage to assess what they have written (Gutiérrez, 2008; Qi and Lapkin, 2001; Sachs and Polio, 2007). On the other hand, it is not clear why learners cannot apply some of the explicit rules that they have learned. As another example, the role of working memory, an issue addressed in the SLA literature, has not been researched in L2 writing, only in the L1 literature (e.g., Kellogg, 1996,

2001) One important issue is whether or not there is a difference in the role of working memory and its limitations between oral and written production. Such a difference could be related to the nature of the inherent differences between the two modalities, as discussed below.

Longitudinal development

Over ten years ago, Wolfe-Quintero et al., (1998) compiled a comprehensive review of measures used in the study of L2 writing development. The majority of the studies that they reviewed were cross-sectional. Since that time, a few studies have examined the longitudinal development of learners' written language. As mentioned previously, Bardovi-Harlig (2000), using a functional analysis, examined L2 learners' narratives as one source of data on learners' overall development of tense and aspect. But as Sasaki (2004) pointed out, studies of writing development tend to be cross-sectional and rarely follow students for more than a semester.

Sasaki (2007) followed 11 Japanese learners of English through their time at university. Six of those students spent two–eight months studying in an English-speaking country during that time. In addition to documenting how their overall proficiency and use of writing strategies changed, Sasaki examined what changed in their overall writing quality (but not specific skill areas) and fluency. She found that all students' writing quality improved after a year, but only the students who had studied abroad continued to improve. Furthermore, although students increased their writing fluency, the increase was not linear and was not evident until 2.5 years after the study began for both groups. With regard to strategies, I mention here the use of translation and, what Sasaki calls *rhetorical refinement*, a focus on small wording changes. Not surprisingly, the students who studied abroad used translation from L1 to L2 less often over time than the EFL group. No significant changes were seen in rhetorical refinement. One possible interpretation is that even after 3.5 years of writing instruction, students did not feel comfortable dealing with language-related issues that were related to minor changes in meaning. Taken together, these results show a slow and non-linear progression of changes with regard to writing, at least for Japanese students at the university level.

In a very different context, Serrano and Howard (2007) presented two case studies from a larger study in which they followed a native English speaker and a native Spanish speaker in a two-way immersion program. They described the development of these learners from grades 3 to 5. They used a rubric, which although divided into components, was too broad to fully detail language development. The grammar component of the rubric included verbs, agreement, placement, and prepositions. They went so far as to suggest that their native Spanish speaker's early rapid improvement in English grammar and mechanics as opposed to composition is because "grammar and mechanics are much easier to teach and learn, as there are specific rules that can be explained and followed" (p. 161). What is problematic is that language development was studied using only a section of an analytical grading rubric. Most likely, raters focused on errors in the above structures as opposed to complexity, the latter being an important component in development (Wolfe-Quintero et al., 1998). Their study is noteworthy in that like Sasaki (2007), they found differences in learning to write in a L2 setting (i.e., the Spanish speaker learning English) and a foreign language setting (i.e., the English speaker learning Spanish).

Byrnes and Sinicrope (2008) studied the longitudinal development of relative clauses among 23 English learners of German. They provided a very clear analysis of the development of relative clauses and challenge the universality of the noun phrase accessibility hierarchy. They do mention that one limitation of their study is that topic was not held constant.

In summary, it is difficult to generalize about longitudinal development particularly when many longitudinal studies are, understandably, case studies. Studies that use a larger number of participants, such as Byrnes and Sinicrope (2008), may focus on only one linguistic feature. Nevertheless, such studies can shed some light on how at least one feature develops over time and may provide insight into some of the differences between speaking and writing. Furthermore, how one chooses to analyze the data should be theoretically motivated, as in the Byrnes and Sinicrope study. Processablity theory is the one approach that makes clear predictions about longitudinal development, but as mentioned earlier, how much the theory is applicable to written language is open to debate.

The effect of different task variables

A large amount and wide variety of research on task variables and L2 writing has been completed by those interested in pedagogy, SLA, and assessment. Some variables studied include task complexity, direct writing vs. translation, and planning time. I describe some example studies below.

The effect of task complexity has been widely studied in speaking (see Robinson, 2005 for an overview) and but only somewhat studied in writing. Students' performance on writing tasks of various types have been compared in the writing assessment literature (see review in Weigle, 2002) but less so in relation to the SLA literature. Two such studies include Zhang (1987) and more recently, Kuikken and Vedder (2008). Zhang (1987) found that cognitively more complex tasks elicited more writing and more syntactically complex writing from L2 learners. Students did not, however, vary in their level of accuracy. Kuikken and Vedder (2008) tested Skehan's limited attentional capacity model and Robinson's cognition hypothesis by comparing how L2 learners of Italian performed on more and less complex tasks. Their findings lent partial support for Robinson's model in that students wrote more accurately on the more complex task.

Some studies have examined differences in learners' writing when translating from their L1 versus composing directly in their L2. Kobayashi and Rinnert (1992) found an improvement for lower proficiency students in terms of grammatical complexity (as measured by clauses per T-unit) if they wrote first in their L1 and then translated. Later Cohen and Brooks (2001) completed a small-scale study comparing native English speakers writing directly in their L2 (French) or translating from English. They found that more of the students did better writing directly, but unlike Kobayashi and Rinnert (1992), they assessed linguistic features using only an holistic rubric. Nevertheless, these studies are important and may help explain on how learners access the L2 when writing and how that process changes for different proficiency levels. Related studies, although not studies of task variables per se, include those that examine the effect of using the L1 or L2 during the prewriting stage (Friedlander, 1990; Lally, 2000; Stapa and Majid, 2009).

Planning time is another task variable that can affect language use in writing. The effects of planning on oral production have been studied extensively (Foster and Skehan, 1996; Mehnert, 1998; Mochizuki and Ortega, 2008; Ortega, 1999; Sangarun, 2005; Wendel, 1997; Wigglesworth, 1997; Yuan and Ellis, 2003) with the general finding that planning increases linguistic complexity but seems to have a variable or no effect on accuracy. With regard to writing, however, few studies have been conducted. Ellis (1987) conducted a study with varying conditions, one of which included having students write as a form of planning. This study, however, confounded planning with modality, so the implications are not clear. Later, Kawauchi (2005) studied the effect of writing as a planning device for speaking and found no effect. Neither of these studies, however, examined the effect of planning on written language, a topic of relevance to teaching and assessing writing. Ellis and Yuan (2004) investigated the effect of different types of planning on writing. They found that pre-task planning increased syntactic variety and fluency, but that online planning increased accuracy.

In summary, these studies may indicate something about the role of attention in producing language. Manipulating task variables often results in differences to where a writer's attention is focused. This is one area in particular where L2 writing research might be able to inform SLA and one area, as addressed below, that has potentially the greatest number of teaching implications.

Relevance of the medium

Several studies (most notably by Swain and her colleagues) have examined the effects of various tasks on learning where those tasks are writing tasks. It is important to consider writing as one type of output that can help students focus on language and perhaps even more so in collaborative writing (Gutiérrez, 2008; Storch, 2005) where students are producing oral output about written output. These studies bring in elements of both the sociocultural and interaction approach (e.g., scaffolding, feedback).

Some researchers have mentioned, mostly in passing, that the written modality is helpful for helping draw learners' attention to form and thus may have a facilitative effect on overall proficiency. Cumming (1990, p. 483) stated:

> Composition writing elicits an attention to form-meaning relations that may prompt learners to refine their linguistic expression—and hence their control over their linguistic knowledge—so that it is more accurately representative of their thoughts and of standard usage. This process appears to be facilitated by the natural disjuncture between written text and the mental processes of generating and assessing it. (Cumming, 1986; Zamel, 1983; also see Olson, 1977)

Wong (2001) showed that in writing, unlike in speaking, learners can pay attention to form and meaning at the same time, and Adams and Ross-Feldman (2008) investigated whether or not written output increases attention to form, as measured by the number of language-related episodes, but their results were not statistically significant. Kim (2008), from a small-scale case study concluded that integrating written language with oral leads to greater gains in oral proficiency. Weissberg (2000) and Harklau (2002) both showed that language may emerge first in the written modality before speaking, while Tarone and Bigelow (2005) have argued that L1 literacy has an impact on the processing of L2 oral language. In a review article, Williams (2008) nicely summarizes the possible benefits of writing on oral language as well as the effect of oral language on written.

Of course, studies outside of L2 learning have investigated oral/written differences that may affect acquisition. In the area of discourse analysis and corpus linguistics, Biber and his colleagues (e.g., Biber, 2006; Biber et al., 2002) have detailed linguistic differences that, given the importance of frequency in SLA, could impact acquisition. From a psycholinguistics perspective, psychologists have examined modality differences. For example, Cleland and Pickering (2006) studied differences in syntactic priming with regard to modality and found no effects. Further studies both in discourse analysis and psycholinguistics could be relevant to the relationship between learning oral and written language.

Ultimately, we need to consider that writing can be slower and more deliberate than speaking and that it can involve a different set of skills. Thus, even those approaches that consider the role of explicit knowledge to be minimal in oral acquisition cannot deny some role for explicit knowledge in learning to write. In fact, studies from the Barcelona Age Factor project, summarized in Celaya and Naves (2009), point to the fact that the benefits of an early start, even in the long term, are not evident in foreign language writing, perhaps because of the cognitive demands of the task. (For a detailed discussion of differences in tasks completed in oral and written modes, see Kuiken and Vedder, Chapter 22, this volume.)

Error correction

The issue of written error correction has dominated the field of L2 writing since Truscott's (1996) polemic against the practice. Since then, many empirical studies have appeared, but most do not directly refute Truscott's original claim. To cover all the studies would take too much space, so instead, I refer readers to discussions of research methods (e.g., Guenette, 2007), meta-analyses (Russell and Spada, 2006; Truscott, 2007), and critiques of the research (Chandler, 2004; Truscott, 2004; Xu, 2009).

To summarize, Truscott (1996) opened the debate about written error correction by claiming that empirical studies showed that error correction was ineffective and that this was to be expected "given the nature of the correction process and the nature of language learning" (p. 328). Since that time, the issue of error correction has been debated on pedagogical grounds (i.e., that learners want and expect error correction, Bitchener *et al.*, 2005; Ferris and Roberts, 2001) and through empirical studies claiming to demonstrate that error correction works (Bitchener, 2008; Bitchener *et al.*, 2005; Chandler, 2003; Ellis *et al.*, 2008; Sheen, 2007). Nevertheless, all of these studies can be refuted on methodological grounds. Chandler (2003) did not control for the amount of writing between the experimental and control groups, and Bitchener *et al.* (2005) did not control for the amount of outside instruction. Sheen (2007) used a grammar test as one measure, and Bitchener (2008), and Ellis *et al.* (2008) examined only the accuracy of articles. All of these studies omitted other measures of learner language including syntactic complexity, thus ignoring one of Truscott's (1996) central points: measures taken to improve accuracy may harm the complexity of written language produced.

In addition, surprisingly few have refuted Truscott's (1996) claim that written error correction should not be expected to work given the nature of language learning. Some theories or approaches discussed above might predict the effectiveness of written error correction. From a sociocultural perspective, Aljareef and Lantolf (1994) argued that one individualized type of correction could work. From an interactionist perspective, Sachs and Polio (2007) argued that certain types of error correction might be effective, particularly given the importance of attention in SLA. Both studies, however, were limited in their conclusion. Aljaafreh and Lantolf (1994) did not show a cause-effect relationship, and Sachs and Polio (2007) studied only short-term changes. In sum, future studies of error correction not only need to be improved in terms of design, but also need to be grounded in SLA theory.

Data and common elicitation measures

Research on L2 writing involves many different methodologies, both quantitative and qualitative (For a comprehensive review of approaches, see Polio, 2003). L2 writing research that focuses on language generally examines writers' texts, but also sometimes their writing process.

Studying the writing process

Some research on the writing process focuses on language-level issues such as composing (e.g., Miller *et al.*, 2008), or editing and dealing with feedback (e.g., Brooks and Swain, 2009; Sachs and Polio, 2007). Like other more general studies of the writing process, process research focusing on language uses a variety of techniques including stimulated recall, think-aloud protocols, and key-stroke logging. In addition, research on collaborative writing can capture these processes as they are verbalized in group work. All of these studies are valuable in that they examine the process of sentence construction while writing, something not seen through text analysis only, as well as the editing process. Furthermore, these techniques are effective for tapping into learners' explicit knowledge because learners can directly comment on what knowledge they are using to make language decisions. Even when that knowledge is not explicit, the researcher can see uses of language that may be attempted orally but that do not make it on to paper. I address the advantages and disadvantages of the various techniques for studying the writing process in Polio (2003) and focus here on studying written texts because research on texts more often involves an analysis of learner language, the focus of this chapter.

Eliciting written texts

Data elicitation for studies related to linguistic features consists mostly of having students write. Of course, as mentioned above, there are a variety of writing task variables, and the specific task used depends on the focus of the study.

The way that these texts are collected is an important issue and there are a number of variables to consider when having participants write. Such variables include time, opportunity for revision, access to and use of outside sources, topic, genre, and so on. The most typical task is to have students respond to a question without the use of outside sources and without prewriting in a limited amount of time. Such procedures ensure internal validity but result in great sacrifices to ecological validity. The issue of limiting research to studies of timed writing without any preparation or revision has not been widely discussed in the literature related to research methodology. It has, however, been addressed at length in the writing assessment literature. For example, the use of timed writing in assessing writing has been criticized (National Council of Teachers of English [NCTE], 2005) and supported (Cumming, 2002) in large-scale assessment. Most studies of L2 writing done within an experimental paradigm do continue to use relatively short timed essays despite problems related to external validity.

Analyzing written texts

How one analyzes written texts is an important topic. Some research attempts to describe features of students' texts (e.g., Hinkel, 2002) while many others attempt to measure certain features to make claims about, for example, an effective treatment or the effect of a task variable. In Polio (2001), I summarized how researchers have measured accuracy, fluency, complexity, the lexicon, and discourse level features. In addition, the previously mentioned Wolfe-Quintero et al. (1998) volume reviewed most of various possible measures.

Generally, as with any measures used in L2 research, the key is operationalizing variables and ultimately choosing a reliable and method for measuring those variables. To take the example of accuracy, there is a constant struggle between reliability and validity (Polio, 1997). When measuring accuracy through general measures such as number of errors or error-free T-units, it can be very easy to achieve interrater reliability. Nevertheless, such measures do not capture differences in error types and thus may not be valid in measuring the construct of accuracy. Tabulating error types is probably a more valid measure, but because of problems of interpreting learner errors, appropriate levels of interrater reliability are difficult to achieve.

Applications

Models of the L2 writing process and longitudinal development. Research in these two areas may not have many implications for the teaching of writing. First, models of L2 writing are not well developed and have not been tested among different groups of writers. Even if the models were better developed, it is not clear what a teacher would do with the knowledge, for example, that working memory is an important factor in composing. Similarly, if we know that students at lower levels rely more on translation, the implications for teaching are not obvious. As for longitudinal studies, again, we do not have a clear picture of language development across languages and learners. But, taking as an example the development of negation, which has been fairly well described for oral language, even a clear picture of development does not inform classroom practices. What it can do is to make teachers aware of why learners may not be progressing. Hinkel's (2002) study of learner writing, which was not a longitudinal study, can serve as a basis for helping teachers decide what structures need to be explicitly addressed. Indeed, Hinkel (2004) is based on her own descriptive work.

Task variables. Research on task variables is highly relevant to both teaching and assessing writing. If it is the case that certain tasks elicit more complex language, then this should inform teachers and writing assessors who may want to vary writing tasks accordingly. The same is true for planning, particularly in testing situations. Also relevant is the role of collaboration in completing writing tasks. Not only is writing one additional form of output, but the research above suggests that collaboration increases attention to form, promoting Swain's (2005) metalinguistic function of output.

Relevance of the medium. Given that writing is a way to get more students on task (i.e., producing output) in large classes, it can be used in various ways in the classroom. For example, by having students freewrite on a topic as a prereading or prelistening activity, every student is engaged. In a teacher-led class discussion, the same may not be true. Freewriting can also be used for five or ten minutes at the end of class to help students produce more language and possibly use new vocabulary from the day's lesson. In addition, the teacher can check all students' comprehension, not just those who were speaking. Written language is both an additional source of input and output. And as discussed earlier, for some students, morphosyntactic structures and vocabulary may emerge first in writing for a variety of reasons.

The effect of using writing as form of planning for speaking is not completely clear. Given the repeated positive results for the effect of planning on syntactic complexity in oral language, however, it is reasonable to assume a positive effect for writing as a form of planning on oral language. Thus, using writing as a prespeaking activity should be beneficial in all language classrooms, even those where oral proficiency is the primary goal.

Error correction. Of all the areas of investigation, this topic should have the greatest impact on teaching. Nevertheless, it has not. First, as discussed above, many of the studies are methodologically flawed. Second, written error correction is ingrained as a teaching practice. Students want and expect error correction, and teachers feel that they are not doing their job if they do not correct (e.g., Ferris, 2002; Lee, 2004). Nevertheless, if we extrapolate from other research on the effectiveness of explicit instruction (for reviews see Norris and Ortega, 2000 and Ellis, 2001), it is certainly tempting to say that written error correction should work. In addition, some of the approaches to SLA discussed above, can be interpreted as suggesting a role for written error correction. Most teachers agree that regardless of the type of feedback (uses of codes, underlining, direct correction), student have to do something that forces them to pay attention to the feedback such as revising their writing or even commenting on the corrections. Ultimately, however, because of the conflicting views and research, teachers should not feel compelled to address all written errors in all writing. Given the other benefits of writing as additional source of output and a possible way to focus on the form of the language, writing even without written feedback should be effective in promoting SLA.

Future directions

How does L2 written development differ from L2 speaking development?

With so few longitudinal studies of speaking or writing, it is not surprising that studies comparing the development of the two skills do not exist. In addition to the difficulties in conducting longitudinal research, problems in measuring development are quite complex. One way to approach the issue is to focus on one specific feature. The Byrnes and Sinicrope (2008) study is useful in that it studied a fairly well-researched phenomenon, relative clauses, and thus comparisons to other studies can be made. Future studies could also compare measures of accuracy, complexity, and fluency with regard to modality.

Can language learned in writing tasks carry over to speaking? What writing tasks best facilitate oral acquisition?

This question is extremely important to language teaching in foreign language contexts where students may not have enough exposure to oral language. Even when students get enough exposure, they may not produce much oral output because of teacher centeredness or large class size. Writing is a way to have students produce more output. One possible way to investigate the matter is to have learners engage in writing tasks that force production of certain structures or vocabulary and then examine whether or not they carry over into oral tasks.

What is the effect of error correction on long-term development?

Despite the plethora of studies, most are methodologically flawed. Often, variables are not controlled in experimental and controlled groups. More often, learners' texts are not examined for a wide range of features. In other words, as discussed above, only measures of accuracy are reported. In order for written error correction to be considered effective, as argued by Truscott (1996), studies must show that other aspects of learners' writing does not suffer, namely complexity. The issue of written error correction is both one of the most widely researched and least understood issues in L2 writing.

Are the results of past studies of L2 writing consistent across languages with non-Roman, syllabary-based, and logographic writing systems?

Of the empirical studies discussed in this chapter, none examined students writing in a L2 using anything other than a Roman script. Although research on learning how to read in other scripts is common, the same is not true for writing. Replication of studies with writers learning new scripts would add to what we know about learning to write. Certainly, learning how to write logographs is a significant challenge. As for learning syllabaries or non-Roman alphabets, the issues are not obvious. For example, are the challenges of learning to write in Arabic trivial (i.e., memorizing a new writing system) or are they qualitatively different than learning to write in other languages?

Notes

1 The interaction approach has been widely applied to synchronous computer-mediated communication. Although the modality investigated is written, I am not considering it here.
2 Nevertheless, Gass and Mackey (2007) state that long-term development is the most important evidence.

References

Adams, R. and Ross-Feldman, L. (2008). Does writing influence learner attention to form? The speaking-writing connection in second language and academic literacy development. In D. Belcher and A. Hirvela (Eds.), *The oral/literate connection: Perspectives on L2 speaking, writing, and other media interaction* (pp. 210–225). Ann Arbor: University of Michigan Press.

Alamargot, D. and Chanquoy, L. (2001). General introduction: A definition of writing and a presentation of the main models. In D. Alamargot and L. Chanquoy (Eds.), *Through models of writing* (pp. 1–32). Dordrecht: Kluwer.

Aljaafreh, A. and Lantolf, J. (1994). Negative feedback as regulation and second language learning in the zone of proximal development. *Modern Language Journal*, 78, 465–83.

Bardovi-Harlig, K. (1997). Another piece of the puzzle: The emergence of present perfect. *Language Learning*, 51, 215–264.

Bardovi-Harlig, K. (2000). *Tense and aspect in second language acquisition: Form, meaning, and use.* Oxford: Blackwell.

Bardovi-Harlig, K. (2007). One functional approach to second language acquisition: The concept-oriented approach. In B. VanPatten and J. Williams (Eds.), *Theories in second language acquisition: An introduction* (pp. 57–76). Mahwah, NJ: Erlbaum.

Belcher, D. and Hirvela, A. (Eds.) (2008). *The oral/literate connection: Perspectives on L2 speaking, writing, and other media interactions.* Ann Arbor: University of Michigan Press.

Biber, D. (2006). *University language: A corpus-based study of spoken and written registers.* Amsterdam: John Benjamins.

Biber, D., Conrad, S., Reppen, R., Byrd, P., and Helt, M. (2002). Speaking and writing in the university: A multidimensional comparison. *TESOL Quarterly*, 36, 9–48.

Bitchener, J. (2008). Evidence in support of written corrective feedback. *Journal of Second Language Writing*, 17(2), 69–124.

Bitchener, J., Young, S., and Cameron, D. (2005). The effect of different types of corrective feedback on ESL student writing. *Journal of Second Language Writing*, 14, 191–205.

Blake, C. (2009). Potential of text-based internet chats for improving oral fluency in a second language. *Modern Language Journal*, 93, 227–240.

Brooks, L. and Swain, M. (2009). Languaging in collaborative writing: Creation of and response to expertise. In A. Mackey and C. Polio (Eds.), *Multiple perspectives on interaction: Second language research in honor of Susan M. Gass* (pp. 58–89). New York: Routledge.

Byrnes, H. and Sinicrope, C. (2008). Advancedness and the development of relativization in L2 German: A curriculum-based longitudinal study. In L. Ortega and H. Byrnes (Eds.), *The longitudinal study of advanced L2 capacities* (pp. 109–138). Mahwah, NJ: Erlbaum.

Ceyala, M. L. and Navés, T. (2009). Age-related differences and associated factors in foreign language writing: Implications for L2 writing theory and school curricula. In R. M. Manchón (Ed.), *Writing foreign language contexts: Learning, teaching, and research* (pp. 130–155). Bristol, UK: Multilingual Matters.

Chandler, J. (2003). The efficacy of various kinds of error feedback for improvement in the accuracy and fluency of L2 student writing. *Journal of Second Language Writing*, 12, 267–296.

Chandler, J. (2004) A response to Truscott. *Journal of Second Language Writing*, 13, 345–348.

Cleland, A. and Pickering, M. (2006). Do writing and speaking employ the same syntactic representations?. *Journal of Memory and Language*, 54, 185–198.

Cohen, A. and Brooks-Carson, A. (2001). Research on direct versus translated writing: Students' strategies and their results. *Modern Language Journal*, 85, 169–188.

Cumming, A. (1990). Metalinguistic and ideational thinking in second language composing. *Written Communication*, 7, 482–511.

Cumming, A. (2002). Assessing L2 writing: Alternative constructs and ethical dilemmas. *Assessing Writing*, 8, 73–83.

Ellis, N. (2005). At the interface: Dynamic interactions of explicit and implicit language knowledge. *Studies in Second Language Acquisition*, 27, 305–352.

Ellis, N. (2007). The associative-cognitivist CREED. In B. VanPatten and J. Williams (Eds.), *Theories in second language acquisition: An introduction* (pp. 77–96). Mahwah, NJ: Erlbaum.

Ellis, R. (1987). Interlanguage variability in narrative discourse: Style in the use of the past tense. *Studies in Second Language Acquisition*, 9, 12–20.

Ellis, R. (2001). Introduction: Investigating form-focused instruction. *Language Learning*, 51 (Supplement 1), 1–46.

Ellis, R., Sheen, Y., Murakima, M., and Takashima, H. (2008). The effects of focused and unfocused written corrective feedback in an English as a foreign language context. *System, 36*, 353–371.

Ellis, R. and Yuan, F. (2004). The effects of planning on fluency, complexity, and accuracy in second language narrative writing. *Studies in Second Language Acquisition, 26*, 59–84.

Ferris, D. (2002). *Treatment of error in second language student writing*. Ann Arbor: University of Michigan Press.

Ferris, D. and Hedgcock, J. (2005). *Teaching ESL composition*. Mahwah, NJ: Erlbaum.

Ferris, D. and Roberts, B. (2001). Error feedback in L2 writing classes: How explicit does it need to be?. *Journal of Second Language Writing, 10*, 161–184.

Flower, L. and Hayes, J. (1980). The cognition of discovery: Defining a rhetorical problem. *College Composition and Communication, 310*, 21–32.

Flowerdew, J. (2001). Attitudes of journal editors to non-native speaker contributions. *TESOL Quarterly, 35*, 121–150.

Flowerdew, J. and Li, Y. (2009). English or Chinese? The trade-off between local and international publication among Chinese academic in the humanities and social sciences. *Journal of Second Language Writing, 18*, 1–16.

Foster, P. and Skehan, P. (1996). The influence of planning and task type on second language performance. *Studies in Second Language Acquisition, 18*, 299–324.

Friedlander, A. (1990). Composing in English: Effects of a first language on writing in English as Second Language. In B. Kroll (Ed.), *Second language writing: Research insight for the classroom* (pp. 109–125). Cambridge: Cambridge University Press.

Gass, S. M. and Mackey, A. (2006). Input, interaction and output: An overview. *AILA Review, 19*, 3–17.

Gass, S. and Mackey, A. (2007). Input, interaction, and output in second language acquisition. In B. VanPatten and J. Williams (Eds.), *Theories in second language acquisition: An introduction* (pp. 175–199). Mahwah, NJ: Erlbaum.

Guenette, D. (2007). Is feedback pedagogically correct? Research design issues in studies of feedback on writing. *Journal of Second Language Writing, 16*(1), 40–53.

Gutiérrez, X. (2008). What does metalinguistic activity in L2 learners' interaction during a collaborative writing task look like? *Modern Language Journal, 92*, 519–537.

Harklau, L. (2002). The role of writing in classroom second language acquisition. *Journal of Second Language Writing, 11*, 329–350.

Hatch, E. (1978). Discourse analysis and second language acquisition. In E. Hatch (Ed.), *Second language acquisition: A book of readings* (pp. 401–435). Rowley, MA: Newbury House.

Hayes, J. R. (1996). A new framework for understanding cognition and affect in writing. In C. Levy and S. E. Ransdell (Eds.), *The science of writing: Theories, methods, individual differences and applications* (pp. 1–27). Mahwah, NJ: Laurence Erlbaum Associates.

Hayes, J. R. and Flower, L. S. (1980). Identifying the organization of writing processes. In L. Gregg and E. R. Steinberg (Eds.), *Cognitive processes in writing* (pp. 3–30). Hillsdale, NJ: Lawrence Erlbaum.

Hinkel, E. (2002). *Second language writers' text*. Mahwah, NJ: Erlbaum.

Hinkel, E. (2004). *Teaching academic ESL writing*. Mahwah, NJ: Erlbaum.

Kawauchi, C. (2005). The effects of strategic planning on the oral narratives of learners with low and high intermediate L2 proficiency. In R. Ellis (Ed.), *Planning and task performance in a second language* (pp. 143–164). Amsterdam: John Benjamins.

Kellogg, R. T. (1996). A model of working memory in writing. In M. C. Levy and S. E. Ransdell (Eds.), *The science of writing: Theories, methods, individual differences and applications* (pp. 57–71). Mahwah, NJ: Laurence Erlbaum Associates.

Kellogg, R. T. (2001). Competition for working memory among writing processes. *American Journal of Psychology, 114*, 175–192.

Kim, Y. (2008). The effects of integrated language-based instruction in elementary ESL learning. *Modern Language Journal, 92*, 431–451.

Kobayashi, H. and Rinnert, C. (1992). Effects of first language on second language writing: Translation vs. direct composition. *Language Learning, 42*, 183–215.

Kuiken, F. and Vedder, I. (2008). Cognitive task complexity and written output in Italian and French as a foreign language. *Journal of Second Language Writing, 17*, 48–60.

Lally, C. (2000). First language influences in second language composition: The effect of pre-writing. *Foreign Language Annals, 33*, 428–432.

Lantolf, J. and Thorne, S. (2007). Sociocultural theory and second language learning. In B. VanPatten and J. Williams (Eds.), *Theories in second language acquisition: An introduction* (pp. 197–220). Mahwah, NJ: Erlbaum.

Lee, I. (2004). Error correction in L2 secondary writing classrooms: The case of Hong Kong. *Journal of Second Language Writing, 13*, 285–312.

Leki, I., Cumming, A., and Silva, T. (2008). *A synthesis of research on second language writing in English.* New York: Routledge/Taylor and Francis.

Levelt, W. (1989). *Speaking: From intention to articulation.* Cambridge: MIT Press.

Long, M. H. (1981). Input, interaction, and second language acquisition. In H. Winitz (Ed.), *Native language and foreign language acquisition: Annals of the New York academy of science, 379*, 259–278.

Long, M. H. (1983). Linguistic and conversational adjustments to non–native speakers. *Studies in Second Language Acquisition, 5*, 177–193.

Mackey, A. and Polio, C. (2009). Introduction. In Mackey, A. and Polio, C. (Eds.), *Multiple perspectives on interaction: Second language research in honor of Susan M. Gass* (pp. 1–10). New York: Routledge.

Manchón, R. M. (2011). The language learning potential of writing in foreign language contexts: Lessons from research. In M. Reichelt and T. Cimasko (Eds.), *Foreign language writing: Research insights* (pp. 44–64). West Lafayette: Parlour Press.

Mehnert, U. (1998). The effects of different lengths of time for planning on second language performance. *Studies in Second Language Acquisition, 20*, 83–108.

Miller, K., Lindgren, E., and Sullivan, K. (2008). The psycholinguistic dimension in second language writing: Opportunities for research and pedagogy using computer key stroke logging. *TESOL Quarterly, 42*, 433–454.

Mitchell, R. and Myles, F. (1998). *Second language learning theories.* London: Arnold.

Mochizuki, N. and Ortega, L. (2008). Balancing communication and grammar in beginning-level foreign language classrooms: A study of guided planning and relativization. *Language Teaching Research, 12*, 11–37.

Nassaji, H. and Cumming, A. (2000). What's in a ZPD? A case study of a young ESL student and teacher interacting through dialog journals. *Language Teaching Research, 4*, 95–121.

National Council of Teachers of English (2005). *The impact of the SAT and ACT timed writing tests.* http://www.ncte.org/library/NCTEFiles/Resources/Positions/SAT-ACT-tf-report.pdf

Norris, J. M. and Ortega, L. (2000). Effectiveness of L2 instruction: A research synthesis and quantitative meta-analysis. *Language Learning, 50*, 417–528.

Norris, J. M. and Ortega, L. (2003). Defining and measuring L2 acquisition. In C. Doughty and M. H. Long (Eds.), *Handbook of second language acquisition* (pp. 717–761). New York: Blackwell.

Ortega, L. (1999). Planning and focus on form in L2 oral performance. *Studies in Second Language Acquisition, 21*, 109–148.

Pienemann, M. (1998). *Language processing and second language development: Processability theory.* Amsterdam: Benjamins.

Pienemann, M. (2005). *Cross-linguistic aspects of processability theory.* Philadelphia: Benjamins.

Pienemann, M. (2007). Processability theory. In B. VanPatten and J. Williams (Eds.), *Theories in second language acquisition: An introduction* (pp. 137–154). Mahwah, NJ: Erlbaum.

Pienemann, M. and Johnston, M. (1987). Factors influencing the development of language proficiency. In D. Nunan (Ed.), *Applying second language acquisition research* (pp. 45–141). Adelaide, Australia: National Curriculum Resource Centre, AMEP.

Pinker, S. (1994). *The language instinct.* New York: William Morrow.

Polio, C. (1997). Measures of linguistic accuracy in second language writing research. *Language Learning, 47*, 101–143.

Polio, C. (2001). Research methodology in second language writing research: The case of text-based studies. In T. Silva and P. Matsuda (Eds.), *On second language writing* (pp. 91–116). Mahwah, NJ: Erlbaum.

Polio, C. (2003). An overview of approaches to second language writing research. In B. Kroll (Ed.), *Exploring the Dynamics of Second Language Writing* (pp. 35–65). Cambridge: Cambridge University Press.

Qi, D. and Lapkin, S. (2001). Exploring the role of noticing in a three-stage second language writing task. *Journal of Second Language Writing, 10*, 277–303.

Robinson, P. (2005). Cognitive complexity and task sequencing. Studies in componential framework for second language task design. *International Review of Applied Linguistics, 43*, 1–32.

Russell, J. and Spada, N. (2006). The effectiveness of corrective feedback for the acquisition of L2 grammar: A meta-analysis of the research. In J. M. Norris and L. Ortega (Eds.), *Synthesizing research on language learning and teaching* (pp. 133–164). Philadelphia: John Benjamins.

Sachs, R. and Polio, C. (2007). Learners' uses of two types of written feedback on an L2 writing revision task. *Studies in Second Language Acquisition, 29*(1), pp. 67–100.

Sangarun, J. (2005). The effects of focusing on meaning and form in strategic planning. In R. Ellis (Ed.), *Planning and task performance in a second language* (pp. 111–141). Amsterdam: John Benjamins.

Sasaki, M. (2000). Toward an empirical model of EFL writing processes. *Journal of Second Language Writing*, *9*, 259–292.

Sasaki, M. (2004). Building an empirically-based model of EFL learners' writing processes. In S. Ransdell and M. -L. Barbier (Eds.), *New directions for research in L2 writing* (pp. 49–80). Amsterdam: Kluwer Academic.

Sasaki, M. (2007). Effects of study-abroad experiences on EFL writers: A multiple data analysis. *Modern Language Journal*, *91*, 602–620.

Schoonen, R., Snellings, P., Stevenson, M., and Van Gelderen, A. (2009). Towards a blueprint of the foreing language writer: The linguistic and cognitive demands of foreign language writing. In R. M. Manchón (Ed.), *Writing foreign language contexts: Learning, teaching, and research* (pp. 77–101). Bristol, UK: Multilingual Matters.

Serrano, R. and Howard, E. R. (2007). Second language writing development in English and in Spanish in a two-way immersion programme. *International Journal of Bilingual Education and Bilingualism*, *10*(2), 152–170.

Sheen, Y. (2007). The effect of focused written corrective feedback and language aptitude on ESL learners' acquisition. *TESOL Quarterly*, *41*, 255–283.

Stapa, S. and Magid, A. (2009). The use of first language in developing ideas in second language writing. *European Journal of Social Sciences*, *7*(4), 41–47.

Storch, N. (2005). Collaborative writing: Product, process, and students' reflections. *Journal of Second Language Writing*, *14*, 153–173.

Swain, M. (1998). Focus on form through conscious reflection. In C. Doughty and J. Williams (Eds.), *Focus on form in classroom second language acquisition* (p. 64–81). Cambridge: Cambridge University Press.

Swain, M. (2005). The output hypothesis: Theory and research. In E. Hinkel (Ed.), *Handbook of research in second language teaching and learning* (pp. 471–483). Mahwah, NJ: Lawrence Erlbaum Associates.

Swain, M. and Lapkin, S. (1995). Problems in output and the cognitive processes they generate: A step towards second language learning. *Applied Linguistics*, *16*, 371–391.

Tarone, E. and Bigelow, M. (2005). Impact of literacy on oral language processing: Implications for second language acquisition research. *Annual Review of Applied Linguistics*, *25*, 77–97.

Truscott, J. (1996). The case against grammar correction in L2 writing classes. *Language Learning*, *46*, 327–369.

Truscott, J. (2004). Evidence and conjecture on the effects of correction: A response to Chandler. *Journal of Second Language Writing*, *13*, 337–343.

Truscott, J. (2007). The effect of error correction on learners' ability to write accurately. *Journal of Second Language Writing*, *17*, 255–272.

Tyler, A. (2011) Usage-based approaches to language and their applications to second language learning. *Annual Review of Applied Linguistics*, *30*, 270–291.

VanPatten, B. and Williams, J. (2007). Introduction: The nature of theories. In B. VanPatten and J. Williams, (Eds.), *Theories in second language acquisition: An introduction*. Mahwah, NJ: Erlbaum.

Wang, W. and Wen, Q. (2002). L1 use in the L2 composing process: An exploratory study of 16 Chinese EFL. *Journal of Second Language Writing*, *11*, 225–246.

Weigle, S. C. (2002). *Assessing writing*. Cambridge: Cambridge University Press.

Weissberg, R. (2000). Developmental relationships in the acquisition of English syntax: Writing vs. speech. *Learning and Instruction*, *10*, 37–53.

Wendel, J. (1997). *Planning and second language narrative production*. Unpublished PhD thesis. Temple University, Japan.

White, L. (2007). Linguistic theory, Universal grammar, and second language acquisition. In B. VanPatten and J. Williams (Eds.), *Theories in second language acquisition: An introduction* (pp. 37–56). Mahwah, NJ: Erlbaum.

Wigglesworth, G. (1997). An investigation of planning time and proficiency level on oral test discourse. *Language Testing*, *14*, 85–106.

Williams, J. (2008). The speaking-writing connection in second language and academic literacy development. In D. Belcher and A. Hirvela (Eds.), *The oral/literate connection: Perspectives on L2 speaking, writing, and other media interaction* (pp. 10–25). Ann Arbor: University of Michigan Press.

Wolfe-Quintero, K., Inagaki, S., and Kim, H. Y. (1998). Second Language Development in Writing: Measures of Fluency, Accuracy, and Complexity. (Technical Report #17). Honolulu: National Foreign Language Resource Center.

Wong, W. (2001). Modality and attention to meaning and form in the input. *Studies in Second Language Acquisition*, *23*, 345–368.

Xu, C. (2009). Overgeneralization from a narrow focus: A response to Ellis *et al.*, (2008) and Bitchener (2008). *Journal of Second Language Writing, 18*, 270–275.

Yuan, F. and Ellis, R. (2003). The effects of pre-task planning and on-line planning on fluency, complexity and accuracy in L2 monologic oral production. *Applied Linguistics, 24*, 1–27.

Zhang, S. (1987). Cognitive complexity and written production in English as a second language. *Language Learning, 37*, 469–481.

Zimmermann, R. (2000). L2 writing subprocesses. A model of formulating and empirical findings. *Learning and Instruction, 10*, 73–99.

20

Second language speech production

Lucy Pickering

Historical discussion

The study of second language (L2) speech production has a long history in second language (SLA) research, both for what it can tell us about the development of the specific skill and how it might illuminate the general processes of SLA. Over time, studies in L2 phonological attainment have become a battleground for perennial issues in SLA research encompassing cognitive, psychological, and socio-cultural factors as varied as age-related constraints on ultimate attainment, and the role of identity in perceptions of accentedness. SLA research has also benefited from the ongoing development of phonological theory which has been consistently applied to L2 production throughout the decades.

The investigation of L2 speech production has been part of second language acquisition research from its beginnings. Following the prevailing linguistic paradigm of the time, researchers employed Contrastive Analysis (CA) (Lado, 1957) and the "difference = difficulty" hypothesis to explain the shape of L2 accents (Weinreich, 1953). Despite this belief that transfer was at the root of non-native accents, it became evident that the prognoses made by CA with regard to L2 phonology, as with other language systems, were not predictive of learner error. Recognizing this difficulty, Eckman supplemented CA with the Markedness Differential Hypothesis (1977) and the Structural Conformity Hypothesis (1991) (for further information, see Chapter 6 by Eckman).

Throughout the 1980s, speech researchers followed the shift in the field of SLA away from CA toward a closer investigation of learner language through Error Analysis (Corder, 1967) and the recognition of stable, transitional grammars, or interlanguages (ILs) (Selinker, 1972). Major's Ontogeny Model (OM) (1987) for example, proposed a three-part structure underlying IL comprising influences from L1, L2 and universal processes. The OM further stated that these influences would be more salient during different phases of learner development in phonology with L1 transfer initially frequent in the IL and then decreasing as developmental processes increased.[1]

During this time, few had challenged the presumption of a critical period (Lenneberg, 1967) for linguistic development, and Scovel (1988) predicted that post-pubescent L2 learners would retain permanently accented speech. In the early 1980s, however, Flege and his colleagues began to question the role of the CPH as the primary explanatory factor for the differences between the production of L2 phonetic segments by children and adults (see later in this chapter for a detailed discussion of the debate regarding the CPH). Based on an ongoing series of studies (Flege, 1981,

1987; Flege and Eefting, 1986; Flege and Hillenbrand, 1984; among others), they posited a relationship between perception and production that operated differently in L2, not because of an age-based constraint but because adult speaker-hearers already have established phonetic categories in their L1. Flege proposed a mechanism termed Equivalence Classification in which adult learners are more likely to identify new phones appearing in the L2 as equivalent to already existing L1 categories. Equivalence classification predicts that learners are likely to be less effective at successfully distinguishing and producing sounds that are similar to sounds in their L1 than they are with sounds that are novel and have no correlate in the L1 sound system. This may be the result of perceptually similar but phonetically distinct sounds in L2 being assimilated into a single category (See Hardison, Chapter 21, in this volume for a discussion of the relationship between perception and production in the L2.). Although the hypothesis predicts that missed perceptual cues will render production inaccurate and that changes in perception should lead to changes in production, Flege notes that not all inaccurate production can or should be explained by perception. In a 1995 study, he discusses output constraints on syllable type as a possible cause of production difficulties such as the word-external epenthesis typically shown by Spanish speakers of English. Over time, Flege has formalized his hypotheses in the Speech Learning Model (SLM) which he describes as follows:

> An assumption we make is that the phonetic systems used in the production and perception of vowels and consonants *remain adaptive over the life span*, and that phonetic systems reorganize in response to sounds encountered in an L2 through the addition of new phonetic categories, or through the modification of old ones.

> *(1995, p. 233)*

The SLM focuses on the production of segments and with a few exceptions, research on the development of suprasegmentals in L2 has traditionally been scarce (see Wenk, 1986 and Juffs, 1990). Taking intonation study as a specific example, Willems (1982) initially reported that Dutch speakers of English demonstrated differences in all aspects of intonation structure including pitch range, pitch prominence, and pitch reset following a boundary. These features have since been confirmed in more recent studies with participants comprising a range of L1s. In investigations of advanced and intermediate Asian and European learners of English, Wennerstrom (1994, 1997) found that speakers did not use pitch variation to signal new or contrastive lexical items, and used less reduction of pitch than L1 speakers on non-prominent words. Japanese, Thai, and Chinese speakers also tended to use low boundary tones between repeated propositions where rising or mid level tones would be anticipated by native speaker (NS) hearers. Pirt (1990) reported similar results in a study of Italian learners, and Pickering (2001) reported equivalent findings for Chinese speakers of English in academic discourse. Hewings (1995) found a preference for the use of falling tones in the discourse of advanced L2 learners from Korea, Greece, and Indonesia in contexts where NSs would use rising or level tones. Both Mennen (1998) and Pickering (2004) report demonstrably narrower pitch ranges in L2 learners as compared to NSs.

In addition to studies addressing different aspects of the phonological system, some of the recent approaches taken to L2 speech production have emerged from current models of phonology such as Optimality theory (OT) (Prince and Smolensky, 1993) and Connectionism (Elman *et al.*, 1996). Optimality theory proposes a universal set of violable constraints accessible to all speakers. Each language ranks these constraints differently and these different rankings account for phonological differences among languages (see Archangeli and Langendeon, 1997, for a complete introduction to OT, and Eckman, Chapter 6, in this volume for a more detailed discussion of OT.). As examples of natural language, ILs may also allow novel structures to surface (i.e., structures that are not present in either the L1 or L2) as a result of learners hypothesizing different constraint rankings. Hancin-Bhatt and Bhatt (1997) account for both Japanese and Spanish learners' difficulties with phonotactic structure in English within the OT framework, and Broselow *et al.* (1998) attribute the preference for Mandarin speakers of English to devoice final obstruents to a specific re-ranking of constraints.

Connectionist frameworks are modeled on computer programming, and propose a network of nodes which have different activation values. Connections between the nodes are weighted, with larger weights indicating stronger connections. A network of connections is built as the learner is exposed to many instances of a given language feature. As an example of its possible application to L2 phonology, Hancin-Bhatt (1992) exemplifies how a connectionist approach to processing may account for the substitution of a dental [t] for the voiceless alveolar fricative by Hindi speakers of English. There continues to be a burgeoning research agenda in the field of L2 speech production with a continued emphasis on model building supplemented by more recent additions such as the investigation of neurological factors in language production (Sereno and Wang, 2007).

Core issues

This part of the chapter discusses the following issues as they relate to L2 speech production: Age-related effects, language-related effects, and socio-affective factors involved in L2 production. The final section reviews research in intelligibility as it pertains to SLA. An additional core area of importance, the relationship between speech production and perception is only briefly addressed, and the reader is referred to Chapter 21 in this volume by Hardison.

Age-related effects on L2 speech production

Often referred to as the "Conrad phenomenon" after the novelist Joseph Conrad, perhaps the most compelling question in L2 phonology research has been the interaction between the Critical Period Hypothesis (CPH) and degree of accent, i.e., the assumption that after a certain age, L2 learners are biologically incapable of achieving a native accent in their second language (See also Chapter 31 by Byrnes and Chapter 27 by DeKeyser in this volume.):

> In its most succinct and theory neutral formulation, the CPH states that there is a limited developmental period during which it is possible to acquire a language be it L1 or L2 to normal, natively levels. Once this window of opportunity is passed, however, the ability to learn language declines.
>
> *(Birdsong, 1999, p. 1)*

With regard to pronunciation specifically, proponents of the CPH have proposed a developmental constraint ranging from five to 15 years old. L2 speech production has been one of the primary testing grounds for the CPH, and the controversy is well illustrated in an open debate that began in the journal *Applied Linguistics* between Flege (1987, 1999) and Patkowski (1990, 1994).

As noted above, Flege (1987) questioned a number of the assumptions underlying traditional acceptance of the CPH. He cites studies in which children do not appear to out-perform adults in the production and perception of L2 speech sounds (Snow and Hoefnagel-Höhle, 1978; Winitz, 1981) and argues that studies show a linear relationship between degree of foreign accent and age as opposed to a noticeable discontinuity which would be expected at the onset of the end of the critical period (Oyama, 1978). He describes the focus on CPH as reductionistic and suggests that differences between adult and child learners may be the result of a number of factors other than (or in addition to) a critical period. Examples of possible confounding factors include previous linguistic experience, affective factors such as motivation, and social factors such as group identity.

In his reply to this paper, Patkowski (1990) argues that proponents of the CHP focus on ultimate L2 proficiency rather than rate of acquisition; thus, evidence of adults showing faster *initial* rates than children are not relevant to the debate. With regard to Flege's contention that there is a lack of research evidence verifying the onset of a marked discontinuity which would mirror the end of the critical period, Patkowski both challenges the design of the studies cited by Flege and cites a study of his own (Patkowski, 1980) in which such a discontinuity was in evidence. In summary, Patkowski states that there is no "convincing rationale for entirely discarding the notion of a biologically based age limitation on the ability to acquire second languages with native fluency" (1990, p. 86).

In a follow-up paper in 1994, Patkowski cites a number of review articles and empirical studies (including most notably Long, 1990 and Patkowski, 1990) to support his position that a biologically based sensitive or critical period somewhere between the ages of 12 and 15 years exists for the ultimate attainment of second language phonology. Flege (1999) responds and cites two studies (Flege *et al.*, 1995; Yeni-Komshian *et al.* 1997) which continue to show a linear relationship between degree of perceived accent and age in subjects between the ages of two and 23 years which does not support an abrupt biologically or neurologically based shift in ability.

The debate continues to expand (for an accessible summary see "The whys and why nots of the CPH-L2A" by Birdsong, 1999); Bongaerts (1999) conducted several studies in which some highly advanced late Dutch learners of English and French were rated by judges as indistinct from native speakers suggesting that the CHP could be nullified. Bongaerts submits that this may be the result of high motivation, high levels of input, and training in the perception and production of L2 speech. Birdsong (2007) reports similar results in a study with late Anglophone learners of French. There continues to be no clear resolution to this controversy. In the first chapter of their 2007 volume, Bohn and Munro cite Flege *et al.* (2006) who find that even very young L2 learners exhibit foreign accents and also report Hakuta *et al.* (2003) whose adult learners exhibit success that correlates negatively with age of arrival.

Language-related effects: Transfer and markedness

Early studies that conceived of transfer through the lens of CA sought straightforward explanations of L2 pronunciation errors in a comparative analysis of the different phonological systems of L1 and L2. As more and more empirical evidence came to light that did not support this thesis, a more moderate version of CA (Oller and Ziahosseiny, 1970) became popular. The original hypothesis was revised to include both similarities and differences between phonological systems, and there was a recognition that perceptual saliency may play a crucial role.

Major (2001) suggests that learners may perceive large differences between the L1 and L2 sound systems but have more difficulty noticing smaller differences. Thus, the learner may be more likely to hit a phonological target if that target is unlikely to be substituted by a similar target in the L1 (see also Flege's SLM above). Major further advanced the notion of similarity and dissimilarity by adding the principle of rate (Major and Kim, 1996). The Similarity Differential Rate Hypothesis suggests that dissimilar features will be acquired at faster rates than similar ones but that markedness will slow rate. Major proposed that this combination of underlying factors results in a surface structure in the IL that does not support simplistic notions of transfer.

In an investigation of the relative contribution of markedness and direct L1 transfer, Carlisle (1994) reviews studies in the area of syllable structure. These studies show a clear preference for L2 learners to transfer syllable structure into IL phonology by resyllabifying to match L1 constraints rather than simplifying to produce a universally less marked structure (e.g., an open CV syllable).

With regard to prosodic structure, overall prosodic profiles of certain groups of learners have resulted in similar suggestions of the primacy of transfer over developmental features (for example, Wennerstrom (1998) for Chinese learners of English and Jilka (2007) for English speakers of German.) However, it is also the case that similar errors in L2 intonation structure by learners of very different backgrounds have been reported (see Mennen, 2007 for a summary). As Mennen notes, however, much of this work is inconclusive. The majority of studies report on L2 acquisition of English only, and the lack of a common framework to describe intonation systems cross-linguistically makes it difficult to assess features that may reflect universal tendencies vs. cases of L1 transfer.

Social and affective factors

Despite a historical focus on both age- and language-related effects, research suggests that there are additional language independent constraints that may affect L2 phonological attainment. Thus far, studies have investigated task variation (Tarone, 1980), attitudes and motivation (Stokes, 2001), concern for pronunciation accuracy (Elliott, 1995), social markings of identity (Dowd et al., 1990; Lybeck, 2002), and extent of L1 and L2 use (Piske et al., 2001) among other socio-affective variables. Two current studies, Moyer (2004) and Hansen (2006) demonstrate a more recent research agenda in which social factors are at the center of the analysis.

Moyer investigates 25 advanced learners of German as a second language from a range of L1 backgrounds. She considers a number of instructional and social factors including level of motivation, self-perceived accentedness, amount of formal language instruction, and amount and context of use of German on a regular basis. The participants completed four language tasks which were recorded and then judged by three NS judges. Participants also completed a questionnaire and semi-structured interviews in which they talked about their personal language-related experiences. Moyer found that although age exerted some independent influence, psychological variables such as intensity of motivation, satisfaction with attainment, and professional motivational orientation accounted for a larger percentage of the variance than age of onset combined with length of residence. Thus, she determines that "the idea that ultimate attainment is *primarily* a function of age must be reconsidered. Instead, the impact of age should be understood as *indirect* as well as possibly direct" (p. 140).

Hansen (2006) conducted a longitudinal study of the development of syllable margins in the emerging L2 of two adult Vietnamese learners of English and considered both linguistic and social constraints in accounting for acquisition. The participants in the study, a husband and wife in their 40s (Nhi and Anh), arrived in the USA from Vietnam one year before data collection began. Like Moyer, Hansen uses interview data to target socio-affective factors. In her discussion of social constraints, she presents a narrative account spanning ten months, partially in her own words and partially in the words of her participants. The reader is introduced to the participants' changing social contexts over the length of the study and given insights into each person's personality, motivations, and frustrations. We learn that Anh adapts very slowly to her new surroundings and by the end of the study, she still struggles to communicate in English. Nhi is a more easy-going learner and significantly less anxious than Anh. He prioritizes his relationships with English speakers and engages in his English language environment at work. In her interpretation of these data, Hansen uses both Schumann's Acculturation Model (1986) and Pierce's (1995) concept of investment to explain how social constraints such as perceptions of cultural identity and extended family dynamics may impact Anh and Nhi's individual phonological development. Although emerging production modifications suggest a shift in developmental patterns that will ultimately favor Nhi (and by extension his approach to learning), it remained to be confirmed in terms of overall change.

Intelligibility

Assessment of intelligibility has long been considered a core area of L2 speech research. Although we can use intelligibility in a broad sense to mean "intelligible production and felicitous interpretation of English" (Nelson, 1995, p. 274), more recently there has been a distinction in the literature between "intelligibility" to mean formal recognition of decoding of words and utterances, and "comprehensibility" to mean the listener's ability to understand the meaning of the word or utterance in its given context. Thus, as Field (2003) suggests, a listener may use contextual understanding to compensate for the fact that a message is unable to be precisely decoded.

Comprehensibility or intelligibility judgments of L2 speech tend to rely on NS listener ratings (Anderson-Hsieh *et al.*, 1992; Piske *et al.*, 2001) and are often accompanied by judgments of accentedness (Derwing and Munro, 1997); as yet, however, no clear relationship has been established between accentedness and comprehensibility. Speakers who succeed in reducing the degree of foreignness in their accents (based on expert NS raters) may still be heard as incomprehensible by lay listeners (Munro and Derwing, 1995). Although accentedness in L2 speech may derive from several different sources, Derwing and Munro (1997) conclude that L2 comprehensibility is improved for NS listeners with enhanced prosodic proficiency, and their position is supported by subsequent studies (e.g., Derwing and Rossiter, 2003; Field, 2005). Prosodic characteristics that have been found to be important include speech rate (Derwing, 1990; Derwing and Munro, 2001), mean length of utterance (Kormos and Dénes, 2004), length and placement of pauses (Anderson-Hsieh and Venkatagiri, 1994; Pickering, 1999; Riggenbach, 1991), and non-standard word stress (Field, 2005; Hahn, 2004).

Most recently, intelligibility studies have expanded to include non-native speaker (NNS) perceptions of comprehensibility in NNS-NNS or learner-learner interactions (for a review of studies within the context of English as a lingua franca see Pickering, 2006). This work suggests that L2 listeners may process phonological features differently from their NS counterparts. While prosodic features appear to be a crucial cue for NS comprehensibility, studies with NNS listeners suggest that they may rely more on segmental features (Deterding, 2005; Field, 2005; Jenkins, 2000). Jenkins suggests that this predominant focus on bottom-up processing (i.e., resorting to acoustic information rather than contextual information) reflects L2 speakers' higher dependency on phonological form as opposed to shared contextual knowledge with their interlocutors.

In addition, L2 speaker-hearers may draw on an "interlanguage speech intelligibility benefit" (Bent and Bradlow, 2003)— an effect resulting from some familiarity with particular non-standard phonological forms. An L2 learner may be better equipped to interpret specific acoustic-phonetic features of a L2 speaker that are matched with her or his own production, and therefore find understanding an L2 speaker from their own L1 background easier than understanding someone from a different L1 background (cf., Major *et al.*, 2002; see also Gass and Varonis, 1984).

Data and common elicitation measures

The types of data utilized and the methods of analysis employed in L2 speech production research reflect the breadth of quantitative and qualitative research possibilities typically found in applied linguistics. Research designs encompass experimental designs comprising a hundred or more participants (Flege *et al.*, 1995) to more naturalistic contexts involving just two participants (Hansen, 2006). Elicitation measures range from native speaker judgments of perceived accent or intelligibility (Munro and Derwing, 1995) to objective measures of acoustic characteristics such as voice onset time (VOT) (Strange, 1995) or fundamental frequency values (Jilka, 2007; Kang et al., 2010). The following discussion addresses issues of data collection and verification in studies of segmental and suprasegmental features of L2 production.

Segmental studies

At the highly experimental end of the research continuum, L2 research focused on segmentals has been dominated by Flege and his colleagues (see earlier discussion). Their goal for the most part has been to find evidence for the claims made by the SLM (1995), namely, that phonetic systems remain adaptive and that L2 learners will be more successful at creating new categories for L2 sounds that are dissimilar from L1 sounds than those that are similar. Thus, studies typically employ late learners who can be exempted a priori from traditional conceptions of the CPH or learners comprising a range of ages. L2 populations have also come from a wide variety of L1 backgrounds including Swedish, Chinese, Spanish, Italian, Dutch, and Japanese speakers. As the focus is on creation of phonetic categories, testing is usually confined to a very small aspect of production such as VOT or vowel duration. In order to limit confounding variables for these heavily statistical designs, spontaneous speech is also eschewed in favor of word lists or utterances read aloud. Certain segmental features have become emblematic of L2 phonological research such as the perception and production of /l/ and /r/ by Japanese learners of English (Bradlow, 2008; Yamada et al., 1996) or the cross-linguistic comparison of formant structures (F1 and F2) or duration in vowels (see Strange, 2007 for a review.) These have allowed researchers to compare findings more easily.

At the opposite end of the continuum, while still focusing on individual elements of L2 phonology, in this case the production of syllable margins, Hansen (2006) adopts a dual design that incorporates both qualitative and quantitative components. Interviews recorded with two participants targeted socio-affective factors and were transcribed and coded for production of syllable onsets and codas. Hansen is able to document detailed production modifications over time that suggest an emerging L2 phonology in which L2 consonants are very gradually acquired by the two learners in similar stages but at different rates. Quantitative findings, however, are difficult to interpret, as there are not enough data to make this kind of analysis work well. At one point, for example, Hansen notes that although it appears that one participant has acquired three-member consonant onsets at 89 percent accuracy, there are too few tokens for this percentage to be meaningful.

Suprasegmental studies

Studies of the suprasegmental characteristics of L2 speech tend to look quite different from work in segmentals. Most notably, they are usually smaller in terms of numbers of participants. Following a review of studies on L2 prosody in major journals over the past 25 years, Gut (2007, p. 145) finds that research on intonation is conducted with an average number of 22.6 participants and research on word stress is based on an average of 7.7 participants. In addition, she notes that most studies comprise artificial speech tasks such as reading aloud and are undertaken in laboratory settings. There is growing evidence that such data are problematic for assessing suprasegmental features such as intonation and rhythm. Tao (1996, p. 34), for example, argues that the proposed pitch register differences suggested between interrogatives and declaratives in Mandarin may be an artifact of studying isolated sentences as opposed to natural discourse. He finds that the theory of register does not account for a large portion of the intonation patterns that may be present in natural speech. Similarly, with regard to rhythmic characteristics, Lai (2002) proposes that misconceptions about the stress patterns of Cantonese derive in part at least from a reliance on experimental production of the language which alters its natural prosodic patterns. Finally, Brazil (1992) recognizes a number of different levels of engagement in reading aloud by a speaker which result in different prosodic compositions depending on the type of reading (i.e., text versus isolated sentences), and the degree of engagement by the speaker with text and listener.

Despite their disadvantages, these research designs often reflect necessary compromises if we want to compare apples to apples; two issues are particularly salient. First, differences between L1 and L2 production of intonational features such as use of contrastive prominence or tonal structure are difficult to assess if participants are saying different things. To address this difficulty, Hewings (1995) asked L2 learners to read scripted dialogs and then compared these readings to NS performances. Wennerstrom (1994) asked all her participants to read the same passage that had been constructed to exemplify specific intonational features. The second issue is the increased use of instrumental data to support findings regarding L2 prosodic structure through programs such as WASP (Huckvale, 2003) and PRAAT (Boersma and Weenick, 2002) which are freely down-loadable, as well as commercially available programs (see Schuetze-Coburn et al., 1991, for a comparison of auditory and instrumental analysis). These tools allow researchers to measure a variety of acoustic features; however, they also demand audio data of a high quality that is difficult to obtain outside of a controlled environment (although see Pickering (1999) and Wennerstrom (1997) for the recording of naturally occurring data).

An alternative approach to data collection lies in recent developments in corpus construction. Currently there are at least two learner corpora that include some annotation of prosodic features of L2 speakers. The LeaP (Learning Prosody in a Foreign Language) corpus comprises more than 12 hours of recording time of second language learners of German and English and includes six manually annotated and two automatically annotated tiers. The Hong Kong corpus of Spoken English has approximately one million words prosodically transcribed (manually) using Brazil's (1997) discourse model. Both corpora have generated studies of L2 speech production (e.g., Cheng et al., 2005; Gut, 2007) which benefit from the large datasets that they are based on.

Applications

There has been a consistent interplay between L2 speech production research and pedagogy throughout the history of this area, most particularly in the teaching of EFL/ESL. English pronunciation materials such as *Drills and Exercises in English Pronunciation* (1967) which focuses on stress and intonation and *English Pronunciation Illustrated* (Trim, 1965) which practices phonemes and minimal pairs reflect the tenets of CA and the belief that practice will instill the good habits needed to conquer L2 pronunciation (O'Connor, 1967). With the onset of research in L2 interlanguage and the recognition of the complexity underlying L1 transfer, some attempts were made to introduce notions of markedness and universal processes to language instruction. For example, Yavas (1994) addressed the finding of a universal tendency toward final devoicing with a set of graded teaching materials for English in which presentation and instruction of bilabial final stops (e.g., tub, cab) precedes more difficult stops and consonant clusters.

During the 1980s, the popularity of the communicative approach encouraged development of pedagogical materials that embraced the full scope of the L2 phonological system including suprasegmentals (Chun, 2002). Materials often explicitly addressed the changing ideologies in SLA. In their introduction to *Teaching American English Pronunciation* for example, Avery and Ehrlich (1992) go beyond linguistic factors in pronunciation instruction to discuss the roles of socio-cultural and personality variables. They further note that teachers should be concerned with comprehensibility rather than accuracy when correcting student pronunciation.

Despite this progress toward a focus on language use, the phonological system still tended to be taught in pieces rather than in a realistic context. This applied particularly to the intonation structure in English where priority was still given to grammatical contrasts of attitudinal effects (Levis, 1999) despite growing recognition that intonation formed part of a speaker's discourse and pragmatic competence (Brazil, 1997; Grosz and Sidner, 1986) and that isolated contours form part of a larger organizational structure through which they acquire their full significance (Pierrehumbert and Hirschberg, 1990). In the past several years, interactive teaching materials such as *Streaming Speech* (Cauldwell, 2003) have begun to incorporate examples of naturally occurring discourse that introduce the characteristics of conversational English. The 1980s also saw the more widespread use of speech visualization technology in prosodic instruction (de Bot, 1980; de Bot and Mailfert, 1982; Weltens and de Bot, 1984). Results suggested that learners who received audio-visual feedback demonstrated improved perception and production of intonational contrasts in the L2. More recently, Levis and Pickering (2004) discuss these applications and expand pedagogical applications to a discourse context.

Instruction in English as a foreign language has also been at the forefront of the paradigm shift prompted by the precipitate growth of English as a global lingua franca (Jenkins, 2002). Traditional conceptions of intelligibility that prioritize the speaker are giving way to those that more explicitly consider the listener, and a review of recent research suggests that we may want to promote very different strategies in L2 learners if they intend to remain in an international context (Pickering, 2006). There is also ongoing debate regarding pedagogical practices that privilege certain varieties of English as exemplified by Walker (2001) who discusses proposals that reconsider traditional target models and move toward pronunciation for international intelligibility.

Most recently, there has been a heartening trend in volumes addressing L2 phonological acquisition to include not only research but instructional implications and practice (see Hansen Edwards and Zampini, 2008; and Trouvain and Gut, 2007, for examples). In their preface, Trouvain and Gut describe their hope for what this kind of cross-pollination may achieve:

> The first part [of the volume] contains contributions by SLA researchers and experts in prosody ... This includes overviews of current theoretical models as well as findings from empirical investigations. In the second part, some of the leading teaching practitioners and developers of phonological learning materials present a variety of methods and exercises in the area of prosody ... On the one hand, research on non-native prosody can help teachers to interpret and make sense of their classroom experiences and to provide them with a broad range of pedagogic options. On the other hand, researchers may be encouraged to investigate aspects of non-native prosody that have shown to be of primary importance in language classrooms.
>
> *(pp. v–vi)*

This synergy between laboratory and classroom will be critical to the continued evolution of L2 speech production research and practice.

Future directions

The future agenda of this area is robust as the extent of the work discussed in this chapter suggests. In this section I identify three areas of particular interest for researchers and teachers:

(1) Perhaps the most promising area of growth is in the new technologies being used to investigate the processes of language production such as fMRI scans (Sereno and Wang, 2007) or ultrasound imaging techniques (Gick *et al.*, 2008). It remains to be seen how much this work will impact our current understanding of L2 acquisition of speech; however, it is likely that increased understanding of neurological factors will illuminate differences between L1 and L2 phonological experience.

(2) Some of the most recent expansions in this area have been as a result of a shift in the research terrain toward an interrogation of what constitutes intelligibility, the native speaker, and possible influences on speech production. We need to continue to fill in these gaps. They include both investigations of language learning outside of an English context, and as Leather (1999) suggests, a broadening of our learner base to include multilingual speaker-hearers in non-Western environments.

(3) Speech production research continues to benefit from methodological innovation. Most recently, the development of learner corpora offer a new and largely untapped resource for researchers to access data which may previously have been unattainable due to limited resources.

Notes

1 For the current revision of this model see Major (2001).

References

Anderson-Hsieh, J., Johnson, R., and Koehler, K. (1992). The relationship between native speaker judgments of non-native pronunciation and deviance in segmentals, prosody, and syllable structure. *Language Learning*, *42*, 529–555.

Anderson-Hsieh, J. and Venkatagiri, H. S. (1994). Syllable duration and pausing in the speech of intermediate and high proficiency Chinese ESL speakers. *TESOL Quarterly*, *28*, 807–812.

Archangeli, D. and Langendoen, D. T. (1997). *Optimality theory: An overview*. Malden, MA/London: Blackwell.

Avery, P. and Ehrlich, S. (1992). *Teaching American English pronunciation*. Oxford: Oxford University Press.

Bent, T. and Bradlow, A. R. (2003). The interlanguage speech intelligibility benefit. *Journal of the Acoustic Society of America*, *114*, 1600–1610.

Birdsong, D. (1999). Introduction: Whys and why nots of the critical period hypothesis for second language acquisition. In D. Birdsong (Ed.), *Second language acquisition and the critical period hypothesis* (pp. 1–22). Mahwah, NJ: Lawrence Earlbaum.

Birdsong, D. (2007). Nativelike pronunciation among late learners of French as a second language. In O.-S. Bohn and M. J. Munro (Eds.), *Language experience in second language speech learning* (pp. 99–116). Amsterdam/Philadelphia: John Benjamins.

Boersma, P. and Weenick, D. (2002). *Praat* [Computer software]. Amsterdam, The Netherlands: Institute of Phonetic Sciences, University of Amsterdam.

Bohn, O. S. and Munro, M. (Eds.). (2007). *Language experience in second language speech learning*. Philadephia: John Benjamins.

Bongaerts, T. (1999). Ultimate attainment in L2 pronunciation: The case of very advanced late L2 learners. In D. Birdsong (Ed.), *Second language acquisition and the critical period hypothesis* (pp. 133–159). Mahwah, NJ: Lawrence Earlbaum.

Bradlow, A. (2008). Training non-native language sound patterns: Lessons from training Japanese students on the English /r/ and /l/ contrast. In J. Hansen Edwards and M. Zampini (Eds.), *Phonology and second language acquisition* (pp. 287–308). Philadelphia: John Benjamins.

Brazil, D. (1992). Listening to people reading. In M. Coulthard (Ed.), *Advances in spoken discourse analysis* (pp. 209–241). London: Routledge.

Brazil, D. (1997). *The communicative value of intonation in English*. Cambridge University Press, Originally published in 1985 by University of Birmingham: English Language Research, UK.

Broselow, E., Chen, S., and Wang, C. (1998). The emergence of the unmarked in second language phonology. *Studies in Second Language Acquisition, 20*, 261–280.

Carlisle, R. S. (1994). Markedness and environment as internal constraints on the variability of interlanguage phonology. In M. Yavas (Ed.), *First and second language phonology* (pp. 223–249). San Diego, CA: Singular.

Cauldwell, R. (2003). *Streaming Speech Student's Book: Listening and pronunciation for advanced learners of English.* Birmingham: Speechinaction.

Cheng, W., Greaves, C., and Warren, M. (2005). The creation of a prosodically transcribed intercultural corpus: The Hong Kong Corpus of Spoken English (prosodic). *International Computer Archive of Modern English (ICAME) Journal, 29*, 47–68.

Chun, D. (2002). *Discourse intonation in L2: From theory to research practice.* Philadelphia: John Benjamins.

Corder, S. P. (1967). The significance of learners' errors. *International Review of Applied Linguistics, 5*, 161–170.

de Bot, K. (1980). The role of feedback and feedforward in the teaching of pronunciation: An overview. *System, 8*, 35–45.

de Bot, K. and Mailfert, K. (1982). The teaching of intonation. Fundamental research and classroom applications. *TESOL Quarterly, 16*, 71–77.

Derwing, T. M. (1990). Speech rate is no simple matter: Rate adjustment and NS-NNS communicative success. *Studies in Second Language Acquisition, 12*, 303–313.

Derwing, T. M. and Munro, M. J. (1997). Accent, comprehensibility and intelligibility: Evidence from four L1s. *Studies in Second Language Acquisition, 19*, 1–16.

Derwing, T. and Munro, M. (2001). What speaking rates do non-native listeners prefer? *Applied Linguistics, 22*, 324–337.

Derwing, T. M. and Rossiter, M. J. (2003). The effects of pronunciation instruction on the accuracy, fluency and complexity of L2 accented speech. *Applied Language Learning, 13*, 1–18.

Deterding, D. (2005). Listening to estuary English in Singapore. *TESOL Quarterly, 39*, 425–440.

Dowd, J., Zuengler, J., and Berkowitz, D. (1990). L2 social marking: research issues. *Applied Linguistics, 10*, 16–29.

Eckman, F. (1977). Markedness and the contrastive analysis hypothesis. *Language Learning, 27*, 315–330.

Eckman, F. (1991). The Structural Conformity Hypothesis and consonant clusters in the interlanguage of ESL Learners. *Studies in Second Language Acquisition, 13*, 23–41.

Elliott, A. (1995). Field independence/dependence, hemispheric specialization, and attitude in relation to pronunciation accuracy in Spanish as a foreign language. *The Modern Language Journal, 79*, 356–371.

Elman, J., Bates, E., Johnson, M., Karmiloff-Smith, A., Parisi, D., and Plunkett, K. (1996). *Rethinking innateness. A connectionist perspective on development.* Cambridge, MA: MIT Press.

English Language Service (1967). *Drills and exercises in English pronunciation. Stress and intonation.* London/New York: McMillan.

Field, J. (2003). Promoting perception: Lexical segmentation in L2 listening. *ELT Journal, 57*, 325–334.

Field, J. (2005). Intelligibility and the listener: The role of lexical stress. *TESOL quarterly, 39*, 399–424.

Flege, J. E. (1981). The phonological basis of foreign accent. *TESOL Quarterly, 15*, 443–455.

Flege, J. E. (1987). A critical period for learning to pronounce foreign languages? *Applied Linguistics, 8*, 162–177.

Flege, J. E. (1995). Second language speech learning. Theory, findings, and problems. In W. Strange (Ed.), *Speech perception and linguistic experience* (pp. 233–277). Baltimore, MD: York Press.

Flege, J. E. (1999). Age of learning and second language speech. In D. Birdsong (Ed.), *Second language acquisition and the critical period hypothesis* (pp. 101–131). Mahwah, NJ: Lawrence Earlbaum.

Flege, J., Birdsong, D., Bialystok, E., Mack, M., Sung, H., and Tsukada, K. (2006). Degree of foreign accent in English sentences produced by Korean children and adults. *Journal of Phonetics, 34*, 153–175.

Flege, J. and Eefting, W. (1986). Linguistic and developmental effects on the production and perception of stop consonants. *Phonetica, 43*, 155–171.

Flege, J. and Hillenbrand, J. (1984). Limits on pronunciation accuracy in adult foreign language speech production. *Journal of the Acoustical Society of America, 76*, 708–721.

Flege, J., Munro, M., and MacKay, I. (1995). The effect of age of second language learning on the production of English consonants. *Speech Communication, 16*, 1–26.

Gass, S. and Varonis, E. (1984). The effect of familiarity on the comprehensibility of non-native speakers. *Language Learning, 34*, 65–89.

Gick, B., Bernhardt, B., Bacsfalvi, P., and Wilson, I. (2008). Ultrasound imaging applications in second language acquisition. In J. Hansen and M. Zampini (Eds.), *Phonology and second language acquisition* (pp. 309–322). Amsterdam: John Benjamins.

Grosz, B. and Sidner, C. (1986). Attention, intentions, and the structure of discourse. *Computational Linguistics, 12,* 175–204.

Gut, U. (2007). Learner corpora in second language prosody research and teaching. In J. Trouvain and U. Gut (Eds.), *Non-native prosody. Phonetic description and teaching practice* (pp. 145–167). Berlin: Mouton de Gruyter.

Hahn, L. D. (2004). Primary stress and intelligibility: Research to motivate the teaching of suprasegmentals. *TESOL quarterly, 38,* 201–223.

Hakuta, K., Bialystok, E., and Wiley, E. (2003). Critical evidence: A test of the critical-period hypothesis for second-language acquisition. *Psychological Science, 14,* 31–38.

Hancin-Bhatt, B. (1992). Toward a forward model of second language phonology: Phonological theory and connectionism. *Papers in Applied Linguistics Michigan (PALM), 7,* 61–81.

Hancin-Bhatt, B. and Bhatt, R. M. (1997). Optimal L2 syllables. Interactions of transfer and developmental effects. *Studies in Second Language Acquisition, 19,* 331–378.

Hansen Edwards, J. and Zampini, M. (Eds.). (2008). *Phonology and second language acquisition.* Philadelphia: John Benjamins.

Hansen, J. G. (2006). *Acquiring a non-native phonology.* London: Continuum.

Hewings, M. (1995). Tone choice in the English intonation of non-native speakers. *International Review of Applied Linguistics, 33,* 251–265.

Huckvale, M. (2003). SFS/WASP Version 1.41 http://www.phon.ucl.ac.uk/resource/sfs/wasp.htm

Jenkins, J. (2000). *The phonology of English and an international language.* Oxford: Oxford University Press.

Jenkins, J. (2002). A sociolinguistically-based, empirically-researched pronunciation syllabus for English as an International Language. *Applied Linguistics, 23,* 83–103.

Jilka, M. (2007). Different manifestations and perceptions of foreign accent in intonation. In J. Trouvain and U. Gut (Eds.), *Non-native prosody. Phonetic description and teaching practice* (pp. 77–96). Berlin: Mouton de Gruyter.

Juffs, A. (1990). Tone, syllable structure and interlanguage phonology: Chinese learners' stress errors. *International Review of Applied Linguistics, 28*(2), 99–117.

Kang, O., Rubin, D., and Pickering, L. (2010). Suprasegmental measures of accentedness and judgments of English language learner proficiency in oral English. *The Modern Language Journal, 94,* 554–566.

Kormos, J. and Dénes, M. (2004). Exploring measures and perceptions of fluency in the speech of second language learners. *System, 32,* 146–164.

Lado, R. (1957). *Linguistics across cultures.* Ann Arbor, MI: University of Michigan Press.

Lai, E. L. Y. (2002). *Prosody and prosodic transfer in foreign language acquisition: Cantonese and Japanese.* Muenchen: Lincom.

Leather, J. (1999). Second-language speech research: An introduction. *Language Learning, 49,* 1–56.

Lenneberg, E. (1967). *The biological foundations of language.* New York: Wiley and Sons.

Levis, J. (1999). Intonation in theory and practice, revisited. *TESOL Quarterly, 33,* 37–64.

Levis, J. and Pickering, L. (2004). Teaching intonation in discourse using speech visualization technology. *System, 32*(4), 505–524.

Long, M. H. (1990). Maturational constraints on language development. *Studies in Second Language Acquisition, 12,* 251–285.

Lybeck, K. (2002). Cultural identification and second language pronunciation of Americans in Norway. *The Modern Language Journal, 86,* 174–191.

Major, R. C. (1987). A model for interlanguage pronunciation. In G. Ioup and S. Weinberger (Eds.), *Interlanguage phonology: The acquisition of a sound system.* Rowley: Mass. Newbury House.

Major, R. C. (2001). *Foreign accent. The ontogeny and phylogeny of second language phonology.* Mahwa, NJ: Lawrence Earlbaum.

Major, R., Fitzmaurice, S., Bunta, F., and Balasubramanian, C. (2002). The effects of non-native accents on listening comprehension: Implications for ESL assessment. *TESOL Quarterly, 36,* 173–90.

Major, R. C. and Kim, E. (1996). The similarity differential rate hypothesis. *Language Learning, 46,* 465–496.

Mennen, I. (1998). Can second language learners ever acquire the intonation of a second language? *Proceedings of the ESCA workshop on speech technology in language learning.* Marholmen: Sweden.

Mennen, I. (2007). Phonological and phonetic influences in non-native intonation. In J. Trouvain and U. Gut (Eds.), *Non-native prosody. Phonetic description and teaching practice* (pp. 53–76). Berlin: Mouton de Gruyter.

Moyer, A. (2004). *Age, accent and experience in second language acquisition.* Clevedon, UK: Multilingual Matters.

Munro, M. and Derwing, T. (1995). Foreign accent, comprehensibility, and intelligibility in the speech of second language learners. *Language Learning, 45,* 73–97.

Nelson, C. (1995). Intelligibility and world Englishes in the classroom. *World Englishes, 14,* 273–79.

Oller, J. and Ziahosseiny, S. (1970). The contrastive analysis hypothesis and spelling errors. *Language Learning, 20,* 183–89.

Oyama, S. (1978). The sensitive period and comprehension of speech. *Working Papers in Bilingualism/Travaux de Recherches sur le Bilinguisme, 61,* 1–17. In S. D. Krashen, R. C. Scarcella, and M. Long, (Eds.) (1982), *Child-adult differences in second language acquisition* (pp. 39–51). Rowley, MA: Newbury House.

O'Connor, J. D. (1967). *Better English pronunciation.* Cambridge: Cambridge University Press.

Patkowski, M. (1980). *The sensitive period for the acquisition of syntax in a secondary language.* Unpublished doctoral dissertation. New York University.

Patkowski, M. S. (1990). Age and accent in a second language: A reply to James Emil Flege. *Applied Linguistics, 11,* 73–89.

Patkowski, M. S. (1994). The critical period hypothesis and interlanguage phonology. In M. Yavas (Ed.), *First and second language phonology* (pp. 205–221). San Diego, CA: Singular.

Pickering, L. (1999). *An analysis of prosodic systems in the classroom discourse of native speaker and nonnative speaker teaching assistants.* Unpublished dissertation. University of Florida.

Pickering, L. (2001). The role of tone choice in improving ITA communication in the classroom. *TESOL Quarterly, 35*(2), 233–255.

Pickering, L. (2004). The structure and function of intonational paragraphs in native and non-native instructional discourse. *English for Specific Purposes, 23,* 19–43.

Pickering, L. (2006). Current research on intelligibility in English as a lingua franca. *Annual Review of Applied Linguistics, 26,* 219–233.

Pierce, B. N. (1995). Social identity, investment, and second language learning. *TESOL Quarterly, 29,* 9–31.

Pierrehumbert, J. and Hirschberg, J. (1990). The meaning of intonation in the interpretation of discourse. In P. Cohen, J. Morgan, and M. Pollack (Eds.), *Intentions in communication* (pp. 271–311). Cambridge MA: MIT Press.

Pirt, G. (1990). Discourse intonation problems for non-native speakers. In M. Hewings (Ed.), *Papers in Discourse Intonation* (pp. 145–156). Birmingham, England: University of Birmingham, English Language Research.

Piscataway, N. J. and Riggenbach, H. (1991). Toward an understanding of fluency: A microanalysis of non-native speaker conversations. *Discourse Processes, 14,* 423–441.

Piske, T., Mackay, I. R. A., and Flege, J. E. (2001). Factors affecting degree of foreign accent in a L2: A review. *Journal of Phonetics, 29,* 191–215.

Prince, A. and Smolensky, P. (1993). *Optimality Theory: Constraint interaction in generative grammar,* RuCCs Technical Report #2, Rutgers University Center for Cognitive Science.

Riggenbach, H. (1991). Toward an understanding of fluency: A microanalysis of non-native speaker conversations. *Discourse Processes, 14,* 423–441.

Schuetze-Coburn, S., Shapley, M., and Weber, E. (1991). Units of intonation in discourse: A comparison of acoustic and auditory analyses. *Language and Speech, 34,* 207–234.

Schumann, J. (1986). Research on the acculturation model for second language acquisition. *Journal of Multilingual and Multicultural development, 7,* 397–92.

Scovel, T. (1988). *A time to speak: A psycholinguistic enquiry into the critical period for human speech.* Rowley, Mass: Newbury House.

Selinker, L. (1972). Interlanguage. *International Review of Applied Linguistics, 10,* 209–231.

Sereno, J. A. and Wang, Y. (2007). Behavioral and cortical effects of learning a second language: The acquisition of tone. In O. Bohn and M. Munro (Eds.), *Language experience in second language speech learning* (pp. 239–258). New York: John Benjamins.

Snow, C. E. and Hoefnagel-Höhle, M. (1978). The critical period for language acquisition: Evidence from second language learning. *Child Development, 49,* 1114–1128.

Stokes, J. (2001). Factors in the acquisition of Spanish pronunciation. *I.T.L. Review of Applied Linguistics, 131/ 132,* 63–83.

Strange, W. (1995). Cross-language studies of speech perception: A historical review. In W. Strange (Ed.), *Speech perception and linguistic experience: Issues in cross-language speech research* (pp. 3–45). Timonium, MD: York Press.

Strange, W. (2007). Cross-language phonetic similarity of vowels: Theoretical and methodological issues. In O. Bohn and M. Munro (Eds.), *Language experience in second language speech learning* (pp. 35–55). New York: John Benjamins.

Tao, H. (1996). *Units in Mandarin conversation: Prosody, discourse, and grammar.* Amsterdam/Philadelphia, PA: John Benjamins.

Tarone, E. (1980). Communication strategies, foreigner talk and repair in interlanguage. *Language Learning, 30,* 417–431.

Trim, J. (1965). *English pronunciation illustrated.* Cambridge: Cambridge University Press.

Trouvain, J. and Gut, U. (Eds.). (2007). *Non-native prosody. Phonetic description and teaching practice.* Berlin: Mouton de Gruyter.

Walker, R. (2001). Pronunciation for international intelligibility. *English Teaching Professional, 21,* 1–7.

Weinreich, U. (1953). *Languages in contact.* New York: Linguistic circle of New York.

Weltens, B. and de Bot, K. (1984). Visual feedback of Intonation II: Feedback delay and quality of feedback. *Language and Speech, 27,* 79–88.

Wenk, B. (1986). Cross-linguistic influence in second language phonology: Speech rhythms. In E. Kellerman and M. Sharwood-Smith (Eds.), *Cross-linguistic influence in second language acquisition* (pp. 120–133). Oxford: Pergamon Press.

Wennerstrom, A. (1994). Intonational meaning in English discourse. *Applied Linguistics, 15,* 399–421.

Wennerstrom, A. (1997). *Discourse intonation and second language acquisition: Three genre-cased studies.* Unpublished PhD Dissertation. University of Washington.

Wennerstrom, A. (1998). Intonation as cohesion in academic discourse: A study of Chinese speakers of English. *Studies in Second Language Acquisition, 20,* 1–25.

Willems, N. (1982). *English intonation from a Dutch point of view.* Dordrecht/Cinnaminson, NJ: Foris.

Winitz, H. (1981). Input considerations in the comprehension of first and second language. In H. Winitz (Ed.), *Native and foreign language acquisition.* New York: New York Academy of Sciences.

Yamada, R. A., Tohkura, Y., and Kobayashi, N. (1996). Effect of word familiarity on non-native phoneme perception: Identification of English /r/, /l/ and /w/ by native speakers of Japanese. In J. Leather and A. James (Eds.), *Second-Language speech: Structure and process* (pp. 103–117). Berlin: Mouton de Gruyter.

Yavas, M. (Ed.). (1994). *First and second language phonology.* San Diego, CA: Singular.

Yeni-Komshian, G., Flege, J., and Liu, S. (1997). Pronunciation proficiency in L1 and L2 among Korean-English bilinguals: The effect of age of arrival in the US. *Journal of the Acoustical Society of America, 102*(5), 3138.

21

Second language speech perception

A cross-disciplinary perspective on challenges and accomplishments

Debra M. Hardison

Historical discussion

It has been well documented that infants are able to discriminate among the phonetic units of a range of languages; however, a significant decline in this ability occurs between 6–8 and 10–12 months of age (e.g., Werker and Tees, 1984). During this period of first language (L1) perceptual attunement, perception of native-language consonants improves, beginning the process of a neural commitment to those auditory patterns (Rivera-Gaxiola *et al.*, 2005). These simultaneous processes of decline in non-native sound discrimination and facilitation of native sound perception have been attributed to the learning of the acoustic and statistical regularities of speech, which serve as the foundation for acquiring more complex patterns as the lexicon develops (Kuhl *et al.*, 2006). This process for the child, the epitome of the "early" language learner, raises the question of the impact of age on second-language (L2) speech perception, and underscores the important role of continued neural plasticity in L2 perceptual category development.

Many studies explored the observation of better L2 performance by individuals whose age at the time of learning was "early" compared to those who began in late adolescence or adulthood. Yamada (1995) found early exposure in childhood versus adulthood to American English (AE) /r/ and /l/, the most commonly studied L2 sounds, resulted in better perception of these sounds by native speakers (NSs) of Japanese. Some researchers linked the effect of age to maturational constraints related to the notion of a critical period for speech acquisition involving a purported loss of neural plasticity (Scovel, 1969); others linked it to differences in the state of development of L1 phonetic categories and perceived L1–L2 phonetic distance (e.g., Flege, 1999). Native Language Magnet theory proposed that the effect of L1 perceptual attunement on L2 perception could be characterized as an L1-conditioned "warping" of speech input due to the effect of L1 "magnets," reducing the perceptual distance between L2 sounds that are attracted by the same L1 prototype (e.g., Kuhl and Iverson, 1995; Kuhl *et al.*, 2008).

In addition, the L1 phonological system was a major consideration in studies exploring the perception of sounds such as /r/ and /l/ by native Japanese and Korean learners of English as a second language (ESL) (e.g., Ingram and Park, 1998; Mochizuki, 1981; Sheldon and Strange,

1982). Studies involving these sounds also revealed better performance with natural versus synthesized speech stimuli (e.g., Mochizuki, 1981), greater experience with the L2 (e.g., Goto, 1971; MacKain *et al.*, 1981), and position of the sound in a word (e.g., initial vs. final, singleton vs. cluster) (e.g., Logan *et al.*, 1991).

More recent research, outlined in the following section, has attempted to investigate a wider range of potential factors impacting L2 speech perception. This research involves the contributions of many disciplines, including phonetics, phonology, cognitive psychology, neuroscience, and second language acquisition.

Core issues

There are several core issues in current L2 speech perception research that will be discussed in the following section:

- Length of residence and L2 input
- L1 and L2 use
- Modifying the adult perceptual system through auditory training
- Modifying the adult perceptual system through auditory-visual input
- Relationship between perception and production

Length of residence and L2 input

Many studies have been conducted to explore the range of factors accounting for the lack of uniform success among L2 learners in speech perception. Length of residence (LOR) in the L2 environment, most often explored as a factor contributing to accented production,[1] was investigated in a study comparing groups of L1 Chinese adults living in the USA on several tasks including perception of word-final English consonants, presented with and without the final release burst, and with and without masking noise, which is used to reduce ceiling effects (Flege and Liu, 2001). Participants were divided into two LOR categories: 0.5–3.8 years ("short LOR") and 3.9–15.5 years ("long LOR"), each of which was subdivided into two occupational categories (i.e., university students and non-students). There was a significant effect of LOR, but only for the students; those with longer LORs had higher scores. The authors concluded "segmental phonetic perception may be influenced most importantly by native-speaker input" (p. 546), which was more readily available to the students than to the research assistants or scientists. Results support the importance of an input- and interaction-rich L2 environment in the development of L2 perception.

L1 and L2 use

In addition to LOR and type of input, studies demonstrated that learners who seldom use their L1 were better able to identify English consonants (MacKay *et al.*, 2001), recognize more English words in noise (Meador *et al.*, 2000), and perceive L2 vowel contrasts (Flege and MacKay, 2004). Flege and MacKay found higher scores on discrimination tasks for two types of participants: early learners (L1 Italian) who immigrated to Canada between two and 13 years of age versus late learners who immigrated between 15 and 26 years, and learners who reported low L1 use (average of 8 percent of the time) versus those with high L1 use (average of 48 percent). Early learners with high L1 use differed from NSs of English, but not from learners of comparable age of arrival (AOA) and low L1 use. Findings suggested that early AOA is not a guarantee of native-like L2 vowel perception, and, importantly, L2 learners with an established L1 phonetic system can still show comparable (though not identical) performance to NSs. Højen and Flege (2006) also point out that identical perception by even early L2 learners and NSs should not be sought as evidence for the continued plasticity of the perceptual system given the variable nature of the statistical properties of individuals' language input.

The above findings are compatible with the Speech Learning Model hypothesis (SLM; e.g., Flege, 1995) that neural plasticity in terms of the ability to establish new perceptual categories exists throughout life. The SLM also predicts that: (a) the development of L2 perceptual categories is dependent on the perceived distance between an L2 speech sound and the closest L1 sound, and (b) as L1 phonetic categories develop throughout life, they are more likely to assimilate perceptually close L2 sounds (see also Best and Tyler, 2007, for a discussion of the Perceptual Assimilation Model for functional monolinguals). Perceived similarity is an important concept as the basis for categorization behavior (e.g., Nosofsky, 1986).

Modifying the adult perceptual system through auditory training

Of both theoretical and pedagogical significance was the series of studies by Pisoni and colleagues (e.g., Lively et al., 1993; Logan et al., 1991) from which emerged a better understanding of the hallmarks of successful adult L2 perception training. Perception of L2 sounds involving spectral differences, such as /r/ and /l/, is generally more challenging than perception of contrasts involving temporal differences (e.g., Bohn, 1995). For example, an early study that trained NSs of English to identify a new voice onset time (VOT) category was accomplished in one session (Pisoni et al., 1982). Initial attempts to train L1 Japanese speakers to discriminate AE /r/ and /l/ had mixed results (Strange and Dittmann, 1984). Pre- and post-test stimuli involved natural speech minimal pairs contrasting the sounds in four word positions (initial singleton, initial cluster, medial, final singleton), and two synthesized speech continua (*rock-lock* and *rake-lake*). Training (14–18 sessions) involved synthesized tokens (*rock-lock* continuum) and a discrimination task. Following training, participants showed more categorical-like perception of the *rock-lock* series, with some generalization to the *rake-lake* series; however, there was no significant improvement in the identification of natural speech tokens.

Using the testing stimuli from the Strange and Dittmann (1984) study, Logan et al. (1991) administered three weeks of training to adult L1 Japanese learners of English who completed forced-choice identification tasks. Training stimuli included 68 minimal pairs contrasting /r/ and /l/ in all word positions (i.e., those noted above plus final clusters) produced by five different NSs of English. Significant improvement was noted between pre- and post-tests, especially for the initial cluster and medial positions, which had the lowest pre-test accuracy. There was also a significant effect of talker. Following the post-test, additional identification tasks revealed that participants were able to generalize performance accuracy to novel words (produced by a familiar talker from training) and to a new voice.

Role of stimulus variability. A subsequent study drawing from the same population tested the hypothesis that multiple- versus single-talker training involving /r/ and /l/ promotes phonetic category development robust across context and talker variability (Lively et al., 1993). In the first experiment, testing stimuli were from Logan et al. (1991); however, training stimuli, spoken by five talkers, were limited to the more difficult word positions for L1 Japanese learners (i.e., initial singleton, initial cluster, medial). Findings revealed moderate but significant improvement in overall identification accuracy with a corresponding decrease in reaction times[2] across three weeks of training. Participants were able to generalize performance to a new voice. In Experiment 2, only one talker was used in training (i.e., the one producing the best scores from Experiment 1), and final singleton and final cluster positions were included. Results indicated no significant improvement with training. Identification accuracy did not generalize well to word-initial /r/ and /l/ spoken by an unfamiliar talker. The authors concluded that participants receiving multiple-talker training showed better generalization to a new voice.

The following emerged as characteristics of successful L2 perception training: (a) multiple exemplars that are representative of the variability the sounds show in the natural language environment, (b) natural (vs. synthesized) speech to preserve all acoustic cues, (c) multiple talkers, (d) relatively implicit training, (e) identification (vs. discrimination) tasks to promote observation of within-category similarities and between-category differences, (f) testing compatible with the training, and (g) feedback during training. Feedback is particularly important for stimuli characterized by considerable variability (e.g., /r/ and /l/) (Homa and Cultice, 1984). Successful perception training should show generalization to novel stimuli and new voices, transfer ability to other tasks/skills such as production, and retention.

In addition to its use in segmental training, a high variability stimulus set was used to train L1 English learners of Mandarin to identify four Mandarin tones over a two-week period. Accuracy showed significant improvement following training, with generalization to new stimuli and talkers, and transfer to production (Wang *et al.*, 2003).

Although the above perception training studies incorporated stimulus variability, it was controlled by using (a) stimuli spoken in citation form, recorded and presented under ideal conditions, (b) intelligible talkers, (c) a consistent rate and style of speech, and (d) stimuli produced by one talker per training session. As Leather (1990) commented, "too much or too little variability at too early a stage may prevent the learner from discovering with sufficient accuracy the prototypical forms that exemplars expound" (p. 96).

Other training techniques. Using a perceptual fading technique, Morosan and Jamieson (1989) trained Canadian Francophones to perceive the English voiced (e.g., this) and voiceless (e.g., thought) interdental fricatives. Training stimuli were synthesized consonant-vowel (CV) syllables on a continuum from voiceless to voiced, involving exaggerated frication, initially set at 140 ms gradually decreasing to 35 ms over a period of 90 minutes (two sessions). Participants completed an identification task with feedback. Results showed that the identification accuracy of synthesized and natural tokens significantly improved, but without generalization to other word positions or contrasts; for example, participants were able to identify the voiced interdental fricative when the alternative was the voiceless one but not the voiced stop /d/.

A similar type of training was used with children exhibiting a temporal processing deficit, which results in difficulty segmenting the speech stream if input is presented too fast. Tallal and colleagues hypothesized that if critical cues (e.g., formant transitions distinguishing /ba/ from /da/) were temporally amplified or exaggerated, stimuli might be more easily identified (e.g., Tallal *et al.*, 1996). Results indicated that some children showed perceptual improvement, but there was variability in performance.

Hyperarticulated/exaggerated speech may also offer some advantages for L2 learners. Exaggerated cues such as an expanded vowel space were found in speech directed toward infants (Kuhl *et al.*, 1997; Uther *et al.*, 2007), and adult non-native speakers of English (Uther *et al.*, 2007). Hyperarticulated vowel sounds may make them better exemplars of their respective categories, making each more distinct.

Exaggerated stimuli were used to train Japanese learners of English to perceive /r/ and /l/ (McCandliss *et al.*, 2002). Using synthesized *rock-lock* and *road-load* continua, the /r/-/l/ distinctions were exaggerated (adaptive training) and compared with fixed training (using good examples of /r/ and /l/ stimuli from each continuum). Participants took the training at home on one continuum (3 sessions, each 20 minutes, 480 trials per session), and were tested on both. Results showed the fixed training with feedback was the best, followed by adaptive training with or without feedback. Fixed training without feedback offered little improvement. Exaggerated stimuli may draw learner attention to critical cues by making them more perceptually salient, resulting in faster gains because more stimuli and variability create competition and challenge in dividing up psychological space. However, such variability is closer to the perceptual challenge of the natural language environment. Transfer to other skills and retention ability are unknown with such approaches.

Modifying the adult perceptual system through auditory-visual input

All of the above studies have involved unimodal (i.e., auditory) input to the adult perceptual system. Yet, in many instances, speech communication involves both visual and auditory sources of input. In fact, some researchers have argued that multimodal speech (e.g., auditory, visual, haptic) is the primary mode of speech perception (e.g., Rosenblum, 2004). Auditory-visual integration in perception has a longer history in the fields of infant speech development (e.g., Dodd, 1987; Meltzoff and Kuhl, 1994) and adult monolingual processing (e.g., Massaro, 1998; McGurk and MacDonald, 1976) than in L2 speech processing (see Hardison, 2007). In an early study on the difficulty adult Japanese speakers face in perceiving AE /r/ and /l/, Goto (1971) stated that for L2 learners, there was the "disadvantage of not being able to read the lips of the speaker" (p. 321). Some years later, the influence of visual cues from a talker's face was explored with L2 learners of English (Hardison, 1996). This study investigated whether learners whose L1s were Japanese, Korean, Spanish, and Malay would experience the McGurk effect (e.g., McGurk and MacDonald, 1976). This refers to a perceptual illusion which arises from mismatched auditory and visual cues; for example, when NSs of English see a talker's face on a monitor whose articulatory gesture represents /ga/ with the dubbed auditory production /ba/, some report they hear /da/. The intermediate-level ESL learners in Hardison's (1996) study were presented with both matched and mismatched CV syllables involving AE /p, f, w, r, t, k/ and /a/. The Japanese speakers showed a significant increase in identification accuracy of /r/ when visual /r/ was present; Korean speakers showed more accurate perception of /r/ and /f/ with corresponding visual cues. For mismatched stimuli, findings revealed that the cue which learners could identify the best contributed more to the percept on each trial. These results suggested visual cues should be explored in L2 perception training.

In a subsequent study using a pre-test-post-test design, auditory-visual (AV) training was compared to auditory-only (A-only) with a focus on /r/ and /l/ for intermediate-level Japanese and Korean ESL learners (Hardison, 2003). Independent variables were word position (initial singleton and cluster, medial, final singleton and cluster), adjacent vowel (varying the dimensions of height and rounding), and training modality (AV vs. A-only). Training involved 15 sessions (each about 30 minutes) over three weeks. Learners began at comparable levels of perceptual accuracy. Comparison of A-only pre- and post-test scores (the shared modality for both training types) revealed AV and A-only training resulted in significant improvement for both L1 groups; however, AV training was significantly more effective. Visual input contributed the most in contexts where L1 phonology would suggest greater difficulty (i.e., initial word position for the Japanese and final position for the Korean learners[3]). Both groups' mean scores on a video-only (V-only) condition showed they also improved their lipreading ability.[4] There were significant effects of talker (in the training data), word position, and adjacent vowel; vowel effects had not been explored in previous studies. Successful generalization obtained for novel stimuli and a new talker, with transfer to improved production of /r/ and /l/.

353

There is variability in the degree to which visual and auditory cues are helpful for L2 learners. In one study using British English, AV training was more effective than A-only in improving the perception of the labial/labiodental contrast (/v/-/b/-/p/) by L1 Spanish speakers, but not the perception of /r/ and /l/ by Japanese speakers (Hazan *et al.*, 2005). Hazan *et al.* concluded that AV training is more effective when the critical visual cues are sufficiently salient. It is worth noting that comparability is difficult to establish across studies such as Hardison (2003) and Hazan *et al.* (2005) due to differences in (a) the discernibility of lip movements in different varieties of English (e.g., American vs. British), (b) articulatory gestures between talkers, (c) learners' linguistic experience, exposure to L2 articulatory gestures, motivation and attention to critical stimulus features, and (d) methodological elements such as period of training, feedback, size of video screen, stimuli, etc.

Computer-animated talking heads such as Baldi (e.g., Massaro, 1998) have been used in the training of L2 learners, and children with language disorders. Because Baldi's exterior surface can be made transparent or eliminated, the internal articulators (e.g., tongue) can be displayed. Massaro and Light (2003) compared training of Japanese learners of English to perceive /r/ and /l/ using the normal view of Baldi and the view showing movement of the articulators. Both approaches resulted in improvement in identification and production; however, seeing the articulators did not provide an additional benefit.

Visual input in speech processing is not limited to human faces or talking heads. Electronic visual displays of pitch contours are helpful for L2 perception and production, and are user-friendly (see Chun *et al.*, 2008 for a review). Waveform displays for visualization of segmental duration with the accompanying speech provided a significant advantage for AE learners of Japanese in the improvement of geminate[5] perception compared to those who received A-only training (no display) although both groups improved with transfer to production (Motohashi Saigo and Hardison, 2009).

Relationship between perception and production

Several studies shed light on other facets of successful training such as retention and transfer to production. Japanese speakers living in Japan significantly improved their identification of /r/ and /l/ with retention of perceptual abilities (i.e., loss of only 2 percent accuracy) when tested three months later (Lively *et al.*, 1994). One might predict that learners in the L2 environment with the advantage of continued input would also show retention although this is often difficult to investigate because of participant availability.

Studies using auditory-only input (Bradlow *et al.*, 1997; Wang *et al.*, 2003) and those using auditory-visual input, both from a talker's face (Hardison, 2003) and an electronic display (Motohashi Saigo and Hardison, 2009) demonstrated that perception training transferred to significant improvement in production in the absence of production training. Hardison (2003) found that the variability in production accuracy of /r/ and /l/ by Japanese and Korean learners of English as a function of word position decreased with perception training. However, these studies also pointed out that performance variability exists between these domains across individual learners. For example, in Wang *et al.* (2003), Mandarin tone 3 became relatively easy for L1 AE learners to perceive after training, but remained difficult to produce. Bradlow *et al.* (1997) and Motohashi Saigo and Hardison (2009) measured *relative improvement* (i.e., improvement as a proportion of the room for improvement)[6] to compare perception and production improvement rates for participants in their studies. In both cases, no significant relationship was found between degrees of learning in perception and production due to individual variation.

Beyond the segmental level. The segmentation of the speech stream generally poses a challenge in the early stages of L2 acquisition when adult learners rely on cues relevant to the L1 (Strange and

Shafer, 2008). Rhythmic categories such as stress units in English, syllables in French, and morae[7] in Japanese play a role in this process (e.g., Cutler and Otake, 2002). A recent auditory study found that with increasing proficiency in L2 Japanese, L1 English learners adopted a segmentation strategy focusing on moraic units (vs. stressed syllables), which increased identification accuracy of Japanese geminates (e.g., moraic obstruents), which contrast in duration with their singleton counterparts (Hardison and Motohashi Saigo, 2010). Perception was facilitated by contexts with greater consonant-vowel sonority[8] difference enhancing the perception of mora boundaries for segmentation.

The question arises as to whether segmental-level perception training can improve learners' word identification processes. Using the gating paradigm, which involves successive presentations of increasing amounts of a target word (e.g., Grosjean and Frauenfelder, 1996), adapted for auditory-visual input, Hardison (2005a) found that L2 learners of English identified words significantly earlier following perception training with minimal pairs, and when visual cues (talker's face) were present. This AV advantage was noted especially for words beginning with /r/ and /l/, the primary focus of the training. Findings suggested that because articulatory movements precede the associated acoustic signal, visual cues play a priming role in the word identification process for a listener-observer in face-to-face situations (see also Hardison, 2005b; Munhall and Tohkura, 1998). Results of a recent study using a gating task revealed that visual cues from a talker's face and sentence context played significant yet independent roles in word identification by L1 Japanese and Korean learners of English (Hardison, 2008). Much as the temporal precedence of an articulatory gesture can give visual cues a priming role in AV spoken language processing, so can comprehensible sentence context.

The trend toward examining the larger context of a speech event leads us to the potential role of a talker's hand-arm gestures in the processing of L2 speech input. Results of a multiple-choice listening comprehension task administered to low-intermediate and advanced ESL learners revealed significantly higher scores when both proficiency levels were able to see the speaker (Sueyoshi and Hardison, 2005). For the low-intermediate level, seeing the face and gestures produced the best results; for the advanced level, seeing only the face produced the highest scores. Hand gestures were primarily related to the semantic component of the stimulus, whereas lip movements were linked to the phonological component, favoring the more proficient learners who had greater experience with L2 communication. Questionnaire responses revealed positive attitudes toward both types of visual cues (see also Gullberg, 2006). Co-speech gestures also facilitated recall of Japanese words learned by L1 English adults with no prior knowledge of the language (Kelly et al., 2009). Based on results of memory tests and event-related potentials (ERPs[9]), Kelly et al. suggested that co-speech gesture "deepens the imagistic memory trace for a new word's meaning in the brain" (p. 330). We will return to the issue of memory traces below (see *Empirical verification*).

Data and common elicitation measures

As noted above, in L2 speech research, synthesized and natural speech have been used as stimuli. Synthesized speech allows researchers to manipulate critical acoustic cues of interest along a continuum in which the end points represent good examples of each of two categories that NSs clearly perceive as different (e.g., /r/ and /l/); the intermediate points are equal physical changes on a set of critical parameters (e.g., Strange and Dittman, 1984). In contrast to NS categorical perception of consonant categories, less experienced L2 learners typically exhibit a more con-tinuous pattern of perception. Synthesized speech is also used to produce techniques such as perceptual fading (e.g., Morosan and Jamieson, 1989), and in its sophisticated form, to contribute to the creation of talking heads such as Baldi. As noted earlier, the use of synthesized speech as training stimuli tended to result in poorer generalization ability compared to natural speech.

Synthesized speech is often used with discrimination tasks. For example, in an AXB discrimination task, three stimuli are presented per trial where "X" is either "A" or "B," and participants determine whether "X" was similar to "A" or "B" (see Højen and Flege, 2006). In an AX (same-different) task, participants determine the similarity of two stimuli. In an identification task, listeners categorize or label the stimulus presented in each trial. Listeners can discriminate between stimuli to the extent that they can identify them as belonging to different categories. Performance on discrimination tasks relies on low-level acoustic-phonetic input, whereas identification tasks direct attention to a phonemic level, matching input to stored representations in memory, and more closely mirror daily language tasks. Researchers may measure both accuracy and reaction time.

Natural speech may be presented in citation form as is often the case with CV syllables (e.g., Hardison, 1996) or minimal pairs used in perception training (e.g., Lively et al., 1993), which may be real words or nonwords. Lively et al. found no significant difference in L2 learners' perception of segments (e.g., /r/ and /l/) in real words versus those in nonwords. In a forced-choice identification task, the word serves as a carrier of phonetic context. In these tasks, participants are shown a minimal pair (on paper or computer screen) and asked to select the one being presented. (See *Other training techniques* for studies using hyperarticulated/exaggerated versus natural speech.)

In tasks of spoken word identification that require access to the mental lexicon (i.e., access to meaning-based representations), the participants' familiarity with the stimulus is an important consideration. Familiarity may be determined objectively based on corpus-based assessments of word frequency, which imply likelihood of familiarity, or subjectively using a familiarity scale. The scale may be administered prior to a study to a peer group of participants (i.e., those similar to the study participants in level of proficiency, etc.) and/or following data collection to the study participants. In addition to familiarity, the density of the lexical neighborhood is a consideration in selecting materials. Words in dense lexical neighborhoods have many neighbors (i.e., words that differ from the target by a one-phoneme addition, substitution, or deletion in any position). These require listeners to attend carefully to the phonetic input to distinguish the target from its neighbors who are competitors in the process (Pisoni et al., 1985). For L2 learners, more exposure to the spoken language appears related to the ability to recognize words from denser neighborhoods (Bradlow and Pisoni, 1999). Fewer studies have examined the relationship between segmental perception and spoken word recognition for L2 learners (see Hardison, 2005a, b). As with segmental perception, both accuracy and reaction-time data can be collected in the assessment of spoken word recognition (see Grosjean and Frauenfelder, 1996 for a review of paradigms). Finally, technological developments including functional magnetic resonance imaging[10] (fMRI), and ERPs have begun to compare the neural organization of L1 and L2 processing (see Perani and Abutalebi, 2005 for a review).

Empirical verification

The studies described earlier that demonstrated variable performance across phonetic contexts and talkers support the view that sources of variability in the speech signal are a part of subsequent neural representations (Goldinger, 1996, 1997). Lively et al. (1993) suggested L2 learners may rely on context-dependent exemplars (vs. abstract prototypes) for input identification. As a result of perception training, learner attention is shifted to relevant stimulus features. These shifts are the "stretching" and "shrinking" of perceptual distances in psychophysical space to make items from different categories (e.g., /r/ and /l/) appear less similar, and within-category variants (i.e., allophones) more similar (e.g., Nosofsky, 1986).

In an adaptation of multiple-trace memory (MTM) theory (e.g., Hintzman, 1986), also referred to as an *episodic* or *exemplar* theory, for auditory-visual L2 speech learning, Hardison (2003) suggested the exemplars of episodic models and the prototypes of an abstractionist approach could co-exist. Multiple-trace memory theory states that the memory encoding of a perceptual event involves storage of the attended details as episodes or traces, preserving aspects of variability. In processing, a retrieval cue or probe generated in primary memory contacts in parallel all stored traces in long-term memory, simultaneously activating each based on similarity to features of the probe. In AV speech perception, the features that comprise the preliminary representation that probes memory depend upon the attention given to the auditory and visual attributes of a stimulus relevant for a given task. Jusczyk (e.g., 1993) viewed the extraction of auditory features in infant speech input as part of the human auditory system's innate guided learning mechanism whose attention-weighting role gives prominence to those features as part of L1 perceptual attunement. One of the challenges for L2 learners is to adopt a weighting scheme based on the critical features of the L2. Perception training can serve to focus learner attention to these stimulus attributes. The probe is then said to return an echo or response to primary memory. The goal for learners is to have the echo from clearly defined L2 traces overshadow that from any similar L1 traces. As a consequence of successful perception training, new L2 traces should be less ambiguous in content and at greater psychological distance to L1 traces.

At the time of information retrieval, abstract knowledge can be derived from a composite of episodic traces. A category is, thus, regarded as an aggregate of individual exemplars activated together at the time of information retrieval. The category prototype concept, as a representation of the shared features of multiple traces, captures the advantage of redundancy. Whereas exemplars preserve detailed relevant information of an event, they may be forgotten over time; however, the prototype concept is retained longer. This may account for the retention capability demonstrated by successful L2 perception training studies using multiple exemplars (e.g., Lively *et al.*, 1994). The more exemplars of a category that are stored, the more likely one or more will generalize to the probe and influence its classification. Goldinger (2007) also provided computational evidence of a reciprocal neural network that includes inter-dependent episodic and abstract representations involved in word perception. This complementary learning systems (CLS) approach combines the advantage of a fast-learning network representing, in neurophysiological terms, the hippocampus (to rapidly memorize specific events), and a more stable network representing the cortex (to slowly learn statistical regularities of the input), replicating behavioral evidence from recognition memory data (e.g., Goldinger, 1996, 1997).

L2 learners may store details of both auditory and visual elements of speech events in memory to facilitate subsequent processing (see Hardison, 2003). In bimodal speech processing, the auditory and visual modalities initially provide separate sources of input to the perceptual system. Recent behavioral and neurophysiological evidence supports the early integration of bimodal information. One view suggests unimodal signals are integrated in multisensory areas of the cortex with feedback pathways to primary sensory areas, accounting for enhanced response of neurons to the presentation of concordant auditory and visual events, and the establishment of a multisensory perceptual representation (e.g., Calvert, 2001; Driver and Spence, 2000). Another view suggests that the contribution of multisensory sites throughout the cortex lies in the predictive role one modality's information can have on the other to reduce stimulus uncertainty and facilitate processing (van Wassenhove *et al.*, 2005). Specifically, visible articulatory movements allow the listener-observer's brain to reduce the set of potential targets the speaker will produce (Skipper *et al.*, 2007). This preliminary representation elicits a cohort of possible targets that are compared against the auditory input and fed back for correction. In the case of informative visual cues or fewer possible targets (e.g., salient articulations of bilabials /p,b,m/), more precise predictions can be made resulting in greater facilitation of processing. Visual speech can speed up the cortical processing of auditory signals by NSs within 100 ms of signal onset (van Wassenhove *et al.*, 2005); however, such findings assume listener-observer knowledge of correspondences between sound and lip movements that begin to develop in infancy (e.g., Meltzoff and Kuhl, 1994). For adult L2 learners, these findings emphasize the value of AV training with feedback that exposes them to the concordance of bimodal cues using multiple exemplars from a variety of talkers, offering greater potential for the creation of an accurate L2 cohort to facilitate spoken language processing (Hardison, 2003).

Results of a recent study of bimodal L2 speech processing involving advanced ESL learners (L1 Korean) provided additional support for an episodic lexicon (Hardison, 2006). If listener-observers store information about a talker's face, then subsequent presentation of only a partial visual stimulus of a familiar talker should serve as an effective memory probe to produce greater word identification accuracy compared to a comparable stimulus from an unfamiliar talker, or to an auditory-only stimulus from either type of talker. Findings revealed that seeing only the eye and upper cheek areas of a talker's face was significantly more informative in L2 word identification compared to just hearing the voice, but *only* when these cues belonged to a familiar talker. Similarly, seeing just the mouth and lower jaw was equivalent to seeing the entire face, but *only* when the talker was familiar. These results suggest that the visual information learners attend to on a talker's face is not limited to lip movements. Initial processing may be more global allowing observers to preserve as many details as possible in memory with subsequent strategic shifts of attention. As proposed in MTM theory, a cue composed of a familiar but only partial stimulus (e.g., the talker's mouth or eyes) can be enhanced by echoes from stored representations of the entire stimulus (e.g., talker's entire face) in memory to fill in missing details in order to facilitate a task such as word identification. This function based on partial input was also modeled computationally in a CLS framework (Norman and O'Reilly, 2003).

Applications

Instructors may very well question whether one can actually teach someone to perceive a sound. For example, telling learners to focus attention on a low third formant frequency (an acoustic cue that distinguishes AE /r/ from /l/) would not be helpful. In contrast, production lends itself to teaching how sounds are produced, and how they can be affected by surrounding sounds, rate and style of speech, etc. Production is also subject to proprioceptive[11] feedback. Nevertheless, instructors can facilitate the perception process by manipulating the input.

Training studies suggest that stimulus variability contributes to development of perceptual categories robust to the variable input of the natural language environment. Taking AE /r/ and /l/ as examples, these sounds show considerable variability depending on vocalic context, word position, and talker. Presenting learners with multiple, auditory-visual exemplars of these sounds in a range of phonetic contexts (e.g., road-load, hear-heal, arrive-alive, crew-clue, etc.), produced by a variety of talkers on a recurring basis would exploit the advantages demonstrated by the afore-mentioned successful training studies. Not all sounds, of course, show the same degree of variability. Although extensive focused training, if needed, may require sessions that are separate from regular classes, zooming in on troublesome sounds in frequent words as they are encountered in communicative activities is beneficial and compatible with an incidental focus-on-form approach. However, incorporation of variability in input raises the question of how much is helpful, and at what point it should be introduced. Decisions must be made in accordance with a learner's interlanguage stage, needs, and tolerance.

Feedback is also important, especially for those perceptual categories that are more difficult to establish because of the variability of the L2 sounds and/or their similarity to L1 sounds. Here it is helpful for instructors to have some knowledge of the phonology of the learners' L1(s).

Given the contribution of visual cues to perception, and their precedence in articulation, instructors should consider pointing out the visible aspects of articulations as part of the knowledge learners can take with them when they leave the classroom to aid both perception and production practice. Visual cues include articulatory gestures related to segmental production and hand gestures that are part of the larger speech event, and may correspond to suprasegmental features of stress, rhythm, and intonation.

Early reference to the visual component of speech can be found in the classic textbook, *Manual of American English Pronunciation* (Prator and Robinett, 1985). It included diagrams of "mouth shapes" for practicing the perception and production of vowels. However, books are not the best medium to help learners take advantage of dynamic visual input, and neither books nor audiotapes provide sufficient variability (e.g., contextual, talker, stylistic). Web-based programs that are currently available are similarly limited and lack the ability to provide feedback on perceptual accuracy, but they do offer some opportunity for auditory-visual segmental input outside the classroom (e.g., http://www.uiowa.edu/~acadtech/phonetics/ for English, German, and Spanish; http://international.ouc.bc.ca/pronunciation/ for English). For instructors who wish to produce and edit their own audiorecordings for learners, *Audacity* is a free cross-platform sound editor (available at http://audacity.sourceforge.net/). There is also *Anvil* (Kipp, 2001; see http://www.anvil-software.de/ for details), a program which provides a screen display integrating the recorded audio and video components of a speech event with the associated pitch track and/or waveform extracted using *Praat* (http://www.fon.hum.uva.nl/praat/).

Future directions

It is evident from studies demonstrating a significant improvement in production as a result of perception training that there is a relationship between these two domains although its exact nature remains elusive. In L2 acquisition, there is a need for studies examining the transfer of production training to perception. Although assessing the retention of abilities following training presents practical challenges for researchers, this also remains an important issue in L2 learning.

In addition, there is a need for L2 studies combining behavioral and neurophysiological evidence. Based on fMRI results, Hickok *et al.* (2003) suggest there is a predominantly left hemisphere network that enables acoustic-phonetic input to guide the acquisition of language-specific articulatory gestures, and underlies phonological working memory in adults, which has become a focus of some studies in L2 production (e.g., O'Brien *et al.*, 2007). In addition, phonetic training studies have demonstrated that learning can be reflected in ERP measures before behavioral measures (e.g., Tremblay and Kraus, 2002), suggesting a direction for L2 research. Finally, eye-tracking studies may indicate which components of a speech event a perceiver attends to and how this changes over the course of the event, and over the course of learning. The convergence of behavioral, neurophysiological, and psychophysical evidence is a promising direction for future research in L2 spoken language processing.

Notes

1 See Chapter 20 (Pickering) for a discussion of L2 speech production.
2 Reaction time is the elapsed time between presentation of a stimulus and the detection of the associated behavioral response as an indication of processing duration.

3 Japanese has a flap in the dental or alveolar region occurring in utterance-initial and intervocalic positions, with acoustic, articulatory, and perceptual similarities to the AE flap. Korean has a nonvelarized or clear /l/ in syllable-final position and a flap intervocalically (or between vowel and glide; see Hardison, 2003).

4 In AV speech research, it is common to assess the contribution from each modality separately (A-only, V-only) as well as both combined (AV).

5 The duration of vowels and consonants is a contrastive feature in Japanese unlike English. In Japanese, singleton consonants contrast with their longer geminate counterparts (e.g., *kite* "coming," *kitte* "postage stamp").

6 Following Bradlow *et al.* (1997), relative improvement is measured as post-test accuracy minus pre-test accuracy divided by 100 minus the pre-test accuracy.

7 A mora is a unit of timing, which plays a role in the temporal organization of speech in production and segmentation of speech in lexical recognition.

8 Sonority is considered an inherent property of a segment, traditionally based on stricture. Generally speaking, the wider the openness of the vocal tract (the smaller the degree of stricture), the greater the energy in the acoustic signal, and the higher the sonority value.

9 ERPs measure the timing of electrical brain responses to a stimulus. The brainwaves correspond to different types of neurocognitive processes.

10 fMRI is a method of capturing and creating an image of the activity in the brain through measurement of the magnetic fields created by the functioning nerve cells in the brain associated with a given task.

11 Proprioception refers to the ability to sense the location and movement of parts of one's own body (e.g., tongue position in the production of sounds).

References

Best, C. T., and Tyler, M. D. (2007). Non-native and second-language speech perception: Commonalities and complementarities. In O. -S. Bohn and M. J. Munro (Eds.), *Language experience in second language speech learning: In honor of James Emil Flege* (pp. 13–34). Amsterdam: Benjamins.

Bohn, O. S. (1995). Cross-language perception in adults: First language transfer doesn't tell it all. In W. Strange (Ed.), *Speech perception and linguistic experience: Theoretical and methodological issues* (pp. 370–410). Timonium, MD: York Press.

Bradlow, A. R. and Pisoni, D. B. (1999). Recognition of spoken words by native and non-native listeners: Talker-, listener-, and item-related factors. *Journal of the Acoustical Society of America, 106*(4), 2074–2085.

Bradlow, A. R., Pisoni, D. B., Akahane-Yamada, R. A., and Tohkura, Y. (1997). Training Japanese listeners to identify English /r/ and /l/: IV. Some effects of perceptual learning on speech production. *Journal of the Acoustical Society of America, 101,* 2299–2310.

Calvert, G. (2001). Crossmodal processing in the human brain: Insights from functional neuroimaging studies. *Cerebral Cortex, 11*(12), 1110–1123.

Chun, D. M., Hardison, D. M., and Pennington, M. C. (2008). Technologies for prosody in context: Past and future of L2 research and practice. In J. G. Hansen Edwards and M. L. Zampini (Eds.), *Phonology and second language acquisition* (pp. 323–346). Amsterdam: Benjamins.

Cutler, A. and Otake, T. (2002). Rhythmic categories in spoken-word recognition. *Journal of Memory and Language, 46*(2), 296–322.

Dodd, B. (1987). The acquisition of lip-reading skills by normally hearing children. In B. Dodd and R. Campbell (Eds.), *Hearing by eye: The psychology of lip-reading* (pp. 163–175). London: Erlbaum.

Driver, J. and Spence, C. (2000). Multisensory perception: Beyond modularity and convergence. *Current Biology, 10*(20), R731–R735.

Flege, J. E. (1995). Second-language speech learning: Theory, findings, and problems. In W. Strange (Ed.), *Speech perception and linguistic experience: Issues in cross-language research* (pp. 229–273). Timonium, MD: York Press.

Flege, J. E. (1999). Age of learning and second-language speech. In D. Birdsong (Ed.), *Second language acquisition and the critical period hypothesis* (pp. 101–131). Mahwah, NJ: Erlbaum.

Flege, J. E. and Liu, S. (2001). The effect of experience on adults' acquisition of a second language. *Studies in Second Language Acquisition, 23*(4), 527–552.

Flege, J. E. and MacKay, I. R. A. (2004). Perceiving vowels in a second language. *Studies in Second Language Acquisition, 26*(1), 1–34.

Goldinger, S. D. (1996). Echoes of echoes? An episodic theory of lexical access. *Psychological Review*, *105*(2), 251–279.

Goldinger, S. D. (1997). Words and voices: Perception and production in an episodic lexicon. In K. Johnson and J. W. Mullennix (Eds.), *Talker variability in speech processing* (pp. 33–66). San Diego, CA: Academic Press.

Goldinger, S. D. (2007, August). *A complementary-systems approach to abstract and episodic speech perception*. Paper presented at the International Congress of Phonetic Sciences (ICPhS XVI), Saarbrücken, Germany. Retrieved August 13, 2010 http://www.icphs2007.de/conference/Papers/1781/1781.pdf

Goto, H. (1971). Auditory perception by normal Japanese adults of the sounds "l" and "r". *Neuropsychologia*, *9*(3), 317–323.

Grosjean, F. and Frauenfelder, U. H. (1996). A guide to spoken word recognition paradigms: Introduction. *Language and Cognitive Processes*, *11*(6), 553–558.

Gullberg, M. (2006). Some reasons for studying gesture and second language acquisition. *International Review of Applied Linguistics in Language Teaching*, *44*(2), 103–124.

Hardison, D. M. (1996). Bimodal speech perception by native and nonnative speakers of English: Factors influencing the McGurk Effect. *Language Learning*, *46*(1), 3–73.

Hardison, D. M. (2003). Acquisition of second-language speech: Effects of visual cues, context, and talker variability. *Applied Psycholinguistics*, *24*(4), 495–522.

Hardison, D. M. (2005a). Second-language spoken word identification: Effects of perceptual training, visual cues, and phonetic environment. *Applied Psycholinguistics*, *26*(4), 579–596.

Hardison, D. M. (2005b). Variability in bimodal spoken language processing by native and nonnative speakers of English: A closer look at effects of speech style. *Speech Communication*, *46*(1), 73–93.

Hardison, D. M. (2006). Effects of familiarity with faces and voices on L2 spoken language processing: Components of memory traces. In *Proceedings of the Ninth International Conference on Spoken Language Processing* (pp. 2462–2465). Bonn, Germany: International Speech Communication Association. Retrieved August 13, 2010 from https://www.msu.edu/~hardiso2/Hardison.ICSLP2006.pdf

Hardison, D. M. (2007). The visual element in phonological perception and learning. In M. C. Pennington (Ed.), *Phonology in context* (pp. 135–158). Basingstoke, England: Palgrave Macmillan.

Hardison, D. M. (2008, March). *The priming role of context and visual cues in spoken language processing by native and non-native speakers*. Paper presented at the American Association for Applied Linguistics Conference, Washington, D.C.

Hardison, D. M. and Motohashi Saigo, M. (2010). Development of perception of L2 Japanese geminates: Role of duration, sonority, and segmentation strategy. *Applied Psycholinguistics*, *31*(1), 81–99.

Hazan, V., Sennema, A., Iba, M., and Faulkner, A. (2005). Effect of audiovisual perceptual training on the perception and production of consonants by Japanese learners of English. *Speech Communication*, *47*(3), 360–378.

Hickok, G., Buchsbaum, B., Humphries, C., and Muftuler, T. (2003). Auditory-motor interaction revealed by fMRI: Speech, music, and working memory in area Spt. *Journal of Cognitive Neuroscience*, *15*(5), 673–682.

Hintzman, D. L. (1986). "Schema abstraction" in a multiple-trace memory model. *Psychological Review*, *93*(4), 411–428.

Højen, A. and Flege, J. E. (2006). Early learners' discrimination of second-language vowels. *Journal of the Acoustical Society of America*, *119*(5), 3072–3084.

Homa, D. and Cultice, J. C. (1984). Role of feedback, category size, and stimulus distortion on the acquisition and utilization of ill-defined categories. *Journal of Experimental Psychology: Learning, Memory, and Cognition*, *10*(1), 83–94.

Ingram, J. C. L. and Park, S. -G. (1998). Language, context, and speaker effects in the identification and discrimination of English /r/ and /l/ by Japanese and Korean listeners. *Journal of the Acoustical Society of America*, *103*(2), 1161–1174.

Jusczyk, P. W. (1993). From general to language-specific capacities: The WRAPSA model of how speech perception develops. *Journal of Phonetics*, *21*(1–2), 3–28.

Kelly, S. D., McDevitt, T., and Esch, M. (2009). Brief training with co-speech gesture lends a hand to word learning in a foreign language. *Language and Cognitive Processes*, *24*(2), 313–334.

Kipp, M. (2001). Anvil - A generic annotation tool for multimodal dialogue. In *Proceedings of the 7th European Conference on Speech Communication and Technology* (pp. 1367–1370). Aalborg, Denmark: Eurospeech.

Kuhl, P. K., Andruski, J. E., Chistovich, I. A., Chistovich, L. A., Kozhevnikova, E. V., and Ryskina, V. L. (1997). Cross-language analysis of phonetic units in language addressed to infants. *Science*, *277*(5326), 684–686.

Kuhl, P. K., Conboy, B. T., Coffey-Corina, S., Padden, D., Rivera-Gaxiola, M., and Nelson, T. (2008). Phonetic learning as a pathway to language: New data and native language magnet theory expanded (NLM-e). *Philosophical Transactions of the Royal Society B, 363*(1493), 979–1000.

Kuhl, P. K. and Iverson, P. (1995). Linguistic experience and the "Perceptual Magnet Effect". In W. Strange (Ed.), *Speech perception and linguistic experience: Issues in cross-language research* (pp. 121–154). Timonium, MD: York Press.

Kuhl, P. K. Stevens, E., Hayashi, A., Degucki, T., Kiritani, S., and Iverson, P. (2006). Infants show a facilitation effect for native language phonetic perception between 6 and 12 months. *Developmental Science, 9*(2), F13–F21.

Leather, J. (1990). Perceptual and productive learning of Chinese lexical tone by Dutch and English speakers. In J. Leather and A. James (Eds.), *New Sounds 90* (pp. 72–97). Amsterdam: University of Amsterdam.

Lively, S. E., Logan, J. S., and Pisoni, D. B. (1993). Training Japanese listeners to identify English /r/ and /l/. II: The role of phonetic environment and talker variability in learning new perceptual categories. *Journal of the Acoustical Society of America, 94*(3), 1242–1255.

Lively, S. E., Pisoni, D. B., Yamada, R. A., Tohkura, Y., and Yamada, T. (1994). Training Japanese listeners to identify English /r/ and /l/. III: Long-term retention of new phonetic categories. *Journal of the Acoustical Society of America, 96*(4), 2076–2087.

Logan, J. S., Lively, S. E., and Pisoni, D. B. (1991). Training Japanese listeners to identify English /r/ and /l/: A first report. *Journal of the Acoustical Society of America, 89*(2), 874–886.

MacKain, K. S., Best, C. T., and Strange, W. (1981). Categorical perception of English /r/ and /l/ by Japanese bilinguals. *Applied Psycholinguistics, 2*(4), 369–390.

MacKay, I., Meador, D., and Flege, J. (2001). The identification of English consonants by native speakers of Italian. *Phonetica, 58*(1–2), 103–125.

Massaro, D. W. (1998). *Perceiving talking faces: From speech perception to a behavioral principle.* Cambridge, MA: MIT.

Massaro, D. W. and Light, J. (2003). Read my tongue movements: Bimodal learning to perceive and produce non-native speech /r/ and /l/. In *Proceedings of Eurospeech (Interspeech), 8th European Conference on Speech Communication and Technology (CD-ROM).* Geneva, Switzerland.

McCandliss, B. D., Fiez, J. A., Protopapas, A., and Conway, M. (2002). Success and failure in teaching the [r]-[l] contrast to Japanese adults: Tests of a Hebbian model of plasticity and stabilization in spoken language perception. *Cognitive, Affective, and Behavioral Neuroscience, 2*(2), 89–108.

McGurk, H. and MacDonald, J. (1976). Hearing lips and seeing voices. *Nature, 264,* 746–748.

Meador, D., Flege, J., and MacKay, I. (2000). Factors affecting the recognition of words in a second language. *Bilingualism: Language and Cognition, 3*(1), 55–67.

Meltzoff, A. N. and Kuhl, P. K. (1994). Faces and speech: Intermodal processing of biologically relevant signals in infants and adults. In D. J. Lewkowitz and R. Lickliter (Eds.), *The development of intersensory perception: Comparative perspectives* (pp. 335–369). Hillsdale, NJ: Erlbaum.

Mochizuki, M. (1981). The identification of /r/ and /l/ in natural and synthesized speech. *Journal of Phonetics, 9*(3), 282–303.

Morosan, D. E. and Jamieson, D. G. (1989). Evaluation of a technique for training new speech contrasts: Generalization across voices, but not word-position or task. *Journal of Speech and Hearing Research, 32*(3), 501–511.

Motohashi Saigo, M. and Hardison, D. M. (2009). Acquisition of L2 Japanese geminates: Training with waveform displays. *Language Learning and Technology, 13*(2), 29–47. Retrieved August 13, 2010 from http://llt.msu.edu/vol13num2/motohashisaigohardison.pdf

Munhall, K. G. and Tohkura, Y. (1998). Audiovisual gating and the time course of speech perception. *Journal of the Acoustical Society of America, 104*(1), 530–539.

Norman, K. and O'Reilly, R. (2003). Modeling hippocampal and neocortical contributions to recognition memory: A complementary learning-systems approach. *Psychological Review, 110*(4), 611–646.

Nosofsky, R. M. (1986). Attention, similarity, and the identification-categorization relationship. *Journal of Experimental Psychology: General, 115*(1), 39–57.

O'Brien, I., Segalowitz, N., Freed, B., and Collentine, J. (2007). Phonological memory predicts second language oral fluency gains in adults. *Studies in Second Language Acquisition, 29*(4), 557–581.

Perani, D. and Abutalebi, J. (2005). The neural basis of first and second language processing. *Current Opinion in Neurobiology, 15*(2), 202–206.

Pisoni, D. B., Aslin, R. N., Perey, A. J., and Hennessy, B. L. (1982). Some effects of laboratory training on identification and discrimination of voicing contrasts in stop consonants. *Journal of Experimental Psychology: Human Perception and Performance, 8*(2), 297–314.

Pisoni, D. B., Nusbaum, H. C., Luce, P. A., and Slowiaczek, L. M. (1985). Speech perception, word recognition and the structure of the lexicon. *Speech Communication*, *4*(1–3), 75–95.

Prator, C. H. and Robinett, B. W. (1985). *Manual of American English pronunciation* (Fourth Edition). Orlando, FL: Harcourt Brace.

Rivera-Gaxiola, M., Silva-Pereyra, J., and Kuhl, P. K. (2005). Brain potentials to native and non-native speech contrasts in 7- and 11-month-old American infants. *Developmental Science*, *8*(2), 162–172.

Rosenblum, L. D. (2004). Primacy of multimodal speech perception. In D. B. Pisoni and R. E. Remez (Eds.), *The handbook of speech perception* (pp. 51–78). Malden, MA: Blackwell.

Scovel, T. (1969). Foreign accents, language acquisition, and cerebral dominance. *Language Learning*, *19*(3–4), 245–253.

Sheldon, A. and Strange, W. (1982). The acquisition of /r/ and /l/ by Japanese learners of English: Evidence that speech production can precede speech perception. *Applied Psycholinguistics*, *3*(3), 243–261.

Skipper, J. I., van Wassenhove, V., Nusbaum, H. W., and Small, S. L. (2007). Hearing lips and seeing voices: How cortical areas supporting speech production mediate audiovisual speech perception. *Cerebral Cortex*, *17*(10), 2387–2399.

Strange, W. and Dittmann, S. (1984). Effects of discrimination training on the perception of /r-l/ by Japanese adults learning English. *Perception and Psychophysics*, *36*(2), 131–145.

Strange, W. and Shafer, V. L. (2008). Speech perception in second language learners: The re-education of selective perception. In J. G. Hansen Edwards and M. L. Zampini (Eds.), *Phonology and second language acquisition* (pp. 153–191). Amsterdam: Benjamins.

Sueyoshi, A. and Hardison, D. M. (2005). The role of gestures and facial cues in second language listening comprehension. *Language Learning*, *55*(4), 661–699.

Tallal, P., Miller, S. L., Bedi, G., Byma, G., Wang, X., and Nagarajan, S. S. (1996). Language comprehension in language-learning impaired children improved with acoustically modified speech. *Science*, *271*(5245), 81–84.

Tremblay, K. L. and Kraus, N. (2002). Auditory training induces asymmetrical changes in cortical neural activity. *Journal of Speech, Language, and Hearing Research*, *45*(3), 564–572.

Uther, M., Knoll, M. A., and Burnham, D. (2007). Do you speak E-NG-L-I-SH? A comparison of foreigner- and infant-directed speech. *Speech Communication*, *49*(1), 2–7.

van Wassenhove, V., Grant, K. W., and Poeppel, D. (2005). Visual speech speeds up the neural processing of auditory speech. *Proceedings of the National Academy of Sciences*, *102*(4), 1181–1186.

Wang, Y., Jongman, A., and Sereno, J. A. (2003). Acoustic and perceptual evaluation of Mandarin tone productions before and after perceptual training. *Journal of the Acoustical Society of America*, *113*(2), 1033–1043.

Werker, J. F. and Tees, R. C. (1984). Cross-language speech perception: Evidence for perceptual reorganization during the first year of life. *Infant Behavior and Development*, *7*(1), 49–63.

Yamada, R. A. (1995). Age and acquisition of second language speech sounds: Perception of American English /r/ and /l/ by native speakers of Japanese. In W. Strange (Ed.), *Speech perception and linguistic experience: Issues in cross-language research* (pp. 305–320). Timonium, MD: York Press.

22

Speaking and writing tasks and their effects on second language performance

Folkert Kuiken and Ineke Vedder

Historical discussion

It is hard to answer the question when the human race started speaking: was it 50,000, 150,000 or 250,000 years ago? And did humanoids start speaking immediately after they were physically able to do so? It is equally hard to tell when we began to write. Was it around 3000 BC judging by the Mesopotamian tablets which date from around that time? Or was it as early as 5000 or 8000 BC if we also include "forerunners" of writing that have been found on small clay objects at sites from Palestine to eastern Iran (Daniels and Bright, 1996)? How difficult these questions may be to answer, what is not contested is that speaking is primary and writing is secondary. This is still the case in modern society: children start to speak first and only later do they learn to write. But writing has become very important nowadays. A human being who cannot write will not be able to participate fully in daily life. And there are situations and contexts in which more importance is attached to the written than to the spoken word.

In second language learning oral and written tasks often go hand in hand. Although it is possible to learn a second language (L2) just by listening and responding orally to the input, within the context of instructed L2 learning most learners will use books or other written documents in order to acquire the target language. So from the very beginning of L2 learning the majority of learners will be submitted to both oral and written language tasks. Recently a lot of research has been done on various factors influencing task performance in a L2 (Ellis, 2003; Robinson, 1995, 2007; Skehan, 1998; among others). These factors include the type of task, the inherent cognitive complexity of the task, the conditions under which the task has to be performed (e.g., the number of participants involved) and the nature of the task (e.g., monologic or dialogic, open or closed). The mode (oral versus written) in which the task has to be completed is another factor that has to be taken into consideration, but surprisingly enough mode has attracted little attention in the L2 research agenda. It is precisely for this reason that in this chapter the focus is on the role of mode in second language acquisition (SLA).

Although their have been many studies which have looked at the effect of task type on linguistic performance, the majority of studies which have investigated the influence of particular task characteristics have concentrated on oral performance (Gilabert *et al.*, 2009; Yuan and Ellis, 2003). Prabhu (1980, 1984, 1987) was one of the first to emphasize the effect of oral information gap tasks. These are tasks in which the participants do not have the same items of information so that they are forced to communicate with each other in order to solve the task. Information gap tasks were introduced to the SLA research context by Long (1980, 1985).

Long (1985) mentions six variables along which tasks can be varied, leading to more and better vs. less and weaker performance. These variables are: motivation, planning time, open versus closed tasks, convergent versus divergent tasks, one-way versus two-way tasks, and information gap tasks. Later research has confirmed many of Long's assumptions. For instance, with respect to planning, there is now ample evidence that almost any kind of planning helps the learners to perform better (Ellis, 2005, 2009). The results for complexity and accuracy are mixed, depending both on the type of planning and the mediating effect of various factors, including task design, implementation variables, and individual difference factors.

Other researchers who have explored the effect of task characteristics on oral performance are Skehan, Foster and Tavakoli (Foster and Skehan, 1996; Skehan and Foster, 1997; Skehan, 2001, 2009; Tavakoli and Foster, 2011; Tavakoli and Skehan, 2005). In these studies the outcomes of three types of tasks have been compared with each other: personal tasks (e.g., explain how to get to one's home to turn off an oven that has been left on), narrative tasks (e.g., making up a story from a series of pictures or a video fragment) and decision-making tasks (e.g., agree on the appropriate sentence for a series of crimes). In an overview study Skehan (2001, 2009) draws the following conclusions: (1) tasks requiring information manipulation lead to higher complexity; (2) interactive tasks favor accuracy and complexity; (3) tasks containing clear structure benefit accuracy and fluency; (4) tasks based on concrete or familiar information also advantage accuracy and fluency. There are, however, differences between the kind of tasks and even within a task: the picture-based narrative for instance yields other results than the video-based narrative. Task design, in other words, can influence the level of complexity, accuracy, or fluency for a particular task.

Whereas numerous studies on the relationship between task characteristics and linguistic output concern oral tasks, not many studies have examined the effects of task type and task complexity on the written performance of L2 learners. There are, however, some exceptions (Kuiken and Vedder, 2007a, b, c; Kuiken et al., 2005; among others). Moreover, there are only a few studies in which the effect of mode on linguistic performance in L2 or L1 has been established and a comparison is made between oral and written task performance (Grabowski, 2005, 2007; Granfeldt, 2007; among others). We have to keep in mind that in these studies, which will be discussed further on, the relationship between the influence of mode and particular task characteristics has often not been systematically explored. Moreover, as will be shown, the results that have been established so far are often contradictory.

Core issues

An important issue regarding the influence of speaking and writing tasks on L2 performance concerns the differences that exist between L2 speaking and writing. A major difference is to be found in the nature of the linguistic knowledge accessed by the learner and the underlying processes required for oral and written production (see the contributions of Pickering on speech production and of Polio on writing, Chapter 19, in this volume). While oral production is generally considered to give evidence of the learner's implicit knowledge, written production seems to allow for the use of explicit knowledge (Towell et al., 1996). Also the underlying language production processes related to speaking and writing differ from each other. As pointed out in several studies, a prerequisite for linguistic and thematic coherence in oral and written text production is to remember what has already been said or written. Compared to speaking, where the information which has already been produced must be maintained exclusively in memory, in writing the already written text can be re-read. Besides that, writing is often five to eight times slower than speaking, since more time is needed for the verbalization of content (Fayol, 1997). As a consequence, cognitive resources can be used for a longer period of time, from which information retrieval from long-term memory as well as planning should benefit. Moreover, while speech production requires continuous progress, language production in writing is self-determined: it is possible for the writer to stop the grapho-motoric process and to concentrate only on retrieval or on planning processes. The cognitive load of writing compared to speaking is therefore lower (Grabowski, 2007, pp. 168–170; Granfeldt, 2007).

In a study on the relationship between oral and written production and memory recall in L1, Grabowski (2005, 2007) investigated the question of how the diverse sub-processes of oral and written language production are related to memory span and whether they offer equivalent possibilities for learners to express their cognitive achievements. In a study, conducted among two groups of university students and primary schoolchildren in Germany, Grabowski found that for university students there was no mode effect on recall performance from working memory, whereas for schoolchildren a significant effect was observed, in favor of the oral mode. In a follow-up study in which the differential effects of oral and written task production in relation to recall from both long-term memory and working memory were examined, a significant difference between the two modes was detected. For adult learners, a robust and stable superiority effect of writing was reported on recall from long-term memory, in so far as the written mode seemed to reflect the underlying knowledge of the students better than the oral mode did. No differences between the oral and written mode, however, could be established with respect to recall performance from working memory (Grabowski, 2007).

Remarkably enough the distinction between oral tasks and written tasks and their effects on language performance has not often been an object of research. This may have to do with the fact that the majority of tasks (personal, narrative, problem solving, decision making, information gap, map tasks) can be performed in both the oral and written mode. This also holds for the variables mentioned by Long (1985): both oral and written tasks can be manipulated with respect to the amount of planning time allowed, and to the degree in which a task is open or closed, convergent or divergent, monologic or dialogic. Some variables, however, inherently seem to be more related to either an oral or a written task. This is, for instance, the case with the planning that learners undertake while they are performing a task (within-talk planning). As speaking is faster than writing, learners can do a lot more within-talk planning during writing, compared to speaking. Another example concerns interaction. In an oral situation there is generally an interlocutor who is present most of the time waiting for some kind of immediate response: in a tête-à-tête, throughout a Skype session, or during a phone call. This is not the case when somebody writes a letter, an SMS- or an e-mail message: although there is always an addressee, the interlocutor is not expected to react right away; except perhaps during a chat session, but even then the addressee may decide to take time to react. In other words, there is not so much of what could be defined as a prototypical oral task or a unique writing task. Nevertheless, some tasks are used more often in an oral situation, while others lend themselves better to the written mode.

To summarize: despite the similarities that exist between some oral and written tasks, there are several differences between speaking and writing, which may possibly lead to a differential influence of mode on linguistic performance. In the following section we will discuss the types of data that are used in studies on the effects of mode, the way the data are collected and analyzed, and the measures used in this type of research.

Data and common elicitation measures

Looking at the relatively small number of studies that have investigated the effects of mode on linguistic performance, one is struck by the enormous variety in the kind of tasks that have been used in these studies, the participants involved, the way the data have been collected and the measures that have been used to analyze the data.

With respect to the focus of the study and the participants involved, most researchers have submitted tasks to adult L2 learners, but with a variety of source languages and target languages, cf., L1 Hungarian—L2 English (Kormos and Trebits, 2009), L1 Spanish—L2 English (Martínez-Flor, 2006), L1 Swedish—L2 French (Granfeldt, 2007), L1 Dutch—L2 French (Bulté and Housen, 2009), L1 Dutch—L2 Italian (Kuiken and Vedder, 2009, 2011). Ferrari and Nuzzo (2009) studied the acquisition of L2 Italian by younger learners of various language backgrounds. The research focus of the studies differed from a single focus on lexical complexity (Bulté and Housen, 2009; Yu, 2009) or pragmatic competence (Martínez-Flor, 2006), to a broader scope regarding grammatical complexity and accuracy (Ferrari and Nuzzo, 2009), or even grammatical complexity, lexical complexity, and accuracy (Granfeldt, 2007; Kormos and Trebits, 2009; Kuiken and Vedder, 2009, 2011).

Given these differences in participants and research focus it is not surprising that there is also much variation in the way the data have been collected and analyzed. Oral retelling and written narrative tasks were used by Ferrari and Nuzzo (2009) and by Kormos and Trebits (2009). Yu (2009) adopted written compositions and interviews, whereas Martínez-Flor (2006) used phone messages and e-mails. The L2 learners in Kuiken and Vedder (2009, 2011) had to fulfill two argumentative tasks. Besides these different tasks, various languages measures, both general and more specific, were employed. With respect to grammatical complexity general and specific measures were used, based on utterance length, the proportion of subordinate clauses (subclause ratio), or the use of cohesive devices. Measures which have often been used for measuring the lexicon are D, establishing lexical diversity (Malvern and Richards, 1997, 2002; Malvern et al., 2004), type-token ratio measures, and lexical profile measures, classifying the vocabulary into frequency bands (Laufer and Nation, 1995, 1999). Accuracy was measured by counting the number of errors, error-free clauses, and first, second, and third degree errors focusing on the seriousness of the errors. Fluency was measured by counting the number of repetitions and paraphrases. Pragmatic competence was established by the occurrence of target language forms for making suggestions.

These different source and target languages, the variety in participants, data collection procedures, and languages measures, make it hard to compare the various studies with each other and to draw unambiguous conclusions. Nevertheless, we will try to do so in the next section.

Empirical verification

Recently several studies have investigated the effect of mode on second language performance (Bulté and Housen, 2009; Ferrari and Nuzzo, 2009; Granfeldt, 2007; Kormos and Trebits, 2009; Kuiken and Vedder, 2009, 2011; Martínez-Flor, 2006; Yu, 2009). With respect to the influence of the oral versus the written mode on linguistic performance the results of the experimental studies which have been found so far are contradictory.

Granfeldt (2007) conducted a study among Swedish university students in which the effect of mode in oral and written L2 French was explored. Data collection took place in two sessions. In the first session the participants had to produce two expository texts. Half of the subjects spoke before writing and half of them wrote before speaking. In the second session the same procedure was repeated with two narrative texts. Due to the fact that writing, compared to speaking, allows more possibilities for control, planning, and monitoring, it was expected that the written L2 production would be characterized by a higher degree of complexity and accuracy than the oral production. Spelling and pronunciation errors were not taken into account. Although lexical complexity in writing turned out to be significantly higher than in speaking, contrary to expectations this was not the case for grammatical complexity, established both by a subclause ratio measure and by the occurrences of "advanced" syntactic structures. Furthermore, there were more errors in writing than in speaking. Although no general effect of mode was found in the study, there was a tendency toward individual differences between the learners, due to mode. A possible explanation could be that learners have preferences for either the oral or the written mode, as suggested by Weissberg (2000), who found that learners have "modality preferences" when it comes to morphosyntactic constructions.

In a study by Ferrari and Nuzzo (2009), a comparison was made of the grammatical complexity and accuracy of the spoken and written production of young L2 learners from various L1 backgrounds and L1 speakers of Italian, in an oral retelling task and a written narrative. Grammatical complexity was measured both by general measures, for example, number of words per clause, number of dependent clauses per AS-unit or T-unit (i.e., the dominant clause and its dependent clauses in respectively spoken and written discourse), and by specific measures (type of dependent clauses and the use of cohesive devices). The native speakers who tended to be more complex in the written mode than in the oral mode, produced longer clauses and more complex T-units. For the L2 learners there were fewer differences in the degree of syntactic subordination between the two modes, in spite of a slight superiority effect of the written mode. While native speakers seemed to use a wider variety of dependent clauses in the written narrative, there turned out to be no differences between the two modes for the non-native speakers. Both native and non-native speakers seemed to employ a wider range of connectors and textual anaphors in the written mode. With respect to accuracy, in line with the findings of Granfeldt (2007), L2 learners, unlike L1 learners, seemed to be more accurate in oral production. What these differences between native and non-native speakers seem to imply is that the superiority of either the oral or the written mode may also be constrained by the level of linguistic competence.

In the studies by Yu (2009) and Bulté and Housen (2009) the focus is on the development of lexical competence in L2. With respect to lexical complexity, there are a number of differences between oral and written task performance. Compared to written production, oral production is generally characterized by a high number of disfluency markers, repetitions, and paraphrases, a small range of clause connectors, lower lexical diversity and the use of more high-frequent words. Yu (2009), in a study on the lexical complexity of spoken and written discourse produced by L2 learners of English from various language backgrounds, compared lexical diversity in written compositions and interviews. The main finding of the study was that the lexical diversity of the writing and speaking performance of the L2 learners, as established by D (Malvern and Richards, 1997, 2002; Malvern et al., 2004), was not only significantly positively related, but also approximately at the same level. On the basis of these results Yu suggests that lexical diversity does not seem to be affected by task types (written compositions vs. spontaneaous interviews) or other task type characteristics such as pre-task planning and time pressure.

Bulté and Housen (2009) examined the development of lexical competence, in L2 speaking and writing in L2 French by native speakers of Dutch in Belgium. Lexical competence was measured by different quantitative and qualitative measures often employed for establishing lexical diversity (type-token ratio measures, D, Guiraud Index of Lexical Richness, Uber, lexical profile measures). The main result of the study was that although most of the measures indicated a significant increase in proficiency, both in the oral and the written task, this development did not seem to run in parallel for spoken and written tasks. Contrary to Yu (2009), but similar to

Granfeldt (2007), the scores on the written tasks were generally higher than the scores on the oral tasks, for all the measures employed, except for the lexical profile measures.

Kormos and Trebits (2009) compared the grammatical and lexical complexity, accuracy and the use of cohesive devices in the written and spoken production of a group of Hungarian L2 learners of English in a Hungarian bilingual secondary school, in two oral and two written narrative tasks (a cartoon description and a story narration). Both general and specific linguistic measures were used. Grammatical complexity and text cohesion were measured by specific measures (occurences and types of coordinate and subordinate clauses; use of grammatical and lexical cohesive devices). Lexical complexity, operationalized as lexical diversity and lexical sophistication, was measured by D and by lexical profile measures (Laufer and Nation, 1995, 1999). Accuracy was established by means of the occurrence of error-free past-tense verbs, relative clauses, and error free clauses. Similar to the findings of Bulté and Housen (2009) and Granfeldt (2007), a superiority effect of the written mode was found for both lexical diversity and lexical sophistication. Contrary to the results of Ferrari and Nuzzo (2009) and Granfeldt (2007), no differences between the oral and the written mode were found with respect to grammatical complexity, while accuracy seemed to be higher in the written mode. In the written mode also the number of lexical cohesive devices was higher, although with respect to grammatical cohesive devices no differences between the two modes could be established.

In a study on the development of pragmatic competence by Spanish learners of English, Martínez-Flor (2006) examined the production of target language forms that had been selected for expressing suggestions in oral and written production tasks (i.e., phone messages and emails) by intermediate university students of English, with Spanish as their L1. In the study a higher number of pragmalinguistic target forms (e.g., modifiers, modals) in appropriate contexts (i.e., equal or higher status situation) was produced by the learners in the written production task. This finding contrasts with previous studies concerning the oral and written production of speech acts in L2, in which a greater amount of target forms in the oral task was found (Houck and Gass, 1996).

Kuiken and Vedder (2009, 2011) investigated the influence of task complexity on grammatical and lexical complexity and accuracy, in relation to the mode in which the tasks were performed. To investigate these effects a study was set up in which two tasks which previously had been submitted to a group of learners of Italian L2 in the written mode, were presented to another group as speaking tasks. In these tasks task complexity was manipulated along two variables of the Multiple Resources Attentional Model (Robinson, 1995, 2007): the number of elements to be taken into account and the reasoning demands posed by the task. The participants in the oral mode were 44 learners of Italian as a second language, with Dutch as their mother tongue. Their performance was compared with that of another group of 91 Italian L2 learners who had performed the same tasks in the written mode. In the study, differences between the oral and written performance of the learners, in relation to the influence of task complexity, were found only with respect to grammatical complexity, as the number of dependent clauses per clause in the complex task turned out to be lower in the oral mode. No differences between the oral and the written mode were detected regarding the number of clauses per T-unit, or with respect to the lexical complexity and accuracy of the output.

The results that have been obtained so far by studies in which the influence of mode on L2 performance was investigated are summarized in Table 22.1. With respect to grammatical complexity Ferrari and Nuzzo (2009) and Kuiken and Vedder (2009, 2011) found a superiority effect of the written mode (more subordination), whereas Granfeldt (2007) and Kormos and Trebits (2009) did not observe a difference between the two modes. Concerning lexical complexity a similar picture emerges: a superiority effect of the written mode was established by Granfeldt (2007), Bulté and Housen (2009) and Kormos and Trebits (2009), while Yu (2009) and Kuiken and

Table 22.1 Studies which have investigated language performance in the oral and written mode

	Superiority of written mode	Superiority of oral mode	No effect of mode
Grammatical complexity	Ferrari and Nuzzo (2009) Kuiken and Vedder (2011)		Granfeldt (2007) Kormos and Trebits (2009)
Lexical complexity	Granfeldt (2007) Bulté and Housen (2009) Kormos and Trebits (2009)		Yu (2009) Kuiken and Vedder (2011)
Accuracy	Kormos and Trebits (2009)	Granfeldt (2007) Ferrari and Nuzzo (2009)	Kuiken and Vedder (2011)

Vedder (2009, 2011) could not detect a difference between the oral and the written mode. The picture tends to become even more diversified if we include findings on accuracy: Kuiken and Vedder (forthcoming) did not find any differences between the two modes, whereas Granfeldt (2007) and Ferrari and Nuzzo (2009) found a superiority effect of the oral mode, contrary to Kormos and Trebits (2009) who observed a superiority effect of the written mode.

All in all, this means that an unequivocal effect of mode with respect to grammatical complexity, lexical complexity and accuracy cannot yet be established. Regarding grammatical and lexical complexity some studies did not observe any effects of mode. Those studies that did find such an influence, observed a superiority effect of the written mode. As far as accuracy is concerned, the results that have emerged so far seem to point in all possible directions: no effect of mode, superiority of the oral mode, or superiority of the written mode.

Applications

In this section we will turn to the practice of language teaching and present some characteristic speaking and writing tasks. We will first discuss two information gap tasks, as examples of speaking tasks eliciting oral output. Then we will present a "typical" writing task, consisting in an argumentative letter to be sent to the editorial board of a newspaper. Next we will discuss a dictogloss task as an example of a task which includes both an oral and a written component. It will be shown how in a dictogloss task, both the oral and written mode may reinforce each other.

Information gap tasks. An information gap task is usally performed orally. Information gap tasks generally ask learners to find differences between (series of) pictures, to order sentences in stories, or to restore portions of incomplete maps and charts. As learners carry out these activities, they engage in functional, meaning-focused use of the target language, and gain acces to input for learning (Pica, *et al.*, 2006). For a typical example of an information gap task see Box 22.1 (based on Ur, 1988, pp. 99–105).

The task presented in Box 22.1 is an example of a convergent task in which interaction leads to a specific goal or outcome, in this case an appointment between the four participants involved. In order to be able to reach this outcome, verbal exchange of information between the participants is required by the task. As Pica *et al.* (2006) note, such tasks are among the most productive for L2 acquisition: they set up conditions for participants to modify their interaction through negotiation of meaning. Moreover, as learners repeat and rephrase utterances (e.g., "Are your free on Monday? No, on Monday I cannot make it") to make sure that their information is accurate and understood, information gap tasks also draw the attention of the learners to the linguistic forms that encode these utterances, in this example question formation and negation.

Making an appointment as presented in Box 22.1 is a task which mostly will be carried out orally, based on an authentic situation: the four participants involved in the task draw their agendas and discuss possible time slots to meet each other. The task, however, is not exclusively and necessarily an oral task. Although the appointment is made orally, the four learners have to consult the written information in their diaries to be able to arrange a meeting. And thanks to electronic diaries, nowadays it would even be possible for just one person (e.g., an office secretary) to perform the whole task on her/his own, without ever speaking a single word, provided that she/he has access to the electronic diaries of the participants. But, as in real life, this would make things much duller, as the buzz of making the appointment is already part of the fun of the whole event.

Box 22.1 Making an appointment

Yolanda's diary

Monday	Tuesday	Wednesday	Thursday	Friday	Saturday
19–20.30	20–22		18–21		
Fitness	Gospel choir		Sue: shopping		

Ron's diary

Monday	Tuesday	Wednesday	Thursday	Friday	Saturday
		19–21	19.15	18–19	20.00
		Soccer	Call Maria	Swimming	Ben: videos

Maxwell's diary

Monday	Tuesday	Wednesday	Thursday	Friday	Saturday
	18.30	18.30		23.00 Salsa	
	Tennis	Pick up Ron		in the Poco Loco	

Vanessa's diary

Monday	Tuesday	Wednesday	Thursday	Friday	Saturday
19–20.30	19–20				20.00
Fitness	Tango lesson				Ben: videos

Source: (Based on Ur, 1988, pp. 99–105)

In an article on the multiple roles of information gap tasks and the contribution these tasks can make to research methodology, Pica *et al.* (2006) present another example of an information gap task. In this task a (written) review of a film is used as a starting point. After having read the original review individually, the learners are grouped into pairs, and each member of a pair receives a slightly modified version of the text. In this spot-the-difference task the learners are asked to discuss, sentence by sentence, which of the two versions is the correct one (e.g., "We see Andrew as a typical workaholic attorney" versus "We see Andrew as one typical workaholic attorney"). The next task is a jigsaw task, in which the sentences of the original review have been shuffled, and together each pair has to put the sentences in the correct order. Finally a grammar communication task has to be completed consisting of a fill-in-the blanks exercise in which the right word to fill in the blanks has to be chosen. Although a lot of written information has to be processed, the real processing occurs during the oral interaction phase, when learners have to work together to detect the differences in the information each of them has been provided with, and to decide which solution is correct and which is not. Besides the filling-in-the blanks activity, there is no writing involved in the task. Even if learners are provided with written textual input to carry out the task, the main focus is thus on the oral processing of particular grammatical structures.

Argumentative writing tasks. The following example of a writing task has been taken from a study by Kuiken *et al.* (2010), in which the relationship in L2 writing between linguistic complexity and communicative adequacy is investigated. The task submitted to the participants consists of an argumentative letter which has to be written to the editorial board of a newspaper. The learners have to convince the editorial board to select, out of three options, a particular topic for the leading article of the monthly supplement of the newspaper. In their letter the participants, who have to take into account a number of criteria, are asked to come up with at least three arguments. Since in this writing task learners are not allowed to interact with each other, they are left to their own devices while conceptualizing the letter and putting their ideas on paper (see Box 22.2).

The task presented in Box 22.2 can be considered semi-authentic, as it may be quite natural for an editorial board of a newspaper to invite its readers once in a month to have a say in the contents. However, instead of asking the readers to come up with a written report of their choice, it might also be possible to organize an oral panel discussion, during which readers express their opinion on what should be the leading article for the monthly supplement. Although the task presented in Box 22.2 can be considered a typical example of a writing task, it is not necessarily the case that this task can only be performed as a writing activity, similarly to the information gap task (e.g., making an appointment) which can be performed both as a speaking and a writing task.

Dictogloss. In a dictogloss task, described by Wajnryb (1990), L2 learners have to reconstruct both in the oral and in the written mode a short text read to them by the teacher at normal speed. This text, either a constructed text or an authentic one, is intended to provide practice in the use of particular linguistic forms or constructions (e.g., the use of passives). While the text is being read, learners first take notes; and then work together in small groups to reconstruct the initial text from their shared resources. After the reconstruction phase, the final version produced by each group is compared with the original text, and analyzed and commented on by the teacher. The dictogloss procedure allows the teacher to compare and to analyze both the oral output of the participants (i.e., the transcripts of the recordings of the interaction going on between the learners) and the written output (i.e., the text produced by the learners). As hypothesized in the literature, while learners interact with each other, as a result of this co-construction of L2 knowledge their language ability will improve, as far as their morpho-syntactic, lexical, and pragma-rhetorical skills are concerned (Swain and Lapkin, 2001; see also the chapter on interaction by Mackey, Abbuhl and Gass Chapter 1, in this volume).

Box 22.2 Writing an argumentative text

Every month your favorite newspaper invites its readers to have a say in what will be the leading article for the monthly supplement. This time the Editorial Board has come up with three suggestions: (1) global warming, (2) physical education, (3) animal experiments.

Out of these three suggestions one has to be selected. The selection is made by a Readers' Committee. Every member of the committee has to write a report to the editors in which she/he states which article should be selected and why. On the basis of the arguments given by the committee members the Editorial Board will decide which article will be published on the front page. This month you have been invited to be a member of the Readers' Committee. Read the brief descriptions of the suggestions for articles below. Determine which article should be on the front page and why. Write a report in which you give at least three arguments for your choice. Try to be as clear as possible and include the following points in your report:

- which article should be selected;
- what the importance of the article is;
- which readers will be interested in the article;
- why the Editorial Board should place this article on the front page of the monthly supplement.

You have 35 minutes available to write your text and you need to write at least 150 words (about 15 lines). The use of a dictionary is not allowed.

Suggestions for articles:

(1) *Global warming*: there is an ongoing political and public debate worldwide regarding what, if any, action should be taken to reduce global warming.
(2) *Physical education*: the government is launching a campaign in order to prevent people from becoming obese and to encourage them to move more.
(3) *Animal experiments*: it is estimated that 50 to 100 million animals worldwide are used annually and killed during or after experiments.

Source: (Kuiken *et al.*, 2010)

This can be illustrated by means of an excerpt in which three Dutch L2 learners of English, Lovella, Fabe, and Hester, are reconstructing a text about a stolen painting, based on Willis (1991, p. 171) (cf., Kuiken and Vedder, 2002a, b, 2005). Box 22.3 contains the reconstructed text produced by the students. We will focus on one particular sentence of the reconstructed version: "At Liverpool airport the exchange took place." Although the reconstructed version contains a couple of errors, the students have succeeded quite well in reproducing the global contents of the text (see Box 22.4).

As can be noted from the excerpt in Box 22.4 the students have considerable trouble in formulating the sentence "At Liverpool airport the exchange took place." They first hesitate about the use of the preposition "in" versus "at": do they have to say "*in* Liverpool airport" or "*at* Liverpool airport"? They quickly opt for "at," as this "sounds more logical" to them. In spite of some doubts concerning the word "exchange," they then decide that "exchange" is probably the correct solution "since it was an exchange." But their main problem resides in the construction of the verbal phrase. Before finally deciding to write down "the

---

Box 22.3 The stolen painting: Reconstructed text

Two men tried to steal a painting who was owned by Mary Jones, aged 84 years old. She said that maybe an anchester showed the painting to the two men. She should have received the painting as a wedding present in 1941, but she didn't receive it untill 1945. Mr X (who's name can't be told for legal reasons) who was accused of stealing it, liked to sell the painting for a cheap price to get rid of it. At Liverpool airport the exchange took place. The buyer was flown in there with the money. At first, he was shown the painting in a banner, then he showed the money in a suitcase to Mr X. But the police had surrounded the airport and they arrested Mr X.

Box 22.4 Excerpt of the discussion between three students during the reconstruction phase[1]

Lovella:	Okay, so it was "in Liverpool airport" or something like that.
Fabe:	Yes.
Lovella:	"At" or "at Liverpool airport" er …
Hester:	"At" sounds more logical.
Lovella:	Yes, "at," okay, but do we say then "at Liverpool airport er the exchange would find place" or something like that?
Fabe:	Yeah, "would taken" er …
Lovella:	"Would ha …"
Fabe:	"Would …"
Lovella:	"Would taken," no, "would take place."
Fabe:	Yeah, is that okay?
Lovella:	Or "the agreement" or so, no "the exchange" for it was an exchange.
Fabe:	Yes, it was an exchange, yeah.
Lovella:	So "at Liverpool airport … the exchange … er would er, would …, no, once more."
Fabe:	Shit.
Lovella:	So it was in any case … for in Dutch it is, so to say, at the airport of Liverpool …
Fabe:	At the airport …
Lovella:	The exchange would, will …, so …, "at Liverpool … airport … the exchange should have been …"
Fabe:	"Taking place."
Lovella:	Yes.
Fabe:	That is a lot of verbs at a row.
Lovella:	Yeah, so "at Liverpool airport the exchange would … take place," yes, it would take place there.
Fabe:	Yeah, "would …"
Lovella:	"Would take place," isn't it?
Fabe:	Yes.

Note:
[1] The discussion was held partly in Dutch, partly in English, but has been translated into English. Words pronounced originally in English have been put between quotation marks.

exchange took place," as shown in the text in Box 22.3, several options are proposed and discussed: "would taken," "would ha ...," "would take place," "would, will ...," "should have been taking place" and again "would take place." The discussion in the excerpt presented in Box 22.4 stops at this point. However, after having completed and re-read the reconstructed version of the text, "would take place" is cancelled once more and finally replaced by "took place."

The excerpt in Box 22.4 illustrates the extensive deliberations going on between the participants before deciding to commit something to paper. It also shows how students are co-constructing sentences and how they hesitate between the use of various structures before a final decision is taken. One may wonder if learners would have used the correct verbal structures in the reconstructed text, if they had not been offered the opportunity to discuss these constructions together. Oral interaction may thus enhance the quality of a written text. This is precisely the aim of dictogloss: a task in which L2 learners have to collaborate, both in the oral and the written mode, in order to complete the task, and as a result the two modes will reinforce each other.

Future directions

As demonstrated by the research findings presented in the preceding sections, a contradictory picture emerges concerning the superiority of either the oral or the written mode with regard to grammatical complexity, lexical complexity, and accuracy. The fact that a straightforward conclusion with respect to the effect of mode cannot be drawn has several reasons. First of all, the number of studies that have investigated the effect of mode is rather small. Secondly, the tasks the participants in the studies were submitted to vary from simple descriptive tasks to more complex reasoning tasks. Thirdly, these studies differ from each other with respect to the kind of learners involved in the experiment, their source and target languages, and the performance measures which have been used. Fourthly, it is possible that learners may have particular preferences for either the oral or the written mode, as suggested by Weissberg (2000) and finally, the superiority of a particular mode may also be constrained by the level of L2 proficiency, as observed by both Granfeldt (2007) and Ferrari and Nuzzo (2009).

With regard to the distinction between oral and written tasks we have presented some examples of so-called "typical" speaking and writing tasks. We should, however, keep in mind, that there is not so much of what could be defined a prototypical oral task or a unique writing task, as a large number of tasks can be performed in both modes, as demonstrated by the dictogloss task. This allows teachers and researchers to compare the oral and written production of their learners and to detect possible differences in task outcomes, depending on whether the task has been carried out orally or in the written mode.

Our overview of studies that have investigated the role of mode in SLA shows that we are left with many questions of what is exactly the effect of speaking and writing tasks on L2 performance. We therefore conclude this chapter by suggesting three research questions which in our view are worth investigating in order to get a a better insight in the effect of mode on L2 performance. These questions are:

(1) How do task type and task complexity relate to the effect of mode?
(2) To which extent is the superiority of either the oral or the written mode constrained by the proficiency level of the learners?
(3) How can preferences of learners for either the oral or the written mode be explained?

References

Bulté, B. and Housen, A. (2009). The development of lexical proficiency in L2 speaking and writing tasks by Dutch-speaking learners of French in Brussels. Paper presented in the colloquium "Tasks across modalities", *Task Based Language Teaching Conference*, Lancaster 2009.

Daniels, P. T. and Bright, W. (Eds.) (1996). *The world's writing systems*. Oxford: Oxford University Press.

Ellis, R. (2003). *Task-based language learning and teaching*. Oxford: Oxford University Press.

Ellis, R. (Ed.) (2005). *Planning and task performance in a second language*. Amsterdam: John Benjamins.

Ellis, R. (2009). The differential effects of three types of task planning on the fluency, complexity and accuracy in L2 oral production. *Applied Linguistics, 30*(4), 474–509.

Fayol, M. (1997). *Des idées au texte. Psychologie cognitive de la production verbale, orale et écrite*. Paris: Presses Universitaires de France.

Ferrari, S. and Nuzzo, E. (2009) Meeting the challenge of diversity with TBLT: Connecting speaking and writing in mainstream classrooms. Paper presented in the colloquium "Tasks across modalities", *Task Based Language Teaching Conference*, Lancaster 2009.

Foster, P. and Skehan, P. (1996). The influence of planning on performance in task-based learning. *Studies in Second Language Acquisition, 18*(3), 299–324.

Gilabert, R., Barón, J., and Llanes, A. (2009). Manipulating cognitive complexity across task types and its impact on learners' interaction during oral performance. *International Review of Applied Linguistics, 47*(3–4), 367–395.

Grabowski, J. (2005). Speaking, writing, and memory span performance: Replicating the Bourdin and Fayol results on cognitive load in German children and adults. In L. Allal and J. Dolz (Eds.), *Proceedings Writing 2004*. Geneva (CH): Adcom Productions (CD-ROM).

Grabowski, J. (2007). The writing superiority effect in the verbal recall of knowledge: Sources and determinants. In G. Rijlaarsdam (Series Ed.) and M. Torrance, L. van Waes, and D. Galbraith (Volume Eds.) *Writing and cognition: Research and applications (Studies in Writing)* (pp. 165–179). Amsterdam: Elsevier.

Granfeldt, J. (2007). Speaking and writing in L2 French: Exploring effects on fluency, accuracy and complexity. In S. Van Daele, A. Housen, F. Kuiken, M. Pierrard, and I. Vedder (Eds.), *Complexity, accuracy and fluency in second language use, learning and teaching* (pp. 87–98). Brussels: KVAB.

Houck, N. and Gass, S. M. (1996). Non-native refusals: A methodological perspective. In S. Gass and J. Neu (Eds.), *Speech acts across culture* (pp. 45–64). Berlin: Mouton de Gruyter.

Kormos, J. and Trebits, A. (2009). Task-related differences across modes of performance. Paper presented at the *Task Based Language Teaching Conference*, Lancaster 2009.

Kuiken, F., Mos, M., and Vedder, I. (2005). Cognitive task complexity and second language writing performance. In S. Foster-Cohen, M. P. García Mayo, and J. Cenoz (Eds.), *Eurosla Yearbook* (Vol. 5, pp. 195–222). Amsterdam: John Benjamins.

Kuiken, F. and Vedder, I. (2002a). Collaborative writing in L2: The effect of group interaction on text quality. In G. Rijlaarsdam, M. L. Barbier, and S. Ransdell (Eds.), *New directions for research in L2 writing* (pp. 168–187). Dordrecht: Kluwer Academic Publishers.

Kuiken, F. and Vedder, I. (2002b). The effect of interaction in acquiring the grammar of a second language. *International Journal of Educational Research, 37*, 343–358.

Kuiken, F. and Vedder, I. (2005). Noticing and the role of interaction in promoting language learning. In A. Housen and M. Pierrard (Eds.), *Investigations in instructed second language acquisition* (pp. 353–381). Berlin/New York: Mouton de Gruyter.

Kuiken, F. and Vedder, I. (2007a). Cognitive task complexity and linguistic performance in French L2 writing. In M. P. García Mayo (Ed.), *Investigating tasks in formal language learning* (pp. 117–135). Clevedon, UK: Multilingual Matters.

Kuiken, F. and Vedder, I. (2007b). Task complexity and measures of linguistic performance in L2 writing. *International Review of Applied Linguistics, 45*(3), 261–284.

Kuiken, F. and Vedder, I. (2007c). Cognitive task complexity and written output in Italian and French as a foreign language. *Journal of Second Language Writing, 17*(1), 48–60.

Kuiken, F. and Vedder, I. (2009). Tasks across modalities: The influence of task complexity on linguistic performance in L2 writing and speaking. Paper presented in the colloquium "Tasks across modalities", *Task Based Language Teaching Conference*, Lancaster 2009.

Kuiken, F. and Vedder, I. (2011). Task complexity and linguistic performance in L2 writing and speaking: The effect of mode. In P. Robinson (Ed.), *Second language task complexity: Researching the Cognition Hypothesis of language learning and performance* (pp. 91–104). Amsterdam: John Benjamins.

Kuiken, F., Vedder, I., and Gilabert, R. (2010). Communicative adequacy and linguistic complexity in L2 writing. In I. Bartning, M. Martin, and I. Vedder (Eds.), Communicative proficiency and linguistic development: Intersections between SLA and language testing research. *Eurosla Monograph Series*: 1, 81–100.

Laufer, B. and Nation, P. (1995). Vocabulary size and use: Lexical richness in L2 written production. *Applied Linguistics*, *16*, 33–51.

Laufer, B. and Nation, P. (1999). A vocabulary-size test of controlled productive ability. *Language Testing*, *13*, 151–172.

Long, M. H. (1980). Input, interaction and second language acquisition. Doctoral dissertation. UCLA. *Dissertation Abstracts International*, *41*, 5082.

Long, M. H. (1985). Input and second language acquisition theory. In S. M. Gass and C. Madden (Eds.), *Input in second language acquisition* (pp. 377–393). Rowley, MA: Newbury House.

Malvern, D. and Richards, B. (1997). A new measure of lexical diversity. In A. Byran and A. Wray (Eds.), *Evaluating models of language* (pp. 58–71). Clevedon: Multilingual Matters.

Malvern, D. and Richards, B. (2002). Investigating accommodation in language proficiency interviews using a new measure of lexical diversity. *Language Testing*, *19*, 85–104.

Malvern, D., Richards, B., Chipere, N., and Durán, P. (2004). *Lexical diversity and language development: Quantification and assessment*. Basingstoke, Englans: Palgrave Macmillan.

Martínez-Flor, A. (2006). Task effects on EFL learners productions of suggestions: A focus on elicited phone messages and emails. *Miscelánea: A journal of English and American Studies*, *33*, 47–64.

Pica, T., Kang, H. -S., and Sauro, S. (2006). Information gap tasks: Their multiple roles and contributions to interaction research methodology. *Studies in Second Language Acquisition*, 28(2), 301–338.

Prabhu, N. S. (1980). *Reactions and predictions (Special issue)*. Bulletin 4(1). Bangalore: Regional Institute of English, South India.

Prabhu, N. S. (1984). Procedural syllabuses. In T. E. Read (Ed.), *Trends in language syllabus design* (pp. 272–280). Singapore: Singapore University Press/RELC.

Prabhu, N. S. (1987). *Second language pedagogy*. Oxford: Oxford University Press.

Robinson, P. (1995). Task complexity and second language narrative discourse. *Language Learning*, *45*(1), 99–145.

Robinson, P. (2007). Task complexity, theory of mind, and intentional reasoning: Effects on L2 speech production, interaction, uptake and perceptions of task difficulty. *International Review of Applied Linguistics*, *43*, 1–31.

Skehan, P. (1998). *A cognitive approach to language learning*. Oxford: Oxford University Press.

Skehan, P. (2001). Tasks and language performance assessment. In M. Bygate, P. Skehan, and M. Swain (Eds.), *Researching pedagogic tasks: Second language learning, teaching, and testing* (pp. 167–185). London: Longman.

Skehan, P. (2009). Modelling second language performance: Integrating complexity, accuracy, fluency and lexis. *Applied Linguistics*, *30*(4), 510–532.

Skehan, P. and Foster, P. (1997). Task type and processing conditions as influences on foreign language performance. *Language Teaching Research*, *1*(3), 185–211.

Swain, M. and Lapkin, S. (2001). Focus on form through collaborative dialogue: Exploring task effects. In M. Bygate, P. Skehan, and M. Swain (Eds.), *Researching pedagogic tasks. Second language learning, teaching and testing* (pp. 99–118). Harlow: Pearson Education.

Tavakoli, P. and Foster, P. (2011). Task design and second language performance: The effect of narrative type on learner output. *Language Learning*, *61*(51), 37–72.

Tavakoli, P. and Skehan, P. (2005). Planning, task structure, and performance testing. In R. Ellis (Ed.), *Strategic planning and task performance in a second language* (pp. 230–273). Amsterdam: John Benjamins.

Towell, R., Hawkins, R., and Bazergui, N. (1996). The development of fluency in advanced learners of French. *Applied Linguistics*, *17*(1), 84–119.

Ur, P. (1988). *Grammar practice activities. A practical guide for teachers*. Cambridge: Cambridge University Press.

Wajnryb, R. (1990). *Grammar dictation*. Oxford: Oxford University Press.

Weissberg, R. (2000). Developmental relationships in the acquisition of English writing vs speech. *Learning and Instruction*, *10*, 37–53.

Willis, D. (1991). *Collins Cobuild Student's Grammar*. London: HarperCollins Publishers.

Yu, G. (2009). Lexical diversity in writing and speaking task performances. *Applied Linguistics Advance Access*. Published on June 4, 2009. doi:10.1093/applin/amp024.

Yuan, F. and Ellis, R. (2003). The effects of pre-task planning and on-line planning on fluency, complexity and accuracy in L2 monologic oral production. *Applied Linguistics*, *24*(1), 1–27.

Part V
Individual differences

23

Language aptitude

Peter Skehan

Introduction

This chapter reviews a wide range of issues in language aptitude. After a contextualizing, historical introduction, sections then cover the role of context in aptitude functioning; the relationship of aptitude and dyslexia; and the wider analysis of memory that is now relevant for aptitude. Then some contemporary aptitude debates are explored, comprising the relevance of aptitude to second language acquisition (SLA), the importance of aptitude in understanding critical period effects, and proposals which have been made for aptitude complexes. A brief survey is provided of developments in aptitude measurement, as well as a discussion of the pedagogic implications of aptitude work. This leads to a conclusion which assesses current perceptions of the nature and relevance of aptitude, and outlines challenges for the future.

Historical discussion

Accounts of foreign language aptitude often start with an historical introduction, as though the study of aptitude is mostly in the past. This review will also, but it will later attempt to justify the claim that aptitude research has recently been one of the revitalized areas in applied linguistics and SLA. It is now changing from a marginal position to one where it is center-stage.

The dominating figure in language aptitude research has been J. B. Carroll. Carroll was a cognitive psychologist (before that term became commonplace), and the approach he took to foreign language aptitude was typical of his wider approach to studying the structure of cognitive abilities (as represented in his life's work, published in 1993, *Human Cognitive Abilities*). The assumptions he gave us were that (a) the constellation of abilities that capture the notion of foreign language aptitude is distinct from other cognitive abilities, including intelligence, (b) aptitude is fairly stable in nature, and (c) is itself componential. Carroll's contributions fall into two areas. First, he has been the most significant theorist of language aptitude with his four factor view of aptitude. The factors are phonemic coding ability (the capacity to retain, through appropriate coding, unfamiliar auditory material); inductive language learning ability (a talent to find generalizations based on language input, and then be able to extrapolate and produce language based on such generalizations); grammatical sensitivity (the ability to identify the functions of words in sentences); and associative learning (the capacity to make links between verbal elements such as first language (L1) and second language (L2) words). His second area of contribution is more practical. He devised a large number of potential foreign language aptitude sub-tests, administered these to large numbers of people, as well as achievement tests in the languages they were learning, and then explored the relationships (a) between the different aptitude tests themselves, and (b) between the aptitude tests and the achievement tests. On this basis he rejected the tests which did not predict achievement, and he also rejected tests that duplicated one another. In so doing, and through exploratory factor analysis, he had empirical support for the four factor view of aptitude outlined above.

This led to the culmination of his more practical work. With Stanley Sapon, he was the creator of the Modern Languages Aptitude Test (MLAT) (Carroll and Sapon, 1957), a practical and comprehensive system, with associated norms, for assessing aptitude. This test battery contains five sub-tests, respectively Number Learning, Phonetic Script, Hidden Words, Words in Sentences, and Paired Associates. Curiously, and rather disappointedly, the focus in this test is on achieving predictive power, rather than explanation (Robinson, 2005). So sub-tests, somewhat ironically, are not always direct measures of the four constructs Carroll proposed, for example, number learning measures both phonemic coding ability and associative memory. In addition, one of the constructs, inductive language learning ability, is not represented in the battery at all. In any case, as prediction goes, the MLAT (and other aptitude batteries (see below)) have been successful. They generally produced correlations of between 0.30 and 0.55 between MLAT scores and subsequent achievement tests. Generally these validity coefficients are higher when instruction is carried out in more controlled conditions, for example, intensive instruction, and with unselected students. These correlations may not seem exceptional, but by the standards of correlations in language learning, these values are about as high as one gets, with only motivation scores being comparable.

Carroll's view of aptitude, and the MLAT as a practical measurement tool, have been dominant since the late 1950s. Other batteries were subsequently developed, for example, Pimsleur's Language Aptitude Battery (PLAB) (Pimsleur, 1966; which targets younger, i.e., school-age, learners and emphasizes a more auditory perspective), the Defense Language Aptitude Battery (DLAB) (Petersen and Al-Haik, 1976) developed by the US military and intended, not particularly successfully, to be more discriminating than the MLAT with high ability learners; and VORD (Parry and Child, 1990), where VORD means *word* in the artificial language which was used in this test. There were also other less comprehensive tests, such as the York Language Aptitude Test (Green, 1975), which only assesses inductive language learning ability. The original MLAT test was for English L1 speakers learning other languages. Now versions are available in other languages. Some of these, such as for French, are fairly directly translated (and validated) forms, while others, such as for Hungarian or Japanese (Sasaki, 1991, 1996), required considerably more modification and validation. More recently developed measurement tools will be covered later in this chapter.

Core issues

Aptitude and learning context

The MLAT and the PLAB especially were constructed largely in relation to the prediction of success in instructed language learning contexts and at a time when the prevailing methodology, at least in the USA, was audiolingualism. Language teaching has changed considerably since then, and the field of SLA has grown hugely. During the 1970s and 1980s, therefore, there was a widespread belief that aptitude was only relevant to a bygone age (Krashen, 1981). A particularly relevant type of aptitude research is therefore anything which explores the potential of aptitude measures for acquisition-rich or informal learning.

One study of this type was conducted in Canada. Wesche (1981) showed that one can use aptitude information to explore interactions between aptitude profiles (analytic vs. memory-oriented learners) and teaching methodology (analytic vs. situational), with matches of learner aptitude profile and methodology leading to satisfaction and higher achievement, and mismatches leading to the reverse. Another early study was that of Reves (1982) who explored whether aptitude is predictive not simply in classroom contexts but also for informal learning. In Israel, she compared L1 Arabic instructed learners of English with comparable informal learners of Hebrew. She showed that aptitude is predictive in both of these situations, and indeed, that aptitude was the strongest predictor of achievement even in the informal situation. These two studies are consistent with aptitude having *general* relevance, not simply relevance to more conventional classroom situations. Related to Wesche's study, Skehan (1986b) explored language learning in the British Army, and demonstrated that, in the context of a communicative approach to Arabic instruction for English L1 learners, aptitude was a high predictor of achievement. He also argued that one should consider aptitude profiles. Like Wesche he distinguished between analysis-oriented and memory-oriented learners, and showed that success could be achieved either by an analytic profile or a memory profile.

There have been other, more recent studies which have examined whether there is any connection between aptitude and instructional options. Harley and Hart (1997) explored whether there were differences in aptitude relevance as a function of age. Researching in Canada with French immersion programs, they used two measures of memory (one paired associates test from the MLAT, and another measure of memory for text) and one of language analysis, the Language Analysis sub-test from PLAB. They researched with two groups of 11th-grade students—those who had had early immersion (i.e., starting in grade 1) and those who had had late immersion (i.e., starting in grade 7). The early immersion children tended to outperform the late immersion children for oral-aural skills, but were in turn outperformed on tests of writing. Other areas showed no significant differences. Interestingly, the early immersion students generated significant correlations between the memory-oriented aptitude scores and achievement, while the late immersion children showed one significant correlation and that was with the language analysis test.

Erlam (2005) also investigated the relevance of aptitude measures to different instructional contexts. She used a phonemic coding ability test, Part 4 of the MLAT (Words in Sentences), and a working memory test emphasizing the phonological buffer (see below). Participants were 60 students in their second year of the study of French. Three different instructional methods were used: deductive instruction, that is, rule presentation followed by form-focused activities; structured input instruction, that is, rule presentation followed by input-based activities based on VanPatten's work; and inductive instruction, that is, practice activities which induced students to identify rules. All methods targeted object pronouns in French. Broadly, the deductive approach was superior to the Structured Input approach, which in turn was superior to the Inductive approach. The lowest correlations between the aptitude and achievement scores were for the deductive group, suggesting that more structured presentation "equalizes" the effects of instruction (an issue raised by Carroll (1965) many years ago). Correlations were slightly more evident with the other two conditions, particularly for the written achievement test.

Kormos and Safar (2008) have also investigated aptitude linked to instructional context. They studied a group of 15–16 year old beginner Hungarian learners of English following a one-year intensive course, in which they received more than 500 hours of instruction. The course was characterized as communicative. Aptitude was measured through a modified forms of the Phonetic Script sub-test of the MLAT, Pimsleur's Language Analysis sub-test, MLAT IV, Words in Sentences, and MLAT-V, Paired Associates. Proficiency was measured through the Cambridge First Certificate test. No reliability or revalidation indices are given for any of these measures. Correlations between aptitude measures and proficiency measures are low, with values for total proficiency scores at 0.34 (Phonetic Script, $p < 0.05$); 0.26 (Language Analysis, ns., although two component proficiency tests, Writing and Listening, do generate significant correlations). The authors interpret these as low correlations where aptitude information is used in communicative contexts.

Quite clearly here the jury is still out on the relationship between aptitude testing and communicative teaching contexts. There are correlations, but these vary in strength from study to study. In any case, studies are not strictly comparable. What we can conclude is that one cannot dismiss aptitude as irrelevant from communicative instructional contexts, and that more, finer-grained research may be useful in resolving such issues. (See also Chapter 33 by (Jessica) Williams, this volume.)

Aptitude and dyslexia

Carroll (1965) proposed the construct of phonemic coding ability for the component of aptitude concerned with the processing of sound, that is, the ability to analyze sound as this influences how sounds can be retained for more than a few seconds. In slight contrast, Pimsleur (1968) proposed a sound–symbol association ability, a simpler ability which only reflects the capacity to learn and operate new sound–symbol mappings. This area has been developed considerably but from a different direction since the initial formulation. Sparks and colleagues (Sparks and Ganschow, 1991; Sparks et al., 1992) have argued that tests of phonemic coding ability bear a close relationship to tests for mild dyslexia. In each case, the focus seems to be on how there are differences in the ways sound is processed and how it is related to symbol. Essentially, Carroll's notion of analyzing sound so that it can be retained is close to how symbols can be used to impose some structure on sound that is heard, in such a way that the dual coding involved enables more robust memory. With L2 learners, problems in this area may *not* mean that there is poorer "raw" discrimination, but rather that sound is not processed efficiently, presumably not being segmented so effectively into words, and certainly not being analysed into a state of distinctness so that it can be more easily retained. With mild dyslexics there is a problem in linking sound representations to the symbols on the page which have to be read. All this seems to argue that it is advantageous to be able to link sound and symbol. With dyslexics, the lack of connection with (well understood native language) sounds means that the symbols on the page have less meaning and processability. With L2 learners it may be the other way around–the sounds do not link with a representational system in another modality. Sparks and Ganschow (1991) propose the Linguistic Coding Deficit hypothesis to account for these two types of difficulty.

Aptitude and memory

The analysis provided of phonemic coding ability and dyslexia suggests that Carroll was extra-ordinarily prescient in this area. Things are not quite the same with memory. The MLAT, practically, and Carroll's four factor theory focus on associative memory, the form of memory dominant in psychology at the time of development of the MLAT. Psychological perspectives on memory have changed radically since that time. For example, Skehan (1982) argued that the capacity to analyze larger quantities of material so that it can be retained more effectively, and the capacity to memorize material lacking in familiarity are also relevant to aptitude.

But easily the most significant development in the area of memory is the importance now attached to working memory (Baddeley, 2007; Miyake and Shah, 1999). In the current volume, Chapter 26 by (John) Williams explicates working memory functioning. For the purposes of the current chapter, we only need to note different measurement procedures for different working memory components. Measures which emphasize the central executive tend to use span tasks where computation is a major influence on the memory score (Waters and Caplan, 2003), whereas measures which emphasize the phonological buffer tend to use nonword repetition tasks, for example, words like "tablus" and "acklar" (Gathercole, 2006). The correlation between working memory scores on each of these measures is generally in the range 0.30 to 0.40 (Wen, 2009), which suggests (a) they are not measuring exactly the same thing, and that to have a high executive working memory does not mean one has a high phonological buffer, and (b) to use just one of these measures in an aptitude study is not enough: both need to be included. Not only does this measurement problem have an impact on psychological studies, but it is also relevant for any assessment of the relevance of working memory for foreign language aptitude.

One can see the relevance of working memory, and its centrality in language aptitude (Miyake and Friedman, 1998) by considering the following stages in L2 processing, linked with potential working memory involvement:

Input processing	More phonological memory enables longer stretches of language to be processed, and parsing therefore to be more efficient
Noticing and handling form and meaning simultaneously	Greater capacity can enable parts of input to be extracted, and enable form-meaning connections to be made
Pattern identification	More input available enables patterns of greater length to be identified
Complexification/restructuring	More capacity enables connections to be made between current working memory and what is held in long-term memory, as well as to enable long-term memory to be changed
Error avoidance	More working memory capacity enables attention to be directed to monitoring and error avoided
Response to feedback	More memory enables attention to be directed to feedback, and the incorporation of feedback into performance, as well as the potential to change long-term memory
Automatization/Lexicalization	More material in working memory enables chunking which can be transferred to long term memory

The suggestions in the table, though, are conjecture. We need next to review the evidence on working memory as aptitude. Interestingly, most research has concerned vocabulary learning. Baddeley *et al.* (1998) propose that the phonological buffer is a "language learning device," particularly important in the learning of new L1 words by children, as evidenced in research such as Gathercole (1999). Service and Kohonen (1995) have extended these L1 claims to L2 vocabulary learning (English words by L1 Finnish learners), as has Cheung, *et al.* (1996), with Cantonese L1 and English L2 learning, and Masoura and Gathercole (1999) with Greek L1 and English L2. Papagno and Vallar (1995) made similar claims for older learners with L1 Italian and L2 Russian.

There are different views on the role of phonological working memory (PWM) with grammar and morphology learning. Ellis and colleagues (Ellis and Sinclair, 1996; Ellis, 1996), on the basis of a theoretical outlook emphasizing chunk learning and the importance of frequency, (see Chapter 12 by Ellis, this volume) report data on PWM correlations with morphological learning and agreement rules. Williams and Lovatt (2003, 2005) report relationships between PWM and the learning of sequences of familiar morphemes important in grammar learning with a semi-artificial language. French and O'Brien (2008) report PWM–L2 grammar learning correlations which are independent of measures of vocabulary learning. Strikingly here, most of the studies reporting correlations with vocabulary or grammar learning have used phonological working memory measures rather than executive working memory (EWM) tests (although EWM tests have figured more in studies of performance, rather than learning (Fortkamp, 1999)). A different approach to relating working memory to acquisition is to explore how larger working memory is associated with a greater capacity to benefit from and incorporate feedback. Mackey *et al.* (2002) investigated this possibility and were able to show that high working memory participants in their study were able to benefit more from feedback, and notice more about the helpful information they were being given incidentally during interaction.

There have also been studies that have examined relationships between (phonological) working memory and L2 development over longer timespans. French (2006) investigated PWM relationships in an L1 French–L2 English five-month intensive program and reported significant correlations at the outset and the end of this program, and also PWM correlated with gain scores but only for the lower proficiency group in the study. O'Brien *et al.* (2006; 2007) also report significant PWM correlations with L2 oral development in a study abroad context for older learners. Kormos and Safar (2008, and see above) report significant PWM correlations with Hungarian secondary school students on a one-year intensive program performing on a battery of tests taken from the Cambridge First Certificate Exam paper.

Taken together, the various studies do indicate that consistent correlations are obtained between working memory measures and language development measures, and so one can consider that working memory is a fundamental component of a foreign language aptitude (Miyake and Friedman, 1998). But an interesting final point is to ask whether we are dealing with a domain-general or a domain-specific measure (DeKeyser and Juffs, 2005). One additional facet of this debate arises from work by Chan *et al.* (2011). Influenced by Levelt and Wheeldon's (1994) claim that in early life children acquire L1 syllabaries, Chan *et al.* (2011) propose that a major task in L2 learning is to acquire the syllable structure of the target language. In effect, this represents the ability to handle and memorize the specific sound sequences of the L2, and goes beyond the more general abilities represented by phonemic coding ability. Chan *et al.* (2011) propose therefore that tests of phonological working memory can be produced more effectively by using nonwords for repetition which reflect the syllable structure of the target language. They are proposing that there is a very domain-specific phonological element in language learning, and phonemic coding ability and phonological working memory can be brought closely together to provide the basis for more effective measures.

Aptitude and second language acquisition

At the beginning of this chapter, claims and evidence were discussed on whether aptitude applies to formal learning and not acquisition. One response would be to try to relate aptitude to developments within SLA theory. If an acquisitional process or stage implicates individual differences, then we have the possibility of an aptitude component.

One can focus on six stages that are involved, notionally separately, in the process of gaining control over a L2. (The stages are adapted slightly from those discussed with working memory.):

- Input processing and noticing
- Pattern identification
- Complexification/restructuring/integration
- Error avoidance
- Repertoire and salience creation
- Automatization/Lexicalization

The first three are concerned with apprehension of the rule-based nature of language, and the capacity to complexify and reorganize these rules as learners are able to move from exemplars to systems (see Chapter 16 by VanPatten on input processing and Chapter 14 by Pienemann and

Keßler on processability theory, this volume). This requires flexibility as an interlanguage system grows, and it also requires a capacity to respond to feedback (see chapters by Loewen (Chapter 2), on feedback, and Mackey *et al.* on interactionist approaches, Chapter 1, this volume). This portrayal clarifies some central questions regarding aptitude. These concern the theories which account for L2 development, and then the ways that any language learning capacity appropriate to acquiring a rule-based system can be sampled and measured. For example, if one subscribes to a Universal Grammar account of SLA, one might use this analysis to clarify what the progression would be for a L2 learner. Similarly, if one takes a cognitive approach, for example, that of Processability Theory (Pienemann, 1998, and Pienemann and Keßler, Chapter 14, this volume), then one would expect developmental progression to be consistent with the stages that Pienemann describes, and so any aptitude test could be organized to follow this sequence (as in Skehan and Chan, ms).

What is interesting in the aptitude field, of course, is that the "sampling frames" used in structure-oriented aptitude sub-tests are not informed by any of the above considerations. The Grammatical Sensitivity (Part 4) sub-test of the MLAT appears to have little sampling progression or organization beyond different word categories in English. The various inductive language learning sub-tests are based on some loose sense of increasing complexity of structures, but that is all. This seems a promising area for research.

Returning now to the six points above, the second set of three stages are radically different in nature and are concerned much more with control and access to material already in long-term memory. The implication for aptitude would be more the need to measure speed of learning and proceduralization. One assumes that learners vary in these areas, and so an important part of aptitude would be how learners convert noticing and pattern insight into fluent and error-free performance. Once again, proposals within L2 learning for chunk learning (Ellis, 2005) and frequency effects (Ellis, 2007, and Chapter 12, this volume) would be highly relevant. It may be that speed of learning and automatization are distinct from speed of pattern identification.

The issue of aptitude and acquisition is not all theorizing. There have been some interesting acquisition-aware studies. For example, Robinson (1995) used aptitude results in a study involving four intervention conditions: instructed (in which learners were given explicit instruction, that is, the non-acquisitional context); rule-search (in which they were given material and told to search for a rule); implicit (in which learners were given material to study, but were not told to search the material for the rule it contained); and incidental (in which learners were given a meaning related task, based on material containing the same target rule, but again were uninformed of this rule). The study involved two rules, one deemed easy and one hard. All conditions generated significant correlations between learning and aptitude, except for the incidental one, and this applied to both easy and hard rules. In other words, aptitude (measured by two sub-tests from the MLAT: paired associates and words-in-sentences) seemed relevant for acquisition-rich as well as acquisition-poor contexts. Similarly, DeGraaf (1997) compared a rule-explanation with a non-explanation condition for the learning of an artificial language, and also of Spanish, and also like Robinson, with a comparison of simple and complex rules. DeGraaf also used aptitude information, and correlated this with test performance. He reports significant correlations for both the rule-explanation condition and the non-explanation condition, for both the artificial language and Spanish, and for both the simple and the complex rules. The conclusion seems to be here that aptitude information is relevant for predicting success both with implicit as well as explicit conditions.

Aptitude and a critical period

The debate on the existence of a critical period for language development, during which language might be learned in a manner qualitatively different from learning in other domains, has raged for many years (Bialystok and Hakuta, 1994; Johnson and Newport, 1989, and see Byrnes, Chapter 31, and also DeKeyser, Chapter 27, this volume). DeKeyser (2000) working with Hungarian immigrants to the USA, proposed that post-critical period arrivals who had high levels of achievement, that is, learners who seemed to defy the existence of a critical period, had high language aptitude. However, Bialystok (2002) criticized DeKeyser's claims on the basis that numbers were very small.

Abrahamsson and Hyltenstam (2008) approached the issue slightly differently. In one of their studies, they identified over 100 Spanish L1 speakers of Swedish who passed for native speakers, from whom they were able to identify two matched groups, distinguished by age on arrival, with the age of 12 set as the cut-off. Both groups were then given aptitude and grammaticality judgment tests, this latter both written and auditory. Abrahamsson and Hyltenstam (2008) show that for arrivals before the age of 12, aptitude is widely distributed, and so lower as well as higher aptitude young arrivals generally meet the "pass for native speaker" criterion. In contrast, all those who arrived in Sweden after the age of 12 but who are able to pass for native speakers have high aptitude; in other words, none of the high achievers in Swedish had low foreign language aptitude. Abrahamsson and Hyltenstam (2008) interpret this to mean that high foreign language aptitude is required in order to compensate for late arrival. Abrahamsson and Hyltenstam (2008) have also explored the role of foreign language aptitude in language attrition and report that higher language aptitude Spanish L1 immigrants to Sweden lost Spanish less than lower aptitude immigrants, suggesting that aptitude here can serve as some sort of compensation for lack of input.

These findings connect with an earlier study by Skehan (1986a). This reported on a follow-up of more than 100 children studied in the Bristol Language Project, whose L1 development was carefully monitored for rate and route (Wells, 1985). Some 12 years after the original L1 data collection, these children were given aptitude tests when they were 13 to 15 years old, and despite the time interval between the collection of the L1 and the foreign language aptitude data, there were significant correlations between rate of L1 development and level of language analytic ability, at around 0.40 to 0.50. In other words, if one assumes that differences in L1 acquisition rate reflect differences in some sort of language endowment, this seems connected with subsequent levels of foreign language aptitude. This is consistent with a speculation of Carroll's that foreign language aptitude is the residue of L1 learning ability (Carroll, 1973).

Aptitude complexes

Earlier there were sections on the linkage between aptitude and context and also on aptitude linked to SLA processes. These insights are developed even further in Robinson's Aptitude Complex Hypothesis (Robinson, 2007). Robinson looks at aptitude abilities not through a componential approach, linked to techniques such as factor analysis, but in terms of acquisition processes. Some of these are similar to the proposals in Skehan (2002), and reflect stages of processing and acquisition. At the most fine-grained level, Robinson proposes *primary cognitive abilities*, which comprise perceptual speed, pattern recognition, PWM capacity, speed of PWM, analogies, the capacity to infer word meaning, memory and speed of memory for text, grammatical sensitivity, and rote memory. Robinson relates each of these to *ability tests*, where these are available. But at a higher level, he relates pairs of primary cognitive abilities to even broader ability factors. Hence perceptual speed and pattern recognition come together to underpin *noticing the gap*, while PWM capacity and speed of PWM underpin *memory for contingent speech*. The other three broad ability factors are *deep semantic processing*, *memory for contingent text*, and *metalinguistic rule rehearsal*.

Robinson builds upon this structure to discuss aptitude complexes, in which these broader ability patterns are linked to different learning contexts. He emphasizes four such learning contexts. These are:

- Learning via recasting (noticing; memory for contingent speech)
- Incidental learning—oral mode (memory for contingent speech; deep semantic processing)
- Incidental learning—written mode (memory for contingent text; deep semantic processing)
- Explicit rule learning (memory for contingent text; metalinguistic rule rehearsal)

Each of these learning contexts is linked to particular aptitudinal complexes as shown in the parenthesized material. In each case the two ability factors interact orthogonally, and generate a two-by-two arrangement. The context of learning from recasting, for example, draws upon the ability factors of *noticing* and *memory for contingent speech* (MCS), so that one can have people who are high in noticing and high in MCS, low in noticing and low in MCS, high in noticing and low in MCS, low in noticing and high in MCS. The other learning contexts are similarly underpinned by the two ability factors shown.

The assumption is that it is interactions which account for learning, and so it is possible to imagine learners who will do well in one context but poorly in others. The approach, in other words, formalizes the relevance of discussing strengths and weaknesses in learning and how they manifest themselves (cf., the earlier work by Wesche, 1981). What is needed next is a research program to validate the testable claims which are being made. This testing needs to address a range of issues:

- The validity of the ability tests as measures of the different primary cognitive abilities
- The existence, relevance, and separation of the different primary cognitive abilities
- The viability of using a median-split approach to characterize high and low levels
- The relevance of the ability factors for the four learning contexts.

Data and common elicitation measures

We now examine some practical measurement concerns. As indicated earlier, the MLAT and PLAB were developed in the 1950s and 1960s respectively. They are omnibus aptitude test batteries, and were easily available at the time of their development. After a time of difficulty in getting hold of them, they are now available again (www.2lti.com). These two tests are still, many years later, distinguished by their comprehensiveness, their accessibility, and the likelihood that they will still be used in research studies. Since their development, there have been other omnibus test batteries (see above), but each has the major disadvantage that it is restricted, as a result of its development in a military context. More recently we have seen the development of the CANAL-F test (Cognitive Ability for Novelty in Acquisition of Language—Foreign). This too has a military history, and is restricted. But it is a little different from the others in the openness and differentness of its rationale (Grigorenko et al., 2002). It was developed with awareness of cognitive psychology, and of attentional function, for example, processes like selective encoding, selective comparison, and selective combination. Its sampling frame includes concern for levels of processing (traditional language levels), modes of input (visual vs. oral), and encoding, storage and retrieval of information, raising the need to have immediate and delayed recall. The test is based on Ursulu, an invented language, and is an integrated test, i.e., the different sub-tests are cumulative in what they assess. There are five sections: learning meanings of neologisms from context, understanding the meaning of passages, continuous paired associates learning, sentential inference, and learning language rules. In validation studies, the CANAL-F scores correlate with MLAT scores, but also indicate distinctness from them, and also generated higher correlation with instructors' ratings on a language course than did MLAT scores (Grigorenko et al., 2002).

A different development is represented by the LLAMA aptitude test (Meara, 2005). First, this is a computer based test. Second, it is available for free download (www.lognostics.co.uk/tools/llama). Third, it is designed so that it is accessible without the L1 being a factor, beyond understanding initial instructions. The four-part test is loosely based on the MLAT. There are sub-tests on paired associates learning, on targetting sound-symbol association, and assessing grammatical inferencing. Finally there is a sub-test probing sound recognition which requires previously heard sound sequences to be identified in new sequences.

These two batteries can be compared with the MLAT, as Table 23.1 shows:

Table 23.1 A comparison of different foreign language aptitude batteries

	MLAT	LLAMA	CANAL-F
Phonemic Coding Ability	+	+	
Grammatical Sensitivity	+		
Inductive Language Learning		+	+
Paired Associates	+	+	+
Working Memory		+	
Attentional Processing			+
Working Memory to Long-term Memory Connections			+

The MLAT seems more limited in coverage, and even omits Carroll's inductive language learning factor. LLAMA is broader, avoids grammatical sensitivity, but adds a receptive interpretation of inductive language ability as well as more focus on working memory. CANAL-F is the broadest battery of all. It focuses on language analysis and memory (although without an overt concern for working memory), downplays sound, but is far more concerned than the other batteries with attentional function and learning.

Applications

In principle, knowledge of foreign language aptitude could have considerable implications for language instruction. In practice, there is almost nothing to be said with any conviction! It is of no small interest to try to resolve the paradox implied in these two statements.

One can imagine aptitude information being used to achieve the following educational aims:

- Selection
- Counseling
- Remediation
- Instructional modification.

The first case would imply administrators being able to make decisions about course admission on the basis of aptitude information. Although, of course, selection is widespread within education, this is not a major application with aptitude. In fact, aptitude researchers have almost all been at pains to stress that aptitude information predicts *time* to achieve a criterion, and should not be used for exclusion purposes. Counseling and remediation are associated with Pimsleur's work with aptitude (Pimsleur, 1968; Pimsleur *et al.*, 1964). Counseling would imply using aptitude information to explain to learners where they might have difficulties, and so which types of methodology would be easiest. In this way, a reading course, rather than an oral-aural course, might be suggested to learners weak in, for example, phonemic coding ability. One could also counsel learners to be realistic about the length of time it will take them to reach particular levels of achievement. Remediation is also a potential rather than real application of aptitude. Again, imagining a learner with auditory difficulties, it might be suggested that pre-course, auditory training might be appropriate so that when instruction proper starts, the sorts of auditory processing difficulties that would otherwise be encountered could be forestalled.

The major potential area for educational application, however, has to be instructional modification. We have seen through Wesche (1981) such a use. This offers the prospect of increasing the overall effectiveness of instruction, as learners are matched with appropriate methodologies. More recently, through Robinson's work (2007), we have seen more theoretical and acquisition-informed proposals for the same thing. The potential is considerable, and as indicated earlier, it is surprising that more research has not been done in this area. Aptitude has been mainly relevant as a predictor in research studies, or has figured in theorizing language acquisition. Practitioners (the military apart) have avoided its use, perhaps because it is too cumbersome or because it does not fit well with textbooks and materials which assume only one kind of learner.

Future directions

The aptitude agenda that Carroll shaped half a century ago is still relevant. The changes that have occurred have been in the nature of our understanding of aptitude components and their inter-relationship, and also the addition of a greater concern for working memory and learning.

Carroll proposed a phonemic coding ability factor. We have seen that Sparks and colleagues (Ganschow et al., 1998) have linked this with similar problems experienced by mild dyslexics. The factor has endured well. But a question does remain. Phonemic coding ability involves unfamiliar sound. Phonological working memory generally uses nonword repetition. There might well be a close correspondence here. Perhaps the difference might be in the nature of the nonwordness (and see Chapter 26 in this volume by John Williams). If these are based on the syllable structure of the L1 then the words may not exist, but they may not be unfamiliar either, as it were. If they are based on the L2, as is proposed by Chan et al. (2011) then phonological nonword repetition working memory tests may be remarkably close to phonemic coding ability. Resolving this issue is the first challenge for the future.

Studies researching aptitude now seem to standardly include a measure of inductive language learning. This, and the grammatical sensitivity sub-test, generate the most consistent correlations in such research. These results indicate that aptitude may be central rather than marginal within SLA. As noted above, Carroll (1973) speculated that foreign language aptitude is the residue of a first language learning ability. To recast this insight in more modern, SLA-oriented terms, the issue is whether Universal Grammar is still available, or whether it is partially available (in the various ways "partial" has been defined (White, 2003)), or not available at all. The partial or not-available options might be consistent with L2 learning, in a post-critical period manner, representing explicit learning, perhaps with some specific language material involvement. This would chime with DeKeyser's (2000) interpretations of aptitude and Sasaki's (1996) proposals about aptitude linkages with intelligence. It would also be supported by studies which report a linkage between aptitude and metalinguistic abilities (Alderson et al., 1997; Elder et al., 1999). Roehr (2008), reporting such a connection, contrasts explicit and implicit knowledge systems, and explicit and implicit learning processes, linking aptitude with explicit knowledge and processes. But these interpretations would not chime with Skehan's (1986a) findings on first to foreign language aptitude correlations. The central point, though, is to explore the nature of L2 development through aptitude test studies. Things are not clear at present. As a later paragraph will indicate, perhaps progress here will be dependent on the development of more theory-oriented tests of inductive language learning ability. Establishing whether inductive language learning concerns implicit or explicit knowledge (Carpenter, 2008) is a second challenge for the future, and connects with the question regarding the relationship of aptitude to a critical period for language learning.

The third aptitude component introduced by Carroll was associative memory. As we have seen, this conceptualization of memory is limited, even if still relevant. Much wider interpretations of memory are now used, and in particular, the centrality of working memory has been recognized. Here there is something of a tension between working memory linked to ongoing performance (and so greater capacity to process input and feedback, and greater capacity to manipulate, through executive working memory, the contents of what is being currently held in consciousness) and working memory linked to long-term memory and the capacity for change. It is clear that both facets are important, and the range of studies showing working memory correlations is impressive. Perhaps in the future though, the connection between working memory and learning will become more important, as reflected, for example in the composition of CANAL-F.

What was not anticipated in the earlier aptitude work is the importance of alternative approaches to learning. This showed itself originally in proposals for learner types which contrasted analysis-oriented learners and memory-oriented learners (Skehan, 1986b; Wesche, 1981). More recently, Robinson (2007) has conceptualized the same approach in terms of aptitude complexes. At a theoretical level, this issue is relatively straightforward and addresses the complexity of language learning, integrates aptitude theorizing and SLA processes, and allows learner individuality to emerge. Empirically, though, this is going to be a difficult line to pursue, and it will be interesting to see how these insights lead to data-based studies, and aptitude tests which probe the speed with which learners can gain control of language material. This represents the third challenge for the future.

Next, if one accepts the argument that aptitude has been revitalized, it is clear that there is an urgent need to develop new measures, and also measures which are widely available. This is particularly the case for theory-based measures of a language analytic ability which incorporate insights from SLA research. It would also be useful to have widely available tests of the different components of working memory, integrated perhaps into wider aptitude batteries. And following the lead of CANAL-F, there is considerable scope to develop more measures of learning and memory, to reflect the greater realization now of the importance of proceduralized memory.

Finally, in terms of future challenges, and most urgently of all, we need research to explore Robinson's proposals on aptitude complexes, or, more generally, interactions between learner aptitude components and variations in learning conditions. Such research would transform the perceived instructional relevance of aptitude.

References

Abrahamsson, N. and Hyltenstam, K. (2008). The robustness of aptitude effects in near-native second language acquisition. *Studies in Second Language Acquisition, 30*(4), 481–509.

Alderson, C. J., Clapham, C., and Steel, D. (1997). Metalinguistic knowledge, language aptitude, and language proficiency. *Language Teaching Research, 1*, 93–121.

Baddeley, A. (2007). *Working memory, thought, and action.* Oxford: Oxford University Press.

Baddeley, A., Gathercole, S. E., and Papagno, C. (1998). The phonological loop as a language learning device. *Psychological Review, 105*, 158–173.

Bialystok, E. (2002). On the reliability of robustness: A reply to DeKeyser. *Studies in Second Language Acquisition, 24*(3), 481–488.

Bialystok, E. and Hakuta, K. (1994). *In other words: The science and psychology of second language acquisition*. New York: Basic Books.

Carpenter, H. (2008). *A behavioural and electrophysiological investigation of different aptitudes for L2 grammar in learners equated for proficiency level*. Unpublished PhD Dissertation. Georgetown University.

Carroll, J. B. (1965). The prediction of success in intensive foreign language training. In R. Glaser (Ed.), *Training, research, and education* (87–136). New York: Wiley.

Carroll, J. B. (1973). Implications of aptitude test research and psycholinguistic theory for foreign language teaching. *International Journal of Psycholinguistics, 2*, 5–14.

Carroll, J. B. (1993). *Human cognitive abilities*. Cambridge: Cambridge University Press.

Carroll, J. B. and Sapon, S. M. (1957). *Modern languages aptitude test*. New York: Psychological Corporation.

Chan, E., Skehan, P., and Gong, G. (2011). Working memory, phonemic coding ability and foreign language aptitude: Potential for construction of specific language aptitude tests—the case of Cantonese. *ILHA Do Desterro, 60*, 34–52.

Cheung, H., Chan, M., and Chong, K. (1996). Use of orthographic knowledge in reading by Chinese-English bi-scriptal children. *Language Learning, 57*(3), 469–505.

DeGraaf, R. (1997). The eXperanto experiment: Effects of explicit instruction on second language acquisition. *Studies in Second Language Acquisition, 19*, 249–275.

DeKeyser, R. (2000). The robustness of critical period effects in second language acquisition. *Studies in Second Language Acquisition, 22*, 499–533.

DeKeyser, R. and Juffs, A. (2005). Cognitive considerations in L2 learning. In E. Hinkel (Ed.), *Handbook of research in second language teaching and learning* (pp. 437–454). Mahwah, NJ: Lawence Erlbaum Associates.

Elder, C., Warren, J., Hajek, J., Manwaring, D., and Davies, A. (1999). Metalinguistic knowledge: How important is it in studying a language at university? *Australian Journal of Applied Linguistics, 22*(1), 81–95.

Ellis, N. (1996). Sequencing in SLA: Phonological memory, chunking, and points of order. *Studies in Second Language Acquisition, 18*, 991–126.

Ellis, N. (2005). At the interface: Dynamic interactions of explicit and implicit language knowledge. *Studies in Second Language Acquisition, 27*, 305–352.

Ellis, N. (2007). Language acquisition as rational contingency learning. *Applied Linguistics, 27*, 1–24.

Ellis, N. and Sinclair, S. G. (1996). Working memory as the acquisition of vocabulary and syntax: Putting language in good order. *The Quarterly Journal of Experimental Psychology, 49A*, 234–250.

Erlam, R. (2005). Language aptitude and its relationship to instructional effectiveness in second language acquisition. *Language Teaching Research, 9*, 147–171.

Fortkamp, M. B. M. (1999). Working memory capacity and aspects of L2 speech production. *Communication and Cognition, 32*, 259–296.

French, L. (2006). *Phonological working memory and L2 acquisition: A developmental study of Quebec francophone children learning English*. New York: Edward Mellen Press.

French, L. and O'Brien, I. (2008). Phonological memory and children's second language grammar learning. *Applied Psycholinguistics, 29*, 463–487.

Ganschow, L., Sparks, R., and Javorsky, J. (1998). Foreign language learning difficulties: An historical perspective. *Journal of Learning Disabilities, 31*, 248–258.

Gathercole, S. E. (1999). Cognitive approaches to the development of short term memory. *Trends in Cognitive Sciences, 3*(11), 410–419.

Gathercole, S. E. (2006). Nonword repetition and word learning: The nature of the relationship. *Applied Psycholinguistics, 27*, 513–543.

Green, P. (1975). *The language laboratory in school: The York study*. London: Oliver and Boyd.

Grigorenko, E. L., Sternberg, R. J., and Ehrman, M. (2002). A theory based approach to the measurement of foreign language learning ability: The Canal-F theory and test. *The Modern Language Journal, 84*(3), 390–405.

Harley, B. and Hart, D. (1997). Language aptitude and second language proficiency in classroom learners of different starting ages. *Studies in Second Language Acquisition, 19*, 379–400.

Johnson, J. and Newport, E. (1989). Critical period effects in second language learning: The influence of maturational state on the acquisition of English as a second language. *Cognitive Psychology, 21*, 60–99.

Kormos, J. and Safar, A. (2008). Phonological short term memory, working memory, and foreign language performance in intensive language learning. *Bilingualism: Language and Cognition, 11*(1), 261–271.

Krashen, S. (1981). Aptitude and attitude in relation to second language acquisition and learning. In Diller K. (Ed.), *Individual differences and universals in language aptitude*. Rowley, MA: Newbury House.

Levelt, W. and Wheeldon, L. R. (1994). Do speakers have access to a mental syllabary? *Cognition, 50*, 239–269.

Mackey, A., Philp, J., Egi, T., Fujii, A., and Tatsumi, T. (2002). Individual differences in working memory, noticing of interactional feedback and L2 development. In P. Robinson (Ed.), *Individual differences and instructed language learning*. Amsterdam: John Benjamins.

Masoura, E. V. and Gathercole, S. E. (1999). Phonological short term memory and foreign language learning. *International Journal of Psychology, 34*, 383–388.

Meara, P. (2005). *LLAMA language aptitude tests: The manual*. Lognostics: University of Swansea. (www.lognostics.co.uk/tools/llama).

Miyake, A. and Friedman, D. (1998). Individual differences in second language proficiency: Working memory as language aptitude. In A. Healy and L. Bourne (Eds.), *Foreign language learning: Psycholinguistic studies on training and retention*. Mahwah, NJ: Lawrence Erlbaum Associates.

Miyake, A. and Shah, P. (1999). *Models of working memory*. Cambridge: Cambridge University Press.

O'Brien, I., Segalowitz, N., Collentine, J., and Freed, B. (2006). Phonological memory and lexical, narrative, and grammatical skills in second-language oral production by adult learners. *Applied Psycholinguistics, 27*, 377–402.

O'Brien, I., Segalowitz, N., Freed, B., and Collentine, J. (2007). Phonological memory predicts second language oral fluence gains in adults. *Studies in Second Language Acquisition, 29*, 557–582.

Papagno, C. and Vallar, G. (1995). Verbal short-term memory and vocabulary learning in polyglots. *The Quarterly Journal of Experimental Psychology, 48A*, 98–107.

Parry, T. S. and Child, J. R. (1990). Preliminary investigation of the relationship between VORD, MLAT, and language proficiency. In Parry, T. S. and Stansfield, C. W. (Eds.), *Language aptitude reconsidered*. Washington, DC.: Center for Applied Linguistics.

Petersen, C. R. and Al-Haik, A. (1976). The development of the Defense Language Aptitude Battery (DLAB). *Educational and Psychological Measurement, 36*, 369–380.

Pienemann, M. (1998). *Language processing and second language development: Processability theory*. Amsterdam: John Benjamins.

Pimsleur, P. (1966). *Pimsleur Language Aptitude Battery (PLAB)*. New York: Harcourt, Brace, Jovanovich.

Pimsleur, P. (1968). Language aptitude testing. In A. Davies (Ed.), *Language testing: A psycholinguistic approach*. Oxford: Oxford University Press.

Pimsleur, P., Sundland, D. M., and McIntyre, R. D. (1964). Underachievement in foreign language learning. *International Review of Applied Linguistics, 2*, 113–50.

Reves, T. (1982). *What makes a good language learner?* Unpublished PhD thesis. Hebrew University of Jerusalem.

Robinson, P. (1995). Learning simple and complex rules under implicit, incidental, rule-search, and instructed conditions. *Studies in Second Language Acquisition, 18*, 27–67.

Robinson, P. (2005). Aptitude and second language acquisition. *Annual Review of Applied Linguistics, 25*, 46–73.

Robinson, P. (2007). Aptitudes, abilities, contexts and practice. In R. M. DeKeyser (Ed.), *Practice in second language learning: Perspectives from applied linguistics and cognitive psychology* (pp. 256–286). Cambridge: Cambridge University Press.

Roehr, K. (2008). Metalinguistic knowledge and language ability in university level L2 learners. *Applied Linguistics, 29*(2), 173–199.

Sasaki, M. (1991) *Relationships among second language proficiency, foreign language aptitude, and intelligence: a structural equation modelling approach*. Unpublished PhD dissertation. University of California at Los Angeles.

Sasaki, M. (1996). *Second language proficiency, foreign language aptitude, and intelligence: Quantitative and qualitative analyses*. New York: Peter Lang.

Service, E. and Kohonen, V. (1995). Is the relation between phonological memory and foreign language learning accounted for by vocabulary acquisition? *Applied Psycholinguistics, 16*, 155–172.

Skehan, P. (1982). *Memory and motivation in language aptitude testing*. Unpublished PhD thesis. University of London.

Skehan, P. (1986a). Where does language aptitude come from? In Meara P. (Ed.), *Spoken language*. London: Centre for Information on Language Teaching.

Skehan, P. (1986b). Cluster analysis and the identification of learner types. In V. Cook (Ed.), *Experimental approaches to second language acquisition*. Oxford: Pergamon.

Skehan, P. (2002). Theorising and updating aptitude. In P. Robinson (Ed.), *Individual differences and instructed language learning*. Amsterdam: John Benjamins.

Skehan, P. and Chan, E. (ms). Rethinking aptitude: developing a theory-based measure of language analytic ability based on second language acquisition theory.

Sparks, R. E., and Ganschow, L. (1991). Foreign language learning differences: Affective filter or native language aptitude differences. *The Modern Language Journal*, 75(1), 3–15.

Sparks, R. E., Ganschow, L., Javorsky, J., and Pohlman, J. (1992). Test comparisons among students identified as high-risk, low-risk, and learning disabled in high-school foreign language courses. *The Modern Language Journal*, 76(2), 142–158.

Waters, G. S., and Caplan, D. (2003). The reliability and stability of verbal working memory measures. *Behaviour Research Methods, Instruments, and Computers*, 35, 550–564.

Wells, G. (1985). *Language development in the pre-school years*. Cambridge: Cambridge University Press.

Wen, Z. (2009). *Effects of working memory capacity on L2 task-based speech planning and performance*. Unpublished PhD dissertation. Chinese University of Hong Kong.

Wesche, M. B. (1981). Language aptitude measures in streaming, matching students with methods, and diagnosis of learning problems. In K. Diller (Ed.), *Individual differences and universals in language aptitude*. Rowley, MA: Newbury House.

White, L. (2003). *Second language acquisition and universal grammar*. New York: Cambridge University Press.

Williams, J. and Lovatt, P. (2003). Phonological memory and rule learning. *Language Learning*, 53, 67–121.

Williams, J. and Lovatt, P. (2005). Phonological memory and rule learning: II. *Language Learning*, 55 (Supplement 1), 177–233.

24

Motivation

Ema Ushioda and Zoltán Dörnyei

Historical discussion

Motivation has been a major research topic within second language acquisition (SLA) for over five decades, ever since it became recognized as an important internal cause of variability in language learning success. Of course, the study of motivation in general has a much longer history across the broader disciplines of mainstream and educational psychology. Second language (L2) motivation research has evolved somewhat independently, however, originating in a concern to address the unique social, psychological, behavioral, and cultural complexities that acquiring a new communication code entails. Over the years, the field has evolved through successive phases reflecting increasing degrees of integration with developments in mainstream motivational psychology, while retaining a sharp focus on aspects of motivation unique to language learning. Dörnyei and Ushioda (2011) have identified these phases as follows:

- The *social-psychological period* (1959–1990), characterized by the work of Robert Gardner and his associates in Canada
- The *cognitive-situated period* (during the 1990s), characterized by work drawing on cognitive theories in educational psychology
- The *process-oriented period* (turn of the century), characterized by a focus on motivational change
- The *socio-dynamic period* (current), characterized by a concern with dynamic systems and contextual interactions.

L2 motivation research owes its origins to two Canadian social psychologists, Robert Gardner and Wallace Lambert, who conducted a series of studies investigating language learning attitudes and motivation dating back to 1959, and published a collective report in 1972 that was to prove seminal in shaping this research area for the next two decades. Gardner and Lambert (1972) theorized that motivation was a significant cause of variability in SLA, and that its effect was independent of ability or aptitude. They speculated moreover that SLA had important social and psychological dimensions which distinguished the motivation to learn a second language from other types of learning motivation, since learners are expected not simply to acquire knowledge of the language but to identify with the target language community and adopt their distinctive speech behaviors and styles. Individuals' attitudes toward the target language community, as well as their ethnocentric orientation in general, were hypothesized to exert a directive influence on their L2 learning behavior, which led Gardner and Lambert (1972) to propose two kinds of motivational orientation in language learning: an *integrative* orientation "reflecting a sincere and personal interest in the people and culture represented by the other group"; and an *instrumental* orientation "reflecting the practical value and advantages of learning a new language" (p. 132).

Founded in the bilingual social context of Canada, L2 motivation research thus originated in a *social-psychological* framework implicating the social context of SLA and attitudes and relations between different communities. This social perspective sharply differentiated L2 motivation research from the individual-cognitive perspectives then dominating mainstream motivational psychology, and as Dörnyei (2005) comments, was radically ahead of its time since socio-contextual perspectives did not really begin to inform motivation research in mainstream psychology until the 1990s (p. 67). Through the 1970s and 1980s, Gardner and Lambert's theory and later models developed by Gardner and his associates generated a wealth of empirical investigation in Canada and beyond (see e.g., Gardner, 1985; Gardner and MacIntyre, 1993).

By the late 1980s and early 1990s, however, there was a sense that the social-psychological line of inquiry had run its course and that alternative research perspectives were needed to complement the existing findings and thus widen the horizon of L2 motivation research. This view was voiced independently by a number of scholars at the turn of the decade (e.g., Brown, 1990; Crookes and Schmidt, 1991; Julkunen, 1989; Skehan, 1989), and prompted a series of discussion papers published in *The Modern Language Journal* in 1994 on broadening the research agenda (e.g., Dörnyei, 1994a, b; Gardner and Tremblay, 1994; Oxford and Shearin, 1994). These discussions marked a shift toward what Dörnyei (2005) has called the *cognitive-situated period* of L2 research. This period was characterized by two interrelated trends: (a) the need to bring L2 motivation research in line with *cognitive* theories in mainstream motivational psychology, and (b) the desire to move from the broad macro perspective of ethnolinguistic communities and learners' general dispositions to L2 learning to a more *situated* analysis of motivation in specific learning settings (e.g., classrooms). Essentially, the cognitive-situated period entailed focusing more on motivation in L2 instructional contexts, integrating cognitive motivation concepts from the education field (e.g., intrinsic motivation, self-efficacy, attributions) and developing more extensive theoretical frameworks (e.g., Dörnyei, 1994a; Williams and Burden, 1997), yet without discarding social-psychological perspectives altogether.

With this more situated analysis of motivation in the classroom setting, attention was also drawn to the unstable nature of motivation during the learning process, whether during engagement in a task, through successive lessons, or across the broader time span of a course of study. Analyzing the temporal structure of motivation has always been a challenge in mainstream motivational psychology, since motivation research has typically relied on theoretical models and corresponding research designs that attempt to measure motivation at a particular point in time and investigate relationships with other variables such as achievement or performance. These approaches do not lend themselves to investigating the complex ebb and flow of motivation. Such snapshot approaches have also dominated L2 motivation research, and it is only relatively recently that we have begun to address temporal perspectives and adopt more *process-oriented* approaches to the analysis of L2 motivation (e.g., Dörnyei, 2002; Dörnyei and Ottó, 1998; Shoaib and Dörnyei, 2005; Ushioda, 1996a, 2001; Williams and Burden, 1997). In this connection, a basic first step in analyzing motivation from a temporal perspective is to clarify the conceptual distinction between motivation to engage in L2 learning (choices, reasons, goals, decisions), and motivation during engagement (how one feels, behaves, and responds during the process of learning). Dörnyei and Ottó's (1998; see also Dörnyei, 2000, 2001b) process model represents the most elaborate attempt to date to delineate the temporal structure of L2 motivation, which it divides into pre-actional (choice motivation), actional (executive motivation), and post-actional (evaluation) phases, each shaped by various internal and contextual motivational influences and regulatory mechanisms. These influences and mechanisms can be enhancing (e.g., sense of self-efficacy, positive teacher feedback), or inhibiting (e.g., competitive pressures, distracting influences), depending on whether they contribute to successful implementation of the goal or dampen the actor's endeavor.

The process model of L2 motivation has two key shortcomings: (a) it assumes that we can define clearly when a learning process begins and ends; (b) it assumes that the actional process occurs in relative isolation, without interference from other actional processes in which the learner may be simultaneously engaged. These shortcomings in fact reflect limitations of most approaches to motivation in SLA to date, which, in the effort to identify explanatory linear models, have not taken adequate account of the dynamic and situated complexity of the learning process or the multiple goals and agendas shaping learner behavior. Within the past decade or so in the broader field of mainstream motivational psychology, there has been a move toward more dynamic contextual paradigms for the analysis of motivation (e.g., Järvelä, 2001), where the relationship between individuals and context is conceived of in terms of complex and dynamic organic systems emerging and evolving over time. Such perspectives have also begun to influence thinking in the L2 motivation field, heralding a shift to the current new *socio-dynamic* phase. This phase is characterized by a focus on the situated complexity of the L2 motivation process and its organic development in interaction with a multiplicity of internal, social, and contextual factors—that is, a move toward relational or dynamic systems perspectives on motivation (e.g., Dörnyei, 2009a; Ushioda, 2009); and characterized by a concern to theorize L2 motivation in ways that take account of the broader complexities of language learning and language use in the modern globalized world—that is, by reframing L2 motivation in the context of contemporary theories of self and identity (Dörnyei, 2005; Dörnyei and Ushioda, 2009a).

It should be noted that complexity theory and dynamic systems perspectives have also begun to pervade discussions across the wider field of SLA (e.g., Ellis and Larsen-Freeman, 2009; Larsen-Freeman and Cameron, 2008a; see also Larsen-Freeman, Chapter 5, this volume). In this regard, the current socio-dynamic phase may represent a period when motivation research contributes to the development of major lines of thinking within SLA. Surprisingly perhaps, this kind of integration of motivation research with the more dominant linguistic traditions that prevail in SLA has been slow in coming. As Dörnyei (2003) comments, motivation research has endured a somewhat isolated and marginalized position within SLA, largely because it has had rather little to say about how the psychology of motivation relates to the actual processes and intricacies of linguistic development, which are the major emphasis in SLA, regardless of the theoretical motivation. The analysis of motivation and its role in SLA has largely been at the level of global learning outcomes or measures of proficiency. Thus while motivation is recognized as a prerequisite for SLA to take place, the relevance of motivation research to understanding the finer detail of how SLA happens has been rather unclear. Despite the moves toward more cognitive-situated and then process-oriented approaches, L2 motivation research has not really succeeded in bridging the gap between psychological and linguistic perspectives in SLA. It will be interesting to see if the current socio-dynamic phase brings about a real change in this respect.

Core issues

Throughout the history of L2 motivation research to date, a central preoccupation has been to develop a theoretical analysis of motivation and its role in SLA. Until the 1990s, the theoretical concept that prevailed was a social-psychological construct, composed of three motivation components (motivational intensity, desire to learn the language, attitudes toward learning the language); and motivational antecedents comprising orientations (i.e., integrative or instrumental reasons for learning) and attitudinal factors (interest in foreign languages, attitudes toward the target language community, attitudes toward the L2 learning situation) (for detailed discussion, see Gardner, 1985, pp. 146–150). In short, the social-psychological tradition established a rigorously articulated analysis of L2 motivation, which distinguished between motivation per se (encapsulating effort, desire, and positive affect toward learning the language) and its social-psychological determinants (orientations and attitudes). While Gardner and Lambert's (1972) original model predicted direct causal links between orientations, attitudes, and L2 proficiency, Gardner's later conceptualization hypothesized that this association was mediated by motivation (Gardner, 1985, p. 150). Empirical investigations largely confirmed this analysis, as well as the independence of motivation and aptitude as causal variables influencing L2 achievement (Gardner, 1985; Masgoret and Gardner, 2003).

Research findings also pointed to the prevalence and significance of a particular constellation of attitudinal-motivational variables reflecting integrative motivation—that is, a combination of integrative orientation, positive attitudes, and motivation, providing empirical support for Gardner's (1985) key claim that L2 motivation "always has an integrativeness component," since even when motivation is instrumental "this has associated with it some level of willingness to interact with other communities" (p. 168). Undoubtedly this claim represents the core issue to emerge from the social-psychological analysis of L2 motivation, provoking critical questions about the nature of integrative motivation, its strong or weak forms (i.e., whether it expresses a desire to identify and integrate with the target language community, or simply positive attitudes and interest), its generalizability and relevance to foreign language (FL) versus L2 learning settings, and its conceptual distinctiveness from instrumental motivation or other possible kinds of motivational orientation (e.g., Clément and Kruidenier, 1983; Dörnyei, 1990; McDonough, 1981).

As the analysis of L2 motivation moved beyond social-psychological perspectives through the 1990s, the integrative and instrumental dimensions of L2 motivation continued to be recognized as important in determining basic learning goals and language choice, but insufficient to explain the processes of motivation shaping engagement in learning, particularly in formal classroom contexts. Intrinsic and extrinsic orientations gained theoretical prominence as motivation concepts more relevant to the analysis of classroom language learning, and more directly amenable to pedagogical influence and to internal as well as external regulation (e.g., Dörnyei, 1994a; Noels, 2001; Ushioda, 1996b; Williams and Burden, 1997). Dörnyei's (1994a) expanded framework analysed L2 motivation in terms of three levels: the *language level* (integrative and instrumental motivational subsystems), the *learner level* (individual motivational characteristics), and the *learning situation level* (situation-specific motives relating to the course and social learning environment). Core issues during the cognitive-situated and process-oriented periods increasingly turned to practical questions of how motivation might be initiated, influenced, supported, or sustained. Attention thus focused on the interaction between the learning situation (e.g., instructional techniques, classroom environment, interpersonal relations), and individual motivational cognitions and behaviors (e.g., goals, attitudes, beliefs, processing of experience, self-regulatory strategies) (Dörnyei, 2002; Dörnyei and Tseng, 2009).

From a conceptual point of view, this interactional focus considerably complicates the analysis of motivation, since its theoretical boundaries are seen to extend beyond the individual to embrace the dynamic interaction between the individual and the social learning environment. A key issue now emerging is how to integrate the individual and context in the analysis of motivation (for a recent overview of the challenging nature of this task, see Dörnyei, 2009d). This issue mirrors similar theoretical concerns in contemporary mainstream motivational psychology, and also reflects broader debates within the SLA field concerning cognitive-psycholinguistic versus social-contextual perspectives on language learning (e.g., Lafford, 2007; Zuengler and Miller, 2006). Where the analysis of motivation is concerned, a further issue is the difficulty of isolating "motivation" (traditionally classified as an affective variable and individual difference characteristic—e.g., Skehan, 1989) from the range of cognitive and emotional processes that interact with one another (and the social environment) to shape engagement in learning. Addressing these issues, Dörnyei (2009a) has recently argued against an individual difference approach to motivation in favor of a dynamic systems framework. Dynamic systems approaches concern the behavior of complex systems that contain multiple interconnected components, where development is characterized by non-linear growth as systems adapt and evolve organically in response to contextual processes and in ways that contribute to shaping context. As Dörnyei (2009a, d) argues, this dynamic systems perspective on SLA processes renders the notion of discrete individual difference variables (such as motivation) rather meaningless, since processes of motivation, cognition, and emotion and their constituent components continuously interact with one another and the developing context, thereby changing and causing change, as the system as a whole restructures, adapts, and evolves. As noted above, complex systems perspectives have also begun to influence thinking across the wider field of SLA (see Larsen-Freeman, Chapter 5, this volume), and it seems likely that a dynamic systems approach to the analysis of motivation will entail much closer integration with other dimensions of SLA than hitherto, given that the focus is across evolving systems of interacting internal and contextual factors shaping engagement in SLA, and given the need to consider the processes of human agency and intentionality that are fundamental to the interactions between individual and context (Sealey and Carter, 2004). However, a key challenge will be to develop workable research designs and analytical tools to investigate such systems in a coherent way (see Larsen-Freeman and Cameron, 2008b).

Returning to the social-psychological dimensions of L2 motivation, the integrative/instrumental motivation concepts have maintained their enduring influence on theorizing about why people learn languages or choose particular languages to learn. Since the turn of the century, however, growing discussions about the global spread of English have provoked a new critical issue in the analysis of integrative motivation. A basic question we have begun to ask is whether it is meaningful to talk about integrative motivation in the case of English as target language, given the status of English as a global language, an international lingua franca, and a basic educational skill in more and more educational curricula. One response has been to broaden the target reference group from a specific geographical community of speakers to a global community, transmuting the notion of integrative motivation to a generalized international outlook or what Yashima (2002) has called "international posture." However, as Ushioda (2006) asks: Precisely because it is a global community, is it meaningful to conceptualize it as an external reference group, or as part of one's internal representation of oneself as a *de facto* member of that global community? (p. 150). This shift in focus from an external reference group to the internal domain of self and identity represents a significant development in current L2 motivation theory, and was prompted in large part by the findings of a major longitudinal survey of Hungarian students' language learning motivation (Dörnyei and Csizér, 2002; Dörnyei *et al.*, 2006). Commenting on the salience and multifaceted composition of an integrative motivation factor in their data, Dörnyei and Csizér (2002) speculated that the process of identification theorized to underpin integrativeness might be better explained as an internal process of identification within the person's self-concept (p. 453).

Based on these findings, Dörnyei (2005, 2009b) has drawn on the psychological theory of "possible selves" (Markus and Nurius, 1986) and developed a new conceptualization of the "L2 Motivational Self System" centered on people's vision of themselves in the future. Its central concept is the *ideal self*, signifying the attributes that one would ideally like to possess (i.e., a representation of personal hopes, aspirations, or wishes). A complementary concept is the *ought-to self*, signifying the attributes that one believes one ought to possess (i.e., a representation of someone else's sense of duty, obligations, or responsibilities). A basic tenet is that if proficiency in the target language is integral to one's *ideal* or *ought-to* self, this will serve as a powerful motivator to learn the language because of our psychological desire to reduce the discrepancy between current and future self states. Key issues for analysis and empirical investigation concern how such self images develop and evolve in interaction with the complex constellations of internal and contextual processes shaping engagement in learning, represented as a third component (L2 learning experience) in the L2 Motivational Self System, and thus relating back to the dynamic systems perspectives discussed above.

Data and common elicitation measures

As an abstract, multifaceted construct subject to various internal, contextual and temporal processes, motivation is notoriously difficult to measure in an objective way. It is not directly observable, since observable behaviors (e.g., how many times students bid for turns in class) may well reflect a variety of underlying motivational factors (e.g., interest in learning, or a desire to display knowledge, outperform others, please the teacher, seek attention or praise). Consequently, motivation research has generally relied on gathering self-report data to access L2 learners' own perspectives, such as, for example, how much they agree or disagree with, rate the importance of, or perceive as true for themselves, certain statements reflecting particular attitudes, intentions or behaviors (e.g., "I don't think that foreign languages are important school subjects," Dörnyei *et al.*, 2006, p. 160).

To minimize the inherent subjectivity of such data, considerable attention has been paid to constructing rigorous measurement instruments with good psychometric properties, as exemplified in particular by the standardized Attitude/Motivation Test Battery (AMTB) developed by Gardner and his associates (see Gardner, 1985, Appendix). In its original form, the AMTB operationalizes the main attitudinal-motivational constituents of Gardner's theory, and also includes measures of language anxiety and parental encouragement. It comprises a number of multi-item Likert, multiple choice, and semantic differential scales, yielding composite indices of attitudinal-motivational variables such as *interest in foreign languages* and *integrative* or *instrumental orientation*. These indices are then entered into statistical analyses of relationships with other independent or dependent variables (e.g., measures of language aptitude or L2 proficiency), typically using factor analytical, correlational, regression analysis, or path analysis methods.

The AMTB has been adapted for use in a variety of L2 contexts (e.g., Clément *et al.*, 1994; Kraemer, 1993). Its psychometric design principles have been applied to the development of measures of other motivational constructs such as intrinsic and extrinsic orientations (e.g., Noels *et al.*, 2000), and have influenced approaches to constructing self-report scales to measure new L2 motivation constructs such as *ideal* and *ought-to* selves (e.g., MacIntyre *et al.*, 2009; Ryan, 2009; Taguchi *et al.*, 2009). In short, there has been a robust tradition of quantitative psychometric measurement in L2 motivation research, reflecting the methodological traditions that have prevailed in mainstream cognitive and social psychology. Strengths of this quantitative approach include rigor and systematicity in data-gathering and analysis, as well as comparability and replicability of data, and generalizability to wider populations.

As noted in our historical review earlier, however, the evolution of L2 motivation research has been characterized by a growing concern with temporal and contextual variability, and with the limitations of linear models in representing the dynamic complexity of motivational processes. Current quantitative methods of SLA inquiry are ill-equipped to investigate these more complex, process-oriented, and contextual perspectives, since such methods typically rely on superficial snapshot measures at an arbitrary point in time, seek to generalize on the basis of statistically representative patterns in the data, and are not sensitive to the particularities of evolving motivational experiences or individual-contextual interactions. Within the last decade or so, more qualitative methods of inquiry have gradually begun to complement the dominant quantitative paradigm, in an effort to address the dynamic and situated complexity of L2 motivation, and also mirroring a general trend in SLA research. In particular, unstructured or semi-structured interview techniques have been used to elicit in-depth self-report data on motivation and motivational experience, with the transcribed data then subjected to thematic analysis based on predetermined codes and categories, grounded or emergent categories (Gibbs, 2007), or a mixture of the two (e.g., Shoaib and Dörnyei, 2005; Ushioda, 2001; Williams *et al.*, 2001).

While interview studies are inevitably limited in scale and scope, the data elicited can offer very rich insights into the process and experience of motivation, particularly when a longitudinal research design is adopted with multiple interviews with participants (e.g., Kim, 2009). Moreover, limitations in the scope of the dataset can be offset by complementing it with more large-scale quantitative data in a mixed methods research design (e.g., a questionnaire survey of attitudes and motivation, combined with follow-up interview data from a sub-sample; or an exploratory interview study followed by a questionnaire survey to generalize the findings to a wider sample). In L2 motivation research as in much SLA research in general, there is increasing recognition that mixed methods approaches can help to capture more of the complexity of the issues under investigation (Dörnyei, 2007a; Larsen-Freeman and Cameron, 2008b). In particular, with current moves toward more socio-dynamic perspectives on motivation, the investigation of contextual factors and individual-contextual interactions is likely to entail triangulation of multiple forms of data from diverse points of view (e.g., interviews with teachers and students, classroom observations, classroom interaction data, focus group discussions, learner journals, written narratives), in order to obtain a rich holistic analysis of motivation-in-context, rather than relying (as traditionally) on a single set of self-report measures (on researching the classroom as a dynamic system, see also Jessica Williams, Chapter 33, this volume). Needless to say, however, such research designs pose some interesting challenges for the analysis and representation of these complex datasets.

We now consider empirical verification. As noted above, the study of L2 motivation has been characterized by a solid tradition of empirical research, beginning with the pioneering investigations conducted by Gardner and Lambert (1972). Attitudinal-motivational, aptitude, and achievement data elicited from various groups of L2 learners in Montreal, Louisiana, Connecticut, and the Philippines were factor analysed to see if independent attitudinal-motivational and aptitude factors would emerge, each with loadings on the criterion variable achievement. The clearly bilingual setting of Montreal produced the strongest evidence of an independent relationship between integrative motivation and achievement, with findings less conclusive for the other settings. Thus, causal relationships (between motivation and achievement) and applicability to different ethno-linguistic settings became key issues during the social-psychological period, leading to critical and empirical analyses of the direction of causality (e.g., Hermann, 1980), of the chains of causation linking attitudes, orientations, motivation, and achievement (Gardner, 1985), and of their generalizability to a range of cultural and linguistic settings (e.g., Clément *et al.*, 1994; Kraemer, 1993).

To investigate causality and test the validity and generalizability of Gardner's theoretical model, sophisticated structural equation modeling techniques became adopted to verify hypothesized causal links between constructs (e.g., *attitudes toward the learning situation* and *motivation*) and between constructs and their constituent components (e.g., *attitudes toward the learning situation*, and its constituent components of Evaluation of the L2 Teacher and Evaluation of the L2 Course) (e.g., Gardner, 1985; Gardner *et al.*, 1983; Gardner *et al.*, 1997; Tremblay and Gardner, 1995). As Masgoret and Gardner (2003) summarize in their meta-analysis of empirical studies involving 75 independent samples and 10,489 L2 learners, the overall evidence underlines positive relationships between L2 achievement and five classes of attitudinal-motivational variables (attitudes toward the learning situation, integrativeness, motivation, integrative orientation, instrumental orientation), with motivation emerging as the strongest predictor of achievement. These composite findings are irrespective of the age of the learners or the availability of the target language in the immediate environment, although it should be noted that most of the studies analysed were conducted in a single country, Canada.

Regarding the claim that L2 motivation "always has an integrativeness component" (Gardner, 1985, p. 168), the empirical evidence has been more mixed depending on cultural setting (Noels *et al.*, 2000). Even in Gardner and Lambert (1972), data from their Philippines study suggested that parental instrumental forms of motivation were more significant, a finding mirrored in more recent investigations in East Asian settings such as Warden and Lin (2000), and Chen *et al.* (2005), where a "required motivation" factor emerged, reflecting culturally valued and internalized motivation to meet social and parental expectations. While factor analytical studies in other settings have often produced a factor reflecting a positive disposition toward native speakers and the cultural values linked to the language, it is not always clearly distinguished from more pragmatic instrumental aspects of motivation or defined with reference to a specific community of speakers (Irie, 2003). Such was the finding in a major longitudinal survey of Hungarian teenagers' language learning attitudes and motivation, spanning the period from 1993 to 2004 and involving 13,391 respondents across three phases of data collection (Dörnyei and Csizér, 2002; Dörnyei *et al.*, 2006). Although an integrative motivation factor did emerge consistently strongly in the data, it was shown to be underpinned by both practical instrumental motivation as well as attitudes to target language speakers, thus raising questions about the conceptual distinctiveness of integrative and instrumental motivation. As we saw earlier, this finding has led Dörnyei (2005, 2009b) to reframe the process of identification theorized to underpin integrativeness as an internal process of identification within the self-concept, leading to his new conceptualization of the L2 Motivational Self System. Recent attempts to operationalize the self system and test its key claims in a diverse range of contexts (China, Hungary, Iran, Japan) with extensive datasets offer cumulative empirical evidence that future self-guides act as powerful motivators for L2 learning (Csizér and Kormos, 2009; Ryan, 2009; Taguchi *et al.*, 2009).

As noted earlier, within the last decade or so L2 motivation research has also been characterized by a growing number of more qualitative studies which seek to explore the process and experience of individual motivation and its dynamic interactions with contextual factors. In these studies, motivation is defined not in terms of measurable attitudes, effort or behavior, but in terms of how learners think about their learning and process relevant experience, and how their thinking affects their motivation and engagement in learning. Qualitative interview studies by Williams and Burden (1999), Williams *et al.* (2001), and Ushioda (1996a, 2001), for example, have provided a rich source of insights into causal attributional processes shaping learner motivation—that is, how L2 learners make sense of positive or negative outcomes in their learning experience, and how their thinking then shapes subsequent motivated engagement in learning. Ushioda's (2001) longitudinal interview study of Irish learners of French also uncovered variation between and within individuals in the temporal frame of reference shaping learner motivation, depending on how strongly motivation was perceived to be shaped by past learning experiences or future goals. Her findings suggested that goal-orientation may be better conceived as an evolving dimension of motivation, rather than as its defining rationale. Examining motivational change on a more extensive timescale, Shoaib and Dörnyei (2005) conducted retrospective qualitative interviews with 25 learners of English ranging in age from 18 to34, and identified a number of recurring temporal patterns and key transformational episodes affecting motivation, such as transitions to new life phases (e.g., leaving school and entering the world of work) or experiences of being in an English-speaking environment. More recently, Kim (2009) has used longitudinal interview data from Korean ESL learners in Canada to provide qualitative evidence in support of Dörnyei's

(2005, 2009b) concepts of the *ideal* and *ought-to selves*, and to elaborate the possible interrelationship between these self-guides by drawing on analytical perspectives from Vygotskian sociocultural theory and activity theory (see Lantolf, Chapter 4, this volume).

Applications

A key criticism of the social-psychological tradition of L2 motivation research was that it provided few genuinely useful insights for teachers, beyond highlighting the desirability of promoting students' positive attitudes to the target language culture (Crookes and Schmidt, 1991). As noted earlier, the shift to more cognitive-situated approaches in the 1990s brought about a stronger emphasis on the classroom context of L2 learning and on pedagogical issues such as how motivation might be generated and sustained. In particular, attention was drawn to the importance of intrinsic motivation and how it could be fostered through engaging students in setting optimal challenges or short-term (proximal) goals and promoting feelings of success and competence (Ushioda, 1996b; Williams and Burden, 1997). Personalizing learning content and making it meaningful and relevant were also emphasized as important strategies for promoting intrinsic motivation (Chambers, 1999). In addition, certain aspects of teacher behavior and teacher–student relations were identified as significant in shaping students' intrinsic motivation. For example, Noels *et al.* (1999) found that teachers who were perceived to adopt an autonomy-supportive (rather than controlling) communicative style and provide informational feedback on students' learning were likely to reinforce students' sense of self-determination and intrinsic enjoyment of learning. This finding has been mirrored in research exploring connections between L2 motivation and learner autonomy (e.g., Ushioda, 1996b, 2003), and points to the importance of adopting a democratic (rather than authoritarian) leadership style in the classroom (Dörnyei, 2007b). Among other things, this means involving students in some of the decision-making processes that shape their learning (Ushioda, 2003), and fostering trust, good interpersonal relations, and a cohesive learner group (Dörnyei, 2007b).

More generally, these and other implications of relevant theory and research have been developed into a comprehensive framework of classroom motivational strategies by Dörnyei (2001a). The framework comprises 35 motivational strategies organized according to four key phases of the teaching-learning process: creating the basic motivational conditions, generating initial motivation, maintaining and protecting motivation, and encouraging positive retrospective self-evaluation. This framework of motivational teaching practice was derived in part from empirical research with Hungarian teachers, which led to the development of an influential set of "ten commandments" for motivating students (e.g., Set a personal example with your own behavior. Increase the learners' linguistic self-confidence) (Dörnyei and Csizér, 1998). More recently, the framework has been used as the basis for large-scale investigations of teachers' motivational strategies in Taiwanese and Korean EFL contexts (Cheng and Dörnyei, 2007; Guilloteaux and Dörnyei, 2008). The research findings provide empirical confirmation that the teachers' motivational instructional practice does have a positive bearing on student motivation, but also suggest that motivational strategies may vary in importance according to cultural setting, and that context-appropriate strategies may indeed be influential in increasing student motivation. However, interesting questions remain about how far teachers can be trained to use motivational strategies or adopt a more motivational teaching practice (Kubanyiova, 2009), as well as whether the impact on student motivation may depend on how strategies used by teachers are actually perceived by students (Bernaus and Gardner, 2008).

While teachers' motivational strategies focus primarily on teacher behaviors and practices for motivating students, a related but separate angle of inquiry has focused on what has been variously called self-motivational strategies, self-regulation of motivation, or motivational thinking (Ushioda, 2008). This angle of inquiry has been shaped by theoretical and research perspectives on the process-oriented dimension of L2 motivation (Dörnyei and Ottó, 1998; Dörnyei and Tseng, 2009; Ushioda, 2001, 2003), and has been informed in particular by theories of action control, self-regulation, and autonomy. Although concerned principally with developing L2 learners' own capacity to sustain, enhance, and protect their motivation (in the face of negative affective experiences and competing distractions), this growing literature on motivational self-regulation has clear implications for instructional practices. In particular, it highlights the important role of teacher feedback and teacher–learner dialog in helping learners to reflect on their learning process, to attribute negative outcomes to factors within their control such as effort or choice of strategies, and to engage in constructive thinking about themselves as active agents of their learning (Ushioda, 2003, 2008).

Most recently, this focus on how L2 learners think about themselves has been developed further in the context of Dörnyei's L2 Motivational Self System, which has led Dörnyei (2009b, c) to speculate about practical pedagogical strategies for helping learners (a) to construct and sustain visions of their future ideal selves as L2 users, using visualization techniques and guided imagery; (b) to develop action plans comprising interim goal-setting and self-regulatory strategies in order to operationalize the vision and build realistically toward it; and (c) to counterbalance this image of their desired self with that of their feared self (i.e., the consequences of not learning the language or failing in one's aspirations), in order to stay firmly committed to their future ideals. These ideas have been developed into a collection of practical classroom activities for teachers and learners by Hadfield and Dörnyei (in press), providing, for example, various visualization scenarios as well as protocols to substantiate the ideal self image by looking at potential obstacles and ways by which certain role models have overcome those.

Future directions

There is no doubt in our minds that future research *should* be moving toward increasing integration between: (a) group-based quantitative approaches representing a macro-perspective and (b) individual-centered social approaches representing a situated, micro-perspective. However, we cannot currently say with certainty that this direction will achieve mainstream status in L2 motivation research because there are certain salient obstacles currently blocking the way. Therefore, in this concluding section we first reiterate the main reasons why such an integration would be desirable and then discuss some obstacles that will need to be overcome by future research.

We have argued recently (Dörnyei and Ushioda, 2009b) that the study of SLA– including L2 motivation research—has been characterized by a "schizophrenic" situation whereby research approaches have been framed through polarizing dichotomies such as positivist-interpretive, quantitative-qualitative, or cognitive-sociocultural, and scholars have by and large occupied "two parallel SLA worlds" (Zuengler and Miller, 2006; see also Lafford, 2007). We have two main concerns with this state of affairs: on the one hand, we believe that both approaches can shed important and unique light on research questions—the history of L2 motivation research outlined earlier offers convincing evidence for this. On the other hand, we also feel that pursuing research agendas in such a demarcated fashion may prevent scholars from doing justice to the complex and dynamic nature of most acquisitional/developmental phenomena within the broad remit of SLA. In an inherently social process such as language acquisition, the learner cannot be meaningfully separated from the social environment within which he/she operates, and therefore the challenge is to adopt a dynamic perspective that allows us to consider simultaneously the ongoing multiple influences between environmental and learner factors in all their componential complexity, as well as the emerging changes in both the learner *and* the environment as a result of this development (Dörnyei, 2009d).

The other side of the coin is, however, that while adopting a complex, dynamic systems perspective to the study of L2 motivation—and more generally, of individual differences—seems so beneficial in theory, it turns out to be a rather challenging task in practice. How can we meaningfully operationalize the dynamic relationship between language, learner, and the environment on the one hand, and motivation, emotion, and cognition on the other, in specific measurement terms? Admittedly, there are no easy answers or simple templates to follow, because what is needed, in essence, is changing our natural and traditional research outlook from trying to identify cause-effect relationships on the basis of selected variables to focusing on overarching processes and changes in a fluid tapestry of interrelated factors. Howe and Lewis (2005) explain that developmental psychology has been grappling with this issue for over a decade, but while many scholars have highlighted the value of dynamic systems-based thinking in theoretical articles, research in the dynamic systems vein remains a clear minority. Their conclusion of why this might be so is not at all optimistic:

> We think this is because the trajectory of developmental psychology, like other dynamic systems, tends toward stability much of the time. Researchers stick to well-established habits of thinking and working, and their students acquire the same habits, often because that is the easiest road to publication and career advancement.
>
> *(Howe and Lewis, 2005, p. 250)*

In sum, the current challenge in the study of L2 motivation appears to be a research methodological one: How can we establish valid "stories of motivation" which are powerful enough to resonate in the audiences and to offer concrete suggestions for application; which are backed by sufficient empirical evidence, whether qualitative or quantitative; and which are comprehensive rather than reductionist so that the complexity of motivation is not treated in a simplistic manner by focusing on one or two selected aspects only? We conclude this chapter by listing three potentially fruitful (and interrelated) research areas for future investigations in this vein:

- How does motivation change over time, and what factors drive this change? This question can be explored with regard to individual learners (i.e., multiple case studies) or whole groups of learners (i.e., longitudinal studies). The emphasis should be on trying to identify constellations of specific learner variables that form optimal patterns with environmental factors, thus constituting powerful channels of progress.
- How are aspects of one's identity/self related to facets of one's motivational intentions or motivated behaviors? The framework offered by the L2 Motivational Self System is obviously helpful in structuring such an investigation, but other self-aspects (e.g., professional or gender-related identities—see in particular the work of Norton, 2000; see also Duff, Chapter 25, this volume) are also likely to interact with motivational factors. A particularly relevant corollary of this issue is how identity changes may reflect motivational changes.
- How do environmental influences and contingencies shape motivational dispositions? From a theoretical point of view, this question concerns the social dimension of motivation and may lead to the exploration of motives rooted in one's situated language identity (see Clément et al., 2007). From a practical perspective, the question concerns conscious attempts to increase motivation by applying various motivational strategies or by generating language-specific vision in the learners.

References

Bernaus, M. and Gardner, R. C. (2008). Teacher motivation strategies, student perceptions, student motivation, and English achievement. *The Modern Language Journal, 92*, 387–401.

Brown, H. D. (1990). M and Ms for language classrooms? Another look at motivation. In J. E. Alatis (Ed.), *Georgetown University round table on language and linguistics 1990* (pp. 383–393). Washington, DC: Georgetown University Press.

Chambers, G. (1999). *Motivating language learners.* Clevedon, UK: Multilingual Matters.

Chen, J. F., Warden, C. A., and Chang, H. T. (2005). Motivators that do not motivate: The case of Chinese EFL learners and the influence of culture on motivation. *TESOL Quarterly, 39*, 609–633.

Cheng, H.-F., and Dörnyei, Z. (2007). The use of motivational strategies in language instruction: The case of EFL teaching in Taiwan. *Innovation in Language Learning and Teaching, 1*, 153–174.

Clément, R., Dörnyei, Z., and Noels, K. A. (1994). Motivation, self-confidence and group cohesion in the foreign language classroom. *Language Learning, 44*, 417–448.

Clément, R. and Kruidenier, B. (1983). Orientations in second language acquisition: 1. The effects of ethnicity, milieu, and target language on their emergence. *Language Learning, 33*, 273–291.

Clément, R., Noels, K. A., and MacIntyre, P. D. (2007). Three variations on the social psychology of biliguality: Context effects in motivation, usage and identity. In A. Wetherall, B. M. Watson, and C. Gallois (Eds.), *Language, discourse and social psychology* (pp. 51–77). Basingstoke: Palgrave.

Crookes, G. and Schmidt, R. (1991). Motivation: Reopening the research agenda. *Language Learning, 41*, 469–512.

Csizér, K. and Kormos, J. (2009). Learning experience, selves and motivated learning behaviour: A comparative analysis of structural models for Hungarian secondary and university learners of English. In Z. Dörnyei and E. Ushioda (Eds.), *Motivation, language identity and the L2 self* (pp. 98–119). Bristol: Multilingual Matters.

Dörnyei, Z. (1990). Conceptualizing motivation in foreign-language learning. *Language Learning, 40*, 45–78.

Dörnyei, Z. (1994a). Motivation and motivating in the foreign language classroom. *The Modern Language Journal, 78*, 273–284.

Dörnyei, Z. (1994b). Understanding L2 motivation. On with the challenge! *The Modern Language Journal, 78*, 515–523.

Dörnyei, Z. (2000). Motivation in action: Towards a process-oriented conceptualisation of student motivation. *British Journal of Educational Psychology, 70*, 519–538.

Dörnyei, Z. (2001a). *Motivational strategies in the language classroom.* Cambridge: Cambridge University Press.

Dörnyei, Z. (2001b). *Teaching and researching motivation.* Harlow: Longman.

Dörnyei, Z. (2002). The motivational basis of language learning tasks. In P. Robinson, (Ed.), *Individual differences and instructed language learning* (pp. 137–158). Amsterdam: John Benjamins.

Dörnyei, Z. (2003). Attitudes, orientations and motivations in language learning: Advances in theory, research and applications. In Z. Dörnyei (Ed.), *Attitudes, orientations, and motivations in language learning* (pp. 3–32). Oxford: Blackwell.

Dörnyei, Z. (2005). *The psychology of the language learner: Individual differences in second language acquisition.* Mahwah, NJ: Lawrence Erlbaum.

Dörnyei, Z. (2007a). *Research methods in applied linguistics.* Oxford: Oxford University Press.

Dörnyei, Z. (2007b). Creating a motivating classroom environment. In J. Cummins and C. Davison (Eds.), *International handbook of English language teaching* (Vol. 2, pp. 719–731). New York: Springer.

Dörnyei, Z. (2009a). *The psychology of second language acquisition.* Oxford: Oxford University Press.

Dörnyei, Z. (2009b). The L2 motivational self system. In Z. Dörnyei and E. Ushioda (Eds.), *Motivation, language identity and the L2 self* (pp. 9–42). Bristol: Multilingual Matters.

Dörnyei, Z. (2009c). Motivation and the vision of knowing a second language. In B. Beaven (Ed.), *IATEFL 2008: Exeter Conference Selections* (pp. 16–22). Canterbury: IATEFL.

Dörnyei, Z. (2009d). Individual differences: Interplay of learner characteristics and learning environment. In N. C. Ellis and D. Larsen-Freeman (Eds.), *Language as a complex adaptive system* (pp. 237–255). Oxford: Wiley Blackwell.

Dörnyei, Z. and Csizér, K. (1998). Ten commandments for motivating language learners: Results of an empirical study. *Language Teaching Research, 2*, 203–29.

Dörnyei, Z. and Csizér, K. (2002). Some dynamics of language attitudes and motivation: Results of a longitudinal nationwide survey. *Applied Linguistics, 23*, 421–62.

Dörnyei, Z., Csizér, K., and Németh, N. (2006). *Motivation, language attitudes and globalisation: A Hungarian perspective.* Clevedon, UK: Multilingual Matters.

Dörnyei, Z. and Ottó, I. (1998). Motivation in action: A process model of L2 motivation. *Working Papers in Applied Linguistics (Thames Valley University, London)*, 4, 43–69.

Dörnyei, Z. and Tseng, W.-T. (2009). Motivational processing in interactional tasks. In A. Mackey and C. Polio (Eds.), *Multiple perspectives on interaction: Second language research in honor of Susan M. Gass* (pp. 117–134). Mahwah, NJ: Lawrence Erlbaum.

Dörnyei, Z. and Ushioda, E. (Eds.) (2009a). *Motivation, language identity and the L2 self.* Bristol: Multilingual Matters.

Dörnyei, Z. and Ushioda, E. (2009b). Motivation, language identities and the L2 self: Future research directions. In Z. Dörnyei and E. Ushioda (Eds.), *Motivation, language identity and the L2 self* (pp. 350–356). Bristol: Multilingual Matters.

Dörnyei, Z. and Ushioda, E. (2011). *Teaching and researching motivation* (Second Edition) Harlow: Pearson Education.

Ellis, N. C., and Larsen-Freeman, D. (Eds.) (2009). *Language as a complex adaptive system.* Oxford: Wiley-Blackwell.

Gardner, R. C. (1985). *Social psychology and second language learning: The role of attitudes and motivation.* London: Edward Arnold.

Gardner, R. C., Lalonde, R. N., and Pierson, R. (1983). The socio-educational model of SLA: An investigation using LISREL causal modeling. *Journal of Language and Social Psychology*, 2, 1–15.

Gardner, R. C. and Lambert, W. E. (1972). *Attitudes and motivation in second language learning.* Rowley, MA: Newbury House.

Gardner, R. C. and MacIntyre, P. D. (1993). A student's contributions to second-language learning. Part II: Affective variables. *Language Teaching*, 26, 1–11.

Gardner, R. C. and Tremblay, P. F. (1994). On motivation, research agendas and theoretical frameworks. *The Modern Language Journal*, 78, 359–68.

Gardner, R. C., Tremblay, P. F., and Masgoret, A.-M. (1997). Towards a full model of second language learning: An empirical investigation. *The Modern Language Journal*, 81, 344–62.

Gibbs, G. (2007). *Analysing qualitative data.* London: Sage.

Guilloteaux, M. J. and Dörnyei, Z. (2008). Motivating language learners: A classroom-oriented investigation of the effects of motivational strategies on student motivation. *TESOL Quarterly*, 42, 55–77.

Hadfield, J. and Dörnyei, Z. (in press). *Theory into practice: Motivation and the ideal self.* London: Longman.

Hermann, G. (1980). Attitudes and success in children's learning of English as a second language: The motivational vs resultative hypothesis. *English Language Teaching Journal*, 34, 247–54.

Howe, M. L., and Lewis, M. D. (2005). The importance of dynamic systems approaches for understanding development. *Developmental Review*, 25, 247–251.

Irie, K. (2003). What do we know about the language learning motivation of university students in Japan? Some patterns in survey studies. *JALT Journal*, 25, 86–100.

Järvelä, S. (2001). Shifting research on motivation and cognition to an integrated approach on learning and motivation in context. In S. Volet and S. Järvelä (Eds.), *Motivation in learning contexts: Theoretical advances and methodological implications* (pp. 3–14). Oxford: Elsevier Science.

Julkunen, K. (1989). *Situation- and task-specific motivation in foreign-language learning.* Joensuu: University of Joensuu.

Kim, T.-Y. (2009). The sociocultural interface between Ideal Self and Ought-to Self: A case study of two Korean students' ESL motivation. In Z. Dörnyei and E. Ushioda (Eds.), *Motivation, language identity and the L2 self* (pp. 274–294). Bristol: Multilingual Matters.

Kraemer, R. (1993). Social psychological factors related to the study of Arabic among Israeli high school students. *Studies in Second Language Acquisition*, 15, 83–105.

Kubanyiova, M. (2009). Possible selves in language teacher development. In Z. Dörnyei and E. Ushioda (Eds.), *Motivation, language identity and the L2 self* (pp. 314–332). Bristol: Multilingual Matters.

Lafford, B. A. (Ed.) (2007). Second language acquisition reconceptualized? The impact of Firth and Wagner (1997) (Focus issue). *The Modern Language Journal*, 91.

Larsen-Freeman, D. and Cameron, L. (2008a). *Complex systems and applied linguistics.* Oxford: Oxford University Press.

Larsen-Freeman, D. and Cameron, L. (2008b). Research methodology on language development from a complex systems perspective. *The Modern Language Journal*, 92, 200–213.

MacIntyre, P., Mackinnon, S., and Clément, R. (2009). Toward the development of a scale to assess possible selves as a source of language learning motivation. In Z. Dörnyei and E. Ushioda (Eds.), *Motivation, language identity and the L2 self* (pp. 193–214). Bristol: Multilingual Matters.

Markus, H. R. and Nurius, P. (1986). Possible selves. *American Psychologist, 41*, 954–69.

Masgoret, A.-M. and Gardner, R. C. (2003). Attitudes, motivation, and second language learning: A meta-analysis of studies conducted by Gardner and his associates. *Language Learning, 53* (Supplement 1), 167–210.

McDonough, S. (1981). *Psychology in foreign language teaching.* London: George Allen and Unwin.

Noels, K. A. (2001). New orientations in language learning motivation: Towards a model of intrinsic, extrinsic, and integrative orientations and motivation. In Z. Dörnyei and R. Schmidt (Eds.), *Motivation and second language acquisition* (pp. 43–68). Honolulu, HI: University of Hawaii Press.

Noels, K. A., Clément, R., and Pelletier, L. G. (1999). Perceptions of teachers' communicative style and students' intrinsic and extrinsic motivation. *The Modern Language Journal, 83*, 23–34.

Noels, K. A., Pelletier, L. G., Clément, R., and Vallerand, R. J. (2000). Why are you learning a second language? Motivational orientations and self-determination theory. *Language Learning, 50*, 57–85.

Norton, B. (2000). *Identity and language learning: Gender, ethnicity and educational change.* Harlow: Longman.

Oxford, R. L. and Shearin, J. (1994). Language learning motivation: Expanding the theoretical framework. *The Modern Language Journal, 78*, 12–28.

Ryan, S. (2009). Self and identity in L2 motivation in Japan: The ideal L2 self and Japanese learners of English. In Z. Dörnyei and E. Ushioda (Eds.), *Motivation, language identity and the L2 self* (pp. 120–143). Bristol: Multilingual Matters.

Sealey, A. and Carter, B. (2004). *Applied linguistics as social science.* London: Continuum.

Shoaib, A. and Dörnyei, Z. (2005). Affect in lifelong learning: Exploring L2 motivation as a dynamic process. In D. Nunan (Ed.), *Learners' stories: Difference and diversity in language learning* (pp. 22–41). Cambridge: Cambridge University Press.

Skehan, P. (1989). *Individual differences in second-language learning.* London: Edward Arnold.

Taguchi, T., Magid, M., and Papi, M. (2009). The L2 Motivational Self System among Japanese, Chinese and Iranian learners of English: A comparative study. In Z. Dörnyei and E. Ushioda (Eds.), *Motivation, language identity and the L2 self* (pp. 66–97). Bristol: Multilingual Matters.

Tremblay, P. F. and Gardner, R. C. (1995). Expanding the motivation construct in language learning. *The Modern Language Journal, 79*, 505–20.

Ushioda, E. (1996a). Developing a dynamic concept of L2 motivation. In T. Hickey and J. Williams (Eds.), *Language, education and society in a changing world* (pp. 239–245). Dublin/Clevedon, UK: IRAAL/Multilingual Matters.

Ushioda, E. (1996b). *Learner autonomy 5: The role of motivation.* Dublin: Authentik.

Ushioda, E. (2001). Language learning at university: Exploring the role of motivational thinking. In Z. Dörnyei and R. Schmidt (Eds.), *Motivation and second language acquisition* (pp. 93–125). Honolulu, HI: University of Hawaii Press.

Ushioda, E. (2003). Motivation as a socially mediated process. In D. Little, J. Ridley, and E. Ushioda (Eds.), *Learner autonomy in the foreign language classroom: Teacher, learner, curriculum and assessment* (pp. 90–102). Dublin: Authentik.

Ushioda, E. (2006). Language motivation in a reconfigured Europe: Access, identity and autonomy. *Journal of Multilingual and Multicultural Development, 27*, 148–61.

Ushioda, E. (2008). Motivation and good language learners. In C. Griffiths (Ed.), *Lessons from good language learners* (pp. 19–34). Cambridge: Cambridge University Press.

Ushioda, E. (2009). A person-in-context relational view of emergent motivation, self and identity. In Z. Dörnyei and E. Ushioda (Eds.), *Motivation, language identity and the L2 self* (pp. 215–228). Bristol: Multilingual Matters.

Warden, C. and Lin, H. J. (2000). Existence of integrative motivation in Asian EFL settings. *Foreign Language Annals, 33*, 535–47.

Williams, M. and Burden, R. L. (1997). *Psychology for language teachers.* Cambridge: Cambridge University Press.

Williams, M. and Burden, R. L. (1999). Students' developing conceptions of themselves as language learners. *The Modern Language Journal, 83*, 193–201.

Williams, M., Burden, R. L., and Al-Baharna, S. (2001). Making sense of success and failure: The role of the individual in motivation theory. In Z. Dörnyei and R. Schmidt (Eds.), *Motivation and second language acquisition* (pp. 171–184). Honolulu, HI: University of Hawaii Press.

Yashima, T. (2002). Willingness to communicate in a second language: The Japanese context. *The Modern Language Journal, 86*, 54–66.

Zuengler, J. and Miller, E. R. (2006). Cognitive and sociocultural perspectives: Two parallel SLA worlds? *TESOL Quarterly, 40*, 35–58.

25

Identity, agency, and second language acquisition*

Patricia A. Duff

Introduction

The processes of learning an additional language and the experiences and backgrounds of language learners have been conceptualized in various ways since the field of second language acquisition (SLA) was established. Each descriptor related to *language learners* has foregrounded certain aspects of their lives, their abilities, their identities and aspirations, and has also reflected certain theoretical assumptions about SLA historically. In SLA theory and practice in recent decades, for example, language learners have been described using the following terms: *interlanguage speakers, fossilized second language (L2) users, immigrants, limited (English) proficient speakers, refugees, non-native speakers, heritage-language learners, Generation 1.5 learners.* These terms and many others like them, typically chosen by researchers or institutions rather than by learners (research participants) themselves, often convey incomplete processes and outcomes of learning and acculturation. In contrast, the terms *bilinguals, multilinguals, advanced L2 users* (not *"learners"*), *multicompetent speakers,* or *lingua franca speakers/users,* to provide just a few alternatives, depict the same individuals, the larger social groups they belong to, and their dispositions and accomplishments—such as their attained L2 or L3 proficiency—quite differently.

How one is defined or described by oneself or by others, whether in research contexts or in life more generally, will of course always be partial, subjective, and situation-dependent. People invariably have a variety of social roles, identities, and characteristics, not all of which may be relevant or salient at the moment of description or easily captured in just one or two words. Whatever labels are used to describe language learners, these naming practices position people and their abilities and aspirations in particular ways, which itself has become a topic of critical reflection and theorizing in applied linguistics (e.g., Block, 2007a, 2007b; Leung *et al.*, 1997; Norton, 1997a, 1997b, 2000; Norton Peirce, 1995; Thesen, 1997).

In what follows, I first present a brief review of identity and agency as described and operationalized traditionally in SLA and sociolinguistics and then proceed to current perspectives. Next I describe research methods and theoretical approaches associated with studies of identity in SLA and finally suggest future directions for work in this area.

Historical discussion

Sociological and social-psychological approaches

In early sociological research, aspects of identity such as gender, first language (L1), and ethnicity tended to be treated as straightforward, easily categorized, relatively homogeneous, and static group variables—an assumption critiqued a generation later. A student or speaker belonged to one social (e.g., ethnolinguistic) group or another, and the relationships (correlations, causal relations) between that group identification and certain traits (e.g., L2 proficiency), behaviors (L2 use), attitudes, or motivations were investigated. Much of the first generation of research in this area took place in Canada, an officially bilingual country with national multicultural policies designed to help minorities retain aspects of their ethnic group identity (e.g., language, culture, traditions; see Edwards, 1985), which in turn led to educational possibilities for majority language (Anglophone) students to study French and Francophone minority students to study English. A great deal of social-psychological research on the attitudes, dispositions, and learning of French by Anglophone Canadians or of English by Francophones ensued. Identity was operationalized as the degree or strength of ethnic or linguistic identification with one's own (L1) group in relation to other groups.

Categories such as ethnicity, L1, or gender served as independent variables in studies investigating how women's speech differs from men's, how working-class people (i.e., those with lower socio-economic status, SES) use language in comparison with people of higher classes or SES, and how identification with one's ethnolinguistic group or the vitality of one's group influenced one's attitudes and behaviors, either fostering or hindering language learning or particular linguistic practices (e.g., Giles and St. Clair, 1979, and issues of the *International Journal of the Sociology of Language* during those same years).

Language use (e.g., code choice, register, genre, accent) itself conveys social information such as group identity: geographical region, language variety, and thus, in some contexts, socio-economic status, or educational background. Linguistic variants therefore mark "insider" (in-group) or "outsider" (out-group) status relative to one's interlocutors or audience. Clear evidence of the relationships between ways of speaking and (ascribed) social identity emerged in experimental studies in Montreal, and later elsewhere, in which bilinguals or multiple-dialect speakers were asked to read a text in different languages or varieties (e.g., Genesee and Holobow, 1989; Lambert *et al.*, 1960). Listeners would react to the different types of language as though they were produced by different people and make judgments about them; for example, the English speaker was judged more "reliable;" the French speaker more "intelligent" or "attractive," and thus inferences were drawn about not just the speakers but the sociolinguistic groups the speakers ostensibly belonged to. This *matched guise technique* indirectly revealed attitudes and biases toward particular linguistic identities, varieties, and social groups, including toward one's own group.

Recent research in social psychology with respect to motivation and SLA describes aspects of language identity in terms of the "self": e.g., the "ought-to self" (see Dörnyei and Ushioda, 2009). Researchers now attempt to view motivation in a somewhat more dynamic, emergent, and socially constructed vein than in earlier accounts, explaining that motivation needed to be "radically reconceptualized and retheorized in the context of contemporary notions of self and identity" and needed to incorporate issues of hybridity in relation to Global English, especially (Ushioda and Dörnyei, 2009, p. 1). The authors also capture notions of future possibilities and imagined identities in chapters on "possible selves"—and not just one's current self—following Norton (2000, and elsewhere).

Patricia A. Duff

Sociolinguistic approaches to identity and agency

Sociolinguistics, according to Edwards (1985), "is *essentially about identity*, its formation, presentation and maintenance" (p. 3, emphasis in original). The first generation of sociolinguists commonly used social categories related to identity, such as age, gender, race, nationality/ethnicity, L1 background, or class (SES). In *Language and Social Identity*, Gumperz (1982) and his colleagues took a more contextualized and interactional perspective on communication examining actual discourse as it unfolds instead of using questionnaire-based surveys of attitudes and practices related to language and social identity. Their qualitative discourse analytic approaches allowed them to study how identity manifests itself in everyday speech events such as job interviews and also how interlocutors—and especially minority group members, such as recent immigrants—may be socially and discursively positioned in various ways, sometimes to their disadvantage (e.g., as reticent, hostile, unforthcoming, evasive, or overly direct), on the basis of their group membership. The researchers' goal was to assist minority-group members, often L2 learners of English, to gain better access to employment and other opportunities in "modern industrial society." As Gumperz and Cook-Gumperz (1982) explained, "to understand issues of identity and how they affect and are affected by social, political, and ethnic divisions we need to gain insights into the communicative processes by which they arise" (p. 1).

Early studies of identity and agency in SLA

In early SLA interlanguage analysis studies, some applied linguists made connections among sociolinguistics, identity, and SLA, such as the variety of language a learner chooses (high prestige, low prestige) as his or her target L2 model. They also highlighted learners' agency in SLA. Zuengler (1989), for example, argued that learners exert their *agency* or choice in selecting a target variety to learn, such as a high-status standard variety or a non-standard variety representing solidarity with a peer group, and that it is not simply a result of exposure: "it could be described as a decision as to who the learner wants to *identify* with" (p. 82). Beebe's (1980) early work on style-shifting in SLA, furthermore, showed how learners' identification with a prestige variety or marker in their L1 (Thai) influenced their L2 production. That work was not about identity *per se* but captured how social identification and status markers indirectly influenced SLA by subtly affecting learners' choice of phonological variants, such choices being an aspect of agency.

Other research suggested that L2 learners might deliberately *not* accommodate to certain target L2 features, revealing aspects of their identities and agency. Women in Siegal's (1994) study of Westerners learning Japanese in Japan typically resisted very honorific, deferential, and feminine Japanese speech patterns because such forms or registers were incompatible with their identities as assertive Western women.

SLA diary studies since the late 1970s (e.g., Bailey, 1983; Kramsch, 2009; Pavlenko and Lantolf, 2000; Schumann, 1997) have analyzed aspects of language learners' identities and self-image based on their status as foreign language learners and teachers, expatriate L2 learners (and, simultaneously, English language educators), or as highly competitive students seeking recognition and distinction in required L2 courses. However, much of the early research saw the issues encountered by learners (anxiety, competitiveness) as internal and psychological more so than fundamentally social or sociological.

Recent studies of identity, agency, and SLA

Recent scholarship in the disciplines of anthropology, sociology, and cultural psychology has contributed a great deal to how identity in L2 learning is viewed and how L2 learners are represented in and through their interactions with others, particularly as a result of the development of sociocultural theory (Lantolf, 2000; Wenger, 1998). Insights from various other theoretical and methodological approaches, such as poststructuralism, critical theory, feminist theory, narrative inquiry, phenomenology, and hermeneutics (which represent different ways of understanding and interpreting human behavior and experience) have all influenced SLA and have addressed issues of identity and agency (e.g., Block, 2003, 2007; Duff, 2002; Kramsch, 2002, 2009; Morgan, 2007; Norton, 2000; Pavlenko, 2002, 2008). Norton (1997a, 1997b, 2000; Norton Peirce, 1995) was particularly influential in her arguments for the centrality of identity and agency in SLA, informed by critical theory, sociology, feminist theory, and poststructuralism. The publication of many book-length language learning memoirs written by non-linguists also addressed issues of identity and agency directly (e.g., Hoffman, 1989; Kaplan, 1993; Lvovich, 1997; Pavlenko and Lantolf, 2000). These memoirs often featured highly literate immigrant women reflecting on their complex experiences and their very mixed feelings and ambivalence about themselves as a consequence of their L2 learning, and loss of aspects of their L1 and former identities (e.g., Norton, 2000; Pavlenko and Norton, 2007). In general, this work examines identity in terms of a learner's unique past, present, and future experiences, desires, trajectories, and opportunities. This body of work, unlike more traditional SLA, has paid relatively little attention to an analysis of what learners are actually observed to do *with* and *in* their L2 or other languages and literacies in their repertoire. The research tends to examine the individual in relation to the social world and affective dimensions of identity. And rather than seek coherent, consistent, and generalizable results, the research considers some of the contradictions conveyed—or performed— by L2 language learners and users about their experiences and the sometimes hybrid notions of identity that result (Kramsch, 2009). In *Selves in Two Languages*, for instance, Koven (2007) pluralizes the language learner self (selves). There has consequently been considerable attention paid to individuals' lives as new immigrants learning an additional language and seeking integration into educational, occupational, and other social spaces in their new society yet experiencing various kinds of internal, interpersonal, and societal struggles and indeterminate trajectories or outcomes in the process. Deterministic accounts of biological or social aspects of identity in SLA have been critiqued in favor of continually *negotiated* identities and the "nonunitary subject" (Norton, 2000, p. 125).

Agency, referred to earlier in relation to Zuengler's (1989) and Siegal's (1994) studies, has become an important theoretical construct in SLA as well, often in combination with *identity*, reflecting the view that learners are not simply passive or complicit participants in language learning and use, but can also make informed choices, exert influence, resist (e.g., remain silent, quit courses), or comply, although their social circumstances may constrain their choices. Such actions or displays of agency, which might be as simple as insisting on speaking one language (one's L2) versus another (others' L2) in a conversation with a language exchange partner, can also be considered acts of identity and the site of power dynamics (Le Page and Tabouret-Keller, 1985). An additional construct introduced by Norton (2000), also connected with agency in SLA, is *investment*, which captures the degree to which people actively put symbolic, material, and other resources into their language learning based on a kind of cost-benefit assessment, and in light of their desires and hopes.

Currently, attention is being focused on how interlocutors' actions, perceptions, and *language use* serve to position language learners/users and their investments in particular ways. That is, the focus is not just the "objective" identities of individuals but how certain aspects of their identities are construed subjectively by others (e.g., as "legitimate" or "illegitimate"; Lave and Wenger, 1991; Wenger, 1998). Morita (2004) provides a detailed study of six female Japanese international students in Canadian university content courses in which the participants had various experiences related to their in-class participation, perceptions of their English L2 proficiency and content knowledge, and the identities imposed on them but also contested by them.

In another study, of Japanese L2 learning in a Canadian university program, Nakamura (2005, Duff *et al.*, 2006) showed how a small-group of Japanese learners negotiated meanings related to the Japanese language and also content, as well as their own identities and histories as L1 and L2 learners. The Japanese (heritage) background student in the group tried to foreground her identity as a Canadian with reasonably good conversational Japanese ability, but one who preferred to speak English in class and showed some resistance to being positioned as Japanese, consistent with her having dropped out of Japanese heritage-language courses as a child. Her lack of Japanese literacy skills, and particularly Japanese characters, *kanji*, was backgrounded. The Chinese Canadian immigrant students, on the other hand, foregrounded their literate identities, as people with expertise in character recognition, based on their proficiency in L1 Chinese characters, drawing attention away from their lack of Japanese oral skills. They were also positioned by the Japanese-Canadian classmate as people who did not know Canadian culture or geography, as relative newcomers to Canada, and they therefore deferred to her knowledge of oral Japanese and the local culture to complete the assigned task.

In a Chinese L2 learning context, Lantolf and Genung (2002) described Genung's unhappy experiences of attempting to fulfill a PhD program language requirement by studying intensive Chinese. Genung, who was multilingual in several European languages and a colonel in the US Army and highly motivated to learn Chinese at the outset, kept a journal and later produced a retrospective account of her experiences as a highly frustrated student in the course. She felt a lack of agency in the course because of the inflexible rules for classroom interaction and the lockstep teaching methods. Classroom greeting and leave-taking routines were "juvenile and demeaning" to her—socializing her into an infantile identity she did not want and especially as a military officer of some rank. She became resigned to enduring the course instruction, however, to obtain the required course credit but did not learn Chinese to the level desired.

The above examples illustrate how students came to their classroom or other interactions with particular kinds of expertise (or lack of expertise), identities, and desires, but these attributes were also constrained or reframed by their classmates or teachers or the curriculum in ways they did not always appreciate and were at cross-purposes with their SLA and identities.

Agency, gendered identities, and SLA

Facile representations of learners and their language-learning-related identities, and especially identities that are too unidimensional and homogenized, are now considered problematic. To assume that all Japanese female graduate students, for instance, will have similar experiences and exhibit similar linguistic behaviors and dispositions in a Canadian university classroom context or across different classroom contexts *essentializes* their identities as Japanese females, downplaying their many other identities, abilities, roles, and potential acts of agency or choice and also denying the role of their interlocutors and contexts in shaping their actions (Morita, 2004). Essentialism in such work is seen to be a reproduction of stereotypes, both negative and positive. As noted earlier, much of the emerging research on identity, particularly from a poststructural perspective, focuses on the dynamics of identity construction and performance and agency, portraying learners as individuals with wants and needs and with multifaceted identities, who may exert themselves and their interests by making deliberate choices with respect to language learning, including the choice to resist learning or perform in the target language in expected ways (Pavlenko, 2007). Alternatively, they may choose other learning approaches, such as participating in virtual or simulated (L2) worlds—and other identities (e.g., *computer nerd, jock, party animal, class clown*)—instead.

Despite such discussions of agency, however, scholars interested in gender and (second) language learning point out that often women or learners from historically disadvantaged socio-economic and socio-cultural backgrounds may have fewer actual choices in SLA and thus limited opportunities to express their agency or realize a fuller range of their (potential) identities due to various social, cultural, and economic constraints (Norton, 2000). These constraints might include domestic duties in the home, restricted opportunities for, or expectations about, their advanced education, or the need to support themselves or their family by working in entry-level positions that do not require or develop higher-level L2 proficiency. In addition, they may experience peer pressure to maintain solidarity with others from similar ethnolinguistic backgrounds and not to leave their primary linguistic communities by becoming too integrated in mainstream society (Goldstein, 1997; Norton, 2000; Pavlenko, 2004; Pavlenko and Blackledge, 2004). That is, the possibility of becoming a student, a lifelong learner, or a proficient speaker and member of the L2 community with many available options and resources may not be welcomed within the home or L1/L2 community. To give another scenario, female learners in study-abroad contexts may find that their agency over their learning may be stymied by sexual harassment in or exclusion from (gendered) public domains where they might otherwise have been able to learn or practice their L2, thus reducing their opportunities to fulfill their potential, their desires, or even their program requirements (e.g., Kinginger, 2008; Polanyi, 1995; see review by Block, 2007a). Their gendered experiences therefore clearly impact their SLA trajectories (Ehrlich, 1997).

On a more positive note, engaging in SLA can enable some learners, such as the Japanese women learning English in McMahill's (1997, 2001) and Kobayashi's (2002) studies, to develop and express aspects of their identity in more egalitarian or empowering ways than would be possible or acceptable in their L1, Japanese. Learning English may therefore be considered an act of resistance to hierarchical and gendered cultural norms within "communities of resistance" and a language with many other possibilities (McMahill, 1997).

Core issues

Definitions of identity and agency

Identity. Issues connected with identity in relation to bilingualism and L2 learning and use have been theorized and researched in various ways over the past several decades. Identity, the focus of this chapter, is crucially related to one's core *self* (or senses of self). Sometimes *identity* is used synonymously with *subjectivities* or *subject positions* in the burgeoning literature in this area, which now includes the *Journal of Language, Identity and Education* and many articles and collections in other journals and books with a focus on identity in second language (L2) or multilingual contexts (see Block, 2007a, 2007b; Dörnyei and Ushioda, 2009; Jackson, 2008; Kramsch, 2009; Menard-Warwick, 2009). *Identity* traditionally was understood in terms of one's connection or identification with a particular social group, the emotional ties one has with that group, and the meanings that connection has for an individual. Tajfel (1974, 1978) is commonly cited in early social-psychological treatments of identity relevant to SLA (see McNamara, 1997, pp. 562–564). Processes of self- and other-categorization, awareness of social identity, social comparison, and social distinctiveness in intergroup relations were central to his conceptualization of identity. Pavlenko and Blackledge (2004), representing a more recent, and quite widely accepted theoretical perspective, describe identity as "a dynamic and shifting nexus of multiple subject positions, or identity options, such as mother, accountant, heterosexual, or Latina" (p. 35). Norton (2000), influenced by feminist poststructuralist theory (Weedon, 1997) and critical sociology (e.g., Bourdieu, 1977, 1991), conceives of identity as follows:

... how a person understands his or her relationship to the world, how that relationship is constructed across time and space, and how the person understands possibilities for the future. I argue that SLA theory needs to develop a conception of identity that is understood with reference to larger, and more frequently inequitable, social structures which are reproduced in day-to-day social interaction. (p. 5)

Thus, scholars increasingly emphasize the *multiple* possible social groups or roles that individuals such as language learners may identify with at any given time and how language (or discourse) itself works to construct those same identities situationally whether in research interviews or in L2 classrooms.

Consider the term *heritage-language (HL) learners*, such as Chinese-Canadians learning Chinese. The assumption that HL learners represent a fairly homogeneous and stable identity category is very problematic for both theory and practice. HL learners' levels of expertise in, and affiliation with, the heritage language and with HL literacy practices, may vary considerably from one HL person to another, at different points in the learner's life, and with different interlocutors, despite their heritage; furthermore, their (home) language may be a different variety than the one taught in educational institutions (Leung *et al.*, 1997; see also Blackledge and Creese, 2008; He, 2004, 2006). To give another example, *Generation 1.5 English language learners/users* typically immigrate to an L2 context as children and experience some or most of their primary/secondary education there, unlike their parents. However, the same students may be construed as hardworking, model minority students (i.e., "good students"), or as students with problems in language or literacy development, attitudes, and in their academic work as well ("the worst") (Harklau, 2000; Talmy, 2008).

Thesen (1997) argued that "educators need to expand the repertoire of identity categories by which they describe and explain the complex and often contradictory stances that students take in the acquisition of academic literacy" (p. 487). McKay and Wong (1996), drawing on earlier work by Norton Peirce (1995), were among the first to examine the intersection of identity and agency in the different "discourses" being negotiated by their Chinese-American high school case study subjects with respect to their identities at school (e.g., model-minority status, gender, and nationality).

Current discussions of identity in SLA textbooks are framed in terms of "social aspects" or "social dimensions" of language learning (e.g., Ellis, 2008, and Ortega, 2009, respectively) rather than as primarily affective or individual factors. Identity is therefore associated with the "social turn" in SLA (Block, 2003) and with particular qualitative approaches to research, such as narrative inquiry, and theory that ranges from interpretive to poststructural to critical (Duff, 2008a). Interpretive research tends to focus on how language learners and others (e.g., teachers) make sense of their experiences and also how researchers in turn make sense of (interpret) data obtained from interviews, observations, narratives, and other sources. Poststructuralism eschews fixed categories or structures, oppositional binaries, closed systems, and stable "truths" and, rather, embraces contradictions and multiple meanings (Pavlenko, 2002, 2008). Critical research is more directly ideological, normally assuming that particular social relations and structures historically disadvantage certain participants, such as language learners, or certain kinds of learners who have less power and control over their conditions than others, based on their race, gender, class, age, immigrant status, and so on. Not coincidentally, perhaps, these research methods and theories have gained some prominence in SLA together along with dynamic systems approaches, complexity theory, and new understandings of social context and the ecology of language learning (e.g., Atkinson, 2011; Block, 2007a, 2007b; Dörnyei and Ushioda, 2009; Kramsch, 2002; Menard-Warwick, 2006; Norton, 2010; Ricento, 2005; Swain and Deters, 2007). A similar shift toward an examination of identity and the incorporation of poststructural perspectives has occurred in L1 and L2 literacy studies (e.g., Ivanič, 1997; Starfield, 2002; Warriner, 2007), in second/foreign/heritage language education (Day, 2002; He, 2004; Kubota and Lin, 2006; McKinney and Norton, 2008; Miller, 2003; Nelson, 2009; Potowski, 2007; Toohey, 2000; White, 2007), and in other fields in the social, human, and applied sciences (e.g., sociolinguistics; Bucholtz and Hall, 2004a, 2004b; Ehrlich, 1997; Omonyi and White, 2006). Other research has examined the intersections between language teacher and language learner identities (e.g., Clarke, 2008; Duff and Uchida, 1997; Kubota and Lin, 2006; Nelson, 2009; Pavlenko, 2003; Varghese et al., 2005). This work, taken together, considers how social/ cultural and professional identity, race, gender, language proficiency, and sexuality, and other aspects of identity (e.g., expertise, non-native vs. native speaker status and thus perceived legitimacy) are (co-)constructed in classroom SLA especially. Language socialization research also places an emphasis on identity and agency in SLA (Duff and Hornberger, 2008; Ochs, 1993; Wortham, 2006) by examining the cultural apprenticeship of newcomers into not only new communities and linguistic and social practices, but also new identities, ideologies and worldviews (Duff, 2010).

Agency. Agency refers to people's ability to make choices, take control, self-regulate, and thereby pursue their goals as individuals leading, potentially, to personal or social transformation. Ahearn (2001), a linguistic anthropologist, defines agency as "the socioculturally mediated capacity to act" (p. 112). A sense of agency enables people to imagine, take up, and perform new roles or identities (including those of proficient L2 speaker or multilingual) and to take concrete actions in pursuit of their goals. Agency can also enable people to actively resist certain behaviors, practices, or positionings, sometimes leading to oppositional stances and behaviors leading to other identities, such as rebellious, diffident student. A perceived lack of agency on the part of learners might lead to similar outcomes as they become passive and disengaged from educational pursuits. Agency, power, and social context (structures) are therefore linked because those who typically feel the most control over their lives, choices, and circumstances also have the power—the human, social, or cultural capital and ability—they need to succeed. Indeed, Pavlenko and Lantolf (2000) argue that:

> ultimate attainment in second language learning relies on one's agency ... While the first language and subjectivities are an indisputable given, the new ones are arrived at by choice. Agency is crucial at the point where the individuals must not just start memorizing a dozen new words and expressions but have to decide on whether to initiate a long, painful, inexhaustive and, for some, never-ending process of self-translation.
>
> *(pp. 169–170)*

Although children, displaced people, or students fulfilling language requirements may have relatively little apparent choice or control over their L2 learning, reaching advanced levels of L2 proficiency arguably requires concerted effort, sustained and strategic practice, and opportunity—all manifestations of personal and social agency (see Flowerdew and Miller, 2008; Gao, 2010).

Data and common elicitation measures

The most common research methods for the design, collection, and analysis of empirical data related to identity and agency in SLA are one or more of the following: (1) case study methods (e.g., Duff, 2008a); (2) ethnographic research with embedded case studies (e.g., Day, 2002; Duff, 2008b; Toohey, 2001); (3) narrative inquiry (Pavlenko, 2007, 2008); (4) mixed-method research involving proficiency interviews and personal narratives (e.g., Kinginger, 2008); and

(5) conversation analysis or discourse analysis to examine interactions in classroom, interview, or other settings (e.g., Talmy and Richards, 2011). However, these methods are not mutually exclusive.

With respect to the first two categories, case studies and ethnographies, Day (2002) conducted an ethnographic case study of a young Punjabi-Canadian boy, Hari (age five when her study began), one of five participants in her larger (dissertation) study of diverse learners in a kindergarten class in a suburb of Vancouver, Canada. Day examined interactions between Hari and his (Anglo) teacher, on the one hand, and Hari and his friends and classmates, on the other, noting how his home language use shifted at school to English even with Punjabi speakers, who deferred to him.

Toohey (1998, 2000, 2001) conducted a similar multi-year ethnographic multiple-case study of ethnolinguistically diverse students in the same contexts, focusing on their disputes, their positioning of one another and positioning by the teacher in both socially/academically advantageous and disadvantageous ways and positioning by other students as well (cf., Norton and Toohey, 2001). Again, the analysis involved a triangulation of data from various sources, including classroom observations, interviews, document analysis, and discourse analysis. Data in the publications included representative classroom discourse excerpts revealing some of the themes that emerged connected with social exclusion, for example.

Other research has been based more on the analysis of learners' narratives about their experiences than on direct observations of their interactions in public spaces (see Pavlenko, 2007, 2008). The narratives take various forms, typically diaries, journals, and often published memoirs produced by the authors/researchers themselves; or narratives elicited from others by means of in-depth interviews or written diaries or journals. The narratives are usually subjected to a content analysis of emerging themes related to identity, agency, and SLA, from various theoretical perspectives—ranging from neurobiology (Schumann, 1997) to poststructuralism (Norton, 2000). In the narrative inquiry tradition, it has been much less common than in more traditional approaches to SLA to document and analyze learners' L2 proficiency. Thus, the narratives have been current and retrospective accounts of learners' experiences and perceptions (e.g., about their identities in relation to SLA), produced either in their L1 or L2, without any independent analysis of their linguistic development or their linguistic profiles.

The fourth approach has been to combine SLA proficiency interviews with narrative traditions to provide a better sense of learners' actual abilities and identities—and changes over time—in the L2. Kinginger (2008) described in some detail the linguistic profiles of a group of American study-abroad learners of French both before and after their sojourn in France. She combined her linguistic description and analysis with a thematic analysis of learners' narratives (journals, interview accounts) produced mostly in their L1 throughout their time abroad.

The fifth approach can take data from a variety of sources and perform an in-depth analysis of interactional features in discourse such as turn-taking, repetition, repair (corrections), questioning strategies by teachers, and so on, thought to be connected with identity, agency and SLA.

Data analysis

Researchers can analyze qualitative data for evidence of identity and agency in SLA in many different ways. For example, pronoun use by speakers (teachers, students, interviewers, and interviewees) might be analyzed and interpreted as a sign of different group affiliations connected with identity: *us* vs. *them, we* vs. *I, the local children* vs. *us, the other workers* vs. *me.* Alternatively, learners may be asked to come up with metaphors to describe themselves, their experiences, and SLA itself, and these metaphors might be analyzed and compared conceptually. Categorical noun phrases used in oral or written texts might also be relevant, especially when they reference the roles, backgrounds, or status of oneself as an L2 learner or of others: *ESL students, White students, non-native speakers, Chinese students* vs. *Canadians, foreigners learning Chinese, outsiders, newcomers,* and other such terms (Duff, 2002). Normally there are no measures, per se, unless quantification of one's identification with a language or group or identity is sought, which is not typically done.

Critical incidents or interactions (e.g., with native speakers in an L2 context) reported by participants or observed by researchers might also be analyzed for how they seemed or were reported to affect language learners' identities, practices, or persistence as L2 learners, for example.

For a more linguistic analysis of agency, the kinds (and mood) of verbs and modal auxiliaries used by speakers might be very telling: e.g., *chose* vs. *was forced to ...*, *conquered / mastered (the language)* vs. *failed (to learn), tried* vs. *did not manage to ...*, *will* vs. *might, can* vs. *cannot.* Other expressions of agency might also be relevant, such as by focusing on adverbials such as *intentionally, persistently,* or *without giving up* or adjectives such as *devastated, disappointed, euphoric, confused, fluent, tongue-tied.* Or the researcher might simply take note of the decisions made by speakers in a content or thematic analysis of data: *took a course, dropped a course, sought out language exchange partners, practiced as often as possible, joined online chat rooms,* or *withdrew from all interactions involving the L2.* What is coded or selected by researchers for analysis and interpretation depends a great deal on the research questions, the constructs, the quantity of data and types of data, the number of participants (e.g., a single case analysis vs. a cross-case analysis) and the length of the study. Whether one codes, quantifies, or pinpoints relevant linguistic expressions or simply chooses highly representative examples of their use and meaning vis-à-vis identity, agency, and SLA again depends on the research approach and theory that is adopted. Non-verbal behaviors, social networks, artistic constructions (photo collages, artwork, plays) or essays created by learners to represent themselves might also be examined more holistically for evidence of how language learners perceive or portray themselves and/or their linguistic and cultural attributes, histories, and futures.

Empirical verification

Empirical verification may take the form of inter-coder reliability checks or quantification, as in other SLA traditions, possibly using qualitative data analysis software, or may be achieved by conducting a systematic and rigorous analysis of multiple texts or datasets pertaining to the same individual as part of the process of triangulation. An analysis of changing perceptions by oneself or others, or even inherent contradictions, tensions, or counter-examples, may be important to include as part of the empirical verification and validation (see Duff, 2008a). Verification or validation in some research on identity and agency is not based on whether the researcher—or the research participant—has produced the "truest" or "best" account of SLA. The work is judged based on whether it is a credible, convincing, or plausible account, and perhaps even presents a novel interpretation of data, but one whose claims or assertions are well supported by evidence and are relevant to existing or new theory. In this way, the reader can also feel confident about the interpretations or, alternatively, may arrive at different conclusions and a sense of how relevant the findings are to other SLA contexts and populations.

Narrative- and interview-based research at present also recognizes that the narratives and other types of data produced by learners—in whatever form—are social constructions, produced in a particular situation, with an intended audience, for particular purposes, and based on the contingencies of the mode and language of production itself. How research participants represent themselves and their histories or experiences may depend to a great extent on their assumptions about what the researcher expects to hear. Therefore, explicit reflection by researchers on the research process and the social context in which recruitment and data collection took place, and their own role in the research and their connection to the research participants is normally included in such research (Talmy, 2010). In summary, the researcher should provide justification of, and explanations for, theoretical, methodological, analytical, and representational decisions to be as transparent and ethical as possible about the research process.

One trend in SLA case study research related to identity is to include several cases, rather than just one, providing some indication of the representativeness of the cases in terms of sampling and findings (see Duff, 2008a, for examples). Other research attempts to include "member checks" in which research participants (if willing and able) can provide feedback on the researcher's interpretation of the data analysis or can offer alternative perspectives.

Applications

Studies of identity and agency in SLA have very clear relevance for both language learners and educators. It is important for teachers and learners to understand their own stances and positionings, and how these affect their engagement with (or participation in) language education. Furthermore, we must better understand how teachers, learners, and language textbook writers (e.g., Shardakova and Pavlenko, 2004) portray or position learners, either inadvertently or intentionally, in classrooms as well as in published instructional materials, or influence the kinds of language students are exposed to in such a way that they may reinforce existing stereotypes or provide an inadequate range of registers and genres through interactions and course materials. We must also consider how such positioning might affect the opportunities the learners have to expand their future L2 repertoires and identities.

Abdi (2009, 2011), for example, in her recent study of Canadian high school Spanish classes with a mixture of heritage and non-heritage language students, found that the well-meaning teacher in that class (non-Hispanic, but formerly married to a Mexican) identified quite closely with some of the Hispanic-background students in her class—and with a very charismatic, outspoken teenaged Hispanic male in particular. She encouraged the HL students to speak Spanish in class to help expose their peers—and her—to authentic Spanish. However, her positioning of some students as Spanish-background (HL students), even when they were not (e.g., in the case of a Portuguese-speaking Brazilian) or, conversely, her lack of recognition of some Spanish-background students as such, when they were, or her sometimes dismissive attitude to the potential contributions and needs of the non-HL students, gave the individuals not only different sorts of validation related to their linguistic or cultural expertise, but also different opportunities to use their Spanish in class and thus to improve by having more opportunities to practice and get feedback. However, as Abdi reported (and Morita (2004), documented in a related study), the teacher was quite oblivious to the sometimes very detrimental effects that her ways of viewing, grouping, and discussing students and their abilities and backgrounds had on students, their learning, identities, and motivation.

Thus it is important for teachers to know learners' cultural and linguistic backgrounds, abilities, and aspirations better, to begin with, as well as other aspects of their identity that are important to them (artistic, academic, or athletic abilities, other interests, or strengths; Cummins, 2006). This knowledge will enable teachers to provide encouragement and support for students and to find suitable topics or projects about which they might wish to communicate in their L2. Finally, teachers can play a crucial role by inspiring students to persist with their L2 development and use, and with their ongoing L2 identity construction, through the use of engaging and pedagogically sound instruction. They can also introduce them to new digital media and platforms enabling students to take more control and responsibility for their own learning (exercising personal agency).

Future directions

Research on identity and agency in SLA shows every sign of becoming a more significant aspect of SLA theorizing. With new means of conducting and disseminating research, especially mediated by new information and communication technologies and multimodal, multilingual graphic interfaces, it is likely that future research will aim to incorporate more languages, images, voices, and sound, visual, and textual data into accessible online research accounts (cf., Swain and Deters, 2007) that can be annotated by participants, by stakeholders, and by other researchers in so-called Web 2.0 (i.e., second-generation, more collaborative, interactive, Web-based) communities and platforms. Accordingly, research questions that could be addressed in the future include these:

(1) How might developments in research on identity and agency transform theory and methodologies in those areas of SLA that have previously not considered those aspects, as in recent developments in motivation research—e.g., Dörnyei and Ushioda's (2009) embrace of selfhood, subjectivity, and dynamicity in social-psychological research? Related to this question, how might more interpretive and critical research, that is, research that applies critical theory by examining power in SLA, together with an examination of identity and agency, be brought to bear on the teaching, learning, and use of languages in contexts of language revitalization, Indigenous languages, postcolonial settings, lingua francas, non-European target languages, and signed languages, all of which have been seriously under-studied in SLA? For example, how might findings in research on Chinese or Japanese as an additional language with Turkish, Ugandan, and Vietnamese L1 learners (in those countries and/or studying in China or Japan) differ from existing work with predominantly White Anglophone learners of European (especially English and French) and Asian languages (mainly Chinese and Japanese) with respect to identity and agency (Duff *et al.*, 2013)? And how might those same results change when diverse populations of learners, with varying race, ethnicity, professional standing, age, and gender backgrounds, are included in the studies?

(2) What new technological and theoretical innovations in identity research and in the multi-modal and multilingual representation of findings, perhaps drawing on fields outside of applied linguistics (semiotics, cultural studies), could inform research in this area so that it continues to produce original new insights and not just print-based, somewhat predictable accounts of people's struggles and negotiations as L2 users? And how might truly longitudinal research be undertaken in such a way that identity and agency can be tracked over time, across contexts and languages, satisfactorily?

(3) How might participants in identity/agency research be more centrally involved in decisions related to the research enterprise and to authorship so that the researcher is not given primary ownership and authority over the collection, analysis, interpretation, representation, and publication of data that is jointly produced?

(4) How might research bring together in innovative, interesting, and multidimensional ways the contingencies and hybridity of teacher, researcher, and student/learner/research participants' experiences with respect to issues of identity and agency in the same study? One possibility, for example, would be to represent their experiences multilingually rather than monolin-gually, through translation, or using code-switching in the research reports themselves (cf., Brogden, 2009).

(5) What new qualitative data analysis tools and insights might be integrated in the analysis and presentation of narrative data so that the results are sufficiently theorized, contextualized, and exemplified, following recent suggestions by Pavlenko (2007, 2008)? For example, how

might corpus research or qualitative data analysis software help tag the linguistic expression of agency or identity in narratives in a systematic and theoretically interesting manner?

(6) How might the technologically sophisticated language learners/users of today and tomorrow engaged in learning and using language in creative new ways via social networking, gaming, simulations, and other virtual experiences that may involve different kinds of identities (e.g., imagined or simulated ones) and agentive acts, help advance SLA theory, empirical research, and educational practice in keeping with new advances in our highly globalized societies? Since practice-based and sociolinguistic approaches to SLA both emphasize that language experience with roles, audiences, interactions, and texts of various types is necessary to effectively expand one's communicative repertoire, how might new media facilitate this in engaging ways?

To conclude, research on identity and agency in SLA—and in many related areas of academia—has made tremendous strides in recent years. This work is now having a major impact on subfields of SLA that previously looked at identity in more simplistic or categorical terms. Identity research now goes well beyond issues of ethnic or linguistic affiliation to other social factors, including gender, race, sexuality, transnationalism, and extends to digital or textual identities. Identity categories once seen as relatively monolithic are now being viewed as much more differentiated, variable, and socially and temporally constructed than before (e.g., *non-native speaker, refugee, Generation 1.5 learner, heritage-language learner, Japanese female learner, immigrant*). With future research combining approaches to identity that include the multiple facets of learners' languages, lives, and modes of expression, SLA research will be enriched and transformed. Finally, as researchers with more intimate knowledge about the symbolic (linguistic, textual, cultural) resources and social/cultural practices, traditions, and linguistic ecologies of different communities of language learners become trained in applied linguistics, our understanding of the creativity and resourcefulness of language users internationally—their symbolic competence—will increase exponentially (see, e.g., Kramsch and Whiteside, 2008).

Note

* I thank Alison Mackey, graduate students at Georgetown University and the University of British Columbia, and anonymous reviewers for their helpful suggestions on an earlier version of this chapter.

References

Abdi, K. (2009). *Spanish heritage language learners in Canadian high school Spanish classes: Negotiating ethnolinguistic identities and ideologies.* Unpublished master's thesis. Vancouver, Canada: University of British Columbia.

Abdi, K. (2011). "She really only speaks English": Positioning, language ideology, and heritage language learners. *The Canadian Modern Language Review, 67(2),* 161–189.

Ahearn, L. (2001). Language and agency. *Annual Review of Anthropology, 20,* 109–137.

Atkinson, D. (Ed.) (2011). *Alternative approaches to second language acquisition.* London: Routledge.

Bailey, K. M. (1983). Competitiveness and anxiety in adult second language learning: Looking at and through the diary studies. In H. W. Seliger and M. H. Long (Eds.), *Classroom oriented research in second language acquisition* (pp. 67–103). Rowley, MA: Newbury House.

Beebe, L. M. (1980). Sociolinguistic variation and style shifting in second language acquisition. *Language Learning, 30(2),* 433–445.

Blackledge, A. and Creese, A. (2008). Contesting "language" as "heritage": Negotiation of identities in late modernity. *Applied Linguistics, 29(4),* 533–554.

Block, D. (2003). *The social turn in second language acquisition.* Washington, D.C.: Georgetown University Press.

Block, D. (2007a). *Second language identities*. London, UK: Continuum.

Block, D. (2007b). The rise of identity in SLA research, post Firth and Wagner (1997). *Modern Language Journal*, *91*(5), 863–876.

Bourdieu, P. (1977). The economics of linguistic exchanges. *Social Science Information*, *16*(6), 645–668.

Bourdieu, P. (1991). *Language and symbolic power* (J. B. Thompson (Ed.), G. Raymond and M. Adamson, Trans.). Cambridge, England: Polity Press (Original work published 1982).

Brogden, L. M. (2009). François, f/Fransask-qui? Franco-quoi? Constructions identitaires d'un enseignant en formation en situation linguistique minoritaire. *Canadian Modern Language Review*, *66*, 73–99.

Bucholtz, M. and Hall, K. (2004a). Language and identity. In A. Duranti (Ed.), *A companion to linguistic anthropology* (pp. 268–294). Oxford: Basil Blackwell.

Bucholtz, M. and Hall, K. (2004b). Theorizing identity in language and sexuality research. *Language in Society*, *33*(4), 501–547.

Clarke, M. (2008). *Language teacher identities: Co-constructing discourse and community*. Clevedon, UK: Multilingual Matters.

Cummins, J. (2006). Identity texts: The imaginative construction of self through multiliteracies pedagogy. In O. Garcia, T. Skutnabb-Kangas, and M. Torres-Guzman (Eds.), *Imagining multilingual schools: Languages in education and glocalization* (pp. 51–68). Clevedon, UK: Multilingual Matters.

Day, E. M. (2002). *Identity and the young English language learner*. Clevedon, UK: Multilingual Matters.

Dörnyei, Z. and Ushioda, E. (Eds.). (2009). *Motivation, language identity and the L2 self*. Bristol, UK: Multilingual Matters.

Duff, P. (2002). The discursive co-construction of knowledge, identity, and difference: An ethnography of communication in the high school mainstream. *Applied Linguistics*, *23*(3), 289–322.

Duff, P. (2008a). *Case study research in applied linguistics*. New York: Lawrence Erlbaum/Taylor and Francis.

Duff, P. (2008b). Language socialization, participation and identity: Ethnographic approaches. In M. Martin-Jones, M. de Mejia, and N. Hornberger, (Eds.), *Discourse and education. Encyclopedia of language and education* (Vol. 3, pp. 107–119). New York: Springer.

Duff, P. (2010). Language socialization. In N. H. Hornberger and S. McKay (Eds.), *Sociolinguistics and language education* (pp. 427–452). Bristol, UK: Multilingual Matters.

Duff, P. and Uchida, Y. (1997). The negotiation of teachers' sociocultural identities and practices in postsecondary EFL classrooms. *TESOL Quarterly*, *31*(3), 451–486.

Duff, P. and Hornberger, N. H. (Eds.). (2008). *Language socialization. Encyclopedia of language and education* (Vol. 8). New York: Springer.

Duff, P., Li, D., and Nakamura, E. (2006). *Multilingual participation in FL classrooms: Agency, identity, and language functions*. Paper presented at the International Pragmatics Association Conference, Riva del Garda, Italy.

Duff, P., Anderson, T., Ilnyckyj, R., Lester, E., Wang, R., and Yates, E. (2013). *Learning Chinese: Linguistic, sociocultural, and narrative perspectives*. Berlin and Boston: De Gruyter Mouton.

Edwards, J. (1985). *Language, society, and identity*. Oxford: Basil Blackwell.

Ehrlich, S. (1997). Gender as social practice: Implications for second language acquisition. *Studies in Second Language Acquisition*, *19*(4), 421–446.

Ellis, R. (2008). *The study of second language acquisition* (Second Edition). Oxford: Oxford University Press.

Flowerdew, J. and Miller, L. (2008). Social structure and individual agency in second language learning: Evidence from three life histories. *Critical Inquiry in Language Studies*, *5*(4), 201–224.

Gao, X. (2010). *Strategic language learning: The roles of agency and context*. Bristol, UK: Multilingual Matters.

Genesee, F. and Holobow, N. (1989). Change and stability in intergroup perceptions. *Journal of Language and Social Psychology*, *8*(1), 17–38.

Giles, H. and St. Clair, R. (Eds.). (1979). *Language and social psychology*. Oxford: Basil Blackwell.

Goldstein, T. (1997). *Two languages at work: Bilingual life on the production floor*. New York: Mouton de Gruyter.

Gumperz, J. (Ed.). (1982). *Language and social identity*. Cambridge: Cambridge University Press.

Gumperz, J. and Cook-Gumperz, J. (1982). Introduction: Language and the communication of social identity. In J. Gumperz (Ed.), *Language and social identity* (pp. 1–22). New York: Cambridge University Press.

Harklau, L. (2000). From the "good kids" to the "worst": Representations of English language learners across educational settings. *TESOL Quarterly*, *34*(1), 35–67.

He, A. W. (2004). Identity construction in Chinese heritage language classes. *Pragmatics*, *14*(2–3), 199–216.

He, A. W. (2006). Toward an identity theory of the development of Chinese as a heritage language. *Heritage Language Journal*, *4*(1), 1–28.

Hoffman, E. (1989). *Lost in translation*. New York: Penguin.

Ivanič, R. (1997). *Writing and identity: The discoursal construction of identity in academic writing.* Amsterdam: John Benjamins.

Jackson, J. (2008). *Language, identity and study abroad.* London, UK: Equinox.

Kaplan, A. (1993). *French lessons.* Chicago: University of Chicago Press.

Kinginger, C. (2008). Language learning in study abroad: Case histories of Americans in France. *Modern Language Journal Monograph, 92* (Supplement 1).

Kobayashi, Y. (2002). The role of gender in foreign language learning attitudes: Japanese female students' attitudes toward learning English. *Gender and Education, 14*(2), 181–197.

Koven, M. (2007). *Selves in two languages: Bilinguals' verbal enactments of identity in French and Portuguese.* Amsterdam: John Benjamins.

Kramsch, C. (Ed.). (2002). *Language acquisition and language socialization: Ecological perspectives.* London: Continuum.

Kramsch, C. (2009). *The multilingual subject: What language learners say about their experience and why it matters.* Oxford: Oxford Press.

Kramsch, C. and Whiteside, A. (2008). Language ecology in multilingual settings. Towards a theory of symbolic competence. *Applied Linguistics, 29*(4), 645–671.

Kubota, R. and Lin, A. (2006). Race and TESOL: Introduction to concepts and theories. *TESOL Quarterly, 40*(3), 471–493.

Lambert, W., Hodgson, J., Gardner, R., and Fillenbaum, S. (1960). Evaluational reactions to spoken languages. *Journal of Abnormal and Social Psychology, 60*(1), 44–51.

Lantolf, J. (Ed.). (2000). *Sociocultural theory and second language learning.* Oxford: Oxford University Press.

Lantolf, J. and Genung, P. (2002). "I'd rather switch than fight": An activity-theoretic study of power, success, and failure in a foreign language classroom. In C. Kramsch (Ed.), *Language acquisition and language socialization* (pp. 175–196). New York: Continuum.

Lave, J. and Wenger, E. (1991). *Situated learning: Legitimate peripheral participation.* Cambridge, England: Cambridge University Press.

Le Page, R. and Tabouret-Keller, A. (1985). *Acts of identity.* Cambridge: Cambridge University Press.

Leung, C., Haris, R. and Rampton, B. (1997). The idealised native speaker, reified ethnicities, and classroom realities. *TESOL Quarterly, 31*(3), 543–560.

Lvovich, N. (1997). *The multilingual self.* Mahwah, NJ: Lawrence Erlbaum.

McMahill, C. (1997). Communities of resistance: A case study of two feminist English classes in Japan. *TESOL Quarterly, 31*(3), 612–622.

McMahill, C. (2001). Self-expression, gender, and community: A Japanese feminist English class. In A. Pavlenko, A. Blackledge, I. Piller, and M. Teutsch-Dwyer (Eds.), *Multilingualism, second language learning, and gender* (pp. 307–344). Berlin: Mouton De Gruyter.

McKay, S. and Wong, S. L. (1996). Multiple discourses, multiple identities: Investment and agency in second-language learning among Chinese adolescent immigrant students. *Harvard Educational Review, 66*(3), 577–608.

McKinney, C. and Norton, B. (2008). Identity in language and literacy education. In B. Spolsky and F. Hult (Eds.), *The handbook of educational linguistics* (pp. 192–205). Malden, MA: Blackwell.

McNamara, T. (1997). Theorizing social identity: What do we mean by social identity? Competing frameworks, competing discourses. *TESOL Quarterly, 31*(3), 561–567.

Menard-Warwick, J. (2006). Both a fiction and an existential fact: Theorizing identity in second language acquisition and literacy studies. *Linguistics and Education, 16*(3), 253–274.

Menard-Warwick, J. (2009). *Gendered identities and immigrant language learning.* Bristol, UK: Multilingual Matters.

Miller, J. (2003). *Audible difference: ESL and social identity in schools.* Clevedon, UK: Multilingual Matters.

Morgan, B. (2007). Poststructuralism and applied linguistics: Complementary approaches to identity and culture in ELT. In J. Cummins and C. Davison (Eds.), *International handbook of English language teaching* (pp. 1033–1052). New York: Springer.

Morita, N. (2004). Negotiating participation and identity in second language academic communities. *TESOL Quarterly, 38*(4), 573–603.

Nakamura, E. (2005). *Language use in Japanese as a foreign language classrooms.* Unpublished master's thesis. University of British Columbia: Vancouver, Canada.

Nelson, C. (2009). *Sexual identities in English language education: Classroom conversations.* New York: Routledge.

Norton Peirce, B. (1995). Social identity, investment, and language learning. *TESOL Quarterly, 29*(1), 9–31.

Norton, B. (1997a). Language, identity, and the ownership of English. *TESOL Quarterly, 31*(3), 409–429.

Norton, B. (1997b). Language and identity. [Special issue]. *TESOL Quarterly, 31* (3).

Norton, B. (2000). *Identity and language learning: Gender, ethnicity and educational change*. London: Pearson/Longman.

Norton, B. (2010). Language and identity. In N. Hornberger and S. McKay (Eds.), *Sociolinguistics and language education* (pp. 349–369). Bristol: Multilingual Matters.

Norton, B. and Toohey, K. (2001). Changing perspectives on good language learners. *TESOL Quarterly*, *35*(2), 307–322.

Ochs, E. (1993). Constructing social identity: A language socialization perspective. *Research on Language in Social Interaction*, *26*(3), 287–306.

Omonyi, T. and White, G. (2006). *The sociolinguistics of identity*. London: Continuum.

Ortega, L. (2009). *Understanding second language acquisition*. London, UK: Hodder Arnold.

Pavlenko, A. (2002). Poststructuralist approaches to the study of social factors in second language learning and use. In V. Cook (Ed.), *Portraits of the L2 user* (pp. 277–302). Clevedon, UK: Multilingual Matters.

Pavlenko, A. (2003). "I never knew I was a bilingual": Reimagining teacher identities in TESOL. In Y. Kanno and B. Norton (Eds.), *Imagined communities and educational possibilities* [Special issue]. *Journal of Language, Identity, and Education*, *2*(4), 251–268.

Pavlenko, A. (2004). Gender and sexuality in foreign and second language education: Critical and feminist approaches. In B. Norton and K. Toohey (Eds.), *Critical pedagogies and language learning* (pp. 53–71). New York: Cambridge University Press.

Pavlenko, A. (2007). Autobiographic narratives as data in applied linguistics. *Applied Linguistics*, *28*(2), 163–188.

Pavlenko, A. (2008). Narrative analysis in the study of bi- and multilingualism. In M. Moyer and L. Wei (Eds.), *The Blackwell guide to research methods in bilingualism* (pp. 311–325). Oxford: Blackwell.

Pavlenko, A. and Blackledge, A. (Eds.). (2004). *Negotiation of identities in multilingual contexts*. Clevedon, UK: Multilingual Matters.

Pavlenko, A. and Lantolf, J. P. (2000). Second language learning as participation and the (re)construction of selves. In J. P. Lantolf (Ed.), *Sociocultural theory and second language learning* (pp. 155–177). New York: Oxford University Press.

Pavlenko, A. and Norton, B. (2007). Imagined communities, identity, and English language teaching. In J. Cummins and C. Davison (Eds.), *International handbook of English language teaching* (pp. 669–680). New York: Springer.

Polanyi, L. (1995). Language learning and living abroad: Stories from the field. In B. F. Freed (Ed.), *Second language acquisition in a study abroad context* (pp. 271–291). Amsterdam: John Benjamins.

Potowski, K. (2007). *Language and identity in a dual immersion school*. Clevedon, UK: Multilingual Matters.

Ricento, T. (2005). Considerations of identity in L2 learning. In E. Hinkel (Ed.), *Handbook of research on second language teaching and learning* (pp. 895–911). Mahwah, NJ: Lawrence Erlbaum Associates.

Schumann, J. (1997). *The neurobiology of affect in language*. Malden, MA: Blackwell.

Shardakova, M. and Pavlenko, A. (2004). Identity options in Russian textbooks. *Journal of Language, Identity and Education*, *3*(1), 25–46.

Siegal, M. S. (1994). *Looking east: Learning Japanese as a second language in Japan and the interaction of race, gender and social context*. Unpublished doctoral dissertation. University of California, Berkeley, CA.

Starfield, S. (2002). "I'm a second-language English speaker": Negotiating writer and authority in sociology one. *Journal of Language, Identity and Education*, *1*(2), 121–140.

Swain, M. and Deters, P. (2007). "New" mainstream SLA theory: Expanded and enriched. *The Modern Language Journal*, *91*(5), 820–836.

Talmy, S. (2008). The cultural productions of the ESL student at tradewinds high: Contingency, multidirectionality, and identity in L2 socialization. *Applied Linguistics*, *29*(4), 619–644.

Talmy, S. (2010). Qualitative interviews in applied linguistics: From research instrument to social practice. *Annual Review of Applied Linguistics*, *30*, 128–148.

Talmy, S. and Richards, K. (Eds.) (2011). Qualitative interviews in applied linguistics: Discursive perspectives [Special issue]. *Applied Linguistics*, *32*(1).

Tajfel, H. (1974). Social identity and intergroup behavior. *Social Science Information*, *13*(2), 65–93.

Tajfel, H. (1978). The social psychology of minorities. (Minority Rights Group Report No. 38). London: Minority Rights Group; reprinted in part in H. Tajfel (1981). *Human groups and social categories*. Cambridge: Cambridge University Press.

Thesen, L. (1997). Voices, discourse, and transition: In search of new categories in EAP. *TESOL Quarterly*, *31*(3), 487–511.

Toohey, K. (1998). "Breaking them up, taking them away": ESL students in Grade 1. *TESOL Quarterly*, *32*(1), 61–84.

Toohey, K. (2000). *Learning English at school: Identity, social relations and classroom practice*. Clevedon, UK: Multilingual Matters.

Toohey, K. (2001). Disputes in child L2 learning. *TESOL Quarterly, 35*(2), 257–278.

Ushioda, E. and Dörnyei, Z. (2009). Motivation, language identities and the L2 self: A theoretical overview. In Z. Dörnyei and E. Ushioda (Eds.), *Motivation, language identity and the L2 self* (pp. 1–8). Bristol, UK: Multilingual Matters.

Varghese, M., Morgan, B., Johnston, B., and Johnson, K. (2005). Theorizing language teacher identity: Three perspectives and beyond. *Journal of Language, Identity, and Education, 4*(1), 21–44.

Warriner, D. S. (Ed.). (2007). Transnational literacies: Immigration, language learning, and identity. *Linguistics and Education, 18* (3–4), 201–214.

Weedon, C. (1997). *Feminist practice and poststructuralist theory* (Second Edition). Oxford: Blackwell.

Wenger, E. (1998). *Communities of practice: Learning, meaning, and identity*. New York: Cambridge University Press.

White, C. (2007). Innovation and identity in distance language learning and teaching. *Innovation in Language Learning and Teaching, 1*(1), 97–110.

Wortham, S. (2006). *Learning identity*. Cambridge: Cambridge University Press.

Zuengler, J. (1989). Identity and IL [interlanguage] development and use. *Applied Linguistics, 10*(1), 80–96.

26

Working memory and SLA

John N. Williams

Introduction

The term *working memory* (WM) refers to a temporary storage system that lies at the core of complex cognition. Everyday tasks such as remembering a phone number, mental arithmetic, or playing chess, place varying levels of demand on the WM system. Remembering an unfamiliar phone number long enough to dial it involves storing the number in short-term memory, and perhaps repeating it silently to oneself. Multiplying 26 by 7 in your head involves storing the digits produced by multiplying 6 and 7 (4 and 2) while multiplying 2 and 7, adding the carried 4 and retrieving the stored 2 to give the final answer of 182. Skilled chess playing involves strategic planning of a sequence of moves whilst retaining multiple piece configurations in short-term memory. These tasks not only require short-term storage of information, but also a high degree of control of that information in order to maintain partial results whilst carrying out further processing, or to resist interference between similar items of information. Thus, WM can be regarded as a system that is used for the temporary maintenance of task-relevant information whilst performing cognitive tasks.

As one would expect, individuals vary a good deal in their ability to carry out such complex cognitive tasks, or even, as it turns out, relatively simple ones like remembering sequences of digits. This gives rise to the notion of working memory capacity as an important dimension of individual difference (see Skehan, Chapter 23, this volume). The question that will concern us here is whether variation in WM capacity (WMC) is related to variation in first and second language processing and learning ability. The answer to this question could not only prove useful in using tests of WM as a predictor of language abilities, but also could illuminate the nature of the processing and learning mechanisms themselves.

Historical discussion

There are two essential components to the WM system. The first is concerned with the temporary storage of information; that is, short-term memory. The second is concerned with the control of that information, as required to carry out complex tasks, and the component responsible for this is variously referred to as the *Central Executive* (Baddeley, 2007) or *executive attention* (Kane *et al.*, 2007). The first model of WM was proposed by Baddeley and Hitch (see 1974 for a review). They postulated two domain-specific short-term memory systems—the phonological loop for the storage of phonological information (as used when remembering a phone number) and the visuo-spatial scratch pad for visual and spatial information (as used when remembering chess configurations). It is the first of these that will concern us most here of course. Information in these systems was assumed to decay rapidly—in the case of information in the phonological store after about two seconds. In order to maintain information for longer it is necessary to refresh its activation through a rehearsal process. Hence the phonological loop contains a passive phonological store, which will be referred to here as *phonological short-term memory* (PSTM), and a subvocal rehearsal process (a metaphorical "loop"). The central executive was conceived as a mechanism for controlling and managing information in the short-term stores. In Baddeley's early work, where the focus was primarily on the functioning of the phonological loop, little attention was paid to the central executive beyond its role in controlling rehearsal processes. The phonological loop was explored using simple random digit and word list recall tasks in which it is natural to employ rehearsal strategies. It was found that recall is poorer for similar sounding items (the "phonemic similarity effect") reflecting interference between representations in the phonological store. Recall was also found to be affected by factors that affect rehearsal rate, such as the length of the items (the "word length effect"), and a person's articulation rate, effects that disappear when rehearsal is prevented by concurrent articulatory suppression tasks (Baddeley, 2007).

Other researchers have developed the original Baddeley and Hitch (1974) conception of WM to make it more relevant to complex cognition in general, focusing directly on the role of the central executive in maintaining task-relevant information (Cowan, 1999; Engle *et al.*, 1999). It is this latter function that is crucially important in the mental arithmetic and chess examples considered earlier. Here the problem is not just the storage of phonological or visuo-spatial information but also the maintenance of specific representations in the face of potential interference from similar items in memory, or stimuli from the environment. Kane *et al.* (2007) provide other everyday examples such as searching for your car in a car park that you use frequently or when driving on the opposite side of the road in a foreign country. In the first case memories of other spaces you have previously used in the car park interfere with your search (a case of "pro-active interference"). In the second, the problem is to manage the competition between automatic responses and the novel ones required by the current context. Thus, the executive component of the WM system is assumed to be involved even in tasks that do not have an obvious short-term storage component. Indeed, there is good evidence that this component of WM is related to general fluid intelligence, as measured by non-verbal figural reasoning tasks (Engle, *et al.*, 1999).

At first sight it may seem that very different notions of WM abound in the literature. Yet these are differences of emphasis rather than overall conception. Most researchers agree that WM is a multi-component system comprising domain-specific storage systems and a domain-general executive component. Whilst the focus of much of Baddeley and colleagues has been on the storage components, the focus of Engle and colleagues has been on executive functions. As we shall see, both of these perspectives can make different, yet complementary, contributions to our understanding of SLA.

This chapter is organized in two parts, the first dealing with PSTM specifically and the second with the operation of the WM system as a whole. It is easiest to understand the various different aspects of WM by considering how they are measured, and so a discussion of elicitation measures and empirical verification will precede discussion of core issues. The chapter will end with a consideration of applications and future directions.

Data and common elicitation measures: Phonological short-term memory and SLA

Traditional measures of verbal short-term memory involve immediate repetition of sequences of varying numbers of random digits, words, or nonwords in the order of presentation. For example, the maximum number of random digits that a person can accurately and reliably repeat back in the correct order is known as their *digit span*. Typically, items are presented at a rate of one per second providing the opportunity to cumulatively rehearse the sequence. Hence the correspondence between digit span and factors that affect rehearsal rate, such as word length. Following the Baddeley and Hitch WM model, performance on this task is predicted to be a function of the decay rate of information in the phonological store (PSTM) as well as the efficiency of the subvocal rehearsal process, as determined by the person's articulation rate. Performance is also dependent upon whether the person chooses to adopt a rehearsal strategy. These factors introduce ambiguity into the interpretation of digit span measures. For example, the fact that children have smaller digit spans than adults could be because of faster decay, slower articulation rate, or failure to use rehearsal. Indeed rehearsal strategies typically do not develop until around age seven (Baddeley *et al.*, 1998).

The *nonword repetition task* is often used as an alternative, and arguably more direct, measure of verbal short-term memory, and may be particularly suitable for use with young children (Gathercole *et al.*, 1994). Participants are simply required to immediately repeat back individual nonsense words of varying lengths (e.g., *ballop, doppelate, empliforvent*). The longer the nonword, the more likely it is that the beginning will have been lost from PSTM before it has ended. The larger a person's PSTM capacity, the longer the nonword that they will be able to repeat successfully. Note that, as operationalized by this task, PSTM "capacity" refers to the duration, rather than the amount, of information in PSTM. The test measures how long phonological information persists in the absence of rehearsal.

An important issue that impacts upon the design and interpretation of the nonword repetition test, however, is that performance is affected by lexical knowledge, such as similarity to known words (Gathercole, 1995). For example, English-French bilinguals are equally good at repeating nonwords conforming to English and French phonotactics, but monolinguals are worse for nonwords conforming to French phonotactics (Thorn and Gathercole, 1999). It has also been argued that nonword repetition only partially reflects short-term memory capacity but also a variety of phonological processing skills such as speech perception, phonological encoding, and assembly of a phonological representation for articulation (Bowey, 2006). Thus, as in the case of immediate serial recall, the test cannot unambiguously be interpreted as a simple, direct, measure of PSTM capacity.

Given the differences between immediate serial recall and nonword repetition tasks it is hard to see how they can both be regarded as tests of the same underlying construct of PSTM. Digit span uses highly familiar items and invites rehearsal strategies, nonword repetition uses unfamiliar items and rehearsal is not possible. Yet performance on the two tasks has been found to correlate (Gathercole *et al.*, 1992; Gupta, 2003). The correlation between the tasks suggests that they share a common component of short-term storage ability, possibly the ability to retain serial order. The problem in a digit span task is not only remembering which digits occurred in the list, but also the order in which they occurred. Likewise, when remembering a nonword the problem is remembering the order of the segments, not just the segments themselves. It has been suggested that short-term memory for item and order information should be regarded as distinct aspects of short-term memory (Gupta, 2003).

Short-term memory tests have been developed that are more sensitive to order than item information. In the *serial nonword recognition* task varying length sequences of single syllable CVC nonwords are constructed (e.g., *mel, guk, vip*) which are either immediately followed by the same sequence, or by a sequence containing a reversal of two adjacent items (e.g., *guk, mel, vip*). The task is simply to indicate whether the two sequences are the same or different. Performance on this task is hardly affected by whether the items are words or nonwords (Gathercole *et al.*, 2001), or whether the words are from a person's L1 or L2 (Thorn *et al.*, 2002) suggesting that it is principally sensitive to memory for sequence, rather than item, information.

Another way of measuring order information independently of item information is by using the *serial order reconstruction task* (Majerus *et al.*, 2008). This is a variant of the digit span task in which instead of recalling the sequence orally the participant is provided with cards corresponding to the digits used in the sequence and is required simply to arrange them into the correct order. The digits used in each sequence are known in advance because, for example, a five-item sequence uses the digits 1 to 5, and a six-digit sequence the digits 1 to 6. Thus there is no requirement to remember the items, only the order in which they occurred.

Core issues: PSTM and language learning

Vocabulary learning

An early indication that PSTM is implicated in language learning came from the short-term memory patient PV (Baddeley *et al.*, 1998). Despite being severely impaired on digit and word span tasks she was able to learn arbitrary associations between pairs of known words in her native Italian. However, she was unable to learn unknown L2 (Russian) words paired with L1 (Italian) translations. This suggested that PSTM plays a specific role in the formation of long-term phonological representations. Subsequently, in a study of normally developing children Gathercole *et al.* (1992) found that both digit span and nonword repetition were correlated with vocabulary size, the relationship being strongest for nonword repetition in four and five year-olds. A similar relationship has been found in adult SLA (Service and Kohonen, 1995) and in laboratory studies of foreign vocabulary learning (Service and Craik, 1993; Speciale *et al.*, 2004; Williams and Lovatt, 2003).

Of course, given that nonword repetition is itself related to vocabulary knowledge there is a potential circularity in using it as a predictor of vocabulary development. The similarity of a novel word to known words could affect both ease of repetition, and also the ease of storage in LTM. However, PV showed impaired novel word learning even though she had unimpaired access to her native vocabulary. Furthermore, digit span has been found to be related to vocabulary learning, even though digit recall makes minimal demands on lexical knowledge (Atkins and Baddeley, 1998). Gupta (2003) even found that digit span was a better predictor than nonword repetition of learning nonword names for pictures of imaginary animals. These are compelling results given that digit span would appear to be a very different task from vocabulary learning.

Gutpa (2003) suggested that the connection between digit span and vocabulary learning is largely due to the serial order component of PSTM. Majerus *et al.* (2008) tested this hypothesis by examining the efficiency of learning pairs of English and French-derived nonwords (a laboratory simulation of vocabulary learning) by English learners of French at varying levels of proficiency. Performance on the serial order reconstruction task correlated highly with word-nonword learning, as did French proficiency, and regression analyses showed that these factors made independent contributions to word-nonword learning. Majerus *et al.* assume that the proficiency measure provides an indication of the extent of support for vocabulary learning from the existing French lexicon. They propose that proficiency relates to item retention in PSTM, whereas the serial order reconstruction task relates to retention of sequence information, and that both factors contribute to vocabulary learning. Evidence for an independent contribution of the efficiency of sequence learning to vocabulary learning is also provided by Speciale *et al.* (2004).

Although there is good evidence for a relationship between PSTM and vocabulary learning it should be noted that this has not always been evident in studies conducted outside the laboratory, particularly when learners already have some familiarity with the language. Gathercole *et al.* (1992) found that nonword repetition is predictive of subsequent vocabulary size only at the very earliest ages tested (between age four and five). Masoura and Gathercole (2005) studied Greek children who had been studying English for three years and found that although there was a strong relationship between nonword repetition (using English-derived nonwords) and current English vocabulary size, nonword repetition ability did not predict the ability to learn new words. Likewise, in a study of learning of English by French children in a five-month intensive program, French and O'Brien (2008) found that nonword repetition ability as measured at the start of the program only explained 3.5 percent of the variance in vocabulary development. These children had already received 100 hours of English instruction prior to the study. Gathercole (2006) suggests that PSTM might be most important at the initial stages of language learning. As the size of the vocabulary develops word learning is affected more by the ease of integrating words into the existing lexicon through words of similar sound and meaning, reflecting LTM contributions to learning of new information. Thus, even individuals with quite poor PSTM ability can eventually develop normal-sized vocabularies through applying these other learning strategies. This does not mean that PSTM is not a relevant consideration in naturalistic language learning, but it is one of many factors that determines vocabulary growth.

Grammar learning

Emergentist and connectionist perspectives on language acquisition imply a close relationship between acquisition of vocabulary and grammar. Learning words involves learning sequences of phonemes, and learning grammar involves learning sequences of morphemes (Ellis, 1996). Formulaic memorized chunks can provide the data for further analysis, leading to the abstraction of rules (Myles *et al.*, 1999). So to the extent that vocabulary acquisition is dependent upon PSTM, and to the extent that learning sequences of morphemes is like learning sequences of phonemes, then PSTM would be predicted to be related to grammar learning.

Indeed there is good evidence for a close relationship between vocabulary size and grammatical development in normal and abnormal populations (Bates and Goodman, 1997). Larger vocabularies provide a richer database from which morphosyntactic regularities can be extracted. And there is experimental evidence that when the operation of the phonological loop is disrupted through articulatory suppression, both the acquisition of vocabulary and grammatical rules are severely affected (Ellis and Sinclair, 1996). But these observations do not necessarily imply a direct relationship between PSTM and grammar learning. For instance, as more vocabulary items are learned, segmentation of grammatical morphemes becomes easier, and these segmented morphemes could trigger learning processes that are not necessarily dependent upon PSTM at all. What is the evidence that PSTM influences grammar learning independently of its effect on vocabulary learning?

One approach to answering this question is to examine grammar learning in situations where knowledge of vocabulary is already well-developed. This was the case in Robinson's (1997) study of various components of aptitude in relation to acquisition of grammatical rules by intermediate-level learners of English. He found that memory ability was related to rule learning, but only in the instructed and rule search training groups. No such relationship was found for the implicit (memory task) and incidental (comprehension task) groups. This study provides evidence of a connection between PSTM and grammar learning that is not mediated by vocabulary learning, at least when explicit learning strategies are being used.

In a study by Williams (1999) participants with no prior knowledge of Italian first learned the vocabulary items to be used in the experiment and then performed a memory task on sentences exemplifying a range of inflectional morphemes and agreement patterns. Rule learning was assessed by a surprise grammaticality judgment task on sentences containing known words in novel combinations. Rule learning was correlated with the speed with which the vocabulary had been learned in the pre-training phase, and also with the accuracy of sentence recall over the first few training trials. Assuming that these measures reflect PSTM ability, this experiment provides indirect evidence for a connection between PSTM and grammar learning.

More direct evidence comes from a study by Williams and Lovatt (2003, Experiment 2) that focused on the induction of arbitrary noun classes. In order to learn the target system participants had to remember which articles had occurred with which nouns in the input; that is, they had to infer the underlying noun class distinction from distributional information alone (there were no semantic or phonological cues to class membership). Participants first learned the form and meaning of all of the articles and nouns to be used in the experiment as isolated units. They were then exposed to grammatical combinations of articles and nouns in a memory task. Learning of the noun class distinction was assessed by cyclic generalization tests on novel combinations of the articles and nouns used in training. Both PSTM (as measured by nonword span) and prior knowledge of gender languages made independent contributions to learning. Presumably PSTM affected the ability to remember article-noun combinations during the training task, and these formed the basis for inducing the underlying noun class distinction.

Given that the above studies are all laboratory-based it is important to obtain evidence for the PSTM-grammar learning link from more natural situations. French and O'Brien (2008) examined the relationship between PSTM, as measured by nonword repetition, and grammar learning in French children in an intensive five-month English immersion program. Nonword repetition at the start of the program was correlated with grammatical knowledge at the end, a relationship that held even when initial grammatical knowledge, nonverbal intelligence, L2 contact, and, crucially, vocabulary knowledge at the end of the program had all been entered into the regression model. French and O'Brien suggest that, although there were improvements in vocabulary knowledge over the program, the independent contribution of PSTM to grammar learning reflects learning sequences of morphemes, as opposed to the morphemes themselves.

Thus, there is good evidence from both laboratory- and classroom-based studies for a contribution of PSTM to grammar learning. This appears to result from a relationship between PSTM function and the ability to store morpheme sequences in LTM, even when the forms of those morphemes are already familiar.

Data and common elicitation measures: Working memory and SLA

Following the psychological construct of WM outlined earlier, tests of WMC need to measure a person's ability to both retain and manage information in short-term memory in the face of potential interference from other cognitive tasks. Daneman and Carpenter (1980) developed a reading span task (RST) in which participants read increasingly longer sequences of unrelated sentences and then have to recall the final word of each sentence in order. A person's reading span is the maximum number of sentence-final words that can be reliably recalled. This is clearly more complex than PSTM tasks because participants are required to maintain increasing numbers of sentence-final words in STM whilst simultaneously processing irrelevant sentences. Performance on the reading span task varies considerably between individuals (between two and six in college students according to Daneman and Carpenter, 1980). Hence working memory capacity, as operationalized by this task, could be an important dimension of individual differences.

However, span tasks of this type can only be used to investigate individual differences if they are reliable. Waters and Caplan (1996) found that the test re-test reliability of the Daneman and Carpenter test was poor, as was the consistency of classification of participants into span groups, even over short time periods. One reason for this may be that participants vary in the resources they devote to the secondary, sentence reading, task. Waters and Caplan found that a variant that required participants to judge each sentence for plausibility, rather than just read it aloud, had higher reliability and stability. In other variants, each sentence is followed by an unrelated word that has to be remembered (Engle *et al.*, 1999), or by a single letter (Kane *et al.*, 2004). This prevents people from using memory for sentence gist to aid recall of sentence-final words.

The Daneman and Carpenter RST was based on a domain-specific view of WM. In this view, the best way to measure the WM resources used in reading comprehension is with a task that involves memorization of verbal material whilst reading sentences. In contrast, for Engle and colleagues (Engle *et al.*, 1999; Engle *et al.*, 1999) the executive component of WM is domain-general and it is only necessary that the task combines a memory component with a demanding processing component. They therefore developed span tasks that do not necessarily involve sentence comprehension. In their operation span task (Turner and Engle, 1989) the sentences of the reading span task were replaced with simple equations that the participants had to verify (e.g., $9/3-2 = 1$, or $9/3-2 = 6$) followed by single words that had to be recalled. In counting span tasks (e.g., Engle *et al.*, 1999) participants have to count the number of target items (e.g., dark circles) in a series of displays containing distracters (dark blue squares and light blue circles). At the end of the series they have to recall the number of target items that were in each display. Conway *et al.* (2005) suggest that the simplicity of the processing component in counting span tasks makes them particularly suitable for a range of populations, including children and brain-damaged patients. The fact that the task is language independent would also appear to make it particularly suitable for use in second language research. See Conway *et al.* (2005) for a discussion of other methodological issues in relation to the administration and scoring of WM tests.

Correlational studies support the contention that WM tasks are primarily sensitive to domain-general executive function and only secondarily sensitive to domain-specific storage abilities, the converse being the case for STM tasks (Caplan *et al.*, 2007). For example, WM tasks predict around 50 percent unique variance in general fluid intelligence (Kane *et al.*, 2005) compared to only 18 percent for PSTM tasks (Conway *et al.*, 2002). Verbal and spatial WM tasks share 70–85 percent of variance, but verbal and spatial STM tasks only 40 percent (Kane *et al.*, 2004).

Core issues: Working memory and language learning

First language ability

Daneman and Carpenter (1980) argued that language comprehension is a prime example of a complex cognitive activity that involves temporary maintenance of task-relevant information during ongoing processing. They found that reading spans of college students were highly correlated with their reading comprehension test scores, with these correlations lying between 0.5 and 0.6 in various experiments. When specific reading abilities were considered, for example the ability to answer a factual question about a passage, or to determine the referent of a pronoun, the correlation with reading span reached 0.9 (see Daneman and Merikle, 1996 for a meta-analysis). In studies of young children WMC has also been shown to be related to anaphor resolution (Oakhill and Yuill, 1986), and to the ability to resolve anomalies when the critical information is distant in the text (Yuill *et al.*, 1989). On the other hand, attempts to relate WMC to on-line syntactic processing have led to largely negative results, leading to the hypothesis that syntactic processing, at least in native speakers, is modularized and does not draw on general verbal working memory capacity (Caplan *et al.*, 2007). Correlations between WMC and tests of language comprehension are attributed to higher-level "post-interpretive" comprehension processes (e.g., anaphor resolution). However, some recent studies have revealed an influence of WMC on syntactic processing when very distant elements have to be integrated (Havik *et al.*, 2009; Roberts *et al.*, 2007), suggesting that WMC limitations are only evident when storage and integration costs (Gibson, 1998) of on-line processing are very high.

Second language ability

A large number of studies have found correlations between L1 and L2 RST performance, with coefficients of 0.39 (Harrington and Sawyer, 1992), 0.48 (Berquist, 1997), 0.61 (Juffs, 2004), 0.84 (Osaka and Osaka, 1992), 0.85 (Osaka *et al.*, 1993). This is hardly surprising, given the assumed domain-generality of the executive component of WM, although what accounts for the variability in strength of association is not clear. For example, both Harrington and Sawyer (1992) and Osaka and Osaka (1992) studied advanced Japanese learners of English, and yet found very different strengths of correlation.

Reading span has also been reported to be lower in the L2 than in the L1 (Berquist, 1997; Havik *et al.*, 2009; Osaka *et al.*, 1993; Walter, 2004) whereas in some studies not significantly different (Harrington and Sawyer, 1992; Osaka and Osaka, 1992). A problem here is to equate the difficulty of RST tests in different languages since when the syntax of the languages differs radically, the sentence-final words will have very different properties (Harrington and Sawer, 1992; Osaka *et al.*, 1993). An obvious solution for obtaining better comparisons would be to require recall of words or letters that follow each sentence.

It seems reasonable to assume that where differences between L1 and L2 reading spans are obtained this is partly attributable to level of L2 proficiency. Indeed, Harrington and Sawyer (1992) found that L2 RST correlated with TOEFL (Test of English as a Second Language) scores at r = 0.54, and Berquist (1997) found a correlation with TOEIC (Test of English for International Communication) scores at r = 0.41. Walter (2004) found that lower intermediate French learners of English had lower English RST scores than upper intermediate learners, and this held even when differences in L1 RST performance were taken into account. Reduced L2 RST performance is to be expected on a single resource view (Just and Carpenter, 1992), since as the processing drains of sentence processing increase the WM resources available for storage of sentence-final words decreases. It could also reflect the influence of differences in domain-specific storage capacity on WM function (Engle, Kane *et al.*, 1999). For example, if L2 representations are of "low quality" (Perfetti, 2007) they may be more subject to interference. Performance on an L2 RST would be reduced, whilst the common domain-general executive attention ability would ensure that L2 and L1 performance is also correlated.

With regard to specific tests of L2 comprehension, Walter (2004) found correlations between an L2 RST and performance on L2 summary completion and anaphor resolution tasks. These correlations were stronger for lower intermediate learners, and not significant at all for the upper intermediate learners on the anaphor resolution task. This pattern is to be expected if WMC constraints are most apparent when the processing system is most challenged (Just and Carpenter, 1992). Kormos and Safar (2008) found a correlation of 0.55 (p < 0.01) between WMC (as measured by L1 reverse digit span) and performance on the Cambridge First Certificate Exam after the first year on an intensive English instruction program. Correlations with WM were also found over the Reading, Listening, Speaking, and Use of English components of the exam.

With regard to on-line syntactic processing, one might expect that increased difficulty, or reduced automaticity, in L2 might make general verbal WMC limitations more evident than in L1. However, studies have either shown no effect of WMC on L2 sentence processing (Juffs, 2004, 2005), or an effect in L1 but not L2 (Felser and Roberts, 2007). One exception is Havik *et al.* (2009) who showed that both L1 and L2 sentence processing are similarly constrained by WMC. In general, though, there is surprisingly little evidence for WMC constraints on on-line L2 syntactic processing. Thus, the mass of evidence for a general relationship between WMC and L2 language skills would seem to be largely attributable to post-interpretive processes beyond the sentence level.

Reasoning, category learning, and artificial grammar learning

There are good reasons to expect that WM should be related to learning in general, but only when learning processes involve intentional control; that is, broadly speaking, explicit, as opposed to implicit learning. First we shall consider evidence from reasoning, category learning, and artificial grammar learning that suggests that this should be the case, before considering studies of SLA in the following section.

Reasoning. WM, as well as IQ, are strongly related to what Evans (2003) dubs explicit "System 2" conscious abstract reasoning and hypothetical thinking, but not implicit "System 1" reasoning, as supported by phylogenetically older and domain-specific associative systems (a distinction that aligns with Reber's distinction between explicit and implicit learning systems (Reber (1993)). Interestingly, the relationship between conscious reasoning and IQ is particularly strong when semantic information has to be ignored in favor of logical form, as for example when verifying the logical correctness of the syllogism "All mammals can walk, whales are mammals, therefore whales can walk" (see Stanovich and West, 2000, for a review). It is reasonable to conclude that this relationship reflects the executive attention component of WM.

Category learning. DeCaro *et al.* (2009; DeCaro *et al.*, 2008) demonstrate a link between WM, as measured by reading and operation span tasks, and inductive learning of rule-based categorizations, where the categories can be stated as easily verbalizable rules (e.g., if the stimulus embedded within the object is a circle then the object belongs to category A). High WMC individuals were also found to be superior on more complex categorizations that involve integrating information over a number of dimensions, although in this case it is not clear whether the effect was due to implicit learning or complex explicit knowledge (DeCaro *et al.*, 2008). Low WM individuals appear to persist with simple learning strategies when faced with complex problems (see also Beilock and DeCaro, 2007). In the case of the category learning problem studied in DeCaro *et al.* (2008, 2009) this could produce above-chance responding, and even superior performance to high WM individuals if a lax criterion for success was adopted. However, only high WM individuals were able to learn the categories according to stricter criteria (DeCaro *et al.*, 2009). Hence the apparent success, or even superiority, of low WM individuals in complex learning tasks can be more apparent than real.

Artificial grammar learning. There is good evidence that learning is related to IQ under explicit, rule discovery, but not implicit, memorize, instructions (Gebauer and Mackintosh, 2007; Reber *et al.*, 1991). In so far as tests of general fluid intelligence are assumed to tap the executive component of the WM system (Engle *et al.*, 1999) then in this sense it can be argued that WM is related to explicit, but not implicit, learning. However, Robinson (2002, 2005) found that low WM was actually associated with more success in artificial grammar learning under instructions to memorize. It is possible that this reflects spontaneous explicit learning in high WM individuals, which may have actually suppressed performance (see Reber, 1976, for evidence that rule search can lead to worse performance than memorization in artificial grammar learning). This is another reason why low WM might lead to superior performance.

John N. Williams

Second language learning

In light of the above findings it certainly makes sense to predict a role for WM in SLA, especially when learning processes toward the explicit end of the spectrum are involved. It is therefore clearly important to consider this question in relation to different learning conditions, as far as the available data allow.

Explicit instruction. Roehr (2008) hypothesizes that working memory should be important in learning from explicit instruction because of the requirement to retain metalinguistic information in memory whilst simultaneously producing and comprehending language, and because explicit rule-based processing should place demands on the central executive. Some evidence for this is provided by Ando *et al.* (1992, described in Mackey *et al.* 2002) who found that L1 WM correlates with L2 learning after 20 hours of explicit form-focused instruction, although only on a two-month delayed post-test.

Task-based learning. Here there is an emphasis on interaction and the role of interactional feedback in prompting learners to briefly focus on form in a meaningful context. WM might be important for rapidly switching attention between form and meaning, for making comparisons between one's own output and a corrective recast, and in general for permitting greater degrees of noticing in communicative situations (Doughty, 2001; Robinson, 2001). A study by Mackey *et al.* (2002) provides initial support for these ideas. They examined the development of question forms in Japanese learners of English. Teaching was through communicative tasks that involved interactional feedback followed up by stimulated recall activities to evaluate noticing. High working memory was associated with more noticing of relevant forms (although the effect was marginally significant over the small sample tested). In subsequent studies WMC has been found to be positively associated with the probability that a learner will modify their utterance in response to feedback whilst engaging in an interactive task with a native speaker (Mackey *et al.*, 2010; Sagarra, 2007). Thus there is good evidence that higher WMC enables greater noticing of feedback and subsequent modification of output. In terms of actual learning gains, Mackey *et al.* (2002) found evidence for more development amongst the high WM group at the delayed post-test (although this analysis is only based on a total of 7 participants). In a computer-based task requiring typed cloze responses Sagarra (2007) found that providing the correct answer as feedback (i.e., recasts) produced high learning gains as measured by immediate and delayed post-tests, and that learning gains correlated with WMC. Although this was not a face-to-face communicative task, the results do suggest that WMC is involved in learning from feedback.

Intentional induction. Brooks *et al.*, (2006) and Kempe and Brooks (2008) examined learning of a Russian inflectional system in which there were associations between noun suffixes and semantic (case) and noun class (grammatical gender) cues. Participants performed comprehension and production tasks with feedback that would have encouraged them to search for regularities. Learning was assessed by performance on old items and generalization to new items. In Brooks *et al.* (2006) both non-verbal fluid intelligence and WM made independent contribution to performance on old items, but only IQ made an independent contribution to new items. Following Engle *et al.* (1999) they argue that tests of general fluid intelligence tap the executive attention component of the WM system, and that this is related to learning the underlying rules of the target system because of the requirement to direct attention to distributional patterns during the training task. The relationship between WM and performance on old items reflected the storage component of the WM system. Similar results were obtained by Kempe and Brooks (2008) using a non-transparent system in which there were no phonological cues to noun class membership.

Incidental learning. Robinson (2002, 2005) examined learning of some syntactic rules of Samoan under "incidental" training conditions that simply involved reading sentences for meaning and answering comprehension questions. There were no effects of WM on grammaticality judgment post-tests that used visually presented sentences. However, there were positive correlations with WM on a listening version of the grammaticality judgment task and a production task, especially in the delayed post-tests. It is not clear whether these correlations reflect the effect of WM on learning, or whether they reflect the effect of WM on test performance. Once again, note that WM correlations were most evident in the post-tests. Also note that according to the question-naire data the participants had high levels of awareness of two of the three target rules, and a high proportion of them said that they had searched for rules during the training task. Thus, it appears that if WM had affected learning it was through the mechanism of intentional induction.

There is mounting evidence for a relationship between WM and second language learning, and this has come from studies that seem to have involved explicit learning, as one would expect from work done in the related areas of reasoning, category learning, and artificial grammar learning.

Applications

Skehan (Chapter 23, this volume) suggests that the broad areas of application of individual differences research relate to selection, counseling, remediation, and instructional modification. In particular, ultimately one would like to see tests of WM being used as a means of directing students to instructional programs that are tailored to their cognitive abilities. For example, students with low PSTM might require a relatively low rate of vocabulary acquisition, with plenty of opportunities for recycling. Students with low WM might struggle with tasks that rely on intentional inductive learning where they are required to discover patterns for themselves, or may have difficulty learning from interactive tasks where rapid switching of attention between form and meaning is necessary. However, it must be born in mind that before WM tests are used in this way we need far more evidence of the relationship between different aspects of WM and specific learning processes (see *Future Directions* below).

Another approach to application lies not in modifying instruction, but in modifying cognitive abilities themselves. There is now evidence that WM can be improved through training (Holmes *et al.*, 2009; Klingberg, 2010). These effects are not confined to specific tasks, but have been shown to generalize from, for example, spatial to verbal memory, and in particular to tasks that involve the executive component of WM, such as Stroop tests. In fact, Holmes *et al.* (2009) found effects of training on WM, but not PSTM, tasks, suggesting that WM training improves the executive, rather than the storage, component of the WM system. Note, however, that most of this work has been carried out on children and special populations (e.g., children with attention-deficit hyper-activity disorder (ADHD)). Also, the fact of being a fluent bilingual appears to be associated with enhanced executive functions, presumably because of the increased control demands of managing two languages (Bialystok, 2009). Apart from providing further evidence that WMC is modifiable by experience, this also illustrates a potential application of WM research in encouraging bilingu-alism and bilingual education.

Future directions

Clearly it is a difficult task to specify exactly how a process as multi-faceted as SLA is related to a psychological construct that is as complex as WM, but some possible ways of homing in more precisely on the basis of their relationship are as follows:

(1) Pay more attention to the nature of the learning targets. For example, in relation to PSTM and grammar learning, do the target rules have to depend on phonological distinctions

(e.g., agreement patterns, distinguishing articles that otherwise have the same meaning)? If PSTM is to have a more general role, say, in learning word order regularities, then retention of sequential information will be critical, and the relevant item information will have to be represented at the more abstract level of meaning or grammatical categories. In general, if we are to understand the precise role of PSTM in grammar learning more attention needs to be paid to the nature of the regularities under investigation, specifically the kind of information required for rule induction, and also to the potential importance of both item and order information as dissociable aspects of PSTM function.

(2) Pay more attention to learning tasks, contrasting in particular implicit and explicit learning modes. We need to be more precise about what learners are actually doing during learning tasks in order to relate learning success to specific cognitive functions. This may be achieved through a combination of more constrained learning tasks and think-aloud and stimulated recall procedures (as used for example by Mackey *et al.*, 2002).

(3) Compare more or less complex (or verbalizable) learning targets, as in the category learning studies of DeCaro *et al.* (2008, 2009) and the inflection learning study of Kempe and Brooks (2008). This will potentially reveal how different learning processes along the explicit-implicit dimension are related to WM.

(4) Pay more attention to specific WM components. The reading span task involves both storage and executive functions and so it is difficult to relate performance to precise learning processes. More direct, non-linguistic, tests of executive function might be more useful, such as counting and calculation span tasks. The use of non-verbal IQ is a step in this direction (Brooks *et al.*, 2006; Kempe and Brooks, 2008), but this appeals to an assumed relationship between IQ and WM.

Conclusion

There are clearly individual differences in WMC, both in relation to PSTM and executive function. We have seen that this variability impacts upon second language *learning* in various ways. PSTM ability affects the efficiency of learning novel word forms, and the retention of sequences of forms. The latter plausibly contributes to grammatical development through processes of analysis. Where analysis depends upon conscious, intentional, explicit learning processes the executive component of WM appears to be implicated. Thus, the construct of WM is undoubtedly an important component of the notion of language learning aptitude, at least in the context of these specific kinds of learning processes. As we gain a greater understanding of how WM is implicated in different learning processes we will be able to have more confidence in using tests of WMC as predictors of language learning success in specific learning contexts. At the same time we will see how individual differences in WMC can be used as a tool for prising apart different aspects of the language learning process.

References

Ando, J., Fukunaga, N., Kurahashi, J., Suto, T., Nakano, T., and Kage, M. (1992). A comparative study on two EFL teaching methods: The communicative and the grammatical approach. *Japanese Journal of Educational Psychology*, *40*, 247–256.

Atkins, P. W. B. and Baddeley, A. D. (1998). Working memory and distributed vocabulary learning. *Applied Psycholinguistics*, *19*, 537–552.

Baddeley, A. D. (2007). *Working memory, thought, and action*. Oxford: Oxford University Press.

Baddeley, A. D., Gathercole, S. E., and Papagno, C. (1998). The phonological loop as a language learning device. *Psychological Review*, *105*, 158–173.

Baddeley, A. D. and Hitch, G. (1974). Working memory. In G. Bower (Ed.), *The psychology of learning and motivation* (Vol. *8*, pp. 47–90). New York: Academic Press.

Bates, E. and Goodman, J. C. (1997). On the inseparability of grammar and the lexicon: Evidence from acquisition, aphasia and real-time processing. *Language and Cognitive Processes, 12*, 507–584.

Beilock, S. L. and DeCaro, M. S. (2007). From poor performance to success under stress: Working memory, strategy selection, and mathematical problem solving under pressure. *Journal of Experimental Psychology: Learning, Memory, and Cognition, 33*, 983–998.

Berquist, B. (1997). Individual differences in working memory span and L2 proficiency: Capacity or processing efficiency? In A. Sorace, C. Heycock, and R. Shillcock (Eds.), *Proceedings of the GALA '97 Gonference on Language Acquisition* (pp. 468–473). Edinburgh: Human Communication Research Centre, University of Edinburgh.

Bialystok, E. (2009). Bilingualism: The good, the bad, and the indifferent. *Bilingualism: Language and Cognition, 12*, 3–11.

Bowey, J. A. (2006). Clarifying the phonological processing account of nonword repetition. *Applied Psycholinguistics, 27*, 548–552.

Brooks, P. J., Kempe, V., and Sionov, A. (2006). The role of learner and input variables in learning inflectional morphology. *Applied Psycholinguistics, 27*, 185–209.

Caplan, D., Waters, G., and Dede, G. (2007). Specialized verbal working memory for language comprehension. In A. R. A. Conway, C. Jarrold, M. J. Kane, A. Miyake, and J. N. Towse (Eds.), *Variation in working memory* (pp. 272–302). Oxford: Oxford University Press.

Conway, A. R. A., Cowan, N., Bunting, M. F., Therriault, D. J., and Minkoff, S. R. B. (2002). A latent variable analysis of working memory capacity, short-term memory capacity, processing speed, and general fluid intelligence. *Intelligence, 30*, 163–183.

Conway, A. R. A., Kane, M. J., Bunting, M. F., Hambrick, D. Z., Wilhelm, O., and Engle, R. W. (2005). Working memory span tasks: A methodological review and user's guide. *Psychonomic Bulletin and Review, 12*, 769–786.

Cowan, N. (1999). An embedded-processes model of working memory. In A. Miyake and P. Shah (Eds.), *Models of working memory: Mechanisms of active maintenance and executive control* (pp. 62–101). Cambridge: Cambridge University Press.

Daneman, M. and Carpenter, P. A. (1980). Individual differences in working memory and reading. *Journal of Verbal Learning and Verbal Behavior, 19*, 450–466.

Daneman, M. and Merikle, P. M. (1996). Working memory and language comprehension: A meta-analysis. *Psychonomic Bulletin and Review, 3*, 422–433.

DeCaro, M. S., Carlson, K. D., Thomas, R. D., and Beilock, S. L. (2009). When and how less is more: Reply to Tharp and Pickering. *Cognition, 111*, 415–421.

DeCaro, M. S., Thomas, R. D., and Beilock, S. L. (2008). Individual differences in category learning: Sometimes less working memory capacity is better than more. *Cognition, 107*, 284–294.

Doughty, C. J. (2001). Instructed SLA: Constraints, compensation and enhancement. In C. Doughty and M. Long (Eds.), *Handbook of second language acquisition*. Oxford: Blackwell.

Ellis, N. C. (1996). Sequencing in SLA: Phonological memory, chunking, and points of order. *Studies in Second Language Acquisition, 18*, 91–126.

Ellis, N. C. and Sinclair, S. G. (1996). Working memory in the acquisition of vocabulary and syntax: Putting language in good order. *Quarterly Journal of Experimental Psychology, 49A*, 234–250.

Engle, R. W., Kane, M. J., and Tuholski, S. W. (1999). Individual differences in working memory capacity and what they tell us about controlled attention, general fluid intelligence, and functions of the prefontal cortex. In A. Miyake and P. Shah (Eds.), *Models of working memory: Mechanisms of active maintenance and executive control* (pp. 102–134). Cambridge: Cambridge University Press.

Engle, R. W., Tuholski, S. W., Laughlin, J. E., and Conway, A. R. A. (1999). Working memory, short-term memory, and general fluid intelligence: A latent variable approach. *Journal of Experimental Psychology: General, 128*, 309–331.

Evans, J. S. B. T. (2003). In two minds: Dual-process accounts of reasoning. *Trends in Cognitive Sciences, 7*, 454–459.

Felser, C. and Roberts, L. (2007). Processing wh-dependencies in a second language: A cross-modal priming study. *Second Language Research, 23*, 9–36.

French, L. M. and O'Brien, I. (2008). Phonological memory and children's second language grammar learning. *Applied Psycholinguistics, 29*, 463–487.

Gathercole, S. E. (1995). Is nonword repetition a test of phonological memory or long-term knowledge – It all depends on the nonwords. *Memory and Cognition, 23*, 83–94.

Gathercole, S. E. (2006). Nonword repetition and word learning: The nature of the relationship. *Applied Psycholinguistics, 27*, 513–543.

Gathercole, S. E., Pickering, S. J., Hall, M., and Peaker, S. M. (2001). Dissociable lexical and phonological influences on serial recognition and serial recall. *Quarterly Journal of Experimental Psychology*, *54*A, 1–30.

Gathercole, S. E., Willis, C., Emslie, H., and Baddeley, A. D. (1992). Phonological memory and vocabulary development during the early school years: A longitudinal study. *Developmental Psychology*, *28*, 887–898.

Gathercole, S. E., Willis, C. S., Baddeley, A. D., and Emslie, H. (1994). The children's test of nonword repetition: A test of phonological working memory. *Memory*, *2*, 103–127.

Gebauer, G. F. and Mackintosh, N. J. (2007). Psychometric intelligence dissociates implicit and explicit learning. *Journal of Experimental Psychology: Learning, Memory, and Cognition*, *33*, 34–54.

Gibson, E. (1998). Linguistic complexity: Locality of syntactic dependencies. *Cognition*, *68*, 1–76.

Gupta, P. (2003). Examining the relationship between word learning, nonword repetition, and immediate serial recall in adults. *The Quarterly Journal of Experimental Psychology Section A: Human Experimental Psychology*, *56*, 1213–1236.

Harrington, M. and Sawyer, M. (1992). L2 working memory capacity and L2 reading skill. *Studies in Second Language Acquisition*, *14*, 25–38.

Havik, E., Roberts, L., van Hout, R., Schreuder, R., and Haverkort, M. (2009). Processing subject–object ambiguities in the L2: A self-paced reading study with German L2 learners of Dutch. *Language Learning*, *59*, 73–112.

Holmes, J., Gathercole, S. E., and Dunning, D. L. (2009). Adaptive training leads to sustained enhancement of poor working memory in children. *Developmental Science*, *12*, F9–F15.

Juffs, A. (2004). Representation, processing and working memory in a second language. *Transactions of the Philological Society*, *102*, 199–225.

Juffs, A. (2005). The influence of first language on the processing of wh-movement in English as a second language. *Second Language Research*, *21*, 121–151.

Just, M. A. and Carpenter, P. A. (1992). A capacity theory of comprehension: Individual differences in working memory. *Psychological Review*, *99*, 122–149.

Kane, M. J., Conway, A. R. A., Hambrick, D. Z., and Engle, R. W. (2007). Variation in working memory capacity as variation in executive attention and control. In A. R. A. Conway, C. Jarrold, M. J. Kane, A. Miyake, and J. N. Towse (Eds.), *Variation in working memory* (pp. 21–48). Oxford: Oxford University Press.

Kane, M. J., Hambrick, D. Z., and Conway, A. R. A. (2005). Working memory capacity and fluid intelligence are strongly related constructs: Comment on Ackerman, Beier, and Boyle (2005). *Psychological Bulletin*, *131*, 66–71.

Kane, M. J., Hambrick, D. Z., Tuholski, S. W., Wilhelm, O., Payne, T. W., and Engle, R. W. (2004). The generality of working memory capacity: A latent-variable approach to verbal and visuospatial memory span and reasoning. *Journal of Experimental Psychology: General*, *133*, 189–217.

Kempe, V. and Brooks, P. J. (2008). Second language learning of complex inflectional systems. *Language Learning*, *58*, 703–746.

Klingberg, T. (2010). Training and plasticity of working memory. *Trends in Cognitive Sciences*, *14*, 317–324.

Kormos, J. and Safar, A. (2008). Phonological short-term memory, working memory and foreign language performance in intensive language learning. *Bilingualism: Language and Cognition*, *11*, 261–271.

Mackey, A., Adams, R., Stafford, C., and Winke, P. (2010). Exploring the relationship between modified output and working memory capacity. *Language Learning*, *60*, 501–533.

Mackey, A., Philp, J., Egi, T., Fujii, A., and Tatsumi, T. (2002). Working memory, interactional feedback and L2 development. In P. Robinson and P. Skehan (Eds.), *Individual differences and second language instruction*. Philadelphia: Benjamins.

Majerus, S., Poncelet, M., Van der Linden, M., and Weekes, B. S. (2008). Lexical learning in bilingual adults: The relative importance of short-term memory for serial order and phonological knowledge. *Cognition*, *107*, 395–419.

Masoura, E. V. and Gathercole, S. E. (2005). Contrasting contributions of phonological short-term memory and long-term knowledge to vocabulary learning in a foreign language. *Memory*, *13*, 422–429.

Myles, F., Hooper, J., and Mitchell, R. (1999). Interrogative chunks in L2 French. *Studies in Second Language Acquisition*, *21*, 49–80.

Oakhill, J. and Yuill, N. (1986). Pronoun resolution in skilled and less-skilled comprehenders: Effects of memory load and inferential complexity. *Language and Speech*, *29*, 25–37.

Osaka, M. and Osaka, N. (1992). Language-independent working memory as measured by Japanese and English reading span tests. *Bulletin of the Psychonomic Society*, *30*, 287–289.

Osaka, M., Osaka, N., and Groner, R. (1993). Language-independent working memory: Evidence from German and French reading span tests. *Bulletin of the Psychonomic Society, 31*, 117–118.

Perfetti, C. (2007). Reading ability: Lexical quality to comprehension. *Scientific Studies of Reading, 11*, 357–383.

Reber, A. S. (1976). Implicit learning of synthetic languages: The role of instructional set. *Journal of Experimental Psychology: Human Learning and Memory, 2*, 88–94.

Reber, A. S. (1993). *Implicit Learning and Tacit Knowledge*. Oxford: Oxford University Press.

Reber, A. S., Walkenfeld, F. F., and Hernstadt, R. (1991). Implicit and explicit learning: Individual differences and IQ. *Journal of Experimental Psychology: Learning, Memory, and Cognition, 17*, 888–896.

Roberts, L., Marinis, T., Felser, C., and Clahsen, H. (2007). Antecedent priming at trace positions in children's sentence processing. *Journal of Psycholinguistic Research, 36*, 175–188.

Robinson, P. (1997). Individual differences and the fundamental similarity of implicit and explicit adult second language learning. *Language Learning, 47*, 45–99.

Robinson, P. (2001). Attention and memory in SLA. In C. Doughty and M. Long (Eds.), *Handbook of second language acquisition* (pp. 631–678). Oxford: Blackwell.

Robinson, P. (2002). Effects of individual differences in intelligence, aptitude and working memory on incidental second language learning: A replication and extension of Reber, Walkenfield, and Hernstadt (1991). In P. Robinson and P. Skehan (Eds.), *Individual differences and second language instruction* (pp. 211–265). Philadelphia: Benjamins.

Robinson, P. (2005). Cognitive abilities, chunk-strength, and frequency effects in implicit artificial grammar and incidental L2 learning: Replications of Reber, Walkenfeld, and Hernstadt (1991) and Knowlton and Squire (1996) and their relevance for SLA. *Studies in Second Language Acquisition, 27*, 235–268.

Roehr, K. (2008). Linguistic and metalinguistic categories in second language learning. *Cognitive Linguistics, 19*, 67–106.

Sagarra, N. (2007). From CALL to face-to-face interaction: The effect of computer-delivered recasts and working memory on L2 development. In A. Mackey (Ed.), *Conversational interaction in second language acquisition: A series of empirical studies* (pp. 229–248). Oxford: Oxford University Press.

Service, E. and Craik, F. I. M. (1993). Differences between young and older adults in learning a foreign vocabulary. *Journal of Memory and Language, 32*, 608–623.

Service, E. and Kohonen, V. (1995). Is the relation between phonological memory and foreign- language learning accounted for by vocabulary acquisition. *Applied Psycholinguistics, 16*, 155–172.

Speciale, G., Ellis, N. C., and Bywater, T. (2004). Phonological sequence learning and short-term store capacity determine second language vocabulary acquisition. *Applied Psycholinguistics, 25*, 293–320.

Stanovich, K. E. and West, R. F. (2000). Individual differences in reasoning: Implications for the rationality debate? *Behavioral and Brain Sciences, 23*, 645–665.

Thorn, A. S. C. and Gathercole, S. E. (1999). Language-specific knowledge and short-term memory in bilingual and non-bilingual children. *Quarterly Journal of Experimental Psychology, 52*A, 303–324.

Thorn, A. S. C., Gathercole, S. E., and Frankish, C. R. (2002). Language familiarity effects in short-term memory: The role of output delay and long-term knowledge. *Quarterly Journal of Experimental Psychology, 55*A, 1363–1383.

Turner, M. L. and Engle, R. W. (1989). Is working memory capacity task dependent? *Journal of Memory and Language, 28*, 127–154.

Walter, H. C. (2004). Transfer of reading comprehension skills to L2 is linked to mental representations of text and to L2 working memory. *Applied Linguistics, 25*, 315–339.

Waters, G. and Caplan, D. (1996). The measurement of verbal working memory capacity and its relation to reading comprehension. *Quarterly Journal of Experimental Psychology, 49*A, 51–79.

Williams, J. N. (1999). Memory, attention, and inductive learning. *Studies in Second Language Acquisition, 21*, 1–48.

Williams, J. N. and Lovatt, P. (2003). Phonological memory and rule learning. *Language Learning, 53*, 67–121.

Yuill, N., Oakhill, J., and Parkin, A. (1989). Working memory, comprehension ability and the resolution of text anomaly. *British Journal of Psychology, 80*, 351–361.

27

Age effects in second language learning

Robert DeKeyser

Introduction

Age effects in first and second language learning are a well-known phenomenon. Any layperson is familiar with stories of immigrant families where, after a few years, the children speak like native speakers of the same age while the parents keep being recognized as non-natives for the rest of their lives. The popular press has also familiarized many with the concept of "feral children," raised in circumstances of extreme neglect, and unable to become full-fledged speakers of any language after being rescued from their situation at an age beyond which first language learning (L1) is largely complete under normal circumstances (see, e.g., Benzaquén, 2006; Rymer, 1992). As is often the case, the media have promoted simplistic implications of these phenomena, such as a presumed impossibility of adults becoming highly skilled in a second language (L2) and the presumed ability of elementary school programs to instill a high level of L2 skill in all children, thus making it seem that age is the one and only determinant of success at language learning.

Historical discussion

In the last half-century, researchers have taken various positions on the role of age in second language development. In 1959, the neurologists Penfield and Roberts advocated early immersion in a second language because they thought that decreasing brain plasticity with increasing age made it much harder to learn a language later on. In 1967, the linguist Eric Lenneberg borrowed the term "critical period" from studies on animal behavior and applied it to language learning in humans, again using brain plasticity as an argument. Ever since then, few have doubted that there is a critical period for first language learning. What remains controversial, however, is whether the age effects commonly seen in second language learning also reflect a critical period; what is still completely unknown is exactly what aspects of brain maturation would be responsible for such a loss of plasticity. Lenneberg's (1967) assumption that increasing lateralization was to blame is no longer viable, as more recent research has shown that lateralization is complete by early infancy if not at birth (Hahn, 1987; Marzi, 1996).

In other respects, however, Lenneberg sounds surprisingly modern, and the seeds of much current debate can be found in this passage from his book:

> [O]ur ability to learn foreign languages tends to confuse the picture. Most individuals of average intelligence are able to learn a second language after the beginning of their second

decade, although the incidence of "language-learning-blocks" rapidly increases after puberty. Also automatic acquisition from mere exposure to a given language seems to disappear after this age, and foreign languages have to be taught and learned through a conscious and labored effort. Foreign accents cannot be overcome easily after puberty. However, a person can learn to communicate in a foreign language at the age of forty. This does not trouble our basic hypothesis on age limitations because we may assume that the cerebral organization for language learning as such has taken place during childhood, and since natural languages tend to resemble one another in many fundamental aspects (…), the matrix for language skill is present.

(1967, p. 176)

Lenneberg clearly realized that adults can learn a foreign language well, but that this does not contradict the critical period hypothesis because (a) these individuals, by definition, have the advantage of having learned a language already, which means that some of the most fundamental principles do not have to be learned at a later age, (b) being cognitively more mature, they are good at learning specific aspects of the L2 through mechanisms that adults or adolescents are good at (explicit learning), even though this means more effort, and (c) in spite of this cognitive maturity and this effort, the results tend to fall short of native-speaker standards, which is especially obvious in the area of pronunciation. Many studies of the last 20 years or so pick up on various threads present in this piece of text: Johnson and Newport's (1989) discussion of the maturation hypothesis vs. the exercise hypothesis, Mayberry's (1993) comparison of age effects on L1 and L2, Bley-Vroman's (1988, 2009) fundamental difference hypothesis, and DeKeyser's (2000), Ullman's (2001, 2005) and Paradis' (2004, 2009) claim that aging implies a shift from implicit/procedural to explicit/declarative learning.

Lenneberg's (1967) and Penfield and Roberts' (1959) work did not exactly provide the spark for much empirical *research* right away (even though it did provide the impulse for Foreign Language in the Elementary School *practice* from the 1960s onward). A few more or less isolated behavioral studies were published in the 1960s, 1970s, and 1980s, involving mostly global ratings of pronunciation and grammar, but the past two decades have seen a burgeoning of research in the area of age effects, both behavioral and neurological, with increasing conceptual and methodological sophistication. Data elicitation techniques have evolved from global pronunciation ratings and grammaticality judgments to tests involving reaction times, acoustic measurements, eye-tracking, electrophysiological measurements, and neuro-imaging; and the effect of age on many aspects of pronunciation and grammar has been scrutinized in great detail, from voice onset time and vowel quality to subjacency and aspectual distinctions. Particularly rich empirical studies, with a large number of participants, encompassing both grammar and pronunciation, and showing that the effects of age of arrival (AoA) and other predictors can be quite different from one domain or subdomain of language to the other, are Flege *et al.*, (1999) and Abrahamsson and Hyltenstam (2009) (see the section on empirical evidence for more detail on those studies). Recent book-length discussions of the age issue can be found in Herschensohn (2007) and Montrul (2008).

Core issues

The wealth of empirical research referred to in the previous section and described in more detail in the next section has not diminished the controversy surrounding the issue. The concept of "critical period" implies a declining learning capacity within a specific age range and a maturational, ultimately biological reason for this decline; both of these characteristics of a true critical period are absent in second language acquisition according to some researchers (e.g., Birdsong, 2005, 2009; Hakuta *et al.*, 2003), and therefore "age effects" is often preferred as a more neutral term, referring to undeniable empirical facts with fewer theoretical implications than the term "critical period."

The main arguments against a "critical period" are the lack of clear causal mechanism of a biological nature (while there are many confounds with age differences, including input differences, increasing role of L1 influence with age, decreasing role of schooling with age, different patterns of socialization, and L1 vs. L2 use as a function of age of immigration) and the lack of agreement on clear onset or offset points for the "critical period."

All these arguments are further complicated by a number of distinctions that are crucial for understanding the existing empirical findings, but that are often forgotten. First and foremost, a distinction needs to be made between speed of learning and ultimate attainment (see Han, Chapter 29, this volume, for the related notion of fossilization). What children are particularly good at is eventually reaching native-speaker levels, NOT learning faster than adults or adolescents. This distinction was clearly made already in Krashen *et al.* (1979) and is generally accepted now by researchers on age effects, yet often ignored in research design. Quite regularly studies are published that claim to "test the critical period hypothesis" but that investigate participants with only a couple of years of exposure to L2. After such a short period of exposure, the learners' linguistic competence is still developing, which means that any measures taken then reflect speed of learning and not ultimate attainment, and hence cannot serve to "test the critical period hypothesis." Particularly interesting, however, are studies that show, *with the same learners tested at different points in time,* how after limited amounts of exposure older learners do better, but after several more years younger starters get further ahead: Jia and Fuse (2007) and Larson-Hall (2008), the former with immigrants in the USA, the latter with classroom foreign language learners in Japan.

Next are two distinctions that overlap in most cases, but are not quite the same: formal ("instructed," "tutored) learning versus naturalistic learning, and explicit versus implicit learning. As the quote from Lenneberg (1967) above suggests, adults are not any worse at learning grammar rules or vocabulary in explicit fashion than children, on the contrary; what they are worse at is learning the language through mere exposure and communicative interaction without reflecting on the language. Most classroom learning tends to rely quite a bit on reflecting on structure, and most non-tutored immigrants tend to do little such reflection; hence the two distinctions tend to coincide. They are not the same, however, as some classroom learners do get large amounts of exposure to and communicative practice in the L2 (particularly in immersion programs) and as some adult or adolescent learners, particularly those with above-average levels of education and/or verbal ability, are likely to do quite a bit of reflection and explicit induction of patterns on their own. Needless to say, when the three distinctions coincide in the sense that research participants are tutored learners in a classroom that encourages explicit learning (learning with awareness of the structures being learned), and if their proficiency is tested after only a couple of years of L2 exposure, often only a few hours a week, then, all that is measured is speed of explicit learning, not ultimate attainment through implicit learning, and the data are irrelevant to the critical period debate (but not to the study of age effects, of course).

Further distinctions need to be made on the side of the dependent variable, proficiency in L2. Linguists traditionally distinguish phonology, morphosyntax, and lexicon (educators may prefer the largely equivalent terms pronunciation, grammar, and vocabulary), and it has often been observed that age effects are stronger in pronunciation than in grammar and barely noticeable in vocabulary; some even hypothesized that age effects were limited to pronunciation. Sufficient empirical evidence has accumulated now for strong age effects in both pronunciation and grammar, and at least some research suggests that (less obvious) effects exist in vocabulary (Abrahamsson and Hyltenstam, 2009; Hyltenstam, 1992; Silverberg and Samuel, 2004; pace Hirsh *et al.*, 2003).

Increasingly, however, research has shown that more fine-grained distinctions need to be made to determine what aspects of language are affected by age of acquisition. Within pronunciation, e.g., Abrahamsson and Hyltenstam (2009) found that voice onset time was more affected by age than global accent rating. Within the area of grammar, e.g., Birdsong (1992), DeKeyser (2000), Johnson and Newport (1989), and McDonald (2006), among others, found that different morpho-syntactic structures showed different degrees of decline with increasing age of acquisition. DeKeyser *et al.* (forthcoming; cf., also DeKeyser, 2000) found that the less salient a morphological structure, the more sensitive it was to age effects; components of salience that interacted most strongly with age were stress on the morpheme to be acquired and distance between morphemes in agreement patterns. Within the area of vocabulary, susceptibility to priming (Silverberg and Samuel, 2004) and knowledge of idioms (Abrahamsson and Hyltenstam, 2009) stand out as being dependent on AoA, while vocabulary as a whole is generally assumed to show little or no effect of AoA.

A final point to keep in mind when reading the empirical literature on age effects is that the notion of nativelikeness is not entirely non-problematic (see esp. Abrahamsson and Hyltenstam, 2009; Birdsong, 2007, 2009). When rather easy tests of basic morphosyntax are used, they may lead to ceiling effects that hide aspects of non-nativeness that would become obvious with harder tests; these ceiling effects become more likely for younger learners, learners with an L1 close to the L2, and highly-educated learners, thus easily providing a distorted picture, because the degree of non-nativeness masked by the easy test depends on all these factors. When much harder tests are used, one may find that native speakers show quite a bit of variability on the structures at issue, as a function of social class, level of education, region of origin, and so on, which makes it very hard to determine the boundaries of nativeness; one will usually find a statistical difference between natives or young learners and older learners, but some of the better older learners are likely to fall "within native range" on some of the items or measures, given that the native range is so wide. Ideally, of course, one should use elements of grammar or pronunciation that are known to be quite hard for second language learners (with a given L1), but where native speaker variability is extremely minimal, such as the use of articles in English or the use of verbal aspect in the Romance or Slavic languages.

Taking all of these caveats into account, what does the empirical literature show? Nobody doubts that a strong negative correlation between AoA and ultimate attainment is found for many aspects of both grammar and pronunciation; nobody doubts either that some individuals often pass for native speakers in everyday interaction, even though they learned a language as an adult. Neither of these two observations have much to say about the existence of a critical period; the second one not even about age effects. In fact, a strong negative correlation between age of acquisition and ultimate attainment throughout the lifespan (or even from birth through middle age), the only age effect documented in many earlier studies, is *not* evidence for a critical period. As pointed out above, the critical period concept implies a break in the AoA-proficiency function, i.e., an age (somewhat variable from individual to individual, of course, and therefore an age range in the aggregate) after which the decline of success rate in one or more areas of language is much less pronounced and/or clearly due to different reasons.

On the other hand, more recent studies often do not calculate AoA-proficiency correlations separately for different age ranges (say, e.g., 0–6, 6–12, 12–18, 18–40, 40–60), but infer from the negative correlation over the lifespan that the correlation is equally negative and for the same reasons for each age range, and hence that there is no critical period. This is equally naïve as inferring there *is* a critical period from the same data. A mere (strong) negative correlation for the whole lifespan is not evidence for either of these inferences at all. Nor does the existence of people who can often pass for native speakers prove automatically that they are immune to critical period effects or any other age effects. Until it is shown that their nativelike appearance holds up under scrutiny, this appearance is just an appearance; in other words it merely shows that they are less strongly affected and/or that they found an alternative path to reaching the same observable skill.

A few studies claim to have found speakers who hold up under such scrutiny, even in the area of pronunciation (Bongaerts *et al.*, 1995; Bongaerts *et al.*, 1997; Bongaerts, 1999; Bongaerts *et al.*, 2000; Birdsong, 2007). These studies have been criticized on a variety of methodological grounds, however (most notably by Long, 2005). Moreover, the largest and most careful study on this topic to date, Abrahamsson and Hyltenstam (2009), with carefully selected learners who were administered a set of difficult tests on grammar, pronunciation, and vocabulary, found that out of 195 participants with varying AoA who said they could pass for natives and 41 who were indeed deemed to be native by a panel of judges listening to a short speech sample, none with AoA > 8 scored within native speaker range on all 10 fine-grained measures (the maximum for any of these "older" learners was 7 measures out of 10); moreover those who passed for native on most tests were all highly educated language professionals, suggesting again that to the extent adult learners even come close to nativelikeness, it is only with the help of large amounts of explicit learning. Further evidence for this point of view comes from DeKeyser (2000) and Abrahamsson and Hyltenstam (2008), who showed that none of their adult learners scored within the native range, even by liberal standards, unless they had high levels of aptitude. Other studies, such as DeKeyser *et al.* (2010), and Harley and Hart (1997), provide evidence that aptitude plays a much larger role for adolescents and adults than for children, again pointing to a larger role for explicit learning in (successful) older learners. A more detailed account of the empirical evidence available is provided below.

Meanwhile, before delving more deeply into the literature, let us mention what is probably the most interesting but also the most contentious question of all, that of the causal interpretation of this whole body of research: are the age effects that are being documented with ever more precision for ever more populations and languages evidence of a maturational phenomenon or not? And if so, is that maturation sufficiently delimited in time to be called a critical period? If yes, what is its biological etiology? It is natural to think that neuro-imaging research and other areas of cognitive neuroscience are crucial for answering these questions, and progress is certainly being made in that area. There are two reasons, however, why the picture that emerges is far from clear. One is that the amount of research that has tried to pinpoint the exact nature of age-sensitive elements of language in (psycho)linguistic terms is quite limited (the vast majority of studies have only used broad distinctions, like phonology versus syntax); as a result, one does not even know exactly what to look for in neuroscience, i.e., what specific aspects of brain maturation may be responsible for changes in the capacity to learn those specific aspects of language. The other reason is that cognitive neuroscience data tend to be extremely variable from study to study and hard to interpret, let alone to predict. Predictive validity is still a distant goal in most neuro-imaging research (see e.g., Vul *et al.*, 2009) and in the neuroscience of second language acquisition in particular (see e.g., de Bot, 2008), even though meta-analyses are beginning to allow some generalization (see e.g., Indefrey, 2006). As a result, the existing neuroscience literature on age effects in L2 (a summary of which can be found in Birdsong, 2006) largely aims at answering the same question as the behavioral research: what is the extent of age effects for specific aspects of language learning, and does any of this suggest a critical period, that is, a maturational, not a contextual, phenomenon? A specific biological etiology for the age effects found is seldom even suggested, let alone tested.

In summary, the core questions are whether there is a specific period of decline in the ability for implicit language learning, and whether any such decline is due to maturational factors. These questions sometimes lead to unnecessary confusion because of the failure to distinguish between implicit and explicit learning, between speed of learning and ultimate attainment, and between various aspects of language; not all aspects of grammar or even phonology are equally sensitive to age effects. In the next section, we discuss the various strands of research on these questions in more detail.

Data and common elicitation measures

While a wide variety of measures have been used to assess L2 proficiency in age effect studies, fairly global measures dominated at first: global accent ratings in the area of phonology (e.g., Asher and García, 1969; Oyama, 1978), grammaticality judgments with a wide variety of structures in the area of morphosyntax (e.g., Johnson and Newport, 1989; Patkowski, 1980). In both areas, more recent research has often narrowed its focus. Specific aspects of phonology have been investigated, such as voice onset time (Abrahamsson and Hyltenstam, 2009), vowel discrimination (Tsukada *et al.*, 2005), and acoustic characteristics of consonant production (Kang and Guion, 2006), as well as specific aspects of grammar, such as subjacency (Johnson and Newport, 1991), verb aspect (Montrul and Slabakova, 2003), and adjective–noun agreement (Scherag *et al.*, 2004).

At the same time, the testing format has often shifted from untimed paper-and-pencil tests to measures of reaction times, not only for priming experiments (e.g., Scherag *et al.*, 2004), but also for grammaticality judgment tests (Abrahamsson and Hyltenstam, 2009). Still other measures have been used in the area of vocabulary, such as lexical decision tasks (Silverberg and Samuel, 2004), and oral fill-in-the-blanks (Abrahamsson and Hyltenstam, 2009).

The last 15 years or so have seen an explosion of research in cognitive neuroscience, in this area as well as in others. Through fMRI and PET, researchers have tried to pinpoint areas in the brain that are maximally active during second language processing by adults who had learned an L2 at different ages (e.g., Perani *et al.*, 1998, 2003; Wartenburger *et al.*, 2003); even more recently, ERP has been used to trace the time course of the brain's reaction to correct and incorrect stimuli in the L2 as a function of AoA (e.g., Hahne, 2001; Weber-Fox and Neville, 1996) or to assess whether adult learners necessarily show different patterns from native speakers (e.g., Friederici *et al.*, 2002; Ojima *et al.*, 2005).

Finally, at the opposite end of the spectrum from the neuroscience research and the more fine-grained behavioral research, there is the census research. Almost all age effect studies that have collected their own data have limited reliability because they have too few subjects, maybe not in a general sense, but definitely for a robust analysis of age effects in narrow age ranges or when a number of covariates have to be partialed out. Therefore, researchers like Chiswick and Miller (2008), Hakuta *et al.* (2003), and Stevens (1999) have taken the opposite approach: use existing census data to establish a more reliable correlation between immigrants' age of arrival and their linguistic proficiency. The problem in this case, of course, is not reliability but validity: self-assessments may have their value for certain types of research, but the extremely coarse scales used by the census, combined with the lack of reference point for the average census participant, casts serious doubts on the usefulness of this approach (DeKeyser, 2006; Stevens, 2004).

We next turn to empirical verification. Even though a variety of methodologies have been used for assessing age effects, as explained in the previous section, three clusters of studies stand out that have used the most frequently used methodologies: oral grammaticality judgment tests, other tests of morphosyntax (esp. written grammaticality judgment tests and global ratings of grammatical accuracy), and global accent ratings. For these three clusters of studies we provide a table with the most important variables and findings of the studies, and therefore provide less detail in the text. For all other methodologies we provide a more detailed discussion.

As Table 27.1 shows, the vast majority of studies that use GJTs (Grammaticality Judgment Tests) as the outcome variable have found large correlations between AoA and GJT scores. Global correlations for the entire lifespan (or at least the part included in the individual studies) range from |0.45| to |0.77| (correlations being negative for test scores, and positive for error rates or reaction time). For the younger groups (varying from study to study between AoA < 12 and AoA < 18) the correlation ranges from |0.24| to |0.87|; for the older groups from |0.04| to |0.69| (the vertical stripes refer to absolute value, and the values are negative where accuracy is concerned and positive where error rate is concerned). In those studies where the two groups are described separately, the correlation is much higher for the younger than for the older group, except in Birdsong and Molis (2001), where there was a ceiling effect for the younger group. This global picture from more than a dozen studies provides support for the non-continuity of the decline in the AoA-proficiency function, which all researchers agree is a hallmark of a critical period phenomenon. In other words, contrary to what some researchers have claimed, there is evidence for an upper age limit to the decline in implicit language learning ability, a limit which all agree is a necessary condition for the claim that the age effects observed are not simply a matter of lifelong decline.

The results for other morphosyntactic measures in Table 27.2 show largely the same picture: where global correlations are given, they range from |0.35| to |0.74|; where group comparisons are made, learners with AoA > 15–16 are significantly worse than younger learners; for some studies there is even no overlap for the older learners with the native speaker range.

Table 27.3 shows that global accent ratings also yield high correlations for the entire lifespan (|0.66| to |0.85|) or for younger learners, the only exception being Flege *et al.* (2006), where AoA was strongly confounded with age at testing for the older, but not the younger group. Where group comparisons are made, younger learners always do significantly better than the older learners. The behavioral evidence, then, suggests a non–continuous age effect with a "bend" in the AoA-proficiency function somewhere between ages 12 and 16.

Further evidence for the effect of AoA on pronunciation comes from more narrowly focused investigations. As Table 27.4 shows, the approach taken in these studies varies widely: they examined production or perception, vowels or consonants, using human judgments or acoustic analyses; they included other variables that differed from study to study, such as length of residence (LOR) or L1/L2 dominance; they examined immigrants in some cases and classroom learners in others; some made group comparisons and others studied individuals' performance. This makes it hard to come to any clear conclusions except that AoA seems to play a very significant role, but that it is often confounded with other variables, and that a few individuals can pass for native on some narrowly constrained tasks. The main point, however, is that there is no evidence of the AoA effect disappearing when other variables are taken into account, or of adult learners passing for native on a wide range of stringent tests.

The evidence from neuroscience is even more ambiguous in its findings and harder to summarize because of the great variety of tasks, measures, and outcomes (see Table 27.5). Some studies found clear qualitative differences between younger and older learners in the details of brain anatomy (Mechelli *et al.*, 2004) or in the nature of L2 processing, as indicated by location and intensity of brain activity (Kim *et al.*, 1997; Perani *et al.*, 1996, 2003; Wartenburger *et al.*, 2003; Weber-Fox and Neville, 1996); others did not find any qualitative differences (Perani *et al.*, 1998), at least not when controlling for proficiency. Most brain studies provide only indirect evidence in the sense that they provide support for differences between L1 and L2 processing, even for advanced late learners, but they do not establish direct correlations with AoA (e.g., Hahne, 2001; Hahne and Friederici, 2001; Ojima *et al.*, 2005; Sabourin and Stowe, 2008, all using ERP). Other studies are even harder to interpret because they deal with instructed learning (e.g., Chen *et al.*, 2007), even short-term instructed learning (e.g., Mueller *et al.*, 2005; Tokowicz and MacWhinney, 2005). Patkowski (2003), on the other hand, does make relevant age comparisons that show a clear difference between AoA < 12 and AoA > 12, but provides only indirect evidence about differential hemisphere involvement (behavioral evidence from a verbal-manual dual-task paradigm).

Table 27.1 Correlations between AoA and L2 proficiency as measured by oral grammaticality judgment tests

Study	L1	L2	LoR range	n	AoA range	r between AoA and L2	remarks
Abrahamsson and Hyltenstam (2009)	Spanish	Swedish	12–42	41	E: 1–11	58% native-like	for score
					L: 13–19	40% native-like	
					E: 1–11	94% native-like	for RT
					L: 13–19	60% native-like	
Bialystok and Miller (1999)	Chinese	English	1–18	33	1–32	−0.82	for AoA<15
						−0.57	for AoA>15
	Spanish	English	2–23	28	3–41	−0.68	for AoA<15
						−0.51	for AoA>15
Birdsong and Molis (2001)	Spanish	English	min. 10	61	3–44	−0.24	for AoA<16
						−0.69	for AoA>16
							for AoA>16
DeKeyser (2000)	Hungarian	English	min. 10 mean 34	57	1–40	−0.63	for all learners
						−0.26	for AoA<16
						−0.04	for AoA>16
DeKeyser et al., in press	Russian	English	> 8	76	5–71	−0.71	for AoA < 18
						−0.17	for AoA > 18
		Hebrew	> 8	62	4–65	−0.51	for AoA < 18
						−0.12	for AoA > 18
Flege et al. (1999)	Korean	English	min. 8	240	1–23	−0.71	for AoA<15
						−0.23	for AoA>15
Jia (1998)	various	English	5–32	105	3–34	−0.68	
Johnson and Newport (1989)	Chinese + Korean	English	3–26	46	5–39	−0.77	for all learners
						−0.87	for AoA<16
						−0.16	for AoA>16
Johnson and Newport (1991)	Chinese	English	5–15	21	4–16	−0.63	all AoA<16
Kim (1993)	Korean	English	min. 3	30	3–35	−0.66	for error rate
						−0.55	for reaction time
Larson-Hall (2008)	Japanese	English	1–9	200	4–13	−0.38 (partial)	foreign language (early-late t: p = .20)
McDonald (2000)	Spanish	English	3–24	28	0–20	−0.61	for test score; for RT late acquirers differ from all others
	Vietnamese	English	9–23	24	0–10	−0.59	for test score; for RT all L2 acquirers differ from L1 acquirers
McDonald (2006)	various	English	1–18	50	12–29	−0.38 (older!)	for GJT? for RT?
Shim (1993)	Korean	English	5–21	60	0–29	−0.45	for error rate
						−0.71	for reaction time

Table 27.2 Correlations between AoA and L2 proficiency as measured by other tests of morphosyntax

Study	L1	L2	LoR range	n	AoA range	r between AoA and L2	remarks
Abrahamsson and Hyltenstam (2009)	Spanish	Swedish	12–42	41	E: 1–11 L: 13–19	65% native-like 50% native-like	for written GJT
Ball (1996)	Greek	English	10–72	102	1–40	0.62	marked decline for AoA>16
Bialystok and Miller (1999)	Chinese Spanish	English	1–18 2–23	33 28	1–32 3–41	n.s.	exact r not reported
Coppieters (1987)	various	French	min. 5.5 mean 17.4	21	min. 18	not reported	no overlap with NS group
Hyltenstam (1992)	Finnish Spanish	Swedish	no info (sound native)	24	<15	not reported	no overlap with NS group
Jia (1998)	various	English	5–72	105	3–34	−0.35	
Jia and Fuse (2007)	Chinese	English	1–3	10	5–16	−0.59	spontaneous speech
Johnson (1992)	Chinese + Korean	English	4–27	46	5–39	−0.54 −0.73	for all learners for AoA<15
Lee and Schachter (1997)	Korean	English	2.2–4.6	76	3–24	not reported	AoA>15 worst AoA 11–15 best
Montrul and Slabakova (2003)	English	Spanish	0.5–10	64	12–24	n.a.	19/64 within native range (no naturalistic learners; some within CP still)
Oyama (1978)	Italian	English	5–20	60	6–20	−0.57	r is for AoA-L2 with LoR removed
Patkowski (1980)	various, mostly Indo-European	English	6–61	67	5–5	−0.74	
Scherag, *et al.* (2004)	English	German	6–33	10	12–49	n.a.	L2 speakers less sensitive to morpho-syntactic priming
Sorace (1993)	English French	Italian	5–15	24 20	18–27	not reported	signif. difference with NS group
Van Boxtel, *et al.* (2005)	German, Dutch French, Turkish		4–50	43	12–35	n.a.	8/43 within native range (1 Turkish) (imitation task and preference task combined)

Table 27.3 Correlations between AoA and L2 proficiency as measured by global phonological ratings

Study	L1	L2	LoR range	n	AoA range	r between AoA and L2	remarks
Abrahamsson and Hyltenstam (2009)	Spanish	Swedish	> 10	175	E: < 11 L: > 12	62% native-like 6% native-like	
Abu-Rabia and Kehat (2004)	various	Hebrew	8–43	13	7–40+	n.a.	Ss selected by author; none native on all tests
Asher and Garcia (1969)	Spanish	English	mean 5	71	1–19	not reported	for AoA>12: only 7% near-native
Birdsong (2007) part 1	various	French	5–32	22	18–61	3/22 are "native-like"	passage reading
Flege et al. (1995)	Italian	English	15–44	240	2–23	not reported	AoA accounts for 60% of variance-AoA>16: none native-like
Flege et al. (1999)	Korean	English	min. 8	240	1–23	−0.62 −0.5	for AoA<12 for AoA>12
Flege et al. (2002)	Italian	English	4–50	E: 36 L: 36	E: 2–13 L: 15–26	not reported	if early AND L2-dominant (n = 18): no accent (delayed repetition)
Flege et al. (2006)	Korean	English	2–6	72	6–38	−0.19 −0.55	for children for adults; (but AOA-age confound for adults, not for children) signif. diff. child-adult
Munro and Mann (2005)	Chinese	English	6–19	32	3–16	strong linear decline	all Ss are within CP
Oyama (1976)	Italian	English	5–20	60	6–20	−0.69 (stories) −0.83 (paragraph)	for error rate; LoR partialed out
Patkowski (1980)	various	English	6–61	67	5–50	−0.76	
Tahta et al. (1981)	various	English	min. 2	109	min. 6	−0.66	for error rate; AoA<6: all perfect
Thompson (1991)	Russian	English	not	36	4–42	−0.81	for error rate
Tsukada et al. (2005)	Korean	English	3–5	72	E: 6–14 L: 21–38		discrimination: early between native and late production (acoustic anal.): early like native
Yeni-Komshian et al. (2000)	Korean	English	min. 8	240	1–23	−0.85	Sign. diff. btw. NS & all Koreans

Table 27.4 Other evaluations of pronunciation

Study	L1	L2	LoR range	n	AoA range	r between AoA and L2	remarks
Abrahamsson and Hyltenstam (2009)	Spanish	Swedish	12–42	41	E: 1–11 L: 13–19 E: 1–11 L: 13–19	74% native-like 40% native-like 71% native-like 20% native-like	VOT perception VOT production
Birdsong (2007) part 2	various	French	5–32	22	18–61	3/22 are native-like	VOT and vowel duration in word reading
Guion (2003)	Quichua	Spanish	not given	20	0–25	if AoA > 15 no native-like L2 vowels	repeat words
Guion *et al.* (2004)	Spanish	English	ave. 23.4 ave. 12.9	10 10	E: 2.5–6 L: 15–33		
Kang and Guion (2006)	Korean	English	10+	40	1–6 & 15–34	n.a.	acoustic measurements of stop conson. Early: separate Late: merged L1-L2 system
Larson-Hall (2008)	Japanese	English	1–9	200	4–13	0.03 (partial)	phoneme discrimination (early-late t: $p = .01$ but eta-sq $=.03$)
Lee *et al.* (2006)	Korean and Japanese	English	E: 10–40 L: 5–26	40	E: 1–6 L: 15–34	interactions between age and L1	vowel duration, intensity, pitch
Tsukada *et al.* (2005)	Korean	English	2–6	72	8–41	n.a.	vowel discrimination; vowel production; children > adults
Yeni-Komshian *et al.* (2001)	Korean	English	min. 8	192	6–23	0.31 (Cons) 0.69 (Vowels)	for error rate

If one accepts the argument that only comparisons between bilinguals are valid (otherwise instead of documenting age effects one may be modeling monolingual vs. bilingual effects, as demonstrated in Proverbio, Çok and Zani's 2002 ERP study; see also Byrnes, Chapter 31, this volume) and that to talk about age effects one should make direct age comparisons, not just compare late L2 learners to L1 speakers, few relevant studies exist. If one further rejects the results from studies that did not have any control for proficiency or years of exposure, one is left with only a handful of studies: Kim *et al.* (1997), Mechelli *et al.* (2004), Perani *et al.* (1998, 2003), Wartenburger *et al.* (2003), Weber–Fox and Neville (1996). All of these found a significant effect of AoA, except for Perani *et al.* (1998). If one adds to that the inescapable argument that not documenting any difference for a couple of structures does not mean there are none for other structures, the scant

Table 27.5 Neuro-imaging and neurophysiological measures

Study	L1	L2	LoR range	n	AoA range	Technique	findings
Chen *et al.* (2007)	Chinese	English	9–14 (instruction)	15	10–13 (instruction)	ERP	L2 diff. from L1 in ERP, not in behavioral data
Hahne (2001)	Russian	German	ave. 66 (range: 12–204) (in mo.)	16	> 10	ERP	no ELAN and delayed P600 in L2
Hahne and Friederici (2001)	Japanese	German	2–78 mo.	12	18–31 (instruction)	ERP	differerence in P600 between L1 and L2
Kim *et al.* (1997)	various	various	not reported	6 6	infancy adulthood	fMRI	late bilinguals show slightly different location
Mechelli *et al.* (2004)							
Study 1	various	various	>5	58	early:< 5; late: 10–15	voxel-based morphometry	early: increased gray-matter density in inferior parietal cortex
Study 2	Italian	English	not reported	22	2–34	voxel-based morphometry	AoA correlates negatively with proficiency (.855) and gray-matter density
Mueller *et al.* (2005)	German	Japanese	n.a.	24	20–26	ERP	P600 same; LAN different
Ojima *et al.* (2005)	Japanese	English	H: 3.75y L: 0.5y	46	around 12	ERP	no P600 in L2 for S-V agreement
Patkowski (2003)	various	English	6.6y	68	early:4–12 late:13–55	dichotic and tachistoscopic	interference from dual task (hand-tapping) shows hemisphere by AoA interaction
Perani *et al.* (1998)	Italian Spanish	English Catalan	>1y at birth	9 12	> 10 < 4	PET	proficiency matters, not age
Perani *et al.* (2003)	Spanish/Catalan Catalan/Spanish			5 6	L1: < 3 L2: > 3	fMRI	both age and proficiency matter
Sabourin and Stowe (2008)	various	Dutch	high proficiency	22	late	ERP	L1-L2 difference in P600
Tokowicz and MacWhinney (2005)	English	Spanish	2–4 terms (instruction)	34	college	ERP	L2 diff. from L1 in behavioral, not in ERP data

(continued on the next page)

Table 27.5 (continued)

Study	L1	L2	LoR range	n	AoA range	Technique	findings
Wartenburger (2003)	Italian	German	ave. 27 ave.10 ave. 5	32	av. 0 ave. 19 ave. 20	fMRI	semantics < profic. grammar < AoA
Weber-Fox and Neville (1996)	Chinese	English	>3: 14.3 >13: 7.8 >16: 7.6	61	1 to adult	ERP	AoA>3: effect in syntax AoA>13: effect in semantics AoA>16: effect in behavior

evidence we have so far does suggests qualitative differences in brain activity as a function of age, even when L1/L2 status and proficiency/exposure are controlled for.

Showing qualitative effects does not necessarily require brain imaging or ERP, however. Other researchers have tried to provide more indirect evidence (and for the learning processes rather than their end result) by investigating the different predictive validity of both learner and language variables in different age ranges. DeKeyser (2000), DeKeyser et al. (2010), and Harley and Hart (1997) all show that aptitude plays a much more important role in L2 acquisition for adolescents and adults than for children; Abrahamsson and Hyltenstam (2008) and DeKeyser (2000) both showed that no adult learners fell within the native proficiency range unless they had high aptitude. Such findings suggest a larger role of explicit/declarative learning in older than in younger learners (cf., also Bley-Vroman, 2009; Montrul, 2009; Paradis 2004, 2009; Ullman, 2001, 2004). The interaction between the salience of linguistic structures and AoA as documented in DeKeyser et al. (forthcoming) also points in that direction, given that salience is known to play a much larger role in explicit than in implicit learning (Reber et al., 1980).

The literature on L1 attrition/incomplete acquisition is also of potential relevance here. Not only does attrition, "the non-pathological decrease in a language that had previously been acquired by an individual" (Köpke and Schmid, 2004), show the reverse pattern of L2 acquisition in the sense that the earlier the switch is made from L1 (dominance) to L2 (dominance), the less remains of L1; it is becoming increasingly clear that this age effect in attrition is a maturational effect in the sense that it is due to lack of input at a critical age (Bylund, 2009a, b; Hyltenstam et al., 2009; Montrul, 2008; Schmid, 2009) rather than lack of continued practice later on.

The attrition research is also relevant to two more specific questions: the issue of the role of L1 "entrenchment" (e.g., MacWhinney, 2006) in the increasingly incomplete acquisition of L2 with increasing AoA/L1 development, and the much-debated issue of the non-continuity of the AoA function. Research with adoptees (Pallier et al., 2003; Ventureyra et al., 2004) is often quoted as showing that when there is zero interference from the L1 (because L1 is completely lost), then L2 is acquired 100 percent, and some have used this as an argument for the interpretation of (the lack of) incomplete acquisition of L2 as due to (the lack of) L1 entrenchment. Oh et al. (2010), however, report traces of phoneme recognition in adults who were adopted at a very young age, and Hyltenstam et al. (2009) show that neither complete L1 loss nor complete L2 acquisition are necessarily found in children adopted at a very young age, but that small traces of L1 do remain, as well as traces of non-nativeness in L2. Perhaps one could argue that this is just another example of L1 and L2 being proportionately lost/acquired, if not 100 percent, as in Pallier et al. (2003) or

Ventureyra *et al.* (2004), then at least close to 100 percent, but that does not account for an important fact from research on sign language acquired as L1 at different ages. Mayberry (1993), e.g., shows that age effects on American Sign Language (ASL) as L1 (in congenitally deaf children of hearing parents) are similar to age effects on ASL as L2 (in those who become deaf later or for some other reason learn ASL as L2). Clearly, age effects in L1, by definition, cannot be due to entrenchment of a previously acquired language, and therefore Occam's razor requires us to think twice before trying to explain age effects in L2 with arguments about L1 interference.

The non-continuity debate has pitted researchers such as Johnson and Newport (1989) and DeKeyser *et al.* (2010), who worked with linguistic data elicited specifically for age effect research and found non-continuous effects of AoA, leveling off in early adolescence, against others such as Bialystok and Hakuta (1994, Hakuta *et al.*, 2003) and Chiswick and Miller (2008), who used self-ratings retrieved from census data and found a continuous, lifelong decline. Here again, research on L1 attrition provides important evidence: Schmid (2002) found no difference in attrition when comparing adolescent learners to adult learners, in contrast with the various aforementioned findings about attrition in pre-puberty learners, suggesting non-continuity in attrition, not just in acquisition.

In conclusion then, the preponderance of the evidence on the acquisition of phonology and morphosyntax, both behavioral and neurological, as well as the literature on attrition, strongly support non-continuous age effects of a qualitative nature. Little is known, however, about the biological aspects of these changes. For discussion of possible explanations in psychological terms, see DeKeyser and Larson-Hall (2005).

Applications

As pointed out in the historical section of this chapter, research on age effects in language learning has always provided a strong impetus for early teaching; the work of Penfield and Roberts (1959) was instrumental in starting the immersion program movement in Canada, soon to be followed by a push for foreign language in the elementary school (FLES) in the USA and many other countries. This push for earlier foreign language teaching is still going on today, particularly in Asia.

It should be pointed out, however, that "earlier is better" when it comes to L2 learning, does not necessarily imply that "earlier teaching is better." Virtually all the research quoted in the previous sections was carried out with immigrants who are fully immersed in a second language environment and who may or may not have received any instruction in it. In a school context we have the opposite situation: plenty of instruction, but very little exposure, except of course in true immersion programs. Moreover, the quality of the input may be diminished by various factors such as the artificiality of classroom interaction (even assuming it is always in the L2, a big assumption for most elementary foreign language instruction) and the often far-from-perfect proficiency of non-native teachers, especially in the area of pronunciation.

We know that children are better than adults at acquiring an L2 (a) in the long run from (b) massive amounts of (c) native-speaker input, but does that mean that (a) after just a few years of instruction (b) provided only a few hours per week and not every week in the year by (c) non-native teachers with sometimes very limited proficiency, children will do better than adults too? Of course, students who have had several years of L2 instruction in grade school and middle school before going on with the same language in high school will know more than those who only start in high school, but that does not say anything about age, only about amount of instruction. Given the same amount of the same kind of instruction at an earlier age, do students learn more? That is a question that has been addressed by surprisingly little research, especially given the enormity of its implications for educational systems worldwide.

Almost all empirical research carried out in an attempt to answer that question has been conducted in Spain. Muñoz (2008) provides a summary and comes to the clear conclusion that "older is better," except perhaps for pronunciation. As always, the picture is not 100 percent clear, because this research almost inevitably suffers from a design flaw in the sense that younger learners being tested after the same amount of instruction as older learners are simply younger when tested, and therefore less adept at taking tests. Given our interpretation of the nature of age effects above, however, i.e., that they reflect a shift from predominantly implicit to predominantly explicit learning processes, the results described in Muñoz (2008) are to be expected.

More indirect evidence also exists for the view that, instead of a mere quantitative change in the sense of declining learning capacity with increasing age of arrival, what really takes place is a qualitative shift from implicit to explicit learning. Studies that provide a broad view on the language development of immigrant children such as Tarone *et al.* (2009) show the important role of metalinguistic awareness and explicit learning in older children, while more focused studies such as White (2008) and Alcón Soler and García Mayo (2008) provide evidence of the efficiency of age-appropriate focus on form.

Future directions

Research on age effects has only begun. We need much more documentation of what aspects of language become harder to learn at what age, and much more research on the immediate and ultimate causes. One avenue to pursue is a wider variety of more sophisticated measures, whether they be of the neurophysiological or neuro-imaging kind or "simply" involve clever use of behavioral measures elicited under laboratory conditions, involving reaction time measurements, priming conditions, eye tracking, and so on.

Two other avenues are less technical in nature, but no less important. We need research with a wider variety of source and target languages, preferably in the same study, in order to be able to generalize in more abstract terms what kinds of features of language become harder to learn with age. Most importantly of all, however, we need much better samples. All participants in AoA studies should have had a fair chance to develop native-like proficiency in L2. That means, among other things, a length of exposure of at least five, ideally ten years, so that we can observe ultimate attainment and not just speed of learning (because empirical evidence shows that learners asymptote after ten years for just about any area of language, except vocabulary), and learners who have spent almost all this time interacting in the L2—a condition virtually no study has met so far, because we all tend to use samples of convenience consisting of participants drawn from sizable immigrant communities (close to our universities), where L1 use is quite common. Combining the requirement of having largely isolated speakers with the obvious statistical requirement of having bigger samples than is typically the case, is one of the greatest challenges in this area. Obtaining large samples of largely isolated learners, preferably native speakers of an L1 that is distant from the L2, should be a goal we can all agree on, whether we think age effects are maturational or not.

References

Abrahamsson, N., and Hyltenstam, K. (2008). The robustness of aptitude effects in near-native second language acquisition. *Studies in Second Language Acquisition, 30*(4), 481–509.

Abrahamsson, N. and Hyltenstam, K. (2009). Age of onset and nativelikeness in a second language: Listener perception versus linguistic scrutiny. *Language Learning, 59*(2), 249–306.

Alcón Soler, E. and García Mayo, M. D. P. (2008). Incidental focus on form and learning outcomes with young foreign language classroom learners. In J. Philp, R. Oliver, and A. Mackey (Eds.), *Second language acquisition and the younger learner: Child's play?* (pp. 173–192). Amsterdam: Benjamins.

Asher, J. J. and García, R. (1969). The optimal age to learn a foreign language. *The Modern Language Journal*, *53*, 334–341.

Ball, J. (1996). *Age and natural order in second language acquisition.* Unpublished Ed. D., University of Rochester.

Benzaquén, A. S. (2006). *Encounters with wild children. Temptation and disappointment in the study of human nature.* Montreal, Canada: McGill-Queen's University Press.

Bialystok, E. and Hakuta, K. (1994). *In other words: The science and psychology of second-language acquisition.* New York: BasicBooks.

Bialystok, E. and Miller, B. (1999). The problem of age in second-language acquisition: Influences from language, structure, and task. *Bilingualism: Language and Cognition*, *2*(2), 127–145.

Birdsong, D. (1992). Ultimate attainment in second language acquisition. *Language*, *68*(4), 706–755.

Birdsong, D. (2005). Interpreting age effects in second language acquisition. In J. F. Kroll and A. M. B. de Groot (Eds.), *Handbook of bilingualism: Psycholinguistic approaches* (pp. 109–127). Oxford, UK: Oxford University Press.

Birdsong, D. (2006). Age and second language acquisition and processing: A selective overview. *Language Learning*, *56* (Supplement 1), 1–49.

Birdsong, D. (2007). Nativelike pronunciation among late learners of French as a second language. In O. -S. Bohn and M. J. Munro (Eds.), *Language experience in second language learning. In honor of James Emil Flege* (pp. 99–116). Philadelphia: Benjamins.

Birdsong, D. (2009). Age and the end state of second language acquisition. In T. Bhatia and W. Ritchie (Eds.), *The new handbook of second language acquisition* (pp. 401–424). Bingley: Emerald.

Birdsong, D. and Molis, M. (2001). On the evidence for maturational constraints in second-language acquisition. *Journal of Memory and Language*, *44*, 235–249.

Bley-Vroman, R. (1988). The fundamental character of foreign language learning. In W. Rutherford and M. Sharwood Smith (Eds.), *Grammar and second language teaching: A book of readings* (pp. 19–30). New York: Newbury House.

Bley-Vroman, R. (2009). The evolving context of the fundamental difference hypothesis. *Studies in Second Language Acquisition*, *31*(2), 175–198.

Bongaerts, T. (1999). Ultimate attainment in L2 pronunciation: The case of very advanced late L2 learners. In D. Birdsong (Ed.), *Second language acquisition and the critical period hypothesis* (pp. 133–159). Mahwah, NJ: Erlbaum.

Bongaerts, T., Mennen, S., and van der Slik, F. (2000). Authenticity of pronunciation in naturalistic second language acquisition: The case of very advanced late learners of Dutch as a second language. *Studia Linguistica*, *54*(2), 298–308.

Bongaerts, T., Planken, B., and Schils, E. (1995). Can late learners attain a native accent in a foreign language? A test of the critical period hypothesis. In D. Singleton and Z. Lengyel (Eds.), *The age factor in second language acquisition* (pp. 30–50). Clevedon, UK: Multilingual Matters.

Bongaerts, T., van Summeren, C., Planken, B., and Schils, E. (1997). Age and ultimate attainment in the pronunciation of a foreign language. *Studies in Second Language Acquisition*, *19*(4), 447–465.

Bylund, E. (2009a). Maturational constraints and first language attrition. *Language Learning*, *59*(3), 687–715.

Bylund, E. (2009b). Effects of age of L2 acquisition on L1 event conceptualization patterns. *Bilingualism: Language and Cognition*, *12*(3), 305–322.

Chen, L., Shu, H., Liu, Y., Zhao, J., and Li, P. (2007). ERP signatures of subject-verb agreement in L2 learning. *Bilingualism: Language and cognition*, *10*(2), 161–174.

Chiswick, B. R. and Miller, P. W. (2008). A test of the critical period hypothesis for language learning. *Journal of Multilingual and Multicultural Development*, *29*(1), 2008.

Coppieters, R. (1987). Competence differences between native and near-native speakers. *Language*, *63*, 544–573.

de Bot, K. (2008). The imaging of what in the multilingual mind? *Second Language Research*, *24*(1), 111–133.

DeKeyser, R. M. (2000). The robustness of critical period effects in second language acquisition. *Studies in Second Language Acquisition*, *22*(4), 499–533.

DeKeyser, R. M. (2006). A critique of recent arguments against the critical period hypothesis. In C. Abello-Contesse, R. Chacón-Beltrán, M. D. López-Jiménez, and M. M. Torreblanca-López (Eds.), *Age in L2 acquisition and teaching* (pp. 49–58). Bern, Switzerland: Peter Lang.

DeKeyser, R. M., Alfi-Shabtay, I. and Ravid, D. (2010). Cross-linguistic evidence for the nature of age effects in second language acquisition. *Applied Psycholinguistics*, *31*(3), 413–438.

DeKeyser, R. M., Alfi-Shabtay, I. and Ravid, D., and Shi, M. (forthcoming). The role of salience in the acquisition of Hebrew as a second language.

DeKeyser, R. M. and Larson-Hall, J. (2005). What does the critical period really mean? In J. F. Kroll and A. M. B. de Groot (Eds.), *Handbook of bilingualism: Psycholinguistic approaches* (pp. 89–108). Oxford: Oxford University Press.

Flege, J. E., Birdsong, D., Bialystok, E., Mack, M., Sung, H., and Tsukada, K. (2006). Degree of foreign accent in English sentences produced by Korean children and adults. *Journal of Phonetics, 34*(2), 153–175.

Flege, J. E., Mackay, I. R. A., and Piske, T. (2002). Assessing bilingual dominance. *Applied Psycholinguistics, 23*(4), 567–598.

Flege, J. E., Munro, M. J., and MacKay, I. R. (1995). Factors affecting strength of perceived foreign accent in a second language. *Journal of the Acoustical Society of America, 97*(5), 3125–3138.

Flege, J. E., Yeni-Komshian, G. H., and Liu, S. (1999). Age constraints on second-language acquisition. *Journal of Memory and Language, 41*(1), 78–104.

Friederici, A. D., Steinhauer, K., and Pfeifer, E. (2002). Brain signatures of artificial language processing: Evidence challenging the critical period hypothesis. *PNAS, 99*(1), 529–534.

Guion, S. G. (2003). The vowel systems of Quichua-Spanish bilinguals. Age of acquisition effects on the mutual influence of first and second languages. *Phonetica, 60*, 98–128.

Guion, S. G., Harada, T., and Clark, J. J. (2004). Early and late Spanish-English bilinguals' acquisition of English word stress patterns. *Bilingualism: Language and Cognition, 7*, 207–226.

Hahn, W. K. (1987). Cerebral lateralization of function: From infancy through childhood. *Psychological Bulletin, 101*, 376–392.

Hahne, A. (2001). What's different in second-language processing? Evidence from event-related brain potentials. *Journal of Psycholinguistic Research, 30*(3), 251–266.

Hahne, A. and Friederici, A. D. (2001). Processing a second language: Late learners' comprehension mechanisms as revealed by event-related brain potentials. *Bilingualism: Language and Cognition, 4*(2), 123–141.

Hakuta, K., Bialystok, E., and Wiley, E. (2003). Critical evidence: A test of the critical-period hypothesis for second-language acquisition. *Psychological Science, 14*(1), 31–38.

Harley, B. and Hart, D. (1997). Language aptitude and second language proficiency in classroom learners of different starting ages. *Studies in Second Language Acquisition, 19*(3), 379–400.

Herschensohn, J. (2007). *Language development and age.* New York: Cambridge University Press.

Hirsh, K., Morrison, C. M., Gaset, S., and Carnicer, E. (2003). Age of acquisition and speech production in L2. *Bilingualism: Language and Cognition, 6*(2), 117–128.

Hyltenstam, K. (1992). Non-native features of near-native speakers: On the ultimate attainment of child-hood L2 learners. In R. J. Harris (Ed.), *Cognitive processing in bilinguals* (pp. 351–368). Amsterdam and New York: Elsevier.

Hyltenstam, K., Bylund, E., Abrahamsson, N., and Park, H.-S. (2009). Dominant-language replacement: The case of international adoptees. *Bilingualism: Language and cognition, 12*(2), 121–140.

Indefrey, P. (2006). A meta-analysis of hemodynamic studies on first and second language processing: Which suggested differences can we trust and what do they mean? *Language Learning, 56*(1), 279–304.

Jia, G. and Fuse, A. (2007). Acquisition of English grammatical morphology by native Mandarin-speaking children and adolescents: Age-related differences. *Journal of Speech, Language and Hearing Research, 50*, 1280–1299.

Johnson, J. S. and Newport, E. L. (1989). Critical period effects in second language learning: The influence of maturational state on the acquisition of English as a second language. *Cognition, 39*, 215–238.

Johnson, J. S. and Newport, E. L. (1991). Critical period effects on universal properties of language: The status of subjacency in the acquisition of a second language. *Cognitive Psychology, 21*, 60–99.

Kang, K.-H. and Guion, S. G. (2006). Phonological systems in bilinguals: Age of learning effects on the stop consonant systems of Korean-English bilinguals. *The Journal of the Acoustical Society of America, 119*(3), 1672–1683.

Kim, R. (1993). A sensitive period for second language acquisition: A reaction-time grammaticality judgment task with Koren-English bilinguals. *IDEAL, 6*, 15–27.

Kim, K. H. S., Relkin, N. R., Lee, K.-M., and Hirsch, J. (1997). Distinct cortical areas associated with native and second languages. *Nature, 388*, 171–174.

Krashen, S. D., Long, M. A., and Scarcella, R. C. (1979). Age, rate, and eventual attainment in second language acquisition. *TESOL Quarterly, 13*(4), 573–582.

Köpke, B. and Schmid, M. S. (2004). Language attrition: The next phase. In M. S. Schmid, B. Köpke, M. Keijzer, and L. Weilemar (Eds.), *First Language Attrition. Interdisciplinary perspectives on methodological issues* (pp. 1–43). Amsterdam: Benjamins.

Larson-Hall, J. (2008). Weighing the benefits of studying a foreign language at a younger starting age in a minimal input situation. *Second Language Research, 24*(1), 35–63.

Lee, B., Guion, S. G., and Harada, T. (2006). Acoustic analysis of the production of unstressed English vowels by early and late Korean and Japanese bilinguals. *Studies in Second Language Acquisition, 28*(3), 487–513.

Lee, D. and Schachter, J. (1997). Sensitive period effects in binding theory. *Language acquisition, 6*(4), 333–362.

Lenneberg, E. H. (1967). *Biological foundations of language*. New York: Wiley.

Long, M. (2005). Problems with supposed counter-evidence to the Critical Period Hypothesis. *IRAL, 43*(4), 287–316.

MacWhinney, B. (2006). Emergent fossilization. In Z. Han and T. Odlin (Eds.), *Studies of fossilization in second language acquisition* (pp. 134–156). Clevedon, UK: Multilingual Matters.

Marzi, C. A. (1996). Lateralization. In J. G. Beaumont, P. M. Keneally, and M. J. C. Rogers (Eds.), *The Blackwell dictionary of neuropsychology* (pp. 437–443). Oxford, UK: Blackwell.

Mayberry, R. I. (1993). First-language acquisition after childhood differs from second language acquisition: The case of American sign language. *Journal of Speech and Hearing Research, 36*, 1258–1270.

McDonald, J. L. (2000). Grammaticality judgments in a second language: Influences of age of acquisition and native language. *Applied Psycholinguistics, 21*(3), 395–423.

McDonald, J. L. (2006). Beyond the critical period: Processing-based explanations for poor grammaticality judgment performance by late second language learners. *Journal of Memory and Language, 55*, 381–401.

Mechelli, A., Crinion, J. T., Noppeney, U., O'Doherty, J., Ashburner, J., and Frackowiak, R. S. (2004). Structural plasticity in the bilingual brain. *Nature, 431*, 757.

Montrul, S. A. (2008). *Incomplete acquisition in bilingualism: Re-examining the age factor*. Amsterdam: Benjamins.

Montrul, S. A. (2009). Reexamining the fundamental difference hypothesis: What can early bilinguals tell us? *Studies in Second Language Acquisition, 31*(2), 225–257.

Montrul, S. and Slabakova, R. (2003). Competence similarities between native and near-native speakers: An investigation of the preterite-imperfect contrast in Spanish. *Studies in Second Language Acquisition, 25*(3), 351–398.

Mueller, J. L., Hahne, A., Fujii, Y., and Friederici, A. D. (2005). Native and nonnative speakers' processing of a miniature version of Japanese as revealed by ERPs. *Journal of Cognitive Neuroscience, 17*(8), 1229–1244.

Munro, M. and Mann, V. (2005). Age of immersion as a predictor of foreign accent. *Applied Psycholinguistics, 26*, 311–341.

Muñoz, C. (2008). Symmetries and asymmetries of age effects in naturalistic and instructed L2 learning. *Applied Linguistics, 29*(4), 578–596.

Oh, J. S., Au, T. K.-F., and Jun, S.-A. (2010). Early childhood language memory in the speech perception of international adoptees. *Journal of Child Language, 37*(5), 1123–1132.

Ojima, S., Nakata, H., and Kakigi, R. (2005). An ERP study of second language learning after childhood: Effects of proficiency. *Journal of Cognitive Neuroscience, 17*(8), 1212–1228.

Oyama, S. (1978). The sensitive period and comprehension of speech. *Working papers in bilingualism, 16*, 1–17.

Pallier, C., Dehaene, S., Poline, J.-B., LeBihan, D., Argenti, A.-M., and Dupoux, E. (2003). Brain imaging of language plasticity in adopted adults: Can a second language replace the first? *Cerebral Cortex, 13*, 155–161.

Paradis, M. (2004). *A neurolinguistic theory of bilingualism*. Philadelphia: Benjamins.

Paradis, M. (2009). *Declarative and procedural determinants of second languages*. Amsterdam: Benjamins.

Patkowski, M. S. (1980). The sensitive period for the acquisition of syntax in a second language. *Language Learning, 30*, 449–472.

Patkowski, M. (2003). Laterality effects in multilinguals during speech production under the concurrent task paradigm: Another test of the age of acquisition hypothesis. *IRAL - International Review of Applied Linguistics in Language Teaching, 41*, 175–200.

Penfield, W. and Roberts, L. (1959). *Speech and brain-mechanisms*. Princeton, NJ: Princeton University Press.

Perani, D., Abutalebi, J., Paulesu, E., Brambati, S., Scifo, P., and Cappa, S. F. (2003). The role of age of acquisition and language usage in early, high-proficient bilinguals: An fMRI study during verbal fluency. *Human Brain Mapping, 19*, 170–182.

Perani, D., Dehaene, S., Grassi, F., Cohen, L., Cappa, S., and Dupoux, E. (1996). Brain processing of native and foreign languages. *Neuroreport, 7*, 2439–2444.

Perani, D., Paulesu, E., Galles, N. S., Dupoux, E., Dehaene, S., and Bettinardi, V. (1998). The bilingual brain: Proficiency and age of acquisition of the second language. *Brain, 121*, 1841–1852.

Proverbio, A. M., Çok, B., and Zani, A. (2002). Electrophysiological measures of language processing in bilinguals. *Journal of Cognitive Neuroscience, 14*(7), 994–1017.

Reber, A., Kassin, S., Lewis, S., and Cantor, G. (1980). On the relationship between implicit and explicit modes in the learning of a complex rule structure. *Journal of Experimental Psychology: Human Learning and Memory, 6*, 492–502.

Rymer, R. (1992). A Silent Childhood. *The New Yorker, 13 April 1992 and 20 April 1992*, Part 1 41–76, Part 42 43–77.

Sabourin, L. and Stowe, L. A. (2008). Second language processing: When are first and second languages processed similarly. *Second Language Research*, 24(3), 397–430.

Scherag, A., Demuth, L., Rösler, F., Neville, H. J., and Röder, B. (2004). The effects of late acquisition of L2 and the consequences of immigration on L1 for semantic and morpho-syntactic language aspects. *Cognition*, 93, B97–B108.

Schmid, M. S. (2002). *First language attrition, use, and maintenance: The case of German Jews in Anglophone countries*. Amsterdam: John Benjamins.

Schmid, M. S. (2009). L1 attrition across the lifespan. In K. de Bot and R. W. Schrauf (Eds.), *Language development over the lifespan* (pp. 171–188). London: Routledge.

Shim, R. J. (1993). Sensitive periods for second language acquisition: A reaction-time study of Korean-English bilinguals. *IDEAL*, 6, 43–64.

Silverberg, S. and Samuel, A. G. (2004). The effect of age of second language acquisition on the representation and processing of second language words. *Journal of Memory and Language*, 51, 381–398.

Sorace, A. (1993). Incomplete vs. divergent representations of unaccusativity in non-native grammars of Italian. *Second Language Research*, 9(1), 22–47.

Stevens, G. (1999). Age at immigration and second language proficiency among foreign-born adults. *Language in Society*, 28, 555–578.

Stevens, G. (2004). Using census data to test the critical-period hypothesis for second-language acquisition. *Psychological Science*, 15(3), 215–216.

Tahta, S., Wood, M., and Loewenthal, K. (1981). Foreign accents: Factors relating to transfer of accent from the first language to a second language. *Language and Speech*, 24(3), 265–272.

Tarone, E., Bigelow, M., and Hansen, K. (2009). *Literacy and second language oracy*. Oxford: Oxford University Press.

Thompson, I. (1991). Foreign accents revisited: The English pronunciation of Russian immigrants. *Language Learning*, 41(2), 177–204.

Tokowicz, N. and MacWhinney, B. (2005). Implicit and explicit measures of sensitivity to violations in second language grammar: An event-related potential investigation. *Studies in Second Language Acquisition*, 27(2), 173–204.

Tsukada, K., Birdsong, D., Bialystok, E., Mack, M., Sung, H., and Flege, J. E. (2005). A developmental study of English vowel production and perception by native Korean adults and children. *Journal of Phonetics*, 33, 263–290.

Ullman, M. T. (2001). The neural basis of lexicon and grammar in first and second language: The declarative/procedural model. *Bilingualism: Language and Cognition*, 4, 105–122.

Ullman, M. T. (2004). Contributions of memory circuits to language: The declarative/procedural model. *Cognition*, 92, 231–270.

Ullman, M. T. (2005). A cognitive neuroscience perspective on second language acquisition: The declarative/procedural model. In C. Sanz (Ed.), *Mind and context in adult second language acquisition* (pp. 141–178). Washington, D.C.: Georgetown University Press.

Ventureyra, V. A. G., Pallier, C., and Yoo, H. -Y. (2004). The loss of first language phonetic perception in adopted Koreans. *Journal of Neurolinguistics*, 17, 79–91.

Vul, E., Harris, C., Winkielman, P., and Pashler, H. (2009). Reply to comments on "Puzzlingly high correlations in fMRI studies of emotion, personality, and social cognition". *Perspectives on Psychological Science*, 4(3), 319–324.

Wartenburger, I., Heekeren, H. R., Abutalebi, J., Cappa, S. F., Villringer, A., and Perani, D. (2003). Early setting of grammatical processing in the bilingual brain. *Neuron*, 37, 159–170.

Weber-Fox, C. M., and Neville, H. J. (1996). Maturational constraints on functional specializations for language processing: ERP evidence in bilingual speakers. *Journal of Cognitive Neuroscience*, 8, 231–256.

White, J. (2008). Speeding up acquisition of his and her: Explicit L1/L2 contrasts help. In J. Philp, R. Oliver, and A. Mackey (Eds.), *Second language acquisition and the younger learner: Child's play?* (pp. 193–228). Amsterdam: Benjamins.

Yeni-Komshian, G., Flege, J. E., and Liu, S. (2000). Pronunciation proficiency in the first and second languages of Korean-English bilinguals. *Bilingualism: Language and Cognition*, 3(2), 131–149.

Yeni-Komshian, G., Robbins, M., and Flege, J. E. (2001). Effects of word class differences on L2 pronunciation accuracy. *Applied Psycholinguistics*, 22(3), 283–299.

van Boxtel, S., Bongaerts, T., and Coppen, P.-A. (2005). Native-like attainment of dummy subjects in Dutch and the role of the L1. *IRAL*, 43, 355–380.

28

The role of educational level, literacy, and orality in L2 learning

Martha Bigelow and Jill Watson

Historical discussion

In the Western academic tradition, inquiry into the influence of literacy on human intellectual processes can be traced to the dawning of the modern science of linguistics. Ferdinand de Saussure's Course in General Linguistics (1916/1959) established foundational approaches to understanding what he called the semiological facts of any human society, including the distinctions of diachronic versus synchronic language studies, paradigmatic versus syntagmatic approaches, linguistic register studies, and the key distinction between written and oral language. Contrastive inquiries into the foundations of orality and literacy have been taken up in various ways by Jousse (1925), Luria (1976), Lévi-Strauss (1966), and Goody (1977), providing initial insight into the characteristic cognitive patterns of non-literate people without formal academic education and a basis for understanding the transformations engendered by the advent of literacy and academic learning. Contributing to this line of work were classics-oriented scholars like Parry (1971), Lord (1975), and Havelock (1963), who explored the structure of what was often termed "oral literature," discovering distinctive characteristics supporting memorization, social stability goals, and mythological functions in works of high orality, and emphasizing the profound historical effect of alphabetic literacy on the functioning of mind and society. In the sociological domain, McCluhan (1964) provided a rich theoretical map of the irrevocable and unavoidable effects of the media of communication, including orality, writing, the printing press, and electronic media, on human cognitive, social, and emotional structure.

Perhaps the landmark work positing specific intellectual characteristics of orality, and how these characteristics are transformed through literacy and immersion in literate academic culture, was Walter Ong's *Orality and literacy: The technologizing of the word* (1982). The significant contributions of this work included a framework for understanding cultures as primarily, residually, or secondarily oral, a taxonomy of characteristics of oral mind and, perhaps most tellingly, the recognition that the transformation from orality to literacy can only go in one direction, is permanent, and always entails a loss: "you have to die [to orality] to continue living [in literacy]" (1982, p. 15). While some researchers focus on the limitations of the orality/literacy distinction for understanding cognitive development (e.g., Gee, 2008), scholarship in the tradition of Ong continues to the present day (e.g., Olson, 2006), and may for the purposes of this chapter be distinguished by its perspective that literacy and formal education create distinct intellectual processes manifested in distinct ways of understanding and acting in the world. Because literacy is so intertwined with formal schooling, this kind of work is foundational to explorations of the role of formal schooling in second language (L2) learning. Indeed, Watson (2010) relates the particular epistemological and axiological affordances of life in a culture of orality versus a culture of literacy to L2 education concerns, arguing that the role of literacy and literacy instruction in the world needs to be understood within the larger fabric of colonial history and western Enlightenment hegemony.

In exploring educational level and L2 learning, it is important to consider how the psychological circumstances of learners' lives may have affected their cognitive and linguistic development. There are many models which could be reviewed here, but for illustrative purposes we may examine Piaget's stages of cognitive development model (1952). Piaget holds that all people go through necessary stages: sensorimotor (ages 0–2), preoperational (2–7), concrete operational (7–11), and formal operations (11–adult). The ages given for each stage are approximate and, crucially for the present discussion, depend on experiential stimuli that provide significant interaction and reasoning opportunities. A person must progress in order through the stages and none can be skipped, meaning that if older children or adults lack the necessary experiences to stimulate development in any stage, they do not progress cognitively beyond the stage they have acquired. This theory is echoed in Vygotsky (1978), who holds that learning occurs primarily through social interaction with others—a skilled partner is needed for a person to acquire the skills that lie beyond his or her independent ability, in the zone of proximal development.

It is during Piaget's preoperational stage, when symbolic thought begins and language development blossoms, that children in many societies are first exposed to the visual codification of language—reading and writing. During the concrete operational stage, individuals develop the classification skills prerequisite to the formal operational stage, which is characterized by the ability to solve abstract problems and think hypothetically. Non-print literate adult L2 learners, on the other hand, have not had the same experiences in oral or written stimuli, nor specific social interaction supporting literacy. Their cognitive development, it may be posited, has progressed in ways promoted by the environmental stimuli they have experienced, that is, those stimuli characteristic of oral culture. Ong (1982) describes the thought processes of orality as characterized by a primary focus on, among other things, relationship, contextual import, and the well-being of the community. These directions are notably distinct from the tradition of abstraction, classification, hierarchicalization, and hypothesis characteristic of successfully educated western adults.

While the foregoing represents a western view, scholars writing from the perspective of the colonized also bear witness to the disparateness of western academic and primarily oral education traditions, chronicling the sometimes devastating effects of literacy and western education on traditional oral knowledge and ways. It is beyond the scope of our chapter to fully review this body of work, however, we refer the interested reader to scholarship on this topic from different contexts including Africa: Achebe (1961), Irele (2001), and Mazrui (2007); India: Nandy (1983) and Visvanathan (1987), and Native America: Ross (1989), DeLoria (1970), and Battiste (2000).

Foundational to this discussion in the field of second language acquisition (SLA) is the Zweitspracherwerb Italienischer und Spanischer Arbeiter (ZISA) project (Clahsen et al., 1983). This language learning study included 45 adult learners with little formal schooling. Participants were Italian or Spanish speakers learning German. The most important outcome of this research was a proposal that learners of German go through fixed acquisitional stages in terms of grammar. However, the researchers added the caveat that "there is sufficient room for the individual to find his or her own [language acquisition] path" (Pienemann et al., 1988, p. 222) in the process. The more schooled group preferred a "standard" orientation, which prioritized accuracy, while the other group had a "simplifying orientation, favoring communicative effectiveness. This finding suggested that level of schooling has an effect on SLA in terms of the way learners approach the experience and the process. Another early study was funded by the European Science Foundation and is often referred to as the ESF project. Researchers collected data from 40 participants learning a variety of minority languages from five different countries, over ten years. The researchers reported that the participants with low levels of education seemed to make slower progress in their classes compared to literate learners (Klein and Perdue, 1992; Perdue, 1993). See also Pienemann and Keßler (Chapter 14, this volume) for an overview of research related to Processability Theory and the Multidimensional Model, both of which are related to this population and the research summarized in this section.

Since the publication of studies related to these projects, most SLA research has been carried out with educated adult participants who have native language literacy. Consequently, we know little about how the variable of degree of formal schooling influences L2 learning processes because there is so little research in L2 studies on the phenomena of limited formal schooling among adults. Therefore, most SLA theories can only be applied responsibly to highly educated individuals (Bayley and Tarone, Chapter 3, this volume, Bigelow and Tarone, 2004). The common assumption is that L2 fluency and education are reciprocal, and some research shows this (e.g., Espinosa and Massey, 1997). It is essential, however, to explore the absence of formal schooling, and presumably literacy, as a learner characteristic that influences language acquisition across all modalities (Tarone et al., 2009). Mathews-Aydinli (2008), in her review of research on adult English language learners points out that "the contextual and individual-level differences between most ESL/EFL students in higher education and adult ESL students in non-academic contexts are so great, that research with one group has often little significance or relevance to the other" (p. 210). This chapter will proceed with an exploration of some of the issues and scholarship related to limited formal schooling among adolescents or adults.

Core issues

Educational level and oral language processing

There is a substantial body of experimental research from the fields of cognitive science and neuroscience exploring how complete lack of alphabetic print literacy affects how adults perceive, repeat, and manipulate oral language in their L1 (e.g., Adrian et al., 1995; Dellatolas et al., 2003; Reis and Castro-Caldas, 1997). This research has shown that even a small amount of literacy can make a difference in certain oral skills. Adults with some print literacy could manipulate language units such as phonemes and syllables, in the oral mode, while adults without print literacy performed significantly worse on these oral skills. For example, dropping the first sound from a word and flipping syllables was much harder for illiterate adults than it was for those with alphabetic print literacy. On the other hand, participants performed similarly on oral tasks involving rhyming or generating lists of semantically related words. It seems that basic alphabetic literacy offers adults a strategy for visualizing encoded oral language in order to manipulate it phonemically. (For a review of this literature see Tarone et al., 2009.) This well-developed body of work done with adults with and without alphabetic print literacy suggests that literacy engenders phonemic awareness, not the reverse, which is the assumption among most literacy researches and practitioners who focus on children.

It is fortunate to have this solid base of research upon which to formulate hypotheses about adult L2 learners, and a thorough test of how applicable these findings are to L2 learners would contribute to the research programs across a number of disciplines such as cognitive science, literacy, and SLA. The idea that a low level of alphabetic print literacy may facilitate performance on some phonemic awareness tasks has many implications for instruction. For example, teachers should expect that adult emergent readers will have much more difficulty manipulating phonemes in oral language than adults with even minimal print literacy. Perhaps those with low literacy will perceive corrective feedback (see Loewen, Chapter 2, this volume) related to the manipulation of phonemes differently than those with more print literacy.

Educational level and school-related tasks

For adult individuals without formal schooling, a classroom learning environment can seem bizarre. Language may be used for reasons other than communication, students may be asked to interact with members of the classroom community in ways that seem unnatural, and materials used for learning may have no resemblance to any documents students have ever seen outside the classroom. Teachers are often sensitive to these issues and thoughtfully introduce literacy to L2 learners who are new to schooling and take steps to teach in ways that build on the students' interests and strengths.

The transition to schooling calls for new skills and behaviors—beyond the different ways of processing oral language—in which lack of prior literacy or schooling seems to matter. For example, studies have shown that adults without formal schooling may perceive or interpret visual materials often used in classrooms (e.g., line drawings, two-dimensional information) in ways schooled adults do not (Bramão et al., 2007; Reis et al., 2001; Rosselli and Ardila, 2003). Again, these studies were not carried out with L2 learners, but rather with participants using their native language(s), thus pointing to another core issue which needs to be explored with L2 learners.

Educational approaches

In cultural environments inundated with text of every imaginable type and format, massive libraries and databases, fantastical internet resources, and bookstores that in earlier ages would have looked like palaces, it would be difficult to overstate the enormity of the abyss that lies between the readers of this chapter and the preliterate L2 learners from oral cultures whose situation we are addressing. Indeed, our manner of address, made possible *and academically necessary* by the deeper legacies of the literate tradition, may be profoundly at odds with the values of the very people we are researching or teaching. As Smith has noted:

> Literary activity itself could be seen as complicit in the current crisis of literacy. The culture of literacy, which Western culture is, has created its own crisis in the sense that a culture oriented by print is one oriented by a particular way of arriving at what should be valued, and how. (1999, p. 71)

From our side of the abyss, we can only begin to discern the chasms that people of orality must cross to achieve literacy, noting that it is impossible for us to make the trip in reverse. We may note the chasm from home to new culture, entailing culture shock and recovery from trauma. There is the chasm from L1 to L2–no mere matter of acquiring new skills but a soul-shaking matter of crossing "the abyss between how languages mean" (Becker, 1992, p. 281). The most demanding of all may be the semiotic chasm (McCluhan, 1994), that projects the learner from traditional orality to codified literacy to the digitacy of technologized culture. Even as we review available research on the issue of educational level and L2 learners, we do so with the recognition that if the learners we discuss in this chapter end up succeeding in their new culture on *its* terms, it is because they will have crossed a great abyss that hyperliterate academic culture cannot truthfully understand nor ever fully describe (Watson, 2010).

Data and common elicitation measures

Although the relationships between educational level, literacy and language processing have yet to be fully explored in SLA research, there is a solid and relevant body of basic research from which to draw. For instance, there is a robust body of research on phonological processing and literacy from the field of cognitive science as well as other work that explores language/conceptual processes and literacy among adults, albeit both without regard to L2 learning (e.g., Ardila, 2004; Castro-Caldas et al., 1998; Duong and Ska, 2001; Ostrosky-Solís and Ramirez, 2004; Reis et al., 2001; Silva et al., 2004). For instance, Silva et al. (2004) examined both literacy and level of formal schooling among monolingual adults from similar socio-cultural backgrounds, except for experiences with formal schooling. The researchers asked participants to generate words that fit into categories of food and animals. Repeated measures of analysis of variance including semantic task scores and literacy found that there is not a substantial difference between literate and illiterate participants in terms of semantic memory, with the caveat that it is important to develop neuropsychological instruments free of educational and cultural influences, or where statistical procedures account for these potential pitfalls.

This line of research should be thoroughly replicated with L2 learners to examine the role of educational level/literacy in oral language development and across a range of oral language skills. For example, in the area of phonemic awareness and cognitive processing, Kurvers and van de Craats (2007) observed that adult language learners of "average literacy" performed significantly better than those with little or no literacy on a digit span task (i.e., repeating a series of number backward or forward) and a pseudo-word repetition task (i.e., repeat words from two to six syllables). Another oral task, marking word boundaries (i.e., recognizing individual words in the speech stream), is particularly problematic for adult language learners without print literacy, a finding consistent with studies cited previously on monolingual adults without print literacy (Kurvers et al., 2007). In another study by Kurvers (2007), beginning word recognition skills in a new language were qualitatively different for non-native speakers than for native speakers. Language learners with emerging print literacy start their learning process with a non-systematic visual strategy in which they try to seek correspondences between visual or context clues and meaning, gradually learning to use the strategy of sequential decoding. This finding corresponds to a number of studies cited previously showing that learning to read itself supports organizational skills needed for academic learning, that adults without print literacy are less systematic than those with print literacy in scanning the visual field (Bramão et al., 2007; Dowse and Ehlers, 2003).

In a series of studies with Somali adolescents and young adults with low print literacy (Tarone et al., 2009) researchers found that literacy level played a role in how participants carried out the oral tasks designed to elicit question forms in English. Participants with higher levels of literacy perceived recasts (targetlike reformulations of errors) and repeated these recasts better than participants with lower levels of literacy. A focal participant, Abukar, accurately imitated stress patterns and attended better to vocabulary items more than to syntactic items (cf., Dowse and Ehlers, 2003). Abukar required multiple corrections to questions such as "Why he is mad?*" or "What he try to write down?*," seemingly unable to invert "he is" or add the auxiliary "is" to these sentences. This difficulty is reminiscent of the syllable and word inversion tasks in studies such as Adrian et al. (1995) done with monolinguals who were not print literate. Abukar preferred processing strategies that relied much more on semantic (meaning) than syntax, again reflecting findings on how adults with low print literacy process language, a finding which mirrors the studies done with monolinguals who were not print literate (Dellatolas et al., 2003; Reis and Castro-Caldas, 1997; Reis et al., 2003). These findings recall the point that scriptural cultures prioritize elaborate syntactics, while oral cultures are more concerned with pragmatics, using whatever works to communicate meaning in context (Ong, 1982, pp. 37–38).

Metalinguistic knowledge and language awareness is another area which promises to yield interesting findings in terms of educational level and L2 learning. A lack of metalinguistic training affects how learners without print literacy or formal schooling are able to think and talk about their oral language (Kurvers *et al.*, 2006). In Gombert's (1994) early study, adult learners with no print literacy appeared to profit from explicit instruction in metalinguistic language and concepts because it gave them an additional tool to talk about language and promoted metalinguistic awareness. Second language acquisition literature often speaks directly to how learners employ, or should employ, conscious language learning techniques, or unconscious ones (that is, exposure to the language through reading, listening, and taking part in language-use activities). The adult learners of Dutch in the study by Kurvers *et al.* (2006) who had no print literacy had significantly more difficulty with language awareness tasks and talked about language in ways qualitatively different from the comparison groups made up of literate children and adults. This again may be related to the preference of oral folk for pragmatic, operational thought as opposed to abstract categorical thinking whose relevance to real life may be vague.

Phonological awareness may intersect with metalinguistic awareness in some ways as well. The important phonological awareness skill of identifying individual words in sentences, which in turn supports the development of concepts such as "word" and "sentence," requires that the learner be able to perceive where words begin and end in sentences (i.e., recognize word boundaries). This task can be difficult because adults may not hear unfamiliar language sounds accurately (Kuhl, 2004). Low awareness of word length can be influenced by the phonological structure of the first (or other) language(s) (Royer *et al.*, 2004). Language, as Kurvers *et al.* (2006) documented, will be concrete, and conceptualization, without abstract learning to extend it, will also seem concrete to individuals without print literacy (Biber, 1988; Biber and Hared, 1991, 1994; Biber *et al.*, 2002).

There is some evidence that even a low level of literacy can greatly improve a language learner's ability to develop language awareness. In a study focusing on developing language awareness among adult participants of different educational backgrounds, those with the lowest levels of formal schooling benefited the most (Lindberg, 2003). One participant, a woman from Morocco with no more than two years of formal schooling, convinced her peers to use the passive voice in their joint task, without using any metalinguistic terms. Their task was to recreate a text together that they heard only orally and had the opportunity to partially write down. She used pen and paper to help her reflect upon the verb forms showing that even a very limited level of literacy is helpful in analyzing a second language. This study also points to the need to uncover linguistic and cognitive strengths among L2 learners without formal schooling. Could they, perhaps, have the potential to hold certain information acquired aurally in short- and long-term memory for longer periods of time? Are they better able to clarify and reinforce complicated information transmitted in the oral mode? Are they more attuned to contextual nuances which bear on communication?

The research exploring this issue from both policy and sociocultural perspectives is becoming more robust as researchers and advocates understand and write about the unique issues facing this population of language learners. There are always larger social structures and policies that impact education, across contexts and learner populations. The field has research showing how understanding literacy in its social context can contribute to a more complete understanding of literacy across cultures and contexts (Reder and Davila, 2005) for adolescent and adult L2 learners without print literacy. For instance, preliterate adult L2 learners' opportunities to learn may be facilitated or hindered by factors far beyond their control. Menard-Warwick's (2005) research with Central American immigrant women shows how immigration laws, welfare policies, and the economy impeded participants' ability to sustain their enrollment in adult literacy programs. The women's motivation was also influenced by their parents' views of education and in materials ways, such as having the opportunity to attend school. Likewise, classrooms and programs are not neutral actors in the process of building literacy among adult L2 learners. Warriner (2007) demonstrates how transnational movement is "conflated with bureaucratic sorting mechanisms that result in heightened surveillance and arbitrary distinctions that have lasting material consequences [...]" (p. 323). Warriner's analysis of students in an adult ESL literacy program shows that while programs may be unfolding exactly as planned (i.e., to train low-wage workers), they inadvertently construct the work identities for students as contributing to, but not benefiting from, the global economy. In this sense, programs and even educators participate in a sort of policy-making enterprise which in turn plays into larger socioeconomic structures.

In some immigrant communities, adults may be hesitant to attend literacy classes because doing so may jeopardize their status in their family or cultural community. For example, the religious beliefs of the Kurdish Yezidis, according to Sarroub (2008), advocate avoiding print literacy. Similarly, Levinson (2007) described resistance to literacy among English Gypsies. A participant in Levinson's study said, "education has divorced me from my community" (p. 30). Education, for this participant, meant that he had betrayed all that his family stood for. Also revealing was that participants said that if they wished to attend adult literacy classes, these classes must be outside their community, so that even their closest relatives would not know they were attending class. Another study focusing on sociocultural issues include Klassen's (1991) ethnographic study of adult Latinos in Canada. He notes that his participants were comfortable navigating life situations in English they developed for that purpose, but felt diminished and uncomfortable only in their ESL classes, where their language was deemed deficient.

There is research which documents the assets of families without formal schooling. For example, Olmedo (1997) describes a Puerto Rican family's funds of knowledge across generations with few formal schooling opportunities "to create a new conceptualization of multicultural education, thus challenging deficit theories that lower expectations and limit possibilities for children of minority groups" (pp. 570–571). This family had many skills that they used to support their families both in Puerto Rico and then later in New York City (e.g., sewing, cabinetry, cooking, rotating credit associations). In another study, Espinoza-Herold (2007) describes how the cultural "dichos" or sayings used by a Mexican immigrant students' mother, who had little formal schooling, supported her in achieving her educational goals. Bigelow (2007) found that a Somali mother with limited formal schooling, little English language proficiency and low native language literacy was able to do many things to help her children succeed in US public schools. For example, she divided household responsibilities among siblings and rearranged chores when children had big projects at school due, sent children to afterschool bilingual homework help, vigilantly monitored their choice of friend, and checked in with teachers to make sure their homework was completed.

In cognitive processing research with this population, data used to study educational level is gathered through the oral modes because participants with low levels of education may have low literacy which in turn delimits the sorts of research questions which can be asked and methods which can be used. As individuals acquire print literacy, researchers can explore the acquisition of literacy and the many consequences of literacy through a wider range of instrumentation, including tests and tasks administered in the reading (see Koda, Chapter 18, this volume) or writing modes across languages.

One of the first tasks for a researcher is to operationalize or consider the meaning of educational level. Some of the ways educational level has been determined are through self-report, transcripts, or by informal teacher evaluation in studies where the research was done in intact classes of particular grade levels or educational institutions. These approaches, when used in lieu of more nuanced measures of linguistic, cognitive, academic, or pragmatic skills, are problematic because educational level does not map flawlessly to any particular skill level (Loureiro *et al.*, 2004). Another common limitation in reporting educational level is the exclusion of the meaning of educational level within specific societies. "Highly educated" is a descriptor that changes across contexts and in terms of availability of schooling and the value placed on different levels of schooling achieved. Educational level is not only located within individuals but is also situated within cultures and sociopolitical or global contexts. As such, the importance of educational level may change or take on different symbolic meaning when individuals or groups of people (im) migrate. Furthermore, it is possible to have acquired L1 and L2 literacy through community practices rather than through formal schooling (Farr, 1994). Sadly, it is also possible to attend school without becoming literate (Serpell *et al.*, 2005). Therefore, because educational level can be interpreted differently across cultures, it must be operationalized in a way that has clear meaning and is complemented/triangulated with measures of language or cognitive skills.

Some of the elicitation measures which have been used with adolescents or adults with limited or no formal schooling, in traditional research paradigms, are the following:

Table 28.1

Instruments/tasks used in studies done in participants' L1	
Socio-demographic inventory	Silva *et al.* (2004)
Semantic verbal fluency tasks	
Generate words corresponding to food items that can be bought at a supermarket	
Generate names of animals	
Phonological processing tasks	Morais and colleagues
Deleting or adding phonemes to create a new word	(Morais and Kolinsky, 2002;
Generating words beginning with a particular first sound (e.g., /p/, /f/)	Morais *et al.*, 1979; 1986;1988)
Identifying rhymes	Loureiro *et al.* (2004)
Inverting syllables	
Repetition of short/long words and nonwords	
Minimal pair phonetic discrimination	
Reading tasks: Letter, syllable, word, sentence recognition	Royer *et al.* (2004)
Letter and word recognition	Durgunoğlu and Öney (2002)
Phonological awareness: phoneme tapping, phoneme blending, deleting initial and final phoneme	
Spelling	
Listening comprehension task (pre-test)	
Reading comprehension task (post-test)	
Instruments/tasks used in studies done in participants' L2	
Native Language Literacy Screening Device	Tarone *et al.* (2009)
Spot-the-difference	
Story completion	
Elicited imitation	
Ethnosurvey questionnaires used to gather family demographic, social and economic characteristics; English language proficiency was self-reported on a 4-point scale	Espinosa and Massey (1997)
Pseudoword reading	Davidson and Strucker (2002)
Diagnostic assessments of reading	
Word recognition	
Silent reading comprehension	
Word attack	
Peabody picture vocabulary test	
Background questionnaire	

As this type of learner is included more often in L2 research, more instrumentation will be produced, and results will be replicated. For instance, the tasks used in L1 studies must be adapted and repeated in L2 studies. Better assessments of L1 literacy are needed. Appropriate research topics may include, among others: (1) techniques supportive of holding large amounts of knowledge in memory, for instance use of assonance, linguistic redundancy, and aggregative fixed expressions; (2) syntactic patterns, for example, additive versus subordinative language; (3) analytic patterns such as situational rather than categorical reasoning; and (4) the development of the auditory sense as contrasted to the visual development characteristic of highly literate societies.

The problematics of research with adolescents or adults who have never been to school include a mismatch between how the researcher and the participants understand the research process. Some individuals may not understand the elicitation tasks because the tasks are so closely tied to culturally bound classroom practices with which they have no experience. Some participants may be hesitant to be audio or video recorded. Other difficulties may include gaining access to the learners through community or classroom venues and then earning their trust in order for them to agree to participate in a study.

Applications

We next turn to instructional relevance. From the perspective of Piaget's stage theory, it may be instructionally useful to consider the extent to which non-literate people may be lodged in preoperational or early concrete operational thought. Indeed, a survey of any manual of adult literacy instruction will reveal the insistence on using concrete objects and real-world examples from daily life. This kind of perspective is obviously a sensitive one, in that it can be misinterpreted to imply that non-literate adults are cognitively puerile. To the contrary, they have highly sophisticated skills typical of the environments in which they have lived, but which do not have the same usefulness in the target culture they now call home. It is possible, we would maintain, to draw from stage theory a constructive understanding of the schooling challenges of orally encultured people without applying it as a terminal diagnosis.

Lack of formal schooling is often accompanied by other circumstances that may affect language learning. Because we know that most immigrants and nearly all refugees entering schools in their host countries have experienced significant physical and emotional trauma, it is important to consider the effects of trauma and deprivation on such learners. The developing field of trauma studies (see, e.g., Sarat *et al.*, 2007) has great relevance for L2 education in general, and adult initial literacy, in particular. In their applied research in countries ravaged by war, Neuner *et al.* (2008) have learned that trauma very negatively impacts the ability of individuals to hold *new* information, particularly symbolic information, in memory, often for many years following the traumatic incidents. A related finding holds that specific trauma triggers—words, places, objects, anything that recalls the original traumatic incident—act on the hippocampus region of the brain, influencing human cognition in such a way as to assign non-standard, exaggerated, or even opposite meanings to actions or linguistic signs. Clearly, interdisciplinary studies investigating trauma experiences and L2 literacy development are an important future direction for research on the instructional needs of these learners.

Of the utmost importance to the issue of educational level and L2 learning is how educators choose to teach learners with interrupted, limited, or no formal schooling. The issue is more pronounced in adolescence and adulthood because the educational gap between this population and other language learners widens with time. Young children have more years of obligatory schooling ahead of them, affording more time to close this gap. Being in a classroom learning context for the first time as an adolescent or adult can be both thrilling and overwhelming. For adolescents and adults seeking to finish a secondary school or college degree, educators are concerned about how to build background knowledge in subject areas quickly while simultaneously developing L2 literacy. A number of books for teachers of under-schooled adolescents or adults focus on this problem and offer programmatic and instructional approaches to integrate content and language learning (DeCapua et al., 2009; DeCapua and Marshall, 2010; Freeman and Freeman, 2002; Mace-Matluck et al., 1998; Short and Fitzsimmons, 2007). Limited formal schooling can be both an instructional and a programmatic challenge. Teachers must have the skills to make academic content comprehensible largely through the oral mode at first. Likewise, programs cannot separate language and content learning because students need both to make progress toward graduation. In contexts typically facing dire shortages of resources, educators are confronted with the following common problems of practice:

- Should newcomers with low levels of education be placed in separate classes to receive focused literacy instruction? Research suggests that separate classes allow for focused attention on basic literacy instruction, recognizing that students may feel inhibited if they are required to learn the most basic literacy concepts with peers who already have basic literacy skills (Hardman, 1999; Klassen, 1991; Skilton-Sylvester, 2002). Classroom assessment must also be different. Students new to literacy should have their progress tracked and communicated to them differently because they are developing far different skills than their literate peers (MacSwan and Rolstad, 2006; Young-Scholten and Strom, 2006).
- Should basic literacy concepts be taught in the native language? Assuming the native language of the students has a written script, whether native language literacy instruction can be offered typically depends on factors such as having enough students who want native language literacy classes, and a teacher able to offer this instruction. L1 literacy instruction facilitates the cognitive leap into the fact that text represents oral language and conveys meaning (Auerbach, 1993; Robson, 1983) as well as having the benefit of encouraging ethnic identity development through native language literacy (e.g., Arthur, 2003).
- Should phonological awareness activities involving manipulation of phonemes occur after students fully grasp the alphabetic principle and can decode words? Other phonological awareness activities such as word games involving rhymes could be early literacy activities because their use does not require prior literacy (e.g., Adrian et al., 1995).

Other issues that seem to go unexplored in the mainstream literature related to teaching adults without prior schooling include the following:

- How can orality be privileged pedagogically as a linguistic strength and cultural norm? What does culturally relevant pedagogy look like with this population (Ladson-Billings, 1995)?
- What is the role of trauma in the L2 acquisition of adults along a continuum of formal schooling (Frater-Mathieson, 2004)?
- How do language and educational policy issues impact L2 learning among adults without prior literacy (e.g., "aging out" of K-12 programs, articulation between secondary and adult programs) (Menard-Warwick, 2005)?

Future directions

Educational level deserves more attention across research in all areas of L2 learning. While educational level has a rich initial base of literature from which to draw, very little is known about how the lack of formal schooling and lack of background in a culture of literacy interact with the L2 learning process. This gap extends to language teacher education: Language teachers are frequently not prepared to teach adolescent or adult learners who have never been to school and do not have literacy in their native language(s).

Some of the broad issues in need of research in the area of L2 learning include the role of educational level in learning across modalities. If, as Tarone *et al.* (2009) found, lower levels of literacy make it more difficult to acquire some grammatical features of the L2, in the oral modes, what other modes or variational features are affected by low literacy? It is important for the fields of second language acquisition to explore the common hypotheses/theories in L2 learning (e.g., noticing hypothesis, interaction hypothesis, Processability Theory) as they apply to learners with limited formal schooling. It is also important to explore how implicit or explicit L2 learning processes unfold when the L2 learner does not possess the metalinguistic knowledge commonly used in classrooms. When L2 learners without literacy are learning in classroom environments, how does educational level/limited formal schooling intersect with investment/motivation and identity? How long does it take L2 learners with limited formal schooling to acquire enough phonemic awareness to engage a wide range of oral language processing strategies (see discussion on input processing by VanPattern, Chapter 16, this volume)? Likewise, how long does it take and what conditions are necessary for learners with limited formal schooling to move from phonemic awareness, to decoding, to meaningful comprehension of a range of relevant texts?

In the area of education and policy, many questions also remain. There is a need to examine, with qualitative and quantitative rigor, the limits and possibilities in educational programming for L2 learners with limited formal schooling. What are or could be alternative paths toward program completion, diplomas, and degrees? It is of pedagogical urgency that researchers explore how the strengths and assets of adolescent and adult learners with limited formal schooling become points of access to other skills that help them reach self-determined goals. Aims of equity and social justice in education need research that uncovers what the experience of having low print literacy as an adolescent/adult in hyper-literate societies is. As educators understand this experience, they will be better able to position themselves in the broader historical and geopolitical landscape of transnational migration. These and so many more issues would benefit from studies done across a broad range research methodologies informed by interdisciplinary perspectives.

Some of the most important dimensions of the issue of educational level and L2 learning may be those hardest for educators and researchers on the hyperliterate side of the abyss to articulate and to face. A true reckoning would remind us that the attitude of global supremacy which underwrote imperialism in times past—with its gruesome legacy of cultural distortion and destruction—marches on still in the neoliberal agenda pursued under a banner of globalization and expressed in the conduct of business and education throughout the occidental world and beyond (Smith, 2006). It is not difficult to see that the presence of L2 learners in the classrooms of industrialized countries is a direct consequence of the exercise of political and military might, coupled with a sense of messianic right. It may be less obvious, however, that the western approach to academic schooling is also an exercise in privileging certain kinds of learning and knowing over others, sponsored by a post-Enlightenment faith in the tenets of science that define much research considered worthy: objectivity, definability of discrete phenomena, and the primacy of method.

It should not fail to impress us that this list of scientific tenets describes item for item the kind of intellectual and life habits foreign to, and fatal to, oral noesis. The scientific stance, ushered in by the objectification of alphabetic literacy (Ong, 1982, p. 112), entails levels of personal, cultural, and natural rupture, that are at the root of widespread suffering in industrialized societies, expressed as depression, loss of belonging, environmental degradation, and senseless violence. As we welcome unschooled immigrants and earnestly seek to guide them into the literacy and academic skills that they also earnestly seek, we unavoidably participate in the extinction of a way of life based on orality, relationality, memory, and context. Is it really unavoidable? Can't we somehow proceed more reciprocally, sharing our different perspectives, rather than wielding one to eliminate the other? That thought alone would represent a true departure. So much depends on how we answer these questions, and whether we are sincerely willing to ask them at all. It may be hard, but is also necessary for the intended audience of this chapter to face such considerations, not just for the survival of the refugees and immigrants who come to learn to read, but for the survival of the highly literate and educated who need to learn to live.

References

Achebe, C. (1961). *No longer at ease*. New York: Ivan Obolensky.

Adrian, J. A., Alegria, J., and Morais, J. (1995). Metaphonological abilities of Spanish illiterate adults. *International Journal of Psychology, 3*, 329–353.

Ardila, A. (2004). There is not any specific brain area for writing: From cave-paintings to computers. *International Journal of Psychology, 39*, 61–67.

Arthur, J. (2003). Baro Afkaaga Hooyo! A case study of Somali literacy teaching in Liverpool. *International Journal of Bilingual Education and Bilingualism, 6*, 253–266.

Auerbach, E. (1993). *Bilingual community literacy training project: Final report*. Boston: University of Massachusetts.

Battiste, M. (Ed.). (2000). *Reclaiming indigenous voice and wisdom*. Vancouver, CA: University of British Columbia Press.

Becker, A. L. (1992). Silence across languages: An essay. In C. Kramsch and S. McConnel-Ginet (Eds.), *Text and context: Cross-disciplinary perspectives on language study*. Lexington, MA: Heath.

Biber, D. (1988). *Variation across speech and writing*. New York: Cambridge University Press.

Biber, D. and Hared, M. (1991). Literacy in Somali: Linguistic consequences. *Annual Review of Applied Linguistics, 12*, 260–282.

Biber, D. and Hared, M. (1994). Linguistic correlates of the transition to literacy in Somalia: Language adaptation in six press registers. In D. Biber and E. Finegan (Eds.), *Sociolinguistic perspectives on register*. Oxford: Oxford University Press.

Biber, D., Reppen, R., and Conrad, S. (2002). Developing linguistic literacy: Perspectives from corpus linguistics and multi-dimensional analysis. *Journal of Child Language, 29*, 458–462.

Bigelow, M. (2007). Social and cultural capital at school: The case of a Somali teenage girl with limited formal schooling. In N. R. Faux (Ed.), *Low-educated adult second language and literacy acquisition proceedings of symposium*. Richmond, VA: Literacy Institute at Virginia Commonwealth University.

Bigelow, M., and Tarone, E. (2004). The role of native language literacy in second language acquisition: Doesn't who we study determine what we know? *TESOL Quarterly, 39*, 689–700.

Bramão, I., Mendonça, A., Faísca, L., Ingvar, M., Petersson, K. M., and Reis, A. J. (2007). The impact of reading and writing skills on a visuo-motor integration task: A comparison between illiterate and literate subjects. *International Neuropsychological Society, 13*, 359–364.

Castro-Caldas, A., Petersson, K. M., Reis, A., Stone-Elander, S., and Ingvar, M. (1998). The illiterate brain: Learning to read and write during childhood influences the functional organization of the adult brain. *Brain and Language, 121*, 1053–1063.

Clahsen, H., Meisel, J. M., and Pienemann, M. (1983). *Deutsch als Zweitsprache: Der Spracherwerb ausländischer Arbeiter*. Tübingen: Narr.

Davidson, R. K., and Strucker, J. (2002). Patters of word-recognition errors among adult basic education native and nonnative speakers of English. *Scientific Studies of Reading, 6*, 299–316.

DeCapua, A., and Marshall, H. (2010). *Breaking new ground: Teaching students with limited or interrupted formal schooling in secondary schools*. Ann Arbor, MI: University of Michigan Press.

DeCapua, A., Smathers, W., and Tang, F. (2009). *Meeting the needs of students with limited or interrupted schooling: A guide for educators*. Ann Arbor, MI: University of Michigan Press.

Dellatolas, G., Braga, L. W., Souza, L. D. N., Filho, G. N., Queiroz, E., and Deloche, G. (2003). Cognitive consequences of early phase of literacy. *Journal of International Neuropsychological Society, 9*, 771–782.

Deloria, V. (1970). *We talk, you listen: New tribes, new turf*. New York: The Macmillan Company.

Dowse, R., and Ehlers, M. S. (2003). The influence of education on the interpretation of pharmaceutical pictograms for communicating medicine instructions. *International Journal of Pharmacy Practice, 11*, 11–18.

Duong, A., and Ska, B. (2001). Production of narratives: Picture sequence facilitates organizational but not conceptual processing in less educated subjects. *Brain and Cognition, 46*, 121–124.

Durgunoğlu, A. Y., and Öney, B. (2002). Phonological awareness in literacy acquisition: It's not only for children. *Scientific Studies of Reading, 6*, 245–266.

Espinosa, K. E., and Massey, D. S. (1997). Determinants of English proficiency among Mexican migrants to the United States. *International Migration Review, 31*, 28–50.

Espinoza-Herold, M. (2007). Stepping beyond *sí se puede: Dichos* as a cultural resource in mother-daughter interaction in a Latino family. *Anthropology & Education Quarterly, 38*, 260–277.

Farr, M. (1994). En los dos idiomas: Literacy practices among Chicago Mexicanos. In B. Moss (Ed.), *Literacy across communities*. Creskill, NJ: Hampton Press.

Frater-Mathieson, K. (2004). Refugee trauma, loss and grief: Implications for intervention. In R. Hamilton and D. Moore (Eds.), *Educational interventions for refugee children: Theoretical perspectives and implementing best practice*. London and New York: Routledge Falmer Taylor and Francis Group.

Freeman, Y. S., and Freeman, D. E. (2002). *Closing the achievement gap: How to reach limited-formal-schooling and long-term English learners*. Portsmouth, NH: Heinemann.

Gee, J. P. (2008). *Social linguistics and literacies: Ideology in discourses (Third Edition)*. London and New York: Routledge.

Gombert, J. E. (1994). How do illiterate adults react to metalinguistic training? *Annals of Dyslexia, 44*, 250–269.

Goody, J. (1977). *The domestication of the savage mind*. Cambridge: Cambridge University Press.

Hardman, J. (1999). A community of learners: Cambodians in an adult ESL classroom. *Language Teaching Research, 3*, 145–166.

Havelock, E. (1963). *Preface to Plato*. Cambridge, MA: Belknap Press of Harvard UP.

Irele, F. A. (2001). *The African imagination: Literature in Africa and the black diaspora*. New York: Oxford University Press.

Jousse, M. (1925). *Le style oral rythmique et mnémotechnique chez les verbo-moteurs*. Paris: Gabriel Beauchesne.

Klassen, C. (1991). Obstacles to learning: The account of low-education Latin American adults. In B. Burnaby and A. A. Cummings (Eds.), *Sociopolitical aspects of ESL in Canada*. Toronto: Ontario Institute for Studies in Education Press.

Klein, W., and Perdue, C. (1992). *Utterance structure: Developing grammars again*. Amsterdam: John Benjamins.

Kuhl, P. (2004). Early language acquisition: Cracking the speech code. *Nature Review: Neuroscience, 5*, 831–843.

Kurvers, J. (2007). Development of word recognition skills of adult L2 beginning readers. In N. R. Faux (Ed.), *Low-educated adult second language and literacy acquisition proceedings of symposium*. Richmond, VA: Literacy Institute at Virginia Commonwealth University.

Kurvers, J., van Hout, R., and Vallen, T. (2006). Discovering features of language: Metalinguistic awareness of adult illiterates. In I. Van De Craats, J. Kurvers, and M. Young-Scholten (Eds.), *Low-educated adult second language and literacy acquisition: Proceedings of the inaugural symposium*. Utrecht, The Netherlands: LOT.

Kurvers, J., van Hout, R., and Vallen, T. (2007). Literacy and word boundaries. In N. R. Faux (Ed.), *Low-educated adult second language and literacy acquisition proceedings of symposium*. Richmond, VA: Literacy Institute at Virginia Commonwealth University.

Kurvers, J., and van de Craats, I. (2007). Memory, second language reading, and lexicon: A comparison between successful and less successful adults and children. In N. R. Faux (Ed.), *Low-educated adult second language and literacy acquisition proceedings of symposium*. Richmond, VA: Literacy Institute at Virginia Commonwealth University.

Ladson-Billings, G. (1995). Toward a theory of culturally relevant pedagogy. *American Educational Research Journal, 32*, 465–491.

Levinson, M. P. (2007). Literacy in English Gypsy communities: Cultural capital manifested as negative assets. *American Educational Research Journal, 44*, 5–39.

Lévi-Strauss, C. (1966). *The savage mind*. Letchworth, Herefordshire, UK: George Weidenfeld and Nicolson Ltd.

Lindberg, I. (2003). Second language awareness: What for and for whom. *Language Awareness, 12*, 157–171.

Lord, A. (1975). Perspectives on recent work in oral literature. In J. Duggan (Ed.), *Oral literature*. New York: Barnes and Noble.

Loureiro, C. D. S., Braga, L. W., Souza, L. D. N., Filho, G. N., Queiroz, E., and Dellatolas, G. (2004). Degree of illiteracy and phonological and metaphonological skills in unschooled adults. *Brain and Language, 89*, 499–502.

Luria, A. R. (1976). *Cognitive development and its cultural and social foundations*. Cambridge: Harvard University Press.

MacSwan, J., and Rolstad, K. (2006). How language proficiency tests mislead us about ability: Implications for English language learner placement in special education. *Teachers College Record, 108*, 2304–2328.

Mace-Matluck, B. J., Alexander-Kasparik, R., and Queen, R. M. (1998). *Through the golden door: Educational approaches for immigrant adolescents with limited schooling*. McHenry, IL: Center for Applied Linguistics and Delta Systems.

Mathews-Aydinli, J. (2008). Overlooked and understudied? A survey of current trends in research on adult English language learners. *Adult Education Quarterly, 58*, 198–213.

Mazrui, A. (2007). Pretender to universalism: Western culture in a globalizing age. In S. H. A. I. Dadi (Ed.), *Unpacking Europe*. Rotterdam: NAI Publishers.

McCluhan, M. (1964/1994). *Understanding media: The extensions of man*. Cambridge, MA: MIT Press.

Menard-Warwick, J. (2005). Intergenerational trajectories and sociopolitical context: Latina immigrants in adult ESL. *TESOL Quarterly, 39*, 165–185.

Morais, J., Bertelson, P., Cary, L., and Alegria, J. (1986). Literacy training and speech segmentation. *Cognition, 24*, 45–64.

Morais, J., Cary, L., Alegria, J., and Bertelson, P. (1979). Does awareness of speech as a sequence of phones arise spontaneously? *Cognition, 7*, 323–331.

Morais, J., Content, A., Bertelson, P., and Cary, L. (1988). Is there a critical period for the acquisition of segmental analysis? *Cognitive Neuropsychology, 5*, 347–352.

Morais, J. and Kolinsky, R. (2002). Literacy effects on language and cognition. In C. V. Hofsten and L. Bäckman (Eds.), *Psychology at the turn of the millennium*. New York: Psychology Press.

Nandy, A. (1983). *The intimate enemy: Loss and recovery of self under colonialism*. Delhi: Oxford University Press.

Neuner, F., Catani, C., Ruf, M., Schauer, E., Schauer, M., and Elbert, T. (2008). Narrative exposure therapy for the treatment of child and adolescent war victims: From neurobiology to field intervention. *Child and Adolescent Psychiatry Clinics of North America, 17*, 641–664.

Olmedo, I. M. (1997). Voices of our past: Using oral history to explore funds of knowledge within a Puerto Rican family. *Anthropology and Education Quarterly, 28*, 550–573.

Olson, D. R. (2006). Oral discourse in a world of literacy. *Research in the Teaching of English, 41*, 136–143.

Ong, W. J. (1982). *Orality and literacy: The technologizing of the word*. London and New York: Routledge.

Ostrosky-Solís, F. and Ramirez, M. (2004). Effects of culture and education on neuropsychological testing: A preliminary study with indigenous and nonindigenous population. *Applied Neuropsychology, 11*, 186–193.

Parry, A. (1971). The making of Homeric verse: The collected works of Milman Parry.

Perdue, C. (Ed.). (1993). *Adult language acquisition: Cross-linguistic perspectives*. Cambridge: Cambridge University Press.

Piaget, J. (1952). *The origins of intelligence in children*. Oxford, UK: International Universities Press.

Pienemann, M., Johnston, M., and Brindley, G. (1988). Constructing an acquisition-based procedure for second language assessment. *Studies in Second Language Acquisition, 10*, 217–243.

Reder, S. and Davila, E. (2005). Context and literacy practices. *Annual Review of Applied Linguistics, 25*, 170–187.

Reis, A. and Castro-Caldas, A. (1997). Illiteracy: A cause for biased cognitive development. *Journal of International Neuropsychological Society, 3*, 444–450.

Reis, A., Guerreiro, M., and Petersson, K. M. (2003). A sociodemographic and neuropsychological characterization of an illiterate population. *Applied Neuropsychology, 10*, 191–204.

Reis, A., Petersson, K. M., Castro-Caldas, A., and Ingvar, M. (2001). Formal schooling influences two- but not three-dimensional naming skills. *Brain and Cognition, 47*, 397–411.

Robson, B. (1983). Hmong literacy, formal education, and their effects on performance in an ESL class. In B. T. Downing and D. Olney (Eds.), *The Hmong in the west: Observations and reports*. Minneapolis, MN: University of Minnesota.

Ross, A. C. (1989). *Metakuye Oyasin: "We are all related."* Ft. Yates, ND: Bear.

Rosselli, M., and Ardila, A. (2003). The impact of culture and education on non-verbal neuropsychological measurements: A critical review. *Brain and Cognition, 52*, 326–333.

Royer, J. M., Abadzi, H., and Kinda, J. (2004). The impact of phonological-awareness and rapid-reading training on the reading skills of adolescent and adult neoliterates. *International Review of Education, 50*, 53–71.

Sarat, A., Davidovitch, N., and Alberstein, M. (2007). *Trauma and memory: Reading, healing*. CA: Stanford University Press.

Sarroub, L. K. (2008). Living "glocally" with literacy success in the Midwest. *Theory into Practice, 47*, 59–66.

Sausurre, F. D. (1959). *Course in general linguistics* (W. Baskin, Trans.). New York: Philosophical Library.

Serpell, R., Baker, L., & Sonnenschein, S. (2005). *Becoming literate in the city: The Baltimore early childhood project*. Cambridge: Cambridge University Press.

Short, D., and Fitzsimmons, S. (2007). *Double the work: Challenges and solutions to acquiring language and academic literacy for adolescent English language learners*. New York: Carnegie Corporation of New York.

Silva, C., Petersson, K. M., Faísca, L., Ingvar, M., and Reis, A. (2004). The effects of literacy and education on the quantitative and qualitative aspects of semantic verbal fluency. *Journal of Clinical and Experimental Neuropsychology, 26*, 266–277.

Skilton-Sylvester, E. (2002). Should I stay or should I go? Investigating Cambodian women's participation and investment in adult ESL programs. *Adult Education Quarterly, 53*, 9–26.

Smith, D. G. (1999). *Pedagon: Interdisciplinary essays in the human sciences, pedagogy and culture*. New York: Peter Lang.

Smith, D. G. (2006). *Trying to teach in a season of great untruth: Globalization empire and the crisis of pedagogy*. Rotterdam, Netherlands: Sense Publishers.

Tarone, E., Bigelow, M., and Hansen, K. (2009). *Literacy and second language oracy*. Oxford: Oxford University Press.

Visvanathan, S. (1987). From the Annals of the Laboratory State. *Alternatives: A Journal of World Policy, 12*, 37–59.

Vygotsky, L. (1978). *Mind in society: The development of higher psychological processes*. Cambridge, MA: Harvard University Press.

Warriner, D. S. (2007). "It's just the nature of the beast": Re-imagining the literacies of schooling in adult ESL education. *Linguistics and Education, 18*, 305–324.

Watson, J. (2010). *Interpreting across the abyss: A hermeneutic exploration of initial literacy development by English language learners with limited formal schooling*. Unpublished PhD dissertation. University of Minnesota, Minneapolis.

Young-Scholten, M. and Strom, N. (2006). First-time L2 readers: Is there a critical period? In I. Van de Craats, J. Kurvers, and M. Young-Scholten, (Eds.) *Low-educated adult second language and literacy acquisition: Proceedings of the inaugural symposium*. Utrecht, The Netherlands: LOT.

29

Fossilization—A classic concern of SLA research*

ZhaoHong Han

Introduction

A frequently noted fact out of a spectrum observed of second language acquisition (SLA) is that in almost all post-pubescent learners, learning stagnates, in spite of all or any favorable conditions that would otherwise propel it (Gass and Selinker, 2008; Sharwood Smith, 1994; Towell and Hawkins, 1994; VanPatten and Williams, 2007). Whereas this fact itself has largely remained a conundrum—notwithstanding abundant speculations that exist, it is further complicated by two additional facets, selectivity and variability. That is, learners do not seem to stabilize prematurely within and across each and every linguistic domain (e.g., phonology, semantics, morphology, syntax), hence selectivity; nor do they all stall on the same linguistic elements, hence variability, even though noticeable overlap does exist, particularly in learners of the same first language background.

The phenomenon of truncated learning was first brought into sharp focus by Selinker (1972). Nearly 40 years have since elapsed. Where are we in terms of identifying the relevant data and theorizing about the lack of learning phenomenon metaphorically known as "fossilization"? In this chapter, I will trace the history of research, focusing, in particular, on the evolution of conceptual changes and the trajectory of empirical research, starting with a brief discussion of the theoretical status of the construct. Along the way, core issues will be highlighted. I will end the chapter with a sketch of future directions as well as with a brief discussion of the implications of fossilization research for second language (L2) instruction.

Historical discussion

The centrality of fossilization to SLA theory construction

The conception of "fossilization" (Selinker, 1972) as a central phenomenon of SLA stems first from a generic, impressionistic observation, as encapsulated in an oft-cited quote from Bley-Vroman (1989):

> Few adults are completely successful; many fail miserably, many achieve very high levels of proficiency, given enough time, input, and effort, and given the right attitude, motivation, and learning environment. (p. 49)

This observation was corroborated by findings of empirical research, notably through data from a large-scale longitudinal study by the European Science Foundation of uninstructed L2 learners

(Perdue, 1993). The observation on the general lack of success in post-pubescent L2 learning was readily affirmed by research on other critical issues, such as the role of biological maturation (e.g., Hyltenstam and Abrahamsson, 2003; Long, 1990, 2005; cf., Byrnes, Chapter 31, this volume; DeKeyser, Chapter 27, this volume).

Researchers have reckoned that the percentage of L2 learners able to achieve native-speaker competence is nil to 5 percent (Bley-Vroman, 1989; Long, 1990; Selinker, 1972; see, however, Birdsong, 1999; Montrul and Slabakova, 2003; White and Genesee, 1996), meaning that the vast majority, that is, 95 percent or more, of L2 learners stop short of that level of attainment. Given the stark asymmetry between the success and the failure rate, it only stands to reason that it is the vast majority of L2 learners, not the small number of "outliers" like a learner named Julie reported in Ioup *et al.* (1994), that should be the source of relevant data for SLA theory construction. Selinker (1972, p. 212) argues that the 5 percent successful learners "may be safely ignored—in a counterfactual sense—for the purposes of establishing the constructs which point to the psychologically-relevant data pertinent to most second-language learners" (see, however, Birdsong, 2004, 2006).

In the earliest conception, the term "interlanguage," referring to an imperfect yet autonomous linguistic system created in the course of L2 learning, was almost synonymous with "fossilization" (Selinker, 1972); many have even claimed that the latter is really what had spurred the field of SLA into existence (Han and Selinker, 2005; Long, 2003). However, the general perception of fossilization has evolved over the years: In the contemporary view, fossilization remains a central characteristic of interlanguage (Bley-Vroman, 1989) and continues to serve as a touchstone for the adequacy of theories of SLA. In Larsen-Freeman's (2006) words, "fossilization provides the stage where issues central to SLA play out ... In order to account for learning, the province of SLA, we should be able to say not only what it is, but also when and why it cannot or does not occur" (p. 193).

By the fossilization "yardstick," then, adequate theories must explain both learning and lack of learning (Gass and Selinker, 2008; VanPatten and Williams, 2007). As Bley-Vroman (2009) points out, "the theory must permit everything from the so-called near-native cases like Julie (Ioup *et al.*, 1994) to cases in which the acquired grammar is dramatically different from that of the input, like Schmidt's (1983) Wes or Schumann's (1978) Alberto" (p. 178). Updating his Fundamental Difference Hypothesis, Bley-Vroman underscores that "addressing the logical problem of foreign language learning[1] requires, in short, postulating an acquisition system that does not work reliably and does not [lead to convergent grammars]" (p. 178).

The sine qua non of fossilization

Given the theoretical import of fossilization, it would seem necessary to attain some uniformity in defining the construct among researchers and across studies. However, doing so has proven quite daunting.

In its inception (Selinker, 1972), the construct of fossilization was both phenomenological and epistemological, thus referring, on the one hand, to observable linguistic units that appear to have stalled short of the aspired targets and, on the other hand, to a cognitive mechanism.

> Fossilization, a mechanism ... underlies surface linguistic material which speakers tend to keep in their interlanguage productive performance, no matter what the age of the learner or the amount of instruction he receives in the target language. (Selinker, 1972, p. 229)

The terminological duality has, over the years, led to a proliferation of uses of the term, with its denotations running the gamut from low proficiency (e.g., Thep-Ackrapong, 1990), to typical error (e.g., Kellerman, 1989), and to systematic use of erroneous forms (e.g., Allwright and Bailey, 1991), while prompting a greater number of speculations on the fossilization mechanism (for review, see Han 2004a). Thus, as Birdsong (2004, 2006) has aptly noted, fossilization has become a "catch-all" term, and as such, is theoretically and empirically vacuous. In a similar vein, Long (2003) indicates that the construct of fossilization conflates *explanandum* with *explanans* and is therefore ambiguous.

Another notable, conceptual development over the years is that by and large, the hypothesized scope of fossilization has expanded from being local to global. Consequently, fossilization is considered to affect not just discrete or isolated linguistic elements, as initially assumed, but rather, the gestalt of the interlanguage system. Selinker and Lamendella (1978), for instance, define fossilization as:

> ... permanent cessation of interlanguage learning before the learner has attained target language norms at all levels of linguistic structure and in all discourse domains in spite of the learner's positive ability, opportunity, and motivation to learn and acculturate into target society. (p. 187)

Bley-Vroman (1989) refers to fossilization as follows:

> It has long been noted that foreign language learners reach a certain stage of learning—a stage short of success—and that learners then permanently stabilize at this stage. Development ceases, and even serious conscious efforts to change are often fruitless. Brief changes are sometimes observed, but they do not "take." The learner backslides to the stable state. (pp. 46–47)

And similarly, Tarone (1994) states:

> A central characteristic of any interlanguage is that it fossilizes—that is, it ceases to develop at some point short of full identity with the target language. (p. 1715)

The term fossilization has, therefore, been utilized to characterize an ultimate stage or an end state of L2 learning (cf., Herschensohn, 2009). Notice, though, that the endstate view does not seem to preclude that fossilization is not ineluctable for some learners. Indeed, in Tarone *et al.* (1976), we can find a sub-categorization of L2 learners into the non-fossilized and the fossilized, suggesting (a) that not all learners will experience fossilization but (b) that some learners are doomed to failure at the outset (see, e.g., Washburn, 1991).

As it turns out, however, neither the endstate nor the fossilized learner view holds up to empirical scrutiny. SLA empirical research to date has shown unequivocal evidence of intra-learner variability; that is, individual learners have been found to achieve differential success across and within linguistic domains and subsystems. Success, in this context, is defined as "acquiring a grammar like that of a native speaker" (White, 2003a, p. 243). Longitudinal studies on fossiliza-tion, in particular, have provided compelling evidence that learning continues even in putatively "fossilized" learners (see, e.g., Lardiere, 1998, 2007). In short, fossilization has demonstrated to be local rather than global. Based on such findings, Han and Odlin (2006) hypothesize:

> L2 acquisition will never have a global end state; rather, it will have fossilization, namely, permanent local cessation of development. (p. 8)

But what counts as local cessation of learning? Most of the definitions of fossilization proposed to date, though quite diverse, have collectively revealed three distinct properties: (a) persistent deviance from the target, (b) resistance to external influence, including explicit instruction and corrective feedback, and (c) being out of the learner's control. Notably, however, most definitions have failed to cognize a fundamental premise on which fossilization was initially predicated. Selinker, from his earliest definition up until his more recent ones, has consistently emphasized the need for a number of learning conditions to be met as a preliminary to any discussion of fossilization. Thus, for determining fossilization, Selinker and Lamendella (1979) have stressed such conditions as the "ability, opportunity, and motivation to learn the target language and acculturate into the target society" (p. 373), which Han (2004a) later reformulates into "three preconditions": (a) abundant exposure to input, (b) adequate motivation to learn, and (c) plentiful opportunity for communicative practice. Upholding these conditions is crucial, as it helps to ensure that the fossilization phenomenon is sufficiently circumscribed to be theoretically, empirically, and practically interesting and productive.

Han (1998, 2004a) offers a two-tier definition:

COGNITIVE LEVEL: Fossilization involves those cognitive processes or underlying mechanisms that produce permanently stabilized interlanguage forms.

EMPIRICAL LEVEL: Fossilization involves those stabilized interlanguage forms that remain in learner speech or writing over time, no matter what the input or what the learner does. (2004a, p. 20)

The purpose of the two-tier definition is to differentiate a theoretical and an empirical level at which fossilization can be described and theorized. Neither endeavor, as will be discussed in the sections that follow, has been quite adequate—notwithstanding that fossilization has been one of the few SLA constructs that have made its popularity, beyond SLA circles, with L2 practitioners.

Core issues

The study of fossilization faces a number of conceptual and empirical challenges. Some of these challenges have been systematically discussed in Long (2003), Lardiere (2007), and Han (2004b): Han (2004b) deals at length with what she sees as five central issues: (a) Is fossilization global or local? (b) Is L2 ultimate attainment isomorphic with fossilization? (c) Is fossilization a product or process? (d) Is stabilization synonymous with fossilization? And (e) Should empirical studies of fossilization span five years or more? Long (2003) poignantly addresses four empirical issues, among others: (a) assuming, not demonstrating, fossilization; (b) selecting inappropriate learners for study; (c) basing findings on insufficient data; and (d) using inadequate analyses. Similarly, Lardiere (2007) takes on several, including volatility.

In this section, I discuss two more. The first issue pertains to the nature of fossilization research, which, to some, showcases a practice of what Bley-Vroman (1983) has referred to as the "comparative fallacy." Fossilization studies are allegedly parasitic on comparison of interlanguage with target language, and more specifically, of L2 learners with monolingual native speakers. A problem with such comparative practice is, as Larsen-Freeman (2006) aptly points out, that it overemphasizes surface deviance while overlooking other, deeper levels of interlanguage such as semantics and usage patterns that do not appear to involve errors of form. Han (2008) concurs and subsequently demonstrates (Han, 2010) that meaning can be a greater source of learning difficulty than form (cf., Bardovi-Harlig, Chapter 9, this volume; Slabakova, Chapter 8, this volume), lending support to Larsen-Freeman's (2006) claim that "because using a language requires using its elements accurately, meaningfully, and appropriately (Larsen-Freeman, 2001), surely inaccurate forms are not the only evidence of fossilization" (p. 194). Indeed, a growing number of studies of very advanced learners, including the oft-cited Ioup *et al.* (1994) study, have offered the insight that meaning and function or, rather, discourse syntax and semantics are the hardest to acquire, suggesting that those should be proper domains for fossilization research.

A paramount concern with the comparative approach, as Larsen-Freeman (2006) further notes, is its predication on "a particular view of language—a view of monolithic, homogeneous, idealized, static end-state competence, where language acquisition is seen to be a process of conformity to uniformity" (p. 194). She advocates, instead, a dynamic view of language which presumes no end and no state. While the no-end/no-state view is highly debatable in the context of L2 learning, fossilization researchers should certainly heed her admonition, namely that "While the concept of fossilization is inherently target-centric, researchers of it must take into account the fact that the target is not monolithic and is always moving, although, of course, different aspects of language change at different rates" (p. 195), and be highly circumspect when determining instances of fossilization.

In a completely different vein, Cook (1992, 1999, 2008) also raises doubts about the comparative approach. The crux of Cook's argument is that the competence developed by L2 learners, dubbed "multi-competence," is necessarily of qualitative difference from that of monolingual speakers. Comparing the two will, therefore, be meaningless and even misleading. Both research and pedagogical practices must therefore reconceptualize the goal of L2 learning, in his view: for research, instead of measuring L2 success against the native speaker norms and assuming that those are what learners have aspired to, profiles should be created of successful L2 learners against which to then evaluate the success or lack thereof of L2 learning in individual learners. For practitioners, Cook's suggestion is that teaching should aim at aligning students with those profiles (see, however, Davies, 2003; Han, 2004c).

Though seemingly orthogonal, the multi-competence view and fossilization research are not entirely out of synch. The former simply rules out native-speaker competence even as a possibility for L2 acquisition, hence averting comparisons, while the latter seeks to document its psychological reality but, more importantly, to find its etiology and does so in reference to the target language. The comparative approach is necessary at times, as some have strongly argued (Birdsong, 2004; Franceschina, 2005; Lardiere, 2003). Han (2004c) suggests that native speaker data should be used only as an aid or a means to elucidate a learning phenomenon, not as an end, say, merely to present native-non-native differences as practiced in Romero Trillo (2002). Franceschina (2005) insightfully points out that to compare or not should be a decision made on the basis of "the aims of individual investigations and not by an *a priori* decision about what SLA researchers should or should not be interested in" (Franceschina, 2005, p. 18).

Still, if fossilization research is not about revealing surface deviance of a given interlanguage from its intended target but about uncovering an underlying mechanism of L2 acquisition, it appears that more attention should be given to the internal logic of interlanguage than to differences, as Bley-Vroman has counseled, and accordingly, that there should be less interlanguage and target language comparison but more within-interlanguage analysis, both in scope and depth.

A second issue that I wish to consider briefly here is whether or not the term fossilization should be extended to forms that have been acquired, and somewhat relatedly, whether or not fossilization and acquisition are driven by the same mechanism. R. Ellis (1985) argues that because fossilization is part of the interlanguage process, occurring at one point in time, there should be both fossilized errors and non-errors (see also, Vigil and Oller, 1976). Most researchers, however, hold that fossilization applies only to non-targetlike forms, conceptualizing fossilization as "a process that may occur in the second language acquisition context as opposed to first language acquisition" (Hyltenstam, 1988, p. 68).

Fundamentally, in tying fossilization to acquired forms, researchers conflate fossilization with stabilization. Their rationale is that just as non-targetlike features can stabilize, so can targetlike features be construed as a form of stabilization. This view is neither theoretically plausible nor empirically and practically desirable (see discussion in the next section of different types of stabilization). At the very least, it masks rather than elucidates the complexity of second language learning, inasmuch as it lumps what may very well be disparate phenomena. SLA research over the past four decades has striven for a greater and finer-grained understanding of the learning process, outcome, and mechanism. Differentiating fossilization from other types of stabilization can therefore be crucial to a more sophisticated understanding of this unique learning and cognitive phenomenon of SLA. It would simply be a hard-sell argument that truncated learning, manifested as persistent deviance from the target, has followed the same cognitive process as for complete acquisition.

Perhaps a more interesting and substantive question with regard to fossilization and acquisition is whether or not they have the same underlying mechanism. Following the above line of thinking, although their processes may very well be different, it would nevertheless seem implausible that fossilization and acquisition each are driven by a different mechanism. Theoretically, it would not be enticing to posit two mechanisms, as doing so would compromise the parsimony of the theory, a well-sought-after virtue by theorists (Jordan, 2004). More important, it is difficult to argue that for a given L2 learner there are two mechanisms, one leading to learning and one to incomplete learning. Empirical findings on fossilization as local rather than global point favorably to the understanding that one mechanism drives two processes, with one "non-contaminated," as in the case of acquisition, and the other "contaminated" or tempered with by the L1 (cf., Lardiere, Chapter 7, this volume), as in the case of fossilization. Fossilization, after all, is not zero learning but incomplete learning.

Such appears to have been the reasoning behind current theoretical approaches to accounting for acquisition and fossilization, such as the generative approach (see, e.g., Hawkins, 2000; Lardiere, 1998, 2007; Sorace, 1993, 2003; White, 2003b) and the connectionist approach (see, e.g., N. Ellis, 2006). From a somewhat eclectic perspective and with fossilization as her main explanandum, Han (2009) recently posited a Selective Fossilization Hypothesis, which proposes a unitary mechanism, made up of L1 markedness and L2 input robustness and their interaction, for both fossilization and acquisition. According to the hypothesis, predictions can be made, by examining the nature of L2 input such as frequency and variability and, similarly, the nature of the corresponding L1 feature such as its frequency and variability, about (a) what is acquirable, (b) not as acquirable, (c) fossilizable, and (d) not as fossilizable. The hypothesis further translates into a numerical model (a set of formulae) that enables the calculation of the interaction of L1 input robustness and L2 markedness vis-à-vis a given target feature and subsequently its fossilizability. Importantly, in this framework, *that* feature is not simply a form, but a unity (or lack thereof) of form, meaning, and function (Larsen-Freeman, 2001).

Data and common elicitation measures

To date, empirical research on fossilization has, primarily, been clinical rather than controlled or statistical, relying heavily on naturalistic data, the goal often being to isolate instances of fossilization. Typically, the methodology employed is a longitudinal case study, though cross-sectional studies exist as well, with the data analyzed more qualitatively than quantitatively.

Earlier studies on fossilization have relied exclusively on natural samples of learner language, drawn primarily from untutored learners (see, e.g., Agnello, 1977; Schumann, 1978; Shapira, 1978; Stauble, 1978). By way of illustration, Shapira (1978), for a year and a half, followed Zoila, a 25-year-old Guatemalan woman, a native speaker of Spanish learning English as the L2 without instruction. Data collected consisted of transcripts of conversation interviews conducted at three points in time, each interview session lasting from 30 to 45 minutes. The data were then analyzed around ten grammatical structures: the plural -s, the third-person singular -s, plural NP subjects followed by the verb BE, BE copula, BE+ V-ing, negation of sentences with BE, negation of sentences with verbs other than BE, Yes/No questions, WH-questions, and possessive -s. Obligatory occasion analysis, which counts tokens of targetlike use, was carried out to assess and compare Zoila's production accuracy vis-à-vis these targeted constructions, both synchronically and diachronically, using 80–85 percent suppliance in all obligatory environments as the benchmark. Results indicated "little or quite insignificant development in the acquisition of any of the ten grammatical categories studied" (p. 248). Shapira then invoked biological, cognitive, affective accounts of a critical period (Lenneberg, 1967) to understand why there was little progress, arguing that (a) the putative biological changes—such as cortical lateralization—around puberty, (b) the cognitive and social changes induced by the onset of formal operations, and (c) psychological distance triggered by language and culture shock all might have been responsible for the fact that little progress had been made except in the area of fluency. In addition, learner strategies such as prioritizing communication over formal accuracy and L1 transfer were offered as potentially confounding factors.

It should be noted, however, that Zoila's learning was not a complete failure: Although little morphosyntactic progress was observed in her during the one and a half years, "a process of 'replacement' of transferred vocabulary by English equivalents" was attested (Shapira, 1978, p. 254), which suggests differential intra-learner interlanguage development. Similar findings were reported by Schmidt (1983, 1984) on Wes, an adult Japanese immigrant to Hawaii, whose ability to communicate displayed a steady and impressive rate of increase but whose grammatical development appeared to have made no progress over a period of three years. Thus, as MacWhinney (2006) has noted, "fossilization is not an across-the-board phenomenon. Rather, we find continual growth in some areas and relative stability of error in others" (p. 135).

The best-known early study on fossilization is that of Schumann (1978), a ten-month longitudinal case study. The subject, Alberto, was an adult native speaker of Costa Rican Spanish, who had resided in the USA for four months. In his home country, Alberto had received six years of instruction in the English language, at the intensity of two to three hours a week. He was reported to be able to "speak only a few words and phrases in English," limited to select topics such as work and shopping, at the onset of the study. The data comprised, primarily, 20 tapes of recordings of spontaneous conversations between Alberto and the researcher. Obligatory occasion analysis of the data, focusing on Alberto's use of the English auxiliary and its related structures, the negative, and the interrogative, showed little development in these areas over the ten-month period. Interestingly, in this study, the lack of progress was revealed also through comparison with other learners of a similar L1 background, shedding light on the idiosyncratic nature of fossilization. According to Schumann, several factors contributed to the lack of learning in Alberto, but two, in particular: social and psychological distance.

To the extent that the early studies such as the ones described above established, via longitudinal data, stabilization of morphosyntactic deviances from the target language, they are invaluable for their contribution to the inception of an empirical basis for fossilization. However, the methodological weaknesses of the early studies are also important, which mitigate their evidential credibility. For one thing, the fact that these studies all focused on early stage learners is enough cause for concern: Had the learners had enough exposure to the target language—one of the three preconditions for empirically determining fossilization? And how had they fared in terms of the two other preconditions, motivation and opportunity for communicative practice? Indeed, what the early studies offered by way of explanations often point to the lack of satisfaction of these conditions. That is, they indicated that the subjects neither had had much contact with the target language nor the opportunity to practice and/or the motivation to strive for accuracy.

Schumann's Acculturation Hypothesis (1978, 1986), for example, precisely claims that social and psychological distance from the target culture and language constricts exposure to input. Hence, it would not be an unreasonable contention that if those learners had had enough exposure and so forth, they might have progressed beyond the observed plateau.

Another major question that can be raised with the early studies is whether or not the observed stabilization equals fossilization. Han (1998; cf., Han, 2004a; Selinker and Han, 2001) distinguishes three underlying forces of surface stabilization. First, stabilization can result from a natural slow-down in the learning process. According to skill acquisition theory, learning (language learning included) is subject to the power law of practice; that is, learning heightens as a result of practice but gradually declines and plateaus, with further, repeated practice (DeKeyser, 2007; Verspoor et al., 2008). Second, stabilization can stem from the initiation of mental activity, as can occur, for instance, in stage two of the well-documented U-shaped learning whereby learning behavior (a) starts out being targetlike as a function of mechanic imitation of stimuli, (b) then turns non-targetlike as a result of inception of a chain of analytic processes, and (c) eventually becomes targetlike again as a result of successful restructuring of mental representations. Finally, a third scenario of surface stabilization is that it can be a result of fossilization, in which case learning has ceased prematurely. Detection and differentiation of these different types of surface stabiliza-tions can be challenging but not impossible. For example, applying multivariate statistical analysis to the data can determine whether learning has indeed come to a halt, as Berdan (1996) has demonstrated. In his reanalysis of Schumann's data using a statistical procedure called logistic regression, Berdan showed that "Alberto is in the process of acquiring negation" (p. 206), one of the structures that Schumann had adjudicated as fossilized. The change was non-dramatic, for sure, but "incontrovertible" (p. 237). It thus seems that what Alberto experienced was not fossilization, but rather, slow learning (see, however, Verspoor et al., 2008).[2] Clearly, how to accurately determine fossilization remains a methodological challenge.

The stabilization/fossilization intricacy is compounded by another phenomenon which Long (2003) has referred to as "volatility." Long's concern is counter-evidence: What constitutes counter-evidence to claims of fossilization? He argues that stabilization and variation are mutually exclusive (cf., Birdsong, 1999). Other researchers, such as Schachter (1996), Lardiere (2007), and Han (2004a, 2006), have argued and demonstrated that there can be fossilized variation.

Unlike the studies conducted in the 1970s and the early 1980s which focused on early- stage, untutored learners, fossilization research conducted in the mid-1980s through the mid-1990s turned its attention to instructed learners. In most cases, researchers would employ corrective feedback as a strategy to gauge fossilization, reasoning that if the efficacy is nil to low for the perceptually persistent interlanguage forms, then those forms may have fossilized (see, e.g., Lin, 1995; Mukattash, 1986; Schouten, 1996; Thep-Ackrapong, 1990; Washburn, 1991). Studies of this nature were liable to the same criticisms leveled at the earlier studies in that they, too, did not ensure that the subjects had been learning under exogenously and endogenously favorable conditions. Furthermore, they operated on premises about corrective feedback that current research has proven false. For example, it was tacitly assumed that corrective feedback is a one-way process involving transactions from a giver to a receiver, and/or that corrective feedback should be equally effective for every linguistic feature.

Since the mid-1990s, researchers have gradually moved away from early-stage learners to so-called endstate learners, that is, learners who, as defined by White (2003a), "have completed their L2 acquisition" and who are "no longer L2 learners but, rather, bilingual (or multilingual) speakers or users of the L2" (p. 241). Two types of endstate learners have been examined thus far: those who have reached a high level of proficiency and subsequently had extended immersion, and those who have been long-term residents (five–ten years), in the target language society but who nevertheless have not reached a high level of proficiency. Because the three preconditions (i.e., input, motivation, and opportunity for practice) can be quite safely assumed with either type of endstate learners, they, arguably, offer the best testing ground for fossilization: Whatever deviance can be found in them is most likely to have persisted for a long time and least likely to change (cf., Sorace, 2003).

Studies focusing on endstate learners are generally either longitudinal or non-longitudinal. The longitudinal studies tend to last longer (≥ten years) than their counterparts in the early days (≤two years). One such study can be found in Lardiere (1998), a single case study lasting nearly ten years focusing on a subject named Patty. A native speaker of Chinese, Patty had resided in the USA for 18 years and was married to a native speaker of American English, the target language. Interview data were collected at three points over time, and the analytical focus was on Patty's use of pronominal case marking and past-tense inflectional morphology. Obligatory analysis with frequency counts over time provided indisputable evidence of fossilization, importantly, as a local phenomenon: Patty's past-tense marking in an eight-year period. However, her pronominal marking was fully target-like. (For analysis of other aspects of Patty's grammar and similar findings, see Lardiere, 2007.)

Unlike the studies undertaken in the 1970s and 1980s, a marked methodological development in the more recent longitudinal studies is the variegation of data. Instead of relying on one type of data, researchers employ a combination of multiple data types, including, but not limited to, natural and clinically elicited samples of learner production (Ellis and Barkhuizen, 2005). For instance, in Han (2000, 2006, 2010) naturalistic writings were sampled from the case subject(s) over time and, concurrently, data were elicited via translation and acceptability judgment tasks. Thus, multiple perspectives were staged for co-constructing and/or co-verifying evidence of fossilization and for elucidating its nature and etiology.

The majority of the contemporary studies on endstate learners are, distinctly, non-longitudinal (see, e.g., Coppieters, 1987; Franceschina, 2005; Hopp, 2004; Liu, 2007; Montrul, 2002; Papp, 2000; Sorace, 1993) and controlled. They typically focus on very advanced learners or so-called "near-native speakers," that is, L2 learners who "have reached a level of surface equivalence with native speakers in language use and proficiency" (Coppieters, 1987, p. 547), using nonlinguistic data such as acceptability judgments and reaction times (Ellis and Barkhuizen, 2005). Sorace (1993), for example, explored near-natives' intuitions regarding constructions associated with Italian unaccusatives, using a methodological procedure called magnitude estimation whereby groups of native speakers of French and English who were near-native speakers of Italian were asked to assign numerical ratings to 48 sentences presented to them one by one, based on their perception of the relative acceptability of each sentence to its previous sentence. The results, similar to those reported from the longitudinal studies, indicated differential attainment, with fossilization being local rather than global.

Overall, research on endstate learners to date has seen an expansion of its scope from morphosyntactic features to phonological features and from mental representations to processing. Liu (2007), for instance, examined phonological recoding in Chinese character recognition by near-native speakers/readers of Chinese. The study had an experimental design that allowed comparisons of native speakers and near-natives vis-à-vis the lexical processing procedure (i.e., how and what types of information are activated during word processing and semantic integration), in particular, the activation of tonal information in processing Chinese characters. Lexical decision and semantic judgment tasks were administered to both the native and the near-native speakers of Chinese. Results showed similarities as well as qualitative and quantitative differences. For example, while both groups activated phonetic information to assist their decoding of Chinese characters and semantic integration of characters at the sentence level, the natives outperformed the near-natives both in terms of efficiency and accuracy, and where qualitative difference is concerned, the natives activated tonal (phonological) information but the near-natives either did not activate it or activated it late. This study was the first to document fossilization in lexical processing.

In summary, research on fossilization has undergone steady and substantive changes over the last four decades. The changes are most visible in the population chosen for study and in the types of data sampled. Importantly, over the years there has been increasing effort to ensure that the selected subjects meet the preconditions of input, motivation, and practice opportunity. The studies so far have collectively shown that fossilization is local and selective, affecting certain domains and/or subsystems only.

Applications

Research on fossilization, though seemingly accentuating a negative aspect of SLA, nevertheless has unique and critical contributions to make to L2 pedagogy. First and foremost, it dispels a long-held assumption that instruction is necessary and helpful, regardless, suggesting, instead, that instruction is helpful sometimes, under certain conditions, and in relation to certain linguistic elements (see, e.g., Han, 2001). Importantly, research on fossilization has pointed to a need to differentiate in SLA study between learning and acquisition (Krashen, 1981); while everything may be learnable, not everything can be acquirable. In this case, acquisition or success is defined as the ability to use language accurately, fluently, and appropriately (cf., Bailey and Tarone, Chapter 3, this volume). Instruction, and explicit instruction, in particular, as delimited by understandings drawn from fossilization research, should subsequently target those that are amenable to it and ignoring those that are not. More specifically, it should focus on those that are explicable via simple, surface rules, giving less attention to those that are not. Though still largely an empirical question, it would seem from extant research that the efficacy of instruction may improve if done implicitly vis-à-vis features bearing complex form-meaning-function relations (see, however, Hulstijn and de Graaff, 1994). In brief, effective instruction should be differential, varying according to the nature of learner difficulty in relation to different features of the target language.

Findings from existing research on fossilization highlight two sets of morphosyntactic features as hard to acquire and to which instruction is not or only partially useful: (1) interface features (Sorace, 2005) closely interacting with semantics and pragmatics, for example, verbs of causative alternation in English or the topic-comment construction in Chinese and (2) grammatical morphemes and functors, such as nominal declensions, verbal inflections, and articles, which encode abstract concepts such as definiteness, tense, and aspect. These features are largely immune to instruction, even though, ironically, they tend to receive most attention in the classroom. The learning of these features requires rich and consistent exposure to contextualized, naturalistic input, something that classroom instruction typically falls short of.

Instruction can sometimes promote or induce fossilization, as demonstrated in fossilization research (see e.g., Han, 2001). Inadequacies in input quality and quantity, pedagogical procedures, and/or opportunities for communicative practice can singly or in combination engender premature stabilization of interlanguage features (cf., Han, 2004a), in which case stabilization may become a harbinger of fossilization. SLA research on classroom learning over the past four decades has produced and reverberated a clear message for teachers, namely that instructional capacity is limited for stimulating acquisition, due largely to the inherent limitations of the classroom, and yet it can be boosted when combined with experience-based learning in naturalistic environments (see, e.g., DeKeyser, 2007; Rifkin, 2005).

Teachers in the past have manifested two polarizing attitudes toward fossilization. While some have embraced it whole-heartedly and thereby have been overgenerous in applying the term to an array of errors including those that either have not fossilized or may never fossilize by a standard interpretation of fossilization, others have shied away from it, refusing to believe that there can ever be such a thing as no learning and therefore to do anything about any potential incidences of fossilization. Clearly, neither attitude helps learning. Fossilization research drives home the message for teachers that it does matter if the teacher has or has no understanding of fossilization: Knowledge would lead to efforts to maximize learning while entertaining realistic expectations about the learning outcome, whereas ignorance would lead to use of non-differentiated strategies, which diminishes rather than enhances learning.

Future directions

Even though fossilization has garnered considerable attention from researchers over the past four decades and a general understanding has been formed about its nature and scope, much of it remains to be explored and substantiated, both empirically and theoretically. As is clear from the discussion in this chapter and elsewhere, the L2 literature on fossilization, though substantially ameliorated in the last 15 years, has for long exhibited an imbalance between data and explanations, with explanations outstripping the empirical data, a scenario which Han and Odlin (2006) have depicted as the "fossilization flip-flop," i.e., explanation before description (cf., Byrnes, Chapter 31, this volume). Therefore, it is necessary that future empirical research continue to build the descriptive database, abiding by the three preconditions for subject sampling, namely, exposure to input, motivation, and opportunity for communicative practice. A longitudinal approach should serve as the primary methodology, for, as Long (2003; cf., Selinker and Han, 2001) has compellingly argued, there is no substitute for it when it comes to empirically determining fossilization (for discussion on duration of longitudinal research, see Han, 2004b). In the meantime, multiple types of data must be sought for greater validity and reliability of the research findings. Only when an adequate database is in place can any theoretical work become meaningful and useful.

On the theoretical front, in spite of the abundance of explanations available in the literature, there have been few attempts to *systematically* explain fossilization (see, e.g, Selinker and Lakshmanan, 1992), and virtually none for both fossilization and acquisition. The overwhelming majority of the existing accounts are random, *post hoc*, atomistic, and non-generalizable. In Han (2004a), about 50 such explanations were listed exhausting almost every factor relevant to language acquisition. However, with insights on fossilization permeating the entire SLA literature, and more importantly, with substantially increased amount of robust descriptive evidence, the time is now ripe for performing theoretical analysis of existing findings relating to fossilization as well as acquisition and to construct hypotheses that can guide further empirical research.

Future research must also strive to substantiate the current understanding of issues, among them (a) the relationship between instruction and fossilization and (b) the idiosyncratic nature of fossilization. Concerning instruction and fossilization, it would be a desirable goal, among others, for fossilization research to not only identify features that do not seem amenable to any kind of instruction, but also build gravity indices for the fossilizable features. Such types of information would prove invaluable to teachers and materials writers, as they can use the research-based information to help organize teaching and select implementation strategies. With respect to the idiosyncratic nature of fossilization, while much has been said about fossilization being intra-learner, which gradually has led to the assumption of fossilization as an individual difference phenomenon, the fact has often been overlooked that where fossilizable features are concerned, there is a great deal of commonality across learners. For example, where L2 acquisition of English articles is concerned, learners from miscellaneous L1 backgrounds tend to exhibit omission of articles in the following linguistic environments: when a noun is (a) modified by an adjective,

(b) in topic position, (c) representing a subsequent- (as opposed to first-) mention referent, and (d) when the referent object is in the immediate environment (for detailed discussion, see Trenkic, 2009). Teasing apart what is idiosyncratic from what is universal is important to achieving a finer-grained understanding of fossilization and its underlying mechanism.

Finally, future research must break new ground. This would require, on the one hand, going beyond the customary domains and units of investigation, such as surface forms, and on the other hand, examining fossilization alongside other major phenomena such as acquisition and attrition. Doing so would not only be theoretically compelling, if uncovering a unitary cognitive mechanism is a goal for SLA research, but also practically beneficial for understanding fossilization itself. As a Chinese saying goes, 触类旁通 (read as chu4 lei4 pang2 tong1), which can be glossed for this context as the following: A better understanding can be achieved of the issue at hand when looking beyond it and into other seemingly remote concerns.

Notes

* I thank the editors and the anonymous reviewers for their insightful comments on an earlier version of this chapter. Any errors are exclusively my own.

1 The logical problem in foreign language learning refers to an overall lack of success in L2 learning, which, in Bely-Vroman's recent formulation, is manifested across the board as (a) lack of reliability (gap between the interlanguage grammar and the grammar underlying the target language input) and (b) lack of convergence (incongruence between individuals' interlanguage grammars).

2 A reanalysis of Cancino et al. (1978) by Verspoor et al. (2008) indicates no change in Alberto's use of negation strategies. This raises an interesting question: Could the reported changes or lack thereof have been artifacts of statistical analysis?

References

Agnello, F. (1977). Exploring the pidginization hypothesis: A study of three fossilized negation systems. In A. Henning (Ed.), *Proceedings of the Los Angeles second language research forum* (pp. 224–234). Los Angeles, CA: University of California at Los Angeles.

Allwright, D. and Bailey, K. (1991). *Focus on the language classroom*. Cambridge: Cambridge University Press.

Berdan, R. (1996). Disentangling language acquisition from language variation. In R. Bayley and D. Preston (Eds.), *Second language acquisition and linguistic variation* (pp. 203–244). Amsterdam: Benjamins.

Birdsong, D. (1999). Introduction: Whys and why nots of the critical period hypothesis for second language acquisition. In D. Birdsong (Ed.), *Second language acquisition and the critical period hypothesis* (pp. 1–22). Mahwah, NJ: Lawrence Erlbaum Associates.

Birdsong, D. (2004). Second language acquisition and ultimate attainment. In A. Davies and C. Elder (Eds.), *The handbook of applied linguistics* (pp. 82–105). Oxford: Blackwell.

Birdsong, D. (2006). Why not fossilization. In Z. -H. Han and T. Odlin (Eds.), *Studies of fossilization in second language acquisition* (pp. 173–188). Clevedon, UK: Multilingual Matters.

Bley-Vroman, R. (1983). The comparative fallacy in interlanguage studies: The case of systematicity. *Language Learning, 33*(1), 1–17.

Bley-Vroman, R. (1989). What is the logical problem of foreign language learning? In S. Gass and J. Schachter (Eds.), *Linguistic perspectives on second language acquisition* (pp. 41–68). Cambridge: Cambridge University Press.

Bley-Vroman, R. (2009). The evolving context of the fundamental difference hypothesis. *Studies in Second Language Acquisition, 31* [Special issue 02], 175–198.

Cancino, E., Rosansky, E., and Schumann, J. (1978). The acquisition of English negative and interrogatives by native Spanish speakers. In E. Hatch (Ed.), *Second language acquisition*. Rowley, MA: Newbury House.

Cook, V. (1992). Evidence for multi-competence. *Language Learning, 42*(4), 557–591.

Cook, V. (1999). Going beyond the native speaker in language teaching. *TESOL Quarterly, 33*(2), 185–207.

Cook, V. (2008). Multi-competence: Black hole or wormhole for second language acquisition research. In Z. H. Han (Ed.), *Understanding second language process* (pp. 16–26). Clevedon, UK: Multilingual Matters.

Coppieters, R. (1987). Competence differences between native and near-native speakers. *Language*, *63*(3), 544–573.

Davies, A. (2003). *The native speaker: Myth and reality*. Clevedon, UK: Multilingual Matters.

DeKeyser, R. (2007). Study abroad as foreign language practice. In R. Dekeyser (Ed.), *Practicing in a second language: Perspectives from applied linguistics and cognitive psychology* (pp. 208–226). New York: Cambridge University Press.

Ellis, N. C. (2006). Selective attention and transfer phenomena in L2 acquisition: Contingency, cue competition, salience, interference, overshadowing, blocking, and perceptual learning. *Applied Linguistics*, *27*(2), 164–194.

Ellis, R. (1985). *Understanding second language acquisition*. Oxford: Oxford University Press.

Ellis, R. and Barkhuizen, G. (2005). *Analyzing learner language*. Oxford: Oxford University Press.

Franceschina, F. (2005). *Fossilized second language grammars: The acquisition of grammatical gender* (Vol. *38*). Amsterdam: John Benjamins.

Gass, S. and Selinker, L. (2008). *Second language acquisition: An introductory course* (Third Edition). New York: Routledge.

Han, Z.-H. (1998). *Fossilization: An investigation into advanced L2 learning of a typologically distant language*. Unpublished doctoral dissertation. University of London, London, UK.

Han, Z.-H. (2000). Persistence of the implicit influence of NL: The case of the pseudo-passive. *Applied Linguistics*, *21*(1), 78–105.

Han, Z.-H. (2001). Fine-tuning corrective feedback. *Foreign Language Annals*, *34*(6), 582–599.

Han, Z.-H. (2004a). *Fossilization in adult second language acquisition*. Clevedon, UK: Multilingual Matters.

Han, Z.-H. (2004b). Fossilization: Five central issues. *International Journal of Applied Linguistics*, *14*(2), 212–242.

Han, Z.-H. (2004c). To be a native speaker means not to be a non-native speaker. *Second Language Research*, *20*(2), 166–187.

Han, Z.-H. (2006). Fossilization: Can grammaticality judgment be a reliable source of evidence? In Z.-H. Han and T. Odlin (Eds.), *Studies of fossilization in second language acquisition* (pp. 56–82). Clevedon, UK: Multilingual Matters.

Han, Z.-H. (2008). On the role of meaning in focus on form. In Z.-H. Han (Ed.), *Understanding second language process* (pp. 45–79). Clevedon, UK: Multilingual Matters.

Han, Z.-H. (2009). Interlanguage and fossilization: Towards an analytic model. In V. Cook and L. Wei (Eds.), *Contemporary applied linguistics* (pp. 137–162). London: Continuum.

Han, Z.-H. (2010). Grammatical morpheme inadequacy as a function of linguistic relativity: A longitudinal study. In Z.-H. Han and T. Cadierno (Eds.), *Linguistic relativity in second language acquisition: Evidence of L1 thinking for speaking* (pp. 154–182). Clevedon, UK: Multilingual Matters.

Han, Z.-H., and Odlin, T. (2006). Introduction. In Z.-H. Han and T. Odlin (Eds.), *Studies of fossilization in second language acquisition* (pp. 1–20). Clevedon, UK: Multilingual Matters.

Han, Z.-H., and Selinker, L. (2005). Fossilization in L2 learners. In E. Hinkel (Ed.), *Handbook of research in second language teaching and learning* (pp. 455–470). Mahwah, NJ: Lawrence Erlbaum.

Hawkins, R. (2000). Persistent selective fossilization in second language acquisition and the optimal design of the language faculty. *Essex Research Reports in Linguistics*, *34*, 75–90.

Herschensohn, J. (2009). Fundamental and gradient differences in language development. *Studies in Second Language Acquisition*, *31*, 259–289.

Hopp, H. (2004). Constraining L2 word order optionality: Scrambling in advanced English-German and Japanese-German interlanguage. *Second Language Research*, *25*(1), 34–71.

Hulstijn, J. and de Graaff, R. (1994). Under what conditions does explicit knowledge of a second language facilitate the acquisition of implicit knowledge? A research proposal. *AILA Review*, *11*, 97–112.

Hyltenstam, K. (1988). Lexical characteristics of near-native second language learners of Swedish. *Journal of Multilingual and Multicultural Development*, *9*, 67–84.

Hyltenstam, K. and Abrahamsson, N. (2003). Maturational constraints in SLA. In C. Doughty and M. Long (Eds.), *The Handbook of second language acquisition* (pp. 539–588). Oxford: Blackwell.

Ioup, G., Boustagui, E., El Tigi, M., and Moselle, M. (1994). Reexamining the critical period hypothesis: A case study of successful adult SLA in a naturalistic environment. *Studies in Second Language Acquisition*, *16*(1), 73–98.

Jordan, G. (2004). *Theory construction in second language acquisition*. Amsterdam: John Benjamins.

Kellerman, E. (1989). The imperfect conditional: Fossilization, cross-linguistic influence and natural tendencies in a foreign language setting. In K. Hyltenstam and L. Obler (Eds.), *Bilingualism across life span* (pp. 87–115). Cambridge: Cambridge University Press.

Krashen, S. (1981). *Second language acquisition and second language learning*. Oxford: Pergamon.

Lardiere, D. (1998). Case and tense in the "fossilized" steady state. *Second Language Research*, *14*(1), 1–26.

Lardiere, D. (2003). Revisiting the comparative fallacy: A reply to Lakshmanan and Selinker, 2001. *Second Language Research*, *19*(2), 129–143.

Lardiere, D. (2007). *Ultimate attainment in second language acquisition: A Case Study*. Mahwah, NJ: Lawrence Erlbaum.

Larsen-Freeman, D. (2001). Teaching grammar. In M. Celce-Murcia (Ed.), *Teaching English as a second or foreign language* (Third Edition). (pp. 251–266). Boston: Heinle and Heinle.

Larsen-Freeman, D. (2006). Second language acquisition and the issue of fossilization: There is no end, and there is no state. In Z.-H. Han and T. Odlin (Eds.), *Studies of fossilization in second language acquisition* (pp. 189–200). Clevedon, UK: Multilingual Matters.

Lenneberg, E. (1967). *Biological foundations of language*. New York: Wiley.

Lin, Y.-H. (1995). *An empirical analysis of stabilization/fossilization: Incorporation and self-correction of Chinese learners*. Unpublished doctoral dissertation. Barcelona University, Spain.

Liu, Y.-T. (2007). *Phonological recoding in sentence-level Chinese character recognition by successful adult L2 Chinese learners*. Unpublished doctoral dissertation. Teachers College, Columbia University, New York.

Long, M. (1990). Maturational constraints on language development. *Studies in Second Language Acquisition*, *12*, 251–285.

Long, M. (2003). Stabilization and fossilization in interlanguage development. In C. Doughty and M. Long (Eds.), *The handbook of second language acquisition* (pp. 487–536). Oxford: Blackwell.

Long, M. (2005). Problems with supposed counter-evidence to the critical period hypothesis. *International Review of Applied Linguistics and Language Teaching*, *43*, 287–317.

MacWhinney, B. (2006). Emergent fossilization. In Z.-H. Han and T. Odlin (Eds.), *Studies of fossilization in second language acquisition* (pp. 134–156). Clevedon, UK: Multilingual Matters.

Montrul, S. (2002). Incomplete acquisition and attrition of Spanish tense/aspect distinctions in adult bilinguals. *Bilingualism: Language and Cognition*, *5*(1), 39–68.

Montrul, S. and Slabakova, R. (2003). Competence similarities between native and near-native speakers: An investigation of the preterit-imperfect contrast in Spanish. *Studies in Second Language Acquisition*, *25*(3), 351–398.

Mukattash, L. (1986). Persistence of fossilization. *International Review of Applied Linguistics in Language Teaching*, *14*(3), 187–203.

Papp, S. (2000). Stable and developmental optionality in native and non-native Hungarian grammar. *Second Language Research*, *16*(2), 173–200.

Perdue, C. (1993). *Adult language acquisition: Cross-linguistic perspectives*. Cambridge: Cambridge University Press.

Rifkin, B. (2005). A ceiling effect in traditional classroom foreign language instruction: Data from Russian. *The Modern Language Journal*, *89*(1), 623–646.

Romero Trillo, J. (2002). The pragmatic fossilization of discourse markers in non-native speakers of English. *Journal of Pragmatics*, *34*, 769–784.

Schachter, J. (1996). Learning and triggering in adult L2 acquisition. In G. Brown, K. Malmkjaer, and J. Williams (Eds.), *Performance and competence in SLA* (pp. 70–88). Cambridge: Cambridge University Press.

Schmidt, R. W. (1983). Interaction, acculturation, and the acquisition of communicative competence: A case study of an adult. In N. Wolfson and E. Judd (Eds.), *Sociolinguistics and language acquisition* (pp. 137–174). Rowley, MA: Newbury House.

Schmidt, R. (1984). The strengths and limitations of acquisition: A case study of an untutored language learner. *Language, Learning, and Communication*, *3*, 1–16.

Schouten, E. (1996). Crosslinguistic influence and the expression of hypothetical meaning. In E. Kellerman, B. Weltens, and T. Bongaerts (Eds.), *EUROSLA 6: A selection of papers. Toegepaste taalwetenschap in artikelen (Applied linguistics in article form)* (Vol. 55, pp. 161–174). Amsterdam: VU Uitgeverij.

Schumann, J. (1978). *The pidginization process: A model for second language acquisition*. Rowley, MA: Newbury House.

Schumann, J. (1986). Research on the acculturation model for second language acquisition. *Journal of Multilingual and Multicultural Development*, *7*(5), 379–392.

Selinker, L. (1972). Interlanguage. *International Review of Applied Linguistics*, *10*(2), 209–231.

Selinker, L. and Han, Z.-H. (2001). Fossilization: Moving the concept into empirical longitudinal study. In C. Elder, A. Brown, E. Grove, K. Hill, N. Iwashita, T. Lumpley, T. McNamara, and K. O'Loughlin

(Eds.), *Studies in language testing: Experimenting with uncertainty* (pp. 276–291). Cambridge: Cambridge University Press.

Selinker, L. and Lakshmanan, U. (1992). Language transfer and fossilization: The multiple effects principle. In S. M. Gass and L. Selinker (Eds.), *Language transfer in language learning* (pp. 190–216). Philadelphia: John Benjamins.

Selinker, L. and Lamendella, J. (1978). Two perspectives on fossilization in interlanguage learning. *Interlanguage Studies Bulletin, 3*(2), 143–191.

Selinker, L. and Lamendella, J. (1979). The role of extrinsic feedback in interlanguage fossilization: A discussion of "rule fossilization: A tentative model". *Language Learning, 29*(2), 363–375.

Shapira, R. (1978). The non-learning of English: Case study of an adult. In E. Hatch (Ed.), *Second language acquisition: A book of readings*. MA: Newbury House: Rowley.

Sharwood Smith, M. (1994). *Second language learning: Theoretical foundations*. Harlow: Longman.

Sorace, A. (1993). Incomplete vs. divergent representations of unaccusativity in non-native grammars of Italian. *Second Language Research, 9*(1), 22–47.

Sorace, A. (2003). Near-nativeness. In C. Doughty and M. Long (Eds.), *The handbook of second language acquisition* (pp. 130–151). Oxford: Blackwell.

Sorace, A. (2005). Selective optionality in language development. In L. Cornips and K. Corrigan (Eds.), *Syntax and variation: Reconciling the biological and the social* (pp. 111–160). Amsterdam: John Benjamins.

Stauble, A. (1978). Acculturation and second language acquisition. In R. Scarcella and S. Krashen (Eds.), *Research in second language acquisition* (pp. 43–50). Rowley, MA: Newbury House.

Tarone, E. (1994). Interlanguage. In R. E. Asher (Ed.), *The encyclopedia of language and linguistics* (Vol. 4, pp. 1715–1719). Oxford: Pergamon.

Tarone, E., Frauenfelder, U., and Selinker, L. (1976). Systematicity/variability and stability/instability in interlanguage systems. *Language Learning, 4*, 93–134.

Thep-Ackrapong, T. (1990). *Fossilization: A case study of practical and theoretical parameters*. Unpublished doctoral dissertation. Illinois State University, Normal, IL.

Towell, R. and Hawkins, R. (1994). *Approaches to second language acquisition*. Clevedon, UK: Multilingual Matters.

Trenkic, D. (2009). Accounting for patterns of article omissions and substitutions in second language production. In R. Hawkins and M. P. G. Mayo (Eds.), *Second language acquisition of articles: Empirical findings and theoretical implications* (pp. 115–143). Amsterdam: John Benjamins.

VanPatten, B. and Williams, J. (Eds.). (2007). *Theories in second language acquisition: An introduction*. Mahwah, NJ: Lawrence Erlbaum Associates.

Verspoor, M., Lowie, W., and van Dijk, M. (2008). Variability in L2 development from a dynamic systems perspective. *The Modern Language Journal, 92*, 214–231.

Vigil, N. and Oller, J. (1976). Rule fossilization: A tentative model. *Language Learning, 26*(2), 281–295.

Washburn, G. (1991). *Fossilization in second language acquisition: A Vygotskian perspective*. Unpublished doctoral dissertation. University of Pennsylvania, Philadelphia, PA.

White, L. (2003a). *Second language acquisition and universal grammar*. Cambridge: Cambridge University Press.

White, L. (2003b). Fossilization in steady state L2 grammars: Persistent problems with inflectional morphology. *Bilingualism: Language and Cognition, 6*, 129–141.

White, L. and Genesee, F. (1996). How native is near-native? The issue of ultimate attainment in adult second language acquisition. *Second Language Research, 12*(3), 233–265.

30

Heritage languages and L2 learning

Olga Kagan and Kathleen Dillon

Historical discussion

The heritage language field began developing in the late 1990s, and "the recognition of heritage language learners as a variable in second language research is recent" (Gass and Selinker, 2008, p. 23). A coherent, commonly held theory of Heritage Language Acquisition (HLA) has yet to be formulated. Scholars in countries where immigrant populations have sought formal study of their home language continue to define the term and the field itself. Since our expertise is largely limited to US issues, we will refer to heritage languages in the USA, but we think that many of the principles are also applicable to home/community language learners in the growing number of other countries with large immigrant populations. In this chapter we focus on heritage language learners (HLLs), that is those speakers of heritage languages who choose to study their home language in a K–16 setting. (In the USA K–16 refers to the primary, secondary, and tertiary levels of education.) We discuss the most commonly used definitions of HLLs, and we situate heritage language discussion in a historical context, within the framework of research on bilingualism and second language acquisition (SLA) as well as instructional practices. We then examine how heritage language (HL) teaching over the past 10–15 years has been tied to an increase in immigration and changing immigration patterns, which have presented the challenge of offering instruction in a "foreign" language to students who already speak that language at home. We describe who these learners are, how they are different from other language learners, and what kind of research has been done to determine their key characteristics. Finally, we recommend some research-based approaches to HL instruction.

The term

The term "heritage language" originated in Canada (Cummins, 2005, p. 585), where it has since been replaced by the term "home-background" language. Australians use the term "community languages" (Lo Bianco, 2008), and in Europe "heritage languages" are referred to as "immigrant," "home," "regional," and "minority" languages (Regional and minority languages may not be considered to be heritage languages in the USA. This is an example of the varying uses and understandings of the term "heritage." In many countries the term "community languages" is the equivalent of "heritage languages" in the USA). (European Commission: Multilingualism, available at http://ec.europa.eu/education/languages/languages-of-europe/doc139_en.htm.)

In Scandinavian countries, dramatic changes in immigration patterns from distant parts of the world have greatly increased their populations' ethnic diversity. Legislation related to mother-tongue instruction guarantees support for first language maintenance and development in the schools to children who speak languages other than the majority language (Hyltenstam, 2002, p. 2120).

Australia has instituted a national policy on languages and has established more than 1,000 community language schools that provide maintenance in 69 languages to more than 100,000 school-age children. Nevertheless, "[t]he family remains for most immigrants and their offspring the main domain for community language use," and therefore much of Australian research on community languages focuses on the family (Pauwels, 2005, p. 124).

In the USA, the term "heritage language" first entered general use after it appeared in the *Standards for foreign language learning in the 21st century* (National Standards in Foreign Language Education Project, 2006.) (Valdes (2001). Despite the argument by some critics (Hornberger, 2005) that the word "heritage" points backward instead of forward, the term has firmly taken root. It is commonly understood that the concept refers to those who live in homes where a language other than English is spoken, but scholars continue to seek more comprehensive explications. For the remainder of this section we chronologically outline the progression of viewpoints on defining the term "heritage." In the section Core Issues below, we examine the interface between the terms "bilinguals" and "heritage speakers."

Definitions

The most frequently quoted definition, which focuses on measurable proficiencies, is from Valdés (2000), who describes heritage speakers as "individuals raised in homes where a language other than English is spoken and who are to some degree bilingual in English and the heritage language." Fishman (2001, p. 81) offers a much broader definition of heritage language as a language of "particular family relevance to the learners."

Polinsky and Kagan (2007) propose paired definitions of HLLs that have direct implications for instruction: broad and narrow. The broad definition applies to those learners who have been raised with a strong cultural connection to a particular language, usually through family interaction (cf., Fishman, 2001; Van Deusen-Scholl, 2003), but who may not be able to speak or comprehend the language. The narrow definition applies to those who were exposed to a particular language in childhood but did not learn it to full capacity because another language became dominant. These latter learners are somewhat proficient in the language, predominantly in speaking and listening (cf., Valdés, 2000), but typically with limited vocabulary and mostly informal register. Heritage learners of the broad definition may differ from second language (L2) learners in their motivation and familiarity with the culture but may not differ in terms of proficiencies. Gass and Selinker (2008) argue that "[f]or research into [heritage] language acquisition, an important issue is the exposure and use of the language in childhood" (p. 23). Expressing support for the term, Lee and Suarez (2009) propose that while in some cases "heritage" expresses a relationship to the language similar to terms like "primary language, home language, mother tongue, first language," it can also "represent a wider spectrum of relationships that linguistic minorities have with a language irrespective of the level of linguistic proficiency" (p. 138).

Development of the field

The vast influx of immigrants to the USA and to many other developed countries beginning in the 1990s had an almost immediate impact on foreign language (FL) classrooms. The pedagogical concerns of teachers of a broad spectrum of languages drove the development of research and pedagogy aimed at this new population of learners.

Landmark events in the development of the heritage language field include:

- 1999—The Center for Applied Linguistics convened the first heritage language conference, "Heritage Languages in America," in Long Beach, CA. The conference underscored the pressing need to design K-16 heritage language programs and to develop multi-disciplinary research that would inform new curricula. Selected papers from the conference were published as "Heritage Languages in America: Preserving a National Resource" (Peyton *et al.*, 2001).
- 2000—The UCLA "Heritage Language Research Priorities Conference" proposed a definition of a heritage learner that underscored the contrast between HLLs and foreign language learners (FLLs), stressing that heritage language learning begins in the home while FL learning typically starts in the classroom (UCLA Steering Committee, 2000).
- 2002—The Center for Applied Linguistics sponsored "Heritage Language in America: The Second National Conference." It aimed to "develop public awareness of the economic, personal, and social benefits of proficiency in heritage languages and promote the inclusion of heritage language issues in the national dialog; to shape a national heritage language policy and share information on best practices; to develop collaboration among all constituent groups; and to devise a plan for moving from rhetoric to action."
- 2006—The US Department of Education deemed the heritage language field important enough to fund the National Heritage Language Resource Center (NHLRC), one of 15 national language resources centers (NLRCs). While the other centers may dedicate some of their efforts to heritage language education, NHLRC is the only one whose mission is to promote and improve heritage language education through research, professional development, curriculum, and materials design.
- Since 2007, the NHLRC has conducted annual Summer Heritage Research Institutes and workshops for HL teachers, and has provided funding for the development of materials.
- February 2010—The first international conference on heritage/community languages, sponsored by NHLRC, was held at UCLA. It forged international collaborations, expanded the scope of research into heritage/community languages, and broadened understanding of issues facing researchers and educators around the world.

There are still few publications dedicated to heritage language education exclusively. The *Heritage Language Journal* began publication in 2003, and several volumes dedicated to heritage languages have been published in the past five years (Brinton *et al.*, 2008; He and Xiao, 2008; Kondo-Brown, 2006; Kondo-Brown and Brown, 2008).

Core issues

A number of linguists focus attention on the distinctions between "bilinguals" and "heritage speakers." The bilingual continuum outlined by Valdés (2000, p. 385) removes the HL and the dominant language from the "either a native speaker-or-not" dichotomy and situates the two in a constantly changing relationship, depending on the generation of immigration and the extent of HL use in daily life. Gass and Selinker (2008, p. 23) assert that "[h]eritage language acquisition is a form of second language acquisition and a form of bilingualism." There are many definitions and understandings of the term "bilingualism" and its interface with definitions and understandings of "heritage speakers."

By contrast, Colin Baker finds ambiguity between the two terms and underscores the complexity of defining a person or a community as bilingual by posing two fundamental questions: "Is someone bilingual if they are fluent in one language but less than fluent in their other language? Is someone multilingual if they rarely or never use one of their languages?" (Baker, 2006, p. 2) Based on our examination of the most current research on HLLs presented at the annual NHLRC Heritage Research Institutes, we conclude that HL speakers are in fact bilinguals because they grow up speaking two languages, even though they usually do so with different and shifting degrees of fluency. For that reason, much of their linguistic development can be analyzed through the lens of research into bilingualism. Heritage speakers are typically unbalanced bilinguals, that is, their proficiencies in the two languages are not equal, with the heritage language being the weaker of the two.

According to the NHLRC Heritage Language Learner Survey (NHLRC Survey, 2009), the majority of respondents speak their HL exclusively up to the age of five, though we can be fairly certain that there are many contexts where even at the pre-school age they interact to some degree with the dominant language (TV, accompanying their parents shopping, playing in the park, etc.) (Baker, 2006, p. 4–6). The NHLRC Survey also confirms that after the age of five, when children start school, use of the HL declines, though it does not disappear completely. Even if attending a community school or working with a tutor, HLLs do not benefit from full exposure to the language, because they are not fully immersed in it and, with rare exceptions, are not within an educational system where the language is used as an instrument of transmitting knowledge. The survey also indicates that college-age HLLs use a combination of heritage language and English with their families. They may watch TV in the HL and attend community events conducted in the HL. In any case, they do not seem to be cut off entirely from their HL. While this exposure and language access is less than that of their peers in the target language country, it is considerably more than L2 learners' access to language. We could thus place heritage learners on a continuum between native speakers and L2 learners. Benmamoun (2010) states that "[F]rom an acquisition point of view, heritage speakers are in some respects similar to native speakers in having been exposed to the target language early in childhood. However, they differ from native speakers in that their L1 exposure ... get[s] interrupted and [is] limited in its scope and domain (usually confined to the home and immediate family and community)."

Data and common elicitation measures

In this section we focus on HL research that most directly impacts HL education. HL research has employed the same methods that are commonly used in linguistic and SLA research (Doughty and Long, 2003; Gass and Mackey, 2007; Gass and Selinker, 2008; Larsen-Freeman and Long, 1991; Mackey and Gass, 2005). Research into HL acquisition only started in the late 1990s, and the body of research is not yet extensive. While proposed classroom-based studies (see Jessica Williams, Chapter 33, this volume) could make a real contribution to the field, they are not yet available.

The baseline comparison groups in most studies comprise either L2 learners, native speakers, or both. The studies are both quantitative and qualitative, and typically the number of respondents is not very high. In collecting data from HLLs, one needs to be especially aware that, for several reasons, responses are "dependent on external variables" (Gass and Mackey, 2007). HL speakers typically use their HL in restricted circumstances for informal interpersonal discourse in the home. They have not studied their HL formally and are not used to making linguistic judgments about their HL. Polinsky (2009) notes, for example, that grammaticality judgments are not a good elicitation technique with HLLs as they are unable to choose one form over another. Forced-elicitation techniques may not yield solid results either, once again because HL speakers are not sophisticated language users. Elicitation needs to be done within the naturalistic boundaries of a familiar context or genre, as in the examples that follow.

(1) The most widespread approach to HL research is analysis of written and oral errors collected in the classroom environment. Such studies are relatively easy to carry out and are very productive because they can help adjust the curriculum. Many researchers compare written and oral errors made by HLLs and their L2 peers on the same assignment. One such study by Xiao (2006) compares the performance of Chinese HLLs and non-HL students in the same class. Xiao's data indicate that, overall, the HLLs performed better than the L2 students on both the oral and written grammar portions of the midterm and final, but L2 students evidenced higher levels of achievement in some aspects. HLLs produced more characters on the essay part of the test, but they made more orthographic mistakes than the non-HLLs. While HLLs' performance was better on the SAT II grammar test, they "did not perform better than their non-heritage peers in reading comprehension, vocabulary learning, and character writing." Kagan and Friedman (2004) made similar findings in their study of Russian heritage speakers. Although these results offer valuable snapshots of students' proficiencies and linguistic gaps, they do not provide a complete picture.

While grammatical accuracy is important, it may not be the best indicator of HLL proficiency or linguistic knowledge. Valdés remarked (personal communication, April 2008) that researchers should spend less time analyzing mistakes and focus instead on drawing broader conclusions from comparisons of HLLs and L2s. Sekerina (2008) observes that accuracy is "the most common measure of HL speakers' linguistic performance, but [it] may mask the participant's level of ability and underestimate the HLL's capacity." These are important considerations for the development of classroom practices. Language instructors frequently focus on grammatical accuracy when they find HLLs in their classes. Such a focus is prompted by an illusion that HLLs are native speakers of the heritage language (cf., courses entitled "Spanish for Native Speakers" at many educational institutions) who just have some gaps in their knowledge of grammar. Kagan and Dillon (2004) and Kagan (2005) analyze Russian HLLs' knowledge and suggest conditions that would allow such speakers to reach high/professional proficiency in the language.

(2) Written tests and studies with intervention measures (Montrul, 2004, 2006; Montrul and Bowles, 2010; O'Grady *et al.*, 2001) typically target written language and compare the morphosyntax of HLLs and non-HLLs before and after an intervention. The results may be used as predictors of how well HLLs will be able to relearn the language and attain more advanced multiple-skill proficiency. Very few studies of this nature have been conducted so far, and they have not proved conclusive.

(3) A number of open-ended studies based on oral story telling (Isurina and Ivanova-Sullivan, 2008; Kagan and Friedman, 2004; Polinsky, 2008) target broad areas of HLLs' oral proficiency and reveal differences between HLLs, L2 learners, and native speakers. All three narration studies are based on Berman and Slobin's (1994) frog pictures. These pictures can be used by respondents of various ages and language competencies, and, because they elicit a large volume of text, can lead to a number of conclusions. For example, Polinsky (2008) used the "frog story" to compare the structure of a narrative by HL speakers and native speakers of Russian. She found lack of embeddings, loss of case marking, and inconsistent use of tenses. She also concluded that HL speakers have difficulty with lexical retrieval.

Isurina and Ivanova-Sullivan (2008) find that Russian HLLs "outperform English-speaking learners of Russian in such linguistic areas as the correct use of aspect/tense and cases, but they fall well behind the native speakers in these same areas." As in other studies (Friedman and Kagan, 2008) the authors find that HLLs' proficiency is situated somewhere between that of L2 learners and native speakers, confirming the collective conclusion that HLLs require a specific curriculum.

(4) Research into language retrieval is best represented by a multi-year project conducted by Au *et al.* (2008), which explores whether exposure to HL in early childhood has an impact on relearning for adult language learners. The study focuses on phonology and morphosyntax, because these are the two areas easily acquired in childhood but difficult for adult L2 learners to master. The data are gathered in several stages: preliminary questionnaires that include self-reports of language competency; interviews to corroborate speakers' proficiencies; a series of stimuli to which respondents have to react. The subjects in the study were two groups of Spanish and Korean heritage speakers, childhood overhearers (those who heard the language in early childhood but did not produce it) and early childhood speakers who stopped speaking the language before the age of seven. The goal was to determine whether early childhood experience helped HL speakers when they started relearning their heritage language as adults. Au and her co-authors have determined that when (re)learning the language in college, overhearers had an advantage over L2 learners in phonology, and those who used their HL till the age of seven had an advantage over overhearers both in phonology and on grammar measures, even though their performance did not equal that of native speakers. The outcomes of Au's studies may have significant implications for teaching practices. Taking note of the patterns of early language use can deepen our understanding of HLLs' overall, if latent, competency.

(5) Surveys and questionnaires provide insight into HLLs' linguistic backgrounds, motivations, and identities. In fact, all studies of heritage speakers include some form of a questionnaire (Au, 2008; Montrul, 2006, 2008; Polinsky, 2000, 2006). Many surveys ask the respondents to self-rate their language proficiencies. The largest current set of survey data, gathered from 1,700 college-level HLLs, is available from a project of the NHLRC (Carreira and Kagan, 2011) and reveals some language specific characteristics of HLLs, as well as similarities and differences across languages. For example, it reveals that 70 percent of respondents were born in the USA. That fact dispels the myth that HLLs are foreigners who are in fact native speakers of the language and need no instruction. The survey also confirms that the use of the HL declines significantly after the age of five, when respondents begin to use their home language in combination with English. The use of the HL in the home varies by language (for example, speakers of some languages indicate that they speak more HL with family than speakers of other languages). The survey also shows that most HLLs are motivated to pursue formal study of the language to learn about their cultural and linguistic roots, though Spanish and Chinese HLLs indicate career goals as their main reason for studying the language. Some of the survey's results and their curricular implications have been discussed in Kagan and Dillon (2009), and in a more extensive study (Carreira and Kagan, 2011). The survey report can be found on the NHLRC website.

(6) Anthropological/ethnographic studies, though few in number, are proving revelatory. One example is Friedberg's (2008) study of students from a Russian Pentecostal community in Oregon—fairly recent immigrants to the USA. By conducting interviews, analyzing essays, and participating in community events, Friedberg developed a sociolinguistic and socio-cultural portrait that illustrates how different a baseline the home language (Polinsky and Kagan, 2007) can be from the language expected by instructors, and from the language of what is generally considered "an educated native speaker." The study also points to the regional nature of HL experience. Even though Friedberg's respondents may have arrived in the USA at the same time as other immigrants from the former Soviet Union (Kagan and Dillon, 2010), they differ significantly from them because of their home environment. While other Russian HLLs typically lack higher speech registers, these speakers feel more comfortable with the language of the Bible than they do with contemporary standard Russian.

(7) Several studies have analyzed (Peyton *et al.*, 2001; Potowski, 2007; Potowski and Carreira, 2004; Wang and Green, 2001; Webb and Miller, 2000) and evaluated HLL programs (Lynch, 2008). Potowski (2003) and Potowski *et al.* (2008) conclude that bilingual Spanish-English programs in Chicago elementary schools do little for Spanish HLLs, because they do not distinguish between the needs of HLLs and L2 English speaking students. The authors propose a new and improved curriculum for the bilingual program that enrolls predominantly Spanish-speaking students. The new curriculum is based on earlier work by Potowski and Carreira (2004) who advocate a curriculum for HLLs that more closely resembles a language arts curriculum than the FL approach. The new curriculum takes into consideration national and local standards, and blends "English Language Arts standards, Foreign Language standards, and Content Area standards whenever possible." The curriculum stresses knowledge of Latino cultures in the USA and around the world, thus making community connections central, and use of community resources vital for the success of the program. This curriculum design situates HLLs at the intersection of first language (L1) and L2 language teaching, and builds on the knowledge they acquired from family and community, rather than viewing HLLs as deficient L2 learners. Similarly, Lynch (2008) recommends including community resources in program evaluation, since he believes that a solid heritage language program should strengthen students' ties to the community. To our knowledge, no such evaluation has yet been carried out by HLL or FLL programs.

Applications

SLA researchers and FL teachers continue to probe the question whether HLA is truly different from L2 acquisition. Lynch (2003) explores the putative difference, and suggests that "the heritage speakers who arrive to secondary and postsecondary classrooms seem not entirely L1 speakers or L2 speakers of the language in question." Lynch's point is the springboard for subsequent studies (Brinton *et al.*, 2008; He and Xiao, 2008; Kagan and Dillon, 2009; Kondo-Brown and Brown, 2007, 2008; Kondo-Brown, 2006) that concur in their findings that there are significant distinctions between HL, L1, and L2 speakers. The differences indicate the need for new approaches to instruction, based on the existing language skills of heritage learners as they enter the classroom, which will promote their attainment of higher levels of proficiency in their first but no longer dominant language.

Since 2000, when the UCLA Heritage Language Priorities Conference (UCLA Steering Committee (2000) mapped out the first directions for research into heritage languages, the accumulated research has laid the foundation for designing curricula aimed at HLLs. Researchers agree that the fundamental difference between L2 and HL learners is in proficiency at the onset of instruction. Montrul (2008) notes that most of the adult Spanish HLLs who grew up in the USA are at the Intermediate or Advanced level of oral proficiency in accordance with the ACTFL (American Council on the Teaching of Foreign Languages) Oral Proficiency Interview (OPI) rating (ACTFL, 1999). The high proficiency of Spanish HLLs can be explained by the large numbers of Spanish speakers in the community, the accessibility of Spanish language media, the proximity of Spanish-speaking countries, and continuing immigration that contributes to daily use of the language. The oral proficiency of learners of other languages may be somewhat lower (Intermediate-Low-Mid-to-Advanced in Kagan and Friedman, 2004 and Sohn and Shin, 2007). Nevertheless even that range of proficiency is higher than that of a typical L2 learner after several years of language study (Rifkin, 2002; Thompson, 2000).

HLLs are heterogeneous with varying levels of proficiency; nevertheless, a comparison of HLLs and L2 learners may allow us to summarize typical proficiencies as found in a college FL class.

Classroom experience and self-assessments by students (NHLRC Survey, 2009) indicate that listening is perceived to be and is in fact HLLs' strongest skill. It is typically followed by speaking, then reading and writing. As for subskills, an HLL's phonology is generally better than that of an L2 learner (Au, 2008; Godson, 2004). Vocabulary is extensive in comparison to L2 learners but is limited to the home realm and the interpersonal, informal register. Grammar comprehension is quite good on the average, but grammar production may be flawed (Schwartz, 2001). The language may display regional traits, dialectal features, and other non-academic, non-formal, non-prestige characteristics. Writing is typically phonetic (Bermel and Kagan, 2000), imprecise, and displays lack of register awareness or ability to use complex sentences (Friedman and Kagan, 2008). Although research is still at an early stage of development, it nevertheless offers us insights that can guide us in formulating heritage language curricula.

Foundations of a heritage language curriculum

We propose three major features that should form the basis of programs designed to meet the specific learning needs of HLLs and serve as foundations of a HL curriculum.

(1) Demographic and geographic relevance. HLLs are rooted in the community. Even a cursory glance at the Modern Language Association linguistic map (MLA, 1990) and US Census Bureau (US Census) data indicates that while speakers of all languages can be found in most areas of the USA, there are concentrations of speakers of certain languages in particular geographic areas. Demographic factors, combined with knowledge of the history of immigration, ought to be primary considerations in administrative decisions concerning the teaching of HLs. Offering courses in local community languages should be a mandate for future language education policy and funding. The Australian model (Pauwels, 2005) can serve as a launching point for planning purposes.

(2) The language in use in the family and community. In a FL course, the language taught is almost universally standard and formal. Vocabulary is textbook-based; grammar is introduced and practiced in small increments, and is in most cases prescriptive, excluding the imperfections and shortcuts of a living contemporary language. It is assumed that students who persist in learning the language will eventually acquire more colloquial registers once they travel to the country and immerse themselves in the language. HLLs' use of language, however, is derived from everyday interactions with non-textbook vocabulary and grammar, and the informal register. Moreover, a HLL's speech may contain dialectal features or other varieties that are not generally taught or even used in the classroom. Some researchers refer to them as non-prestige varieties, and note that they may be a source of friction between the teacher and the students (Valdés, 2001). Because the HL is a language in contact, code-switching between the HL and the dominant language can be expected. Andrews (1998) analyzes the vocabulary of Russian immigrants, and finds that even adults fully educated in Russian code-switch when they talk about job-related or other everyday life issues. HLLs' baseline language is impoverished in vocabulary, grammar, and register, despite parental language proficiency. While some of the differences may be minor, others may have a profound effect on instruction and on the school's relationship with the community. For example, Lam (2006) points out that Contemporary Standard Vietnamese is based on the dialect spoken in northern Vietnam, and Vietnamese textbooks reflect the standard. However, most residents of the largest concentration of Vietnamese speakers in Orange County, California, speak the southern dialect. If a school hires an instructor who speaks and teaches the northern dialect, it may lead to a conflict with the local Vietnamese community. In sum, the baseline language

of the family and community may differ considerably from the language taught in the classroom. HL curricula need to bridge this divide.

(3) Learner characteristics that separate HLLs from FLLs. Some of these characteristics span across languages while others are language-specific. The broad and narrow definitions of heritage learners mentioned earlier in this chapter can be illustrated with examples of language-specific studies. Kagan and Dillon (2001/2003) divide Russian HLLs into four groups. The most proficient group has completed or almost completed high school in the former Soviet Union, and their language proficiency is on a par with educated native speakers. It may be a misnomer to label them "heritage speakers." The second group attended or completed junior high school or its equivalent in the former Soviet Union, and while there may be lacunae in their lexical development, they have fully acquired the grammatical structure of the language. The third group attended or completed elementary school in the former Soviet Union, and they switched to English earlier than the other two groups. Consequently, there are more lacunae in their language, their performance in the language is typically uneven, and their knowledge of Russian culture is limited. Their proficiency in Russian is measurable, however. The fourth group emigrated at a pre-school age, or were born outside the former Soviet Union. Their competency in Russian will be the weakest of all the four groups, and they may be more akin to L2 learners. Their proficiencies depend on the use of language at home and also on individual characteristics and motivations that are discussed below.

Placement and proficiency assessment

The question of how to assess heritage learners awaits more extensive probing and would benefit from an exploration of new assessment approaches suggested by Norris and Ortega (Chapter 35, this volume). Research to date has produced limited data supporting the use of certain assessment instruments for determining HLLs' proficiency levels for placement purposes: (1) questionnaires to collect linguistic biographies; (2) oral proficiency testing. Many practitioners use biographical questionnaires for placement purposes (Kagan and Dillon, 2001/2003). They elicit information about the learner's place of birth, age of arrival, schooling in the target language country, attending community schools, and use of language with family members. The purpose is to develop a learner profile based on a linguistic biography. Carreira and Kagan (2011) find that linguistic questionnaires serve as good predictors of students' initial competencies. The most important factors are age of arrival in the USA, daily use of language, exposure to community and media, and motivation. These factors may be quite sufficient for placement at a starting point, since "language retrieval will occur during relearning" (Au, 2008).

The Oral Proficiency Interview (OPI), despite its drawbacks (Bachman and Savignon, 1986; Valdés, 1989), can serve as a broad assessment tool for HLLs. However, the tester and rater need to be aware of the peculiarities of HLLs' linguistic abilities. In administering OPI interviews to Russian HLLs, Kagan and Friedman (2004) find that even students in Groups 3 or 4 (see above), perform across the spectrum from Intermediate-Low to Advanced (ACTFL Proficiency Guidelines, 1999). The majority of students in their study tested at an Intermediate or above level of proficiency. According to the ACTFL OPI Guidelines, an Intermediate level speaker is limited to "predictable and concrete exchanges." FLLs' knowledge is predictable, since it is textbook-based. HLLs' knowledge is also limited and predictable to some degree, if we are aware of their baseline language level, and what errors, especially in grammar and register (Polinsky and Kagan, 2007), they can be expected to make. It is more difficult to predict their vocabulary and fluency range.

Phonetically, HLLs resemble native speakers, (Godson, 2004), and their rate of speech may also be close to native-like (Kagan and Friedman, 2004). These similarities at first produce the false impression of a native speaker's ease and fluidity, a phenomenon that could be called "the heritage learner illusion." HLLs are generally understood by native speakers, even though their language can cause annoyance or even resentment due to the inappropriate register typical of their speech. While there may be considerable differences in performance between FLLs and HLLs, the OPI's level descriptors may be appropriate for HLLs, although certain features need to be adjusted or understood differently. HLL-specific guidelines currently being developed by the ACTFL may resolve some of these problems.

A matrix for a HLL curriculum

With appropriate instruction, HLLs are capable of reaching higher levels of proficiencies in a shorter period of time than typical L2 learners. They will not progress significantly if offered a L2 curriculum that starts by focusing on the everyday vocabulary with which they are already familiar, and if tested and graded in ways that do not measure their competence. Valdés (2000) suggests a metalinguistic framework that would focus on raising awareness of dialects, speech registers, etc., but as far as we know, few programs implement these recommendations.

Kagan and Dillon (2001/2003, 2009) propose a macro approach that includes content-based, task-based, and project-based curricula. They suggest a matrix for the HLL curriculum that incorporates proper placement and stresses the significant amount of time that HLLs require in order to relearn and expand their language. The matrix includes programmatic rigor, HL-specific instructional materials, community-based curriculum, and instructors trained in HL teaching methodologies and approaches.

Few existing HL programs adhere to these principles (Potowski, 2003; Potowski *et al.*, 2008). Most HLL programs are offered at a beginning level, to teach literacy. They are not committed to HLL development as a long-term, multi-level, and rigorous enterprise. There are some exceptions, such as the three-year collaboration between the Hunter College Department of Curriculum and Teaching, Hunter College High School, and ACTFL. The goal of the project was to develop effective teaching practices for HLLs. The resulting model led to the development of courses that became an official part of the undergraduate and graduate teacher certification programs at Hunter College (Webb and Miller, 2000).

Future directions

As we stated in the introduction, the HL field is so new that a cohesive theory remains to be formulated. More questions remain unanswered than have been answered. Similar to bilingualism, which researchers (Grosjean, 2003; Hakuta, 1986) see as multidisciplinary, HLA needs to be rooted in research across numerous disciplines, including demography, psychology, linguistics, psycholinguistics, neuroscience, and education. Some work by linguists, psychologists, and demographers is already available, but neurological and cognitive research is still in its infancy.

The following topics for future research may lead to improvements in our understanding of HLLs' needs.

(1) In the NHLRC Survey (2009), a large number of students mentioned that they combine and even prefer to combine use of English and their HL in everyday life. An interesting question to explore would be what students mean by a "combination of English and HL." Under what conditions do they code-switch? Only when speaking their weaker (heritage) language? Or do they also code-switch when speaking the dominant language?

(2) Future research should establish the HLL's baseline language, i.e., the language a learner was exposed to during childhood, in the home. This "requires knowledge of demographic patterns" and an "understanding of dialectal and/or register differentiation in a given language" (Polinsky and Kagan, 2007, p. 373).

(3) Polinsky (1997, 2000, 2006; Polinsky and Kagan, 2007) suggests that vocabulary knowledge may be the strongest indicator of HLLs' proficiency. This approach is also stressed by Kondo-Brown (2003, p. 13), who writes that efforts must be made to determine the most efficacious approaches "for enhancing bilingual HL learners' vocabulary, which needs to go beyond the domain of immediate personal use." A research project to validate the connection between vocabulary and overall proficiency would be of practical value to the field.

(4) Using neurological and cognitive methodologies (eye tracking, Magnetic Resonance Imaging, Positron Emission Tomography, and others) that have been used successfully for research into bilingualism (DeKeyser, Chapter 27, this volume; Marian, 2007, p. 30) would be a fruitful direction for HL research. Very little has been done thus far, but some work has begun (Sekerina, 2008, Sekerina and Brooks, 2007)

(5) Exploration of the issue of "relearning" is essential for future development of successful instructional practices. If retrieval is best achieved through relearning (Au, 2008), what are the best instructional approaches for HLLs?

(6) Vygotsky's (1978) Zone of Proximal Development (ZPD) is "the distance between the actual development level as determined by independent problem solving and the level of potential development as determined through problem solving under adult guidance or in collaboration with more capable peers." Exploring this concept as a cornerstone of the HLL curriculum may be a fruitful direction for research that would ideally involve a collaboration of educational psychologists, linguists, and educators (Moll, 1990; Wells, 1999; Wertsch, 1991).

(7) Vygotskian ZPD theory also has consequences for assessment. HLLs' language proficiencies are difficult to assess, because some of their knowledge may be "dormant" and not immediately retrievable. Poehner and Lantolf's work suggests possibilities for L2 learner assessment (Poehner and Lantolf, 2003; see also Poehner, 2008). The authors note (p. 5) that while static testing "taps into already matured abilities," dynamic testing "promotes functions that are maturing." A research project to determine whether dynamic testing could be used with HLLs to capture the process of language learning could result in changing approaches to HLL teaching.

(8) The question instructors most frequently ask is how they can successfully teach HLLs and FLLs together. Since at most academic institutions the administrative reality requires that HLLs and FLLs be taught together at least some of the time, we need to determine at what level and with what curriculum the two groups could study most comfortably and productively together.

Some language teaching methodologies—for example, differentiated learning (Tomlinson *et al.*, 2008)—have been proposed for such a scenario, but only future research findings, including experimental classroom research studies, can definitively support or reject the practice of combined L2 and HL classes.

Conclusion

Twenty years ago, Valdés (1989) described the heritage language field as "atheoretical," and today it remains a field of study in search of a theory. The surge in research since the late 1990s promises continued growth and, eventually, the establishment of a solid theoretical base. It is our hope that even while an overarching theory is being formulated, research will lead to efficacious developments in curriculum and instructional approaches.

References

American Council on the Teaching of Foreign Languages. (1999). Proficiency guidelines—speaking. *Foreign Language Annals, 33*(1), 13–18.

Andrews, D. (1998). *Sociocultural perspectives on language change in diaspora: Soviet immigrants in the United States. (*Vol. 5). IMPACT: Studies in language and society*. Amsterdam and Philidelphia: John Benjamins.

Au, T. K. (2008). Salvaging heritage languages. In D. Brinton, O. Kagan, and S. Bauckus (Eds.), *Heritage language education: A new field emerging* (pp. 337–351). New York: Routledge.

Au, T. K., Oh, J. S., Knightly, L. M., Jun, S., and Romo, L. F. (2008). Salvaging a childhood language. *Journal of Memory and Language, 58*, 998–1011.

Bachman, L. and Savignon, S. (1986). The evaluation of communicative oral proficiency: A critique of the ACTFL oral interview. *The Modern Language Journal, 70*, 380–390.

Baker, C. (2006). *Foundations of bilingual education and bilingualism* (Fourth Edition). Clevedon, UK/Buffalo, NY: Multilingual Matters.

Benmamoun, E. with Albirini, A., and Saadah, E. Grammatical features of Egyptian and Palestinian Arabic Heritage Speakers' oral production. *Paper at the 4th NHLRC Heritage Research Institute, June 2010, University of Hawaii at Manoa*. Retrieved July 30, 2010 http://www.nhlrc.ucla.edu/2010summer/presentations/Tuesday/Abbas.pdf.

Berman, R. and Slobin, D. I. (1994). *Relating events in narrative: A cross-linguistic developmental study*. Hillsdale, NJ: Lawrence Erlbaum.

Bermel, N. and Kagan, O. (2000). The maintenance of written Russian in heritage speakers. In B. Rifkin, O. Kagan, and S. Bauckus (Eds.), *The learning and teaching of Slavic languages and cultures* (pp. 405–436). Bloomington, Indiana: Slavica.

Brinton, D., Kagan, O., and Bauckus, S. (Eds.) (2008). *Heritage language education: A new field emerging*. New York: Routledge.

Carreira, M. and Kagan, O. (2011). The results of the national heritage language survey: Implications for teaching, curriculum design, and professional development. *Foreign Language Annals, 44*(1), 40–64.

Cummins, J. (2005). A proposal for action: Strategies for recognizing heritage language competence as a learning resource within the mainstream classroom. *The Modern Language Journal, 89*(4), 585–592.

Doughty, C. and Long, M. (2003). *The handbook of second language acquisition*. Oxford: Blackwell Publishing. European Commission: Multilingualism. Retrieved from http://ec.europa.eu/education/languages/languages-of-europe/doc139_en.htm

Fishman, J. A. (2001). 300-plus years of heritage language education in the United States. In J. K. Peyton, D. A. Raynard, and S. McGinnis (Eds.), *Heritage languages in America: Preserving a national resource*. Washington, D.C.: CAL, ERIC; McHenry, IL: Delta Systems Co., Inc.

Friedberg, N. (2008) Religious language as everyday life: Genre and register in the speech of Russian Pentecostal heritage speakers. Power Point presented at The Second Heritage Language Summer Research Institute at Harvard University. Also available at http://nhlrc.ucla.edu/events/institute/2008/presentations/friedberg_june_27.pdf

Friedman, D. and Kagan, O. (2008). Academic writing proficiency of Russian heritage speakers: A comparative study. In D. Brinton, O. Kagan, and S. Bauckus (Eds.), *Heritage language education: A new field emerging*. New York: Routledge.

Gass, S. M. and Mackey, A. (2007). *Data elicitation for second and foreign language research*. Mahwah, NJ: Erlbaum.

Gass, S. M. and Selinker, L. (2008). *Second language acquisition: An introductory course*. New York: Routledge.

Godson, L. (2004). Vowel production in the speech of western Armenian heritage speakers. *Heritage Language Journal, 2*(1). Retrieved from http://www.heritagelanguages.org

Grosjean, F. (2003). Studying bilinguals: Methodological and conceptual issues. *Bilingualism: Language and Cognition, 1*(2), 131–149.

Hakuta, K. (1986). *Mirror of language: The debate on bilingualism*. New York: Basic Books.

He, A. W. and Xiao, Y. (Eds.). (2008). *Chinese as a heritage language: Fostering rooted world citizenry*. Honolulu, HI: National Foreign Language Resource Center/University of Hawaii.

Hornberger, N. (Ed.), (2005). Heritage/community language education: U.S. and Australian perspectives. [Special issue]. *International Journal of Bilingual Education and Bilingualism, 8*(2–3), 101–108.

Hyltenstam, K. (2002). Linguistic minorities in Scandinavia II: Immigrant minorities. In O. Bandle, K. Braunmüller, E. H. Jahr, A. Karker, H.-P. Naumann, and U. Teleman (Eds.), *An international handbook of the history of the North Germanic languages* (pp. 2120–2127). New York: Walter de Gruyter.

Isurina, L. and Ivanova-Sullivan, T. (2008). Lost in between: The case of Russian heritage speakers. *Heritage Language Journal, 6*(1), 72–104.

Kagan, O. (2005). In support of a proficiency-based definition of heritage language learners: A case of Russian. *International Journal of Bilingual Education and Bilingualism, 8*(2–3), 213–221.

Kagan, O. and Dillon, K. (2001/2003). A new perspective on teaching Russian: Focus on the heritage learner. *Slavic and East European Journal, 45*(3), 507–518. Reprinted in *Heritage Language Journal, 1*(1). Retrieved from http://www.heritagelanguages.org

Kagan, O. and Dillon, K. (2004). Heritage speakers' potential for high-level language proficiency. In H. Byrnes and H. Maxim (Eds.), *Advanced foreign language learning: A challenge to college programs* (pp. 99–112). Boston, MA: Heinle/Thomson.

Kagan, O. and Dillon, K. (2009). The professional development of teachers of heritage language learners: A matrix. In M. Anderson and A. Lazarton (Eds.), *Bridging contexts, making connections: Selected papers from the Fifth International Conference on Language Teacher Education* (pp. 155–175). Minneapolis, MN: University of Minnesota, CARLA.

Kagan, O. and Dillon, K. (2010). Russian-speaking immigrants in the United States. In K. Potowski (Ed.), *Language diversity in the US*. New York: Cambridge University Press.

Kagan, O. and Friedman, D. (2004). Using the OPI to place heritage speakers of Russian. *Foreign Language Annals, 36*, 536–545.

Kondo-Brown, K. (2003). Heritage language instruction for post-secondary students from immigrant backgrounds. *Heritage Language Journal, 1*(1), 1–25.

Kondo-Brown, K. (Ed.). (2006). *Heritage language development: Focus on East Asian immigrants* (Vol. 32). Studies in bilingualism. Amsterdam: John Benjamins.

Kondo-Brown, K. and Brown, J. D. (Eds.) (2007). *Teaching heritage students in Chinese, Japanese, and Korean.* Mahwah, NJ: Lawrence Erlbaum Associates.

Kondo-Brown, K. and Brown, J. D. (Eds.) (2008). *Teaching Chinese, Japanese and Korean heritage language students: Curriculum needs, materials, and assessment* (ESL and Applied Linguistics Professional series). New York: Lawrence Erlbaum Associates/Taylor and Francis.

Lam, M. B. (2006). The cultural politics of Vietnamese language pedagogy. *Journal of Southeast Asian Language Teaching, 12*(2), 1–19.

Larsen-Freeman, D. and Long, M. H. (1991). *An introduction to second language acquisition research.* New York: Longman, Inc.

Lee, J. S., and Suarez, D. (2009). A synthesis of the roles of heritage languages in the lives of immigrant children. In T. G. Wiley, J.-S. Lee, and R. Rumberger (Eds.), *The education of language minority Immigrants in the USA.* Clevedon, UK: Multilingual Matters.

Lo Bianco, J. (2008). Policy activity for heritage languages: Connections with representation and citizenship. In D. Brinton, O. Kagan, and S. Bauckus (Eds.), *Heritage language education: A new field emerging* (pp. 53–69). New York: Routledge.

Lynch, A. (2003). The relationship between second and heritage language acquisition: notes on research and theory building. *Heritage Language Journal, 2*, 1.

Lynch, B. (2008). Locating and utilizing heritage language resources in the community: An asset-based approach to program design and evaluation. In D. Brinton, O. Kagan, and S. Bauckus (Eds.), *Heritage language education: A new field emerging* (pp. 321–333). New York: Routledge.

Mackey, A. and Gass, S. (2005). *Second language research: Methodology and design.* Mahwah, NJ: Lawrence Erlbaum Associates.

Marian, V. (2007). Bilingual research methods. In A. Mackey (Ed.), *Conversational interaction in second language acquisition: A collection of empirical studies* (pp. 13–39). Oxford: Oxford University Press.

MLA (n.d.) The Modern Language Association language map: A map of languages in the United States. Retrieved from http://www.mla.org/census_main.

Moll, L. C. (Ed.). (1990). *Vygotsky and education: Instructional implications and social applications of socio-historical psychology.* New York: Cambridge University Press.

Montrul, S. (2004). Subject and object expression in Spanish heritage speakers: A case of morpho-syntactic convergence. *Bilingualism, Language and Cognition, 7*, 125–142.

Montrul, S. (2006). On the bilingual competence of Spanish heritage speakers: Syntax, lexical- semantics and processing. *International Journal of Bilingualism, 10*(1), 37–69.

Montrul, S. (2008). *Incomplete acquisition in bilingualism: Re-examining the age factor.* Amsterdam: John Benjamins.

Montrul, S. and Bowles, M. (2010). Is grammar instruction beneficial for heritage language learners? Dative case markings in Spanish. *Heritage Language Journal*, 7(1), 47–73. Also available at http://www. heritagelanguages.org/.

National Standards in Foreign Language Education Project. (2006). *Standards for foreign language learning in the 21st century* (Rev. Third edition). Lawrence, KS: Allen Press.

NHLRC Survey. (2009). *The heritage language learner survey: Report on the preliminary results.* UCLA: National Heritage Language Resource Center. Retrieved from

O'Grady, W., Lee, M., and Choo, M. (2001). The acquisition of relative clauses by heritage and non-heritage learners of Korean as a second language: A comparative study. *Journal of Korean Language Education*, 12, 283–294.

Pauwels, A. (2005). Maintaining the community language in Australia: Challenges and roles for families. *International Journal of Bilingual Education and Bilingualism*, 8(2–3), 124–131.

Peyton, J. K., Lewelling, V., and Winke, P. (2001). *Spanish for native speakers: Developing dual language proficiency.* Washington, D.C.: Center for Applied Linguistics. Retrieved from http://www.cal.org/ resources/digest/spanish_native.html.

Poehner, M. E. (2008). *Dynamic assessment: A Vygotskyan approach to understanding and promoting second language development.* New York: Springer Publishing.

Poehner, M. E. and Lantolf, J. P. (2003). *Dynamic assessment of L2 development: Bringing the past into the future.* (CALPER Working Paper Series, No. 1). The Pennsylvania State University, Center for Advanced Language Proficiency Education and Research.

Polinsky, M. (1997). American Russian: Language loss meets language acquisition. In W. Brown, E. Dornisch, N. Kondrashova, and D. Zec (Eds.), *Formal approaches to Slavic linguistics* (pp. 370–407). Ann Arbor, MI: Michigan Slavic Publications.

Polinsky, M. (2000). A composite linguistic profile of speakers of Russian in the U.S. In O. Kagan, B. Rifkin, and S. Bauckus (Eds.), *The learning and teaching of Slavic languages and cultures* (pp. 437–465). Bloomington, IN: Slavica.

Polinsky, M. (2006). Incomplete acquisition: American Russian. *Journal of Slavic Linguistics*, 14, 161–219.

Polinsky, M. (2008). Heritage language narratives. In D. Brinton, O. Kagan, and S. Bauckus (Eds.), *Heritage language education: A new field emerging.* New York: Routledge.

Polinsky, M. (2009). Presentation at Research Institute of the National Heritage Language Resource Center, University of Illinois, Urbana-Champaign. Retrieved from http://www.international.ucla. edu/languages/nhlrc/2009summer/powerpoint.asp.

Polinsky, M. and Kagan, O. (2007). Heritage languages: In the "wild" and in the classroom. *Language and Linguistics Compass*, 1(5), 368–395. Retrieved from http://www.fas.harvard.edu/~lingdept/Offprint.pdf.

Potowski, K. (2003). Chicago's "heritage language teacher corps": A model for improving Spanish teacher development. *Hispania*, 86(2), 302–311.

Potowski, K. (2007). *Language and identity in a dual immersion school.* Clevedon, UK: Multilingual Matters.

Potowski, K. and Carreira, M. (2004). Towards teacher development and national standards for Spanish as a heritage language. *Foreign Language Annals*, 37(3), 421–431.

Potowski, J. B., Clark, A., and Hammerand, A. (2008). Spanish for K-8 heritage speakers: A standards-based curriculum project. *Hispania*, 91(1), 25–41.

Rifkin, B. (2002). A case study of the acquisition of narration in Russian: At the intersection of foreign language education, applied linguistics, and second language acquisition. *Slavic and East European Journal*, 46(3), 465–481.

Schwartz, A. M. (2001). Preparing teachers to work with heritage language learners. In J. K. Peyton, D. A. Ranard, and S. McGinnis (Eds.), *Heritage languages in America: Preserving a national resource* (pp. 229–252). McHenry, IL: Center for Applied Linguistics; Washington, D.C.: CAL, ERIC; McHenry, IL: Delta Systems Co., Inc.

Sekerina, I. A. (2008). *Online spoken language processing in heritage speakers: Evidence from eye movements.* Presentation at Research Institute of the National Heritage Language Resource Center, Cambridge, MA. Retrieved from http://www.international.ucla.edu/languages/nhlrc/2008summer/presentations/ sekerina_6_25.pdf.

Sekerina, I. A. and Brooks, P. J. (2007). Eye movements during spoken-word recognition in Russian children. *Journal of Experimental Child Psychology*, 98, 20–45.

Sohn, S.-O. and Shin, S.-K. (2007). True beginners, false beginners, and fake beginners: Placement strategies for Korean heritage learners. *Foreign Language Annals*, 40, 353–364.

Thompson, I. (2000). Assessing foreign language skills: Data from Russian. In O. Kagan, B. Rifkin, and S. Bauckus (Eds.), *The learning and teaching of Slavic languages and cultures* (pp. 255–282). Bloomington, IN: Slavica.

Tomlinson, C. A., Brimijoin, K., and Narvaez, L. (2008). *The differentiated school: Making revolutionary changes in teaching and learning*. Alexandria, VA: Association for Supervision and Curriculum Development.

UCLA Steering Committee. (2000). Heritage Language Research Priorities Conference Report. *Bilingual Research Journal, 24* , 333–346. Also available at http.www.cal.org/heritage U.S. Census. n.d. Retrieved from http://www.census.gov/.

Valdés, G. (1989). Teaching Spanish to Hispanic bilinguals: A look at oral proficiency testing and the proficiency movement. *Hispania, 72*(2), 392–401.

Valdés, G. (2000). *Introduction. Spanish for native speakers*. Vol. 1. AATSP professional development series handbook for teachers K-16. New York: Harcourt College Publishers.

Valdés, G. (2001). Heritage language students: Profiles and possibilities. In J. K. Peyton, D. A. Ranard, and S. McGinnis (Eds.), *Heritage languages in America: Preserving a national resource* (pp. 37–77). McHenry, IL: Center for Applied Linguistics; Washington, D.C.: CAL, ERIC; McHenry, IL: Delta Systems Co., Inc.

Van Deusen-Scholl, N. (2003). Toward a definition of heritage language: Sociopolitical and pedagogical considerations. *Journal of Language, Identity, and Education, 2*(3), 211–230.

Vygotsky, L. S. (1978). *Mind in society: The development of higher psychological processes*. Cambridge, MA: Harvard University Press.

Wang, S. and Green, N. (2001). Heritage language students in the K-12 education system. In J. K. Peyton, D. A. Ranard, and S. McGinnis (Eds.), *Heritage languages in America: Preserving a national resource* (pp. 167–196). Washington, D.C. and McHenry, IL: Center for Applied Linguistics and Delta Systems.

Webb, J. and Miller, B. (Eds.). (2000). *Teaching heritage learners: Voices from the classroom*. New York: ACTFL.

Wells, G. (1999). *Dialogic inquiry: Towards a sociocultural practice and theory of education*. New York: Cambridge University Press.

Wertsch, J. V. (1991). *Voices of the mind: A sociocultural approach to mediated action*. Cambridge, MA: Harvard University Press.

Xiao, Y. (2006). Heritage learners in the Chinese language classroom: Home background. *Heritage Language Journal, 4*(1), 47–56.

31

Advanced language proficiency

Heidi Byrnes

Historical discussion

The inclusion of "advanced language proficiency" in this *Handbook* is a first even as a concern for "advancedness" is hardly new. Two views of language have influenced existing research, particularly in the USA: an earlier cognitive, psycholinguistic "acquisition" orientation and a more recent social, "use" orientation. Concurrently, European scholarship pursued a blended, semantically, and textually oriented approach that focused on linguistic phenomena in inter-ethnic discourse and used a longitudinal methodology (e.g., Perdue, 1993). The two orientations have thus far not been linked. As a consequence, the field does not yet have a sufficiently comprehensive theoretical basis for understanding advanced language, much less advanced language use.

Core issues

This section addresses past approaches and remaining challenges in terms of three interrelated themes: (1) probing the capacity for advanced second language (L2) proficiency, (2) describing L2 advanced proficiency, and (3) exploring a semiotic dimension for understanding advanced L2 performance.

Probing the capacity for advanced L2 proficiency

While describing advanced L2 proficiency should have conceptual priority over understanding an adult learner's capacity for attaining it, applied linguistics initially focused on "capacity," defining it cognitively and psycholinguistically. For a long time, this line of inquiry substituted for a description of advanced L2 performance abilities.

The critical period hypothesis and constraints on native-like L2 attainment. Specifically, a lively strand of inquiry proposed a critical period for language learning past which later (i.e., second) language learners, due to maturation roughly circumscribed by puberty, could no longer process linguistic stimuli in the fashion that enables earlier learners to reach ability levels associated with nativeness. Its strong version claimed a discontinuity in learning outcomes manifested either as a cessation of learning or a significant down-turn in the learning slope. The critical period hypothesis (CPH) initially arose in the 1960s within a cognitivist orientation toward the human language capacity, had a particularly lively period in the 1990s, but lingers to the present (DeKeyser, Chapter 27, this volume). Its core claims are most plausible when second language acquisition (SLA) research operates within a monolingual framework and recognizes L2 users' shortcomings as defining L2 learning. Translating the CPH's theoretical position into empirically verifiable questions and pondering its real-life implications proved to be difficult (see DeKeyser, 2000 and the response by Bialystok, 2002). Nevertheless, the theory continued to highlight innate constraints even under favorable learning conditions and retained its theoretical tenets despite counter-evidence from successful L2 learners and, more important, successful L2 users.

For example, Bongaerts (1999) found that highly motivated learners with access to massive L2 input and intensive training in the perception and production of L2 speech sounds attained nativelike abilities even in pronunciation, an area predicted to be subject to strong maturational constraints. Similarly, a large-scale study by Abrahamsson and Hyltenstam (2009) of Swedish learners of Spanish found a not insignificant subset passing for native speakers. Because a concurrently administered battery of tests with highly complex, cognitively demanding tasks showed none of the late learners performing in the native speaker range the authors concluded that "nativelike ultimate attainment of a second language is, in principle, never attained by adult learners" (p. 250). That position was taken although research also revealed that native-like performance was "much less common among child learners than has previously been assumed" (p. 250). Further ambivalences arose from research on age, an important aspect of the CPH, when it determined that factors independent of age, particularly socio-psychological, experiential, and instructional variables, influenced ultimate attainment (Moyer, 2004).

Fundamental for this research orientation is Chomsky's seminal distinction between a highly valued underlying competence and a considerably less relevant observable performance or use. Some researchers probing for underlying intuitions regarding grammar (e.g., Coppieters, 1987) established competence and performance as independent from each other while researchers espousing a use orientation (e.g., Piller, 2002) proposed that native-like performance was more appropriately described as a temporary, context-, audience-, and medium-specific phenomenon. Taking an even stronger counter-position, Herdina and Jessner (2002) altogether rejected Universal Grammar-inspired approaches and advocated a dynamic systems approach, particularly under the condition of learning several non-native languages.

Such variant stances raise at least these questions: (1) Exactly what constitutes native-like success in language learning when passing for a native speaker is deemed insufficient? (2) What legitimates privileging monolingual native performance over multilingual non-native performance, the foundation of critical period claims? (3) What is the theoretical and empirical value of invariable, rule-based notions of competence in light of the evident variability of language learning and language use, and the importance of learner agency in learning an L2 to very advanced levels? In time, such questions undermined long-held claims by exposing their often implicitly held, conceptually flawed and ethically and socially irresponsible notions of bilingualism (Birdsong, 2005). On that account, L2 learners should be valued as inherently multicompetent speakers: not only are they under "no obligation" to process and use language as native users do, they bring unique features to language use that deserve to be recognized as falling outside categories of native performance and judgments of deficits (Cook, 2008; Ortega, 2010).

Fossilization and stabilization in relation to advanced learning capacity. Related research investigated ultimate levels of attainment and fossilization (see also Han, Chapter 29, this volume) or, at least, stabilization in language acquisition. First proposed by Selinker (1972), the notion of a non-native like unchangeable end-state in grammatical learning rapidly gained acceptance in the field. However, as Long (2003) pointed out, the construct of fossilization is fundamentally flawed when research begins by assuming that it exists rather than first convincingly demonstrating the existence of the postulated phenomenon. Moreover, under stringent research requirements (e.g., selecting appropriate learners; collecting sufficient data over extended periods of time; referring to individual data rather than group means; and using stability/change measures rather than accuracy ranges), indisputable evidence becomes quite thin. Finally, because use of the term is unusually varied, Long concluded that "researchers would do better to focus on describing and explaining the well-attested phenomenon of stabilization" (p. 487) rather than postulating fossilization.

Grammatical categories and L2 ultimate attainment. By comparison with these cognitivist approaches, a number of European studies pursued a functional or meaning-oriented approach. Their goal was to understand the creation of knowledge in texts, their point of interest the role of language structure in that process, especially grammaticized formal categories of language (Carroll and Lambert, 2006; Carroll *et al.*, 2000). Because these categories vary significantly across languages, differentiated research evidence can contribute insights both to the long-standing debate about the relationship between language and thought and to the nature of language learning to very advanced ability levels.

For example, following a perspective-driven semantic model of information organization, Carroll *et al.* (2000) investigated questions such as these: what do advanced L2 learners deem worthy of being reported, in what order do they provide information in the linear organization of speaking and writing, what perspective do they take, into what propositional units do they translate information, within which macro-genres, with what communicative goals? Related research focused on L2 event construal (von Stutterheim and Nüse, 2003), the expression of time and place (von Stutterheim *et al.*, 2003) and the expression of motion and duration, including bounded and unbounded events (von Stutterheim and Carroll, 2006).

These studies illuminated another well-known phenomenon: many advanced speakers can handle the L2 in seemingly flawless ways and yet prompt native speakers to comment that they "wouldn't put it that way." For example, the textual organization of very advanced learners of L2 German with L1 English or Spanish backgrounds shows that "an object-based organization plays a central role in information structure in descriptions in English, whereas information is typically organized in spatial terms in German" (Carroll *et al.*, 2000, p. 445). Taken together, the research seems to support the conclusion "that the central factor impeding the acquisitional process at advanced stages ultimately is grammatical in nature, in that learners have to uncover the role accorded to grammaticized meanings and what their presence, or absence, entails in information organization" (von Stutterheim and Carroll, 2006, p. 51).

That position shows strong affinity to cognitive semantics, which investigates how language organizes central conceptual domains: space and time, motion and location, causation and force interaction, and attention and viewpoint. It also echoes Slobin's (1996a) conclusions that languages learned in childhood provide "a subjective orientation to the world of human experience, and this orientation **affects the ways in which we think while we are speaking**" (p. 91, original emphasis). Finally, it tracks well with Slobin's observations (1996b) on the difficulty of translating texts from typologically different languages with their different functional resources for textual meaning-making. These resources are extraordinarily difficult to learn because they "cannot be explained by a single feature; they are determined by a coalition of grammaticized features" (Carroll and Lambert, 2006, p. 71), that is, they act variably across the strata of the lexicogrammatical system of a language, from morpheme, word, phrase, clause, sentence, to discourse levels (see also Choi and Lantolf, 2008). As a result, if the notion of "transfer" is at all to be invoked, it should not be limited to syntactic phenomena but, for advanced learners in particular, should investigate the domain of information structure and information organization (Bohnacker and Rosén, 2008).

Describing advanced L2 proficiency

The previous discussion of learners' capacity for learning a second language already included descriptors for advanced levels of ability. This section puts advanced proficiency directly in focus.

"Fluency" and advanced levels of proficiency. Non-technical treatments customarily refer to an advanced L2 speaker as "fluent," thereby highlighting effortless and continuous performance. That emphasis also pervades language assessment where valued performances at any proficiency level and also at higher proficiency levels are described in terms of smooth and flowing execution. Much more technical understandings are associated with the work of Schmidt (e.g., 1992). While he, too, focused on temporal phenomena of fluency he positioned them within a number of well-researched psychological learning mechanisms, such as the contrast between automatic and controlled processing, the distinction between declarative and procedural knowledge (the latter further refined in terms of knowledge compilation and fine tuning through generalization, discrimination, and strengthening), or in terms of various forms of memory-retrieval. For an automatic procedural skill like fluency, debate ultimately revolves around the importance of well-practiced instances vs. the assumption of increasingly skillful application of abstract rules. Both options were particularly prominently and productively investigated in conjunction with notions of planning with different tasks under different task conditions (e.g., Ellis, 2009; Foster and Skehan, 1996).

But fluency can also refer to proficiency in and of itself or to good management of the entire language code (Koponen and Riggenbach, 2000). Such broader understandings were proposed early on by Carroll (1968) who distinguished fluency by the levels of the system where it was operative: from word, to ideational, to expressional fluency. Researchers like Segalowitz (2000) added the notion of cognitive fluency as distinct from performance fluency in order to foreground "the efficiency of the operation of the cognitive mechanisms underlying performance" (p. 202). A critical position toward viewing competence as non-variable had earlier on been taken by Fillmore (1979). Among sources of fluency differences he identified features like knowledge of fixed linguistic forms; control of processes for creating new expressions (e.g., word formation, syntactic devices); differences in speakers' habitual use of certain devices, as well as differential knowledge of the cognitive or semantic schemata for which the language has provided linguistic encodings; knowledge of the various interactional schemata for conversations and discourse schemata, and knowledge of the appropriateness of words, forms, or syntactic constructions to particular settings with their respective genres and registers (cf., pp. 94–98).

Such thinking was elaborated in a prominent article by Pawley and Syder (1983) that circumscribed language learning in terms of native-like selection and native-like fluency. Specifically, the authors differentiated clause-chaining behaviors, which string together relatively independent clauses, from clause-integrating behaviors, which require speakers to consider larger stretches of speech retrospectively and prospectively, therefore demanding certain levels of planning. As a result, they highlighted the role played by lexicalized sentence stems as a site where syntax, lexicon, individual processing demands, and social convention regarding language use as a cultural phenomenon intersect in larger units of salient meanings and language form.

Cognitively oriented theoretical and pedagogical treatments have frequently opposed fluency to accuracy and complexity, where all are interpreted as aspects of advancedness. Skehan (see Skehan and Foster, 2001) assumed attentional limitations in processing whereby L2 learners will engage in a trade-off between fluency on the one hand and accuracy and complexity on the other. By contrast, Robinson (2001) postulated a differentiation between resource-directing dimensions of complexity, which might increase attention to the code (and therefore foster learning of accurate morpho-syntax), and resource-depleting dimensions of tasks, which make additional demands, such as through removing prior knowledge support.

A recent special issue of *Applied Linguistics* (Housen and Kuiken, 2009) demonstrated the longevity and influence of that line of research, including notions of advancedness, even as it also uncovered serious theoretical and empirical limitations. These arise when its central constructs operate independently from each other, from individual users, and from specific contexts, and without a well-theorized longitudinal trajectory (Larsen-Freeman, 2009; Norris and Ortega, 2009).

Capturing advanced language performance: diverse practical approaches. In many educational contexts considerably less rigorous notions of advancedness have tended to dominate. Thus, collegiate foreign language programs in the USA regularly accord advanced status according to seat time to learners past the language requirement of three–four semesters. In effect, "more" and "better," perhaps "longer," more "complex" and "more fluent" use of grammar and lexicon become the privileged qualities of advanced speaking, reading, and writing abilities. Another route to specifying advanced ability levels is through assessment regimes, such as the American Council on the Teaching of Foreign Languages (ACTFL) proficiency guidelines (ACTFL, 1999), the Foreign Service Institute/Interagency Language Round Table (FSI/ILR) scale, and the Test of English as a Second Language (TOEFL). Here advancedness is captured by the relationship between cut-off scores or ratings and access to licenses (e.g., ACTFL Intermediate or Advanced Low for teacher licensure in many states in the USA), to job opportunities (e.g., the ILR professional ratings of 3 and above) or to educational opportunities in US higher education institutions (a score of 600 on the TOEFL). At the same time, their "use-in-context" approach remains general, almost commonsensical. Malone *et al.* (2003) demonstrate that public education may demand precise statements of learning outcomes and accountability, yet provides surprisingly little specification for advanced language performance. Remarkably, such tests not only tend to be one-shot and often one-sided determinations of language abilities, a problematic matter in and of itself (Shohamy, 2006); they make little reference to the concrete instructional programs for which they function as high-stakes gate-keeping events.

Describing advanced levels of proficiency in ESL/EFL contexts. By contrast, college-level ESL/EFL instructional programs in particular have expressed advancedness in highly contextualized terms, especially through the academic language abilities needed by international students who seek admission to undergraduate study; wish to pursue diverse disciplinary majors or minors; and engage in graduate study with its high performance demands in a range of spoken and written genres, including theses and dissertations, case studies reports in business, lab reports in science and engineering, interpretations of literary work in the humanities, or comparative policy analyses.

In that effort, EFL/ESL programs increasingly proposed curricular progressions and pedagogical activities based on needs analyses (e.g., Reid, 2001). These generally take a holistic approach regarding language use to be crucial for attaining advancedness, a stance that contrasts with the emphasis on discrete grammatical features that characterizes EFL instruction in many countries. From an initial interest in different modalities of use—listening, reading, speaking, and writing— (Belcher and Hirvela, 2001; Connor, 1996; Ferris and Tagg, 1996; Hyland, 2004; Hyon 2001; Johns, 1997; Silva and Matsuda, 2001; Spack, 1997; Swales and Feak, 1994; Ventola and Mauranen, 1996), followed by diverse, but general aspects of English for Academic Purposes (EAP), research has moved to highlighting the discipline-specific nature of advancedness (e.g., Belcher and Braine, 1995; Flowerdew, 2002; Hyland, 2006; Hyland and Bondi, 2006; Johns, 1997; Spack, 1997; Swales, 2004; Swales and Feak, 1994; Zamel and Spack, 1998).

In that trajectory, the notion of genre has become central, especially for advanced level writing (e.g., Berkenkotter and Huckin, 1995; Bhatia, 2002; Johns, 2002). In particular, Swales'(1990) analysis of the research article in terms of an Introduction-Method-Results-Discussion (IMRD) structure and his positing of genre-specific textual moves have attained near-canonical status. Other analyses have addressed citation practices, tense and aspect use, ways of posing questions and raising problems, contrasting opinions and drawing logical conclusions; forms of hedging one's claims and evaluating extant findings, as well as writers' metadiscursive comments as a way of creating an authorial voice (Ädel, 2008; Francis, 2006; Hyland, 2005; Jessner, 2006).

English for Specific Purposes (ESP) contexts, too, rely on genre analysis to capture advanced ability levels, especially for language use in business (e.g., Bhatia, 1993; Bhatia and Gotti, 2006). Importantly, these discussions foreground social relationships, identities, and power structures characteristic in attorney–client or doctor–patient relationships or in the nature of negotiations, sales, or job interviews, over more language-based interpretations of the construct genre.

By contrast, contrastive rhetoric (Connor, 1996), one of the earliest and most prominent research strands addressing issues of advancedness, had focused on different rhetorical traditions and their effect on learners' ability to acquire the patterns valued in L2 literacy. Because that interest can fall prey to (out)dated notions of texts, of writing, and of learning (Kubota and Lehner, 2004), more recent scholarship highlighting the social situatedness of writing draws on diverse methodologies and data sources (e.g., genre analysis, corpus analysis, qualitative historical and ethnographic approaches) in order to create what is called an intercultural rhetoric (Connor *et al.*, 2008).

Finally, a broadly textual approach to describing advancedness in ESL contexts is that chosen by Biber and researchers inspired by him (Biber, 1992; Biber and Finegan, 1994). Building on his extensive investigations of textual variation through multi-feature/multi-dimensional analyses, Biber (2006) characterized diverse university registers by drawing on computerized corpora and computational analytical tools. Analysis included the description of prevalent vocabulary patterns; the use of lexico-grammatical and syntactic features; the expression of stance; the use of lexical bundles; and a multi-dimensional analysis of the overall patterns of register variation. Applied to ten registers (four written and six spoken) that range from informationally dense prose to interactive and involved spoken registers occurring in university settings, the research provided crucial information for teaching and testing at the advanced level that is explicitly language oriented (Biber *et al.*, 2002).

Advanced proficiency as situated language use toward a multicompetent literacy. Characterizing advanced abilities in terms of situated language use in context (e.g., through register and genre) opened the door to a second prominent research strand, namely that highlighting sociocultural and sociolinguistic considerations of appropriateness. An area directly implicated is pragmatics, which investigates the interaction with/relation between social and linguistic phenomena, most recently expanding from a focus on speech acts to utilizing discourse-analytical approaches. Furthermore, learner discourse is now understood as reflecting the pragmatic conventions neither of the L1 nor of the L2 community (Bardovi-Harlig and Hartford, 2005) but as creating its own space, particularly through the interaction among advanced communicative participants (e.g., Kinginger and Belz, 2005).

Other central qualities of advanced proficiency are addressed through such related notions as literacy, situated discourse abilities, and, more generally, the dialogical nature of advanced language performance. Thus, Byrnes *et al.* (2010) propose a multicompetent literacy in order to foreground the humanistically oriented educational concerns and learning goals of collegiate foreign language programs, both of which require advanced L2 abilities. Recognizing that the content foci of public, institutional, and disciplinary language use are realized in certain preferred genres, they envision an evolving genre-based literacy as learners progress toward and also within the considerable expanse of what is called advanced L2 performance (Byrnes *et al.*, 2006; Crane, 2006).

The considerable performance range within advanced proficiency might then be imagined through the following progression: (1) recounting, reporting, and narrative or story genres that focus on the verbal system and express Participants, Processes, and Circumstances in real-life situations, first in simplex, then in complex clauses that move from paratactic to hypotactic and embedded clauses; (2) genres that privilege more metaphorical construals of life, realized through increasing lexical density and greater syntactic complexity, with human participants engaging with public and institutional concerns, values, and beliefs that express comparative, contrastive, and issue-oriented stances in terms of logical relationships; (3) genres that feature both human and abstract actors in created textual spaces by using verbal processes, chunks, collocations, and phrasal stems that can lay out logical arguments in an increasingly greater range of genres and disciplinary and content areas (see Byrnes, 2009a).

Advanced abilities can also be described through two major forms of dialogicality. Oral language use manifests the overt dialogicality of conversations; in addition, advanced abilities comprise the covert dialogicality of intratextual aspects of coherence and cohesion, and of various forms of intertextual reference. In line with Bakhtin's notion of the centrally dialogical nature of language, Wertsch (2006) characterizes advanced forms of language performance by referring to language users' ability to incorporate the complex intertextualities that make up what is commonly referred to as cultural literacy. Even more, advancedness involves the ability to "reflect the voice of others, including entire groups, who are not present in the immediate speech situation" (p. 61). Advanced forms of language use can therefore also be seen as a multivoiced language performance, a notion that is only heightened in a multilingual and multicultural world.

Both conceptualizations provide a basis for comprehensive curricular trajectories toward advanced ability levels. Their realization in educational settings with their particular educational philosophies and human and material resources, and, most important, their particular learners who themselves can vary greatly, requires informed pedagogical decision-making. But as Byrnes *et al.* (2010) have shown, the very existence of situated, long-range curricular thinking that is also embedded in a principled pedagogy and carefully conceived assessment practices, can significantly enhance the likelihood that learners in fact develop advanced L2 ability levels. This is true inasmuch as such a conceptual framework is entirely compatible with the kind of dynamic, variable, and non-linear view of language development that recent SLA research has begun to foreground (Norris and Ortega, Chapter 35, this volume); it is also compatible with emergent notions of multicompetent language use—in fact what advanced multicompetent L2 abilities might be depends on just such contexts. In other words, research has yet to obtain trustworthy evidence for the capacity of instructed L2 learners to attain advanced multilingual abilities.

Exploring a semiotic dimension for understanding advanced L2 performance

Perhaps the most serious impediment in that regard is that mainstream theorizing, research, and educational practice have not addressed the relationship between contexts of language use and textually oriented formal features of language. While that deficit has no debilitating consequences for teaching and learning at lower ability levels, the social-semiotic and textual quality of language is central to fostering advanced abilities. To date, the only comprehensive account of language as a textually oriented meaning-making resource, one that furthermore espouses educational concerns, comes from systemic-functional linguistics (SFL) as elaborated by M. A. K. Halliday and researchers inspired by him (representative publications are Halliday and Matthiessen, 2004; Halliday and Webster, 2009; Hasan *et al.*, 2005/2008; Martin and Rose, 2003, 2008). From this extensive literature, I highlight two particularly fecund areas: (1) the semiotic shift central to the language of schooling and, by implication, advanced language abilities; and (2) a set of dimensions that can help conceptualize advanced language proficiency as a long-term process.

A central claim in SFL is that meaning-making through and in and with language takes place from two perspectives. What is called a congruent form of semiosis makes sense of our physical and social environment in the most direct way from experience to language: Participants are expressed mostly with human identifiable actors (*My friend*), Processes as verbs (*visited*), and Circumstances through lexical items or prepositional phrases (*for the first time*). By contrast, in non-congruent/ metaphorical or synoptic semiosis, the same meanings are remapped to a different grammatical category, while yet retaining, in this fused state, some of the process-meaning of the verb: *My friend's recent visit to Berlin* restructures information through nominalization both from the stand-point of meanings and of syntax. At the same time it adds layers of meaning: the original human actor has now become an abstract actor in conceptual space, *visit*, and an entire clause has been reduced to a single noun phrase available for new syntactic roles in new clausal structures.

This semiotic shift is one way to describe the difference between what Halliday (2002) terms the "choreographic complexity" of oral language and the "crystalline complexity" of written language (cf., pp. 335–337). Accompanied by greater lexical density (pp. 327–331), the relation-ship between grammatical and content words, this semiotic shift *as* lexicogrammatical shift, most especially nominalizations of verbal processes, enables textual meaning-making capacities that are fundamental to the genres of public discourse, institutions, the professions, and disciplinary ways of knowing. This is so because this semiotic shift–SFL aptly refers to as grammatical metaphor (GM)– is fundamental to the creation of new, textual worlds: it helps create coherence and cohesion over longer textual stretches (cf., Byrnes, 2009b; Ryshina-Pankova, 2008), ways of structuring larger meaning chunks, it marks foregrounding and backgrounding of information and theme-rheme progressions, and establishes the kind of cause and effect relationships typical for advanced language use (e.g., Coffin, 2006; Martin and Rose, 2003; Schleppegrell, 2004, 2006; Teruya, 2006).

SFL explicitly links the human meaning-making capacity in texts to a context of situation and, ultimately, a context of culture through a number of conceptual and analytical tools.

(1) *The hierarchy of stratification* refers to the fact that language is stratified into a system of "meanings," its semantics, and a system of "wordings," manifested in the lexicogrammar of a language. The L2 learner's task is therefore to learn to look at the language system trinocularly from all stratal angles: "from below," in terms of the available L2 resources along the continuum of lexicon and grammar; "from above," in terms of resources available for signaling meaning in context; and, "from within," to come to appreciate the internal organization of a given stratum (cf., Matthiessen, 2006, pp. 35–37).

(2) *The spectrum of metafunction* refers to three central metafunctional modes of meaning in language: the ideational metafunction construes our experience of the world as meaning; through the interpersonal metafunction language enacts social roles and relations; and the textual metafunction organizes the flow of information in language use.

(3) *The cline of instantiation* recognizes that a given text is but a specific instance of the meaning-making potential available in the entire language system; the goal is to enable learners to become aware of the system's resources so as to be able to make their own situated choices of meaning-making.

Combining the three foundational dimensions of the language system with the semiotic trajectory delineated above, Ortega and Byrnes (2008b, p. 293) describe advanced L2 users as being engaged in "the complex task of instantiating the system in a particular text and, in reverse, coming to understand that each text is but a particular realization of the system that provides certain glimpses into the system's potential ... the cline of instantiation is perhaps the key way in which one might describe how far an advanced learner has advanced or, for that matter, can advance." Research with an SFL orientation has well substantiated the progression outlined above for charting L1 literacy development (Christie and Derewianka, 2008). It appears that the same semiotic progression, precisely because it is based on evolving lexicogrammatical, that is, meaning-making capacities, applies to adult L2 learners (Byrnes, 2009b). For that reason, it can serve to circumscribe a principled curricular and pedagogical framework toward advanced abilities over long periods of time (cf., Byrnes *et al.*, 2010 for an application to writing).

Data and common elicitation measures

Knowledge regarding the nature of advanced abilities is seriously constricted by the fact that prevailing research primarily uses cross-sectional methodologies, tends to investigate isolated features without a comprehensive *language-based* theoretical framework, and essentializes "L2 learning" by not considering how previous instruction might have influenced both its attainment and its particular profile. By implication, research has been unable to consider how an instructional approach that would explicitly target advanced abilities right from the start might change existing assumptions about instructed L2 learning, including the attainment of advanced abilities (Byrnes 2009; Byrnes *et al.*, 2010; Larsen-Freeman, 2009; Larsen-Freeman and Cameron, 2008; Ortega and Byrnes, 2008b).

The following external and internal factors come into play. For a number of reasons, it is uncommon for programs to develop and follow agreed-upon principled proposals regarding the development of advanced L2 abilities: (1) they do not have the instructional time necessary for advancedness to be realistically attainable; (2) they separate language learning from content learning, thereby creating their own educational dead-ends; (3) they craft course-based instructional proposals rather than articulated, multi-year curricula; (4) their learners often hail from instructional cultures that emphasize formal accuracy, have varied literacy backgrounds, and performance profiles, and enroll for short time periods. All these factors directly and indirectly influence subsequent pedagogies and create a glass ceiling for attaining advancedness.

The first two characteristics predominate with FL programs, one explanation for the scarcity of data for non-English advanced L2 learning. The noteworthy exception is heritage language instruction, in the USA primarily Spanish. The latter two apply to collegiate ESL programs, many of which are driven by test-derived assumptions regarding L2 learning. Finally, in mainstream education, the demand that English language learners perform the same tasks as native learners complicates obtaining differentiated data.

In order to overcome these limitations, several recommendations merit attention:

- Detailed information about learning histories, a kind of ecology of learning, for individuals and groups in terms of curricular and instructional realities. It would be akin both to the microgenetic focus in socioculturally oriented studies (e.g., Lantolf and Thorne, 2006) and the recent proposals in dynamic systems theory, which treats language learning as highly varied according to exposure history (Beckner *et al.*, 2009; Verspoor and Lowie, 2008);
- Case studies probing the interconnectedness of linguistic subsystems and also larger macro-contextual factors (Duff, 2008) in order to be able document the highly variable development of advanced learners in terms of interactions over time as well as their perceptions, beliefs, and attitudes (aspects of learner agency), and to trace recurring features in social context (Harklau, 2008);
- Research that foregrounds how learners negotiate choices in meaning-making in oral and written texts, particularly in light of the differences between L1 and L2 in concept structures, event construal and ordering;
- Corpus-based research that is textually oriented, for instance by foregrounding genre (Flowerdew, 2005), explores the relation between system and textual instance and back

(cf., Thompson and Hunston, 2006), or investigates the dynamic shifts within lexicogrammar between more lexically or more grammatically inclined features (cf., Moon, 2009).

Applications

Fostering advanced L2 abilities requires learners to be highly aware language users, with regard to language as a culturally embedded system for making meanings and with regard to diverse approaches toward language learning. Research increasingly suggests that such meta-awareness will itself need to be created in instruction. Indeed, it is considered to be at the heart of continuing development toward very advanced literacies, often a life-long project. Similarly, it seems that advanced L2 abilities are possible in instructed settings when instruction presents content that is worth learning and, in turn, requires learners to create content worth thinking and communicating about. Not least among the consequences of such a stance is the motivating force for language learning and identity construction when a multicompetent speaker is taken seriously and valued for being able to work with several language systems. In such a hybrid third space learners can find an intellectual and affective environment that is conducive to developing a new authorial voice and, as desired, new situated identities (see Duff, Chapter 25, this volume).

For advanced abilities that third space involves various aspects of literacy, including learning to appropriate several collective dialogs, to use Wertsch's term for learners' moving comfortably in several language systems as dialogic meaning-making environments. As mentioned, instruction must focus on enabling them to extrapolate from particular textual instances to the system and, in reverse, on deploying the system's resources to create and interpret instances of oral or written texts. Development toward advanced L2 proficiency can then be described as continued expansion of registerial domains that themselves reflect bundles of language features in line with the major functions of language. Less abstractly, it is about learners expanding their generic repertoires, where genres reflect texts as typified social action. Importantly, both registerial and generic expansion will take place at the intersection of highly probable and valued discursive conventions and learners' desire and ability to expand those conventions creatively in line with their own interests and intentions, including judiciously subverting and playing with them. The capacity toward simultaneously learning language and learning content as new ways of being and knowing is a local phenomenon, with learners engaging with the language in the trinocular dimensions mentioned earlier on. Finally, at the advanced level, learning language "from within" is about developing a sizable repertoire of fixed phrases and chunked language within the central dynamic of that language system, its lexicogrammatical resources (Rinner and Weigert, 2006).

Such learners characteristics and needs, of course, relate directly to desirable features for an instructional program. Worth reiterating is the need for a principled curricular progression that begins by envisioning the very possibility of advanced L2 learning. By embracing an explicitly text-based instructional approach it can model the lexicogrammatical resources of the language in terms of the functional domains of field (the content being construed and conveyed), tenor (the social relations being enacted), and mode (the role played by the textual language itself) (cf., Byrnes *et al.*, 2010; Martin, 2009; Rothery, 1996). Given the intimate and intricate relationship between linguistic resources and their development and use in various texts, instruction toward advancedness must assure textual variety in order to let learners encounter the range of options made available by the language system. Instruction will need to favor a semantically oriented cognitive focus that starts with the intent to mean. In movement that Samuda (2001) describes as meaning–form–meaning in task-based language instruction, learners can first become aware of the intricate interweaving of meaning-form relationships that are available as semiotic choices and then progress to deploying those resources that best convey their own intentions and judgments.

Finally, linking curricular, pedagogical, and assessment practices right from the start, and doing so variably with sensitivity toward the local context in a transparent fashion is crucial for conveying an articulated and consistent educational philosophy, itself a basis for facilitating learners' progress toward attaining advanced L2 proficiency (Byrnes *et al.*, 2010; Norris, 2006; Shohamy, 2006).

I conclude by referring to an area traditionally associated with advanced L2 abilities, indeed deemed indispensable for attaining them,—namely study abroad. While there is little dispute about the overall benefits of a study abroad sojourn, recent research has shown that an in-country stay in and of itself in no way guarantees the development of advanced abilities (Kinginger, 2008). Equally important is learners' willingness to be "oriented toward this goal in a profound and enduring way" (p. 108), as is their ability to "derive coherence from their study abroad experiences and the interpretive resources they recruit for this purpose" (p. 108). That conclusion is both a healthy antidote to overstated expectations for study abroad and welcome recognition of the substantial contributions of well-conceived instructional programs.

Future directions

In light of the previous representations the following directions should prove particularly useful for future substantive and substantial engagement with the phenomenon of advanced L2 proficiency:

(1) *A push toward theorizing advancedness through functionally and textually oriented approaches to language analysis.* Because of the extended developmental nature of advancedness such theorizing would ideally include further specification of diverse developmental dimensions, in terms of performance profile and in terms of processing characteristics;

(2) *Explicit linking of advancedness to multilingualism.* In line with the bilingual turn in applied linguistics, this research will engage in "non-normative comparisons with multilingual natives and other multiple-language learning profiles" and will analyze L1/L2 users' multiple repertoires (Ortega, 2010);

(3) *Expansion of research contexts into additional domains.* This will serve such interrelated purposes as describing and researching advancedness beyond the classroom, most likely in the interplay between naturalistic and instructed learning, and investigating rigorously the nature of teaching and learning toward advancedness. Ultimately, it should facilitate systematizing what we know about the capacity for advanced L2 learning;

(4) *Expansion of the domains of inquiry regarding advancedness.* Beyond the current heavy emphasis on largely academic and written norms, it will address advanced performance in multimodal contexts (Tardy and Swales, 2008);

(5) *Longitudinal studies investigating diverse aspects of instructed language learning*, particularly with regard to measurable aspects of efficiency and effectiveness of learning; the development of language in the professions; the determination of thresholds of language ability at the advanced level that would be relatively immune to language loss and, in reverse, enable rapid revitalization of upper level language use after extended periods of non-use (see contributions in Ortega and Byrnes, 2008a);

(6) *Research on learning multiple languages to advanced levels.* Research findings would benefit such diverse areas as translation and interpretation and the increasingly prominent language needs in government, including the diplomatic service, security, and the military, for example with regard to the possibility of cross-training across typologically related languages;

(7) *Development of corpora that use to greatest advantage the capacities of corpus-based analyses.* These would serve to research the nature of advanced learner language in different modalities and different domains;

(8) *Further specification of research methodologies suited for investigating the development of advanced L2 abilities.* This means working through challenges presented not only by longitudinal studies, but by the highly varied and dynamic nature of language learning, the active role of learners, and the textual and meaning-focused quality of advanced L2 performance.

References

Abrahamsson, N. and Hyltenstam, K. (2009). Age of onset and nativelikeness in a second language: Listener perception versus linguistic scrutiny. *Language Learning, 59*(2), 249–306.

Ädel, A. (2008). Metadiscourse across three varieties of English: American, British, and advanced-learner English. In U. Connor, E. Nagelhout, and W. V. Rozycki (Eds.), *Contrastive rhetoric: Reaching to intercultural rhetoric* (pp. 45–62). Philadelphia/Amsterdam: John Benjamins.

American Council on the Teaching of Foreign Languages (ACTFL). (1999). *Proficiency guidelines revised.* Yonkers, NY: Author.

Bardovi-Harlig, K. and Hartford, B. (Eds.). (2005). *Interlanguage pragmatics: Exploring institutional talk.* Mahwah, NJ: Lawrence Erlbaum.

Beckner, C., Blythe, R., Bybee, J., Christiansen, M. H., Croft, W., and Ellis, N. C. (2009). Language is a complex adaptive system. Position paper. *Language Learning, 59* (Supplement 1), 1–26.

Belcher, D. and Braine, G. (Eds.). (1995). *Academic writing in a second language: Essays on research and pedagogy.* Norwood, NJ: Ablex.

Belcher, D. and Hirvela, A. (Eds.). (2001). *Linking literacies: Perspectives on L2 reading-writing connections.* Ann Arbor, MI: The University of Michigan Press.

Berkenkotter, C. and Huckin, T. (1995). *Genre knowledge in disciplinary communication: Cognition/culture/power.* Hillsdale, NJ: Lawrence Erlbaum.

Bhatia, V. K. (1993). *Analysing genre: Language use in professional settings.* New York: Longman.

Bhatia, V. K. (2002). A generic view of academic discourse. In J. Flowerdew (Ed.), *Academic discourse* (pp. 21–39). Harlow, England: Longman.

Bhatia, V. K. and Gotti, M. (Eds.). (2006). *Explorations in specialized genres.* Frankfurt: Peter Lang.

Bialystok, E. (2002). On the reliability of robustness. *Studies in Second Language Acquisition, 24*(3), 481–488.

Biber, D. (1992). On the complexity of discourse complexity: A multidimensional analysis. *Discourse Processes, 15*(2), 133–163.

Biber, D. (2006). *University language: A corpus-based study of spoken and written registers.* Philadelphia/Amsterdam: John Benjamins.

Biber, D., Conrad, S., Reppen, R., Byrd, P., and Helt, M. (2002). Speaking and writing in the university. *TESOL Quarterly, 36*(1), 9–48.

Biber, D. and Finegan, E. (Eds.). (1994). *Sociolinguistic perspectives on register.* Oxford: Oxford University Press.

Birdsong, D. (2005). Nativelikeness and non-nativelikeness in L2A research. *International Review of Applied Linguistics in Language Teaching, 43*, 319–328.

Bohnacker, U. and Rosén, C. (2008). The clause-initial position in L2 German declaratives: Transfer of information structure. *Studies in Second Language Acquisition, 30*(4), 511–538.

Bongaerts, T. (1999). Ultimate attainment in L2 pronunciation. The case of very advanced L2 learners. In D. Birdsong (Ed.), *Second language acquisition and the critical period hypothesis* (pp. 133–159). Mahwah, NJ: Lawrence Erlbaum.

Byrnes, H. (Guest Ed.). (2009a). Instructed foreign language acquisition as meaning-making: Systemic-functional reflections. *Linguistics and Education, 20*(1), 1–79.

Byrnes, H. (2009b). Emergent L2 German writing ability in a curricular context: A longitudinal study of grammatical metaphor. *Linguistics and Education, 20*(1), 50–66.

Byrnes, H., Crane, C., Maxim, H. H., and Sprang, K. A. (2006). Taking text to task: Issues and choices in curriculum construction. *ITL: International Journal of Applied Linguistics, 152*, 85–110.

Byrnes, H., Maxim, H. H., and Norris, J. M. (2010). Realizing advanced FL writing development in collegiate education: Curricular design, pedagogy, assessment. *The Modern Language Journal, 42*, S-1.

Carroll, J. B. (1968). The psychology of language testing. In A. Davies (Ed.), *Language testing symposium: A psycholinguistic approach* (pp. 46–69). London: Oxford University Press.

Carroll, M. and Lambert, M. (2006). Reorganizing principles of information structure in advanced L2s: French and German learners of English. In H. Byrnes, H. Weger-Guntharp, and K. A. Sprang

(Eds.), *Educating for advanced foreign language capacities: Constructs, curriculum, instruction, assessment* (pp. 54–73). Washington, D.C.: Georgetown University Press.

Carroll, M., Murcia-Serra, J., Watorek, M., and Bendiscioli, A. (2000). The relevance of information organization to second language acquisition studies: The descriptive discourse of advanced adult learners of German. *Studies in Second Language Acquisition, 22*(3), 441–466.

Choi, S. and Lantolf, J. P. (2008). Representation and embodiment of meaning in L2 communication: Motion events in the speech and gesture of advanced L2 Korean and L2 English speakers. *Studies in Second Language Acquisition, 30*(2), 191–224.

Christie, F. and Derewianka, B. (2008). *School discourse: Learning to write across the years of schooling.* London: Continuum.

Coffin, C. (2006). *Historical discourse: The language of time, cause and evaluation.* London: Continuum.

Connor, U. (1996). *Contrastive rhetoric: Cross-cultural aspects of second-language writing.* Cambridge: Cambridge University Press.

Connor, U., Nagelhout, E., and Rozycki, W. V. (Eds.). (2008). *Contrastive rhetoric: Reaching to intercultural rhetoric.* Philadelphia/Amsterdam: John Benjamins.

Cook, V. (2008). Multi-competence: Black hole or wormhole for second language acquisition research? In Z. Han (Ed.), *Understanding second language process* (pp. 16–26). Clevedon, UK: Multilingual Matters.

Coppieters, R. (1987). Competence differences between native and near-native speakers. *Language, 63*(3), 544–573.

Crane, C. (2006). Modelling a genre-based foreign language curriculum: Staging advanced L2 learning. In H. Byrnes (Ed.), *Advanced language learning: The contribution of Halliday and Vygotsky* (pp. 227–245). London: Continuum.

DeKeyser, R. M. (2000). The robustness of critical period effects in second language acquisition. *Studies in Second Language Acquisition, 22*(4), 499–533.

Duff, P. A. (2008). *Case study research in applied linguistics.* New York: Lawrence Erlbaum.

Ellis, R. (2009). The differential effects of three types of task planning on the fluency, complexity, and accuracy in L2 oral production. *Applied Linguistics, 30*(4), 474–509.

Ferris, D. and Tagg, T. (1996). Academic oral communication needs of EAP learners: What subject-matter instructors really require. *TESOL Quarterly, 30*(1), 31–58.

Fillmore, C. J. (1979). On fluency. In C. J. Fillmore, D. Kempler, and W. Wang (Eds.), *Individual differences in language ability and language behavior* (pp. 85–101). New York: Academic Press.

Flowerdew, J. (2002). *Academic discourse.* Harlow, England: Longman.

Flowerdew, L. (2005). An integration of corpus-based and genre-based approaches to text analysis in EAP/ESP: Countering criticism against corpus-based methodologies. *English for Specific Purposes, 24*(3), 321–332.

Foster, P. and Skehan, P. (1996). The influence of planning and task type on second language performance. *Studies in Second Language Acquisition, 18*(3), 299–323.

Francis, N. (2006). The development of secondary discourse ability and metalinguistic awareness in second language learners. *International Journal of Applied Linguistics, 16*(1), 37–60.

Halliday, M. A. K. (2002). Spoken and written modes of meaning. In J. J. Webster (Ed.), *On grammar* (pp. 323–351). London: Continuum.

Halliday, M. A. K. and Matthiessen, C. M. I. M. (2004). *An introduction to functional grammar* (Third Edition). London: Edward Arnold.

Halliday, M. A. K. and Webster, J. J. (Eds.). (2009). *Continuum companion to Systemic Functional Linguistics.* London/New York: Continuum.

Harklau, L. (2008). Developing qualitative longitudinal case studies of advanced language learners. In L. Ortega and H. Byrnes (Eds.), *The longitudinal study of advanced L2 capacities* (pp. 23–35). New York: Routledge.

Hasan, R., Matthiessen, C. M. I. M., and Webster, J. J. (Eds.). (2005/2008). *Continuing discourse on language: A functional perspective* (Vol. *1 and 2*). London: Equinox.

Herdina, P. and Jessner, U. (2002). *A dynamic model of multilingualism: Perspectives of change in psycholinguistics.* Clevedon, UK: Multilingual Matters.

Housen, A. and Kuiken, F. (Guest eds.) (2009). Complexity, accuracy and fluency (CAF) in second language acquisition research. *Applied Linguistics, 30*(4), 461–606.

Hyland, K. (2004). *Genre and second language writing.* Ann Arbor, MI: University of Michigan Press.

Hyland, K. (Ed.). (2005). *Metadiscourse: Exploring interaction in writing.* London: Continuum.

Hyland, K. (2006). *English for Academic Purposes: An advanced resource book.* London: Routledge.

Hyland, K. and Bondi, M. (Eds.). (2006). *Academic discourse across disciplines*. Frankfurt: Peter Lang.

Hyon, S. (2001). Long-term effects of genre-based instruction: A follow-up study of an EAP reading course. *English for Specific Purposes, 20* (Supplement 1), 417–438.

Jessner, U. (2006). *Linguistic awareness in multilinguals: English as a third language*. Edinburgh: Edinburgh University Press.

Johns, A. M. (1997). *Text, role, and context: Developing academic literacies*. Cambridge: Cambridge University Press.

Johns, A. M. (2002). *Genre in the classroom: Multiple perspectives*. Mahwah, NJ: Lawrence Erlbaum.

Kinginger, C. (2008). Language learning in study abroad: Case studies of Americans in France. *The Modern Language Journal, Supplement to Volume 92*, Monograph, 2008.

Kinginger, C. and Belz, J. A. (2005). Socio-cultural perspectives on pragmatic development in foreign language learning: Microgenetic case studies from telecollaboration and residence abroad. *International Pragmatics, 2–4*, 369–421.

Koponen, M. and Riggenbach, H. (2000). Overview: Varying perspectives on fluency. In H. Riggenbach (Ed.), *Perspectives on fluency* (pp. 5–24). Ann Arbor, MI: University of Michigan Press.

Kubota, R. and Lehner, A. (2004). Toward critical contrastive rhetoric. *Journal of Second Language Writing, 13*(1), 7–27.

Lantolf, J. P. and Thorne, S. L. (2006). *Sociocultural theory and the genesis of second language development*. New York: Oxford University Press.

Larsen-Freeman, D. (2009). Adjusting expectations: The study of complexity, accuracy, and fluency in second language acquisition. *Applied Linguistics, 30*(4), 579–589.

Larsen-Freeman, D. and Cameron, L. (2008). Research methodology on language development from a complex systems perspective. *The Modern Language Journal, 92*(2), 200–213.

Long, M. H. (2003). Stabilization and fossilization in interlanguage development. In C. J. Doughty and M. H. Long (Eds.), *The handbook of second language acquisition* (pp. 487–535). Malden, MA: Blackwell.

Malone, M. E., Rifkin, B., Christian, D., and Johnson, D. E. (2003). *Attaining high levels of proficiency: Challenges for language education in the United States*. Paper presented at the Conference on Global Challenges and U.S. Higher Education at Duke University, January 23–25, 2003. http://www.duke.edu/web/cis/globalchallenges/pdf/malone-rifkin.pdf.

Martin, J. R. (2009). Genre and language learning: A social semiotic perspective. *Linguistics and Education, 20*(1), 10–21.

Martin, J. R. and Rose, D. (2003). *Working with discourse: Meaning beyond the clause*. London: Continuum.

Martin, J. R. and Rose, D. (2008). *Genre relations: Mapping culture*. London: Equinox.

Matthiessen, C. M. I. M. (2006). Educating for advanced foreign language capacities: Exploring the meaning-making resources of languages systemic-functionally. In H. Byrnes (Ed.), *Advanced language learning: The contribution of Halliday and Vygotsky* (pp. 31–57). London: Continuum.

Moon, R. (Ed.). (2009). *Words, grammar, text: Revisiting the work of John Sinclair*. Philadelphia/Amsterdam: John Benjamins.

Moyer, A. (2004). *Age, accent and experience in second language acquisition: An integrated approach to critical inquiry*. Clevedon, UK: Multilingual Matters.

Norris, J. M. (2006). Assessing advanced foreign language learning and learners: From measurement constructs to educational uses. In H. Byrnes, H. Weger-Guntharp, and K. A. Sprang (Eds.), *Educating for advanced foreign language capacities: Constructs, curriculum, instruction, assessment* (pp. 167–187). Washington, D.C.: Georgetown University Press.

Norris, J. M. and Ortega, L. (2009). An organic approach to investigating complexity, accuracy, and fluency in instructed SLA: The case of complexity. *Applied Linguistics, 30*(4), 555–578.

Ortega, L. (2010). *The bilingual turn in SLA*. Plenary delivered at the 2010 conference of the American Association for Applied Linguistics, Atlanta, GA, March 8, 2010. http://www2.hawaii.edu/~lortega/.

Ortega, L. and Byrnes, H. (Eds.). (2008a). *The longitudinal study of advanced L2 capacities*. New York/London: Routledge.

Ortega, L. and Byrnes, H. (2008b). Theorizing advancedness. Setting up the longitudinal research agenda. In L. Ortega and H. Byrnes (Eds.), *The longitudinal study of advanced L2 capacities* (pp. 281–299). New York/London: Routledge.

Pawley, A. and Syder, F. (1983). Two puzzles for linguistic theory: Nativelike selection and nativelike fluency. In J. Richards and R. Schmidt (Eds.), *Language and communication* (pp. 191–226). London: Longman.

Perdue, C. (Ed.). (1993). *Adult language acquisition: Cross-linguistic perspectives. Vol I. Field methods. Vol. II: The results*. Cambridge: Cambridge University Press.

Piller, I. (2002). Passing for a native speaker: Identity and success in second language learning. *Journal of Sociolinguistics*, 6(2), 179–206.

Reid, J. (2001). Advanced EAP writing and curriculum design: What do we need to know? In T. Silva and P. K. Matsuda (Eds.), *On second language writing* (pp. 143–160). Mahwah, NJ: Lawrence Erlbaum.

Rinner, S. and Weigert, A. (2006). From sports to the EU economy: Integrating curricula through genre-based content courses. In H. Byrnes, H. Weger-Guntharp, and K. A. Sprang (Eds.), *Educating for advanced foreign language capacities: Constructs, curriculum, instruction, assessment* (pp. 136–151). Washington, D.C.: Georgetown University Press.

Robinson, P. (2001). Task complexity, cognitive resources and syllabus design: A triadic framework for examining task influences on SLA. In P. Robinson (Ed.), *Cognition and second language instruction* (pp. 287–318). New York: Cambridge University Press.

Rothery, J. (1996). Making changes: Developing an educational linguistics. In R. Hasan and G. Williams (Eds.), *Literacy in society* (pp. 86–123). London: Longman.

Ryshina-Pankova, M. (2008). Creating textual worlds in advanced learner writing: The role of complex theme. In H. Byrnes (Ed.), *Advanced language learning: The contribution of Halliday and Vygotsky* (pp. 164–183). London: Continuum.

Samuda, V. (2001). Guiding relationships between form and meaning during task performance: The role of the teacher. In M. Bygate, P. Skehan, and M. Swain (Eds.), *Researching pedagogic tasks: Second language learning, teaching and testing* (pp. 119–140). Harlow, England: Pearson Education Limited.

Schleppegrell, M. J. (2004). *The language of schooling: A functional linguistics perspective*. Mahwah, NJ: Lawrence Erlbaum.

Schleppegrell, M. J. (2006). The linguistic features of advanced language use: The grammar of exposition. In H. Byrnes (Ed.), *Advanced language learning: The contribution of Halliday and Vygotsky* (pp. 134–146). London: Continuum.

Schmidt, R. (1992). Psychological mechanisms underlying second language fluency. *Studies in Second Language Acquisition*, 14(4), 357–385.

Segalowitz, N. (2000). Automaticity and attentional skill in fluent performance. In H. Riggenbach (Ed.), *Perspectives on fluency* (pp. 200–219). Ann Arbor: University of Michigan Press.

Selinker, L. (1972). Interlanguage. *International Review of Applied Linguistics*, 10, 209–231.

Shohamy, E. (2006). Rethinking assessment of advanced language proficiency. In H. Byrnes, H. Weger-Guntharp, and K. A. Sprang (Eds.), *Educating for advanced foreign language capacities: Constructs, curriculum, instruction, assessment* (pp. 188–208). Washington, D.C.: Georgetown University Press.

Silva, T. and Matsuda, P. K. (Eds.). (2001). *Landmark essays on ESL writing*. Mahwah, NJ: Hermagoras Press.

Skehan, P. and Foster, P. (2001). Cognition and tasks. In P. Robinson (Ed.), *Cognition and second language instruction* (pp. 183–205). New York: Cambridge University Press.

Slobin, D. I. (1996a). From "thought and language" to "thinking for speaking". In J. J. Gumperz and S. C. Levinson (Eds.), *Rethinking linguistic relativity* (pp. 70–96). Cambridge: Cambridge University Press.

Slobin, D. I. (1996b). Two ways to travel: Verbs of motion in English and Spanish. In M. Shibatani and S. A. Thompson (Eds.), *Grammatical constructions: Their form and meaning* (pp. 195–219). Oxford: Clarendon Press.

Spack, R. (1997). The acquisition of academic literacy in a second language: A longitudinal case study. *Written Communication*, 14(1), 3–62.

Swales, J. M. (1990). *Genre analysis: English in academic and research settings*. Cambridge: Cambridge University Press.

Swales, J. M. (2004). *Research genres: Explorations and applications*. New York: Cambridge University Press.

Swales, J. M. and Feak, C. B. (1994). *Academic writing for graduate students: Essential tasks and skills: A course for nonnative speakers of English*. Ann Arbor, MI: University of Michigan Press.

Tardy, C. M. and Swales, J. M. (2008). Form, text organization, genre, coherence, and cohesion. In C. Bazerman (Ed.), *Handbook of research on writing: History, society, school, individual, text* (pp. 565–581). New York: Lawrence Erlbaum.

Teruya, K. (2006). Grammar as a resource for the construction of language logic for advanced language learning in Japanese. In H. Byrnes (Ed.), *Advanced language learning: The contribution of Halliday and Vygotsky* (pp. 109–133). London: Continuum.

Thompson, G. and Hunston, S. (2006). *System and corpus: Exploring connections*. London: Equinox.

Ventola, E. and Mauranen, A. (Eds.). (1996). *Academic writing. Intercultural and textual issues*. Philadelphia/Amsterdam: John Benjamins.

Verspoor, M. and Lowie, W. (2008). Variability in L2 development from a dynamic systems perspective. *The Modern Language Journal, 92*(2), 214–231.

von Stutterheim, C. and Carroll, M. (2006). The impact of grammatical temporal categories on ultimate attainment in L2 learning. In H. Byrnes, H. Weger-Guntharp, and K. A. Sprang (Eds.), *Educating for advanced foreign language capacities: Constructs, curriculum, instruction, assessment* (pp. 40–53). Washington, D.C.: Georgetown University Press.

von Stutterheim, C., Carroll, M., and Klein, W. (2003). Two ways of construing complex temporal structures. In F. Lenz (Ed.), *Deictic conceptualisation of space, time, and person* (pp. 97–133). Berlin: de Gruyter.

von Stutterheim, C. and Nüse, R. (2003). Processes of conceptualization in language production: Language-specific perspectives and event construal. *Linguistics: Special Issue: Perspectives in Language Production, 41*(5), 851–881.

Wertsch, J. V. (2006). Generalized collective dialogue and advanced foreign language capacities. In H. Byrnes (Ed.), *Advanced language learning: The contribution of Halliday and Vygotsky* (pp. 58–71). London: Continuum.

Zamel, V. and Spack, R. (Eds.) (1998). *Negotiating academic literacies: Teaching and learning across languages and cultures.* Mahwah, NJ: Lawrence Erlbaum.

Part VI

The setting for learning

32

Learning through immersion during study abroad*

Sally Sieloff Magnan and Barbara A. Lafford

Historical discussion

Input and interaction are recognized as essential for language learning (see Mackey, Abbuhl, and Gass, Chapter 1, this volume). Because it can provide large amounts of authentic input and interaction with native speakers, immersion in the target country has been considered the ideal context for language learning. This branch of second language acquisition (SLA) research has focused on the effects of a study abroad (SA) experience on foreign language learning. Research on SA thus fits into studies that investigate the context of learning. The SA context is often compared with learning in foreign language classrooms or in immersion programs in the native country, in an attempt to demonstrate advantages of the abroad experience or, more recently, to consider whether this context is more conducive to language learning than others.

For several decades research in SA has asked two basic questions: What do sojourners learn? What factors facilitate that learning? The way researchers have approached these questions relates to their SLA theoretical perspectives.

In line with interactionist theories of language learning, early SA research focused on linguistic outcomes to demonstrate the advantage of the abroad immersion setting for language acquisition. Often it used quantitative analysis to measure language gain and relate it to specific programs or behaviors of learners abroad. As this line of research progressed, the definition of what constitutes language broadened from grammar, vocabulary, and pronunciation features to include pragmatic and certain sociolinguistic features, which has led to a change in focus for SA research.

Issues surrounding factors that facilitate learning have become the focus of a second wave in SA research, dating from the mid-1990s. Looking primarily at individual and social factors, this research responds to the "social turn" in second language (L2) studies (Block, 2003), which has stimulated interest in investigating issues of identity, gender, and the effects of social networks on SLA. This body of research, which increasingly uses qualitative techniques such as diary studies and interviews, has presented case studies that cast light on curious results from language gain studies done in quantitative frameworks. For example, insights into the individual nature of family stays helps explain differences in language gain among learners who all participate in homestay programs.

Certain early aspects of this research (e.g., interaction studies) relate to cognitive psychology (psycholinguistics). Other more recent aspects (e.g., work on identity, gender, and learner choice of behavior) relate to more socially based theories, including especially Vygotskian-based work in sociocultural and activity theory. The trajectory of SA research has thus followed the development of SLA theoretical approaches, with each contributing to our understanding of how input and interaction enable language learning.

Core issues

The primary issue in SA research today is to determine relationships between language gain and social factors. Research looking at these two areas has rarely connected them in systematic ways. Language gain studies have typically worked with many learners in order to enable the use of statistical analysis, whereas the studies of social factors which seek to examine the depth of experience of an individual, have needed to use case studies on small numbers of learners. The different foci and scope of studies in these two paradigms has made it difficult to consider findings together and thus to come to a comprehensive picture of learning in a SA setting.

A most compelling issue then is how individual and social factors affect linguistic gain outcomes, that is, to make the connection between the first question, "What do sojourners learn?" and the second question "What factors facilitate that learning?" Once we understand this crucial connection, we can address the practical issue of how programs, instructors, and individuals might enhance the immersion experience abroad. We can only then also address the related questions that have occupied much research to date: Who should go abroad, and when in the learning trajectories? What length and type of programs are best? During the programs what should learners do abroad? What is the role of native hosts in the learners' SA experience? What goals are achievable during a SA experience? How do individual differences affect learners' outcomes and satisfaction with SA?

Findings to date have provided partial answers that point toward the following notions: language acquisition is best fostered by longer study before the SA experience, by longer stays abroad, by intense social contacts with native hosts and native social networks and by the avoidance of native language (L1) peer social networks. Yet, language gain is no longer seen as the only goal of SA: personal growth and learning strategy development, identity shifts, and broadened motivations and attitudes are also now viewed as positive outcomes. The crucial nature of the interaction between individual and situational variables is becoming evident as research demonstrates repeatedly how different students shape experiences in unique and personal ways.

More nuanced examinations of these outcomes and the factors fostering them will help researchers compare language learning gains in immersion settings abroad with those in country, in both US immersion settings and classrooms. The SLA field needs to go in the direction of making ties between different theoretical perspectives and their diverse data sets, between the questions of what learners acquire and what facilitates their learning. These ties need to be made through both investigations of large data sets using statistical analysis as well as closer examinations using qualitative methods.

In this chapter, we will focus primarily on the individual and social factors that facilitate learning during SA. However, to situate that discussion, we will also consider briefly the work on linguistic gain. Respecting the chapter's length limitations, we have selected certain studies as touchstones to demonstrate the major issues, research methodologies, and findings. We look exclusively at languages other than English, which stands apart in its global use today, and focus mostly on learners in European countries, consistent with the dominance of Europe as a SA location (Gore, 2005). Beyond Europe, we include some studies from Asia, especially Japan, where the number of SA students has been growing (Gore, 2005).

Data and common elicitation measures

Research on SA has used a variety of data types, research designs, data collection instruments, and qualitative, quantitative, or mixed methods analytical approaches. The choices scholars make limit what we know about the data, and determine what other kinds of data are needed in future research.

Elicitation measures

Types of data. The types of data elicited in SA research are reviewed under the *Instruments* section below.

Research designs. Both experimental and qualitative/descriptive research designs are common in SA research. Experimental designs incorporate both single (SA) group pre-post test designs (O1 X O2) (O1= first observation [pre-test], X=treatment [SA experience], O2= second observation [post-test]), and quasi-experimental designs, which use pre- and post-tests with experimental (SA) and control (AH=at home) groups. These designs have been used to study changes over time in linguistic outcomes (e.g., Brecht *et al.*, 1995; Ife *et al.*, 2000; Kinginger, 2008; Segalowitz and Freed, 2004), sociolinguistic and intercultural competence (e.g., Allen *et al.*, 2006; Elola and Oskoz, 2008; Jones and Bond, 2000; Kinginger, 2008), learning and communication strategies (e.g., Adams, 2006; Lafford, 1995, 2004), and attitude and motivation (e.g., Chieffo and Griffiths, 2004; Isabelli-García, 2006). Although the size of these studies varies considerably with some being quite large (e.g., Brecht *et al.*, 1995; Davidson, 2010), a general weakness of these experimental studies relates to sample size. In addition, these studies cannot use random samples because they work with the limited number of students who self-select to study abroad, which must also be considered when interpreting statistical results (noted much earlier by Freed, 1995).

Qualitative/descriptive SA research includes case studies of individual learners as well as group studies using agglomerated data from several learners (outside of a pre-post test format). This type of research has complemented experimental designs in its investigation of attitudes and motivation (e.g., Isabelli-García, 2006; Kinginger, 2008), intercultural competence (Elola and Oskoz, 2008), and learning strategies (Paige *et al.*, 2004). Such contextualized case studies have also provided unique insights into changes in self-perceptions of identity (e.g., Iino, 2006; Kinginger, 2008; Miyahira and Petrucci, 2006; Pearson-Evans, 2006; Pellegrino-Aveni, 2005), the role of gender and race in language acquisition (e.g., Polanyi, 1995; Siegal, 1995; Talburt and Stewart, 1999), learners' attitudes and motivations (e.g., Brecht and Robinson, 1995; Isabelli-García, 2006; Kinginger, 2008), and information about the social networks in which learners operate while abroad (e.g., Isabelli-García, 2006; Kinginger, 2008; Knight and Schmidt-Rinehart, 2002; Magnan and Back, 2007; Papatsiba, 2006; Pearson-Evans, 2006). What is typically missing here, however, is a quantitative component on the larger data set from which the case studies were drawn (see Kinginger, 2008, as a noted exception), which would allow researchers to combine a broader view of the SA experience to complement the restricted lens of the case study.

Standardized and other objective tests used to study language gain. The research on SA includes the use of large-scale standardized tests. Such tests have been used for diverse languages to measure growth in different linguistic skills: listening and reading abilities in Russian (Educational Testing Service Listening/Reading, Brecht *et al.*, 1995); general proficiency in Japanese (Japanese Proficiency Test, Huebner, 1995); and general proficiency in French (Test de français international, Kinginger, 2008). Objective tests have also been used in a pre-post test format to measure gains in vocabulary (French: Language Awareness Interview, Kinginger, 2008; Spanish: Lexical Association Test, Ife *et al.*, 2000), and in grammar (French: Test de français international, Kinginger, 2008; Spanish: cloze tests [Schell, 2001] and grammaticality judgment tests [Isabelli, 2004]).

A common instrument used in SA research to collect oral data has been the American Council on the Teaching of Foreign Languages (ACTFL) Oral Proficiency Interview (OPI). Using this tool, SA scholars have investigated changes in oral proficiency (Brecht *et al.*, 1995; Guntermann, 1992a, b; Kinginger, 2008; Magnan and Back, 2007; Segalowitz and Freed, 2004), grammatical knowledge (Collentine, 2004; Isabelli, 2004), pronunciation (Simoes, 1996); fluency (Segalowitz and Freed, 2004), communication strategies (DeKeyser, 1991; Lafford, 1995, 2004), and lexical abilities (Guntermann, 1992a, b; Lafford and Ryan, 1995). Although the OPI has been used quite often in SA research to study these factors , criticisms against the OPI as not representing a natural form of interaction (e.g., Johnson and Tyler, 1998) need to be kept in mind when relying on this measure in SA research. In addition, more SA studies should use multiple measures to document linguistic abilities before and after a sojourn abroad in order to triangulate results and gain a greater understanding of the effects of the SA experience.

Instruments used to study individual and social factors. In contrast to SA studies investigating linguistic gains (products), instruments used to gather data about factors influencing the learning process are more open-ended and personalized in nature. They range from written surveys and personal diaries to in-person interviews and direct observations.

Surveys and questionnaires. Surveys and questionnaires have gathered valuable information on several variables that might influence the trajectory of target language acquisition. The Language Contact Profile (LCP, Segalowitz and Freed, 2004) and other demographic questionnaires have been used to record learners' personal information (age, sex), linguistic backgrounds, and language contact with the native and target languages through media and hours spent with host families (Spanish: Lafford, 2004; Segalowitz and Freed, 2004; French: Kinginger, 2008; Magnan and Back, 2007; French/Italian/Spanish: Allen *et al.*, 2006; Japanese: Miyahira and Petrucci, 2006; Russian: Pellegrino-Aveni, 2005). In these studies, the LCP and other such measures are sometimes used retrospectively (e.g., Magnan and Back, 2007), which leads scholars to question the accuracy of data they present.

Surveys and questionnaires have also been used to collect data on learners' attitudes and motivations, and how they might change over time in a SA context (e.g., Chieffo and Griffiths, 2004; Isabelli-García, 2006; Pellegrino-Aveni, 2005). Other surveys and questionnaires have been used to study learning strategies (e.g., Strategic Inventory for Language Learning, SILL [Adams, 2006; Huebner, 1995] and a languages strategy survey [Paige *et al.*, 2004]), perceptions of identity and personality (Allen *et al.*, 2006; Bakalis and Joiner, 2004; Miyahira and Petrucci, 2006), adaptation or acculturation to the target culture (e.g., Strategic Inventory for Learning Culture, SILC [Paige *et al.*, 2002] and the Intercultural Development Inventory, IDI [Allen *et al.*, 2006; Elola and Oskoz, 2008]) and the impact of SA on learners years after their sojourn [Dwyer, 2004].

Discourse completion task questionnaires, in which learners complete a dialog with appropriate rejoinders, have been used to gauge gains in pragmatics (Speech Act Measure of Language Gain [Cohen and Shively, 2007]). An extended version of this task (Free Discourse Completion Task [Barron, 2006]), in which the learner has to write both sides of a dialog, has been used to study the acquisition of pronouns of address. These tasks can be criticized for artificiality, but are widely used because they can be administered relatively easily in a fairly controlled manner. Lafford (2010) points out how methodological variations in interlanguage pragmatics studies (e.g., research designs; instruments [oral and written discourse completion tasks (DCTs), roleplays, verbal reports, naturalistic data] for data collection; learner characteristics [pre-treatment language levels, living conditions]; pragmatic instructional interventions; data analysis) used in SA studies to date could directly affect our (mis) understanding of how L2 pragmatic competence is acquired.

Journals/diary studies. This method of data solicitation has been quite prominent in the study of learners' perceptions of identity, race, and gender (e.g., Russian: Pellegrino-Aveni, 2005; Polanyi, 1995; French: Kinginger, 2008; Japanese: Iino, 2006; Miyahira and Petrucci, 2006; Pearson-Evans, 2006; Siegal, 1995; Spanish: Isabelli-García, 2006; Talburt and Stewart, 1999). Journals and diaries have also been used to study learners' attitudes and motivation (Russian: Polanyi, 1995; French: Douglass, 2007; Kinginger, 2008; Spanish: Isabelli-García, 2006), social networks (Pearson-Evans, 2006), learning strategies (Adams, 2006), and pragmatic abilities (Siegal, 1995). The intimate, personal nature of diary and journal entries provide a unique window to an individual learners' thought processes and attitudes and how these may change over time in reaction to "rich points" (Agar, 1996)—meaningful experiences that promote new understandings of the target culture.

Social network logs. The number and depth of social relationships that learners establish and maintain abroad has been studied with social network logs. Researchers have used these logs to record both contact with natives and with compatriots from the home country, other foreigners, and (virtually) with people back home. For example, Isabelli-García's (2006) groundbreaking study of the establishment of first- and second-degree social networks chronicled learners' interactions with various people in the SA environment.

Learner corpora and blogs. Written data from SA students have often taken the form of learner corpora and blogs. Researchers have analyzed corpora of student reports and texts to study identity issues (Miyahira and Petrucci, 2006; Papatsiba, 2006; Russian: Pellegrino-Aveni, 2005). Other SA scholars have leveraged learner engagement with internet-based social technologies by using their blogs to study both identity (Japanese: Miyahira and Petrucci, 2006) and intercultural competence (Spanish: Elola and Oskoz, 2008). Like diaries and journals, learner blogs often provide access to learners' perceptions of themselves and members of the target culture as well as their reactions to experiences in the SA setting. However, the public nature of blogs often invites commentary and interaction with those who read them (e.g., native speakers of the target language or other learners).

Oral interviews and roleplays. In addition to measuring linguistic gain, the ACTFL OPI has been used frequently to gather information about changes in learners' self-perceptions of identity, as well as adjustments in their attitudes and motivation during the SA experience (Huebner, 1995; Kinginger, 2008; Pellegrino-Aveni, 2005; Polanyi, 1995). A modified version of the OPI, the Simulated Oral Proficiency Interview (SOPI), was used by Isabelli-García (2006) to investigate the influence of social networks on L2 acquisition in an SA context.

In addition to the OPI, several SA scholars have used ethnographic, sociolinguistic, and open interviews to study learner reactions to issues of gender, race, identity, attitudes, motivation, and sociolinguistic/pragmatic competence (Brecht and Robinson, 1995; Douglass, 2007; Iino, 2006; Isabelli-García, 2006; Kinginger, 2008; Miyahira and Petrucci, 2006; Pellegrino-Aveni, 2005; Shively, 2008; Siegal, 1995; Talburt and Stewart, 1999; Twombly, 1995). Focus group interviews involving the interchange of ideas among SA students have sometimes been used to complement individual interviews in the study of identity, race, and gender (Miyahira and Petrucci, 2006; Talburt and Stewart, 1999). Alred and Byram (2006) used semi-structured oral interviews with British L2 French-speaking SA alumni to gauge the long-term effects of SA ten years after the experience. To get a better picture of the context in which SA learners operate, scholars have interviewed faculty, host families, and program coordinators (Iino, 2006; Knight and Schmidt-Rinehart, 2002; Shively, 2008; Talburt and Stewart, 1999). Roleplays have also been used to study sociolinguistic competence (Kinginger, 2008) and communication strategies (Lafford, 1995, 2004).

Observations and field notes. Several SA studies complemented the use of other instruments with observations and field notes. Joining the learners in various activities, some researchers used a participant observation approach (Shively, 2008) whereas other investigators served as outside observers (Kinginger, 2008; Talburt and Stewart, 1999). Studies of L2 learners in Japan have also videotaped or audiotaped SA learners in conversations with host families and friends to study the joint construction of folk beliefs (Cook, 2006), norms of interaction with homestay families (Iino, 2006), and gender roles (Siegal, 1995).

To get a broader picture of the language learning experiences, scholars have observed students as they interact in classroom situations in the SA context. For instance, investigators have examined the value of formal instruction (Brecht and Robinson, 1995) and the nature of native speaker-non-native speaker (NS-NNS) interactions (McMeekin, 2006) using data collected in SA classroom settings. Pellegrino-Aveni (2005) observed SA classroom interaction to gain insights into the strategies learners used to manage their language use and to study the effects of the observation process on learners' interactions. Wilkinson (2002) noted that learners brought SA classroom-type interaction into their conversation with host families.

Data analysis

Quantitative, qualitative, and a mixed method approach have all been used in SA research. In SA research quantitative approaches have been used mostly to investigate possible gains in linguistic outcomes (pronunciation [Simoes, 1996], fluency [Segalowitz and Freed, 2004], grammar [Collentine, 2004], lexical abilities [Collentine, 2004; Kinginger, 2008; Lafford and Ryan, 1995], and communication strategies [DeKeyser, 1991; Lafford, 1995, 2004]). These studies often involve a substantial number (25–100) of university undergraduates (mostly aged 18–21) in order to make generalizations from the analysis. In addition, scholars using a quantitative approach normally use parametric measures such as ANOVAs, Repeated Measures, and correlations (Pearson's r) to test for significant changes in SA learners' linguistic performance over time and for significant correlations of linguistic gain with learner attitudes or amount of language contact. Although there are several advantages of quantitative research (systematicity, generalizability, relatively short time for statistical analysis, prestige factor), this decontextualized mode of inquiry averages responses from the entire group of subjects, thus obscuring individual differences and eliminating possible explanatory social and environmental factors that could be captured using a qualitative case-study approach.

Even though the first in-depth qualitative case studies of SLA in a SA context appeared in the early to mid-1990s (e.g., DeKeyser, 1991; Polanyi, 1995; Siegal, 1995) SA qualitative research has gained notable momentum only recently. Most recent case studies of the social aspects of SLA in a SA setting have been carried out on data from learners of Russian (Pellegrino-Aveni, 2005; Polanyi, 1995), Japanese (Cook, 2006; Miyahira and Petrucci, 2006; Siegal, 1995), French (Kinginger, 2008), and Spanish (DeKeyser, 1991; Isabelli-García, 2006). These studies typically investigate data from a small number of subjects (four–six), which limits the generalizability of their findings, but allows more opportunity for scholars to carry out "thick" descriptions of the complex interrelationships of various social, cognitive, and situational factors.

Qualitative analyses provide insights into an individual's situated experience in a given environment. To understand the complexity of language learning in SA environments, qualitative SA studies almost always triangulate data from various instruments (interviews, observations/field notes, journals/diaries), and occasionally also with quantitative data. For instance, Kinginger (2008) was the first SA study done in a sociocultural theoretical framework that tied quantitatively-measured linguistic outcomes (e.g., TFI scores, Language Awareness Interview) to social and contextual factors (e.g., attitudes, self-perceptions, social networks) investigated with the use of qualitative data (e.g., interviews, journals/diaries, observations, roleplays). The triangulation of these different types of data provides insights into the diverse factors that can lead to notable differences in individual linguistic achievement during a sojourn abroad.

This type of mixed methods approach, in which several data sources are analyzed and the results are triangulated to strengthen the validity of the findings, has been used primarily to investigate social factors including identity, race, and gender motivation, attitude, learning styles and strategies, and intercultural competence (e.g., Allen *et al.*, 2006; DeKeyser, 1990; Douglass, 2007; Elola and Oskoz, 2008; Hokanson, 2000; Iino, 2006; Isabelli-García, 2006; Jones and Bond, 2000; Kinginger, 2008; Miyahira and Petrucci, 2006; Pellegrino-Aveni, 2005; Siegal, 1995; Talburt and Stewart, 1999; Twombly, 1995; Wilkinson, 1998).

Empirical verification: Language gain

There is now substantial empirical evidence that learners improve their linguistic and socio-linguistic abilities through studying abroad. In recent reviews, Collentine and Freed (2004) and Churchill and DuFon (2006) emphasized the breadth of learning demonstrated: improvement in pronunciation and fluency; gain in vocabulary and grammatical accuracy; enhancement in interaction skills, including listening, speaking, and narrative ability; increases in literacy skills; development of pragmatic abilities, including politeness strategies, routines, terms of address, and manipulation of speech acts and registers; intercultural sensitivity; and the development of learning and communicative strategies. These gains vary by language, learning situation, and the learners themselves. Gains often appear in a U-shaped progression, where learners make marked improvement early, appear to stop progressing for a while, and then resume a rapid trajectory of improvement (Pearson-Evans, 2006).

Juxtaposing this language gain against learning in the classroom, research generally shows an advantage for the abroad experience; however, this advantage does not always hold when SA learners are compared with students in domestic immersion settings (Collentine and Freed, 2004, special issue *Studies in Second Language Acquisition*). The editors explained that these studies "provide no evidence that one context of learning is uniformly superior to another for all students, at all levels of language learning, and for all language skills" (p. 164).

Most of these studies, however, do not examine individual or social factors in tandem with linguistic gain. Thus, the disconnect is striking between the two questions, What do learners gain? and What factors influence that gain?

Empirical verification: Individual and social factors

More recent studies associated with the social turn in SLA, which have relied heavily on qualitative methodological approaches, have provided insight into the individual nature of learning abroad, and the complexity of the social situations in which it occurs. These findings help researchers nuance empirical findings on linguistic gain and probe into long-held assumptions regarding programmatic and individual variables.

Programmatic variables. As Churchill and DuFon (2006) pointed out, the design of SA programs has an explicit—and sometimes unintended—impact on the learner's experience. Of particular interest are the effects of program length, living conditions, and social networks, both with the host community and with compatriots on the program or from home.

Length of program. Although "the research of the effect of program length is relatively scare and inconclusive" (Churchill and DuFon, 2006, p. 23), studies that compared gain over time revealed greater gains for longer stays (for Spanish grammar and/or vocabulary: Ife *et al.*, 2000; Isabelli, 2004; for French pragmatics: Hoffman-Hicks, 1999). Dwyer's (2004) 50-year retrospective of SA reported gains in increased confidence and commitment to language study that favored the year and even the summer program, over the semester program. Other studies have shown learners improving aspects of their language skills in programs of a few weeks (for listening: Cubillos *et al.*, 2008; for pronunciation: Simoes, 1996; for self-perceived ability: Cubillos *et al.*, 2008; for intercultural and personal growth: Jones and Bond, 2000). SA studies typically make conclusions about the effect of length of stay using a cross-sectional approach to compare the outcomes of different groups of students participating in programs of varying lengths. In order to understand more fully the effects of time on linguistic abilities in a SA context, more longitudinal research is needed to measure the effects of time spent abroad on the linguistic abilities of given groups at various time intervals in specific contexts.

Participants' language learning backgrounds. The relationship between program length and language gain may be sensitive to the language learning background or the initial proficiency level of the learner. The level of linguistic background needed for success has been studied as the *threshold hypothesis* (cf., Lafford, 2006). Regan (2003) reviewed findings to suggest that lower-level students make the most advances because they have the most to gain, a finding recognized by Churchill and DuFon (2006) with the caveat that advanced learners may enter more readily than beginning learners into contact situations that facilitate language development. Providing evidence to support this contention, Magnan and Back (2007) demonstrated that students with more course work, but the same ACTFL level, made greater gains in speaking proficiency than students with less coursework. They speculated that the increased coursework might have prepared the learners to benefit from aural and written input and given them more confidence, all of which drove their social networking, leading to their linguistic gain (cf., Churchill and DuFon, 2006). This suggestion recalls the finding of Brecht *et al.* (1995) that preprogram reading and grammar skills could predict success abroad.

Initial proficiency level also influences how students learn. Students at lower proficiency levels appear to benefit more from social, especially oral, interaction (Freed, 1990) than from other types of input. In contrast, students at upper levels may profit more than students at lower levels from involvement with written and aural media (Freed, 1990) and from sociolinguistic (Kasper, 1996) and cultural (Pearson-Evans, 2006) aspects of the language.

Living conditions. For years, the home stay was considered the *sine quo non* recommendation because, according to the *Contact Hypothesis*, it provided the social and cultural interaction conducive to language learning (Allen *et al.*, 2006; Knight and Schmidt-Rinehart, 2002; Rivers, 1998). In Schmidt-Rinehart and Knight (2004) and Knight and Schmidt-Rinehart (2002) host mothers assisted American students linguistically, culturally, and psychologically. Other studies have found that interaction with host families has helped increase cultural understanding (Cook, 2006) and learner confidence (Magnan and Back, 2007). Iino (2006) illustrated how conversation in the home can be particularly useful in cultures where different linguistic norms are expected of foreigners (e.g., Japan); however, as Iino pointed out, the home stay also complicates learning foreigner patterns because there is typically no foreigner linguistic model in the household other than the learner him or herself.

Recent ethnographic research, however, points to problems with home stays, such as those described poignantly by Kinginger (2008) and Pellegrino-Aveni (2005). According to Knight and Schmidt-Rinehart (2002), the major problem areas were incompatibility of personalities, lack of interaction, interaction patterns that are not beneficial to language acquisition, or highly stressful living situations.

Program length may also play a role in students' relationships with host families. For example, Schmidt-Rinehart and Knight (2004) and Knight and Schmidt-Rinehart (2002) revealed that students had fewer problems with home stay when they were on longer programs, which might be explained by both the commitment made between students and host families and the time available to work through cultural differences.

Quantitative results also question the superiority of home stays. In a large study, Rivers (1998) found that dormitory students gained more in their Russian language proficiency than home stay students. Magnan and Back (2007) found no significant difference between American students in France who lived with French families or apartment-mates and those who lived in international dormitories or apartments alone or with other Americans. In contrast to these findings, Allen *et al.* (2006) found that their home stay participants reported significantly higher target language linguistic abilities than their non-home-stay peers. These findings may be influenced by the learners' initial proficiency level, however. In all three studies, the group making the greatest gain had either higher initial proficiency levels or more language course work, a variable that might be more influential than living condition.

Social networks and language contact. Beyond the family environment, research has recently considered other social networks, which include three types of communities: those composed primarily of host culture natives, those composed of fellow nationals on the program, and those made virtually with friends and family at home. Lybeck (2002) explained that the first is vital to the SA experience because learners who engage in exchange networks with native speakers feel connected in the host culture. Providing examples of students participating in sports clubs, church groups, community service, and other curricular activities, Kinginger (2008) and Isabelli-Garcia (2006) attested to how students with such networks made the most gain in language ability and cultural insight.

The opposite picture occurs when the social network is with members of the home culture. Magnan and Back (2007) found a negative correlation between language gain and contact with fellow Americans. Research demonstrates how learners often regret they did not interact more with members of the host country because they spent time with the compatriot group (Kinginger, 2008; Wilkinson, 1998).

A social network with people from home is formed increasingly via technology (Pearson-Evans, 2006). In several studies, students who remained connected with friends and family at home through email, English music on iPods, blogs, cell phones, IMs, and internet social networks such as Facebook (eg., Kinginger, 2008; Knight and Schmidt-Rinehart, 2002) demonstrated fewer linguistic gains and less satisfaction with their abroad experience than others who relied less on these virtual contacts. In addition, people from home visit and travel with learners, creating a space where the native language is used, and generally taking the learner from the target culture (e.g., Kinginger's Liza).

A few researchers have pointed to positive effects of technological connections. Pearson-Evans (2006) and Papatsiba (2006) explained how virtual attachments help learners through initial adjustments abroad, build confidence, and reduce loneliness. Elola and Oskoz (2008) demonstrated how blog exchanges between SA students in Spain and classroom students in the USA fostered intercultural competence in both groups.

Contact through media. Many learners mention how they used media (e.g., radio, television, newspapers) to improve their language abilities and gain cultural insights (Kinginger, 2008; Pellegrino-Aveni, 2005). Because media provides authentic input, which should feed language learning, it is surprising that Magnan and Back (2007), using the LCP, did not find a significant relationship between improvement in speaking proficiency and amount of contact with aural and written media. Also using the LCP, Segalowitz and Freed (2004) suggested that learners' initial oral abilities played a role in determining the learners' extracurricular L2 contact. Individual factors (initial language ability and individual learner difference) interact with situational factors (access to media) to affect language gain.

Individual variables. Learners' personal backgrounds and preferences influence how they approach the SA experience, and are also amplified by it (Kinginger, 2008). The most common individual variables treated in research are identity and gender, motivation, attitude, and learning and communicative styles and strategies.

Identity and gender. Identity has many dimensions related to internal factors of an individual, such as race and physical characteristics, gender, age, social class, personal motivations, goals and attitudes, personal history, and even attractiveness of personality, all of which affect a learner's access and reception in foreign communities (Churchill and DuFon, 2006; Iino, 2006; Pellegrino-Aveni, 2005). For example, Miyahira and Petrucci (2006) demonstrated how Okinawan heritage students from Brazil and Peru were expected to speak and act like host nationals and met with disapproval when they did not.

Identity is responsive to external factors, such as expectations of the learner by members of the host society. Taking a post-structural perspective, many studies (e.g., Kinginger, 2008; Pellegrino-Aveni, 2005) examined how perceived power relationships evolve between learners, peers, and natives, and how these relationships influence learners' willingness, and ability, to communicate in the L2.

The role of gender seems particularly influential for women during SA. Siegal's (1995) American women studying in Japan resisted learning honorifics because they perceived a conflict between their self-images as powerful women and the Japanese view of humility. Polanyi (1995), Twombly (1995), and Talburt and Stewart (1999) recounted the alienating experiences of American women in Russia, Costa Rica, and Spain, respectively, who expressed discomfort with ritual flirtation and sexual remarks made by host culture men. Gender issues also affect males, who have been recorded as assuming a protector role for their female compatriots (e.g., Kinginger's [2008] Bill) or as avoiding social male relationships (Isabelli-García, 2006) because they did not want to be associated with male target culture behavior.

The dynamics of gender and cultural behavior may help explain a discrepancy between the linguistic achievement of males and females. Brecht et al. (1995) and Polanyi (1995) suggested that men may make greater linguistics gains abroad than women, because, in line with the Contact Hypothesis, women have less access to meaningful social interaction (Kinginger, 2008).

Pellegrino-Aveni (2005) studied the interplay of internal and external identity factors in terms of learners' perceptions of their ideal self and their actual self. When there is too great a contrast between the ideal self and the actual self the learner's self-image is destabilized. Researchers have found explanations for this destabilization in discourses of power (Gore, 2005) and sociocultural approaches and activity theory (Kinginger, 2008).

Differences between images of the ideal self and the actual self are strongly related to learners' motivation and goals for SA. Learners with a history of doing well in language classes and whose academic success is important to their self-esteem may be frustrated or even depressed when expectations are too high (e.g., Douglass' [2007] Claire; Pellegrino-Aveni's [2005] Rebeccah). Others may feel infantilized, such as Pellegrino-Aveni's Bob, who objected to classroom games, or Jim, when his host father persisted in explaining to him how to boil water.

As a social mirror of self, identity is not monolithic. Kinginger (2008) demonstrated how learners and hosts co-created new identities daily: changes in social situations led to evolution in learners' self concepts, which, in turn, led to more L2 use, and to a further change in their identities. For example, the behavior of Pellegrino-Aveni's (2005) Bob was influenced by his self-comparison to compatriot peers. Because they did not understand social rituals and hierarchies, Pearson-Evans' (2006) Lucy rejected initiatives of her host family, and Kinginger's (2008) Beatrice missed rich points in cultural interaction.

Goals and motivation. Learners go through stages of adjustment leading toward the convergence of the ideal and actual self. Part of this adjustment is often a shift in motivation for language study and in goals for the SA experience. For example, Pellegrino-Aveni's (2005) Rebeccah, who first did not want to be perceived as a foreigner, later used the foreigner personae to foster interaction with native hosts.

Gore (2005) classified goals for SA into two types of discourse: (a) a dominant Grand Tour discourse that is particularly prevalent among women who view SA as a finishing step in a liberal education, and (b) an alternate discourse, which covers a wide variety of goals including inter-cultural competence and academic advantage. Research (e.g., Kinginger, 2008) has shown that, although most students express their goals in terms of the alternate discourse as they begin their SA programs, many of them change to a Grand Tour approach when they become frustrated with language learning and cultural differences that threaten the self. Students' goals also relate to the personal backgrounds they bring to the SA experience. For example, Kinginger's Deidre's lack of travel experience and goal of finishing off her French studies encouraged her to take a Grand Tour approach and to not invest in language learning, whereas Louis's previous reading of the French author Céline and family travel fostered his alternate discourse approach and heavy investment in class work and community service.

Attitude. Attitude change appears to be an inherent part of the abroad experience. Although research has demonstrated that SA does not always bring tolerance or understanding of other cultures (Papatsiba, 2006), Allen *et al.* (2006) demonstrated how, after only an eight-week summer session in France, Italy, or Spain, high school students significantly decreased their identification with their native cultures and significantly increased their identification with the target culture.

Learners also increase their appreciation of their home country, sometimes to the point of becoming its defender (Alred and Byram, 2006; Papatsiba, 2006). In the case of heritage learners returning to the ancestral homeland, SA affects how they view their identity in relation to the diaspora (Miyahira and Petrucci, 2006).

It may be the attitude toward others and the self that evolves the most during the SA experience. Learners have reported less fear of new situations, greater comfort with inabilities, increased self-awareness, and more confidence (Alred and Byram, 2006; Magnan and Back, 2007; Pellegrino-Aveni, 2005), and a better ability to manage a variety of sociocultural tasks (Allen *et al.*, 2006). In fact, Kinginger (2008) questioned the common assumption that SA is about language learning and even that all participants are language learners. Gore (2005) contended that identity development is now a major outcome of the SA experience.

Personalities, cognitive styles, and strategies. Research in SA, as well as in SLA generally, is increasing focus on personality and learning styles and particularly on learning and communication strategies. Bakalis and Joiner (2004) argued that students who have personalities characterized by receptivity to diversity and change are more likely to participate in a SA program than other students. Once abroad, Knight and Schmidt-Rinehart (2002) discussed how personality type was related to problems with home stays, noting difficulties when students were shy, hesitant to interact, or were perceived as non-communicators. In fact, most host families in their study felt that personality was more important in adjusting to the home stay environment than language ability.

Hokanson (2000) used cognitive styles to relate the activity preferences of American students in Guatemala to language acquisition. She found that different types of learners gravitated toward different activities: extroverts spent time with instructors exploring markets, museums, and cafes, while introverts studied mostly at school. After one month, the extroverts were more fluent in oral production, and the introverts were more prolific and expressive in writing. Such activity choices can become purposeful learning strategies, as demonstrated by Kinginger (2008) and Pellegrino-Aveni (2005). In addition to social choices, research has considered learners' use of metalinguistic strategies, such as self-monitoring and repair (Lafford, 1995), as ways to build language proficiency.

Personal background can also affect the choice and use of learning strategies. Adams (2006) found that previous instruction in mnemonic devices had a significant effect on the use of memory strategies at the beginning of the SA period, a difference that was not maintained throughout the abroad experience. Preferences for different learning strategies are related to other factors of identity, especially to gender, as shown by Adams (2006) who found that males used more cognitive strategies than females throughout the abroad program. Lafford (1995) showed that the SA experience broadens the repertoire of communicative strategies of L2 learners. Dekeyser (1990) and Guntermann (1992a, b) found that language learners in Spain and Latin America, respectively, simply avoided using grammatical structures they did not control.

Many authors have suggested instructing students in learning and communicative strategies as a way to enhance their language acquisition while abroad (e.g., Adams, 2006; Magnan and Back, 2007). Exploring curricular interventions with a training manual (Paige *et al.*, 2002), Paige *et al.* (2004) and Cohen and Shively (2007) found that SA students increased their strategy use in many areas (speaking, listening, pragmatic performance in making requests and apologies, non-verbal communication strategies, interpreting culture, and coping with cultural shock), but were unable to relate this growth statistically to the curricular intervention.

In summary, empirical findings have verified common thinking—the SA environment is rich with opportunity for linguistic and cultural learning and for self-growth. More important, however, is that this empirical verification has demonstrated the complexity of the experience, and how it essentially depends on individual and social factors that shape interaction. What continues to elude researchers is a neat relationship between outcome gains and individual experience. Experience responds to individual volition as well as to situational constraints, and, as such, is highly mutable and fluid.

Applications

It is thus no small challenge for practitioners to draw applications from SA research, either for individuals or for programs at home or abroad. The SA research reviewed here could imply the following to facilitate student linguistic success abroad: (a) require a basic knowledge of the target language before studying abroad including the use of authentic oral and written materials to build language and intercultural competence (*threshold hypothesis*); (b) encourage students to study abroad for longer periods of time; (c) set up email exchanges and opportunities for prospective SA students to engage in social computing networks with their future host families to facilitate the establishment of first- and second-level social networks before they arrive on site; (d) provide extensive pre-departure training for SA learners in which they learn about the target language culture, L2 pragmatics, and strategies for learning and communicating in the L2 abroad; (e) require students to live in an interactive home stay situation (without other English speakers) or with native speakers of the target language in other situations; (f) encourage participation in service learning and internships in which learners can use their L2 naturally with NSs of the target language; (g) discourage contacts among co-nationals such as those made through in-country orientations, group trips, and common courses; and (h) discourage virtual connections and extended visits with people back home.

These recommendations are primarily to foster language learning and intercultural competence. However, recent research on SA students (Gore, 2005) has shown that most students who spend time abroad are not language majors and may not even have language learning as their primary goal. The recognition that different learners have different personal goals should make programmatic decision-makers wary of a "one program fits all" approach. As identity growth becomes a more recognized, and valued, outcome of SA, and as individual differences are better understood, it will become increasingly possible to match students with programs developed toward a range of learning goals.

Future directions

Traditional SA research in the 1990s focused heavily on linguistic gains in a SA context (What do sojourners learn?). Recent trends in SA research have shown a strong interest in exploring how social and contextual variables (e.g., length of program, living situation, social networks) interact with individual learner factors (e.g., identity, attitudes, gender, and race issues) during SA. We now need to explore systematically the impact of the interaction of these sociocontextual factors on linguistic gains in a SA context (What factors facilitate learning?). Using as a model such studies as Kinginger (2008) with its quantitative and qualitative dimensions investigating the experience of the same SA students, this impact needs to be front and center on the SA research agenda in both the short and long term. It is only when this tie is made between linguistic abilities and individual and contextual factors that the field of SA research can make a more solid contribution to the field of SLA as a whole.

The preceding review of SA research has pointed to the need for more studies that would give investigators insight into the complex factors contributing to changes in learner performance and perceptions during a SA experience. Research questions could include the following:

- How does the establishment and maintenance of various types of first- and second-degree social networks with native speakers by SA learners affect their linguistic progress and attitudes toward the target culture?
- In homestay situations, how does the composition of the family, the number of students in a home, the orientation for both students and host families, and family interaction affect learners' linguistic gains, attitudes, and perception of self?
- What role do electronic communication pathways (e.g., Skyping, texting, emailing, blogging, Facebooking, Twittering) play in determining or facilitating the amount and type of contact SA learners have with NSs of the target language abroad and with speakers of the learners' native language at home or in the SA environment?
- What types of interactions and feedback do learners experience in formal classroom environments in the host country taught by local or home institution faculty? How do these interactions compare to those in classroom settings in the learners' home institutions?
- What factors in the individual predispose a learner to a successful SA experience? To what degree are those factors responsive to instructional intervention either before or during the SA experience?

In addition to these areas of research, there remain pressing questions about what different methodologies can bring to our understanding.

- What types of insights can be provided by observations of interactions between learners and host families, instructors, and program administrators, or by interviews with these same individuals?
- What new insights can be gained by using concordance programs to analyze learner corpora of oral texts in order to understand interaction patterns between NS-NNS and NS-NS, and also between NS-NNS and NNS-NNS individuals?

The current social turn in SLA research encourages investigation of these questions, especially within qualitative research frameworks. As we move forward, we need to blend the interactionist focus on linguistic outcomes, with its frequent quantitative analyses capable of making generalizations, with the in-depth qualitative examination of individual experience. These two routes to understanding the SA experience may appear incompatible: the individual nature may always defy group analysis. Nonetheless, by investigating the relationship between the questions "What do sojourners learn?" and "What factors influence that learning?" we are enriching our understanding of the complexity of the immersion experience in a SA setting.

Notes

* We would like to recognize and thank Seungyeon Lee and Michelle Petersen for their work with Barbara Lafford and Jacques Arceneaux and Alice Astarita and for their work with Sally Magnan. These four graduate students offered an essential contribution to this article through their careful bibliographic work.

References

Adams, R. (2006). Language learning strategies in the SA context. In M. A. DuFon and E. Churchill (Eds.), *Language learners in SA contexts* (pp. 259–92). Clevedon, UK: Multilingual Matters.

Agar, M. (1996). *The professional stranger: An informal introduction to ethnography* (Second Edition). New York: Academic Press.

Allen, H., Dristas, V., and Mills, N. (2006). Cultural learning outcomes and summer SA. In M. Mantero (Ed.), *Identity and second language learning: Culture, inquiry, and dialogic activity in educational contexts* (pp. 187–214). Charlotte, NC: Information Age Publishing.

Alred, G. and Byram, M. (2006). British students in France: 10 years on. In M. Byram and A. Feng (Eds.), *Living and studying abroad* (pp. 210–231). Clevedon, UK: Multilingual Matters.

Bakalis, S. and Joiner, T. (2004). Participation in tertiary SA programs: The role of personality. *International Journal of Educational Management, 18,* 286–291.

Barron, A. (2006). Learning to say "you" in German: The acquisition of sociolinguistic competence in a SA context. In M. A. DuFon and E. Churchill (Eds.), *Language learners in SA contexts* (pp. 59–88). Clevedon, UK: Multilingual Matters.

Block, D. (2003). *The social turn in second language acquisition.* Edinburgh: Edinburgh University Press.

Brecht, R., Davidson, D., and Ginsberg, R. (1995). Predictors of foreign language gain during SA. In B. F. Freed (Ed.), *Second language acquisition in a SA context* (pp. 37–66). Amsterdam: Benjamins.

Brecht, R. and Robinson, J. L. (1995). On the value of formal instruction in SA: Student reactions in context. In B. F. Freed (Ed.), *Second language acquisition in a SA context* (pp. 317–334). Philadelphia, PA: John Benjamins.

Chieffo, L. and Griffiths, L. (2004). Large scale assessment of student attitudes after a short-term study-abroad program. *Frontiers, 10,* 165–178.

Churchill, E. and DuFon, M. (2006). Evolving threads in SA research. In M. DuFon and E. Churchill (Eds.), *Language learners in SA contexts* (pp. 1–27). Clevedon, UK: Multilingual Matters.

Cohen, A. D., and Shively, R. L. (2007). Acquisition of requests and apologies in Spanish and French: Impact of SA and strategy-building intervention. *The Modern Language Journal, 91*(2), 189–212.

Collentine, J. (2004). The effects of learning contexts on morphosyntactic and lexical development. *Studies in Second Language Acquisition, 26,* 227–248.

Collentine, J. and Freed, B. (Ed.) (2004). *Studies in Second Language Acquisition, 26,* 2 [Special issue].

Cook, H. (2006). Joint construction of folk beliefs by JFL learners and Japanese host families. In M. A. Dufon and E. Churchill (Eds.), *Language learners in SA contexts* (pp. 120–173). Clevedon, UK: Multilingual matters.

Cubillos, J., Chieffo, L., and Fan, C. (2008). The impact of short-term SA programs on L2 listening comprehension. *Foreign Language Annals, 41,* 157–185.

Davidson, D. (2010). Study abroad: When, how long, and with what results? New data from the Russian front. *Foreign Language Annals, 43,* 6–26.

DeKeyser, R. M. (1990). From learning to acquisition? Monitoring in the classroom and abroad. *Hispania, 70,* 238–247.

DeKeyser, R. (1991). Foreign language development during a semester abroad. In B. F. Freed (Ed.), *Foreign language acquisition research and the classroom* (pp. 104–199). Lexington, MA: D.C. Heath.

Douglass, K. B. (2007). *Climbing the Eiffel Tower: An activity theoretic analysis of motives in an individual learner of French.* Unpublished doctoral dissertation. Pennsylvania State University, University Park.

Dwyer, M. (2004). More is better: The impact of SA program duration. *Frontiers, 10,* 151–164.

Elola, I. and Oskoz, A. (2008). Blogging: Fostering intercultural competence development in foreign language and study abroad contexts. *Foreign Language Annals, 41,* 454–477.

Freed, B. (1990). Language learning in a SA context: The effects of interactive and non-interactive out of class contact on grammatical achievement and oral proficiency. *Linguistics, language teaching and language acquisition.* Georgetown University Round Table on Languages and Linguistics.

Freed, B. (1995). Introduction. In B. Freed (Ed.), *Second language acquisition in a study abroad context* (pp. 3–34). Philadelphia: John Benjamins.

Gore, J. (2005). *Dominant beliefs and alternate voices*. New York: Routledge.

Guntermann, G. (1992a). An analysis of interlanguage development over time: Part I, *por* and *para*. *Hispania*, 75, 177–187. http://www.jstor.org.ezproxy1.lib.asu.edu/stable/pdfplus/344777.pdf.

Guntermann, G. (1992b). An analysis of interlanguage development over time: Part II. *ser and estar*. *Hispania*, 75, 1294–1303.

Hoffman-Hicks, S. (1999). *The longitudinal development of French foreign language pragmatic competence: Evidence from SA*. Unpublished doctoral dissertation. Indiana University, Bloomington.

Hokanson, S. (2000). Foreign language immersion homestays: Maximizing the accommodation of cognitive styles. *Applied Language Learning*, 11, 239–264.

Huebner, T. (1995). The effects of overseas language programs: Report of a case study of an intensive Japanese course. In B. Freed (Ed.), *Second language acquisition in a SA context* (pp. 171–193). Philadelphia: John Benjamins.

Ife, A., Vives Boix, G., and Meara, P. (2000). The impact of SA on the vocabulary development of different proficiency groups. *Spanish Applied Linguistics*, 4, 55–84.

Iino, M. (2006). Norms of interaction in a Japanese homestay setting: Toward a two-way flow of linguistic and cultural resources. In M. DuFon and E. Churchill (Eds.), *Language Learners in SA Contexts* (pp. 151–173). Clevedon, UK: Multilingual Matters.

Isabelli, C. A. (2004). The acquisition of null subject parameter properties in SLA: Some effects of positive evidence in a natural learning context. *Hispania*, 87(1), 150–162.

Isabelli-García, C. (2006). SA social networks, motivation, and attitudes: Implications for SLA. In M. DuFon and E. Churchill (Eds.), *Language learners in SA contexts* (pp. 231–258). Clevedon, UK: Multilingual Matters.

Johnson, M. and Tyler, A. (1998). Re-analyzing the OPI: How much does it look like natural conversation? In R. Young and A. He (Eds.), *Talking and testing* (pp. 28–47). Amsterdam: John Benjamins.

Jones, M. and Bond, M. (2000). Personal adjustment, language acquisition, and cultural learning in short-term cultural immersion. *International Review*, 10, 33–49.

Kasper, G. (1996). The development of pragmatic competence. In E. Weltens, and T. Bongaerts (Eds.), *Eurosla* (Vol. 6, pp. 103–120). Amsterdam: UV Uitgeverij.

Kinginger, C. (2008). Language learning in SA: Case studies of Americans in France. *The Modern Language Journal*, 92, Monograph. Oxford: Blackwell.

Knight, S. and Schmidt-Rinehart, B. (2002). Enhancing the homestay: SA from the host family's perspective. *Foreign Language Annals*, 35, 190–201.

Lafford, B. (1995). Getting into, through and out of a survival situation: A comparison of communicative strategies used by students studying Spanish abroad and "at home". In B. Freed (Ed.), *Second language acquisition in a SA context* (pp. 97–121). Amsterdam: Benjamins.

Lafford, B. (2004). The effect of context of learning on the use of communication strategies by learners of Spanish as a second language. *Studies in Second Language Acquisition*, 26(2), 201–226.

Lafford, B. (2006). The effects of study abroad vs. classroom contexts on Spanish SLA: Old assumptions, new insights and future research directions. In C. Klee and T. Face (Eds.), *Selected proceedings of the 7th conference on the acquisition of Spanish and Portuguese as first and second languages* (pp. 1–25). Somerville, MA: Cascadilla Proceedings Project.

Lafford, B. (2010). *Variation in the acquisition of Spanish L2 pragmatic competence "at home" and abroad: Context, methods, and outcomes*. Presentation given at the annual meeting of the Hispanic Linguistics Syposium. Indiana University, October, 2010.

Lafford, B. A. and Ryan, J. M. (1995). The acquisition of lexical meaning in a SA context: The Spanish prepositions *por* and *para*. *Hispania*, 78(3), 528–547.

Lybeck, K. (2002). Cultural identification and second language pronunciation of Americans in Norway. *The Modern Language Journal*, 86, 174–191.

Magnan, S. and Back, M. (2007). Social interaction and linguistic gain during SA. *Foreign Language Annals*, 40, 43–61.

McMeekin, A. (2006). Negotiation in a Japanese SA setting. In M. A. DuFon and E. Churchill (Eds.), *Language learners in SA contexts* (pp. 177–202). Clevedon, UK: Multilingual Matters.

Miyahira, K. and Petrucci, P. (2006). Going home to Okinawa: Perspectives on heritage language speakers studying in the ancestral homeland. In M. Mantero (Ed.), *Identity and second learning* (pp. 257–282). United States: Information Age Publishing.

Paige, R., Cohen, A., Kappler, B., Chi, J., and Lassegard, J. (2002). *Maximizing SA*. Minneapolis, MN: CARLA.

Paige, R., Cohen, A., and Shively, R. (2004). Assessing the impact of a strategies-based curriculum on language and culture learning abroad. *Frontiers*, 10, 253–276.

Papatsiba, V. (2006). SA and experiences of cultural distance and proximity: French Erasmus students. In M. Byram and A. Feng (Eds.), *Living and studying abroad* (pp. 108–133). Clevedon, UK: Multilingual Matters.

Pearson-Evans, A. (2006). Recording the journey: Diaries of Irish students in Japan. In M. Byram and A. Feng (Eds.), *Living and studying abroad* (pp. 38–64). Clevedon, UK: Multilingual Matters.

Pellegrino-Aveni, V. (2005). *SA and second language use: Constructing the self.* Cambridge: Cambridge University Press.

Polanyi, L. (1995). Language learning and living abroad: Stories from the field. In B. Freed (Ed.), *Second language acquisition in a SA context* (pp. 271–291). Amsterdam: Benjamins.

Regan, V. (2003). Sociolinguistics and language learning in a SA context. *Frontiers, 4,* 61–90.

Rivers, W. (1998). Is being there enough? The effects of homestay placements on language gain during SA. *Foreign Language Annals, 31,* 492–500.

Schell, K. (2001). *Functional categories and the acquisition of aspect in L2 Spanish: A longitudinal study.* Unpublished doctoral dissertation. University of Washington, Seattle.

Schmidt-Rinehart, B. and Knight, S. (2004). The homestay component of SA: Three perspectives. *Foreign Language Annals, 37,* 254–262.

Segalowitz, N. and Freed, B. (2004). Context, contact, and cognition in oral fluency acquisition: Learning Spanish in at home and SA contexts. *Studies in Second Language Acquisition, 26,* 173–199.

Shively, R. (2008). *Politeness and social interaction in SA: Service encounters in L2 Spanish.* Unpublished doctoral dissertation. University of Minnesota, Twin Cities.

Siegal, M. (1995). Individual differences and SA: Women learning Japanese in Japan. In B. Freed (Ed.), *Second language acquisition in a SA context* (pp. 225–244). Amsterdam: Benjamins.

Simoes, A. (1996). Phonetics in second language acquisition: An acoustic study of fluency in adult learners of Spanish. *Hispania, 79,* 87–95.

Talburt, S. and Stewart, M. (1999). What's the subject of SA? Race, gender and "living culture". *The Modern Language Journal, 91,* 163–175.

Twombly, S. (1995). Piropos and friendship: Gender and cultural clash in SA. *Frontiers, 1,* 1–27.

Wilkinson, S. (1998). SA from the participants' perspective: A challenge to common beliefs. *Foreign Language Annals, 31,* 23–39.

Wilkinson, S. (2002). The omnipresent classroom during summer SA: American students in conversation with their French hosts. *The Modern Language Journal, 86,* 157–173.

33

Classroom research

Jessica Williams

Historical discussion

Most surveys of classroom second language research (Allwright and Bailey, 1991; Chaudron, 1988; Nunan, 2005) begin with comparative methods studies of the late 1960s and 1970s, which were considered failures because they showed little difference among different teaching methods. These studies simply looked at inputs, such as materials and how language was presented, and outputs—essentially test scores—in hopes of determining a causal relationship between them. The general conclusion is that the studies failed because classrooms are too complex to be compared as unitary phenomena. This heralded a new era of classroom studies, in which the classroom itself, dubbed "the black box" by Long (1980), became the focus. This tradition of "input-output" research continues, recently with more tightly controlled studies (Lightbown *et al.*, 2002; VanPatten and Sanz, 1995). In the past 30 years, however, researchers have also investigated what happens between input and output, that is, what actually goes on in second language classrooms, addressing many different questions, and using a variety of approaches.

Early classroom studies were primarily of two types: first, descriptive studies attempting to provide a global view of teaching orientation (Fröhlich *et al.*, 1985; Mitchell, 1989), or documenting the presence of specific aspects of classroom input and/or interaction thought to be important in second language learning (Seliger and Long, 1983), and second, ethnographic studies of classrooms (Duff, 1995; Harklau, 1994; Watson-Gegeo, 1988) that examined classroom interaction and learning, and cultural constructions of behavior within a broader social and political context. These took a variety of theoretical perspectives, including language socialization, ethnography of communication, and critical theory.

Core issues

What is Classroom Second Language Research? Language learning researchers are interested in classroom learning contexts for what they can reveal about language learning processes in general, but also for quite practical reasons. They want to know how instruction can be made more effective and more efficient. Thus, classroom second language research is located at the nexus of theoretical and practical concerns. It is research in contexts with the following characteristics:

- the purpose is educational
- an instructor is present
- more than one learner is present.

These parameters thus exclude experimental studies outside of the classroom in which learning opportunities are created solely for the purpose of research. Classroom research highlights the role of the teacher and of inter-learner dynamics and investigates questions such as:

- What do teachers do and say?
- How do they respond to learners?
- How do learners respond to the teacher?
- How do they respond to one another?
- What are the patterns of interaction in the classroom?
- How does the language of instructed learners change in the short-term and long-term?
- How does what happens in the classroom relate to learners' lives outside of the classroom?

These questions have been investigated from a variety of theoretical perspectives, among others, ethnomethodology, ethnography of communication, communities of practice, sociocultural theory, and critical theory. The most common framework for the investigation of classroom second language learning, however, has been the Input, Interaction, Output Approach (Gass and Mackey, 2007; Long, 1996; Mackey, Abbuhl, and Gass, Chapter 1, this volume; see Block, 2003, for a critique). This approach examines the nature of input to learners, learner output, and how interaction can direct attention and lead to modifications of both input and output. Two meta-analyses have shown that interaction is indeed facilitative of acquisition (Keck *et al.*, 2006; Mackey and Goo, 2007).

It is important to distinguish between classroom research and other similar research, which may have implications for classroom learning, for example, studies of interaction between dyads or among groups outside of the classroom (Lyster and Izquierdo, 2009; Mackey, 1999, 2002; McDonough, 2005; Nassaji, 2007, 2009). These studies may be considered *classroom-oriented research* rather than classroom research. Such studies outnumber those conducted in classrooms—perhaps because they are easier to conduct and control—despite the greater ecological validity of the latter. The extent to which research outside the classroom reflects what happens inside real classrooms remains an important question (Foster, 1998; Gass *et al.*, 2005; Li, 2010; Lyster and Izquierdo, 2009; Mackey, 2002). Gass *et al.* (2005) showed there was little difference in interactional patterns between a laboratory and a classroom setting. Their results suggested that task, rather than setting, had the greatest impact on how learners interacted, and by implication, how and what they learned. Thus, although this chapter will be limited to classroom research, the questions that such research addresses spans a broader range of contexts. Two major categories of classroom second language research will be discussed in this chapter.

Studies that involve researcher intervention

Typically in these studies, the researcher specifies tasks, participant structures, or interactional moves by the teacher. Often these are quasi-experimental studies in which the researcher is attempting to manipulate or control these variables in order to determine their contribution to learning. Many have a pre-test/post-test design as well as a control or comparison group. Although these controls make results more generalizable, such interventions inevitably move the classroom and the learners away from their natural state.

Research in intact classrooms

Typically, the researcher in these studies simply observes and/or records what happens in all or part of the class. These studies have greater face validity than studies in which researchers intervene, but the trade-off is that it is harder to make general claims based on the results. Participants may be asked to reflect on their thoughts or behavior, often in a stimulated recall (Nabei and Swain, 2002; Mackey *et al.* 2007; Zyzik and Polio, 2008), but there is no intervention during instruction. Most qualitative studies belong in this category (Canagarajah, 1993; Duff, 1995; Waring, 2009).

In these studies, the goal is often simply to describe: What kinds of feedback do teachers provide? How do teachers and/or learners focus on matters of form versus meaning? When do learners use their first language? Most studies have not made the leap to actual learning; rather, they focus on how learning opportunities are created and structured. In some studies, however, there is an attempt to match variables to outcomes: What kind of feedback is most likely to lead to a change in learner output? Under what circumstances do learners notice or use explicit information about language form or use? Where claims have been made about learning, they have tended to be about immediate or short-term change, rather than long-term gains in proficiency.

Data and common elicitation measures

How is classroom learning investigated?

A wide range of tools and techniques has been used in classroom research to collect and analyze classroom data. In some cases, it is possible to separate these data collection techniques from theory. For example, audio and video-recordings have been used in studies from a variety of theoretical perspectives. However, in other instances, it is difficult to disentangle the theoretical stance of the study from its methodology. In sociocultural research and in conversational analysis, data collection methods are embedded in theory and often cannot be separated. For example, Waring (2009) uses a single case analysis, which is typical of a conversation-analytic framework. Therefore, both data collection and approaches to analysis are in some cases presented together.

Direct observation. Many studies have used direct observation as at least one form of data collection. These have ranged from audio-recording (Ellis *et al.*, 2001a; Lyster and Ranta, 1997; Ohta, 2000; Zhao and Bitchener, 2007) and video-recording (Nabei and Swain, 2002; Zyzik and Polio, 2008) to observational schemes, such as the Communicative Orientation to Language Teaching (Ammar, 2008; Lyster and Ranta, 1997; Sheen, 2004), to records of computer-mediated communication (de la Fuente, 2006). The techniques used in these studies have the advantage of providing the closest approximation of what happens in classrooms when no research is being conducted.

Interaction analysis. Classroom research has included observations of both intact classes (Antón, 1999; Foster and Ohta, 2005; Loewen and Philp, 2006) and those that have been manipulated by the researcher in order to examine a specific aspect of interaction (Doughty and Varela, 1998; Kim and McDonough, 2008; Swain, 1998). The focus of these studies has included feedback moves, teacher questions and responses, form-focused episodes, and inter-learner negotiation.

Introspective methods. Introspective methods ask learners and teachers to reflect on their performance, behavior, knowledge, and beliefs. These techniques allow researchers to verify their own findings against the views of the participants in interaction. Especially relevant to classroom research are stimulated recall protocols, in which participants and researchers review the interaction together and the participants are asked to elaborate retrospectively on their interaction or perspectives (Egi, 2010; Mackey, 2002, 2006; Nabei and Swain, 2002; Zyzik and Polio, 2008). Other studies have used more informal interviews and questionnaires to gain a deeper perspective on participants' thoughts during interaction and on their learning (Kim and McDonough, 2008; Lyster and Izquierdo, 2009; Williams, 1999; Zyzik and Polio, 2008). These usually complement other methods. Finally, in some studies, learners are asked to write down their thoughts about their learning processes using a diary or learning log (Mackey, 2006; Simard, 2004).

Ethnography/social construction and communities of practice. Studies that take an ethnographic, social constructionist, or community of practice perspective often go beyond the classroom to examine how the classroom fits into a larger social, political, or cultural context (Crago, 1992; Duff, 1995; Haneda, 2006). Ethnographies aim to provide a rich description of learners' experiences in the classroom beyond specific interactions. Some social constructionist studies, making use of critical theory, examine power relationships in classrooms and how these reflect issues of identity and power that extend beyond the classroom (see Duff, Chapter 25, this volume). For example, Toohey (1998), in her study of English language learners in primary school, found that specific classroom practices had the effect of reinforcing these students' marginalization and reifying community stratification.

Sociocultural analysis. Sociocultural theory posits that mental processes are mediated by cultural artifacts and activities, and perhaps above all, by language. These processes develop as a result of social interaction (Lantolf and Thorne, 2007; Lantolf, Chapter 4, this volume). Data collection therefore seeks to capture evidence of the development of these mental processes in the course of interaction. This includes investigations of assistance provided by learners to one another (Foster and Ohta, 2005; Ohta, 2000; Swain and Lapkin, 1995), or by the teacher (Antón, 1999; Waring, 2009), and of private speech, that is, learners addressing themselves in low-volume oral rehearsal (Ohta, 2001).

Conversation analysis/micro-analysis. Conversation analysis offers a micro-analytic moment-by-moment orientation to talk in interaction. It examines how conversation is managed, how participants orient themselves to conversation, and how they co-construct their roles in those conversations as well as opportunities for learning. It requires painstaking transcription of utterances, including suprasegmental features, turn sequences, overlaps, interruptions, and in some studies, even gesture (Mori, 2004; Waring, 2009). The main claim of conversation analysis is that these very close transcriptions allow us to see second language learning as it unfolds. Analysis is limited to what is found in these data; the approach does not permit speculation about processes or contexts beyond the conversation.

Empirical verification

Feedback. Perhaps the most widely researched topic in classroom second language research is feedback (Loewen, Chapter 2, this volume). Early studies focused on patterns of feedback, including what teachers respond to. In general, the trigger for teacher feedback is a real or perceived error of content or form. Later studies began to address the range of feedback that teachers give in response to learner error, as well as its effectiveness. A variety of terms have been used, but there are two broad categories of feedback on error: (1) moves in which the teacher revises the non-target-like utterance in a target-like form, providing positive evidence (as well as implicit negative evidence), and (2) moves in which learners are given more explicit negative evidence and prompted to use their own resources to formulate a more target-like utterance. The first are generally called *recasts* or *reformulations* and the second, *prompts* or *elicitations*. Recasts vary in the degree to which they inform the learner of their error, that is, in the explicitness of negative evidence they provide. Prompts may also vary, specifically, in the amount and type of guidance they provide regarding the target form.

The final topic addressed by these studies is the effect of feedback. An immediate learner response to a feedback move is usually referred to as *uptake*. This response may contain an attempt at repair, an acknowledgment, or simply a repetition of the feedback move. Alternatively, the learner may appear to ignore the feedback. Several studies have addressed factors that influence uptake, repair, and/or signals of noticing. These factors include the focus of feedback, pedagogical approach, learner proficiency, working memory, and anxiety (Ammar and Spada, 2006; Ellis, 2007; Lyster and Mori, 2006; Sheen, 2004, 2006, 2008). In addition, a few classroom studies have looked beyond the post-feedback turn and have sought to determine if there is any long-term impact on acquisition of various types of feedback, as well as the factors that might influence this (Ammar, 2008; Ellis *et al.*, 2006; Loewen and Phlip, 2006; Lyster and Izquierdo, 2009; Sheen, 2007, 2008).

Many studies of feedback are largely descriptive. They show when and how teachers respond to error. Most studies across a variety of classroom contexts and learners (foreign language, second language, immersion, children, adults) have demonstrated that recasts are the dominant form of feedback (Ellis *et al.*, 2001b; Loewen and Philp, 2006; Lyster and Mori, 2006; Lyster and Ranta, 1997; Nassaji, 2007; Panova and Lyster, 2002; Sheen, 2004). One reason for this is that recasts are the least intrusive; they allow interaction to continue unimpeded. Indeed, proponents of recasts claim this as their fundamental advantage—consistency with an overall communicative orientation to teaching and learning. In addition, several studies suggest that teachers are more likely to provide feedback on grammatical errors than other types of errors.

Learners may respond to feedback in a variety of ways. In order to repair their errors, they must perceive the teacher's move as corrective. It has been argued that that prompts are more likely to be clearly perceived as corrective than are recasts (Ammar, 2008; Lyster, 1998b; Nassaji, 2007). However, this conclusion hinges on the measure of noticing, which is generally uptake. Yet this spot is not always available for repair (Oliver, 1995; Zhao and Bitchener, 2007). The teacher may recast a learner's utterance and continue, not offering any opportunity for repair. It is possible that the impact is only evident in a later turn (Mackey and Philp, 1998). Indeed, research outside of classrooms has demonstrated that a simple analysis of subsequent turns offers a skewed picture of the impact of feedback (McDonough and Mackey, 2006).

When no uptake occurs, other evidence may show that learners have noticed the feedback, a step that could lead to further processing. Mackey demonstrates that learners do notice even implicit feedback, such as recasts, although these results differ depending on the type of form being recast. Mackey's use of learner logs and stimulated recalls provides evidence that learner noticing does take place even in the absence of overt evidence (2006; Mackey *et al.*, 2007).

Conflicting evidence of the relative effectiveness of these kinds of feedback in the classroom and the variation in definitions of terms such as *recast* have led researchers to examine teachers' and learners' language and interactional moves in more detail. The feedback moves themselves have come under the closest scrutiny, with a focus on the following factors: (1) explicitness of the corrective nature of the move, (2) the length and complexity of the move, and (3) whether the feedback is extensive or intensive, that is, whether just one form (or very few forms) are the focus of feedback or if the teacher simply responds to whatever errors emerge.

Studies have also shown the conflicting findings regarding the relative effectiveness of recasts and prompts when the measures of effectiveness are uptake and repair. As noted, part of the reason for this disparity is how results are counted. A count of subsequent turns is likely to favor feedback that allows or requires the learner to take the next turn. Studies that have used this method of counting have generally found prompts to be more effective (Lyster, 1998a; Lyster and Mori, 2006; Lyster and Ranta, 1997; Panova and Lyster, 2002). However, when repair rates are compared only on the basis of available turns, the rate of repair following recasts is much closer to that of prompts (Sheen, 2004). It should also be noted that since prompts, unlike recasts, do not provide any positive evidence about the target form, their success depends on the learners' current knowledge of the form being corrected. Thus, Lyster and Izquierdo (2009) explain their results by concluding that learners who received recasts benefited from the positive evidence they received whereas learners who received prompts benefited from the clearer negative evidence they contain. Within sociocultural theory, the move that follows a recast is an important transition point. Even if the uptake is simply an imitation, this may still represent learning. This transition from feedback to uptake occurs in the learner's zone of proximal development, a site of collaborative activity where imitation can spur development. This feedback-imitation sequence helps learners to internalize the new knowledge (Lantolf, Chapter 4, this volume).

Nicholas *et al.* (2001), in their review of recast studies, conclude that the most effective recasts are narrow and explicit. In other words, the feedback addresses a single form and is clearly corrective. This claim has generally been substantiated by both classroom and classroom-oriented research. Both Nassaji (2007, 2009) and Sheen (2006) found that more explicit recasts were more likely to lead to uptake and repair. Mackey *et al.* (2007) demonstrated that learners were more likely to perceive more explicitly corrective feedback. However, Li (2010), in a meta-analysis of corrective feedback, found the impact of implicit feedback is more likely to endure than that of explicit feedback. Ellis and Sheen (2006) argue that the picture is more complicated, in that explicit and implicit knowledge may develop separately, even as they may influence each other. They suggest that explicit forms of feedback are more likely to affect explicit knowledge, but that they may also affect implicit knowledge indirectly.

The use of uptake and repair as evidence of acquisition has been the subject of some debate. As a result, several researchers have chosen to use other assessments, principally pre-test/post-test designs of various types, including measures of developmental stage and tests of implicit and explicit knowledge (Norris and Ortega, Chapter 35, this volume). As in the studies that used uptake and repair as a measure of noticing or learning, these studies generally found that more explicit feedback was more effective. Specifically, prompts were generally found to be more effective than recasts (Ammar and Spada, 2006; Lyster, 2004; Lyster and Saito, 2010; Russell and Spada, 2006; Yang and Lyster, 2010, although see Mackey and Goo, 2007). Ellis *et al.* (2006) and Sheen (2007) go even further, showing that metalinguistic information (e.g., "you need to use past tense") was particularly effective in developing explicit knowledge, but also indirectly, implicit knowledge. In those studies where recasts were found to be effective using measures beyond immediate uptake or repair, the recasts generally included negative evidence, that is, some clear signal to the learner that an error had been made, such as stress or rising intonation (Doughty and Varela, 1998; Loewen and Philp, 2006).

Beyond feedback moves and responses to them, classroom characteristics may play an important role in determining the effectiveness of various types of feedback. Several studies suggest that feedback choices should be made in concert with the overall pedagogical orientation of the classroom (Ellis and Sheen, 2006; Lyster, 1998b, 2007; Lyster and Izquierdo, 2009; Lyster and Mori, 2006; Mackey *et al.*, 2007; Panova and Lyster, 2002). In meaning-oriented classrooms, form-oriented feedback may be most appropriate because it clearly calls learner attention to form. In contrast, in form-oriented settings, even somewhat more implicit feedback, such as recasts, may be an adequate form of negative evidence. In the end, much will depend on what aspects of the feedback are perceived by the learner.

Focus on form. Another major topic that has been extensively investigated in classroom research is Focus on Form. This topic overlaps with feedback but includes other aspects of classroom interaction as well. Researchers have sought to answer the following questions:

- Do teachers and learners in communicative classrooms focus on formal aspects of language? If so, which aspects?
- Does a focus on form have any demonstrable effect on acquisition?
- What factors influence whether participants focus on form?
- If focus on form is effective, can it be facilitated by the teacher or specific interactional activities?

One difficulty in reporting on focus-on-form research is the variation in terms and definitions used in the literature. All definitions share the notion that a form-focused episode (in some studies called an language-related episode) is one in which, for a relatively brief time, participants focus on language as object, but the overall focus is on the communication of meaning. Where they differ is: (1) whether the episode can be preemptive rather than in response to a learner's problem and (2) how explicit a move can be in order to still qualify as focus on form (that is, still part of an interaction that is largely focused on meaning.

Classroom research shows that both teachers and learners do sometimes focus on form during otherwise meaning-focused interaction. However, findings vary widely as to how much, from a study by Pica (2002), which showed focus on form to be a relatively rare feature of a content-based ESL class, to classes in which a form-focused episode occurs every few minutes (Basturkmen *et al.*, 2002; Loewen, 2003). Leeser (2004) and Williams (1999, 2001) found the number of form-focused episodes, particularly those initiated by learners, to be related to language proficiency, with more advanced learners choosing to focus on form more frequently. Williams (2001), Loewen (2003), and Zhao and Bitchener (2007) all found the majority of such episodes had a lexical focus whereas Leeser (2004) found this to be an effect of proficiency, with lower proficiency learners more frequently choosing a lexical focus and higher proficiency learners, a grammatical focus. Kim and McDonough (2008) found more grammatically than lexically focused episodes across all proficiency levels but a rise in lexical episodes with increasing proficiency. The considerable variation in these findings may well be related to varying task demands.

A smaller number of classroom studies have addressed the effects of form-focused episodes. Most have examined how the variables in these episodes—their initiator, resolution, length, and focus—affect uptake and learning. Uptake shows how a learner responds to the form-focused episode, as in this example from Basturkmen *et al.* (2002, p. 6):

Student 1: **PRE**diction
Student 2: I think the second syllable is stressed.
Student 1: Pre**DICT**ion ←uptake

It is easier to assess this impact if the focus of the episode is known in advance, as in the case of intensive recasts and some preemptive focus on form. However, several studies have also examined reactive and/or extensive focus on form, using tailor-made tests to determine its impact (e.g., Ellis *et al.*, 2006; Sheen, 2007; Swain, 1998; Williams, 2001). Most of these studies have addressed the narrower issue of teacher feedback. Only a few have also looked at student-initiated form-focused episodes, but one study (Zhao and Bitchener, 2007) suggests that the level of successful uptake in teacher-learner and learner-learner episodes is very similar.

Basturkmen *et al.* (2002) distinguished between reactive form-focused episodes, which include error correction and other kinds of feedback, and pre-emptive episodes, in which participants initiate a focus on form in the absence of an error or overt problem in communication. In particular, they were interested in the use of metalinguistic language in these exchanges. They found that students frequently used metalanguage in pre-emptive form-focused episodes and that this was significantly related to uptake. This was not the case with reactive form-focused episodes, where, metalanguage was rarely employed. Several other studies have also found that the impact is greater, as measured by uptake (Ellis *et al.*, 2001a, 2001b) and post-tests (Loewen, 2005; Williams, 2001), when learners, rather than the teacher, initiate a form-focused episode.

Negotiation. Feedback is a frequent feature of form-focused episodes, but it is possible for learners to focus on form in the absence of feedback on error, usually in response to a problem in communication. Research on interaction has posited a major role for learner negotiation in promoting noticing and by extension, in facilitating acquisition both in and outside of the classroom (Keck *et al.*, 2006; Mackey and Goo, 2007). Learner participation in such negotiated interaction is thought to facilitate comprehension, but also to highlight what learners do not know and increase the salience of novel or problematic elements in the input. The facilitating effect of negotiation on noticing or recognition of novel input is particularly likely with lexical items (Kuiken and Vedder, 2005; Swain, 1998; Williams, 2001). Similar findings regarding the benefits of negotiation on noticing have emerged from studies of computer-mediated communication (Lai and Zhao, 2006; Shekary and Tahririan, 2006; Smith, 2004). In spite of these positive findings on the connection between negotiation and noticing, some classroom research suggests noticing of forms during negotiation does not always lead to acquisition (Kuiken and Vedder, 2005).

Even if the direct connection between negotiation and acquisition still needs more empirical verification, negotiation has been shown to have an effect on modification of output by classroom learners. Modification of output has been claimed to promote metalinguistic reflection and deeper linguistic processing (Lyster and Izquierdo, 2009; Swain, 1998). Following a breakdown in communication, learners may strive to bring their production closer to the target.

At the same time, the role of negotiation remains problematic for classroom research. Most studies of the effect of negotiation have been carried out in experimental settings outside of the classroom (McDonough, 2005; Muranoi, 2000). This may be because negotiation is not frequent in second language classrooms (Foster, 1998; Foster and Ohta, 2005; Pica, 1997, 2002; Williams, 1999). Pica (1997) notes that, in particular, learners rarely negotiate morphosyntactic features. She suggests that this is because most classroom tasks do not require it. As a result, there has been considerable effort to discover what sorts of tasks maximize the need for learners to negotiate formal aspects of language (Loschky and Bley-Vroman, 1993; Pica et al., 1993; Kuiken and Vedder, Chapter 22, this volume) and further, to integrate such tasks naturally in the classroom.

This assumed positive—either direct or indirect—role for negotiation in the classroom has spurred investigation into negotiation beyond the design of interactive tasks. Several studies have specifically examined the nature of collaborative interaction, focusing on the characteristics of interaction and interactants that lead to successful task and learning outcomes. Within theoretical perspectives that see language acquisition as a primarily social process, such as sociocultural theory, these investigations are particularly significant. It may be the collaborative aspect of such interaction, rather than its potential to direct learner attention to form, that is most important. Several classroom studies have demonstrated that when learners collaborate, they can create new knowledge that none of the interactants holds individually (Ohta, 2001; Swain, 1998; Swain and Lapkin, 2002).

This is especially clear in comparison studies of the same participants working alone and in collaboration with other learners, in which the collaborative pairs were more successful (Kim, 2008). Not all collaboration is equally useful, however; success depends on a variety of factors. Leeser (2004) and Williams (1999) both found the higher-proficiency learners were more likely to engage in negotiation during form-focused episodes. They also found, along with Kim and McDonough (2008), that such negotiations were more likely to lead to a successful resolution of the episode with more advanced learners.

Storch (2002a, 2002b) investigated the dynamics of interaction in collaborative tasks. She examined participants' interaction along two dimensions: mutuality and equality. Equality refers to the degree of control over the direction and content of the interaction, and mutuality refers to the level of engagement, as seen in responses and sharing moves. She found that the pairs demonstrating a high level of mutuality were the most successful in task completion. Closer examination of the interaction showed active problem solving and co-construction of knowledge among these pairs.

From a sociocultural perspective, collaboration is far broader than the limited negotiation triggered by miscommunication or lack of comprehension (Lantolf, Chapter 4, this volume). Learners may assist one another to create and internalize new knowledge in a variety of other ways. Foster and

Ohta (2005) showed that negotiation of meaning was just one of the many features of collaborative interaction, and in fact, not a particularly frequent one. Learners were able to assist one another and co-construct knowledge in the course of interaction by using prompts, repairing their own utterances and those of their classmates, as well as showing interest and offering encouragement.

These three areas of investigation: corrective feedback, focus on form, and negotiation have been at heart of classroom second language research in the last two decades. All three have been found to be facilitative of acquisition.

Applications

In early classroom research, the reference point for classroom interaction tended to be conversation and other naturally occurring speech events. The overarching pedagogical goal was to make the second language classrooms more like the real world, with rich input and opportunities for interaction and output. Classroom studies were replete with criticisms of classrooms that focused too much on the formal aspects of language with little regard to learners' communicative needs. The past 25 years of research has substantiated the importance of the role of interaction. However, recent research has also raised doubts about pedagogical approaches that focus exclusively on communication.

Probably the most substantial criticism of such approaches has revolved around the development of accuracy. Such criticisms led to the current trend in research related to linguistic accuracy. This renewed focus on form has resulted in more finely grained investigations of feedback practices and of instruction that focuses on language as object in the context of communicative language teaching, and finally, in the perhaps inevitable swing of the pendulum, a reexamination of explicit knowledge and its role in second language development (DeKeyser, 2003; Hulstijn and Ellis, 2005). These issues have been pursued mostly in experimental studies and will now need to be investigated more thoroughly in classrooms settings, but they suggest that teachers are justified in maintaining a focus on form in their instruction. In a recent meta-analysis, Spada and Tomita (2010) concluded that explicit instruction had an advantage over more implicit instruction both in the short and long term. Their results indicate that this advantage goes beyond the development of explicit knowledge and simple rules; it extends to the complex forms as well. Even the role of metalinguistic knowledge and processing, long shunned in many communicative classrooms, has once again come into focus (Basturkmen et al., 2002; Ellis, 2007; Ellis et al., 2006; Sheen, 2007; Simard, 2004), with findings generally pointing to a positive instructional role for such knowledge.

A final important trend in classroom second language research has been the inclusion of broader social aspects of the classroom interaction and the social context of learning. This review has focused on the more cognitive aspects of classroom research, but like so much of second language research (Atkinson, 2011; Block, 2003; Duff, Chapter 25, this volume; Firth and Wagner, 2007; Swain and Deters, 2007, Lantolf, Chapter 4, this volume), investigations of classrooms have also recently taken a social turn. This area of research will help teachers to consider the broader context of language learning and to understand how meaning is interactionally achieved in the classroom.

Future directions

Future research in classroom second language research is likely to pursue both the cognitive and social aspects of language learning in a more unified way (Zuengler and Miller, 2006). This will involve movement away from single variable-driven cause-and-effect research, that is, investigations of the impact of a controlled variable (e.g., type of recast) on another (e.g., uptake). Because classrooms are complex and dynamic systems, current approaches may prove to be overly simplistic (Larsen-Freeman, Chapter 5, this volume). Research designs will increase in complexity and become more interdisciplinary.

The learning sciences offer possible avenues for future classroom research. The learning sciences combine the cognitive tradition of quantitative, variable-driven, experimental research with more qualitative approaches that draw on a variety of traditions, including ethnography and sociocultural theory. In part, this approach is in the response to one drawback of traditional approaches for studying classroom interaction, namely, that it is almost impossible to control rigorously all the variables in a learning environment. The learning sciences take a broader view of the learning environment, of how the myriad factors in the environment contribute to learning, and how these factors might be changed to improve learning. It shares much with complexity theory (Larsen-Freeman, Chapter 5, this volume) in that classrooms and language learning are complex systems whose properties emerge from the interaction of multiple variables, not all of which can be predicted, still less, controlled.

A major advantage of such an approach is that it attempts to break down the division between research and pedagogy, between researchers and teachers, and between experimental rigor and ecological validity. One strand of the learning sciences, *design-based research*, may be of particular interest to second language classroom researchers, in that it focuses recursively on learning processes and learning environments rather than exclusively on learning outcomes. The goal is not to test a specific theory. Rather, design and theory are developed simultaneously and revised continuously through the research process. This approach, more widely used in science and mathematics education, "simultaneously pursues the goals of developing effective learning environments and using such environments as natural laboratories to study learning and teaching" (Sandoval and Bell, 2004, p. 200; for a more detailed description, see A Peer Tutorial for Design-Based Research, 2006).

Finally, there will be a need for longer-term investigations of classroom learners. Because classrooms are dynamic systems and language learning is a complex and non-linear process, short-term studies can offer only a limited perspective on the process and the impact that we, as researchers and teachers, can have on this process. Some studies have already shown important differences between short and long term impact of classroom activities and instruction (Li, 2010; Lyster and Saito, 2010; Mackey and Goo, 2007). Only with more longitudinal studies of classrooms and classroom learners will we be able to deepen and elaborate our knowledge.

References

A Peer Tutorial For Design-Based Research. University of Georgia. http://projects.coe.uga.edu/dbr/tutorial.htm. Retrieved July 24, 2010.

Allwright, R. and Bailey, K. (1991). *Focus on the language classroom: An introduction to classroom research for language teachers*. Cambridge: Cambridge University Press.

Ammar, A. (2008). Prompts and recasts: Differential effects on second language morphosyntax. *Language Teaching Research, 12*, 183–210.

Ammar, A. and Spada, N. (2006). One size fits all? Recasts, prompts and L2 learning. *Studies in Second Language Acquisition, 28*, 543–574.

Antón, M. (1999). The discourse of a learner-centered classroom: Sociocultural perspectives on teacher-learner interaction in the second language classroom. *The Modern Language Journal, 83*, 308–318.

Atkinson, D. (Ed.). (2011). *Alternative approaches to second language acquisition*. New York: Routledge.

Basturkmen, H., Loewen, S., and Ellis, R. (2002). Metalanguage in focus on form in the communicative classroom. *Language Awareness, 11*, 1–13.

Block, D. (2003). *The social turn in second language acquisition*. Washington, D.C.: Georgetown University Press.

Canagarajah, S. (1993). Critical ethnography of a Sri Lankan classroom: Ambiguities in student opposition to reproduction through ESOL. *TESOL Quarterly, 27*, 601–626.

Chaudron, C. (1988). *Second language classrooms: Research on teaching and learning.* Cambridge: Cambridge University Press.

Crago, M. (1992). Communicative interaction and second language acquisition: An Inuit example. *TESOL Quarterly, 26*, 487–505.

DeKeyser, R. (2003). Implicit and explicit learning. In C. Doughty and M. Long (Eds.), *Handbook of second language learning* (pp. 313–348). Oxford: Blackwell.

de la Fuente, M. (2006). Classroom L2 vocabulary acquisition: Investigating the role of pedagogical tasks and form-focused instruction. *Language Teaching Research, 10*, 263–295.

Doughty, C. and Varela, E. (1998). Communicative focus on form. In C. Doughty and J. Williams (Eds.), *Focus on form in classroom second language acquisition* (pp. 114–138). Cambridge: Cambridge University Press.

Duff, P. (1995). An ethnography of communication in immersion classrooms in Hungary. *TESOL Quarterly, 29*, 505–537.

Egi, T. (2010). Uptake, modified output and learner perceptions of recasts: Learner responses as language awareness. *The Modern Language Journal, 94*, 1–21.

Ellis, R. (2007). The differential effects of corrective feedback on two grammatical structures. In A. Mackey (Ed.), *Conversational interaction in second language acquisition* (pp. 339–360). Oxford: Oxford University Press.

Ellis, R., Basturkmen, H., and Loewen, S. (2001a). Preemptive focus on form in the ESL classroom. *TESOL Quarterly, 35*, 407–432.

Ellis, R., Basturkmen, H., and Loewen, S. (2001b). Learner uptake in communicative ESL lessons. *Language Learning, 51*, 281–318.

Ellis, R., Loewen, S., and Erlam, R. (2006). Implicit and explicit corrective feedback and the acquisition of L2 grammar. *Studies in Second Language Acquisition, 28*, 339–368.

Ellis, R. and Sheen, Y. (2006). Reexamining the role of recasts in second language acquisition. *Studies in Second Language Acquisition, 28*, 575–600.

Firth, A. and Wagner, J. (2007). On discourse, communication and (some) fundamental concepts in SLA research. *The Modern Language Journal, 91*, 757–772.

Foster, P. (1998). A classroom perspective on the negotiation of meaning. *Applied Linguistics, 19*, 1–23.

Foster, P. and Ohta, A. (2005). Negotiation for meaning and peer assistance in second language classrooms. *Applied Linguistics, 26*, 402–430.

Fröhlich, M., Spada, N., and Allen, P. (1985). Differences in the communicative orientation of classrooms. *TESOL Quarterly, 19*, 27–56.

Gass, S. and Mackey, A. (2007). Input, interaction, and output in second language acquisition. In B. VanPatten and J. Williams (Eds.), *Theories in second language acquisition* (pp. 175–199). Mahwah, NJ: Erlbaum.

Gass, S., Mackey, A., and Ross-Feldman, L. (2005). Task-based interactions in classroom and laboratory settings. *Language Learning, 55*, 575–611.

Haneda, M. (2006). Classrooms as communities of practice: A reevaluation. *TESOL Quarterly, 40*, 807–817.

Harklau, L. (1994). ESL and mainstream classes: Contrasting second language learning contexts. *TESOL Quarterly, 28*, 241–272.

Hulstijn, J. and Ellis, R. (2005). Theoretical and empirical issues in the study of implicit and explicit second-language learning. *Studies in Second Language Acquisition, 27*(2).

Keck, C., Iberri-Shea, G., Tracy-Ventura, N., and Wa-Mbaleka, S. (2006). Investigating the empirical link between task-based interaction and acquisition: A meta-analysis. In J. Norris, and L. Ortega (Eds.), *Synthesizing research on language learning and teaching* (pp. 91–131). Amsterdam: Benjamins.

Kim, Y. (2008). The contribution of collaborative and individual tasks to the acquisition of L2 vocabulary. *The Modern Language Journal, 92*, 114–130.

Kim, Y. and McDonough, K. (2008). The effect of interlocutor proficiency on the collaborative dialogue between Korean as a second language learners. *Language Teaching Research, 12*, 211–234.

Kuiken, F. and Vedder, I. (2005). Noticing and the role of interaction in promoting language learning. In A. Housen and M. Pierrard (Eds.), *Investigations in instructed second language acquisition* (pp. 353–381). Berlin: Mouton.

Lai, C. and Zhao, Y. (2006). Noticing and text-based chat. *Language Learning and Technology, 10*, 102–120.

Lantolf, J. and Thorne, S. (2007). Sociocultural theory and second language acquisition. In B. VanPatten and J. Williams (Eds.), *Theories in second language acquisition* (pp. 201–224). Mahwah, NJ: Erlbaum.

Leeser, M. (2004). Learner proficiency and focus on form during collaborative dialogue. *Language Teaching Research*, *8*, 55–81.

Li, S. (2010). The effectiveness of corrective feedback in SLA: A meta-analysis. *Language Learning*, *60*, 309–365.

Lightbown, P., Halter, R., White, J., and Horst, M. (2002). Comprehension-based learning. The limits of "do-it-yourself." *The Canadian Modern Language Review*, *58*, 427–464.

Loewen, S. (2003). Variation in the frequency and characteristics if incidental focus on form. *Language Teaching Research*, *7*, 315–345.

Loewen, S. (2005). Incidental focus on form and second language learning. *Studies in Second Language Acquisition*, *27*, 361–386.

Loewen, S. and Philp, J. (2006). Recasts in adult English L2 classrooms: Characteristics, explicitness and effectiveness. *The Modern Language Journal*, *90*, 536–555.

Long, M. (1980). Inside the "black box": Methodological issues in classroom research on language learning. *Language Learning*, *30*, 1–42.

Long, M. (1996). The role of the linguistic environment in second language acquisition. In W. Ritchie and T. Bhatia (Eds.), *Handbook of research on second language acquisition* (pp. 413–468). New York: Academic Press.

Loschky, L. and Bley-Vroman, R. (1993). Grammar and task-based methodology. In G. Crookes and S. Gass (Eds.), *Tasks and language learning* (pp. 123–167). Clevedon, UK: Multilingual Matters.

Lyster, R. (1998a). Negotiation of form, recasts, and explicit correction in relation to error types and learner repair in immersion classrooms. *Language Learning*, *48*, 183–218.

Lyster, R. (1998b). Recasts, repetition and ambiguity in L2 classroom discourse. *Studies in Second Language Acquisition*, *20*, 51–80.

Lyster, R. (2004). Differential effects of prompts and recasts in form-focused interaction. *Studies in Second Language Acquisition*, *26*, 399–432.

Lyster, R. (2007). *Learning and teaching languages through content: A counterbalanced approach*. Amsterdam/Philadelphia: John Benjamins.

Lyster, R. and Izquierdo, J. (2009). Prompts versus recasts in dyadic interaction. *Language Learning*, *59*, 453–498.

Lyster, R. and Mori, H. (2006). Interactional feedback and instructional counterbalance. *Studies in Second Language Acquisition*, *28*, 269–300.

Lyster, R. and Ranta, L. (1997). Corrective feedback and learner uptake: Negotiation of form in communicative classrooms. *Studies in Second Language Acquisition*, *19*, 37–66.

Lyster, R. and Saito, K. (2010). Oral feedback in classroom SLA: A meta-Analysis. *Studies in Second Language Acquisition*, *32*, 265–302.

Mackey, A. (1999). Input, interaction and second language development: An empirical study of question formation in ESL. *Studies in Second Language Acquisition*, *21*, 557–587.

Mackey, A. (2002). Beyond production: Learners' perceptions about interactional processes. *International Journal of Educational Research*, *37*, 379–394.

Mackey, A. (2006). Feedback, noticing and instructed second language learning. *Applied Linguistics*, *27*, 405–430.

Mackey, A., Al-Khalil, M., Atanassova, G., Ham, M., Logan-Terry, A., and Nakatsukasa, K. (2007). Teachers' intentions and learners' perceptions about corrective feedback in the L2 classroom. *Innovation in Language Learning and Teaching*, *1*, 129–152.

Mackey, A. and Goo, J. (2007). Interaction research in SLA: A meta-analysis and research synthesis. In A. Mackey (Ed.), *Conversational interaction in second language acquisition* (pp. 407–452). Oxford: Oxford University Press.

Mackey, A. and Philp, J. (1998). Conversational interaction and second language development: Recasts, responses and red herrings? *The Modern Language Journal*, *82*, 338–356.

McDonough, K. (2005). Identifying the impact of negative feedback and learner responses on ESL question development. *Studies in Second Language Acquisition*, *27*, 79–103.

McDonough, K. and Mackey, A. (2006). Responses to recasts, repetitions, primed production and linguistic development. *Language Learning*, *56*, 693–72.

Mitchell, R. (1989). Second language learning: Investigating the classroom. *System*, *17*, 192–210.

Mori, J. (2004). Negotiating sequential boundaries and learning opportunities: A case from a Japanese language classroom. *The Modern Language Journal*, *88*, 536–550.

Muranoi, H. (2000). Focus on form through interaction enhancement: Integrating formal instruction into a communicative task in EFL classrooms. *Language Learning*, *50*, 617–673.

Nabei, T. and Swain, M. (2002). Learner awareness of recasts in classroom interaction: A case study of an adult EFL student's second language learning. *Language Awareness*, *11*, 43–63.

Nassaji, H. (2007). Elicitation, reformulation and their relationship to learner repair in student-teacher dyadic interaction. *Language Learning*, *57*, 511–548.

Nassaji, H. (2009). Effects of recasts and elicitations in dyadic interaction and the role of feedback explicitness. *Language Learning*, *59*, 411–452.

Nicholas, H., Lightbown, P., and Spada, N. (2001). Recasts as feedback to language learners. *Language Learning*, *51*, 719–758.

Nunan, D. (2005). Classroom research. In E. Hinkel (Ed.), *Handbook in second language teaching and research* (pp. 225–240). Mahwah, NJ: Erlbaum.

Ohta, A. (2000). Rethinking recasts: A learner-centered examination of corrective feedback in the Japanese language classroom. In J. K. Hall and L. Verplaetse (Eds.), *Second and foreign language learning through classroom interaction* (pp. 47–71). Mahwah, NJ: Erlbaum.

Ohta, A. (2001). *Second language acquisition processes in the classroom: Learning Japanese*. Mahwah, NJ: Erlbaum.

Oliver, R. (1995). Negative feedback in child NS-NNS conversations. *Studies in Second Language Acquisition*, *17*, 459–481.

Panova, I. and Lyster, R. (2002). Patterns of corrective feedback and uptake in the adult ESL classroom. *TESOL Quarterly*, *36*, 573–595.

Pica, T. (1997). Second language teaching and research relationships: A North American view. *Language Teaching Research*, *1*, 48–72.

Pica, T. (2002). Subject-matter content: How does it assist the interactional and linguistic needs of classroom language learners? *The Modern Language Journal*, *86*, 1–19.

Pica, T., Kanagy, R., and Faludon, J. (1993). Choosing and using communicative tasks for second language research and instruction. In S. Gass and G. Crookes (Eds.), *Tasks and language learning: Integrating theory and practice* (pp. 9–34). Clevedon, UK: Multilingual Matters.

Russell, J., and Spada, N. (2006). The effectiveness of corrective feedback for the acquisition of L2 grammar: A meta-analysis of the research. In J. Norris and L. Ortega (Eds.), *Synthesizing research on language learning and teaching* (pp. 133–162). Amsterdam: John Benjamins.

Sandoval, W. and Bell, P. (2004). Design-based research methods for studying learning in context: Introduction. *Educational Psychologist*, *39*, 199–201.

Seliger, H. and Long, M. (1983). *Classroom oriented research in second language acquisition*. Rowley, MA: Newbury House.

Sheen, Y. (2004). Corrective feedback and learner uptake in communicative classrooms across instructional settings. *Language Teaching Research*, *8*, 263–300.

Sheen, Y. (2006). Exploring the relationship between characteristics of recasts and learner uptake. *Language Teaching Research*, *10*, 361–392.

Sheen, Y. (2007). The effects of corrective feedback, language aptitude, and learner attitudes on the acquisition of English articles. In A. Mackey (Ed.), *Conversational interaction in second language acquisition* (pp. 301–322). Oxford: Oxford University Press.

Sheen, Y. (2008). Recasts, anxiety, modified output and L2 listening. *Language Learning*, *58*, 835–874.

Shekary, M. and Tahririan, M. (2006). Negotiation of meaning and noticing in text-based online chat. *The Modern Language Journal*, *90*, 557–573.

Simard, D. (2004). Using diaries to promote metalinguistic reflection among elementary school students. *System*, *13*, 34–48.

Smith, B. (2004). Computer-mediated negotiated interaction and lexical acquisition. *Studies in Second Language Acquisition*, *26*, 365–398.

Spada, N. and Tomita, Y. (2010). Interactions between type of instruction and type of language feature: A meta-analysis. *Language Learning*, *60*, 263–308.

Storch, N. (2002a). Patterns of interaction in ESL pair work. *Language Learning*, *52*, 119–158.

Storch, N. (2002b). Relationships formed in dyadic interaction and opportunity for learning. *International Journal of Educational Research*, *37*, 305–322.

Swain, M. (1998). Focus on form through conscious reflection. In C. Doughty and J. Williams (Eds.), *Focus on form in classroom second language acquisition* (pp. 64–81). Cambridge: Cambridge University Press.

Swain, M. and Deters, P. (2007). "New" mainstream theory: Expanded and enriched. *The Modern Language Journal*, *91*, 820–836.

Swain, M. and Lapkin, S. (1995). Problems in output and the cognitive processes they generate: A step toward second language learning. *Applied Linguistics*, *16*, 371–391.

Swain, M. and Lapkin, S. (2002). Talking it through: Two French immersion students' response to reformulation. *International Journal of Educational Research*, *3/4*, 285–304.

Toohey, K. (1998). "Breaking them up, taking them away": ESL students in grade 1. *TESOL Quarterly*, *32*, 61–84.

VanPatten, B. and Sanz, C. (1995). From input to output: Processing instruction and communicative tasks. In F. Eckman, D. Highland, P. W. Lee, J. Mileham, and R. Weber (Eds.), *Second language acquisition theory and pedagogy* (pp. 169–185). Mahwah, NJ: Erlbaum.

Waring, H. Z. (2009). Moving out of IRF (Initiation-Response-Feedback): A single case analysis. *Language Learning*, *59*, 796–824.

Watson-Gegeo, K. (1988). Ethnography in ESL: Defining the essentials. *TESOL Quarterly*, *22*, 575–592.

Williams, J. (1999). Learner-generated attention to form. *Language Learning*, *49*, 583–625.

Williams, J. (2001). The effectiveness of spontaneous attention to form. *System*, *29*, 325–340.

Yang, Y. and Lyster, R. (2010). Effects of form-focused practice and feedback on Chinese EFL learners' acquisition of regular and irregular past tense forms. *Studies in Second Language Acquisition*, *32*, 235–263.

Zhao, S. and Bitchener, J. (2007). Incidental focus on form in teacher-learner and learner-learner interactions. *System*, *35*, 431–447.

Zuengler, J. and Miller, E. (2006). Cognitive and sociocultural perspectives: Two parallel worlds? *TESOL Quarterly*, *40*, 35–58.

Zyzik, E. and Polio, C. (2008). Incidental focus on form in university Spanish literature courses. *The Modern Language Journal*, *92*, 53–70.

34

Language learning through technology

Trude Heift and Carol A. Chapelle

Historical discussion

Many second language teachers and researchers may think of the use of computer technology in language learning as a phenomenon arising in the mid-1990s with the advent of the World Wide Web. In fact, however, the idea of harnessing the capabilities of technology for language instruction was acted upon in the 1960s by individual teachers and a few researchers at universities. For the first two decades (1960s–1980s), researchers in this area were preoccupied with the question of whether learning might be better accomplished through computer-assisted instruction than in the classroom by, for example, measuring the acquisition rate and mastery of grammar and vocabulary taught in a computer-based language learning environment compared to a teacher-led classroom. Although such comparisons are relevant in some contexts, research attempting to understand what, why, how, and to what end technology leads to successful learning outcomes is the challenge for most applied linguists working in this area today. In addition to these comparative studies, some teachers, in contrast, were interested in developing programs that provided learners with some added features such as individualized instruction, interactivity, and record keeping. For instance, the PLATO project developed in the early 1970s included a reading course with interactive vocabulary and grammar drills and translation tests that measured students' progress. It remains clear why such capabilities were of interest, but the materials from that period reflect the structural view of language dominant in North America at that time, and therefore, the beginnings of computer-assisted language learning (CALL) are typically shown as text-based interactive programs intended to teach grammar and vocabulary (Hart, 1981).

Such materials spanned the period when large mainframe computers were used (1960s–1980s), but the introduction of the microcomputer created an important sociological function of widening dramatically the number of teachers who had access to computer technology and therefore the creativity in thinking about the question of how computers might be used in language teaching (Ahmad *et al.*, 1985). During this period, for example, Johns (1986) introduced the idea that learners' might benefit by using computers to conduct their own corpus-based investigations—an idea that continues to grow in its relevance in view of the corpus of language data learners have access to on the Web and the growing corpus-based research in applied linguistics. Overall, CALL evolved through application of ideas from communicative language teaching to include interactive language games, and other activities in which language was not evaluated but rather interaction and conversation was stimulated (Higgins and Johns, 1984; Underwood, 1984).

Such CALL activities extended beyond computer-learner interactions to include interactions among learners working together and using the computer as a catalyst for their conversation (Mohan, 1992).

Despite the creativity applied to the issues during this period, the fact remained that the first microcomputers were painfully lacking in the basic capabilities needed for teaching language such as adequate presentation of language characters on the screen, coordinated presentation of video with interactivity and sufficient processing size to conduct analyses of learners' production beyond the word and phrase. By the late 1980s, microcomputers had become more sophisticated, making possible the introduction of multimedia materials and natural language processing (NLP) which aims at automated understanding and generation of natural human languages. With this genera-tion of computers, authors were able to create interactive CALL programs with images, video, and sound thus providing opportunities for learners to obtain input from and practice with carefully selected and sequenced audio and video materials. Such technologies made it possible to develop input-based instruction, whereas the NLP capabilities allowed for the computer to provide an analysis of learners' language and relevant feedback. The best examples of both types of CALL materials included interactive help for learners as well.

In the early 1990s, local area networks (LANs) had been established in many language learning centers and some teachers and researchers were exploring the possibilities for computer-mediated communication (CMC) among students within classrooms (Swaffar et al., 1998). Such commu-nication, conducted using text chat, seemed to provide an effective addition to face-to-face conversation that was so painful for many students in the foreign language classroom. The written medium provided opportunity for useful reflection on linguistic form while prompting more even participation in classroom discussion. Moreover, evidence suggested that the linguistic functions students performed in interactive written communication expanded the scope and number of linguistic functions that students engaged in during class (Chun, 1994).

At the same time that LANs were being used in university laboratories, most university teachers had access to the next generation of electronic communication—the Internet. Before the Web popularized electronic communication, some teachers saw the potential of the electronic version of the pen pal, i.e., the key pal (e.g., Sanaoui and Lapkin, 1992). Such communication evolved beyond the face-to-face talk at the keyboard to CMC across distance and time (Thorne and Payne, 2005). Today, technology is used to connect learners with each other and other speakers of the target language through a variety of stationary and mobile devices (Sharples et al., 2007). These include asynchronous modes which function as electronic mailboxes where users can deposit text, audio, and video messages for each other to pick up at their convenience as well as synchronous interactive modes of conversing in real time through text, audio, and video, or some combination of the three. An important aspect of today's technology, called Web 2.0, is the participation of the users in creating and designing their own place in an ever more flexible and accessible virtual space of the Web. Beyond the language classroom, the Web of today is well populated and heavily traveled whereby students might work collaboratively with their peers or remain alone at the computer, which may be at an Internet café or at their home. The Web therefore provides an unprecedented amount and quality of target language opportunities for input, help, information, and interaction for learners who know how to use them.

The technology practices that have evolved throughout this period are important for under-standing current practices and options, which today include various combinations of all facets of historically developed approaches including including "traditional" CALL, multimedia, artificial intelligence, communications software, Web 2.0 applications. Thus the acronym CALL nowadays refers to any environment in which a learner, alone or collaboratively with peers, uses technology in a second or other language. Throughout these changes in technological capabilities and teaching practices, however, several core issues have remained important from the perspective of studying how technology can help learners develop their language ability.

Core issues

Computer technology represents a significant extension of the types of language experiences that learners engage in, and therefore researchers are keen to understand through research and development the extent to which computer technology can contribute to language learning. The research issues are numerous but we have clustered them into three areas of investigation that are related to and extensions of research issues in other areas of language learning research—the role of interaction, the challenge of individual differences, and the goals of autonomous learners.

Interactions through technology

Since interaction has been shown to be important for second language acquisition (SLA) (see the opening chapter of this volume), how beneficial are the interactions learners engage in through technology for language learning? Clearly, learners' use of technology involves various forms of interaction, between the learner and the computer and between the learner and other people in CMC. Ellis (1999) takes a broad view of the ways in which interaction might benefit language learners by examining cognitive and social benefits of both interpersonal and intrapersonal interaction, and Chapelle (2003) extends that framework to include human–computer interaction as well. Of all of the types of interactions that occur, particularly interesting in CALL research are the instances where learners are able to get help with or feedback on their language as well as to engage in conversation and negotiation of meaning with another speaker of the language.

A first type of interaction occurs when learners ask for help in their comprehension and production of the language (Rost and Fuchs, 2004). Such interactions can take place as learners read any electronic texts or use word processing software and consult interactive CALL materials. For example, learners who are reading online can move back and forth between the text and an online dictionary to get help with word meaning. Similarly, learners writing at the computer have the option of checking an electronic dictionary when they need help in choosing the wording that they need to express particular meanings or accessing a concordance which provides a means for learners to encounter and explore words in a variety of contexts by listing segments of texts containing the word. Such help is accessed while students are engaged in meaning-making, and therefore can be conceptualized similarly to the potentially valuable interactions that occur between students and teachers during face-to-face interactions (Gass, 2003). In a CALL environment such interactions can take place when learners ask for repetitions, modifications, or elaborations. Developers of CALL materials can intentionally provide these opportunities for learners, but learners who are able to use strategies for getting help on the Internet and in word processing software can create valuable computer-learner interactions beyond pedagogical software.

A second type of interaction in CALL appears when learners' performance is followed by computer-generated feedback. Such feedback can come from instructional materials containing explicit exercises aimed at providing learners with practice on particular grammatical forms and meanings (e.g., Heift, 2010). Such materials, which can focus on specific areas of grammar or vocabulary, reading or listening, are aimed at providing learners with immediate feedback about the correctness of their responses to questions in a manner that engages learners in focused interactions that illuminate their gaps in their knowledge. For instance, this can be achieved with NLP software. CALL software that provides pronunciation feedback also exists and has shown promising results; however, feedback on learners' spoken language is not yet sufficiently reliable to allow for free conversations. Important interactions can also occur if learners are able to use the feedback provided by word processing programs—both the word-level spelling mark-up and the sentence-level grammatical mark-up.

A third type of interaction occurs as students communicate with other learners through CMC. The study of learners' interaction in oral and written CMC both in and outside the classroom has demonstrated expanded opportunities for interaction for language learners beyond face-to-face tasks. Some teachers and researchers have developed and investigated tasks for electronic communication based on the guidelines that come from work on face-to-face communication tasks (e.g., Blake, 2000). Others have expanded the types of tasks and perspectives on interaction studied (e.g., Belz, 2001; Lamy and Goodfellow, 1999). However, investigations based on each of these perspectives on interaction with and through technology do not suggest that students left on their own will engage in productive interactions through technology; instead, the research suggests the important role the teacher plays in demonstrating to students how to make the most out of such opportunities for interaction.

Individual learner differences and assessment

The second research issue is the evaluation of learner performance particularly in environments where the computer program can provide appropriate feedback or instructional decision-making. How can the computer be used to analyze learners' language and behavior in a manner that increases capacity for assessment of individual characteristics beyond what can be done with current testing methods? In view of the variability in the abilities of any like-designated group of learners, the need for means of analyzing and recording specific learners' knowledge is crucial in order to attempt to provide appropriate instruction. For instance, Heift (2008) investigated learner variability by examining learner usage of a variety of grammatical constructions in a beginner second language (L2) course for German. Her longitudinal data which were collected and analyzed by a NLP program emphasize the dynamic aspects, complexity, and non-linearity of interlanguage and, more generally, the variability of SLA: students not only acquire L2 constructs at a different rate but they also exhibit differences and variation in their own patterns of acquisition. Her study outcomes suggest an individualized learning environment capable of making distinctions at a very fine-grained level. While this is an issue that appears to be solvable only through the use of technology, in view of the complexity of analysis of learners' language as well as the possibilities for individualization in instruction, much more research is needed, with regards to the kind of language analysis that needs be performed to achieve an individualized environment most conducive to language learning.

Learner autonomy and identity

The third research issue in CALL arises from the dynamic that is evident if one considers the learner as an agent who chooses learning options, selects strategies, and constructs his or her own version of self in the target language (see Dörnyei and Ushioda, 2009). The study of possibilities the learner constructs for himself or herself is potentially as rich as the technologies themselves because these issues extend beyond the classroom to the life-long process of language learning. This fact creates both the need for learners to develop their autonomous strategies for language learning (Benson, 2001) and the opportunity for researchers to study how these strategies play out. Although the concept of autonomy does not have to be tied to technology, the reality today is that if autonomous learners are to take advantage of the resources and tools available for language learning, for example in a self-access lab (e.g., Milton, 1997), they are going to be working with technology.

Learners' use of technology for language learning beyond the classroom raises another issue—the construction of their identity through participation in particular communities on the Web (Lam, 2000). This is a rich area for research as language learners of all ages see the Web as the natural place to get information, communicate with like-minded people, and learn things. The study of the role of learners' identity and their use of the Web as a context for access to target language forums suggest the utility of a broad theoretical lens for viewing, describing, and explaining learners' technology use (Warschauer, 2005).

Data and common elicitation measures

In addition to computers providing a wide range of learning opportunities for language learners, they also constitute a powerful means for computer-aided data elicitation and collection for researchers. As such, they have had a significant impact on the study of language acquisition and use. Hulstijn (2000, p. 39), for instance, states that "until some 20 years ago, empirical research on language acquisition and use was restricted to the observation and measurement of language input and output. With these computer-aided tools, however, researchers have the means to get closer to the *processes* of language acquisition and use." Ayoun (2000) summarizes the advantages of computer-based data elicitation and notes that, for example, a computer environment will expose all study participants to the stimuli and/or study treatment in the same way. Moreover, it eliminates or minimizes human error in data collection and facilitates data analysis and organization. Finally, it ensures a more complete data set because computer-based studies are generally designed in such a way that they require a response from study participants.

Interaction-based research

Cognitive interactionist and socio-cultural SLA theories have provided the theoretical background and thus departure point for interaction-based research, that is, CALL studies that focus on aspects of human-computer interaction and CMC. Interaction-based research methods in CALL generally manipulate the types of interactions in which language learners are involved (see Chapelle, 2005a).

Learner-computer interactions. Data gathered automatically as learners interact with computers allow researchers to heed the advice of Swain (1998, p. 80) who recommends that researchers examine "what learners actually do, not what the researcher assumes instructions and task demands will lead learners to do" (see also Chapelle, 2001, 2005b). In a CALL environment, software features are designed with a particular pedagogical goal in mind but, due to a number of reasons, they may not be exploited to their best potential or, in the worst case, students may not even use them at all. For instance, Cobb and Stevens (1996) reported that even after students had learned in training sessions that certain help options in reading courseware were beneficial to their learning, they did not take advantage of the options when using the courseware outside of class (see also Grgurovic and Hegelheimer, 2007).

These important observations are made through the use of tracking procedures such as computer log files. A visit to a Website may be recorded in the server log with the date and time of the request, the originating Internet address, and the system response. More importantly, however, are the user selection of software features (e.g., frequency and sequence of access) and learner responses during task completion that can also be recorded and analyzed. For instance, a study on incidental vocabulary learning by Laufer and Hill (2000) investigated learner look-up preferences of additional information about new words and how well these words are remembered. The help options for the test items included an audio recording of the word, its first language (L1) translation, an L2 explanation of the test item as well as different types of morphological information. The CALL program recorded learners' look-up behavior by means of a computer log file which then was examined and correlated with learner performance on a meaning recall test of the target words. Study results indicate that the additional information provided about the new words was useful, however, individual learner differences in look-up preferences were also noted.

In addition to computer log files that record learner-computer interactions, video-screen recordings and/or eye-tracking also provide insight into interaction-based learner behavior in CALL. For instance, Pujolà's (2001) study with adult learners of Spanish examined learners' use of various help facilities using *ImPRESSions*, a multimedia program for teaching listening and reading comprehension. In addition to observation and retrospection questions about the use of help facilities, learners' screen movements were recorded and used to analyze learner responses to different types of system feedback. Due to eye-tracking technology, the study was able to determine whether students read, skimmed and/or ignored the feedback that was provided to them.

Computer-mediated interactions with peers. Researchers have also emphasized the importance of combining different data collection tools for interaction-based research (e.g., computer log files with video screen captures) to assess student learning behavior in computer-mediated interactions. For instance, Smith (2008) examined the use of self-repair among learners of German in a task-based synchronous computer-mediated communication (SCMC) environment. Using the chat function in Blackboard, paired study participants engaged in six jigsaw tasks over the course of one semester. For data collection, the chat sessions were not only recorded in a printed computer log file but, in addition, a video file of the screen captured the entire interaction. Study results indicate that by only considering the written computer log file one may gain the impression that learners do not self-correct very often in an SCMC environment. However, by also examining the video file, the data suggest that self-correction increased by over eight-fold of the amount of self-correction that was recorded by the written transcripts.

In addition to examining task types between individual learners, Lee (2004), for example, combined a number of data collection tools to examine the necessary learning conditions for satisfactory networked collaborative interaction between groups of learners. Lee collected data from online discussions, end-of-semester surveys, and final oral interviews between non-native and native speakers of Spanish. The combination of the distinct data sets provides evidence that network collaborative interaction, at the same time offering advantages and benefits, also causes notable difficulties for the non-native speakers with respect to finding a common time to be online and getting access to the network at the host institution in addition to age differences, learners' language, and computer skills.

Interaction with corpora. Another application of interaction-based research can be found in the area of corpus analysis. In CALL research, we can distinguish between two main types of language corpora: *Native* corpora that have been collected from written and/or oral data of native speakers and *learner* corpora that provide a collection of data produced by language learners. Studies that employ native corpora primarily focus on learner interactions with concordancing tools with the ultimate goal to provide insight into teachers' and learners' use of corpora. For instance, Braun's (2007) case study with 25 EFL learners in Germany investigated the conditions and challenges of integrating corpus materials and corpus-based learning activities into secondary education. For data collection, Braun used a number of quantitative and qualitative data sources: a pre-test for overall proficiency assessment, computer log files, a post-study questionnaire, and comments and observations made by students and teachers during the study as well as during the final discussion of the teaching unit. Study results show that the experimental group outperformed the control group in their acquisition of lexical knowledge and proficiency. At the same time, the study highlights a number of challenges (e.g., skill-related as well as methodological and logistical problems) that have to be resolved in order to integrate learner corpora into the language learning classroom successfully.

In addition to interaction-based research that involves native corpora, CALL researchers have also examined learner corpora. The two main methodological approaches employed here are studies of Contrastive Analysis and Error Analysis, both ultimately aiming at testing and/or contributing to some aspect of SLA theory (see Granger et al., 2002). For studies of Contrastive Analysis, researchers investigate features present in learner language and compare and contrast them with those found in native language. On the contrary, studies of Error Analysis investigate interlanguage phenomena, for example, the order of acquisition and/or particular use of morphemes. For instance, Granger (2006) investigated the use of verb forms by L2 learners of English for Specific Purposes. By comparing the top 100 used words in two corpora (a learner and a native corpus), Granger found that the differences in learner usage of these words are less characterized by their frequency of use but more so by a distinctive lexico-grammatical patterning of these words, notably with respect to active-passive alternation.

Surveys and questionnaires

In CALL research, Hubbard (2005) found that questionnaires have decreased in use over the past decade. This shift in data collection tools since the mid-1990s (see Jung, 2005) might be, at least partly, due to the fact that research in CALL has shown significant discrepancies between tracked learner use of software in the form of computer log files and learner self-reports of system use (see e.g., Fischer, 2004). Hubbard (2005) reviewed 78 studies reported in CALL journals from 2000 to 2003 and found that only 15 percent of the studies he surveyed relied exclusively on questionnaire or survey sources for student data (compared with 75 percent that included behavioral data). For instance, Chen et al. (2004) investigated the effectiveness of mode of interaction for listening comprehension tasks in a Web-based course, *Academic English*, with the aim to measure learning outcomes and learners' attitudes toward the Web-based course. Learning outcomes were measured by means of computer log files and a pre-treatment questionnaire that examined participants' prior knowledge of the topic of instruction. A post-treatment questionnaire rated participants' attitudes toward the Web-based course. The combination of interaction-based research methods with questionnaires allowed the researchers to not only assess learners' performance during system interaction in a quantitative way but also to determine learners' motivation and attitudes toward the Web-based course.

Retrospective interviews and think-alouds

CALL studies also make use of introspective methods—retrospective interviews and think-alouds to examine students' and teachers' perceptions and attitudes toward learning materials during and/or after CALL use. According to Mackey and Gass (2005), one advantage of conducting interviews is the fact that they provide an opportunity for the researcher to observe phenomena that are not readily observable by other research methods. For instance, Meskill et al. (2002) studied the "technology talk" of novice and expert teachers of language and literacy in kindergarten and grades 1 through 8 (K-8). Interview data with eight teachers provided insights into the conceptual and practical differences between teachers with varying degrees of experience with technology. Study results show that classroom experience has a stronger impact on the prediction of teachers' comfort level with implementing technology than training in classroom technologies.

Think-alouds aim to provide insights into learners' mental processes and strategies that they employ when using a CALL program. For example, in a study by Vinther (2005) students were asked to verbalize their thoughts while using a CALL program to learn English syntax. By considering both learners' think-alouds and quantitative data, the study provides evidence that, in the case of low-achieving students, the computer can help learners to improve their cognitive strategies.

Computer-aided research allows us to examine aspects of SLA and use that goes beyond the possibilities found with classroom-based research. The degree of control over instructional and testing decisions, the minimization of human error rate in data collection as well as the vast data samples that can be elicited, collected, and analyzed contribute to making this a unique research environment.

Applications

Instructional relevance is the *raison d'être* for CALL research, which aims to discover and demonstrate how technology can be used to create optimal instructional practices. In view of the range of factors involved in second language learning, and the challenge in finding evidence that learners' language competence has improved as the result of any one particular instructional intervention, the overall objective is addressed from a number of different angles. This leads to a wide range of claims about CALL use. Researchers tend to state their claims in terms of factors that are expected to create a positive learning experience, particularly drawing on constructs, such as interaction, individualization, and autonomy, that we outlined above (*Core Issues*). Whereas claims about learning conditions in terms of CALL design and its learning outcomes are the most commonly found in research in this area, some researchers are also concerned with claims about the relative value of CALL when compared with classroom learning.

Technology-classroom comparisons

The claim that some CALL researchers want to be able to make is that the use of technology for language learning or a technology-plus-classroom blend is at least as—if not more—effective than use of classroom instruction alone. Nutta (1998), for instance, conducted a study on the acquisition of verb tenses by post-secondary ESL students to determine the impact of two distinct methods of instruction, computer-based and teacher-directed. Study results indicate that for all proficiency levels, the computer-based students significantly outperformed the teacher-directed students on open-ended tests. No significant differences, however, were found between the computer-based and teacher-directed student scores on multiple choice or fill-in the-blank tests. Similarly, Torlakovic and Deugo (2004) studied ESL learners in their acquisition of the positioning of adverbs by comparing a teacher-fronted group with a CALL group. Study results show a significant improvement for the computer group on both learners' performance and confidence in positioning adverbs while no significant gains for the teacher-fronted group were recorded.

Whereas these comparative questions are of interest for making particular curricular decisions, researchers interested in better understanding CALL, pointed out years ago that such research is limited because the findings cannot be generalized due to the lack of specification of what the technology consists of (e.g., Pederson, 1987). A more pointed approach to investigating learning outcomes in CALL is to examine the effects of various design and activity features (e.g., help options) on CALL use and learning.

Activity features and learning

Research on specific features of design yields evidence aiming to increase professional knowledge in CALL that can inform materials developers, teachers, and learners. For example, if evidence suggesting that the help and feedback learners get from the computer is beneficial for comprehension, learning, or both, then developers know that this feature is worthwhile to add to CALL tasks, and teachers know that they should encourage students to use help and feedback if they are available. In fact, such evidence has been found to support the value of learners' interaction with the computer while working on CALL tasks online. An examination of both help options and feedback shows that research yields evidence about even more specific claims about the types of help and feedback.

Help with comprehension. With respect to students' aural comprehension, many studies have shown that pictorial or written information enhances students' comprehension of a written text (e.g., see Chun and Payne, 2004; Guillory, 1999; Jones and Plass, 2002; Lavine, 1992; McGrath, 1992; Plass *et al.*, 1998, 2003; Weinberg, 2002; Zhao, 1997). These studies have also shown that help with comprehension in reading can assist students to understand the text and learn vocabulary; moreover, in studies comparing different modes of help (e.g., L1, L2, images, text, aural, written), the finding is that the more modes the help appears in the better for vocabulary learning.

The claims one can make about the role of help on comprehension and learning of aural input are less clear. Gruba (2004), however, found that the importance of visual information on students' aural comprehension changes dependent upon students' comprehension of the material presented. Moreover, if left to their own devices, students exhibit preferences for certain help options over others and learner differences exist in the use of help options. Grgurovic and Hegelheimer (2007), for instance, designed a multimedia listening activity that contained a video of academic lectures with the goal to offer help in the form of target language subtitles and lecture transcripts in cases of comprehension breakdowns. Study results indicate that overall, participants interacted with the subtitles more frequently and for longer periods of time than with the transcript, but some students used only subtitles, only transcripts, both, or none at all. These results also support previous findings by Hoven (2003), for example, who found that high proficiency learners used multimedia-based help tools more often than did low or medium proficiency learners (see also Cárdenas-Claros, 2005; Desmarais *et al.*, 1998; Hegelheimer and Tower, 2004; Jones, 2003, 2006; Pujolà, 2002). These results suggest that help options are generally beneficial to the learner, but the studies also show that learner training is central, in particular, in the case of low proficiency learners.

Feedback. Research has sought evidence that feedback in CALL makes a difference, and more specifically what kind of feedback makes a difference. One of the early studies investigating different feedback types for Japanese grammar instruction found that "intelligent" feedback (with a metalinguistic explanation) was more effective than traditional feedback (e.g., *wrong, try again!*) (Nagata, 1993). A number of studies followed (e.g., see Bowles, 2005; Brandl, 1995; Clariana and Lee, 2001; Gaskell and Cobb, 2004; Heift, 2002, 2004, 2010; Murphy, 2007; Nagata and Swisher, 1995; Nagata, 1996; Petersen, 2010; Pujolà, 2002; Rosa and Leow, 2004; Vinther, 2005) and the results generally support the claim that students benefit from explicit feedback because they subsequently perform better on particular target language structures and/or because students' grammatical awareness is subsequently raised. Evidence for effects of computer-generated feedback has also been sought in studies examining learner error correction behavior, referred to as learner uptake (Lyster, 2007), in response to distinct feedback types (e.g., Heift and Rimrott, 2008). Here, the findings report significantly more learner uptake for feedback that provides detailed corrections.

Effects of feedback obtained from interlocuters during CMC tasks have also been investigated. For example, Sauro (2009) examined the impact of two types of computer-mediated corrective feedback, recasts and metalinguistic feedback, on the development of adult ESL learners' during task-based interaction via text-chat. While study results indicate an improvement in mean scores for both feedback groups compared to the control group, only the metalinguistic group showed significant gains (see also e.g., Loewen and Erlam, 2006; Ware, 2008).

Meaning-based communication with metalinguistic reflection

Researchers seek to test the claim that learners engage in meaning-based communication in written CMC including tasks with opportunities for beneficial metalinguistic reflection on the language. Fernández-Garciá and Martínez-Arbelaiz (2002), for instance, investigated whether or not negotiation of meaning would take place in text chat discussion among third-year university students studying Spanish. The authors found some instances of L2 negotiation as learners discussed questions about readings, but they also found many instances of resolution of communication breakdown through the use of the L1 (see also Fernández-Garciá and Martínez-Arbelaiz, 2003; Jepson, 2005). Research in CMC has also examined different task types to determine their impact on learner's discourse with respect to negotiation of meaning. For instance, Blake (2000) compared types of communication tasks constructed in accordance with those designed by researchers investigating face-to-face communication. In his study, dyads of L2 learners of Spanish carried out a series of online tasks (jigsaw, information-gap, decision-making) using a synchronous chat program. The study found that the jigsaw tasks in written synchronous CMC seem to prompt negotiation of meaning best thus confirming previous results found in face-to-face communication (see also Pellettieri, 2000; Warschauer, 1996).

Individual learner needs

That CALL activities can meet the individual needs of learners is a claim that has been made since the earliest work on CALL. The goal was to use the computer to support classroom instruction in a way that would provide individualization to meet learners' needs by identifying specific areas of knowledge (e.g., placement of the indirect object in French), providing exercises on these areas of knowledge for learners to complete, and tabulating learners' successes and errors within the knowledge categories. This work has become more sophisticated as CALL developers explored more sophisticated exercise types requiring NLP (Heift and Schulze, 2007). A more delicate and potentially more useful analysis can be made with NLP software that can analyze learners' language rather than simply categorizing their responses on selected-response items. Such a program is also useful for modeling what the student knows based on the evidence found in his or her writing, and such models can be used for making suggestions about useful areas of instruction.

Learner autonomy and intercultural competence

It has been claimed that learners expand their autonomous learning strategies and opportunities for development of their intercultural competence as they work on some CALL tasks. Many language learners look to the Web for language resources such as dictionaries and concordances, language and cultural materials to read, listen to, and watch (e.g., newspapers and YouTube), and conversations to participate in (e.g., special interest forums). As a result, learners have many opportunities to engage in collaborative development of language (e.g., wikis) and cultural content. Teachers who struggle to get students to use the target language in the classroom see students participating in the social world of the Web through wikis, blogs, and social bookmarking (e.g., Facebook). There is much in this domain to be studied if researchers are to get a better understanding of the new contexts of linguistic input for learners provided by computer technology.

In view of the scope of such claims about technology use, research framed in socio-cultural theory has been useful in seeking evidence concerning how collaborative CMC activities can support language development and intercultural understanding in telecollaborative language learning (Belz, 2002, 2003; Kern, 2000; Meskill and Anthony, 2005; Thorne, 2003; Thorne and Payne, 2005; Ware and Kramsch, 2005). Warschauer (1998, p. 760), for example, notes that in order "to fully understand the interrelationship between technology and language learning, researchers have to investigate the broader ecological context that affects language learning and use in today's society, both inside and outside the classroom" (see also Chapelle, 2000; Salaberry, 1999, 2000). Belz (2006), for instance, investigated the kinds of interactional patterns and norms that are jointly constructed by L2 learners, finding that while learners construct their learning contexts as active social agents, the teacher, nevertheless, plays an important role in determining the appropriateness of a selected CMC tool for the purpose of an activity (see also Fiori, 2005).

Future directions

This brief overview of CALL reveals a rich new set of opportunities for language learners, teachers, and second language researchers. For learners, there are new options for accessing the target language, connecting with users of the language in virtual spaces, and obtaining online help. These opportunities radically change the language learning landscape. As for teachers, their involvement can trigger, stimulate, monitor, and guide online as well as offline activities conducive to learning. The primary goal for researchers in CALL is to better understand the new landscape with its implications for language teaching and impact on language learning. The research findings suggest some instructional practices that can guide materials developers, teachers, and learners and it is to these we turn next.

At least two large issues underlie the suggestions. One concerns the type of professional knowledge required of language teachers in view of the changed landscape for L2 learning. A new set of teaching competencies is required for helping learners to take advantage of technology as well as to plan and work within new types of language curricula. Language teaching, like other professions, is changing as the result of pervasive use of technology and therefore teachers need to be able to use and develop technology-based learning materials most conducive to language learning.

A second large issue pertaining specifically to SLA is the significant change in the environments in which language is learned today. The precious, and in many contexts rare, face-to-face conversations that formed the basis of important theoretical perspectives on SLA have been supplemented, diversified, and extended beyond the physical boundaries that separated learners from their target language in the past. Perspectives on the psycholinguistic dimensions of SLA can be expanded to theorize and study the new types of interactions that learners engage in and their effects on the learners' language and identity. Perspectives on the social contexts of SLA need to encompass computer technology as an important player in these contexts. Despite the utility of existing knowledge and research directions in SLA for the study of CALL, the need exists to better understand the new conditions for SLA brought about by the real language-related capabilities of technologies that many learners have access to on a daily basis.

References

Ahmad, K., Corbett, G., Rogers, M., and Sussex, R. (1985). *Computers, language learning, and language teaching.* Cambridge: Cambridge University Press.

Ayoun, D. (2000). Web-base elicitation tasks in SLA research. *Language Learning and Technology*, *3*(2), 77–98.

Belz, J. A. (2001). Institutional and individual dimensions of transatlantic group work in network-based language teaching. *ReCALL*, *13*(2), 213–231.

Belz, J. A. (2002). Social dimensions of telecollaborative foreign language study. *Language Learning and Technology*, *6*(1), 60–81.

Belz, J. A. (2003). Linguistic perspectives on the development of intercultural competence in telecollaboration. *Language Learning and Technology*, *7*(2), 68–117.

Belz, J. A. (2006). ESL students' computer-mediated communication practices: Context configuration. *Language Learning and Technology*, *7*(2), 65–84.

Benson, P. (2001). *Teaching and researching autonomy in language learning*. Harlow, England: Pearson Education.

Blake, R. (2000). Computer-mediated communication: A window on L2 Spanish interlanguage. *Language Learning and Technology*, *4*(1), 120–136.

Bowles, M. (2005). *Effects of verbalization condition and type of feedback on L2 development in a CALL Task*. Washington, D.C.: Georgetown University.

Brandl, K. K. (1995). Strong and weak students' preferences for error feedback options and responses. *The Modern Language Journal*, *79*(ii), 194–211.

Braun, S. (2007). Integrating corpus work into secondary education: From data-driven learning to needs-driven corpora. *ReCALL*, *19*(3), 307–328.

Cárdenas-Claros, M. (2005). *Field dependence/field independence: How do students perform in CALL-based listening activities?* Unpublished MA thesis. Iowa State University, Ames.

Chapelle, C. (2000). Is network-based learning CALL? In M. Warschauer and R. Kern (Eds.), *Network-based language teaching: Concepts and practice* (pp. 204–228). New York: Cambridge University Press.

Chapelle, C. A. (2001). *Computer applications in second language acquisition: Foundations for teaching, testing, and research*. Cambridge: Cambridge University Press.

Chapelle, C. A. (2003). *English language learning and technology: Lectures on applied linguistics in the age of information and communication technology*. Amsterdam: John Benjamins.

Chapelle, C. A. (2005a). Interactionist SLA theory in CALL research. In J. Egbert and G. Petrie (Eds.), *Research perspectives on CALL* (pp. 53–64). Mahwah, NJ: Laurence Erlbaum Associates.

Chapelle, C. A. (2005b). Computer-assisted language learning. In E. Hinkel (Ed.), *Handbook of second language teaching and learning* (pp. 743–755). Mahwah, NJ: Lawrence Erlbaum.

Chen, J., Belkada, S., and Okamoto, T. (2004). How a web-based course facilitates acquisition of English for academic purposes. *Language Learning and Technology*, *8*(2), 33–49.

Chun, D. M. (1994). Using computer networking to facilitate the acquisition of interactive competence. *System*, *22*(1), 17–31.

Chun, D. C. and Payne, J. S. (2004). What makes students click: Working memory and look-up behavior. *System*, *32*(4), 481–503.

Clariana, R. B. and Lee, D. (2001). The effects of recognition and recall study tasks with feedback in a computer-based vocabulary lesson. *Educational Technology Research and Development*, *49*(3), 23–36.

Cobb, T. and Stevens, V. (1996). A principled consideration of computers and reading in a second language. In M. Pennington (Ed.), *The Power of CALL* (pp. 115–136). Houston, TX: Athelstan.

Desmarais, L., Laurier, M., and Renie, D. (1998). The analysis of navigation patterns in CALL. *Computer Assisted Language Learning*, *11*(3), 309–315.

Dörnyei, Z. and Ushioda, E. (Eds.) (2009). *Motivation, language identity and the L2 self*. Bristol: Multilingual Matters.

Ellis, R. (1999). *The study of second language acquisition*. Oxford: Oxford University Press.

Fernández-Garciá, M. and Martínez-Arbelaiz, A. (2002). Negotiation of meaning in nonnative speaker-nonnative speaker synchronous discussions. *CALICO Journal*, *19*(2), 279–294.

Fernández-Garciá, M. and Martínez-Arbelaiz, A. (2003). Learners' interactions: A comparison of oral and computer-assisted written conversation. *ReCALL Journal*, *15*(1), 113–136.

Fiori, M. L. (2005). The development of grammatical competence through synchronous computer-mediated communication. *CALICO Journal*, *22*(3), 567–602.

Fischer, R. (2004). How do we know what students are actually doing? Monitoring students' behavior in CALL. *Computer Assisted Language Learning*, *20*(5), 409–442.

Gaskell, D. and Cobb, T. (2004). Can learners use concordance feedback for writing errors? *System*, *32*(3), 301–319.

Gass, S. (2003). Input and interaction. In C. J. Doughty and M. H. Long (Eds.), *The handbook of second language acquisition* (pp. 224–255). Malden, MA: Blackwell Publishing.

Granger, S. (2006). Lexico-grammatical Patterns of EAP verbs: How do learners cope? *Paper presented at the exploring the lexis-grammar interface conference*, Hanover (Germany), 5–7 October, 2006.

Granger, S., Hung, J., and Petch-Tyson, S. (Eds.). (2002). *Computer learner corpora, second language acquisition, and foreign language. Vol. 6: Language Learning and Language Teaching*. Amsterdam and Philadelphia: John Benjamins.

Grgurovic, M. and Hegelheimer, V. (2007). Help options and multimedia listening: Student's use of subtitles and transcripts. *Language Learning and Technology, 11*(1), 45–66.

Gruba, P. (2004). Understanding digitized second language video text. *Computer Assisted Language Learning, 17*(1), 51–82.

Guillory, H. G. (1999). The effect of keyword captions to authentic French video on learner comprehension. *CALICO Journal, 15*(1–3), 89–108.

Hart, R. S. (Ed.). (1981). *Studies in language learning. special issue on the PLATO system and language study* (Vol. 3). Urbana, IL: Language Learning Laboratory, University of Illinois at Urbana-Champaign.

Hegelheimer, V. and Tower, D. (2004). Using CALL in the classroom: Analyzing student interactions in an authentic classroom. *System, 32*(2), 185–205.

Heift, T. (2002). Learner control and error correction in ICALL: Browsers, peekers and adamants. *CALICO Journal, 19*(3), 295–313.

Heift, T. (2004). Corrective feedback and learner uptake in CALL. *ReCALL, 16*(2), 416–431.

Heift, T. (2008). Modeling learner variability in CALL. *Computer-Assisted Language Learning, 21*(4), 305–321.

Heift, T. (2010). A longitudinal study of learner uptake. *The Modern Language Journal, 94*(2), 198–216.

Heift, T. and Rimrott, A. (2008). Learner responses to corrective feedback for spelling errors in CALL. *System, 36*(2), 196–213.

Heift, T. and Schulze, M. (2007). *Errors and intelligence in computer-assisted language learning: Parsers and pedagogues*. London: Routledge.

Higgins, J. and Johns, T. (1984). *Computers in language learning*. Reading, MA: Addison-Wesley.

Hoven, D. (2003). Strategic uses of CALL: What learners use and how they react. *Australian Review of Applied Linguistics, 17*(1), 125–48.

Hubbard, P. (2005). A review of subject characteristics in CALL research. *Computer Assisted Language Learning, 18*(5), 351–368.

Hulstijn, J. (2000). The use of computer technology in experimental situations of second language acquisition: A survey of some techniques and some ongoing studies. *Language Learning and Technology, 3*(2), 32–43.

Jepson, K. (2005). Conversations—and negotiated interaction—in text and voice chat rooms. *Language Learning and Technology, 9*(3), 79–98.

Johns, T. (1986). Micro-Concord, a language learner's research tool. *System, 14*(2), 151–162.

Jones, L. (2003). Supporting student differences in listening comprehension and vocabulary acquisition with multimedia annotation: The Students Voice. *CALICO Journal, 21*(1), 41–65.

Jones, L. (2006). Effects of collaboration and multimedia annotations on vocabulary learning and listening comprehension. *CALICO Journal, 24*(1), 33–58.

Jones, L. and Plass, J. (2002). Supporting listening comprehension and vocabulary acquisition in French with multimedia annotations. *The Modern Language Journal, 86*(4), 546–561.

Jung, U. (2005). CALL: Past, present and future—A bibliometric approach. *ReCALL, 17*(1), 4–17.

Kern, R. (2000). *Literacy and language teaching*. Oxford: Oxford University Press.

Lam, W. S. E. (2000). L2 literacy and the design of the self: A case study of a teenager writing on the internet. *TESOL Quarterly, 34*(3), 457–482.

Lamy, M. -N. and Goodfellow, R. (1999). "Reflective conversation" in the virtual language classroom. *Language Learning and Technology, 2*(2), 43–61.

Laufer, B. and Hill, M. (2000). What lexical information do L2 learners select in a CALL dictionary and how does it affect word retention? *Language Learning and Technology, 3*(2), 58–76.

Lavine, R. (1992). Rediscovering the audio language laboratory: Learning through communicative tasks. *Hispania, 75*(5), 1360–1367.

Lee, L. (2004). Learners' perspectives on networked collaborative interaction with native speakers of Spanish in the U.S. *Language Learning and Technology, 8*(1), 83–100.

Loewen, S. and Erlam, R. (2006). Corrective feedback in the chatroom: An experimental study. *Computer Assisted Language Learning, 19*(1), 1–14.

Lyster, R. (2007). *Learning and teaching languages through content: A counterbalanced approach*. John Benjamins.

Mackey, A. and Gass, S. (2005). *Second language research: Methodology and design*. New Jersey: Lawrence Erlbaum Associates.

McGrath, D. (1992). Hypertext, CAI, paper, or program control: Do learners benefit from choices? *Journal of Research on Computing in Education, 24*(4), 513–532.

Meskill, C. and Anthony, N. (2005). Foreign language learning with CMC: Forms of online instructional discourse in a hybrid Russian Class. *System, 33*(1), 89–105.

Meskill, C., Mossop, J., DiAngelo, S., and Pasquale, R. K. (2002). Expert and novice teachers talking technology: Precepts, concepts, and misconcepts. *Language Learning and Technology, 6*(3), 46–57.

Milton, J. (1997). Providing computerized self-access opportunities for the development of writing skills. In P. Benson and P. Voller (Eds.), *Autonomy and independence in language learning* (pp. 237–248). London: Longman.

Mohan, B. (1992). Models of the role of the computer in second language development. In M. Pennington, and V. Stevens (Eds.), *Computers in applied linguistics: An international perspective* (pp. 110–126). Clevedon, UK: Multilingual Matters Ltd.

Murphy, P. (2007). Reading comprehension exercises online: The effects of feedback, proficiency and interaction. *Language Learning and Technology, 11*(3), 107–129.

Nagata, N. (1993). Intelligent computer feedback for second language instruction. *The Modern Language Journal, 77*, 330–338.

Nagata, N. (1996). Computer vs. workbook instruction in second language acquisition. *CALICO Journal, 14*(1), 53–75.

Nagata, N. and Swisher, M. V. (1995). A study of consciousness-raising by computer: The effect of metalinguistic feedback on second language learning. *Foreign Language Annals, 28*(3), 337–347.

Nutta, J. (1998). Is computer-based grammar instruction as effective as teacher-directed grammar instruction for teaching L2 structures? *CALICO Journal, 16*(1), 49–62.

Pederson, K. M. (1987). Research on CALL. In W. F. Smith (Ed.), *Modern media in foreign language education: Theory and implementation* (pp. 99–132). Lincolnwood, IL: National Textbook Company.

Pellettieri, J. (2000). Negotiation in cyberspace: The role of *chatting* in the development of grammatical competence in the virtual foreign language classroom. In M. Warschauer and R. Kern (Eds.), *Network-based language teaching: Concepts and practice* (pp. 59–86). Cambridge: Cambridge University Press.

Peterson, K. (2010). *Implicit corrective feedback in computer-guided interaction. Does mode matter?* PhD dissertation. Georgetown University, Washington, D.C., USA.

Plass, J., Chun, D., Mayer, R., and Leutner, D. (1998). Supporting visual and verbal learning preferences in a second language multimedia learning environment. *Journal of Educational Psychology, 90*(1), 25–36.

Plass, J., Chun, D., Mayer, R., and Leutner, D. (2003). Cognitive load in reading a foreign language text with multimedia aids and the influence of verbal and spatial abilities. *Computers in Human Behavior, 19*(2), 221–243.

Pujolà, J. -T. (2001). Did CALL feedback feed back? Researching learners' use of feedback. *ReCALL, 13*(1), 79–98.

Pujolà, J. -T. (2002). CALLing for help: Researching language learning strategies using help facilities in a web-based multimedia program. *ReCALL, 14*(2), 235–262.

Rosa, E. and Leow, R. (2004). Computerized task-based exposure, explicitness and type of feedback on Spanish L2 development. *The Modern Language Journal, 88*, 192–217.

Rost, M. and Fuchs, M. (2004). *Longman English interactive*. New York: Pearson Education.

Salaberry, M. R. (2000). L2 morphosyntactic development in text-based computer-mediated communication. *Computer Assisted Language Learning, 13*, 5–27.

Salaberry, R. (1999). CALL in the year 2000: Still developing the research agenda. A commentary on Carol Chapelle's CALL in the year 2000: Still in search of research paradigms. *Language Learning and Technology, 3*(1), 104–107.

Sanaoui, R. and Lapkin, S. (1992). A case study of an FSL senior secondary course integrating computer networking. *The Canadian Modern Language Review, 48*(3), 525–552.

Sauro, S. (2009). Computer-mediated corrective feedback and the development of L2 grammar. *Language Learning and Technology, 13*(1), 96–120.

Sharples, M., Taylor, J., and Vavoula, G. (2007). A theory of learning for the mobile age. In R. Andrews and C., Haythornthwaite (Eds.), *The Sage handbook of E-learning research* (pp. 221–247). Los Angeles: Sage Publications.

Smith, B. (2008). Methodological hurdles in capturing CMC data: The case of the missing self-repair. *Language Learning and Technology, 12*(1), 85–103.

Swaffar, J., Romano, S., Markley, P., and Arens, K. (Eds.). (1998). *Language learning online: Theory and practice in the ESL and the L2 computer classroom*. Austin, TX: Labyrinth Publications.

Swain, M. (1998). Focus on form through conscious reflection. In C. Doughty and J. Williams (Eds.), *Focus on form in classroom second language acquisition* (pp. 64–81). Cambridge: Cambridge University Press.

Thorne, S. L. (2003). Artifacts and cultures-of-use in intercultural communication. *Language Learning and Technology*, 7(2), 38–67.

Thorne, S. L. and Payne, J. S. (2005). Evolutionary trajectories, internet-mediated expression, and language education. *CALICO Journal*, 22(3), 371–397.

Torlakovic, E. and Deugo, D. (2004). Application of a CALL system in the acquisition of adverbs in English. *Computer-Assisted Language Learning*, 17(2), 203–235.

Underwood, J. H. (1984). *Linguistics, computers, and the language teacher: A communicative approach*. Rowley, MA: Newbury House.

Vinther, J. (2005). Cognitive processes at work in CALL. *Computer Assisted Language Learning*, 18(4), 251–271.

Ware, P. (2008). Peer feedback on language form in telecollaboration. *Language Learning and Technology*, 12(1), 43–63.

Ware, P. and Kramsch, C. (2005). Toward an intercultural stance: Teaching German and English through telecollaboration. *The Modern Language Journal*, 89(2), 190–205.

Warschauer, M. (1996). Comparing face-to-face and electronic discussion in the second language classroom. *CALICO Journal*, 13(2and3), 7–25.

Warschauer, M. (1998). Researching technology in TESOL: Determinist, instrumental, and critical approaches. *TESOL Quarterly*, 32(4), 757–761.

Warschauer, M. (2005). Sociocultural perspectives on CALL. In J. Egbert and G. Petrie (Eds.), *Research perspectives on CALL* (pp. 41–51). Mahwah, NJ: Laurence Erlbaum Associates.

Weinberg, A. (2002). Virtual misadventures: Technical problems and student satisfaction when implementing multimedia in an advanced French listening comprehension course. *CALICO Journal*, 19(2), 331–357.

Zhao, Y. (1997). The effects of listeners' control of speech rate on second language comprehension. *Applied Linguistics*, 18(1), 49–68.

Part VII

Conclusion

Assessment of L2 knowledge

35

Assessing learner knowledge

John M. Norris and Lourdes Ortega

Introduction

Second language acquisition (SLA) researchers are interested in understanding how learners acquire an additional language (henceforth L2) after they have acquired a first language (L1) or languages. The topics investigated vary widely and focus primarily on factors that are thought either to enable or inhibit the rate, route, and ultimate attainment of L2 acquisition. Particular questions posed in SLA are shaped by the theoretical lenses that a given researcher chooses to adopt, the increasing diversity of which is well-reflected in the chapters in this *Handbook*. Nevertheless, despite SLA's theoretical breadth, most L2 research involves the assessment of learner knowledge. In this chapter, we examine key issues SLA researchers face in utilizing assessments of learner knowledge. By "assessment" we mean a systematic and replicable technique that allows researchers to elicit, observe, and interpret indicators of L2 knowledge (however defined), with underlying standards of practice that govern its development and use.

Clearly, the particular focus and theoretical approach to a study—along with associated traditions of practice—will play an important role in determining the assessment methods employed. This means that there is no single "best" way to assess learner knowledge. Nevertheless, current assessment practices must be evaluated so as to muster disciplinary consensus regarding the design, interpretation, and reporting of assessments within SLA. In pursuit of this goal, the chapter embarks from the following overarching assumptions:

(1) The choice of assessment method in SLA should be guided by three concerns: (a) *what* gets assessed, or the L2 knowledge constructs researchers want to know about; (b) *how* to assess, or the ways of eliciting and analyzing phenomena related to these constructs; and (c) *who* gets assessed and *why*, or the clearly specified learners and populations that researchers investigate and the explicitly considered purposes for assessing them.
(2) Individual SLA researchers must attend to two primary challenges when assessing learner knowledge: (a) defining the specific L2 knowledge constructs of interest from their theoretical perspective; and (b) proceduralizing data collection through assessment such that interpretable light is shed upon them. Attention to these issues is needed anew in each study context, and simultaneously contrasted against the disciplinary backdrop of collectively accumulated knowledge.

Historical discussion

SLA researchers utilize assessments for a variety of purposes: to make inferences about learners' grammatical representations, to describe what L2 features are being acquired in what patterns over time, to determine what has been acquired (or not) at the onset of study, to document changes in learners (or the lack thereof) as a result of conditions introduced during a study, and for other reasons. Historically, SLA has imported assessment methods from the antecedent disciplines of linguistics, psychology, and education, with other more recent influences coming from psycholinguistics, neurolinguistics, sociology, and anthropology. Given the relative youth of the field, this intense interdisciplinary borrowing comes as no surprise, and imported methods certainly shed light on distinct dimensions of L2 acquisition. Of these interdisciplinary influences, however, the predominant tendency has been to approach the task of "assessing" learner knowledge in quantifiable measurement terms that are associated with experimental epistemologies. In this vein, Loewen and Gass (2009) examined three flagship journals (*Language Learning, Second Language Research*, and *Studies in Second Language Acquisition*) and found a steady decrease between 1965 and 2006 in publications where no statistics or only descriptive statistics are reported, coupled with a dramatic rise in the use of inferential statistics since the mid-1980s. Likewise, Benson *et al.* (2009) uncovered a contrast in publication patterns over the last ten years of *Language Learning* and *Studies in Second Language Acquisition*, whose pages featured only a handful of qualitative studies, in comparison with eight other applied linguistics journals, which hosted a larger proportion of qualitative studies, ranging between 20 percent and 40 percent of empirical articles. These patterns in empirical publications found in core SLA journals reflect an increasing dependence on experimental methodologies and associated statistical techniques, all of which in turn has influenced approaches to—and critical gaps in—SLA assessment practices.

One clear pattern has been a reliance on the language testing community as translators and disseminators of both quantitative research methods and assessment practices. Telling in this respect are the papers published in Bachman and Cohen (1998), which revealed important interfaces between the two fields but also challenges that have their roots, as these authors noted, in the distinctiveness of disciplinary goals. SLA researchers pursue theoretical explanations of the development of L2 grammars—although "grammar" may be defined by different SLA research strands in quite different ways, as we will see in the next section. By contrast, most language testers are interested in capturing, through the shortcut of tests, what learners can do in the L2 outside the test situation, when faced with varying communication demands. Moreover, SLA research may need to feature a wider range of data elicitation procedures and analytic methods, by comparison to the more restricted response formats employed in the language testing field. Despite such differences, language testing practices have persistently shaped the design of assessments for SLA research, with an emphasis on tests that elicit repeated (items) or extended (tasks) performances related to a single, typically broad, construct of interest and generating a score which can be interpreted along a linear scale of ability and subjected to statistical analysis. However, and perhaps reflecting the fact that SLA is interested in distinct phenomena with characteristics not captured by such tests, it has been repeatedly observed that quantitative assessments in SLA research often fail to meet the strict criteria for variables to be included in inferential analyses (Lazaraton, 2005; Norris and Ortega, 2000, 2003; Shohamy, 2000).

Another major legacy of the historical predilection for quantitative and inferential statistics-centered assessments is the paucity of agreed upon methodological standards or examples of assessment practice coming specifically from within the SLA field and reflecting the unique learners and knowledge constructs that are at stake. Assessments measuring complex, developmental, and non-linear SLA phenomena (i.e., those that fit with difficulty into inferential statistical analyses; see Larsen-Freeman and Cameron, 2008) have received insufficient attention. Publications addressing the interface between assessment and SLA also have been minimal, and fewer still are carefully developed research programs that have followed requisite design steps, from construct definition through to data collection and interpretation. Problematic in this regard is the tendency to assume—rather than build an empirical case for—the validity of whatever assessment method is adopted, regardless of the L2 learner population of interest (e.g., child versus adult, naturalistic versus instructed) or the SLA-theoretical interpretations to be made about learner knowledge (e.g., reflective of what stage of the acquisition process, indicating what type of implicit/explicit/metalinguistic knowledge). While assessment innovation, research, and development are not unheard of within SLA (see below), to date the assessment of learner knowledge has consisted mostly of either appropriated or idiosyncratic methods, rather than carefully designed and validated techniques for illuminating core L2 phenomena as defined and valued within various types of SLA theories.

Core issues

In this section, we examine critical issues surrounding the conceptualization of L2 knowledge *constructs*, which pertain to *what* gets assessed (e.g., "ability to recognize a grammar rule" or "automatic, fluent performance with the target form"). The careful conceptualization of constructs and the behaviors they help to explain provide the premises upon which L2 theories are built, with the ultimate goal of rendering warranted interpretations about learner knowledge. It is only after construct conceptualization that the *how* of assessments—that is, the proceduralization of instruments and techniques for eliciting and analyzing construct-relevant data—is possible. Indeed, the standard assessment concerns of validity (i.e., the extent to which an assessment provides sound evidence about a particular construct) and reliability (i.e., the consistency with which assessments produce trustworthy findings) can be addressed only in the context of well-conceptualized constructs.

Defining what is acquired, or learner knowledge as a construct

If asked what aspects of learner knowledge need to be assessed, many SLA researchers will answer that they need to assess what is acquired, and most will mention grammar. Many may also qualify grammar as language knowledge that is implicit or explicit, a distinction which in lay terms can be understood as a difference between knowledge *of* language (i.e., implicit) versus knowledge *about* language (i.e., explicit). Yet, the construct definition of what may count as grammar varies widely across SLA theories, as do the roles that implicit and explicit knowledge play in attributing theoretical interpretations to empirical evidence. We turn to an examination of these two issues across theoretical SLA perspectives, from narrowest to broadest positions.

From a formal linguistic SLA perspective (Lardiere, Chapter 7, this volume), what is acquired is grammar construed as mental *representations* of morphosyntactic rules, defined via theoretically specialized knowledge constructs which have been categorized successively at the level of parameters, functional categories, features, and interfaces. Under this lens, implicit, intuitive knowledge must be assessed, whereas explicit knowledge has no theoretical status. The object of inquiry here is highly abstract core linguistic knowledge believed to be available prior to any linguistic experience and encapsulated in a language-specific processing module impervious to any other kind of knowledge. Determining the extent to which implicit linguistic knowledge might be involved in L2 (as opposed to L1) acquisition, or the question of whether Universal Grammar constrains L2 acquisition, is one of the ultimate goals of inquiry in this line of SLA research. Another goal is to specify the L1-based reconfigurations and new learning that must be accomplished if convergence with licit L2 configurations is to be achieved or is even possible. The nature of observable indicators relevant for these highly mentalistic interpretations has attracted much debate. For example, some scholars have argued that the choice of L2 grammar phenomena to be targeted for investigation needs to satisfy certain theoretical requirements, such as ensuring that what is studied is so subtle and abstract that it could not possibly be known solely on the basis of experience with the target input, knowledge of the L1, or explicit knowledge accrued during language instruction (Schwartz and Sprouse, 2000, but see Hawkins, 2001, for a different opinion). In the end, though, the indicators favored from this perspective are grammaticality judgment tasks which ask learners to judge by "feel" whether certain language exemplars are legal.

For researchers working from a usage-based, emergentist, and probabilistic perspective (Ellis, Chapter 12, this volume; MacWhinney, Chapter 13, this volume), grammar is also in focus, but the construct refers to a wide range of layered inventories of form-meaning mappings known as *constructions*, in which both grammar and lexis are intertwined; thus, degrees of lexico-grammatical knowledge must be assessed (e.g., N. Ellis and Ferreira-Junior, 2009). As in formal linguistic SLA theories, implicit knowledge matters most for understanding L2 development, but the construct interpretations and observable indicators have very little in common with those of formal linguists. Instead, implicit knowledge is defined as intuitive but general-cognitive knowledge of constructions, including information regarding frequency, distribution, and contextual dependencies. Implicit knowledge is thought to be abstracted bottom-up (that is, inductively) by mandatory automatic tallying upon repeated experience with the L2 input, and it reflects the sum of the actual history of language use for a given learner. Factors that are thought to complicate L2 acquisition include the amount and quality of exposure to L2 input, established knowledge of L1 constructions and associated attunement to particular cues when processing the target input, and attentional capacities of individuals. Relevant observable indicators must capture the interaction of the linguistic environment with the learner's cognitive capacities, and they include estimated input frequencies for lexico-grammatical features, computer-based models of what learning should look like under diverse environmental conditions, experimental memory measures, and learner L2 exposure "histories."

From the perspective of cognitive-interactionist SLA (Long, 1990; Mackey, Abbhul, and Gass, Chapter 1, this volume), additional language learning is a cognitive process (involving attention, memory, and awareness, i.e., internal to the learner) shaped and constrained by variables and conditions associated with immediate learning contexts, such as the types of responses interlocutors provide in communication, the things learners try to do with words in the classroom or in the real world, and so on (i.e., external to the learner). The definition of grammar is broader than that of either formalist or usage-based approaches, as it encompasses the L2 nuts and bolts of *communicative ability*, such as morphosyntax, lexis, phonology, pragmatics, and some areas of interactional and discourse competence. These multiple dimensions are assessed either in isolation or in interaction with one another. Under this theoretical perspective, both implicit and explicit knowledge are considered important in any SLA explanations. The crux of inquiry is to elucidate empirically how they are interconnected, or the so-called interface question (R. Ellis, 2004): Can what is learned via explicit attention to the language code eventually influence a learner's implicit mental representations? While the jury is still out, the theoretical importance that is placed on this controversy leaves researchers with the challenge of demonstrating in each study whether it is indeed implicit or explicit knowledge (or both) that is being engaged. Relevant indicators may run the gamut from what the learner does in communicative L2 performance, to what the learner can consciously state about L2 rules or patterns, to how and how quickly the learner responds to different kinds of linguistic stimuli.

For socially minded SLA researchers (see Bayley and Tarone, Chapter 3, this volume; Duff, Chapter 25, this volume), what is acquired includes also knowledge of sociolinguistic variation (Kinginger and Blattner, 2008) and semiotic resources that are symbolic, cultural, and historical (Kramsch, 2006); knowledge of the makeup of academic registers and genres (Schleppegrell,

2004); social and interactional resources (Young, 2009); and knowledge of the social practices and even values of the target community (Rymes, 2008). Critically inclined researchers from the wider field of applied linguistics would include other non-linguistic aspects of what is acquired, such as the "ability to claim the right to speak" (Norton Peirce, 1995, p. 23) and "an awareness of how to challenge and transform social practices of marginalization" (p. 25). With respect to the interpretation of implicit-explicit knowledge, there is no agreed upon view among social theories of L2 learning. Thus, Vygotskian sociocultural SLA researchers (Lantolf, Chapter 4, this volume) place explicit knowledge at the center stage of their research program, as they are most interested in investigating higher-order cognition and human consciousness. In terms of L2 knowledge, they value conceptual (i.e., metalinguistic and explicit) knowledge of grammar, which can develop through mediation with tools such as the L1, grammar explanations, interactional support from more linguistically capable others, and private speech or languaging. Indicators typically include a combination of: (a) discourse data where the microgenesis of learning can be captured; (b) think-aloud or interview data in which learners reveal their metacognitive insights about intentions, histories, goals, motives, and chosen means to attainment; and (c) product learning data assessed via tailor-made tests created for each learner, depending on targets that each experiences during interaction or instruction (Swain, 2001). By contrast, conversation analysis (Markee and Kasper, 2004) concentrates on the implicit knowledge, or perhaps more precisely "performed" knowledge, that allows interactants to maintain or repair social order during communication. Legitimate evidence here is confined to the publicly available record of details that are linguistic (discourse contributions and sequences), paralinguistic (silence, stress, speech rate, etc.), and peri-linguistic (gaze, gesture, etc.), always in relation to naturally occurring interaction. Yet a third social approach to the study of L2 learning, language socialization (Duff, Chapter 25, this volume), places equal importance on implicit or performative knowledge and on explicit or metacognitive knowledge, and makes use of a wide range of indicators that tap both, typically drawing on the rich tradition of ethnography in linguistic anthropology.

Clearly, the variegated ways of conceptualizing "acquired knowledge" span a very broad range in scope and granularity (i.e., type and extent of knowledge in focus) from what learners sense or understand about discrete elements of the target language, to what they say (and, although less often investigated in SLA, what they write or sign), what they do, even what they believe and feel, and possibly what they have the power, capacity, or disposition to do. Even when researchers across theoretical perspectives might agree that language proper should be the focus of SLA inquiry, the language dimensions to be acquired and therefore in need of assessment in SLA have expanded in recent years and might include gestures (Gullberg and McCafferty, 2008), thinking-for-speaking (Slobin, 1996), and other kinds of conceptual-semantic knowledge (Jarvis, 2007). Naturally, the assessment methodologies that can elucidate what is being acquired will differ considerably across this palette of constructs (see below, *Data and common elicitation measures*).

Interpreting acquisition: Targets and benchmarks

Fundamentally, the A in SLA is about changes in the L2 system and factors that contribute to or delimit such change. Acquisition has been variously qualified along a developmental continuum from initial noticing and awareness of form-meaning connections, to incipient and "chunked" production, to expansion and destabilization followed by restructuring, and ultimately to automatic and fluent communicative performance. Moreover, researchers increasingly conceive of L2 targets in multi-dimensional ways, for example, not just the acquisition of a single morphological rule, but the simultaneous development of a whole subsystem of interrelated rules or nested inventories of constructions. These interpretive realities complicate matters considerably. In order for assessments to adequately inform such multi-dimensional and dynamic interpretations about changes in L2 knowledge, they clearly call for more than an isolated snapshot of what a learner knows or can do with a particular rule or form in the target language. This reality translates into the need to choose meaningful benchmarks for interpretation of learners' L2 knowledge en route.

Benchmarking (i.e., providing a stable frame of reference for interpreting L2 development) requires some kind of a legitimate target or sequence for comparison, and the choice of fitting benchmarks has led to considerable debate. Most researchers working from a formal linguistic perspective find it imperative to adopt assessments that compare learners' grammaticality judgments of particular rules with those of a baseline group of L1 speakers, in the belief that native competence offers the only theoretically plausible interpretive benchmark on what is or is not licensed in the grammar (e.g., Lardiere, 2003). By contrast, researchers working from the perspective of L2 learners as emerging bilinguals whose two grammars interact have suggested that the best comparison is an early, balanced bilingual baseline group (Cook, 2008; Singleton, 2003) or they have called for the elicitation of performances by the same learners across both their L1 and L2 to fully understand what L2 behaviors mean (Ortega and Carson, 2010). Other researchers, operating within a processability framework (Pienemann, 2005), must look across broad spectrums of learner L2 production—at best, collected persistently over considerable spans of time—in order to identify the initial emergence of ability to use a given target form and to locate the learner along precedented sequences of L2 development. Still other researchers working from socialization and critical perspectives (e.g., Duff, Chapter 25, this volume) might define benchmarks as successful enculturation into given L2 practices without oppressive assimilation. Evaluations of how these various choices contribute to adequate interpretations of assessments of learner knowledge and its acquisition are much needed.

Data and common elicitation measures

In this section we review four families of data elicitation options, associated with the identification of observable behaviors that should tell SLA researchers something meaningful about their constructs of interest. These families are by no means exhaustive of existing possibilities nor comprehensive in covering SLA constructs and their associated theoretical diversity (as reviewed above). Nevertheless, they are representative of the majority of assessment practices within the domain.

Assessment as a window into the mind/brain

One of the earliest and most widely employed assessment techniques in SLA is commonly referred to as the grammaticality judgment task (GJT; see R. Ellis, 1991). In a GJT study, participants are asked to judge, often on a scale of relative certainty, whether large numbers of carefully designed language exemplars are acceptable, licit, or grammatical in the target grammar. These judgments are thought to open a window onto how grammar rules are represented in the learners' mental L2 system. Similar assessments are used in other theoretical approaches to SLA for the elicitation of user intuitions about constructs such as frequency, prototypicality, or idiomaticity of L2 exemplars (e.g., N. Ellis and Ferreira-Junior, 2009). Methodological weaknesses of GJTs have been widely discussed in both linguistics and SLA, particularly the fact that they elicit a type of performance influenced by non-linguistic factors, such as learners' varying attention or willingness to make such judgments. The major question here is the extent to which GJTs tap the actual implicit knowledge that is being interpreted by researchers. Proposals to improve GJTs have been offered for procedure and stimuli design (R. Ellis et al., 2009) and response formats (Sorace and Keller, 2005). Analytically, GJTs are also tricky in that they produce both learner agreements and disagreements with both licit and illicit exemplars; converting these discrete and often conflicting item responses into interpretable approximations of an overall level of "nativelikeness" has proven challenging from both a scoring and statistical analysis point of view (Paolillo, 2000).

In order to get at a more refined understanding of how the mind deals with language, SLA researchers have begun to adopt, often in conjunction with GJTs, a rich suite of experimental measures developed in the field of psycholinguistics. With a primary focus on latency data, that is, the timing of behavioral responses to L2 stimuli on the order of milliseconds, these include self-paced reading tasks, computer-based reaction times, cross-priming techniques, and eye tracking, among others. Dörnyei (2009) offers an in-depth evaluation of these methods, together with a review of other experimental techniques from the field of neurolinguistics that directly measure brain activity during language processing tasks. This range of both psycholinguistic and more recent neurolinguistic evidence holds the promise of opening up new insights into SLA phenomena in coming years. Any of these elicitation procedures clearly exceeds participants' capability for conscious inspection of their explicit L2 knowledge during performance, offering an advantage not only in formal linguistic investigations, in that they get much closer to underlying tacit knowledge of grammar, but also in SLA investigations of general cognitive phenomena such as attention and memory, since the data provide evidence of below-consciousness mental operations. Perhaps the major challenge for such techniques is the extent to which measured cognitive attributes can be linked to any kind of meaningful L2 patterns; for example, it is unclear how measures of extremely short-termed phenomena (the milli-second firing of neurons) might be eventually related to the acquisition of very large-scope and longitudinally acquired L2 targets like words, sentences, discourse behaviors, and so on.

Psychology has also influenced SLA assessments into attitudes and perceptions, with a focus both on language operations per se and on correlated phenomena. Learner introspection and retrospection (Gass and Mackey, 2000) is one such set of techniques in which learners are asked to think aloud (concurrently) or comment on (retrospectively) what they are/were thinking about as they engage/engaged with communicative tasks such as reading, writing, or interacting with others. The objective here is to open a largely conscious window onto what is occurring in the mind (and what may be already known, noticed as new, or learned). A major interpretive challenge has to do with what learners are able and willing to say about their mental activities and the issue of reactivity, or how the procedure may alter the natural cognitive operations that it is designed to tap (Bowles, 2010).

Another strongly psychological tradition is SLA correlational research that seeks to clarify why distinct learners acquire the same target L2 knowledge differently and with differential success, by assessing psychological constructs (e.g., personality, motivation, learning strategies) through learner self-reports via questionnaires (Brown, 2001). These assessments yield data that are expressed numerically via Likert-scale response formats (e.g., from 1 = strongly disagree to 5 = strongly agree). The obtained evidence is then typically submitted to correlational analyses in which the strength of association between variables—rather than a relationship between cause and effect, as is typical of more experimental evidence—is measured. Challenging for these assessments is the extent to which often broadly metaphorical constructs (e.g., "Willingness to Communicate") can be captured by a handful of self-report items, as well as the question of what correlational magnitude might indicate what kind of influence on acquisition (e.g., what does a Pearson correlation of $r = 0.35$ really tell us about potential influence on L2 learning?).

Educationally oriented SLA assessments of learner knowledge

Educational measurement practices (i.e., those derived from educational uses of tests to determine learner differences and learning outcomes) have also influenced the design of learner knowledge assessments, principally in the strand of research on instructed SLA, which is devoted to under-standing how learners may benefit from a variety of types of instruction, typically operationalized at the scale of task, activity, or lesson. Here, assessment is called upon to detect often subtle, and very immediate, changes in learner knowledge and behavior vis-à-vis whatever language forms comprise the focus of instruction. Most of these assessments are designed by researchers—though often derived from teacher-made tests—and they typically take the form of relatively short sets of discrete items, either selected-response (e.g., multiple choice) or constrained-constructed-response (e.g., fill-in-the-blank), though they may occasionally extend to freer communicative-oriented language production (Norris and Ortega, 2000). Proportion correct of total items on the test is the primary approach to scoring, and such scores are frequently produced in a pre-test, post-test experimental design, with inferential analysis of mean differences serving as the primary interpretive mechanism. The most serious criticism of these assessments is that test performances may yield indicators unrelated to the constructs of interest in L2 instruction research, since they often measure explicit, metalinguistic, or immediate recall (i.e., memorized) knowledge, rather than development of implicit knowledge or ability for communicative language use, and they often lead to an overestimation of L2 learning or "acquisition" for this reason (Doughty, 2003; Norris and Ortega, 2003).

Learners' global proficiency is another construct that figures centrally in SLA research and for which a variety of educational test instruments and frameworks exist. Some form of assessed global proficiency is often needed, though unfortunately less frequently used, in order to justify the sampling of participants into a study or to assign participants to distinct groups. Measuring and reporting learner proficiency can also aid readers of research when deciding the extent to which findings can be generalized to other samples and populations (Norris and Ortega, 2006; Shohamy, 2000). A major challenge for proficiency assessment is the sheer size of the construct, covering essentially all of language ability, and the diversity of assessment options available, ranging from lengthy and in-depth measures of academic (e.g., Test of English as a Foreign Language) or spoken foreign language (e.g., Oral Proficiency Interviews based on the American Council on the Teaching of Foreign Languages Guidelines) proficiency, to very short-cut estimates based on principles of reduced redundancy testing (e.g., cloze tests, C-tests, elicited imitation), to simple self-report indices such as length of study or residence within a target-language context (see Thomas, 2006). While the reporting of any L2 proficiency estimate is better than none, it is also the case that one major limitation to the generalizability of SLA research findings is the lack of domain-specific standardized proficiency assessments.

Profiling learner knowledge acquisition by assessing L2 production

Together with GJTs, the most popular family of assessment techniques in SLA involves the elicitation of extended oral or written discourse production that is communicative in nature albeit relatively contrived through researcher-imposed elicitation situations or devices. Elicitation techniques include structured spoken interviews, tasks involving information-sharing or problem-solving, story-retelling tasks probed by pictures or silent movie clips, and role plays, among others. Generally speaking, these assessments seek to engage learners in meaningful communication activities that ostensibly reveal internalized and automated aspects of L2 knowledge spanning multi-componential models of competence (e.g., Canale and Swain, 1980).

Extended production data may be analyzed in a variety of ways, depending largely on the theoretical questions at stake. Early efforts in SLA applied variationist sociolinguistic tools to the detailed micro- and macro-analysis of individual learner interlanguage development and particularly conversation (e.g., Sato, 1990). Another early and influential example in SLA came from the ZISA project in Germany, where data were collected from international guest workers learning German in a variety of on-the-job and social settings (Meisel *et al.*, 1981). This project eventually inspired Pienemann's (2005) Processability Theory (Pienemann and Keßler, Chapter 14, this volume) and fueled the development of an associated suite of elicitation measures designed to rapidly profile learners' emerging development levels. More recent work, issuing from socially oriented theories of SLA, has used extended discourse data to explore ways of operationalizing such phenomena as interactional competence and the "interactional complexity" of tasks (Young, 2009).

Learner production data have also been submitted to analyses derived from corpus linguistics, heralded in particular by usage-based L2 researchers, who view learner corpora as central to assessing learner knowledge, given the possibility of tracing the emergence and deployment of constructions in large amounts of learner data. For example, N. Ellis and Ferreira-Junior (2009) traced early proto-typical and generic usages of three types of argument structure in English (Verb + Locative, Verb + Object + Locative, and Verb + Object + Object), first in strong association with certain high-frequency core verbs or "islands" (*go*, *put*, and *give*, respectively) followed later by the gradual spread of relevant uses with a wider range of frames and different (less prototypical and more specific) verbs. From more general cognitive-interactionist perspectives, as well, learner production corpora have gained in importance, although they are mostly analyzed by comparing L2 learners' usage of forms with those of L1 users (e.g., Granger, 2002). Methods adapted from L1 acquisition for observing and characterizing language development have also made their way into SLA in the form of various indices that are applied to extended L2 discourse, with the aim to measure task-related variation or development-related longitudinal change in syntactic complexity, lexical sophistication, target-like accuracy, or idiomatic fluency in learner production (Housen and Kuiken, 2009).

Major challenges for production-based L2 assessments involve, first, the extent to which data may be assumed to capture the constructs of interest; for example, where first emergence of a particular token is sought, it may be necessary to look across numerous possible language use contexts to be sure that it has or has not emerged. Second, unless sufficient data are collected repeatedly from the same learners, what is observed may be misinterpreted as acquisition or the lack thereof (Tomasello and Stahl, 2004). Third, tasks or other elicitation devices may themselves constrain or facilitate the use of certain language forms (as, for that matter, might the context of performing them), so the apparent lack of sought-after L2 forms in production may not necessarily indicate the lack of learner knowledge of them. Finally, all learner production data must be subjected to coding and analysis for various L2 forms of interest, and the reliability with which that coding takes place (e.g., within or across raters) may limit the trustworthiness of extracted evidence, though the increasingly viable automation of such codings has improved matters considerably (e.g., through automatic grammar tagging, e.g., Biber, 2006; or through automated counts of lexical and grammatical features, as in the CHILDES suite of applications, MacWhinney, 2000).

Authentic, naturalistic data as a basis for assessment of L2 knowledge

Rather than relying on the targeted elicitation of discourse data, some SLA researchers prefer to look for their evidence about learner knowledge in naturalistic data from authentic social settings, drawing on methods from sociology and linguistic or educational anthropology. Seeking evidence of instructional effectiveness, classroom SLA researchers record and investigate interactions naturally occurring in formal academic settings, often in classrooms but sometimes in other educational contexts, such as advising sessions, or they may collect and analyze assignments done for instructional purposes. It is also common for these researchers to gather other types of complementary data, for example, through classroom observation instruments (e.g., Lyster and Mori, 2006) or teaching logs (e.g., Bardovi-Harlig, 1994). Conversation Analysts, on the other hand, tend to study casual conversations and public encounters and less often classrooms, and they submit such data to detailed qualitative analyses following highly specified analytical procedures (Markee and Kasper, 2004) which may shed light on critical moments in L2 knowledge acquisition. Depending on the purposes for analysis and the interpretations to be made, naturally occurring L2 data would seem to bring with them some intrinsic or ecological validity, the argument being that only under such naturalistic conditions can true language knowledge be captured (i.e., all other assessments are to some extent contrived). However, special ethical challenges arise with naturalistic data, since the language to be treated as data pre-exists the research context and thus belongs by definition to the language users, not the researchers. Further, what assessments sacrifice in ecological validity, they gain in terms of controlling various factors that may undermine construct interpretations. For naturalistic assessments, the principal challenge remains what precisely may be interpreted about learner knowledge based only on observing what happens to emerge within the particular interaction and/or social setting.

Applications

Given such a variety of approaches to assessing learner knowledge in SLA, it is crucial for researchers to consider the extent to which the assessments they work with are indeed appropriate for their interpretive purposes (why they assess) and the populations or individuals under investigation (who they assess). Inquiry into these aspects of assessment is the object of validation (Messick, 1989) or validity evaluation (Norris, 2008), and the need for sustained research programs that investigate the validity of assessments of L2 knowledge cannot be overstated (see repeated critiques of SLA research over the years in Bachman and Cohen, 1998; Chapelle, 1998; Douglas, 2001; Lazaraton, 2005; Norris and Ortega, 2000, 2003; Shohamy, 2000). Historically within applied linguistics, validation work has been the domain of language testers, and validation methodologies have been applied to a range of educational assessments. An extensive example of validation within this milieu is the multi-year Test of English as a Foreign Language 2000 (subsequently dubbed New TOEFL) project, which included needs assessment, discourse analysis, item and task design, pilot-testing, computerization, test-score calibration, expert reviews, test user reviews, and other phases (Chapelle *et al.*, 2008).

While such examples provide useful models for how to go about validation in general, validity inquiry for SLA assessments is distinct in that it focuses not on the decisions and actions that are associated with educational tests but much more closely on the nuanced theory-based interpretations that researchers and research communities make about particular L2 knowledge constructs. At stake in the validation of L2 knowledge assessments is the well-worn question: To what extent is the assessment measuring what it is purported to measure? Answers derive from ascertaining the extent to which SLA constructs are adequately represented in instrument design and the degree to which methods are not rife with variance unaccounted for. An equally crucial question, and one that often goes unnoticed in the field, is considering who gets assessed, that is, whether or not interpretations about SLA are warranted for distinct populations of learners and the contexts in which they are acquiring the L2.

L2 assessment validation programs in SLA

What might validation of theory-based SLA assessments, intended for research purposes, look like? One example comes from the work of Rod Ellis and colleagues, who have been seeking to define, operationalize, and validate assessments of explicit versus implicit L2 knowledge (see R. Ellis *et al.*, 2009). Beginning in earnest with R. Ellis (2004), the first step was to distill, from the extensive theoretical and empirical literature, a likely set of agreed-upon definitions for the constructs of explicit and implicit L2 knowledge. Key here was the fact that the relevant research domain had generated a substantial amount of discussion and debate, such that targeted construct interpretations could be synthesized by the assessment developers; that is, rather than creating a definition from intuition, the definition emerged as a consensus from the work of numerous researchers and theoreticians. For R. Ellis and colleagues, then, explicit L2 knowledge is conscious, declarative, actively controlled, verbalizable, and learnable, whereas implicit L2 knowledge is intuitive, procedural, automatically accessible, behavioral but not verbalizable, and developmentally constrained (R. Ellis, 2004; R. Ellis *et al.*, 2009). Building from these construct definitions, the next step was to operationalize assessments that could tap the complex array of phenomena that constitute explicit versus implicit L2 knowledge. Accordingly, they designed not a single instrument for each construct, but a battery of elicitation devices, each attuned to particular observable phenomena that the research domain associated with the construct, including: (a) elicited imitation, (b) oral narrative, and (c) timed grammaticality judgment tasks (all tapping implicit phenomena); vs. (d) untimed grammaticality judgment tasks, and (e) metalinguistic knowledge tests (both tapping explicit phenomena). Moving beyond careful operationalization of constructs in assessment instruments, validation studies then ensued, primarily through the testing of hypotheses implied within the theoretical definitions of explicit versus implicit L2 knowledge, such as the apparent influence on test behaviors of factors like awareness, timing, certainty, learnability, etc. (see, e.g., Elder, 2009). These investigations have adopted primarily correlational, factor analytic, and analysis of variance techniques to explore the hypothesized relationships between test performances and theoretically related factors, and they have provided initial evidence in support of the construct interpretations being made on the basis of these assessments.

Several characteristics of this example might guide future inquiry into assessments used in other domains of SLA research (see related recommendations in Douglas, 2001; Norris and Ortega, 2003). First, the constructs that get assessed take the form of agreed upon definitions for particular aspects of L2 knowledge, and these definitions emerge through the synthesis of a broad base of antecedent work. Assessable construct definitions are not the creation of particularly insightful SLA theoreticians, rather they seem to be more the collective conscience of research communities as compiled by individuals or groups with a keen sense of the domain. Second, assessment instruments are deliberately designed based on these commonly shared construct definitions in order to shed light on behavioral indicators that say something of meaning to the research community. For most L2 knowledge constructs, that means the development of multiple assessments as reflective of the complex nature of L2 knowledge and its acquisition. Third, validation involves the examination of hypothesized relationships between assessments so designed and a variety of criteria, such as pre-existing differences among language user populations, responses to interventions, diverse factors that theory tells us should play a role in determining assessment outcomes, other assessments or measures, and so on. Key here is that these hypotheses are not idiosyncratic, rather they too reflect the theorized expectations of the domain for the nature of the construct and how it might manifest in observable behaviors.

Perhaps the main point to be drawn from what we might term L2 assessment validation *programs* is that validity has much to do with figuring out the common language and expectations of a particular SLA domain, first, and then investigating the possibilities by which researchers within that domain can communicate with each other in shared and trustworthy terms (i.e., through particularly meaningful assessments).

Instructional relevance and the importance of considering who gets assessed

It may be argued that the SLA research uses of assessments take the common purpose of informing theories, as opposed to decisions or actions about individual students or educational programs, which is the focus of validation efforts in educational assessment (Messick, 1989; Norris, 2008). However, it is also the case that L2 knowledge assessments are used to inform claims about the relative effectiveness of language instructional techniques within the broad domain of instructed SLA research (Norris and Ortega, 2000). Though there is no reason why all SLA research should be forced to exhibit educational relevance, in those cases where researchers do make claims about instruction, it is critical for assessment-based interpretations to be validated for the learners and the learning settings in question.

Under instructional research circumstances, validation is called upon to investigate the extent to which assessments can inform consistent interpretations about theoretical constructs as they exist and are measured across diverse and potentially distinct types of learners. Cultural, cognitive, demographic, proficiency, literacy, motivational, first language, educational experience, and other individual or group variables may all play a role in determining how learners respond to assessment techniques; it is therefore critical that SLA researchers refrain from assuming the validity of a given assessment (even one that has been "validated" in another study) when it is being applied to a new group of learners. For example, written production- or comprehension-based and metalinguistic assessments of specific features may function well for tapping knowledge of L2 forms with adolescent or adult learners who have been exposed to substantial amounts of schooling, but the same assessments will likely tell us very little about younger, bi- or multilingual learners who have been raised in cultures that emphasize oral literacy, strongly narrative traditions of education, and/or the value of multilingual register-based code switching (e.g., Tarone et al., 2009). In tapping constructs such as oral proficiency, language development, or mastery of certain forms in the language of these learners, it is clear that alternatives must be sought and validated, such as the development of picture-based oral elicitation tasks that are: (a) culturally relevant, (b) provide ample opportunity for learners to demonstrate language knowledge through performance, and (c) account for the possibility that knowledge may be evident in one, another, or multiple language systems (e.g., Sánchez, 2006).

It is also important that what SLA researchers interpret as an effect (or the lack of an effect) for instructional interventions not be predicted simply on the basis of an unobserved moderating variable in the form of learner proficiency differences. Thus, in the case of a grammatical sub-system like syntactic complexity, considerable evidence has emerged that measures of subordination will demonstrate initial linear growth over beginning to intermediate levels of L2 proficiency, followed by a decrease at upper levels of proficiency, when more complex behaviors such as nominalization take over (e.g., Byrnes et al., 2010). If researchers do not understand this particularly important link between learner proficiency and subordination (or other syntactic phenomena), they may mistakenly interpret lower amounts of subordination to indicate lack of effect of an instructional intervention, when in fact the opposite might be true. For these examples and others, then, it is a major job of validation research to doggedly pursue possible alternative explanations for observed assessment behaviors, especially when a variety of learner differences not related to the construct may in fact be the primary cause underlying the assessment results.

Finally, a major challenge that remains virtually unacknowledged in the assessment of L2 knowledge within instructed SLA research has to do with the fundamental disconnect between educational-level decisions and the scope and focus of L2 knowledge assessments. Language teaching and learning take place in broad strokes, over very extended periods of time, with language proficiency development as the primary goal, yet the vast majority of L2 instructional research is focused on very short-term gains on very circumscribed targets, typically assessed in educationally uninteresting or even irrelevant terms. If the assessment of L2 knowledge, and by extension research into instructed SLA, is in fact intended to make some kind of impact on L2 education, then dramatic changes in practice, at least for this subfield of SLA, will be required.

Future directions

The future of assessing learner knowledge within SLA will depend on a variety of factors, including the training and conduct of individual researchers, the continued improvement of reporting and editorial practices within the main SLA journals, and investment by researchers in longer-term validation of their assessments. We close the chapter with a few optimistic predictions on the directions that assessments will take, and we identify a handful of high-priority questions.

A principal line of work will involve the expansion, refinement, and clarification of *what* gets assessed, that is, the increasingly variegated theoretical L2 knowledge constructs which form the focus of SLA research. The major practices in assessing L2 knowledge represented by formal linguistic, usage-based, and cognitive-interactionist approaches will continue along well-established lines. However, new socially oriented theoretical approaches will make new demands on construct elucidation and validation. For all of these divergent lines of SLA work, it will be incumbent upon researchers to develop conceptual clarity regarding the interpretations they intend to make about L2 knowledge, including not just what it looks like, but also what it looks like as it emerges over time and along detailed developmental continua, how and when it is acquired, and what factors are particularly salient in fostering or constraining its learning for particular learner populations.

New suites of research methodologies will help determine *how* to assess what is being acquired across this broad palette of theoretically relevant SLA constructs. This methodological diversification will need to account for learning that is non-linear and longitudinal, and for outcomes that are complex and multi-dimensional (Norris and Ortega, 2009), and new technologies will be called upon to elicit, analyze, and share the variety of data implied in such assessments, from a host of cognitive and physiological measurement tools (e.g., event-related potentials, eye-tracking), to large-scale models and simulations (e.g., neural networks), to increasingly automated mechanisms for capturing, coding, and analyzing L2 speech and writing (e.g., CHILDES, MacWhinney, 2000). Moreover, as Larsen-Freeman and Cameron (2008) have argued, assessments will be expected to track variability-centered growth (e.g., from initial noticing and awareness of L2 forms through to their automatic deployment in communication) of multiple inter-related phenomena (e.g., syntactic complexity as it interacts with morphosyntactic accuracy and communicative fluency). This tracking must also be done from multiple perspectives, for example, the learner's own insights on acquisition in comparison with contextually determined opportunities to learn.

With the accumulation of larger amounts of L2 assessment data, there will be greater need for the use of sophisticated inferential statistical procedures, such as structural equation modeling, path analysis, and latent trait analysis (Bachman, 2004). At the same time, we hope SLA researchers will develop a more refined appreciation for descriptive and non-parametric statistics (Corder and Foreman, 2009), innovative graphic displays (Verspoor *et al.*, 2011), and the meaningful use and interpretation of effect sizes (Norris and Ortega, 2006). Similarly, mixed methods research will be called upon to "weigh the two types of evidence against each other [... and] to combine quantitative and qualitative methods in ways that do have an influence on the findings" (Benson *et al.*, 2009, p. 87). Key also will be the development within SLA of proprietary standards for assessment design and use that are rigorous enough to produce trustworthy indications of L2 knowledge, replicable from one study to the next, and facilitative of non-reductionist methods.

A final, important direction in research will have to do with *who* is being assessed and the kinds of claims about them that may or may not be warranted. Rather than assuming generalized findings for all learners, assessments will be designed to get at individual learner variability, including techniques for determining how learners respond to assessment tasks or other stimuli (e.g., introspection, think aloud, retrospection) as well as measures of moderating variables (e.g., aptitude, motivation, proficiency). It will become increasingly important to provide descriptive assessments of learner demographic characteristics as well (e.g., first language, age, instructional setting), given heightened awareness that these factors may shade assessment performance as well as acquisition itself. Particularly critical will be the development of benchmarks for interpreting assessment findings, where combinations of learner factors can be related to levels of assessment performance such that researchers will have a richer foundation for understanding what a score on a particular assessment means in terms of degree, quality, or extent of L2 knowledge.

These predictions might be summarized in a handful of guiding questions for assessment in the service of SLA research:

(1) To what extent do current definitions of diverse aspects of learner knowledge, across SLA theories, provide a sufficient foundation for identifying relevant observable phenomena within research? In other words, do our theories provide clearly defined constructs that can be assessed?

(2) To what extent do current assessment techniques provide a sufficient empirical window into diverse theories and their claims about learner L2 knowledge?

(3) Which technologies can facilitate the automation, reliability, and sharing of both L2 data elicitation and its analysis, and what are the benefits and drawbacks of using them?

(4) What do L2 assessment findings really mean and what don't (or can't) they mean, in the context of a given study and vis-à-vis the targeted population of learners, and how can researchers incorporate meaningful benchmarks into their interpretations about L2 acquisition?

(5) How should each assessment of learner L2 knowledge be validated, by whom, for what purposes, and against what criteria? To what extent can assessments be utilized, and their results generalized, across learning contexts?

Clearly, each of these "big" questions implies a full research program involving the cooperation of SLA researchers with others such as statisticians, language testers, software specialists, and with continued input from other feeder disciplines. At the same time, it would seem incumbent upon the SLA research community to embark upon a synthetic shift (Norris and Ortega, 2006), that is, a move away from individual researchers pursuing their own versions of assessing learner knowledge and toward the realization of research as a cumulative and cooperative endeavor. What we learn about learner knowledge from any given assessment depends greatly on what we already know from other studies; how we go about assessing should therefore help researchers to situate their findings within the broader spectrum of related research. It is in this shared and cumulative sense that construct definition becomes essential (providing a common frame of reference), that standards for assessment design and use enable consistency from one study to the next (reducing construct under-representation and irrelevant variance), and that the full and careful reporting of assessments and their findings is crucial (enabling benchmarking, replication, and generalization).

References

Bachman, L. F. (2004). *Statistical analyses for language assessment*. New York: Cambridge University Press.

Bachman, L. F. and Cohen, A. (1998). *Interfaces between second language acquisition and language testing research*. New York: Cambridge University Press.

Bardovi-Harlig, K. (1994). Reverse-order reports and the acquisition of tense: Beyond the principle of chronological order. *Language Learning*, 44, 243–282.

Benson, P., Chik, A., Gao, X., Huang, J., and Wang, W. (2009). Qualitative research in language teaching and learning journals: 1997–2006. *The Modern Language Journal*, 93, 79–90.

Biber, D. (2006). Corpus-based parsing and grammatical description. In K. Brown (Ed.), *Encyclopedia of language and linguistics* (second Edition). (Vol 9, pp. 197–205). Oxford, UK: Elsevier.

Bowles, M. (2010). *The think-aloud controversy in second language research*. New York: Routledge.

Brown, J. D. (2001). *Using surveys in language programs*. Cambridge: Cambridge University Press.

Byrnes, H., Maxim, H., and Norris, J. M. (2010). Realizing advanced foreign language writing development in collegiate education: Curricular design, pedagogy, assessment. *The Modern Language Journal*, 94 (Supplement 1). Monograph Series.

Canale, M. and Swain, M. (1980). Theoretical bases of communicative approaches to second language teaching and testing. *Applied Linguistics*, 1, 1–47.

Chapelle, C. (1998). Construct definition and validity inquiry in SLA research. In L. F. Bachman and A. D. Cohen (Eds.), *Second language acquisition and language testing interfaces* (pp. 32–70). Cambridge: Cambridge University Press.

Chapelle, C., Enright, M., and Jamieson, J. (Eds.). (2008). *Building a validity argument for the Test of English as a Foreign Language*. New York: Routledge.

Cook, V. (2008). Multi-competence: Black hole or wormhole for second language acquisition research?. In Z. Han (Ed.), *Understanding second language process* (pp. 16–26). Clevedon, UK: Multilingual Matters.

Corder, G. W. and Foreman, D. I. (2009). *Nonparametric statistics for non-statisticians: A step-by-step approach*. Malden, MA: Wiley.

Dörnyei, Z. (2009). *The psychology of second language acquisition*. Oxford: Oxford University Press.

Doughty, C. J. (2003). Instructed SLA: Constraints, compensation, and enhancement. In C. J. Doughty and M. H. Long (Eds.), *The handbook of second language acquisition* (pp. 256–310). Malden, MA: Blackwell.

Douglas, D. (2001). Performance consistency in second language acquisition and language testing: A conceptual gap. *Second Language Research*, 17, 442–456.

Elder, C. (2009). Validating a test of meta-linguistic knowledge. In R. Ellis *et al.* (Eds.), *Implicit and explicit knowledge in second language learning, testing and teaching* (pp. 113–138). Clevedon, UK: Multilingual Matters.

Ellis, N. C. and Ferreira-Junior, F. (2009). Construction learning as a function of frequency, frequency distribution, and function. *The Modern Language Journal*, 93, 370–385.

Ellis, R. (1991). Grammaticality judgments and SLA. *Studies in Second Language Acquisition*, 13, 161–186.

Ellis, R. (2004). The definition and measurement of explicit knowledge. *Language Learning*, 54, 227–275.

Ellis, R., Loewen, S., Elder, C., Erlam, R., Philp, J., and Reinders, H. (2009). *Implicit and explicit knowledge in second language learning, testing, and teaching*. Clevedon, UK: Multilingual Matters.

Gass, S. M. and Mackey, A. (2000). *Stimulated recall methodology in second language research*. Mahwah, NJ: Lawrence Erlbaum.

Granger, S. (2002). A bird's-eye view of computer learner corpus research. In S. Granger, J. Hung, and S. Petch-Tyson (Eds.), *Computer learner corpora, second language acquisition and foreign language teaching* (pp. 3–33). Amsterdam: John Benjamins.

Gullberg, M. and McCafferty, S. G. (Eds.). (2008). Gesture and SLA: Toward an integrated approach. *Studies in Second Language Acquisition*, 30(2) [Special issue].

Hawkins, R. (2001). The theoretical significance of Universal Grammar in second language acquisition. *Second Language Research*, 17, 345–367.

Housen, A. and Kuiken, F. (Eds.). (2009). Complexity, accuracy, and fluency in second language acquisition: Theoretical and methodological perspectives. *Applied Linguistics*, 30(4) [Special issue].

Jarvis, S. (2007). Theoretical and methodological issues in the investigation of conceptual transfer. *Vigo International Journal of Applied Linguistics (VIAL)*, 4, 43–71.

Kinginger, C. and Blattner, G. (2008). Histories of engagement and sociolinguistic awareness in study abroad: Colloquial French. In L. Ortega and H. Byrnes (Eds.), *The longitudinal study of advanced L2 capacities* (pp. 223–246). New York: Routledge.

Kramsch, C. (2006). From communicative competence to symbolic competence. *The Modern Language Journal*, *90*, 249–252.

Lardiere, D. (2003). Revisiting the comparative fallacy: A reply to Lakshmanan and Selinker, 2001. *Second Language Research*, *19*, 129–143.

Larsen-Freeman, D. and Cameron, L. (2008). *Complex systems and applied linguistics*. Oxford: Oxford University Press.

Lazaraton, A. (2005). Quantitative research methods. In E. Hinkel (Ed.), *Handbook of research in second language teaching and learning* (pp. 209–224). Mahwah, NJ: Lawrence Erlbaum.

Loewen, S. and Gass, S. M. (2009). Research timeline: The use of statistics in L2 acquisition research. *Language Teaching*, *42*, 181–196.

Long, M. H. (1990). The least a second language acquisition theory needs to explain. *TESOL Quarterly*, *24*(4), 649–666.

Lyster, R. and Mori, H. (2006). Interactional feedback and instructional counterbalance. *Studies in Second Language Acquisition*, *28*, 321–341.

MacWhinney, B. (2000). *The CHILDES project: Tools for analyzing talk. Volume I: Transcription format and programs* (Third Edition), Mahwah, NJ: Lawrence Erlbaum.

Markee, N. and Kasper, G. (2004). Classroom talks: An introduction. *The Modern Language Journal*, *88*, 491–500.

Meisel, J. M., Clahsen, H., and Pienemann, M. (1981). On determining developmental stages in natural second language acquisition. *Studies in Second Language Acquisition*, *3*, 109–135.

Messick, S. (1989). Validity. In R. L. Linn (Ed.), *Educational measurement* (Third Edition). (pp. 13–103). New York: Macmillan.

Norris, J. M. (2008). *Validity evaluation in language assessment*. New York: Peter Lang.

Norris, J. M. and Ortega, L. (2000). Effectiveness of L2 instruction: A research synthesis and quantitative meta-analysis. *Language Learning*, *50*, 417–528.

Norris, J. M. and Ortega, L. (2003). Defining and measuring SLA. In C. J. Doughty and M. H. Long (Eds.), *Handbook of second language acquisition* (pp. 717–761). Malden, MA: Blackwell.

Norris, J. M. and Ortega, L. (2006). The value and practice of research synthesis for language learning and teaching. In J. M. Norris and L. Ortega (Eds.), *Synthesizing research on language learning and teaching* (pp. 3–50). Amsterdam: John Benjamins.

Norris, J. M. and Ortega, L. (2009). Towards an organic approach to investigating CAF in instructed SLA: The case of complexity. *Applied Linguistics*, *30*, 555–578.

Norton Peirce, B. (1995). Social identity, investment, and language learning. *TESOL Quarterly*, *29*, 9–31.

Ortega, L. and Carson, J. G. (2010). Multicompetence, social context, and L2 writing research praxis. In T. Silva and P. Matsuda (Eds.), *Practicing theory in second language writing*. (pp. 48–71). West Lafayette, IN: Parlor Press.

Paolillo, J. (2000). Asymmetries in Universal Grammar: The role of method and statistics. *Studies in Second Language Acquisition*, *22*, 209–228.

Pienemann, M. (Ed.). (2005). *Cross-linguistic aspects of processability theory*. Amsterdam: John Benjamins.

Rymes, B. (2008). Language socialization and the linguistic anthropology of education. In P. A. Duff and N. H. Hornberger (Eds.), *Encyclopedia of language and education* (Second Edition). (Vol. *8* pp. 29–42). New York: Springer.

Sánchez, L. (2006). Bilingualism/second-language research and the assessment of oral proficiency in minority bilingual children. *Language Assessment Quarterly*, *3*, 117–149.

Sato, C. (1990). *The syntax of conversation in interlanguage development*. Tübingen: Gunter Narr.

Schleppegrell, M. J. (2004). *The language of schooling: A functional linguistics perspective*. Mahwah, NJ: Lawrence Erlbaum.

Schwartz, B. D. and Sprouse, R. A. (2000). When syntactic theories evolve: Consequences for L2 acquisition research. In J. Archibald (Ed.), *Second language acquisition and linguistic theory* (pp. 156–185). Malden, MA: Blackwell.

Shohamy, E. (2000). The relationship between language testing and second language acquisition, revisited. *System*, *28*, 541–553.

Singleton, D. (2003). Critical period or general age factor(s)? In M. P. García Mayo and M. L. García Lecumberri (Eds.), *Age and the acquisition of English as a foreign language* (pp. 3–22). Clevedon, UK: Multilingual Matters.

Slobin, D. I. (1996). From "thought and language" to "thinking for speaking". In J. J. Gumperz and S. C. Levinson (Eds.), *Rethinking linguistic relativity* (pp. 70–96). New York: Cambridge University Press.

Sorace, A. and Keller, F. (2005). Gradience in linguistic data. *Lingua*, *115*(11), 1497–1524.

Swain, M. (2001). Examining dialogue: Another approach to content specification and to validating inferences drawn from test scores. *Language Testing, 18*, 319–346.

Tarone, E., Bigelow, M., and Hansen, K. (2009). *Literacy and second language oracy*. Oxford: Oxford University Press.

Thomas, M. (2006). Research synthesis and historiography: The case of assessment of second language proficiency. In J. M. Norris and L. Ortega (Eds.), *Synthesizing research on language learning and teaching* (pp. 279–298). Amsterdam: John Benjamins.

Tomasello, M. and Stahl, D. (2004). Sampling children's spontaneous speech: How much is enough? *Journal of Child Language, 31*, 101–121.

Verspoor, M. H., de Bot, K., and Lowie, W. (Eds.). (2011). *A dynamic approach to second language development: Methods and techniques*. Amsterdam: John Benjamins.

Young, R. (2009). *Discursive practice in language learning and teaching*. Malden, MA: Wiley-Blackwell.

Glossary

Accentedness   the production of segmental and suprasegmental features in L2 speech that fall outside L1 speaker norms.

Action research   teacher conducted research designed to critically and systematically investigate instructional issues within teachers' own classrooms.

Age of arrival   the age at which individuals arrive in the country where the target language is spoken and could in principle start acquiring the target language. Commonly used term as an imprecise proxy for age of onset (*see age of onset*).

Age of onset   the age at which second language learning begins, which may or may not coincide with age of arrival (*see age of arrival*).

Agency   the view that language learners play an active rather than passive role in language learning by self-regulating and making choices in their production of target forms.

Allophone   a variant of a phoneme; one of the phonetic realizations in which a phoneme in a language can be pronounced (*see phoneme*).

Aptitude complexes   frameworks to examine how combinations of aptitude components, such as grammatical sensitivity and phonemic coding ability, interact with different learning contexts in a non-linear manner to account for language learning success.

Assessment   a systematic and replicable technique that allows researchers to elicit, observe, and interpret indicators of language knowledge and/or ability constructs, with underlying standards of practice that govern its development and use.

Assessment reliability   the consistency of the assessment in producing trustworthy findings across different sets or administrations of a test.

Attention (in language processing)   the aspect of the cognitive system underlying language processing responsible for the selectivity of processing goals (e.g., focusing on particular words or relations between words).

Automaticity (of language processing)   highly efficient processing that, beyond being fast, is unstoppable once triggered and does not require conscious cognitive effort (e.g., recognition of familiar words).

Categorical perception   listeners' ability to discriminate between two stimuli equal to their ability to identify them as belonging to different categories.

Central Executive or Executive Attention   a component of the working memory system concerned with the management and control of information, and hence closely related to attentional processes. This component regulates the distribution of attentional resources when more than one cognitive task requires attention (*see working memory*).

Classroom research   research conducted in language classrooms on activities that have an educational purpose.

Co-adaptation   a phenomenon that occurs when the language resources of two or more interlocutors are altered in adaptive imitation of one another.

Cognitive and social approaches to SLA   theories that focus on understanding how language acquisition takes place in the mind of the learner (cognitive) or as a result of social interaction (social).

Cognitive linguistics   a branch of linguistics which analyzes language in terms of the concepts which underlie its forms. It holds that language is learned by general cognitive processes, that grammar can be understood in terms of conceptualization, and that language is learned from usage.

Collocations   commonly occurring lexical combinations characterized by restricted co-occurrence of elements and relative transparency of meaning. For example, *follow instructions, heavy traffic,* and *completely satisfied.*

Competition   a basic cognitive process that takes account of contrasting perceptions and motives to reach optimal decisions in language processing.

Competition model   a functional approach that claims sentence-level comprehension occurs through the use of linguistic cues and cue strengths, in other words, the probability with which linguistic cues can be reliably used.

Component skills approach   a term used in reading. This approach measures in tandem, closely related mental operations in an attempt to clarify their functional and developmental relationships.

Comprehensible input   language exposure that L2 learners can understand.

Comprehensible output   learner produced utterances that are understandable to the interlocutor.

Computer-assisted language learning   any environment or application in which a learner, alone or collaboratively with peers, uses technology in a second or other language.

Concordancer   a computer program that allows learners to encounter and explore words in a variety of contexts by listing segments or lines of texts containing the target word.

Construct validity   the extent to which an assessment or a data elicitation procedure provides accurately interpretable evidence about a particular construct.

Construction Grammar   a theory that holds that the primary unit of grammar is the grammatical construction (*see constructions*).

Constructions   form-meaning mappings, conventionalized in the speech community, and entrenched as language knowledge in the learner's mind. They are the symbolic units of language relating the defining properties of their morphological, syntactic, and lexical form with particular semantic, pragmatic, and discourse functions.

Contact Hypothesis   an hypothesis that states that learners who establish more target language contact (e.g., social networks, opportunities for aural and written second language input) make greater linguistic gains than those who do not.

Context of learning   the context in which the second language is acquired (e.g., at home, foreign language classroom, second language naturalistic context, target language domestic immersion program, or study abroad program).

Conversation analysis   type of analysis that uses conversation as a medium to describe how patterns of interaction, such as turn-taking or adjacency pairs, relate to changes in the participants' knowledge.

Corpora   a collection of more than one corpus consisting of written and/or oral data of native speakers and/or language learners (*see corpus*).

Corpus   a systematic collection of naturally occurring spoken or written language that is selected to be a balanced representation of a particular type of language (e.g., American or British

English), genre (e.g., academic writing or conversation), or population (e.g., native speaker or language learners).

Corrective feedback (negative feedback)   information provided to learners about the ill-formedness of their L2 production. Feedback may supply the correct form or it may prompt learners to try to do so on their own *(see also feedback)*.

Cortex (cerebral)   the layer of neural tissue ("gray matter") that covers the cerebrum and plays a role in higher-level cognitive functions.

Critical period   the age where language is claimed to be learned easily, through input and interaction with native speakers, followed by marked decline (maturational in nature and only modulated, not caused, by contextual factors) of this learning ability and eventual stabilization at a lower level.

Critical Period Hypothesis   an hypothesis that proposes there is an age-related barrier to achieving native-like ultimate proficiency in a second language. During the critical period, learners are claimed to be able to readily acquire a second language and attain native-like performance, while after this period acquisition becomes more difficult.

Cue validity   a measure of the extent to which a given linguistic form leads uniformly to the correct interpretation.

Declarative memory   the memory system for knowledge of facts and personal experiences. Evidence suggests that this knowledge is largely, though not completely, available to conscious awareness.

Design–based research   a research methodology that addresses the complexity of learning processes and learning environments rather than simply outcomes. Design and theory are developed simultaneously and revised continuously throughout the research process.

Dialectic   the necessary unity or synthesis of two interacting opposites to form a whole. For example, a tapestry is held together by threads running in opposite directions.

Discourse completion task (DCT)   usually written, an indirect means for assessing spoken language through written production; if oral, also called a closed role play. Often used in pragmatics research, DCTs are frequently designed to elicit specific speech acts, such as compliment responses, by describing the situation and asking learners to imagine what they might say.

Dyslexia   a reading disability that occurs when the brain does not properly recognize and process certain symbols. Also known as developmental reading disorder.

Educational level   a characteristic of adult language learners that is often associated with low levels of print literacy. Educational level may play a role in how learners process oral language, including feedback.

EEG (Electroencephalogram)   scalp-based recording of the brain's ongoing electrical activity.

Emergentism   an approach proposing that language is a complex adaptive system which emerges from usage.

Entrenchment   a basic neuronal process operating across development that leads to the proceduralization and speeding-up of specific linguistic forms.

ERP component   a characteristic ERP wave form (e.g., the N400) that is found consistently under particular experimental conditions.

Explicit knowledge   knowledge of a language that a learner is aware of and can articulate.

Factor analysis   a statistical procedure to identify patterns and underlying constructs in large datasets which cannot otherwise be identified.

Feature unification   one of the key processes in Lexical-Functional Grammar utilized in Processability Theory. The process ensures that the features of two constituents match *(see Processaility Theory)*.

Feedback   information that is provided to a learner that a prior utterance is correct or incorrect (*see also corrective feedback*).

Focus on form   the allocation of focal attention to language form during an otherwise meaning-focused interaction.

Formant   a concentration of acoustic energy corresponding to the resonating frequency of the air in the vocal tract (e.g., vowels are distinguished by three formants).

Fossilization   the phenomenon of learning stagnating permanently in spite of abundant exposure to input, adequate motivation to learn, and plentiful opportunity for communicative practice.

Functional category   A formal grammatical feature or bundle of features that participates in a system of grammaticalized contrasts in a language, such as case, number, gender, definiteness, tense, aspect, mood, voice, etc. and that may also play a role in syntactic relations (such as agreement) and operations (such as movement).

Fundamental Difference Hypothesis   the hypothesis that second language acquisition is fundamentally different from first language acquisition.

General nativism   this approach holds that general cognitive processes, such as those used for pattern detection, probabilistic inference and category formation, subserve the process of language acquisition as well as the child's development in other cognitive domains (*see nativism and specific nativism*).

Genre   used variably in such traditions as New Rhetoric, language for special purposes, and literacy education to capture qualities of particular texts; also used to refer to recurrent configurations of meanings that enact social practices in a given culture.

Grammatical meanings (of function words or affixes)   a concept that has to do with basic ontological categories such as number, tense, aspect, or pointing to the word's function in the sentence, for example, case. These are more abstract and general compared to lexical meanings.

Grammatical metaphor   form of semiosis that involves a shift from direct (i.e., "congruent") forms of meaning-making to more indirect (i.e., "non-congruent") or metaphorical forms of meaning-making. Nominalization of more "normal" verbal processes involves grammatical metaphor in the ideational realm.

Hemodynamic   related to blood circulation. Certain functional neuroimaging techniques such as functional Magnetic Resonance Imaging (fMRI) and Positron Emission Tomography (PET) are based on the hemodynamic response to neural activity in particular experimental conditions.

Heritage language (HL)   a language other than a country's official or dominant languages that speakers have been exposed to at home, but have not fully acquired because of their switch to another more dominant language, usually the one in which they are educated.

Heritage language acquisition (HLA)   heritage language speakers' re/acquisition of their home language.

Heritage language learner (HLL)   a heritage language speaker who studies the home language formally, typically in a community school or in K-16.

Heritage language speaker   An individual who was exposed to a language at home but did not fully acquire it because of a switch to another language.

Hypothesis Space   a metaphor illustrating the constraints that Processability Theory places on development and variation in SLA. These constraints create a space within which the learner can entertain hypotheses about the L2 (*see Processability Theory*).

Ideal L2 self   the L2-specific facet of one's ideal self, that is, the possible future self one desires to become.

Identity personalized aspects that make up an individual language learner (e.g., gender, ethnicity, age).

Implicational scaling a statistical technique which assumes that success at one level implies success at lower levels of the scale (e.g., active word knowledge presupposes passive word knowledge).

Implicit knowledge knowledge of a language that a learner is unaware of and cannot articulate.

Input the language that is available to learners; that is, exposure.

Input processing making a connection between form and meaning/function during comprehension.

Instrumental orientation reasons for learning the L2 pertaining to the potential pragmatic benefits and value of being proficient in the language, such as a higher salary or improved employment opportunities.

Integrative orientation a positive disposition toward the L2 group reflecting a desire to interact with and even integrate into their community.

Intelligibility the ability of the listener to decode the form of words or utterances and understand their meaning in a given context.

Interaction approaches approaches that consider conversational interaction as a locus of learning.

Interlanguage the linguistic system a learner creates in the course of developing a second language.

Internalization the process of learning to use a second language in one's own inner speech and thinking.

Interphonology the sub-system of the interlanguage that governs the L2 learner's production and perception of the TL sound patterns.

Introspective methods research methods that ask study participants to reflect on their own experiences, responses or feelings. For example, think-alouds or language diaries.

Language related episodes (LREs) any part of an interactional dialog in which learners talk about or monitor their production and use of the L2.

Learner characteristics (individual variables) characteristics of learners that can affect their second language acquisition (e.g., age, sex, social and physical characteristics, personality, learning styles, attitudes/motivation, pre-departure language levels for study abroad learners).

Lexical meaning the idiosyncratic denotation of a word as an entry in the mental lexicon. Words may either be taken to denote things in the world, or concepts, depending on the particular approach to lexical semantics.

Lexicon an inventory of the words and morphemes of a language; in most linguistic discussions a lexicon refers to a mental inventory of words and morphemes.

Markedness a relationship used to show that a linguistic feature is in some way privileged or preferred relative to other features in that it is more widely distributed, both within a language and cross-linguistically.

Mediation the central concept of sociocultural theory, which holds that mental functioning is organized in accordance with the signs created by a culture.

Meta-analysis a statistical technique that combines the results of multiple studies that all have similar or related hypotheses. The goal is to make a more robust claim than is possible with a single study.

Metafunctions of language the most general functions served by language, typically broken down into the ideational (with their experiential and logical subtypes), the interpersonal, and the textual metafunctions.

Metalinguistic knowledge   knowledge about language itself. Metalinguistic abilities relate to the ability to talk about, analyze, and even manipulate this knowledge.

Modern Language Aptitude Test (MLAT)   an assessment designed to predict a learner's likelihood of ease and success at learning a foreign language.

Modified output   the learner's production of rephrased or reformulated original utterances.

Motivation   the attribute that explains the direction and magnitude of human behavior, that is, the choice of a particular action, its instigation, and the persistence with which it is sustained, as well as the effort expended throughout the process.

Nativism   the view that children are genetically predisposed to acquire language (*see specific nativism and general nativism*).

Natural language processing   a field of computer science and linguistics concerned with automated understanding and generation of natural human languages.

Negative feedback   (*see corrective feedback*).

Neural plasticity   ability of the brain to change to adapt to new conditions.

Obstruent   a consonant whose salient phonetic characteristic is that its production involves a partial or complete obstruction of the airstream.

Operationalize   to provide a concrete definition of a construct so that it can be measured.

Orality   a way of thinking and communicating in societies where verbal expression prevails over print-based expression; a reliance on oral over written language often occurring in societies where writing and print are uncommon.

Ought-to L2 self   the L2-specific facet of one's ought-to self, that is, the possible future self one ought to become to meet others' expectations and avoid negative consequences.

Output   learner's production of forms and utterances in the target language.

Output Hypothesis   a hypothesis stating that the production of language, particularly that which results from the learner being "pushed" to produce output in order to make themselves understood, is a necessary condition for SLA (*see comprehensible output*).

Parameters   a set of innately pre-specified grammatical options whose values are fixed by learners on the basis of exposure to utterances in the language being acquired.

Parsing (in processing)   the moment-by-moment syntactic processing of sentences during comprehension.

Phoneme   an abstract unit of phonology that functions to distinguish the pronunciation of words or morphemes in a language; as an abstract construct, a phoneme in a language is always pronounced as one or more variants, known as allophones (*see allophone*).

Phonological awareness   phonological awareness refers to the ability to analyze a word into its phonological constituents. The ability is one of the most powerful predictors of reading development.

Phonological processing   the way in which individuals process auditory language, including phonemes, syllables, words, and rhymes. Phonological processing may be influenced by alphabetic print literacy.

Phonological short-term memory   a component of the working memory system specialized for the short-term storage of phonological information. Implicated mainly in vocabulary learning, but also in grammar learning.

Poverty of the stimulus   the claim that language learners end up with knowledge of language (especially complex formal knowledge of what is *not* possible in the language they are acquiring) that could not have been learned from the utterances they are exposed to in the linguistic environment.

Pragmalinguistic (competence)   the strategies and linguistic forms used to realize communicative acts, including making a statement vs. asking a question, grammatical knowledge (e.g., question formation, modals, imperative, subjunctive), lexicon and conventional expressions.

Pragmatic competence   The knowledge of how to say what to whom, when.

Pragmatics   the study of situated uses of language, the study of language in relation to the users of language, and the study of linguistic communication as a social activity.

Praxis   the dialectic unity of theory and practical goal-directed activity whereby each component depends necessarily on the other.

Private speech   derived from interaction in social communication, speech directed at the self that mediates an individual's mental activity.

Procedural memory   rooted in brain circuits passing through the basal ganglia and frontal cortex, this memory system underlies the learning and control of motor and cognitive skills such as riding a bicycle. The knowledge stored in procedural memory seems to be entirely implicit.

Processability Theory   a theory that posits that learner comprehension and production can take place only when the linguistic processor is ready. There exists a hierarchy of activation in processing procedures that leads to implicational sequencing in the acquisition of forms.

Processing (of language)   the cognitive activities that underlie different aspects of language learning and use (e.g., retrieving or recognizing the meaning of a word or producing a sentence).

Processing instruction   a particular type of pedagogical intervention that attempts to alter learner strategies for processing input.

Processing research (on language)   behavioral/neurocognitive research aimed at uncovering the mental activities and procedures—and supporting brain mechanisms—underlying language learning and use, typically using the techniques of experimental psychology.

Prompt   also known as elicitation, this type of corrective feedback indicates that an error has occurred, but it requires learners to produce the correct form on their own.

Psycholinguistics   a branch of cognitive science which draws upon the experimental methods and findings of cognitive psychology to explain the mental processes that underlie the acquisition, representation, and processing involved in the production and understanding of spoken and written language.

Pushed output   learner output that is at the limits of their linguistic abilities (*see comprehensible output and output hypothesis*).

Rapid profile   a computer-based procedure that permits a trained analyst to rapidly determine the developmental features of a given sample of learner language.

Reading universals   properties of reading that are shared across languages.

Recast   a type of corrective feedback that reformulates a learner's erroneous L2 utterance while maintaining the meaning of the utterance.

Register   a variety of language that is closely associated with a particular social setting and its common functions and forms of language use (e.g., academic register, formal/informal register).

Second language acquisition (SLA) methodologies   the combination of research designs (e.g., ethnographic case studies, experimental), instruments, and qualitative and/or quantitative data analyses used to carry out empirical SLA studies

Selective Fossilization Hypothesis   this hypothesis highlights the nature of fossilization as being local and selective, pertaining to certain interlanguage subsystems only, and attributes fossilization or acquisition to an interaction between native language and target language input characteristics (i.e., frequency and variability).

Self-organization   a process whereby order emerges from the interaction of components of a system without guidance from an external source or any innate plan.

Semantics   the study of literal, context-independent meaning in language; the constant meaning that is associated with a linguistic expression in all of its occurrences.

Semiosis   activity involving the use of signs, in particular the ways in which signs carry meaning by establishing relationships between different systems of signs. Language is often taken to be the prototypical sign system.

Sociolinguistic variable   a variable linguistic form that is systematically constrained by features of the linguistic environment, the social situation, and the characteristics of the speaker, such as age, gender, or socio-economic status.

Sociopragmatic (competence)   knowledge linking cultural and contextual information to language use; allows speakers to recognize culturally determined contexts. For example, knowing in which situations it is appropriate to thank vs. apologize, complain vs. request.

Soft-assembly   an individual's real-time response to the variable and dynamic features of a particular task.

Specific nativism   this approach holds that some kinds of linguistic knowledge (e.g., attunement to possible feature contrasts and/or constraints that are exclusively dedicated to language) are available to the child in advance of experience (*see nativism and general nativism*).

Stabilization   the phenomenon of learning that reaches a temporary plateau (hence distinct from fossilization). Often a product of development in which L2 learning incubates, and then continues to develop at a later point.

Study abroad (SA)   a context in which learners are exposed to a combination of formal second language instruction and naturalistic second language input/interaction while living in the target culture.

Study abroad programmatic variables   characteristics of study abroad programs that may affect second language acquisition (e.g., length of stay, living conditions [homestays/dorms/apartments], opportunities to form social networks with native speakers, and cultural travel).

Style-shift   movement from one style of speech (e.g., careful to casual). Styles can be represented on a continuum ranging from casual speech to interview style to reading passage style to word lists and finally to minimal pairs.

Suprasegmental features   features whose domain extends beyond the individual segment. Also described as prosodic features, they typically include pitch, stress, and pause structure.

Systematic variation   variation in linguistic form that is correlated with linguistic and/or social factors.

Teachability Hypothesis   an hypothesis that states that the effect of teaching is constrained by the learner's current level of acquisition.

Threshold Hypothesis   an hypothesis that states that those learners with a well-developed cognitive, lexical, and grammatical base will be best able to process and produce grammatical forms more accurately after a study abroad experience.

Truth value judgment task   a psycholinguistic task in which participants judge the truth or falsity of a test sentence with respect to a context acted out with toys or described in a story.

Ultimate attainment   often interchangeable with "end state," the term refers to the final, steady state of the interlanguage system. The term is neutral in the sense that the final state can be target-like, non-target-like, or a combination of both.

Unmarked alignment   the process which permits language learners to align the intended message (argument structure) and its grammatical form at the initial state, resulting in canonical word order.

VARBRUL   a specialized application of the statistical procedure of logistic regression, designed to analyze variable linguistic data. VARBRUL allows the researcher to consider all of the potential influences on variable simultaneously, even in cases where the numbers of tokens are highly unbalanced.

Voice onset time (VOT)   the interval between the release of a closure (e.g., release of a stop consonant) and onset of vocal cord vibration.

Word family   a base word with its inflected forms and regular, transparent and productive derived forms (e.g., avoid, avoids, avoided, avoiding, avoidance, avoidable, unavoidable).

Working memory   a system that is used for the temporary maintenance and storage of task-relevant information whilst performing cognitive tasks.

Working memory capacity   the ability to both retain and manage information in short-term memory in the face of potential interference from other cognitive tasks.

Zipf's law   describes how the highest frequency words account for the most linguistic tokens. The frequency of words decreases as a power function of their rank in the frequency table, with the most frequent word occurring approximately twice as often as the second most frequent word, which occurs twice as often as the fourth most frequent word, etc.

Zone of Proximal Development   the difference between what an individual or group can accomplish alone versus what they can do with mediation. It is the mechanism of psychological development.

Index

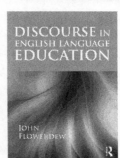

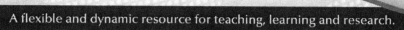